Environmental Strategies Handbook

Other McGraw-Hill Environmental Engineering Books of Interest

Environmental Strategies Handbook

Rao V. Kolluru, DrPH

Editor in Chief

McGraw-Hill, Inc.

New York   San Francisco   Washington, D.C.   Auckland   Bogotá
Caracas   Lisbon   London   Madrid   Mexico City   Milan
Montreal   New Delhi   San Juan   Singapore
Sydney   Tokyo   Toronto

Library of Congress Cataloging-in-Publication Data

Environmental strategies handbook / Rao V. Kolluru, editor in chief.
     p.   cm.
    Includes bibliographical references and index.
    ISBN 0-07-035858-3
    1. Environmental policy—United States—Handbooks, manuals, etc. 2. Management—
Environmental aspects—United States—Handbooks, manuals, etc. 3. United States—
Industries—Environmental aspects— Handbooks, manuals, etc. 4. Environmental
protection—United States—Handbooks, manuals, etc. 5. Environmental law—United States.
6. Liability for environmental damages—United States. I. Kolluru, Rao V.
HC110.E5E4997   1993
658.4'08—dc20   93-20520
                                                           CIP

1 2 3 4 5 6 7 8 9 0 DOC/DOC 9 9 8 7 6 5 4 3

ISBN 0-07-035858-3

*The sponsoring editor for this book was Gail F. Nalven, the editing supervisor was Peggy Lamb, and the
production supervisor was Suzanne W. Babeuf. This book was set in Palatino. It was composed by
McGraw-Hill's Professional Book Group composition unit.*

Printed and bound by R. R. Donnelley & Sons Company.

This book is printed on acid-free paper.

Contents

Contributors

Matthew B. Arnold   President and Founder, Management Institute for Environment and Business, Washington, D.C. (CHAPTER 19)

Stuart Bacher   Director, Development Technology, Merck Research Laboratories, Rahway, New Jersey (CHAPTER 6 APPENDIX)

David M. Benforado, P.E.   3M Company, St. Paul, Minnesota (CHAPTER 6)

Steve M. Boden   Partner, Deloitte & Touche, New York, New York (CHAPTER 9)

Gary Brayton   Partner, Deloitte & Touche, San Francisco, California (CHAPTER 9)

Robert P. Bringer, Ph.D.   Vice President, 3M Company, St. Paul, Minnesota (CHAPTER 6)

Paul N. Cheremisinoff, D.E.E., P.E.   Professor, Department of Civil and Environmental Engineering, New Jersey Institute of Technology, Newark, New Jersey (CHAPTER 5)

Walter Coddington   Coddington Environmental Management, New York, New York (CHAPTER 15)

Walter H. Corson, Ph.D.   Global Tomorrow Coalition, Washington, D.C. (CHAPTER 2)

Vincent T. Covello, Ph.D.   Professor, School of Public Health, Columbia University, New York, New York (CHAPTER 13)

Richard A. Denison, Ph.D.   Senior Scientist, Environmental Defense Fund, Washington, D.C. (CHAPTER 8)

Erik A. Dienemann, Ph.D.   Merck Research Laboratories, Rahway, New Jersey (CHAPTER 6 APPENDIX)

James A. Fava, Ph.D.   Project Director, Roy F. Weston, Inc., West Chester, Pennsylvania (CHAPTER 14)

Carl Frankel, J.D.   Green Market Alert, Bethlehem, Connecticut (CHAPTER 15)

Harris Gleckman, Ph.D.   United Nations Division of Transnational Corporations and Management, New York, New York (CHAPTER 18)

J. Ladd Greeno   Senior Vice President and Managing Director, Arthur D. Little, Cambridge, Massachusetts (CHAPTER 3)

Michael W. Hansen   United Nations Division of Transnational Corporations and Management, New York, New York (CHAPTER 18)

Carl L. Henn, C.P.L., C.F.P.   Fellow, Society of Logistics Engineers, New Brunswick, New Jersey (CHAPTER 14)

Joel S. Hirschhorn, Ph.D.   President, Hirschhorn and Associates HGCL, Lanham, Maryland (CHAPTER 2)

Ravi K. Jain, Ph.D., P.E.   Associate Dean, University of Cincinnati, Cincinati, Ohio (Formerly Director, Army Environmental Policy Institute) (CHAPTER 4)

Rao V. Kolluru, DrPH   Director, Environmental Health Services, CH2M Hill, Reston, Virginia (CHAPTERS 4, 11, 12, and 16)

George P. Korfiatis, Ph.D.   Director, Center for Environmental Engineering, Stevens Institute of Technology, Hoboken, New Jersey (CHAPTER 5)

Frederick J. Long   Executive Director, Management Institute for Environment and Business, Washington, D.C. (CHAPTER 19)

Gary E. Marchant, Ph.D., J.D.   Kirkland & Ellis, Washington, D.C. (CHAPTER 10)

Morton L. Mullins   Vice President, Chemical Manufacturers Association, Washington, D.C. (CHAPTER 7)

Henry R. Norman, J.D.   President, Volunteers in Technical Assistance, Arlington, Virginia (CHAPTER 22)

Ann C. Pizzorusso   Director, Environmental Affairs, North American Philips, New York, New York (CHAPTER 4)

James E. Post, Ph.D., J.D.   Professor of Management, Boston University, Boston, Masschusetts (CHAPTER 1)

Jackie Prince   Staff Scientist, Environmental Defense Fund, Washington, D.C. (CHAPTER 8)

Vincent A. Rocco, P.E.   Chairman and CEO, TRC Companies, Inc., Windsor, Connecticut (CHAPTER 17)

Allan Rosenfield, M.D.   Dean, Columbia University School of Public Health, New York, New York (CHAPTER 21)

Stephan Schmidheiny, J.D.   Chairman, Business Council for Sustainable Development (and Unotec), Geneva, Switzerland (LOOKING FORWARD)

Michael E. Silverstein   President, Environmental Economics, Philadelphia, Pennsylvania (CHAPTER 16)

Andrew Steer   Deputy Director, Environment Department, The World Bank, Washington, D.C. (CHAPTER 20)

Will Wade-Gery   Consultant, Environment Department, The World Bank, Washington, D.C. (CHAPTER 20)

Scott A. Weiner, J.D.   Commissioner, New Jersey Department of Environmental Protection and Energy, Trenton, New Jersey (CHAPTER 4)

Reviewers

Michael S. Baram, J.D.   Boston University School of Law, Boston, Massachusetts.

A. W. Bazemore, Ph.D.   Director, Executive Training Concepts, Cedar Grove, New Jersey

Paul Brandt-Rauf, Sc.D., M.D., DrPH.   Director, Occupational Medicine, Columbia Presbyterian Medical Center and School of Public Health, New York, New York

John V. Conner, Ph.D.   Woodward-Clyde Consultants, Franklin, Tennessee

Hans Ebenfelt   Chairman, Board of Directors, Systecom A.B., New York, New York

Daniel C. Esty   Deputy Assistant Administrator, U.S. Environmental Protection Agency, Washington, D.C.

Alan L. Farkas   Managing Director, Farkas Berkowitz & Co., Washington, D.C.

Grant Ferrier   President, Environmental Business International, San Diego, California

Jeffrey Himmelberger, Ph.D.   Clark University, Worcester, Massachusetts

Jon C. Holtzman   Vice President-Communications, Chemical Manufacturers Association, Washington, D.C.

Robert F. Housman, J.D.   Law Fellow, Center for International Environmental Law, Washington, D.C.

Ronald A. Lang   President, American Industrial Health Council (AIHC) and SOCMA, Washington, D.C.

William J. Librizzi   Director, Technical Services, OHM Corporation, Princeton, New Jersey

Trevor Russel   Communications Director, Business Council for Sustainable Development, Geneva, Switzerland

W. Leigh Short, Ph.D.   Vice President, Woodward-Clyde Consultants, Wayne, New Jersey

Bruce Smart   Senior Fellow, World Resources Institute, Washington, D.C.

H. Michael Utidjian, M.D.   Corporate Medical Director, American Cyanamid Co., Wayne, New Jersey

Preface

This handbook is about our environment—the air, the water, the land, the energy, the biosphere—the fundamental resources that sustain human life and economic development. Paraphrasing a DuPont commercial, one might ask: What in the world isn't environmental?

A quiet and yet profound transformation is occurring in the environmental field: from a traditional approach focusing predominantly on pollution control, *end-of-pipe* treatment and compliance costs to one that emphasizes long-range capital investments for prevention, income, and competitive advantage; from an awkward appendage of the business plan to an integral part of the strategic planning process, occasionally fortified by life-cycle thinking; and from preoccupation with efficiency (doing things right) to increasing emphasis on effectiveness (doing the right thing).

On the regulatory side, the fractionated media (air, water, land) programs are beginning to yield to more unified multi-media approaches; *command-and-control* and confrontational tactics to market-based incentives and cooperation among the stakeholders; purely technology-based standards to a combination of technology and health-based standards; and human-centered policies to those aimed at protecting ecological resources in their own right, independent of their economic value to humans (*Homo sapiens*, after all, is only one of perhaps a hundred million species inhabiting this planet).

Abraham Lincoln said public opinion in a democracy counts for everything. In a sense, the global environmental movement is an egalitarian expression. It is the poorer members of society who have more to gain from improved environmental quality; they cannot "buy out" of pollution problems. Further, it is poverty or "socioeconomic status" that presents the greatest public health and environmental threat, concomitant with population growth and density. For the environment, as well as public health, the optimal course of action is to balance restoration, preservation, conservation, and prevention.

This handbook explores these concepts and strategies within the framework of resource management, stewardship, and sustainable development. As Stephan Schmidheiny observes in "Looking Forward," what we are seeking here is to promote a pattern of economic and social development that meets our needs today without compromising the capacity of future generations to fulfill their own aspirations.

A preoccupation with the environment is not what this book is about—rather, it is about expanding the stakeholders and the time horizon (by at least two generations) and incorporating environmental, health, and safety (EHS) priorities in management thinking along with other strategic issues.

This volume is without precedents in its scope and reach. Most publications in the environmental field have addressed a single or a few topics such as air or water pollution control, remediation technologies, risk assessment, or eco-marketing. What you will find in this handbook are many traditional topics, but some *bottom line* issues as well. These are presented in eight parts and 22 chapters, written by more than 30 distinguished authors from industry, consulting firms, government, and educational institutions. The coverage ranges from regulatory framework to pollution prevention, to liability and financial issues to risk assessment and public health, to life-cycle analysis and resource mangement, to environmental business strategies, to global perspectives—supplemented by numerous cases and illustrations.

In developing the contents, we sought a balance between concepts and "how-to," between technical and business information, between U.S. and global issues. The main objective has been to offer guidance to decision makers within and outside the corporate world for developing and implementing resource-effective environmental, health, and safety strategies. We hope the handbook will serve as a comprehensive reference for technical and business executives alike, as well as for graduate students in environmental science and business programs.

I would like to express my gratitude to the authors for completing their chapters expeditiously to allow timely publication of the handbook, despite their extraordinarily busy schedules. The ideas expressed and the writing styles are those of the individual authors, with only minor editing performed to achieve consistency. I also want to express my appreciation to those who reviewed chapters and offered valuable comments.

I would also like to thank Woodward-Clyde Consultants for providing support and secretarial assistance; the handbook chapters were written and edited while I was with that firm. Thanks are also due to CH2M Hill, with which I am now associated, for support with the follow-up tasks during the production process.

A handbook such as this would not be possible without the contribution of colleagues, friends, and students, and the forbearance of our families. Special thanks go to McGraw-Hill Professional Book Group, in particular Gail F. Nalven, Senior Editor, for her guidance and perseverance; and to Sybil Parker, Publisher, Peggy Lamb, Editing Supervisor, and Suzanne Babeuf, Production

Supervisor, who transformed the weighty manuscript into this handbook on a fast track.

The success of the book of course depends on how useful it actually proves to be. We welcome your comments on what you have found of interest and what additional topics you would like to see included in future editions.

Rao V. Kolluru

Acknowledgments

When this handbook was in the early conceptual stage in the fall of 1991, in order to identify what it should address and how best it could serve its intended audience (technical and business management), a cursory survey was conducted eliciting the views of those listed below. These valuable responses were considered in developing the content of this handbook, but the final decision on what was included was, of course, that of the editor and the authors. Here is a collective interpretation of the responses; some of these are reflections on the current situation, while others are suggestions for strategic change.

Observations

- Until the 1980s, the environmental movement was largely compliance driven (tactical phase), now it is moving into voluntary initiatives and heading toward strategic integration (e.g., life-cycle planning). By and large, the environment has not yet become integral to the strategic planning process.

- Pervasive fear of environmental liabilities and civil and criminal penalties detract from routine business management (although initially necessary in some cases).

- The Right-to-Know (more) laws have been a potent force for change in the way business is conducted in North America and Europe.

- Competition for funds—there is no question that funds will be available for compliance. Voluntary initiatives compete with other projects; the CEO, however, can preempt financial hurdles (which are based on conventional capital budgeting and accounting).

- A significant convergence of interests of various stakeholders is beginning to occur: organizational managers, employees/labor, owners/investors, communities, consumers, governments, environmentalists, public health professionals, trade advocates, and future generations (while the debate continues on international competitiveness and cross boundary concerns). Interdisciplinary convergence within organizations is also occurring in parallel.

Suggested Actions

- Industry should preempt regulations by foresight, enlightened self-interest, and offering sound scientific bases for legislation. Chemical Manufacturers Association (CMA) Responsible Care® Codes of Management Practices are a vital part and illustrative of such initiatives.

- Abolish or restructure Superfund. Eliminate RCRA's more onerous provisions. Some 70 to 90% of remediation expenditures are not actually going into clean-up actions, in part due to the adversarial relationships between government, industry, and environmentalists.

- Stop chasing imaginary risks and focus on proven public health risks. Prioritize problems and needs, and allocate resources on the basis of health and safety risks; focus on risk reduction rather than *background levels*.

- Allow flexibility in the means of achieving environmental goals, where appropriate, through economic incentives and market based approaches.

- Coordinate and harmonize environmental, health, and safety (EHS) policies and programs with international bodies such as the Organization for Economic Cooperation and Development (OECD), and United Nations Environment Programme (UNEP) and World Health Organization (WHO).

- Almost unanimously expressed sentiment: What is the *right* thing to do? How can we determine the right thing? How should we communicate that we are doing the right thing?

Among the many executives who shared their ideas and insights, we would especially like to thank the following:

Dorothy P. Bowers
Vice President
Merck & Co., Inc.

Albert J. Costello
President
American Cyanamid Company

David Eastman
Vice President
Lonza, Inc.

Thomas Hellman
Vice President, Corp. Environmental Affairs
Bristol-Myers Squibb Company

Robert T. Jackson
Director, Environmental Affairs
Union Carbide Corporation

Jack S. Kace
Assistant Vice President
Hoffmann-LaRoche, Inc.

James C. Lime
Vice President, Environmental Affairs
Warner Lambert Company

Joseph F. Terenzi
Vice President
American Cyanamid Company

Looking Forward:

Our Common Enterprise

Stephan Schmidheiny*

In 1990, Maurice Strong, the secretary general of the United Nations Conference on Environment and Development (UNCED), asked me to serve as his principal adviser on business and industry. Seeking safety and wisdom in numbers, I asked 47 other chief executive officers and board chairmen and chairwomen to join me in a Business Council for Sustainable Development (BCSD). We planned to draft a report from business to the conference, held in June 1992.

The Plan

We began our work with two things in common. First, we were all overwhelmed by the uncertainty and controversy surrounding so many of the crucial environmental issues, such as climate change, ozone depletion, and loss of species. Second, we all agreed that the broad concept of "sustainable development" was a worthy goal for society in general and business in particular.

It is difficult to be against a pattern of economic and social development meant to meet the needs of those living today without compromising the ability of future generations to meet their own needs. From both a political and a busi-

*Stephan Schmidheiny is a Swiss industrialist and chairman of the Business Council for Sustainable Development. He served as principal adviser for business and industry to the secretary general of the UN Conference on Environment and Development (UNCED), Rio de Janeiro, June 1992. Mr. Schmidheiny, with the Council, wrote *Changing Course: A Global Business Perspective on Development and the Environment* (MIT Press, Cambridge, Massachusetts), the Council's report to UNCED, now available commercially in seven languages.

1

ness point of view, it makes a great deal of sense to avoid damaging spillovers between generations, and also between regions and social groups.

But as we debated, we realized that any real move toward sustainable development will not be merely environmental; it will mean change in economic, social, and political systems. It will require a revolution, a change in civilization from one based on consumption and short-term competition to one based on conservation and equity between generations.

I think that revolution is already under way. But it is by no means clear that we shall be able to change fast enough and efficiently enough to prevent a great deal of human suffering and damage to major natural systems. We are challenged as a species to implement economic and social changes of great magnitude and to innovate in our technology, social organization, and the dissemination of know-how.

Sustainable development must be adapted to local conditions. Different cultural and historical backgrounds create different perceptions and interpretations of facts. Different knowledge and experience may lead to different proposals on ways and means. Different personal values may create a different order of priorities in addressing problems and in seeking solutions.

Yet, in the interests of sustainable development, patterns of conflict and cooperation between business leaders, politicians, public administrators, and conservationists will have to change. A common vision must motivate a common enterprise. For sustainable development can be achieved only through a new and strong partnership between governments, business, citizens' groups, and the broader society that comprises consumers, voters, and those who through their daily actions are the planet's true environmental decision makers.

Business has a great deal to offer to the search for sustainable development. The World Commission on Environment and Development, which in its 1987 report *Our Common Future* called for the holding of such a conference as UNCED, identified among the prerequisites for sustainable development an environmentally sound production system that fosters sustainable patterns of trade and finance. Given the key roles of business and industry in production, technology, trade, and finance, it is crucial that we offer leadership in the search for sustainability.

Business is, after all, the world's foremost creator of wealth, employment, trade, and technology, as well as the controller of tremendous human and financial resources. It is the system by which value is added to resources, and the major system through which basic human needs are met. It is also a culture which transcends and binds other cultures, in that businesspeople from different continents and backgrounds can deal, through business, with one another. What is more, the multinational companies are among the few private organizations powerful enough to influence international environmental and development problems. They often take a longer term and more international view than governments themselves.

Businesspeople are often more experienced than politicians in the practice of weighing risks and making decisions based on uncertainty. We do it daily.

Political and economic decisions with far-reaching consequences must be made quickly; and they will of necessity be based on incomplete scientific evidence and knowledge. The risks implied by such decisions must be weighed against the risks implied by no decisions. We must work with governments and the general public to see that the right alternatives are chosen.

The challenge for business is to use its capabilities and resources in a responsible and sustainable way. The fundamental problem—from a business and perhaps from any other perspective—lies in the fact that market prices for energy and raw materials tend to reflect only their direct costs—or even less than their direct costs if they are subsidized. Prices reflect neither ecological costs, in terms of the damage goods and services do to the environment, nor the depletion of natural capital when a nonrenewable resource is being used.

The cost of environmental damage must be internalized into the prices of goods and services. In fact this was agreed upon by OECD countries in the early 1970s in the "polluter pays principle." When we started discussing our report, many BCSD members doubted the wisdom of calling for prices that reflect environmental as well as economic reality. But we gradually realized that this was the key to changing both technology and consumption patterns toward sustainability.

From a business perspective, sustainable development implies a fundamentally new approach not only to the relationship between the economy and the environment, but also to the very nature of economic development itself. It implies:

- A shift from growth to *development*. Growth means simply that things get bigger. But when systems develop they get better, more efficient. Certainly, growth will be necessary to meet the needs of growing populations and of the one-fifth of the present global population that lives in poverty. But we have to decouple growth from environmental degradation.

- A shift toward more *efficiency* in the use of natural resources, especially energy. This implies resources, investments, development, training, and venture capital.

- A shift toward an economy of *opportunity*, one that facilitates entrepreneurial access to markets and technological capacities. This includes better access to credit, to markets, and to appropriate technologies, both for individuals and for nations.

- A shift toward an economy of *conservation*, with incentives to integrate environmental values into business practices. This means recycling, remanufacturing, and a repair economy in which the developing world would enjoy many advantages.

- A shift toward an economy promoting *long-term investment* and capital gains, rather than short-term profit maximization. This means new approaches to taxation, and a new corporate vision which extends beyond the next quarterly dividend.

- A shift to a *savings* culture, rather than one built on immediate consumption. This applies equally to individuals, corporations, and governments.

These changes require a quick but intensive learning process. Business has proved itself capable of adapting to rapidly changing circumstances, and can do so in the present circumstances.

Changing the Rules

More efficiency, opportunity, and innovation are needed but will be possible only if set within national and international policy frameworks that open markets and allow free competition. These are the best systems in which businesses can minimize resource use, in the interests of remaining competitive, and can minimize pollution, in the interests of reducing waste.

But these markets and that competition have become distorted by faults of omission and commission. First, as I noted, we have omitted to include in our cost calculations the costs of environmental degradation. Most of the errors of commission center around the range of environmentally damaging subsidies which have grown up in an illogical, ad hoc way over the years. These include subsidies to over-use pesticides, fertilizers, and water, to clear forests, and to squander various forms of energy.

Business has to support governments in changing market frameworks so that full environmental costs are reflected and distorting subsidies are phased out.

More open markets will require better "rules of the game" and more efficient public institutions. In developing countries with weak or no traditions of open markets, improving the rules of the game will demand far-reaching institutional reforms.

Clear and consistent rules of the game are also important at the microeconomic level. The practice of environmental management must expand from local pollution control to an integrated responsibility for the total life cycle of the product and all of the effects of producing it.

Governments have two types of options in encouraging industries toward cleaner habits. One is straight regulation—the old "command and control" approach. There will always be a need for regulations to maintain minimal standards and to handle situations of acute risk. But we know from experience that enforcement is expensive and that it tends to stifle technical innovations that might encourage companies to surpass minimal standards.

So business favors greater reliance on the use of economic instruments— incentives, taxes, tradable permits, user charges, deposit refund systems, etc. There is far less experience with these, but they proved their ability to encourage industry to use its creativity to surpass regulatory norms. They are less costly to enforce, and compliance is cost-effective.

There is also great scope for self-regulation. This may seem a self-serving recommendation on the part of industry and it is; but the best companies have already found that setting—and announcing—tough environmental targets for themselves is good business. It also means that business can play a bigger role in setting the agenda for the transition toward sustainable development, rather than leaving the agenda setting to governments.

A New "Developing World"

On the one hand, environmental destruction has become ever more visible and menacing. Urgent change is now essential to avoid irreparable damage to the global environment. On the other hand, it has become widely recognized that a halt to growth is economically and morally indefensible, particularly for the developing countries and in the former Eastern Bloc.

At least a billion people live in poverty in the developing world. These unfortunate people can hardly be denied the benefits of economic growth. Furthermore, the reconstruction of eastern Europe and the Soviet Union will require huge amounts of capital. Growth is essential to improve the quality of human existence, especially considering that the global human population is expected to at least double next century, and that more than 90 percent of this growth is expected to occur in the developing world.

If the developing countries fail to generate sufficient growth, there are risks of massive population displacements. Already hundreds of thousands flee poverty each year. Most of the migrations of the poor take place inside the developing world, but not all of them.

Not only is this developing world poverty morally unjustifiable, it is environmentally destructive. One of the major threats to the global environment is caused by people living in poverty, who have virtually no real choice except to burn their forests and over-use their land and their resources just to secure a livelihood. This is not to blame the poor, but to blame the policies and social organizations that keep so many people poor. Unfortunately, much of the conventional development process also poses a danger to nature, because of the almost unchecked growth of many pollution-intensive industries.

In industrialized nations, improving the quality of the natural environment is perceived as a way of improving the quality of life. Industrialized nations also have democratic mechanisms to change government policies and have the necessary resources at their disposal to act systematically. Too often in developing countries, "quality of life" is primarily a question of having enough food and basic shelter.

There can be no doubt that, in global terms, those who are better off economically will have to make a relatively larger contribution to resolving common problems. This notion was broadly accepted long ago within national boundaries. No citizen of a European country would seriously dispute the fact that someone who has a bigger income must pay more taxes—taxes that are spent, among other things, for the preservation of the natural environment. Following the well-accepted principle of national solidarity, we have to establish a new base for international solidarity with the less developed parts of the world.

Among other things, we need to reexamine the current pattern of global capital flows that has had such a devastating effect on developing world countries: in 1991, developing country debts increased to almost $1500 billion. Many of these debts have performed no valid economic function in the debtor countries. A substantial part of the money has been wasted or siphoned off overseas by elites.

As a result of the debt burden, developing countries are now forced to deplete more and more of their resources and sell them at decreasing world market prices. This vicious and depressing cycle sadly enough sets the general conditions under which a rapidly growing population must pursue its legitimate objective of raising its standard of living. But the developing countries have been unable to escape this fate by their own efforts. It is therefore our obligation in the wealthier parts of the world to create a new vision of global solidarity by which we will actively contribute to sustainable development in the developing world and help provide the basis for better lives for their children as well as our own.

A Vision for the Next Millennium

The BCSD held more than 50 meetings in 20 countries. As we met, we sought a common denominator that could link business, the environment, and the increasing human needs of this generation and the larger generations of the future. We found that the concept of *efficiency* offers that link. Efficiency keeps companies competitive; it adds most value with the least use of natural resources; and it is crucial in the fight against mass poverty in the world. (Of course, one must always be sure that one is effective or "doing the right thing" before one becomes concerned with "doing it right"—or efficiently.)

We coined the term "eco-efficiency" to describe those corporations that produce ever more useful goods and services while continuously reducing resource consumption and pollution.

Some governments, and many businesspeople, fear that business excellence and environmental concern cannot be combined. We found the opposite; they cannot be separated. We all agreed, after studying worldwide business trends, that tomorrow's winners will be those who make the most and the fastest progress in improving their eco-efficiency. Why?

- Customers are demanding cleaner products.
- Banks are more willing to lend to companies that prevent pollution rather than pay for cleanup.
- Insurance companies are more amenable to covering clean companies.
- Employees prefer to work for environmentally responsible corporations.

- Environmental regulations are getting tougher.

- New economic instruments—taxes, charges, and tradable permits are rewarding clean companies.

All these trends, which will accelerate as science offers more evidence of environmental damage, mean that investments in eco-efficiency will help, rather than hurt, profitability. It is the eco-efficient companies that will emerge more competitive as these trends take hold.

This is also true of the eco-efficient nations. Professor Michael Porter, at Harvard Business School, reported after a global study that it was the nations with the most rigorous environmental standards at home that often led in the export of the very products affected by those standards. He mentioned the success of Germany and Japan, and also the success of the chemicals, plastics, and paints industries of the United States.

Sustainable development is today a vision which must be made real. Open markets can help in this transformation, but only if business plays its proper leadership role. This will require new and more intense working partnerships between business, government, and nongovernmental organizations (NGOs). Sustainable development is a challenge for innovation in institutions, organizations, communications, and politics.

The prospect of a world in 2025 of over eight billion people, hopefully enjoying a higher standard of living, requires a fundamental reorientation of the quality and quantity of economic development to ensure that it is less environmentally damaging and more equitable. This reorientation would make existing definitions of whether countries are "developed" or "developing" obsolete; all are unsustainable to a lesser or greater degree. All countries now need to set in motion the process of developing anew.

The complexity of the challenges, and the diversity of circumstances of nations, mean that there can be no static blueprint for sustainable development. Rather, sustainable development is a dynamic process of constant improvement.

Two major efforts are needed over the short term:

- To reduce the environmental impacts of the affluent countries, which contribute the bulk of current pollution problems such as ozone depletion and climate change

- To improve the economic opportunities of the developing world

Only through improved standards of living in developing countries, which mean improved chances of survival for children, can population growth be slowed and the environmental consequences of poverty be avoided.

Trends in population size, economic growth, and resource use show, however, that in the long run the issue will become one of managing the capacity of this globe of ours to carry the environmental demands placed upon it. The onus is on the affluent North to take the lead in establishing new economic frameworks and new technologies that foster globally sustainable development. Only in this way can developing countries avoid making the same mistakes we have already made in the North and define a new quality of lasting development.

There are two well-known statistics which, taken together, sum up the challenge facing the world in the next millennium. First, the roughly 20 percent of the world's population which lives in the wealthy industrial countries consume about 80 percent of the world's resources, leaving the four-fifths of the people who live in the poorer, developing countries only one-fifth of the resources. Second, over 90 percent of future population growth is expected to be in the poorer, resource-starved nations.

Therein lies the ultimate, double-edged challenge for business and industry: to be a part of the solution, rather than part of the problem, of pollution and wasteful consumption in the North, while devising ways to turn the rapidly growing needs of the South into markets in which those needs can be met.

We in business are slowly coming to see sustainable development as "our common enterprise," one which unites the goals of all the many businesses from the many nations of the world into one effort to protect our common future.

PART 1

Business, Environment, and Stewardship

1

Environmental Approaches and Strategies: Regulation, Markets, and Management Education

James E. Post, Ph.D., J.D.
School of Management,
Boston University

In this chapter:

- Government regulation
- Market incentives
- Education-oriented policies
- Costs of a clean environment
- Environmentalism after the Earth Summit
- Role of Business and Management Education

This chapter outlines some of the approaches and strategies nations use to develop and achieve environmental goals. National programs to protect air, water, land, and biological resources (the "global commons") range from highly authoritarian to highly voluntary efforts, with widely varying degrees of government involvement. Even a cursory comparison of how the world's most industrialized nations such as the United States, Japan, and Germany pursue their environmental objectives discloses an array of policy approaches. The range and variety of such efforts underscore what one public policy expert observed years ago: "There are many paths to Nirvana."

Three distinct approaches guide environmental management in most industrialized nations. To a great extent, newly industrializing nations mirror these same approaches, although the mix may be quite different in individual political settings. Some place heavy emphasis on the role of government as a standard setter and executor of environmental action programs. Others rely on the "magic of the marketplace" and emphasize incentives or other inducements

Government Regulation	Market Incentives	Education-Oriented
Key assumptions		
Pollution is an externality problem	"Carrots" are more effective than "sticks"	People will act in environmentally responsible ways if educated
Government must set rules for all to follow	Incentive systems can be created within regulatory frameworks	Knowledge and information are the key tools to changing behavior
Approaches		
Set quality standards	Pollution charges	Right-to-know information programs
Set emissions standards	Carbon taxes on fuel use	Green seals, eco-logos, or other designations of preferred products
"Bubbles" and other aggregate concepts	Buying and selling pollution rights	
Pollution taxes		Environmental awards, citations, or other recognition
		"Partnership" programs among voluntary participants

Figure 1-1. Three basic approaches to environmental management.

that will lead organizations and individuals to behave in environmentally desirable ways. Finally, there are initiatives that emphasize voluntary behavior by organizations and individuals as part of their normal, routine ways of operating and living. These approaches are discussed below as (1) regulation-oriented, (2) market-oriented, and (3) education-oriented policies and programs. While individual nations tend generally to favor one or another of these approaches to environmental policymaking, it is noteworthy that many nations are developing combinations of programs that draw on all three approaches. These integrated approaches may be the policy wave of the future in light of the discussions at the 1992 Earth Summit in Rio de Janeiro and the consensus that new ideas must be tried if the world is to respond effectively to the urgency of our environmental problems. As the mid-1990s approach, environmental policy has become the crucible for innovative and imaginative collaboration among business, government, environmentalists, and the public.

Government Regulation

Government can apply pollution controls in a variety of ways even though one of the most widely used methods of regulation is to impose standards based on the implementation of best available or demonstrated technology. This is intended to bring state-of-the-art technology to bear on pollution problems. In order to address different pollutants, pollution sources, economic conditions, and technological features, governments need to use alternative approaches. Some of the alternative approaches that have been employed on a limited basis with good results are economic incentives, environmental standards, pollution charges, and the creation of a market for the buying and selling of pollution rights.

Incentives for Environmental Improvement

Governments may offer various types of incentives to firms that reduce their pollution. Sometimes these incentives work toward standards that may eventually be required. At other times they work for any improvement. For example, the government may decide to purchase only from those firms that meet certain pollution standards, or it may offer aid to those installing pollution-control equipment. Tax incentives, such as faster depreciation for pollution-control equipment, may also be used.

A major advantage of incentives is that they encourage voluntary improvement without the stigma of governmental force. They allow different industries and businesses to proceed at a pace that is best for their individual situation. Further, some businesses may be encouraged by incentives to go beyond the minimum standards of compliance that a regulation would have been able to achieve.

The main disadvantage of incentives is that what is voluntary may not be accomplished at all. The incentives may be too small, or there may be side effects, such as expensive product or process redesign, that reduce the appeal of such action for companies. In such instances, a better incentive can be offered or government can use its regulatory powers to require compliance.

Environmental Standards

One of the long-standing and most common approaches to environmental protection has been the issuance of environmental standards. The U.S. Congress has often passed legislation that directs the Environmental Protection Agency (EPA) or other regulatory body to set standards that will secure a broad, albeit vague, legislative objective, such as to "protect public health." Directives of this sort permit the agency to determine which of several types of standards it will use. For example, an *environmental quality standard* defines the level of a particular pollutant in the air or water, possibly in terms of volume or a concentration level. The setting of ambient-air standards, for example, applies this environmental quality standard approach.

Alternatively, regulators may choose to develop an *emission standard,* which specifies the amount of a type of emission from a particular source to the environment. The setting of such standards requires an understanding of the real risk posed to the environment by the emission and also an understanding of the complexity or difficulty that the polluter will have in reaching the emission standard.

Regulators actually use combinations of environmental quality and emission standards in dealing with air and water pollution. Federal officials often set national environmental quality standards, with local implementation undertaken by local or state officials through the application of emission controls (e.g., filters, scrubbers) that help achieve the national environmental quality goals.

One advantage of environmental standards is that they are enforceable in the courts. This helps assure that their requirements will be met. Moreover, the standards must be applied across-the-board to all polluters, and there is a greater likelihood that the broad environmental goals will actually be met than if the compliance was left to voluntary action. One disadvantage is that the national standard may be difficult or impossible to implement adequately across diverse industries, geographic locations, and technologies. These obstacles may lead to either a watering down of the standard or a series of variances or rulings that permit exceptions from the standard.

A second disadvantage is the heavy reliance on the administrative agency that is charged with enforcing the law. Regrettably, laws are often weakened or undermined by poor administrative enforcement which may itself be the result of limited resources, enthusiasm, or political will. Across-the-board standards also may cause inequity and suffering because each business faces a different pollution-control problem. Older, less efficient plants, for example, face problems because it is often costly to renovate them, while building a new, nonpolluting plant may not be justified because of capital costs or market conditions (see Box 1-1).

Box 1-1. "Regulatory Roulette": A Case Example

The paper and pulp industry is one of EPA's "big five" industries when it comes to pollution-control spending. Pulp and paper mill operations involve significant air and water emissions. Moreover, mill operations require enormous volumes of water each day, thereby necessitating the location of mills near rivers, lakes, and oceans.

The Clean Water Act established a framework for setting national water quality standards. The Environmental Protection Agency has broad authority to grant permits for operations like paper mills that use water resources and discharge effluent. This authority often overlaps that of state agencies to grant operating permits.

The Pigeon River runs from the mountains of western North Carolina into the eastern portion of Tennessee. Since 1913, Champion International Corporation has operated a pulp and paper mill facility in Canton, N.C., on the banks of the Pigeon River. The effluent from Champion's mill enters the Pigeon, affecting the river's color, odor, and composition. For most of its history, the chlorine bleaching processes at the mill resulted in a discharge of dioxin into the Pigeon River. In the 1980s, as the effects of dioxin became more widely understood, pressure mounted on all paper companies to limit their dioxin discharges. In North Carolina, Champion's operating permit renewal was held up until North Carolina officials were satisfied that the company had a plan to address environmental issues.

North Carolina's acceptance was not enough, however. The state of Tennessee, responding to concerns from citizens who lived near the Pigeon River, and to economic interests which sought to expand the recreational potential of the area, insisted that North Carolina not grant the permit until Champion satisfied Tennessee officials that the environmental plan was acceptable. Champion was caught in a cross fire of litigation, regulatory maneuvering, and state-to-state and federal-state negotiations. The company was operating on a temporary permit, needed to make very substantial investments in the facility (estimated at more than $200 million), but could not be certain that approvals would be granted after the investment was made.

Champion's senior management made the decision to go forward with the Canton modernization project after being unable to resolve the uncertainties. More than $300 million will be spent by 1994 to address water quality, water conservation, and air and water discharge issues. The modernized mill will use nearly one-third less water for operations, will significantly decrease air and water discharges, and will eliminate dioxin releases by changing its bleaching processes.

Champion has been involved in a process of "regulatory roulette" which could have been very costly. The inability of the states of North Carolina and

---

(Continued)

Tennessee to agree on water quality standards, and the difficulties facing EPA in addressing the problem, nearly created a situation in which the mill closed and more than 1000 jobs lost. Although a few Tennessee residents would prefer that outcome, most agree that such an economic impact would hurt the company, the communities, and the people of the region. The need to balance environmental requirements and economic realities is often torturous to achieve. But as this case illustrates, the challenge for environmental regulation, and regulators, is to facilitate that balance.

The "Bubble Concept"

In order to allow flexibility and facilitate compliance with environmental rules while still protecting the public, regulators introduced the "bubble concept." Large industrial complexes have many potential sources of pollution from numerous smokestacks, production processes, and pipes that carry liquid and gaseous products. At one time, environmental rules required that each one of these pollution sources conform to mandated standards. This requirement exacerbated the enforcement problems mentioned above, and often made compliance a virtual impossibility. Under the bubble concept, regulators treat the entire facility as if it were surrounded by an invisible "bubble," and they measure only the pollution arising from the whole bubble. This approach means that one or more of the smokestacks or discharge pipes may actually exceed the standards of the law but be allowable because emissions from the other discharge points are low enough to keep total emissions below the overall standard.

Environmental groups sometimes express concern that concepts such as bubbles and other aggregated emissions ideas give business too much flexibility and discretion. The argument that governments should not relinquish such decision-making authority to the regulated has generally failed in the face of cost-benefit calculations that show the benefits to the firm and the public of a more flexible approach. Of special value is the opportunity to phase in pollution-control expenditures (e.g., smokestack cleanups) on a planned basis over time.

Pollution Taxes

The need to meet environmental goals and do so through a system that enables firms to adapt flexibly to their special competitive and market circumstances has led to the development of various taxation proposals. As in the case of the much-discussed "carbon tax," advocates believe that such taxes will, when applied to a predetermined group of polluters (i.e., an industry that emits CO_2, for example, or disposes of toxic waste through incineration), encourage those firms to rationalize their behavior based on the costs of various alternatives. By raising the tax on CO_2 emissions or toxic incineration, an economic incentive is created for the firm to find alternative ways of managing without incurring the cost of the tax.

Pollution taxes can be designed to achieve revenue as well as regulatory objectives, and this has been a political problem for the approach. Some legislators are concerned that expansion of a pollution tax system would simply add to the fiscal problems of the nation and those industries such as petroleum and chemicals which already bear a heavy environmental tax revenue burden. Political problems notwithstanding, pollution taxes remain a middle ground alternative between regulatory standards and market-based incentives. For this reason, they are likely to remain one of the basic methods of achieving regulatory objectives in the future.

Market Incentives

Pollution Charges

An increasingly popular theme in environmental politics, and hence environmental management, is "the polluter pays" principle. Pollution charges are the obvious expression of that principle in operating terms. Governments often establish charges such as "tipping fees" (fees for the dumping of solid waste at landfills) which become a cost of doing business in an industry that generates wastes and pollution. Unlike pollution taxes, where the tax need not bear any relation to the actual expense involved, the amount of a pollution charge is normally related to the actual costs of disposal. Pollution charges must be set high enough to accomplish the desired level of pollution reduction, thereby encouraging each firm to work out its least-cost relationship for waste release or abatement according to its unique circumstances.

The advantage of pollution charges is the flexibility they provide for firms to achieve an environmental goal in ways that best mesh with other competitive realities. The principal disadvantage is expressed by critics as a "license to pollute." Many environmentalists believe it is wrong to permit some organizations to continue to foul the environment simply by paying a charge to do so. Further, some critics of the approach fear that the charges themselves may be too low to effectively discourage present polluters from changing their behavior.

Buying and Selling Pollution Rights

An especially interesting market incentive approach involves the buying and selling of pollution rights. Although it sounds contradictory to environmental goals to allow someone the right to pollute, this approach may work as effectively as others and save money at the same time.

In the Clean Air Act of 1990, Congress endorsed a major market incentive innovation when it embraced a system for buying and selling tradable pollution rights. The law established emission levels and permitted companies whose emissions were below the standard to sell their "rights" to the remaining permissible amount to firms with emissions above the standard that hence faced a penalty. The entire "system" would thereby meet the emissions reduction target but would work to encourage the most economic responses from industry.

Box 1-2. Using the Market

In October 1991, President George Bush signed an executive order creating the President's Commission on Environmental Quality (PCEQ). Twenty-five chief executives, half drawn from the private sector and half from nonprofit foundations, research institutes, and environmental organizations, were commissioned to advise the president on ways in which the private sector could be engaged in the national effort to achieve environmental goals. The commission developed or endorsed several dozen specific projects as an effort to demonstrate the possibilities for intersectoral cooperation, voluntary action, and the use of market incentives.

One of the PCEQ market-oriented efforts was an "accelerated vehicle retirement project" to demonstrate the efficacy of generating air emission credits through accelerated vehicle retirement (AVR). The project was done in cooperation with U.S. Generating Company (USGen) which was committed to building a clean-coal cogeneration facility in southern New Jersey. Supplying coal to the USGen facility meant more tugboat and barge traffic on the Delaware River and, therefore, more air emissions that could affect air quality in the state of Delaware. In response, USGen developed a program to scrap high emitting vehicles in northeastern Delaware by paying owners a $500 fee for old, high polluting vehicles. The volume and type of emissions reductions achieved in the program can then be used to offset or balance the increased emissions from barge and tugboat traffic. The use of a market incentive (payment) to owners of older, high polluting vehicles proved extremely effective, with more vehicles being offered to the program than the sponsors could accept. The project has been assessed as a highly effective example of how market incentives—and an offset concept—can be used to permit industrial activities without deterioration of air quality.

Education-Oriented Policies

Throughout the past several decades, a variety of nonregulatory, nonmarket initiatives have found expression in environmental law and policy. A unifying theme that connects these actions is a belief that individual consumers, communities, companies, managers, and employees have the capacity to influence the behavior of the businesses with which they deal. Thus consumer-oriented programs tend to empower citizens and encourage them to change their own purchasing, employment, or civic behavior in ways that will send clear signals to firms that pollute or create other environmental risks.

Right-to-Know Laws

One of the most basic and powerful policies is that of a citizen's right to know what environmental risks are present in his or her community or workplace.

Various federal, state, and local statutes now require firms to disclose various types of health and safety risks associated with operations and emissions. The assumption that underpins these efforts is that people will respond to knowledge and information regarding environmental hazards and risks. As U.S. Supreme Court Justice Louis Brandeis commented in a different era, "sunlight is the best disinfectant." At a minimum, right-to-know laws encourage people to take steps to avoid further risk exposure. Or they may be able to effectively pressure the company to change its practices. In either event, policymakers hope that by broadening and extending the public's right to know, pollution reductions will be effected.

Right-to-know laws are implemented in a variety of ways, ranging from placement of notices in publicly visible places to the publication of facility-specific data regarding toxic emissions to air, water, and land. Companies have publicly acknowledged that the mere collection and publication of such information led them to change the practices or processes that were generating the pollution discharges. As the environmental affairs manager of one Fortune 200 company said, "We tell employees that (our company) cares about them. How could we publish these data and not be committed to acting?"

Right-to-know programs are relatively inexpensive to implement and do not require the same level of enforcement of other programs. Because employees quickly learn of their rights, they are often quite vigilant about ensuring that the disclosures are made. Labor unions are also important to the enforcement of right-to-know legislation. A disadvantage of these programs is that they normally do not have the punitive sanctions necessary to mandate remedial action by the reporting firm. Some jurisdictions have responded to this problem by using right-to-know statutes in conjunction with other regulatory statutes.

"Green Seals" and Eco-labeling

A number of nongovernmental organizations have begun programs of product analysis and labeling. Through the identification and publication of "environmentally friendly" products, advocates believe the public will be better equipped to "vote with their pocketbooks." The assumption is that consumers need better information about the true characteristics of the products they purchase and that, once given, consumers will act on those data. Product-labeling systems have sprung up in Europe and Canada and are also beginning to take hold in the United States. In a number of states, efforts have been undertaken to make disclosure labeling a mandatory requirement for manufacturers and/or packagers. Most of these labeling initiatives have failed, although the margin of defeat has been small in a number of instances. The legislative future of such proposals may brighten as the public becomes more familiar with the idea and manufacturers' objections are addressed. (See Chap. 15, Environmental Marketing, for details.)

Environmental Awards and Designations

The number of awards and special designations given to organizations for exemplary environmental performance has greatly increased in recent years. These recognitions serve the purpose of publicizing environmentally positive actions, rewarding the organization involved through public relations and image enhancement. Awards are almost always a source of pride for employees and may also have some effect on stockholders, customers, and suppliers. In some instances, companies have taken to advertising their success (this has happened most clearly with the Malcolm Baldrige Quality awards). While the data on consumer responses to such environmentally recognized companies are still uneven, there seems to be a consensus that awards are always "nice to receive" and may be quite helpful to managers who are trying to find ways of leveraging environmental commitments into environmental action within the firm.

Voluntary and Partnership Programs

The Environmental Protection Agency has initiated a number of voluntary programs by which industry has committed to meeting environmental goals. For example, the "Green Lights" and "33/50 Toxics Reduction" programs have enlisted hundreds of U.S. companies into programs designed to reduce energy consumption in the first instance and reduce toxic emissions in the latter. The incentives to participate include technical assistance and cooperation, membership in a network of like-minded companies with commitments to environmental protection, and a "halo effect" that is said to be taken into account in the event of EPA enforcement actions. EPA has sought to publicize these programs, and it is expected that consumers will be educated as to the benefits being received from the participating companies.

Costs of a Clean Environment

One of the central issues of pollution control and environmental protection is its cost. In the past, the question was whether the nation could afford to clean up its environment and keep it clean. In the two decades of the modern environmental movement, the United States has invested heavily in cleaning up the environment. Figure 1-2 shows how much the Environmental Protection Agency estimates has been spent on pollution control in the United States. In 1990, more than $100 billion—or 2 percent of gross national product—was spent for environmental protection. The report points to three critical realities that shape environmental spending and policy choices.

1. Spending on environmental problems is rising significantly for governments at all levels and for businesses. Projections through the end of the century suggest nearly a doubling of pollution-control outlays between 1990 and 2000 in constant dollars. (See Chap. 16, Environmental Business, for detailed projections.)

Box 1-3. Voluntary Action: Education and Values in Action at the Boston Park Plaza Hotel

The application of environmental management techniques to service businesses trails comparable efforts in manufacturing and resource management industries. The hotel industry is an example of an important sector of the economy which has, until very recently, largely ignored its environmental impact. Today, recycling programs, energy and water conservation, and solid waste management are becoming frontier issues for the hotel business.

In 1989, Tedd Saunders was named director of environmental programs at the Boston Park Plaza Hotel, a 977-room landmark property in the heart of Boston's commercial and cultural district. Built in the 1920s, the hotel was designed by Elsworth Statler, one of America's leading hotel architects. But a hotel property—especially an older hotel property—presents many challenges for a modern environmental management program. The Saunders family has owned the Park Plaza property since 1976, rehabilitating and upgrading the hotel into a three-star property that is one of Boston's leading convention hotels.

Beginning with a program to upgrade the hotel's 1600 windows with energy-efficient thermopane installations, Tedd Saunders has engaged the hotel's staff in finding dozens of ways to reduce environmental impacts. The housekeeping staff has made it possible to move from aerosol container cleaners to refillable pump spray bottles that replace more toxic forms of cleaning fluids and reduce solid waste from throwaway containers. Numerous water-conservation measures have been taken in guest rooms and "back of the house" hotel operations such as the laundry, kitchen, and food service areas. All paper, glass, metal, and packaging materials are recycled. Plastic foam products have been eliminated, glass and china have replaced disposable plastic and paper products, and even the plastic swizzle sticks in the hotel's food and beverage operations have been replaced with wooden sticks. In total, nearly one hundred distinct environmental initiatives have been started.

Employee involvement has been a key to the success of the environmental program. Tedd Saunders has worked through the heads of the hotel's departments (e.g., engineering, purchasing, housekeeping, communications). All new employees receive orientation training; all continuing employees are involved in discussions with supervisors, managers, and the environmental program staff. Employees are increasingly enthusiastic and involved in finding new opportunities for environmental management. Incentives, awards, and effective employee communications help reinforce the message

The hotel has documented significant cost savings from the waste reduction, energy, and water-conservation programs. Moreover, Tedd Saunders can point to nearly $1 million of additional business from organizations that want to do business with the Park Plaza because of the hotel's environmental program and reputation.

(Continued)

Since the early days of the program, there has been a strong commitment to educate guests about the hotel's efforts. Printed information is present in the room, explaining the measures taken. Guests are urged to save energy and water through messages on elegant brass "eco plaques" near switches. Most importantly, guests will notice that the usual disposable plastic bottles of shampoo, lotion, and soap have been replaced by refillable dispensers. This eliminates the two million one-ounce bottles that previously went to landfills each year. Replacement has also given the hotel a big cost saving which has been used to upgrade the quality of the soap, lotion, and shampoo that are provided in the dispensers. According to Tedd Saunders, this is a classic "win win win" outcome—the guests get better quality, the hotel saves money, and the environment has less solid waste.

The hotel has received considerable recognition for its efforts. A highlight was receipt of the 1992 President's Environmental and Conservation Challenge Award for environmental quality. And the hotel is continuing its educational outreach efforts by working with industry organizations to establish workshops, programs, and models for effective environmental management in the service industry.

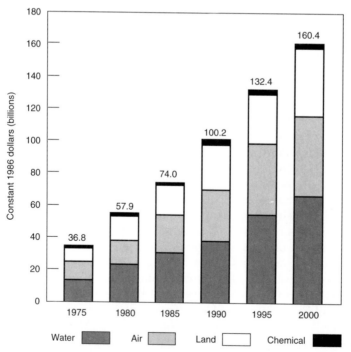

Figure 1-2. (*a*) The costs of a clean environment, and (*b*) who paid them in 1990. Estimates are in constant 1986 dollars. For more detailed projections, see Chap. 16, Environmental Business. (*Source: EPA.*)

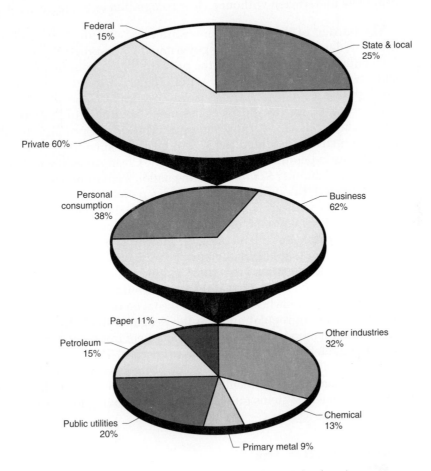

Who paid $100 billion to protect the environment in 1990

Industry invested $10.9 billion in new pollution control equipment

(b)

Figure 1-2. (*Continued*)

2. The allocation of pollution spending is shifting. Historically, the United States has spent heavily to address pollution problems in water and air media. Increasingly, land-protection issues (especially involving landfills) and multi-media pollution will demand larger portions of the pollution-control budget.

3. The costs of pollution control are rising at a time when unmet needs remain quite large. Moreover, public expectations are creating pressures for more environmental spending at the same time scientific knowledge is leading to the identification of whole new areas of environmental risk, especially global

the nation's budget deficit looms large, expansion of environmental programs cannot be undertaken without a clear recognition of the price involved.

The burden of the nation's environmental cleanup falls on both government—federal, state, and local governments accounted for about 40% of the $100 billion spent in 1990, with the private sector accounting for the remaining 60% according to EPA analysis. Within the private sector, business accounted for slightly more than 62% and personal consumption the other 38%. Five industries accounted for two-thirds of business spending: utilities (20%), petroleum (15%), chemicals (13%), pulp and paper (11%), and primary metals (9%). All other industries accounted for 32% of business spending. (These data do not include any expenditures attributable to the Clean Air Act, which has been projected to add another $25 billion to the nation's environmental bill.)

In retrospect, the 1970s and 1980s were a period in which the nation began to come to grips with years of environmental neglect. The huge expenses, plant closings, and employee layoffs were part of the "bitter medicine" business and society had to take to reclaim the environment. The nation has lived through the time when rivers could actually burn because of the toxins within them.

The 1980s demonstrated that costs had to be considered in shaping a realistic environmental agenda, one that the nation could afford. The research for more cost-effective approaches might not have taken place had there not been steadfast opposition to regulation from the Reagan administration. The insistence that market methods be tested and that all environmental initiatives meet the test of budgetary effectiveness has clearly enriched the range of options which policymakers now consider. The legacy of the past two decades is a high level of environmental commitment tempered by the need to find the most cost-effective and efficient systems for cleaning up and moving forward.

Environmentalism After the Earth Summit

The Earth Summit produced enormous global awareness of environmental risks and a mandate for action by governments, industries, nongovernmental organizations, and individuals. There is recognition that sustainable development requires aggressive new actions to achieve proper balance between economic and environmental concerns, and that nations simply must speed up their efforts to stabilize untenable situations such as the depletion of the earth's ozone layer or increases in the emission of greenhouse gases. The agenda is large, formidable in terms of obstacles to be overcome, and ingrained in the ways institutions and people behave. Yet, in the face of a global population that may double from 5 to 10 billion within the next 50 years, there is no choice but to aggressively pursue change. Indeed, many observers of global environmental trends believe that the window of opportunity of time in which action can be taken to stabilize and reverse mankind's most dangerous environmental problems is exceedingly short. That sense of urgency is being felt increasingly in national capitals in the developing and industrialized world alike.

The commitments made at the Rio meeting will lead national governments to reassess the mix of regulatory, market-based, and educational policies and programs being employed to address the environment. As always, national governments will find favor with packages that emphasize some elements and deemphasize others. In general, however, the following predictions seem safely within the framework of national diversity:

1. Remedial action to redress the worst environmental problems, and immediate environmental crises in particular, will remain the responsibility of national governments.

2. There will be increasing support for international adoption of "the polluter pays" liability principle.

3. The sharing of environmental risk information and data will become more widespread. The concept of employee and community "right to know" will be internationally accepted as the twenty-first century unfolds. The media and international scientific community will be important conduits for dissemination of global environmental risk data.

4. Market incentives (and disincentives) will be more widely employed as "carrots" to encourage individuals, organizations, and national governments to take action on environmental matters.

5. Industrialized nations, in particular, will encourage the development of their environmental technology and service industries as a form of industrial development. The global market for environmental products, technologies, and services will easily surpass $500 billion by the first decade of the next century, and could approach one trillion dollars if cleanups of military facilities and the severe problems in eastern Europe are aggressively pursued.

6. Waste reduction and elimination will continue to be the number one environmental priority for business through the early twenty-first century. By the first decade of the new century, major product design improvements will have created a generation of "waste-free" computers, manufacturing systems, and processing operations. Energy conservation will continue to be stressed, whether or not global oil prices sharply rise. Carbon taxes will reinforce the environmental message that energy conservation is a national—and global—priority.

7. National governments will experiment with educational and voluntary action programs. Public education about the importance of environmental issues to all facets of life on earth will reinforce the need for action. Public values will continue to shift in favor of environmental conservation and protection. This public support will continue to translate into marketplace decisions that stimulate companies to accelerate efforts to redress their negative environmental effects. Meanwhile, voluntary stewardship programs to protect natural

resources in industrialized and developing nations will grow in number and variety. Partnerships and other intersectoral collaborations will increase as businesses, environmental organizations, and governments recognize that shared values increase the possibilities for responding to the needs of the planetary ecosystem.

8. Scientific research will continue to expose new risks in the environment and disclose new risks *to* the environment from human industrial activity. The availability of new (instrumentation) and expanded (satellites) scientific technologies will enable researchers to identify and analyze the global aspects of environmental risk more readily and effectively.

These predictions are, in some measure, already occurring since the 1992 Earth Summit. The remainder of the 1990s will see a significant increase in their development along the lines mentioned above. In general, two principles will guide this evolution: (1) cooperation is a necessary and desirable form of interaction to address environmental concerns; and (2) at every level of action—individual, organizational, and national—incentives are being sought to encourage voluntary behavior that responds to environmental needs.

The Role of Business and Management Education

Since the 1970s, when the modern environmental era began, many areas of professional education have responded to the need for environmental understanding. Most of the nation's law schools have offered courses and seminars in environmental regulation for nearly two decades; engineering programs have increasingly focused on chemical, industrial, civil, and materials engineering challenges; a new generation of interdisciplinary programs in "environmental science" have integrated biological, chemical, and ecological knowledge; and a number of universities have created institutes, centers, and programs in energy and environmental studies. Such discipline-based and interdisciplinary programs have provided much of the technical education foundation for business to address the environmental challenges it faces. Ironically, however, business and management education itself has been woefully negligent in addressing the challenges of the environment.

Prior to 1989, there was virtually no graduate or undergraduate business school program or coursework focused on environmental problems. Some business school faculty discussed environmental problems as a topic in "business, government, and society" or "business ethics" courses, but such treatment was inevitably cursory. Change began to occur in the late 1980s when the National Wildlife Federation/Corporate Conservation Council (NWF/CCC) focused on business education as one of its "outreach program" projects. The council, consisting of 20 corporations with large environmental involvements and progressive environmental management programs (including AT&T, ABB-Asea Brown

Boveri, BFI, Dow Chemical, Du Pont, Johnson & Johnson, 3M, Monsanto, USX, and Waste Management), was concerned that no American business schools were teaching about the environmental imperatives that so seriously affected their businesses. The council members conducted a series of discussions with business school faculty and in 1988 launched a program with three universities (Boston University, Loyola of New Orleans, and the University of Minnesota) to develop pilot courses in environmental management. The first course was offered at Boston University in the fall 1989 semester; the Loyola and Minnesota courses followed in the spring 1990 term. By the end of 1992, each of these schools had offered the courses to several hundred business school students (graduate and undergraduate) and shared course information, teaching materials, and environmental management case studies with hundreds of faculty from the United States, Europe, Japan, and at least 15 other countries. The NWF/CCC curriculum project has proved to be the "right idea at the right time" in bringing environmental management into business education.

EPA also sponsored a project to create an infrastructure for continued environmental education at the collegiate and university level by encouraging the development of the Management Institute for Environment and Business (MEB). MEB has established a clearinghouse for case studies and other resource materials, launched a research and case writing program, and established curriculum-development partnerships with eight leading business schools: Northwestern, Stanford, Texas, Duke, NYU, Yale, Michigan, and Virginia. In each, faculty are working with MEB staff to introduce environmental management concepts into basic business courses such as accounting, operations management, marketing, strategic management, and in some instances to create modules or courses dealing exclusively with environmental and natural resource issues. Each partnership is also expected to yield an additional stock of teaching materials and case studies that will be available to faculty throughout the United States and abroad.

These efforts have helped propel environmental management education toward the mainstream business school curriculum. In addition to the schools named above, by 1992 such leading public and private universities as UCLA, Harvard, Massachusetts Institute of Technology (MIT), Pennsylvania (Wharton), Indiana, Emory, Wisconsin, and Tennessee had established an "environmental beachhead" in their business schools. Many of these universities also have environmental education programs in engineering, law, and natural sciences that provide collegial and academic support to the business school faculty.

This form of cross-disciplinary cooperation and collaboration is basic to the future of effective environmental management. Universities such as Tufts, which has a Center for Environmental Management but no business school, have provided leadership through across-the-curriculum initiatives. Tufts, for example, has been especially proactive in drawing together faculty from the natural sciences, humanities, and other disciplines to share ideas on how environmental awareness and issues are affecting all aspects of human existence from philosophy to art to industry. There are abundant possibilities for colleges and universities to use their intellectual resources to pioneer new ways for society to understand, respond to, and influence environmental prospects.

In 1990, Tufts University President Jean Mayer convened 22 university presidents from 13 countries in Talloires, France, to discuss the role of universities in working toward an environmentally sustainable future. The conference resulted in a declaration of actions to make environmental education and research a principal goal of universities around the world (see accompanying box).

University Presidents' Environmental Action Agreement
The Talloires Declaration (excerpt)

University heads must provide the leadership and support to mobilize internal and external resources so that their institutions respond to this urgent challenge. We, therefore, agree to take the following actions:

1. Use every opportunity to raise public, government, industry, foundation, and university awareness by publicly addressing the urgent need to move toward an environmentally sustainable future.

2. Encourage all universities to engage in education, research, policy formation, and information exchange on population, environment, and development to move toward a sustainable future.

3. Establish programs to produce expertise in environmental management, sustainable economic development, population, and related fields to ensure that all university graduates are environmentally literate and responsible citizens.

4. Create programs to develop the capability of university faculty to teach environmental literacy to all undergraduate, graduate, and professional school students.

5. Set an example of environmental responsibility by establishing programs of resource conservation, recycling, and waste reduction at the universities.

6. Encourage the involvement of government (at all levels), foundations, and industry in supporting university research, education, policy formation, and information exchange in environmentally sustainable development. Expand work with nongovernmental organizations to assist in finding solutions to environmental problems.

7. Convene school deans and environmental practitioners to develop research, policy, information exchange programs, and curricula for an environmentally sustainable future.

8. Establish partnerships with primary and secondary schools to help develop the capability of their faculty to teach about population, environment, and sustainable development issues.

9. Work with the U.N. Conference on Environment and Development, the U.N. Environment Programme, and other national and international organizations to promote a worldwide university effort toward a sustainable future.

10. Establish a steering committee and a secretariat to continue this momentum and inform and support each other's efforts in carrying out this declaration.

Jean Mayer
Tufts University, U.S.A.

Pablo Arce
Universidad Autónoma de Centro America,
  Costa Rica

L. Ayo Banjo
University of Ibadan, Nigeria

Boonrod Binson
Chulalongkom University, Thailand

Robert W. Charlton
University of Witwatersrand, Union of South
  Africa

Constantine W. Curris
University of Northern Iowa, U.S.A.

Michele Gendreau-Massaloux
l'Académie de Paris, France

Adamu Nayaya Mohammed
Ahmadu Bello University, Nigeria

Augusto Frederico Muller
*Fundaçao Universidade Federal de Mato
  Grosso, Brazil*

Mario Ojeda Gómez
Colegio de Mexico, Mexico

Calvin H. Plimpton
American University of Beirut, Lebanon

Wesley Posvar
University of Pittsburgh, U.S.A.

T. Navaneeth Rao
Osmania University, India

Moonis Raza
University of New Delhi, India

Pavel D. Sarkisov
*D. I. Mendeleev Institute of Chemical Technology
  C.I.S.*

Stuart Saunders
University of Cape Town, Union of South Africa

Akilagpa Sawyerr
University of Ghana, Ghana

Carlos Vogt
Universidade Estadual de Campinas, Brazil

David Ward
University of Wisconsin—Madison, U.S.A.

Xide Xie
Fudan University, People's Republic of China

Source: Anthony Cortese, "Education for an Environmentally Sustainable Future," *Environmental Science and Technology*, vol. 26, no. 6, 1992.

Summary

Nations seek to achieve environmental goals through the use of regulation, market incentives, and consumer-oriented policies of education and information sharing. As it becomes increasingly difficult to assure the quality of air, water, and land resources in the face of a growing United States population that may reach 400 million by 2050, and a global population that will pass 6 billion by 2000 and may exceed 10 billion by 2050, sustainable practices are essential. Can they be achieved?

The bedrock of national policy in industrialized and developing nations alike is more evidently becoming that of environmental education. Children must learn from an early age the importance of conservation and diligent use of the earth's resources; adults must learn how to alter wasteful patterns of behavior in order to save resources and respect nature; and organizations must learn that waste reduction, energy conservation, stewardship of natural resources, and aggressive remediation of existing environmental problems are the practical definitions of sustainable development. Nations too must learn that economic development policies that are forged in the crucible of environmental destruction are doomed to fail in all but the very short term. Societies do not prosper when their futures are bargained away for short-term gains. As the twentieth century closes, there is a prevailing sense of pessimism about the ecological support systems that make all life possible on earth. The twentieth century has been a century of progress and economic development. It has been an epoch in which humans created the means to end life on the planet; hopefully, it is also the time in which humans discovered the means, and the wisdom, to save it.

Bibliography

Brown, Lester, et al., *State of the World, 1992,* W. W. Norton and Worldwatch Institute, New York, 1992.

Buchholz, Rogene, Alfred Marcus, and James E. Post, *Managing Environmental Issues: A Casebook,* Prentice-Hall, Inc., Englewood Cliffs, New Jersey, 1992.

Cortese, Anthony, "Education for an Environmentally Sustainable Future," *Environmental Science and Technology,* vol. 26, no. 6, 1992.

Meadows, Donella H., Dennis L. Meadows, and Jorgen Randers, *Beyond the Limits: Confronting Global Collapse, Envisioning a Sustainable Future,* Chelsea Green Publishing, Post Mills, Vermont, 1992.

Schmidheiny, Stephan, and Business Council for Sustainable Development, *Changing Course: A Global Business Perspective on Business and the Environment,* MIT Press, Cambridge, Massachusetts, 1992.

Smith, Emily, ed., *Managing for Environmental Excellence,* Island Press, Washington, D.C., 1993 forthcoming.

Stead, W. Edward, and Jean Garner Stead, *Management for a Small Planet: Strategic Decision Making and the Environment,* Sage Publishing, Newbury Park, California, 1992.

Wilson, Edward O., *The Diversity of Life,* Belknap Press of the Harvard University Press, Cambridge, Massachusetts, 1992

Acknowledgments. The author gratefully acknowledges the research assistance of Jennifer W. Griffin and William W. Wubbenhorst, III.

2
Business and the Environment

Joel S. Hirschhorn, Ph.D.
President, Hirschhorn & Associates, Inc.,
Lanham, Maryland

In this chapter:

- The pollution-prevention approach
- Challenges for industry
- The meaning of environmental quality
- Measurement is key
- Becoming proactive and positive
- A total environmental opportunities business strategy
- Environmental credibility
- Planning for the next century

The United States and many other industrialized and developing countries are on a path to a new environmental protection strategy based on pollution prevention, clean technologies, and environmentally responsible products. The strategy requires the full participation and aggressive technological innovation by every business and industry sector. In return, companies that participate will profit from new environmentally driven markets. Globally, the new environmental strategy is also necessary for sustainable economic development and growth.

In the future it is absolutely essential to recognize that there is, indeed, an explicit strategy choice to be made by both government and industry. A sea change in thinking in industry has already begun, with many companies seeing the beginning of an environmentally driven market of historic proportions. While the demand for information has been shaping the service sector, the demand for environmental protection will increasingly influence durable and nondurable products.

Examples of important new business ventures which capitalize on new environmental thinking are given in Boxes 2-1 to 2-3. These companies have overcome what is often an implementation gap between concepts and policies on the one hand and solid business commitments and actions on the other. All three companies have combined technological innovation with a marketing approach based on understanding public attitudes about environmental issues.

Box 2-1. Novon Product Division, Warner-Lambert Company (Morris Plains, New Jersey)

An excellent illustration of a company making a major investment in a new environmentally driven business, outside of its current products and markets, is the case of Warner-Lambert's decision to capitalize on an invention by their research and development group. In seeking to find a new material to substitute for gelatin capsules, the company invented new technology to make materials made primarily from starch derived from such renewable resources as corn and potatoes.

The result is the commercialization of a family of Novon materials which can be engineered to serve a variety of applications. Warner-Lambert sells resins to fabricators and manufacturers, and is working with some 200 firms to test and formulate new applications for its Novon specialty polymers. Some Novon grades can be made to replace common plastics. Environmentally, Novon polymers are truly biodegradable and therefore ideal for recycling through composting after products are discarded. They do not contain toxic materials. From a life cycle perspective, Novon materials offer various environmental advantages over plastics and paper. Overall, Novon materials have the ease of manufacture of plastics but use annually renewable resources instead of petroleum, and pose fewer solid waste problems than plastics. And they have some of the recycling advantages of paper.

Warner-Lambert opened its 100 million pound production facility in Rockford, Illinois, in early 1992. Early commercial uses of Novon materials include loose-fill packing peanuts, golf tees, pharmaceutical capsules, and holders for votive candles. There is an enormous potential to use Novon specialty polymers in a host of packaging applications. Novon products are being marketed worldwide.

Box 2-2. Hunter Environmental Services, Inc.
(Southport, Connecticut)

This company illustrates the high risks some companies are willing to take because they believe in their innovative technologies. In this case, the company believes it has a more environmentally responsible method of managing various kinds of hazardous wastes by using a combination of chemical stabilization and engineered cavities in carefully selected salt domes. The company sold a prosperous environmental consulting business to focus entirely on this new waste management technology.

The first project is in Texas. The use of salt domes offers an alternative to incinerators, injection wells, and landfills, all of which the public vehemently opposes because of perceived risks and uncertainties. Although industrial waste reduction is the preferred priority, increasing regulation of wastes and other factors is leading to increasing volumes of wastes requiring commercial management. Also, many waste-treatment methods produce solid residues which require safe management. Hunter is optimistic that salt dome repositories will be seen as more acceptable hazardous waste facilities and also offer a more cost-effective solution than incineration and disposal alternatives. The company is also examining salt dome opportunities in other countries.

Box 2-3. Baroid Drilling Fluids, Inc.
(Houston, Texas)

As one of the world's leading producers of drilling fluids for petroleum wells, Baroid has spent considerable resources developing a new product which has substantial environmental benefits to complement its current line of drilling fluids. Research and actual field use has demonstrated that the new high-performance product called Petrofree virtually eliminates a number of environmental problems. Such environmental problems have contributed to public opposition to drilling in sensitive marine environments.

Because Petrofree is free of toxic chemicals and biodegrades quickly in aerobic and anaerobic conditions, adverse effects on marine life around offshore wells are not a problem. Conventional drilling fluids are made from petroleum-based materials, while Petrofree is made from vegetable oil, another life cycle advantage. Use of Petrofree can also avoid expensive land disposal of solid wastes from drilling operations. Moreover, it also avoids the occupational exposure of workers to toxic chemicals. The product has already been used in various places around the world with considerable success. Global environmentalism should help build demand for Petrofree because it offers a way to meet the most stringent drilling needs of petroleum companies while offering proven environmental advantages.

The Pollution-Prevention Approach

Too few Americans have an awareness of the Federal Pollution Prevention Act of 1990 (PL 101-508). If the national commitment to pollution prevention prevails, this act is of historic importance. The basic concept is deceptively simple: Changing how society uses materials and technologies to manufacture products and accomplish other tasks is better than trying to control pollutants and manage wastes after they are created. The vision is a highly industrialized society that uses clean technologies, nontoxic raw materials, and green products to reduce and eliminate threats to natural resources, human health, and the life-support capabilities of the planet. The EPA statement (chapter Appendix) provides a succinct description of the pollution-prevention approach.

It took Congress about 4 years to pass the legislation. This happened after some key studies, including the Congressional Office of Technology Assessment report *Serious Reduction of Hazardous Waste* and INFORM's *Cutting Chemical Wastes* in 1986. Congress and others had already prodded EPA into giving pollution prevention some significant attention. Also, several major companies, such as 3M, Polaroid, Chevron, and IBM, had already demonstrated successful programs.

Moreover, by the time Congress passed the law, a number of states had already passed laws that are more ambitious; these state laws have various names in addition to pollution prevention, including toxics use reduction and waste reduction. There are now about 25 such state laws, and their passage indicates strong grass roots support for pollution prevention nationwide. However, all federal pollution-prevention efforts remain at a small scale in terms of funding, and the same can be said about state pollution-prevention programs. Traditional end-of-pipe programs in both government and industry still get most of the funding, which in turn directs most industrial spending on pollution control rather than prevention. The problem is that end-of-pipe pollution control and waste management is what industry must do because of laws and regulations, while pollution prevention is what they should do because it offers better environmental protection and improved profits and competitiveness. But more flexibility is being built into the regulatory system to more effectively allow companies to move upstream and solve environmental problems through modernization and innovation that also makes good business sense.

Challenges for Industry

For American industry, the significance of the Pollution Prevention Act of 1990 is in its basic message rather than in its detailed requirements. The passage of the federal law is just one of a multitude of important events that have defined the national and international pollution-prevention movement. The pollution-prevention movement and its impacts on business in the United States have moved from awareness, to commitment, and now to the early stages of expansion. And one can expect the same historical development worldwide.

The message to industry is that the public and government agencies demand comprehensive reduction and elimination of *all* kinds of nonproduct waste outputs, pollutants, and toxic chemicals. For industry, it means a fundamental rethinking of what environmental problems, laws, and regulations impose on business. In the past it was strictly costs and liabilities which were seen as threats to business. Now it is new business opportunities in the global marketplace.

The act and the state laws also signal the beginning of the transition away from a voluntary system to a regulated approach to industrial waste reduction. Legislation has also appeared to regulate environmental marketing claims for products. The twin messages of the global pollution-prevention movement are that preventive actions will provide improved protection of health and environment, as well as improved efficiency, profitability, and competitiveness for industry. This author's book, *Prosperity without Pollution: The Prevention Strategy for Industry and Consumers* (Van Nostrand Reinhold, Princeton, N.J., 1990), articulates these messages in great detail.

Historically, there is no turning back. Traditional end-of-pipe pollution control and waste management tactics will have to be justified to a much greater degree, and their costs will increase continuously. So will civil and criminal liabilities, which are best defended against by prevention programs, not traditional compliance efforts.

For industry, the most important part of the federal act is Sec. 6607 that covers source reduction and recycling data collection. Facilities that file annual toxic chemical release forms under Section 313 of Superfund Amendments and Reauthorization Act (SARA) must now file information on past and future source reduction and recycling. To make amounts of chemicals significant, the act requires use of a production ratio, which can be very difficult to develop, however. Companies must use new ways of defining their products and outputs to accurately and fairly describe their waste-reduction performance, or face public criticism.

Many of the state laws have more complex and demanding reporting requirements for industrial facilities, especially requirements for detailed waste reduction or toxics use reduction plans that, in some cases, can become public documents. The ultimate impacts of such plans may dwarf the impact of Section 313 Toxic Release Inventory reporting seen thus far. That is, the general public and environmental groups will have more opportunities to scrutinize industrial actions and commitments. Previously, the public became outraged by learning what was coming out of industrial facilities. Now, they will become outraged about what is or is not going on inside plants.

The real and as yet largely ignored issue is that reporting and planning requirements have become costly burdens imposed on all companies, as if all are equally guilty of too little commitment to pollution prevention. The challenge is to modify reporting and planning requirements so that they are incentives and rewards for demonstrable company commitments and performance. Otherwise, limited resources diverted to planning and reporting deprive spending on actually implementing pollution-prevention projects.

It will take several years to see the full impact of the federal and state prevention and reduction laws. Progressive companies with superior management will understand the historical shift in emphasis from reaction and control to prevention. The global prevention movement includes the "green consumer" movement also. Indeed, it would be useful for industrial managers to understand that there are three levels to the global prevention movement, in order of decreasing importance:

1. Products: changing their design, composition, and packaging to offer environmental benefits, and creating totally new products to replace old ones.

2. Materials: changing materials used in industry to reduce use of toxic substances that may only be used in processing and that may reside in products.

3. Manufacturing: making improvements in all processes, technologies, operations, and procedures to reduce and eliminate the generation of *all* wastes at their sources. Other sectors must also change, including energy production, agriculture, and transportation.

Many environmentalists and business managers believe that the 1990s will be not only the decade of pollution prevention but also the historic time when consumer and industrial products drive the most substantial environmental improvements and industrial changes. Those people in business who are willing to believe that the global pollution-prevention movement will be a major stimulus to a global restructuring and modernization of industry—a kind of industrial revolution—will be the ones who profit from it.

Many people speak of sustainable economic growth. To be sustainable is to avoid self-destruction through pollution, contamination by toxic substances, and depletion of nonrenewable resources. The specific advantages of pollution prevention and clean technologies allow sustainability to be reached, so that global population and industrial growth can occur with minimal harm to health and environment. Green products, innovative new materials, such as polymers made from crop materials that substitute for petrochemical-based plastics, and new clean technologies for manufacturing are the three legs upon which sustainable growth will be based. Industry needs to recognize the business opportunities offered by the prevention movement, and it needs to creatively redefine its products, as well as reorganize itself and retrain its work force.

The Meaning of Environmental Quality

No one can dispute the remarkable increase in industrial attention to environmental issues and in particular to environmental "quality." Total Quality Management has quickly spun off Total Environmental Quality Management. There is, however, a critical need to distinguish fluff from substance, and intention from performance. Not all claims of corporate environmental responsibility and commitment, which are intrinsically linked to success in the marketplace, reflect either a well-developed strategy or technical substance.

One problem in the environmental quality arena is the confusion between a pollution-prevention strategy, with its emphasis on clean technologies and clean products, versus traditional end-of-pipe thinking with its heavy emphasis on regulatory compliance. Achieving true corporate success means recognizing that quality must be linked primarily to pollution-prevention performance. Regulatory compliance is the least of what is expected by the public. Pollution prevention, when properly defined, is a sea change in environmental thinking. Proactive prevention is a much more difficult and complex challenge to corporate management than compliance.

Companies committed to pollution prevention have embarked on a path to reexamine and reshape their entire enterprise, from the products they make, to the technologies they use to make them, to the raw materials they base production on, and even on how they market products and think about new acquisitions and investments. Total Quality Environmental Management (TQEM) practitioners need to completely integrate pollution-prevention thinking into absolutely every part of a company but they may not have the power to do so if they are in traditional environmental departments with a focus on regulatory compliance.

A Zen Vision of Quality

To turn public demand for quality into solid business benefits, it will help to think zen.

The zen of quality ultimately means a system where there is no person or department in charge of TQM. Zen quality is everywhere, silent, effortless, and real to those who produce it and those who buy it. Perhaps not a state of perfection with zero defects, but at least a system that no longer has to convince itself or anyone else about what is right. People just do *it*. Getting closer and closer to zero defects in every way for everything by everyone. Having found the path, staying on *it* individually, communally, and organizationally. Continuous improvement.

The zen of environmental quality means a quest to eliminate every ounce of toxic chemical, waste, pollution, and threat to public health and nature. Zen environmental quality is in everyone's head and heart, guiding every thought, plan, and action to reach a goal of zero impact on health, safety, and environment for the whole life cycle of products. Doing *it* because *it* must be done, because *it* is right. Creating new technology to make *it* so. Pollution prevention. Not fearing Greenpeace. Becoming more profitable because of *it*. Smart business.

Even if zero impacts have not yet been achieved, it must be clear to even the most skeptical of environmental activists that something right is going on. Workers and customers must believe that they are producing and buying environmental quality. The public must see clean technology and clean products in harmony with nature. There are already some, mostly smaller companies that seem to have mastered the zen of environmental quality.

Environmental quality is the sound of one hand preventing pollution....

Measurement Is Key

Environmental quality practitioners must measure what must be improved. Some companies, though, emphasize process more than results and measure the wrong things. Soft social science information is no substitute for hard technological realities. With misplaced criteria for success and measurement, advocates of environmental quality will fool no one but themselves. Often, they seem to be competing with each other rather than concentrating on real-world environmental improvement. Consumers who need to be convinced about environmental performance and responsibility won't buy process or simplistic efforts.

Companies which have enormous environmental problems and costs need to do a lot more than talk about tree planting programs, for example. Spare me the details of your benchmarking process; show me measured improvement and results! Don't expect credit for internal processes. Invest in actual engineering projects which produce tangible results. Keep it simple. Think zen.

Pollution-prevention performance must be measured if it is to be improved, and it must be improved if it is to be praised. But what is to be measured? Not mere regulatory compliance. Not how many audits are being done. Not the level of activity of corporate programs. Not endorsements of sustainable economic development. Not how much money has been spent on environmental compliance. Not the office paper recycling program. Not participation in EPA programs.

Hard facts and numbers are needed for the reduction in the use of toxic chemicals and the reduction in the generation of every form of nonproduct waste output (whether regulated or not) as some credible function of production output. The redesign, reformulation, and repackaging of existing products and the development of innovative new products are also top priorities. Products must be proved through accurate and credible life cycle analysis that they offer solid, measurable improvements for specific environmental problems. The methodology will always have limits, but there is no alternative. Companies need to tell the public what fraction of disposable cameras are actually being recycled. Stop misleading the public about degradable plastics that do not biodegrade. Please don't say it is recyclable if there are no available recycling systems for the material.

Becoming Proactive and Positive

Industry professionals need to remember why there are environmental issues and programs. While the word "proactive" is often used, the fact is that industry has been reactive. The forces which have driven environmentalism lie outside industry. Whether corporate environmentally responsible behavior is successful will be determined by those forces which have shaped the agenda. Those forces are the environmental activists, angry and fearful people, the news media, and politicians who respond to environmentally concerned citizens. Environmental quality will be determined by tough judges. Don't underestimate them.

As unsettling as it may be, the customers to be satisfied with environmental performance include Greenpeace, the National Toxics Campaign, the Citizens

Clearinghouse for Hazardous Waste, Environmental Action, the PIRGs, and a myriad of other grass roots groups. The recent rush to market "green" products has achieved some success because of environmentally conscious consumers who translate their environmental values and fears (determined largely by what environmental groups say is truth) into purchase decisions. A host of global and local environmental threats are increasing the number of those consumers. Developing countries need green products also and companies need green products to make their products green. Opportunities abound!

Is TQEM grounded in technological realities? Or has this young movement already been co-opted by public relations doublespeakers and slick management mavens? The test of environmental responsibility is in the numbers, not the words. Every major American corporation has formulated an environmentally "correct" company policy while trade associations have their correct codes of conduct. That's the easy part, compared to producing results. The arbiters of environmental quality will not be satisfied with words. Environmental activists have brilliantly shifted public policy away from reliance on conventional regulations to requirements for reporting information and plans for waste reduction.

From the Toxics Release Inventory (TRI) reporting under Title III of SARA, to the Pollution Prevention Act of 1990, to a multitude of state pollution-prevention kinds of laws, environmentalists have found the lever to force industry to give them and the general public improved quality. It is data, and more data, especially about chemical use, manufacturing operations, products, and environmental claims. Data that might even be useful to competitors. Data that feed more demands such as take back your waste, stop using chlorine, no more pollution, change your products and your packaging, change your production technology. Not regulatory compliance data, but data which relate to pollution prevention, clean technologies, toxics use reduction, and environmentally responsible products. With this new environmentalism, the old-time regulatory compliance will be remembered fondly. Any enlightened business strategy which builds on environmental issues must include a heavy emphasis on data if it is to be a successful strategy. But company departments with regulatory compliance responsibility are not able to obtain the new kind of necessary data.

A Total Environmental Opportunities Business Strategy

Companies have a crucial strategic choice to make: to stay defensive and reactive, or to identify and capitalize on the unlimited business opportunities from growing global demand for environmental quality. Holding on to existing market shares for existing products made with existing technologies is a formula for failure.

Greenpeace and other environmental groups are creating new demands. The issue is not merely environmental strategy. Managers must recognize that environmental issues require a new business strategy, which I call Total Environmental Opportunities (TEO). TEO translates a technological pollution-prevention strategy into a new corporate culture which then drives a new business strategy. Paramount to this change and future industrial competitiveness will be measurable environmental quality and performance.

An environmentally driven industrial revolution is beginning with inevitable winners and losers. Companies that delude themselves about their own environmental success, or underestimate environmental demands today will be the business failures of tomorrow. Environmental quality means reconfiguring the industrial economy to make it a protector of planetary survival rather than a threat. Being proactive means using technological innovation for environmental progress that can be measured, communicated, and used effectively as a marketing tool.

A new corporate culture is also needed, and that means a major commitment to retooling work forces. In-house education and training programs are essential to teach every employee—not just those with environmental jobs—about environmental issues, pollution prevention, environmental marketing, and responsibility. Environmental managers must work effectively with marketers. You cannot do that by adding a few hours to a TQM course. Senior managers also need critical third-party evaluations of corporate pollution-prevention programs, environmental business strategies, and of course TQEM programs. Company programs must be evaluated through the critical eyes of skeptical environmentalists.

Some companies have begun to understand the inevitability of environmentally driven markets and their business opportunities. Total quality has succeeded when it delivered physical improvements which translated into financial benefits. For environmental management to succeed, it too must translate into physical improvements that are correctly measured, honestly communicated, and routinely used to obtain financial benefits.

Currently there is a major "implementation gap" between what many companies say about their environmental programs, and often their environmentally responsible products, and what they are able to demonstrate with quantitative measurements. It is not at all clear that senior managers and CEOs recognize the new business opportunities. Clean technologies and clean products bring competitive advantage. Words do not. Measurement, education and training, restructuring research and development, and life cycle analysis of products are the substantive paths to business success which results from serving environmental needs. This must be done quickly. Companies that choose to wait for more certainty will face stiff competition from new startups based on true technological innovations and also from foreign firms.

Environmental Credibility

Capitalizing on environmental business opportunities through TEO requires environmental credibility. However, industry has a heavy burden to overcome because it has been presumed environmentally guilty and therefore has little environmental credibility.

It matters less that this public view may be wrong (e.g., consumers themselves may be just as responsible) than that it requires an even stronger commitment to comprehensive, accurate, and trustworthy measurements of real environmental progress through new manufacturing technologies and new industrial and consumer products. It will take a lot of positive, substantiated environmental good news to offset the bad news that is preferred by the news media and used so effectively by environmental groups to obtain more laws and regulations.

The environmental crime of the future will be a failure to act preventively and proactively and a failure to measure performance, not failure to comply with regulations. The court of public opinion will issue the harshest judgments which will be translated into actions in the marketplace. Future competitive advantage will increasingly require company and product differentiation on the basis of measured environmental performance.

The cynicism and skepticism of environmental groups and the general public will only be overcome by corporate environmental integrity and credibility beyond anything to date. Documented pollution-prevention performance and documented environmental claims for products must exceed the rhetoric of environmental and social responsibility if both the public and companies are to benefit financially and environmentally from a stronger, sustainable economy and a safer world.

Planning for the Next Century

What should business managers do for the next century to ensure that they are the benefactors of the new global environmentalism? Here are some key steps:

1. Develop a detailed in-house training program to improve the environmental literacy of the entire work force and build a new corporate culture that includes a strong environmental ethic. Shift environmental responsibilities from special departments to all personnel in the company. Place special emphasis on training for people in marketing.

2. Think seriously about changes in products, raw materials, and production systems that can concretely improve the life cycle environmental performance of products and the whole company. Develop creative measurement systems to be accountable to the public with credible data. Better data on continuous pollution-prevention performance also enhance management. See the whole pollution-prevention area as a permanent company effort that requires sustained support by senior management.

3. Assess totally new products which can satisfy both market needs and public demands for more effective solutions to environmental problems. Use new criteria and priorities for research and development or acquisitions to commercialize true technological innovations with environmental competitive advantages.

4. Become active in public policy discussions to ensure that government policies and programs reflect business needs and opportunities. Replace confrontation and litigation with government agencies and environmentalists with proactive participation and cooperation.

5. Aim for the global marketplace. There are constant new opportunities to become involved in public and private sector programs, such as ones focusing on pollution prevention and clean technologies for developing countries in the U.S. Agency for International Development. Be sensitive to different kinds of environmental problems and priorities in different countries.

In conclusion, develop an attitude that what's good for the environment is good for business. But also be prepared to make the case that what's good for business is actually good for the environment.

Appendix

Pollution Prevention: EPA Statement of Definition

Pursuant to the Pollution Act of 1990 and the Pollution Prevention Strategy

Under the Pollution Prevention Act of 1990, Congress established a national policy that:

- Pollution should be prevented or reduced at the source whenever feasible;
- Pollution that cannot be prevented should be recycled in an environmentally safe manner whenever feasible;
- Pollution that cannot be prevented or recycled should be treated in an environmentally safe manner whenever feasible; and
- Disposal or other release into the environment should be employed only as a last resort and should be conducted in an environmentally safe manner.

Pollution prevention means "source reduction," as defined under the Pollution Prevention Act, and other practices that reduce or eliminate the creation of pollutants through:

- increased efficiency in the use of raw materials, energy, water, or other resources, or
- protection of natural resources by conservation.

The Pollution Prevention Act defines "source reduction" to mean any practice which:

- reduces the amount of any hazardous substance, pollutant or contaminant entering any waste stream or otherwise released into the environment (including fugitive emissions) prior to recycling, treatment, or disposal; and
- reduces the hazards to public health and the environment associated with the release of such substances, pollutants or contaminants.

The term includes: equipment or technology modifications, process or procedure modifications, reformulation or redesign of products, substitution of raw materials, and improvements in housekeeping, maintenance, training or inventory control.

Under the Pollution Pevention Act, recycling, energy recovery, treatment, and disposal are not included within the definition of pollution prevention. Some practices commonly described as "in-process recycling" may qualify as pollution prevention. Recycling that is conducted in an environmentally sound manner shares many of the advantages of prevention—it can reduce the need for treatment or disposal, and conserve energy and resources.

Pollution prevention approaches can be applied to all pollution-generating activity: energy, agriculture, federal, consumer, as well as industrial sectors. The impairment of wetlands, groundwater sources, and other critical resources constitutes pollution, and prevention practices may be essential for preserving these resources. These practices may include conservation techniques and changes in management practices to prevent harm to sensitive ecosystems. Pollution prevention does not include practices that create new risk for concern.

In the agricultural sector, pollution prevention approaches include:

- reducing the use of water and chemical inputs;
- adoption of less environmentally harmful pesticides or cultivation of crop strains with natural resistance to pests; and
- protection of sensitive areas.

In the energy sector, pollution prevention can reduce environmental damages from extraction, processing, transport and combustion of fuels.

- increasing efficiency in energy use;
- substituting environmentally benign fuel sources; and
- design changes that reduce the demand for energy.

3

Corporate Environmental Excellence and Stewardship

J. Ladd Greeno*
*Senior Vice President
and Managing Director
Arthur D. Little, Inc.*

In this chapter:

- Driving forces
- Senior management involvement
- Five critical tasks
- Potential hurdles
- Planning initiatives for the next century

---

*J. Ladd Greeno, Senior Vice President of Arthur D. Little, Inc., is Managing Director of the firm's Environmental, Health, and Safety Consulting Practice. A recognized authority on environmental management and auditing, Mr. Greeno is frequently called on to advise corporate management and boards of directors regarding ways to increase the level of assurance provided by their environmental, health, and safety programs. Mr. Greeno graduated from the University of Oklahoma and received an M.B.A. from the Harvard Graduate School of Business Administration. He is a founding member and past chairman of the Environmental Auditing Roundtable and is the author of numerous papers and books on environmental management and auditing.

The trouble with our time is that the future is not what it used to be.
PAUL VALÉRY, 1871–1945

…particularly when it comes to corporate environmental management. Most of us now accept the fact that we can no longer rely on the earth's extraordinary resilience to make up for the spoils of our progress. What we took for granted now shows major signs of devastation, loss, and nonrecovery. Similarly, companies can no longer look at how they manufactured products, packaged them, or managed pollution in the past to make plans for the future. Incremental changes, such as the end-of-pipe solutions to reduce pollution in recent years, will not be sufficient to meet new public, regulatory, and competitive pressures. Instead, an entire "rethink" of how companies operate and manufacture is necessary.

At the same time, senior management no longer has the option of delegating ultimate environmental accountability to a completely separate management function. Environmental management—with all its consociate issues—is becoming one of the most important strategic matters to develop in decades. Moreover, as corporations have discovered, the strategic, regulatory, liability, and competitive issues are all entangled and will become even more so.

One of the most important challenges facing business is shaping the role of senior management in corporate environmental performance. In some leading companies, the CEO or chairman takes the initiative to carefully define his or her role because of a strong personal commitment, a keen grasp of the business incentives, in response to past problems, or because of a combination of these. In other companies, even where corporate policies genuinely support and promote corporate environmental, health, and safety programs, there may still be inaction or reluctance on the part of top management to participate or get involved. This management posture may work for a few more years, but no longer than that—and could quickly become a major detriment to any company's ongoing market success or viability.

This discussion will focus on a strategy for getting top management involved in your company's programs and, where they are already involved, for sharing some insights we have gained from our work with a number of companies where top management has taken a strong role in their companies' environmental issues and has established precedence for what can work well.

Driving Forces

Today's environmental driving forces are beginning to have an important impact on how companies reshape strategy and competitive success—and thus are causing senior management to take notice.

1. *The threat of significant legal and financial liability and resulting loss of personal or corporate reputation—as the result of regulatory infringements, or a major environmental, health, or safety crisis.*   A major oil spill, for example, may cost many

millions of dollars in legal fees—in addition to cleanup costs and fines. Furthermore, courts are more likely now to hold officers and staff managers liable for civil damages resulting from environmental issues. Also, there are reported criminal cases where corporate officials have gone to jail without proof that they knew of the illegality of their own or their subordinates' actions. The threat of legal and financial liability is real—and court actions likely to become more common.

2. *The growing pressure of regulations on the company, and the resultant costs.* As laws and regulations become more stringent, and as companies continue to commit to tougher internal standards, compliance costs increase. Robert Kennedy, chairman and CEO of Union Carbide, estimates chemical industry spending on environmental, health, and safety protection will reach 3 to 4 percent of sales per year in the developed world. In the United States, that is $10 billion a year in a $250 billion industry. If we also look to broader industry spending in the United States, that of the Fortune 500, for example, the amount spent on environmental, health, and safety protection may be as great as $46 billion a year, or 2 percent of sales, which were $2.3 trillion in 1990. And these environmental expenditures are likely to grow.

There are some estimates, for example, that the 1990 Amendments to the Clean Air Act could cost U.S. industry some $25 billion annually. Moreover, in a report prepared by the U.S. Environmental Protection Agency for Congress in December 1990, EPA estimates that U.S. industry and government are spending as much as $115 billion a year in current dollars to protect and restore the nation's air, water, and land. The report estimates further that this figure could reach more than $170 billion by the year 2000 at the present level of implementation of existing programs (Table 3-1).

For individual companies, these issues get at the heart of long-term financial commitments and, as such, must draw on management to formulate long-term objectives and strategies—including how much to invest in personnel and systems that will help keep the company in compliance with growing regulations, and when to hold back on these operational investments with an eye on the bottom line.

There is also a time dimension to this spending: top management has to make choices about what to spend, what not to spend, and when. There are legitimate choices to be made based on company need, regulatory compliance, and future

Table 3-1. Total Annualized Costs for All U.S. Pollution-Control Activities

Total annualized costs	1972	1987	1990
In billions of estimated 1990 dollars	30	98	115
As percentage of GNP	0.9	1.9	2.1

SOURCE: *Environmental Investments: The Cost of a Clean Environment—A Summary*, U.S. Environmental Protection Agency, December 1990.

objectives. Top management must also analyze the payback on these investments—the kinds of environmental, health, and safety (EHS) systems and programs that leading companies put in place can also help increase productivity
and decrease downtime.

Last, there are decisions to be made about whether or not to invest in environmental opportunities. How does investing in corporate environmental stewardship, or diversifying into environmental businesses, fit into your overall
corporate strategy? What is best for your corporation, for your employees, for
your shareholders? What are your near- and long-term goals? Top management
has a critical role in formulating the answers to questions like these.

3. *Intense public scrutiny and media attention directed toward corporate management of environmental matters.*   This is increasingly of high importance to management because of the visibility, both good and bad, it can bring the
corporation, and sometimes with a consequential influence on revenues. As
windows of information continue to open much wider than in the past, the public is in a better position to assess and compare the environmental performance
of individual companies and their product lines. In the United States, for example, provisions under Section 313 of the Superfund Amendments and
Reauthorization Act essentially provide the public unprecedented access to
environmental information about individual industrial plants, companies, and
their products. This is a trend that is also growing in Europe and elsewhere
around the world. Prominent among European measures is the EC's recently
passed Eco-Management and Audit Scheme, which outlines a voluntary environmental management program for companies, including implementing an
audit program and reporting on environmental progress results.

The public is beginning to consider corporate environmental performance criteria in their evaluation of companies. An Arthur D. Little affiliate, Opinion
Research Corporation has been surveying the public about individual corporate
reputations for more than 30 years. In recent years, that study has included
analysis about corporate environmental image. In a 1990 study, Opinion
Research Corporation found that reputational elements describing a company's
environmental attitude carry as much weight on public opinion as do traditionally influential elements, such as dependability, honesty and ethics, and value.
Virtually all of the environmental statements received importance ratings that
were not substantially different from other traditional crucial issues (Table 3-2).

Perhaps not surprisingly, extraordinary circumstances such as major environmental incidents—even those as long ago as 5 years—can cause the public to
have a nonfavorable impression—despite how well a company may be handling
its environmental, health, and safety activities. And, as we have all witnessed,
adept handling of such an incident can enhance a corporate reputation. Johnson
& Johnson is one classic example: Here is a company with an already excellent
public reputation, which probably solidified that perception through its exemplary management of the Tylenol incident. Johnson & Johnson continues to
appear near the top of public image studies—in the top ten of the recent *Fortune*

Table 3-2. Public Attitudes Toward Corporate Reputational Elements

(Percentage of Respondents Selecting These Attributes as of *Highest* Importance)

Corporate issues:	
Is honest and ethical in its dealings with others	51
Lives up to its guarantees and promises	51
Is honest in the conduct of its business	48
You can depend on its products and services	46
Its products and services give good value for the money	44
General environmental concern:	
Its policies demonstrate a definite concern for the environment	46
Is responsive to public concerns about the environment	44
Does a good job of environmental self-regulation	44
Actively works to minimize the generation of wastes	44

SOURCE: Opinion Research Corporation.

survey of "America's Most Admired Companies." On the flip side, any negative opinion with respect to environmental concerns about a company or one of its products may also begin to carry over to consumer purchasing behavior.

The Michael Peters Group, as in other surveys we have seen, reports that over half of those surveyed (53 percent) declined to buy a product in 1991 because they were concerned about its effect on the environment. This, of course, also suggests that there is an opportunity here: If they decline to buy one product, they may buy another they consider more environmentally sound.

4. *Corporate environmental, health, and safety (EHS) posture vis-à-vis the competition.* What are your competitors doing about environmental issues? Which opportunities are they pursuing? Which are likely to be related to success factors for the future in your industry? We will discuss some of these issues later. Suffice it to say here that business and strategy issues are the strongest influence on top management involvement in the EHS arena and underlie each of the issues just discussed: looking at what the competition is doing about environmental issues or about getting into environmental businesses, examining the place for environmental performance in long-term business planning, understanding the costs and their impact on financial performance, and examining the potential impact of public influence on your products and your long-term viability.

Senior Management Involvement

Company officers and directors alike are beginning to confront the need to adapt to these changing influences, to protect their companies from unwarranted liabilities, to help ensure corporate stability and growth, and also to protect their own self-interests. Where top officers are not yet making these commitments, increasingly EHS staffs are trying to promote that involvement.

We see a critical and visible role for the CEO or chairman in environmental, health, and safety management and positioning, as well as an extension of that involvement to the corporate board of directors. A 1991 *Conference Board* study on "Managing Environmental Affairs" asked respondents to indicate the role their CEO played in environmental issues. The CEO was seen to personify the company's philosophy and position on environmental issues and problems in 50 percent of U.S., 44 percent of Canadian, and 57 percent of European respondents (Table 3-3).

These percentages are probably far higher than they would have been even 3 years ago and are likely to continue to grow significantly in the next few years. Increasingly, we will see top management—CEO and others—take a key role in making certain that appropriate EHS systems are in place and functioning smoothly.

The CEO can play two roles here: internal and external. Within the company, the CEO is in a particularly powerful position to convince all employees, as well as the company's other constituencies, that environmental excellence is a corporate priority. In more of an external role, the CEO works with the board of directors and other constituencies to convey the company's position on environmental issues to the shareholders and, ultimately, to the broader public. Shareholders have become very vocal in recent years, beginning to demand greater accountability for environmental programs and performance. One indication is the jump in the number of shareholder resolutions presented for vote in major U.S. corporations. According to the Investor Responsibility Research Center, prior to 1990 there were only two or three such votes a year, generally stemming from a major environmental incident. In 1990, however, 15 environmental-related resolutions came to vote; in 1991, 37; and in the first half of 1992, 32—the bulk of which were driven by the CERES Principles. While these resolutions have not yet passed, they have received enough votes to be counted again the following year. As such, boards of directors need to be in a position to respond to these concerns. Because of this, and their responsibilities as "overseers," the board of directors must determine whether or not the environmental programs and safeguards put in place are effective.

Table 3-3. The External Role of the CEO (Percentage of Respondents)

Role	Aggregate	U.S.	Canada	Europe
Personification of company philosophy	50	50	44	57
Policymaker and participant with outside groups	32	35	26	31
Maintains a hands-off policy	17	14	26	10

Remaining respondents checked some combination of the three views.

SOURCE: The Conference Board; reprinted with permission.

In recent years, we have witnessed a trend toward an increasing number of outside participants on corporations' boards of directors. A 1990 *Conference Board* study on "Membership and Organization of Corporate Boards" surveyed 589 companies about how today's boards are being chosen, elected, and organized. They found that the boards of 89 percent of the companies surveyed have a *majority* of outside directors. The comparable figure in 1972 for manufacturers was only 71 percent.

Increased outside representation on the board has developed for a variety of reasons. For one, it ensures a greater degree of objectivity—a help to management in addressing touchy issues, but also helpful in shaping the perception of the shareholder. This outside representation also enables the chairman and CEO to pull extraordinary talent into the fold of the organization. Traditionally, that expertise has often been financial, legal, or from academia. We expect to see an increasing number of board committees with an environmental, health, and safety agenda—perhaps as part of a public policy agenda, but evident nonetheless. This kind of representation is likely to increase in the next few years, as top management draws on the talents of its boards to help monitor progress and chart direction in environmental stewardship and its business implications for the company. The Investor Responsibility Research Center's (IRRC) 1992 survey of corporate environmental practices of the S&P 500 shows that two-thirds of the responding companies have a board of directors' committee responsible for addressing environmental issues.[1]

Directors need to keep themselves informed about company environmental, health, and safety issues and programs. The courts and experts also say that directors are entitled—even expected—to rely on information and reports by company officers, staff, and outside experts whom they reasonably believe to be competent. This principle will increase the requests from the board for environmental, health, and safety information because, as mentioned, officers and directors increasingly face significant exposure to both public scrutiny and costly litigation with regard to environmental performance.

Five Critical Tasks

What is realistic to expect from corporate officers and directors as participants in the company's thrust for environmental excellence? We have seen again and again what works for successful firms. The company's senior management—generally the CEO, often supported by the board of directors—commits to making sure they have in place environmental programs and systems that are consistent with the objectives and culture of the company and the expectations of shareholders. For some companies, this may be attention to developing and

---

[1] *Investors Environmental Report*, vol. 2, no. 2, 1992 (Investor Responsibility Research Center, Washington, D.C.).

implementing the first corporatewide program in the company's history, or for upgrading existing programs. Yet, for others, this commitment may be to become an environmental leader, both in how the company manages its own internal environmental, health, and safety affairs, and in how the company positions itself to take advantage of the environmental business opportunities and competitive advantages available. To accomplish this, top management makes certain they have among them, or reporting to them, people with the expertise to deal with environmental regulatory, technical, and marketing issues. A corporate officer or director who does not believe that he or she has the information necessary for corporate protection should be seriously concerned.

Moreover, in these progressive companies, top management wants confirmation that there are environmental management systems in place to provide management and the board with ongoing assurance that:

- Knowable EHS risks and opportunities associated with the company's operations and products have been identified.

- Risks to the environment and consequent risks to the company are being appropriately managed.

- Environmental laws, regulations, and permit requirements are being adhered to by the company.

- Appropriate environmental control, quality assurance, and verification systems are in place to ensure that company policies, standards, and procedures are being followed.

- Products do not present unreasonable actual or perceived risks to the environment.

These may sound like the "apple pie" of environmental assurance—and, in a way, they are—but each of them implies the extensive organization and commitment of people, equipment, and financial resources it takes to protect the company and its constituencies.

To ensure excellence, a corporation must address five critical tasks (Fig. 3-1): *positioning, learning, communications, personal involvement,* and *catalyzing progress.* The number is not important; you could present this same information as three or six. But it is the responsibility of the company's EHS professionals to strive to provide the right information and tools to help management fulfill these responsibilities. Certainly these tasks will be more readily addressed if you have the commitment and active involvement of the CEO; but, if not, then it falls to the EHS staff to provide the energy and incentives to make sure they happen—and also to find other high-level management within the company to take on the kind of support we are discussing.

Sixty-six percent of the S&P 500 companies surveyed by IRRC indicated that the senior executive responsible for environmental affairs was an executive vice president or senior vice president (22 percent) or, more frequently, a vice president (44 percent). In fact, we have seen environmental management move

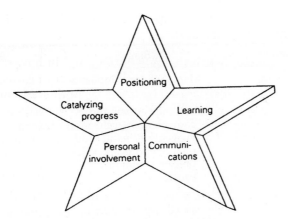

Figure 3-1. Five critical tasks to address for environmental, health, and safety excellence.

quickly up the corporate ladder in the last few years. An Arthur D. Little study shows that in 1991 almost half (44 percent) of the Fortune 100 companies had a vice president or senior vice president in charge of environmental affairs, up from 38 percent a year earlier. Moreover, the industries with the greatest change were not the chemical or oil industries (over 70 percent of which already had environmental vice presidents in 1990) but rather industries that were in the past perceived as presenting lower environmental risk, such as the forest industry and the electronics industry.

Positioning

We define the *first task,* positioning, as specifying the company's environmental, health, and safety management posture. What is your company's environmental, health, and safety baseline—where you stand today? Where do you want to be in 1 year, 5 years, 10 years? What constitutes the right pieces of a sound, far-reaching environmental, health, and safety management program? How do you develop and position your products and services in the context of your environmental, health, and safety posture? We use a three-stage framework for characterizing corporate environmental, health, and safety management posture (Table 3-4).

- *Stage 1* companies pursue a general thrust of "problem solving" and are oriented at trying to define basic goals and directions and solve immediate problems. They tend to be reactive. Their environmental management values stem largely from avoiding "burdensome" costs.

- *Stage 2* companies manage their operations and systems for compliance, building systems and competence to achieve goals, and coordinate compli-

Table 3-4. Framework for Characterizing a Company's Posture Concerning Environmental, Health, and Safety Management

	Stage 1	Stage 2	Stage 3
General thrust	Problem solving	Managing for compliance	Managing for assurance
Primary purpose	Defining basic goals and directions; solving immediate problems	Building systems and competence to achieve goals; coordinating compliance efforts and solutions to common problems	Basic organization and management systems in place for ongoing management of risks
Primary motivations	Avoid burdensome costs	Use resources effectively; avoid large changes in the way things are done	Protect internal resources and external environment from harm
Vulnerabilities	Surprise events that have material impact	More attention to compliance than to future liability	Increased investment in environmental assurance without obvious immediate payback

SOURCE: *State-of-the-Art Environmental, Health, and Safety Programs: How Do You Compare?* Center for Environmental Assurance, Arthur D. Little, Inc.

ance efforts to solve common problems. They use resources efficiently, avoiding large changes in the way things are done.

- *Stage 3* companies actively manage all environmental, health, and safety risks and opportunities. They have well-developed management systems that reinforce line management responsibility for EHS performance. Importantly, their monitoring programs utilize audits that independently assess hazards, verify compliance, and confirm the effectiveness of environmental, health, and safety management systems.

Currently, most major corporations with environmental, health, and safety programs in place are stage 2 companies. We estimate the distribution of EHS postures among the larger industrial companies both in North America and increasingly in Europe to be a bell-shaped curve, with roughly 10 to 15 percent falling in stage 1, 10 to 15 percent in stage 3, and the remainder in the middle (Fig. 3-2). Importantly, we find that facility EHS posture tends to lag somewhat behind corporate programs, standards, and goals. Other corporate performance goals, such as profitability, can—at least over the short term—seem at odds with EHS performance goals and overshadow them.

This stage 1-2-3 framework can be used by a company to evaluate where the company stands with respect to EHS management and where it wants to be. A variety of mechanisms help a company judge where it tends to be in EHS man-

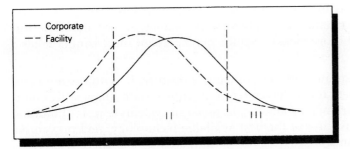

Figure 3-2. Distribution of environmental, health, and safety posture—corporate versus facility. (*Source: Arthur D. Little, Inc.*)

agement. These include environmental audits, environmental management assessments, assurance letters, benchmarking methodologies, . . . , and others.

The *environmental audit*—and particularly the written audit report—is an important vehicle for providing assurance and information to corporate officers about the company's EHS progress or lack thereof. Audit reports are not the only source of information regarding the company's EHS performance. However, they are often among the most visible and, as such, provide EHS professionals with an opportunity for sharing valuable information with top management—getting right back to the thrust of this discussion. Once you know what information management needs and wants, it is important to examine whether your audit approach and audit reports are sensitive to and complement those needs.

Some leading companies have also begun to use a *benchmarking* approach to identifying companies with outstanding environmental management practices and then interviewing those companies with the aim of coming to a greater understanding of their approach and adapting it for use in their own companies. General Electric, for example, is taking this approach.

Another tool used by a growing number of companies to evaluate their performance, and to reinforce the basic line management role, is the *assurance letter*. Typically initiated by the CEO, the letter is a top-down, bubble-up mechanism to identify and communicate matters of noncompliance and to facilitate the correction of significant deficiencies. Allied-Signal and Hoechst-Celanese are two companies that have used this mechanism successfully.

Once you use these kinds of tools to understand the current state of the company's EHS programs, it is possible to define a desired state. If that desired state is to be state of the art, such programs are characterized by a kind of pyramid (from top to bottom):

- Clear, constant top management commitment and support—Unless the entire organization understands management's needs and expectations, everyone will waste a lot of effort second guessing.

- High reporting levels for environmental, health, and safety personnel—As environmental performance, competitive performance, and economic performance become tied more closely, senior management increasingly takes a leading role.

- Resources commensurate with the company's posture, in both quantity and quality—Environmental excellence requires appropriate financial commitments; top-quality, trained professionals; physical systems (e.g., for pollution prevention) that make use of the best available technology; and preventive maintenance programs.

- Ongoing awareness and training programs—Effective programs include an ongoing communication effort that takes the form of safety awareness training, as well as documents and presentations that articulate the company's expectations for good EHS management. All employees, from operating personnel on the floor to senior executives, become aware of the need to be responsible for environmental management.

- Line responsibility for EHS performance—Whether it is the foreman, the operator on the floor, or the materials manager who may be handling hazardous waste, each individual knows that he or she has direct accountability and responsibility for making things happen right.

- Continuous improvement—Because the pressures on companies will continue to increase, it is critical to improve, redesign, and rethink EHS programs.

In addition, a state-of-the-art environmental, health, and safety management program generally has 12 elements as shown in Table 3-5. Not all leading companies have all characteristics and elements soundly in place, but they tend to have most of them well developed (Fig. 3-3).

The most critical aspect of positioning for those charged with managing their company's environmental posture—and certainly involving top management should a change in that posture be warranted—is to determine where they want the company to be. Influencing factors on this decision include:

- The company's culture
- Issues of reality—such as financial condition, public image, and available resources
- External forces—for example, regulatory pressures and consumer expectations
- The need to reevaluate expectations in light of ever-changing demands

Learning

The *second critical task* for the corporation, that of learning, covers two important bases of knowledge: a personal knowledge base to develop and cultivate, and a

Table 3-5. Elements of a State-of-the-Art Environmental, Health, and Safety (EHS) Management Program

---

1. Environmental policies and procedures are clearly defined, broadly communicated, and have the support of senior management
2. An effective EHS organization is in place, functioning smoothly, and is congruent with corporate structure. Roles, responsibilities, and accountabilities are clear to all
3. Day-to-day management systems have been established to identify and correct problems, investigate incidents, provide training, operate and maintain control equipment, document performance, manage compliance, and report results
4. A communication system is in place to ensure appropriate information sharing about progress and problems with all stakeholders, both internally and externally
5. A formalized long-range planning system is in place to identify emerging issues and assure adequate corporate resources. This system is part of, or at least congruent with, the business planning system
6. A formal risk management system has been established to identify hazards and assess risks, set priorities, and track performance
7. Emergency preparedness programs have been implemented, which are reviewed and tested regularly
8. Regulatory surveillance is routinely carried out to both track emerging laws and regulations and influence new laws and regulations at the national, regional, and local level
9. An automated management information system assists line managers and environmental staff to understand requirements and document and report performance
10. Project and program reviews—for capital projects, maintenance modifications, and research and development programs—take environmental issues into consideration
11. Issue-specific programs are carried out to improve environmental performance and manage environmental risks. Examples include programs for waste minimization, assessment of commercial disposal facilities, underground storage tanks, and cleanup of past disposal sites
12. Oversight and control mechanisms provide management with assurance that environmental risks and opportunities are being appropriately managed. These mechanisms include inspections, management system assessments, audits, and other assurance programs

---

SOURCE: Arthur D. Little, Inc.

kind of information bank about the company's performance to have always available to draw upon for examining progress.

EHS professionals readily understand the kinds of knowledge that they must cultivate, but they must also help ensure that both management and every employee of the company develops his or her own knowledge base as appropriate.

Management's personal knowledge should include information about current environmental, health, and safety issues; pertinent regulatory directions and their implications; the company's current environmental posture; how the company is performing against the regulations and corporate goals; an understanding of how peer companies are doing in the same or related industries; and a solid understanding of how the company's products and services fare in the context of environmental, health, and safety issues. The officer develops this knowledge through personal networks, associations within the industry, communications channels up and down the organization, and particularly through formal reporting networks with the corporate EHS staff.

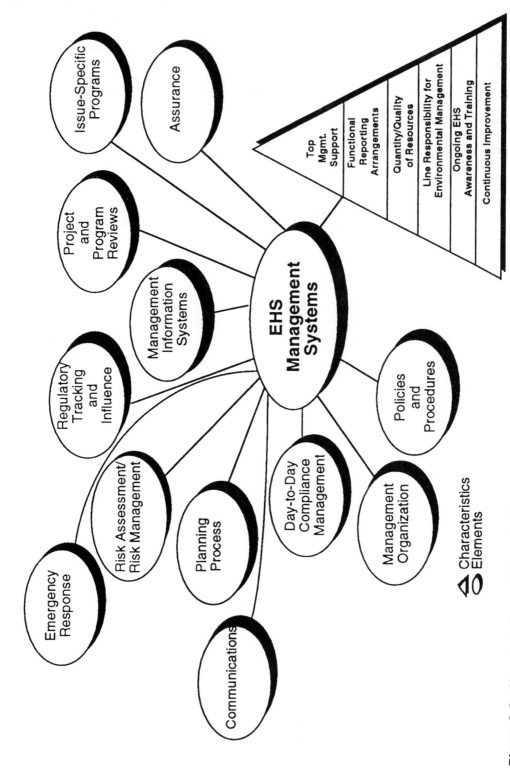

Figure 3-3. Characteristics and elements of a state-of-the-art environmental, health, and safety management program. (*Source: Arthur D. Little, Inc.*)

Enlightened companies are pioneering systems for measuring environmental progress against requirements and goals—primarily because they recognize that *what gets measured gets managed*. These sophisticated measurement programs, much like other continuous improvement initiatives, can help correct shortfalls and improve environmental performance overall. For some, these measurement programs have the added benefit of providing information for corporate disclosure when appropriate. Overall, the key benefit is the *education* of each line manager about the importance of environmental performance. In many of these companies, individual measures of performance, based on broader corporate or business unit measures, are put in place to further reinforce the message.

Environmental performance measurement is an embryonic discipline. Because there are many ways to measure and track progress, it is critical for each company to determine the best measurement system for meeting its particular needs. As shown in Table 3-6, various aspects of EHS performance can be measured—and there are benefits and drawbacks to each approach. However, as the corporate need to measure performance increases dramatically in the next few years, companies will begin to find certain measurement choices much more beneficial to their needs than others. These will vary by company and industry. It is particularly important to choose a system that will stand the test of time for reliable, year-over-year progress measurement in areas such as emissions reduction, waste minimization, and pollution prevention.

Communications

Closely tied to learning is the *third corporate task* of communication. A variety of formal and informal mechanisms are particularly useful to sending and receiving messages. Occasional visits in the field, meetings with line management, and oral communications in staff meetings about environmental, health, and safety issues can send, or reinforce, top management's message throughout the organization that this is a particularly important issue for the company to address. As mentioned earlier, assurance letters, environmental audits, and

Table 3-6. Environmental Performance Measurement Choices

- Compliance with regulations, internal standards, and good management practices
- Progress in implementing EHS programs
- Amount of emissions, discharges, and waste released to the environment, and year-over-year trends
- Impact of operations upon health, safety, and the environment
- Use of renewable and nonrenewable natural resources
- Episodic events, and personnel safety and property damage accidents or incidents
- Level of risk faced by the company and year-over-year trends
- Environmental, health, and safety costs

SOURCE: Arthur D. Little, Inc.

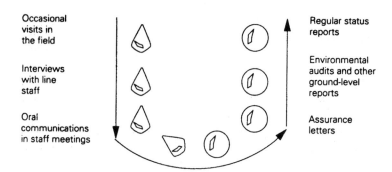

Occasional
visits in
the field

Interviews
with line
staff

Oral
communications
in staff meetings

Regular status
reports

Environmental
audits and other
ground-level
reports

Assurance
letters

Figure 3-4. Examples of formal and informal environmental communication mechanisms. (*Source: Arthur D. Little, Inc.*)

other ground-level reports, as well as regular status reports enable management
to hear back from the field about progress and problems. This sending and
receiving of messages is reflective of a top-down, bubble-up approach to communication (Fig. 3-4).

It is important to acknowledge here the growing concept of a "seamless" corporation: Corporations are increasingly accountable to, and communicating to,
a growing world of constituencies. These include not only employees in all divisions of the company, but also customers, suppliers, local communities, the
board of directors, the shareholders, and, increasingly, the public at large.
Consequently, companies are developing ways to communicate with all these
constituencies via appropriate mechanisms. Here are some examples.

First, companies are talking to their shareholders through both their annual
reports and other reports to the shareholders and the public at large. Dow
Chemical's 1989 annual report, for example, focuses on the company's environmental commitment. Since then, certain companies, including Chevron,
Monsanto, Norsk-Hydro, and Polaroid, have issued environmental reports to
their "stakeholders," highlighting environmental programs and progress; and
as another example, WMX (formerly Waste Management) has committed itself
to 14 principles of environmental excellence, including a thorough and substantive annual review and report to the public on performance against each of
the 14 principles.

In looking at the annual reports of the top industrial chemical companies, we
found that prior to the last 5 years, these companies were often likely to mention health and safety issues in the context of their overall commitment to their
employees' welfare—sometimes as a closing kind of comment in the letter from
the CEO. In the last few years, that statement has become more frequent in the
letter and has been expanded to include, for example, commitment to the environment, and sometimes to discuss environmental expenditures. Moreover,
environmental issues are often addressed elsewhere in the annual report: in

Dow Chemical's 1989 report, previously mentioned, for example, the cover's focus and feature discussion are Dow's commitment to the environment as the "one issue, more than any other, (that) will affect Dow's prospects in the '90s and beyond."

As a second example of communication, some companies are making bold public statements about environmental goals that they have established for themselves. These companies began specifying timetables to meet these goals that, once achieved, would be replaced by even tougher goals for the future. Monsanto's 1988 commitment to reduce toxic air emissions to zero with a benchmark of 90 percent by 1992, and its chemical division's more recent commitment to reduce organic and toxic inorganic wastes by 70 percent by the end of 1995, are examples, as is Polaroid's commitment to reduce toxic use and waste, per unit of production, by 10 percent per year over 5 years, with 1988 as the base year. Still other examples include AT&T's program to end all use of ozone-depleting CFCs by 1994, and 3M's commitment to reduce its air emissions worldwide by 70 percent by 1993, and to reduce all its emissions worldwide by 90 percent by 2000. There are obvious risks involved with this kind of stance, but for companies that are committed to environmental excellence and realistic about their prospects for success, the rewards of this kind of commitment—and public communication about it—can be great.

Third, associations are playing a vital and unique role in helping companies communicate with each other about problems and progress, establish industry or global standards, and, ultimately, establish and communicate about viable expectations. A prime example is the Responsible Care Program first developed in the Canadian Chemical Producers Association—and serving as a model for similar programs by the Chemical Manufacturers Association and more than a dozen other associations around the globe.

An important example of this kind of shared role in commitment and communication was the second World Industry Conference on Environmental Management (WICEM II), which took place in Rotterdam in April 1991. At the conference, 800 business leaders endorsed the Business Charter for Sustainable Development. Underpinning this document are 16 principles developed by the International Chamber of Commerce, which are designed to place environmental management high on corporate agendas and encourage policies and practices for carrying out operations in an environmentally sound manner (Table 3-7). The first principle sets the tone: "to recognize environmental management as among the highest corporate priorities."

The extraordinary gathering of government and industry leaders from around the world at the Earth Summit in Brazil in June 1992 broadened avenues for industry-government communication. Building on the U.N. Conference on the Human Environment in Stockholm in 1972, representatives from nearly 170 nations, including 60 heads of state, gathered in Rio de Janeiro to debate the link between major environmental issues and global development. As part of the UNCED agenda, the delegates signed the Rio Declaration on Environment and Development—a set of underlying principles for future sustainable develop-

Table 3-7. The 16 Principles of the Business Charter for Sustainable Development

1. **Corporate priority.** To recognize environmental management as among the highest corporate priorities and as a key determinant to sustainable development; to establish policies, programs, and practices for conducting operations in an environmentally sound manner

2. **Integrated management.** To integrate these policies, programs, and practices fully into each business as an essential element of management in all its functions

3. **Process of improvement.** To continue to improve corporate policies, programs and environmental performance, taking into account technical development, scientific understanding, consumer needs and community expectations, with legal regulations as a starting point; and to apply the same environmental criteria intentionally

4. **Employee education.** To educate, train, and motivate employees to conduct their activities in an environmentally responsible manner

5. **Prior assessment.** To assess environmental impacts before starting a new activity or project and before decommissioning a facility or leaving a site

6. **Products and services.** To develop and provide products or services that have no undue environmental impact and are safe in their intended use, that are efficient in their consumption of energy and natural resources, and that can be recycled, reused, or disposed of safely

7. **Customer advice.** To advise, and where relevant educate, customers, distributors, and the public in the safe use, transportation, storage, and disposal of products provided; and to apply similar considerations to the provision of services

8. **Facilities and operations.** To develop, design, and operate facilities and conduct activities taking into consideration the efficient use of energy and materials, the sustainable use of renewable resources, the minimization of adverse environmental impact and waste generation, and the safe and responsible disposal of residual wastes

9. **Research.** To conduct or support research on the environmental impacts of raw materials, products, processes, emissions, and wastes associated with the enterprise and on the means of minimizing such adverse impacts

10. **Precautionary approach.** To modify the manufacture, marketing, or use of products or services or the conduct of activities, consistent with scientific and technical understanding, to prevent serious or irreversible environmental degradation

11. **Contractors and suppliers.** To promote the adoption of these principles by contractors acting on behalf of the enterprise, encouraging and, where appropriate, requiring improvements in their practices to make them consistent with those of the enterprise; and to encourage the wider adoption of these principles by suppliers

12. **Emergency preparedness.** To develop and maintain, where significant hazards exist, emergency preparedness plans in conjunction with the emergency services, relevant authorities, and the local community, recognizing potential transboundary impacts

13. **Transfer of technology.** To contribute to the transfer of environmentally sound technology and management methods throughout the industrial and public sectors

14. **Contributing to the common effort.** To contribute to the development of public policy and to business, governmental, and intergovernmental programs and educational initiatives that will enhance environmental awareness and protection

15. **Openness to concerns.** To foster openness and dialogue with employees and the public, anticipating and responding to their concerns about the potential hazards and impacts of operations, products, wastes, or services, including those of transboundary or global significance

16. **Compliance and reporting.** To measure environmental performance; to conduct regular environmental audits and assessments of compliance with company requirements, legal requirements, and these principles; and periodically to provide appropriate information to the board of directors, shareholders, employees, the authorities, and the public

SOURCE: International Chamber of Commerce.

ment. Delegates also committed to the "Agenda 21," setting the global environmental agenda for the next few decades. For corporations, the major effect of UNCED is likely the hastening of a number of changes already in motion: the growing involvement of senior management, recent strides toward environmental excellence, development of management tools, attention to the needs of corporate stakeholders, and a new focus on environmental issues across key business processes.

Personal Involvement

The *fourth critical task* for corporations to address is best accomplished through senior management—ideally by the CEO, who can be the single most important driver of environmental, health, and safety excellence throughout the company. However, some CEOs, despite their strong commitment and support of the company's environmental programs, are simply not comfortable with this role and may delegate it to a manager they believe will carry that "champion" role better. As the strategic issues associated with environmental management become more apparent in the coming years, heretofore "reluctant" CEOs will get involved.

Catalyzing Progress

The *final critical task* for the organization—through the CEO or the top EHS executive—is that of catalyzing progress. Sometimes that may mean a commitment to change if there are problem areas that warrant correction. Other times, commitment to progress may mean building on what is already good—always looking for a more effective way to ensure and improve performance.

Some leading companies are beginning to recognize that in order to meet their overall goals for growth and profitability, they must consider the "green dimension" of doing business—satisfying stakeholders' environmental concerns, managing business processes with minimum risk to the environment, and aligning resources and organizational issues to meet these objectives. They are taking an integrated approach to managing environmental, health, and safety issues as part of their overall processes of doing business—no longer managing environmental issues as a stand-alone, separate function.

The key to successful corporate performance is stakeholder satisfaction—i.e., setting a strategy that explicitly meets the needs of *all* stakeholders by continuously improving critical business processes. When it comes to the environment, important stakeholders include customers, owners, employees, local communities, the public, and some might argue, the regulators as well as the environment itself. Balancing the needs of these multiple stakeholders will require innovation and change on the part of corporations, and a commitment to improving key business processes. Traditional business processes have developed over time, usually with only secondary consideration given to the environmental implications. In the area of pollution prevention, for example, during the last decade a great deal of time, effort, and resources have gone into end-of-pipe control technology to clean up manufacturing and distribution processes. But, as environmental pressures escalate, companies are recognizing they must go beyond incremental improvement and commit to total "rethink" approaches—significant new processes designed at initial cost and risk, but highly rewarding if successful. However, this kind of major change—because of the initial high development costs and risks, and more importantly because of the potential impact on corporate performance—depends on complete understanding and involvement by top management.

Potential Hurdles

When it comes to change, top management and key players in environmental, health, and safety performance should be alert to some typical hurdles:

Resistance to Change.   Paradoxically, this hurdle most often appears when things are running smoothly (or at least appear that way). "Why should we change anything when everything is going well?" "Why risk it?" The answer to these questions is that the competitive environment constantly changes—and EHS programs must change in response. To counter resistance to change, companies should first insist on environmental reviews of potentially adverse effects of all major proposed changes to facility operations. Second, ongoing attention to operations review—for example, by means of audits—and to product reviews through life cycle analysis will help identify areas requiring improvement or change.

Hierarchical Impediments.   If management is listening to employees and maintaining an open-door policy, internal barriers shouldn't be a problem. But sometimes differences of opinion can inhibit an employee's coming forward with a potentially valuable idea. Management should make sure mechanisms are in place to enable every employee to get his or her idea to someone who can help think it through. Mechanisms range from a "suggestion box" that collects ideas for the facility head to incentive programs that reward the employee and his or her manager.

Vague Responsibilities.   Many organizations have not yet developed clear understanding about roles, responsibilities, and accountabilities in environmental management. To be effective, the location of functional responsibility for environmental management should be clearly identified, along with lines of authority and accountability. Where possible, environmental performance expectations should be built into job descriptions and performance reviews.

Prolonged Planning.   All the best intentions and plans can stay right on the launchpad if no one puts them into action. The tendency to plan rather than act can be a major hurdle. To avoid this, a company should provide both a clear sense of the company's goals and objectives regarding environmental performance and the right organizational incentives and resources to meet those commitments.

Planning Initiatives for the Next Century

Industry has come a long way in the past three decades:

- The 1970s—Industry was pugnacious and resistant to regulatory pressures.
- The 1980s—Industry began to accommodate.
- The 1990s—Industry is beginning to take a leadership role.

There is no better time than right now for EHS managers to draw senior management into the process, as well as every employee in the organization. Certainly external pressures have never been higher. But, perhaps more importantly, there is an opportunity today to take a leadership role, both within the company and within industry, to help shape the future and the nature of excellent environmental performance.

Moreover, while a global responsibility, environmental stewardship is pursued on individual, local, regional, national, and multinational levels. Around the world leading companies are addressing the same issues and pursuing similar strategies to reach their EHS objectives. And, finally, excellence in EHS performance is achievable if you really believe it is the right thing to pursue.

The Earth Summit in Brazil likely set into motion significant new initiatives to raise the consciousness of the public and industry to the genuine needs of sustainable development—that heretofore buzzword that is quickly becoming part of an acceptable business and consumer ethic. The world push for improved environmental performance will be further energized as we move into the next century. Increased sensitivity to the need for more effective industrial environmental management will result in the development of a new set of tools for measuring environmental impact and sustainability, and new approaches to manufacturing and delivering products or providing services while eliminating any negative impact on the environment or health and safety of its inhabitants. As we move forward, companies will put their attention to these initiatives, in particular:

- *Choosing top corporate leaders for environmental, health, and safety management.* Some companies such as Dow Chemical are drawing on line managers from their successful operating companies and moving them into these top environmental roles. Some EHS heads are now sitting on corporate operating committees—Monsanto is a notable example. Senior management is making certain that the environmental "issue" is being given sufficient clout and depth to command the attention of the entire company.

- *Investigating and understanding the full impact of their operations, products, and services on EHS*—and allocating appropriate resources to eliminate any problem areas. The use of tools such as environmental audits, life cycle assessments, and risk analysis can enable a company both to uncover immediate problems to be corrected, and to begin to shape processes and products with little or no impact on the environment.

- *Developing and using EHS performance measurement systems* to evaluate and improve overall corporate environmental management. Environmental performance measurement is an embryonic discipline. Because there are many ways to measure and track progress, it is critical for each company to determine the best measurement system for meeting its particular needs. Choose a system that will provide reliable, year-over-year progress measurement in areas such as emissions reduction, waste minimization, and pollution prevention.

- *Designing and building new business processes across the entire organization* that set aside previous biases and recognize the fundamental relationship of EHS issues to basic business processes—such as developing new products, manufacturing products, managing logistics, and managing customer relations. Incremental environmental improvements of the past will give way to process redesign and, ultimately, rethinking and rebuilding entirely new processes for the future—at high initial cost and risk, but highly rewarding when successful.

Enlightened companies recognize that they must take charge of their own EHS destinies. A key component is understanding their many stakeholders' needs. Although environmental management in the past has not received the broad attention that quality has, for example, the movement is building. Environmental priorities will be recognized as critical to all functions of the organization. The organization's need to satisfy its many stakeholders' environmental concerns is a key driving force for this change in vision.

PART 2

Regulation, Compliance, and Prevention

4

Regulatory Framework: United States, Canada, and Mexico

Ravi K. Jain, Ph.D., P.E., D.E.E.*

*Associate Dean for Research and
International Engineering
College of Engineering, University of Cincinnati
Formerly Director, Army Environmental Policy
Institute*

In this chapter:

- Rationale for environmental legislation
- Legislative data systems
- Overview of U.S. environmental legislation
- Environmental protection in New Jersey
- Canadian environmental regulatory framework
- Mexican environmental legislation
- Industry and environmental regulation
- Balancing economic and environmental costs

*Scott Weiner, J.D., Commissioner, New Jersey Department of Environmental Protection and Energy, contributed the section on Environmental Protection in New Jersey. Rao Kolluru outlined some aspects of the Canadian regulatory scene. Ann Pizzorusso of North American Philips prepared the section on Mexican Environmental Laws. Chris Demeroukas, Fellow Army Environmental Policy Institute, reviewed the manuscript and added information related to OSHA, RCRA, CERCLA, and Federal Food, Drug, and Cosmetics Act. William Librizzi of OHM Corporation also reviewed this chapter. Some of the information included here was summarized by the author from recently published material in the McGraw-Hill book *Environmental Assessment* by R. K. Jain et al.

This chapter is about the regulatory framework of the United States, Canada, and Mexico. While detailed information is provided about major United States environmental legislation, only a synoptic overview is included for Mexico and Canada. In the United States, some states are considered "bellwether" states from the perspective of environmental regulations and related concerns. New Jersey is one such state. Consequently, we have summarized some of the innovative initiatives undertaken by New Jersey in environmental compliance and policy areas.

Much environmental legislation in the United States was initiated at the federal government level. Some states have enacted legislation to protect unique environments within their jurisdiction, e.g., coastal areas, wetlands, and cultural and historic sites. Environmental regulations, which form an action-forcing mechanism for implementing the intent of the enabling legislation, are then issued by the regulatory agencies of the government. With the emphasis on giving states the responsibilities for enforcing such regulations, increasingly states are issuing and are responsible for enforcing many of the environmental regulations.

Environmental legislation, and resulting regulations, are continually evolving. Information presented here is designed to provide a broad perspective on environmental legislation. Clearly, environmental regulations can have a profound effect on economic activity, and these effects should be included in assessment of the implementation of these regulations.

Rationale for Environmental Legislation and Regulations

The following discussion of the basis for promulgating environmental legislation and regulations focuses on the role of the market economy, the problem of the commons, and long-term viability of the environment.

Since labor and capital are scarce resources, their consumption is minimized by industry. Since the environment is, or rather has been in the past, an essentially free resource, its consumption has typically been ignored. Consequently, there has been considerable environmental degradation with attendant economic and social costs. Simply put, some economic and social costs are ignored in the ordinary marketplace exchange of goods and services. Also, one cannot ignore the third-party interests when looking at two-party transactions of the buyer and the seller (existence of externalities). This, in fact, is the case for many environmental control problems, and thus the transaction results in "market failure."

Basically, market failure could result from high transaction costs, large uncertainty, high information costs, and existence of externalities (Schultze, 1977, p. 32). In order to correct market failure, two choices exist. One can try to isolate the causes of the failure and restore, as nearly as possible, an efficient market process (process-oriented) or alternatively bypass the market process and promulgate regulations to achieve a certain degree of environmental protection (output-oriented).

Some environmental legislation and regulations are needed to protect the health and welfare of society, and market incentives alone will probably never work. For example, it would be very difficult to put a dollar value on discharge of toxic materials, such as PCBs or mercury, to the environment.

Another reason for environmental legislation and regulations is that long-term protection of the life-support systems is important for sustained economic development. Investment decisions can rarely be made to take into account long-term protection of the life-support systems which belong to everyone—a property ultimately leading to the problems of the commons.

Some projects involve exploitation of energy and other natural resources at an unprecedented rate. A question of temporal optimality of market allocations arises. In such cases, a market economy is unable to properly account for all long-term economic and social benefits and costs. As Solow has pointed out, "there are reasons to expect market interest rates to exceed the social interest rate of time preference..." (Solow, 1977, p. 368). As a result, the market will tend to encourage consumption of exhaustible resources too fast. Consequently, a corrective public intervention—or regulations aimed at slowing down this consumption—needs to be structured. This can be accomplished through compulsory conservation, subsidies, or a system of graduated severance taxes.

Shortcomings of Environmental Legislation and Regulations

Many public administrators, engineers, planners, industrialists, and other decision makers recognize the need for environmental legislation and related regulations to protect the environment. They also recognize the importance of economic efficiency and utility. There are, indeed, a number of concerns regarding many environmental regulations. These concerns are shared by many who feel that environmental regulations can be structured so that they minimally affect efficiency and productivity of the industry, minimally interfere with essential federal programs such as national defense, and still achieve reasonable environmental protection goals. Some concerns related to environmental regulations are:

- Regulations seem to be structured in such a way that the costs are often excessive compared with the benefits they generate.

- In general, the regulations are command-and-control type; i.e., they contain few or no economic incentives for compliance. Consequently, in a free-market economy, they are ineffective and do not preserve elements of voluntary choice.

- Regulations are ineffective because they lack properly structured incentives for achieving social goals.

- It is widely believed that command-and-control regulations generate inefficiencies at both the micro- and macroeconomic levels.

- Some environmental regulations require unnecessary paperwork and cause unnecessary delays in completion schedules which, in turn, create additional costs.

- Many regulations at different government levels, such as federal, state, and local, are duplicative and, at times, incompatible with each other; consequently, they create unnecessary work and inefficiencies.

Legislative Data Systems

New amendments to major environmental legislation are continually being enacted by the U.S. Congress and regulatory agencies are continually modifying environmental regulations. Because of this, a number of environmental legislative data systems have been developed. Described here are some of the existing legislative data systems which readers may want to use, depending on their specific needs.

Federal Legal Information through Electronics (FLITE)

The FLITE system operates as an information retrieval and analysis service. While FLITE does not exist as an actual computerized system, it does provide access to other computerized full-text legal systems such as JURIS, LEXIS, and WESTLAW (discussed below). Lawyers trained in information retrieval techniques field reference questions from federal agencies and conduct searches. This service is backed up by services such as information analysis, abstracting, and legal research. It operates in a "batch mode" with searches run overnight. The user, seeking the information, does not actually perform the search but relies on trained legal staff to perform that service. Its major drawbacks are the cost and possible time delays involved in using the batch mode approach.

Justice Retrieval and Inquiry System (JURIS)

JURIS is a U.S. Department of Justice computer-based storage and retrieval system for federal legislative and litigators' information. It is specifically designed to serve federal lawyers. It is a full-text system and is designed for use by legal personnel. Information from the system could be rather voluminous and, consequently, difficult to use for environmental assessment (EA) purposes.

Computer-Aided Environmental Legislative Data System (CELD)

This system contains abstracts of environmental regulations and is designed for use in environmental impact analysis and environmental compliance. The abstracts are written in a relatively informal narrative style, with all legal jargon and excessive verbiage removed. Characteristics of this system are:

1. Legislative information is indexed to a hierarchical key word thesaurus, in addition to being indexed to a set of environmental attributes, which number approximately 700.

2. Information can be obtained for federal and individual state environmental regulations, as well as regulatory requirements related to the key words or environmental attributes.

3. Appropriate reference documents, such as enactment and effective date, legislative reference, administrative agency, and bibliographical reference, are also included.

The system is structured in order to satisfy the specific needs of the user agency (U.S. Department of Defense) for environmental regulations; consequently, needs of other agencies may not be completely satisfied by this system. Recent augmentations to the system include mining regulations of concern to the U.S. Environmental Protection Agency.

LEXIS

LEXIS is a full-text, proprietary commercial system from Mead Data Central. It is a database with a family of files that contain the full text of the following:

1. *United States Code*—a codification by major title of the body of United States statutes

2. *Code of Federal Regulations*—a codification by major titles of current effective administrative agency regulations

3. *Federal Register* (July 1980 to the present)

4. Supreme Court decisions since 1960

5. State court decisions—courts of last resort, intermediary courts, lower courts

WESTLAW

Like LEXIS, this is a full-text, commercial retrieval system from West Publishing Company, a publisher of legal reference works. It provides access to the text of the:

1. *United States Code*

2. *Code of Federal Regulations*

3. *Federal Register*

4. Supreme Court decisions as found in the *Supreme Court Reporter*, a West publication

5. State court decisions

6. *Shepard's Citations*—a publication providing cross references for court litigation and establishing legal precedents

Both LEXIS and WESTLAW are recommended for use primarily by legal and paralegal researchers with interest in relevant decisions, specific citations, and relevant case law which may relate to a specific issue.

Overview of United States Environmental Legislation

An overview of United States (also referred to as federal) environmental legislation is provided here. State environmental legislation and regulations have been patterned after the federal programs. Information on selected major federal environmental laws is organized under Basic Objective and Key Provisions.

National Environmental Policy Act (NEPA) (42 U.S.C. 4341 et seq.) 1969/70

Basic Objectives.   Main objectives of this act are: "To declare a national policy which will encourage productive and enjoyable harmony between man and his environment; to promote efforts which will prevent or eliminate damage to the environment and biosphere and stimulate the health and welfare of man; to enrich the understanding of the ecological systems and natural resources important to the Nation; and to establish a Council on Environmental Quality."

President's Council on Environmental Quality (CEQ) has the main responsibility for overseeing federal efforts to comply with NEPA. In 1978, CEQ issued regulations to comply with the procedural provisions of NEPA (40 CRF 1500-1508-Appendix D). Provisions of NEPA apply to major federal actions significantly affecting the quality of the human environment.

This act requires federal agencies to assess the environmental impact of implementing their major programs and actions early in the planning process. For those projects or actions which are either expected to have a significant effect on the quality of the human environment or are expected to be controversial on environmental grounds, the proponent agency is required to file a formal environmental impact statement (EIS).

Key Provisions.   Key provisions of this act are summarized as follows:

Title I: Declaration of National Environmental Policy.   Section 101 contains substantive and policy requirements of the act. It emphasizes "...the critical importance of restoring and maintaining environmental quality...declares that it is the continuing policy of the Federal Government...to use all practicable means and measures,...to create and maintain conditions under which man and nature can exist in productive harmony,..." to fulfill the needs of present and future generations.

Section 102 describes the procedural requirements of the act. For every federal action significantly affecting the quality of the human environment a detailed environmental impact statement (EIS) is required to be prepared by the responsible official. CEQ has issued regulations outlining the content and coordination requirements for an EIS. These regulations also describe other documents such as an environmental assessment, finding of no significant impact, and record of decision that may need to be prepared.

Title II of the act describes the makeup of the President's Council on Environmental Quality and its responsibilities.

Clean Air Act (42 U.S.C. 7401 et seq.) 1970, 1977, 1990 Amendments

Basic Objective. The Clean Air Act of 1970, which amended the Air Quality Act of 1967, was established "to protect and enhance the quality of the Nation's air resources so as to promote public health and welfare and the productive capacity of its population." Since 1970, the basic act has been significantly amended to reflect national concern over air quality. Support for cleaner air has come from both environmentalists and the general public, although legislation has been politically controversial because of its impact on industry and economic growth.

The major provisions of the act are intended to set a goal for cleaner air by setting national primary and secondary ambient air quality standards. These standards define levels of air quality necessary to protect public health, while secondary standards define levels necessary to protect the public welfare from any known or anticipated adverse effects of a pollutant.

The basic objectives of the Clean Air Act Amendments of 1977 were to define issues related to significant deterioration and nonattainment areas, to implement a concept of a mission offset, to encourage use of innovative control technologies, to prevent industries from benefiting economically from noncompliance with air pollution control requirements, to state that using tall stacks to disperse air pollutants not be considered a permanent solution to the air pollution problem, to state that federal facilities must comply with both procedural and substantive state pollution control requirements, and to establish guidelines for future EPA standard setting in a number of areas.

The 1990 Clean Air Act Amendments (CA 90) represent another major effort by the U.S. Congress to address many complex and controversial issues related to clean air legislation. CA 90 is expected to have profound and far-reaching effects on federal facilities and industry. One indication of the magnitude of efforts commanded by these amendments is their estimated cost. Expenditures to meet the new requirements are projected to be $20 to $25 billion per year.

Basic objectives of CA 90 are to overhaul the nonattainment provisions, to create an elaborate technology-based control program for toxic air pollutants, to address acid precipitation and power plant emissions, to mandate the phaseout of CFCs, and to greatly strengthen enforcement powers of regulatory agencies.

Key Provisions.   Key provisions of the seven titles of the act are summarized as follows:

Title I: Attainment and Maintenance of the National Ambient-Air Quality Standards.   This title describes air pollution control requirements for geographic areas in the United States which have failed to meet the National Ambient Air Quality Standards (NAAQS). These areas are known as nonattainment areas. Ozone is currently the most pervasive nonattainment pollutant in the United States, and this title is directed at controlling the pollutants (volatile organic compounds and nitrogen oxides) which contribute to ground-level ozone formation. Title VI of this act discusses stratospheric ozone issues.

Title II: Mobile Sources.   This title deals with revised tailpipe emission standards for motor vehicles. Requirements under this title compel automobile manufacturers to improve design standards to limit carbon monoxide, hydrocarbon, and nitrogen oxide emissions. Manufacturers must also investigate the feasibility of controlling refueling emissions. For the worst ozone and carbon monoxide nonattainment areas, reformulated and oxygenated gasolines will be required.

Title III: Hazardous Air Pollutants.   This title deals with control of hazardous air pollutant emissions and contingency planning for accidental release of these pollutants. Requirements of this title are, perhaps, the most costly aspects of CA 90.

Title IV: Acid Deposition Control.   The amendments establish a totally new control scheme for addressing the acid rain problem. The exclusive focus is on power plant emissions of sulfur dioxide and nitrogen oxide. Sulfur dioxide emissions are to be reduced by approximately 10 million tons annually in two phases—the first to take effect in 1995, the second in 2000. It is important to note that these reductions are to be achieved through a new market-based system under which power plants are to be allocated "emissions allowances" that will require plants to reduce their emissions or acquire allowances from others to achieve compliance. The target for the reduction of nitrogen oxide is established at 2 million tons per year.

Title V: Permits.   This title provides for the states to issue federally enforceable operating permits to applicable stationary sources. The permits are designed to enforce the ability of the federal EPA, state regulatory agencies, and private citizens to enforce the requirements of CA 90. These permits will also be used to clarify operating and control requirements for stationary sources.

Title VI: Stratospheric Ozone Protection.   This title limits emissions of chlorofluorocarbons (CFCs), halons, and other halogenic chemicals which contribute to the destruction of stratospheric ozone. Provisions of this title closely follow the control strategies recommended in June 1990 by the second meeting of parties to the Montreal protocol.

Title VII: Enforcement.   Requirements of this title completely replace existing enforcement provisions in the Clean Air Act Amendments of 1977. New enforcement actions include higher maximum fines and terms of imprisonment. Seriousness of violations has been upgraded and liabilities are now targeted at senior management rather than on-site operators.

Pollution Prevention Act of 1990 (PL 101-508, Title VI, Subtitle F, Sections 6601–6610)

Basic Objective.   Traditionally, environmental legislation in the United States has focused on an end-of-pipe-control approach for minimizing discharge of pollutants to the environment. By using this approach, considerable progress has been made in reducing the total discharge of pollutants to the environment. However, this often has resulted in transferring pollutants from one medium to the other and in many cases is not cost-effective. The basic objective of the Pollution Prevention Act is to establish a national policy of preventing or reducing pollution at the source wherever feasible, and it directs the federal EPA to undertake certain steps in that regard. Prior to this act, RCRA Hazardous and Solid Waste Amendments of 1984 had established a program of waste minimization through many provisions including requiring large-quantity generators to certify on their waste manifests that they have a program in place to minimize the amount and toxicity of wastes generated to the extent economically feasible.

Key Provisions.   The Pollution Prevention Act of 1990 established as national policy the following waste management hierarchy:

- Prevention—The waste management priority is to prevent or reduce pollution at the source whenever feasible.
- Recycling—Where pollution cannot be prevented, it should be recycled in an environmentally safe manner whenever feasible.
- Treatment—In the absence of feasible prevention and recycling, pollution should be treated to applicable standards prior to release or transfers.
- Disposal—Only as a last resort are wastes to be disposed of safely.

The Pollution Prevention Act further directed the EPA to:

- Establish a prevention office independent of the agency's single-medium program offices (EPA added pollution prevention to the existing function of Assistant Administrator for Pesticides and Toxic Substances); Congress appropriated $8 million for each of the fiscal years 1991, 1992, and 1993 for the new office to fulfill the functions delineated in the act.

- Facilitate the adoption by business of source reduction techniques by establishing a source reduction clearinghouse and a state matching grants program; Congress further appropriated $8 million for each of the fiscal years 1991, 1992, and 1993 for state grants, with a 50 percent state match requirement.

- Establish a training program on source reduction opportunities for state and federal officials working in all agency program offices.

- Identify opportunities to use federal procurement to encourage source reduction.

- Establish an annual award program to recognize a company or companies which operate outstanding or innovative source reduction programs.

- Issue a biennial status report to Congress (initial report to be issued October–November 1992).

- Require an annual toxic chemicals source reduction and recycling report for each owner or operator of a facility already required to file an annual toxic chemical release form under section 313 of the Superfund Amendments and Reauthorization Act (SARA) of 1986.

The EPA is pursuing integrating pollution prevention into all its programs and activities and has developed unique voluntary reduction programs with public and private sectors. The EPA 33/50 program, through voluntary enrollment and direct action by industry, seeks to reduce the generation of high-priority wastes from a target group of 17 toxic chemicals by 50 percent by 1995, with an interim goal of 33 percent reduction by 1992. This reduction is measured against a 1988 baseline.

Noise Control Act (42 U.S.C. 4901 et seq.)

Enacted: 1972 (PL 92-574)
Major amendments: 1976 (PL 94-301); 1978 (PL 95-609)

Basic Objective.   Noise pollution is one of the most pervasive environmental problems. A report to the President and Congress on noise indicates that between 80 and 100 million people are bothered by environmental noise on a daily basis, and approximately 40 million people are adversely affected (*Report to the President and Congress on Noise*, 1971).

Since noise is a by-product of human activity, the extent of exposure increases as a function of population growth, population density, mobility, and industrial activities. Acts such as NEPA also have an effect on noise control requirements and related land uses.

In congressional hearings regarding federal aviation noise policy (Federal Noise Policy, 1990), it was pointed out that aviation noise is a serious environmental problem for those who live near airports. The Federal Aviation

Administration has authority to regulate aircraft noise emissions, and classifies aircraft into three categories based on their noise levels. Stage 1 aircraft, with the highest emissions, are planes manufactured in the 1960s and 1970s. The original 707 and DC-8 are examples. Stage 2 aircraft represent newer designs, such as the 737 and later models of the 727. Stage 3 aircraft are the newest designs, mostly of mid-1980s production, such as the MD80 and 767, and are notably quieter than older designs.

Since 1988, operation of stage 1 aircraft has been flatly prohibited at many urban airports, which has reduced the number of persons seriously affected by noise from an estimated 7 million in the mid-1970s to 3.2 million in 1990 (Federal Aviation Noise Policy, 1990). Stage 2 aircraft may continue to be operated, though their proportion in the fleet is decreasing through natural attrition, and all are expected to drop out of use after the year 2000. Many citizens' groups and airport authorities are requesting even faster phaseout of stage 2 aircraft. The European Community prohibits the purchase of new stage 2 aircraft, even as replacements, and plans to phase out their use well before 2000. The business and economic implications of this regulation of aircraft type are serious. The mix of stage 2 and stage 3 aircraft varies widely among airline companies, with some of the highest proportions of older aircraft being held by companies in relatively poor financial condition, who may not be able to afford the purchase of new aircraft.

The Noise Control Act has four basic objectives:

1. New product noise emission standards directed principally at surface transportation and construction noise sources
2. The utilization of "in-use" controls directed principally at aviation, interstate motor carriers, and railroad noise sources
3. The labeling of products for protection against voluntary high-level individual exposure
4. The development of state and local programs to control noise

Key Provisions. The act mandates the EPA to promulgate standards for noise emissions from the following new products:

1. Portable air compressors
2. Medium- and heavy-duty trucks
3. Earth-moving machinery
4. Buses
5. Truck-mounted solid waste compactors
6. Motorcycles
7. Jackhammers
8. Lawn mowers

Additionally, the act specifies that the following sources will be regulated via performance standards:

1. Construction equipment
2. Transportation equipment (with the aid of the Department of Transportation)
3. Any motor or engine
4. Electrical or electronic equipment
5. Any other source which can feasibly be regulated

Section 7 of the act also amends the Federal Aviation Act and regulates aircraft noise and sonic booms. The Federal Aviation Administration (FAA) is given the authority to regulate such noise after consultation with and review by the EPA.

In 1987, the Noise Control Act was amended by the Quiet Communities Act. This amendment provided for greater involvement by state and local authorities in controlling noise. Its objectives are:

1. The dissemination of information concerning noise pollution
2. The conducting or financing of research on noise pollution
3. The administration of the quiet communities program, which involves grants to local communities, the monitoring of noise emissions, studies on noise pollution, and the education and training of the public concerning the hazards of noise pollution
4. The development and implementation of a national noise environmental assessment program to (*a*) identify trends in noise exposure, (*b*) set ambient levels of noise, (*c*) set compliance data, (*d*) assess the effectiveness of noise abatement
5. The establishment of regional technical assistance centers

The EPA is further given the authority to certify a product as acceptable for low noise emission levels. These certified products are to be used by federal agencies in lieu of a like product that is not certified.

Safe Drinking Water Act (42 U.S.C. 300f et seq.)

Enacted: 1974 (PL 93-523)
Major amendments: 1977 (PL 95-190); 1986 (PL 99-339)

Basic Objectives.   The primary objectives of the act are twofold: (1) to protect the nation's sources of drinking water, and (2) to protect public health to the maximum extent possible, using proper water-treatment techniques. The act establishes the need to set contaminant levels to protect public health. These levels were established in regulations issued pursuant to the act, which requires the EPA to develop regulations for the protection of underground sources of drinking water. Any underground injection of wastewater must be authorized by a permit. Such a permit is not issued until the applicant can prove that such disposal will not affect drinking water sources. Finally, the act requires procedures for inspection, monitoring, record keeping, and reporting.

Key Provisions.   Key provisions of the act can be summarized as:

1. The establishment of national primary drinking water standards based on maximum contaminant levels (MCLs).
2. The establishment of treatment techniques to meet the standards.
3. The establishment of secondary drinking water standards.
4. The establishment of those contaminants for which standards are set, based on studies conducted by the National Academy of Sciences. The EPA requests comments from the Science Advisory Board, established under the Environmental Research, Development, and Demonstration Act of 1978, prior to proposals on new or revised MCLs.
5. The establishment of state management programs for enforcement responsibilities. States must submit regulatory programs to the EPA for approval. These programs must set primary and secondary drinking water standards which meet or better the national standards. They must also regulate by permit facilities which treat drinking water supplies.
6. The protection of underground sources of drinking water.
7. The establishment of procedures for development, implementation, and assessment of demonstration programs designed to protect critical aquifer protection areas located within areas designated as sole or principal source aquifers.
8. The requirement for state programs to protect wellhead areas from contaminants which may have adverse effects on public health.

Clean Water Act (33 U.S.C. 1251 et seq.)

Enacted: 1948 (Ch. 758, 62 Stat. 1155)
Major amendments 1956 (Ch. 518, §1, 70 Stat. 498); 1972 (PL 92-500); 1977 (PL 95-217); 1987 (PL 100-4)

Basic Objective.   The Clean Water Act is the primary authority for water pollution control programs with emphasis on surface waters. The objective of these programs is to "restore and maintain the chemical, physical, and biological integrity of the Nation's waters." The act set national goals to:

1. Eliminate the discharge of pollutants into navigable waters by 1985
2. Set interim goals of water quality which will protect fish and wildlife and will provide for recreation by July 1, 1983
3. Prohibit the discharge of toxic pollutants in quantities that might adversely affect the environment
4. Construct publicly owned waste-treatment facilities with federal financial assistance
5. Establish waste-treatment management plans within each state
6. Establish the technology necessary to eliminate the discharge of pollutants
7. Develop and implement programs for the control of nonpoint sources of pollution to enable the goals of the act to be met

The goals are to be achieved by a legislative program which includes permits under the National Pollutant Discharge Elimination System (NPDES). Effluent limitations imposed under the initial legislation required the existing sources of pollution to use the "best practicable" treatment technology by 1977 and the "best available" technology by 1983; amendments provided means for modification of compliance dates. It requires an independent set of effluent limitations of new sources.

Key Provisions.   Development of effluent standards and permit systems and state and local responsibilities are key provisions of the act.

Effluent standards for existing and new sources of water pollution are established. These are source-specific limitations. Also, the act lists categories of point sources for which the EPA must issue standards of performance for new sources. States must develop and submit to the EPA a procedure for applying and enforcing these standards.

The EPA may establish a list of toxic pollutants and establish effluent limitations based on the best available technology economically achievable for point sources designated by the EPA. The EPA has also issued pretreatment standards for toxic pollutants.

Anyone conducting an activity, including construction or operation of a facility, which may result in any discharge into navigable waters must first obtain a permit. Permit applications must include a certification that the discharge meets applicable provisions of the act, under NPDES. Permits for a discharge into ocean water are issued under separate guidelines from the EPA. The Corps of Engineers issues permits for the discharge of dredged or fill material in ocean water, based on criteria established by the Corps.

The act makes provision for direct grants to states to help them in administering pollution-control programs. It also provides grants to assist in the development and implementation of waste-treatment management programs, including the construction of waste-treatment facilities. The federal share of construction costs was to be no more than 55 percent after October 1, 1984.

To be eligible for these grants, states must develop waste-treatment management plans that are based upon federally issued guidelines. These programs must be approved by the EPA and must include:

1. Regulatory programs to assure that the treatment facilities will include applicable pretreatment requirement.
2. The identification of sources of pollution and the process by which control will be achieved.
3. A process to control sources of groundwater pollution.
4. The control of pollution from dredged or fill material into navigable waters; this must meet Section 404 requirements of this act.

Waste-treatment management was on an areawide basis, providing for the control of pollution from all point and nonpoint sources. In addition, the states are required to develop implementation plans for EPA approval to meet minimum water quality standards established by the EPA.

Other provisions of the act state that federal facilities must comply with all federal, state, and local requirements for the abatement and control of pollution. Also, the act provides grants to conduct a national wetlands inventory.

In November 1990, the EPA issued regulations setting forth the NPDES permit application requirements for stormwater discharges associated with industrial activities, discharge from municipal storm sewer systems which serve urban areas of 250,000 population or greater, and discharges from municipal storm sewer systems serving populations between 100,000 and 250,000.

Enforcement Responsibilities; Federal-State Relationship. Except for issuing permits for the discharge of dredged or fill material, the EPA has no enforcement responsibilities for the act. The Corps of Engineers has the responsibility of issuing permits for specific categories of activities involving discharge of dredged or fill materials if the discharge will cause only minimal adverse effects. Sites for the discharge of dredged or fill material are specified by EPA guidelines.

Like many other major environmental statutes, the Clean Water Act emphasizes eventual state primacy and enforcement responsibilities. When the state has plans for preserving or restoring water quality, and the EPA has approved those programs, the state will then assume enforcement responsibilities. Both these programs are based upon a minimal federal regulatory involvement. The federal role is also one of providing grants to states for the implementation of these programs.

Resource Conservation and Recovery Act (RCRA) (42 U.S.C. 6901 et seq.)

Enacted: 1976 (PL 94-580) (as an amendment that completely revised the Solid Waste Disposal Act)

Major amendment: 1984 (PL 98-616) (Hazardous and Solid Waste Amendments of 1984)

Basic Objective.   RCRA, as it exists now, is the culmination of a long series of pieces of legislation, dating back to the passage of the Solid Waste Disposal Act of 1965, which address the problem of waste disposal. It began with the attempt to control solid waste disposal and eventually evolved into an expression of the national concern with the safe and proper disposal of hazardous waste. Establishing alternatives to existing methods of land disposal and to conversion of solid wastes into energy are two important needs noted by the act.

The RCRA of 1976 gives the EPA broad authority to regulate the disposal of hazardous wastes; encourages the development of the solid waste management plans and nonhazardous waste regulatory programs by states; prohibits open dumping of wastes; regulates underground storage tanks; and provides for a national research, development, and demonstration program for improved solid waste management and resource conservation techniques.

The control of hazardous wastes will be undertaken by identifying and tracking hazardous wastes as they are generated, ensuring that hazardous wastes are properly contained and transported, and regulating the storage, disposal, or treatment of hazardous wastes. A major objective of the RCRA is to protect the environment and conserve resources through the development and implementation of solid waste management plans by the states. The act recognizes the need to develop and demonstrate waste management practices that are not only environmentally sound and economically viable but also conserve resources. The act requires the EPA to undertake a number of special studies on subjects such as resource recovery from glass and plastic waste and managing the disposal of sludge and tires. An Interagency Resource Conservation Committee has been established to report to the President and the Congress on the economic, social, and environmental consequences of present and alternative resource conservation and resource recovery techniques.

Key Provisions.   Hazardous wastes are identified by definition and publication. Four classes of definitions of hazardous waste have been identified—ignitability, reactivity, corrosivity, and toxicity. The chemicals that fall into these classes are regulated primarily because of the dangerous situations they can cause when landfilled with typical municipal refuse. Four lists, containing approximately 1000 distinct chemical compounds, have been published. (These lists are revised as new chemicals become available.) These lists include waste chemicals from nonspecific sources, by-products of specific industrial processes, and pure or off-specification commercial chemical products. These classes of chemicals are regulated primarily to protect groundwater from contamination by toxic products and by-products.

The act requires tracking of hazardous wastes from generation, to transportation, to storage, to disposal or treatment. Generators, transporters, and operators of facilities that dispose of solid wastes must comply with a system of record keeping, labeling, and manufacturing to ensure that all hazardous waste is designated only for authorized treatment, storage, or disposal facilities. The EPA must issue permits for these facilities, and they must comply with the standards issued by the EPA.

The states must develop hazardous waste management plans which must be EPA-approved. These programs will regulate hazardous wastes in the states and will control the issuance of permits. If a state does not develop such a program, the EPA, based on the federal program, will do so.

Solid waste disposal sites are to be inventoried to determine compliance with the sanitary landfill regulations issued by the EPA. Open dumps are to be closed or upgraded within 5 years of the inventory. As with hazardous waste management, states must develop management plans to control the disposal of solid waste and to regulate disposal sites. EPA has issued guidelines to assist states in developing their programs.

As of 1983, experience and a variety of studies dating back to the initial passage of the RCRA legislation found that an estimated 40 million metric tons of hazardous waste escaped control annually through loopholes in the legislative and regulatory framework. Subsequently, Congress was forced to reevaluate RCRA, and in doing so found that RCRA fell short of its legislative intent by failing to regulate a significant number of small-quantity generators, regulate waste oil, ensure environmentally sound operation of land disposal facilities, and realize the need to control the contamination of groundwater caused by leaking underground storage tanks. Major amendments were enacted in 1984 in order to address the shortcomings of RCRA. Key provisions of the 1984 amendments include

- Notification of underground tank data and regulations for detection, prevention, and correction of releases
- Incorporation of small-quantity generators (which generate between 100 and 1000 kg of hazardous waste per month) into the regulatory scheme
- Restriction of land disposal of a variety of wastes unless EPA determines that land disposal is safe from human health and environmental points of views
- Requirement of corrective action by treatment, storage, and disposal facilities for all releases of hazardous waste regardless of when the waste was placed in the unit
- Requirement of the EPA to inspect government-owned facilities (which handle hazardous waste) annually, and other permitted hazardous waste facilities at least every other year
- Regulation of facilities which burn wastes and oils in boilers and industrial furnaces

Liability.   As with funding, liability under RCRA is not specifically mentioned. It can be assumed that joint and several liability under RCRA will be determined under regular business organization law or CERCLA; that is, if officers of an organization pursue policies or otherwise allow for a release of hazardous wastes under RCRA, liability will hold to those persons under business law or CERCLA joint and several liability provisions as interpreted by the courts.

The following are those significant civil and criminal liabilities that are expressly included in RCRA:

Civil.   RCRA 3008(a):

- Penalty for violation of compliance order is not greater than $25,000 per day of noncompliance with each violation of the order.

     RCRA 3008(g):

- Any person who violates any requirement of Subtitle C is liable to the United States for a civil penalty in an amount not to exceed $25,000 for each violation where each day of violation constitutes a separate violation.

Criminal.   RCRA 3008(d):

- Persons are criminally liable who knowingly transport, treat, store, or dispose of specified hazardous wastes to a facility which does not have a permit or in knowing violation of the conditions of the permit or applicable interim status regulations or standards.
- Persons are liable who knowingly omit material information or make false material statements concerning an application, label, manifest, record, report, permit, or other document used to determine compliance.
- Knowing endangerment is a violation for persons who knowingly transport, treat, store, dispose of, or export any specified hazardous waste who know at that time that they thereby place another person in imminent danger of death or serious bodily injury; they are subject to a fine of not more than 15 years or not more than $250,000 or both. Organizations which are defendants are subject to a fine of not more than $1 million.

Comprehensive Environmental Response, Compensation and Liability Act (CERCLA) (42 U.S.C. 9601 et seq.)

Enacted: 1980 (PL 96-510)
Major amendment: 1986 (PL 99-499) (Superfund Amendments and Reauthorization Act)

Basic Objective.   The act, known as Superfund or CERCLA, has four objectives:

1. To provide the enforcement agency the authority to respond to the releases for hazardous wastes (as defined in the Federal Water Pollution Control Act,

Clean Air Act, Toxic Substances Control Act, Solid Waste Disposal Act, and by the administrator of the enforcement agency) from "inactive" hazardous waste sites which endanger public health and the environment.

2. To establish a hazardous substance Superfund.

3. To establish regulations controlling inactive hazardous waste sites.

4. To provide liability for releases of hazardous wastes from such inactive sites.

The act amends the Solid Waste Disposal Act. It provides for an inventory of inactive and "orphan" hazardous waste sites and for appropriate action to protect the public from the dangers possible from such sites. It is a response to the concern for the dangers of negligent hazardous waste disposal practices.

Key Provisions

1. The establishment of a hazardous substance Superfund based on fees from industry and federal appropriations to finance response actions.

2. The establishment of liability to recover costs of response from liable parties and to induce the cleanup of sites by responsible parties.

3. The determination of the number of inactive hazardous waste sites by conducting a national inventory. This inventory includes coordination by the Agency for Toxic Substances and Disease Registry (ATSDR) of the Public Health Service for the purpose of implementing the health-related authorities in the act.

4. The provision of the authority of the EPA to act when there is a release or threat of release of a pollutant from a site which may endanger public health. Such action may include "removal, remedy, and remedial action."

5. The revision, within 180 days of enactment of the act, of the National Contingency Plan for the Removal of Oil and Hazardous Substances (40 CFR, Part 300). This plan must include a section to establish procedures and standards for responding to releases of hazardous substances, pollutants, and contaminants and abatement actions necessary to offset imminent dangers

Superfund Amendments and Reauthorization Act (SARA) (42 U.S.C. 11001 et seq.)

Enacted: 1986 (PL 99-499)

Basic Objective.   This act revises and extends CERCLA (Superfund authorization). CERCLA is extended by the addition of new authorities known as the Emergency Planning and Community Right-to-Know Act of 1986 (also known as Title III of SARA). Title III of SARA provides for "emergency planning and preparedness, community right-to-know reporting, and toxic chemical release reporting." This act also establishes a special program within the Department of Defense for restoration of contaminated lands, somewhat similar to the Superfund under CERCLA.

Key Provisions.   There are key provisions which apply when a hazardous substance is handled and when an actual release has occurred. Even before any emergency has arisen, certain information must be made available to state and local authorities, and to the general public upon request. Facility owners and operators are obligated to provide information pertaining to any regulated substance present on the facility to the appropriate state or local authorities (Subtitle A). Three types of information are to be reported to the appropriate state and local authorities (Subtitle B):

1. Material safety data sheets (MSDSs), which are prepared by the chemical manufacturer of any hazardous chemical and are retained by the facility owner or operator (or if confidentiality is a concern, a list of hazardous chemicals for which MSDSs are retained can be made available). These sheets contain general information on a hazardous chemical and provide an initial notice to the state and local authorities.

2. Emergency and hazardous chemical inventory forms, which are submitted annually to the state and local authorities. Tier I information includes the maximum amount of a hazardous chemical which may be present at any time during the reporting year, and the average daily amount present during the year prior to the reporting year. Also included is the "general location of hazardous chemicals in each category." This information is available to the general public upon request. Tier II information is reported only if requested by an emergency entity or fire department. This information provides a more detailed description of the chemicals, the average amounts handled, the precise location, storage procedures, and whether the information is to be made available to the general public (allowing for the protection of confidential information).

3. Toxic chemical release reporting, which releases general information about effluents and emissions of any "toxic chemicals."

In the event that a release of a hazardous substance does occur, a facility owner or operator must notify the authorities. This notification must identify the hazardous chemical involved; amounts released; time, duration, and environmental fate; and suggested action.

A multilayer emergency planning and response network on the state and local government levels is to be established, also providing a notification scheme in the event of a release.

CERCLA/SARA

Funding. Superfund. EPA is authorized to draw upon Superfund to finance response activities. The EPA is to replenish this fund through action taken against persons liable for response costs. In practice, a fund must be maintained through a mix of specified taxes and general revenues until and unless the responsible parties are made to pay.

Originally, CERCLA was to be funded from specified taxes and general revenues to a level of $1.6 billion over 5 years through industry taxes (87.5 percent) and general revenues (12.5 percent). The industry taxes were levied mainly on the petrochemical and crude oil industries.

Under Title V of SARA, this level was increased to $8.5 billion. Congress authorized the appropriation of $212 million out of general revenues for each of the 5 fiscal years from 1986 to 1991 and the rest of the money was to be gained from special taxes on industry. Under the Omnibus Budget and Reconciliation Act of 1990 (PL 101-508), Congress extended the taxing authority under this program without modification through December 1995.

Liability. CERCLA establishes strict liability (liability without proof of fault) for the cleanup of facilities on "responsible parties." The courts have found under CERCLA that these parties are "jointly and severally" liable; that is, each and every ascertainable party is liable for the full cost of removal or remediation, regardless of the level of "guilt" a party may have concerning a particular cleanup action. In practice, since it is hard in some cases to identify responsible parties, or those parties have no assets with which to pay response costs, the EPA goes after a few big responsible parties with "deep pockets." Under SARA, there is a right of contribution (responsible parties can sue each other) to recuperate cost incurred based on the responsible parties' relative levels of "guilt." All the responsible parties are then liable for the costs of response actions taken by others, and for damages to natural resources, when hazardous substances are released or there is a substantial threat of their release into the environment. The following is a simplified list of those potentially responsible parties for CERCLA remediation actions:

- Owner and operators of vessels and facilities
- Owner or operator of facilities at time of hazardous waste disposal
- Any person who arranged for transport, disposal, or treatment of hazardous waste
- Any person who accepted for transport hazardous waste to a site from which hazardous waste was released

Under several recent cases, the list of responsible parties grew to include (in some cases) individual corporate officers, shareholders, or employees at a hazardous waste facility, a secured creditor of a hazardous waste facility, and even individual states.

Persons in these groups, with very limited exceptions, are held liable for removal or remediation costs, any other necessary costs of response, damages for "injury to, destruction of, or loss of natural resources," and the costs of related health assessments or health effects studies.

Some classes of persons are excluded from the class of "responsible parties" under CERCLA 107. These include holders of federally authorized permits (for most of those releases authorized by the permits), and applicators of pesticides properly listed under the Federal Insecticide, Fungicide, and Rodenticide Act (FIFRA). In addition, no liability is imposed if the release or threat of release of hazardous waste was due to an act of God, an act of war, or certain acts or omissions by third parties.

Significant civil and criminal liabilities under CERCLA/SARA include:

Civil Penalties.   CERCLA 107:

- Response and damage costs: full liability for all necessary response costs for all responsible parties for willful or negligent conduct, or if primary cause of the release was a violation of applicable safety, construction, or operating standards or regulations.

CERCLA 109:

- Administrative penalties: penalties of not more than $25,000 per violation for those violations relating to notice, destruction of records, financial responsibility, settlement agreements, administrative orders, consent decrees, or other applicable agreements. For certain of these penalties, a second or subsequent violation may result in a fine of not more than $75,000 for each day during which the violation continues.

Criminal Penalties.   CERCLA 103:

- Failure to give notice of release of hazardous substance: penalties of imprisonment of not more than 3 years (or 5 years for subsequent violations).

- Failure to give notice of existence of specified hazardous waste facilities: penalties of not more than $10,000 or imprisonment of not more than 1 year, or both, for knowing failure to provide appropriate notice.

Federal Insecticide, Fungicide, and Rodenticide Act (FIFRA) (7 U.S.C. 136 et seq.)

Enacted: 1947 (Ch. 125, 61 Stat. 163)
Major amendments: 1972 (PL 92-516); 1978 (PL 95-396); 1988 (PL 100-532); 1991 (PL 102-237)

Basic Objective. FIFRA is designed to regulate the use and safety of pesticide products within the United States (which is in excess of 1 billion pounds). The 1972 amendments, a major restructuring which established the contemporary regulatory structure, are intended to ensure that the environmental harm resulting from the use of pesticides does not outweigh the benefits.

Key Provisions

- The evaluation of risks posed by pesticides (requiring registration)
- The classification and certification of pesticides by specific use (as a way to control exposure)
- The restriction of the use of pesticides which are harmful to the environment (or suspending or canceling the use of the pesticide)
- The enforcement of the above requirements through inspections, labeling, notices, and state regulation

Marine Protection, Research, and Sanctuaries Act (33 U.S.C. 1401 et seq.)

Enacted: 1972 (PL 92-532)
Major amendments: 1984 (PL 98-498); 1988 (PL 100-627)

Basic Objective. This act regulates the dumping of all types of materials into the ocean. It prevents or severely restricts the dumping of materials adversely affecting human welfare, the marine environment, ecological systems, or economic potentialities. It provides for a permitting process to control the ocean dumping of dredged material.

The act also establishes the marine sanctuaries program, which designates certain areas of the ocean waters as sanctuaries, when such designation is necessary to preserve or restore these areas for their conservation, recreation, ecology, or aesthetic values. States are involved in the program through veto powers to prohibit a designation.

Key Provisions. The EPA is responsible for issuing permits for the dumping of materials in ocean waters except for dredged material (regulated by the Corps of Engineers), radiological, chemical, and biological warfare agents, and high-level radioactive waste for which no permits are issued.

The EPA has established criteria for reviewing and evaluating permit applications (40 CFR, Subchapter H). These criteria consider:

1. The need for the proposed dumping
2. The effect of such dumping on human health and welfare, including economic, aesthetic, and recreational values

3. The effect of such dumping on marine ecosystems

4. The persistence and permanence of the effects of the dumping

5. The effect of dumping particular volumes and concentrations of such materials

6. Locations and methods of disposal or recycling, including land-based alternatives

7. The effect on alternate uses of oceans such as scientific study, fishing, and other living resource exploitation

The Secretary of the Army is responsible for issuing permits for the transportation and disposal of dredged material in ocean waters. The Secretary applies the same criteria for the issuance of permits as the EPA uses and will issue permits in consultation with the EPA. Permits issued by the EPA or the Corps of Engineers designate:

1. The type of material authorized to be transported for dumping or to be dumped

2. The amount of material authorized to be transported for dumping or to be dumped

3. The location where such transport for dumping will be terminated or where such dumping will occur

4. The length of time for which the permits are valid

5. Any special provisions

The other major provision of the act is the establishment of the Marine Sanctuaries program.

Toxic Substances Control Act (TSCA) (15 U.S.C. 2601 et seq.)

Enacted: 1976 (PL 94-469)
Major amendments: 1986 (PL 99-419); 1988 (PL 100-551)

Basic Objective.   This act sets up the toxic substances program which is administered by the EPA. If the EPA finds that a chemical substance may present an unreasonable risk to health or to the environment and that there are insufficient data to predict the effects of the substance, manufacturers may be required to conduct tests to evaluate the characteristics of the substance, such as persistence, acute toxicity, or carcinogenic effects. Also, the act establishes a committee to develop a priority list of chemical substances to be tested. The committee may list up to 50 chemicals which must be tested within 1 year. However, the EPA may require testing for chemicals not on the priority list.

Manufacturers must notify the EPA of the intention to manufacture a new chemical substance. The EPA may then determine if the data available are inadequate to assess the health and environmental effects of the new chemical. If the data are determined to be inadequate, the EPA will require testing. Most importantly, the EPA may prohibit the manufacture, sale, use, or disposal of a new or existing chemical substance if it finds the chemical presents an unreasonable risk to health or the environment. The EPA can also limit the amount of the chemical that can be manufactured and used and the manner in which the chemical can be used.

The act also regulates the labeling and disposal of polychlorinated biphenyls (PCBs) and prohibited their production and distribution after July 1979.

In 1986, Title II, "Asbestos Hazard Emergency Response," was added to address issues of inspection and removal of asbestos products in public schools and to study the extent of, and response to, the public health danger posed by asbestos in public and commercial buildings.

Key Provisions. Testing is required on chemical substances meeting certain criteria to develop data with respect to the health and environmental effects for which there are insufficient data relevant to the determination that the chemical substance does or does not present an unreasonable risk of injury to health or the environment.

Testing includes identification of the chemical and standards for test data. Testing is required for the following:

1. Manufacturers of a chemical meeting certain criteria

2. Processors of a chemical meeting certain criteria

3. Distributors or persons involved in disposal of chemicals meeting certain criteria

Test data required by the act must be submitted to the EPA, identifying the chemical, listing the uses or intended uses, and listing the information required by the applicable standards for the development of test data.

The EPA will establish a priority list of chemical substances for regulation. Priority is given to substances known to cause or contribute to cancer, gene mutations, or birth defects. The list is revised and updated as needed.

A new chemical may not be manufactured without notification to the EPA at least 90 days before manufacturing begins. The notification must include test data showing that the manufacture, processing, use, and disposal of the chemical will not present an unreasonable risk of injury to health or the environment. Chemical manufacturers must keep records for submission to the EPA as required. The EPA will use these reports to compile an inventory of chemical substances manufactured or processed in the United States.

The EPA can prohibit the manufacture of a chemical found to present an unreasonable risk of injury to health or the environment or otherwise restrict a chemical. The act also regulates the disposal and use and prohibits the future manufacture of PCBs, and requires the EPA to engage, through various means, in research, development, collection, dissemination, and utilization of data relevant to chemical substances.

National Historic Preservation Act
(16 U.S.C. 470-470t)

Enacted: 1966 (PL 89-665)
Major amendments: 1973 (PL 93-54); 1976 (PL 94-422); 1980 (PL 96-515)

Basic Objective.   The act declares a national policy of preserving, restoring, and maintaining cultural resources. The Advisory Council on Historic Preservation is given responsibility under the act to implement this national policy. The National Register of Historic Places is the mechanism by which historic properties can be protected. Any property in the National Register or eligible for inclusion is protected from certain types of activities and can receive funding for restoration and maintenance. Amendments to the act gave the National Park Service the responsibility for determination of eligibility for inclusion in the National Register. State historic preservation officers are ultimately given enforcement responsibilities within the state.

Key Provisions

1. Regulations for determination of eligibility in the National Register of Historic Places.
2. A federal agency must take into account the effect of a project on any property included in or eligible for inclusion in the National Register.
3. The advisory council must be given an opportunity to comment on a federal project.
4. Federal agencies must inventory all property and nominate any eligible properties to the National Register.
5. Federal agencies must provide for the maintenance of federally owned registered sites.
6. Agencies must coordinate projects with the state historic preservation officer of the state in which the project is located.
7. States can qualify for federal grants for the protection, restoration, and maintenance of properties in the National Register.

Wild and Scenic Rivers Act
(16 U.S.C. 1271 et seq.)

Enacted: 1968 (PL 90-542)
Major amendment: 1974 (PL 93-279)

Basic Objective. This act establishes the Wild and Scenic River System. It essentially protects rivers designated for their wild and scenic values from activities which may adversely impact those values. It provides for a mechanism to determine if a river can meet certain eligibility requirements for protection as a wild and/or scenic river.

Key Provisions. In planning for the use and development of water and land resources, federal agencies must give consideration to potential wild and scenic river areas. This potential must be discussed in all river basin and project plans submitted to Congress. No federal agency is allowed to assist in any way in the construction of a water resources project having a direct and adverse effect on the values for which a river was designated as part of the Wild and Scenic River System.

Likewise, no agency is allowed to recommend authorization or request appropriations to begin construction of a project on a designated river without informing the administering secretary (Secretary of the U.S. Department of Interior or Agriculture) in writing, 60 days in advance, and without specifically reporting to Congress on how construction would conflict with the act and affect values of the river being protected by the act.

No agency is permitted to recommend authorization of, or request appropriations to initiate, construction of a project, on or directly affecting a river designated for potential addition to the system during the full 3 fiscal years after the designation, plus 3 more years for congressional consideration, unless the Secretary of Interior or Agriculture advises against including the segment in the system in a report that lies before Congress for 180 in-session days. The comparable time limit for state-promised additions is 1 year.

Agencies must inform the Secretary of any proceedings, studies, or other activities which would affect a river that is designated as a potential addition to the system. Agencies having jurisdiction over lands which include, border upon, or are adjacent to any river within or under consideration for the system protect the river with management policies and plans for the lands as necessary.

Coastal Zone Management Act
(16 U.S.C. 141 et seq.)

Enacted: 1972 (PL 92-583)
Major amendments: 1976 (PL 94-370); 1980 (PL 96-464); 1985 (PL 99-272); 1990 (PL 101-508)

Basic Objective. The act was passed in response to the public's concern for balanced preservation and development activities in coastal areas. It was designed to help states manage these competing demands and provided funding to states participating in the federal program.

The legislation emphasized the state leadership in the program, and allowed states to participate in the federal program by submitting their own coastal zone management proposals. The purpose of these state programs, which are federally approved, is to increase protection of coastal areas while better managing development and government activities at all levels. The act established the Office of Coastal Zone Management (OCZM) in the National Oceanic and Atmospheric Administration (NOAA). Once the OCZM has approved a state program, federal agency activities within a coastal zone must be consistent "to the maximum extent practicable" with the program.

Key Provisions.   Federal agencies must assess whether their activities will directly affect the coastal zone of a state having an approved program.

The 1980 amendments included, as part of coastal areas, wetlands, floodplains, estuaries, beaches, dunes, barrier islands, coral reefs, and fish and wildlife and their habitat. The act also provides public access to the coast for recreational purposes.

States are encouraged to prepare special area management plans addressing such issues as natural resources, coastal-dependent economic growth, and protection of life and property in hazardous areas. Federal grants are available to the states to cover 80 percent of the costs of administering their federally approved coastal zone management programs. They may use 30 percent of their grants to implement the 1980 amendment provisions.

The states are also encouraged to inventory coastal resources, designate those of "national significance," and establish standards to protect those so designated.

Endangered Species Act (16 U.S.C. 1 531-1 542)

Enacted: 1973 (PL 93-205)
Major amendments: 1978 (PL 95-632); 1982 (PL 97-304); 1988 (PL 100-478)

Basic Objective.   This act seeks to conserve endangered and threatened species. It directs the Fish and Wildlife Service of the U.S. Department of Interior to promulgate a list of endangered and threatened species and designate critical habitat for those species. Amendments also created the Endangered Species Committee to grant exemptions for the act.

Federal agencies must carry out programs for the conservation of listed species and must take actions to ensure that projects they authorize, fund, or carry out are not likely to jeopardize the existence of the listed species or result in the destruction or modification of habitat declared to be critical.

The act divides procedures for those projects begun before and after November 10, 1978. For those not under construction before November 10, 1978, agencies must request the Fish and Wildlife Service to furnish information as to whether any species listed, or proposed to be listed, are in the area. If such species are present, a biological assessment must be completed by the proponent agency within 180 days.

If the biological assessment or other project information reveals that a species may be affected, the agency must consult with the Fish and Wildlife Service (or National Marine Fisheries Service). Consultation must be completed by the service within a 90-day period. The Department of the Interior provides the agency with an opinion as to how the action will affect the species or its critical habitat, and suggests reasonable alternatives. The agency may apply for an exemption to the act to the Endangered Species Committee.

Key Provisions.   Of major significance is the promulgation of a list of species which have been found to be either threatened or endangered and the protection of species on the list from activities which may impact their continued protection and survival. Also, the act provides for the designation of habitat from activities which may harm the delicate ecological balance necessary for the existence of a listed species. Federal agencies are required to perform a biological assessment before undertaking a project to determine the impact of a project on a listed species or its habitat. If that impact is negative, the agency must undertake mitigation procedures or the project must be halted. An important provision of the act is the establishment of an Endangered Species Committee to grant exemptions from the act. A federal agency must consult with the Fish and Wildlife Service if the results of the biological assessment show a listed species may be affected by a project. The Fish and Wildlife Service will suggest alternatives to the agency. A process is established whereby a species can be determined to be threatened or endangered, and thus eligible for the list, or cannot be removed from the list.

Fish and Wildlife Coordination Act (16 U.S.C. 661 et seq.)

Enacted: 1934 (Ch. 55, 48 Stat. 401)
Major amendments: 1946 (Ch. 965, 60 Stat. 1080); 1958 (PL 85-624); 1965 (PL 89-72)

Basic Objective.   This act provides that wildlife conservation be given equal consideration and be coordinated with other aspects of water resource development programs. It establishes the need to coordinate activities of federal, state, and private agencies in the development, protection, and stocking of wildlife resources and their habitat. Also, the act provides procedures for consultation between agencies with the purpose of preventing loss of and damage to wildlife resources from any water resource–related project. Any such consultation includes the Fish and Wildlife Service, the head of the agency having administrative control of state and wildlife resources, and the agency conducting the project.

Key Provisions.   The act requires officers of the agency conducting the project to give full consideration to Fish and Wildlife Service recommendations of the state agency. "Full consideration" includes mitigation measures.

Any report recommending authorization of a new project must contain an estimate of wildlife benefits and losses and the costs and amount of reimbursement. Adequate provision must be made for the use of projects lands and water for the conservation, maintenance, and management of wildlife resources, including their development and improvement.

Lands to be measured by a state for the conservation of wildlife must be managed in accordance with a plan which must be jointly approved by the federal agency exercising primary administrative responsibility, the Secretary of the Interior, and the administering state agency.

Occupational Safety and Health Act (OSHA) (29 U.S.C. 651 et seq.)

Enacted: 1970 (PL 91-596)

Major amendment: 1990 (PL 101-508, Title III, §3101)

Basic Objective.   OSHA is designed to reduce injuries in the workplace by setting standards that would enhance safe and healthful working conditions in places of employment throughout the United States. The purpose of the act is "to assure so far as possible every working man and woman in the nation safe and healthful working conditions and to preserve our human resources." The reach of OSHA is different from the EPA in that OSHA is limited to actual workplace hazards. However, OSHA covers both safety and health while the EPA is concentrated on health issues almost exclusively. It covers every nongovernmental employer engaged in a business affecting commerce who has employees. Federal and state employees are excluded from coverage, but under the act, federal and state governments are authorized to adopt occupational safety and health programs for the benefit of their employees. Each of the covered employers has a duty under the act to furnish employees a place of employment free from recognized hazards that are causing or likely to cause death or serious physical harm and to comply with the standards promulgated under the act. OSHA is very much enforcement-oriented.

Key Provisions.   Sections 6(a) Standards: Promulgated in 2 years after the passage of the act, they are the ones most widely used today and basically codified those standards that were "consensus" and "established federal" standards at the time of the passage of the act.

Section 6(b) Standards: Except for the emergency standards authority given to the Secretary under section 6(c), this is the only current authority for promulgating standards. The act details an elaborate process for promulgating standards under this section. The length and number of challenges made under this process result in the fact that most of the current OSHA standards are section 6(a) standards and there are relatively few section 6(b) standards.

Section 6(c) Standards: Promulgating under these standards is a rarely used authority. Mainly, this section allows the Secretary to adopt "emergency temporary standards" when the Secretary determines that a "grave danger" exists as a result of employee exposure to toxic substances or "new hazards" or harmful physical agents and when this emergency temporary standard is needed to protect employees. It lasts for 6 months unless it is properly promulgated under the rules of the act. Under the act the Secretary can allow for limited variances in order to give the employer sufficient time to comply with OSHA standards.

To help enforce the act, each employer must maintain and provide (when required) to the Department of Labor and to the Department of Health and Human Services a detailed and accurate record of work-related illnesses, injuries, and deaths.

States are encouraged to devise and implement their own occupational safety and health programs. Currently, just under half of the states administer and enforce the act. If an employer is believed to be violating the act, he or she receives from an inspector a citation specifically noting the alleged violation. The citation in most cases will specify what needs to be done to eliminate the violation, and gives the employer a specific time in which he or she must make the necessary workplace improvements. For those employers disputing the violation, the act created the Occupation Safety and Health Review Commission (OSHRC) to review contested OSHA citations and penalties. In terms of civil penalties, willful or repeated violations may result in fines of up to $70,000 for each violation. An employer who does not correct a violation (and who fails under the OSHRC process) may be fined up to $7000 for each day the violation goes uncorrected. Criminally, the act provided that an employer who makes a willful violation of the regulations promulgated under the act which results in an employee death can be fined up to $10,000 and imprisoned for up to 6 months.

Recently, the focus of OSHA has been on workplace ergonomics and specifically on those respective types of actions which result in injuries known as cumulative trauma disorders (CTDs). To help prevent the occurrence of these injuries, guidelines have been promulgated which suggest that employers, among other things:

- Devise written ergonomic programs to reduce CTDs
- Redesign the workstation layouts, tools, and other instruments which create CTDs to reduce or eliminate the number and severity of CTDs
- Conduct surveys to identify the workplace CTD problems
- Establish health and safety committees which then will have the power to eliminate conditions and practices which lead to CTDs
- Require that expansion and remodeling operations be reexamined to ensure proper changes are made to reduce or eliminate the risk of CTDs

Federal Food, Drug, and Cosmetic Act
(21 U.S.C. 301 et seq.)

Enacted: 1938 (Ch. 675, 52 Stat. 1040)

Major amendments: 1958 (PL 85-929); 1976 (PL 94-295); 1988 (PL 100-607); 1990: (PL 101-635)

Basic Objective. With the advance of industrialization and the explosion in the number and kinds of foods, drugs, and cosmetics, Congress decided to act to protect the unwary consumer by passing an act to regulate those items of wide distribution to the consumer. Thus this act is designed to, among other things, "keep interstate channels from deleterious, adulterated and misbranded articles of specified types to the end that public health and safety might be advanced." In addition, the act is to "effect the purpose of securing the purity of food and drugs and informing purchasers of what they are buying."

Key Provisions. The major provisions set by the act or authorized in regulations promulgated under the act are arranged by section and listed as follows:

Prohibition of Certain Acts

- The introduction into commerce of misbranded or adulterated food, drugs, and cosmetics
- Forging, counterfeiting, simulating, or falsely representing any mark, stamp, tag, label, or other identification device required by regulations

Imposition of Penalties

- For doing the prohibited acts listed above (and others), a person can be fined not more than $1000 or imprisoned for less than 1 year or both.
- If a person is convicted for a second time for doing a prohibited act, that person can be fined not more than $10,000 or imprisoned for not more than 3 years or both.

Food

- Sets definitions and standards for food, including but not limited to descriptions of adulterated and misbranded food
- Sets tolerances for poisonous or deleterious substances in food
- Sets tolerances for pesticide chemicals in or on raw agricultural commodities
- Sets conditions for the use of food additives

Drugs and Devices

- Regulates drugs and devices, including strength and quality
- Prohibits misrepresentations of strength
- Prohibits the misbranding of drugs and devices
- Allows for exemptions for certain drugs and devices

- Provides for the process of approving new drugs
- Sets performance standards for specified drugs and devices
- Sets performance standards for electronic product radiation

Imports and Exports

- Sets regulations for these to ensure that consumers both here and abroad are protected.

The act also details the role of the Food and Drug Administration within the Department of Health and Human Services in implementing the provisions of this act.

Environmental Protection in New Jersey*

Geography, population density, and a legacy of high industrial productivity have placed New Jersey at the forefront of environmental protection over the past 20 years. But the state can no longer be sure that the old policies will meet the challenges of a new century.

New Jersey recognizes that regulatory oversight of industrial pollution has reached a turning point. In fact, New Jersey has already enacted restructuring measures that will be hallmarks of a new era of environmental protection, where agencies will promote pollution prevention, public access, efficiency, and a "holistic" environmental awareness.

These are a few of the common threads that run through the comprehensive program of regulatory reform implemented by the Department of Environmental Protection and Energy (DEPE). Another is to make sure regulators work to ensure compliance with regulations that protect the environment, not just penalize those who violate them. The state is striving to reach a point where 100 percent of permit holders are meeting high environmental standards, allowing DEPE to redirect resources now used for enforcement to other desperately needed areas.

But while state environmental protection efforts were originally designed to protect and preserve our natural resources, programs and overall organization became unwieldy and unresponsive over the years, often forcing staff, the public, and members of the regulated community to negotiate a bureaucratic maze and experience protracted permit reviews and costly delays.

In early 1991, DEPE restructured largely along functional lines of permitting, enforcement, and site cleanup. This replaced a system that was organized according to the separate environmental media—air, water, land—each with duplicate permitting, enforcement, and cleanup efforts that lacked coordination and often worked at cross-purposes.

*By Scott A. Weiner, Commissioner, New Jersey Department of Environmental Protection and Energy (Sept. 1992).

Part of the reorganization, for example, consolidated 10 major permit programs under one assistant commissioner for environmental regulation. The new structure creates an agency that is designed to ensure clean air and clean water, preserve our natural resources, be more open and accessible to the public, operate efficiently, issue regulations that are fair and predictable, and firmly enforce state environmental standards.

Changing Focus: Stressing Compliance over Enforcement

One important new goal for New Jersey is to achieve 100 percent compliance with all environmental laws. In recent years, success of regulatory programs was measured by ever-increasing amounts of penalties *assessed* against polluters. But now DEPE judges the success of its regulatory efforts by whether we can achieve ever-increasing rates of *compliance* with environmental standards.

New Jersey should see a steady decrease in the amount of penalty assessments as more and more permit holders are encouraged to meet state regulations. This trend became apparent in 1991 when for the first time the department saw penalty assessments *decline* to $55.3 million from a record $95.9 million in 1990, while the amount collected actually increased to $22.7 million compared with $15.7 million the previous year.

Central to this new approach to compliance is a shift toward reducing the amount of hazardous substances and other pollutants used and generated in the first place before they are released, eliminating or minimizing the need for control and cleanup measures—the concept of "pollution prevention."

More than 15 states have enacted pollution-prevention laws, and in autumn 1990 a national Pollution Prevention Act was passed. Despite the flurry of state and federal legislative activity, pollution prevention has a long way to go to achieve widespread success. The challenge for policymakers is to make sure pollution prevention becomes the centerpiece of a coordinated, long-term environmental policy rather than just an attractive-sounding but empty term.

New Jersey is working to achieve this goal by promoting increased recognition by industries that decisions that make good environmental sense can also make good, cost-effective business sense.

Policy into Action: Implementing the Pollution Prevention Act

DEPE is infusing a pollution-prevention ethic and philosophy throughout its organizational structure. The Office of Pollution Prevention is promoting a "whole facility" regulatory perspective that is designed to improve environmental protection and administrative efficiency. Additionally, the program is located administratively with the multimedia permitting programs to help integrate pollution-prevention principles into regulatory permitting.

Several key premises form the basis for New Jersey's Pollution Prevention Act, including:

Pollution prevention planning "up front"   Environmental protection should be incorporated into the design of industrial processes and products, rather than as an afterthought.

Building it into existing regulatory programs   Pollution prevention should be built into existing regulatory programs rather than become a new regulatory level.

Relying on companies' know-how   Industrial facilities know their processes best and should have regulatory flexibility to tailor their own pollution-prevention plans.

The state first began to focus on pollution prevention in 1984 when the Hazardous Waste Facilities Siting Commission, a state advisory agency charged with investigating policies for reducing the generation of hazardous wastes, created the Source Reduction and Recycling Task Force.

Representatives of environmental groups, industry, labor, and academia focused on "source reduction"—the original name for what is now known more generally as "pollution prevention." New Jersey's law developed after an early debate over whether the focus would be on pollution "prevention" or "control." The legislature concluded that the traditional system of separately regulating air, water, and hazardous waste pollution was fragmented—an approach that potentially allowed pollution to be shifted from one environmental medium to another. While this former system has helped improve the state's environment, it did not adequately address the impact of hazardous substances or the need to achieve greater levels of environmental protection in the future.

In January 1990, Governor Jim Florio took office and made pollution prevention a priority. The legislature passed the Pollution Prevention Act with broad-based public and private support just over a year later and Governor Florio signed it into law on Aug. 1, 1991.

Pollution prevention in New Jersey is aimed at chemicals listed under the federal Toxic Release Inventory and businesses covered by the state Right-to-Know Program. Initial implementation affects about 800 major industrial facilities and all release reporting will be coordinated to serve both the pollution-prevention and Right-to-Know programs.

Anticipating that the Pollution Prevention Act would mandate a facility-wide permit pilot program, DEPE initiated a prepilot project to help address technical and policy issues likely to arise as the law is implemented. Three companies—Schering-Plough, Fisher Scientific, and Sybron Chemicals—volunteered to develop pollution-prevention plans and have had their existing permits consolidated into facility-wide documents.

Funding secured through EPA will help DEPE develop a cooperative training program for permit and enforcement staff that will focus on the relationship between pollution-prevention planning and facility-wide permitting.

Challenges for Implementation

The department has confronted several obstacles to implementing pollution prevention through the existing regulatory structure. In many cases state regulators and the regulated community are making a slow transition from a medium-specific, end-of-the-pipe focus to a holistic view of the environment.

The reasons are complicated. Industries already have significant administrative infrastructures designed to comply with the former regulatory system, so there is a lamentable but understandable reluctance to convert technology and retrain armies of engineers. Opposition is often rooted in disbelief in the concept, doubt that it will survive politically or in practice, a general reluctance to abandon "command and control" and deal with possible new demands on financial resources and personnel.

There is also a nagging perception that pollution prevention is just another regulatory burden rather than a productive tool in corporate decision making. Industry typically considers environmental protection as an add-on to process and product design rather than an inherent, "upfront" feature. Because of this add-on approach, accountants rarely assess how compliance is factored into the total cost of a product. The costs of pollution, which is often caused by waste of raw materials, and savings through pollution prevention rarely become part of a company's "bottom line."

Most federal and state laws and regulations were written and adopted with an "end-of-the-pipe" pollution-control focus. It will take time for these statutes and standards—and the viewpoints of those administering them—to reflect a recognition that pollution prevention must be the first choice.

Unfortunately, all too often there is still an adversarial relationship between industry and environmentalists that does not promote dialogue or trust about improving the status quo.

All these obstacles are related to the legal, technical, and cultural framework that evolved from decades of implementing end-of-the-pipe, medium-specific regulations. The existing infrastructure is enormous and involves not only regulatory agencies and industry but consulting businesses, academic engineering curriculums, trade groups and journals, and a host of other factors. The transition toward pollution prevention cannot occur overnight but is proceeding steadily with a mix of education and regulation.

Streamlining the Permit Review Process

Pollution prevention's success as a tool for environmental protection will be enhanced as it becomes integrated into DEPE's comprehensive effort to streamline permitting operations. DEPE has consolidated permitting, reduced costly delays, and encouraged its regulatory offices to communicate closely.

A new Office of Permit Information and Assistance provides the public with information on permit applications, coordinates conferences for applicants with project proposals, and uses a new database to track individual permit applications as well as permit trends and decisions. This office is also working to eliminate unwieldy procedures and requirements that do not directly work to improve the environment.

DEPE is also planning to employ various strategies for reducing permit backlogs. One would increase the use of "general" permits, which are drafted to cover similar, recurring regulated situations at facilities. This option maintains environmental safeguards but also helps save time and reduce unnecessary paperwork.

A Breakthrough: Cleanup Standards

New Jersey's economy owes much to a century-old legacy of prodigious industrial output. This legacy, however, has produced an unfortunate by-product—contaminated sites. Many sites have been cleaned up around the state, but there is a persistent, overriding concern: How can we know for sure that health and safety are protected from contamination in neighborhoods, offices, and schoolyards?

Up to now, answers were achieved in a painstaking, case-by-case manner often involving lengthy negotiations with the party or parties responsible for the cleanup. This process has yielded many successful cleanups but is too cumbersome for a state like New Jersey where 600 major contaminated sites have already been identified and areas requiring action potentially number in the thousands.

DEPE has proposed a three-pronged regulatory strategy that for the first time ever will establish consistent standards for assessing cleanups:

- *Cleanup standards* that will provide a consistent measure to determine "how clean" a site must be to protect public health and the environment

- *Technical requirements* that will provide a consistent "how to" manual that will guide the process of investigating and conducting cleanups

- *Voluntary cleanup program* that will encourage parties responsible for limited contamination to enter into an agreement with DEPE and clean up sites faster

Under the proposed cleanup standards, New Jersey will be able to answer a key question for cleanup projects—"How clean is clean?"—in a fair and predictable manner. The new cleanup regulations apply to surface and subsurface soils and groundwaters for areas in and around where we live and work and they set stringent standards for controlling exposure to more than 100 of chemicals produced and used in the state.

The technical requirements and cleanup standards will detail specific minimum measures for investigating a site, identifying an appropriate cleanup method, starting the actual cleanup, and ensuring thoroughness and consistency while providing sufficient flexibility for varying site conditions. In addition, property owners can clean up their sites faster and with less red tape by signing a "memorandum of agreement" offered by DEPE to reduce time-consuming and costly legal negotiations for companies that want to "do the right thing" and quickly clean up less seriously contaminated sites.

By opening the way to clean up more contaminated sites more quickly, the new program will enhance efforts to protect public health and the environment from hazardous substances. In addition, greater use of voluntary agreements will free up DEPE staff to devote more time to the most serious cleanup problems.

Conclusion

In 1992, a nationwide survey in *City and State* magazine gave New Jersey the highest marks in the country for its recycling, hazardous waste management, air and water pollution, and wetlands and open space preservation programs and per capita environmental spending. The EPA has lauded New Jersey coastal monitoring programs as the most stringent. But these successes have also taught a valuable lesson. With the benefit of roughly two decades' hindsight we now know how programs and policies come up short when they narrowly focus on air, water, and land use and are designed only to control pollution that has already been generated. Pollution prevention as an overall philosophy and policy will increasingly govern the decisions we make on implementing new measures for protecting our environment. And where at one time the main issue for policymakers was, "How do we clean?" today the question has a subtle but profound new twist as we ask, "How clean is clean?"

Along these lines, DEPE will increase efforts to become more responsive to the public and show the regulated community how best to comply with state standards. Greater compliance with regulatory standards—not more and more pollution penalties—will be the best way to improve our environment. And as we enter a new century—and a new era of environmental protection—New Jersey will continue to show the way.

Major New Jersey Environmental Laws—Models

| 1954 | Air Pollution Control Act: The first statewide air-pollution control act in the country |
| 1976 | Spill Compensation and Control Act: This was the model for the Federal Comprehensive Environmental Response, Compensation, and Liability Act (commonly referred to as Superfund) |

1983	Environmental Cleanup Responsibility Act: The first and only law in the nation to protect prospective innocent landowners from buying into hidden liability for hazardous contamination
	Safe Drinking Water Act Amendments (A-280): The only program in the nation to test public water systems for toxic, as opposed to bacterial, contaminants
	Worker and Community Right-to-Know Act: The first statewide Right-to-Know Program in the country—catalyst for the new OSHA regulations protecting workers
1985	Toxic Catastrophe Prevention Act: The first in the nation providing proactive, rather than reactive, protection against a "Bhopal-like" chemical accident
1987	Fresh Water Wetlands Protection Act: The strongest, though not the first, state wetlands act
	Statewide Mandatory Source Separation and Recycling Act: The first statewide mandatory recycling act in the country. Others have since followed
1991	Pollution Prevention Act: The most comprehensive, though not the first, pollution-prevention act in the country

Legislation Overview of Canada*

The purpose of this overview is to identify the principal federal regulatory agencies, to summarize some of the provisions of the Canadian Environmental Protection Act (CEPA), and to offer guidance on finding the sources of further information.

Compared with those of the United States, Canadian environmental regulations are more pragmatic and better integrated; there is more effective cooperation between government and industry, so that a much higher proportion of environmental expenditures are actually devoted to prevention, control, or remedial actions.

The two main federal agencies responsible for environment and health regulations are: (1) Environment Canada and (2) Health and Welfare Canada. Environment Canada is responsible for developing and enforcing regulations and for administering CEPA. Health and Welfare Canada is responsible for assessing the potential impact of substances on human health and for recommending controls or ban on the use of toxic substances.

*By Rao V. Kolluru, DrPH.

Canadian Environmental Protection Act (CEPA)

CEPA, enacted in June 1988, is the cornerstone of federal environmental legislation. It is a comprehensive law that incorporates and rolls over former legislation including:

- Environmental Contaminants Act
- Clean Air Act
- Ocean Dumping Control Act
- Canada Water Act
- Department of the Environment Act

CEPA gives Environment Canada (and Health and Welfare Canada) broad powers to define national standards for toxic substances and to regulate the entire life cycle of these substances—from development and manufacture through various stages of transportation, distribution, storage, and use, to their ultimate disposal (Environment Canada: CEPA Report for the Period Ending March 1990). Codes of Practice and Guidelines are also developed and promulgated under CEPA, as for national ambient-air quality objectives and thermal power generation emissions.

An innovative feature of CEPA is The Environmental Choice Program (Section 8) established by the Minister of the Environment to identify and promote environmentally preferable products. An independent board of Canadians determines the criteria products and services must meet so that, once certified, they can use the EcoLogo.

Federal-Provincial Roles.   CEPA is national in scope and offers the basis for a consistent approach across Canada. The Minister of the Environment has the authority to enter into two types of agreements with provincial and territorial governments. The "administrative agreements" encompass a range of administrative activities including inspection, monitoring, reporting, and enforcement. "Equivalency agreements" are specific to individual regulations and, as the name implies, give provinces the option to develop and apply their own statutes if they are equivalent in effect to the federal program (as in the United States).

Priority Substance List.   When CEPA was promulgated, an advisory panel was formed to identify, from among some 20,000 chemical substances used in Canada, those that might warrant early assessment because of their effects on human health or environment. Forty-four chemicals or families of compounds were selected for the priority substances list (see box) on the basis of the following criteria:

- Potential adverse effects on humans or environment (e.g., benzene, dioxins)
- Persistent (e.g., chromium)

- Accumulate in environmental media (air, water, soil, sediment), or bioaccumulate in tissues of biota (e.g., PCBs, hexachlorobenzene)

- Widely used and already present or can be released into the environment in significant quantities (e.g., paper pulp mill effluents, chlorinated solvents)

Sources of Further Information

The addresses and phone numbers of Environment Canada and Health and Welfare Canada, along with those of related organizations, are given below. You may also want to refer to some key reports: Environment Canada annual reports; CEPA Fiscal Year progress reports; Health and Welfare's *A Vital Link: Health and the Environment in Canada* (1992); and Canada's Green Plan (government of Canada, 1990).

"Canada's Green Plan for a Healthy Environment" is an eminently readable document that presents a coordinating framework for prudent resource management and sustainable development. In December 1990, the Minister of the Environment launched a comprehensive $3 billion action plan. The goal is to balance the use of regulations and market-based approaches. As Jean Charest, Minister of the Environment, noted, "A fundamental principle of the Green Plan is that the environment must become integral to the decisions we all make—governments, businesses, and individual Canadians. The Plan...also recognizes that market incentives can be an effective alternative or complement to our traditional approach to regulation...decision-makers would be allowed more flexibility in the measures they take to meet our environmental goals. This would be an incentive to creativity in finding innovative and cost-effective means of meeting our targets, with continued economic incentive to develop and implement cleaner technology and processes." (Economic Instruments for Environmental Protection, Discussion Paper, 1992.)

"Canada's Green Plan represents our commitment to our children and to future generations. The Green Plan will help Canada become a country which is both economically prosperous and environmentally healthy." (Brian Mulroney, former Prime Minister of Canada.)

Environment Canada
10 Wellington Street
Hull, Quebec, K1A 0H3
Canada
Phone (819) 997-2800

Canadian Council of Ministers of the Environment (CCME)
326 Broadway
Winnipeg, Manitoba R3C 0S5
Canada
(204) 948-2090

Health and Welfare Canada
Tunnui's Pasture
Ottawa, Ontario K1A 0K9
Canada
Phone (613) 957-2991/1615

Environmental Protection Publications
Conservation and Protection
Environment Canada
Ottawa, Ontario K1A 0H3
Canada
(819) 997-2800

The Priority Substances List

Group 1
Arsenic and its compounds
Benzene
Effluents from pulp mills using bleaching
Hexachlorobenzene
Methyl tertiary-butyl ether
Polychlorinated dibenzodioxins
Polychlorinated dibenzofurans
Polycyclic aromatic hydrocarbons
Waste crankcase oils

Group 2
Cadmium and its compounds
Chlorinated wastewater effluents
Chlorobenzene
Chromium and its compounds
Creosote-impregnated waste materials
Dibutyl phthalate
1,2-Dichlorobenzene
1,4-Dichlorobenzene
1,2-Dichloroethane
Dichloromethane
Di-*n*-octyl phthalate
bis (2-Ethylhexyl) phthalate
Inorganic fluorides
Nickel and its compounds
Pentachlorobenzene
Styrene
Tetrachlorobenzenes
1,1,2,2-Tetrachloroethane
Tetrachloroethylene
Toluene
Trichlorobenzenes
1,1,1-Trichloroethane
Trichloroethylene
Xylenes

Group 3
Aniline
Benzidine
Chlorinated paraffin waxes
bis (2-Chloroethyl) ether

bis (Chloromethyl) ether
Chloromethyl methyl ether
3,3-Dichlorobenzidine
3,5-Dimethylaniline
Methyl methacrylate
Mineral fibers
Organotin compounds (nonpesticidal uses)

Mexican Environmental Legislation*

Mexico's first environmental law, Federal Law to Prevent and Control Environmental Pollution, went into effect in 1972, just 2 years after the founding of the U.S. EPA. Subsequently, regulations pertaining to air, water, and noise pollution were enacted throughout the 1970s. A lack of central authority and unequal enforcement caused most of the regulations to be ignored.

In 1982, the Federal Environmental Protection Law was adopted to try to remedy some of the deficiencies of the 1972 law. Unfortunately, by this time, Mexico's economic problems overshadowed environmental issues. In looking at economic development plans, however, the United States–Mexican border zone was identified as an area of future growth. Anticipating environmental problems should rapid industrial development take place, the United States and Mexico entered into a 1983 Border Environmental Agreement, also called the La Paz Agreement. This agreement set forth a policy on border environmental programs as well as setting forth procedures for handling hazardous materials as they are transported from one country to another.

President Miguel de la Madrid's election in 1986 set the stage for active enactment of laws and promulgation of regulations to protect the environment. In 1988, the General Law of Ecological Equilibrium and Environmental Protection (General Ecology Law) was enacted. This is Mexico's comprehensive environmental statute which addresses pollution, environmental impact and risk assessment, resource conservation, and enforcement. Since enactment of the law, many regulations have been promulgated to implement programs involving air, soil, and water protection. Further, 27 of the 31 states in Mexico have enacted local environmental laws. Sanctions were also adopted, including heavy fines, plant closures, and criminal penalties including arrest.

The most critical element of the program, however, was the establishment of SEDUE, the Secretariat of Urban Development and Ecology. This cabinet-level

*By Ann C. Pizzorusso, North American Philips.

office was responsible for administering and enforcing environmental programs throughout the country.

President Carlos Salinas de Gortari continued in the tradition of former President de la Madrid by giving his full support to environmental initiatives. Since 1988, Mexico has increased its environmental budget by 700 percent, committed $460 million to infrastructure improvement and enforcement along the Mexico–United States border, suspended the operating licenses of 1926 facilities for noncompliance, permanently closed more than 100 facilities, including the March 1991 closing of an oil refinery in Mexico City at a cost of $500 million in Mexican government revenues.

President Salinas also declared that Mexico does not accept investments, foreign or domestic, that have been rejected by other nations as harmful to the environment or that do not meet Mexico's environmental regulations. This may come as a surprise to companies seeking to relocate, but as they exist, Mexico's environmental regulations are tougher than those of the United States. Companies seeking to build or expand must file an environmental impact statement. They must install state-of-the-art pollution-prevention equipment and comply with regulations for managing hazardous waste. Violations of the regulations can result in a plant's being shut down and not reopening until the violations are remedied.

In February 1992 Presidents Salinas and Bush announced the first phase of the Integrated Border Environmental Plan (IBEP) for the next decade. The plan calls for comprehensive assessment and remedy for the most pressing border environmental issues, among them air, soil, and water pollution. The proposed budget for the border programs for Mexican and U.S. environmental agencies totals over $326 million. Additional efforts include increasing the number of border environmental inspectors, shutting down 134 maquiladora (Mexico-U.S. border) plants in 1991 for failing to meet environmental regulations, developing technology transfer programs and jointly building water treatment plants, sewage facilities, and air quality monitoring equipment.

In May 1992, SEDUE's name was changed to reflect its added authority. SEDESOL, Secretariat of Social Development, Environmental Regulation and Enforcement, was approved by the Mexican Congress. SEDESOL is responsible for environmental policy formulation and enforcement, urban planning, and the administration of the National Solidarity Program, Mexico's most important social program. Through this organization, Mexico can address environmental protection and its relation to poverty and urban planning. SEDESOL's environmental functions are divided between two autonomous agencies, the National Institute of Ecology, whose activities include formulation of Mexico's environmental protection policies, implementation of environmental protection programs, and conserving natural resources, and the Office of the Attorney General for Protection of the Environment, responsible for enforcement.

President Carlos Salinas de Gortari has identified environmental protection as one of the top priorities of his administration. Toward that end, he has given SEDESOL the mandate to speed up the programs set forth in the IBEP, tighten environmental laws and their enforcement, and modernize Mexico's environmental action program through the privatization of infrastructure projects. As part of a federal and state environmental action plan for 1992–1994, the president proposes to eliminate highly polluting activities, rehabilitate areas showing ecological deterioration, and establish water conservation policies and land reserves.

In addition to Mexico's national laws, it has signed and ratified nearly all international treaties and agreements for the protection of the world's environment and natural resources; these include protection for endangered species and protection of the dolphin population, marine turtles, and gray whales. Mexico was the first country to ratify the Vienna Convention and Montreal Protocol agreements for the protection of the ozone layer and is eliminating use of ozone-depleting chlorofluorocarbons on the same timetable as industrialized nations. It is also aggressively addressing air pollution in Mexico City by prohibiting residents from driving one day a week and using catalytic converters and unleaded gasoline.

Over the past decade, environmental activity has increased both in the government and in the communities, where environmentalists have lobbied for increased government funding and enforcement. The Salinas administration believes that once Mexico's citizens begin to experience the benefits of improved environmental quality, rising levels of expectation will drive the process forward.

A HISTORY OF MEXICAN ENVIRONMENTAL LAW

1972	Federal Law to Prevent and Control Environmental Pollution
1970s	Various regulations pertaining to air, water, and noise pollution
1982	Federal Environmental Protection Law
1983	Border Environmental (La Paz) Agreement
1988	General law of Ecological Equilibrium and Environmental Protection (General Ecology Law)
	■ Creation of the Secretariat of Urban Development and Ecology (SEDUE)
1992	First phase of the Integrated Border Environmental Plan (IBEP)
	■ SEDUE's name changed to SEDESOL, Secretariat of Social Development, Environmental Regulation and Enforcement
	North American Free Trade Agreement approved

In summary, any business wishing to establish a facility in Mexico should incorporate environmental compliance in the initial planning phases. An environmental impact statement is needed before any facilities can be constructed or expanded. Permits are needed before operations can be started. When operating in the border zone as a maquiladora, special regulations govern the importation and use of hazardous materials.

To establish an operation with the least risk, a business should hire an environmental consulting firm and law firm with experience in Mexican environmental requirements. They can help technically and legally in obtaining approvals and permits, and completing all forms in the requisite Spanish.

With the proper planning, operations can be implemented in an expeditious, environmentally responsible manner.

Industry and Environmental Regulations

Discussed here are three major points: costs, challenges, and business opportunities.

Costs

Environmental regulations impose four kinds of costs on industry. First, there are the administrative costs of environmental regulatory compliance; second, there are direct compliance costs by industry in order for them to meet the environmental regulatory requirements; third, indirect costs are incurred because environmental regulations are likely to induce industry to seek less than optimal location for their plants and often encourage industry to maintain older, less economical plants and equipment; and, fourth, taxes are increased to pay for running federal and state regulatory agencies.

Challenges

Numerous inefficiencies exist in all four areas of costs associated with environmental regulations. Industry leaders, with their wealth of experience in running businesses efficiently, can help regulatory agencies reduce these costs. Administrative costs of regulatory compliance can be reduced in many ways. Various permitting requirements could be combined and simplified and unnecessary and duplicative paperwork eliminated. Direct compliance costs could be reduced by using innovative economic incentive approaches and other costs could be reduced by meaningfully balancing environmental benefits, economic costs, and societal needs for jobs and economic growth. Regulatory agency costs should require the same discipline that is imposed on other federal agencies or businesses. Again benefits need to be balanced against regulatory costs and burdens that regulatory agencies place on industry and costs agencies incur internally.

Opportunities

Environmental requirements spawn numerous business opportunities for industry (see Chap. 16, Environmental Business). Examples of opportunities relate to designing and building treatment facilities, hazardous waste site cleanup, and international environmental projects, i.e., global opportunities.

Treatment Facilities.   Driven by the combination of public demand and government regulation, there is a growing market for municipal and industrial wastewater treatment facilities. The EPA's Needs Survey, published in 1988, indicated that 2000 new municipal treatment facilities are needed, and several thousand need to be upgraded in order to comply with the 1987 Clean Water Act revisions. Compliance with the act will cause municipal facilities to raise user fees and thus motivate industry to follow the less costly alternative of pretreating their wastewater in their own treatment plants. William T. Loranz & Co. predicts that industry will spend from $600 to $700 million per year on wastewater treatment between 1991 and 1995. The 1986 revision of the Safe Drinking Water Act, which will require additional plants and upgrades to existing plants, will also expand the construction market for treatment facilities, estimated at $1.8 to $2.6 billion per year over the next 10 years (Saffran, 1990).

New regulations in the petroleum refining industry are expanding opportunities for construction firms. Because of the EPA's ruling requiring petroleum product manufacturers to limit sulfur in diesel fuel to 0.05 percent by weight, the industry will have to alter many of its operations. This will require considerable investment in construction owing to the need to provide facilities for diesel hydrotreaters at refineries (Snow, 1990).

Hazardous Waste Site Cleanup.   Public concerns about the environment and growing government regulations have increased the need to develop new means of dealing with hazardous and toxic wastes. New regulations cover the cleanup of existing hazardous wastes and the management of present and future hazardous wastes. The two most important pieces of legislation which address hazardous waste are the Resource Conservation and Recovery Act (RCRA) which deals with wastes currently being produced, and the Comprehensive Environmental Response, Compensation, and Liability Act (CERCLA), which created the Superfund program to clean up closed and abandoned facilities.

Cleaning up hazardous waste sites and managing hazardous wastes have made the environmental service market one of the most dynamic industries in the world. Many companies are showing large profits. According to a 1989 report from Frost & Sullivan, the hazardous waste market will triple by 1993. Expenditures for 1989 were estimated at $8.6 billion, with a forecast of $23.2 billion for 1993 (JAWMA, 1990).

The multibillion-dollar Superfund program provides opportunities for major contracts to the construction industry. Private contractors are heavily relied upon to provide permanent technologies as solutions at the sites; contractors have received 80 to 90 percent of the funds appropriated each year (OTA, 1989, p. 3). Construction activities include building pumping stations and groundwater treatment plants, capping hazardous sites, and installing containment liners (GAO, 1988, p. 10).

The Superfund program has proved very profitable to contractors. In the years 1984–1988, contractors that are public companies showed growths in annual revenues of 200 to 300 percent (OTA, 1989, p. 11). Personnel trained in this area are in very short supply and are regularly drained from the EPA into private industry positions. Management of hazardous waste sites is presently a field with many opportunities and little competition. As the OTA report states, "To a large extent, the billions of dollars rapidly spent on Superfund have provided an opportunity for many contractors to start new businesses and to learn the new business of toxic waste cleanup." Furthermore, because Congress has capped the amount of appropriated funding available to the EPA for oversight (10 to 20 percent), private industry has gained substantial influence over the direction of the program. Again, this trend is expected to continue during the nineties.

Although Superfund was originally intended as a short-term project, it has become apparent that cleanup efforts must be sustained over many decades, thus providing opportunities for the private industry well into the future. Some officials estimate that the program will be required for at least the next 60 years. Currently, over 35,000 sites are identified in the CERCLIS inventory maintained by the EPA, but the number may eventually reach 300,000 to 400,000. In these first years of the program, costs to treat one site have averaged $20 to $30 million (IIT, 1989, p. 2). Approximately 1270 sites have been placed on the National Priorities list of the most dangerous sites; even if only these sites are treated, the total expenditure for cleanup efforts will far exceed the $10.1 billion presently authorized. As the hazardous waste industry moves from studying the waste-treatment problem into managing hazardous waste, the potential for business for contractors is unlimited.

Global Opportunities.   In the past decades, eastern European countries and the Soviet Union have focused on industrial development to the exclusion of concern for its environmental impact. As a result, environmental conditions are now seriously degraded; air pollution, water pollution, hazardous wastes, and extensive impairment of agricultural land and forests are at extreme levels and among the highest in the world. It has been estimated that environmental degradation is costing Poland 10 to 20 percent of its GNP annually, Czechoslovakia 5 to 7 percent, and the Soviet Union 11 percent (French, 1990, p. 10). Conditions are such that life expectancies for some regions are recognized to be 3 to 5 years less than in cleaner areas, with higher incidence of cancers, respiratory diseases, liver disease, birth defects, and other serious illnesses.

Air in the region is polluted by exceptionally high levels of sulfur dioxides due to dependence on coal burning for energy, few pollution controls, and extremely inefficient energy usage. Rivers, lakes, and seashores are heavily contaminated by industrial discharge and agricultural runoff; 80 percent of Romania's river water is polluted, and half of Slovakia's rivers can no longer support aquatic life (French, 1990, p. 17).

Water pollution is compounded by inadequate treatment of industrial wastewater and household sewage, which is far behind western standards. Large amounts of wastewater are inadequately treated, and many large cities in Poland and the Soviet Union have no sewage treatment facilities.

Solutions to correct these problems would require undertaking major projects at a massive scale, and cost estimates for these projects run into hundreds of billions of dollars. Most of these estimates are not reliable. Just as an example, costs of such projects for Germany alone (formerly East Germany) are estimated at $200 to $300 billion over 10 years (French, 1990, p.40).

Opportunities presented here for the United States private businesses and industry are truly enormous, especially when these projects are funded by the International aid agencies such as the World Bank or the U.S. Agency for International Development.

Balancing Economic and Environmental Costs

The common theme of the environmental movement is that good environmental quality is good for the economy in the long run. The short-run economic dislocation problems with this philosophy were largely ignored in the 1970s. Corporations and municipalities were expected to pay whatever was needed to correct the past environmental problems and to provide future environmental protection, no matter what the price. Federal laws and regulations established ambitious compliance schedules, which occasionally were relaxed but which for the most part committed industry and public to considerable expenditures.

Opposition to the "spend what it takes" approach was often stated ineffectively, mostly because the arguments advanced tended to overstate the problem. Too often decisions to close companies or shut down plants were attributed solely to the cost of environmental regulations. No doubt these were important factors, and they may have been the sole factor in several instances, but not to the extent that was often claimed. Among many environmental activists, who may believe a typical business has "excessive" profits anyway, any such statement of cost sensitivity was summarily dismissed as an attempt to maintain these profit margins at the expense of the common good.

The national priority of the 1980s was renewal of the economy and a trend toward cost-effective regulations. There is, and will be, a requirement on regulators and enforcers to collect the facts before imposing major and costly requirements. The philosophy of the 1970s was that all potential problems imaginable had to be prevented. Now it is recognized that the possibilities that could be safeguarded are too numerous for this approach to be affordable.

Another manifestation of the recognition that priority must be given to the economy will be reduced paperwork requirements for industry. A theme of the environmental regulators in the 1970s was that industry was a source of extensive potentially useful and interesting information on a variety of environmental topics and that a proper role for the regulator was to ask industry to submit such information whether or not immediate need was apparent. This placed an extensive and costly burden on industry which is gradually being relaxed. In summary, the trends toward environmental regulations and environmental protection may be stated as follows:

1. Adjustments in the federal and nonfederal roles are likely to increase state participation in the enforcement and administration of the environmental regulations.

2. Balancing of economic and environmental goals is likely to take the form of moderation in achieving some environmental goals which adversely affect economic activities.

3. Public support for environmental protection and related life-support systems is expected to continue, especially in the industrialized countries.

4. In the United States, midcourse correction to major environmental legislation is expected to be made by the legislative bodies. This midcourse correction will be based on benefits (environmental protection and enhancement) and costs associated with environmental requirements.

5. To the extent possible, regulations will move away from the command-and-control type of approach presently used in most cases. The reason for this is that in a free market economy, command-and-control regulations are inefficient and do not preserve elements of voluntary choice. To the extent technologically practical, future regulatory approaches will focus on the use of economic incentives, such as marketable discharge licenses or permits and effluent charges.

6. With increasing experience in the pollution-control technology area, regulatory controls will move away from the "hothouse" types of control technologies that deteriorate rather quickly and end up contributing large amounts of pollutants and incurring high operation and maintenance costs during the life cycle of the control devices. Instead, more practical emissions standards, with built-in economic incentives, will be established so that cost-effective pollution control technology which provides overall lower pollutants during the life cycle of the equipment could be used.

7. Vigorous public support for incorporating environmental concerns into the decision-making process as embodied in the provisions of legislation, such as the National Environmental Policy Act (NEPA), is expected to continue.

References

Clean Air Act, 42 U.S.C. 7401 et seq. (1963–1983).
Clean Water Act, 33 U.S.C. 1251 et seq. (1948–1987).
Coastal Zone Management Act, 16 U.S.C. 1451 et seq. (1972–1986).
Comprehensive Environmental, Response, Compensation and Liability Act, 42 U.S.C. 9601 et seq. (1980–1987).

Endangered Species Act, 16 U.S.C. 1531–1542 et seq. (1973–1984).

Federal Insecticide, Fungicide, and Rodenticide Act (U.S.C. 136 et seq. (1972–1978).

Fish and Wildlife Coordination Act, 16 U.S.C. 661 et seq. (1958–1965).

French, Hilary F., *Green Revolutions: Environmental Reconstruction in Eastern Europe and the Soviet Union*, Worldwatch Institute, Washington, D.C., 1990.

General Accounting Office, *Superfund: Cost Growth on Remedial Construction Activities: Report to Congressional Requestors*, U.S. General Accounting Office, Washington, D.C., 1988, GAO/RCED-88-69.

"Hazardous Waste Services Market Seen Tripling in Four Years," *Journal of the Air & Waste Management Association*, vol. 40, p. 286, March 1990.

IIT Research Institute, Center for Hazardous Waste Management, *Coalition on Superfund Research Report: Submitted to Coalition on Superfund*, Illinois Institute of Technology, Chicago, 1989.

Jenkins, Tom, "Tapping Hazardous Waste Employment Opportunities," *The Management of World Wastes*, vol. 32, p. 67, July 1989.

Marine Protection, Research and Sanctuaries Act, 33 U.S.C. 1401 et seq. (1972–1980).

National Environmental Policy Act (PL 91-190; 83 Stat. 852), 42 U.S.C. 4321 et seq. (1970–1975).

National Historic Preservation Act, 16 U.S.C. 470–470t et seq. (1966–1980).

Noise Control Act, 42 U.S.C. 4901 et seq. (1972–1978).

Office of Technology Assessment, *Assessing Contractor Use in Superfund: A Background Paper of OTA's Assessment on Superfund Implementation*, Office of Technology Assessment, Washington, D.C., 1989, OTA-BP-ITE-51.

Pollution Prevention Act, PL 101-508, Title VI, Subtitle F.

Report to the President and Congress on Noise, U.S. Environmental Protection Agency, December 1971.

Resource Conservation and Recovery Act, 42 U.S.C. 6901 et seq. (1976–1986).

Rubin, Debra K., *Environmental Firms Seek Size, ENR*, vol. 226, pp. 36–39, Apr. 8, 1991.

Safe Drinking Water Act, 42 U.S.C. 300f et seq. (1974–1986).

Saffran, Edward, "Environmental Rules Can Help Mechanical `Clean Up'," *Contractor*, vol. 37, pp. 19–21, December 1990.

Schultze, C. L., *The Public Use of Private Interest*, The Brookings Institute, Washington, D.C., 1977, p. 32.

Snow, Nick, "Tide of Engineering and Construction Work Rises with Regulations," *Oil Daily*, Oct. 3, 1990, p. B3.

Solow, R. M., "The Economics of Resources or the Resources of Economics," in R. Dorfman (ed.), *Economics of Environment*, 2d ed., W.W. Norton, New York, 1977, p. 368.

Superfund Amendments and Reauthorization Act, 42 U.S.C. 11001 et seq. (1986).

Toxic Substances and Control Act, 15 U.S.C. 2601 et seq. (1976–1986).

Welsh, R. L., "User Manual for the Computer-Aided Environmental Legislative Data System," *Technical Report* E-78, Construction Engineering Research Laboratory, Champaign, Illinois, November 1975.

Wild and Scenic Rivers Act, 16 U.S.C. 1271 et seq. (1968–1987).

5

Environmental Technology and Engineering*

George P. Korfiatis, Ph.D.

Professor and Director
Center for Environmental Engineering
Stevens Institute of Technology
Hoboken, New Jersey

Paul N. Cheremisinoff, DEE, P.E.

Professor of Civil and Environmental
Engineering
New Jersey Institute of Technology
Newark, New Jersey

In this chapter:

- Overview of environmental control technologies
- Air pollution control
- Water pollution control
- Remediation of hazardous waste sites

Overview of Environmental Control Technologies

Concern for protecting and preserving the environment has led to increased regulation which in turn has led to the rapid development and implementation of

*Christos Christodoulatos, Ph.D., of Stevens contributed to this chapter. W. Leigh Short, Ph.D., of Woodward-Clyde reviewed the chapter.

waste-treatment and -control technologies. Because of strict environmental standards and cost of pollution control, such problems have received a great deal of attention from the business community. Corporate managers are often called upon to make costly decisions on the basis of current and anticipated regulations and available pollution-control methods. It is therefore essential that they are well informed on the status of environmental technology and available options.

Pollution-control strategies have had a tremendous impact on business policies and practices as well as engineering practice since the early 1970s. It was not, however, until the early 1980s that industry came under enormous pressure not only to implement pollution controls but also to remediate various sites that have been contaminated over the past several decades. This has prompted the scientific and engineering community to move rapidly toward the development of new cost-effective waste-control and -treatment technologies.

Some noteworthy points about environmental technology development and application within the existing regulatory framework are as follows:

- For the most part, the development of maximum allowable levels of environmental contaminants is not technology-driven. One implication is that current technologies may not be able to achieve the mandated cleanup levels.

- In many situations, regulatory agencies may not allow the field testing of new technologies, making it difficult to establish their effectiveness and viability.

- The pressure to develop new environmental control and waste-treatment techniques at a rapid pace has resulted in investing significant amounts of money pursuing technologies which may ultimately be of little commercial value.

- The potential liability that can result from misapplication of various technologies may prevent engineers from trying new ideas.

- A well-established framework for the transfer of new technologies from the research level to field application and subsequent commercialization has not yet been developed.

This chapter presents an overview of selected technologies for environmental control and waste treatment. Representative established and emerging technologies have been selected on the basis of the type of pollution they address. With more emphasis placed on industrial applications, the following pollution categories are summarized:

- Air pollution from point sources
- Water pollution
- Soil and groundwater remediation

The following summary of the technologies covered in this chapter represents the major methods that are used in pollution control at the present time. Comparisons are made on a qualitative basis since actual values will depend on the specific application and further details are included in the body of the text. Table 5-1 shows a summary of air-pollution-control devices and their relative effectiveness and costs.

Wastewater control treatment includes a wide range of processes to treat various pollutants with a wide range of removal efficiencies. Table 5-2 shows selected wastewater treatment technologies and their efficiency for specific types of contaminants.

Environmental technologies employed in treatment of solid wastes also cover a wide range of engineering practices. A large number of materials fall into the solid waste category and can generally be divided into a number of subdivisions as shown in Table 5-3, with the more commonly employed treatment technology options shown.

A summary of treatment technologies for hazardous wastes is shown in Table 5-4.

Air-Pollution Control

Air quality has become over the years an issue of great concern. This is particularly true in highly urbanized and industrialized areas. The sources of air pollution are numerous and of variable impact. The primary law regulating air emissions is the Clean Air Act passed by Congress in 1963. Since that time, the law has been strengthened by a series of amendments, the latest one being in 1990. The 1990 Clean Air Act Amendments establish new federal permitting procedures for air toxics and acid rain programs and significantly enhance

Table 5-1. Air-Pollution Control from Stationary and Point Sources

Particulate Control				
Control device	Pressure drop	Particulate control, μm	Capital investment	Operating and maintenance costs
Gravity settling	Low	>40	Low	Low
Cyclones	Low	>10–20	Low	Low
Fabric filters	Low–moderate	<1	Moderate	Low–moderate
Electrostatic precipitators	Low	<1	Moderate	Moderate
Combustion	Low	<1	Moderate	Moderate–high
Wet scrubbers (varies with type)	Moderate–high	<1–40	Moderate–high	High

Gaseous Contaminant Control			
Control device	Pressure drop	Capital investment	Operating and maintenance costs
Wet scrubbers (varies with type)	Moderate–high	Moderate–high	Moderate–high
Carbon adsorption	Moderate	Moderate	Moderate–high
Combustion	Low	Moderate–high	Moderate–high

Table 5-2. Wastewater Treatment Processes

Pollutant removal	Treatment process and efficiency range, %
Coarse solids	Screening (90–100)
Suspended solids	Coagulation (70–80)
	Flotation (40–60)
	Microstraining (50–60)
	Sedimentation (50–60)
Soluble organics	Biological (40–60)
	Activated carbon (65–75)
Oils	Activated carbon (90–95)
	Air flotation (80–90)
	Gravity separation (70–80)
Acids and bases	Neutralization (90–95)
Pathogens	Chlorination (98–99)
	Ozone (98–99)
Colloidal solids	Coagulation (70–80)
	Filtration (80–90)
	Microstraining (30–40)
	Ultrafiltration (95–98)
Ammonia	Air stripping (75–85)
	Ion exchange (90–95)
	Nitrification (75–85)
$NO-NO_2$	Denitrification (85–95)
Trace organics	Activated carbon (90–95)
	Biological systems (25–35)
	Air stripping (90–98)
	Ozone (70–80)
Heavy metals and inorganics	Activated carbon (to 95)
	(Chemical precipitation) (90–95)
	Ion exchange (90–95)
	Membrane processes (90–95)
	Ultrafiltration (0–75)

Table 5-3. Solid Waste Disposal and Treatment Alternatives

Type of waste	Treatment or disposal option
Municipal waste	Landfilling
	Incineration, energy and resource recovery
Industrial waste	Landfilling into specially designed sites
	Incineration
Toxic and hazardous:	
Industrial	Incineration, fixation, and land disposal
Medical	Incineration
Animal and farm wastes	Biogasification
Mining wastes	Land disposal

Table 5-4. Alternative Technologies for Hazardous Waste Treatment

Technology	Description of Process or equipment	Example applications	Status	Considerations	Relative cost
Physical treatment: Magnetic processes	Magnetic-separation devices	Debris presort	Commercial	Limited applications	Low
Screening and classification	Standard manufactured units	Separation of over-size materials	Commercial	Reprocessing or disposal of miscellaneous material	Low
Crushing and grinding	Standard manufactured units	Size reduction of solid material for further processing	Commercial	Fugitive emissions	Low
Liquid-solid separation, sedimentation (with or without flocculation), filtration, centrifugation, flotation, belt presses, filter presses	Standard manufactured units	Remove particles from liquids Remove excess moisture from solids or sludges	Commercial	Solid still contains some liquid	Low
Drying	Standard manufactured units	Sludge drying	Some experimental, some commercial	Mechanical problems air emissions	Expensive
Distillation	Multitray or packed column with heating and condensing device	Solvent purification for reuse	Commercial	Scaling and/or fouling, flammability hazard with some solvents	Medium
Evaporation	Single-stage, multi-stage, or vapor-compression evaporators that may include crystallization step	Nuclear wastes Electroplating wastes	Commercial	Scaling and/or fouling, condensate is sometimes contaminated Disposal of concentrate	Moderately high
Stripping, steam, air, other gas	Multitray or packed column with gas injection	Sulfide stripping Trichloroethylene stripping	Commercial	Limited to volatile components, air emissions	Low to medium
Absorption	Multitray or packed column with appropriate solvent	Usually for emission control	Commercial	Disposal of scrubbing liquor	Low
Solvent extraction, liquid-liquid, solid-liquid, supercritical fluid	Standard process (supercritical fluid under development)	Extracting contaminants from soil Extracting metals from liquid	Commercial (supercritical fluid under development)	Contaminated solvent requires further processing for disposal	Moderately high
Adsorption, carbon, resin (ion exchange, others); proprietary systems	Batch or continuous adsorption beds, usually with regeneration	Organic adsorption onto carbon Heavy-metal adsorption onto resins	Commercial	Limited to low concentrations, disposal of regenerate	Medium

Table 5-4. Alternative Technologies for Hazardous Waste Treatment (*Continued*)

Technology	Description of Process or equipment	Example applications	Status	Considerations	Relative Cost
Physical treatment (*Cont*):					
Membrane processes, ultrafiltration, reverse osmosis, dialysis, electrodialysis	Standard manufactured units with appropriate pretreatment facilities to prevent membrane fouling and/or deterioration	Removal of heavy metals or some organics from groundwater	Recently commercial	Separations are imperfect, pretreatment is complex	Medium
Freezing, crystallization, freeze drying, suspension freezing	Many types of units	Suspension-freezing ponds for hydrous metal hydroxides	Experimental other than drying and freezing beds	Not commercially developed	Low for drying beds, high for others
Chemical treatment:					
Neutralization	Chemical addition and mix tanks	Neutralization of acid and alkaline wastes	Commercial	Heat release in concentrated, control complex	Low
Precipitation	Chemical addition, to produce an insoluble solid	Heavy-metals removal	Commercial	Solubility laws interfering substances	Low
Electrochemical processes	DC power and plating apparatus	Copper removal	Some commercial, some experimental	Impurities can upset process	Medium
Oxidation, chlorine-containing reagents, ozone, permanganate, peroxide, others	Chemical addition and contacting tanks	Trace-organic destruction	Some commercial, some experimental	Side reactions may generate other hazardous constituents	Medium to high
Reduction, dechlorination, sulfonation, other	Chemical addition and contacting tanks	Reduction of hexavalent chrome, dechlorination of dioxin	Some commercial, some experimental	Side reactions may generate hazardous constituents	Medium to high
Photolysis, ultraviolet light, natural light	Photolamps and contacting devices	Dioxin destruction Cyanide destruction	Semicommercial	Fouling of photochemical devices, kinetics	Low for natural, high for UV
Gamma irradiation	Shielded irradiator	Pesticide destruction	Experimental	Sophisticated irradiator design	High
Miscellaneous chemical treatments, catalysis, hydrolysis, others	Chemical additions and contacting tanks	Pesticide destruction	Experimental	Side reactions may generate other hazardous constituents	Varies
Biological treatment:					
Activated-sludge lagoons: aerated facultative, anaerobic	Common commercial system designs	Removal of organic materials from water	Commercial	Only effective on biodegradable or bioadsorbable constituents subject to toxic inhibition	Low
Anaerobic digestion, composting, trickling filters, aerobic biofilters, fermentation, waste-stabilization ponds	Common commercial system designs	Removal of organic materials from water	Commercial	Only effective on biodegradable or bioadsorbable constituents subject to toxic inhibition	Low

Table 5-4. Alternative Technologies for Hazardous Waste Treatment (*Continued*)

Technology	Description of Process or equipment	Example applications	Status	Considerations	Relative Cost
Biological treatment (*Cont*):					
New biotechnologies, enzyme, cultured bacteria, gene splicing	Biochemical addition system		Experimental	Field is new, so considerations are not well understood	Low to medium
Thermal treatment:					
Established incineration processes, fluidized bed, multiple hearth, rotary kiln, liquid injection, shipboard	Standard commercially marketed units	Industrial incinerators, contract hazardous-waste incinerators	Commercial	Fuel value, destruction efficiency, disposal of ash and scrubber blowdown	Medium to high
Evolving incineration processes, molten salt, microwave plasma, plasma arc	Developmental units	Dioxin destruction	Experimental	Technology not well developed	High
Codisposal incineration processes, industrial boiler, cement kiln, lime kiln	Standard units	Waste-solvent burning	Commercial	Fuel value, effects on emissions-control equipment	Low to medium
Pyrolysis, conventional temperature, ultra high temperature	Proprietary units	Organics destruction	Mostly experimental	By-products generated may be hazardous	Medium
Wet-air oxidation, autoclave, U-tube reactor, vertical-tube reactor	Proprietary units	Organics destruction	Many commercial, but mostly in non-hazardous-waste applications	Process is only 85–95% efficient	Medium
Fixation and encapsulation:					
Sorption, flyash, kiln dust, lime, limestone, clays, vermiculite, zeolites, alumina, carbon, imbiber beads, proprietary agents	Stabilizing materials and contacting methods	Solidifying hazardous wastes	Commercial	Long-term effectiveness	Medium
Pozzolanic reaction, lime-flyash, portland cement	Mechanical equipment for mixing and reaction	Solidifying hazardous wastes	Commercial	Organic agents sometimes interfere with reaction	Medium
Encapsulation, organic polymers, asphalt, glassification, proprietary agents	Stabilizing materials and mechanical equipment for encapsulation	Solidifying hazardous wastes	Some experimental	Long-term effectiveness	Medium to high

SOURCE: J. T. Valdirio, "Alternatives to Hazardous Wastes," *Pollution Engineering,* July 1990.

enforcement by setting severe noncompliance penalties. Most importantly, however, these amendments set new air quality standards and attainment deadlines and mandate technology-based control measures for nonattainment areas. Air-pollution-control technology therefore has become an issue of primary concern to the industry.

Classification of Air Pollutants

Air pollutants can be classified by their physical and chemical characteristics. Once the type of pollutant is broadly defined, the engineer can decide which system will handle the problems best. The more common and major types of industrial air pollutants are as follows:

Noxious gases Examples of these substances are hydrogen chloride, nitrous oxides, and sulfur dioxide. These are normally emitted in a gaseous or vapor state.

Entrained liquids Liquid particles, usually 10 microns in size or larger, are generated by sprays, agitation, or bubbling and are absorbed into exhaust-air streams.

Mists Usually mists are liquid particles formed by condensation of molecules from the vapor phase. The size of these particles is less than 10 microns.

Dusts Disintegration or grinding of solids will produce solid particles 5 microns and larger.

Fumes Fumes are composed of extremely small solid particles, normally 1 micron or smaller in diameter, produced by condensation, sublimation, or oxidation of metallic vapors.

Entrained particles Particles of liquids, dusts, mists, or fumes are picked up by an air stream through an exhaust ventilation process.

Air-Pollution-Control Systems

The removal of contaminants from a gas stream necessitates special equipment which may include scrubbers, fine-fabric filters, catalytic equipment, and electrostatic precipitators. The following criteria may influence the choice of the proper air-pollution-control unit:

1. Capital investment
2. Minimum space requirement
3. Trouble-free continuous operation
4. High chemical or particulate recovery efficiency
5. Maximum heat recovery

The most frequently used air-pollution-control equipment and systems are described below.

Packed-Tower Wet Scrubbers.   Aqueous absorption systems using either water or chemical-liquid mixtures are frequently used as a solution to air-pollution problems. A packed-bed scrubber may be designed to remove gas and liquid particulates. Scrubbing is done by causing particulate matter in the gas to stick to a large wetted area of the packing and washing the contaminant away. Molecules of a soluble gas mixed with the flue or exhaust to be scrubbed also come into contact with the moist surface and are washed or dissolved away.

To remove contaminants from the gas stream, they must come in contact with the liquid surface by either turbulence or diffusion and may or may not enter the liquid phase, depending upon the solubility or amount already dissolved. This process, known as absorption, depends largely on vapor pressures and temperatures. When the solubility limit of a gas in the liquid phase has been exceeded, the scrubber will not remove it. To be successful, it is necessary that the pressure of gas to be removed in the gaseous phase exceed the pressure of the gas trying to leave the liquid phase.

A variety of packed scrubbers are on the market presently; generally, these can be divided into three categories, based on the gas to scrubbing liquid direction of flow:

1. Cocurrent flow
2. Cross flow
3. Countercurrent flow

Cocurrent-Flow Scrubber.   In a cocurrent-flow scrubber, both gas and liquid move in the same direction. Usually this is downward, owing to gravitational considerations. However, horizontal cocurrent-flow scrubbers are becoming more common. Their primary use is in the removal of particulates and gases of relatively low concentrations, or of high degree of chemical reactivity. The cocurrent system is the most stable and has the greatest capacity of the three.

Cross-Flow Scrubber.   The cross-flow scrubber is primarily used in the removal of coarse solids of 5 microns or larger and liquid mists. The scrubbing liquid flows in from the top edge of the bed of packing while gas moves horizontally through it. This system has limitations because liquid and gas contact is poor, but this method is satisfactory for washing off accumulated contaminants or good-sized packing-surface particles. One advantage of the cross-flow scrubber over the cocurrent one is that it requires a lower liquid flow rate.

Stability of the cross-flow unit is high. Limitations in this system occur when liquid is carried horizontally by gas flow through the packing. However, this limit can be raised by increasing the depth of the entrainment separation zone.

Countercurrent-Flow Scrubber.   In the countercurrent-flow scrubber, as the name implies, liquid and gas travel in opposite directions. Incoming contaminated gas first comes in contact with contaminated liquid, and the output stream of clean gas encounters the pure liquid. Gas flows upward while liquid flows downward. This mode has the greatest contact area; the most contaminated gas contacts the most contaminated liquid. For this reason, it has the highest removal efficiency of the three and is the most widely used. The main flaw in this system is that opposing streams produce eddy currents which diminish either stream's velocity significantly. Solids may be deposited and built up at points of low velocity.

Venturi Scrubbers.   The venturi scrubber is a relatively low capital-investment system, which requires minimum space for operation and offers good chemical and particulate recovery efficiencies.

Venturi scrubbers have handling capacities ranging from 50 to 250,000 cubic feet per minute. They differ from wet packed towers as they rely on pneumatic pressure of a high-velocity gas stream rather than hydraulic pressure for atomization of the scrubbing liquid. Coarse jets of water are introduced into the venturi at relatively low pressures through nozzles located at the throat. Contaminated gas enters the throat restrictions at velocities ranging from 200 to 400 feet per second, instantaneously atomizing the jets into a mass of very fine droplets. Concentration of these droplets combined with the high-velocity difference between the particles and droplets greatly enhances the likelihood of impaction and agglomeration.

Several different mechanisms describe the collection of aerosols in a venturi. These include inertial force, electrostatic attraction by charges, electrostatic attraction by induction, and diffusion by brownian motion.

Dry Collection Systems.   Dry collection systems are predominantly composed of fabric filters. A fabric filter is a device similar to a large vacuum-cleaner bag for separating suspended impurities from process fluids. Wide use of cloth filters is made in industrial dust- and fume-control systems designed for air-pollution control, product processing, or product recovery. As the cake of particles separated from contaminated gas builds up on the cloth, resistance to gas flow increases. Deposits must be removed periodically by vigorous cleaning of the cloth. Cloth filters can be used to control dust concentrations from the submicron-range fumes to powders 200 microns in diameter.

Filter bags come in two major designs:

1. The flat or envelope bag captures dust from the airstream on the outside of the bag. Internal frames prevent it from collapsing. This design offers the greatest surface area contact between cloth and air. Occasionally, dust tends to bridge or plug the spacing between the envelopes, necessitating removal of every other bag.

2. Tubular bags are open at one end and closed at the other. Generally, they are sewn together in groups to form a multibag system. A major disadvantage is limited bag adjustment and bag-replacement cost. A unibag tubular design is also available with gas entering from either the top or the bottom.

Electrostatic Precipitators. Electrostatic precipitators are unique among particulate-collection units in the fact that they apply a collecting force only to the particles, not to the entire gas stream. Consequently, individual units can handle large volumes of gas with relatively negligible pressure drop and low power consumption. Units are available with efficiencies up to 99.9 percent. An electrostatic precipitator operates like a glass rod that is rubbed with a silk cloth, giving the rod an electrostatic charge and making it capable of attracting uncharged bits of lint and paper. In electrostatic precipitators, it is the collecting surfaces that are grounded and the charge is created on the particulates to be collected.

Air-pollution applications of electrostatic precipitators include the following:

- *Ventilation*   Low-operating-temperature processes or vessels exposed to heavy fumes and dust may require ventilation. Applications include asphalt saturators and converters, glass melting, aluminum-reduction pot lines, and carbon-plant ventilation.

- *Grinding*   Precipitators are used to collect pollution generated during grinding operations, such as cement or gypsum grinding.

- *Drying*   Cement, gypsum, bauxite, and various ores may be dried. Before such ores enter the contaminated gas stream in the precipitator, free moisture must be driven off by heating in a rotary kiln.

- *Calcining*   Processing of materials such as cement, gypsum, alumina, and magnesite requires electrostatic precipitators for air-pollution control. High temperatures drive off moisture and also break down materials chemically and drive off gases.

- *Nonferrous metals*   Tail gases from roasters, converters, reverberatory furnaces, blast furnaces, cupolas, and sinter machines are treated in processing. Ores of copper, zinc, lead, tin, nickel, chromium, molybdenum, and precious metals are reduced. Precipitators are used primarily for product recovery.

- *Acid recovery*   Sulfuric and phosphoric acid are generally recovered by electrostatic precipitators. Collected material is generally added to product material, while cleaned gases are either discharged to the atmosphere or sent to a scrubber for removing the remaining SO_2.

- *Power generation*   Used extensively for recovery of flyash from coal-burning boilers.

Cyclones. Cyclones make use of centrifugal force for the separation of dust, liquid droplets, and gas. They are the cheapest form of dust control for dusts containing a high portion of particles greater than 10 microns in size. There are many variations of the basic cyclone, and because of its simplicity of construction and lack of moving parts, a wide variety of construction materials can be used to cover high operating temperature of up to 2000°F. Cyclones are efficient handling devices for particles ranging in size from 10 to more than 2000 microns, with inlet loadings from less than l to more than 100 grains per cubic foot per minute (cfm). There are three main flow patterns in their methods of operation:

- Descending spiral flow—carries the separated dust down the walls of the cyclone to a dust hopper.

- Ascending spiral flow—rotates in the same direction as the descending spiral, but the cleaned gas is carried from the cyclone or the dust receptacle to the gas outlet.

- Radially inward flow—feeds the gas from the descending to the ascending spiral.

Direct-Flame and Catalytic Combustors in Fume Control.   Various gas-pollution applications to control odors, organic vapors, and unburned carbon particulates can be treated by one of two types of fume-incineration systems, catalytic or direct-flame incineration. In both systems, organic pollutant present in the exhaust gases is oxidized to form nonpolluting by-products. The principal by-products emitted are carbon dioxide and water vapor.

Numerous processes make use of incinerators for the abatement of combustible by-products. Applications include burnoff ovens, chemical processing, coil and strip coating, dry cleaning, fat rendering, food processing, metal finishing, mold burnout, paint baking, paper printing and impregnating, rubber and plastic processing, sewage disposal, treating towers, and wire enameling.

Gas Adsorbers.   Adsorption operations use the ability of certain solids to concentrate specific substances from the gas stream on their surfaces. Success has been obtained in the removal of carbon dioxide. This is applied in both the gas and liquid phases. The process is run at low temperatures, since an inverse relationship exists between the capacity of adsorbents for carbon dioxide and temperature.

Although the nature of adsorption is not fully understood, water molecules undergo a process in adsorptive driers similar to condensation. The amount adsorbed decreases with increasing temperature. Several adsorbents are successful in removing water vapor. Probably the largest application of adsorbers has been in the removal of condensable impurities from air prior to liquefaction and distillation (i.e., adsorptive drying). Two major condensable impurities to be removed are carbon dioxide and water vapor.

As gas is passed through the adsorber, the adsorbate becomes slowly saturated and a point is reached where the concentration of solids in the gas effluent is suddenly raised. This point is designated the breakpoint. It indicates when the unit must be shut down and the adsorbate reactivated. Continuous operation may be ensured by installing a pair of driers so that one can be rejuvenated before the adsorptive capacity of the other is exceeded.

Water-Pollution Control

Water-quality objectives call for effective design and operation of wastewater-treatment facilities, using the best available, practicable, or demonstrated technologies. Accurate measurement of pollutants in water is the critical factor in operating or maintaining wastewater-treatment systems. Regulatory limitations imposed on polluted-water discharge to receiving streams make it necessary to analyze contaminants accurately and with speed. While industrial wastes have an almost infinite variety of characteristics, which makes accurate measurement difficult and painstaking, most wastewaters should be analyzed for BOD, COD, color, amount of suspended and dissolved solids, pH, specific organic compounds, and turbidity. Table 5-5 lists further parameters of concern in water treatment.

Waste characterization is the first step in instituting a water-treatment process. Close checks on each waste source will indicate whether or not flow is intermittent or continuous, and analysis of the treated effluent will indicate the final discharge quality. Sampling techniques can be broadly classified into two groups, spot or grab sampling, and continuous or composite sampling. Grab sampling makes it possible to keep track of variations in pollutants. By combining data of spot samples with flow, one can arrive at an accurate description of average conditions. Whenever flow rates vary, a weighted composite can be collected.

Table 5-5. Typical Parameters That May Be Required in Wastewater Effluent Testing

pH	Cyanide
Alkalinity or acidity	Nickel
Color	Lead
Conductivity	Cadmium
Turbidity	Mercury
Temperature	Arsenic
Suspended solids	Zinc
Settleable solids	Hexavalent chromium
Total organic carbon (TOC)	Total chromium
Biochemical oxygen demand (BOD)	Total phosphate
Chemical oxygen demand (COD)	Total nitrogen
Sulfate	Ammonium nitrate
Calcium	Oil and grease
Magnesium	Phenol
Hardness	Surfactants
Aluminum	Chlorinated hydrocarbons
Iron	Pesticides
Copper	Fecal streptococci bacteria
Fluoride	Coliform bacteria
Manganese	

Continuous sampling gives a running record of conditions at a given point. Sampling points should be placed where flow conditions encourage thorough mixing. Velocity of the stream at these points should be high enough so that there is no deposition of solids.

Once tested, concentration of impurities must be correlated with average, minimum, and maximum flows of waste encountered. Many times toxic or unusual impurities may generate adverse effects on standard treatment techniques.

Areas to be considered in the design of industrial water-pollution-control processes include:

1. Quantity of wastewater discharge
2. Major source of discharge within the facility
3. Wastewater composition
4. Treatment options

Selected wastewater treatment processes are summarized here.

Filtration

Filtration is one of the earliest methods of pollution control. It is still an important method and is becoming increasingly sophisticated. Processes of separating solid particulates from liquids depend upon the particular characteristics of the solids and the proportion of solid to liquid to be separated. When there is a relatively small amount of solid compared with liquid, the principal process employed is filtration.

Purification of a liquid containing solids through filtration is accomplished by passing the mixture through a porous filter. The process is sometimes preceded by coagulation and sedimentation or settling. A variety of filter media are available on the market including cloth, porous metals, porous stone and diatomaceous earth, and graded beds of sand or anthracite coal.

Through proper treatment only the smaller and lighter suspended particles and coagulated matter are left in the discharge stream. When these particulates are brought on a clean filter bed, they will be retained in the top few inches of the bed. They then build up on the bed surface. A mat is formed there which serves as a fine-grain filter and affords a finer screening than when the filter bed is initially operated.

Aeration

Aerators are utilized for handling wastewater pollution problems and have two primary functions:

1. To provide air or oxygen by moving large volumes of water through the aeration unit and breaking the mass of water into droplets. This increases the

area available for oxygen transfer for biological treatment in the aerobic process. A secondary transfer zone is generated as the droplets return to the parent body of water.

2. To provide a good mixing pattern within a basin, as in the activated-sludge process.

Aeration systems commonly used in treatment plants are as follows:

Surface aerators are devices which bring quantities of wastewater to the surface for direct contact with air. Oxygen transfer occurs through two different mechanisms. One is through direct transfer to the water while being sprayed through the air. The second is air entrainment, occurring both at the impeller and throughout the area around the unit as a result of splashing liquid impinging into the bulk liquid.

Surface aerators offer lowest operating costs for given oxygen requirements, providing efficiencies highly competitive with other systems. Combination units positioning a surface aerator on a common shaft with a submerged-turbine aerator have proved successful.

Submerged-turbine aerators have been widely used for high-horsepower requirements and relatively short detention times, and to increase oxygen input where existing diffused air systems have reached the limit of their capacity. They provide

1. Sufficient shear to generate fine distribution of bubbles through mechanical and fluid detention

2. A proper fluid region to maximize the air holdup in the system through a hydraulic system

The most common design consists of a *radial-flow impeller* situated above a large-orifice sparge ring or an open pipe. It distributes the air throughout the tank.

Carbon Adsorption Systems

Activated carbon can be utilized in the reduction of the pollution load of many kinds of waste in water as well as in air-pollution control, including a variety of dissolved organic materials. Not all dissolved organics can be handled by carbon, and the exact degree of removal from the liquids is dependent upon the following:

1. Size and polarity of molecules. Small or highly polar molecules are not readily adsorbed.

2. Chemical characteristics of the wastewater.

3. Wastewater pH; a very high pH inhibits adsorption.

An important aspect of carbon adsorption is its ability to eliminate organics which are not completely removed by conventional biological treatment.

Biodegradable organics are also adsorbable. Therefore, carbon can be used in either of two ways: to upgrade conventional biological treatment or to replace it.

The method of contact between the polluted water and the carbon involves two separate steps. First, the contaminated stream is passed through a vessel with either carbon granules or a slurry. Impurities are removed by adsorption when sufficient contact time is provided for the process. Contactors for granular carbon also function as filters which remove suspended particles from the influent stream. The carbon system generally consists of a number of columns or basins used as contactors.

The second step is a rejuvenation process after the carbon adsorptive capacity becomes exhausted. The contactor must then be shut down and the carbon removed for service to be thermally regenerated by combustion of the organic adsorbate. Some carbon is lost during hydraulic transport and regeneration. A recurring maintenance function is routinely to add fresh carbon to the system. Carbon treatment of wastewater has been demonstrated for both municipal and industrial applications. Several options are available in handling various situations:

Downflow carbon columns are used for both adsorption and filtration of contaminated water. Hydraulic loadings of 2 to 10 gallons per minute (gpm) per square foot are recommended. Suspended solids in wastewater are generally collected on the carbon bed surface at the lower flow rates. At higher rates, some of these particulates penetrate some distance into the carbon.

It is necessary to provide periodic backwash of downflow beds to relieve the pressure drop generated by the plugging in the bed by the suspended solids. If the bed becomes compacted or fouled, it becomes difficult to expand without an excessive quantity of backwash. Biological growth frequently occurs on the surface of carbon granules, tending to clog the bed. More frequent backwashing as well as other methods may be required for removal of these growths and control of their activity. To ensure existence of an aerobic condition, dissolved oxygen should be maintained in the feed and backwash water, to prevent formation of sulfides.

Upflow carbon columns pass wastewater upward through the carbon at low hydraulic loadings, less than 2 gpm per square foot. The carbon bed will remain substantially packed at the bottom of the column. At higher flow rates, 4 to 7 gpm per square foot, the bed becomes partially expanded. Rates higher than 7 gpm per square foot will tend to lift the carbon and pack particles against the top of the column. If little or no freeboard is available, the bed operates as a packed bed at any velocity. When this system is operated as a packed bed, suspended particulates present in the contaminated stream will be filtered out on the bottom of the bed and can become a problem.

A "pulsed-bed" system passes wastewater in an upflow direction through the bed. Proper maintenance procedure is to shut down the column periodically and withdraw a portion of the carbon in the bottom of the bed. A fresh equal charge of carbon is forced into the top of the bed.

Gravity and pressurized-flow carbon columns can be operated either downflow or upflow. Large pumps are not necessary; in addition, high capital costs for nonpressurized vessels are eliminated. Because of the limited available head, it is usually necessary to remove suspended solids by chemical clarification or filtration pretreatment.

A gravity-flow-system upflow as a partially expanded bed has more advantages than a packed bed. Pressure drop across the bed remains constant and can provide sustained operation for long periods of time. Usually, a pre- or post-treatment step for supplementary solids removal is included.

Pressurized flow allows the carbon bed to be operated at a higher flow rate and over a greater range of pressure buildup before backwashing is required. The height of the carbon-contacting vessels should be limited to the adsorbent bed depth plus an additional 50 percent for expansion during backwash.

Single and multistage systems are both possible for carbon-contacting beds. Inclusion of adequate piping and valving in the design allows switching from one mode of operation to the other if changes in the treatment objective are anticipated.

Series or multistage systems provide a higher degree of treatment with maximum use of carbon and greater removal of organics. A number of single-stage parallel contactors, staggered in their status operation or degree of exhaustion, can produce an acceptable product by mixing individual exit streams.

Ion-Exchange Columns

Ion exchangers are used in removing dissolved minerals from aqueous solutions by the use of specialized insoluble, inorganic complexes (called zeolites) or by synthetic organic materials (ion-exchange resins). This process is called demineralization.

Any substance to be removed from solution in an ion-exchange system must first be ionized. Most organic compounds are nonionized and are therefore excluded from this process, which is basically a two-step method. Cations (positively charged ions) are removed first by an ion exchanger called a cation exchanger. The negatively charged ions (anions) are removed in the second step by another ion exchanger known as an anion exchanger. When water contaminated with sulfates, chlorides, or nitrates of calcium, magnesium, sodium, or potassium is passed through a hydrogen-cation exchanger, the metallic cations are removed and held by the ion-exchange resin.

After some use, the useful exchange capacity of the hydrogen-cation exchanger becomes exhausted and must be regenerated with acid, which removes accumulated metals. At the same time, the cation exchanger takes on an equivalent amount of hydrogen ions. This exchange restores it to the original hydrogen form. Usually, dilute sulfuric acid or bihydrochloric acid is used for this regeneration.

The anion exchanger is periodically rejuvenated by an alkali which removes the accumulated anions in the form of their soluble salts and restores the anion exchanger to its original state. Chlorides, nitrates, bicarbonate, and silicate are removed by regeneration with caustic soda, which removes the acid in the form of their sodium salts. Simultaneously the anion exchanger is restored.

Carbonic acid is usually created by treatment of water containing alkalinity with a cation exchanger. This can be removed by anion exchange in a process similar to the removal of other acids or by degasification.

Anion and cation resins can be mixed (mixed bed) in a series of two-step demineralizers capable of producing a product of nearly theoretical chemical purity.

Ion-exchange resins are insoluble solids in bead form. The solution to be treated flows through the resins placed in vessels. Cations will be adsorbed onto the resin by exchange and released into the solution. The cation is usually hydrogen. Similarly an anion resin charged with an anion will effect an exchange with anions in the solution passing through the bed.

A variety of ion-exchange resins are commercially available. Two major types of anion resins are the weakly basic type, including aliphatic polyamide epoxy-poly-amine, and polystyrene with tertiary amine functionality; and the strongly basic type, including polystyrene with quaternary ammonium functionality, type I, and polystyrene with quaternary ammonium functionality, type II.

Cation-exchange resins are likewise divided into the weakly acidic type, including carboxylic acid with cross-linked acrylic matrix; and the strongly acidic type, including sulfonated polystyrene with divinyl benzene cross linking, and the carbonaceous type (sulfonated coal).

Air Stripping

Air stripping is a proven technology for the removal of volatile organic compounds (VOCs) from contaminated wastewater and groundwater. Stripping is a physical separation process during which volatile organic compounds are transferred from a liquid phase to a gaseous phase. A number of designs have been used over the years, but the packed-tower design is the most common in environmental engineering applications. Packed towers are continuous contact equipment that bring two phases in close contact with each other and allow mass to be transported across the boundaries of the two phases. They usually operate in a countercurrent mode with the water trickling down the packing by gravity and the air being forced upward through the bed.

Important parameters for the design of air strippers are contaminant type and levels of contamination, the higher the volatility of a compound the more easily it is stripped by aeration; type of packing and packing height, packing should provide large wetted surface, should be inert, and should have a large void volume to minimize serious pressure drop; air to water ratio, which is a function of contaminant type and temperature, typical values are 30:1 for volatile compound and 200:1 for highly soluble compounds; the liquid loading, which is typically 25 to 30 gpm per square foot; and the water temperature. Pilot studies may be necessary to obtain mass-transfer coefficients and Henry's constants if these data are not available.

Air strippers can efficiently and economically remove VOCs such as vinyl chloride, trichloroethane (TCA), trichloroethylene (TCE), and tetrachloroethylene (PCE); pesticides such as chlordane, dibromochloropropane, and aldicarb; and chlorinated aromatics such as dibromobenzene. Less volatile compounds can also be removed by steam stripping at higher temperatures. Removal efficiencies of 99.99 percent have been achieved in many cases.

Membrane Separation

Membranes have been used for many years to separate organic and inorganic species from solutions. A membrane can be loosely defined as a selective barrier between two phases. In other words, a membrane allows preferred passage (permeation) of certain compounds while rejecting others. The mechanism responsible for this permeation phenomenon is usually molecular diffusion within the membrane pores. Other mechanisms that can cause permeation of certain species through a membrane are pressure and electric potential gradients.

Processes that utilize some kind of membrane to separate a mixture of organic or inorganic substances include:

- Reverse osmosis (RO)
- Ultrafiltration (UF)
- Electrodialysis

Consider the case where two solutions that contain a solute of different concentrations are separated by a semipermeable membrane. The semipermeable membrane allows only solvent passage but blocks the passage of solute across the membrane pores. The concentration gradient that exists across the membrane induces a spontaneous transport of solvent in the direction of the more concentrated side. This flow of solvent across the membrane exerts a pressure on the dilute side of the membrane that is known as osmotic pressure. The flow of solvent stops when osmotic equilibrium is established between the two compartments. If a pressure is exerted on the dilute side of the membrane that exceeds the osmotic pressure of the solution, the flow of solvent is reversed and as a result the solute concentration in the concentrated side of the membrane increases. This phenomenon constitutes the basis for reverse osmosis.

Membranes are constructed from a variety of organic materials (synthetic polymers). The most widely used membranes in environmental applications are made out of cellulose acetate films and have a typical thickness of 100 microns. The coefficients of water and solute permeation are characteristics of a particular membrane. Both of these coefficients are temperature-dependent. The rate of hydrolysis of membranes and therefore their rate of deterioration is a function of temperature and pH. This limits the use of many membranes to applications where the hydrolysis rate is minimal.

Solute rejection is a very important parameter that is related to the efficiency of the membrane and its ability to achieve high degrees of separation. Solute rejection is defined as the ratio of the concentration difference across the membrane to the bulk concentration of the concentrate stream. The higher the solute rejection the higher the purity of the solvent in the product stream. Build-up or depletion of some chemical species in the thin layer adjacent to the membrane phase (concentration polarization) reduces the separation efficiency of the process and may result in fouling or deterioration of the membrane. Pretreatment of the feed may, in some cases, be necessary in order to remove turbidity and suspended solids, to adjust the pH, to inhibit precipitation, to disinfect to prevent bacterial growth, and to remove oils to prevent fouling.

Membrane systems are usually of modular design and can be connected in series to produce a treated effluent of high purity. Typical designs are:

- Large tube
- Plate and frame
- Spiral wound
- Hollow fiber

Membrane modules should be able to sustain high pressures [300 to 1500 pounds per square inch gauge (psig)], to avoid pressure drops in the feed and to minimize membrane replacement costs. Because RO is a concentrating process, it can be applied to reduce the volume of a waste, to recover valuable materials, and to concentrate pollutants to improve treatment efficiencies. RO is mainly used for the purification of brackish water that contains high concentrations (10,000 ppm) of dissolved solids, and for the treatment of wastes with high organic loadings.

Ultrafiltration is similar to RO but it operates at lower pressures and is unaffected by osmotic pressure. UF can remove solutes with molecular weights ranging from 500 to 500,000. Colloidal particles may also be removed from waste streams provided the proper membrane is selected. UF also suffers from concentration polarization effects, and pretreatment may be necessary. The difference between UF and RO is not clearly defined, and the terms are interchangeably used in many cases.

Electrodialysis is a process in which the application of an electric current across a series of membranes induces partial separation of the ionic species in solution. The applied electrical energy causes the transport of electrolytes from the dilute to the concentrated solution. Membranes selected for electrodialysis should be good electrical conductors and have low water-permeation coefficients. Separation in these systems is accomplished by placing alternately cation- and anion-selective membranes in the current path.

It should be noted that membrane systems have high energy and maintenance requirements and that pretreatment, which may be necessary, can add significantly to the initial capital and operating costs. The economics, however, for operation and maintenance of membrane systems become favorable when higher water fluxes and longer membrane lives can be obtained.

Precipitation

Precipitation of sparingly soluble metal oxides and hydroxides provides a method for the removal of heavy metals such as cadmium, chromium, lead, and copper from industrial wastewaters. The concentrations of heavy metals in metal-plating wastewater and other waste streams often reach objectionable levels and therefore must be removed prior to discharge.

Various processes are currently in use for the removal of heavy metals from wastewaters such as ion exchange, chemical oxidation, and chemical precipitation. Precipitation of heavy metals is accomplished by pH adjustments. The pH is adjusted by adding other chemical species that bring the concentration of the hydronium ions (H_3O^+) to the desired operating level. The solubility of the solids formed, usually metal oxides and hydroxides, is a function of temperature and pH. In the presence of a solid phase an equilibrium is established between the constituent ions and the solid itself. For instance, when an amount of calcium carbonate, in excess of its solubility limit, is placed in water, the following equilibrium is established between the aqueous and solid phases:

$$CaCO_{3(s)} \Leftrightarrow Ca^{2+} + CO_3^{2-}$$

Addition of any substance that, directly or indirectly, increases the concentration of the ionic species results in precipitation of calcium carbonate and subsequent reduction of the ionic species concentration in the aqueous phase. The product of the activities of the ionic species, in this example calcium and carbonate ions, defines the solubility product constant. When this product is exceeded, precipitation is spontaneous. The stable metal oxides and hydroxides settle to the bottom of a sedimentation tank and are removed for disposal. The produced sludge must be properly disposed of in order to reduce the risk of soil or groundwater contamination due to leaching of the heavy metals.

In addition to the precipitation reactions, certain species (ligands) have the ability to bind the metal ions and form soluble metal complexes. Complexation reactions increase the solubility of the solid, and higher total metal concentrations are observed than those predicted by the solubility product. However, the toxicity of the complexed forms is often lower than the toxicity of the original free ion.

Heavy metals such as trivalent chromium, iron, copper, and lead can be easily removed by lime or sodium hydroxide precipitation. Hexavalent chromium, however, must be reduced to trivalent chromium using a reducing agent prior to lime precipitation. Sulfur dioxide, sodium metabisulfite, and sodium bisulfite are commonly used reducing agents. Chromium hydroxide, which is produced during the precipitation process, exhibits its lowest solubility in the pH range of 7.5 to 10. Chromium hydroxide solubility drops near zero between a pH range of 8.5 to 9.0.

The pertinent complexation and precipitation reactions for most heavy metals in aqueous solutions are not well understood. Lack of this information makes estimation of the required chemical dosages (acids or bases to be added) difficult and in some cases impossible. Chemical dosages are, in most cases, experimentally determined by performing jar tests.

Chemical precipitation is generally a three-step process. In the first step the pH is adjusted by the addition of acids or bases; in the second step a solid phase is formed as fine crystallites aggregate to form larger crystals; and in the final step heavier crystals are removed by gravity in a sedimentation tank. An added advantage of the process is that soluble organics that may be present are adsorbed on the solid surface or enmeshed in the precipitate and consequently removed from solution. A disadvantage is the addition of chemicals for pH adjustments, which may add significantly to the capital and operating costs of the process.

Biological Treatment Processes

Biological treatment is applicable to aqueous streams with organic contaminants. The influent waste stream may contain either dissolved or insoluble organics amenable to biodegradation. The microorganisms rely on enzymes for organic decomposition; the enzymes require water to remain active. In aerobic biological treatment, simple and complex organics are eventually decomposed to carbon dioxide and water; oxygen is essential in the hydrocarbon decomposition. In anaerobic biological treatment only simple organics such as carbohydrates, proteins, alcohols, and acids can be decomposed.

Biological treatment processes do not destroy or alter inorganics. Concentrations of soluble inorganics should be low so as not to inhibit enzyme activity. Traces of inorganics may be partly removed from liquid waste streams as a result of adsorption on microbial cell coating. Microorganisms typically have a net negative charge and undergo cation exchange with soluble metal ions. Anions such as chlorides or sulfates are not affected by biological treatment. The most frequently used biological treatment processes are:

- Activated sludge
- Trickling filter
- Rotating biological contactors (RBCs)
- Aerated lagoon
- Enzyme treatment
- Waste-stabilization pond

- Anaerobic digestion
- Composting

All these biological systems except enzyme treatment contain living organisms.

Most wastewater-treatment plants use primary sedimentation to remove readily settleable solids from raw wastewater. In a typical plant with primary sedimentation and a conventional activated-sludge process for secondary treatment, the dry weight of primary sludge solids is roughly 50 percent of that for the total sludge solids. Primary sludge is usually easier to manage than biological and chemical sludges. Primary sludge is readily thickened by gravity, either within a primary sedimentation tank or within a separate gravity thickener. In comparison with biological and many chemical sludges, primary sludge with low conditioning requirements can be mechanically dewatered rapidly. The dewatering device will produce a drier cake and give better solids capture than it would for most biological and chemical sludges.

Primary sludge production is typically within the range of 800 to 2500 pounds per million gallons [100 to 300 milligrams per liter (mg/L)] of wastewater. A basic approach to estimating primary sludge production for a particular plant is by computing the quantity of total suspended solids (TSS) entering the primary sedimentation tank and assuming an efficiency of removal based on previous experience.

When chemicals are added to the raw wastewater for removal of phosphorus or coagulation of nonsettleable solids, large quantities of chemical precipitates are formed. The quantity of chemical solids produced in chemical treatment of wastewater depends upon the type and amount of chemicals added, chemical constituents in the wastewater, and performance of the coagulation and clarification processes. It is difficult to predict accurately the quantity of chemical solids that will be produced. Classical jar tests are favored as a means for estimating chemical sludge quantities. Conditions that influence primary sludge concentration include the following:

- If wastewater is not degritted before it enters the sedimentation tanks, the grit may be removed by passing the raw primary sludge through cyclonic separators. However, these separators do not function properly with sludge concentrations above 1 percent.
- If the sludge contains large amounts of fine nonvolatile solids, such as silt, from storm inflow, a concentration of well over 6 percent may sometimes be attained.
- Industrial loads may strongly affect primary sludge concentration.
- Primary sludge may float when buoyed up by gas bubbles generated under anaerobic conditions. Conditions favoring gas formation include warm temperatures, solids deposits within sewers, strong septic wastes, long detention times for wastewater solids in the sedimentation tanks, lack of adequate prechlorination, and recirculating sludge liquors.

- To prevent the septic conditions that favor gas formation, it may be necessary to strictly limit the storage time of sludge in the sedimentation tanks. This is done by increasing the frequency and rate of primary sludge pumping.

- If biological sludges are mixed with wastewater, a lower primary sludge concentration will generally result.

Biological sludges are produced by treatment processes such as activated sludge, trickling filters, and rotating biological contactors. Quantities and characteristics of biological sludges vary with metabolic and growth rates of the various microorganisms present in the sludge. The quantity and quality of sludge produced by the biological process is intermediate between that produced in no-primary systems and that produced in full-primary systems in cases when fine screens or primary sedimentation tanks with high overflow rates are used.

Biological sludge containing debris such as grit, plastics, paper, and fibers will be produced at plants lacking primary treatment. Plants with primary sedimentation normally produce a fairly pure biological sludge. The concentrations and therefore the volumes of waste biological sludge are greatly affected by the method of operation of the clarifiers. Biological sludges are generally more difficult to thicken and dewater than primary sludge and most chemical sludges.

Thermal Treatment and Incineration

Methods used to treat hazardous wastes previously destined for landfilling include incineration or some form of thermal treatment. Incinerators and alternate thermal treatment methods are achieving great interest in waste management. Ideally incineration of wastes to carbon dioxide and inorganic constituents offers a flexible and economical detoxification method for a wide variety of nonrecoverable hazardous wastes. There are concerns, however, about this method for emission of toxic combustion by-products such as polychlorinated dioxins and furans and the various metals in residues.

Total incineration can be defined as the conversion of waste to a solidified residue and slag or ash and flue gases which consist mainly of carbon dioxide, oxygen, nitrogen, and water vapor. While energy recovery may be an option, most systems must include adequate air-pollution control. In conventional incineration temperatures are on the order of 1800°F; total incineration operates at temperatures approaching 3000°F. Incineration objectives include:

- Maximum volume and weight reduction

- Complete oxidation or combustion of all combustibles with a resultant residue that is sterile, free of putrescibles, compact, dense and strong, and as free of leachable materials as possible

- A minimal and environmentally acceptable residue disposal operation

■ Complete oxidation of gaseous products of combustion, with an atmospheric discharge after adequate air-pollution control

Incineration, combustion, and thermal treatment processes in use and under continued development include:

Liquid injection incineration This method is limited to destruction of pumpable wastes of viscosities less than 10,000 SS. Usually designed to burn specific waste streams and also used in conjunction with other incinerator systems as a secondary afterburner for combustion of volatiles.

Rotary kilns Usually involve a high capital cost, have economy of scale, can accommodate a great variety of waste feeds: solids, sludges, liquids, some bulk waste contained in fiber drums. Combustion chamber rotation enhances waste mixing.

Cement kilns Attractive for destruction of harder-to-burn waste, owing to very high residence times, good mixing, and high temperatures. Alkaline environment neutralizes chlorine.

Boilers Usually a liquid injection design; has energy value recovery and fuel conservation. The availability on site of waste generators reduces spill risks during transportation.

Multiple hearth Waste passage onto progressively hotter hearths can provide long residence time for sludges and good fuel efficiency. Disadvantages include inability to handle fusible ash, high maintenance due to moving parts in high-temperature zone, and cold spots that inhibit even and complete combustion.

Fluid-bed incinerators Offer large economy of scale. Turbulent bed enhances uniform heat transfer and combustion of waste. Mass of bed is large relative to mass of injected waste.

Pyrolysis Air-pollution-control requirements are minimal; air-starved combustion avoids volatilization of inorganic compounds, and these and heavy metals go into insoluble solid char. This process has potential for high capacity. Disadvantages are that some wastes produce a tar hard to dispose of and the method has potentially high fuel maintenance costs.

Emerging thermal processes include:

Molten salt The molten salts act as catalysts and promote heat transfer which reduces energy and maintenance costs. Units are compact and potentially portable. Air-pollution-control requirements appear minimal since combustion products ash and acidic gases are retained in the melt. Regeneration or ash disposal of contaminated salt appears to be a potential problem making the method unsuitable for high-ash wastes. Chamber corrosion can be a problem.

Plasma arc   Very-high-energy radiation breaks chemical bonds directly without a series of chemical reactions. Operation is simple, with low energy costs, and mobile units are feasible. Principal limitations are limited throughput and high NaOH requirements for scrubbers.

Wet oxidation   Applicable to aqueous wastes too dilute for incineration and too toxic for biological treatment. Lower temperature requirements, no air emissions, and released energy by some wastes are some of the advantages. The process is not applicable to highly chlorinated organics and some wastes may require further treatment.

Supercritical water   Applicable to chlorinated aqueous wastes which are too dilute to incinerate. The process takes advantage of water's excellent solvent properties above the critical point for organic compounds. Injected oxygen decomposes smaller organic molecules to carbon dioxide and water.

High-temperature liquid wall   Waste can be efficiently destroyed as it passes through the cylinder and is exposed to radiant-heat temperatures of about 4000°F. The cylinder is electrically heated; heat is transferred through an inert gas blanket to waste. Mobile units are possible. To date only limited laboratory and pilot units have been available and scale-up remains to be seen. A disadvantage appears to be the potentially high costs for electrical heating.

Other Technologies Used in Waste and Wastewater Treatment

Table 5-6 is a pollutant-process matrix for the processes presented in this chapter as well as some other technologies that were omitted owing to space limitations. The efficiency of both biological and physicochemical processes depends on a large number of parameters. However, if the appropriate technology is selected for the treatment of a particular waste, high removal and destruction efficiencies are possible.

Processes that were not discussed here but appear in Table 5-2 are:

Chlorination and ozonation   Chlorination is currently being used for the destruction of ammonia, but a major problem is the production of odorous gases. Ozonation is being utilized for destruction of organic pollutants such as phenols and other organic acids. Both chlorination and ozonation are used for the disinfection of water and wastewater.

Flotation and dissolved air flotation (DAF)   Flotation can effectively remove solid and liquid particles with densities lower than the density of water. Dissolved air flotation, a modification to flotation, enhances the overall removal efficiency by passing fine air bubbles through the water column. Fine particles, which are suspended in the solution, adhere to the rising bubbles and are carried to the surface. This enables the process to remove particles with densities higher than the water density.

Table 5-6. Removal Efficiencies of Selected Treatment Processes for Various Pollutants, Percent

Processes	Coarse solids	Suspended solids	Soluble organics	Oils	Acids and bases	Pathogens	Colloidal solids	NH_3	NO_2-NO_3	P	Trace organics	Inorganics and heavy metals
Activated carbon			65–75	90–95							90–95	0–95
Aerobic biosystems			50–60							25–35	25–35	
Air stripping								75–85			90–98	
Anaerobic biosystems			40–50								25–35	
Chemical precipitation										90–95		90–95
Chlorination						98–99						
Coagulation and flocculation		70–80					70–80					
Denitrification									85–95			
Dissolved air flotation				80–90								
Electrodialysis											50–60	85–90
Filtration				80–90			80–90					
Flotation		40–60										
Gravity separation				70–80								
Ion exchange								90–95	90–95	90–95	70–80	90–95
Microstraining		50–60					30–40					
Neutralization					90–95							
Nitrification								75–85				
Ozonation						98–99						
Reverse osmosis											70–80	90–95
Screening	90–100											
Sedimentation		50–60										
Ultrafiltration							95–98				0–75	0–75

145

Screening and microscreening   Screening is utilized for the removal of coarse solids whereas microscreening is capable of removing smaller particles and particles of colloidal size.

Coagulation and flocculation   In coagulation and flocculation systems a chemical coagulant is added to the wastewater to accelerate the rate of particle agglomeration. Once the flocs are formed, they are removed by gravity settling in a sedimentation tank. Turbidity, imparted to the water by clays and other suspended solids, can be effectively removed by coagulation and flocculation.

Nitrification and denitrification   Nitrification and denitrification is a two-step process for the removal of ammonia and nitrates from wastewater. The process exploits two genera of bacteria, the nitrifiers and the denitrifiers, for the oxidation of ammonia. Removal of nitrogen prior to discharge is essential since nitrogen is a nutrient and contributes to eutrophication phenomena in lakes and rivers.

Remediation of Hazardous Waste Sites

Hazardous wastes are defined as wastes that pose special hazards to human health. There are two general approaches to defining hazardous waste: by listing and by identification. EPA has published a list of hazardous substances. Any waste that is not included in this list must be identified based on the following criteria:

1. *Corrosivity*   A liquid waste is characterized as corrosive if it has a pH less than 2 or greater than 12.5 and corrodes a plain carbon steel (carbon content of 0.2 percent) at the rate of 6.35 millimeters or greater per year at 55°C.

2. *Toxicity*   A waste is characterized as hazardous on the basis of the toxicity characteristic leaching procedure (TCLP). The TCLP test is a leaching test in accordance with the EPA published protocol (*Federal Register,* March 29, 1990). If the leachate from the TCLP test contains chemicals in excess of the regulatory limit (Table 5-7), the waste is characterized as hazardous.

3. *Ignitability*   If a liquid waste (other than an aqueous solution containing less than 24 percent alcohol by volume) has a flash point of 60°C as determined by ASTM D93-79 or ASTM D93-80 it is characterized as ignitable. A solid waste is characterized as ignitable if it causes fire at 0°C and at a pressure of 1 atmosphere through friction, moisture absorption, or spontaneous chemical reactions.

4. *Reactivity*   Substances that are unstable and can undergo violent changes, form explosive mixtures with water, or create toxic gases are characterized as reactive.

In general, hazardous waste should not be disposed in landfills without first undergoing some kind of pretreatment. As waste disposal in landfills is becom-

Table 5-7. Toxicity Characteristic Constituents and Regulatory Levels

EPA HW No.*	Constituent	CAS No.†	Chronic toxicity reference level, mg/L	Regulatory level, mg/L
D004	Arsenic	7440-38-2	0.05	5.0
D005	Barium	7440-39-3	1.0	100.0
D018	Benzene	71-43-2	0.005	0.5
D006	Cadmium	7440-43-9	0.01	1.0
D019	Carbon tetrachloride	56-23-5	0.005	0.5
D020	Chlordane	57-74-9	0.0003	0.03
D021	Chlorobenzene	108-90-7	1	100.0
D022	Chloroform	67-66-3	0.06	6.0
D007	Chromium	7440-47-3	0.05	5.0
D023	o-Cresol	95-48-7	2	200.0§
D024	m-Cresol⁻	108-39-4	2	200.0§
D025	p-Cresol	106-44-5	2	200.0§
D026	Cresol		2	200.0§
D016	2,4-D	94-75-7	0.1	10.0
D027	1,4-Dichlorobenzene	106-46-7	0.075	7.5
D028	1,2-Dichloroethane	107-06-2	0.005	0.5
D029	1,1-Dichloroethylene	75-35-4	0.007	0.7
D030	2,4-Dinitrotoluene	121-14-2	0.0005	0.13‡
D012	Endrin	72-20-8	0.0002	0.02
D031	Heptachlor (and its hydroxide)	76-44-8	0.00008	0.008
D032	Hexachlorobenzene	118-74-1	0.0002	0.13‡
D033	Hexachloro-1,3-butadiene	87-68-3	0.005	0.5
D034	Hexachloroethane	67-71-1	0.03	3.0
D008	Lead	7439-92-1	0.05	5.0
D013	Lindane	58-89-9	0.004	0.4
D009	Mercury	7439-97-6	0.002	0.2
D014	Methoxychlor	72-43-5	0.1	10.0
D035	Methyl ethyl ketone	78-93-3	2	200.0
D036	Nitrobenzene	98-95-3	0.02	2.0
D037	Pentachlorophenol	87-86-5	1	100.0
D038	Pyridine	110-86-1	0.04	5.0‡
D010	Selenium	7782-49-2	0.01	1.0
D011	Silver	7440-22-4	0.05	5.0
D039	Tetrachloroethylene	127-18-4	0.007	0.7
D015	Toxaphene	8001-35-2	0.005	0.5
D040	Trichloroethylene	79-01-6	0.005	0.5
D041	2,4,5-Trichlorophenol	95-95-4	4	400.0
D042	2,4,6-Trichlorophenol	88-06-2	0.02	2.0
D017	2,4,5-TP (Silvex)	93-72-1	0.01	1.0
D043	Vinyl chloride	75-01-4	0.002	0.2

*Hazardous waste number.

†Chemical abstracts service number.

‡Quantitation limit is greater than the calculated regulatory level. The quantitation limit therefore becomes the regulatory level.

§If o-, m-, and p-cresol concentrations cannot be differentiated, the total cresol (D026) concentration is used. The regulatory level for total cresol is 200 mg/liter.

ing more and more restrictive, the environmental industry has launched an enormous effort to develop innovative cost-effective site remedial technologies.

Site contamination has resulted from improper disposal or accidental release of industrial and other chemicals in the subsurface environment. For the most part, site remediation involves the treatment of contaminated soil and groundwater. Depending on the mode of application, technologies are classified as in situ or ex situ. In situ technologies are applied in the field with minimum disturbance to the soil matrix. Ex situ technologies require that the soil be excavated or the groundwater pumped and treated aboveground. Such treatment may be accomplished on-site or at an off-site facility.

One of the most comprehensive programs for the development and evaluation of site remediation technologies is the EPA Superfund Innovative Technology Evaluation (SITE) program. SITE was established by EPA in 1986 and is administered by the Office of Research and Development, Risk Reduction Engineering Laboratory in Cincinnati, Ohio. The SITE program includes the following components (EPA, 1991):

- *Emerging technology program*   Provides financial support to researchers to investigate emerging technologies in the bench and pilot scales.

- *Monitoring and measurement technologies program*   Develops technologies in the areas of monitoring and measurement of hazardous and toxic substances.

- *Demonstration program*   Conducts demonstrations and evaluates the technical performance and cost-effectiveness of promising innovative technologies.

- *Technology transfer program*   Disseminates technical information concerning technologies supported by the SITE program.

The SITE program has adopted a three-tier approach for the development of innovative technologies from conceptualization to commercialization as shown in Fig. 5-1.

As of 1991, EPA had supported 44 projects in the emerging technology program and 76 in the demonstration program grouped in the categories shown in Table 5-8.

A summary of selected innovative soil and groundwater remedial technologies follows.

Soil Vapor Extraction (SVE)

Soil vapor extraction is a technology which has been used extensively over the past 10 years to remove volatile organic components (VOCs) from contaminated soils in the vadose (unsaturated) zone. The principle of SVE operation is that VOCs can be transferred readily from the undissolved contaminant (nonaqueous phase), contaminated soil moisture (aqueous phase), and the soil grains (solid phase) to the air contained in the soil pores (gaseous phase). In SVE appli-

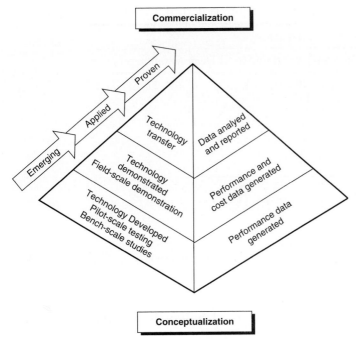

Figure 5-1. Development process of innovative technologies.
(*Source: EPA/540/5-91/008.*)

cations air flow is induced through the soil matrix by applying vacuum in an extraction well with or without the assistance of air injection wells. Contaminated vapors are then pumped out of the soil and are treated aboveground, usually by activated-carbon adsorption columns.

Key factors influencing SVE are contaminant distribution at the site, the site hydrogeologic properties, and contaminant properties. SVE can be employed:

- When the soil contains contaminants with vapor pressure greater than 0.5 mmHg
- When large volumes of contaminated soil need treatment.
- When the soil has air permeability in the range of 10^{-2} to 10^{-5} cm/sec.
- When biological degradation of the contaminant may need enhancement.

SVE has many advantages over other in situ soil remediation processes as follows:

- Requires few mechanical parts.
- Has low operating and maintenance costs.

Table 5-8. Innovative Technologies in the EPA Site Program

	Number of technologies	
Technology group	Emerging program	Demonstration program
Solidification and stabilization	2	11
Biological	10	15
Physical and chemical	21	24
Thermal destruction	7	8
Thermal desorption	0	13
Materials handling	4	3
Radioactive wastes	0	2

SOURCE: EPA 1991.

- Employs conventional equipment, labor, and materials and can be installed rapidly.

- Provides permanent remediation.

- May be used to remediate soils underneath buildings and other structures.

SVE's applicability and usefulness are limited by several factors including:

- Contaminants with low vapor pressures will exhibit low removal efficiencies.

- Soil heterogeneities and the presence of silt and clay layers will prolong treatment times.

- The toxicity of the contaminants may not be altered if biological activity is absent.

- Vapors must be treated to meet applicable air quality standards prior to release.

The cost of remediation using SVE can range from as low as $50 per cubic yard of soil to as high as $200/c.y. depending on the type of contaminant and soil conditions.

SVE has also been used in ex situ applications where soil is excavated and stockpiled. A perforated pipe network system is embedded in the soil pile and air is exhausted by a pump connected to the header pipe.

The SVE technology has been extended to treat contaminated soil and groundwater below the groundwater table by a technique called air sparging. In this process air is injected below the groundwater table and vapors are recovered by an extraction well located above in the unsaturated zone.

In addition, thermally enhanced SVE applications have been reported. In most cases, hot air injection will result in a more rapid and effective removal of contaminants.

Stabilization and Solidification (SS) Technologies

Stabilization and solidification refer to treatment processes that are designed to accomplish one or more of the following:

1. Improve the handling and physical characteristics of the waste

2. Decrease the surface area of the waste mass across which transfer or loss of contaminants can occur

3. Limit the solubility of hazardous constituents of the waste

Contaminated soils and sludges can be treated in situ or ex situ.

Stabilization and solidification of hazardous wastes and contaminated soils encompass a broad and overlapping description of a wide array of treatment processes. To describe the technology, it is best to define the terms stabilization and solidification independently of one another. Even though the two terms are often used interchangeably, the EPA defines them as follows:

Stabilization refers to those techniques that reduce the hazard potential of a waste by converting the contaminants into their least soluble, mobile, or toxic form. The physical nature and handling characteristics of the waste are not necessarily modified by stabilization.

Solidification refers to techniques that encapsulate the waste in a monolithic solid of high structural integrity. The encapsulation may be of fine waste particles (microencapsulation), or coarser waste agglomerated particles or even large waste blocks (macroencapsulation). Solidification does not necessarily involve reagents but may mechanically bind the material into a monolith. Contaminant migration is restricted by decreasing the surface area exposed to leaching and/or isolating the wastes within an impervious capsule.

The term fixation has fallen in and out of favor, but it is widely used in the waste-treatment field to mean any of the stabilization and solidification processes just described. "Fixed" wastes are those that have been treated in this manner. The term "immobilization" refers to those techniques that tend to decrease the concentration of toxic compounds by attaching them onto the surfaces of the solid particles.

To understand fixation, we need to look at the leaching process and the tests by which it is measured. If ground or surface water contacts or passes through a material, each constituent dissolves at some finite rate. Therefore, when a waste, treated or not, is exposed to water a rate of dissolution can be measured. We call this process leaching, the water with which we start leachant, and the resulting contaminated liquid leachate. The capacity of the waste material to leach is called leachability.

The following are the most frequently used SS techniques.

Cement-Based SS. Cement-based stabilization and solidification is a process in which waste materials are mixed with portland cement. Water is added to the mixture, if it is not already present in the waste material, to ensure proper hydration reactions necessary for cement bonding. The wastes are incorporated into the cement matrix and, in some cases, undergo physical-chemical changes that further reduce their mobility in the waste cement matrix. Typically, hydroxides of metals are formed, which are much less soluble than other ionic species of the metals. Small amounts of fly ash, sodium silicate, bentonite, or proprietary additives are often added to the cement to enhance processing. The final product may vary from a granular, soil-like material to a cohesive solid block, depending on the reagent added and the types and amounts of wastes stabilized and solidified.

Cement-based stabilization and solidification has been applied to wastes containing various metals such as arsenic, cadmium, chromium, copper, lead, nickel, and zinc. Cement has also been used with complex wastes containing PCBs, oils, and oil sludges; wastes containing vinyl chloride; resins; stabilized and solidified plastics; asbestos; sulfides; and other materials. The effectiveness of this process on organics has not been established adequately.

Lime-Based Stabilization and Solidification.   Lime-based SS involves the same mechanisms as cement-based SS, the difference being the generally higher pH resulting from lime treatment. Lime is a rather broad term for a variety of calcium-bearing compounds. Various forms of lime have been successfully utilized as a soil-stabilizing agent for many years, including products with various degrees of purity. However, the most commonly used products are hydrated high-calcium lime, monohydrated dolomitic lime, and calcitic quicklime.

Lime has been known to be effective in stabilizing both organic and inorganic wastes. It is generally more effective than cement-based SS, as materials that interfere with cement setting and hardening may do the same with lime, but the effects are not as common. In addition, the volume increase resulting from treatment is generally of a lesser magnitude when lime is the additive. Furthermore, using lime results in better control of the pH increases over a wider range than with cement. Finally, when in situ pressure injection techniques are used for treatment of deeper layers, lime slurry grouts have a viscosity similar to that of water, as lime is readily soluble in water. On the other hand, cement involves particulate grouts that have much smaller mobilities in porous media. However, interestingly enough, lime is not as widely used as cement-based SS techniques are.

Pozzolanic Stabilization and Solidification.   Pozzolanic SS involves siliceous and aluminosilicate materials, which do not display cementing action alone but form cementitious substances when combined with lime or cement and water at ambient temperatures. The primary containment mechanism is the physical entrapment of the contaminant in the pozzolan matrix. Examples of common pozzolans are clay, fly ash, pumice, lime-kiln dusts, and blast-furnace slag. Pozzolanic SS is generally slower than cement or lime SS and involves larger volume increases.

Thermoplastic Techniques. Thermoplastic SS is a microencapsulation process in which the waste materials do not react chemically with the encapsulating material. In this technology, a thermoplastic material, such as asphalt (bitumen) or polyethylene or paraffin, is used to bind the waste constituents into a stabilized and solidified mass. The asphalt binder may be heated before it is mixed with the dry waste materials, or the asphalt may be applied as a cold mix. In the latter case water is being removed by subsequent compaction of the solidified material. Inclusion of water-bearing soluble salts in the waste can create problems in the final product, as water may diffuse through the matrix and cause swelling and cracking.

The process requires trained operators and specialized equipment and is extremely energy-intensive. The elevated process temperature also limits the types of materials which can be incorporated into the matrix, citrates and certain plastics being examples. There is also a fire risk associated with working on organics at high temperatures. Among the benefits of thermoplastic techniques is the reduction of waste volume because water is removed from the matrix, associated leach rates that are very low, and satisfactory long-term performance of the stabilized matrix under water and microbial exposure.

Macroencapsulation. This solidification process involves the encapsulation of waste products by sealing them in an organic resin or binder (overpack drum). The waste is generally thermoplastically solidified prior to macroencapsulation. High-density polyethylene (HDP) and polybutadiene are used to perform the encapsulation. The materials are commercially available and chemically stable, as they show very good resistance to biodegradation. They are also mechanically tough yet flexible. The waste product geometry can be optimized during the molding phase to suit transportation, storage disposal, or burial requirements. Skilled labor is required for molding and the process is again energy-intensive.

Organic Polymerization. Organic polymerization SS relies on polymer formation to immobilize the constituents of concern. Urea formaldehyde is the most commonly used organic polymer for this purpose. Organic polymerization has been primarily used to solidify radioactive wastes. This technology, however, as well as other organic polymerization systems, is believed to be obsolete at this point, at least in the United States. This is because of their relative high costs, their tendency to throw off free water during the condensation reaction, and more importantly recent environmental concern over formaldehyde. However, various nuclear plants that have installed and used such systems in the 1970s, may still have them in use.

Vitrification. This is a method well suited for dangerous or radioactive materials. It may be performed ex situ, typically using an electric furnace, or in situ using the Battelle developed process. The waste is processed by fusing it with silica into a glasslike material with an extremely low leach rate that is safe for disposal without some secondary treatment.

The Battelle process employs an array of four electrodes placed into the soil to the desired treatment depth. A conductive path is put in place to initiate the process, and the current acts as the driving force establishing a thermal gradient in the soil. As the temperature rises above 1600°C organics present in the soil are vaporized and then pyrolyzed. The released gases are collected for further treatment. Inorganics thermally decompose or enter into the melt reaction. The resulting product is a monolithic glasslike microcrystalline structure which is inert and stable. The process is extremely energy-intensive, requires skilled labor and specialized equipment, and may produce large volumes of organic vapors.

Soil Washing and Soil Flushing Technologies

Soil washing refers to a process in which excavated contaminated soils are scrubbed in an aqueous stream to remove undesired contaminants. Soil flushing, on the other hand, refers to a similar process applied in situ.

Soil washing is a volume-reduction process for treating excavated soils. The soil is prepared for the washing process by screening to remove large objects like pieces of wood, concrete, and other debris. The screened soil is mixed thoroughly with water and sometimes other cleaning agents to strip the contaminants from the soil. The process takes place in devices which resemble washing machines.

During the washing process the soils are segregated by size to separate the coarser components from the fine particles. Most of the time the coarser grains can be washed free of contaminants by mixing and mechanical scrubbing and can ultimately be returned to fill in the excavation.

Silt, clay, and other fine soils require additional treatment such as bioremediation, incineration, or landfilling. The water and extraction agent mixtures used to wash the contaminated soils need to be treated prior to disposal.

Soil flushing is an in situ treatment process for removing organic and/or inorganic contaminants. In this process mixtures of water and extraction agents are pumped or sprayed into the contaminated soil zones. The wash fluid is then pumped out by recovery wells and is treated aboveground.

Surfactants are frequently used as extracting agents. Surfactants are substances which have the property of adsorbing onto surfaces or interfaces, reducing the interfacial energy that keeps the contaminants bound in the soil matrix. Several surfactants are commercially available. They have been used to remove chlorinated organics from soils. Other flushing agents include:

- Acidic aqueous solutions such as sulfuric, hydrochloric, and nitric acids. These have been used for removal of certain metals and some basic organic constituents such as amines, ethers, and anilines.

- Basic solutions such as sodium hydroxide have been used to remove metals and various complexing and chelating agents.

Since soil washing and soil flushing is used in conjunction with other technologies to treat the recovered contaminants, its cost is highly variable. Overall, compared with other alternatives, the costs are considered moderate. Problems associated with in situ flushing include:

- Regulatory restrictions may prohibit the injection of various washing agents into the ground.
- Inadequate hydraulic control may result in contaminants traveling away from the capture zone, contaminating the aquifer further.
- Large volumes of waste may be created if the washing agents cannot be separated easily from the waste and reinjected.

Low-Temperature Thermal Desorption

Low-temperature thermal desorption is an ex situ process which uses heated air in combination with agitation to remove contaminants from soils. The contaminants are volatilized and transferred in the airstream, which in turn is recovered and treated before discharge to the atmosphere. The process has proved to be most effective with volatile organic compounds. The basic principle of operation is the transfer of contaminated mass from the soil grains and moisture to the airstream. This mass transfer is assisted by heating the waste to relatively low temperatures. The most effective temperature range is waste-specific. It must be high enough for volatilization to occur but low enough so that combustion of the waste off-gases is avoided. Treatment of the off-gases is necessary and sometimes troublesome. This is particularly true in the cases where the soil matrix contains several elements which may not be treatable by only one technology. The effectiveness of the process will depend on the type of soil and contaminant, the degree of mixing, temperature, and airflow rate. In addition, the physical properties of the contaminated soil such as grain-size distribution, moisture content, organic carbon content, and heating value will influence the performance of the process.

Bioremediation

Bioremediation refers to the application of natural microbial metabolic processes to remediate hazardous wastes. The technology has been applied both in situ and ex situ to remediate soils, groundwater, and soil slurries.

This technology takes advantage of the ability of certain types of bacteria to degrade chemical compounds. The mechanism is the metabolic transformation of organic compounds into energy, biomass, and carbon dioxide. The conversion of organic carbon to inorganic carbon is called mineralization and takes place by enzymatic oxidation in the presence of oxygen (aerobic degradation) or nitrite or sulfite (anaerobic degradation).

Environmental applications of biodegradation utilize either single isolated cultures or mixed colonies of bacteria. Most field applications utilize indigenous mixed cultures. In addition to bacteria, other life forms such as algae and fungi have been used.

Bacteria cells in the subsurface environment are either attached to the soil grains or held in suspension in the soil moisture or groundwater. Bacterial growth in such matrices is sensitive to various factors including toxicity of the contaminant, pH, temperature, and moisture conditions. To sustain bacterial growth it is often necessary to enhance the system by adding nutrients. The most common nutrient amendment is the addition of either phosphate or a reduced nitrogen source such as ammonia.

Bioremediation in situ can be either active or passive. Passive remediation relies totally on natural processes to restore the environment. In this case, indigenous bacteria metabolize the contaminants without intervention with the exception of monitoring. Active techniques involve the enhancement of the process to obtain optimum conditions and improve effectiveness.

Bioremediation has been found to be effective at sites contaminated with a variety of organics as shown in Table 5-9.

In situ application of bioremediation, as in the case of other technology applications, is preceded by a thorough site investigation. The objective of this investigation is to determine if the site conditions are such as to render the process effective. The most important parameters that need to be evaluated for in situ application of bioremediation are shown in Table 5-10.

The effectiveness of in situ biotreatment relies on the ability to deliver oxygen and nutrients to the soil matrix. Nutrients like nitrogen and phosphorus are usually added on a batch mode, while monitoring microbial activity. In some cases, a one-time nutrient enhancement may be adequate; in other cases a continuous enhancement may be required.

Oxygen can be introduced through injection wells in the subsurface in various forms including oxygen, saturated water, peroxide, and air-saturated water. The amount of oxygen and nutrient input is highly variable and depends on site-specific conditions. Laboratory treatability studies are often performed to determine these requirements and the overall effectiveness of the method.

Ex situ application of bioremediation involves excavating of soil and treatment aboveground. The soil can be treated as a slurry in bioreactors or by land farming. Several soil slurry biotreatment processes exist in various stages of development. They involve the treatment of the soil slurry in controlled reactors with either isolated or mixed cultures. Land farming entails the biotreatment of excavated soils or sludges on controlled open areas. Soil is placed in areas which have been designed to prevent migration of the contaminants into the ground or surrounding surface waters. The soil is placed in lifts 2 to 3 feet thick. Biological activity is enhanced by providing the necessary nutrients and oxygen to the soil-

Table 5-9. Bioremediation Effectiveness for Contaminated Soil

Compounds	Effectiveness
Nonpolar halogenated aromatics	Medium
PCBs, halogenated dioxins, furans	High
Halogenated phenols, cresols, amines, thiols, and other polar aromatics	Medium
Halogenated aliphatics	Very high
Nitrated compounds	High
Heterocyclics and simple nonhalogenated aromatics	Very high
Polynuclear aromatics	High
Polar-nonhalogenated organics	Very high

Key:

Effectiveness	Average removal efficiency, %
Very high	>95
High	80–95
Medium	50–80

SOURCE: EPA PB92-963351, June 1990.

Table 5-10. Important Parameters to Be Evaluated for In Situ Application of Bioremediation

Microbiological parameters	Physical and chemical parameters
Bacteria type	Soil grain-size distribution
Total cell count	Hydraulic conductivity
Nitrifiers	Soil moisture content
Denitrifiers	Groundwater flow direction and velocity
Oxygen and nutrient demand	Contaminant concentrations
Degradation rates	pH
	Redox conditions
	Temperature
	Total suspended solids
	Total organic carbon
	Dissolved organic carbon
	Chemical oxygen demand (COD)
	Biological oxygen demand (BOD)
	Nitrate and phosphate concentrations
	Total nitrogen

treatment area. Land treatment has also been applied in situ when surficial soil layers have been contaminated. Regulatory air-quality concerns may require that the land-treatment areas be covered to capture any contaminants escaping to the atmosphere. This is particularly true when volatile organic contaminants are to be treated or due process results in volatile toxic by-products.

The most important limitations and obstacles in the application of bioremediation of contaminated soils and groundwaters include:

- High contaminant concentrations may be toxic to the bacteria.

- Soil heterogeneities may not allow oxygen and nutrients to reach all contaminated areas.

- By-products of the bioremediation process are difficult to identify and in some cases may be more toxic than the treated contaminant.

- Monitoring the effectiveness of the process may be difficult in in situ applications.

- Time for remediation is difficult to predict and is sometimes long.

Despite these limitations, soil biotreatment is a rapidly evolving technology with several advantages. The most important include:

- No excavating and transportation of soils is required for in situ applications.

- Total destruction of the contaminant may be attained.

- Minimizes long-term liability.

- Ecologically acceptable solution.

- Generally cost-effective and competitive with other available technologies.

Additional techniques for treating contaminated soils and groundwater at various stages of development include:

Dechlorination   This is a process in which chemical reactions are used to facilitate the replacement of chlorine atoms in chlorinated aromatic compounds with a hydroxyl or an ether group. This process results in less toxic compounds with higher solubility in water which facilitates their removal from the soil matrix by flushing.

Electroosmosis   This is an emerging technology for extraction of organics and heavy metals from soils of low permeability. It entails the application of an electrical potential drop between two electrodes embedded in the soil. This electrical gradient creates a flow and simultaneous contaminant movement from the anode to the cathode. The contaminants are then collected and treated.

Thermal destruction   Incineration of contaminated soils is a well-developed demonstrated technology. This method has been described in the previous section.

Radio-frequency heating   This is an emerging technology which utilizes ISM band radio frequencies to heat large volumes of soil in situ. The process has been shown to volatilize chlorinated solvents and the aliphatic and aromatic fractions of jet fuel. The contaminant vapors are collected and treated subsequently.

Pneumatic fracturing extraction and catalytic oxidation   This emerging technique uses high-pressure air to fracture contaminated geologic formations of low permeability and facilitates the extraction of organic vapors. The vapors are subsequently treated aboveground by a catalytic oxidation unit.

The effectiveness of various technologies for which laboratory and field data exist has been evaluated by the EPA. A summary of this evaluation is presented in Fig. 5-2. The technologies have been evaluated on the basis of the following ratings (EPA, 1990):

- *Demonstrated effectiveness*   A significant percentage of the data (20 percent) is from pilot and full-scale operations, the average removal efficiency for all the data exceeds 90 percent, and there are at least 10 data pairs.

- *Potential effectiveness*   The average removal efficiency for all the data exceeds 70 percent.

- *No expected effectiveness*   The average removal efficiency for all the data is less than 70 percent, and no interference is expected to this process as a result of this group; adverse effects to the environment or to the treatment process may occur.

Remediation of Petroleum-Contaminated Soils.   Petroleum products are used extensively by industry and the public in large quantities. The frequency of their use has resulted in ubiquitous environmental problems. Accidental surface spills and leaks from underground storage tanks and pipelines have resulted in extensive contamination of the subsurface environment. The most frequently used petroleum hydrocarbon products and the ones that present common contamination problems follow:

- Gasoline
- Kerosene
- Jet fuel
- Heating oils
- Industrial oils
- Motor oils

Petroleum products are derived from crude oil, a highly heterogeneous liquid consisting of hydrocarbons which are comprised almost exclusively of carbon

Treatability group \ Technology	Thermal destruction	Dechlorination	Bioremediation	Low temperature thermal desorption	Chemical extraction and soil washing	Immobilization[4]
Nonpolar halogenated aromatics (W01)	●	◐	◐[3]	●◐[3]	◐	◐[2]
PCBs, halogenated dioxins, furans, and their precursors (W02)	●	◐	◐	○[1]	◐	◐[1]
Halogenated phenols, cresols, amines, thiols, and other polar aromatics (W03)	●[3]	◐	◐	◐	◐	◐[3]
Halogenated aliphatic compounds (W04)	●	◐[2]	◐[2,3]	●	◐	◐[2]
Halogenated cyclic aliphatics, ethers, esters, and ketones (W05)	●	◐[1]	◐[1]	○[1]	◐[1]	◐[1]
Nitrated compounds (W06)	●	○[1]	◐	○[1]	◐	◐[1]
Heterocyclics and simple non-halogenated aromatics (W07)	●	○[2,3]	◐[2,3]	●	◐	◐[2]
Polynuclear aromatics (W08)	●	○[2,3]	◐	◐[3]	◐	◐
Other polar non-halogenated organic compounds (W09)	●	○[2,3]	◐[2,3]	◐	◐	◐[2]
Nonvolatile metals (W10)	○[1]	○[1]	○✕[1]	○[1]	◐	●[3]
Volatile metals (W11)	✕[1]	○[1]	○✕[1]	○[1]	◐	●[3]

● Demonstrated effectiveness
◐ Potential effectiveness
○ No expected effectiveness (no expected interference to process)
○ No expected effectiveness (potential adverse effects to environment or process)
✕ No expected effectiveness (potential adverse effects to environment or process)

1. Data were not available for this treatability group. Conclusions are drawn are from data for compounds with similar physical and chemical characteristics.
2. High removal efficiencies implied by the data may be due to volatilization or soil washing.
3. The predicted effectiveness may be different than the data imply, due to limitations in the test conditions.
4. These technologies may have limited applicability to high levels of organics.

Figure 5-2. Predicted treatment effectiveness for contaminated soil. (*Source: EPA PB02-963361.*)

Table 5-11. Summary of Remedial Technologies

Technology	Exposure pathways*	Applicable petroleum products†	Advantages	Limitations	Relative costs‡
In situ:					
Volatilization	1–7	1, 2, 4	Can remove some compounds resistant to biodegradation	VOCs only	Low
Biodegradation	1–7	1, 2, 4	Effective on some nonvolatile compounds	Long-term time frame	Moderate
Leaching	1–7	1, 2, 4	Could be applicable to wide variety of compounds	Not commonly practiced	Moderate
Vitrification	1–7	1, 2, 3, 4		Developing technology	High
Passive	1–7	1, 2, 3, 4	Lowest cost and simplest to implement	Varying degrees of removal	Low
Isolation and containment	1–7	1, 2, 3, 4	Physically prevents or impedes migration	Compounds not destroyed	Low to moderate
Not in situ:					
Land treatment	1–7	1, 2, 3	Uses natural degradation processes	Some residuals remain	Moderate
Thermal treatment	1–6	1, 2, 3, 4	Complete destruction possible	Usually requires special facilities	High
Asphalt incorporation	1–6	1, 2	Use of existing facilities	Incomplete removal of heavier compounds	Moderate
Solidification	1–6	1, 2, 3, 4	Immobilizes compounds	Not commonly practiced for soils	Moderate
Groundwater extraction and treatment	1–6	1, 2, 4	Product recovery, groundwater restoration		Moderate
Chemical extraction	1–6	1, 2, 3, 4		Not commonly practiced	High
Excavation	1–6	1, 2, 3, 4	Removal of soils from site	Long-term liability	Moderate

SOURCE: Remedial Technologies for Leaking Underground Storage Tanks, EPRI CS-5261.

*Exposure pathways: 1 = vapor inhalation; 2 = dust inhalation; 3 = soil ingestion; 4 = skin contact; 5 = groundwater; 6 = surface water; and 7 = plant uptake.

†Applicable petroleum products: 1 = gasolines; 2 = fuel oils (No. 2, diesel, kerosenes); 3 = coal-tar residues; and 4 = chlorinated solvents.

‡Costs are highly dependent on site conditions.

and hydrogen. Hydrocarbons are generally divided into four groups: paraffins, naphthalenes, olefins, and aromatics.

Aromatics are the fractions of crude oil that have received the greatest attention in environmental problems. The main compounds are benzene, toluene, ethylbenzene, and xylenes (BTEX).

The behavior of petroleum products in the subsurface environment is somewhat unique; owing to their very low solubility in water, they migrate through the soil pores as a separate phase. Following a spill, hydrocarbons migrate through the unsaturated zone where they partition into four phases:

- Immiscible phase (pure hydrocarbon)
- Dissolved phase (contaminated soil moisture)
- Adsorbed phase (components attached to the soil grains)
- Gaseous phase (components volatilizing in the pore space occupied by air)

When hydrocarbons come into contact with groundwater, they spread and float on the top of the groundwater table because they are predominantly lighter than water. At the same time, they begin to dissolve slowly, contaminating the aquifer. This behavior and the fact that petroleum products remain trapped in the soil pores for very long periods of time make their remediation difficult and very time consuming.

There are several available technologies for sites contaminated with petroleum hydrocarbons. Some of these have been described in the previous section. A summary of remedial technologies is presented in Table 5-11. It is important to note that the effectiveness and cost of each of these remedial options is highly site-specific.

Bibliography

Canter, L. W., and R. C. Knox, *Groundwater Pollution Control,* Lewis Publishers, 1985.

Corbitt, R. A. (ed.), *Standard Handbook of Environmental Engineering,* McGraw-Hill, 1990.

Grady, G. P. L., Jr., and H. C. Lim, *Biological Wastewater Treatment,* Marcel Dekker, 1980.

Hwang, S. T., and Kammermeyer, *Membranes in Separations, Techniques of Chemistry,* vol. III, Robert E. Krieger, 1984.

Kostecki, P. T., and E.J. Calabrese, *Petroleum Contaminated Soils,* vols. I, II, III, Lewis Publishers, 1989.

Metcalf & Eddy, Inc., *Wastewater Engineering, Treatment Disposal Reuse,* McGraw-Hill, 1991.

Montgomery, J. M., *Consulting Engineers, Water Treatment Principles and Design,* Wiley, 1985.

Noonan, D. C., and J. T. Curtis, *Groundwater Remediation and Petroleum: A Guide to Underground Storage Tanks,* Lewis Publishers, 1990.

Pankow, J. F., *Aquatic Chemistry Concepts,* Lewis Publishers, 1991.

Testa, S. M., and D. L. Winegardner, *Restoration of Petroleum Contaminated Aquifers,* Lewis Publishers, 1991.

U.S. EPA, "Summary of Treatment Technology Effectiveness for Contaminated Soil," EPA-PB92-963351, June 1990.

U.S. EPA, "The Superfund Innovative Technology Program: Technology Profiles," EPA/540/5-91/008, November 1991.

U.S. EPA, "Handbook for Stabilization Technologies for RCRA Corrective Actions," ORD, EPA/625/6-91/026, August 1991.

U.S. EPA, "Handbook for Stabilization/Solidification of Hazardous Wastes," Hazardous Waste Engineering Research Laboratory, Cincinnati, Ohio, EPA/540/2-86/001, June 1986.

U.S. EPA, "Handbook for In-Situ Treatment of Hazardous Waste Contaminated Soils," EPA/540/2-90/011, January 1990.

U.S. EPA, "Engineering Bulletin, Soil Washing Treatment," EPA/540/2-90/017, September 1990.

U.S. EPA, "Bioremediation in the Field," EPA/540/2-91/007, March 1991.

Weber, W. J., Jr., *Physicochemical Processes for Environmental Control*, Wiley, 1972.

6

Pollution Prevention and Total Quality Environmental Management

Impact on the Bottom Line and Competitive Position

Robert P. Bringer, Ph.D.
Vice President
3M Environmental Engineering and
Pollution Control

David M. Benforado, P.E., DEE
Senior Environmental Specialist
3M Environmental Engineering and
Pollution Control

In this chapter:

- Building In More Intellect and Less Material
- Strategic Shift in National Policy
- Pollution Prevention Pays (3P) and 3P Plus
- Bottom Line Impact on Competitive Position
- Opportunities into the Next Millennium

Building In More Intellect and Less Material

The past two decades have seen a sea change in the way global corporations approach environmental issues. At first, corporate policies were guided by the exponential increase in environmental regulations, coupled with the public's demand for strict enforcement. Over time, managers realized that environmentally sound products and manufacturing processes can have many benefits, such as lower costs, higher quality, more marketable products, less regulatory impact, fewer liabilities, better employee morale, and an enhanced corporate image. The organization of operations to achieve these benefits and reduce regulatory exposure is called total quality environmental management (TQEM).

The long-term goal of TQEM is sustainable development, which combines economic growth with environmental protection. In today's business climate, it is a must. "Progress towards sustainable development makes good business sense because it can create a competitive advantage and new opportunities" (Stephan Schmidheiny).

For 3M, the pursuit of TQEM involves an ongoing process of environmental improvement, using fewer resources to satisfy customer needs and reducing the environmental impact of products and manufacturing processes. In other words, we are trying to build more intellect and less material into our products. 3M's experience in environmental management, in a manner that has improved its competitiveness, can serve as a model for other companies interested in practicing pollution prevention and achieving sustainable development.

This chapter discusses general strategies for TQEM, as well as specific 3M policies and practices proved over the past two decades. Based on our experience, moving a company toward sustainable development requires:

- *Recognition* that it is in the corporation's best interest to do so
- *Commitment* of resources to publicly stated environmental *goals*
- Understanding that this is a *continuous process*

Obviously, any environmental management program must be designed to ensure compliance with all environmental laws and regulations. This will minimize fines and other penalties for noncompliance and assure a continued ability to operate facilities. However, if the program stops there, the company can also be assured of continually rising regulatory costs, decreasing manufacturing flexibility, and in the long run, a poorer competitive position. Compliance programs protect the corporation in the short term, are very expensive, and usually have no return on the investment.

3M's environmental management program has two components, both of which address risk management. They answer management's concern about protecting the corporation but do so in different ways. The first part of the program addresses compliance with a sophisticated set of checks and balances. This ensures that all regulations are dealt with in a way that protects the corporation from penalties but also preserves operating flexibility and minimizes compliance costs.

The second part of the program addresses environmental risk management proactively. It anticipates future regulatory and environmental trends. It also seeks to lower regulatory costs and future liabilities by designing the environmental impact out of its products and processes. These cleaner products and processes are generally simpler and more consolidated, and use more intellect and less material in their development and design. Quite often they lead to lower production costs, higher quality, and improved marketability. In other words, they become more competitive.

Thus proactive environmental risk management seeks a return on its investment in product and process development and design. This return is most likely a long-range return, as are most investments in research and development. Management, therefore, must have the long-range vision and patience to invest now for future returns. There must be a recognition that cleaner products and processes will also require a long-range commitment of resources, since the development of these new products and processes may take 5 to 15 years. That kind of commitment demands courage as well as foresight, given the short-term financial horizons.

The strict compliance approach to command and control regulations will only lead to higher and higher costs chasing smaller and smaller environmental benefits. This is true whether it's the whole world, one country, one company, or even one household under consideration.

On the other hand, the proactive pollution-prevention approach seeks more lasting and complete solutions to environmental problems. The proactive approach to environmental management *is* the essence of sustainable development.

Strategic Shift in National Policy

The pollution control laws adopted by Congress in the 1970s, such as the Clean Air Act and the Clean Water Act, were "command and control laws" with little or no flexibility. They required companies to reduce releases by installing control equipment.

The Resource Conservation and Recovery Act (RCRA) of 1976, which started regulating hazardous waste, introduced one of the most ambitious federal environmental programs. Congress realized that while they had achieved control over air and water pollution, some of the controlled contaminants became waste materials and went right back into the environment, causing environmental damage through the landfill disposal of such wastes. RCRA was designed to correct this and ensure that the disposition of waste materials would be environmentally sound.

It was not until 8 years later that Congress passed laws that were designed to prevent pollution through waste minimization. The Hazardous and Solid Waste Amendments (HSWA) of 1984, which amended RCRA, began shifting the country's efforts from "control and command" to *reducing the generation* of hazardous waste, by requiring companies to develop waste-minimization programs.

Through HSWA, Congress intended that waste minimization be fostered in a practical manner. For example, the 1986 U.S. EPA Report to Congress stated: "The present requirements are not restrictive; the generator determines whether any particular waste minimization approach that might apply to his or her process is *economically practicable*." [Emphasis added.] Also, HSWA instituted a statutory requirement for every hazardous waste generator to certify on each waste manifest that: "I have a program in place to reduce the volume or toxicity of such waste to the degree determined by the generator to be *economically practicable*." [Emphasis added.] The legislative history shows it was Congress's intent that waste minimization be accomplished by companies themselves, without government intrusion in manufacturing operations.

Six years later, with the passage of the Pollution Prevention Act of 1990, Congress expanded the scope of the prevention concept in RCRA to include air and water. It also adopted a national policy on pollution prevention. The policy affirmed a pollution-prevention hierarchy as follows:

1. Pollution should be prevented or reduced at the source whenever feasible.
2. Pollution that cannot be prevented should be recycled in an environmentally safe manner.
3. Pollution that cannot be prevented or recycled should be treated in an environmentally safe manner whenever feasible.
4. Disposal or other release into the environment should be employed only as a last resort and should be conducted in an environmentally safe manner.

The act promotes pollution-prevention practices, which focus on source reduction—preventing the generation of releases at the source—by requiring the U.S. EPA to:

- Incorporate pollution-prevention principles into programs at each EPA office and other federal agencies.
- Review federal regulations for opportunities to apply pollution-prevention principles.
- Facilitate adoption of pollution-prevention practices by businesses through information exchange, technical assistance, and grants.
- Try to standardize a method of measurement.
- Assure public access to environmental data.
- Identify barriers and look for incentives to eliminate them.
- Establish an annual pollution-prevention award program.

Congress intended that the Pollution Prevention Act of 1990 would create a shift toward prevention and foster the widespread adoption of the pollution-prevention ethic. It should be noted that many companies have already adopted this ethic and are looking for opportunities to move up the pollution-prevention hierarchy toward preventing the generation of all releases at the source.

Pollution Prevention Pays (3P) and 3P Plus

In the early 1970s, 3M became concerned that the increasing number of environmental laws and regulations—and their related costs—would adversely affect the corporation's competitiveness. In response to those concerns, 3M formulated its *first* comprehensive environmental policy in 1975. This policy shifted 3M from a reactive position to a stance of positive action and self-control. Under the policy, which remains current in 1992, all employees are directed to:

- Solve our own environmental pollution and conservation problems
- Prevent pollution at the source whenever possible
- Develop products that have a minimal effect on the environment
- Conserve natural resources through reclamation and other methods
- Assure that our facilities and products meet and sustain the regulations of all federal, state, and local environmental agencies
- Assist government agencies and other official organizations engaged in environmental activities

In 1975, before there were pollution-prevention laws or regulatory drivers, 3M became the first company to initiate an organized, companywide application of the pollution-prevention concept with its Pollution Prevention Pays (3P) program. 3P was originally conceived to protect the environment while providing economic benefits to the company. Its goal was to shift the focus from traditional "end-of-the-pipe" controls to preventing pollution by not generating it in the first place.

In the 1980s many other companies adopted similar pollution-prevention programs. A sampling of these can be seen in Table 6-1, which shows the scope, goals, and accomplishments of these programs. The creation of the 3P program and its evolution into a total quality environmental management umbrella program, called 3P Plus, provides a useful lesson in proactive environmental management.

Introduction of 3P within 3M

In 1975, 3M introduced its 3P program throughout the company with presentations to corporate officers and managers of the operating business units, to corporate staff engineering departments, to research and development laboratories, and to all manufacturing personnel at 3M headquarters and plant locations worldwide.

Table 6-1. Companywide Pollution-Prevention Programs and Goals*

Company and program	Scope	Goal	Accomplishments
Allied Signal waste-reduction program	Includes waste minimization under RCRA, as well as nonhazardous waste, and evaluates various disposal alternatives and methods for detoxification. Plant and project basis	Reduce the quantity and toxicity of hazardous waste that must be stored, treated, or disposed of as much as economically practicable	The amount of cyclohexylamine waste produced in 1987 was only 15% of the volume of the same waste produced in 1984 The amount of waste finish oil was reduced nearly 90% from 1984 to 1987
Amoco waste-minimization program (1983)	Primary focus on minimizing hazardous-waste disposal, also minimize and track nonhazardous wastes	Eliminate the generation and disposal of hazardous wastes	Between 1983 and 1988, Amoco reduced its hazardous waste by 86%, saving the company about $50 million
AT&T environmental program	Industrial source reduction and toxic chemical use substitution are priorities	Achieve a 50% reduction of CFCs by 1991, and 100% by 1994. Eliminate toxic air emissions of all types by the year 2000, with a 50% reduction by 1993 and a 95% reduction by 1995 Decrease disposal of total manufacturing process wastes by 25% by 1994	Substituted a derivative of citrus fruits and other organic compounds, called BIOACT, for solvents that are used to clean electronic equipment. Eliminated CFC use in circuitboard manufacturing processes through use of the AT&T low solid fluxer
BASF	Toxic air emissions reduction	Decrease toxic air emissions (lb/year) by 89% by December 1992 (base year July 1989)	
Boeing waste-minimization program	Focus is on process changes which reduce the volume and/or toxicity of hazardous materials used in operations	Reduce use of hazardous materials Minimize the generation of hazardous waste Ensure proper handling and disposal of all wastes	Case study: a chemical substitution in one photoresist stripping operation has increased stripping speeds by 50% and, because of its longer useful life, should reduce annual hazardous waste generation by 50%
BP America waste-minimization program (1989)	Adopts EPA's environmental management hierarchy, with source reduction preferred	All facilities are to have annual waste-minimization goals	One refinery operates a Podbielniak unit which processes spent caustics into acids, which are then sold. The unit paid for itself in less than 8 months

Table 6-1. Companywide Pollution-Prevention Programs and Goals* (*Continued*)

Company and program	Scope	Goal	Accomplishments
Chevron save money and reduce toxics program (SMART, 1987)	SMART adopts EPA's hierarchy, with an emphasis on industrial source reduction, toxic chemical use substitution, and recycling for hazardous and nonhazardous solid wastes	Reduce hazardous waste generation by 65% by 1992 and recycle what is left Find nontoxic alternatives to toxic materials and processes Devise safer operating procedures to reduce accidental releases Ensure that pollution reductions in one area don't transfer pollution to another	From 1987 to 1990, Chevron reduced hazardous waste by 60% and saved more than $10 million in disposal costs Case study: Chevron used to dispose of tank bottoms in landfills. It now uses a centrifuge to separate oil from water; it reuses the oil and treats the water, leaving only a small amount of solid to be landfilled (less than 5% of the original sludge)
Dow waste reduction always pays (WRAP, 1986)	Industrial source reduction and on-site recycling	Increase management support for waste-reduction activities, establish a recognition and reward system for individual plants, compile waste-reduction data, and communicate information on waste-reduction activities Decrease SARA 313 air emissions by 50% by 1995, when compared with 1988 Decrease toxic air emissions (lb/year) 71% by December 1992 (base year December 1988)	SARA 313 overall releases are down from 12,252 tons in 1987 to 9659 tons in 1989, a 21% reduction. Off-site transfers are down from 2855 tons in 1987 to 2422 tons in 1989, a reduction of 15%. Air emissions for 1989 showed a 54% decrease from 1984
Exxon	Toxic air emissions reduction	Decrease toxic air emissions (lb/year) by 14% by January 1991 (base year December 1988)	
General Dynamics zero discharge (1985)	Industrial source reduction, toxic chemical use substitution, recycling, treatment, and incineration	Have no RCRA manifested wastes leaving company facilities	Nearly 40 million lb of hazardous-waste discharge eliminated from 1984 to 1988 (approx. 72%), while sales increased from $7.3 billion to $9.35 billion over same period

Table 6-1. Companywide Pollution-Prevention Programs and Goals* (*Continued*)

Company and program	Scope	Goal	Accomplishments
General Electric pollution, waste, and emissions reduction program (POWER, 1989)	Program encompasses all waste streams (e.g., hazardous, nonhazardous, packaging, and ultimate disposal of product) and adopts EPA's hierarchy which places source reduction first	Prevent or minimize "the generation or release of wastes and pollutants, to the extent technically and economically feasible, throughout the life cycle of the product, including its design, production, packaging and ultimate fate in the environment" Decrease toxic air emissions (lb/year) by 90% by December 1993 (base year December 1988)	GE Appliances' Louisville plant has reduced its production of hazardous wastewater-treatment sludge by 95%; GE Plastics' Ottawa plant has reduced its butadiene emissions by more than 90%; GE Medical Systems' E. Dale Trout plant has reduced its generation of hazardous waste by 74%; businesswide, GE Power Delivery has reduced its CFC usage by 72%; and, companywide, GE has reduced its SARA 313 reported releases by 11% from 1987 to 1988
Goodyear toxic air emissions reduction	Industrial source reduction	Decrease toxic air emissions (lb/year) by 71% by January 1991 (base year December 1988)	Decreased air emissions from operations through improved maintenance and monitoring of equipment and through decreased use of acrylonitrile, butadiene, and styrene
Hoechst Celanese toxic chemical emission reductions	Adopts EPA's hierarchy, which makes source reduction a priority, with a main focus on substituting cleaner production processes for those generating high volumes of waste	An average 70% cut in emissions of TRI chemicals (with 80% reductions at 9 plants with the highest emissions) by 1996, with 1988 TRI emissions as comparison	
IBM	Industrial source reduction and toxic chemical use substitution are priorities, followed by recycling, reuse, and reclamation, incineration, detoxification, and disposal in a secure or sanitary landfill, in that order	Pledged to eliminate ozone-depleting chemicals from IBM products and processes by end of 1993 and to recycle 50% of solid waste by 1992	Hazardous waste generation was reduced 38% from 1984 to 1988; 84% of IBM's hazardous waste was recycled in 1988; 28% of all solid waste from IBM U.S. operations was recycled in 1988; IBM U.S. emissions were reduced 20% from 1987 to 1988; and IBM U.S. had a decrease of 25% in its CFC emissions between 1987 and 1988

Table 6-1. Companywide Pollution-Prevention Programs and Goals* (*Continued*)

Company and program	Scope	Goal	Accomplishments
3M pollution prevention pays (3P, 1975) and 3P Plus (1989)	Eliminate pollution sources through product reformulation, process modification, equipment redesign, recycling, and recovery of waste materials for resale	By 2000, cut all hazardous and nonhazardous releases to air, land, and water by 90% and reduce the generation of hazardous waste by 50%, with 1987 as the base year	From 1975 to 1989, the 3P program has cut 3M pollution in half, per unit of production, with implementation of 2511 recognized 3P projects throughout the company from 1975 to 1990
Monsanto priority one (TRI wastes)	Source reduction, reengineering, process changes, reuse, and recycling to reduce hazardous air emissions and TRI solid, liquid, and hazardous wastes	A 90% reduction in hazardous air emissions from 1987 to 1992 A 70% reduction in TRI solid, liquid, and gaseous wastes from 1987 to 1995	From 1987 to 1990, Monsanto achieved a 39% reduction in hazardous air emissions
Northrup, B-2 Division zero discharge pollution prevention	Primary focus on hazardous-waste minimization; goals have been set for other solid-waste reduction; program includes projects to reduce water usage, stationary air pollutants, and water pollution; targeted areas include elimination of ozone-depleting chemicals and toxic chemicals	Eliminate the generation and disposal of hazardous waste by 1995; reduce solid waste disposal by 25% by 1995 and by 50% by 2000; reduce water usage by 20%; reduce mobile air pollution by 25% by 1992; eliminate ozone-depleting chemical (ODC) use by 1993; eliminate toxic chemical use and risk by 1995	Over 50% reduction in hazardous-waste generation in last 18 months; reduced ODC emissions by 50% in the last 12 months through substitution; reduced mobile air pollution by approx. 280 tons/year; reduced water usage by an average of 28% in each of the last 6 months; reduced solid-waste disposal by 70% in 30 months
Occidental	Toxic air emissions reduction	Decrease toxic air emissions (lb/year) by 78% by December 1992 (base year December 1988)	
Polaroid toxic use and waste-reduction program (TUWR, 1987)	Industrial source reduction and toxic chemical use substitution are priorities, followed by recycling and reuse	Reduce toxic use at the source and waste per unit of production by 10% per year in each of the 5 years ending in 1993 and, as a corollary, emphasize increased recycling of waste materials within the company	Using 1988 as the base year, Polaroid's Environmental Accounting and Reporting System (EARS) reported an 11% reduction in toxic use and waste during 1989
Raytheon	Toxic chemical use substitution	Pledged to eliminate CFC-113 and methyl chloroform from its printed circuit board operations in five states by 1992	

Table 6-1. Companywide Pollution-Prevention Programs and Goals* (*Continued*)

Company and program	Scope	Goal	Accomplishments
Scott Paper	Integrated and multi-faceted approach, including source reduction, recycling and reuse of materials, and landfilling of unusable residual waste	Design products and packaging to reduce volume of waste material, which Scott terms "source reduction" Decrease dioxin levels at paper mills by reducing chlorine usage or altering its method of application, or by adopting new technologies or replacements for chlorine bleaching	By the end of 1989, about 20% of the pulp used for sanitary tissue products was made from recycled fiber, and Scott plans to approximately double its recycled capacity The Duffel, Belgium, mill uses a process that uses less water and less fiber Developed a system for source reduction known as "precycling" in which paper products are packaged in larger quantities, thus saving materials which would otherwise have been wasted
Sheldahl (Northfield, Minn.)	Industrial source reduction and toxic chemical use substitution for hazardous air pollutants	Pledged for methylene chloride: 90% emissions reduction by 1993, and 64% use reduction by 1992	
Texaco	Toxic air emissions reduction	Decrease toxic air emissions (lb/year) by 92% by February 1991 (base year July 1990)	
Xerox	Toxic chemical use substitution, materials recovery, and recycling	Reduce hazardous waste generation by 50% from 1990 to 1995	Substituting *d*-Limonene for chlorinated solvents allowed Xerox to reduce the amount of solvents emitted to the atmosphere from about 200,000 lb in 1982 to an estimated 17,000 lb in 1990 A high-pressure water strip operation has enabled Xerox to recycle 800,000 lb nickel and 2 million lb of aluminum tubes per year, and to return 160,000 lb of selenium to suppliers for reuse

*A number of companies were reviewed but not included in this table because their pollution-prevention programs have not been expressed in terms of quantifiable goals or accomplishments.
Source: "Pollution Prevention 1991, Progress on Reducing Industrial Pollutants," U.S. EPA, October 1991, EPA-21P-3003.

Program Structure

3P is a voluntary program designed to motivate employees to look for innovative ways to eliminate pollution at the source. Employees who develop projects that prevent pollution at the source and provide cost savings become eligible for a 3P award. A submittal form was developed to standardize the project evaluation and selection process. A 3P logo was developed to publicize the program and identify program materials, correspondence, and awards.

3M's staff vice president of environmental engineering and pollution control (EE&PC) is responsible for implementing 3P within the company. This responsibility was assigned by the chief executive officer and the board of directors, all of whom have enthusiastically endorsed the program. Within EE&PC, environmental engineers are responsible for implementing 3P within the division to which they have been assigned.

Project Selection and 3P Awards

Any 3M technical employee or group of employees can nominate a project for a 3P award by filling out the standard submittal form (Fig. 6-1). The application is then reviewed by a 3P Coordinating Committee made up of representatives from all the technical groups (engineering, manufacturing, and research and development). Thus judging is done by a group of one's peers. The coordinating committee meets quarterly to review the entries from 3M's U.S. locations and select those that meet the following criteria:

1. Environmental benefit

2. Innovative technology

3. Cost savings

Once a project is approved, managers of the business units identify the personnel who made measurable contributions to the project. Managers and supervisors are recognized only if they were directly involved in the project. EE&PC personnel are generally not eligible. Awards are presented by business unit vice presidents at a special luncheon or other important function.

Pollution-Prevention Methodologies

The technologies considered acceptable for the 3P award are consistent with the preferred hierarchy for waste management:

Step 1. Generation prevention

Step 2. Recovery and recycling

Step 3. Treatment to reduce volume and toxicity

Step 4. Proper disposal of any residual waste that cannot be prevented, recycled, or further treated

Pollution Prevention
Pays (3P) Submittal

See instructions on reverse side.

Form 34508

Environmental Engineering
and Pollution Control/3M
Bldg. 2-3E-09
P. O. Box 33331
St. Paul, MN 55133-3331

Project Name		Submittal Date
Division/Dept.	Product Affected	Plant Location
Project Contact		EE&PC Contact

Project Origin
(Check one or more) ➤   1 ☐ Lab   2 ☐ Engineering   3 ☐ Manufacturing   4 ☐ Other (List) _____

Project Description *(Be concise)*

Technical Accomplishment *(Describe)*

Project Measurement Criteria

Type of Pollution Prevented *(Check one or more)*	First Year Quantity Prevented
☐ Air Pollution	Tons
☐ Water Pollution	Tons
☐ Wastewater	Million Gallons
☐ Solid Waste/Hazardous Waste/Sludge	Tons

Method Used to Prevent Pollution

1 ☐ Product Reformulation   3 ☐ Equipment Redesign
2 ☐ Process Modification   4 ☐ Recovery and/or Reuse
5 ☐ Quality Improvement

Monetary Benefit
Include All First Year Savings

Capital _____

Additional Considerations

Capital Cost of Implementation

Annual Estimated Operating Cost

Related Challenge Program

Additional Information

Operation & Maintenance _____

Energy _____

Disposal Cost Eliminated _____

Sales _____

Other _____

Total _____

Project Commitment
(Signed AFE, etc.) _____

Implementation Date _____

For Office Use Only

Resolution	Review Date	Publicity ☐ Internal ☐ External	Application in This Division OUS _____ Other Divisions _____
	Project Status ➤ 1 ☐ Accepted ☐ Level I ☐ Level II 2 ☐ On Hold 3 ☐ Rejected		
	Comments		

Figure 6-1(a). Standard submittal form for 3P award.

— INSTRUCTIONS —

Pollution Prevention Pays (3P) Submittal
See instructions on reverse side.

Environmental Engineering
and Pollution Control/3M
Bldg. 2-3E-09
P. O. Box 33331
St. Paul, MN 55133-3331

3M

Enter information as specified.

Include person(s) responsible for the project.

Indicate project origin. (Check at least one.)

Briefly describe the project and why it was implemented.

Briefly explain the results of project implementation, especially if the project was technically innovative or if it involved significant technical accomplishment.

Indicate the types(s) and amount(s) of pollution prevented.

Indicate method used. (This must be checked.)

Enter name of related Challenge Program and the dollar amount.

Indicate first year savings due to project implementation.

Include date implemented.

3P Project Submittal Form

Figure 6-1(b). Instructions for standard submittal form for 3P award.

Only projects that accomplish steps 1 or 2 of the hierarchy are considered for the award. However, it is realized that "treatment" and "proper disposal of residuals" will always be an important part of any waste-management program.

Examples of generation prevention:

1. *Raw material substitution*—eliminating or reducing a hazardous constituent used either in the product or during manufacture of the product.

2. *End product substitution*—producing a different product that accomplishes the same function with less pollution than the original product.

3. *Process modification*—changing the process design to reduce waste generation.

4. *Equipment redesign*—changing the physical design of the equipment to reduce waste generation.

5. *Direct recycling*—reusing materials directly in the manufacturing process without prior treatment. These materials would otherwise become wastes.

6. *Good housekeeping*—instituting new procedures, such as preventive maintenance, to reduce waste generation.

7. *Inventory control*—minimizing the quantities of raw materials or manufactured product in stock, to eliminate surplus that could become waste when the product is changed or discontinued.

Examples of recovery and recycling:

1. Recovering a solvent from a waste air stream by carbon adsorption and recycling it into the manufacturing process.

2. Recovering a solvent from a liquid waste stream by distillation and recycling it into the manufacturing process.

Informing and Motivating Employees

Because 3P is voluntary, motivating individuals to participate is essential to its success. Success depends on individual initiative in identifying pollution-prevention potential and then making it a reality with a 3P project.

Certainly, selection and recognition by one's peers for 3P awards are important motivators. Meeting group goals, and receiving rewards and exposure through promotional materials on the 3P program are factors too. For example, some business units voluntarily set annual 3P goals for dollar savings and the number of projects accepted. Entire departments—and the involved EE&PC staff—are rewarded when goals are achieved. Rewards to EE&PC staff, who are generally not eligible for 3P awards, have taken the form of dinners with spouses and special outings.

Cash awards were considered but rejected as a motivator for 3P projects. This approach was rejected because of concern that it would inhibit the sharing of ideas. However, successful 3P projects are usually reviewed in performance appraisals.

To keep the program as a priority for our technical people, EE&PC staff present 3P seminars companywide to share information about the value of various technologies. Also, we hold 3P laboratory workshops to emphasize pollution prevention in new product design. As an ongoing effort, we post and circulate among employees written materials (including external public communication materials) that tell the story of 3P. Internally, this effort includes regular articles on 3P in company publications, such as the *Environmental Report* (a quarterly newsletter from EE&PC) and the *Stemwinder* (a Twin Cities 3M weekly), and the quarterly distribution of 3P summaries to EE&PC staff.

To foster technology transfer, we regularly distribute idea sheets (Fig. 6-2), one-page summaries that describe the methods and results of 3P projects and identify the people involved. We have also produced a 3P brochure, a 3P sound and slide show, and several pollution-prevention videos. For program promotion throughout industry, we supplement our print materials by presenting papers at technical conferences and by publishing articles in national trade magazines. With the U.S. Environmental Protection Agency, we have cosponsored conferences highlighting the environmental and cost-saving benefits of 3P. This external communications effort improves 3M employee's morale by gaining recognition from industry and from the public for our pollution-prevention efforts.

Program Changes

Since 1975, several changes have been made to keep 3P fresh and alive within the company. The major changes are a new 3P logo, a broadening of 3P project criteria, and a greater emphasis on laboratory efforts. The new logo, with the tag line "Managing for a Better Environment," ties 3P more closely to 3M's environmental policy and has been incorporated into the idea sheets (Fig. 6-2).

Under the original 3P criteria, an application of existing technology to prevent pollution was not eligible for an award. These criteria were broadened to encourage the application of such technology. Today, projects are recognized by two tiers of awards:

1. Project teams that achieve environmental benefit and cost savings through *new innovative* technologies receive a handsome walnut plaque at a special function.

2. Project teams that achieve environmental benefit and cost savings by a *new application of existing* technology receive a certificate at a special function.

In both cases the award is presented by the business unit vice president.

In recent years, we have placed more emphasis on pollution prevention at the product-design stage. Research and development laboratory employees have been asked to develop pollution-free products and, where feasible, to reformulate existing products to eliminate pollutants. A video, "Challenge to Innovation: Pollution Prevention by Waste Minimization," was produced in

ideas

A Compendium of 3P Success Stories

Pollution Prevention Pays

Managing for a better environment

Coating Worth Noting
Riker Innovation Meets Air Regulation

Problem

Riker Laboratories, 3M's pharmaceutical plant in Northridge, California, coated medicine tablets with solvents. Solvent emissions had the potential to exceed air pollution limits of a forthcoming state regulation.

Solution

A water-based coating was developed to replace the solvent coating. Different spraying equipment was installed in the coating machine, which resembles a clothes dryer. Spray guns inside the drum dispense the aqueous mixture as tablets are tumbled through it.

The pumping mechanism and control systems were also modified. Changing the spraying system from airless to air permitted quick and precise application of coating. Too much coating would result in soggy tablets. The same problem would arise if tablets were not dried fast enough since water does not evaporate as quickly as organic solvents. Therefore, the heating capacity of the process was increased.

Medicine tablets with a water-based coating get quality check from Byron J. Seelig.

Riker kept California environmental authorities fully informed of changes being made. Tests confirmed the quality and stability of the new tablet coating and the U.S. Food and Drug Administration approved it. Riker's no-pollution solution met the regulatory deadline.

Payoff

- Changes cost $60,000 but eliminated the need to buy $180,000 in pollution control equipment.

- Solvents used in the old coating process were no longer needed, saving $15,000 a year.

- 24 tons of air pollution prevented annually.

- Less cleanup time required. Unpleasant fumes of solvent mixture eliminated, contributing to worker comfort.

The Idea Team

The technical employees who conceived and implemented the new tablet coating process:

Byron J. Seelig
Florence N. Wong
  Laboratory, St. Paul, MN

Kirk Wong
  Manufacturing, Northridge, CA

12845M/R3891M/11902M 10912M   Printed on Recycled Paper.

Environmental Engineering and Pollution Control Dept./3M
P.O. Box 33331, Bldg. 21-2W
Saint Paul, Minnesota 55133
(612) 778-4791

3M

Figure 6-2. Idea sheet.

1988 to motivate and inform laboratory personnel regarding this effort. Additionally, in an effort to motivate all employees to participate in pollution prevention, a video and brochure, "3M and the Environment: An Individual Effort," were produced in 1992.

A Cumulative Success

The early years of 3P, 1975 through 1980, were a period of moderate savings and accomplishment. During those years, much time and money were expended to educate the company and to establish the program and get it off the ground. Results improved as the program became a regular feature of 3M life and became more visible inside and outside the company. By 1992, 3M had undertaken a worldwide total of more than 3500 successful projects. Altogether, 3M's 3P projects have prevented more than 575,000 tons of pollution, with cumulative first-year savings of more than $550 million (Fig. 6-3). This savings total includes costs avoided and the value of sales retained.

The following examples indicate the variety of successful 3P projects and show the savings and pollution prevented during the first year:

- Scientists at 3M laboratories in St. Paul reformulated a 3M chemical treatment product to help a customer reduce the opacity of plant stack emissions. (*Opacity* is a measure of the visibility of air emissions.) The customer had been using the product in a fabric-coating process that produced stack emissions exceeding state air regulations for opacity. The reformulated product reduced stack opacity by 80%, eliminating the customer's need for costly pollution-control equipment. The customer's energy bill was also reduced, owing to the

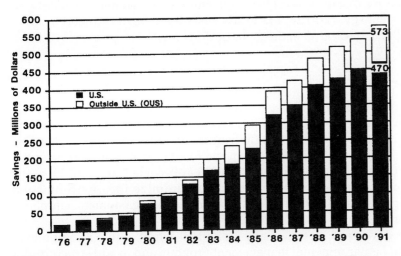

Figure 6-3. Program global savings, 1976–1991 (cumulative "first-year only" savings).

lower drying temperature of the reformulated product. By meeting this customer's needs, 3M retained a $1 million annual account. *Pollution prevented:* 6 to 9 tons of air pollution.

- At the Chemolite Center production facility in Minnesota, evaporation equipment was installed to recover diluted ammonium sulfate from wastewater created in the manufacture of magnetic oxides. The recovered ammonia, concentrated in a 40% solution, is used by local farmers as fertilizer. The vapor compression evaporator cost $1.5 million but eliminated the need for $1 million in water-pollution-control equipment. *Pollution prevented:* 677 tons of wastewater.

- At an Office Systems Division Plant in White City, Oregon, software was developed to put startup temperatures in a paper coating and drying process under computer control. Previously, temperatures were too low after downtime, resulting in some product of inferior quality that had to be discarded. With an investment of only $16,000, startup waste (silver, paper, solvents, and labor) was eliminated, saving $533,200. *Pollution prevented:* 137 tons of solid waste; 53 tons of air pollution.

- A plant made an adhesive from a polymer and a 100% solid polyester resin. The adhesive was difficult to filter, causing a low product yield and the generation of hazardous scrap. Reformulation of the adhesive to use polyester in solution (rather than as a resin) solved the filtering problem and increased the yield by 15%. Material, operating, and maintenance costs were reduced by $270,000. *Pollution prevented:* 42 tons of hazardous solid waste.

- Inventory management procedures at a 3M facility were modified to accommodate the short shelf life of a particular adhesive. Previously, the adhesive at the workstation often "set up" before it could be used. This waste adhesive was destined for disposal. With better inventory management—resulting in less waste—energy and raw materials costs have been reduced by over $15,000. *Pollution prevented:* 6 tons of hazardous waste.

Evolution of 3P into 3P Plus

Over the years an evolution has been taking place within the 3M culture. The Pollution Prevention Pays program has gradually merged into the corporate culture in a manner consistent with the worldwide philosophy of sustainable development. With strong guidance from the EE&PC group the company has moved toward a holistic pollution-prevention approach. Called 3P Plus, the program emphasizes 3M's ongoing effort to minimize the environmental impact of its products, facilities, operations, employees, customers, suppliers, and contractors.

3P Plus was developed to unite many individual activities into a comprehensive total quality environmental management program and to add structure and goals to our voluntary efforts. 3M programs organized under the umbrella of 3P Plus include:

1. The *3P program* itself, which was created in 1975 to eliminate pollution at the source.

2. *Air emission reduction program,* instituted in 1987 as a short-term, voluntary effort to reduce air emissions, primarily using pollution-control systems. The program will result in the elimination of more than 65,000 tons of pollutants worldwide by 1993, and involves an expenditure of more than $170 million.

3. *Challenge 95 program* has set short-term productivity goals for 1995, compared with 1990. They include a 20% reduction in energy use and a 35% reduction in waste generation.

4. *Year 2000 goals,* with a 1987 baseline—a long-term program that will rely to a large degree on pollution prevention to achieve a 90% reduction in all releases to air, water, and land and a 50% reduction in waste generation.

5. *Corporate product responsibility staff group* was formed to provide guidance and support to 3M business units, especially in creating and using environmentally compatible materials, products, and processes.

6. *Environmental management plans* address short-range and long-range environmental issues facing 3M business units and provide resources for their resolution. These plans are developed for each business unit and coordinated by a professional environmental staff. *Environmental goals* are developed by each business unit and included in the environmental management plans. These are translated into individual goals, which motivate employees to become directly involved in achieving the business unit goals.

7. *Internal compliance auditing,* which reviews 3M operations worldwide to ensure that their procedures, practices, and programs comply with corporate policies and governmental regulations.

8. *Energy management* for energy efficiency has become a 3M strategy for long-term growth and competitiveness. Improving energy efficiency reduces emissions and helps conserve natural resources.

9. *Resource recovery program* recovers metals, plastics, solvents, papers, and other materials for reuse or sale.

10. *Environmental marketing claims review committee* was established to ensure that 3M's environmental claims are accurate, clear, documented, and not misleading.

11. *Phaseout of ozone-depleting chemicals,* far in advance of the Montreal Protocol—with a limited exemption for selected essential health-related products—was achieved in 1992.

12. *Employee environmental recognition.* Besides 3P project awards, 3M has instituted the "Chairman's Environmental Leadership Award" and awards for excellence in product responsibility.

13. Other proactive activities include an underground tank and pipe upgrade program, an asbestos abatement policy, PCB elimination, and improvement of hydrofluoric acid storage and handling.

All these programs are voluntary and exceed government regulatory requirements.

Top Management Support

To repeat a cliché, support of top management is critical. 3P Plus and the new corporate culture are grounded in a tradition of senior management support and direct involvement in environmental programs. This support can be noted especially in the following areas:

1. *Commitment of resources.* This is the true proof of a dedicated management. 3M's environmental programs have become part of its long-term business strategy. Each year 3M commits more than $150 million for research and development related to environmental issues.

2. *Total quality environmental management process.* What began as a series of projects aimed at preventing pollution and reducing costs has evolved into an ongoing TQEM improvement process at 3M. (*a*) Senior managers are required to incorporate 3M environmental policies, objectives, and standards into their operations. This includes long-range planning, research and development, and capital and operating budgets. Status reports of environmental issues affecting 3M are submitted quarterly to the board of directors and presented monthly to the corporate operations committee by the EE&PC staff vice president. (*b*) In each business unit, one executive is designated to promote responsible product stewardship. Also, each business unit is required to promote product life cycle analysis, in which every aspect in the life cycle of a product—from initial development through manufacturing, packaging use, and disposal—is evaluated to identify practical ways to reduce its environmental impact cost effectively.

Bottom-Line Impact on Competitive Position

The 3M total quality environmental management program, including responsible product stewardship, makes good business sense—in other words, our environmental strategies complement our business strategies.

Good environmental management means anticipating trends that can affect the environment and the bottom line. It also means having proactive programs to take advantage of the opportunities those trends present, rather than just succumbing to them. This means taking the long-term view. Environmental programs don't always have a short-term payoff, and sometimes not even an obvious or quantifiable payoff.

If we want to remain competitive, we need to be quick in responding to business opportunities but be a low-cost manufacturer. To do that we have to cut the use of regulated materials and cut waste.

People ask, "Why spend all this effort and money protecting the environment on programs not required by law?" The answer is that it's good for the environment and it's good for business. Specifically, the benefits are:

1. New business opportunities are created from new technology spin-offs, which are shared with 3M business units worldwide.

2. Business opportunities are also created by improving the environmental performance of our products.

3. Eliminating pollution reduces future liabilities, thereby improving our competitive position.

4. A good environmental program improves morale because employees feel good about helping to protect the environment.

5. Improving the environment benefits the community and enhances the company's reputation.

Here are a few examples of how 3P and other major 3P Plus programs have benefited the environment and at the same time contributed substantially to improving 3M's competitive position:

1. *Overall results of Pollution Prevention Pays program.* Since 1975, more than 3500 3P projects have resulted in the prevention of over 575,000 tons of pollution:

Air emissions:	134,000 tons
Water pollutants:	16,900 tons
Wastewater:	1.65 billion gallons
Sludge and solid waste:	426,000 tons

   The economic benefits of 3P have evolved into an important factor in 3M's business plans. Since 1975, 3M programs have provided worldwide savings of more than $550 million (cumulative first-year-only savings).

2. *Benefits of the energy management program.* Since 1973, 3M's energy usage has been cut by 50% per unit of production and associated carbon dioxide emissions have been cut by almost 4 billion pounds. This has resulted in savings of more than $730 million in energy costs. Here is an example of how one project conserved energy, eliminated air emissions, and saved dollars in energy costs:

   At a 3M manufacturing plant in Iowa, the mix of air for the drying ovens has been changed to use less outside air. By installing oven-room fans, more warm oven-room air is now mixed with cool air from the outside, reducing the need to heat the incoming air. Ventilated and cooled by the new fans, the oven room is more comfortable. For an investment of $50,000 the facility saved $35,500 in energy costs the first year, conserved 8 billion BTUs in energy, and eliminated 900,000 pounds of air emissions (carbon monoxide, carbon dioxide, and sulfur and nitrogen compounds).

3. *Resource recovery (commodity recycling).* In 1991, more than 188 million pounds of metals, plastics, solvents, papers, and other materials having a value of $26 million were recovered and either reused or sold for reuse. Since 1985, 3M has saved more than $120 million from its resource recovery operations.

Opportunities Into the Next Millennium

According to Livio DeSimone, 3M's Chairman and CEO, "American industry needs to meet environmental goals in such a way as not to weaken the national economy or jeopardize our competitive position in the world." In order to do this and take advantage of environmental opportunities, companies need to make a change:

1. From one that only keeps up with compliance with environmental regulations, to one that establishes its own proactive environmental goals and programs.

2. From one that looks on environmental protection as part of the cost of doing business, to one that creates business opportunities from its programs developed to protect the environment.

3. From one that addresses environmental issues separately, to a company that merges environmental interests with business interests.

3M management has established aggressive environmental goals and programs for this decade and beyond the year 2000, as can be seen in the 3P Plus program goals box. "At 3M, we see our commitment to the environment as part of who we are and how we do business now and in the future" (Allen Jacobson, former 3M Chairman and CEO).

The greatest opportunities for pollution prevention in 3M still lie ahead, in new and improved products, and processes with reduced environmental impact.

And our greatest opportunities to make pollution prevention *really* pay—in new sales, reduced costs, higher quality, less regulatory impact, fewer liabilities—should lie in those same new, environmentally improved products and

---

3P Plus program goals: Allen Jacobson (former 3M CEO)

- By 1993: Cut air emissions 70%.
- By 1995: Reduce energy consumption 20% per unit of production.

     Cut generation of waste 35%.
- By 2000: Reduce all releases 90%.

     Cut generation of waste 50%.
- Beyond the year 2000: Approach zero pollution and achieve sustainable development.

processes. Already, a great deal is going on in 3M laboratories. The use of recycled or recyclable materials is being investigated. More environmentally compatible materials are being developed. The use of materials that trigger regulation is being reduced. For example, solvent-based coatings are being replaced with new solventless coating processes.

The whole movement toward pollution prevention in our products and processes needs to be emphasized, externally and internally, especially now in the early 1990s. Many of these improvements will require fairly long R&D efforts. Those efforts must be in place now if we are to meet our year 2000 goals, if we are to truly become a "sustainable development" company by the year 2000, and if we are to capitalize on the opportunities presented by the emerging market for so-called green products.

Externally, we have an important opportunity *to help customers* address environmental concerns. This will improve both customer relations and the company's competitive position.

For example, 3M and Printing Industries of America (PIA) are jointly sponsoring an environmental management program for the graphic arts industry. This unique training and certification program is designed to educate printers and others in the graphic arts about environmental management, in order to minimize the impact of printing operations on the environment. Like our 3P Plus program, it will help facilities prevent pollution throughout the nation.

Small to medium-sized printing companies are finding it difficult to keep up with the ever-expanding new environmental regulations. Small printers in particular cannot afford to hire the personnel needed to oversee their environmental activities. So 3M is helping these customers identify and address environmental concerns. This environmental management program is one way for 3M to help the customer and to improve our competitiveness.

Internally, it is important for companies to provide all employees the opportunity to make a contribution to protecting the environment in a cost-effective manner. 3M's environmental leadership committee is developing a new employee recognition program to further encourage employees to look for opportunities for environmentally improved products. It will be based on the product life cycle approach. Every stage in the life cycle of a product—from concept and design, to manufacturing, packaging, and distribution, on through to use, reuse, and disposal—is assessed to look for opportunities to reduce environmental impact.

Product life cycle assessment involves examining the raw material and energy inputs and outputs in all stages of the product life cycle. The objective is to identify major opportunities to eliminate or reduce environmental impact using the methodologies in the pollution-prevention hierarchy. For more information on the assessment process, see Chap. 14, Life Cycle Analysis and Resource Management.

The adoption of this product life cycle approach to our product research and development will fill in the largest gap in our "holistic" pollution-prevention process. It will bring all aspects of our business into play when decisions have to be made about what environmental improvements make corporate sense.

In summary, moving a corporation to that new level of performance called "sustainable development" or "sustainable growth" will require:

Recognition that such a move is not only in the world's best interests but in the corporation's best interest

Commitment to becoming a "sustainable growth" company and allocating the necessary resources

Goals that are publicly stated with deadlines for reaching them

A process that is preferably part of an ongoing, never-ending process of continuing improvement such as total quality environmental management

3M's 3P Plus program has all those elements. We have started a process that truly has no end.

References and Additional Reading

Benforado, D. M., "Waste Minimization: Imperatives and Practicalities," 3M, Keynote Address, Hazardous Waste Minimization Course, Government Institutes, Inc., April 1988.

Bringer, R. P., and D. M. Benforado, 3M, "Pollution Prevention as Corporate Policy: A Look at the 3M Experience," *The Environmental Professional*, vol. II, pp. 117–126, 1989.

Buchholz, R. A., A. A. Marcus, and J. E. Post, *Managing Environmental Issues—A Case Book*, Corporate Conservation Council, National Wildlife Federation, Prentice-Hall, Englewood Cliffs, N.J., 1992.

DeSimone, Livio, 3M chief executive officer, in *Today*, Special Report, March 1992, p. 4.

Freeman, H., *Hazardous Waste Minimization*, McGraw-Hill, New York, 1990.

Freeman, H., et al., "Industrial Pollution Prevention: A Critical Review," *Journal of Air & Waste Management Association*, May 1992, September 1992.

Jacobson, Allen, former 3M chairman and CEO, *3M and the Environment*, vol. 1, 1991.

Pollution Prevention Act of 1990, 42 USCode13101.

Quarles, J., *Federal Regulation of Hazardous Wastes—A Guide to RCRA*, Environmental Law Institute, 1982.

Schmidheiny, Stephan, with the Business Council for Sustainable Development, *Changing Course—A Global Perspective on Development and the Environment*, MIT Press, Cambridge, Massachusetts, May 1992.

U.S. EPA Office of Pollution Prevention, *Pollution Prevention 1991, Progress on Reducing Industrial Pollutants*, October 1991, EPA-21P-3003.

U.S. EPA Office of Research & Development, *Facility Pollution Prevention Guide*, May 1992.

U.S. EPA Office of Research & Development, *Industrial Pollution Prevention Opportunities for the 1990s*, August 1991.

U.S. EPA Office of Research & Development, *Pollution Prevention Case Studies Compendium*, April 1992.

U.S. EPA Office of Solid Waste, *Report to Congress—Minimization of Hazardous Waste—Executive Summary*, October 1986, NTIS-PB87-114351.

U.S. EPA Risk Reduction Engineering Laboratory, *Waste Minimization Opportunity Assessment Manual*, Cincinnati, Ohio, 1988.

Appendix

Pollution-Prevention Case Studies:

Waste-Minimization Strategies during Pharmaceutical Process Development

Erik A. Dienemann, Ph.D.
Engineering Associate

Stuart Bacher
Director, Developmental Technology
Merck Research Laboratories*

In this appendix

- Introduction
- Waste-Minimization Strategy
- Case Studies 1 and 2
- Summary of Results

New drug research and development is a complex, costly, and time-consuming endeavor. The best opportunities for incorporating waste-minimization initiatives occur during the process-development phase. This paper focuses on development and implementation of rational waste-minimization strategies during pharmaceutical process development at Merck & Co. The general approach consists of several steps. First, a complete process material balance is calculated

---

*David Wolf, Karen Larson, and E. S. Venkataramani, of the Merck Research Laboratories, contributed to the case studies.

in order to generate detailed descriptions of all prospective waste streams; computerized process simulation is an important tool in this effort. Second, an environmental assessment is conducted to screen all prospective waste streams for possible waste-minimization opportunities. Third, specific waste-minimization initiatives are tested and evaluated, and, if feasible, incorporated into the process design. Finally, the process material balance is updated to incorporate and document successful waste-minimization initiatives. Highlights from two recent case studies illustrating the application of this strategy during process development include the following: for Case 1, technology was developed to recover and reuse 85% of all process solvents, and for Case 2, methylene chloride was engineered out of the process, and 53% of all other solvents will be recovered and reused within the process.

Introduction

An environmental protection strategy based on pollution prevention and waste minimization is more effective than the current strategy which is largely based on protecting specific environmental media via end-of-pipe pollution controls.[1,2] In general, waste minimization results in lower materials usage and inventory costs, leading to more efficient and economic processes, and reduces the amount of process wastes that require treatment and disposal.

The momentum behind the pollution-prevention movement has led to the recent enactment of numerous state and federal pollution-prevention statutes, including the Pollution Prevention Act of 1990.[3] This statute spurred EPA to develop its Industrial Toxics Project, better known as the 33-50 Program. This program calls for industry to voluntarily reduce emissions of 17 high-volume, high-release, high-toxicity chemicals. Emissions of these chemicals have been tallied since 1987 as part of the Toxics Release Inventory (TRI, which includes some 280 other chemicals) mandated by Title III of the Superfund Amendments and Reauthorization Act (SARA) of 1986. The agency's goal is to cut environmental emissions of these 17 chemicals 33% by the end of 1992 and 50% by the end of 1995, using 1988 reported emission levels as a baseline. Merck is one of many companies that have subscribed to this program. In addition, Merck, in 1988, announced a corporate goal of reducing by 90% worldwide all environmental releases of TRI-listed toxic chemicals by the end of 1995, using 1987 as a baseline. (See box "Waste-Minimization Initiatives at Merck.") Thus process-development efforts have become a focal point for evaluating pollution-prevention and waste-minimization initiatives for incorporation into new bulk pharmaceutical processes.

Waste-Minimization Strategy

New drug research and development is a complex, costly, and time-consuming endeavor. It has been estimated that it requires 7 to 10 years and over $200 mil-

---

Waste-Minimization Initiatives at Merck

- By 12/91, reduce by 90% worldwide air emissions of carcinogens and suspect carcinogens

- By 12/93, eliminate carcinogen air emissions or apply best available technology

- By 12/95, reduce by 90% worldwide all environmental releases of toxic chemicals
  - Toxic chemicals defined as those on the SARA 313 list
  - Baselines for reductions are 1987 release levels reported to EPA under SARA

---

lion (industrywide averages) to bring a new drug from discovery through U.S. Food and Drug Administration (FDA) approval.[4] This includes, on average, 18 to 24 months of preclinical safety testing, 4 to 6 years of phased clinical testing to establish drug efficacy and safety, and 2 years for FDA to review and approve the new drug application. Generally, it can be well into the clinical testing phase that a new drug process undergoes intense process development. During this period, significant process modification and optimization are usually required to develop a safe, reliable, cost-effective, and environmentally sound manufacturing process.

Process development presents the best opportunity to incorporate waste-minimization initiatives. By the time process development nears completion, clinical efficacy has likely been established and process modifications (including those intended to effect waste minimization) become more difficult to incorporate, owing to regulatory constraints (see Case Study 1). Therefore, it is important that waste-minimization initiatives be evaluated early in the process-development phase.

The waste-minimization strategy for the two case studies discussed consists of several steps. (See box "Waste-Minimization and Process-Development Strategy.") First, complete process material balances are calculated in order to provide detailed descriptions of all prospective waste streams. This can be difficult, considering that, especially early in process development, reaction stoichiometries and partitioning of various chemical species during mass transfer operations may be poorly understood. Often, one must rely on "educated guesses" until the process streams and waste streams have been analyzed and characterized.

Second, after obtaining estimated waste stream compositions, an environmental assessment is conducted to screen these prospective waste streams for possible waste-minimization opportunities. Typical waste-minimization initiatives considered include materials substitution, materials use reduction, materials recovery and reuse, and a variety of production technology and operations improvements. Usually, the most important waste-minimization technique considered is solvent recovery and reuse, since for Merck and most of the pharma-

---

Waste-Minimization and Process-Development Strategy

1. Calculate initial process material balance to estimate prospective waste streams

   - Computerized batch process simulation is an important tool in this effort

2. Perform environmental assessment of process; evaluate waste-minimization options

3. Where feasible, incorporate waste-minimization options into process design

4. Update process material balance, incorporating waste-minimization initiatives

5. Iterative strategy: repeat steps 1 to 4, as necessary

6. For waste-minimization residuals and nonminimized wastes, evaluate treatment and disposal

Important considerations

   - Requires collaboration among chemists, engineers, and environmental staff
   - May involve significant process changes; usually requires lab and pilot validation
   - Must maintain product quality; safety and economic concerns must be evaluated
   - Early intervention is critical, before process becomes "locked in"

---

ceutical industry, organic solvents account for 75% or more of reported SARA emissions.[5]

The third step in the waste-minimization strategy involves testing and evaluation of specific waste-minimization initiatives which, if feasible, are incorporated into the process design. This usually involves extensive laboratory and pilot-plant evaluation over several months or more and must be demonstrated not to compromise product quality. Finally, the process material balance is revisited and updated to incorporate all process modifications; the update thus reflects and documents waste-minimization results. An important tool in calculating these process material balances is a computerized process simulator. PROVAL, an in-house UNIX-based batch process simulation and design system, was used to calculate the material balances for the two case studies.

Case Study 1

This case study focuses on a multistep alternate chemical synthesis of an intermediate in the production of imipenem, a component of the broad-spectrum antibiotic Primaxin, approved in 1985. The alternate synthesis led to a more simplified process and resulted in the elimination of methylene chloride as a process solvent. However, this case study will focus on the waste minimization achieved in the alternate process, after the methylene chloride had been replaced. The first iteration of the computerized (PROVAL) process simulation indicated that approximately 64 kg of total spent solvent would be generated per kilogram of intermediate. Specifically (all figures are per kilogram of intermediate): (1) step 1 would generate a waste liquor containing 14 kg toluene; (2) step 2 would generate a waste liquor containing 3.5 kg toluene and a waste distillate containing 10 kg toluene and 1.2 kg acetonitrile*; (3) step 4 would generate a waste liquor containing 13 kg toluene and 3.7 kg methanol; and (4) step 5 would generate a waste liquor containing 8.9 kg heptane and 5.1 kg methyl acetate. Given these prospective solvent waste loads, development of solvent-recovery schemes became the primary waste-minimization objective of the development team.

Case Study 1: Solvent-Recovery Overview

- **Step 1:** Sequential aqueous extractions to remove water-soluble species from a waste liquor, followed by distillation to recover 99% pure toluene

- **Step 2:** Sequential aqueous extractions to remove water-soluble species from both a waste liquor and a waste distillate, recovering 99% pure toluene from each*

- **Step 4:** Sequential aqueous extractions to remove water-soluble species from a waste liquor, recovering 99% pure toluene

- **Step 5:** Sequential batch distillation of a waste liquor, recovering reusable distillate (92% methyl acetate/8% heptane) and bottoms (6% methyl acetate/94% heptane)

- Overall, 85% of process solvents will be reused; also, aqueous wastes from solvent recovery are biodegradable and unlikely to upset activated-sludge treatment plant

*Step 3 has no associated waste.

Over the next year, viable solvent-recovery schemes were developed and incorporated into each step in the alternate synthesis. For the first step, the waste liquor was extracted with dilute acid to remove water-soluble organics that would otherwise compromise recovered solvent purity, and then batch-distilled in the presence of water to recover 99% pure toluene. In the second step, the waste liquor was extracted sequentially with dilute base, dilute acid, and neutral water, and the waste distillate was extracted sequentially

*Step 3 has no associated waste.

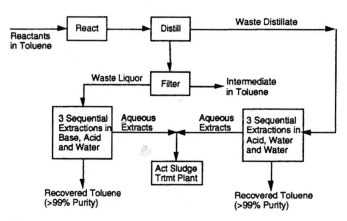

Figure 6A-1. Solvent-recovery schemes for step 2, Case Study 1.

with dilute acid, neutral water, and neutral water again. As an example of what a flow sheet for a solvent-recovery scheme looks like, see Fig. 6A-1, which illustrates the solvent-recovery scheme for step 2. These sequential extractions served to remove water-soluble organics, such as acetonitrile, that would otherwise compromise recovered solvent purity, resulting in 99% pure toluene in both cases. For the fourth step, the waste liquor was subjected to four sequential aqueous extractions, once again to remove water-soluble organics, resulting in recovery of 99% pure toluene. Also, in this step, a second waste liquor containing toluene, methanol, heptane, and methyl acetate is generated, but because of its complexity will be incinerated. For the fifth step, the waste liquor was batch-distilled to generate a distillate containing 60% heptane and 40% methyl acetate, which was, in turn, batch-distilled to generate two reusable streams containing (1) 92% methyl acetate and 8% heptane in the distillate, and (2) 94% heptane and 6% methyl acetate in the bottoms (the bottoms from the first distillation will be incinerated). For an overall summary of the fate of all process solvents, see Table 6A-1.

At the manufacturing scale, it is envisioned that all the 99% toluene streams will be pooled for final distillation to recover reusable-purity

Table 6A-1. Summary of Fate of Process Solvents, Case Study 1
Basis: per Kilogram of Intermediate Produced

Solvent	Total solvent, kg	Waste solvent recovered, %	Solvents to treatment plant, %	Solvents to be incinerated, %
Heptane	11	72	—	28
Toluene	42	98	<1	1
Methyl acetate	6	85	—	15
Methanol	4	—	5	95
Acetonitrile	1	—	99	<1
Total	64	85	3	12

toluene. In addition, it should be noted that all the aqueous waste extracts generated are biodegradable and will be sent to the on-site activated-sludge treatment plant. Finally, this case study illustrates that it is possible to develop and implement process modifications, including waste minimization, *even after a process has been approved by the U.S. FDA.* However, it has been a complex, costly, and time-consuming procedure, in which it had to be demonstrated that final product quality had not been compromised; also, it necessitated filing a supplemental new drug application (NDA) with the FDA.

Case Study 2

The second case study focuses on the development of finasteride, which is targeted for treatment of benign prostatic hypertrophy (enlarged prostate). This process involves a complex, multistep chemical synthesis, and the final drug substance is active at low doses, requiring strict manufacturing and environmental controls. The initial (1989) computer simulation of this process indicated that approximately 70 kg of methylene chloride spent solvent would be generated per kilogram of final product. Therefore, the initial waste-minimization thrust for this process focused on the replacement of methylene chloride as a process solvent. Development of replacements for methylene chloride, used in three process steps, involved many months of laboratory and pilot-scale testing and evaluation.

Case Study 2: Elimination of Methylene Chloride

- **Step 2:**   Sequential $MeCl_2$ extractions replaced by single toluene and isopropanol extraction

- **Step 3:** $MeCl_2$ extraction replaced by toluene and isopropanol extraction

- **Purification Step:**   Alumina and carbon treatment in $MeCl_2$ and a $MeCl_2$-HCl extraction replaced by carbon treatment in tetrahydrofuran and crystallization from THF-HCl

- Overall, eliminated use of 70 kg $MeCl_2$ per kg drug; process yield was significantly improved, and product quality was not compromised

---

The original second process step involved a reaction in methanol and H_2SO_4, followed by sequential extractions of the step intermediate into methylene chloride. This treatment was replaced by a single extraction of the step intermediate into a mixture of toluene and isopropanol. The original third step involved a reaction in toluene followed by two aqueous extractions (to remove certain species) and then an extraction of the step intermediate into methylene chloride. The replacement third step simply eliminates the methylene chloride extraction, keeping the step intermediate in the toluene layer, which also contains isopropanol. Finally one of the final product-purification steps involved alumina and carbon treatment of the product in methylene chloride. This was replaced by an activated-carbon treatment of the product in tetrahydrofuran. Overall, these modifications resulted in the elimination of the use of 70 kg methylene chloride per kilogram of final product; furthermore, process yield was improved significantly, and product quality was not compromised.

After substituting for methylene chloride, the waste-minimization focus shifted to developing solvent recovery and reuse schemes for the remaining solvents, since the updated process simulation (reflecting the replacement of methylene chloride) showed that the overall process would generate approximately 449 kg spent solvents per kilogram of final product. In the first process step, 66 kg acetic acid distillate is generated per kilogram of final product, and the process-development team demonstrated that approximately 95% of this stream can be directly reused within the step. In the second step, 33 kg of mixed toluene, isopropanol, and methanol distillate is generated per kilogram of final product, and it has been demonstrated that approximately 75% of this stream can be directly reused within this step. In one of the purification steps, 153 kg tetrahydrofuran distillate is generated per kilogram of final product, and it has been demonstrated that approximately 95% of this stream can be directly reused within this step.

Case Study 2: Solvent-Recovery Overview

- **Step 1:**   95% of acetic acid distillate will be reused within the step
- **Step 2:**   75% of toluene, isopropanol, and methanol distillate will be reused within the step
- **Purification Step:**   95% of tetrahydrofuran distillate will be reused within the step
- Overall, 53% of total process solvents will be reused

Overall, approximately 53% of all process solvents will be reused within the process. These represent solvents that did not require major purification before reuse; the remaining process solvent wastes are more complex and would require significant purification before reuse is feasible. Initially, these solvent waste streams will be incinerated. As production levels increase, the expectation is that recovery schemes will be developed for many of these solvents.

A small fraction of the solvents used, a small amount of active compounds (including final product), and most of the inorganic salts used in the process partition to the aqueous extractants used in various steps in the process. Currently, a variety of waste-treatment technologies are being considered for these aqueous wastes, including wet-air oxidation and carbon adsorption, but most of these wastes will be incinerated in the interim. For an overall summary of the expected fate of the process solvents, see Table 6A-2.

Table 6A-2. Summary of Fate of Process Solvents, Case Study 2

Basis: per Kilogram of Finasteride Produced

Solvent	Total solvent, kg	Waste solvent recovered, %	Solvents to treatment plant, %	Solvents to be incinerated, %
Tetrahydrofuran	264	55	—	43
Toluene	39	47	—	53
Acetic acid	78	81	10	8
Methanol	8	16	—	84
Isopropanol	16	33	—	67
Isopropyl acetate	20	—	—	100
n-Butyl acetate	24	—	—	100
Total	449	53	2	45

Summary of Results

A rational waste-minimization strategy for pharmaceutical process development described here focuses on constructing overall process material balances to estimate the quantity and composition of prospective process waste streams, and using that information to spur development and implementation of waste-minimization studies. The major waste-minimization accomplishment for Case Study 1 has been the development and incorporation of solvent-recovery schemes which will result in the on-site recovery and reuse of approximately 85% of total process solvents used. The primary waste-minimization accomplishments for Case Study 2 have been the replacement of methylene chloride as a process solvent and development and incorporation of schemes to directly reuse approximately 53% of other process solvents. It should also be reiterated that a successful waste-minimization strategy requires close collaboration among chemists, chemical engineers, and environmental professionals, and is most effective when performed early in the development cycle, since process modifications are difficult to implement later, owing to regulatory and economic constraints.

References

1. U.S. Congress, Office of Technology Assessment, *Serious Reduction of Hazardous Waste*, Washington, D.C., 1986.

2. H. Freeman, *Hazardous Waste Minimization*, McGraw-Hill, New York, 1990.

3. T. Foecke, "A New Mandate for Pollution Prevention," *Pollution Prevention Review*, winter 1990/1991, Executive Enterprises, Inc., 1991.

4. M. Mathieu, *New Drug Development: A Regulatory Overview*, PAREXEL International Corp., Cambridge, Massachusetts, 1990.

5. U.S. EPA, SARA 313 Toxics Release Report.

PART 3

Corporate Management and Public Interest Perspective

7

Industry Perspective: Environmental Health and Safety Challenges and Social Responsibilities*

Morton L. Mullins

Vice President, Regulatory Affairs
Chemical Manufacturers Association (CMA)

In this chapter:

- Introduction/Historical Perspective
- Industry Initiatives
- Responsible Care®
- Codes of Management Practices
- Figures and Tables

*Jon C. Holtzman, vice president, communications, Chemical Manufacturers Association reviewed this chapter. Emily Currie Moses has also contributed to the chapter.

Introduction

In this chapter we discuss U.S. corporate behavior regarding environmental, health, and safety (EH&S) matters; some recent changes in that behavior; and future challenges for American industry. We make no claim to be independent or objective observers. Our views have been biased by lifelong association with the chemical industry. We attempt, however, to convey fairly the views, concerns, distrust, and cynicism that critics express toward this subject, for today, "perception is reality," and it was ignoring thoughtful and well-intentioned criticism in the past that led us to where we are today.

No two corporate cultures are the same, but obvious trends are emerging in how corporate America sees itself and its roles and responsibilities in environmental, health, and safety issues. No longer is it good enough simply to comply with regulations or produce the best goods or create the most jobs. The public expects corporations to be socially responsible as well. That is, the public has demanded and will increasingly expect continuous improvement in EH&S performance by industry. An optimist can find a lot of good news in the cultural revolution that's happening in American industry. This chapter is intended to spread that good news and to suggest to those companies that are on the "EH&S fence" or "lying in the weeds of social responsibility" that becoming a player in this arena not only makes good business sense, it could mean the difference between staying in or going out of business.

The chemical industry makes a large and essential contribution to the economic vitality of the United States. The chemicals produced in the United States are integral to nearly every sector of the nation's economy and are the building blocks or essential ingredients for nearly every product used by our society. The chemical industry is often termed a "basic" industry because 41% of its products are essential to the production processes of other industries such as the automobile, textile, pharmaceutical, high-technology, and service industries. The chemical industry in the United States plays a critical role in the international competitiveness of American manufacturing. It is one of the few industries with a positive balance of trade. Through surpluses in trade and international investments, the chemical industry contributes greatly to the nation's international balance of payments.

The Chemical Industry

Gross National Product (GNP)   The chemical industry is the third largest manufacturing industry in the United States. It accounted for almost 2% of the GNP and over 8% of all U.S. manufacturing in 1990.

Jobs   Collectively, over 30% of U.S. workers are engaged in the production or use of chemical products. The chemical industry employs over one million Americans. Another 33 million people across more than 100 major industrial and service sectors directly depend on chemicals to do their jobs.

Trade   Despite a $66 billion U.S. trade deficit in 1991, the U.S. chemical industry leads all other manufacturing goods in export value. Worldwide, the U.S. chemical industry is second only to Germany's chemical industry in total exports, accounting for nearly 13% of the $280 billion in total world exports of chemicals in 1990.

Capital Spending   The prominent role of U.S. chemicals in world markets reflects an overall industry commitment to innovation and modernization. In 1990, U.S. chemical firms invested almost $21 billion in new capacity, plant, and equipment here in the United States. About $1.6 billion of that total was spent on pollution abatement and control.

Research and Development (R&D)   The U.S. chemical industry is research-intensive. It is consistently among the leading industrial sectors in yearly R&D expenditures.

Data on the chemical industry, including emissions and expenditures for abatement, are shown in tables and figures at the end of this chapter.

In 1988, the Chemical Manufacturers Association (CMA) launched the most ambitious and comprehensive self-improvement effort ever attempted by an American industry—the Responsible Care® initiative. Dedicated to improving the chemical industry's health, safety, and environmental performance—and ultimately its reputation with a soured and skeptical public—Responsible Care not only committed CMA's members to doing a better job, it continues to challenge them to make fundamental changes in the way they deal with the public's concerns about the safety of their operations and products. CMA is a nonprofit trade association representing 90% of the productive capacity of basic industrial chemicals in the United States. So why would some of America's industrial giants join an initiative that requires changing their behavior from the status quo to becoming leaders in proactive volunteerism? The simple answer is that it's good business.

> With all the strengths of the chemical industry, we face some serious challenges: problems pushing the industry from the inside out and problems from outside the industry, pushing in. These challenges have the potential of shaking the operating foundation of the chemical industry and of eating away at its core.
>
> *David J. D'Antoni, president, Ashland Chemical, Inc.*

Historical Perspective

Looking at U.S. industry following World War II is like recounting the stages of death: denial, anger, grief, and confrontation. America came out of World War II bullish on American manufacturing. American manufacturers produced goods valued the world over, created millions of well-paying jobs, and increased the standard of living worldwide. To most Americans, industrial smokestacks meant secure employment, new and useful products, and of course, profits. And industrial management's attitude toward the public was more than a little arrogant. Management presumed it knew what was good for the public (whatever was good for the company), and the public tended to agree. Industry didn't expect to be questioned or held accountable for its actions.

By the early 1960s, environmental incidents such as rivers catching fire, the reported death of Lake Erie, and the early characterizations of acid rain caught the attention of the public. Already weary from a decade of Vietnam and disillusioned by the Watergate scandal, the public's perception of American industry began to erode. In 1962, Rachel Carson's book, *Silent Spring,* alerted the public to and raised fear about the possible cumulative effects of chemicals on the environment. Some critics began to question whether America needed production industries at all. Earth Day I came and went, and—perhaps most significant—the media and the Congress learned that negative environmental news sold copy and captured votes. Industry, by and large, slept through the early days of this revolution but awoke to find itself the target of public outrage. A few companies had the foresight to initiate EH&S efforts far ahead of their time, but most were critical of the "howling jackals" whose demands for expensive pollution control were viewed as unreasoned and intended to force industry out of the United States. Many industrial leaders had grown up accepting pollution as a natural by-product of productivity, and assumed that the environment had unlimited assimilative capacity to accommodate our mess. Few industry leaders shared the vision of a global ecology that was proclaimed on early bumper stickers such as "passengers on planet earth" and "we have met the enemy and it is us." Although workplace safety was generally taken seriously, many industrial leaders viewed EH&S efforts like taxes: They should be properly prescribed by government—and going beyond compliance with the minimum prescribed by law was unnecessary.

Anger and denial generally describe the industry's reaction to the early environmental movement, not because of any intrinsic mean spirit, but because industry leadership did not understand that the emotions of the then embryonic public interest sector were fueled by a sense of distrust, betrayal, and fear of the unknown. Few in industry realized that the blind faith which had been entrusted to them by its stakeholders (neighbors, employees, shareholders, government officials, etc.) had evaporated during the 1960s, along with the trust of the rest of the "establishment."

By the early 1970s, industry began to take the environmental movement and EH&S issues more seriously, but most companies were too busy protecting themselves from new environmental laws and regulations to think about proactive or voluntary actions. Congress had enacted the first Clean Air Act—which was largely a state-run program—and the first Clean Water Act (of 1970 and 1972, respectively). The newly formed Environmental Protection Agency (1970) rapidly began issuing regulations. Much of the attention was on auto and utility emissions, particulate control from industry's stacks, and achieving the equivalent of secondary wastewater treatment. But the financial burden to industry was large, and some basic industries became extinct or endangered in this country (e.g., foundries, steel, smelting).

It became evident by the early 1980s that the public interest and grass roots forces which were focused on environmental issues had gained in both strength and sophistication. Congress enacted more environmental laws. The Resource Conservation and Recovery Act (RCRA), the statute governing waste management, and Superfund, designed to clean up waste sites, were central to the environmental debate, and two unexpected events forever altered the EH&S issue.

The first was a Superfund scandal involving EPA Administrator Anne Burford and Assistant Administrator Rita Lavelle. Following an investigation into EPA's Superfund program, Congress charged that EPA's failure to begin cleaning up waste sites under Superfund was in violation of the intent of Congress. This event gave the lawmakers new license—not only to tell EPA what to do but also to tell the agency how to do it—and when—and how much. The agency's previous discretion to develop thoughtful, cost-effective regulations was eroded. This Superfund scandal also spawned the passage of the 1986 Superfund amendments, which, in the minds of many, sealed the fate of this program to its current characterization of being broken and unable to achieve any degree of effectiveness, efficiency, or equity. The second event was the passage of Title III, or the Community Right-to-Know provisions of the Superfund amendments. Substantively unrelated to the Superfund program, Title III marked a signal turning point in industrial behavior. A response, in part, to the tragic leak of MIC, a highly toxic chemical, from a Union Carbide plant in Bhopal, India, on December 4, 1984, Title III simply called for industry to report its emissions of a 300+ list of "toxic chemicals" and gave the public a scorecard by which to measure industry's pollution. With it came an inferred obligation to reduce the numbers on that scorecard, regardless of whether the chemical posed any calculable risk to health or the environment. Equally, if not more importantly, Title III awakened industry leaders to how much product was potentially being lost or wasted.

For years industry had concerned itself with assuring safe levels of chemical exposure within the workplace and at the fenceline. When industry converted its emission concentrations from parts-per-million (ppm) to pounds per year to meet the Title III reporting requirements, the numbers were surprisingly big— not only in terms of lost product and substantial cost savings but also in terms of credibility. It was clear that explaining those numbers to the public would be difficult. No matter how comfortable a company or plant had become with the safety of a part-per-million concentration at the fence, the emission of hundreds of thousands or even millions of pounds per year was tough to explain—even if it was only a fraction of a percent of the company's throughput.

This revelation caused most plant managers—often for the first time—to put themselves in their neighbors' place and consider what other people might be thinking about the perceived safety of a plant's operations. Real confrontation of issues began. Risk communication experts were retained and plant managers learned about the importance of listening to their neighbor's concerns, recognizing voluntary versus involuntary risk issues (e.g., smoking versus being subjected to toxic air emissions) and about how to understand and deal with an outraged public. When the first Title III reports were submitted in July 1987, real change in industrial thinking and behavior had begun.

Although many companies such as 3M had established pollution-prevention programs before Title III, the angst caused by the need to articulate to the public how much each plant was emitting, what it really meant, and how we were going to respond to the public's expectations that we do something about it, elevated these issues—often for the first time—to the boardroom. Many companies such as Monsanto, Dow and DuPont committed themselves to reduction goals—some based on carefully considered identification of opportunities, others based on what the public might expect or demand.

At about the same time, CMA conducted a public opinion survey which asked the public what it thought about the chemical industry and its value to society. The results were sobering. Not only was the industry held in low esteem, its reputation was worsening. If a window of opportunity existed to reverse the trend, that window was closing. Something had to be done. In 1988, CMA's Board adopted Responsible Care, an initiative aimed at improving the performance and eventually the reputation of the industry. This industry initiative, modeled after a Canadian prototype, has served as a model for other chemical associations worldwide and is being replicated by other industry segments.

Traditionally, the chemical industry's attitude has been to first satisfy the legal requirements placed upon it. Given their choice, the majority of industry executives and managers preferred to stay out of sight and out of the headlines. The public has been a secondary concern, and any statement to it was typically out of necessity. Over the years, the industry's credibility plummeted after heavily publicized toxic waste dumps, spills, releases, and explosions. The public also was alarmed by reports of the millions of pounds of hazardous materials that plants routinely and legally discharged into the environment. To balance the story, the chemical industry tried to educate the public by promoting the industry's health and safety record, economic contributions, and beneficial products. It didn't work. By the mid-1980s, the idea that the industry had an unwarranted image problem was replaced by the realization that its image suffered because of its performance. Chemical company executives recognized changing public opinion depended on restoring confidence in the industry's ability to operate safely, without threatening health or the environment, and on giving people the opportunity to talk to someone in the industry.

Industry Initiatives

Social Responsibility and the Bottom Line

Most companies with well-developed EH&S initiatives and programs consider these efforts part of a broader "social responsibility." Social responsibility might be defined as those initiatives taken by a firm—apart from their primary production of products or providing of services—that are directed at enhancing the company's performance or image in matters of corporate citizenship. These efforts might vary from philanthropic gestures to employment diversity to community leadership to bold initiatives such as Responsible Care.

> Responsible Care represents a radical departure from past practices and marks an end to the old mindset that as long as we were complying with environmental laws and regulations, then the government and the public should keep off our backs. It begins with the premise that our industry has serious environmental and safety performance problems, and that we have to dramatically improve that performance.
>
> *John Johnstone, president and CEO, Olin Corporation.*

Most candid executives will admit that many of these initiatives are driven in part, if not entirely, by "enlightened self-interest." This simply means that while individual executives, and often the corporate culture, may seek to do the right thing for noble or ethical reasons—it's OK and in fact necessary to identify and understand some of the "bottom line" reasons behind your initiative.

Nearly every industrial leader has asked the questions, "Why should I go beyond compliance?" or "Why should I spend enormous sums of money on a new initiative when that money could be spent on new product development or plant improvement?" If you are asking yourself these questions, consider this:

- *Staying in business.* Profits. Absent profit, jobs, products, and services will cease to exist. The high cost of complying with EH&S laws and regulations is ever-increasing. The export of basic industries which occurred in the last few decades hurt the U.S. economy. The United States must keep its producing industries and regain some of those that have been lost. Service industries alone will not sustain the economy or our quality of life. Successful use of voluntary initiatives may be the last opportunity to break the "regulatory spiral" and preserve the ability to compete.

- *Shareholders.* Increasingly conscious of EH&S performance, groups of institutional investors have banded together to identify responsible companies. They offer mutual funds of "green" stocks. Religious investors do likewise. Individual stockholders are increasingly strident. Just read the letters to management after an environmental incident.

- *Government regulation.* The only way to curb the trend toward overly prescriptive, burdensome regulation that goes further than regulation can efficiently go is to build a level of confidence within the public and the lawmakers. Industry has to prove that its own programs can and will pick up where regulation leaves off if the tide of overregulation is ever going to turn.

- *Liabilities.* Via environmental statutes (e.g., RCRA or Superfund) or tort law (product liability or negligence in assuring employee safety), liabilities are ever-increasing.

- *Right-to-operate concerns.* Community opposition has made it increasingly difficult to stay in business. These concerns heighten each time a facility is unable to obtain a permit because of community opposition or when a business is booed out of a prospective location where the local citizenry once would have embraced the prospect of new jobs.

- *Limited resources.* There are limits to the resources available to deal with EH&S issues—whether those resources come from government, industry, or the consumer. Whether resources come from government or industry, the cost to society is ultimately borne by the public (the consumer) whether it comes in the form of higher-priced goods, fewer jobs, or increased taxes. We have to put our money and talent where they will do the most good for the most people. Priorities must be set and resources allocated on the basis of risk avoided.

- *Enhanced public image.* The public is environmentally conscious and will make purchasing decisions based on EH&S performance. A firm with a poor EH&S record or image will simply lose its customer base and market share. As more companies include EH&S considerations in their Total Quality Management efforts, the EH&S performance and reputation of their suppliers, contractors, and even customers will receive greater scrutiny. Even those firms that sell to other industries will look at the EH&S performance record of their customers.

- *Global competition.* The marketplace for manufacturing is global and we must be active players in the marketplace. Where our trading partners have less of a EH&S burden, we operate at a competitive disadvantage, and our ability to support EH&S programs is, in turn, reduced. In 1991 alone, the United States spent 120 billion dollars on environmental protection, or 2% of Gross National Product (GNP). Even so, at the extreme, where jobs are exported, so too may be the EH&S concerns. To the extent that EH&S concerns have global effects, they may become worse in a less sophisticated or nurturing environment. If one considers the total impact on quality of life, a net loss will probably occur as a result of exporting jobs.

- *Recruiting.* The ability to attract and retain the best people is increasingly impacted by a company's EH&S reputation. Few new graduates want to work for a company that is viewed by their peers as a dinosaur or irresponsible.

- *Regulatory discretion.* Sometimes regulatory discretion and/or the benefit of the doubt will be given to a company with a history of being open, honest, and dedicated to EH&S stewardship. Today's regulations are open to reasonable interpretations, and a regulator may be more willing to work with a respected company.

- *Competitive advantage.* Sometimes a real advantage can be gained by firms that are leaders in the voluntary EH&S arena. Any of the above advantages of stewardship are doubly applicable to those who not only practice but lead by innovation and creativity.

Although there are a multitude of reasons to embark on an EH&S initiative, asserting that a responsible action is taken solely for the greater good convinces no one and will detract from the perceived value of the initiative. Don't shy away from letting people know how the initiative fits into your overall business plan. You can be up-front and honest about the good business reasons for voluntarily reducing your emissions or changing your processes and, in the long run, actually contribute to the credibility of your action.

Regulatory Compliance vs. Voluntary Initiatives

An often asked question is how industry initiatives fit with compliance—that which is required by law. In general, initiatives pick up where regulations leave off. While no one likes laws and regulations, the truth is, our society would be short-lived if we didn't have them. The same premise holds true for EH&S regulations. Absent an effective regulatory "safety net," incidents and abuses would undoubtedly occur and the public would be moved toward more prescriptive regulation. And the truth is that a well-reasoned, effective, efficient, and appropriately enforced EH&S regulatory scheme is sometimes necessary to provide the industrial community with a floor—a level playing field—upon which to compete. Without this floor, there would be no baseline for behavior. Without this baseline, the financial performance of those companies that choose to develop innovative EH&S programs or provide leadership on EH&S stewardship would be severely undermined by those who don't. However, compliance itself can undermine EH&S initiatives. As discussed above, regulators today look at not only what industry should do but also at how it should be done—often at the expense of "performance-based" regulations which tell the regulated community what to achieve—and let industry decide how to do it. However, many critics of industry argue that regulations should leave nothing to chance, that every technical detail should be specifically codified in order to assure compliance, and that no room should be left for performance-based initiatives. Unfortunately, government resources, as evidenced by recent regulatory history, simply cannot accommodate the sophisticated level of detail needed to develop comprehensive "command and control" regulations. To accommodate the vast differences in various types of processes to the level of detail believed necessary would consume more of our GNP than compliance itself.

There is a point of diminishing return beyond which the resources necessary to identify a problem, consider appropriate solutions, and define regulatory requirements outweigh the benefits of the remedy. Recent regulatory history tends to bear out this precept. Thus the nation must seek an optimum balance between regulation and incentives for creative, voluntary initiatives. To gain acceptance that regulation can't do the whole job, industry must demonstrate that voluntary initiatives, EH&S "stewardship" or "leadership," can and will pick up the baton and take us further than mere compliance with regulations can go. Where regulation is appropriate—it should, as much as possible, be performance-based so as to allow the regulated community the opportunity to be creative and competitive in seeking the most cost-effective way to comply.

> Under the Clean Water Act, for example, EPA labored for 20 years to develop limits for certain chemicals found in virtually dozens of categories and sub-categories of sources, i.e., types of manufacturing processes. The amount of effort expended to complete this arduous task has not been cost-effective. Similarly, regulations under RCRA, the law which regulates waste-management standards, have left little to chance. RCRA is a classic command and control program. It is complex beyond belief and a nightmare for both the regulators and the regulated community as opposed to the alternative "generic" approach of requiring a percent reduction in effluent concentration over time.

Critical to performance-based initiatives is the issue of compliance assurance. The credibility of a firm's EH&S program cannot survive enforcement actions that bring into question whether the basic requirements of law were addressed. Millions of dollars of potential goodwill from voluntary initiatives can be lost if it is found that the most mundane technical regulatory requirement was over-looked, ignored, or circumvented. Total compliance must be the standard. Attention to detail must be the norm. The time to question requirements which are too prescriptive or too burdensome or which appear to lack benefit is during the rule making—not after a violation has been filed.

Advocacy

Industry plays a key role in both legislative and regulatory EH&S advocacy because it alone can provide a realistic perspective on its operations, the activity being regulated, and the impact and effectiveness of a proposed law or regulation. Industry's credibility is often held suspect by some critics when it opposes legislation or regulations for the sake of promoting effective and equitable regulatory consistency. This generally stems from a conclusion that opposing even a bad bill or regulation is antienvironmental. Proponents of particular legislative initiatives or regulatory programs often subscribe to the notion that more is always better, whereby efforts are made to enact laws that require far more regulation than is actually needed to solve an EH&S concern. This has led to the "environmental brinksmanship" that has become ingrained in the law-making and rule-making process. Given this reality, industry is challenged to achieve "congruence" between its advocacy positions and its EH&S steward-ship initiatives. Even in the face of EH&S initiatives, cost-effectiveness, risk justification, and competitiveness issues continue to be critical in legislative and regulatory debates. Too often the absence of industry data or involvement results in the development of poor laws and regulations.

> Advocacy and Responsible Care are meant to be mutually fulfilling. If Responsible Care is the new home that we've built for ourselves, then advocacy is its foundation. They function in support of one another.

Responsible Care obliges us to participate with the government and others in creating responsible laws, regulation, and standards to safeguard the community, the workplace, and the environment. That does not mean we must meekly accept laws and regulations that are poorly conceived or are meant to be harshly punitive.

Robert Roland, president, CMA.

Industry Programs

For all practical purposes even the concept of industry EH&S initiatives is less than a decade old and still evolving. There are a lot of opportunities in industry for creative initiatives. The more common initiatives are:

- *Pollution prevention*—practices which lead to reduced wastes or releases to the environment. This can include improved controls on air or water pollution; recycling, process changes to eliminate wastes, etc. This has been the most popular category owing to its close relationship with the Title III reporting.

  Companies practice pollution prevention in a number of ways, and it's important to note that steps taken to prevent pollution work best when they are self-imposed. Those who know an operation best also know best how to improve it. There are many good examples of the kinds of innovations occurring every day across the country.

  For example, in 1992, the Texas Eastman Division of Eastman Chemical Company won an award from EPA for its reduction in its toxic release inventory (TRI) emissions. The award was based on the company's energy-conservation and pollution-prevention efforts at its Longview, Texas, petrochemical plant. The plant was able to reduce its emissions by recycling, using a process furnace, and redesigning and installing process control valves.

- *Product stewardship*—steps taken to reduce risks or problems resulting from products in commerce including postconsumer waste issues. These can range from improved labeling to reducing the amount of packaging on certain items to return programs for spent materials.

- *Energy-conservation initiatives*—energy conservation or development of renewable sources of energy increase in attractiveness as the tie between global atmospheric concerns and energy generation is understood.

- *Habitat conservation*—safeguarding of biodiversity through land or forest management or other means is often an opportunity for plant involvement.

- *Policy leadership*—from the plant employee who serves on the waste-disposal planning board to the CEO who provides leadership through participation on a national commission on the environment, some companies have found that the lending of time and expertise is often more effective in solving an EH&S problem than simply throwing money at it (which is usually more costly and seldom appreciated).

Elements of Corporate Programs

As varied as the types of initiatives can be, there are a number of common elements in those that have succeeded:

- *Top management commitment*—from the CEO and delegated in such a way that it's clear that it's everyone's job—not just an individual staff person's assignment. Too often, the CEO and the EH&S staff are committed, but middle management has no direct stake in the outcome. This commitment must include giving the initiative the priority and resources necessary to get the job done.

- *Understanding the issues*—both the science and the perceptions of the various publics. Too often industry embraces the science but rejects the perceptions. And sometimes we bank too much on science that isn't all that key to the issue at hand or is shaky in its validity or has been rejected already by a constituency that isn't ready to believe you or your science. "Perception is reality" to us all, and understanding the perception can help find a solution. Preaching science never does.

- *Policy, plans, vision statements, objectives, rewards, Total Quality Management*— all the "bells and whistles" used to engage the organization in its regular business issues are needed to give EH&S initiatives an equal footing. An EH&S initiative is a long-range undertaking. It must be planned for and kept alive as such.

- *Dialogue, dialogue, dialogue*—it can't be overdone if it's open, honest, and two-way. Dialogue with critics, neighbors, employees, experts, regulators—anyone with a stake and an opinion. Have a communications plan for each constituency and pay attention to them all. Look at your program critically, through the eyes of your critics and ask tough questions. Is it credible?

- *Train, staff, organize, and allocate resources to meet the needs*—EH&S initiatives often need new or different skills than were required in the past. Few plant managers came into the 1980s with the communications skills necessary to dialogue with the community or respond to the media.

- *Take whatever help you can get, but get it*—EH&S initiatives are still in their infancy. The experts are few and still learning. Work through trade associations or others to identify the experts; get whatever you can for free and pay for the rest.

- *Be a missionary*—learn by helping others. As Mercedes says in its commercial, "Some things are too important not to share." Share your knowledge and expertise and remember: If a competitor's plant blows up, you will be tarred by the same brush.

  We have obviously said to ourselves that we don't want to be dragged, kicking and screaming, into the Age of the Environment by government or an angry public. Instead, we dare to believe we can lead, rather than follow, change. We can do a better job than the bureaucrats in making our operations safe for employees, the public and the environment. And in doing so we have a chance to convince the public that the world's resources are safe for future generations.

> *Robert D. Kennedy, chairman and chief executive officer, Union Carbide Corporation (Remarks to the First International Responsible Care Workshop, Rotterdam, The Netherlands, April 9, 1991).*

Public Involvement

If there is one "must" in designing or evaluating EH&S initiatives, it is involving the public in a meaningful way. The only thing worse than not involving them is doing so in a token or contrived way. Early in this chapter we referred to fear of the unknown. Neighbors of industrial plants have lived in the shadow of production units for a lifetime and have not known what materials were used, what products were made, or why.

Public involvement requires community outreach. There's plenty of room for innovative ideas in community outreach. Plants have held open houses (one company will host a tour for anyone, anytime), published newsletters, installed "hot lines," established community advisory panels (CAPs), provided science teacher training, and held dialogues with the community whenever there's something to report.

"Chemistry is Cool" is an innovative outreach program targeted at middle school students, grades 5 through 8, and their teachers who by their own admission are not comfortable teaching science. It's a day-long workshop that comes right into the students' school. It helps battle the epidemic of "science-phobia" in middle schools and explodes the notion that chemistry is for nerds. During the school day workshop, students discover how chemistry impacts their lives in obvious and subtle ways. They have an opportunity to learn more about the products they eat and use, and they make and take home their own concoctions such as toothpaste and lipstick. "Chemistry is Cool" does not end when the last school bell rings that day. Each teacher is given a set of curriculum materials to be used in the classroom as post-lab activities. These activities and resources encourage and support the ongoing study of chemistry.

This innovative science outreach program will reach a couple of hundred thousand middle school students mainly in Ohio over the next few years, and should help keep their interest in and understanding of chemistry alive.

When we cannot get students to our facilities, we take our people to the students. By adopting area high schools and middle schools, we are able to find opportunities for our employees to share their time and talents within the classroom setting. They serve as excellent ambassadors for the field of chemistry and science. This is also where we as individuals can make an important contribution.

Education and public opinion are the major challenges of the chemical industry in the coming years.

> *David J. D'Antoni, president, Ashland Chemical, Inc.*

Accountability

Tracking and reporting progress is one of the toughest, most critical issues to be faced in an EH&S initiative, and there are no easy answers. In the early years of EH&S initiatives, the public offered encouragement and even some recognition for industry efforts. As these initiatives matured, the public began to ask how to track industry progress on their own (short of just accepting industry data and reports). To respond to this public concern, many companies are publishing detailed environmental annual reports and looking at ways of having these reports independently audited. It is obvious, however, that quality validation techniques such as the ISO 9000 European quality system or other ways to involve community groups more intimately in the assessment of your progress are essential to building credibility.

Criticism

Public interest groups are at best supportive of the expressed intent of voluntary initiatives and remain to be shown whether voluntary industry initiatives are all that they purport to be. Some groups seem threatened by these initiatives, and a few have focused their efforts on discrediting them. These groups appear to be concerned that any public relaxation of pressure on industry in EH&S matters will slow or stop legislative and regulatory pressures (based on a belief that industry is being sufficiently self-regulating to preclude the need for more mandates). There is also the reality that public interest groups are dues-funded, and any regeneration of public confidence in industry would almost certainly be followed by a decline in revenues.

> Public Concern about the environment has continued for many years now. The environmental issue has not proven to be a transient one. It is not a fad. It will not go away. Continuous Improvement is being driven by the continuously increasing expectations of the public.
> *John D. Ong, chairman and chief executive officer, The BFGoodrich Company (Remarks to the Chemical Industry Council of New Jersey, April 23, 1991).*

Most industry officials associated with either company or association initiatives avoid using stewardship as a reason not to regulate but instead keep the focus on performance improvement. It is clear, however, that the regulatory spiral is fed by perceived or actual performance failures; therefore, one cannot deny at least an indirect relationship. Indeed, if the performance and openness of a company improves, so too will its reputation. In turn the public, legislators, and regulators will be more likely to allow for increased self-regulation and to allow corporate stewardship to pick up where effective regulation stops.

Boardroom Concerns

Justifying EH&S stewardship is not difficult if the full societal cost of current behavior and practices is realized and internalized. This often requires a long-term view not always characteristic of most boards of directors. If management is preoccupied with the next quarter's results, it takes real leadership to invest in a stewardship program that might not pay off for a decade. Continuous improvement, whether it is fostered by an EH&S initiative or simply by a need for organizational change, takes time, money, and in most cases, a total commitment to change. To be successful, it must be done slowly, with a well-thought-out, well-orchestrated plan of action, and plenty of follow-through. Goals must be set and milestones established. A structure for both internal and external communication must be put into place. Continuous improvement requires continuous dedication. And the stumbling blocks are real. If your competitors are not spending on EH&S programs, your stockholders may question why you did. Just as there are shareholder groups that advocate EH&S stewardship, there are also those (Evelyn Davis et al.) who don't. Many companies have added people considered socially conscious to their boards in order to attain greater insight into EH&S matters. These members can provide a board of directors with a vastly different perspective than the one offered by a company's own directors and officers.

> Those of us charged with managing our businesses recognize that these environmental responsibilities do not displace other priorities. They are in addition to such long standing fundamental obligations of operating our plants competitively in an increasingly global market and earning a fair share for our shareholders.
> *John D. Ong, chairman and chief executive officer, The BFGoodrich Company*
> *(Remarks to the Chemical Industry Council of New Jersey, April 23, 1991).*

Challenges for the Future

As American industry moves into the twenty-first century it will continue to face EH&S challenges, from public opinion to global competition. To remain a vital, thriving competitor, American industry must gear up to meet the material needs of the next generation of consumers. A few key elements necessary to sustain industry in the next millennium are:

- Public confidence must be restored and continually nurtured. It may be decades before the American public renews its faith in industry and it won't happen unless industry accepts responsibility for its past actions and voluntarily facilitates changes in its EH&S behavior.

- We must be champions of education. America is ranked twenty-first in the world in education. Math and science skills must be improved drastically throughout the American population if the United States is to be a competitor in the global marketplace. The surest way to remain competitive in the global marketplace is to foster the level of education here at home. We cannot improve the confidence of the public or the government if only the best and brightest students have basic math and science skills.

- We must dispel the myth that a zero-risk society is achievable. The cost of complying with overly prescriptive, burdensome EH&S laws and regulations adversely impacts on our ability to compete, both domestically and internationally. We must learn to set priorities and allocate our money and talent where it will do the most good for the most people. Resources are limited, and they need to be balanced among the many critical needs of society.

By working with governments and the environmental community in a voluntary, proactive, productive and cooperative manner, we can make sustainable development a reality.

Frank P. Popoff, chairman and chief executive officer,
The Dow Chemical Company.

Responsible Care®: A Case Study

The introduction of this chapter mentions the Chemical Manufacturers Association's initiative called Responsible Care: A Public Commitment. The initiative commits CMA's member companies not only to improve the quality of their performance in health, safety, and environmental matters, but also to listen to public concerns about chemicals and respond to them. The initiative has six elements, discussed in detail below:

1. Guiding Principles
2. Codes of Management Practices
3. Public Advisory Panel
4. Member Self-Evaluation
5. Executive Leadership Groups
6. Obligation of Membership

The association's bylaws obligate member companies to subscribe to the Guiding Principles, to participate in the development of the codes and programs, and to make good-faith efforts to implement the program elements of the Responsible Care Initiative. When plans were made for Responsible Care, members of the board of directors recognized the eventual need to report performance to the public. To be consistent and useful, reports need to be based on standard measures that can be applied to every company and be easily understood by the public. As Responsible Care was developed, CMA began preliminary planning for performance measures. In 1990, CMA asked every code development task group to start working on reporting systems. Some of those groups were able to find systems quickly in existing government reporting requirements. Others have had more difficulty. CMA's goal is to define measures for all codes by 1993.

Responsible Care is far from being at a point where the chemical industry can claim victory or even success. Progress is, however, being made and the association remains firmly committed to the concept. All six Codes of Management Practices are in various stages of implementation. At the urging of the Public Advisory Panel, CMA launched an advertising campaign to tell the public about the initiative and to invite questions. This approach, of telling the public what we intend to do rather than waiting for results before we talk, has drawn fire from some critics—particularly the slogan "don't trust us, track us" (i.e., see if we do what we've said we will do). The advisory panel felt this approach was necessary to put our commitment on the line and to accept accountability for results. In addition to the six elements outlined above, CMA has expanded its Responsible Care efforts to include a Partnership Program, whereby affiliated associations, both foreign and domestic, and nonmember firms can adopt the program or create look-alike versions. CMA has also developed a Mutual Assistance Program for members needing help to implement the initiative.

Any effort made by the chemical industry to meet public expectations won't be successful without finding out what those expectations are. Dialogue with the public has become such an important task for the chemical industry that it is the first of the 10 Guiding Principles of Responsible Care. CMA expects member companies to provide opportunities for the public to say what concerns them about the chemical industry. The member companies are expected to listen and respond to these concerns.

The association, speaking for its member companies, has gone on record inviting the public to participate in this dialogue. It stresses that dialogue must occur at the local level, where the industry's operations have their greatest impacts on people. Through a Public Outreach Program unveiled in June 1991, CMA is publicizing the industry's commitment and asking people to get involved.

This program will get the message of Responsible Care to 10 audiences: the general public, employees, plant communities, educators and students, local interest groups, national interest groups, federal officials, state officials, company shareholders, and the news media.

One part of the program is an advertising campaign built around some of the fundamental questions people have about chemicals and the chemical industry. The ads try to respond to these questions. But when people want more information, they can call a toll-free phone number.

Advertising is only part of the program, however. More than 50 other activities are being implemented. They carry the same message: CMA members are working to improve their operations and are inviting public scrutiny. CMA and member company representatives are briefing congressional delegations and the news media. Sample surveys designed for employees and plant neighbors are being prepared to help facility managers define important local issues. To assist teachers, the association has published a guide to member companies' science education assistance programs. Progress for the industry will depend on the work of individual companies. Each can offer anecdotal accounts of what they have done or are doing under Responsible Care: meetings between plant managers and members of the community, training chemical industry emergency responders, working closely with communities to be prepared for any incident involving chemicals. Chemical emissions are declining. Companies are working with transporters of their products to make shipments safer. Safety experts are inspecting plants annually and recommending that processes be redesigned or procedures be rewritten to make operations safer for employees and the community.

These are only the first steps. Companies are making progress, but CMA doesn't expect full implementation of every code at every facility to be accomplished overnight. Realistically, it could take years. And because improvement will be continuous, there is no "cutoff" in sight when companies can say "we are finished."

1. The Ten Guiding Principles

The Guiding Principles of Responsible Care are statements of the philosophy and commitment by each member company regarding environmental health and safety responsibilities in the management of chemicals. Each member company has pledged to operate according to the Guiding Principles and has signed a statement to that effect. Ascribing to the Guiding Principles is considered an obligation of membership in CMA. Member companies of the Chemical Manufacturers Association are committed to support a continuing effort to improve the industry's responsible management of chemicals. They pledge to manage their businesses according to these principles.

Responsible Care® Guiding Principles

- To recognize and respond to community concerns about chemicals and operations
- To develop and produce chemicals that can be manufactured, transported, used, and disposed of safely
- To make health, safety, and environment considerations a priority in planning for all existing and new products and processes
- To report promptly to officials, employees, customers, and the public, information on chemical-related health or environmental hazards and to recommend protective measures
- To counsel customers on the safe use, transportation, and disposal of chemical products
- To operate plants and facilities in a manner that protects the environment and the health and safety of employees and the public
- To extend knowledge by conducting or supporting research on the health, safety, and environmental effects of products, processes, and waste materials
- To work with others to resolve problems created by past handling and disposal of hazardous substances
- To participate with government and others in creating responsible laws, regulations, and standards to safeguard the community, workplace, and environment
- To promote the principles and practices of Responsible Care by sharing experiences and offering assistance to others who produce, handle, use, transport, or dispose of chemicals

---

2. The Six Codes of Management Practices

In 1989, work began on developing the Responsible Care Codes of Management Practices. The impetus for developing a specific code came from either a public concern or a substantive need to voluntarily improve performance, or both. The codes, which were developed by technical experts on various CMA committees and approved by CMA's membership, define a series of objectives for continuous improvement in operating practices rather than prescribe absolute or quantitative standards. They are:

Code	Date approved
Community Awareness and Emergency Response (CAER)	November 6, 1989
Process Safety	September 11, 1990
Pollution Prevention	April 6, 1990
Expanded	September 6, 1991
Distribution	November 5, 1990
Employee Health and Safety	January 14, 1992
Product Stewardship	April 14, 1992

In addition to these six, CMA has, in cooperation with the Association of American Railroads, implemented an extension of CAER and the Distribution Code called TransCaer. This program extends the concepts of community awareness and emergency response to the many communities through which chemicals are transported by railroad. Since the codes are intended to serve as objectives, they complement existing member company programs or practices that achieve the same goals. Some of the changing attitudes Responsible Care promises are becoming evident as the Codes of Management Practice are implemented.

The CAER Code

The Responsible Care Codes of Management Practices build on the success of the voluntary Community Awareness and Emergency Response (CAER) program that CMA initiated in 1985 to respond to public concern about accidental chemical releases. Within 2 years, more than 1100 facilities had CAER activities to improve joint community and industry emergency response efforts. This voluntary program received praise and broad support among public emergency response groups and was the first area targeted for code development. On November 6, 1989, CMA's board approved CAER as the first of Codes of Management Practices under Responsible Care.

The CAER code is a dual-purpose code intended to bring the chemical industry and local communities together through communication and cooperative emergency planning. It requires companies to communicate with the public about their operations and respond to the community's concerns. It requires companies to have a joint emergency response plan with community responders and to test it annually.

As part of CAER, companies are organizing community advisory panels. In the Houston Ship Channel, where the industry is concentrated, 25 companies have joined forces in convening a panel. Companies are providing tours of facilities to the public. One Connecticut plant took a group of children interested in the environment on a special tour. Other companies regularly hold neighborhood nights and send newsletters to plant neighbors so residents are better informed of plant operations. In emergency response, a group of companies in the Delaware River Valley sponsored a training class on polyvinyl chloride, which they manufacture, for volunteer firefighters in the area. In Michigan, CMA members and other companies worked with the state in building a hazardous materials training center for public and private emergency responders. At the local level, companies are holding drills with fire and rescue companies, are donating time and materials to local emergency planning commissions, and are responding to requests for assistance when firefighters and other responders need specialists and equipment in handling chemical incidents.

> The first Responsible Care code was Community Awareness and Emergency Response (CAER). This code requires companies to work closely with local emergency responders—police, firemen, civil defense personnel, hospitals—to plan and prepare for possible chemical emergencies. The skills learned in the mock disasters and tabletop drills are also useful for responding to natural disasters.
>
> The value of such CAER training was proven in dramatic fashion several years ago in Charleston, Tennessee, the site of a major Olin plant that produces chlorine-based swimming pool sanitizing chemicals. Working with numerous state and local emergency-response agencies, Olin staged a mock train derailment at night involving leaking chlorine rail cars and Olin employees feigning injuries. The elaborate drill included cordoning off the accident scene and stopping the spill, giving first-aid to the "injured" and transporting them to area hospitals, and alerting the surrounding community to the emergency situation. The outside agencies involved in the drill included the local sheriff's department, the Tennessee Highway Patrol, Bradley County Memorial Hospital, the Charleston and Cleveland (Tennessee) fire departments, and state and local emergency management personnel. The drill was followed by a critique by all involved to pinpoint problems and propose ways of improving response. Several months after that drill, a train carrying chemical products from another company derailed one night in Charleston within two miles of our simulated accident scene! The agencies which responded to the derailment said Olin's CAER drill was of enormous help in their successful efforts to contain and clean up the spilled material and to prevent the accident from turning into a tragedy. In fact, although half the population of Charleston was evacuated in the wake of the derailment, no one was injured during the entire incident.
>
> Joining the agencies in responding to the actual accident were members of OCEAN—the Olin Corporation Emergency Action Network, our emergency-response "SWAT team." This team, which also conducted the CAER drill, is trained and equipped to respond to emergencies involving Olin products or even chemicals from other companies. OCEAN teams are in place at key Olin sites across America.
>
> *John Johnstone, Olin Corporation (Reprinted with Permission from CMA).*

Finding a measuring system for the CAER code has been difficult because it is a code with two purposes. Methods such as recording either the number of community outreach and emergency response activities or the number of hours employees spent in such activities have been considered.

A major challenge for CMA members is to convince employees and residents of communities that their commitment to Responsible Care and the Codes of Management Practices is sincere and unwavering. Public understanding and support is crucial to Responsible Care's success. Employee enthusiasm for and involvement in Responsible Care will determine the rate of progress. Residents of plant communities will judge whether the industry is really willing to be accountable.

One encouraging sign that dialogue is developing can be found in the growing number of community advisory panels across the country. For the public, panels are a signal that companies are beginning to listen and take community opinions into account. Every panel is an opportunity to build dialogue between industry managers and the communities they work and live in. Member companies are discussing goals for implementation of Responsible Care openly with panels and are reporting progress to them. They are also inviting local panels to participate in helping them set goals and to follow their facilities' progress.

Responsible Care and CMA have been criticized. Not everyone accepts it as a true change. Some point to the lack of third-party audits of companies' claims of progress as evidence that the initiative is little more than a public relations campaign. CMA is responding to this criticism by encouraging member companies to organize community advisory panels and to share their work in Responsible Care with the panels so they can judge the company's performance.

Dow Chemical's plant in Plaquemine, Louisiana, opened dialogue with the community by inviting town residents to serve on a community advisory panel. The panel and plant management meet regularly and discuss issues surrounding the plant's operations. These discussions give panel members the chance to voice their thoughts and feelings about the plant. Having heard townspeople's opinions, the plant management can move to solve problems that arise.

During one meeting, panel members suggested more needed to be done to publicize the parish emergency warning system and that citizens needed better understanding of what to do in a chemical emergency. The feedback was shared, and chemical companies in the Iberville Parish jointly worked with parish emergency preparedness officials to publish more information about emergency response, train students in area schools, and make door-to-door visits to homes near the plant. In addition, the companies bought equipment to broadcast alerts and instructions over the local cable TV system in an emergency. Other equipment was purchased that would call residents and deliver emergency messages by phone.

The Process Safety Code

The Process Safety Code applies to the manufacturing plants and processes of the chemical industry and is designed to prevent fires, explosions, or chemical releases. The code requires safety audits, inspection and maintenance programs, and safety training for employees and contract workers.

One Texas plant formed eight teams to conduct safety audits and assigned each team to an area of the plant. As part of its safety review process, that company conducts monthly safety reviews of each section of the plant. Items needing repairs are routed to a special maintenance team. Another company discusses safety issues with its community advisory panel, and their concerns are considered in designing process safety systems. That company also annually reviews safety of highly hazardous processes. At another company's Texas facility, contractors are integrated into the plant's employee safety training programs to make them aware of plant procedures.

American Cyanamid Company began implementing the Process Safety Code by issuing a process safety management guideline in 1990. The guideline outlined 13 process safety management functions, which were used in developing a plan with specific goals for implementation.

Each month all of Cyanamid's plants report their progress to senior management. Most of the company's major chemical plants put 85% of the plan in place by the end of 1991. To check the plants' work, the company expanded an existing audit program to include the guidelines and created computerized tracking systems that can issue summaries of progress to plant management or to those responsible for corrective action. In addition to the tracking system, American Cyanamid has put computerized maintenance systems in place at many of its plants. This software is often designed to automatically generate work or inspection orders according to a schedule and can be used to document irregularities found during inspections.

Many companies have collected data on fires, explosions, and accidental chemical releases occurring at their sites. No one has collected these data on an industrywide basis, but using a database known as the Process Safety Performance Tracking, or PROSPECT, CMA intends to gather information on incidents at member company sites. Every accident that meets certain criteria for severity, location, and chemical involvement will be recorded. PROSPECT will be able to create reports on the rates or types of incidents—fires, for example—within various segments of the industry.

The Pollution Prevention Code

The objective of the Pollution Prevention Code is to decrease the amount of pollution and hazardous waste generated by the chemical industry. Where waste cannot be eliminated, the code is designed to promote sound management of it. The code requires companies to look for ways to curb the release of wastes to air, land, and water. Where waste cannot be reduced, companies have to consider ways to safely manage and dispose of it. Methods companies use in reducing emissions can range from recycling, substituting raw materials, or redesigning manufacturing processes to better maintenance procedures or installing new pollution control equipment. The Pollution Prevention Code supersedes many chemical industry waste reduction programs and policies that were in effect prior to Responsible Care. CMA members that are subject to Section 313 of SARA are required by law to report emissions of those chemicals to the government on an annual basis. Under the Pollution Prevention Code, member companies are required to file duplicate reports with the association. From the list of 330 chemicals, CMA has culled a core group of 320 that have been on the list since the law went into effect in 1987. This core list allows CMA to measure emissions consistently and establish trends in performance. Between 1987 and 1990, the year for which the latest information is available, CMA members reported cuts of 35% in releases of the core group of chemicals. Shipments of these chemicals to other facilities for treatment or disposal were down 33% for the same period. CMA also plans to require its members to submit data on the generation, treatment, and disposal of hazardous wastes.

An indicator that the Pollution Prevention Code is changing the way industry views its responsibility came when EPA Administrator William Reilly called on 600 industrial companies to join his voluntary Industrial Toxics Reduction Project (ITP). Under this program, companies who pledge to reduce their emissions of 17 high-priority ITP compounds by 50% by 1996 are given considerable flexibility in determining how to achieve those reductions. Of the 81 CMA members asked to join the ITP effort, 77 immediately agreed to do so. By contrast, of the remaining 519 companies asked from other industries only 40% volunteered.

One Tennessee company set up a comprehensive waste-minimization program that systematically reviews and records waste-minimization improvements in 250 manufacturing processes. A company in Massachusetts discovered that a waste from its operations could be sold as a product that makes concrete stronger and more resistant to chemicals. One company designed a pollution control device that controls vapor releases that occur when barges are loaded. It has volunteered to share the technology with other companies. (Check with CMA for details.)

One company installed a scrubbing system that collects chlorine (once vented into the air), neutralizes it, and returns it to the manufacturing system.

Monsanto Company began pollution-prevention planning prior to code adoption in 1990. In 1988, Monsanto voluntarily announced a goal of reducing air emissions of toxic chemicals by 90% from 1987. The company set the end of 1992 as its deadline. After 3 years, Monsanto has cut its U.S. emissions from 18.4 to 7.8 million pounds, a drop of 58%. The company has plans and programs in place to meet its goals.

These reductions have been achieved at facilities throughout the United States. In Nitro, West Virginia, for example, a modification in raw materials used in a rubber chemicals process reduced the facility's air emissions by more than a third. At its nylon fibers plant in Pensacola, Florida, engineers modified two pollution-control systems that reduced emissions by 95%.

The company's agricultural and chemical units broadened this goal to target reductions of waste releases to all environmental media. Monsanto's preferred solution is to avoid generating waste in the first place.

The Distribution Code

The Distribution Code's objective is to make the transportation of chemicals safer, regardless of the carrier or mode of shipment. As part of this code, companies must evaluate the risks associated with distribution of their products and reduce them. They must set up a qualifying process for carriers that emphasizes safety performance and regulatory compliance. They must review the performance of the people who transport and handle their products, whether they are employees, carriers, distributors, or contractors, to make sure they meet the company's expectation and regulatory standards. And they have to advise and assist responders at an emergency involving their products. In implementing the code, one Ohio company has set standards for carriers of its products. In reviewing carriers' performance, the company has excluded those that did not meet its standards from carrying its products. A Pennsylvania company hosted a two-part drill that simulated accidents involving a tank truck, train, and towboat and "spills" onto land and into water. One company has redesigned its tank trucks to make them safer and less susceptible to rollovers that cause tanks to rupture. Another company has modified one of its distribution centers in Florida so that it can contain any accidental releases of a chemical during loading or unloading.

FMC Corporation used the Distribution Code as a guide in transportation planning for a new business—the sale of liquid sodium cyanide to mining companies. Developing transportation operations in accordance with the Distribution Code resulted in equipment that exceeded regulatory standards for safety and more rigorous training for employees and emergency responders. The liquid sodium cyanide is shipped in railroad tank cars and tank trucks that exceed the U.S. Department of Transportation standards. The shell of the tank trucks, for example, is twice as thick as the law requires. Safety rollovers surrounding the tanker are designed to right it in an accident. Trucks are tracked via satellite to monitor their location.

Drivers have been thoroughly trained in the procedures for the safe handling and delivery of the product. Part of their training includes how to handle an emergency. Railroad supervisors were also trained, and they in turn met with all their crews that handle sodium cyanide.

Before any deliveries were made, FMC personnel trained customers' employees, and FMC gave customers safety manuals and videos about the product. FMC will also lead refresher training and conduct safety audits for customers.

Delivery routes pass through several towns between FMC's plant and its terminal. In keeping with the Responsible Care philosophy of listening to community concerns, teams of FMC and Union Pacific Railroad employees went to every town along delivery routes and met with local officials before any of the product was shipped. The company then led training for firefighters, police officers, and members of the local emergency response commissions in those towns.

The most promising measurement appears to be adapting statistics compiled by the U.S. Department of Transportation, the National Response Center, or some states. Any measuring system would also have to take into account member companies' shipments hauled by other companies.

The Employee Health and Safety Code

The Employee Health and Safety Code's objective is to continuously improve the protection of the more than 1.1 million people who work for the chemical industry. Contract workers working at member company sites and visitors are protected under the code as well. Employees at 60 companies reviewed the code before it was adopted to ensure it addresses employee concerns. The code requires companies to better communicate health and safety information to employees and involve them in making the workplace safer. Training programs that teach employees how to work more safely and better protect themselves are expected to be developed. Companies will review facilities, operations, and processes for potential hazards and, where hazards are present, monitor employees' health. The code also requires that hazards be prevented or controlled through use of health and safety equipment, preventive maintenance programs, and quick investigation of illnesses, injuries, and accidents. When incidents do occur, companies are expected to take corrective action. To track member progress with the Employee Health and Safety Code and to determine whether occupational injury and illness rates among companies are rising or falling, records required by government will be filed with CMA.

The Product Stewardship Code

Product Stewardship, the final Code of Management Practices, encompasses every aspect of a company's products, from proposal to disposal. Its objective is to reduce product risks to health, safety, and the environment. The code extends the principles of Responsible Care beyond the product manufacturer to suppliers, customers, and distributors. Member companies are expected to work with those they do business with to foster proper use and handling of the chemical products. The code, among other things, encourages members to increase customer education programs, gather information about how customers use their products, and revise health and safety recommendations accordingly.

In anticipation of the Product Stewardship Code, ARCO Chemical organized a product stewardship committee responsible for implementing the code within the company. The committee is working on new procedures under the code for reviewing new products and processes. These reviews are intended to identify risks. They will be conducted on the entire life cycle of ARCO's existing products and on all new products and new applications of existing products.

---

3. Public Advisory Panel

The Public Advisory Panel is an important element in the Responsible Care initiative. Comprised of approximately 15 citizens who are considered to be thought leaders in health, safety, or environmental issues, the Public Advisory Panel is a CMA effort. The panelists represent a broad range of viewpoints on Responsible Care, act as a sounding board for the association, and assist in identifying programs that are responsive to public concerns. Since its inception in 1989, the panel has played a key role in advising the industry on Responsible Care, in particular, on the development of the Codes of Management Practices. More generally, the panel has broadened CMA's understanding of public concerns about chemicals in our society. The panel meets five times a year, and often tours local chemical industry sites. During its meetings, the panel critiques the initiative and suggests ways CMA member companies can better communicate with the public. Their recommendations are published in CMA's Responsible Care Annual Report.

4. Member Self-Evaluation

Effective performance evaluation is a critical element of Responsible Care. Each Code of Management Practices includes a Self-Evaluation Form that measures a company's progress in implementing the code. Member companies submit annually to CMA a self-evaluation on each element of each code (almost 100 in all). After compiling the results, CMA reports the industry's collective implementation progress to the public. Each company is expected to report continued progress, although CMA does not expect every company to be at the same level of performance for each Code of Management Practices.

5. Executive Leadership Groups

Executive Leadership Groups (ELGs) are another important element of the Responsible Care initiative. They were formed to help facilitate and support each member company's continual progress and improvement with implementation of the initiative. In periodic regional meetings, senior officials of member companies look at the Code of Management Practices requirements, the progress members are making implementing the codes, and identify areas where individual companies may need help from CMA or other member companies.

6. Obligation of Membership

Participation in the Responsible Care initiative is an obligation of membership in CMA. A member company's obligation to Responsible Care extends to all of its chemical businesses. As part of its commitment to Responsible Care, each member company is obligated to (a) sign the Guiding Principles of Responsible Care; (b) communicate the commitment to Responsible Care to employees; (c) make good-faith efforts to implement the Codes of Management Practices, participate in the self-evaluation process, and meet the expectations of the Responsible Care programs; and (d) use the Responsible Care name and logo in accordance with CMA's guidelines.

In addition, each member company is expected to take part in the development of programs under the initiative. In extreme circumstances, where a member company has consistently failed to conduct its business in accordance with the tenets and objectives of Responsible Care, CMA will pursue corrective measures with the company that could include the disassociation of the company from membership.

The Partnership Program

In 1990, CMA opened Responsible Care to affiliated associations and nonmember companies. Chemical Industry Councils in 10 states have become partners, with the Chlorine Institute and the Florida Phosphate Council joining as allied associations. Several companies are under consideration to become partners. To become a partner company, an applicant must meet the same obligations as CMA member companies. Its senior management must sign the Guiding Principles and communicate Responsible Care to employees. The company has to make good-faith efforts to implement all of the Codes of Management Practices and complete self-evaluations. CMA representatives will evaluate applicants as part of the application process. These evaluations will give the association an opportunity to review the applicant's understanding of and commitment to Responsible Care. The applicant must demonstrate that it is prepared to go beyond the law's requirements and that it will communicate information to employees. It must also be prepared to provide the personnel and financial resources needed to implement Responsible Care.

The Mutual Assistance Program

CMA's Mutual Assistance Program for Responsible Care is designed to facilitate assistance from the association, and the sharing of information between member companies. CMA has designed a computer bulletin board which can be accessed by member companies looking for help with Responsible Care. Members can use it to locate experts within or retired from other member companies who are willing to work as consultants on code implementation. Member companies themselves have listed guides, training programs, and other Responsible Care–related information they are willing to lend. The association has compiled "networking" lists of facilities located near each other. Grouping sites which are close to each other is the first step in helping facility managers exchange information about Responsible Care or pool resources for implementing it.

Responsible Care's Global Growth

In only a few years, the principles of the Responsible Care initiative have traveled across the globe. The Canadian Chemical Industry, which originated the concept, and CMA have joined in promoting the international spread of the initiative. CMA is one of many national chemical associations that are part of the International Council of Chemical Associations (ICCA). ICCA is encouraging more executives of international companies to accept the challenges of the Responsible Care initiative. Responding to the spread of the initiative, ICCA has formed a Responsible Care Leadership Group, which is designing a review process for countries interested in starting their own programs. It aims to assure common commitments and obligations of the initiative. The programs have similar objectives: to develop continuous improvement goals, to increase communication with the public and between member companies, to protect and ensure the long-term growth of the industry, to monitor performance, to build credibility, and to be accountable to the public.

In addition, with assistance from CMA, the United Nations Environment Program (UNEP) has launched APELL (Awareness and Preparedness for Emergencies at Local Level), a project aimed at developing an emergency preparedness program and handbook. APELL's goals are to (1) promote community awareness about possible risks from hazardous materials and the steps taken by authorities and industry to protect the community; and (2) based on this community awareness, to develop response plans for the community to follow in the event of an accident. The handbook is targeted at an international audience and describes elements of CMA's CAER Program, in addition to other programs. APELL calls for communities to form

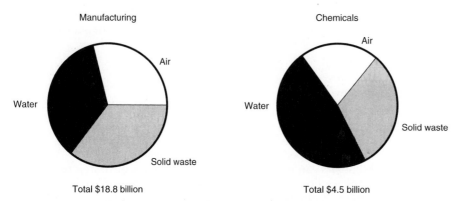

Figure 7-1. Composition of 1991 pollution abatement costs.

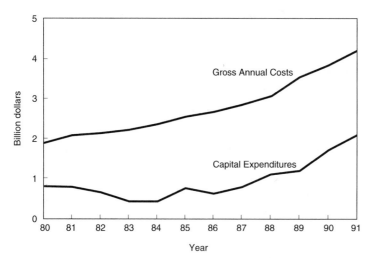

Figure 7-2. Chemical industry pollution abatement.

coordinating groups where government, citizen's groups, and industry can work together.

Responsible Care is not a quick fix program. Once we reach one set of goals, we'll ratchet up the objectives and strive to meet them in turn. Our ultimate goal is to regain the respect and trust of the American public. In doing so, we hope that the chemical industry can continue to play its natural role as one of the main engines of America's economic growth as well as the source of solutions to some of our nation's most challenging environmental problems.

It started with a revolutionary idea—that chemical companies, large and small, can come together to improve their collective environmental performance. And do it in partnership with the public.

Robert D. Kennedy, chairman and chief executive officer, Union Carbide Corporation (Remarks to the First International Responsible Care Workshop.)

Table 7-1. U.S. Spending for Pollution Abatement and Control (Billion Dollars)

Item	1980	1990	1991
Gross domestic product	2708.0	5513.8	5672.6
Pollution abatement and control	1.98%	1.86%	1.97%
Pollution abatement and control spending	53.54	102.80	111.50
Business	32.28	63.30	68.50
Government and other	21.26	39.50	43.00

SOURCE: Bureau of Economic Analysis. 1990 and 1991 data are CMA estimates based on EPA data.

Table 7-2. Pollution Abatement Gross Annual Costs by Media (Million Dollars)

Item	1980	1990	1991
Manufacturing	8,142	17,070	18,825
Air	3,298	5,011	5,550
Water	3,193	6,416	6,975
Solid waste	1,651	5,643	6,300
Chemicals and allied products	1,852	3,944	4,450
Air	540	842	950
Water	943	1,799	2,000
Solid waste	369	1,303	1,500

SOURCE: Bureau of the Census; 1991 data are CMA estimates based on BEA, Census, and EPA data.

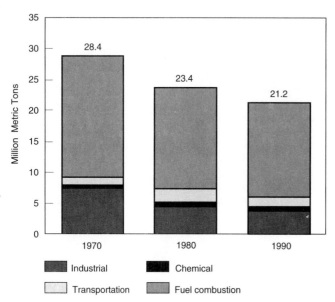

Figure 7-3. U.S. emissions of sulfur oxides by source.

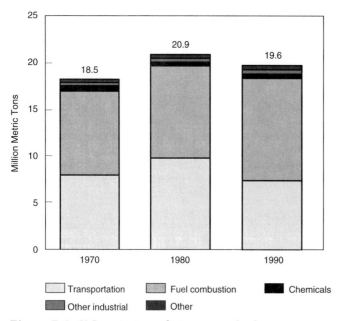

Figure 7-4. U.S. emissions of nitrogen oxides by source.

Table 7-3. U.S. Emissions of Sulfur Oxides by Source (Million Metric Tons)

Item	1970	1980	1990
Total sulfur oxide emissions	<u>28.4</u>	<u>23.4</u>	<u>21.2</u>
Transportation	0.6	0.9	0.9
Fuel combustion	21.3	18.7	17.1
Industrial processes:	6.4	3.8	3.1
Chemicals and allied products	0.5	0.3	0.3
Other industrial	5.9	3.5	3.1
Chemicals as a % of total emissions	1.9%	1.1%	1.5%

SOURCE: Environmental Protection Agency.

Table 7-4. U.S. Emissions of Nitrogen Oxides by Source (Million Metric Tons)

Item	1970	1980	1990
Total nitrogen oxide emissions	<u>18.5</u>	<u>20.9</u>	<u>19.6</u>
Transportation	8.0	9.8	7.5
Fuel combustion	9.1	10.1	11.2
Industrial processes:	0.7	0.7	0.6
Chemicals and allied products	0.2	0.2	0.2
Other industrial	0.5	0.5	0.4
Solid waste	0.4	0.1	0.1
Miscellaneous	0.3	0.2	0.3
Chemicals as a % of total emissions	1.3%	1.0%	0.8%

SOURCE: Environmental Protection Agency.

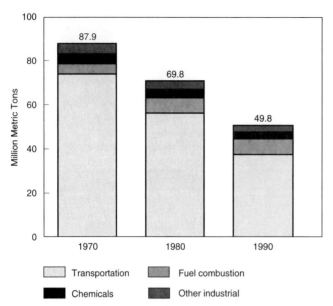

Figure 7-5. U.S. carbon monoxide emissions by source (excluding solid waste and miscellaneous).

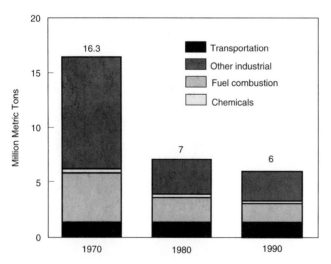

Figure 7-6. U.S. emissions of particulates by source (excluding solid waste and miscellaneous).

Table 7-5. U.S. Emissions of Carbon Monoxide by Source (Million Metric Tons)

Item	1970	1980	1990
Total carbon monoxide emissions	101.4	79.6	60.1
Transportation	74.4	56.1	37.6
Fuel combustion	4.5	7.4	7.5
Industrial plant	9.0	6.3	4.7
Chemicals and allied products	3.1	2.0	1.7
Other industrial	5.9	4.3	3.0
Solid waste	6.4	2.2	1.7
Miscellaneous	7.2	7.6	8.6
Chemicals as a % of total emissions	3.0%	2.5%	2.9%

SOURCE: Environmental Protection Agency.

Table 7-6. U.S. Emissions of Particulates by Source (Million Metric Tons)

Item	1970	1980	1990
Total particulate emissions	18.5	8.5	7.5
Transportation	1.2	1.3	1.5
Fuel combustion	4.6	2.4	1.7
Industrial processes:	10.5	3.3	2.8
Chemicals and allied products	0.2	0.1	0.1
Other industrial	10.3	3.2	2.7
Solid waste	1.1	0.4	0.3
Miscellaneous	1.1	1.1	1.2
Chemicals as a % of total emissions	1.2%	1.6%	1.3%

SOURCE: Environmental Protection Agency.

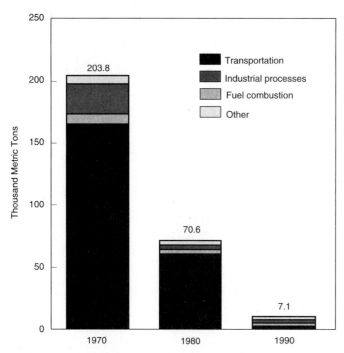

Figure 7-7. U.S. emissions of lead by source.

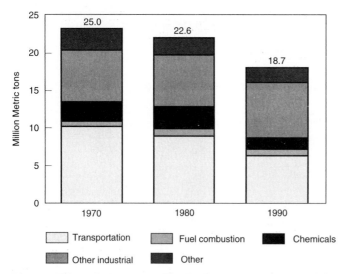

Figure 7-8. U.S. emissions of volatile organic compounds by source.

Table 7-7. U.S. Emissions of Lead by Source (Thousand Metric Tons)*

Item	1970	1980	1990
Total lead emissions	203.8	70.6	7.1
Transportation	163.6	59.4	2.2
Fuel combustion	9.6	3.9	0.5
Industrial processes	23.9	3.6	2.2
Solid waste	6.7	3.7	2.2

SOURCE: Environmental Protection Agency.
*The EPA does not break out the chemical industry separately.

Table 7-8. U.S. Emissions of Volatile Organic Compounds (VOCs) by Source (Million Metric Tons)

Item	1970	1980	1990
Total VOC emissions	25.0	22.6	18.7
Transportation	10.3	9.0	6.4
Fuel combustion	0.6	0.9	0.9
Industrial processes:	8.9	9.2	8.1
Chemicals and allied products	1.6	1.8	1.9
Other industrial	7.4	7.4	6.2
Solid waste	1.8	0.6	0.6
Miscellaneous	3.3	2.9	2.7
Chemicals as a % of total emissions	6.2%	8.1%	10.1%

SOURCE: Environmental Protection Agency.

Table 7-9. Occupational Injury and Illness Rates (per 100 Full-Time Employees)

Item	1980	1990
Total private sector:		
Total cases	8.7	8.8
Lost workday cases	4.0	4.1
Lost workdays	65.2	84.0
Manufacturing:		
Total cases	12.2	13.2
Lost workday cases	5.4	5.8
Lost workdays	86.7	120.7
Chemicals and allied products:		
Total cases	6.8	6.5
Lost workday cases	3.1	3.1
Lost workdays	50.3	61.6

SOURCE: Bureau of Labor Statistics.

Table 7-10. Transportation Incidents, Injuries, and Fatalities Involving Hazardous Materials

Item	1980	1990
Total incidents	15,737	8,687
Total injuries	626	390
Total fatalities by material:	19	4
Gasoline	n/a	3
Other petroleum products	n/a	0
Chemicals	n/a	1
Other materials	n/a	0

SOURCE: Department of Transportation.

Table 7-11. Risks and Cost-Effectiveness of Selected Regulations Affecting the U.S. Chemical Industry

Regulation*	Year issued	Health or safety	Agency	Baseline mortality risk per million exposed	Cost per premature death averted ($ millions 1990)
Underground Construction Standards†	1989	S	OSHA	38,700	0.1
Trihalomethane Drinking Water Standards	1979	H	EPA	420	0.2
Hazard Communication Standard†	1983	S	OSHA	1,800	1.6
Benzene NESHAP (Original: Fugitive Emissions)	1984	H	EPA	1,470	3.4
Ethylene Dibromide Drinking Water Standard	1991	H	EPA	NA	5.7
Benzene NESHAP (Revised: Coke By-Products)†	1988	H	EPA	NA	6.1
Asbestos Occupational Exposure Limit†	1972	H	OSHA	3,015	8.3
Benzene Occupational Exposure Limit†	1987	H	OSHA	39,600	8.9
Arsenic Emission Standards for Glass Plants	1986	H	EPA	2,660	13.5
Ethylene Oxide Occupational Exposure Limit†	1984	H	OSHA	1,980	20.5
Arsenic/Copper NESHAP	1986	H	EPA	63,000	23.0
Haz Waste Listing for Petroleum Refining Sludge	1990	H	EPA	210	27.6
Benzene NESHAP (Revised: Transfer Operations)	1990	H	EPA	NA	32.9
Acrylonitrile Occupational Exposure Limit†	1978	H	OSHA	42,300	51.5
Asbestos Occupational Exposure Limit†	1986	H	OSHA	3,015	74.0
Arsenic Occupational Exposure Limit†	1978	H	OSHA	14,800	106.9
Asbestos Ban	1989	H	EPA	NA	110.7
Diethylstilbestrol (DES) Cattlefeed Ban	1979	H	FDA	22	124.8
Benzene NESHAP (Revised: Waste Operations)	1990	H	EPA	NA	168.2
1,2-Dichloropropane Drinking Water Standard	1991	H	EPA	NA	653.0
Haz Waste Land Disposal Ban (1st 3rd)	1988	H	EPA	2	4,190.4
Municipal Solid Waste Landfill Standards (Proposed)	1988	H	EPA	<1	19,107.0
Formaldehyde Occupational Exposure Limit†	1987	H	OSHA	31	86,201.8
Atrazine/Alachlor Drinking Water Standard	1991	H	EPA	NA	92,069.7
Haz Waste Listing for Wood Preserving Chemicals	1990	H	EPA	<1	5,700,000.0

SOURCE: John F. Morrall III, "A Review of the Record," *Regulation,* vol. 10, no. 2 (1986), p. 30. Updated by Morrall et al.

*70-year lifetime exposure assumed unless otherwise specified.

†45-year lifetime exposure.

NA = not available.

A form of cost-benefit analysis, cost-effectiveness analysis attempts to determine the least cost of achieving a regulatory objective, in most cases the value of saving a statistical life. Baseline risks generally reflect the mortality risk per million of statistical lives exposed. In most cases the actual number of persons exposed is much less. Further, a 70- or 45-year lifetime exposure is often assumed. Given the mobility of the American labor force, actual exposure is often much lower. The cost per premature death averaged, or prevented, is based on the cost per estimated statistical life saved from regulatory policies. Because the actual risk is often lower, the actual costs per estimated life saved are generally much higher than original estimates.

References

Rayport, Jeffrey F., and George C. Lodge, *Responsible Care*, Harvard Business School, Boston, Mass., 1991.

Schmidheiny, Stephan, with the Business Council for Sustainable Development, *Changing Course: A Global Business Perspective on Development and the Environment*, MIT Press, 1992.

Safety Manager's Guide, Bureau of Business Practices, 1992.

Listening and Responding through Community Advisory Panels, Chemical Manufacturers Association, Washington, D.C., 1992.

Preventing Pollution in the Chemical Industry: 1987–1990, Chemical Manufacturers Association, Washington, D.C., 1992.

Corporate Environmental Excellence, Arthur D. Little, Inc., 1991.

PRISM, Third Quarter, 1991, Arthur D. Little, Inc., 1991.

Smart, Bruce, editor, *Beyond Compliance: A New Industry View of Compliance*, World Resources Institute, 1992.

Turning Commitment to Action: 1992 Responsible Care Progress Report, Chemical Manufacturers Association, Washington, D.C., 1992.

8

Developing an Environmental Action Plan for Business:*

Environment as a Standard Operating Practice—A Case Study

Jackie Prince

Richard Denison, Ph.D

Environmental Defense Fund (EDF)

In this chapter:

- Origins of EDF-McDonald's Task Force
- Task Force Activities and Results
- Task Force Process: A Retrospective View
- Integrating Environmental Considerations
- Emphasizing Continuous Improvements
- Environmental Quality and Cost
- McDonald's Leverage as a Customer
- New EDF Initiatives

---

*The EDF-McDonald's case description originally appeared in the article by Jackie Prince and Richard Denison, "Launching a New Business Ethic: Making the Environment a Standard Operating Procedure at McDonald's and Other Companies," *Industrial Management*, vol. 34, no. 6

To develop a strong environmental management program, companies must integrate environmental considerations into all operations ranging from design specifications and purchasing to quality reviews. This case study provides a summary of both the process and the accomplishments of the Environmental Defense Fund (EDF)–McDonald's waste-reduction task force. The EDF-McDonald's task force catalyzed a fundamental change in McDonald's business operations so that environmental considerations will now be considered on par with other business goals. The task force offers a concrete model for environmental protection efforts on several fronts. The tangible actions developed by the project, and now being implemented by McDonald's, serve as a model for reducing packaging and solid wastes. Together with the problem-solving process formulated by the task force, they also serve more broadly as models for how companies can institutionalize environmental ethics into everyday business decision making and how businesses can manage for environmental quality. Improved environmental management will add value to the company over the long term, not cost.

Finally, by bringing together diverse parties, this case can be used as a paradigm for future cooperative projects that rely on joint problem solving rather than filing a lawsuit or promulgating a regulation. While such efforts cannot replace traditional approaches to environmental protection, it is a strategy that should be added to the many tools already in use.

Public Reactions

When first announced, *The New York Times* called the EDF-McDonald's waste-reduction task force an "unusual deal" and said "if it works, it could change the way environmental groups interact with corporate America."[1] But some environmentalists were more skeptical: Ralph Nader commented that "Grassroots environmentalists aren't convinced that McDonald's is serious about creating a better environment."[2]

Then, at the halfway point, McDonald's announced that it would phase out polystyrene foam in favor of less bulky paper wraps. Now it was environmentalists who reacted favorably. Citizens Clearinghouse for Hazardous Waste, the grassroots group started by Lois Gibbs after Love Canal, officially ended its 3-year "McToxics" campaign. But makers of plastics were less

---

(November/December, 1992). For a more detailed description of the EDF-McDonald's agreement and the project in the context of solid waste management policies, see Jackie Prince, "Managing Materials to Conserve Resources: Re-Designing Solid Waste Management at McDonald's," *Duke Environmental Law & Policy Forum,* vol. II, Duke University School of Law, Durham, N.C., 1992. Finally, the results of the waste-reduction task force appear in EDF-McDonald's Waste Reduction Task Force, *Final Report,* Environmental Defense Fund and McDonald's Corporation, Washington, D.C., 1991.

pleased: *Plastics News,* a trade publication of the plastics industry, awarded EDF a "Televangelist Power-of-Persuasion Award" for "getting invited into McDonald's Boardroom and virtually overnight convincing the McDirectors to reverse their stance on polystyrene packaging."[3]

When the task force completed its work, a *Washington Post* editorial entitled "Less McWaste" concluded: "Waste reduction has become an explicit goal of a company that is a symbol of American popular culture. The process has been voluntary and is not just PR. If there are costs involved, the company seems to think there may also be consequential savings. The plan sets an excellent example. Good for McDonald's and EDF both."[4]

Ad Week opined that McDonald's was "rapidly transforming itself from the villain to the hero of the Green Decade" through actions sure to "make its outlets a regular pitstop for the `enviro' crowd."[5] An editorial in the *Minneapolis Star-Tribune* suggested that "the success of the unlikely partnership proves that Earth-lovers and profit-seekers need not be foes."[6] But it was perhaps *Rolling Stone,* of all places, that summed it up best in a feature article entitled "The Greening of the Golden Arches": "For years, corporate executives have argued that environmental considerations were a luxury they couldn't afford. McDonald's, nudged and advised by EDF, has adopted a strategy based on the opposite notion. Environmental action was something it could ill afford not to do."[7]

Origins of EDF-McDonald's Task Force

In 1989, EDF first approached McDonald's to discuss its solid waste problems. Right or wrong, McDonald's had come to symbolize the nation's solid waste problem. Through its early attempts to establish in-store recycling programs, McDonald's had demonstrated a desire to find practical solutions, but the issue remained unresolved. EDF recognized McDonald's role as an industry leader and saw an opportunity for developing a "blueprint" for other related businesses. EDF also saw the potential for a ripple effect that could extend positive results upstream to McDonald's more than 600 suppliers and downstream to its 18 million customers. Subsequently, EDF suggested the formation of a joint task force to study the materials used and solid wastes generated by McDonald's U.S. restaurants. A joint examination of McDonald's solid waste problems would also offer EDF's experts a chance to road-test its ideas in 8500 laboratories across the country: McDonald's restaurants.

McDonald's, recognizing EDF's solid waste expertise and the importance of seeking expert advice, agreed to EDF's suggestion to form a joint task force. Both parties also viewed the work as an opportunity to test a new approach to environmental problems through collaborative problem solving. But forming a task force involved substantial risks for both parties. For EDF, it was an unprecedented move to work with an entity that had long been criticized by environmental groups across the country as a sign of our disposable society—was EDF selling out to the enemy? On McDonald's side, the task force exposed the company to a great deal of scrutiny by an environmental organization, traditionally a thorn in its side. Thus a formal written agreement set the scope of work for the task force and included provisions intended to protect the independence and credibility of both parties. For example, the agreement stated that EDF would independently cover its expenses without compensation from McDonald's and included provisions intended to protect confidential information. The agreement provided an early assurance that all issues were on the table and included a commitment that EDF and McDonald's would jointly and publicly release a final report.

The stated goal of the task force was to produce the greatest possible reduction in the materials used and solid wastes generated by McDonald's in a manner consistent with its business—a high volume, quick-service restaurant. In pursuing this goal, the task force was committed to focusing on the preferred materials management methods of source reduction, reuse, recycling, and organic composting.[8] The press release announcing the formation of the task force noted that discussions had already led to "McDonald's decision to indefinitely suspend research and not pursue use of on-site incineration of restaurant wastes, and to instead focus on the preferred options of source reduction, reuse, recycling, and composting."[9]

Task Force Activities and Results

Over a period of 8 months, the seven-member task force met more than 30 times to gather data, study McDonald's operations, and examine waste-reduction opportunities. The task force undertook a top-to-bottom examination of materials improvement and waste-reduction opportunities throughout the McDonald's system, from suppliers to the individual restaurant. EDF members of the task force each worked in a restaurant for a day, a requirement that McDonald's insisted on. The task force learned firsthand about the McDonald's system by meeting with more than 50 McDonald's staff from a dozen departments and visiting distribution centers and packaging and food suppliers. On select issues, EDF invited outside experts to task force meetings. For example, EDF organized a meeting on paper bleaching issues where Greenpeace and other EDF staff discussed the issue with McDonald's task force members.

With an agreement to put all issues on the table, the task force directly tackled tough issues like use of polystyrene and reusable dishware. It meant long hours of sometimes difficult and even contentious discussion. But the result was an ability to break down these issues into their parts and chip away at what both sides have traditionally viewed as all-or-nothing, black-or-white issues.

The composition of the task force was also an important element of its success. Members of the task force from McDonald's worked in core areas of the company—operations development, packaging, etc. Their expertise in company operations was invaluable. McDonald's top management also granted them the authority to act, enabling the task force to move forward on certain issues quickly and successfully. EDF's solid waste experts also had diverse training in the areas of economics, biochemistry, business, and chemical engineering.

The results of the task force far exceeded expectations and original goals. In April 1991, EDF and McDonald's announced several major products of the task force's work, which have been adopted by McDonald's in a new corporate environmental strategy: (See also the *McDonald's Corporation/Environmental Defense Fund Waste Reduction Task Force Final Report.*[10])

1. A strong corporatewide environmental policy that focuses on waste reduction and sets forth the commitment and direction of the company (Fig. 8-1).

2. A 42-step waste-reduction action plan targeting all levels of the company, to be implemented during 1991 and 1992. Together, these initiatives have the potential to cut the waste stream at the chain's 8500 U.S. restaurants by more than 80% (Fig. 8-2).

3. A set of mechanisms that incorporate waste-reduction criteria directly into the core of McDonald's standard operating procedures, to ensure accountability and to institutionalize the environmental commitment embodied in the policy and action plan.

Specific waste-reduction steps include the following:

Source Reduction.   In a source-reduction step endorsed by the task force, McDonald's switched from polystyrene foam "clamshells" to thin paper-based wraps for packaging its sandwich items. The wraps provide a 70 to 90% reduction in packaging volume, resulting in significantly less space consumed in landfills. Compared with the polystyrene foam boxes they replaced, the new sandwich wraps also offer a substantial savings in energy used and substantial reductions in pollutant releases measured over the full life cycle of the package, according to Franklin Associates, an independent consulting firm.[11]

Source reduction also means reduced environmental impacts in the production of materials, such as paper packaging. McDonald's is systematically reviewing its use of chlorine-bleached paper products with the intention of reducing the use of this type of paper wherever feasible. Because the practice of chlorine bleaching in the manufacture of paper and paper products is a significant source of water pollution from paper mills, considerable environmental benefits can result from a shift to brown, unbleached paper, or paper bleached with more benign chemical processes. McDonald's has phased in 100% recycled (50% postconsumer content) brown paper carry-out bags in all its restaurants. The new wrap for the Big Mac is also made with unbleached paper.

Reuse.   Behind-the-counter restaurant supply operations provide the greatest near-term opportunities to cut waste by replacing disposable containers or

Figure 8-1. McDonald's waste-reduction policy.

McDonald's: Our Commitment to the Environment

McDonald's believes it has a special responsibility to protect our environment for future generations. This responsibility is derived from our unique relationship with millions of consumers worldwide—whose quality of life tomorrow will be affected by our stewardship of the environment today. We share their belief that the right to exist in an environment of clean air, clean earth, and clean water is fundamental and unwavering.

We realize that in today's world, a business leader must be an environmental leader as well. Hence our determination to analyze every aspect of our business in terms of its impact on the environment, and to take actions beyond what is expected if they hold the prospect of leaving future generations an environmentally sound world. We will lead, both in word and in deed.

Our environmental commitment and behavior is guided by the following principles:

Effectively managing solid waste.   We are committed to taking a "total life cycle" approach to solid waste, examining ways of reducing materials used in production and packaging, as well as diverting as much waste as possible from the solid waste stream. In doing so, we will follow three courses of action: reduce, reuse, and recycle.

- *Reduce.* We will take steps to reduce the weight and/or volume of packaging we use. This may mean eliminating packaging, adopting thinner and lighter packaging, changing manufacturing and distribution systems, adopting new technologies, or using alternative materials. We will continually search for materials that are environmentally preferable.

- *Reuse.* We will implement reusable materials whenever feasible within our operations and distribution systems as long as they do not compromise our safety and sanitation standards, customer service and expectations, nor are offset by other environmental or safety concerns.

- *Recycle.* We are committed to the maximum use of recycled materials in the construction, equipping, and operations of our restaurants. We are already the largest user of recycled paper in our industry, applying it to such items as tray liners, happy meal boxes, carry-out bags, carry-out trays, and napkins. Through our "McRecycle" program, we maintain the industry's largest repository of information on recycling suppliers, and will spend a minimum of $100 million a year on the use of recycled materials of all kinds. We are also committed to recycling and/or composting as much of our solid waste as possible, including such materials as corrugated paper, polyethylene film, and paper. We will change the composition of our packaging, where feasible, to enhance recyclability or compostability.

Conserving and protecting natural resources.   We will continue to take aggressive measures to minimize energy and other resource consumption through increased efficiency and conservation. We will not permit the destruction of rainforests for our beef supply. This policy is strictly enforced and closely monitored.

Encouraging environmental values and practices.   Given our close relationship with local communities around the world, we believe we have an obligation to promote sound environmental practices by providing educational materials in our restaurants and working with teachers in the schools.

We intend to continue to work in partnership with our suppliers in the pursuit of these policies. Our suppliers will be held accountable for achieving mutually established waste-reduction goals, as well as continuously pursuing sound production practices which minimize environmental impact. Compliance with these policies will receive consideration with other business criteria in evaluating both current and potential McDonald's suppliers.

Ensuring accountability procedures.   We understand that a commitment to a strong environmental policy begins with leadership at the top of an organization. Therefore, our environmental affairs officer will be given broad-based responsibility to ensure adherence to the environmental principles throughout our system. This officer will report to the board of directors on a regular basis regarding progress made toward specific environmental initiatives.

On all of the above, we are committed to timely, honest, and forthright communications with our customers, shareholders, suppliers, and employees. And we will continue to seek the counsel of experts in the environmental field. By maintaining a productive, ongoing dialogue will all of these stakeholders, we will learn from them and move ever closer to doing all we can, the best we can, to preserve and protect the environment.

products with reusable bulk storage systems. For example, McDonald's is testing reusable shipping containers for condiment packets, bulk storage containers for cleaning supplies, durable shipping pallets in distribution centers, and reusable coffee filters. For in-store customer service, McDonald's is testing pump-style condiment dispensers in place of individual packets and a system for filling customers' reusable coffee cups.

Recycling.   According to waste-composition studies, 34% by weight of the solid waste generated at a typical McDonald's restaurant consists of corrugated shipping containers. McDonald's is working to recycle all its corrugated boxes nationwide. Other behind-the-counter materials such as polyethylene used for inner wraps and shipping packages (e.g., the plastic bags that contain sandwich buns) and jugs and other containers will be included in recycling tests and

Figure 8-2. McDonald's waste-reduction action plan.

REDUCE

Elimination of packaging; reduced use of material in packaging; use of alternate materials which reduce production impacts.

1. Complete the conversion from polystyrene clamshells to paper-based wraps by April 1991.

2. Use paper products which utilize more benign bleaching processes, or use unbleached paper products wherever feasible.

   As a part of its ongoing action in this area, McDonald's has made the following changes in 1991:

   - Convert to unbleached paper carry-out bags by spring 1991.
   - Introduce unbleached Big Mac wrap in March 1991.
   - Complete conversion to oxygen-bleached coffee filters by April 1991.

   McDonald's will explore other opportunities in such areas as napkins, cups, and other wraps, and continue to set annual objectives.

3. Annually evaluate all food service products and packaging items to identify opportunities and establish goals for source reductions. As examples:

   - Reduce the amount of paper used in napkins by 21% through reducing their size, by April 1991.
   - Eliminate individual cutlery packaging where not required by local health regulations or concerns.
   - Test the elimination of lids served on cold drinks for in-store customers.
   - Complete pilot test for the use of paper bags in place of paperboard containers for medium and large french fries by May 1991.

4. Annually analyze all shipping packaging to determine items which could be eliminated or reduced.

   - Eliminate inner-pack dividers in shipping containers for cleaning supplies.
   - Continue to examine ways to reduce the amount of corrugated needed in boxes.

REUSE

The substitution of reusable items for disposable items in shipping, handling, storage, and restaurant operations both behind and over the counter.

1. Continue the development and use of reusable shipping containers to replace disposable corrugated containers wherever possible.

- Complete testing of reusable shipping containers for ketchup packets by December 1991, to determine the operations, economic, and logistical impact from this type of shipping container.
- Implement the use of durable, washable containers to replace heavy-duty corrugated shipping boxes with plastic liners for delivering meat and poultry products to McDonald's suppliers where appropriate.

2. Complete testing of bulk cleaning supplies in place of single-portion packets by March 1992.

3. Develop and test durable shipping pallets for use in the movement of goods in 3 to 5 distribution centers by December 1991.

4. Test and evaluate reusable coffee filters by June 1991.

5. Test and evaluate reusable lids for salad and breakfast entrees in several restaurants by September 1991.

6. Develop and test a refillable coffee mug by December 1991.

7. Develop and test bulk condiment dispensers for customer use by December 1991.

RECYCLE/COMPOST

The following action steps address ways McDonald's will recycle and/or compost waste generated in all aspects of its business; and increase its use of recycled materials of all kinds in its operations, thus helping to develop markets for recycled products nationwide.

1. Complete the implementation of corrugated recycling in U.S. McDonald's restaurants by the end of 1991.

2. Develop and test a pilot program for recycling postconsumer, food-contact paper in 30 northeast restaurants during spring 1991 in order to determine its feasibility and effectiveness in a quick service restaurant, both operationally and economically.

3. Work within the emerging polyethylene recycling infrastructure to establish a comprehensive low-density polyethylene film recycling program in at least one region (approximately 200 restaurants) by the end of 1991.

4. Conduct a controlled compost test of key packaging items to assess their compostability.

5. Initiate, in March 1991, a composting test using waste from 10 northeast restaurants in order to determine the feasibility of composting McDonald's waste.

6. Evaluate all packaging annually to identify potential changes that will enhance either recycling or composting initiatives as they develop.

(Continued)

Figure 8-2. (*Continued*).

- Aggressively seek alternatives to the present wax coatings used on meat shipping boxes to enhance their recyclability.
- Conduct a one-restaurant test of a starch-based material for consumer cutlery to replace present plastic cutlery in order to evaluate its functionality and compostability.
- Maximize use of a single type of plastic film—low-density polyethylene film—for bags and inner wraps to enhance recyclability of that portion of the waste stream.
- Explore alternatives to the polyethylene component of the present layered wrap to enhance its recyclability and/or compostability.

7. Continue to evaluate the total waste sorting and materials recovery approach currently in test with McDonald's restaurants in southern California through 1991, as a means to recover as much of the waste stream as possible.

8. Complete the phase-in of brown, recycled content carry-out bags with a minimum of 50% postconsumer content by April 1991. Increase the total recycled content of carry-out bags to 100% by September 1991.

9. Increase the amount of recycled content in napkins to 100%, with a minimum of 30% postconsumer material, by August 1991.

10. Ensure that all McDonald's suppliers are using corrugated boxes that contain at least 35% recycled content by December 1991.

11. Review recycled content targets for corrugated boxes annually and establish new targets as technology and increased supply permit.

12. Maximize the use of postconsumer recycled content wherever possible, available and allowable under regulations. McDonald's will work with suppliers on an ongoing basis to develop and seek approval for the use of postconsumer recycled materials in direct food-contact applications.

ACCOUNTABILITY

Systemize solid waste reduction and management practices into McDonald's standard operating procedures and its packaging and product specifications.

1. Incorporate waste reduction and management goals into the annual supplier business reviews and evaluate progress toward them with each supplier.

   - Ensure all suppliers meet McDonald's 1989 directive to reduce overall solid waste by 15%, by December 1991.

2. Incorporate waste-reduction goals and audits into the annual distribution center evaluations ("full fields").

3. Continue to conduct annual supplier environmental conferences held by McDonald's and Perseco to highlight new opportunities for waste reduction as well as other important environmental issues.

4. Incorporate the solid-waste-reduction criteria developed by the task force into all packaging specifications by April 1991.

5. Incorporate the waste-reduction packaging specifications into the packaging decision-making process to be considered equivalent to the existing criteria of functionality, cost, and availability. The new specifications will be formalized and communicated to all suppliers by June 1991.

6. Track source reductions, increase use of recycled products and materials, and the status of recycling and composting initiatives on a quarterly basis, and make this information available upon request.

7. Continue to conduct annual waste-characterization studies to establish waste-reduction goals for the upcoming year.

developing programs. To facilitate polyethylene recycling, McDonald's is working to "homogenize" its use of this material, using only one type of plastic film for wraps and bags. Since April 1990, McDonald's has supported recycling by helping to "close the loop" through purchasing products made from recycled materials. Through the McRecycle U.S.A. program, McDonald's has committed to purchasing over $100 million worth of recycled materials for restaurant construction and renovation annually, a goal that was exceeded in each of the program's first 2 years. McDonald's also directed its nearly 600 suppliers to use corrugated boxes that contain at least 35% recycled materials, a target considerably higher than the industry average. Take-out bags contain 50% postconsumer content, and the 100% recycled napkins used in all restaurants contain at least 30% postconsumer recycled content.

Composting.   About 34% of McDonald's on-premise waste consists of organic materials such as eggshells, coffee grounds, and other food scraps. Used paper items such as discarded napkins represent another essentially organic component of McDonald's waste. McDonald's is conducting a series of pilot tests for composting these materials in the northeast.

Task Force Process: A Retrospective View

In retrospect, the work of the task force can be described as encompassing five different steps. Interestingly, the elements of the task force's work reveal many parallels with the tools and steps underlying total quality management practices. These similarities will be discussed in further detail below. The five steps are summarized as:[12]

1. *Inventory*   To set a baseline for measurement and to understand the materials being used and discarded, a full materials and waste inventory is a critical first step. The data should include information on both the amount and the type of material used, for example, whether the paper is bleached or unbleached or how much recycled material is used in a product or package. For large processes or production facilities, it may be helpful to narrow the range of possible areas for action in order to limit the amount of data that must be gathered.

In examining McDonald's system, four sets of data were used: (*a*) a summary of all packaging purchased (quantified and described); (*b*) an on-premise waste-characterization study, based on sorting of waste from two restaurants; (*c*) a packaging materials audit to quantify all secondary and tertiary packaging, e.g., materials used in shipping and delivery; and (*d*) distribution center audits to characterize waste at distribution centers that serve McDonald's.

2. *Brainstorming*   Effective brainstorming should be relatively unconstrained and convey to participants that all options are open for discussion. To bring a fresh perspective to the process, individuals with different training and job responsibility should be included in this step, drawing in outside experts to assist in developing a long list of options. EDF's perspective as a nonprofit environmental advocacy group brought many new ideas to McDonald's. In addition to numerous discussions, the task force used a matrix to develop a full list of options and ensure that options were evaluated systematically for applicability to all relevant aspects of operations.

3. *Evaluation*   To develop priorities for action, the process must include an evaluation phase. Here, the task force developed a set of evaluation criteria early in the process to assist members in articulating key factors in evaluating options and explicitly weighing the relative importance of environmental factors in relation to traditional business considerations such as cost. EDF and McDonald's agreed upon five evaluation criteria: consistency with the waste-management hierarchy, magnitude of environmental impact, public health and safety, practicality, and economic costs and benefits.[13]

4. *Modifying existing management tools*   To build environmental considerations into standard operating procedures and practices and to ensure that the process of environmental improvement is continuous, management mechanisms must be modified. Environmental concerns must be considered during the design phase of developing products and packages and reevaluated periodically.

All too often, stand-alone procedures for environmental reviews are developed that result in considering environmental factors at a stage late in product development. The task force therefore worked to integrate waste reduction and efficient materials use criteria into existing management systems, such as packaging specifications given to all suppliers. McDonald's has traditionally selected its packaging based on specifications that take into account three factors: availability, functionality, and cost. The task force added a fourth primary consideration—waste reduction—to be weighted equally with the other criteria. As one example, detailed packaging waste-reduction specifications were developed to address the following areas:

- reduction in materials use
- reduction in production impacts
- reusable materials
- recyclable materials
- recycled content
- compostable materials

McDonald's own purchasing department and its allied packaging purchasing company, Perseco, now uses this document to evaluate existing and select new packaging. McDonald's also sent the specifications to all its packaging suppliers to provide them with a detailed description of the environmental factors McDonald's considers most important. Developing these specifications enabled McDonald's to shape the direction of the packaging development efforts of its suppliers. During 1992, McDonald's established an optimal packaging team (OPT) to more directly oversee the continuous improvement of its packaging.

The task force also identified means to incorporate waste-reduction considerations into other management mechanisms such as McDonald's annual distribution center audits and supplier business reviews.

5. *Accountability*　To put teeth into a stated commitment to environmental improvements, goals must be combined with clear measurement systems and assignment of responsibility and authority. Accountability and measurement are critical to gauging progress and internally instilling a waste-reduction ethic. Tracking and publicly reporting progress toward company goals are integral parts of a credible environmental management program. Measurement systems ("metrics") should be able to provide information to a variety of audiences and users of the information: management, employees, local community members, and environmental organizations.

In the EDF-McDonald's task force, EDF offered advice on the types of information that would be of interest to solid waste professionals and environmental groups. EDF and McDonald's also worked to establish a clear baseline inventory. Then, McDonald's developed new measurement systems that track progress on ongoing waste-reduction projects and record relevant information on the waste-reduction characteristics of each package. The tracking system covers the areas of source reduction, use of recycled products and materials, and recycling and composting operations. McDonald's will make summaries of this information available to the public on request as well as releasing an annual update on its progress.

In EDF's view, the McDonald's waste-reduction strategy offers a broader model for how companies can institutionalize environmental ethics and practices into their everyday business decision making. What makes McDonald's efforts unique to date is a coupling of a long-term vision and direction with immediate aggressive and accountable actions. The McDonald's waste-reduction plan is *comprehensive* in that all aspects of McDonald's system and operations and all materials were examined for improvement (including McDonald's network of more than 600 suppliers and its national distribution system). The plan is also *incremental* in that it is through the combined impacts of 42 different source-reduction, reuse, recycling, and composting initiatives that significant waste reduction is achieved; there is no silver bullet here. McDonald's is working to start the process of waste reduction on all fronts, whether through pilot tests or immediate actions. Finally, McDonald's waste-reduction plan is designed to stimulate *continuous improvement*. A commitment to a continuous improvement process is a strong indicator of progressive corporate environmental management.

Integrating Environmental Considerations

To achieve continuous improvement, companies must institutionalize environmental thinking throughout the company. A commitment from top management is a critical first step, but corporate environmental policies are often vague. The challenge for corporations today is to develop management mechanisms and other tools to systematically translate corporate policies, which are common, into action and establish practices. Corporate environmental policies need to be supported by detailed, comprehensive strategies and action plans for implementing such policies. In a recent interview, Anita Roddick, founder of The Body Shop, was asked how environmental issues have shaped her business philosophy. Roddick responded as follows:

> Well, it's neither the first nor the last, it just is. It's like breathing. Every decision is made, every new act or every new movement or whatever we do has an environmental consciousness. The most important thing is environmental management. On the company's board, we have a member who is absolutely responsible for the environmental education and management for the company. Then we have an environmental department manned by very strong environmental scientists and workers who have come out of the environmental movement. Then each department within our company has a representative for the environment who is responsible for an environmental audit every six months.[14]

Emphasizing Continuous Improvements

Rarely does a quick fix solve environmental problems, but incremental improvement is almost always feasible. The sum of many different activities and building upon changes can produce significant environmental improvements. Such results, however, depend on a long-term commitment to change.

Environmental factors are not fleeting concerns. To achieve ongoing change, environmental considerations must be built into the standard operating procedures of a company and employees, and considered in purchasing.

McDonald's first annual report on progress toward implementing its action plan demonstrates that improvements are continuing at McDonald's. During 1991, McDonald's completed 19 of the original 42 action steps. Another 12 are in progress and the remaining are ongoing in nature. Most importantly, McDonald's has added 20 new initiatives to the plan, including new management mechanisms such as the optimal packaging team (OPT) mentioned above. The OPT consists of representatives from all relevant departments, and its mandate is to systematically and continuously review all existing packaging to identify areas for further improvement.

The quality revolution laid the foundation for the concept of continuous improvement. Many parallels exist between an environmental quality management (EQM) process and total quality management (TQM), beyond just the emphasis on continuous improvement. TQM emphasizes paradigm and culture shifts, innovative solutions, systems analysis, metrics, and accountability. The tools used are data gathering, brainstorming, checklists, cost-benefit evaluations, measuring and monitoring, etc. TQM also emphasizes involving all employees in the process. To develop an environmental quality management program that is integrated into everyday decisions, environmental considerations must be taken out of the environmental affairs department and built into marketing, research, operations, engineering, etc.

Developing environmental quality programs, however, offers new challenges beyond TQM. Numerous "customers" exist, including a key customer that is silent—the environment—as well as others in the public domain: community residents and environmental groups. With these different types of customers, communication and public reporting become key issues. Only by successfully communicating activities in an open and direct manner can these customers judge whether a program is providing improved environmental quality. The EDF-McDonald's final report, for example, presents extensive data on the materials used and solid wastes generated by McDonald's restaurants and outlines in detail the 42 initiatives in McDonald's action plan. The report is available to the public, and McDonald's sends out an annual letter updating activities related to the waste-reduction plan.

Environmental Quality and Cost

In promoting quality, W. Edwards Deming destroyed the conventional wisdom that high quality meant high cost. Deming proved that quality was not expensive in the short run and saved money in the long run. Companies cannot afford to ignore quality. Nor can companies afford to ignore the environment. Improvements in environmental quality often produce cost savings and increase efficiency, but strong countertraditions still prevail in much of the business arena. As noted in a recent business editorial, "The challenge for the Green Deming will be to show that designing ecology right into the process can be similarly cost-effective."[15]

Whether impacting costs or revenues, the environment is emerging as a long-term strategic issue. It impacts revenues because the environment is a growing concern for consumers in making purchasing choices. A *Wall Street Journal*/NBC poll conducted in July 1991 reports that 46% of those surveyed purchased a product during the past 6 months because the product or the manufacturer had a good reputation for protecting the environment. Fifty-three percent avoided purchasing a product specifically because of environmental concerns about the product or its manufacturer. Over half of the respondents stated that they bought more expensive products because they were better for the environment.[16]

Such concerns are growing. In a poll released July 8, 1992, an overwhelming 90% of all respondents said they agree with the statement that "there need to be stricter laws and regulations to protect the environment," and 67% of those surveyed agree with the statement that "people should be willing to pay higher prices to protect the environment."[17] This information should send a clear signal to businesses that environmental considerations must be part of operations, strategic planning, and product and packaging design.

Companies with good environmental reputations also are discovering improvement in the bottom line. Natural product companies such as Tom's of Maine (body care), The Body Shop (body care), and Earth's Best (baby foods) show terrific growth. For example, Earth's Best sales have been growing at a rate of 70% per year and the company has captured 20% of the competitive market for baby food. Tom's of Maine has annual sales of $17 million for its natural care products.[18]

On the cost side, strong environmental management programs can save money by reducing costs in the areas of disposal fees, raw material purchases, and energy and water bills and can decrease liabilities. Large companies are proving that cost savings can result from waste-reduction and other pollution-prevention initiatives. For example, Chevron reports that its SMART program ("Saves Money And Reduces Toxics") has saved $3.8 million in hazardous waste disposal costs during one year.[19] The 3M Company program, "Pollution Prevention Pays," has saved the company $480 million since 1975. Du Pont cites a savings of $1 million per year through reduced consumption of raw materials and Du Pont's chairman, Edgar Woolard, states that he now views waste reduction as providing a competitive advantage.[20]

A 1992 study by Inform showed that source reduction—reducing or preventing use of problematic materials at the front end—is saving money and even increasing productivity for chemical companies. The study found that six of the largest plants in its study reported that source-reduction efforts resulted in a reduction of 10 million pounds of waste annually. Two of these plants, Aristech's Haverhill, Ohio, plant and Du Pont's Deepwater, N.J., facility, reported annual savings of $3.8 million each. The study also showed that for at least two-thirds of the facilities, payback periods for investments in source-reduction projects were generally 6 months or less.[21]

In developing the McDonald's waste-reduction plan, the company and its suppliers have faced start-up costs for some of the changes and will continue to incur research and development costs. Yet McDonald's anticipates that most of its waste-reduction accomplishments will ultimately prove to be economic winners, providing savings through reductions in the amount of packaging materials purchased and solid waste disposed. For example, a McDonald's restaurant in St. Cloud, Minn., saved $269 per month by instituting recycling; a Vermont restaurant cut its monthly garbage-collection costs by 50%, from an original cost of $1250 to $626, after initiating a corrugated and polystyrene recycling program.

McDonald's Leverage as a Customer

McDonald's McRecycle program and its efforts to increase the amount of recycled material used to manufacture the corrugated boxes it uses demonstrate the ability of a major purchaser to influence the types of materials purchased and to play a more proactive role in setting specifications that benefit the environment.

As part of an overall commitment to purchase recycled materials, McDonald's explored the feasibility of requiring a minimum of 35% recycled content in all corrugated boxes used by its suppliers to ship materials to McDonald's. Large corrugated suppliers claimed it could not be done without making the boxes weaker, more expensive, and heavier. However, one small supplier approached McDonald's with a new box that met the goal and all performance specifications. This achievement enabled McDonald's to feel confident that a directive to use corrugated boxes with 35% recycled content could be met by all suppliers. That directive has now been met by all suppliers. More importantly, McDonald's directive has had the effect of sending a signal throughout the industry: Corrugated manufacturers making the higher-recycled-content boxes for McDonald's now offer that box to their other customers, raising the standard industrywide.

McDonald's is also using its purchasing power to create markets for recycled materials. Its commitment to purchasing recycled materials is extensive, and the company has set an explicit goal of reducing the use of virgin materials in all packaging and products. As part of its "McRecycle" program which calls for the company to purchase at least 100 million dollars annually on recycled products for the construction, renovation, and equipping of McDonald's U.S. restaurants, McDonald's has compiled a database (accessible to the public upon request) on available recycled products, organized by product type and geographic area of the country. This direct approach of affirmatively committing to purchasing a definite amount of recycled materials sends a far stronger signal to manufacturers considering investments that would allow use of more recycled materials than does the more indirect approach used by the federal government of establishing only procurement guidelines for procurement officers and a price preference.[22]

Project Milestones	
July 1989	EDF first contacted McDonald's to suggest a meeting to discuss solid waste issues
October 1989	First meeting of EDF's Fred Krupp and McDonald's Ed Rensi
August 1990	Announcement of the EDF-McDonald's waste-reduction task force
September 1990	Development of EDF-McDonald's waste-reduction task force work plan
November 1990	McDonald's decision to phase out polystyrene sandwich packaging in favor of a thinner paper-based wrap
April 1991	Task force releases final report with a 42-step action plan

New EDF Initiatives

In July 1992, EDF announced another unique project in which EDF and General Motors (GM) will engage in a technical and policy dialogue aimed at the speedy development of potential new policies, incentives, strategies, and technologies to address a broad range of air-pollution issues. EDF approached GM because of the belief that a dialogue, along with quick implementation of the Clean Air Act and EDF's ongoing research, education, and advocacy efforts, can speed up solutions to air-pollution issues. These issues include both the air-quality problems plaguing cities and longer-term problems like global warming. Vehicle emissions play a crucial role in urban air quality, and EDF is interested in finding new ways to protect air quality.

As with McDonald's, EDF and GM have a signed agreement which states that EDF will not accept any monetary or in-kind support from GM at any time. The agreement states that EDF will continue its vigorous advocacy and public education efforts on behalf of a broad range of environmental policies with complete independence and continue to state its own views. The agreement also states that EDF will pursue its own interests and goals, with respect to any matter or activity included in, or related to, the dialogue.

References

1. John Holusha, "Talking Deals: Unusual Alliance for McDonald's," *New York Times*, August 9, 1990, p. D2.
2. Rose Gutfeld, "Big Mac Joins with Big Critic to Cut Trash," *The Wall Street Journal*, August 2, 1990, p. B1.

3. "PN's 1990 `Plastic Globe Awards,'" *Plastic News,* December 24, 1990, p. 8.

4. "Less McWaste," *Washington Post,* April 30, 1991.

5. David Kiley, "McDonald's Repaints the Arches Green," *AdWeek's Marketing Week,* April 22, 1991.

6. "Negotiating for a Green Future," *Star-Tribune,* Minneapolis, Minnesota, May 4, 1991.

7. Bill Gifford, "The Greening of the Golden Arches," *Rolling Stone,* August 22, 1991, p. 34.

8. For a discussion of efficient materials use concepts and solid waste management approaches, see Jackie Prince, "Managing Materials to Conserve Resources: Re-Designing Solid Waste Management at McDonald's," *Duke Environmental Law & Policy Forum,* vol. II, 1992.

9. EDF-McDonald's Press Release, August 1, 1990, EDF, Washington, D.C.

10. See also the *McDonald's Corporation/Environmental Defense Fund Waste Reduction Task Force Final Report,* April 1991. The 160-page report is available upon request from EDF's Washington, D.C., office or McDonald's Corporation in Oak Brook, Illinois.

11. The new wraps offer significant reductions in energy use and pollutant releases relative to polystyrene foam packaging even under the highly optimistic assumption that 50% of the polystyrene is recycled. A summary of the Franklin Associates report documenting these benefits is available from EDF or McDonald's Environmental Affairs Department, McDonald's Plaza, Oak Brook, Illinois.

12. See Jackie Prince and Richard A. Denison, "Launching a New Business Ethic: The Environment as a Standard Operating Procedure at McDonald's and at Other Companies," paper prepared for the Halpren Memorial Symposium on Business Ethics, November 21–22, 1991, at the Amos Tuck School of Business Administration, Dartmouth College, Hanover, New Hampshire. Available from EDF's Washington, D.C., office.

13. See the *McDonald's Corporation/Environmental Defense Fund Waste Reduction Task Force Final Report,* April 1991, pp. 9–10.

14. *Greenwire* Electronic News Service, "Interview: Body Shop's Roddick and the `Second Bottom Line,'" vol. 1, no. 119, October 21, 1991.

15. Michael Schrage, "Going `Green' in Industrial Ecosystems," *San Francisco Examiner,* December 1, 1991.

16. *Wall Street Journal*/NBC Survey conducted by Hart Teeter on July 26–29, 1991. Poll surveyed 1004 randomly selected registered voters nationwide. Reported in *Greenwire* Electronic News Service, vol. 1, no. 67, Falls Church, Virginia, August 6, 1991, as originally reported in the *Wall Street Journal,* August 1, 1991.

17. *Times-Mirror* survey conducted on May 2–June 10, 1992. Poll surveyed 3517 randomly selected registered voters nationwide. Reported in *Greenwire* Electronic News Service, vol. 2, no. 49, Falls Church, Virginia, July 10, 1992, from a *Times-Mirror* July 8, 1992, release.

18. Udayan Gupta, "Natural-Products Makers Discover Power of an Image," *Wall Street Journal,* June 23, 1992.

19. Chevron Corporation, *Save Money and Reduce Toxics,* company brochure, San Francisco, California, 1991.

20. Scott McMurray, "Chemical Firms Find That It Pays to Reduce Pollution at the Source," *Wall Street Journal,* June 11, 1991, pp. A1, A6.

21. Martha Hamilton, "Firms Saving Money by Preventing Pollution," *Washington Post,* June 17, 1992, p. A20.

22. Richard A. Denison, EDF testimony before the Subcommittee on Oversight of Government Management, Senate Committee on Governmental Affairs, on Lessons from the EDF-McDonald's Waste Reduction Task Force for the Federal Procurement Program, November 8, 1991.

PART 4

Financial and Legal Implications and Control

9

Financial Issues in Environmental Liabilities and Decision Making*

Steven M. Boden

Deloitte & Touche
New York, New York

Gary Brayton

Deloitte & Touche
San Francisco, California

In this chapter:

- Summary
- Introduction
- Accounting for Environmental Liabilities for SEC Companies
- Disclosure of Environmental Liabilities for SEC Companies
- Environmental Decision Making: Why It's So Hard and What to Do about It
- Case Study 1: Compliance with the Clean Air Act Acid Rain Standards
- Case Study 2: Selecting Competing Environmental Capital Projects

*John Rafter, formerly of Deloitte & Touche, also contributed to the chapter. This chapter is intended to offer background information on financial accounting and reporting of environmental liabilities in general. Deloitte & Touche is not, by means of this chapter, rendering legal, tax,

Summary

Reporting of existing and potential environmental liabilities represents a challenging business problem facing financial management. Uncertainties in the financial reporting process are caused by the nature of our legal system as well as by problems of estimating cleanup costs and establishing responsible parties. The national bodies that establish financial accounting and reporting rules have been active in recent years, attempting to more clearly define a company's obligation to report environmental problems.

Accounting for environmental contamination treatment costs is an area where financial management is faced with exercising significant judgment. The critical issue faced by management is whether these costs have a future economic benefit, thereby allowing them to be capitalized. The alternative to capitalization is immediate expense recognition, which can adversely impact a company's profitability. Costs incurred for asbestos removal, for example, are an area where future economic benefit has been established.

The users of financial information are particularly interested in knowing when an environmental liability should be recorded on a company's books and records. Accounting guidance in this area classifies the likelihood of recording an environmental contingency into three categories: probable, possible, and remote. Furthermore, the ability to estimate reasonably the amount of the contingency will have a significant impact on the decision to record the liability.

How and when to account for environmental liabilities is only part of the problem; communicating the required environmental information to the users of financial statements is critical. The rules and regulations of the Securities and Exchange Commission (SEC) put a great burden of disclosure on public companies. The SEC has mandated disclosures within public documents filed with the SEC, including Superfund liabilities.

Likewise, executives must make decisions about compliance strategies today which will determine their business' financial well-being in the next century. Sound decision making for managers is all the more challenging owing to numerous uncertainties and the fact that industry is becoming increasingly regulated.

Obviously, compliance will be a complex and costly problem. There is an approach to the problem, however, that can help managers better understand the uncertainties and mitigate their potential risks. The methodology starts by documenting and quantifying assumptions for available options and by applying traditional quantitative decision analysis to determine possible outcomes. Using the results of this work, executives can make knowledgeable decisions relative to the regulations which are consistent with their risk preferences and their expectation about the likelihood of future events.

Introduction

The results of a national survey titled "The Environmental Transformation of U.S. Industry," conducted jointly by Deloitte and Touche and Stanford University's Graduate School of Business, were released in the fall of 1990.[1] This study, the first of its kind since 1973, measured the attitudes of American business on environmental issues. The study analyzed input from 80 companies in 13 business sectors. The most powerful conclusion of the survey is that, since 1973, environmental expenditures have grown from an "expensive annoyance" to a "normal cost of doing business" to an "essential component of a healthy corporate image." Some of the other critical conclusions include:

- Regulatory issues are still dominating the U.S. corporate approach to the environment, and enforcement is getting tougher.

- Those heaviest hit by environmental compliance costs include utilities, heavy manufacturing, and oil companies. Approximately 75 percent of surveyed companies have been penalized for incidents of noncompliance.

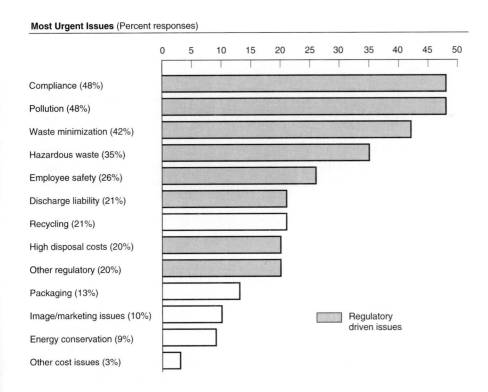

Most Urgent Issues (Percent responses)

© Deloitte & Touche Stanford University Survey, 1990

Comparative Industry Expenditures

Industry	Average environmental expenditures* (annual $million)	Average percent of revenues†
Utilities	$340	6.1
Steel and metals	50	2.9
Oil	430	1.9
Paper	76	1.6
Chemical	56	1.3
High-technology	2	0.4
Food processing	8	0.3
Consumer goods	6	0.1
Automobiles	5+	n/a
Pharmaceuticals	n/a	n/a
Real estate and development	n/a	n/a
Construction	n/a	n/a
Airlines	n/a	n/a
Overall average	**120**	**1.8**

SOURCE: Deloitte & Touche Stanford University Survey, 1990.

*Many firms spend over $5 million, but exact figures were not available. There is a variation in the components of the expenditures reported (e.g., capital costs), so these estimates should be used for illustrative purposes only.

†A simple average of expenditure share of revenues for the companies interviewed.

- In order to deal with complex regulations, firms devote high-level attention to environmental issues.

- Approximately 91 percent of respondents said they now evaluate environmental performance of potential business partners and 70 percent evaluate such performance of suppliers.

- Most companies also seek improvements in their management systems and organizational structures—risk quantification and modeling, waste minimization, operations improvements, technology assessments, and information systems.

- Over one-half of the companies surveyed believe the present trend of heightened environmental concern will significantly increase over the next 10 years.

The financial accounting and reporting implications of managing environmental risks must be considered in a total corporate strategy. The financial consequences for a company that does not properly account for or disclose environmental problems can be devastating. In other words, environmental issues can profoundly affect a company's profitability and even its ultimate value in the marketplace. Likewise, executives must make decisions about compliance strategies today which will determine their business' financial well-being in the next century. Sound decision making for managers is all the more challenging owing to numerous uncertainties, and the fact that industry is becoming more regulated. Some examples of the most critical considerations include:

Share of Companies Equipped with High-Level Environmental Management Structures

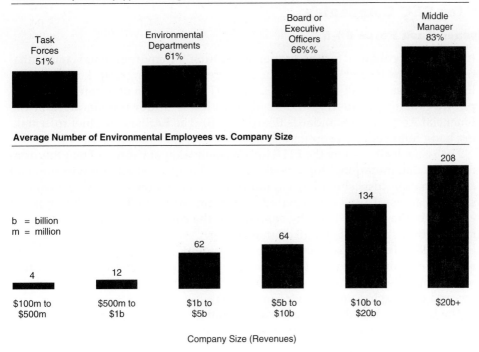

Task Forces 51%

Environmental Departments 61%

Board or Executive Officers 66%%

Middle Manager 83%

Average Number of Environmental Employees vs. Company Size

b = billion
m = million

| 4 | 12 | 62 | 64 | 134 | 208 |
| $100m to $500m | $500m to $1b | $1b to $5b | $5b to $10b | $10b to $20b | $20b+ |

Company Size (Revenues)

© Deloitte & Touche Stanford University Survey, 1990

- Portions of the Clean Air Act Amendments are still undefined or unclear. These will likely evolve only with time, much like the Superfund law.

- Many technologies are available, but most have some degree of uncertainty surrounding their costs and effectiveness.

- The market for emissions allowances, provided for by the Clean Air Act, is embryonic. No one knows what fair market prices will be set or whether a market will develop at all.

- Future compliance choices of competing managers will influence the outcome of today's compliance options.

- In the end, decisions will still depend on the risk sensitivities of the decision makers themselves.

This chapter outlines the critical issues in accounting for and disclosures of environmental liabilities and environmental decision making.

Accounting for Environmental Liabilities for SEC Companies

Emerging Issues Task Force 90-8

In July 1990, guidance for the proper accounting for environmental contamination costs was issued. The guidance was released by a group known as the Emerging Issues Task Force (EITF). The EITF is a group of accountants from public practice, industry, and academia that is under the auspices of the Financial Accounting Standards Board (FASB). The FASB is the chief rule-making body followed by accountants.

The issue dealt with by the EITF in "Capitalization of Costs to Treat Environmental Contamination," topic 90-8 ("Issue 90-8"),[2] is whether environmental contamination costs should be capitalized and shown on a company's balance sheet as an asset (and depreciated over time) or immediately shown as an expense in the period. Thus, by capitalizing the cost, the company can avoid a large income statement charge all in one year.

The EITF defined contamination "treatment" costs as costs incurred to remove, contain, neutralize, or prevent existing or future environmental contamination. These costs may be voluntary or involuntary, and also include penalties and fines levied under environmental laws.

The EITF concluded that these costs should generally be charged to expense; however, there are exceptions in the following cases:

1. Costs incurred that increase an owned asset's life, improve safety or efficiency, or increase capacity. In applying this "improvement" criterion, the condition of the property after the costs are incurred must be improved as compared with the condition of the asset when originally constructed or when acquired, if later.

2. The costs mitigate or prevent environmental contamination costs that have yet to occur. These costs must improve the property compared with its condition when constructed or acquired.

3. The costs are incurred in preparing a property for sale.

An interesting and slight departure from the general rule of expensing cleanup costs concerns asbestos treatment.

Emerging Issues Task Force 89-13

Guidance concerning asbestos costs was issued in October 1989 by the EITF in "Accounting for the Costs of Asbestos Removal," topic 89-13 ("Issue 89-13").[3] In particular, three issues were dealt with by the EITF:

1. Whether the costs incurred to treat asbestos when a property with a known asbestos problem is acquired should be capitalized or charged to expense.

2. Whether the costs incurred to treat asbestos in existing property should be capitalized or expensed.

3. If it is deemed appropriate to charge asbestos treatment costs to expense, whether they should be reported as an extraordinary item.

The EITF consensus was that under scenario 1 or 2 above, costs may be capitalized, assuming that such costs would eventually be recovered in the use or sale of the property. These costs would not be treated as extraordinary items in a company's income statement to the extent these costs were charged to expense.

In essence, a distinction has been drawn between asbestos treatment costs and other contamination treatment costs. Many accountants are not comfortable with this discrepancy. They claim that when new, the asbestos fibers are bound in such a way that they cannot be released into the air and, with the passage of time, the fibers are more likely to be released into the air. Thus treatment of asbestos only restores the building from an unsafe to a safe state. Hence these costs would not qualify for capitalization. However, the EITF was persuaded by the evidence of the unsafe nature of asbestos, and believes treatment renders a structure safer, easier to finance, rent, or sell, and gives the structure a longer useful life.

Statement of Financial Accounting Standards No. 5

The accounting standard that provides the authoritative guidance in answering the question of when an environmental liability needs to be recorded or disclosed is a standard issued by the FASB, Statement of Financial Accounting Standards No. 5, "Accounting for Contingencies" ("Statement No. 5").[4]

Statement No. 5 defines a contingency as an existing condition, situation, or set of circumstances involving uncertainty as to possible gain or loss to an enterprise that will ultimately be resolved when one or more future events occur or fail to occur.

By definition, a future event(s) will determine the exact amount of the liability to be recorded. However, in the preparation of financial statements, management is required to determine whether a liability currently exists and whether an estimate can be made of the future liability.

Statement No. 5 provides the following guidance:

1. If the loss is probable (i.e., likely to occur) and the loss can be reasonably estimated, the loss must be accrued for in the financial statements.

2. If the loss is reasonably possible, the event must be disclosed in the notes to the financial statements only (regardless of whether the eventual outcome can be quantified). Also, disclosure is required in the financial statements if the loss is probable and estimable. If potential liability cannot be estimated, it must be so stated.

3. If there is a remote likelihood of a loss occurring (i.e., slight) then no accrual or disclosure is required.

In a recent survey by Price Waterhouse, titled *Environmental Accounting: The Issues, The Developing Solutions—A Survey of Corporate America's Accounting for Environmental Costs*, 1991[5] (the "PW Survey"), the 125 respondents surveyed differed greatly when asked when liabilities were recorded for hazardous waste remediation resulting from prior activities.

Timing of recording liability for cleanup of prior-period waste	Number of respondents
Provided through charges to income over useful life of property	10
Upon notification of cleanup through internal company procedures	3
Upon initial notification by relevant regulatory authority	16
Upon signing of consent to conduct a remedial investigation/ feasibility study ("RI/FS")	7
Upon completion of RI/FS	28
Upon settlement offer made by company	20
Expensed as incurred during cleanup	25
At sale, disposal, or abandonment of facility	28
Total	137

SOURCE: Price Waterhouse Survey, 1991.

NOTE: Some respondents provided two or more responses to this question. The survey did not specifically address whether the practice of expensing costs as incurred related to material, as well as immaterial, amounts.

An example of the application of Statement No. 5 could be when a company has recently been ordered by a state environmental agency to treat residential well water contaminated by chemicals that leaked into those wells. The company has estimated the cost to neutralize the water in the wells to be $5 million. In this scenario, the liability is likely to occur and the amount of loss can be estimated. The liability should be recorded, expensed, and disclosed in the financial statements.

However, such estimates may be difficult to make. To deal with this issue the FASB issued an interpretation of Statement No. 5. That FASB interpretation, No. 14, requires accrual of the most likely estimate of the loss if it is possible to determine a range.[6] It requires recording at least the lowest point in that range when no amount within the range is a better estimate than any other amount. Obviously, if one amount within the relevant range of loss is more likely than any other estimate within the range, that amount should be accrued.

The PW Survey also questioned companies on the variables considered in developing reliable estimates for recording remediation costs.

The importance of unasserted claims is also addressed in Statement No. 5. An unasserted claim is a potential liability that has not been raised, of which management is aware, but may be asserted at a future date. Disclosure of an unasserted claim or assessment is not required unless it is probable that the

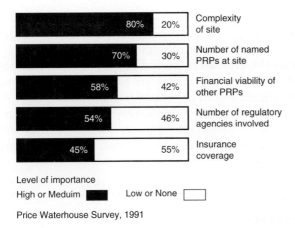

80%	20%	Complexity of site
70%	30%	Number of named PRPs at site
58%	42%	Financial viability of other PRPs
54%	46%	Number of regulatory agencies involved
45%	55%	Insurance coverage

Level of importance

High or Meduim ▮ Low or None ▯

Price Waterhouse Survey, 1991

claim will be asserted and there is a reasonable possibility that the outcome will be unfavorable. By not requiring disclosure unless it is probable that the claim will be asserted, the FASB is attempting to limit situations whereby disclosure of a contingency increases the likelihood of assertion.

Purchase Accounting Transactions

Current accounting rules require that when a business combination is accounted for as a purchase, the assets required and liabilities assumed must be recorded at their fair value at the date of the transaction.

Potential environmental problems may represent liabilities that may need to be recorded in the beginning balance sheet of the acquired company. If fair value of the contingency can be readily determined, the purchase price allocation to all assets and liabilities should be adjusted to include the environmental problems identified. If fair value cannot be determined, contingent liabilities should be recorded when two conditions are met:

- It is probable that the contingent item existed at the transaction or consummation date.

- The amount of the contingent liability can be reasonably estimated.

Generally, it takes time for a buyer to identify and quantify the fair value of all assets and liabilities that should be included in the opening balance sheet of an acquired company. This period of time is known as the "allocation period," which is 1 year from the consummation date.

The authoritative accounting literature is Statement of Financial Accounting Standards No. 38, "Accounting for Preacquisition Contingencies of Purchased Enterprises."[7]

If the above conditions are met, a portion of the total acquisition cost may be allocated to the contingency. This is especially important if the purchaser has agreed to be responsible for the environmental costs.

The importance of the allocation period is that any adjustments resulting from a preacquisition contingency that are identified during the allocation period result in an adjustment to the purchase accounting allocations, which usually means an adjustment to goodwill. However, any adjustments resulting from preacquisition contingencies that are identified after the end of the allocation period will impact the combined companies' net earnings during that period.

Disclosure of Environmental Liabilities for SEC Companies

Requirements under generally accepted accounting principles, applicable for all companies, are set forth in Statement No. 5, discussed earlier. However, rules of the Securities and Exchange Commission (SEC) are significantly more detailed and in-depth and put a great burden of disclosure on the public companies. There are generally three areas within SEC rules where disclosure of environmental issues is addressed. These areas are included in a company's annual public filings (i.e., annual report). The annual or quarterly report is where the majority of companies disclose environmental problems.

Item 101(c) (1) (xii) (Description of the Business) of SEC Regulation S-K ("Item 101")[8]

In this section, companies describe their operations in some detail, including products, markets, competition, and other important information.

This section also requires disclosure of material effects of compliance with environmental legal provisions on the company's capital expenditures, earnings, and competitive position.

1. Includes material estimated capital expenditures on environmental control facilities for the current and succeeding fiscal year. This includes pollution-control facilities, lining tanks, and other major items. This requirement could also require estimates of capital expenditures for additional years if expected to be materially higher than those which otherwise would be expected.

2. Note that, as a general matter, possible effects of any proposed environmental regulations could present a compliance problem with Item 101. For example, the new Clean Air Act Amendments have serious implications for the

auto industry. These matters should be discussed in a company's annual filing with the SEC, if deemed material.

An example of an Item 101 disclosure is set forth below. The company is engaged in the manufacture of glass, coating, resins, and chemicals. The disclosure is derived from the company's 1990 Form 10-K.

Item 1. Description of Business—
An Illustration

Environmental Matters.   Like other companies, the company is subject to the existing and evolving standards relating to the protection of the environment. Capital expenditures for environmental control projects were approximately $23 million in 1990, $15 million in 1989, and $27 million in 1988. It is estimated that expenditures for such projects in 1991 will approximate $60 million. Future capital expenditures cannot be forecast accurately because the regulatory standards are constantly changing, but it can be anticipated that environmental control standards will become increasingly stringent. The company is negotiating with various government agencies concerning various National Priorities List (NPL) and other cleanup sites. The company has been named by the U.S. Environmental Protection Agency (EPA) as a potentially responsible party (PRP) at 53 NPL and other federal sites, and by various state agencies as a possible contributor at nine other sites. While the company is not generally a major contributor of wastes to these sites, each PRP or contributor may face agency assertions of joint and several liability. Generally, however, a final allocation of costs is made based on relative contribution of wastes to the site. There is a wide range of cost estimates for cleanup of these sites, owing largely to uncertainties as to the nature and extent of their conditions and the methods which may have to be employed for their remediation. Additionally, remediation projects have been or may be undertaken at certain of the company's plant sites.

The company has established reserves for those sites where it is probable a liability exists and the amount can be reasonably estimated. Charges against income for environmental remediation projects totaled approximately $34 million in 1990 (including a reserve for XYZ environmental matters), $36 million in 1989, and $21 million in 1988.

The company's experience to date regarding environmental matters leads the company to believe that it will have continuing expenditures for compliance with provisions regulating the protection of the environment and for present and future remediation efforts at waste and plant sites. However, management believes such expenditures will not have a material adverse effect on the financial condition of the company and its consolidated subsidiaries as a whole. In management's opinion, the company operates in an environmentally sound manner and is favorably positioned, relative to environmental matters, within the industries in which it operates.

Instruction 5 to Item 103 (Legal Proceedings) of SEC Regulation S-K ("Item 103")[9]

This rule requires disclosure of pending or threatened legal proceedings by government. This section is fairly mechanical.

1. Includes environmental proceedings that are material to a company's business or financial condition, and includes proceedings involving over 10 percent of the company's current assets on a consolidated basis.

2. Includes proceedings involving potential monetary sanctions in which the government is a party, but a company need not disclose information if it reasonably believes the fine will not exceed $100,000.

3. The SEC finds that costs incurred pursuant to a remedial agreement entered into in the normal course of negotiation with the EPA (i.e., cleanup costs) are not sanctions.

An example of Item 103 disclosure follows. The disclosure is from an oil company's 1990 Form 10-K.

Item 3.   Legal Proceedings.   Eight proceedings instituted by governmental authorities are pending against the company and certain of its subsidiaries under federal, state, or local air, waste, and water-pollution control and nuisance laws, each of which could result in monetary sanctions in excess of $100,000. These proceedings are not material in relation to the company's consolidated financial position.

Item 303 of SEC Regulation S-K: Management's Discussion and Analysis ("MD&A")[10]

In this section, management describes the reasons for the company's financial results, including material changes in current balances and earnings.

1. Management discussion and analysis mandates disclosure where a trend, demand, commitment, event, or uncertainty is both presently known to management and reasonably likely to have a material effect on the financial condition or results of operations.

   ▪ If the known trend, commitment, or uncertainty is not reasonably likely to occur, no financial statement disclosure is required.

   ▪ If that determination cannot be made, management must evaluate objectively the consequences of the known trend, commitment, or uncertainty, on the assumption that it will occur. Disclosure is required unless management determines that a material effect on the financial condition or results of operations is not reasonably likely to occur. It is significant to note that management has the burden of proof to determine that there is *not* a material problem.

2. Under *Superfund,* once the EPA designates a company as a PRP, disclosure of the effects of PRP status, quantified to the extent reasonably practicable, would be required where management has determined the effect on the future financial condition or results of operations is not reasonably likely to occur.

3. The SEC has indicated that companies should disclose significant exposure for asbestos treatment costs in their MD&A.

An example of an Item 303 disclosure follows. The company is a global petrochemical and industrial gas concern. The disclosure was derived from the company's 1990 annual report.

Management's Discussion and Analysis

Worldwide costs relating to environmental protection continue to grow, owing both to increasingly stringent laws and regulations and to the corporation's ongoing commitment to rigorous internal standards. In 1990, worldwide expenses related to environmental protection, including cash expenditures and accruals for waste site remedial activities, totaled $169 million. Expenditures in 1989 and 1988 totaled $167 million and $148 million, respectively. During the last three years, approximately 84 percent of the total expense related to, and has been charged against, chemicals and plastics operations. In addition, worldwide capital expenditures relating to environmental protection in 1990 aggregated $69 million, an increase of $22 million over the prior year.

    The corporation, like other companies in the United States, has periodically received notices from the U.S. Environmental Protection Agency, as well as from state environmental agencies, alleging that the corporation is a PRP under the Comprehensive Environmental Response, Compensation and Liability Act (CERCLA/Superfund) and equivalent state laws for past and future cleanup costs at hazardous waste sites. The corporation has received requests for information, notices, and/or claims with respect to approximately 150 waste sites at which the corporation has no ownership interest. At a substantial majority of these sites, it is our belief that the corporation will incur either no liability or a small liability, since, in general, final allocation of responsibility is made based on each PRP's relative contribution of hazardous waste to the site. Environmental investigatory and remediation projects are also being undertaken at waste sites located on property presently owned by the corporation. The corporation has established accruals for those sites where it is probable that a loss will be incurred and the amount of the loss can be reasonably estimated.

    Estimates of future costs of environmental protection are necessarily imprecise owing to numerous uncertainties, including the impact of new laws and regulations (such as the Clean Air Act of 1990), the availability and application of new and diverse technologies, the eventual outcome of insurance coverage litigation in which the corporation is engaged, the identification of new hazardous waste sites, and in the case of Superfund sites, the ultimate allocation of costs among PRPs. Nevertheless, the corporation estimates that worldwide expenses for environmental protection, expressed in 1990 dollars, should average about $200 million annually over the next 5 years. Worldwide capital expenditures for environmental protection, also expressed in 1990 dollars, are expected to average about $120 million annually over the same period.

SEC Areas of Concern

Within the last year the SEC has been looking closely at the manner in which companies treat proceeds from insurance companies resulting from environmental claims. The issue is straightforward—companies are assuming a *probable* liability (i.e., environmental problem), will be "covered" by a *reasonably possible* asset (i.e., insurance proceeds), thereby effectively offsetting the liability with the asset, where no legal right of offset exists. The result is, at a minimum, that necessary financial statement disclosure may be erroneously omitted and, in a worst-case situation, liabilities that should have been accounted for remain unrecorded in a company's financial statements. The SEC insists that all environmental liabilities be accounted for in accordance with Statement No. 5 and that insurance proceeds not be assumed unless their receipt is probable and estimable. Of course, adequate and complete financial statement disclosure must be followed.

The SEC has recently expressed concern that companies are delaying the accrual of environmental loss contingencies until the ultimate liability is fixed or determinable. At a minimum, FASB Interpretation 14 requires a company to accrue the minimum in a range of estimates.

The SEC also believes that public companies have an obligation to consider the ability of the other PRPs to pay their portion of any joint and several liability. If it is probable that an additional liability will be assessed to the company and the amount can be reasonably estimated, then Statement No. 5 requires the company to accrue the additional liability.

Recently, the SEC has been monitoring the adequacy of environmental disclosures in connection with its review of public filings. In an effort to ensure appropriate disclosure, the SEC staff receives from the EPA lists of all entities that have been named as PRPs as well as information concerning entities subject to the cleanup requirements under the Resource Conservation and Recovery Act (RCRA).

In summary, by focusing on areas of regulatory compliance, risk management, marketing and strategy, improved accounting, and disclosure of environmental problems will inevitably result. Part of the challenge facing the accounting profession is to develop measures of positive environmental actions taken by private enterprise. These actions, such as avoiding pollution and maintenance of higher than required standards, will allow management to tell the full story on how the company is impacting the environment.

Before issues of accounting and disclosure are considered, environmental decisions are made every day that have a significant impact on operations.

Environmental Decision Making: Why It's So Hard and What to Do about It

Many companies have a hard time making environmental decisions. The symptoms are easy to spot: environmental management departments and capital programs that cost fortunes but don't seem to stem the tide of compliance problems and environmental incidents; environmental decision "teams," assembled to address complex decisions, that travel in circles and get nowhere; and environmental managers who never have time to get in front of the environmental "power curve" because they're always fighting the next fire. The underlying disease is harder to see: burdensome and faulty environmental decision making. Why are environmental decisions so hard? To answer this, we should first recognize environmental decisions for what they are.

Environmental Decisions Are Complex.   More so than most business decisions, environmental decisions are multidisciplinary and multifunctional. If there isn't at least an engineer, financial analyst, lawyer, environmental program manager, health and safety manager, manufacturing manager, and (sometimes) marketing manager involved, an environmental decision probably isn't being made. A group this size must be involved because environmental decisions are made in a world of enormous legal, regulatory, and technological complexity.

Environmental Decisions Are Risky.   Uncertainty surrounds almost every aspect of environmental decisions. New control and compliance technologies emerge every day, but no one is completely sure of their ultimate operating costs or effectiveness. The regulatory landscape is ever-changing, and even static regulatory structures are open to interpretation. Add to this the uncertain effect of many substances and processes on human health and safety and it's no wonder environmental decisions are such risky business.

Environmental Decisions Have Potential for Enormous Financial Impact.
Between remediation of environmental accidents, and resulting fines, penalties, litigation, and damages, the costs of bad environmental decisions, and the cost savings that result from good environmental decisions, have risen to shocking heights in the last two decades. For the first time, the potential financial impact of environmental disasters threatens the life of every business in the United States.

Given this anatomy of environmental decisions, it's no surprise they can be difficult to resolve. In fact, burdensome decision making and sometimes outright decision failure follow directly from the very nature of environmental decisions. For example, because the complexity of these decisions requires that they be addressed by larger, multidisciplinary teams, the decision-making process is often bogged down by troublesome group dynamics. Candidate courses of action are sometimes presented with "love me, love my dog" dynamics, where individuals try to see their ideas and themselves as a package deal, betting that other group members would rather accept their views than reject a fellow team member personally. These teams also fall prey to "groupthink."

This riskiness of environmental decisions also contributes to faulty decision making. Traditional financial analysis employs simple point estimates of the outcomes of future uncertain events or, at best, "worst case, most likely, best case" analyses. By collapsing what are naturally continuous probability distributions of possible outcomes into point estimates, these analyses destroy valuable information that might otherwise be accessible to decision makers. Since traditional financial analysis ignores the riskiness of decision components, it also cannot address the risk preferences of decision makers themselves, further increasing the odds that bad decisions will result.

Finally, the potentially crippling financial impact of environmental decisions means they must be scrutinized carefully by financial analysts. But environmental decisions makers are confounded by lack of a common, well-understood language to enhance communication with financial managers. Traditional financial analysis of capital investment alternatives can't capture the significance of environmental risk mitigation projects, but environmental managers also don't often make an effort to communicate in terms financial decision makers can understand. To make matters worse, environmental projects often compete for scarce firm capital with "sexier" projects promising big cost savings.

The ideal decision-analysis framework, then, provides environmental decision makers with three important things:

1. *Structure.*   The complexity of environmental decisions and the troublesome group dynamics of environmental decision-making teams demand a highly structured approach. By dissecting tough decisions into their component parts and by placing a premium on rigorous analysis supported by careful research, structured decision analysis goes a long way toward fighting bad decision making.

2. *Robust analysis.*   When uncertainty dominates decisions, analysis that ignores variability and risk is a dangerous tool. To make good environmental decisions, economic analysis must embrace all available information about alternatives, not just point estimates and expected values.

3. *Communication.*   All the analysis in the world won't compensate for poor communication. Environmental managers must be able to convey the significance of projects that mitigate environmental risk, for example, in a way that recognizes the tenets of traditional financial analysis. In turn, financial managers must learn to read this new language and give environmental projects their fair chance to compete for scarce firm capital.

The two case studies that follow demonstrate application of environmental decision analysis. The first, analysis of an electric utility's decision surrounding Clean Air Act compliance, focuses on the importance of *structure* and *analysis of uncertainty*. The second, a decision between two environmental capital investment alternatives, highlights the power of effective *communication*. Both case studies, however, contain some elements of all three criteria for good environmental decision making.

Case Study 1:

Compliance with the Clean Air Act Acid Rain Reporting Standards

Imagine a utility operating a 500-MW coal-fired generating unit that must comply with the acid deposition provisions of the Clean Air Act. SO_2 emissions must be cut to 2.5 lb/millionBtu by 1995 (Phase I) and to 1.2 lb/millionBtu by 2000 (Phase II). The unit's current emission rate is 3.5 lb/millionBtu, or 50,000 tons of SO_2 per year. How will the utility comply?

This is a complicated decision. Alternatives for compliance include almost infinite combinations of technologies (stack scrubbers, clean coal technologies, etc.) and business strategies (emission allowance sales or purchases, fuel switching, etc.). The decision team is also likely to be large, including engineers, financial analysts, operations managers, regulatory specialists, and corporate counsel. This is also a risky decision. Here is a small sample of the sources of uncertainty:

- How accurately can the team predict scrubber operating and capital costs?
- What will future emission allowances cost?
- What will happen to alternative fuel prices?
- Will the industry develop new technology that could affect the decision?

Defining Alternatives.   First, the decision team should carefully define the compliance options they wish to consider. Usually a large number of options can be discarded from the start as a result of technological or business constraints. Once a manageable number of options emerge, they must be broken down into individual, independent cost components assembled in a structured "decision tree."

Here are qualitative descriptions of four compliance options the decision team decides are worth further investigation:

1. *Install Phase I scrubber: Meet the minimum requirements now and retrofit to meet Phase II requirements in the year 2000.* The utility installs a scrubber that complies with Phase I requirements now. The scrubber has a known capital cost but an uncertain incremental operating cost. In 2000, the utility will retrofit the original scrubber to meet Phase II requirements. The retrofit will have uncertain capital and incremental operating costs.

2. *Install Phase II scrubber: Meet Phase II requirements immediately and free up emission allowances.* The utility installs a scrubber that complies with Phase II requirements now. The scrubber has a known capital cost but an uncertain incremental operating cost. Over the period from 1995 to 2000, the utility will free up a number of emission allowances, which they will sell for an uncertain price, subject to the development of an active air credits market. In this example, the development of an emission allowance market is given a 70 percent

possibility of occurrence. If an emission allowance market does not develop, the utility will not be able to realize value from its allowances.

3. *Switch fuel: Meet Phase II requirements now by switching to low-sulfur coal despite technological uncertainty.* The utility opts to switch to burning coal low enough in sulfur content to comply with Phase II requirements now. The utility can either purchase low-sulfur coal on the open market or continue to buy high-sulfur coal and clean it sufficiently. The coal cleaning option is subject to development of a technically feasible clean-coal technology (presently available technology cannot clean high-sulfur coal sufficiently to meet Phase II requirements for our hypothetical utility) and, if available, will have uncertain capital and incremental operating costs. In this example, development of effective technology is given an 80 percent likelihood of occurrence. If the utility opts (or is forced) to buy low-sulfur coal, it will do so at an uncertain price. In either case, the utility will free up a number of air emission allowances that it will sell for an uncertain price, subject to the development of an emission allowance market.

4. *Buy allowances and postpone decision: Meet Phase I requirements by purchasing emission allowances and delaying Phase II plans.* The utility will purchase emission allowances in sufficient quantities to meet Phase I requirements until 2000. If an emission allowance market develops, it will buy allowances on the open market at an uncertain price. If a market does not develop, it will be forced to buy allowances at EPA auction for an uncertain (most likely different) price. In 2000, it will be faced with the same decision to comply with Phase II requirements either by installing a Phase II scrubber or by switching to low-sulfur coal. We assume here that by delaying its decision, critical time is lost and the option to use clean-coal technology is no longer feasible.

Now the decision team can define individual cost components and arrange them into a decision tree. Figure 9-1 shows the tree for this decision, and it's immediately apparent that even greatly simplified compliance decisions can quickly generate complex decision trees. At this point, the decision tree has gone a long way toward controlling the ill effects of complexity and counterproductive group dynamics. The structure they've imposed on this problem won't allow individual team members much latitude to muddy the waters. Moreover, with a clear picture of the proposed analysis in mind, team members can now focus on collecting information in support of the needed cost probability distributions.

Analyzing Possible Costs.   There are a number of ways to establish probability distributions for individual cost components of any decision. They are too numerous and involved to describe in great detail here but include a variety of intensive interviewing techniques and analyses of historical, technical, and environmental data. The most important aspect of these analyses, though, is that probability information about *all possible cost outcomes* is collected and retained. Best estimates or expected values will not support decision models that highlight optimal decision when risk and uncertainty are significant. Detailed quantitative assumptions for this case example are shown in Tables 9-1 and 9-2.

The decision team can now build a decision model that incorporates cost and probability data. Using Monte Carlo simulation (in which a computer simulates the outcome of a series of uncertain events), the decision makers

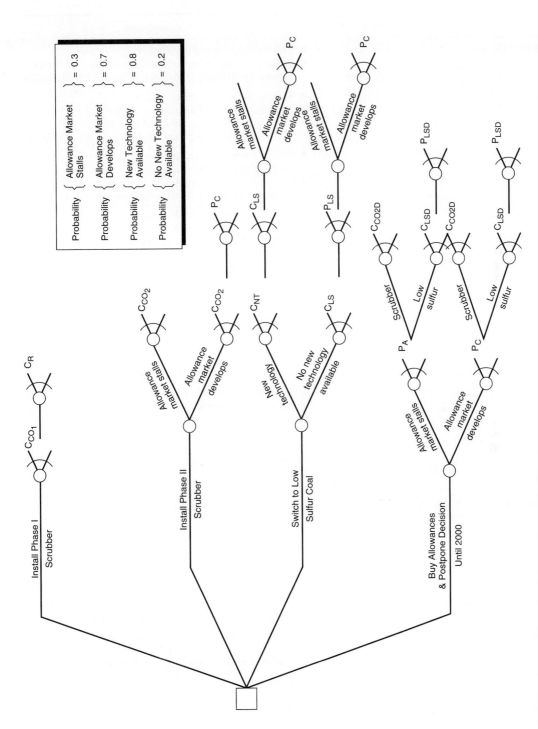

Figure 9-1. Clean Air Act compliance decision tree.

Table 9-1. Clean Air Act Capital and Incremental Operating Cost Assumptions

Variable description	Variable name	Assumptions
Phase I (1995)	C_{CO1}	■ $100 million capital investment ■ $33 million mean incremental operating cost,* with normal probability distribution, sigma = $6.5 million
Phase II (1995)	C_{CO2}	■ $125 million capital investment ■ Accumulate 18,571 allowances/year ■ $50 million mean incremental operating cost,* with normal probability distribution, sigma = $10 million
Phase II (2000)	C_{CO2D}	■ $160 million mean capital investment, with normal probability distribution, sigma = $30 million ■ $64 million mean incremental operating cost,* with normal probability distribution, sigma = $20 million
Retrofit to Phase II	C_R	■ Capital investment with triangular probability distribution, minimum = $40 million, most likely = $50 million, maximum = $60 million ■ $16 million mean incremental operating cost,* with normal probability distribution, sigma = $4 million
Switch fuels (1995)	C_{LS}	■ $30 million capital investment ■ $10 million mean incremental operating cost,* with normal probability distribution, sigma = $2.5 million
Switch fuels (2000)	C_{LSD}	■ $38 million capital investment with normal probability distribution, sigma = $9 million ■ $13 million mean incremental operating costs,* with normal probability distribution, sigma = $5 million
New clean-coal technology	C_T	■ $25 million capital investment ■ $43 million–$86 million mean incremental operating costs,* with uniform probability distribution

*Present value over 15 years.

Table 9-2. Clean Air Act Emission Credits and Fuel Price Assumptions

Variable description	Variable name	Assumptions
Price of emissions allowance on open market	P_C	■ $400–$800/allowance, with uniform probability distribution
Price of emissions allowance at EPA auction	P_A	■ $700 mean price per allowance, with truncated normal probability distribution, sigma = $200, minimum = $200, maximum = $1000
Low- and high-sulfur coal price differential (1995)	P_{LS}	■ $150.9 million mean fuel cost increase,* with triangular probability distribution, minimum = $100.9 million, maximum = $250.9 million
Low- and high-sulfur coal price differential (2000)	P_{LSD}	■ Same as P_{LS}

*Present value over 15 years.

Table 9-3.

Option	Expected (mean) cost	Range of results
1. Phase I scrubber	$174.0 million	$151–$201 million
2. Phase II scrubber	$136.1 million	$75–$200 million
3. Switch fuels	$102.1 million	$36–$283 million
4. Buy allowances and postpone decision	$196.3 million	$123–$305 million

can calculate probability distributions of the possible outcomes of each alternative. The expected (mean) cost and range of costs of each alternative are shown in Table 9-3.

Using traditional analysis of expected cost, the decision team would most likely choose Option 3 (switch fuels). But the range of potential costs illustrated in the table for Option 3 is also very wide (with a maximum of $283 million). By considering the *variability* of costs *within the range* of possible costs, a more sophisticated decision may emerge. Here are the results for each option in ascending order of preference based on potential risks.

Selecting the Best Option

Option 4: Buy Allowances and Postpone Decision. The expected cost of this option is $196 million (see Fig. 9-2). But there is also a 20 percent probability of an outcome with a cost in excess of $217 million. These high-cost outcomes occur when unfavorable events occur together; in this case, when the emission allowance market stalls and costs for both the scrubber and low-sulfur coal options emerge from the upper region of their expected distributions.

Option 1: Install Phase I Scrubber. Figure 9-3 shows that a Phase I scrubber has a set of potential outcomes with an expected value of $174 million. Like Option 4, this distribution of outcomes is mostly normal, but with a smaller standard deviation. There is still a 20 percent probability of an outcome with a cost in excess of $180 million.

Option 3: Switch Fuels. This option has the lowest expected (mean) cost at $102 million. The distribution of outcomes also has a minimum value—$36 million—lower than any other of the options (see Fig. 9-4). But the distribution of likely outcomes has a long tail which extends as high as $280 million. This is almost the same maximum value as the "worst decision" (Option 4). This long tail is driven by the unpredictability surrounding both the development of feasible clean-coal technology and the development of an emission allowance market.

Option 2: Install Phase II Scrubber. Because of the uncertainty surrounding the development of an active market for SO_2 emissions allowances, this option generates outcomes that fall into two ranges of values (see Fig. 9-3). There is a relatively high probability of an outcome in this case of *either* costs in the neighborhood of $115 million *or* costs around $175 million. Moreover, the probability that costs will not exceed $171 million is relatively high (80 percent).

Whereas traditional (point estimate) economic analysis suggests Option 3: switch fuels as the best decision, more thorough decision analysis points to Option 2: install Phase II scrubber as significantly less risky. Given the marginal risk aversion of many corporate decision makers, it's fair to say that, in this case, traditional economic analysis leads to the wrong answer.

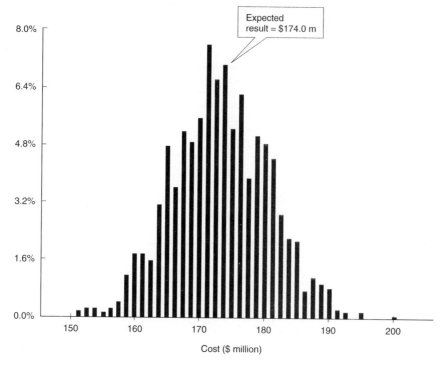

Figure 9-2. Clean Air Act Option 1 cost probability distribution.

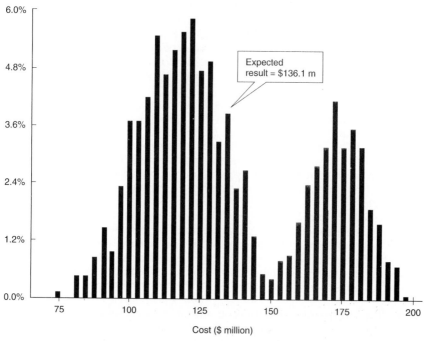

Figure 9-3. Clean Air Act Option 2 cost probability distribution.

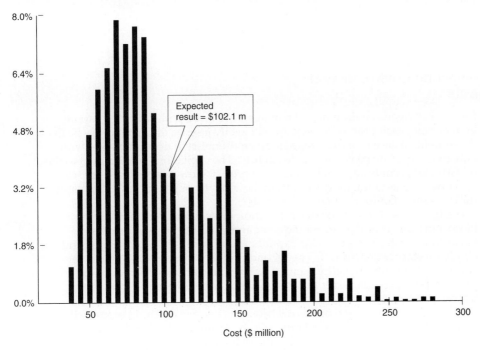

Figure 9-4. Clean Air Act Option 3 cost probability distribution.

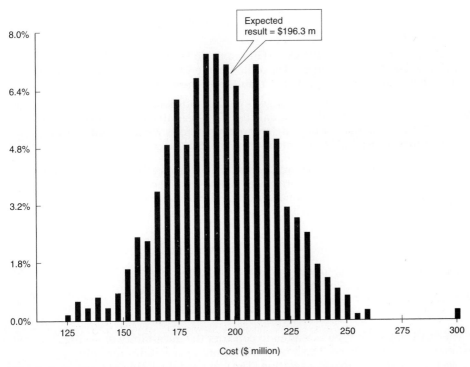

Figure 9-5. Clean Air Act Option 4 cost probability distribution.

Case Study 2:

Selecting Competing Environmental Capital Projects

Like all managers, environmental managers are faced with restricted capital budgets and, each year, must request and justify a series of capital projects. In this simplified case example, imagine an environmental decision maker with only two candidate projects on a "wish list." The capital budget allocated to the department permits approval of only one project. How can the manager select the correct project and, more important, how can he or she successfully justify the decision to company financial analysts?

The first project is a rainwater mitigation project. Rain currently falls on a hazardous waste storage impoundment and runoff must be treated as hazardous waste. The proposed capital expenditure is to roof the area and eliminate stormwater runoff. The second project proposes to engineer the substance MEK (methyl ethyl ketone) out of the company's production process. Both projects result in savings about which there is substantial uncertainty.

The most important step in this decision process is to create an organized, financially rigorous analysis of both projects. A sample analysis is shown in Fig. 9-6. Notice that this analysis contains the following information for each project:

1. *Fully developed cash flows.* Each project's cash flows are shown with specific disclosure of yearly savings anticipated. Also true (but not apparent in Fig. 9-6) is that savings have been modeled as probability distributions, with their inherent uncertainties included. This ensures that valuable information held by the decision maker is not lost.

2. *Present value at risk ("PVAR").* This variable is calculated like the traditional financial "present value." The added name "at risk" acts as a reminder that incremental savings expected to result from these projects are uncertain.

3. *Risk index.* Risk index is analogous to the traditional profitability index (risk index = PVAR divided by capital cost). This variable is more useful than net present value at risk for ranking competing projects when capital is scarce. Larger values of risk index indicate more desirable projects.

This structured analysis of environmental capital projects forces the decision maker to think carefully about anticipated savings and about the uncertainty of those savings. With no additional analysis, the environmental manager can communicate at least the following to corporate financial analysts:

	MEK project	Rainwater project
Capital cost	$250,000	$700,000
PVAR	$387,000	$1.001 million
Risk index	1.55	1.43

The analysis can then be extended to consider the uncertainty of savings estimates. Figures 9-7 and 9-8 show distributions of risk index for both projects and add valuable information: The standard deviation of the

Figure 9-6. Case 2. Cash flow projections and risk index.

Project description: 1. Rainwater mitigation project

Capital cost	Project life, years	Average annual savings	Payback, years	PVAR at 10.00%	IRR	Salvage value	Risk index
700,000	8	275,000	2.5	1,000,700	18.8%	1	1.4296

	Year 0	Year 1	Year 2	Year 3	Year 4	Year 5	Year 6	Year 7	Year 8	Year 9	Year 10
Capital cost	(700,000)										
Expense	0										
Inc. savings		100,000	150,000	200,000	250,000	300,000	350,000	400,000	450,000		
Taxes		(38,500)	(57,750)	(77,000)	(96,250)	(115,500)	(134,750)	(154,000)	(173,250)		
After-tax savings		61,500	92,250	123,000	153,750	184,500	215,250	246,000	276,750		
Depreciation		87,500	87,500	87,500	87,500	87,500	87,500	87,500	87,500		
Dep. tax shield		33,688	33,688	33,688	33,688	33,688	33,688	33,688	33,688		
Other investment		0	0	0	0	0	0	0	0		
Salvage value		0	0	0	0	0	0	0	1		
Net cash flow	(700,000)	95,188	125,938	156,688	187,438	218,188	248,938	279,688	310,439		

Project description: 2. Replace MEK in production process

Capital cost	Project life, years	Average annual savings	Payback, years	PVAR at 10.00%	IRR	Salvage value	Risk index
250,000	10	96,582	2.6	386,522	19.2%	1	1.5461

	Year 0	Year 1	Year 2	Year 3	Year 4	Year 5	Year 6	Year 7	Year 8	Year 9	Year 10
Capital cost	(250,000)										
Expense	0										
Inc. savings		39,558	51,047	64,194	77,186	90,094	102,985	115,868	128,749	141,628	154,506
Taxes		(15,230)	(19,653)	(24,715)	(29,717)	(34,686)	(39,649)	(44,609)	(49,568)	(54,527)	(59,485)
After-tax savings		24,328	31,394	39,479	47,469	55,408	63,336	71,259	79,181	87,101	95,021
Depreciation		25,000	25,000	25,000	25,000	25,000	25,000	25,000	25,000	25,000	25,000
Dep. tax shield		9,625	9,625	9,625	9,625	9,625	9,625	9,625	9,625	9,625	9,625
Other investment		0	0	0	0	0	0	0	0	0	0
Salvage value		0	0	0	0	0	0	0	0	0	1
Net cash flow	(250,000)	33,953	41,019	49,104	57,094	65,033	72,961	80,884	88,806	96,726	104,647

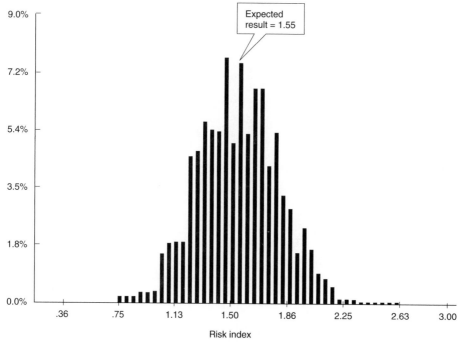

Figure 9-7. Distribution of risk index—MEK project. Standard deviation = 0.26.

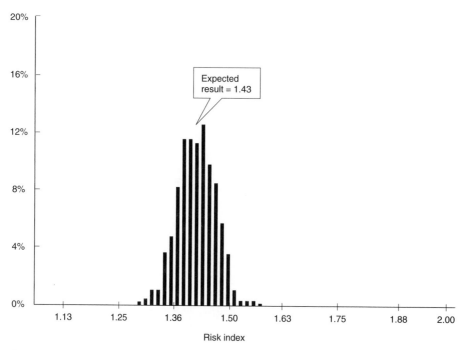

Figure 9-8. Distribution of risk index—rainwater project. Standard deviation = 0.04.

distribution of risk index for the rainwater project is substantially smaller than that of the MEK project. The decision maker is much more certain that rainwater project savings will actually be achieved. With this added information, we might well choose the rainwater project despite its lower risk index.

With a detailed analysis of environmental capital projects like the one described here in our arsenal, an environmental manager can combat nagging communication problems that have hobbled so many environmental capital programs. Financial analysts can no longer complain that they can't understand how environmental projects are selected. And environmental managers have a medium with which they can communicate the financial significance of their candidate projects—one that both recognizes the critical importance of uncertainty in environmental-financial decisions and that forces them to justify their requests in traditional financial terms.

In summary, other benefits of these decision analysis–based approaches can contribute to healthier environmental decisions:

Decision "road maps" are drawn. Structured analysis and documentation provide a record of complex decisions, which helps justify them to interested parties such as boards of directors.

Consensus is built. Decision team members that disagree are driven to reach consensus on complex technical and business issues. Frequently, team members come away knowing much more about the details of technology or their business.

Valuable financial performance data are collected. Once detailed analyses of environmental projects are assembled, actual resulting savings can be measured and compared. Decision makers then have a way to learn from their successes and failures.

There's no doubt that these methods are time-consuming and demanding. But the investment pales in comparison with the potential cost of a bad decision. As all costs—litigation, fines, remediation, compliance—of environment management skyrocket, it makes sense to make a modest investment up front to help make the best decisions possible.

References

1. Deloitte & Touche and Stanford University, *The Environmental Transformation of U.S. Industry,* Deloitte & Touche, San Francisco, California, November 1990.

2. Emerging Issues Task Force, *Accounting for Environmental Contamination Costs,* Financial Accounting Standards Board, Norwalk, Connecticut, 1991.

3. Emerging Issues Task Force, *Accounting for the Costs of Asbestos Removal,* Financial Accounting Standards Board, Norwalk, Connecticut, 1991.

4. Financial Accounting Standards Board, Statement of Financial Accounting Standards No. 5, "Accounting for Contingencies," Norwalk, Connecticut, March 1975.

5. Environmental Accounting: *The Issues, The Developing Solutions—A Survey of Corporate America's Accounting for Environmental Costs,* 1991, Price Waterhouse.

6. Financial Accounting Standards Board, Statement of Financial Accounting Standards Interpretation No. 14, "Reasonable Estimation of the Amount of Loss," Norwalk, Connecticut, September 1976.

7. Financial Accounting Standards Board, Statement of Financial Accounting Standards No. 38, "Accounting for Preacquisition Contingencies of Purchased Enterprises," Norwalk, Connecticut, September 1980.

8. SEC Regulation S-K, Item 101, *SEC Handbook,* Commerce Clearing House, Chicago, Illinois, 1991.

9. SEC Regulation S-K, Item 103, *SEC Handbook,* Commerce Clearing House, Chicago, Illinois, 1991.

10. SEC Regulation S-K, Item 303, *SEC Handbook,* Commerce Clearing House, Chicago, Illinois, 1991.

10
Environmental Legal Liabilities: Prevention and Control

Gary E. Marchant, Ph.D., J.D.*
Kirkland & Ellis, Washington, D.C.

In this chapter:

- Regulatory Noncompliance Liabilities
- Defense and Avoidance Strategies
- Common Law Liabilities
- Major Common Law Doctrines
- Common Law Defenses

Companies face a rapidly growing spectrum of potential environmental legal liabilities. The number and stringency of environmental regulations have steadily increased over recent years at both the federal and state levels, and now require a major commitment of resources and effort for compliance. A growing emphasis by enforcement agencies on more aggressive enforcement of these

---

*The author acknowledges the helpful suggestions of Michael S. Baram, J.D., of Bracken & Baram and the University of Boston School of Law, who reviewed this chapter.

regulatory requirements has also increased the potential for environmental liabilities. Independent of these regulatory requirements and attendant liabilities, companies are also subject to liability for environmental harms under the common law. Novel toxic tort and product liability theories continue to increase the liability exposure of companies.

This chapter reviews the basic theories and forms of regulatory and common law liabilities for environmental conduct. It also discusses many of the strategies and defenses that companies can pursue to limit environmental liabilities. Because there are important differences between regulatory and common law liabilities, regulatory noncompliance liability and its defenses are discussed first, followed by a discussion of common law liability and its defenses.

Part 1.
Regulatory Noncompliance
Liabilities and Defenses

Compliance with the burgeoning tangle of statutory and regulatory environmental requirements is a very expensive undertaking and a major burden for most companies. However, noncompliance with environmental requirements can be even more expensive. The frequency and magnitude of fines and penalties for environmental violations have been growing as rapidly, if not more so, as the adoption of new regulatory requirements that give rise to such violations in the first place.

Box 10-1. Legal Primer

Administrative. Relating to a government agency. For example, an administrative penalty is a fine or sanction imposed by an agency such as EPA.

Civil. Relating to any type of court action other than a criminal proceeding. For example, a civil penalty is a fine imposed by a court in a noncriminal case.

Common law. The body of principles and rules established by judicial case law and enforced by the courts. A common law action is one brought under judicially created causes of action rather than the law created by the legislature.

Criminal. Relating to an act that is in violation of the penal law. A criminal action is brought by the state against an individual or organization for violation of the penal code. Prison sentences can only be imposed in criminal cases.

Guidance. A nonbinding document produced by an administrative agency that is intended to assist regulated entities in complying with regulations. Although an entity cannot be penalized for violation of a guidance, the guidance can provide persuasive authority to a court on an agency's interpretation of its regulations.

Law. A rule of action or conduct that is established by a statute, regulation, or judicial decision. A rule that has the status of "law" is binding and can be enforced in the courts.

Liability. A penalty, debt, or obligation incurred as a result of a violation of statutory or regulatory requirements or the common law.

Preemption. Doctrine established the Supremacy Clause of the Constitution that provides for federal law to take precedence over conflicting or inconsistent state law.

Products liability. The liability of manufacturers, distributors, and sellers of products to compensate persons injured by such products. A product liability action is a lawsuit brought by a person allegedly injured by a product against the manufacturer, distributor, or seller of the product.

Regulation. A rule or order adopted by an administrative agency under the authority of a statute enacted by the legislature. A federal regulation has the force of law when adopting by notice-and-comment rule making.

Rule making. The process for adopting a regulation. A federal regulation is adopted by notice-and-comment rule making which involves publication of the proposed regulation in the *Federal Register*, providing an opportunity for public comment, and publication of the final regulation with a supporting statement.

Standard. A rule of conduct or restriction on an activity established by a statute or regulation. For example, a regulation may establish a specific numerical standard or limitation on the discharge of a pollutant.

Statute. An act of the legislature that regulates conduct or activities. A statute may directly regulate the activity in question, or it may authorize an administrative agency to adopt regulations consistent with the statute to regulate conduct.

Toxic tort. A lawsuit brought under the common law to recover for an injury allegedly caused by exposure to a toxic substance. A "tort" is an injury or wrong that can be remedied by a court.

Liabilities

Types of Regulatory Requirements

The ultimate source of most legal environmental requirements is a complex matrix of federal and state statutes, most of which regulate a specific environmental medium or product type. A list of the major federal environmental and health statutes is provided in Table 10-1. Most facilities and products will be subject to a number of complementary and overlapping statutes. Under each statute is a massive set of agency regulations, guidelines, policy statements, decisions, and orders that provide additional specifics and guidance on the requirements imposed on companies by a particular statute. Only regulations adopted by notice and comment rule making and statutes are federal law for

Table 10-1. Major Federal Health and Environmental Statutes

Statute	Citation	Subject matter
National Environmental Policy Act (NEPA)	42 U.S.C. §§ 4321–4370c	Environmental impact statements
Comprehensive Environmental Response, Compensation, and Liability Act (CERCLA)	42 U.S.C. §§ 9601–9675	Cleanup of abandoned hazardous waste sites
Emergency Planning and Community Right-to-Know Act (EPCRA)	42 U.S.C. §§ 11001–11050	Disclosure of toxic releases
Resource Conservation and Recovery Act (RCRA)	42 U.S.C. §§ 6901–6992k	Solid and hazardous waste disposal
Clean Air Act (CAA)	42 U.S.C. §§ 7401–7611q	Air pollution
Clean Water Act (CWA)	33 U.S.C. §§ 1251–1387	Water pollution
Toxic Substances Control Act (TSCA)	15 U.S.C. §§ 2601–2671	Toxic substances
Federal Insecticide, Fungicide and Rodenticide Act (FIFRA)	7 U.S.C. §§ 136–136y	Pesticides
Safe Drinking Water Act (SDWA)	42 U.S.C. §§ 300f–300j-26	Drinking water
Occupational Safety & Health Act (OSH Act)	29 U.S.C. §§ 651–678	Worker safety and health
Federal Food, Drug and Cosmetic Act (FFDCA)	21 U.S.C. §§ 301, *et seq.*	Drugs and food additives
Consumer Product Safety Act (CPSA)	15 U.S.C. §§ 1261–1274	Consumer products

which compliance is compulsory. However, the various policy statements, guidances, and other materials produced by agencies offer important insights on the agency's views and positions and should also be carefully monitored and considered in compliance programs.

This matrix of statutes, regulations, and other documents imposes a set of specific duties and requirements on regulated companies. These obligations can be of several forms. The most common type of requirement is a specific limit on the discharge of a pollutant from a source. These emission or effluent limitations can be a performance standard that sets a quantitative limit on the discharge of particular pollutants and allows the company to choose the most cost-effective technology or method to achieve the specified limit. For example, a Clean Water Act effluent limitation may set a numerical upper limit on the concentration of phosphorus that is permitted in the effluent discharged by a wastewater-treatment plant. Alternatively, the statute or regulation may itself specify the technology or method of compliance. Such a design standard may, for example, require an electric utility to use a scrubber to reduce sulfur dioxide emissions. Pollution discharges from a facility may also be controlled by process-oriented controls that regulate specific manufacturing processes to prevent or limit leaks and other discharges. Examples include requiring leak-detection systems for process equipment and regulating the chemicals that are used in the manufacturing process. These process-oriented controls, which are becoming increasingly popular under various pollution-prevention programs, usually involve a greater degree of regulatory intrusion in the company's manufacturing and business decision making than do traditional end-of-pipe controls.

Many environmental statutes also impose various types of monitoring and notification requirements on companies. For example, under the Resource Conservation and Recovery Act (RCRA), facilities must notify EPA of any accidental spills or discharges of hazardous chemicals. Workers must be provided information about hazardous substances in the workplace under OSHA's hazard communications standard promulgated under the Occupational Safety and Health Act (OSH Act). The Emergency Planning and Community Right-to-Know Act (EPCRA) of 1986 requires companies to report data on annual releases of hazardous chemicals to the general public. These and other notification requirements impose substantial paperwork burdens on companies and require careful diligence to ensure that all requirements and deadlines are met.

Various statutes and their implementing regulations also impose requirements or restrictions on the production, testing, sale, use, or disposal of specific types of products. For example, new pesticides must be approved by EPA under the Federal Insecticide, Fungicide and Rodenticide Act (FIFRA) before they can be put on the market. New drugs must undergo an extensive review process under the Federal Food, Drug and Cosmetic Act to ensure that they are safe and effective. Labeling requirements are frequently imposed on consumer products by the Consumer Product and Safety Commission to ensure that such products are used safely. Some products, such as PCBs, may be completely banned by regulation or statute.

Environmental statutes and regulations may also impose remediation and compensation requirements to help clean up past environmental problems. The Comprehensive Environmental Response, Compensation and Liability Act (CERCLA), or Superfund, requires responsible parties to pay for the cleanup of abandoned hazardous-waste disposal sites. Although Congress did not expressly require strict liability for CERCLA recovery actions, most courts have interpreted the statute to impose strict liability. Since liability is also retroactive, a company may have exercised all due care in lawfully disposing its wastes and yet still be liable under CERCLA. Liability under the statute is also joint and several, and so one company can be held accountable for the entire cost of cleaning up a site even if it was a relatively minor contributor to the contamination.

The most recent type of regulatory requirements are market mechanisms such as pollution taxes or tradable permit programs. These approaches require companies to pay a tax or buy a permit for each unit of pollution they discharge, and provide the greatest flexibility for how pollution reductions will be achieved both within and between companies. An example is the acid rain provisions of the 1990 Clean Air Act Amendments, which allow utilities and other emitters of sulfur dioxide to buy and sell emission credits.

These various types of requirements imposed by environmental statutes and regulations are often applied to individual facilities through permits. For example, companies are required to obtain permits for discharges into waterways, for emissions into the air, and to generate, transport, or dispose of hazardous wastes. A permit usually includes quantitative limits on pollution discharges, as well as other requirements such as notification and monitoring requirements. Violation of permit conditions is treated as a violation of statutory requirements.

In addition to being liable for its own actions, a company can be liable under statutes such as CERCLA or RCRA for the unlawful conduct of other companies with which it has a business relationship. For example, a company can be held liable for the cleanup of any contaminated property that it has purchased, even though it was not responsible for or aware of the past practices that caused the contamination. Such liabilities, which can amount to many millions of dollars, can arise from acquisitions of real property, corporate acquisitions, mergers, restructurings, loans, and long-term leases. A company can also be liable for the conduct of the waste-disposal company with which it has a contractual relationship to remove and properly dispose of wastes.

Enforcement of Regulatory Requirements

Environmental agencies have a number of options available for enforcing environmental regulations. An agency that finds a company in noncompliance with a regulatory requirement can send a warning letter, issue an administrative order to require corrective action, initiate an administrative penalty proceeding to impose fines, file a civil action in the courts to obtain monetary or injunctive relief, or bring criminal charges against the violator. In addition, private citizens can file "citizen suits" under many environmental statutes to require compliance with regulatory requirements and to impose penalties on violators. In addition, most federal environmental statutes provide for citizen awards of up to $10,000 to any individual who comes forward with information leading to the arrest and conviction of any person or company for violation of the statute.

Box 10-2. Citizen Suits

Every major federal environmental statute authorizes private citizens to bring "citizen suits" under certain circumstances to require a company or the agency to comply with the statutory requirements. The citizen suit provisions that have been utilized the most are those of the Clean Water Act, which were recently construed by the U.S. Supreme Court in *Gwaltney* v. *Chesapeake Bay Foundation*, 484 U.S. 49 (1987).

Section 505(a) of the CWA authorizes a private citizen, in the absence of federal or state enforcement, to commence a civil action against any person "alleged to be in violation" of a federal or state discharge permit. If the citizen prevails in such an action, the court may enjoin the activity and/or order the illegal discharger to pay a fine to the U.S. treasury. The statute also allows the court to award attorney fees and costs to the private citizen that brought the suit.

In *Gwaltney*, a meatpacking plant repeatedly exceeded the effluent limitations in its discharge permit. Two environmental organizations brought a citizen suit based on the company's permit violations. Although the district court and federal appeals court held in favor of the environmental organizations, the Supreme Court remanded because there had been no finding that the company was continuing to violate its permit. The Supreme Court acknowledged that EPA can bring actions for past violations of the act, but held that the citizen suit provisions are prospective and therefore can be used only to abate an ongoing violation. The court stated that "the citizen suit is meant to supplement rather than to supplant governmental action."

In the past few years, both federal and state authorities have significantly increased environmental enforcement efforts, resulting in both increased civil and criminal sanctions. For example, in the period from 1989 to 1991, EPA assessed $200 million in civil penalties and criminal fines, which is more than it assessed in the entire previous 17-year history of the agency (1972–1988). See also Fig. 10-1. The rationale for the increased emphasis on aggressive enforcement of environmental compliance was stated recently by EPA in developing a more rigorous enforcement policy under RCRA:

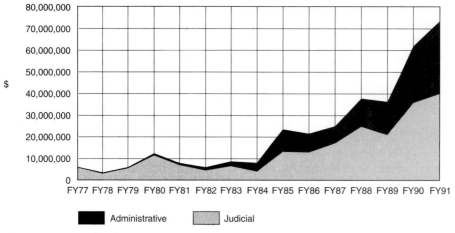

Figure 10-1. Federal, judicial, and administrative penalties assessed fiscal year 1977 to fiscal year 1991. (*EPA, "Enforcement Accomplishments Report FY 1991," April 1992.*)

> An effective enforcement program must detect violations, compel their correction, ensure that compliance is achieved in a timely manner, and deter other violations. The RCRA enforcement program will obtain substantial voluntary compliance only if the regulated community perceives that there is a greater risk and cost in violating a requirement than in complying with it.*

The increased emphasis on enforcement has been facilitated by new reporting requirements and computer databases that allow agencies to collect and evaluate data submitted by companies. In recent years, many health and environmental statutes have imposed increased recordkeeping and reporting requirements on companies, providing a large set of data that enforcement officers can use to detect and prove noncompliance. For example, EPCRA requires manufacturing facilities with more than 10 employees to annually report releases of some 300 chemicals to the environment. The Pollution Prevention Act of 1990 requires companies to file a toxic chemical source-reduction and recycling report for each of these 300 reportable chemicals that the company uses.

The federal government and to a lesser extent the states have recently begun to emphasize cross-program, multimedia enforcement. Instead of just monitoring a company's compliance with a media-specific law such as the Clean Air Act or the Clean Water Act, EPA enforcement officials are now reviewing a company's total compliance activities with respect to all environmental and related regulations. The goal is comprehensive identification and remediation of prob-

---

*EPA, *The Nation's Hazardous Waste Management Program at a Crossroads,* July 1990.

lems at a facility. As part of this emphasis on multimedia enforcement, EPA recently entered into an enforcement Memorandum of Understanding with OSHA to help coordinate EPA and OSHA enforcement efforts. EPA also entered into a Memorandum of Understanding with the FBI in 1982 under which the FBI has agreed to provide investigative manpower when requested by EPA for criminal environmental investigations.

An enforcement action by a state or federal agency is usually initiated by a complaint from workers or nearby citizens, as a result of a failure to comply with reporting requirements or on the basis of the information contained in reports to the agency, or following a random inspection. Once a facility has been targeted, the agency will usually conduct an inspection of the facility. (See Box 10-3.) If violations are found, the agency will normally issue an administrative order requiring corrective action and possibly imposing penalties. If the violations are serious, the agency may refer the case to the Justice Department for civil or criminal prosecution.

Box 10-3.   What to Do When the Inspector Knocks

The major investigative tools of environmental enforcement officials are inspections, subpoenas for documents, and employee interviews. A company's rights with respect to each of these enforcement tools are summarized below:

Inspections. Government inspectors may show up to inspect a facility with or without a search warrant, and with or without advance notice. Although a company can refuse entry to inspectors without a search warrant, such a strategy may be counterproductive because inspectors can usually obtain a warrant quickly and will be more hostile and adversarial as a result of the initial denial of entry. A few statutes provide for inspections without a search warrant, but the constitutionality of mandatory searches without a warrant has not yet been decided by the courts. A search warrant gives the inspector the right to search specified places and seize specified objects, but it does not give the right to interview employees. The company should designate an official to accompany the inspector and document the details of the search. The inspector must furnish a receipt for any documents or other materials that are seized. If the inspector takes samples, the company should request a split sample so that it can verify the government's sampling and test results.

Subpoenas for documents. Agencies such as EPA have been granted authority to issue subpoenas for documents. A grand jury acting at the request of a

---

(Continued)

prosecutor in a criminal case may also issue a subpoena. A subpoena allows an investigator access to a company's records and documents. The company should keep a record of any documents turned over to the government inspectors. Documents covered by the attorney-client privilege or some other privilege should be withheld. A subpoena can be quashed by a court if it is unreasonable or calls for the production of privileged documents.

Employee interviews. Government investigators are increasingly relying on interviews with a company's employees to establish the factual basis for an enforcement action. Companies should notify employees of their rights in such interviews, which includes the right to decline to be interviewed, the right to have counsel present, and the right to terminate the interview at any time. Company counsel should debrief any employee who has been interviewed by enforcement officials in order to collect information and maintain a record of an ongoing investigation.

SOURCE: Chemical Manufacturers Association, *The Knock on the Door: Preparing for and Responding to a Criminal Investigation*, 1991.

A company that has been issued an administrative order can consent to the order and negotiate the corrective measures and any assessed penalties recommended by the agency. Alternatively, the company can contest the order, in which case an administrative law judge (for an administrative action) or a judge (for a civil or criminal referral) will decide the merits of the case.

Administrative and Civil Liability

A company that has been found to be in violation of the requirements of environmental statutes or regulations is subject to civil penalties of thousands of dollars per violation per day. Every major federal environmental statute provides for such civil penalties. Once EPA determines a facility is in violation of one or more environmental regulations, it can initiate its own administrative action or refer the matter to the Justice Department for a civil trial. Administrative actions are more frequent and on average result in smaller penalties than judicial actions. For example, in 1991, approximately 89 percent of all EPA cases with penalties were administrative actions while 11 percent were judicial actions. However, 56 percent of all EPA federal penalty dollars came from the relatively smaller number of judicial actions. The highest administrative penalty in 1991 was $3.4 million for an action brought under RCRA, whereas the highest judicial civil penalty was $6.2 million for a case brought under the Clean Water Act. The distribution of administrative and judicial penalties by size is shown for 1991 in Fig. 10-2.

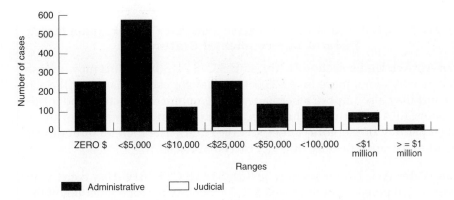

Figure 10-2. Distribution of civil and administrative penalties—all programs—for environmental violations, fiscal year 1991. (*EPA, "Enforcement Accomplishments Report FY 1991," April 1992.*)

Table 10-2. EPA Administrative and Civil Actions 1982–1991

Year	EPA administrative actions initiated	EPA civil referrals to Justice Department
1982	864	112
1983	1848	165
1984	3124	251
1985	2609	276
1986	2626	342
1987	3194	304
1988	3085	372
1989	4136	364
1990	3804	375
1991	3925	393

SOURCE: EPA, *Enforcement Accomplishments Report FY 1991,* April 1992.

The number of both administrative and civil judicial actions has increased substantially over the last decade. As shown in Table 10-2, the annual number of administrative actions initiated by EPA rose from 864 in 1982 to approximately 4000 per year in each of the years from 1989 to 1991. Similarly, the number of civil referrals from EPA to the Justice Department increased from 112 in 1982 to almost 400 in 1991. Moreover, the size of penalties imposed has also increased dramatically. In 1991 alone, the EPA collected 23 percent of all civil penalty dollars collected in the history of EPA. The civil and administrative penalty provisions of some of the major federal environmental statutes are summarized in Box 10-4.

Box 10-4. Civil and Administrative Penalties under Some Major Federal Environmental Statutes

Clean Air Act. Under section 113(b), 42 U.S.C. § 7413(b), a court may impose a civil penalty of not more than $25,000 per day for each violation of the act. The court may also impose a permanent or temporary injunction under this provision. EPA is authorized to impose administrative penalties of up to $25,000 per day of violation under section 113(d). The total amount of any such administrative penalty may not exceed $200,000.

Clean Water Act. Under section 309(d), 33 U.S.C. § 1319(d), a court may impose a civil penalty not to exceed $25,000 per day for each violation of the act. A court may also permanently or temporarily enjoin an activity that violates the act. The act also provides for administrative penalties assessed by EPA under section 309(g). EPA may assess a penalty of up to $10,000 per violation for a class I civil penalty, and a penalty of up to $25,000 per violation for a class II violation. The maximum amount of any penalty shall not exceed $25,000 for a class I penalty and $125,000 for a class II penalty.

RCRA. Section 3008(g), 42 U.S.C. § 6928(d), provides for civil penalties that are not to exceed $25,000 per day for each violation.

CERCLA. Unlike most other environmental statutes that regulate a company's current environmental practices, a central purpose of CERCLA is to impose liability for past conduct. Most courts have interpreted CERCLA to impose strict, joint, and several liability on responsible parties for the cleanup of abandoned hazardous-waste sites. In addition, CERCLA provides for civil penalties of up to $25,000 per violation of the notification and other requirements of the act.

Several factors are important in determining the size of an administrative or civil penalty that is imposed by EPA or a court for a particular violation. For example, under the new RCRA Civil Penalty Policy issued by EPA in October 1991, penalties for RCRA violations are calculated in a four-step analysis. First, an appropriate "gravity-based penalty," or "GBP," is calculated based on the "probability of harm" posed by the violation and its "extent of deviation from regulatory requirements." Next, a multiday component is factored in based on the duration of the violation. Third, the overall GBP is adjusted based on case-specific factors. Finally, the penalty is assessed to ensure that the economic benefits of noncompliance are recouped. Section 309(d) of the Clean Water Act requires consideration of similar factors in assessing civil penalties, including "the seriousness of the violation or violations, the economic benefit (if any) resulting from the violation, any history of such violations, any good-faith efforts to comply with the applicable requirements, the economic impact of the penalty on the violator, and such other matters as justice may require." Other statutes identify similar factors that are to be considered in setting the amounts of administrative or civil penalties.

Criminal Liability

The major federal environmental statutes provide for criminal liability for many of the same offenses that are subject to civil liability. Criminal sanctions tend to apply to a narrower range of violations, however, and can be significantly more severe than civil sanctions. The criminal enforcement provisions of many of the major statutes are summarized in Box 10-5. Although many of the major environmental statutes have provided for criminal sanctions since they were enacted in the early 1970s, these provisions were used very infrequently prior to 1982. In that year, EPA established an Office of Criminal Investigations and the Department of Justice created the Environmental Crimes Section. With these units in place, criminal environmental enforcement began in earnest in 1982 and has been steadily increasing in importance since that time. As shown in Table 10-3, the number of EPA criminal referrals to the Justice Department rose from 20 in 1982 to 81 in 1991, and the number of defendants convicted rose from 11 to 82 in the same time period. The total number of months that defendants in federal cases were sentenced to jail for environmental violations increased from zero in 1982 to 963 months in 1991.

Box 10-5. Criminal Sanctions under Some Major Federal Environmental Statutes

Clean Air Act. Under section 113(c), 42 U.S.C. § 7413(c), any person who knowingly violates many provisions of the act is subject to a fine, imprisonment for 1 to 5 years, or both. A person who knowingly releases a hazardous air pollutant into the air, placing another person in imminent danger of death or serious bodily injury, is subject to a fine, up to 15 years of imprisonment, or both. A person who negligently releases such a pollutant and places another person in imminent danger is subject to a fine, up to 1 year of imprisonment, or both. These penalties for release of hazardous air pollutants can be doubled for subsequent violations.

Clean Water Act. Section 309(c), 33 U.S.C. § 1319(c), provides for fines of from $2500 to $25,000 per day of violation, imprisonment for up to 1 year, or

---

(Continued)

both for negligent violations of permit conditions or limitations. A knowing violation can result in a fine of from $5000 to $50,000 per day, imprisonment for up to 3 years, or both. These penalties can be doubled for subsequent violations. A person who knowingly violates the act and places another person in imminent danger of death or serious bodily injury is subject to a fine of up to $250,000, imprisonment for up to 15 years, or both. A company or other organization that commits such a violation is subject to a fine of up to $1 million. The doubling provision applies to subsequent violations.

RCRA. Under section 3008(d), 42 U.S.C. § 6928(d), any person who knowingly transports, stores, treats, or disposes of hazardous waste in violation of the act's provisions is subject to a fine of up to $50,000 per day of violation, imprisonment for 2 to 5 years, or both. Subsequent violations are subject to doubled penalties. A person who knowingly endangers another person by violating the act is subject to a fine of up to $250,000, imprisonment for up to 15 years, or both. A company that is convicted of such a violation is subject to a fine of up to $1 million.

Table 10-3. EPA Criminal Enforcement 1982–1991

Year	Referrals to Justice Department	Defendants convicted	Months sentenced
1982	20	11	
1983	26	28	
1984	31	26	6
1985	40	40	78
1986	41	66	279
1987	41	58	456
1988	59	50	278
1989	60	72	325
1990	65	55	745
1991	81	82	963

SOURCE: EPA, *Enforcement Accomplishments Report FY 1991*, April 1992.

Several factors are responsible for the increasing emphasis on criminal environmental enforcement. A key factor is public opinion, which has been driving more aggressive criminal enforcement activities by authorities. The *Wall Street Journal* reported on July 23, 1991, the findings of a public opinion survey by Arthur D. Little, Inc., which found that "Americans rank corporate environmental crimes more serious than insider trading, antitrust violations, and worker health and safety violations. Some 74 percent of 1000 people surveyed said executives should be held personally liable for their companies' environmental offenses."

Congress, no doubt responding to public sentiment, has been actively promoting a greater emphasis on criminal sanctions for environmental violations. For example, Congress has recently upgraded certain violations under statutes such as the Clean Water Act and RCRA from misdemeanors to felonies, helping to make these violations a greater priority for prosecutors. Congress has also authorized funding for much larger criminal environmental enforcement efforts. Section 202 of the Pollution Prosecution Act of 1990 authorizes EPA to increase the number of criminal investigators to 200 by 1995, which is three times larger than the current force.

Another important change in criminal environmental enforcement is that corporate officers and not just corporations are now being prosecuted. For many years, most criminal sanctions for environmental violations involved fines imposed on the corporation. However, there has been a growing emphasis in recent years on the use of prison terms as a penalty and deterrent for environmental violations. Since corporations cannot be sentenced to prison terms, prosecutors have been focusing more on corporate officers or employees who can be sentenced to prison terms.

The Federal Sentencing Guidelines, required by the Sentencing Reform Act of 1984, have also contributed to more and longer prison sentences for environmental violations. In the past, judges had broad discretion in imposing criminal sentences and routinely suspended the sentences for most convicted environmental violators. The Sentencing Guidelines for individuals enacted in 1987 prescribe a sentencing formula with a predetermined range of sentences that take into account various mitigating or aggravating factors. The guidelines prohibit the routine suspension of sentences. The 1987 Sentencing Guidelines include a specific section for environmental crimes. Sentences under the guidelines are calculated by a three-step process: (1) identify the base offense; (2) consider any mitigating or aggravating circumstances; and (3) determine the final sentence, taking into account criminal history. The categories of environmental violations and range of sentences for individuals provided by the Sentencing Guidelines for environmental crimes are summarized in Table 10-4. Sentencing Guidelines for corporations are also under development for environmental violations.

The key issue in most criminal environmental cases is whether the defendant "knowingly" violated the statute or regulation at issue. Most federal environmental statutes require a "knowing" violation before criminal sanctions can be imposed. A few provisions, such as section 309(c) of the Clean Water Act, provide for misdemeanor convictions for a "negligent" violation of statutory requirements. An act is negligent if the actor failed to take reasonable care. A few statutes, such as the Federal Food, Drugs and Cosmetic Act, impose strict liability which provides for criminal sanctions for violations even if the defendant took due care.

Table 10-4. Categories of Environmental Crimes under Federal Sentencing Guidelines

Sentencing guideline	Category of violation	Months of imprisonment
2Q1.1	Knowing endangerment resulting from mishandling hazardous or toxic substances	51–63
2Q1.2	Mishandling hazardous or toxic substances, pesticides, record keeping, tampering, and falsification	0–6
2Q1.3	Mishandling other environmental pollutants, record keeping, tampering, and falsification	0–6
2Q1.4	Tampering or attempted tampering with public water system	27–33
2Q1.5	Threatened tampering with public water system	6–12

The requirement that the prosecution must demonstrate a "knowing" violation under many environmental statutes has not been applied rigorously by many courts. It is well established that the defendant need not know that the activity in question violated a regulation or statute. Ignorance of the law is no defense. Rather, the prosecution need only show that the defendant knew that a particular act was being committed, such as the discharge of effluent into a waterway or the storage of drums of waste at a facility. If such acts turn out to violate regulatory or statutory requirements, the defendant will have been found to have committed a "knowing" violation. As one court recently described the current law, "'knowledge' as used in such regulatory statutes means knowledge that one is doing the statutorily prescribed acts, not knowledge that the statutes or potential health hazards exist." *United States* v. *Buckley,* 934 F.2d 84 (6th Cir. 1991). Under this standard, a person can be convicted of a criminal offense without any wrongful intent or awareness of wrongdoing, and it is immaterial whether the defendant acted in good faith.

The "responsible corporate officer" doctrine may also expand the criminal liability of corporate managers. This doctrine originated in strict liability statutes such as the Federal Food, Drug and Cosmetic Act. (See Box 10-6.) A corporate official, who by position and authority within the company had the power to prevent a violation but did not, is presumed to be culpable even if the official had no personal knowledge of the violation.

Box 10-6. The Origins of the Responsible Corporate Officer Doctrine

The "responsible corporate officer" doctrine, which can impose liability on a company official simply on the basis of his or her position within the corporation, arose under strict liability statutes such as the Federal Food, Drug and Cosmetic Act. The leading case establishing this doctrine is *United States v. Park*, 421 U.S. 658 (1975), in which a company and its president and CEO, Mr. Park, were charged with violations of the FFDCA for allowing rodent infestation of its food warehouses. The company pleaded guilty but Mr. Parks did not, contending that he had properly directed subordinates to correct the problem.

The U.S. Supreme Court rejected this delegation argument and concluded that Mr. Park, because of his position within the company, had a duty to seek out and remedy violations. In upholding the conviction of Mr. Park, the Court stated: "The requirements of foresight and vigilance imposed on responsible corporate agents are beyond question demanding, and perhaps onerous, but they are no more stringent than the public has a right to expect of those who voluntarily assume positions of authority in business enterprises whose services and products affect the health and well-being of the public that supports them."

While some courts have come close to applying the responsible corporate officer doctrine under environmental statutes that require a "knowing" violation, courts have so far stopped short of such an application. The courts have held that an officer's position and duties within an organization may be probative as to whether he or she "knew" or was willfully ignorant of the violation, and therefore liable. However, the courts have generally not adopted the responsible corporate officer doctrine in its pure form, which would impose automatic liability based solely on an officer's position within the organization. (See Box 10-7.) Nevertheless, both prosecutors and judges have demonstrated an increased zeal to pursue criminal liability for corporate officers on the grounds that they could have prevented the noncompliant conduct but did not. In one widely publicized case, *United States v. Pennwalt Corp.*, a federal judge did not allow Pennwalt's counsel to enter a guilty plea on behalf of the corporation but rather demanded that the company's president personally appear and enter the guilty plea even though he had no direct involvement in the unlawful conduct. Accordingly, corporate managers are unlikely to escape personal criminal liability by delegating responsibility for environmental compliance responsibility to lower-level officials.

Box 10-7. The Responsible Corporate Officer Doctrine and "Knowing" Violations

Most of the major federal environmental statutes require that a violation be "knowing" before criminal liability can be imposed. The courts have generally held that this knowledge requirement precludes application of the responsible corporate officer doctrine under such statutes. However, the courts still treat an officer's position within the company as probative of the officer's knowledge of the violation.

A good example is *United States* v. *MacDonald & Watson Waste Oil Co.*, 933 F.2d 35 (1991), in which a company that transported and disposed of hazardous wastes, several of its employees, and its president were convicted under RCRA by a jury of illegally disposing hazardous wastes.

The statute required a "knowing" violation, and the district court judge instructed the jury that such knowledge could be proven for the company's president, in the absence of proof of actual knowledge by the defendant, if the evidence did "establish that the defendant was what is called a responsible officer of the corporation committing the act. In order to prove that a person is a responsible corporate officer three things must be shown. First, it must be shown that the person is an officer of the corporation, not merely an employee. Second, it must be shown that the officer had direct responsibility for the activities that are alleged to be illegal. Simply being an officer or even the president of a corporation is not enough. The government must prove that the person had a responsibility to supervise the activities in question. And the third requirement is that the officer must have known or believed that the illegal activity of the type alleged occurred."

The jury found the company, the employees, and the president guilty. The appeals court, in reversing the conviction of the president, stated "that knowledge may be inferred from circumstantial evidence, including position and responsibility of defendants such as corporate officers, as well as information provided to those defendants on prior occasions. Further, willful blindness to the facts constituting the offense may be sufficient to establish knowledge. However, the district court erred by instructing the jury that proof that a defendant was a responsible corporate officer, as described, would suffice to conclusively establish the element of knowledge expressly required under [the statute]. Simply because a responsible corporate officer believed that on a prior occasion illegal transportation occurred, he did not necessarily possess knowledge of the violation charged. In a crime having knowledge as an express element, a mere showing of official responsibility under [the responsible corporate officer doctrine] is not an adequate substitute for direct or circumstantial proof of knowledge."

The bottom line of this and similar decisions is that the same evidence used to establish liability under the responsible corporate officer doctrine can be used as "circumstantial evidence" to establish actual knowledge, as long as the responsible corporate officer doctrine is not expressly referred to by name.

In addition to the individual liability of corporate officers and employees, a corporation itself can be held liable if any of its employees did have the requisite knowledge, because a corporation is presumed to be liable for the acts of any of its employees within the scope of employment. Moreover, a corporation can be held to have "knowingly" violated a statute or regulation even if no single individual had the necessary knowledge of the violation. Under the "collective knowledge" doctrine, liability can be imposed if the collective knowledge of all its employees created sufficient knowledge of the violation. Thus corporate liability could be imposed if one employee knew that a given pollutant was being discharged at a particular level and another employee knew that such a discharge would violate the applicable standard.

In addition to the substantial corporate and individual liabilities that can result from a criminal conviction for noncompliance with environmental regulations, there are other potential collateral consequences. Criminal convictions and penalties can result in disbarment from federal contracts, higher insurance premiums, common law liability, and even stockholder derivative suits. For example, both the Clean Water Act and the Clean Air Act have mandatory "listing" provisions that bar a facility from receiving any government contract, loan, or grant if the company or the facility operators have been convicted of a criminal violation. These potential consequences can be very harmful to a company's competitive position, and are further inducements to ensure full regulatory compliance.

State Requirements

In addition to federal regulatory requirements, states and municipalities may adopt their own environmental statutes and regulations that apply to certain activities and products. These state and local requirements can impose additional requirements on regulated companies. In the past, most state environmental requirements implement programs established by federal statutes. For example, under the federal Clean Water Act, EPA delegates authority for issuing and enforcing discharge permits to states with approved permitting programs. States also set water quality standards under the act, subject to EPA approval. Similarly, under the Clean Air Act, states are responsible for adopting and implementing "state implementation plans" (SIPs) designed to achieve compliance with federal ambient standards for air pollutants. Under these and other statutes, EPA has delegated authority to most states to implement the programs required by federal law, and performs only an oversight function to ensure that the state programs meet minimum federal criteria.

In recent years, states have been more aggressive in adopting independent state programs that are not based on or that exceed federal requirements. Examples include state laws requiring an environmental assessment or cleanup before property can be sold or transferred, and laws mandating reductions in the use of packaging materials or toxic chemicals. These state requirements usually include their own enforcement provisions, along with provisions for civil and criminal penalties. As these independent state requirements become more prevalent and stringent, they are assuming an increasingly central focus of industry compliance efforts and costs.

Most states also have some type of criminal environmental enforcement. The courts have ruled that the right against "double jeopardy" does not protect a company against separate enforcement actions by state and federal authorities for the same conduct. *United States* v. *Louisville Edible Oil Products*, 926 F.2d 584 (6th Cir. 1991). Accordingly, a company can be subject to federal and state criminal actions and sanctions for the same actions. Some state criminal laws impose requirements that are broader or more stringent than federal requirements. For example, the California Corporate Criminal Liability Act imposes criminal liability on corporate managers who fail to disclose product dangers to workers or consumers.

Local and municipal requirements are also becoming increasingly prevalent and important to corporate compliance efforts. With the renewed interest in environmental activism in recent years, many local governments are enacting environmental ordinances and other requirements that companies must comply with. These municipal laws typically focus on problems of local concern such as discharges into municipal wastewater-treatment plants, the siting of waste-disposal facilities, emergency planning, and recycling.

Box 10-8.   The State and Local Police Power

State and local governments have traditionally had a broad "police power" to protect the safety and health of their citizens. This authority, which extends beyond any specific state or local environmental statute or ordinance, can be applied in a very broad and unpredictable manner to regulate environmental conduct. The exercise of this state or local police power has great potential to conflict with or disrupt federal regulatory programs, but courts have historically been very reluctant to find preemption of such state or local actions.

A recent example is the U.S. Supreme Court's decision in *Wisconsin Public Intervenor* v. *Mortier*, 111 S.Ct. 2476 (1991). The small Wisconsin village of Casey adopted an ordinance requiring a permit for the use of pesticides, and authorized the town board to "deny the permit, grant the permit, or grant the permit with...any reasonable conditions on a permitted application related to the protection of the health, safety and welfare of the residents of the Town of Casey." The ordinance was enacted under a Wisconsin statute that accords villages with general police, health, and taxing powers.

Ralph Mortier applied for a permit to apply pesticides to a portion of his land but was denied approval by the town board to conduct the spraying program for which he had applied. He appealed the decision through the courts up to the U.S. Supreme Court on the ground that the town ordinance was preempted by the Federal Insecticide, Fungicide, and Rodenticide Act (FIFRA). Even though the Supreme Court recognized that FIFRA represented a "comprehensive regulatory statute" for the control of pesticides, it nevertheless upheld the town ordinance on the "assumption that the historic police powers of the states [and municipalities] were not to be superseded by the Federal Act unless that was the clear and manifest purpose of Congress."

Defenses and Avoidance Strategies for Liability from Regulatory Noncompliance

A number of strategies can help minimize the potential for regulatory noncompliance and the consequent environmental liabilities. Some of these strategies are discussed below, followed by a discussion of defenses that can prevent or mitigate liabilities if a company is found to be in noncompliance.

Avoidance Strategies

Compliance Audits.   The most effective way of avoiding liability for regulatory noncompliance is to ensure that a facility is in full compliance with all statutory and regulatory requirements. A periodic and comprehensive compliance audit can be very helpful in monitoring compliance and identifying any compliance problems that need to be corrected. EPA has published a policy statement on environmental audits that defines an audit as "a systematic, documented, periodic, and objective review of entities with relation to their meeting all environmental requirements."

The Department of Justice issued a policy document in July 1991 intended to encourage environmental auditing. The policy document identified factors that would affect criminal prosecutions for environmental violations, which are summarized in Box 10-9. The policy document states that self-auditing and voluntary disclosure of environmental violations by companies would be mitigating factors that the department would consider in exercising its prosecutorial discretion under environmental statutes. In other words, the existence of self-audits reduces the possibility of a criminal prosecution. Moreover, in setting civil penalties under most statutes, EPA considers good-faith efforts to comply as a mitigating factor, and a record of self-auditing is evidence of good-faith efforts to comply and therefore can also help reduce the size of any penalties that are imposed.

Box 10-9.   Department of Justice Policy Document for Environmental Criminal Prosecutions

In July 1991, the Department of Justice (DOJ) issued a policy document that was intended "to encourage self-auditing, self-policing and voluntary disclosure of environmental violations by the regulated community." The policy document listed "mitigating factors" that federal prosecutors would consider in exercising its enforcement discretion. No single factor would be dispositive in determining whether or not to prosecute, but rather all relevant factors will be considered "and given the weight deemed appropriate in the particular case." The following mitigating factors, which were not intended to be exclusive, were identified by the DOJ policy document as factors weighing in favor of greater leniency by prosecutors:

- Voluntary disclosure of noncompliance
- Cooperation with prosecutors
- Existence of comprehensive environmental compliance program and/or environmental compliance audits
- Nonpervasiveness of noncompliance (i.e., noncompliance is of limited obviousness, seriousness, duration, history, or frequency)
- Effective internal disciplinary system within company
- Subsequent compliance efforts, including prompt good-faith efforts to reach environmental compliance agreements with authorities

SOURCE: U.S. Department of Justice, Factors in Decisions on Criminal Prosecutions for Environmental Violations in the Context of Significant Voluntary Compliance or Disclosure Efforts by the Violator (July 1, 1991).

One down side to auditing is that some types of environmental violations or problems that may be discovered may have to be reported by law to authorities. Moreover, there has been considerable concern that an environmental compliance audit would aid prosecutors by providing a "road map" of the company's compliance status. One way to minimize this risk is to carefully document the actions taken to correct any violations identified in the self-audit. Companies can also attempt to protect the confidentiality of compliance audits by utilizing the attorney-client privilege, which protects confidential communications between a company and its counsel made in the context of the attorney-client relationship. While the attorney-client privilege does not protect the underlying facts about a company's noncompliance, it can be used to protect documents that are generated by a compliance audit. Protection afforded by the attorney-client privilege is often unpredictable and open to challenge, but certain steps can increase the likelihood that documents will be found by a judge to be privileged. The attorney-client privilege is more likely to apply if the audit is undertaken at the instruction of the attorney and is presented as a legal opinion. The documents should also be clearly labeled "privileged and confidential." Moreover, since the privilege only applies to documents that the parties intended to keep confidential, distribution of the documents should be limited to the extent possible to avoid waiver of the privilege. The documents may also be protected from disclosure by the attorney work product doctrine if the audit was conducted in anticipation of possible litigation.

Corporate Environmental Compliance Program. A written corporate environmental compliance program that clearly sets out the company's policies and responsibilities for environmental performance can also help prevent liability. Such a program should establish clear expectations and procedures for employees with respect to compliance with environmental requirements, set out a clear structure and chain of command within the corporation for responsibility for environmental performance, and establish effective mechanisms for detecting and communicating problems that could lead to potential environmental noncompliance. The program should also include worker training programs, written materials setting forth the company's environmental policies, and guidances for workers that cover common compliance problems or situations.

Record Retention Program. Maintaining careful records of all environmental compliance programs can be very helpful in demonstrating that the company is usually in compliance and has exercised due care. Documents should be easily accessible in case of a surprise inspection, and there should be a file management system in place to locate and retrieve any files currently being used. Records that should be retained include waste manifests, permits and permit applications, emergency preparedness plans, records of process or product changes or testing, inventory and storage records, waste process logs, maintenance and repair logs, and employee training records. In addition, all communications with regulatory agencies, environmental consultants, and waste-disposal contractees should be memorialized in writing and retained. Compilations of data on employee exposure levels and other monitoring results should also be retained for use in rule-making proceedings or lawsuits. A company should have a written records-retention policy that has been reviewed by counsel, and documents should only by destroyed consistent with this policy. As a general matter, all environmental records should be retained for a period of at least 10 years. The file management system should also identify and permit easy segregation of privileged documents.

Product Stewardship. A product stewardship program attempts to incorporate health, safety, and environmental concerns at all stages of a product's life cycle. Such "cradle to grave" stewardship promotes more environmentally friendly design, production, use, and disposal of products. Product stewardship begins with product design and makes environmental risk reduction and the design of safer products an important criterion in performance evaluation of new products at the research and development stage. At the production stage, a product stewardship program attempts to find ways to lower the use of energy and raw materials in the manufacturing process and to reduce pollution discharges. A key focus of product stewardship programs is to encourage the safe use and disposal of products after they leave the manufacturer's facility in order to reduce any manufacturer liabilities resulting from "downstream" injuries. A product stewardship program will therefore establish criteria for subcontractors and distributors to ensure that these business partners have adequate environmental protection practices. Inspections, seminars, and other educational efforts directed at subcontractors and distributors can help promote safer practices in such companies. Finally, a product stewardship program includes design factors, incentives, educational efforts, and/or recycling efforts to promote the safe disposal of a manufacturer's products.

A manufacturer should expressly indicate in its own written product stewardship program, and any agreements it enters with distributors or subcontractors pursuant to such a program, that the efforts to promote safe use and disposal of products is not an acceptance of legal liability for injuries resulting from misuse or improper disposal by downstream customers or users. However, because plaintiffs injured by a product almost always include the product manufacturer in any lawsuit, even if downstream misconduct or negligence was responsible for the injuries, a manufacturer's attempt to prevent such injuries through product stewardship will reduce the manufacturer's liabilities.

Transactional Due Diligence.   As discussed above, a purchaser of real property may assume the environmental liabilities incurred by the previous owners. Such transfers of liabilities may also occur under other transactions such as mergers and acquisitions. To avoid such liabilities, a purchaser or lender should conduct an environmental due diligence audit of the property in question. The environmental due diligence effort should include (1) an evaluation of the facility's current compliance status with applicable federal, state, and local environmental regulations; (2) an assessment of the history of the site and any environmental problems that may still remain from past uses; (3) an inspection of the site for the existence of potential environmental problems; (4) an investigation of the surrounding area for any environmental problems that may affect or implicate the property in question; and (5) a review of the past off-site waste-disposal practices of the facility. This audit should include a site assessment by qualified consultants.

Environmental due diligence serves two purposes. First, it informs the purchaser or lender of the potential liabilities associated with the transaction property, and this information can be used in valuing the property and setting the transaction price. Second, CERCLA provides an "innocent purchaser defense" that exempts a land purchaser from responsibility for past environmental liabilities if the purchaser can demonstrate that it did not know of such liabilities after undertaking "all appropriate inquiry."

A purchaser of real property should also insist on an indemnification clause in the purchase agreement that would require the original owner to indemnify the purchaser for any liability for environmental cleanups resulting from past activities at the facility. Although such an indemnification agreement will not protect the purchaser from liability imposed by the government, it would allow the purchaser to seek indemnification for such liability from the previous property owner. Companies should also insist on indemnification agreements and adequate environmental liability insurance from any waste-disposal service it employs.

Regulatory Participation.   In enacting environmental statutes, Congress usually provides general frameworks for regulatory programs but leaves the details to be filled in by the agency that has been delegated authority to administer the statute. Agencies such as EPA fill in the details of a regulatory program primarily through notice and comment rule-making under the Administrative Procedure Act (APA). The APA or the particular regulatory statute involved require the agency to publish its proposed regulation in the *Federal Register*, to provide an opportunity for public comment on the proposal, and in many cases to convene a hearing to provide for further public comment.

These opportunities for public participation provide an important chance for regulated interests to influence the agency to adopt reasonable regulations. Cost estimates, exposure data, and other evidence submitted by industry often play a key role in an agency's standard-setting process. It is usually much easier for an industry to persuade an agency such as EPA to adopt a reasonable position at the outset in the original rule making than to try to get the agency to change course after its regulations are finalized. Moreover, participation in rule-making proceedings is often required to preserve one's right to challenge the regulations in a future court action. Accordingly, full and effective participation in rule-making proceedings is critical to minimizing compliance problems in the future from unreasonable or infeasible regulatory requirements.

Defenses to Avoid or Mitigate Liabilities

The liability avoidance strategies summarized above should form a company's primary program for protecting against environmental liability. However, if these strategies fail and a company is charged with noncompliance with environmental statutes or regulations, there are several additional defenses a company can assert to protect against liability.

Challenging the Feasibility or Validity of Regulations.   Many regulations can be challenged at the enforcement stage on the grounds that they are infeasible or otherwise invalid. As one federal court of appeals recently stated, "[a]bsent an explicit withdrawal of jurisdiction, we will entertain affirmative defenses attacking the validity of an administrative regulation that is brought to us for enforcement," and indeed such review of standards at the enforcement stage remains "the ordinarily preferred method." *Atlantic & Gulf Stevedores, Inc.* v. *Occupational Safety & Health Review Comm'n*, 534 F.2d 541, 551 (3d Cir. 1976). Accordingly, unless expressly precluded by statute, a company may challenge the validity of a regulation at the enforcement stage. Grounds for such a challenge include a claim that the regulation is inconsistent with the requirements of the statute under which it was enacted, that procedural requirements were not met in the promulgation of the regulation, that compliance with the regulation is not feasible, or that the regulation is otherwise arbitrary and capricious.

Enforcement review of some regulations is, however, expressly precluded by statute. For example, section 509(b)(1) of the Clean Water Act provides for judicial review of many regulations promulgated under the act in the courts of appeals within 120 days of promulgation. Section 509(b)(2) states that an "[a]ction of the Administrator with respect to which review could have been obtained under paragraph (1) of this subsection shall not be subject to judicial review in any civil or criminal proceeding for enforcement." Similar provisions are found in other federal environmental statutes. These provisions preclude any challenge to regulations at the enforcement stage that could have been raised at the time the regulations were promulgated, and therefore underscore the importance of challenging the feasibility or legality of many regulations at the time they are adopted. Other statutes have been interpreted to allow some types of challenges to the validity of the regulation at the enforcement stage, while other challenges can only be brought in the preenforcement review stage. For example, procedural challenges to occupational health and safety standards adopted by OSHA may only be brought within 60 days of the date of enactment, whereas substantive challenges to the validity of the regulation may be brought at the preenforcement or enforcement stages. *National Industrial Constructors, Inc.* v. *Occupational Safety & Health Review Comm'n*, 583 F.2d 1048 (8th Cir. 1978).

Preemption.   A defense for failure to comply with a state statute or regulation is that the state law is preempted by federal law. The Supremacy Clause of Article VI of the U.S. Constitution requires the invalidation of any state law that conflicts with federal law. Preemption of state requirements can be expressed when Congress or a federal agency expresses a clear intent to preclude any state regulation in a particular subject area. Preemption can also be implied if there is a conflict between the state and federal law. Such implied preemption is found when it is impossible to comply with both the federal and state requirements, where Congress has "occupied the field" by regulating an area comprehensively, leaving no room for state regulation, or where the state law is an obstacle to the accomplishment and execution of the full objectives of Congress.

Therefore, any time the federal government has regulated a given subject matter, different or more stringent state regulations may be subject to a preemption challenge. A company that is charged with violating a state requirement will frequently be able to assert such a preemption defense, although courts are often reluctant to invalidate state regulations on this ground unless the federal government has indicated a clear preemptory intent.

Lack of Standing. Under the U.S. Constitution, courts are only authorized to act where a "case or controversy" exists. To meet this constitutional requirement, a party bringing a lawsuit must have a sufficient interest in the outcome of the litigation to present a true "case or controversy." To show such an interest or "standing," a party bringing a lawsuit must show that it will be injured in fact by the activity it is contesting, and that such injury is within the "zone of interests" that the applicable statute was intended to protect. The Supreme Court defined the "injury" requirement in *Sierra Club* v. *Morton*, 405 U.S. 727, 735 (1972), as follows:

> Abstract injury is not enough. The plaintiff must show that he has sustained or is immediately in danger of sustaining some direct injury as the result of the challenged conduct and the injury or threat of injury must be both real and imminent, not conjectural or hypothetical. [Citations omitted.]

Citizen suits and other actions brought by environmental organizations often encounter standing problems under the standard enunciated by the Supreme Court.

Consent Agreements. A company facing liability for environmental violations can often reduce the penalties by entering into a consent order with the agency. Enforcement officials are often willing to accept a lower penalty as part of a settlement to avoid the burden and uncertain outcome of a contested proceeding. EPA has been increasingly willing in recent years to mitigate penalties as part of a settlement agreement in return for a company's commitment to undertake supplemental pollution-reduction projects. These projects include company commitments to reduce the use of toxic substances in manufacturing processes, reduce pollutant discharges beyond the levels required by regulation, undertake restoration projects in the surrounding environment to clean up contamination caused by the unlawful conduct, conduct an environmental audit and correct any discovered problems, or to undertake public awareness campaigns on the importance of environmental compliance. The project agreed to by the violating company and the agency must have a sufficient nexus to the underlying violation. Although an agreement to undertake such a supplemental project may result in a significant penalty reduction, it will not eliminate the penalty entirely and may commit the company to ongoing requirements that may themselves be quite burdensome.

Part 2. Common Law
Liabilities and Defenses

"Common law" environmental requirements refer to judge-made rules and doctrines that are applied and enforced by the courts. Both civil and criminal liabilities are possible under the common law. Civil cases are usually brought by private citizens, while criminal cases are brought by government prosecutors. Common law rules derive from judicial precedent, and therefore are much less defined and fixed than statutes or regulations adopted by legislatures or regulatory agencies. Judges have considerable flexibility in the application of common law legal doctrines to a particular set of facts, and are free to expand or mold the doctrines to fit new sets of facts or other changes. Environmental lawsuits under the common law are often tried by juries. For these reasons, regulated parties face much greater unpredictability and uncertainty about the requirements imposed by common law than those imposed by statutes or regulations.

Major Common Law Doctrines

Common law doctrines for environmental liabilities can be grouped into the three categories discussed below: "toxic torts," products liability, and criminal liability.

Toxic Torts

"Toxic tort" cases are typically lawsuits brought by individuals or groups of individuals that have allegedly been injured from exposure to hazardous substances that have been discharged or have leaked from the defendant's facility or other property. The plaintiff in such actions will often pursue claims under a variety of legal theories, including nuisance, negligence, and strict liability. Nuisance arises from the unreasonable use of one's property that causes injury or annoyance to a neighbor. A public nuisance is defined by the Second Restatement of Torts as "unreasonable interference with a right common to the general public." Private citizens require some type of distinctive special injury to have standing to bring a public nuisance action.

Negligence is an unreasonable act or omission that causes harm to another person. Negligence and nuisance are both "fault" theories in that liability is only imposed if the defendant's actions are found to be unreasonable. Strict liability, on the other hand, applies even if the defendant has acted reasonably. Strict liability is usually limited to abnormally dangerous activities, which are defined by the six factors listed in Box 10-10. The manufacture or handling of toxic substances and hazardous wastes are frequently found to meet the criteria for abnormally dangerous activities, and thus are often subject to strict liability.

Box 10-10.   Abnormally Dangerous Activities

The Second Restatement of Torts identifies six factors that must be considered in determining whether an activity is "abnormally dangerous" and thus subject to strict liability. The six factors are:

1. Existence of a high degree of risk of some harm to the person, land or chattels, or others

2. Likelihood that the harm that results from it will be great

3. Inability to eliminate the risk by the exercise of reasonable care

4. Extent to which the activity is not a matter of common usage

5. Inappropriateness of the activity to the place where it is carried on

6. Extent to which its value to the community is outweighed by its dangerous attributes

Based on these six factors, most courts have treated the handling, storage, or disposal of toxic substances as an abnormally dangerous activity.

Even under strict liability in which there is no required showing of fault, the plaintiff must show that the defendant's product or activities was the proximate cause of his or her injuries. Proving medical or scientific causation in toxic tort actions is often the major hurdle for plaintiffs to overcome in such actions. Causation is particularly difficult to demonstrate for low-level exposure to toxic substances that does not result in any unique or "signature" diseases. The plaintiff must show both that the toxic substance in question was capable of causing the plaintiff's illness at the alleged exposure level and that such exposure resulting from defendant's action did indeed cause the disease in that particular case.

Courts have applied different standards for proving causation. Traditionally, courts have applied a "but for" standard, which requires the plaintiff to show that its injuries would not have occurred "but for" the defendant's actions. For example, in *In re Agent Orange Litigation,* Judge Weinstein held that "under either a strict liability or a negligence theory, plaintiffs must establish by a preponderance of the evidence a but-for causal connection between their claimed injuries and exposure to Agent Orange." 611 F. Supp. 1223, 1236 (D.C.N.Y. 1985). In contrast, many courts in recent years have rejected the "but for" test in favor of a more lenient "substantial factor" test. See, e.g., *Allen* v. *United States,* 588 F. Supp. 247 (D.Utah 1984), *rev'd* 816 F.2d 1417 (10th Cir. 1987). Under this test, plaintiffs can recover damages if they can show that the defendant's actions were likely to be a substantial factor in causing the injury. Once a plaintiff has shown that the defendant's actions are capable of causing the injury in question and may indeed have done so, the burden shifts to defendants under this standard to show that some other factor or party was responsible for the particular injury in that case.

In recent years, plaintiffs have brought claims to recover damages for nontraditional "injuries" allegedly resulting from exposure to toxic chemicals. Examples include claims for increased risk of future cancer, emotional distress resulting from fear of cancer, or "cancerphobia," and the costs of future medical surveillance. (See Box 10-11.) Although many courts have rejected such claims on doctrinal or evidentiary grounds, some courts have allowed substantial monetary damages for such claims and have thereby encouraged plaintiffs to continue to bring such claims in the future.

Box 10-11. Recovery for Increased Risk of Cancer

Under traditional tort law, plaintiffs must have suffered a "present injury" before they can bring a lawsuit. However, once a present injury has been demonstrated, the plaintiff may recover for all harm, past, present, and future. In recent years, many plaintiffs who have been exposed to toxic substances but have not yet developed any observable symptoms of disease have alleged that they nevertheless have a present injury consisting of an increased risk of developing cancer in the future. Although many courts have rejected such claims, some courts have allowed plaintiffs to recover damages under such theories.

A leading precedent is *Ayers* v. *Township of Jackson*, 525 A.2d 287 (N.J. 1987), in which plaintiffs' well water was contaminated by toxic pollutants that leached from a landfill owned and operated by the township of Jackson. The plaintiffs did not allege any specific illnesses caused by their exposure but rather sought recovery for emotional distress, increased risk of cancer, and future medical surveillance. The New Jersey Supreme Court held that recovery for emotional distress in such circumstances was precluded by state statute. The court stated that "an enhanced risk of disease caused by significant exposure to toxic chemicals is clearly an `injury.'" But because the plaintiffs had failed to quantify their increased risk of cancer, the court declined "to recognize plaintiffs' cause of action for the *unquantified* enhanced risk of disease." (Emphasis in original.)

In upholding the jury's award of over $8 million to plaintiffs to cover the future cost of medical surveillance, however, the court held that such costs were "a compensable item of damages where the proofs demonstrate, through reliable expert testimony predicated upon the significance and extent of exposure to chemicals, the toxicity of the chemicals, the seriousness of the diseases for which the individuals are at risk, the relative increase in the chance of onset of disease in those exposed, and the value of early diagnosis, that such surveillance to monitor the effect of exposure to toxic chemicals is reasonable and necessary."

Products Liability

Products liability actions are cases brought by persons allegedly injured by a company's products. Most product liability claims can be grouped into three general categories: (1) product defects, (2) failure to warn, and (3) breach of warranty. An injured plaintiff will often bring claims under all three of these categories. Most states have adopted a strict liability standard for "defective" products. This doctrine is based on § 402(a) of the Second Restatement of Torts, which imposes liability on a seller of "any product in a defective condition unreasonably dangerous to the user or consumer" and that such liability applies even if the seller "has exercised all possible care in the preparation and sale of his product." This strict liability for a defective product has been applied to manufacturers, component manufacturers, wholesalers and retailers of the product, as well as successor corporations. A product can be defective if there was a mistake in the manufacture of the particular unit that allegedly caused the injury, or if the product generally was improperly designed. Manufacturing defects are proved by comparing the individual unit with the company's own design or specifications. A design defect is demonstrated by comparison of the product's design with those of competing manufacturers, by the results of risk-utility and cost-benefit analyses, and with reference to consumer expectations.

Product liability can also be imposed for injuries resulting from a manufacturer's failure to adequately warn about the dangers inherent in the product. Most courts have applied a negligence standard to this doctrine and only impose liability if the manufacturer failed to warn of dangers it knew or should have known to exist. However, some courts have applied a strict liability standard by assuming that the manufacturer knew of the risks even if no evidence has been introduced of such knowledge. The final major category of product liability causes of action is breach of warranty, which involve an injury resulting from a breach of the manufacturer's express or implied warranty that the product will be fit for the ordinary purposes for which such goods are used.

A company that has been found liable in a product liability action may be subject to substantial punitive damages as well as compensatory damages. Punitive damages are intended to punish a particularly egregious act and to deter others from similar misconduct in the future. Most states require a standard such as "conscious disregard of the safety of others" or "willful, wanton, malicious or reckless acts" for the imposition of punitive damages. The size of a punitive damages award is left to the discretion of the jury in many states, based on the nature of the defendant's conduct, the nature and extent of the harm, and the defendant's wealth. (See Box 10-12.) Punitive damages can impose a tremendous financial burden on manufacturers, especially if a company is subject to repeated punitive damages awards for the same product. In recent years, punitive damages awards have become more frequent and sizable, and several states have responded by imposing caps on punitive damages to prevent unreasonable awards.

Box 10-12.   Constitutionality of Punitive Damages

The Supreme Court recently addressed the constitutional limits of punitive damages in *Pacific Mutual Life Insurance Co.* v. *Haslip*, 111 S.Ct. 1032 (1991). In *Haslip*, a licensed agent for an insurance company contracted to provide life and health insurance for some municipal employees, but unknown to the insurance company, the agent misappropriated the premiums paid by the municipal workers. When the insurance company failed to receive the premiums, it sent a notice via its agent that it was canceling the policies of the workers. However, the agent did not pass on the notices to the workers. When one of the workers got sick, the fraud by the agent was discovered and the workers brought a lawsuit against the agent and the insurance company. The jury found the insurance company liable under a theory of *respondent superior*, because the agent was acting within the scope of his apparent authority. The jury awarded approximately $200,000 in compensatory damages and over $800,000 in punitive damages.

The insurance company appealed to the Alabama Supreme Court and the U.S. Supreme Court on the ground that such a large punitive damages award was a violation of due process, but the judgment was upheld. The U.S. Supreme Court held that allowing juries to assess punitive damages was not unconstitutional per se, and that the constitutionality of punitive damages awards must be examined on a case-by-case basis. The court stated: "We need not, and indeed we cannot, draw a mathematical bright line between the constitutionally acceptable and the constitutionally unacceptable that would fit every case." The punitive damages award was upheld in *Haslip* because the jury was given "objective criteria" to assess such damages that were reasonably related to the goals of retribution and deterrence, and because postverdict review by the Alabama Supreme Court was available to ensure that "punitive damages awards are not grossly out of proportion to the severity of the offense and have some understandable relationship to compensatory damages."

Criminal Liability

Criminal liability for environmental damages most often arises under the criminal sanctions provisions of environmental statutes. However, environmental criminal sanctions can and sometimes are imposed under criminal "common law," which has mostly been codified in state criminal codes. For example, state murder statutes have occasionally been applied to environmental crimes resulting in death. State or federal conspiracy laws also have application to environmental crimes.

Common Law Defenses

Many of the avoidance strategies for liabilities for environmental noncompliance discussed above will also help protect against common law liability as well. Indeed, the need to protect against common law liability is good reason for going beyond regulatory compliance in self-audits, environmental compliance programs, and product stewardship programs, and to reduce pollution levels as low as can be justified economically. Such preventive programs help to predict and avoid potential problems that could result in common law liabilities. The existence of such programs will also be helpful evidence of a company's due care if it is the subject of a lawsuit for environmental injuries. Other potential common law defenses are discussed below.

Failure to Prove Causation

Plaintiffs' inability to show that the defendant's acts were the proximate cause of their injuries is the major obstacle to recovery in many lawsuits. A company sued in a toxic tort or product liability action can often defend itself by introducing evidence rebutting the plaintiffs' evidence that the company's activities or products are capable of causing, and indeed did cause, the injuries in question. Defendants can also support a lack of causation defense by introducing evidence that some other factor was capable of causing, or did cause, the plaintiffs' injuries.

Defendants can also defend on causation grounds by showing that some superseding or intervening event was the proximate cause of the injuries. If the superseding or intervening event was not reasonably foreseeable to the defendant, the defendant could not have anticipated the injury that resulted and therefore will usually not be held culpable.

The scientific validity and reliability of the evidence and expert opinions relied on by plaintiffs to prove causation is often suspect. For example, instead of relying on human epidemiologic data, plaintiffs' experts often rely on extrapolations from high-dose animal experiments, which may not present a realistic or reliable estimate of human risk. Accordingly, plaintiffs' experts may not be qualified to testify under Federal Rule of Evidence 702 or the equivalent state rule, and therefore the admissibility of such testimony may be subject to a challenge on evidentiary grounds.

Regulatory Compliance

Regulatory compliance is not a complete defense against common law liability. Nevertheless, compliance with applicable environmental statutes and regulations can have some persuasive value with a judge or jury in showing that a company has exercised due care. This is especially true when an expert federal or state agency has carefully examined the complex scientific data relating a hazardous substance or activity in promulgating the regulations that the company has complied with. While regulatory compliance is not a complete defense, regulatory noncompliance will almost always provide sufficient evidence of negligence. Indeed, violation of an environmental statute or regulation is negligence per se in most states, and the plaintiff will need to make no other showing of fault.

Compliance with Industry Standards and Custom

A company's compliance with voluntary standards and industry custom is also not a complete defense in tort or product liability cases but is usually admissible to show due care or that a product is not defective. Consistency with industry custom or usage can be demonstrated by showing that the defendant's practices or products are at least as protective as those of other companies in the same or similar industries. There are also usually many voluntary standards or codes of conduct that apply to a particular industry, and demonstrated compliance with these standards or codes can be effective in showing that the company exercised due care or produced products that are not defective.

A showing that a company has complied with industry custom and voluntary standards may therefore be helpful to defend against both negligence and strict liability causes of action. Almost all courts will allow a defendant to introduce such evidence to show due care, although such evidence will not be conclusive in demonstrating that the company was not negligent. Some courts have prohibited the introduction of such evidence in a strict liability product action, but most courts have permitted such evidence to be introduced on the issue of whether the product was defective. Of course, evidence that a company has not complied with industry custom or standards will usually be very damaging to a company's defense.

State of the Art

A defense that is similar to the industry custom defense is the state-of-the-art defense. This defense asserts that the manufacturer's conduct was at the highest level capable of achievement as a practical matter, and therefore was the "state of the art." A manufacturer's possible knowledge of the hazards or risks presented by a particular product may also be limited by the state of the art of scientific or technical achievement. The state-of-the-art defense is only available for negligence actions in many states, but the state-of-the-art evidence may be admissible even in strict liability cases on the question of whether a manufacturer's design was defective.

Preemption

Tort and product liability common law is primarily state law and therefore can be preempted by federal legislation, in the same way that state legislation and regulation can be preempted. In diverse areas such as vehicle safety, cigarette warnings, prescription drug warnings, and pesticide labeling, courts have held that state product liability actions are precluded or limited by Congress' intent to establish uniform federal standards. In each case, the critical factor is whether Congress intended to allow states to impose their own requirements.

Contributory Negligence and Comparative Fault

A traditional defense in a negligence case was that the plaintiff also failed to take due care and that such negligence contributed to the injury. A showing of such contributory negligence would bar any recovery by the plaintiff. Most states have now abandoned this "all-or-nothing" approach and have adopted a rule that diminishes a plaintiff's recovery based on comparative fault or responsibility. A "pure" comparative fault system allows a plaintiff to recover some damages provided that his or her own culpable conduct was not 100 percent to blame for the injury. Other states have adopted a "modified" comparative fault rule that allows a plaintiff to recover in proportion to the defendant's fault only if the plaintiff's own fault was less than 50 percent. Although the contributory negligence and comparative fault defense originally applied only to negligence actions, most states have now allowed a comparative fault defense in strict liability actions.

Assumption of Risk

The assumption of risk defense requires the defendant to show that the person who was injured voluntarily engaged in an activity or used a product with actual knowledge and appreciation of the dangers presented by that activity or product. If the defendant can make such a showing, the plaintiff will be found to have assumed the risks associated with the conduct in question. The assumption of risk can be either implicit or explicit. Implicit assumption of risk occurs when the plaintiff voluntarily exposed himself or herself to a known risk. Explicit assumption of risk occurs when the plaintiff contracts in advance to undertake an activity with a known risk.

Unlike contributory negligence, the assumption of risk defense can only be used when the injured person can be shown to have actually known of the risk that was assumed. The defense does not apply when the injured person should have known the risk he or she was assuming but in actual fact did not. When successfully asserted, the assumption of risk defense has traditionally acted as a complete bar to recovery. In some jurisdictions now, however, the plaintiff must have assumed at least 50 percent of the risk for the defense to apply. In other jurisdictions with a pure comparative negligence system, a showing of assumption of risk will only reduce damages proportionally and will not act as a complete bar to recovery. Because exposure to low-level pollutants in groundwater or other media is usually not known at the time of such exposure, the assumption of risk defense rarely applies in toxic tort cases and is more frequently asserted in product liability or occupational injury cases.

Statute of Limitations

A lawsuit must be brought within a specified time after the injury was incurred. The statute of limitations usually runs from the time of injury and in most states is from 1 to 6 years for tort or product liability actions. The application of the statute of limitations in many environmental cases involving latent injuries is controversial because of the delay between exposure, the initiation of injury or the disease process, and the manifestation of injury. Most states have now adopted a "discovery" rule under which the statute of limitations starts running when the injured person discovers, or should have discovered, the injury. A few states still begin the period of limitations at the time the injury occurs.

In summary, a variety of strategies, such as those identified here, can be adopted by companies and management to prevent and limit their environmental liabilities.

References

Cahill, Lawrence C., and Kane, Raymond W., *Environmental Audits*, 6th ed., 1989.

Chemical Manufacturers Association, *The Knock on the Door: Preparing for and Responding to a Criminal Investigation*, 1991.

EPA, Enforcement Accomplishments Report (annual).

Friedman, Frank B., *Practical Guide to Environmental Management*, Environmental Law Institute, 1991.

Government Institutes, *Environmental Law Handbook*, 11th ed., 1991.

U.S. Department of Justice, "Factors in Decisions on Criminal Prosecutions for Environmental Violations in the Context of Significant Voluntary Compliance or Disclosure Efforts by the Violator" (July 1, 1991).

PART 5

Protecting Public Health and the Environment

11

Risk Assessment and Management

Rao V. Kolluru, DrPH*

Director, Environmental Health Services,
CH2M Hill

In this chapter:

- The Continuing Debate about Risk: Setting Environmental Priorities and Allocating Resources
- Safety Hazard Analysis (Probabilistic and Quantitative Risk Assessment)
- Health Risk Assessment (Human Health Risk Analysis)
- Ecological Risk Assessment (Environmental Evaluation)
- Vision for the Next Millennium

The publication by the U.S. Environmental Protection Agency of two landmark reports, "Unfinished Business: A Comparative Assessment of Environmental Problems" and "Reducing Risk: Setting Priorities and Strategies for Environmental Protection," launched a national debate on risk and its role in setting priorities for environmental protection. The concept of environmental risk is at once elegant, complex, and controversial. Given that the "bottom line" for environmental laws, regulations, and actions is the protection of human health, risk criteria offer a scientific and valid basis for resource-effective strategies.

*This chapter was written while the author was at Woodward-Clyde Consultants.

327

In this chapter, you will find three major types of risk assessment—safety hazard, human health, and ecological—and a wide range of possible applications by corporations and other organizations to address diverse problems with a common language. In addition, some guidelines are presented for estimating corporate environmental risk and a strategy for reducing aggregate financial risk. Informed decision makers can achieve substantial cost savings by using risk criteria in conjunction with technology-based or other regulatory approaches and targeting resources toward action-sensitive hazards and exposures. Cases, "points to consider," and examples throughout the chapter illustrate the possibilities, the methods, the rationale, the advantages, as well as the limitations of risk assessment.

The Continuing Debate about Risk:
Setting Environmental Priorities and Allocating Resources

The Unfinished Business: Comparative Assessment of Problems

Amid the growing complexity of environmental issues and conflicting demands for its limited resources, the U.S. Environmental Protection Agency (EPA) commissioned a special task force in 1986 to compare the risks related to major environmental problems. The task force of senior managers and technical experts first divided environmental concerns into 31 problem areas such as air pollutants, contaminants in drinking water, and hazardous-waste sites. Then they considered different types of risk for each problem area: cancer and noncancer health risks, ecological effects, and welfare effects (e.g., visibility impairment, property damage). The task force findings were published in the landmark report "Unfinished Business: A Comparative Assessment of Environmental Problems" (EPA, 1987).

Acknowledging limitations in data and risk-assessment methods, the EPA experts ranked environmental problems as follows (Fig. 11-1):

- High or at least medium in all types of risk: criteria air pollutants, stratospheric ozone depletion, pesticide residues on food, and other pesticide risks

- High in health risks but low in ecological and welfare risks: hazardous air pollutants, indoor radon and other indoor air pollution, exposure to consumer products, and worker exposure to pesticides and other chemicals

- High in ecological and welfare risks but low in health risks: global warming, point and nonpoint sources of surface water pollution, and alteration of aquatic habitats (e.g., estuaries and wetlands)

- Low or medium in all types of risk: groundwater

These observations revealed that EPA's program priorities and resource allocation did not correspond well with the risk rankings. For example, indoor radon and other indoor air pollutants and stratospheric ozone depletion, considered high risk by the EPA experts, were low on EPA program priorities. Conversely, areas of low risk but high EPA priority include sites regulated by the Resource Conservation and Recovery Act (RCRA) and the Superfund. (These probably account for fewer than 100 cancer cases with possible double counting of drinking water and toxic air pollutants.) In other cases, EPA shared jurisdiction with agencies with more direct responsibility such as the Consumer

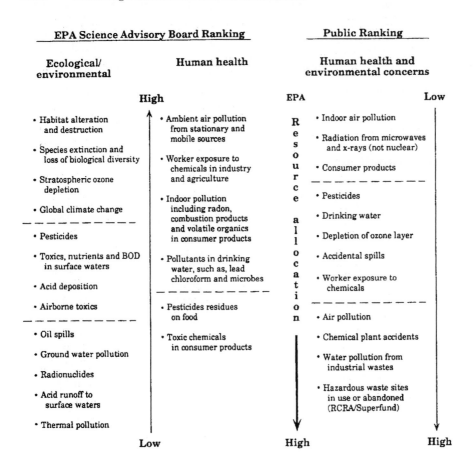

Note: The order of problems listed in each group does not imply a relative ranking.

Figure 11-1. Risk ranking versus resources allocation. (*"Unfinished Business: A Comparative Assessment of Environmental Problems," EPA. February 1987; "Reducing Risks: Setting Priorities and Strategies for Environmental Protection," EPA, September 1990.*)

Products Safety Commission (CPSC) and the Occupational Safety and Health Administration (OSHA). Overall, EPA's priorities appear more closely aligned with public opinion than with estimated risks. National polling data revealed the following ranking by the public:

■ High: chemical waste disposal, water pollution, chemical accidents, air pollution

■ Medium: oil spills, worker exposure, pesticides, drinking water

■ Low: indoor air pollution, consumer products, radiation (except nuclear power), global warming

Thus "Unfinished Business" made an important contribution in that the environmental problems were viewed across the EPA program boundaries (air, water, solid waste, etc.), pointing to the dichotomy between the seriousness of risk and the application of resources. This set the stage for a fundamental shift in national environmental policy.

Reducing Risk: Setting Priorities and Developing Strategies

Early in 1989, in one of his first actions as EPA Administrator, William Reilly asked EPA's Science Advisory Board to review Unfinished Business and suggest ways to improve the process of identifying, assessing, and reducing risks. The Science Advisory Board, established by Congress in 1978 to provide independent advice to EPA and congressional committees on environmental matters, consists of about 60 scientists, engineers, and technical experts who serve 2-year terms.

In September 1990, the Science Advisory Board submitted the report titled "Reducing Risk: Setting Priorities and Strategies for Environmental Protection." The board, noting some past successes from public and private expenditures of about $100 billion a year (approximately 2 percent of GNP), pointed to the fragmentary nature of U.S. environmental policy in laws, in programs, and in tools. Following are some excerpts from the report:

> Given the diversity, complexity, and scope of the environmental problems of concern today, it is critically important that U.S. environmental policy evolves in several fundamental ways. Essentially, national policy affecting the environment must become more integrated and more focused on opportunities for environmental improvement than it has been in the past.... One tool that can help foster the evolution of an integrated and targeted national environmental policy is the concept of environmental risk. Each environmental problem poses some possibility of harm to human health, the ecology, the economic system, or the quality of human life.... Risk assessment is the process by which the form, dimension, and characteristics of that risk are estimated, and risk management is the process by which the risk is reduced.
>
> The concept of environmental risk, together with its related terminology and analytical methodologies, helps people discuss disparate environmental problems with a common language. It allows many environmental problems to be measured and compared in common terms, and it allows different risk reduction options to be evaluated from a common basis. Thus the concept of environmental risk can help the nation develop environmental policies in a consistent and systematic way.
>
> Scientists have made some progress in developing quantitative measures for use in comparing different risks to human health. Given sufficient data, such comparisons are now possible within limits. Although current ability to assess and quantify ecological risks is not as well developed, an increased capacity for comparing different kinds of risks more systematically would help determine which problems are most serious and deserving of the most urgent attention. That capacity would be even more valuable as the number

and seriousness of environmental problems competing for attention and resources increase.

An improved ability to compare risks in common terms would have another value as well: it would help society choose more wisely among the range of policy options available for reducing risks. There are a number of ways to reduce the automobile emissions that contribute to urban smog; there are a number of ways to decrease human exposure to lead. The evaluation of relative risks can help identify the relative efficiency and effectiveness of different risk reduction options.

There are heavy costs involved if society fails to set environmental priorities based on risk. If finite resources are expended on lower-priority problems at the expense of higher-priority risks, then society will face needlessly high risks. If priorities are established based on the greatest opportunities to reduce risk, total risk will be reduced in a more efficient way, lessening threats to both public health and local and global ecosystems....

This report, together with its three appendices, suggests steps that the Environmental Protection Agency should take to improve its own efforts— and to involve Congress and the rest of the country in a collective effort— to reduce environmental risk. We strongly believe that the Agency should take steps to ensure that this nation uses all the tools at its disposal in an integrated, targeted approach to protecting human health, welfare, and ecosystem.

Along these lines, the Science Advisory Board (SAB) made 10 recommendations for EPA to:

1. Target environmental protection efforts on the basis of opportunities for the greatest risk reduction.

2. Attach as much importance to reducing ecological risk as to reducing human health risk.

3. Improve the data and analytical methodologies that support the assessment, comparison, and reduction of different environmental risks.

4. Reflect risk-based priorities in strategic planning processes.

5. Reflect risk-based priorities in the budget process.

6. Make greater use of all the tools available to reduce risk, along with the nation as a whole.

7. Emphasize pollution prevention as the preferred option for reducing risk.

8. Increase efforts to integrate environmental considerations into broader aspects of public policy in as fundamental a manner as are economic concerns.

9. Work to improve public understanding of environmental risks and train a professional work force to help reduce them.

10. Develop improved analytical methods to value natural resources and to account for long-term environmental effects in economic analyses.

These recommendations and related criteria are reflected in the EPA's new 4-year strategic plans (personal communication with R. Morgenstern, EPA):

- Comparative risk as a guiding principle for setting priorities
- Pollution prevention as a strategy of first choice
- Preference for market-based incentives or voluntary action over traditional command and control approaches
- Technological innovation and transfer
- International leadership
- The importance of state and local capacity to the success of EPA's efforts

The Office of Research and Development, one of EPA's principal cross-media support offices, revamped its research planning process to focus on key areas of health and environmental risk in its most recent strategic plan to:

- Ensure that the research program reflects the highest risk areas
- Improve methods for determining relative risks
- Place greater emphasis on ecological research and ecological risk assessment
- Examine innovative approaches to risk reduction, for both pollution prevention and pollution control

It will undoubtedly take time for this strategic shift in thinking to translate into implementation at the local level. The SAB recommendations, though, offer an equally persuasive framework for the policies and practices of business organizations at the national and even global level.

Risk Assessment: Emergence, Concepts, Application

Risk assessment as a formal discipline emerged in the 1940s and 1950s paralleling the onset of nuclear industry. Listed in Table 11-1 are selected milestones in the evolution of risk assessment. Safety hazard analyses have been used since at least the 1950s in the nuclear, petroleum refining, and chemical process industries, and in aerospace. The health risk assessments, on the other hand, are of more recent vintage, having made their debut in 1976 with EPA's publication of Carcinogenic Risk Assessment Guidelines, and subsequently propelled by the Superfund and RCRA programs in the 1980s. The science of ecological risk assessment is still in its infancy but the growing public interest in ecological resources and the Science Advisory Board's ranking of these issues at the top of the list of national concerns have provided further impetus for evaluating ecological risks.

Table 11-1. Emergence of Risk Assessment—Selected Milestones

1938	Federal Food, Drug, and Cosmetic Act
1940s–50s	General principles for atomic energy operations: Hazop, failure mode, fault tree risk analyses
1958	Food, Drug and Cosmetic Act amendments—Delaney Clause
1975	WASH-1400 Reactor Safety Study (Rasmussen), U.S. Nuclear Regulatory Commission
1976	EPA's publication of carcinogenic risk assessment guidelines (first quantification of chemical cancer risks)
1980	Supreme Court ruling that OSHA should prove health benefit of lowering benzene limit from 10 ppm
1980s	Renewed emphasis on protecting human health, especially from carcinogenic risks, e.g., EPA's water quality criteria based on 10^{-7} to 10^{-5} risk, 95 percentile upper bound risk, linearized multistage dose-response model
1981	First publication of the journal *Risk Analysis*
1983	NAS/NRC Report, Risk Assessment in the Federal Government—Managing the Process
1986	Formalized risk assessment guidelines Superfund Public Health Evaluation Manual (SPHEM) The Exposure and Risk Assessment Guidelines of 1986 (including mutagenic, carcinogenic, developmental, and chemical mixtures) Mounting importance of risk communications in risk management (SARA Title III, 1986)
1987	EPA's publication of Unfinished Business: A Comparative Assessment of Environmental Problems
1989	EPA's Risk Assessment Guidance for Superfund (RAGS), *Human Health Evaluation Manual; Environmental Evaluation Manual*
1990	EPA Science Advisory Board publication of Reducing Risk: Setting Priorities and Strategies for Environmental Protection Clean Air Act Amendments (air toxics, accidental release provisions)
1990s	OSHA Process Safety Management (29CFR1910.119) Increasing use of pharmacokinetic models (bioavailability) Growing emphasis on noncancer (e.g., reproductive) effects Refinements in exposure modeling Dioxin study as a new paradigm for PAHs/carcinogens (toxicity equivalence) Increasing attention to ecological impacts New guidelines for exposure; developmental, reproductive, and neurotoxicities; carcinogenic risk; and ecological risk assessments Increasing international coordination of risk issues through OECD, UNEP, etc.

Concepts and Definitions

Although difficult in concept, risk is inherent in everyday life and in all decision making. The caveman had to weigh the risk to life and limb from hunting large animals for food and clothing. Treatises on the strategies of war and its risks, including the humiliation of the loss of wives to the victor, date back thousands of years.

Risk assessment or analysis means different things to different people: the financial risks of Wall Street, the actuarial risks of the insurance industry, the fatalities from a nuclear plant accident, the cancer risks associated with industrial emissions, the habitat loss from human activities—all these seemingly disparate notions have in common the concept of a measurable phenomenon called risk. In a "unified approach," risk assessment can be defined as the process of estimating the probability of occurrence of an event and the probable magnitude of adverse effects—economic, human safety or health, or ecological—over a specified time period. This is a "scientific" and simple definition of risk in that the magnitude is only one dimension; societal definitions tend to rest on equity, control, trust, etc. (sometimes referred to as a "soft" version of risk-based paradigm; see also Chap. 13). Among the many facets of risk are financial exposure from a Superfund site; probability of a bridge failure and consequent loss of life; probability of a chemical reactor or tank failure and the effect of sudden release of contents in terms of injuries and property loss; or the incidence of cancer in a community exposed to carcinogens in air and water, or pesticide residues in food.

Different Types/Expressions of Risk

■ Safety hazard	■ Acute
■ Human health	■ Subchronic
■ Environmental/ecological	■ Chronic
■ Financial	
■ Organizational image/"franchise"	
■ Occupational/worker	■ Cancer (nonthreshold) risk
■ Environmental/public	■ Non-cancer/systemic (threshold) effects
■ Consumer	

Note: See examples and definitions in text and glossaries.

Financial risk and liability related to environmental actions are discussed briefly here and in other chapters. The three major types of risk assessment discussed here are (Fig. 11-2, Table 11-2):

1. Safety hazard analysis: Typically low-probability, high-consequence accidents; acute, immediate effects. Obvious cause-and-effect relationships. Focus is on human safety and loss prevention, mainly within workplace boundaries.

2. Health risk assessment: Typically high-probability, low-consequence, ongoing, chronic exposures; long latency, delayed effect. Cause-effect relationship not easily established. Focus is on human health, mainly outside the workplace or site.

3. Ecological risk assessment: Myriad interactions among populations, communities, and ecosystems (including food chains) at micro and macro levels;

Risk: A measure of likelihood of occurrence and magnitude of consequences

Risk: hazard + public perception

Types of Risk Assessment:

Risk Assessment (Risk Analysis)

- **Financial risk analysis**
  insurance, liability exposure, property loss
  (economic focus)

- **Safety hazard analysis**
  low probability, high consequence,
  accidental, acute
  (human safety focus)

- **Health risk assessment**
  high probability, low consequence,
  ongoing, chronic
  (human health focus)

- **Ecological/environmental risk assessment**
  subtle changes, latency, complex
  interactions, macro impacts
  (habitat/ecosystem focus)

Figure 11-2. Risk assessment: definitions and scope.

great uncertainty in cause and effect. Focus is on habitat and ecosystem impacts that may be manifest far away from the sources of concern.

Table 11-2 presents an overview of these risk assessments including major process steps, outcomes of interest, and typical applications. Each type of risk assessment is discussed in more detail later. All the assessments start with hazard identification or problem definition (Fig. 11-3). A hazard is a chemical, biological, or physical agent (including electromagnetic radiation) or a set of conditions that present a source of risk but not risk per se. The definitions vary to some degree depending on the context. For example, safety hazard analysis in the nuclear and petrochemical industry generally refers to all the steps from hazard identification through risk evaluation. On the other hand, in health risk assessment, hazard analysis is considered the first step involving data evaluation and selection of chemicals of concern. Risk assessment and risk analysis are often used synonymously as in this chapter, but risk analysis is sometimes used broadly to include risk management aspects as well. Risk assessment has its share of acronyms, sometimes confusing; for example, HEP stands for hazard evaluation procedures in process industries but for habitat evaluation procedures in ecological assessment.

After the hazards are defined, the next step is to identify potential receptor populations and exposure locations; exposure occurs when someone comes into contact with a hazard, that is, joint occurrence in time and space of a hazard and a receptor. (In other words, a hazard constitutes a risk only if there is such contact.) Subsequently, in the risk characterization step, the nature and magnitude of the consequences from the exposure are characterized. In safety hazard analysis,

Table 11-2. Overview and Comparison of Three Types of Risk Analyses

Safety hazard analysis	Human health risk assessment	Ecological risk assessment
Process steps:		
1. Hazard identification	1. Data analysis and hazard identification	1. Problem formulation
Materials, equipment, procedures, e.g., inventories size and location, flammable, reactive or acutely toxic materials, and initiating events, e.g., equipment malfunction, human error, containment failure	Quantities and concentrations of chemical, physical, and biological agents in environmental media at a site or study area	Resident and transient flora and fauna, especially endangered or threatened species; aquatic, terrestrial surveys; contaminants and stressors of concern in study boundary
2. Probability and frequency estimation	2. Dose response or toxicity assessment	2. Exposure assessment
Likelihood of initiating events and accidents (internal and external causes)	Relationship between exposure and dose and adverse health effects	Pathways, habitats, or receptor populations, especially endangered or threatened species; exposure concentrations
3. Consequence analysis	3. Exposure assessment	3. Ecological effects and toxicity assessment
Nature and magnitude of adverse effects, e.g., fires, explosions, sudden release of toxic materials	Pathways and routes, potential receptors including sensitive subgroups, exposure rates, and timing	Aquatic, terrestrial, and microbial tests, e.g., LC_{50}, field studies
4. Risk determination and evaluation	4. Risk characterization	4. Risk and threat characterization
Integration of probabilities and consequences for quantitative estimates of safety risks	Integration of toxicity and exposure data for qualitative or quantitative expression of health risks; uncertainty analysis	Integration of field survey, toxicity and exposure data for characterizing significant ecological risks, causal relationship, uncertainty
Typical endpoints:		
Fatalities, injuries Economic loss	Human health, e.g., individual and population cancer risks, noncancer hazards	Ecosystem or habitat impacts, e.g., population abundance, species diversity
Typical applications:		
Chemical and petrochemical process safety Hazardous materials transport OSHA Process Safety Management New Jersey TCPA, California	Hazardous-waste sites (Superfund, RCRA) Air and water permitting Food additives, drugs (FDA) Fish and shellfish safety	Environmental assessments, NRDA Superfund/RCRA sites Facility siting, wetland studies Pesticide registration TSCA premanufacture

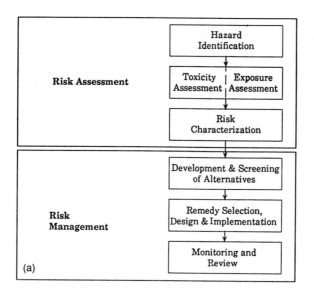

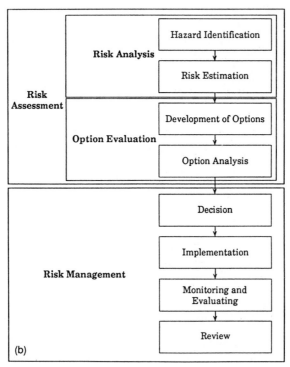

Figure 11-3. Generalized risk assessment and management models: (*a*) American model. (*Adapted from U.S. EPA, "Risk Assessment Guidance for Superfund," 1989.*) (*b*) Canadian model. (*Health and Welfare Canada, "Health Risk Determination," 1989/90.*)

the endpoints are well defined: fatalities, injuries, and economic losses. The impact is immediate and transparent; the cause-effect relationship is generally clear. Well-known examples of catastrophic accidents are Seveso, Bhopal, and Chernobyl. In contrast, considerable uncertainty pervades health risk analyses because of multifactorial causation, background noise, and long latency periods, the cause-effect relationship being at best tenuous. For example, we are all exposed to thousands of chemicals every day, most of which are not likely to cause disease at the low concentrations to which we are generally exposed; some diseases, especially cancers, have a long latency of 10 to 20 or more years.

Ecological risks are perhaps an order of magnitude more complex and orders of magnitude more uncertain; the effects may not be evident except in retrospect, if at all. Despite these differences, the risks are interrelated. The Chernobyl accident, for instance, resulted in a few immediate deaths but the radiation exposure continues to affect the health of thousands more. Since humans are part of an ecosystem, human health could be affected indirectly by, for example, consumption of contaminated fish, especially in cases of high bioaccumulation of pesticides or other fat-soluble compounds in edible fish tissues found in contaminated waters.

Uses of Risk Assessment

Major federal agencies that routinely use risk analyses include FDA, EPA, OSHA, and others (see accompanying box). Keep in mind also that the Toxic Substances Control Act (TSCA) requires companies to notify EPA whenever they develop knowledge of a significant risk that may not be known to the agency. Such reports usually stem from results that show up in a new testing program. Most large companies have an "8e committee" to which new information on risks is referred so that a decision can be made on its reportability to EPA.

U.S. federal agencies that use risk assessments

- Food and Drug Administration (FDA)
- Environmental Protection Agency (EPA)
- Occupational Safety and Health Administration (OSHA)
- Consumer Products Safety Commission (CPSC)
- U.S. Department of Agriculture (USDA)
- Department of Energy (DOE)
- Department of Defense (DOD)
- Department of Transportation (DOT)
- Nuclear Regulatory Commission (NRC)

The passage of federal and state laws to protect public health and the environment sharply expanded the application of risk analyses in the 1970s and 1980s. The strategic shift in EPA's policies and programs discussed earlier will further extend the application of risk analyses. They can be used in a variety of situations, for example, to:

- Assess benefits (therapeutic effects) vs. risks (side effects or toxic effects) of new drugs
- Appraise benefits (higher yields, less spoilage) vs. risks (environmental media contamination, residues on food) of pesticide use
- Evaluate facility siting, process safety, and transportation hazards to help select sites and improve design
- Conduct baseline analysis of a site or facility to determine the need for remedial action and the extent of cleanup required
- Develop cleanup goals for contaminants where numerical standards have not been promulgated by federal or state authorities or to seek variance from the standards and guidelines (e.g., alternate concentration limits)
- Construct what-if scenarios, for example, to compare the potential impact of remedial alternatives and to set priorities for corrective action
- Evaluate existing and new technologies for effective prevention, control, or mitigation of hazards and risks
- Develop scientific framework for closing down or decommissioning facilities
- Address community public health concerns and provide a consistent basis for public health expectations among different locations
- Provide a scientific basis for a corporate risk reduction and management program
- Identify emerging ecosphere hazards and galvanize global action

Advantages of Risk Assessment

As EPA's Science Advisory Board pointed out, risk criteria provide an effective framework for prioritizing problems, allocating resources, and reducing risks. Using the results of hazard and risk analyses, resources for prevention, remediation, or control can be targeted toward *action-sensitive hazards,* that is, areas, sources, or situations where the greatest reductions in risk can be achieved from unit deployment of resources. In financial terms, resources can be leveraged; empirical evidence to date suggests that well-designed, targeted risk analyses can yield savings of 5–20% of total project costs by focusing on the highest sources of risk and reducing associated uncertainty.

Table 11-3. Examples of Risk Assessment Applications

Safety Hazard Analysis

- Regulatory compliance:
    Federal: EPA's CAA; OSHA's process safety management (29CFR1910.119)
    State: TCPA, AHMRMA, EHSRMA
- Worker and public safety, process safety
- Loss prevention, insurance, liability
- Facility siting, design, technology selection

Human health risk assessment

- Regulatory compliance: EPA's CERCLA/Superfund, SARA Title III, RCRA/HSWA, CAA, TSCA; FDA; CPSC; state programs, e.g., ECRA
- Facility siting, design, technology selection (waste storage, disposal)
- Public health and community health concerns; public image
- Aggregate financial risk estimates (from environmental situations) to target corporate risk reductions

Ecological risk assessment

- Regulatory compliance: Superfund, RCRA, FIFRA
- Pesticide registration: OECD protocols for exports to Europe
- Environmental impact assessments
- Siting, construction (e.g., wetlands)
- Global policies, e.g., climate change, ozone depletion, acid rain, habitat alteration

AHMRMA	California's Acutely Hazardous Materials Risk Management Act
CAA	Clean Air Act Amendments, 1990
CERCLA and SARA	Comprehensive Environmental Response, Compensation, and Liability Act of 1980, also known as Superfund; followed by Superfund Amendments and Reauthorization Act (SARA) of 1986
CPSC	Consumer Product Safety Commission
ECRA	New Jersey Environmental Cleanup Responsibility Act
EHSRMA	Delaware's Extremely Hazardous Substances Risk Management Act
FDA	Food and Drug Administration
FIFRA	Federal Insecticide, Fungicide, and Rodenticide Act, 1972
NRC	Nuclear Regulatory Commission
OSHA	Occupational Safety and Health Administration
RCRA and HSWA	Resource Conservation and Recovery Act, 1976 followed by Hazardous and Solid Waste Amendments, 1984
TCPA	New Jersey's Toxic Catastrophe Prevention Act ("Bhopal Act")
TSCA	Toxic Substances Control Act, 1976

Table 11-4. Examples of Risk Assessment Firms and Professional Organizations

Safety Hazard Analysis	
Private firms	Professional and nonprofit organizations
Arthur D. Little	American Institute of Chemical Engineers Center for Chemical Process Safety (AIChE-CCPS)
Decision Focus	
DuPont Safety & Environmental Services	American Petroleum Institute (API)
	Battelle Columbus
JBF Associates	Chemical Manufacturers Association (CMA)
Pickard, Lowe, & Garrick	SRI International
Primatech	United Nations Environment Programme (UNEP) (awareness and preparedness for emergencies at local level "APELL")
SAIC	
Stone & Webster	
Technica	

Health and Ecological Risk Assessment	
More specialized firms	Diversified environmental firms
Chem Risk/McLaren Hart	ABB Environmental
Clement/ICF	Camp Dresser & McKee (CDM)
Dynamac	CH2M Hill
EA Engineering, Science and Technology (ecological emphasis)	Dames & Moore
	Ebasco
Environ	ENSR
Gradient	ERM Group
Lawler, Matuskly & Skelly (ecological emphasis)	Geraghty & Miller
Life Systems	IT Corp.
Terra	NUS/Halliburton/Brown & Root
Versar	Roy F. Weston
	Woodward-Clyde

The above list provides only examples of organizations offering risk assessment services and is not all-inclusive. The division between specialized and diversified firms is somewhat arbitrary and is intended to indicate original emphasis and/or that a substantial part of total revenues is derived from risk assessment services.

Limitations

Perhaps the most crucial limitation to realizing the full potential of risk assessments is the paucity of professionals who have the broad training and the perspective needed to transcend the cookbook approach and focus on the critical issues. Nor is there a scientific consensus on the approach and the purpose that risk analyses should serve. The magnitude of uncertainty sometimes tends to detract from the science of risk assessment. For example, in engineering, the designer of a reactor vessel may build in a two- or threefold safety factor, and a bridge may have a five- or sixfold safety factor. In contrast, risk estimates typically have two to three *orders of magnitude* uncertainty. For this and other reasons, many believe that risk expressions are an attempt to obfuscate responses to a simple question: "Is it safe or unsafe?"

Worse still, some sponsors of risk assessment believe that it is a tool to prove that there is little or no risk, and may seek second and third opinions if the reported results are unanticipated. Moreover, risk assessment professionals have to serve multiple clients with diverse interests—the paying client, the EPA or other federal agencies, the state agency, the lawyers, the peer reviewers, public interest groups, and others. In this scheme of things, the ultimate objective—public health—could easily be overlooked.

Risk Assessment and Risk Management

The commonly used health risk assessment model, especially for Superfund sites, is based on EPA guidelines in "Risk Assessment Guidance for Superfund" (EPA, RAGS, 1989). These guidelines are based in part on the National Research Council report "Risk Assessment in the Federal Government: Managing the Process" (NRC, 1983). The council recommended that risk assessment contain some or all of four steps: (1) hazard identification, (2) dose-response assessment, (3) exposure assessment, and (4) risk characterization. Another recommendation is to keep risk assessment separate from risk management; the latter involves consideration of the risk data, as well as political, social, technical, and economic issues for the development of alternative options for responding to health hazards. However, the NRC committee goes on to say: "Risk assessment and risk management functions are analytically distinct, but in practice they do—and must—interact.... For example, to complete risk characterization, risk assessors must know what policy options are to be used to calculate alternative projected exposures, and new options may develop as the risk management process proceeds.... Separation could also impair the risk manager's ability to obtain assessments that are timely and in a useful form" (NRC, p. 152).

While the intent of the NRC recommendation to keep risk assessment separate from management issues is to avoid prejudgment of the results by cost implications and value judgments (isolate science from politics and policy), the assessment and management phases suffer from this disjunction in practice. In the Superfund remedial process, for example, risk assessment is expected to provide a key link between remedial investigation (RI) of site and contaminant characterization and the feasibility study (FS) of remedial action. And yet the site and contaminant data collection and presentation are seldom adequate to devise a remedy. The problem is worsened by the long study phase and the time lag between study phase and action phase (5 to 10 years or more), changes in consultants, and changes in EPA and state agency personnel. In the Canadian risk assessment model, shown in Fig. 11-3, development of remedial options begins early in the process and the assessment and management phases are better integrated. The NRC launched a 15-month study in January 1992 to improve the scientific basis for environmental risk assessment and regulatory policy.

Risk Measures, Indices, or Descriptors

The measures or indicators of risk for safety hazards are fatalities, injuries, disabilities, and economic loss. Human health risks are expressed in terms of cancer risks and noncancer hazards such as reproductive, respiratory, and neurological effects. Risks can be expressed as both individual and population risks, as the examples later will illustrate. Individual risk is the probability of injury or disease in the case of a highly exposed individual in a population. (An individual cancer risk of 10^{-6} or 1E-6 means, for example, one incremental chance in a million of developing cancer from exposure to the hazard at the same level over an assumed 70-year lifetime.) Population risk is an estimate of the incidence in the total population that is potentially exposed.

Risk Acceptability

Zero-Risk Ideal.   According to the zero-risk principle, no risk can be tolerated no matter how small and whatever the benefits to society. In practice, however, we do not and cannot live in a risk-free world. There is always the background risk from natural sources, and a "small" risk would seem preferable if a much larger risk could be avoided. Examples of such risk may be the risk of toxicity from a food additive to prevent spoilage versus the risk of food poisoning from contaminated food; the benefits of preventing childhood diseases by immunizations versus the risk of adverse reactions; or the risk of tissue damage and cancer from diagnostic x-rays versus the benefit of early detection of cancer.

The Alar Scare

The ambivalence in assessing and managing risk can be illustrated by the Alar scare. Alar (daminozide) is a growth-regulating chemical and fungicide used on apple trees. The environmental group Natural Resources Defense Council (NRDC) charged that children exposed to Alar residues were at increased risk of cancer. After much media attention, the chemical was pulled from the market. Its manufacturer stopped selling it, and the EPA proposed to phase out all allowable residue levels.

Yet, according to Bruce Ames, chairman of biochemistry and director of the Department of Environmental Health Sciences at the University of California at Berkeley, the human cancer risk from Alar is about the same as that from tap water, which contains the carcinogen chloroform, and lower than from peanut butter, which can contain aflatoxin, a potent natural carcinogen. Our intake of natural carcinogens typically exceeds that of "synthetic" carcinogens by orders of magnitude. (We are thus faced once again with the dilemma of environmentalists highlighting adverse consequences, while businesspeople point to the underlying uncertainty and the media play up the controversy.)

Interview with a Risk Expert

SCIENCE: Dr. Noitall, you are the ultimate world authority on all types of risks, a revered figure who has just appeared in national television.

NOITALL: A vast understatement of my true value.

SCIENCE: You must have a large laboratory to uncover so many facts not available to the regulatory agencies.

NOITALL: Facts are no longer created in laboratories, they are created by the media. Any pronouncement of mine repeated in three periodicals, four newspapers, or one television program is considered a fact. My appearance on three talk shows is enough to qualify me as an expert. It is no longer necessary to have a laboratory in my profession.

SCIENCE: Could you give examples of how to avoid risk?

NOITALL: Stay out of the home. More than 3 million people in the United States were injured in 1987 in home accidents; 90% of all automobile accidents occur within 10 miles of home. It is imperative that you stay away from home.

SCIENCE: But I've heard that many accidents occur on highways.

NOITALL: That is true. There is one fatality for every 10 minutes of driving on the highways in the United States. I have developed a rigorous formula that shows that the more time spent on the highway, the greater the chance of an accident. Therefore, I recommend driving 80 miles per hour as a way of reducing the time spent on highways and thus reducing your chance of an accident.

SCIENCE: If one stays away from home, is there not an increased chance of infectious diseases?

NOITALL: One has to give up sexual intercourse entirely. The danger of disease from that source is far greater even than from eating an apple, and it should be avoided at all costs.

SCIENCE: Are there other dangers about which the Environmental Protection Agency has failed to advise us?

NOITALL: Breathing. All breathing generates oxygen radicals, which are the main sources of mutations in DNA, leading to cancer, birth defects, and very peculiarly shaped molecules in the urine. Breathing has been observed three minutes before death in 100% of all fatalities. We urge everyone to

(Continued)

stop breathing until the proper research has been carried out. The EPA has been told about this relation and has failed to act on it, a scandalous display of irresponsibility.

SCIENCE: What about hazards from crime?

NOITALL: A third of all homicides are committed on intimates, about a third on acquaintances, and about a third on strangers. Hence, it is imperative to avoid intimates, acquaintances, and strangers in order to reduce your risk of homicide significantly.

SCIENCE: Can one ever completely eliminate a given risk?

NOITALL: One can reduce a risk to essentially zero by adopting what I call "the riskier alternative strategy." For example, one could take up hang gliding, as it has been conclusively demonstrated that fewer hang gliders die of passive cigarette smoke than those who never participate in the sport. People who bicycle without a helmet need not worry about a little nuclear reactor nearby. People who have a cocktail before dinner or wine with a meal need never worry about a little trichloroethylene in their drinking water. By the proper choice of alternative strategies, it is possible to reduce one's chance of dying of any particular disorder to any desired level. It has relieved many people of risk anxiety syndrome.

SCIENCE: This seems so sensible, I am surprised people don't follow your advice.

NOITALL: Most ignoramuses are in fact following my formula without knowing it. Millions of people commute 20 miles to work, take airplanes, and choose hopelessly short-lived grandparents and still worry about clean drinking water. These people are secret admirers of peptic ulcers.

SCIENCE: We can't thank you enough for the time you are spending with us, but I have one last question. Do you practice what you preach?

NOITALL: Sadly, the answer is no. My family on the paternal side has a hereditary weakness whose clinical manifestation is the "eat, drink, and be merry" psychosis. As a result, all my ancestors on that side of the family have died prematurely, in their early nineties. I doubt whether I will escape the family curse.

SOURCE: Daniel E. Koshland, *Science*, June 30, 1989, vol. 244, p. 1529, copyright 1989 by AAAS.

De Minimis and De Manifestis Risks

The de minimis principle means that there are some levels of risk that are so trivial that they are not worth bothering about ("the law does not concern itself with trifles"). While an attractive concept, it is hard to define a de minimis level acceptable to an entire society. Understandably, regulatory authorities are reluctant to be explicit about an acceptable risk, but lifetime risk on the order of one in a million (or in the range of 10^{-6} to 10^{-4} for Superfund and RCRA) for the general public is often considered acceptable throughout much of the industrial world and is used by the EPA, FDA, and CPSC. The origins of one in a million acceptable risk and the meaning of such a risk remain obscure, but the impacts on product choices, operations, and costs are very real (running, for example, into hundreds of billions of dollars in site cleanup decisions alone). Levels of risk at the higher end of the range (10^{-4} rather than 10^{-6}) may be acceptable if only a few people are exposed versus the entire country as would be the case for food additives, for instance. Also, higher levels of risk are considered acceptable for workers than for the general population because workers tend to be a more homogeneous, healthier group, and because of the voluntary nature of employment, benefits, etc.

At the other end of the spectrum is de manifestis risk, i.e., such an obvious risk that it must be controlled irrespective of cost. Risk of more than one in a thousand (10^{-3}) is in this category and will almost certainly trigger regulatory action (Fig. 11-4).

> Passage of the Clean Air Act in 1990 may be a harbinger of changes in the way government deals with some aspects of risk in the future. Based on the assumption that the public wants *no* exposure to toxic air pollutants, regardless of whether the exposures represent any meaningful health risk, the law requires companies to achieve the lowest level of emissions technologically achievable (MACT) without regard to whether or not those levels are needed to protect the public. Eventually, Congress will have to decide how it will determine if the remaining emissions still represent an unacceptable risk (the residual risk issue) and has asked the National Academy of Sciences for recommendations on how to evaluate such risks. Whatever decision is eventually made in this regard is likely to change the way risk assessment is done throughout the government.

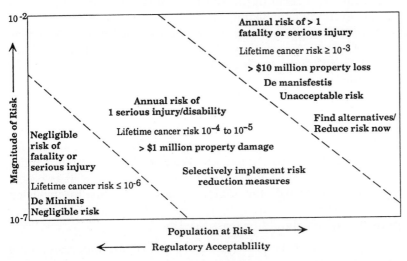

Figure 11-4. Risk management framework—an illustration.

Points to Consider

1. In parallel with national priorities, and in keeping with the concept of opportunity costs of alternative investments, individual organizations should consider adopting risk criteria to get the "biggest bang for the buck."

    Organizations that have multiple sites and facilities (DOE, DOD, multinational corporations, for example) can evaluate environmental, health, and safety (EHS) risks across sites, facilities, divisions, and the like, and prioritize them for remedial action. Corporations can also develop "aggregate environmental risk," i.e., expected financial costs for the corporation that reflect the magnitude of the various problems, probabilities of occurrence, and time frames during which particular problems might develop. This process helps guide investments toward targets that would yield the highest overall reduction in risk.

2. Be wary of the traditional discounted cash flow (DCF) business perspective that may hinder effective environmental decision making.

    In the DCF method (or a variation thereof) that traditionally anchored business investment decisions, the effect of what happens in 20 or 30 years is of little present value. Businesspeople tend to deal with uncertainty by shortening the time frame for anticipated results, where linear extrapolations tend to hold true. In contrast, in the environmental arena, what seems trivial today can assume monumental dimensions tomorrow with crucial impact (as in Superfund, for example). The unprecedented decision to phase out CFCs, as part of the Montreal Protocol of 1987 and the subsequent London agreement in 1990, demonstrates that concerted action is possible even in the face of scientific uncertainty, economic conflicts, and long lag times.

3. Shift resources toward prevention programs consistent with EPA policy shift. Reevaluate groundwater cleanup strategy.

    The EPA's SAB ranked groundwater to be of low or medium concern in all types of risk. A General Accounting Office report on groundwater (GAO, 1992) urges EPA to shift focus to preventive programs such as the Wellhead Protection Program which costs about $10 million, or less than the cost of groundwater cleanup at a single NPL site. Some would argue that the 1 to 5 ppb groundwater cleanup requirement in some states for such common, relatively low toxicity chemicals as tetrachloroethylene and trichloroethylene represent an "overkill," providing only marginal health benefits, if at all, for a cost of $5 to $20 million or more per site. We need to develop an aquifer classification system that takes into account water quality as well as potential use and capacity. Moreover, the original weighting scheme for inclusion in Superfund NPL accorded a high share to groundwater relative to other media, especially air, and should be reassessed.

4. Consider the opportunity cost of overestimating risk versus underestimating existing or residual risk.

Risk estimates that represent implausible situations in the name of prudent avoidance impose high costs on society and divert resources from more important public health concerns (remedial costs tend to grow exponentially). The well-known 80-20 Pareto's law, or perhaps the 90-10 rule, probably applies to risk reduction as well—90% of the risk could be reduced for 10% of the cost, and should be achieved first with minimal transaction costs. (Public policy should also seek to balance "worst sites first" and "highest risk reduction per unit cost first" because they are not always the same.)

5. Examine the basis for risk estimates—are the risks real or do they stem from the methodology and the uncertainty?

A high degree of uncertainty pervades the data and assumptions that typically form the basis of risk assessments. The underlying uncertainty is at the root of gross overestimates of risk. The risk assessment method mandated by EPA "guidance" involves repeated use of default parameters that magnifies the risk manyfold, perhaps orders of magnitude, giving it a fictional character and misleading the public into believing that the estimate is real. The expressions of uncertainty, if any, seldom get a second look. (Some scientists, including Gio Batta Gori of the Health Policy Center in Bethesda, believe that any connection between science and typical risk assessments is incidental.)

6. Are we overemphasizing cancer risks to the exclusion of others, succumbing to the "looking for the keys by the lamp post" syndrome?

While cancer presents a clear endpoint that reflects public dread, environmental pollutants are estimated to cause less than 5% of human cancers (detailed discussion in Chap. 12 under Public Health). Are we neglecting others such as reproductive, neurological, and respiratory effects? What are the implications of 10^{-6} (one in a million) upper bound cancer risk as a basis for environmental decisions? The background risk of developing some form of cancer in the United States is one in three (33%), and of death one in four (25%) over a lifetime. The 10^{-6} risk would increase the risk to 0.250001; a 10^{-5} risk to 0.25001, etc. Should we distinguish between less and more serious types of cancer? What level of incremental cancer risk as a basis for environmental regulation is likely to lead to the optimum mix of resource allocation?

7. Risk assessment and risk management should be separate but not independent or disjointed activities. Position risk assessments to link with action phase and improve the heretofore 80-20 transaction-remediation cost ratio.

Nearly 80 to 85% of environmental expenditures in the United States have been devoted to the investigation, study, and argument phase, leaving 15 to 20% for actual remediation. (In Europe and Canada this is reversed.) Admittedly, remediation requires 7 to 10 times more money than study, but the temporary advantage of postponement could be offset by higher costs, liability exposure, and negative image.

For the majority of risk reduction projects, such as hazardous-site remediation, the Canadian model that links hazards and risks directly with remedial options would be more effective in terms of lower costs and shorter time frames. The recent pronouncements by the EPA seem to signal movement in this direction.

8. Recognize explicitly the magnitude of resource requirements and the trade-offs between treatment and prevention in formulating national policy for environmental risk reduction.

The remediation of the 1275 hazardous waste sites in the Superfund National Priorities List (including federal facilities) and the additional 36,000 on CERCLIS inventory are estimated to cost more than $200 billion. Overall, there may be as many as a half million hazardous-waste sites in the United States that may entail aggregate cleanup costs in the range of $1 to $2 trillion in the next 20 to 30 years. In light of the enormity of the problem, resources should be directed toward those projects, and the degree of cleanup, that yield the highest reduction in risk per unit investment (present and future). These decisions should be guided by the "polluter pays" principle and the recognition that preventive programs tend to be much more effective, perhaps by an order of magnitude, than rehabilitation to "background" levels. Also, national risk reduction programs should emphasize, in addition to command-and-control, economic incentives and market-based strategies (Project 88—Round II).

9. Build scientific consensus based on "good science" and harmonize risk approaches with international agencies.

The wide disparities in risk concepts and analytical framework within the U.S. federal agencies (e.g., EPA, FDA) and among international agencies (e.g., OECD, EC, UN/WHO/IARC) further complicate risk management issues. The situation in the United States is characterized by (*a*) a lack of public trust in government and experts, (*b*) preoccupation with cancer vs. broad public health perspective, (*c*) conceptual separation of risk assessment and management, and (*d*) adversarial relationships between government, industry, and environmentalists (W. Farland, EPA).

Corporate Environmental Risk: A Strategy for Quantifying and Reducing Aggregate Financial Risk

The Need

Multinationals and other large companies have repositories of environmental data of varying quantity and quality on their assorted facilities, including site conditions, contaminant levels, pollutant emissions, compliance status, etc. What does all this mean in terms of long-term financial risks or liabilities to company stakeholders? How does one know that the money is being well spent in reducing the aggregate risk, i.e., the total expected financial liabilities from environmental situations of the operations of a firm, or a division, or a group of facilities in a country?

Such information is of more than academic interest. It is of value for:

1. Linking environmental management with corporate strategic planning

2. Targeting financial resources at action-sensitive operations to minimize aggregate risk

3. Acquiring and managing different types of insurance that match the type of risk

4. Asset restructuring, acquisitions, and divestitures (opportunity-oriented rather than liability-oriented); information for investment bankers

5. SEC (Securities and Exchange Commission) reporting, and to establish contingency reserves if there is material effect on equity

The aggregate financial risks hinge on environmental, health, and safety risks (discussed in the following pages), but these have to be translated into financial costs of reducing such risks, or the probable costs of consequences if the actions are deferred (see Fig. 11-5 for a simple illustration). What to spend and when, and when not to, is a legitimate corporate management concern. The approach outlined here combines the corporate environmental policy with environmental science and engineering expertise, database management, and financial risk analysis for strategic management of decisions under uncertainty. (As Peter Drucker has said: the more the uncertainty, the more the need for planning. Risk management, after all, is planning for and managing the future.)

The Method and Inputs

The process starts with a review and articulation of corporate philosophy and environmental policy, and the development of a unified corporate environmental plan. This presents the framework for expectations and operating practices

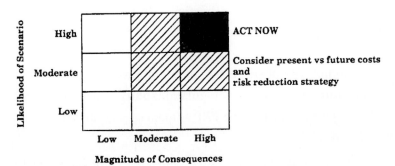

Figure 11-5. Environmental liability analysis—an illustration.

(e.g., "environment as a standard operating practice"), levels of acceptable risk to protect shareholders' investments, and the data and level of confidence required to support the decisions.

The quantification of short-term costs and long-term costs (future liability or risk) involves the following steps:

- Identify the universe of environmental problems, usually through facility audits, assessments, and monitoring programs; distinguish between sudden and accidental release potential (e.g., failure of a reactor or tank) and long-term gradual contamination (e.g., aquifer contamination from a leak).

- Estimate the present costs of avoiding potential accidents and correcting existing environmental problems as a probability distribution (using, for example, low, medium, and high cost estimates).

- Estimate, if applicable, company share of remedial costs as for Superfund potentially responsible party (PRP), also as probability distribution.

- Project the likely course of development of the problem (e.g., from a spill or leak to aquifer contamination) if action is deferred, and the time frame during which it would reach maximum liability (taking into account natural attenuation by biodegradation, etc.).

- Estimate magnitude of future costs (if any) for correction, litigation, penalties, and compensation (including toxic torts and natural resource damage) using probability distribution.

- Combine these estimated costs (short-term and long-term) and their probabilities to yield expected costs at a specified level of confidence for a single facility or two or more facilities (aggregate risk) using decision trees and flowcharts.

- Organize and present the data to portray aggregate risk as expected costs by division, product line, geographic unit, class of problem, present vs. future costs, etc. The expected short-term costs are the likely costs of correcting the problem now; the expected long-term costs represent future financial liability or long-term financial risk, discounted to present value.

Obviously, there is more uncertainty in estimating long-term liability than in estimating the cost of immediate action. The sources of financial uncertainty include:

- Cost of action now (complexity of site, extent of migration)
- Cost of action in the future (including new regulations and agencies involved)
- Share of costs (e.g., Superfund PRP, other PRP's financial viability)
- Time frame of cash flows
- Discount rate

- Insurance coverage and recoverability (commercial or state guaranty fund)
- Costs of litigation

The degree of uncertainty may be reduced to some extent by collecting additional data and using expert panels. For example, the financial solvency of the insurance company and other PRPs, and recovery of costs, can be important decision inputs. Estimates of the insurance industry's potential liability and cleanup insurance costs are in the range of $40 to $50 billion over the next 10 years (personal communication with F. Kloman et al. of Tillinghast/Towers Perrin Co.).

Output and Decision Making

The environmental and financial data can be combined and sorted for the whole firm, as well as by division, geographic unit (region or country), operating unit, business unit, facility, etc. Costs are estimated as probability distributions and aggregate risk is represented by expected cost.

Example 1. There is an 80% probability that the corporate aggregate environmental risk is $250 million or less, and a 50% probability that it is $150 million or less.

Example 2. The Superfund exposure as a PRP for 50 sites is likely to be $100 million or less at 90% confidence level.

Example 3. The company needs x dollars of liability insurance for property damage from specific accidents plus y dollars for cleanup liability arising out of gradual pollution.

Example 4. Comparison of estimated costs of action now versus liability if action is deferred.

	Present cost, million $	Future cost, NPV million $	Ratio, future/present
1	10	12	1.2
2	14	20	1.4
3	10	60	6.0

Assuming similar contexts and confidence levels, investment in unit 3 now yields the highest reduction in long-term financial risk and is clearly the action-sensitive opportunity.

In summary, this is a commonsense and powerful approach that combines technical and financial data with database and decision techniques, to construct a macrocorporate perspective for environmental decisions. By prudent extrapolation, the underlying principles can yield the elements of a national environmental strategy as well. (For case studies of environmental decision making, see Chap. 9.)

Safety Hazard Analysis
(Probabilistic and Quantitative Risk Assessment)

Concepts and Definitions

The tragic accidents at Seveso, Bhopal, and Chernobyl, and more recently Pasadena (Texas) and Guadalajara (Mexico) heightened concerns about public safety worldwide. These developments renewed interest in preventive and mitigative approaches; safety hazard analysis is such an approach used for identifying industrial and other safety hazards and preventing or minimizing their consequences. Unlike health risk assessment, the focus of safety hazard analysis is acute hazards—chemical and physical conditions that have the potential to cause human injury or economic loss from instantaneous or short-duration exposure to an accident. (Related concepts are discussed in more detail in the next section on Health Risk Assessment.) Acute hazards may be associated with a range of operations including manufacture, storage, transportation, use, and disposal involving materials, equipment, and procedures.

Safety hazard analysis centers on four basic questions:

- What can go wrong and why?
- How likely is it?
- How bad could it be?
- What can we do about it?

These four questions provide the framework for hazard analysis. Broadly defined, hazard analysis includes the identification of hazards, estimation of the likelihood of events occurring that would cause an accident, potential consequences of such an accident, and the likelihood that mitigation systems and response measures would prevent or reduce the consequences (AIChE, 1985 and 1989). Safety hazard analysis is also referred to as a predictive hazard evaluation, quantitative risk assessment, chemical process quantitative risk analysis, and probabilistic risk assessment; it was originally used in the nuclear industry and in aerospace manned space flight programs. In this section, all these labels are used interchangeably to represent a set of core principles and processes as illustrated in Figs. 11-6 and 11-7.

Hazard Analysis Process Steps

The four major steps of safety hazard analysis are:

1. Hazard identification

2. Probability/frequency estimation

3. Consequence analysis

4. Risk determination and evaluation

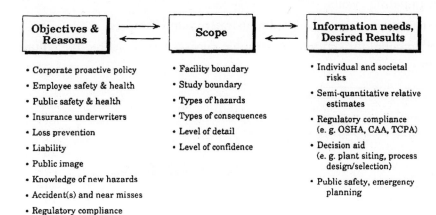

	Safety Review	Checklist/ What-if	Relative Ranking	PHA	Hazop	FMEA	FTA/ETA	HRA
R & D			X	X				
Conceptual Design		X	X	X				
Pilot Plant Operations		X		X	X	X	X	X
Detailed Engineering		X			X	X	X	X
Construction/Start-Up	X	X						X
Routine Operation	X	X			X	X	X	X
Expansion or Modification	X	X	X	X	X	X	X	X
Incident Investigation					X	X	X	X
Decommissioning	X	X						

Figure 11-6. (*a*) Safety hazard analysis: objectives and scope. (*Adapted from Chemical Manufacturers Association, "Evaluating Process Safety in the Chemical Industry," 1989.*) (*b*) Typical applications of hazard evaluation techniques. See glossary for definitions. (*Adapted from American Institute of Chemical Engineers, "Guidelines for Hazard Evaluation Procedures," 1992.*)

Hazard Identification

A hazard is a characteristic of a system or process that represents the potential for an accident (fire, explosion, toxic release). In the fundamental hazard identification step, the hazards inherent in or related to the facility operation and existing practices are explored. The methods and techniques range from qualitative, and yet powerful, what-if scenarios to more quantitative FMEA and HAZOP procedures (see Fig. 11-6 and the glossary at the end of this section). In the hazard identification step, risk assessors:

- Define analytical boundaries
- Identify hazards generally associated with the industry, facility, and operation
- Determine hazardous material inventories, location, transport, and handling
- Identify initiating events
- Review current engineered and administrative safety features
- Identify potential for sudden catastrophic releases based on credible failure scenarios

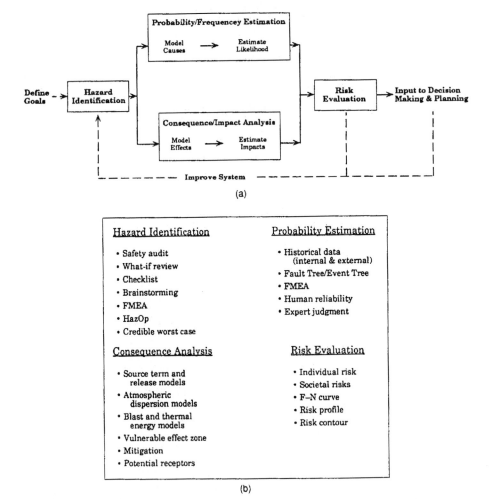

Figure 11-7. Safety hazard analysis: (*a*) process and procedures and (*b*) procedures, models, and outputs. (*Adapted from Chemical Manufacturers Association, "Evaluating Process Safety in the Chemical Industry," 1989.*)

Sources of process hazards and initiating events are shown in Table 11-5. Typical examples are:

- Loss of containment of flammable, reactive, or acutely toxic materials during storage, handling, or processing
- None, less, more, etc., of reactants and energy
- Hazardous release or unsafe condition because of mechanical failure or human error (e.g., pump A stops working while valve B is open)

Probability or Frequency Estimation

This step involves the estimation of the likelihood of occurrence of the events and situations identified in the previous step. This can sometimes be accomplished readily by extrapolating industry accident data and experience. Chemical process industry component failure databases are being expanded by the AIChE, API, and other industry organizations. Typically, the development of expected frequencies requires synthesis of historical data, models (e.g., event tree and fault tree), and expert judgment:

- Develop accident scenarios
- Collect industry and facility data
- Quantify frequency of various scenarios
- Delineate key contributors and influences

Examples of probability estimates are:

- The probability of loss of cooling water to an oxidation reactor (initiating event) is 10^{-4} per year.
- The likelihood of failure of a safety system (designed to respond to the initiating event) is 10^{-3} per year.
- The probability of a 1000-lb ammonia release is 2×10^{-4} in a one-year period.

Consequence Analysis

Consequence analysis involves five activities that seek to link hazard sources with potential receptors:

- Characterize source term, i.e., quantity, form, and rate of material and energy released to the environment.
- Estimate, by measurements and/or models, material transport and energy propagation through the environment toward receptors of interest.
- Assess safety and health effects related to projected exposure levels, especially atmospheric concentrations
- Identify environmental impacts
- Estimate property loss and other economic impacts

Table 11-5. Dynamics of Incidents and Accidents

| | | Intermediate events | | |
Process hazards	Initiating events	Propagating factors	Mitigating factors	Outcomes/consequences
Significant inventories of:	Process upsets	Equipment failure	Control/operator responses	Fires
Flammable materials	Process deviations	Safety system failure	Alarms	Pool fires
Combustible materials	Pressure	Ignition sources	Control system response	Jet fires
Unstable materials	Temperature	Furnaces, flares, incinerators	Manual and automatic ESD	BLEVEs
Corrosive materials	Flow rate	Vehicles	Fire/gas detection system	Flash fires
Asphyxiants	Concentration	Electrical switches	Safety system responses	Explosions
Shock-sensitive materials	Phase/state change	Static electricity	Relief valves	Confined explosions
Highly reactive materials	Impurities	Hot surfaces	Depressurization systems	Unconfined vapor cloud explosions (UVCE)
Toxic materials	Reaction rate/heat of reaction	Management systems failure	Isolation systems	Physical explosions (PV)
Inerting gases	Spontaneous reaction	Usefulness	High-reliability trips	Dust explosions
Combustible dusts	Polymerization	Timeliness	Backup systems	Detonations
Pyrophoric materials	Runaway reaction	Human errors	Mitigation system responses	Condensed phase detonations
	Internal explosion	Omission	Dikes and drainage	Missiles
Extreme physical conditions:	Decomposition	Commission	Flares	Analysis
High temperatures	Containment failures	Fault diagnosis	Fire-protection systems (active and passive)	Discharge
Cryogenic temperatures	Pipes, tanks, vessels, gaskets/seals	Decision making	Explosion vents	Flash and evaporation
High pressures	Equipment malfunctions	Domino effects	Toxic gas absorption	Dispersion
Vacuum	Pumps, valves, instruments, sensors, interlock failures	Other containment failures	Emergency plan responses	Neutral/positively buoyant gas
Pressure cycling		Other material releases	Sirens/warnings	Dense gas
Temperature cycling	Loss of utilities	External conditions	Emergency procedures	Consequences
Vibration/liquid hammering	Electrical, nitrogen, water, refrigeration, air, heat transfer fluids, steam, ventilation	Meteorology	Personnel safety equipment	Effect analysis
		Visibility	Sheltering	Toxic effects
Reaction rates sensitivities:	Management systems failure		Escape and evacuation	Thermal effects
Impurities	Design		External events	Overpressure effects
Process parameters	Communication		Early detection	Damage assessments
	Human error		Early warning	Community
	Design		Specially designed structures	Work force
	Construction		Training	Environment
	Operations		Other management systems	Company assets
	Maintenance			
	Testing and inspection			
	External events			
	Extreme weather conditions (floods, winds)			
	Earthquakes			
	Nearby accidents' impacts			
	Vandalism/sabotage			

SOURCE: Adapted from American Institute of Chemical Engineers, Guidelines for Chemical Process Quantitative Risk Analysis, 1989.

To predict potential exposures to accidental releases, the direction and rate of dispersion in the atmosphere are important considerations. The dispersion estimates and concentration profiles are quite sensitive to source term variations. A number of models exist for source term characterization, as well as for passive and nonpassive (dense gas) atmospheric dispersion. Passive dispersion is modeled by Gaussian models: plume (steady, continuous release—point source or line source) or puff (instantaneous release). The industrial source complex (ISC) short-term and long-term models are among the more commonly used Gaussian models. For dense gases, lateral spread by gravity and decreased vertical mixing are important considerations; DEGADIS is an example of dense gas dispersion models.

To understand the nature of potential threats to public safety, the atmospheric concentrations in the vulnerable or effect zone can be compared with toxicity indicators and short-term exposure limits shown in the following box.

Examples of Toxicity Indicators and Exposure Limits

Acute toxicity (lethal concentration or dose)
    Inhalation: LC_{LO}, LC_{50}
    Oral: LD_{50}

Exposure limits (time-weighted average and short-term)
    ACGIH: TLV, STEL
    OSHA: PEL, STEL
    NIOSH: REL, IDLH
    AIHA: ERPG

Short-term exposure limits:
    STEL—short-term exposure limit;
    maximum 15-min concentration limit for workers under OSHA regulations and ACGIH guidelines
    IDLH—immediately dangerous to life or health;
    maximum concentration from which one could escape within 30 minutes without experiencing any escape-impairing or irreversible health effects [IDLH values are available from National Institute for Occupational Safety and Health (NIOSH)]

    ERPG—emergency response planning guidelines;
    being developed by American Industrial Hygiene Association (AIHA) industry task force; ERPG-2 is maximum airborne concentration below which, it is believed, nearly all receptors could be exposed up to 1 hour without experiencing serious health effects that could impair an individual's ability to take protective action (ERPGs have been developed for a few chemicals)

Examples of consequences are:

- Under this conservative scenario, 1000 lb of ammonia would be released and 10 people would be exposed to concentrations exceeding IDLH (500 ppm for ammonia) or ERPG limits.
- One fatality and five serious injuries are expected outside facility boundary.
- Expected economic loss from property damage and interrupted production is $5 million.

Health effects from chronic toxicity are discussed under Health Risk Assessment. Although acute and chronic effects overlap to some extent, what distinguishes acute hazards is the timing of response, which is critical to thwart an accident or mitigate its effects.

Risk Determination and Evaluation

To arrive at the risk estimates, the results of probability and consequence analyses are integrated. Risk estimates are generally developed for both individual and population or societal risks.

A great deal of uncertainty pervades probability and consequence estimates, and therefore the risk estimates, especially for very low probability accidents with very high consequences. The uncertainty in risk estimates should be characterized in order to understand (1) major sources of uncertainty and (2) assumptions and variables that have the most effect on the risk estimates. Sensitivity analysis can be used for this purpose to gain insights into the most influential variables; their values can be further refined and resources targeted toward major contributors of risk (e.g., production, storage, transfer).

Examples of risk estimates:

- The risk of a worker fatality from boiling liquid expanding vapor explosion (BLEVE) is 1 in 10 years.
- The risk of injury outside the facility boundary is 2×10^{-5} per year (chance of two injuries per year in a population of 100,000).
- Failure of safety system B contributes 60% of total risk for this process.
- The economic risk of operating this unit is $2 million during its lifetime.

Risk Measures and Presentation.   Risk measures should be developed for individual as well as societal risks and presented in simple language. Risk to people is generally presented in terms of severe injuries and fatalities, although it is difficult to define the degree of injury and make comparisons in advance. The three most common forms of risk expression are:

1. Risk contour plot (Fig. 11-8) around a facility (source of risk) showing isorisk lines of injuries or fatalities

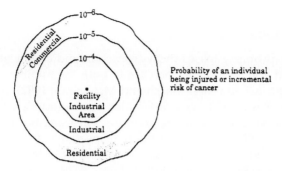

Figure 11-8. Individual risk contour example.

2. Risk profile, either individual or population, showing expected frequency vs. distance from a source, or frequency vs. magnitude of consequences

3. *F-N* (frequency-number) curve that is a logarithmic plot of cumulative frequency vs. consequences, e.g., cumulative frequency of events causing N or more fatalities or other effects (Fig. 11-9).

Any plan to reduce risk should of course consider both reduction in frequency of events and mitigation of expected consequences. In theory, high-frequency, low-consequence accidents and low-frequency, high-consequence risks are equivalent if they have the same risk numbers, but they generate entirely different levels of public and political concern. Risk reduction programs thus require a judicious balancing of public perceptions, as well as individual and societal risks, with the conservative nature of basic assumptions.

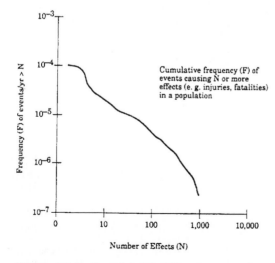

Figure 11-9. Societal risk *F-N* curve example.

Hydrocarbon and Chemical Industry Property Losses and Causes

An analysis of large property losses in hydrocarbon and chemical industries indicates a continued and significant increase in both the number and magnitude of losses over the last 30 years (Marsh and McLennan, 1992). In the 5-year period 1987–1991, there were 41 large property losses amounting to $2.94 billion compared with 36 and $1.23 billion in the previous 5-year period. Total losses in 1990 and 1991 are $170 million and $527 million, respectively. (The loss amounts include property loss and cleanup costs but not the costs of business interruption, penalties, employee injuries, or liability claims.) The increase in the magnitude of losses is partly due to the trend toward larger-capacity, more compact plants (concentration of assets in a smaller area), and higher cleanup costs related to asbestos, PCBs, and oil and chemical spills.

The types and causes of hydrocarbon and chemical property losses are shown in Table 11-6. Examples of major accidents, causes, and consequences are in Table 11-7; the LPG accident in Mexico City, just before Bhopal, is described in the following box. Catastrophic accidents such as these led to the landmark safety legislation, notably OSHA's process safety management standard, and the EPA's risk management plan discussed in the following pages.

Table 11-6. Large Hydrocarbon and Chemical Property Losses

Type of Loss by Facility				
	Explosions, %	Fires, %	Vapor cloud explosions, %	Other, %
Refineries	15	48	31	6
Petrochemical plants	46	17	37	0
Terminals	22	44	28	6
Gas processing plants	0	40	60	0
Miscellaneous	7	50	36	7

Cause of Loss and Relative Importance		
Cause	Percent of losses	Average loss, $ million
Mechanical failure	41	39.0
Operational error	20	51.8
Unknown	18	38.6
Process upset	8	51.1
Natural hazard	6	45.4
Design error	4	57.6
Sabotage and arson	3	26.2

SOURCE: Marsh and McLennan, 1992. Large Property Damage Losses in the Hydrocarbon-Chemical Industries.

Table 11-7. Examples of Major Accidents, Causes, and Consequences (Rough Estimates)

Date	Location	Cause	Fatalities	Injuries	Loss*	Comments
April 1992	Guadalajara, Mexico	Hexane leak exploding in sewer system	100+	Several hundred	?	
October 1989	Pasadena, Texas	Ethylene-isobutane leak at petrochemical plant	23	132	>$700 million	Largest onshore loss of hydrocarbon and chemical industries
July 1988	North Sea	?	167	?	$1 billion	Loss of entire oil platform
April 1986	Chernobyl nuclear plant	Sudden power surge and core meltdown	30 during event	500+	>$5.5 billion (by end of 1989)	Widespread contamination from ~50 million curies released; long-term death toll in thousands
December 1984	Bhopal, India	Methyl isocyanate gas leak from pesticide plant	4000	200,000+	?	$470 million paid toward damage claims
November 1984	Mexico City, Mexico	LPG line rupture and fire	650	2700	$20 million equipment loss	Five massive BLEVEs, secondary fires and explosions
March 1979	Three Mile Island nuclear plant	Cooling system failure	0	0 (~15 curies released)	$1.3 billion	Plant damage was serious enough not to operate again

*Losses shown are for property damage only and do not include loss of production and business interruption, penalties, and liability claims.

Example of a Catastrophic Accident: Mexico City, November 1984

The massive explosion and fire that occurred at a government-owned and -operated LPG terminal is perhaps the most devastating such incident ever. Three refineries supplied the facility with up to 1.3 million gallons of LPG daily. This was stored in six spheres and 48 bullets with a combined capacity of 4.2 million gallons. Tanks were about 90% full at the time of the loss.

Product for storage was being received at 341 psig via a 12-inch pipeline from a refinery 250 miles distant. The two largest spheres (630,000-gallon capacity each) and the 48 cylindrical tanks had been filled. The four remaining spheres, each with capacity for 420,000 gallons, were receiving product and were about one-half full when an 8-inch line to one of the spheres ruptured. The pressure drop was immediately sensed by the refinery operators. Attempts to contact the terminal by telephone were unsuccessful and since the flow could only be stopped at the terminal it continued. About 10 minutes later the large vapor cloud which had formed was ignited by a grade-level burn pit-flare. Within five minutes of ignition the first of a series of five massive BLEVEs occurred, producing a fireball estimated to be 1200 feet in diameter. The radiated heat from the rupturing tanks and the missile damage allowed the release of more fuel from other tanks.

Eventually, the four smaller spheres and 44 of the bullets BLEVE'd or were ruptured by missiles. Some tanks weighing 20 tons skyrocketed, landing 3900 feet away. The terminal's fire water system was disabled in the initial blast. Water transported to the scene by 100 tank cars was used by fire fighters in keeping the two large spheres sufficiently cool to prevent their failure. These spheres developed leaks in their vapor spaces which allowed them to depressure and burn under controlled conditions. (SOURCE: Marsh and McLennan, 1992.)

The above incident resulted in as many as 650 fatalities and 2700 injuries. There has been a buildup of low-income housing around the facility after it was first built, as is typical in developing countries, which aggravated the human impacts.

Regulatory Driving Forces

Employee and societal safety is of course good business and a key element of corporate environment, health, and safety programs. In addition to being the "right thing to do," and economic incentives for preventing injuries and property losses, state and federal regulations mandate the application of safety hazard analyses.

In response to the Bhopal accident and the resulting worldwide concern about public safety, New Jersey's Toxic Catastrophe Prevention Act (1986), California's Acutely Hazardous Materials Risk Management Act (1986), and

Delaware's Extremely Hazardous Substances Risk Management Act (1988) followed in quick succession.

At the federal level, OSHA recently issued its Final Rule: Process Safety Management of Highly Hazardous Chemicals, Explosives and Blasting Agents (29 CFR 1910, February 24, 1992). This rule, which became effective May 26, 1992, established procedures for process safety management to protect employees by preventing accidents or minimizing their consequences. In a move that would blur the line between OSHA and EPA domains, the 1990 Clean Air Act requires EPA to propose a risk management plan and promulgate within three years regulations governing accidental release prevention and chemical process safety management. Employees will benefit by the merging of OSHA Standard and EPA risk management plan requirements.

OSHA's Process Safety Management

The process management of highly hazardous chemicals (OSHA 29CFR 1910.119), also known as process safety management (PSM) standard, is far-reaching in its technical scope, administrative detail, and economic implications. OSHA estimates annual compliance costs of about $890 million and savings from improved safety and productivity of $720 million, with net costs of $170 million. The industry estimates of costs of compliance are 10 to 20 times higher, but there seems to be a consensus that such a preventive and formalized safety program is needed.

The standard applies to manufacturing industries (chemical, petroleum, pulp and paper, food processing, and electronics, among others) and processes that deal with more than 130 highly hazardous chemicals, toxics, and reactives in amounts larger than specified threshold quantities (Appendix A to 1910.119). It also applies to flammable gases and liquids except those stored only for workplace consumption as a fuel under specified pressure and temperature conditions. A process is defined as "any activity involving a highly hazardous chemical including using, storing, manufacturing, handling, or moving such chemicals at the site, or any combination of these activities. For purposes of this definition, any group of vessels that are interconnected, and separate vessels located in a way that could involve a highly hazardous chemical in a potential release, are considered a single process" (OSHA 3132.1992, p. 5).

The standard contains the following 14 provisions:

1. Process safety information
2. Process hazard analysis
3. Operating procedures
4. Employee participation
5. Training: initial training; refresher training; training documentation
6. Contractors: application; employer responsibilities; contract employer responsibilities

7. Pre-startup safety review

8. Mechanical integrity

9. Hot work/nonroutine work permit

10. Management of change

11. Incident investigation

12. Emergency planning and response

13. Compliance audits

14. Trade secrets

The process hazard analysis is the cornerstone of the standard and involves the following (excerpt from Process Safety Management, OSHA 3132.1992):

> The process hazard analysis is a thorough, orderly, systematic approach for identifying, evaluating, and controlling the hazards of processes involving highly hazardous chemicals. The employer must perform an initial process hazard analysis (hazard evaluation) on all processes covered by this standard. The process hazard analysis methodology selected must be appropriate to the complexity of the process and must identify, evaluate, and control the hazards involved in the process.
>
> First, employers must determine and document the priority order for conducting process hazard analyses based on a rationale that includes such considerations as the extent of the process hazards, the number of potentially affected employees, the age of the process, and the operating history of the process. All initial process hazard analyses should be conducted as soon as possible, but at a minimum, the employer must complete no fewer than 25 percent by May 26, 1994; 50 percent by May 26, 1995; 75 percent by May 26, 1996; and all initial process hazard analyses by May 26, 1997. Where there is only one process in a workplace, the analysis must be completed by May 26, 1994.
>
> Process hazard analyses completed after May 26, 1987, that meet the requirements of the PSM standard are acceptable as initial process hazard analyses. All process hazard analyses must be updated and revalidated, based on their completion date, at least every 5 years.
>
> The employer must use one or more of the following methods, as appropriate, to determine and evaluate the hazards of the process being analyzed:
>
> - What-if
> - Checklist
> - What-if/checklist
> - Hazard and operability study (HAZOP)
> - Failure mode and effects analysis (FMEA)
> - Fault tree analysis
> - An appropriate equivalent methodology
>
> A discussion of these methods of analysis is contained in the companion publication, OSHA 3133, *Process Safety Management—Guidelines for*

Compliance. Whichever method(s) are used, the process hazard analysis must address the following:

- The hazards of the process
- The identification of any previous incident that had a potential for catastrophic consequences in the workplace
- Engineering and administrative controls applicable to the hazards and their interrelationships, such as appropriate application of detection methodologies to provide early warning of releases. Acceptable detection methods might include process monitoring and control instrumentation with alarms, and detection hardware such as hydrocarbon sensors
- Consequences of failure of engineering and administrative controls
- Facility siting
- Human factors
- A qualitative evaluation of a range of the possible safety and health effects on employees in the workplace if there is a failure of controls

OSHA believes that the process hazard analysis is best performed by a team with expertise in engineering and process operations, and that the team should include at least one employee who has experience with and knowledge of the process being evaluated. Also, one member of the team must be knowledgeable in the specific analysis methods being used.

Hazard Evaluation Methods

Safety hazard analysis methods, procedures, and techniques, including those recommended by OSHA for process safety, are presented in many professional and industry publications (AIChE, CMA, API) listed under the references. See, for example, AIChE/CCPS *Guidelines for Hazard Evaluation Procedures,* 2d ed., with worked examples, 1992.

Safety Hazard Glossary and Definitions

Checklist: A detailed list of requirements or steps to assess the status of a system or operation and to ensure compliance with standard operating procedures (SOPs).

Event Tree Analysis (ETA): A graphic model and technique for identifying the sequence of events, following initiating event(s), that result in accidents.

Failure Modes and Effects Analysis (FMEA): A systematic tabular method for identifying failure modes of components or features of a system and corresponding outcomes.

Fault Tree Analysis (FTA): A deductive technique that helps in determining the causes of failure or accident (top event).

Hazard and Operability (HAZOP) Studies: A widely used method to identify potential operating problems that might cause a deviation from design intent. A series of guide words are used (e.g., no, more, other than, as well as) at specific "study nodes" (e.g., no-flow, high pressure).

Human Reliability Analysis (HRA): A method to evaluate whether necessary human actions and tasks will be performed or completed successfully within a required time; estimation of the probability of successful performance of a task.

Preliminary Hazard Analysis (PHA): A precursor to detailed hazard analysis, used to recognize hazards early in conceptual and developmental phases, and in site selection.

Process Safety Management (PSM): A systematic program involving management principles and scientific data to ensure safety of processing units and facilities.

Relative Ranking: Analysis that allows comparison of hazardous characteristics of alternative siting, design or layout options, and ranking of risks. The two widely used methods are Dow fire and explosion index (F&EI) and ICI Mond index.

Safety Review and Loss Prevention Review: An inspection of plant process units, drawings, procedures, emergency plans, etc., by an experienced team; this review is often oriented toward problem solving and as such may differ from audits by independent teams that emphasize prevention.

Sustance Hazard Index (SHI): Equilibrium vapor concentration of a substance at 20°C divided by acute toxicity concentration "ATC" (ATC is the lowest reported concentration that will cause permanent injury or death to humans after a single exposure of 1 hour or less).

What-if Analysis: A brainstorming technique to explore possibilities and consider the results of undesired or unexpected events (e.g., what if the wrong material or wrong concentration material is delivered; what if the operator opens the wrong valve?).

Health Risk Assessment*

Planning Is Critical

In health risk assessment, our focus is on long-term exposures to hazardous substances and related chronic health effects. The risk assessment process illustrated in Fig. 11-10 is based on the guidelines issued by the National Academy of Sciences and National Research Council (NAS, NRC) and adopted by the EPA.

Critical to the success of risk assessments is upfront planning. This requires clear articulation and understanding of situation or site-specific objectives:

1. What types of decisions are being considered? What is at stake? What is driving the decision? (Human health or ecological risks?)

2. What are the uses and who are the users of risk assessment data? What is the scope of the assessment?

Among the driving forces are:

- Regulatory compliance
- Voluntary action for commercial reasons
- Public health concerns
- Public concerns other than health, e.g., property values
- Financial liability, toxic torts
- Natural Resource Damage Assessment (NRDA) compensation
- Public goodwill "franchise"

Examples of users and applications include:

- Sponsoring company, related operations, and consultants
- EPA
- State agencies (departments of environment and health)
- Environmental groups
- Community residents
- Lawyers
- Public health professionals, researchers
- Natural resource trustees and NRDA
- Media

*Ronald A. Lang of the American Industrial Health Council reviewed this Health Risk Assessment section.

Research Data
- Laboratory
- Field
- Clinical
- Occupational
- Epidemiological

....

Risk Assessment

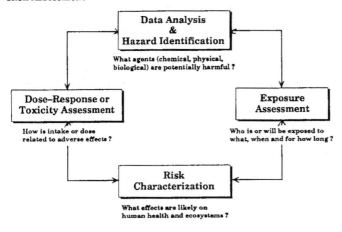

Figure 11-10. Risk assessment and management model.

Risk Management
- Regulatory & non-regulatory options
- Value judgments & policy considerations
- Economic analyses
- Communication, acceptability
- Decisions and Actions

The objectives of risk assessment, expected output, its use, and proposed analytical approach should be defined, discussed, and agreed upon with the client, regulatory agencies, and other stakeholders involved. This is carried out preferably before, or at least in conjunction with, the development of project budget and time schedule. This initial investment of time yields rich dividends from clearly defined objectives (including data quality objectives) and strategy, because risk assessment suffers from a "black box" image and inferred promise of "all things to all people."

Risk Assessment Process

Risk assessment starts off with an initial phase of research and data collection. In the context of assessing risks from a contaminated site, the hazard data come from sampling of environmental media (soil, groundwater, surface water, sediment, air) on and off site. The toxicity data may come from a variety of sources:

animal experiments, worker occupational exposures, epidemiological studies, medical or clinical records, and structure-activity relationships.

The risk assessment method described here is oriented toward quantifying risks associated with contaminated sites such as Superfund and RCRA sites. The same principles could of course be applied to assessing health risks in similar situations, including hazardous-waste storage facilities, resource recovery facilities, new incinerators, and operating permits. Subsequent risk management phase involves remediation goals, screening of alternatives, and implementation of selected course of action.

The four major steps in a baseline risk assessment (BRA) are shown below. The baseline risks are those that are related to existing site conditions under the no-action or minimal action scenario, e.g., fencing and access restrictions. (See also the Ecological Risk Assessment section for additional discussion of these steps.)

1. Data evaluation and hazard identification (selection of chemicals of concern or "indicator chemicals")

2. Toxicity or dose-response assessment

3. Exposure assessment

4. Risk characterization (including uncertainty analysis)

Data Evaluation and Hazard Identification

What is of concern?

Data Quality Objectives (DQOs)

DQOs are statements that specify the quality and quantity of data required to support regulatory and nonregulatory decisions. Risk assessors occasionally have the opportunity to specify in advance their data needs, rather than try to "retrofit" existing data. The DQOs should reflect all identified uses, including risk assessment (human, ecological), treatability studies, ARARs, and remedial actions. Key questions are:

1. What are the expected uses of the data and who will use them?

2. Should the data be collected, analyzed, and validated according to the EPA contract laboratory program (CLP) or other applicable protocols? Is it legally defensible?

3. What kind of sampling program is appropriate to the site—purposive, biased (near "hot spots"), random, systematic, or a combination?

4. Is the list of analytes appropriate to the site? Does only a subset need to be analyzed based on site production and use history? What is the level of confidence required? How many samples are needed?

5. Are sufficient samples collected and are they close to potential exposure points (e.g., top 6 inches or 2 feet of surface soil)?

6. Are quantitation or detection limits of analytical methods sufficiently low, i.e., below health-based reference concentrations and potential ARARs?

7. Are background (upgradient, upstream, upwind, reference) and off-site (downgradient, downstream, downwind) samples to be collected?

Chemicals of Concern (COCs) and Site-Specific Chemistry

The data evaluation and COCs identification process should include a review of site history (chronology of land use) and activities. A site map that shows major areas of concern and site boundaries should also be included. A site assessment (of the "air bubble" and the "inverted subsurface bubble") usually yields a large quantity of data—thousands of data sets on hundreds of chemicals including volatiles, semivolatiles, metals, pesticides, and other hazards. We are surrounded by numerous chemical, physical, and biological hazards, both natural (e.g., bacteria, radon) and synthetic (e.g., chlorinated solvents). A hazard is a source of risk but not a risk itself; i.e., its presence is a necessary but not sufficient condition for health and safety risks. This distinction needs to be made because in the public perception: hazard = exposure = risk = personal injury.

Volatile organics, petroleum hydrocarbons, chlorinated solvents, pesticides, secondary transformation products, and metals are among the most common contaminants found at Superfund and other waste sites. From scores of such compounds, a subset of chemicals that pose the greatest risks is selected. These chemicals of potential concern, sometimes referred to as indicator chemicals, are selected on the basis of:

- Toxicity, e.g., carcinogen slope factors, noncarcinogen reference doses
- Concentration in media compared with background levels (quantity, abundance)
- Concentration in media vs. federal and state standards and criteria
- Frequency of detection
- Fate and transport characteristics, e.g., potential for off-site migration, transformation, persistence, and bioaccumulation (Henry's law constant, octanol-water partition coefficient K_{ow}, half-life, bioconcentration factor)
- Pathways: air, groundwater, surface water, sediments (are exposure pathways complete?)

The number of detected chemicals can be reduced to a manageable size for further analysis by an initial qualitative screening and a more quantitative concentration-toxicity screening. In the initial step, some chemicals can sometimes be excluded from further consideration on the basis of:

- Chemical concentration in the range of local background levels
- Low frequency of detection (e.g., <5% of samples)
- Common laboratory contaminant (e.g., sample concentration <10 times blank)
- Low intrinsic toxicity (low slope factors, high reference doses)
- Essential nutrient, below recommended daily allowance (RDA)
- Concentration below federal and state standards (e.g., MCLs for water)
- Incomplete exposure pathways

Concentration-Toxicity Screening

The purpose of this screening procedure is to identify the chemicals (carcinogens and noncarcinogens) by each medium or pathway (e.g., air, water) most likely to contribute to health risks because of their toxicity and abundance. The risk factor R for each medium can be computed by a simple formula:

$$R = \sum (C_i)(T_i)$$

where R = risk factor for the medium

C = concentration of specific chemical in medium, maximum or 95% upper confidence limit value, whichever is lower

T = toxicity value for specific chemical in medium, slope factor for carcinogens, or $1/RfD$ for noncarcinogens [slope factors and reference doses (RfD) are explained in the next section].

The ratio of individual chemical risk factors to the total risk factor for each medium represents an approximation of the chemical's relative risk. Separate risk factors should be calculated for carcinogenic and noncarcinogenic risks and for each medium. A chemical that contributes less than a specified fraction of the total risk factor (say, less than 1%) would not be considered further in risk assessment. The reduction in the number of chemicals makes the quantitative risk assessment more manageable, while at the same time focusing attention on chemicals that are likely to contribute the most risk.

Toxicity Assessment (Dose-Response Assessment)

Dosis solus denenum facit "Dose is what makes the poison"

The purpose of the toxicity assessment is to evaluate available evidence about the potential for selected chemicals to cause adverse effects in exposed populations, and to provide an estimate of the relationship between the extent of exposure and the increased likelihood of adverse effects, i.e., dose-response relationship. (See Glossary of Toxicology Terms at the end of this section.)

Obviously, not all contaminants or chemicals are created equal in their capacity to cause adverse effects. The toxicity data are derived largely from animal experiments where the animals, mostly mice and rats, are exposed to increasingly higher concentrations or doses, and corresponding effects are observed. The dose-response relationship for a chemical thus indicates the degree of toxicity to exposed species (Fig. 11-11 *a* and *b*). Dose is normalized as milligrams of substance ingested, inhaled, or absorbed through the skin per kilogram of body weight per day (mg/kg-day). Responses or effects can vary widely—from no observable effect to temporary and reversible (such as enzyme depression caused by some pesticides) to permanent injury to organs (liver and kidney effects of chlorinated solvents and heavy metals) to chronic functional impairment (bronchitis, emphysema from smoke) and finally death. In addition to animal experiments, toxicity data are derived from occupational, clinical, and epidemiological studies.

For the purposes of health risk assessment, we classify health effects as cancer effects and noncancer effects. The two principal indices of toxicity are known as Carcinogenic Slope Factor (SF) and Reference Dose (RfD). Toxic

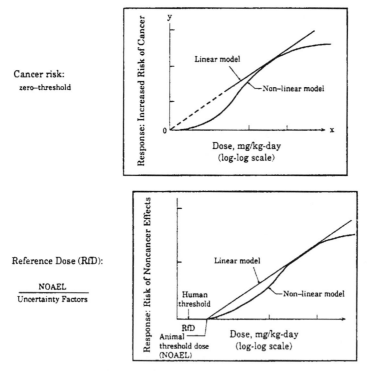

Cancer risk:
  zero–threshold

Reference Dose (RfD):

$$\frac{\text{NOAEL}}{\text{Uncertainty Factors}}$$

Figure 11-11. (*a*) Cancer zero-threshold dose-response curves (illustration). (*b*) Noncancer threshold dose-response curves (illustration).

responses are generally classified as nonthreshold (zero-threshold) effects and threshold effects. Cancer is a multistage process with long latency periods. For cancer effects of carcinogens, the EPA assumes zero threshold; that is, there is some risk no matter how small the dose. The cancer slope factor, also called the potency factor, is a conservative estimate of the incremental probability of cancer from a unit intake of a chemical over a lifetime. A second important factor for carcinogens is the weight of evidence whereby carcinogens are classified into groups depending on the quality and quantity of data that underlie their designation as potential human carcinogens. (Although only a fraction of nearly a hundred thousand chemicals in commercial use have so far been tested, available evidence to date indicates that fewer than one hundred, such as arsenic, asbestos, benzene, and vinyl chloride, are proven human carcinogens.) Both the slope factor and the weight of evidence are considered for permissible exposure levels and residual risks.

The threshold-response effects, represented by Reference Dose (RfD), allow for the existence of thresholds; that is, a certain quantity of a substance or dose is needed below which there is no observable toxic effect (no observable adverse effect level "NOAEL") by virtue of the body's natural repair and detoxifying capacity. An RfD for a substance is the intake or dose of the substance per unit body weight per day that is likely to be without appreciable risk to human populations, including sensitive groups (e.g., children). The threshold concept was first advanced in the Middle Ages by Philippus Aureolus Theophrastus Bombast von Hohenheim (who called himself Paracelsus!). His then-revolutionary view that "Dose is what makes the poison" remains axiomatic and an integral part of present-day toxicology. In general, substances with relatively high slope factors and low reference doses tend to be associated with higher toxicities.

Safe or Unsafe? Spectrum of Effects: Aspirin Example

Threshold?	Children under 12, possible factor in Reye's syndrome
165 to 325 mg/day (1/2 tablet to 1 tablet)	Preventive maintenance—against blood clotting, second heart attack, and stroke (anticoagulant)
650 mg (2 tablets) two to four times/day	Therapeutic—usual adult dose against headache and pain (analgesic), fever (antipyretic), and inflammation
10,000 to 20,000 mg (10 to 20 g)	Toxic—stomach ulcers, bleeding, ringing in ears (tinnitus), liver and kidney damage
20,000 to 40,000 mg (a bottle of about 100 tablets)	Fatal dose (if taken in a short time)

Hierarchy of Toxicity Data Sources

Because of frequent changes and updates in toxicity information, the EPA recommends the following hierarchy of preferred sources:

1. EPA integrated risk information system (IRIS) on-line database (updated monthly)
2. Health effects assessment summary tables (HEAST), hard copy with verified and interim data (updated periodically)

Some other toxicity information sources are:

- Agency for Toxic Substances and Disease Registry (ATSDR) toxicological profiles
- Hazardous Substances Databank (HSDB) available through National Library of Medicine (NLM)

Extrapolation from Mice to Men

Chemical toxicity data are derived largely from animal experiments where the animals, mostly mice and rats, are exposed to increasingly higher concentrations or doses, and corresponding effects are observed. Responses can vary widely—from no observable effect to temporary and reversible to permanent injury to organs, to chronic functional impairment, to malignant tumors, and finally death. High doses are administered to compensate for the small number of animals, about 50 per test group, and the low statistical sensitivity of the bioassays. The tests, even with mice and rats, cost hundreds of thousands to millions of dollars.

Typically, animal experiments are conducted with sensitive species (usually B6C3F1 mice), with single chemicals, at high doses, and over short time spans instead of chronic low-level and complex mixture exposure typical of humans. For carcinogens, EPA uses linearized, multistage no-threshold model where responses at high doses are extrapolated to low doses by a straight line to the origin, i.e., zero threshold.

The reference dose (RfD) and reference concentration (RfC) for noncarcinogens or for noncarcinogenic effects of carcinogens in humans are derived by dividing the no observed adverse effect level (NOAEL) by an uncertainty factor (UF) and/or a modifying factor (MF):

$$\text{RfD or RfC} = \frac{\text{NOAEL}}{\text{UF} \times \text{MF}}$$

In extrapolating the results of animal experiments to predict effects in humans, uncertainty or safety factors of 10 to 1000 are generally used to allow for intraspecies and interspecies differences in sensitivities and to account for differences in exposure periods and routes of exposure.

Carcinogen Classification. On the basis of tests conducted by the National Toxicology Program (NTP) of National Institute of Environmental Health Sciences (NIEHS) and others, the EPA classifies chemicals into the following groups according to the weight of evidence from animal experiments, clinical experience, and epidemiological studies. The International Agency for Research on Cancer (IARC) has a similar classification used by many countries.

EPA	IARC	Characterization
A	1	Human carcinogen (sufficient evidence of carcinogenicity in humans)
B	2A	Probable human carcinogen (B1—limited evidence of carcinogenicity in humans; B2—sufficient evidence of carcinogenicity in animals with inadequate or lack of evidence in humans)
C	2B	Possible human carcinogen (limited evidence of carcinogenicity in animals and inadequate or lack of human data)
D	3	Not classifiable as to human carcinogenicity (inadequate or no evidence)
E	4	Evidence of noncarcinogenicity for humans (no evidence of carcinogenicity in adequate studies)

Implications. The classification of a chemical as a carcinogen, the estimate of slope factor, and then its grouping by weight of evidence have enormous health and economic implications (as exemplified by the Delaney Clause). The zero-threshold concept, the "upper-bound" estimate of risk, and the use of maximum tolerated dose (MTD) have been subject to much controversy.

The zero-threshold for carcinogenic effects means that thresholds for low doses, however small, do not exist (even for promoters)—which seems to contradict actual human experience. Also, many scientists contend that EPA's upper-bound estimates of risk are misleading in that they do not actually predict risk but are only statistical estimates of the upper limits of risk. According to the EPA, "The true value of risk is unknown and may be as low as zero."

Another point of controversy has been the use of MTD, an artificially high dose that keeps the animals barely alive; the size of dose is considered grossly out of proportion and irrelevant to human exposure. Many toxicologists believe that perhaps two-thirds of NTP classified carcinogens would not be classified as such if the MTD were not used.

During 1991–1992, the NTP has gone through some changes and is reported to be moving away from MTD toward biologically effective dose, also taking into account nutritional factors (K. Olden, NTP/NIEHS).

OECD Investigation of the Safety of High-Production-Volume Chemicals

Nearly 100,000 chemicals are in commercial use worldwide, but we have sufficient toxicity data on only a small fraction of these chemicals. Through an OECD (Organization for Economic Cooperation and Development) Council decision, the 24 member countries including the United States have jointly undertaken the investigation of approximately 600 high-production-volume (HPV) chemicals. These chemicals are produced in one OECD member country in quantities above 10,000 metric tons (22 million pounds) per year or above 1000 metric tons in two or more OECD countries. These countries will cooperatively:

- Select the chemicals to be investigated
- Collect information from government and industry files
- Complete the agreed upon screening information data set (SIDS) testing
- Make an initial assessment of the potential hazards and risks of each chemical
- Identify possible future priority effects for these chemicals

The stages involved in the SIDS process are the following:

1. Priority setting based on (lack of) readily available data—the "working" list
2. Allocation of chemicals from the working list to potential sponsor countries
3. Collection of data
4. Review of the quality of data, preparation of SIDS dossiers, and SIDS testing plans
5. Circulation of SIDS dossiers and SIDS testing plans to all sponsor countries
6. Cooperative agreement on SIDS testing plans at the SIDS review meeting
7. SIDS testing
8. Preparation of recommendation for initial hazard assessment based on a complete SIDS by the sponsor country
9. Cooperative initial hazard assessment

Screening data set is to include:

- Chemical identity and physical-chemical data
- Sources and levels of exposure including production volumes and types of use

- Environmental fate and pathways
- Ecotoxicological data including acute and chronic effects on aquatic and terrestrial species
- Toxicological data including acute and chronic genetic and reproductive toxicities

The U.S. chemical and related industries, through CMA and EPA, are voluntarily participating in the program because of its many benefits: (1) potential impacts of common chemicals on human health and environment will be better understood and controlled; (2) financial costs are shared among companies and countries and duplication minimized; and (3) use of animals in testing is reduced. SIDS dossiers on the 600 priority chemicals are expected to be available before the end of the decade. The results will be made available worldwide through the United Nations International Program on Chemical Safety (IPCS) and the International Register of Potentially Toxic Chemicals (IRPTC).

SOURCE: EPA, CMA.

Exposure Assessment

Who is, or is likely to be, in contact?

Exposure is the process by which an organism comes into contact with a hazard; exposure or access is what bridges the gap between a hazard and a risk. Exposure to contaminants from a source can occur via inhalation of air, ingestion of water or food, or absorption through the skin via dermal contact. Most of us are exposed to varying degrees by multiple pathways and routes (Fig. 11-12). Contaminant sources, release mechanisms, transport and transformation characteristics, as well as the nature, location, and activity patterns of exposed population are important aspects of exposure assessment.

Exposure assessment should consider both current and future land use, including possible residential use. As can be expected, the level of cleanup will depend in part on whether the land would be restricted to industrial use or developed into a commercial or residential property. The key steps in exposure assessment are identification of potential receptor population, evaluation of exposure pathways and routes, and quantification of exposures.

Exposure Setting and Potential Receptors

In this step, the physical attributes of a site (hydrogeologic, climatic) and population at or near the site are characterized. As in real estate, location is the key; a map of the site and surroundings, and positions of potential receptors, should

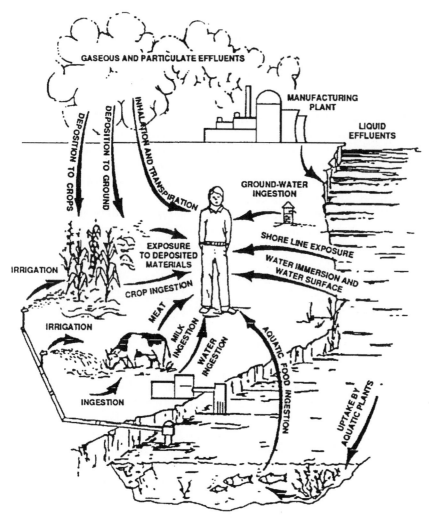

Figure 11-12. Multiple exposure pathways. (*National Research Council,* *"Frontiers in Assessing Human Exposure," 1991.*)

be included. The populations that may come into contact because of their locations or activity patterns include:

- On-site long-term workers
- On-site temporary maintenance or construction workers (subchronic exposures)
- Visitors
- Trespassers
- Area residents

- Recreational visitors (including fishermen to nearby streams, rivers)
- Sensitive subpopulations or locations (e.g., schools, hospitals, parks)
- Ecological receptors

We can use a site conceptual exposure model such as that in Fig. 11-13 as a checklist of potential receptors and pathways for exposure assessment, and to delineate complete pathways.

Exposure Pathways and Contaminant Fate and Transport

An exposure pathway is the course that a hazardous agent takes from a source to a receptor via environmental carriers or media, generally air (volatile compounds, particulates) or water (soluble compounds). (An exception is electromagnetic radiation which does not need a medium.) Exposure route is how the transfer occurs, i.e., by inhalation, ingestion, and dermal contact (Fig. 11-14). Dermal contact can result in a local effect at the point of entry and/or systemic effect by percutaneous absorption.

An exposure pathway to be complete must consist of four elements: (1) a source and a release mechanism, (2) a transport medium for released constituents, (3) a point of contact with contaminated medium, and (4) intake routes at the point of contact by a receptor. Without all these four elements, an exposure pathway would be considered incomplete and therefore not contributing to risk by that pathway. Exposure pathways are identified on the basis of contaminant sources, releases, and transport media in the context of the locations and activities of potential receptors.

Contaminant Fate and Transport Screening

Atmosphere. Volatilization, dispersion, airborne dust, transfer to other environmental media by wind and precipitation

Surface water and sediments. Exchange with groundwater, sediment adsorption, transfer to biota

Soil and groundwater. Percolation through unsaturated soils, transfer to surface water downgradient, transfer to humans or biota

Examples of Fate and Transport Processes

Physical. Volatilization, dispersion, advection, sorption

Chemical. Hydrolysis, reduction-oxidation (redox), photolysis

Biological. Biodegradation, biouptake, bioaccumulation

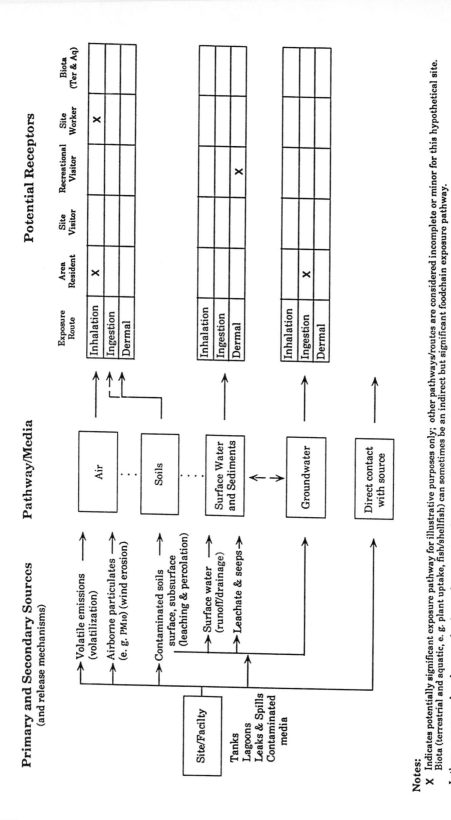

Figure 11-13. Site conceptual exposure model: contaminant sources, pathways, and potential receptors.

Respiratory Route

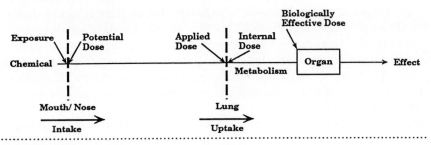

Oral Route

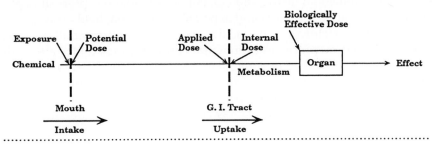

Dermal Route

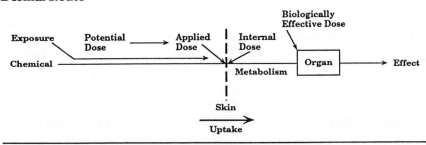

Exposure: Contact of medium with outer boundary of a person or organism, e.g. nose, mouth, skin
  Example units: (Concentration) x (Time) e.g. ug/m³ x days of contact

Potential Dose: Amount of chemical contained in air breathed, material ingested or applied to skin
  Units of dose are Mass of chemical (concentration represents level, dose represents quantity)

Applied Dose: Amount of chemical in contact with primary absorption boundaries – lungs,
  gastrointestinal tract, skin – and available for absorption

Internal Absorbed Dose: Amount of chemical penetrating across exchange boundary or absorption
  barrier via physical or biological processes

Delivered Dose (Biologically Effective Dose): Amount of chemical avaible for interaction with
  particular organ, tissue or cell

Figure 11-14. Schematic of exposure and dose. (*Adapted from "EPA Guidelines for Exposure Assessment," Federal Register, May 29, 1992.*)

Exposure Quantification

The next step in the exposure assessment process is the quantification of the magnitude, frequency, and duration of exposure for all the pathways that are considered complete and significant. This step involves estimation of exposure point concentrations for chemicals of concern, and calculation of intake or dose. The quantification of exposure, intake, or potential dose involves equations with three sets of variables: (1) chemical concentrations in media; (2) exposure rates (magnitude, frequency, duration); and (3) biological characteristics of receptors (body weight, absorption).

Exposure point concentrations are derived from measured, monitored, and/or modeled data (see example of calculating concentration term). Ideally, exposure concentrations should be measured at the points of direct contact between the environmental media and current or potential receptors. It is possible to identify potential receptors and exposure points from field observations and other information. However, it is seldom possible to anticipate all potential exposure points and measure environmental concentrations under all conditions. In practice, a great deal of professional judgment and a combination of monitoring and modeling data will be required to estimate exposure concentrations. As to exposure rates and receptor biological data, site-specific values should be used to the extent feasible; otherwise, conservative default values suggested by the EPA can be used (Table 11-8). The *Exposure Factors Handbook* (EPA, 1990) also provides equations and a range of values for exposure calculations. Exposures can be chronic (e.g., residential) or subchronic (e.g., maintenance workers, trespassers). It is important to make this distinction for noncarcinogenic effects because subchronic reference doses tend to be higher than chronic, often by an order of magnitude, due to shorter exposure periods. (This distinction is not made for carcinogenic effects.)

Exposure Data Hierarchy: Approximation to Actual Exposure

Exposure surrogates → Indirect measurements → Personal monitoring
    residence location,   media exposure point   dosimetry,
    employment,   concentrations—models   biological markers,
    census data   and measurements   clinical data

Exposure Assessment Output

The output of the exposure assessment process generally consists of two profiles: average case, and reasonable maximum exposure (RME) scenario. The average exposure is estimated using average conditions that may be typical of an individual with normal activity patterns (50th percentile). The RME is loosely defined as the 90th or 95th percentile exposure, meaning fewer than 5 to 10% of potential receptors are likely to exceed the RME exposure or risk. The

Table 11-8. EPA Standard Default Exposure Factors*

Land use	Exposure pathway	Daily intake	Exposure frequency, days/year	Exposure duration, years	Body weight, kg
Residential	Ingestion of potable water	2 liters/day	350	30	70 (154 lb)
	Ingestion of soil and dust	200 mg (child) 100 mg (adult)	350	6 24	15 (child) 70 (adult)
	Inhalation of contaminants	20 cu m (total) 15 cu m (indoor)	350	30	70
Industrial and commercial	Ingestion of potable water	1 liter	250	25	70
	Ingestion of soil and dust	50 mg	250	25	70
	Inhalation of contaminants	20 cu m (workday)	250	25	70
Agricultural†	Consumption of homegrown produce	42 g (fruit) 80 g (veg.)	350	30	70
Recreational	Consumption of locally caught fish	54 g	350	30	70

SOURCE: EPA Supplemental Guidance, March 25, 1991 (OSWER Directive 9285.6-03).
*Factors presented are those that should generally be used to assess exposures associated with a designated land use. Site-specific data may warrant deviation from these values; however, use of alternate values should be justified and documented in the risk assessment report. Listed pathways may not be relevant for all sites and other exposure pathways may need to be evaluated owing to site conditions.
For dermal exposure, chemical-specific permeability coefficients or absorption factors would also be needed. If permeability is less than 10^{-1} cm/h for water, or absorption less than 10% for soil, dermal route may not be important (EPA Dermal Exposure Assessment, 1992).
†Agricultural ingestion of water and soil, and inhalation of contaminants same as Residential.

RME is based on the 95% upper confidence limit on the arithmetic mean concentration estimate, and other factors that are representative of high-end exposures. The intent is to identify a conservative exposure case, cumulatively well above average, that is still within the range of possible exposures, instead of an absolute worst-case scenario. The average and RME cases provide point estimates but also an idea of the plausible range of exposures from a source. Exposure and risk estimates are illustrated on the following pages.

In risk assessment literature, we find references to worst-case scenarios and theoretical maximum exposed individual (MEI). The question is whom are we trying to protect: "jogging asthmatic," "couch potato," or lifelong resident of a hazardous-waste landfill? These concepts are intuitively attractive but actually do little to protect public health. There is no such thing as a worst case—only a lack of imagination. Nor is there even a remote possibility of an MEI, an individual who is conceived to be in direct contact with the pollutants all his or her life. The RME, at least in theory, is a more defensible concept, though quite often outside the range of plausible exposures.

Risk Characterization

What are the likely effects?

In risk characterization, the results of toxicity assessment (slope factors, reference doses) and exposure assessment (estimated intake or dose of potentially exposed populations) are integrated to arrive at quantitative estimates of cancer risks and hazard indices. (See examples of estimates toward the end of this section.) Risk characterization is an iterative process and is a bridge between risk assessment and risk management. According to American Industrial Health Council (AIHC), "Risk characterization is the interactive process of extracting and integrating decision-relevant information from hazard, dose-response and exposure evaluations and rendering it comprehensible to a diversity of users." Risk estimates should be thought of not as a single number but as a composite picture or a mosaic (D. Patton, EPA).

Cancer Risks

Cancer risk is the probability of an individual's developing cancer from exposure to specified hazards, estimated as follows:

$$\text{Incremental cancer risk} = \underset{\text{(mg/kg-day)}}{\text{(chronic daily intake)}} \times \underset{\text{(mg/kg-day)}^{-1}}{\text{(slope factor)}}$$

The incremental cancer risk is expressed, for example, as 3×10^{-6} (three chances in a million), 1×10^{-5} (one chance in one hundred thousand), etc. Because the slope factor in cancer risk generally represents the 95th percentile probability of response based on animal data using a linearized multistage model, the risk estimate tends to be an upper-bound estimate. According to the EPA, "Such an estimate, however, does not necessarily give a realistic prediction of the risk. The true value of the risk is unknown, and may be as low as zero. The range of risks, defined by the upper limit given by the chosen model and the lower limit which may be as low as zero, should be explicitly stated." (*The Risk Assessment Guidelines of 1986*, EPA 1987.) Even with this acknowledgment of uncertainty, cancer risk estimates higher than 10^{-6} to 10^{-4} are generally considered to be of regulatory concern.

Noncancer Hazard Quotient and Hazard Index

Noncancer risk is expressed in terms of hazard quotient (HQ) for a single substance or hazard index (HI) for multiple substances and/or exposure pathways. These are ratios of chemical exposure to reference doses (RfD) as shown below.

The ratio of exposure level, intake, or dose to RfD for the same route of exposure (inhalation, oral), and the same exposure period (chronic, subchronic) is called a hazard quotient:

$$\text{Hazard quotient (HQ)} = \frac{\text{Exposure or intake} \quad \text{(mg/kg-day)}}{\text{RfD} \quad \quad \text{(mg/kg-day)}}$$

If the exposure or intake is less than the corresponding RfD (HQ less than 1), the hazards are not considered to pose a threat to public health including sensitive subgroups. If the exposure level of a substance exceeds the corresponding RfD (if the hazard quotient exceeds 1), there may be concern for potential noncancer effects. In general, the greater the value of the hazard quotient above 1, the greater the level of concern. However, hazard quotient does not represent a statistical probability of an effect's occurring.

As a screening step, the overall potential for noncarcinogenic effects from simultaneous exposure to multiple chemicals and multiple routes can be estimated by summing up hazard quotients for the same individual or subgroups. The resulting sum is referred to as the hazard index. This approach assumes that multiple subthreshold exposures to several chemicals could cumulatively result in an adverse health effect. The HI is computed as follows:

$$\text{Hazard Index (HI)} = E_1/\text{RfD}_i + E_2/\text{RfD}_2 + \cdots + E_i/\text{RfD}_i = \sum_i E_i/\text{RfD}_i$$

where E_i = exposure level (intake or dose) for the ith toxicant, mg/kg-day
 RfD_i = reference dose for the ith toxicant, mg/kg-day

The RfD is either chronic or subchronic for the specific route of exposure depending on exposure duration. For Superfund risk assessment, exposures ranging from 2 weeks to 7 years are considered subchronic, and beyond 7 years chronic. Subchronic RfDs tend to be higher than chronic, often by an order of magnitude, because of shorter exposure duration. Chronic and subchronic RfDs for inhalation and oral routes can be found in EPA's IRIS and HEAST. In assessing dermal exposures, because RfDs have not been developed for the dermal route, oral RfDs can be used, adjusted by an absorption factor to account for the difference between administered and absorbed dose (dermal absorption tends to be a fraction of oral absorption, generally assumed to be 100%).

Where a population may be exposed to selected chemicals via multiple pathways (e.g., inhalation of particulates, soil ingestion, and dermal contact with soil), individual HIs from all relevant pathways can be added to obtain the total HI for that population. If the sum of the ratios is less than 1, cumulative exposure to the substances of interest at a site is judged unlikely to result in an adverse effect. If the sum is greater than 1, a more detailed and critical evaluation of the risks, including consideration of specific target organs and toxic mechanisms, would be required.

In summary, risk assessments should include estimates of RME (a measure of upper-bound exposure), and average (a measure of central tendency) cancer risks and noncancer hazards for individuals, and for populations, if possible.

The assessments should consider both current and future land uses, and characterize sources of uncertainty.

Uncertainty Analysis

Uncertainty is inherent in every step of the risk assessment process. In order to appreciate the limitations and significance of the risk estimates, it is important to have some understanding of the nature and magnitude of uncertainty. Sources of uncertainty in risk assessment include:

- Sampling and analysis, e.g., statistical validity of sampling program, identity and concentration of substances just above and below method detection limits

- Toxicity data, e.g., time period, dose, and species extrapolations

- Exposure assessment, e.g., receptor populations, exposure parameters, contaminant fate and transport, exposure point concentrations, intake or dose, overall assumptions for average case, and RME

- Risk estimates, e.g., multiple exposures and complex interactions, sensitivities, uncertainty magnification

As discussed before, in the Superfund and related health risk assessments, a series of average and conservative assumptions are made to derive "average" and "RME" risk estimates. These conditional point estimates in themselves are not very meaningful without an explanation of the likelihood of these cases and the degree of confidence in the estimates, which is required as part of risk assessment reports.

To compensate for the uncertainty in risk assessment, EPA and other regulatory agencies recommend upper-bound biased values as a prudent public health policy. However, there is no way of knowing the degree of cumulative conservatism built into the point estimates. For example, the use of 95th percentile value for contaminant concentration, and again for just one other exposure parameter (e.g., ingestion of soil), would result in 99.75% $(1 - 0.05^2)$ rather than the implied 95% confidence level. This can make a significant difference in the risk estimates and remedial costs.

Two approaches that could be used to characterize uncertainty are sensitivity analyses and Monte Carlo simulations, briefly described below.

Sensitivity and Probability Distribution Analyses

The purpose of sensitivity analysis is to identify influential variables and the extent of change in dependent variables relative to that of independent variables. For example, each parameter that influences the exposure estimates is changed from its "average case" value to a low and a high value (e.g., ±20%), with all other parameters remaining at their average case value. In this way, the sensitivity of the exposure estimates to each parameter assumption can be estimated. The sensitivity analysis can be used to guide future data acquisition—data that reduce the uncertainty associated with variables to which exposure estimates are most sensitive and thereby refine the risk estimates. However, sensitivity analysis in the Superfund context may not be all that helpful since many of the input variables are near their upper-bound values.

Monte Carlo Simulation

Monte Carlo-type techniques offer a means of quantifying uncertainty in exposure and risk estimates. Because the "95th percentile RME case" generally incorporates several "high" or "reasonable maximum" assumptions, it is very unlikely to be the "true value"; i.e., the probability that the actual exposures would be that high is much less than 5%. To provide a more reasonable estimate of the probable range of exposures, instead of varying input parameters one at a time, all parameters are assumed to be random or uncertain and probability density–distribution function (PDF) for each variable is generated. The computer program selects randomly from each distribution every time the model equations are solved, and the procedure is repeated many times. From the resulting output distribution of exposure or risk, we can identify the value corresponding to a specified probability, e.g., 50th percentile, 95th percentile, or the likelihood of the RME case. (For details, refer to, for example, Salhotra et al. and Thompson et al. listed in the references.)

Advantages and Limitations of Risk Assessments

Advantages

- Address "bottom line" public health and safety concerns with a common language
- Provide framework for problem prioritization and resource allocation
- Allow for situation-specific factors (rather than highly conservative default values)
- Provide scientific and consistent bases for risk management
- Resource-effective—often save costs by directing efforts toward action-sensitive hazard sources and exposure channels

Example. Superfund-type contaminated site, possible savings from application of risk assessment principles

Costs of RI/FS, $1 to $4 million

Site remediation total cost, $20–$40 million

(Continued)

Human health risk assessment, $150,000 to $200,000

Ecological risk screening, $50,000 to $150,000

Savings could amount to 5 to 20% of project costs, attractive return on investment (ROI)

Examples: Sources of possible savings

- Study and action phases—linking baseline risk assessment to the development of remedial objectives and cleanup levels

- Sampling and analytical costs—selecting sampling program by site history, required degree of confidence, detection limits

- Modeling and measurement—reducing uncertainty in site parameters, often the primary cause of risk overestimates

- Exposure pathways and future scenarios—applying the basic principle "no exposure–no risk"

- Points of compliance—characterizing subareas and media (and delineating hot spots) in a way that would permit remedial action flexibility

- Managing risk, not concentration—shifting focus from single chemical "action levels" to risk associated with contaminant mix

Limitations

- No broad consensus on the purpose, the approach, or the results

- Key role of human factors in safety hazard analyses not well understood

- Large variability in health and ecological assessments, subjective, no consensus

- Orders-of-magnitude uncertainty

- Few qualified professionals with needed range of skills

- Inadequate data, fictional nature of assumptions

- Creditability and perception of "pulling wool over one's eyes"

- Unrealistic expectations

- Multiple clients, diverse interests

Risk Assessment, Cleanup Criteria, and Remedial Options

There are five basic approaches, and many more combinations, for developing site remediation criteria and cleanup levels:

1. Federal and state standards and guidelines

2. Technology-based or performance-based levels
3. Cost-benefit (value) analysis
4. Risk analyses
5. Industry standards, norms, or precedents

Regulatory Guidelines

As a first step in determining the need for and the extent of cleanup, site contaminant levels can be compared with federal and state standards and guidelines (such as air quality standards, or MCLs for water) which are intended as a general guidance for unrestricted use of a site. Such standards and guidelines may be risk-based; alternatively, inorganic contaminant criteria may correspond with background levels and organic contaminant limits may be set at close to, or multiples of, detection limits. These criteria do not reflect site-specific factors and can be applied when relatively little is known about a site. Because of uncertainty in such situations, the guidelines tend to be conservative.

Technical Feasibility

Technology options provide crucial input to remedial decisions. Available technologies for treating and controlling contaminants at a site range from proven to best demonstrated available technology (BAT), maximum achievable control technology (MACT), as low as is reasonably achievable (ALARA), best available technology not entailing excessive costs (BATNEEC), experimental, speculative, and so on. An example of a performance-based standard is the "Four 9s," e.g., 99.99% destruction of organics in incinerators. A performance standard can also be an emission or effluent limit on discharge. The selection of a remedial program, whether technology-based or performance-based, is a balancing act, heavily weighted toward proven treatment and containment technologies that are implementable in a timely manner, with a high degree of confidence in the outcome.

Cost-Benefit (Value) Analysis

Costs are inevitably a factor, whether implicit or explicit, whether immediate cash outlays or long-term societal costs. Projections of risk and cleanup requirements should be scientifically supportable and an optimal balance should be sought between risks and costs of risk reduction.

Risk Analyses

As discussed earlier, risk analysis is a tool to aid prioritization and decision making. Various types of risk analyses can be used to identify, reduce, and manage human health, environmental, and financial risks. In the development of remedial criteria, risk assessments (1) allow the use of site-specific factors rather than default values, and (2) provide the basis for developing cleanup levels when there are no regulatory standards, or to seek variance from such standards. In evaluating remedial alternatives for Superfund and related feasibility studies, the two "threshold" criteria are overall protection of human health and the environment, and compliance with ARARs. Other criteria include: long-term and short-term effectiveness, reduction in toxicity, volume or mobility, implementability, cost, and state and community acceptance.

Industry Standards, Norms, or Precedents

Regulatory requirements vary with the type of industry, such as mining. A review of the standards and operating practices of an industry, and discussion with an industry association, can help expand the array of remedial options.

Points to Consider

1. Plan for risk assessment at the beginning, even if it does not appear on the horizon.

    More often than not, risk assessments turn out to be afterthoughts trying to "retrofit" data already collected. For risk assessments to be meaningful and effective, we should define the decision types, users and uses, and data quality objectives upfront with the participation of the project sponsor, consultant, EPA, and state agencies.

2. Beware of "cookbook" approach results. Are the risks real or due to the assumptions and the methodology?

    Consider the tradeoff between the cost of reducing the degree of uncertainty and refining risk estimates vs. potential savings. Use of source- and receptor-specific parameters could make two or more orders of magnitude difference in risk estimates, especially important in the 10^{-4} to 10^{-6} gray area. In this respect, some points to keep in mind are:

    a. What are the major contributors to risk? What are the variables (inputs) that the risk estimates are most sensitive to?

        For example, are the soil and groundwater data adequate to delineate the sources and areas of concern with confidence? The cost of additional samples that would permit statistical analysis may be more than offset by pinpointing and limiting areas that would require cleanup. Groundwater modeling using site factors could reduce estimated risk severalfold, perhaps an order of magnitude. In case of air, actual measurements off-site may give air concentrations four- or fivefold below modeled values. Is measurement necessary and the cost justified?

    b. Select indicator chemicals of concern judiciously and document key assumptions. Consider site-specific chemistry.

Are the chemicals site-related? What is the site elevation? What are background levels, especially metals? Are site data properly screened and validated? To assess, for example, whether chemicals in the atmosphere off-site are site-related, we could use a variety of techniques: identification of what is emitted at the site (using emission isolation flux chambers and the like); ratio analysis (e.g., ratio of benzene to methane) on-site vs. off-site; modeling with site data; statistical analysis to determine if there is a significant difference between upwind and downwind concentrations; use of tracers, etc. (Similar techniques could also be used for water.)

c. Estimate exposure concentrations at plausible exposure points. Are pathways complete? Is the future scenario unrestricted residential use? Are risks from existing pathways clearly distinguished from potential future exposures (e.g., child resident)? Is the information on spatial distribution of hazards retained and used to provide linkages to remedial phase?

The highest detected concentration in soil, groundwater, surface water, and air should not be picked automatically for exposure values. (A contaminant 6 feet below surface, for example, would not be meaningful for inhalation and dermal contact but may be relevant for groundwater if soluble and mobile.) Ideally, representative chemical concentrations closest to the exposure locations should be used whenever available. In the case of groundwater pathway, if the shallow aquifer is contaminated, is it now or will it likely be used for drinking water? Is the aquifer yield sufficient for it to be a source of drinking water supplies? Is the receptor behavior likely to change? Does zoning permit unrestricted use in an industrial area? Is there a high fence, coupled with site security, that would render an oral exposure of children implausible? These questions are helpful in determining whether a pathway is complete and contributes to risk now or in the future.

d. What is the exposure value—media concentration or internal dose? Are adjustments made in calculating intake to reflect absorption and bioavailability?

Are toxicity data, e.g., slope factors and reference doses, for the selected chemicals of concern based on administered dose or absorbed dose? Default exposure values generally assume 100% of ambient contaminant is absorbed and available via inhalation and oral routes. This could be especially significant for inhalation and dermal routes, the latter extrapolated from oral. Pharmacokinetic data, often available from literature for individual compounds, can make a two- or threefold difference in risk estimates, and the tradeoff is their contribution to risk vs. the additional time requirement to refine the estimates.

e. Ascertain the additivity of diverse risks in making risk estimates.

In developing hazard indices, for example, the mechanisms of toxicity and the target organs involved should be examined before multiple exposures by multiple pathways and routes are simply added up to predict cumulative effects.

 f. Are individual as well as population risks expressed?

   Population risks generally provide a better and more meaningful basis for risk reduction than the theoretical maximum exposed individual (MEI).

3. For site remediation, the cost of initial study phase should generally not exceed 15% of total project cost. The project team should be led by a "generalized specialist" who has an overall perspective.

   Despite the "one-stop-shop" and integrated capability claims, many environmental consulting and engineering firms have become discipline- and procedure-oriented (like medical practice) which tends to deflect from the ultimate objective of remedial actions and risk reduction. The key questions are: will the additional studies, samples, and data reduce the uncertainty in, or the costs of, remedy selection, design, or implementation? Will it make any difference in postremedy program requirements?

4. For remedial decisions, consider the advantages of learn-as-you-go observational method compared with the traditional "study-design-build" sequential method.

   The hazardous-waste site remediation process is invariably beset with a high degree of uncertainty because of subsurface complexity and related factors. The marginal value of further studies declines rapidly. The conventional method for coping with the uncertainty is to base the design on excessive safety factors or on "average" conditions. The first is wasteful; the second could be dangerous. In the learn-as-you-go observational or experimental method, the remedial process begins with the use of site data to construct a conceptual model based on probable conditions and reasonable deviations (alternative scenarios), coupled with preestablished contingency plans to respond to these deviations. This method does not actually reduce uncertainty, but it enables the scientists and engineers to enter the implementation phase better prepared to respond to the uncertainties as they are uncovered (Wallace and Lincoln, 1989).

5. Set goals in terms of health and environmental risks rather than contaminant levels or specific means of achievement. Manage risk, not concentration.

   Limits for specific contaminants (rather than a mix), and methods or means to be employed (e.g., BAT, MACT) are simpler for regulatory agencies to enforce but tend to stifle innovation and increase costs. In remedial decisions, we are often preoccupied with contaminant concentrations, losing sight of the fact that it is the risk we are concerned with. We need to focus on high-concentration, high-exposure combinations rather than averages so that, for example, an entire site doesn't have to be excavated and massive volume treated or transported. Also, if a remedial scheme, such as groundwater pump-and-treat to remove volatile organics, reaches an asymptotic relationship, a review of residual risks may be warranted.

6. If the contaminants are of low toxicity or in low concentrations and biodegradable or immobile, consider in-place containment of plume and waste materials.

After the source of contamination is discontinued or is removed and any free product (e.g., floating oil) recovered, the containment option makes sense for at least three reasons: (1) off-site migration can be monitored and controlled by "sentinel" wells downgradient of the contaminant plume or other early warning signals; (2) digging and handling (or pumping and treating) and transportation create their own "competing" risks on-site and off-site and often merely transfer them to a different setting; and (3) the public opposition to the building and operation of incinerators and landfills makes this option more viable as we move from the NIMBY (not in my backyard) to the BANANA (build absolutely nothing anywhere near anybody) syndrome.

7. Express exposure and risk as a range with confidence limits. Express uncertainty with sensitivity analysis and/or probability distributions. Have risk assessments peer reviewed by credible parties.

Although the EPA states that "The true value of the risk is unknown...," the point risk estimates based on 95th percentile values are generally perceived to be "true risks." As discussed earlier, a series of 95th percentile assumptions actually distort risk predictions. Such estimates could have a costly impact on remedial programs and risk reduction because cleanup costs tend to increase exponentially as we approach residual contaminant levels of parts per billion (ppb) range or residual risks on the order of 10^{-5} to 10^{-7} (Fig. 11-15). There have been recent indications that at least some EPA regions will tolerate, if not endorse, probability distributions, although they do complicate the decision process by moving away from pass-fail decisions directed by single risk numbers.

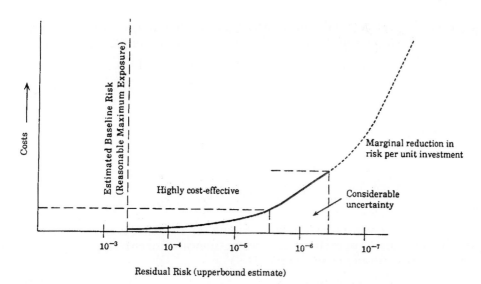

Figure 11-15. Risk reduction vs. costs: cost-effective range (illustration).

Simple Examples of Risk Estimates

- General equations for risk: (media concentration) (exposure factors) (biological factors) (toxicity)

- Incremental or excess risk of cancer (carcinogens):

$$\underset{\text{(from exposure assessment)}}{\text{(Chronic daily intake)}} \times \underset{\text{(from IRIS or HEAST)}}{\text{(Slope factor)}} = CDI \times SF$$

- Hazard quotient (noncancer effects):

$$\frac{\text{Intake or exposure}}{\text{Reference dose}} = \frac{E}{RfD} \quad \begin{array}{l} \text{(from exposure assessment)} \\ \text{(from IRIS or HEAST)} \end{array}$$

- General equation for exposure, intake, or potential dose:

$$\text{Intake, mg/kg-day} = C \times \frac{CR \times EF \times ED}{BW} \times \frac{1}{AT}$$

where C = chemical or contaminant concentration in media (e.g., water, soil, air in mg/L, mg/kg, mg/m^3, etc.)
  CR = contact rate per unit time or event, L/day, mg/day
  EF = exposure frequency, days/year
  ED = exposure duration, years
  BW = body weight, kg
  AT = averaging time (days, i.e., ED × 365 days/year for noncarcinogenic effects, and lifetime, i.e., 70 years × 365 days/year for carcinogenic effects)

Example. Cancer risk from a carcinogen in drinking water. Residential exposure to 10 µg/L (ppb) trichloroethylene (TCE) in water (B2 carcinogen):

$$\text{CDI, mg/kg-day} = \frac{CW \times IR \times EF \times ED}{BW \times AT}$$

Using default exposure factors (Table 11-7):

$$CDI = \frac{(0.01 \text{ mg/L}) (2L/day) (350 \text{ days/year}) (30 \text{ years})}{(70 \text{ kg}) (70 \text{ years} \times 365 \text{ days/year})} = 1.2E - 4 \text{ mg/kg-day}$$

Excess cancer risk = (CDI) (SF)
$$= (1.2E - 4) (1.1E - 2) = 1.3E - 6 \text{ (in the acceptable range)}$$

Example. Noncancer hazard from toluene in drinking water. Residential exposure to 1 mg/L (ppm) toluene in water (noncarcinogen):
Using default exposure factors (Table 11-7):

$$\text{Intake} = \frac{(1 \text{ mg/L}) (2L/day) (350 \text{ days/year}) (30 \text{ years})}{(70 \text{ kg}) (365 \text{ days/year}) (30 \text{ years})} = 2.7E - 2 \text{ mg/kg-day}$$

$$\text{Hazard quotient} = \frac{\text{Intake}}{\text{RfD}} = \frac{0.028}{0.2} = <1 \therefore \text{considered safe}$$

Example. Permissible residual level for cleanup: carcinogen. Groundwater cleanup for TCE based on $E - 6$ acceptable cancer risk:

$$\text{Cleanup level (action level)} = \frac{(\text{acceptable risk}) (\text{body weight})}{(\text{SF}) (\text{intake})}$$

$$= \frac{(E - 6) (70 \text{ kg})}{1.1E - 2 \, (\text{mg/kg-day})^{-1} \, (2\text{L/day})}$$

$$= 3.2E - 3 \text{ mg/L} = 3 \text{ ppb}$$

Example. Permissible residual level for cleanup: noncarcinogen. Groundwater cleanup for toluene based on RfD:

$$\text{Cleanup level (action level)} = \frac{(\text{RfD}) (\text{body weight})}{(\text{intake}) (\text{absorption})}$$

$$= \frac{(0.2) (70)}{(2) (100\%)} = 7 \text{ mg/L} = 7 \text{ ppm}$$

Note the three orders of magnitude difference in acceptable levels between a carcinogen and a noncarcinogen—ppb vs. ppm for this example.

Unit Risks and Aggregate Population Risks

Unit risk: risk per unit concentration of contaminant in environmental medium.

Air unit risk = risk per $\mu\text{g/m}^3$ (incremental risk of cancer from inhaling 1 μg of substance per cubic meter of air over a lifetime)

Water unit risk = risk per $\mu\text{g/L}$ (incremental risk of cancer from ingesting 1 μg of substance per liter of water over a lifetime)

Example 1. Benzene unit risk in air = $8.3 \, E - 6 \, (\mu\text{g/m}^3)^{-1}$ (from EPA's IRIS or HEAST).

Individual lifetime cancer risk from 1 $\mu\text{g/m}^3$ = (units in air) (unit risk)
$$= (1) (8.3 \, E - 6) = 8.3 \, E - 6$$

This indicates approximately eight incremental cases of cancer per million population from lifetime exposure to 1 $\mu\text{g/m}^3$ benzene in air.

Example 2. Ten thousand people in a community exposed to 20 $\mu\text{g/m}^3$ of benzene in air over lifetime.

$$\text{Aggregate population risk} = (20)\,(8.3E - 6)\,(10,000) = 1.7 \text{ cases}$$

$$\text{Average annual incidence} = \frac{1.7}{70} = 0.02 \text{ cases in 10,000 population}$$
$$\text{or 2 cases in a million } (2E - 6)$$

Unit Risks and Slope Factors

Unit risks can be converted to slope factors and vice versa by using air inhalation rate of 20 m^3/day, or water consumption rate of 2 liters/day, human body weight of 70 kg, and accounting for any differences in absorption rates.

Slope factor = risk per unit dose = risk per (mg/kg-day)
(Incremental risk of cancer from a dose of 1 mg of substance per kilogram of body weight per day over a lifetime)

Unit risk per μg/m^3 air (inhalation exposure)

$$= \frac{\text{slope factor} \times 20 \text{ m}^3/\text{day} \times 10^{-3} \text{ mg/μg}}{70 \text{ kg body weight}}$$

Unit risk per μg/L water (oral exposure)

$$= \frac{\text{slope factor} \times 2L/\text{day} \times 10^{-3} \text{ mg/μg}}{70 \text{ kg}}$$

Example.   Arsenic exposure. If inhalation unit risk is $4.3E - 3$ μg/m^3, what is the slope factor?

$$4.3E - 3 \text{ μg/m}^3 = \frac{(SF?) \times 20 \text{ m}^3/\text{day} \times 10^{-3} \text{ mg/μg}}{70 \text{ kg}}$$

Solving for slope factor: 15 (mg/kg-day)$^{-1}$ without absorption adjustment. If we factor in 30% absorption of inhaled arsenic (HEAST, 1992):

$$\frac{15}{0.3} = 50 \text{ (mg/kg-day)}^{-1}$$

The unit risk of $4.3E - 3$ μg/m^3 means that the incremental lifetime risk of respiratory cancer from inhaling 1 μg/m^3 of air could be as high as 4 in 1000 (compared with the population background risk of 6 in 100). In recent years, the EPA has been tending to publish only unit risks for the inhalation route and not slope factors. This is based on the premise that the site of action is the respiratory route (although this may underestimate the risk for other sites). The extrapolation from inhalation to the oral route is not always straightforward because the absorption depends on the proportion of respirable particles, breathing rates, and so on. For the oral route, on the other hand, virtually 100% of the contaminants are assumed to be absorbed, although this is not always true. (See also the Arsenic Dilemma, following.)

The Arsenic Dilemma

Arsenic is unique in many ways, but its regulation epitomizes environmental decision making under conflicting requirements and considerable uncertainty.

Arsenic has a long and colorful history and is of considerable toxicological interest. Arsenic toxicity has been recognized for centuries and put to extensive use. It was Agatha Christie's favorite murder weapon; the French called it inheritance insurance. The remains of Zachary Taylor, the twelfth president of the United States, were exhumed in 1991 after 140 years on suspicions that he might have been poisoned by arsenic (available as rat poison at the time).

Arsenic is a naturally occurring element distributed throughout the environment. There are a number of medicinal, agricultural, and industrial uses for arsenic compounds. Arsenic was used extensively in medicine (Fowler's solution) for the treatment of leukemia, psoriasis, asthma, and in the formulation of antiparasitic drugs.

Arsenic's toxicity depends on valence, solubility, and route of exposure. Trivalent compounds include arsenic trioxide, sodium arsenite, and arsenic trichloride; the pentavalent compounds, generally less toxic than trivalent, are arsenic pentoxide, arsenic acid, and arsenates. There is ample evidence of arsenic's carcinogenicity in humans in terms of respiratory and skin cancer (classified group A). But it is one of those rare chemicals that proved embarrassingly difficult to induce cancer in animal studies.

On the basis of a Taiwanese drinking water study (Tseng et al., 1977), the EPA proposed oral exposure unit risk of $5E - 5$ $(\mu g/L)^{-1}$; and on the basis of occupational studies, an inhalation unit risk of $4.3E - 3$ $(\mu g/m^3)^{-1}$ was established.

Under the Safe Drinking Water Act, the maximum contaminant level (MCL) and the maximum contaminant level goal (MCLG) are both set at 0.05 mg/L. The nonzero MCLG for a carcinogen (which does not take into account technical or economic feasibility) reflects arsenic's role as an essential nutrient. At the MCL or MCLG of 0.05 mg/L (50 µg/L), the carcinogenic risk would be

$$\text{Incremental cancer risk} = (\text{contaminant units in water}) \times (\text{unit risk})$$
$$= (50 \ \mu g/L) \times 5 \times 10^{-5} \ (\mu g/L)^{-1} = 2.5 \times 10^{-3}$$

In other words, two to three people in a thousand could contract cancer at the drinking water limit, a risk level that would not ordinarily be acceptable for the general public. Actual experience with arsenic over a long time does not indicate a risk level anywhere near as high as that. And yet such an apparent result should not be surprising in light of arsenic's wide distribution in nature, use, and high background levels; technical difficulty and expense of treating arsenic in water; high unit risk values and upper-bound estimates inherent in EPA approach; and arsenic's nutritional value. In practice, the "target risk" for arsenic regulation varies by orders of magnitude.

Calculating Concentration Term for Exposure and Intake: Superfund and RCRA Normal and Lognormal Distribution Assumptions

Superfund

The concentration of a contaminant is a key input to risk estimates. The Superfund risk assessments now call for two estimates of exposure: (1) average, and (2) reasonable maximum exposure (RME) that represents the high end of exposure or intake. Because of the uncertainty involved in exposure concentration estimates, EPA recommends for RME, the 95% upper confidence limit (UCL) on the arithmetic mean, i.e., a value that equals or exceeds the true mean 95% of the time (and should not be confused with a 95th percentile of site concentration data). (For the average scenario, consult with the particular EPA region on the use of arithmetic or geometric average, or 95% UCL.) The formula for calculating the UCL depends on whether the underlying distribution of the data is normal or lognormal (more common).

$$\text{UCL for lognormal distribution} = e^{(\bar{x} + 5s^2 + sH/\sqrt{n-1})}$$

$$\text{UCL for normal distribution} = \bar{x} + t\,(s/\sqrt{n})$$

where e = constant (base of the natural logarithm, equal to 2.718)
  $\bar{x}$ = mean of the data (transformed data in case of lognormal)
  s = standard deviation of the data (transformed data in case of lognormal)
  H = H-statistic for lognormal (e.g., from table published in Gilbert, 1987)
  n = number of samples
  t = student statistic for normal (e.g., from table published in Gilbert, 1987)

Example of Data Transformation and Calculation of UCL.   This example shows the calculation of a 95% UCL of the arithmetic mean concentration for chromium in soil at a Superfund site. This example is applicable only to a scenario in which a spatially random exposure pattern is assumed. The concentrations of chromium obtained from random sampling in soil at this site (in mg/kg) are 10, 13, 20, 36, 41, 59, 67, 110, 110, 136, 140, 160, 200, 230, and 1300. Using these data, the following steps are taken to calculate a concentration term for the intake equation:

1. Plot the data and inspect the graph. The plot shows a skew to the right, consistent with a lognormal distribution.

2. Transform the data by taking the natural log of the values [determine $\ln(x)$]. For this data set, the transformed values are 2.30, 2.56, 3.00, 3.58, 3.71, 4.08, 4.20, 4.70, 4.70, 4.91, 4.94, 5.08, 5.30, 5.44, and 7.17.

3. Apply the UCL equation for a lognormal distribution, where

$$\bar{x} = 4.38 \qquad s = 1.25 \qquad H = 3.163 \text{ (based on 95\%)} \qquad n = 15$$

The resulting 95% UCL of the arithmetic mean is thus found to equal $e^{(6.218)}$, or 502 mg/kg, whereas a simple average of the concentration data is 176 mg/kg. (SOURCE: EPA Publication 9285.7-081, MAY 1992.)

In the above example, if the distribution is incorrectly assumed to be normal and the Student t-test statistic is used, the UCL would be 325 mg/kg vs. 502 mg/kg of lognormal distribution. The same statistical procedures would be used for contaminants in groundwater. For example, if the above concentrations were observations over time from a water supply well, or from different wells, the value of 502 ppm should be used for estimating exposure and risk.

RCRA

It is interesting to see the implications of the above site concentration data in the context of a RCRA SWMU (solid waste management unit) single-well compliance. We can use the tolerance interval procedure (Interim Final Guidance, EPA5:30-SW-89-027 and Addendum to Interim Final Guidance, Draft, July 1992). A 95% tolerance interval is designed to contain, on average, 95% of all possible sample measurements with a probability of 95%. For the data set above, this interval would be 8 to 775 mg/kg, implying that this well would be out of compliance with a regulatory limit of 774 mg/kg or lower. This procedure would apply unless the regulatory limit was based on the average of on-site background data, in which case a 99% lower confidence limit (LCL) on the geometric mean is constructed (34 mg/kg for the data set above). Under these circumstances the well would only be out of compliance for a regulatory limit of 34 mg/kg or lower!

Glossary of Toxicology Terms

Absorption: The movement of a substance into the bloodstream (systemic absorption) after entering the body through lungs, gastrointestinal tract, or skin.

Acute Exposure/Effect: A single exposure to a substance (generally in high concentrations lasting no longer than a day) that results in severe biological harm, usually evident in a short time.

Antagonistic Effect (Antidote): The effect of two or more chemicals when they counteract each other's actions; the combined effect is less than the sum, e.g., 3 + 4 = 1 (see also Synergistic Effect).

Bioavailability: The degree to which a chemical has access or becomes available to the target tissues after exposure or administration (for positive or negative effect).

Cancer and Carcinogen: A disease characterized by uncontrolled cell growth and malignant tumors; a carcinogen is any agent (chemical, biological, radiological) that can cause or contribute to the induction of cancer in a series of steps.

Chronic Exposure and Effect: Repeated exposure (generally in low concentrations) over a long time or persistence of effects over a long time; the effect(s) may not be apparent for a long time after initial exposure. Subacute and subchronic exposures and effects are intermediate between acute and chronic (generally lasting a few weeks to several months).

Dose: A measure of exposure usually expressed as amount of substance per unit body weight of subject per unit time; e.g., mg/kg-day. (See also Fig. 11-14 for further explanation.) Maximum tolerated dose (MTD) is the highest dose that is compatible with survival of most test animals.

Dose-Response Relationship/Curve: A graphical representation of the relationship between the amount of dose and the extent of adverse health effects.

Effect/Endpoint: Biological response due to exposure to a substance. Local effect occurs at the site of first contact; systemic effects require absorption and distribution of toxicant, the effects occurring at sites or organs distant from the initial entry point.

Excess or Incremental Lifetime Risk: Additional risk (over background) from exposure over an individual's lifetime.

Exposure: Contact of an organism's outer boundary with chemical, biological, or physical agents.

LC_{50} and LD_{50} (Median Lethal Concentration and Median Lethal Dose): The concentration (mg/m^3, mg/L) or dose (mg/kg) at which 50% of test organisms die when exposed to the substance in a specified time period.

Latency Period: The time between initial induction of a health effect and its clinical manifestation; cancer latency varies from a few years (leukemia) to decades (asbestosis).

Metabolism and Metabolites: Biochemical changes that a chemical undergoes in the body producing metabolites that may be less or more toxic than the original substance.

No-Observed-Adverse-Effect Level (NOAEL): An exposure level at which there are no statistically significant increases in the frequency or severity of adverse effects.

Pharmacokinetics and Physiologically Based Pharmacokinetic (PB-PK) Models: Absorption, distribution, metabolism, and excretion characteristics of a substance (a drug or pollutant) in the body. PB-PK models are useful in predicting specific tissue dose under a range of exposure conditions.

Reference Dose (RfD), Reference Concentration (RfC), and Acceptable Daily Intake (ADI): An estimate (with uncertainty spanning perhaps an order or magnitude) of a daily exposure to the human population, including sensitive subgroups, that is likely to be without appreciable risk of deleterious effects during a lifetime. (Virtually safe dose or tolerable daily intake.)

Risk: A measure of the likelihood and magnitude of adverse effects, including injury, disease, or economic loss.

Routes of Exposure: Contact via inhalation, ingestion (oral), or dermal absorption.

Slope Factor or Carcinogen Slope Factor (CSF): The slope of the dose-response curve in the low-dose region, usually assumed to be linear and expressed as 1/(mg/kg-day).

Synergistic Effect: Cooperative interaction of two or more chemicals or other phenomena that result in an effect greater than the sum of individual effects, e.g., 3 + 4 = 40 (also see Antagonistic Effect).

Threshold: The dose or exposure below which a significant adverse effect is not expected.

Toxicology: The study of the adverse effects of chemical, biological, and physical agents on living organisms.

Unit risk: The upper bound (plausible upper limit) excess lifetime cancer risk expected to result from continuous exposure to an agent at a concentration of 1 $\mu g/L$ in water, or 1 $\mu g/m^3$ in air.

Ecological Risk Assessment (Environmental Evaluation)*

Basic Concepts and Definitions

A Complex Process

In the past, society believed that the supply of natural resources was unlimited, that ecosystems not harvested were of no benefit to society, their exploitation was harmless until the evidence became direct and dramatic, and that technological advances would correct any problem resulting from destruction of natural resources (Cairns, Niederlehner: Predicting Ecosystem Risk, 1992). In recent years, the growing public interest in ecological issues such as global climate, biological diversity, and habitat loss ("global commons"), and EPA Science Advisory Board's ranking of these issues at the top of the list of national concerns, as well as regulatory requirements, provided the impetus for evaluating ecological risks. Human beings are of course a vital part of ecosystems, and human effects are a subset of ecosystem risks, perhaps the most obvious links being food chains and commercial and recreational aspects.

Ecological risk assessment (ERA), also called environmental evaluation, is a qualitative or quantitative analysis of actual or potential impacts of hazards or stressors on plants and animals (including birds), other than people and domesticated species (USEPA, Risk Assessment Guidance for Superfund, vol. 2, *Environmental Evaluation Manual*, 1989). Although the 1992 EPA "Framework for Ecological Risk Assessment" includes natural phenomena among stressors, this section will focus on anthropogenic hazards, especially chemical contaminants in environmental media at contaminated sites. At NPL and other hazardous waste sites, the emphasis in RI/FS risk assessments has been on human health effects (including indirect exposure through fish and vegetation), but increasingly ecological receptors are being viewed as valuable resources deserving protection for their intrinsic value independent of human interaction.

Ecological assessment is far more complex than human health risk assessment, and surrounded by even more uncertainty. Unlike human health assessments that involve single species, ecological assessments involve many levels of biological organization, from single species to communities to entire ecosystems, and multiple endpoints that reflect complex interactions of anthropogenic hazards and natural stresses. There is no single set of ecological values to be protected, and a variety of stressors need to be addressed, including chemical, physical, and biological entities that can induce adverse responses on popula-

---

*John V. Conner, Ph.D., of Woodward-Clyde reviewed and contributed to this section.

tions, communities, or ecosystems. (According to Edward Wilson of Harvard University, the total number of species on earth including plants, animals, and microorganisms could be close to 10 million or as high as 100 million. Only about 1.4 million of these have been given scientific names.)

Primer on Ecology

The ecosphere is composed of individual organisms, populations, communities, and ecosystems. The effects of stressors on individual organisms are quite different from, and often less important than, the effects on the structure and functioning of ecological assemblages.

Ecology is a unifying subject that addresses the relationships of organisms to their surroundings, i.e., their environment. Ecologists draw on all the basic natural sciences (biology, chemistry, physics, geology) in attempting to understand how organisms relate, functionally, to one another and abiotic (nonliving) factors. Four levels of organization are generally recognized in ecology—individual organisms, populations, communities, and ecosystems. It is important to recognize that stressors act directly upon individual organisms, producing indirect effects at the higher levels of organization. Typically, however (and in contrast to studies of human health), ecological information is communicated in terms of the higher organizational levels.

A population is an assemblage of individuals of the same species, capable of interbreeding, and generally occupying a contiguous area. The size and structure (e.g., ratio of sexes or of juveniles to adults) of a population depend on processes such as birth and death rates, and immigration and emigration. Those processes, in turn, are influenced by numerous factors which, depending on the context, may be adverse and thus "stressors."

In nature, populations virtually never exist in isolation. Logical assemblages of populations are termed communities. Ecologists are especially interested in structural attributes of a community, such as diversity, which is basically the number of different species comprising the assemblage. Diversity may be expressed in several ways, e.g., richness or evenness, and is often used as an indication of the relative "health" or well-being of a community. Communities, like their component populations, are in constant flux and change seasonally or over longer cycles in response to natural or human factors.

An ecosystem is a logical association of communities continuously interacting among themselves and with the abiotic components of the environment in complementary relationships involving transfer and circulation of energy and nutrients. Because each ecosystem is unique in terms of physical, chemical, and biological relationships, and may respond uniquely to external stimuli, an ecosystem is often considered the fundamental unit of ecology.

The intricate pathways for transfer of energy and nutrients in ecosystems are known as food chains or food webs. A given food chain consists of hierarchical "trophic" levels:

- Primary producers (green plants) that capture solar energy and convert carbon dioxide and water into carbohydrates through photosynthesis

- Consumers which in complex systems are categorized as primary (e.g., herbivores), secondary, and tertiary

- Decomposers such as bacteria and fungi that feed on dead and decaying matter, producing simple organic molecules and nutrients that are recycled in the system

Habitat is a generic term used to refer to the structural setting in which an organism exists. Many organisms occupy different habitats during different seasons or during successive phases in their lives. For example, some mammals (bears) hibernate in winter, and toads begin life as tadpoles in water. Availability and quality of habitats are significant environmental factors. Natural resource managers, who may be thought of as applied ecologists, typically manipulate habitats to produce the desired responses in plant or animal populations. Sometimes the manipulation involves introduction of a stressor, e.g., a herbicide, to suppress certain populations and thus enhance others. (However, such manipulations should be approached with caution. For example, the deliberate introduction of game fish into U.S. territorial waters for sport has led to a sharp decline in North America's 850 native fish species.)

Bioaccumulation is a general term describing the process by which chemicals are taken up by aquatic organisms by all routes, i.e., by a combination of ingestion and direct transfer across membranes, as across the gills. Bioconcentration is a more specific term describing the process by which chemicals are taken up by aquatic organisms directly from the water, e.g., via transfer across gill surfaces. Bioconcentration factor (BCF) thus becomes the ratio of concentration in the organism to the concentration of the chemical in solution in water at steady state. Biomagnification refers to the phenomenon of increasingly higher concentrations of a chemical at higher trophic levels because of food chain transfer.

Diverse Ecosystems and Their Functions

Ecosystems vary with climatic, geological, and biotic factors, ranging from Arctic tundras to deserts to tropical rain forests. There are three basic types of ecosystems: terrestrial (land), wetlands, and aquatic (freshwater, marine, estuaries), as discussed below, with excerpts from RAGS, vol. 2.

Terrestrial ecosystems are distinguished by the dominant vegetation types that determine the structure of their communities. Deciduous (leaf-shedding) forests and grasslands are two common ecosystems in temperate North America.

Wetlands, the subject of much recent controversy, represent a zone of transition and a vital link between terrestrial and aquatic environments created by topography and hydrology. Wetlands are often or always covered by shallow water sufficient to support vegetation, and include swamps, marshes, and bogs. There were an estimated 100 million acres of wetlands in the contiguous United States (mostly in Louisiana and Florida) in the mid-1970s. In the last two decades, 11 million acres were lost, primarily due to agricultural drainage, and secondarily due to urban development. Such natural threats as erosion, sea level rise, and overgrazing by wildlife also had an adverse effect.

Rich in biological diversity, wetlands perform several functions and offer many benefits:

- Flood attenuation, erosion control, and groundwater aquifer recharge
- Water quality improvement by removal or settling of inorganic and organic matter and microbes (uv light from sun destroys bacteria and viruses)
- Wildlife habitat and food and drinking water for animals (including migratory birds)
- Aesthetic and recreational benefits, ecotourism
- Possible venue for treatment of contaminated sites

According to the U.S. Fish and Wildlife Service, the majority of endangered species in this country are dependent on wetlands for their survival. In this era of intensive resource management, wetlands offer a compelling case for leaving things alone, or "as they are."

Freshwater ecosystems such as rivers, streams, and lakes, though much smaller in area than marine ecosystems, are also a valuable resource since they provide a readily accessible source of water for agricultural, domestic, and industrial uses; fish and other species of commercial value; and recreational resources.

Marine ecosystems are critical to maintaining global environment and sustaining life. The sea covers 70% of the earth's surface and supports a great diversity of life at all depths, especially near the continental shelves. Most fishing grounds are on or near the continental shelves because of abundance of nutrients deriving from both land and sea bottom. Circulating ocean waters replenish nutrients and dissolved oxygen vital to marine life. The oceans typically have a pH of 8 and salinity of 3.5% vs. less than 0.05% average for fresh water.

Estuaries are partly open bodies of water related to coastal zones including river mouths and bays. They are strongly influenced by saltwater tides and freshwater drainage from land; the tides play a key role in supplying food and removing wastes. Estuarine systems are highly productive, especially as breeding and nursery grounds for fish, shellfish, and birds.

Examples of Ecological Stresses

Local scale

- Thermal pollution (e.g., effluent discharges)
- Chemical contaminants (e.g., pesticides)
- Nutrients (e.g., eutrophication)

Regional scale

- Acid rain
- Altered habitats

Global scale

- Ozone depletion (electromagnetic radiation)
- Climate change (warming and cooling)

Regulatory Basis for Ecological Risk Assessment

Ecological risk assessment is an essential component in the process of determining overall risk from hazardous-waste sites and other sources. Through CERCLA/SARA and other statutes, EPA is authorized to:

- Protect fisheries, wildlife, endangered and threatened species, and valued habitats
- Ensure compliance with applicable or relevant and appropriate requirements (ARARs) based on federal and state laws and regulations designed to preserve and protect natural resources.

CERCLA (Section 104b2) calls on the EPA to notify federal and state natural resource trustees about potential threats to natural resources. The federal natural resource trustees include:

- U.S. Fish and Wildlife Service (USFWS), National Park Service (NPS), and Bureau of Land Management (BLM) of the Department of the Interior
- National Oceanic and Atmospheric Administration (NOAA) of the U.S. Department of Commerce
- U.S. Department of Agriculture Forest Service

Data from ecological risk assessments may be used by the natural resource trustees for Natural Resource Damage Assessments.

Natural Resource Damage Assessment (NRDA). The NRDA rule was adopted under CERCLA/SARA; the CERCLA/SARA and the Clean Water Act (CWA) regulations are used to assess injury and damage to natural resources caused by release of hazardous materials or discharge of oil. In this context, an injury is a measurable adverse change in the chemical or physical quality or viability of a resource, while damage is the amount of money sought as compensation. Injury could be to any of these resources: air, geologic (soil, rocks), groundwater, surface water, and biological resources. An NRDA may be conducted by natural resource trustees to determine the compensation from a responsible party if a response action does not sufficiently restore or protect the natural resources damaged by a release. NRDAs have been initiated, or can be initiated, at Superfund and RCRA sites; mining, refining, or manufacturing locations; oil spill sites; waste disposal, and other sites where releases of hazardous substances have occurred.

In planning ecological assessments, the uses and users of data (along with liability issues) and corresponding data quality objectives must be carefully considered. Ecological risk assessment approaches and technologies are outlined in Fig. 11-16 and Table 11-9.

Ecological Risk Assessment Process: Major Steps

The four major phases or steps in ecological assessment, as illustrated in Fig. 11-16 are:

1. Problem formulation and hazard identification
2. Exposure assessment
3. Ecological effects/toxicity assessment
4. Risk characterization

The following guidance includes extracts from USEPA's Eco Update Ecological Assessment of Superfund Sites: An Overview (1991, Publication 9345.0-051); and USEPA Framework for Ecological Risk Assessment, 1992.

Problem Formulation and Hazard Identification (Ecological Risk Screening)

Problem formulation defines the objectives and scope of the ecological assessment. This involves a review of existing data, including previous studies of the site, such as the preliminary assessment, field investigation, and other sources. The problem formulation step can itself serve as a desktop screening study to

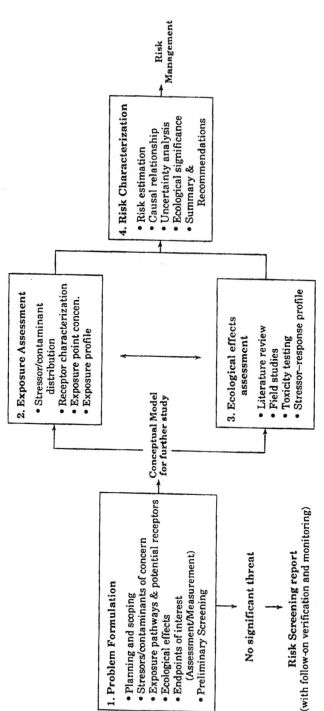

Figure 11-16. Ecological risk assessment process.

Table 11-9. Ecological Risk Assessment: Approaches, Techniques, and Endpoints

Approaches	Techniques	Endpoints	Information provided	Information not provided
Comparison of measured and/or projected contaminant concentrations to ecological benchmark levels	Measured concentrations Projected concentrations (quotient method)	Mortality Reproduction Growth Community structure AWQC NOELs/LOELs	Yes-no information as to whether impacts are likely; impacts resulting from direct exposures as well as indirect exposure via food chains; ecologically based cleanup criteria for single contaminants	Quantitative measures of severity of impacts if benchmarks are exceeded; impacts to communities or ecosystems (unless benchmarks specifically account for these)
Estimate of exposure potential (no benchmark)	Measured concentrations Projected concentrations Qualitative evaluation	Mortality Reproduction Growth Community structure	Types of ecosystems and receptors potentially exposed to contaminants; identification of potential exposure pathways	Likelihood or severity of impacts; aerial extent and reversibility of impacts; uncertainty of the characterization
Estimate of hazard potential (media toxicity tests)	Laboratory toxicity tests In situ toxicity tests	Mortality Reproduction Growth Tissue residue level	Quantification of likelihood and severity of impacts to populations of test organisms; identification of hazards to site-specific populations; aerial extent of impacts (if media tested at sufficient number of locations); ecologically based cleanup criteria for mixtures of contaminants	Impacts to communities or the ecosystem; interpretation of test results can be difficult (e.g., basis for the toxic response)
Quantitative risk modeling	Fault-tree analysis Probabilistic pathway analysis Multiple attribute ranking (linear models)	Reproduction failure	Specific probabilistic prediction of the likelihood of specific impacts to individual organisms, populations, communities, or the ecosystem; severity and aerial extent of impacts; quantification of ecological risks for risk management decisions	Not known (major disadvantage can be cost to implement)
Evaluation of biotic community structure	Quantitative sampling	Diversity indices	Identify large, major, readily apparent impacts	Subtle impacts; impacts to populations; severity of impacts
	Qualitative surveys Aerial photography	Description of community	Aerial extent of impacts; identify small subtle impacts; potential exposure pathways and contaminant effects	Minor impacts; likelihood, severity, or ecological significance of such impacts
Evaluation of individual morphology or physiology	Field sampling Histopathology, necropsy Records of mortality	Tissue residue levels Disease and abnormalities Reproduction	Direct evidence of injury to individuals; aerial extent of major impacts to individuals	Impacts to populations, communities, or the ecosystem
	Detailed field studies	Same	Quantification of small, subtle impacts to individuals or populations	Impacts to communities or the ecosystem
Comparison of contaminant concentrations to ecological benchmarks	Field sampling	Contaminated media Hazard indices	Nature and aerial extent of contamination and/or contamination above benchmarks; identification of exposure benchmarks	Direct evidence of actual impacts

SOURCE:. EPA

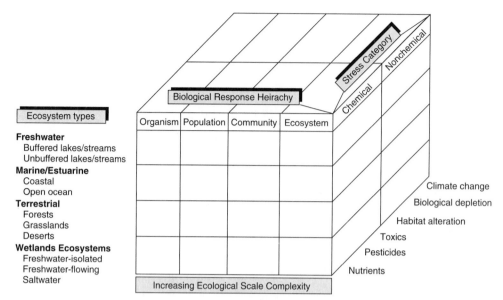

Figure 11-17. Ecological risk assessment organizing principles: the cube. (*EPA Report on the Ecological Risk Assessment Guidelines Strategic Planning Workshop.*)

quickly determine whether a contaminated site, for example, poses a significant ecological threat. If the threat is judged to be insignificant, then only a screening report may be necessary, with monitoring for a period of time. If further studies are needed, this step provides a conceptual, qualitative model that identifies the environmental values to be protected, the data needed, and the analyses to be used.

Planning and Scoping

The first step in a meaningful ecological assessment is to define the need, the objectives, the scope, and the design for such an assessment. As in human health, it is crucial to invest the time up front in planning for the collection of the right data—data necessary and usable in the risk assessment. The following framework is based largely on USEPA guidance for Superfund sites.

An ecological assessment is required under CERCLA (Superfund), RCRA, and other regulations as part of remedial investigation and feasibility studies. Pesticide registration under FIFRA and premanufacture notification under TSCA (as also OECD protocols for export to Europe) require ecological assessments. In the CERCLA/RCRA context, a typical objective is to determine and document actual or potential effects of contaminants on ecological receptors and habitats as a basis for evaluating remedial alternatives in a scientifically defensible manner.

> ### Should ecological risk be based on risks to individuals, populations, or ecosystems?
>
> Ecological risk assessments (ERAs) can evaluate risk to an individual, a population, or an ecosystem. An individual endpoint indicates that the intent is to protect individual members of a species from harm. A population endpoint allows the evaluation of risk in terms of harm to the population of a species, with the intent of protecting the species as a whole from decline but not necessarily protecting individual members of the species. The use of an ecosystem endpoint will allow the evaluation of risk to the ecological unit that encompasses all species within a community, with the intent of maintaining the number of species but not necessarily the types of species within the ecosystem. The EPA pulp and paper mill ERA estimates risk to individual members of a species. However, the risk to the most sensitive species in that assessment was evaluated in terms of reduced hatchability of eggs and other embryological defects. This endpoint could be thought of as both an individual and a population endpoint because reduced hatchability affects population size.
>
> SOURCE: Travis and Morris, *Risk Analysis,* 1992.

Factors to Consider in Planning Ecological Assessment

- The need for, and scope of, ecological studies, including programmatic goals, uses and users, framework and requirements; and agreement with regulatory agencies on the scope and the method
- Data quality objectives and sampling protocols
- The habitat and sensitive populations (including rare or endangered species) potentially affected now or by future remedial actions
- Boundaries of site or source of the problem "edge of the plume," and a comparable reference area
- Prior studies of the site or surroundings
- Time and resource requirements (budget and schedule, e.g., cost and time of sampling vs. value of incremental data)
- Level of effort appropriate to the objectives
- Stressors and contaminants of concern
- Ecological receptors and indicator species
- Significant exposure pathways
- Assessment and measurement endpoints
- Form of output or end product needed for risk management decisions

- Environmental media to be sampled both on-site and off-site (reference area), spatial and temporal considerations (e.g., seasonal changes in water flows, temperature), and confidence limits (all relevant media including soil, surface water, and sediments covered? Number of samples for required confidence level? Locations close to exposure points?)

- Contaminants to be analyzed and detection limits (sufficiently low for both human and ecological receptors?)

- Transport processes and off-site migration (valid models?)

- Toxicity tests of media and species, and ecological effects (population, community, or ecosystem) to be measured, diagnosed, or predicted (proper extrapolation factors?)

Stressors/Contaminants

Examples of chemical stressors at hazardous-waste sites include polycyclic aromatic hydrocarbons (PAHs), pesticides, PCBs, and metals. Some metals that are essential human nutrients, such as copper, zinc, and selenium, can elicit toxic responses in ecological receptors. Dissolved oxygen, pH, and temperature also influence toxicity. Physical stresses may result from hydrologic changes (e.g., floods), fires, and harvesting of fishery or forest resources. A subset of stressors that are likely to contribute the most risk are selected for analysis as discussed under contaminants of concern.

Contaminated Media, Release, Migration, and Fate

Included here are what is known about contaminated media, movement, and the geographical extent of current and future contamination, such as:

- Groundwater discharge to surface water and wetlands
- Transport of contaminated soils and sediments
- Runoff from and erosion of contaminated soils
- Biodegradation, transformation, and partitioning
- Bioaccumulation and bioconcentration

If sediments are a medium of concern, sediment characteristics such as particle-size distribution and organic carbon are important; for example, fine particles bind chemicals strongly, thus reducing their bioavailability.

Contaminants of Concern (COCs)

Not all contaminants warrant equal attention with regard to risk. Further, not all contaminants that pose human health risks are important with respect to ecological risk, and vice versa. Factors to consider in identifying contaminants of ecological concern are:

- Concentration in environmental media (soils, surface water, groundwater, sediments, air, and biota) representing viable exposure pathways
- Frequency of occurrence, indicating the prevalence or quantity of the contaminant in site media
- Background or reference area levels, indicating the concentrations that cannot be attributed to the site
- Physical-chemical properties, such as volatility, solubility, bioavailability, temperature, dissolved oxygen, and pH
- Potential for bioaccumulation or bioconcentration, based on its physical-chemical properties, e.g., octanol-water partition coefficient
- Potency, or the amount of toxicant capable of producing adverse effects
- Effects, such as acute lethality (LC_{50}) or sublethal responses, e.g., reproductive impairment

As with human health, contaminant concentration and toxicity are critical factors; in addition, bioconcentration can be important in ecological risk (e.g., food chain and reproductive effects). Bioconcentration factors (BCFs) higher than 300 are generally considered significant. The number of years to reach the maximum concentration can vary from less than 1 for DDT/DDE in foliage to 5 or more years in birds.

Exposure Pathways

An exposure pathway is the link between a contaminant source and a receptor. In evaluating exposure pathways, we need to consider all media (groundwater, surface water, sediments, soils, air, and biota) that are or could be contaminated. Exposure may be the result of direct contact with contaminated media (e.g., dermal contact, uptake through gills, ingestion) or indirectly through the food chain. If a pathway is incomplete, there is no exposure and hence no risk.

Potential Receptors

Receptors are individual organisms, populations, or communities that can be exposed to contaminants. Receptors can be identified from a review of the fate, migration, and potential release of contaminants. Ecologists begin by identifying potentially exposed habitats on or near the site using a wide variety of methods, including field reconnaissance, aerial photography, satellite imagery, and a review of previous studies. Identification of receptors should include:

- Species considered essential to, or indicative of, the healthy functioning of the habitat
- Rare, endangered, or threatened species on or near the site
- Species protected under federal or state law, e.g., Migratory Bird Treaty Act, and Marine Mammal Protection Act
- Species of commercial or recreational value

Ecological Response and Effects

The effects data sources include field observations (e.g., fish or bird kills), field tests (microcosm tests), laboratory tests (single species or microcosm tests), and structure-activity relationships. Toxic effect on an individual organism can affect the population size by changes in mortality, birth, and immigration/emigration rates, which in turn can lead to changes in community structure and function. The community-level shifts in species diversity, food webs, and competitive advantages can eventually disrupt ecosystem dynamics and productivity. Productivity is the rate at which new biomass is produced. The productivity of an ecosystem is indicated by oxygen production by the plant community or by respiration rates measured by carbon dioxide output. The ratio of production to respiration (P/R ratio) per unit time is a measure of an ecosystem's efficiency.
    Examples of ecosystem responses to stress are:

- Reduction in species diversity or richness
- Shortened life spans and smaller-sized organisms
- Shortened food chains and disruption of nutrient dynamics
- Reduction in vulnerable or sensitive species vs. tolerant species
- Decline in bellwether species (that may signal threat to entire ecosystem and provide early warning)
- Changes in standing crop biomass
- Changes in production/respiration ratio

Endpoints

An endpoint is an expected effect of a stressor on an ecological component, such as increased fish mortality. Two types of endpoints are generally distinguished. Assessment endpoints are actual environmental values to be protected—in other words, they are recognized and valued by the public and drive the decision making. Measurement endpoints are measurable responses to stressors that are related to and predictive of assessment endpoints (surrogates). When an assessment endpoint can be measured directly, both the endpoints are the same; but in most cases, direct measurement of environmental effects would not be practical. For example, a decline in sport fish population such as trout (assessment endpoint) can be evaluated using laboratory studies on the survival, growth, or reproduction of surrogate species such as fathead minnow (measurement endpoint).

Examples of Measurement and Assessment Endpoints	
Assessment Endpoints	**Measurement Endpoints**
Population:	
Abundance of preferred species	Abundance
Endangered, extinct	Reproduction and fecundity
Structure (ages, ratios)	Morbidity, mortality
Community:	
Commercial value	Species diversity
Recreational quality	Community structure
Changes to less desired species	
Ecosystems:	
Productivity	Biomass or standing crop
Human health concerns	Nutrient dynamics
(e.g., food chain quality)	Fish tissue concentrations

Exposure Assessment

Exposure assessment quantifies the magnitude and type of actual and/or potential exposures of ecological receptors to site contaminants and other stressors. The key elements in exposure assessment are:

- Quantification of contaminant release, migration, and fate
- Characterization of receptors
- Measurement and/or modeling of exposure point concentrations
- Development of exposure profile

Quantification of Release, Migration, and Fate

In the exposure assessment phase, estimates of current and future contaminant levels in affected media, including all relevant spatial and temporal characteristics of the contamination are developed. These estimates can then be used to determine exposure point concentrations.

Direct sampling of media yields information on the current location and concentration of contaminants. Fate-and-transport models predict the movement of contaminants from the source and between media. Sampling design, sample placement and timing, and the selection of models applicable to the site are considered in estimating exposure point concentrations.

Characterization of Receptors and Indicator Species

Most sites requiring ecological assessments contain a large number of species, populations, and communities—from microbes to mammals, from algae to trees. To develop a reasonable and practicable evaluation, the investigation should focus on a limited number of receptors called indicator species or representative species based on the endpoints of concern and specific characteristics of the site under study. In characterizing receptors, information should be collected (primarily from published literature) on the species' feeding habits, life histories, habitat preferences, and other attributes that could affect their exposure or sensitivity to contaminants.

Exposure Point Concentrations

The concentrations of contaminant(s) in the media to which the receptors are exposed, known as the exposure point concentration, are measured in the environmental medium or estimated using fate-and-transport modeling. The amount of contaminant a receptor takes in depends on such factors as:

- The properties of the contaminant
- The way the organism assimilates contaminant, e.g., direct absorption or ingestion
- The nature of the receptor, e.g., behavior, life history
- The physical and chemical properties of the media, e.g., pH, organic carbon content

If a contaminant is known or expected to bioconcentrate, it may be necessary to collect and analyze samples from biota at two or more trophic levels (e.g., plant, herbivore, carnivore) along with surrounding media. This information is used in two ways:

- Directly, as exposure point concentrations for dietary exposure pathways for ecological receptors
- Indirectly, for calculating site-specific bioconcentration factors (BCFs) or bioaccumulation factors (BAFs) to predict the food-chain transfer of contaminants to organisms at higher trophic levels

Exposure Profile

Exposure profile quantifies the magnitude and spatial and temporal patterns of exposure (acute, sporadic or pulsed, chronic) for input to risk characterization.

Exposure effects can be expressed in dose units (mg substance/kg body weight/day) at the individual organism level, or in units of concentration/unit area/time for higher levels of organization such as an ecosystem.

Ecological Effects/Toxicity Assessment

This step provides the link between concentrations of contaminants and adverse effects in receptors, e.g., suppression of plant growth, reduction in fish populations. Literature reviews, field studies, and toxicity testing provide this dose-response or stressor-response information; that is, how much toxicant is associated with how much of an adverse effect.

Literature Reviews and Field Studies

Literature reviews and databases can provide specific dose-response information for the species under study. This information is useful in risk characterization through comparison of measured concentrations of contaminants in site media with literature values for adverse effects.

Ecological field studies offer direct or corroborative evidence of a link between contamination and ecological effects. Such evidence, in comparison with a reference area, could include:

- Reduction in population sizes of species
- Absence of species normally occurring in the habitat
- Presence of species associated primarily with stressed habitats
- Changes in community diversity or trophic structure
- Incidence of lesions, tumors, or other pathologies

Toxicity Testing

Toxicity bioassays in the laboratory evaluate the effects of contaminated media on the survival, growth, reproduction, and metabolism of test organisms. Review of test results along with data on chemical concentrations of media and biological observations from field studies can point to the effects that may be attributable to the presence of hazardous substances from a site.

Stressor-Response Profile

Ideally, the stressor-response profile should depict the relationship between the magnitude, frequency, and duration of exposure to a stressor and the magnitude of response (assessment endpoint). Most often, such relationships have to be inferred through extrapolations. Common extrapolations include those between species (e.g., bluegill sunfish mortality to rainbow trout mortality), between responses (e.g., from bobwhite quail LC_{50} to NOEL or from acute to chronic effects), and from laboratory to field.

Risk Characterization

The science of risk assessment in ecology has not evolved to the point where scientists can make standard risk calculations for common risk scenarios as in human health evaluations. Risk characterization in ecological assessment is a process of applying professional judgment to determine whether adverse effects are occurring or likely to occur as a result of contamination associated with a site.

Risk Estimation

Ecologists estimate risk by comparing exposure and stressor-response profiles. Typically, single-effect values are compared with predicted or measured values of stressors, e.g., contaminant concentrations. The effect values from stressor-response profile can be used directly or extrapolated with an uncertainty or safety factor (generally 10 or 100). In the commonly used quotient method, the quotient or ratio of exposure estimate to effect value provides the risk estimate. For instance, exposure concentration can be compared with or divided by a toxicity reference value (TRV) similar to human reference dose (HQ = exposure/TRV). If the quotient is more than one, adverse effects are expected to occur (as in human health) based on the threshold. In more probabilistic approaches, single-species or multispecies (e.g., aquatic food web) simulation models can be used to evaluate both direct and indirect effects.

Many sources, including databases and publications, contain information on ecological effects of contaminants. For example, EPA's Ambient Water Quality Criteria (AWQC) documents, and Aquatic Toxicity Information Retrieval (AQUIRE) database contain peer-reviewed data describing effects of contaminants on aquatic organisms. AWQC tend to be either ARARs or "to be considered" (TBCs) in risk management decisions; EPA guidance can be used to make the values site-specific. State fish (and wildlife) consumption advisories and FDA action levels can also provide points of reference.

AQUIRE database was established in 1981 by the EPA Environmental Research Laboratory in Duluth, Minnesota, and has information on 5500 chemicals and nearly 2400 organisms as of August 1992. Where appropriate, data on chemicals similar but not identical to site contaminants can help characterize likely effects. Modeling techniques, such as Quantitative Structure Activity Relationships (QSAR), sometimes help in identifying surrogate chemicals for data collection. (See also accompanying box.)

Eco-Risk Characterization: Methods, Procedures, and Approaches

- Sediment-water equilibrium partitioning (EP) or water quality approach (Long and Morgan, 1990)

- Screening level concentration approach (Long and Morgan, 1990)

- Apparent effects threshold (AET) or species approach (Long and Morgan, 1990)

- Bioeffects and contaminant cooccurrence analyses (COA) approach (Long and Morgan, 1990)

- Sediment quality triad and criteria approach (Chapman, 1989)

- Bioassay approach (toxicity tests) (EPA, 1989)

- Diversity indices (Pielou, 1975)

- Hazard indices

- Quotient method (Barnthouse and Suter, 1986)

- Species richness and relative abundance indices

- Contaminant monitoring operations methodology (USFWS, in development)

- Wetland evaluation technique (WET) (USCOE, 1987)

- Indices of biological integrity (IBI) (Karr et al., 1986)

- Habitat evaluation procedure (HEP) (USFWS, 1987)

- Exposure pathway analysis (Fordham and Reagan, 1991)

- Probabilistic, sensitivity, and uncertainty analysis

- Linear structural modeling (Johnson et al., 1991)

SOURCE: Woodward-Clyde Consultants.

Causal Relationship

Four types of data are needed to establish a causal link between a hazard such as a waste site and ecological effects: (1) chemical analysis of the media (e.g., water, sediments) to identify presence and concentrations; (2) field surveys to determine that ecological effects have occurred; (3) tissue analyses of selected species to estimate bioconcentration, and implications to higher trophic levels; and (4) toxicity tests to establish the link between the toxicity of the hazardous source and the adverse ecological effects. It is also useful to have a reference area for comparison. A nearby area upstream or upgradient with no apparent source of contamination (if one could be found) that is similar in geophysical setting to the site of concern should be selected for comparative analysis. Without all these data, it would be difficult to rule out the possibility of natural variability and habitat alterations unrelated to a given hazard.

Uncertainty Analysis

The uncertainty in data, models, and assumptions in each phase of risk assessment is carried through and often magnified in risk estimates. The level of confidence in the estimates should be expressed and should include a discussion of the weight of evidence such as adequacy and quality of data and corroborative evidence of causality.

Ecological Significance

The interpretation of the meaning of the risk estimates and the ecological context provides the link between the risk assessment and risk management. The key aspects of ecological significance to be considered include the nature and magnitude of effects, spatial and temporal patterns, and the potential for recovery with or without further action. (The Alaskan oil spill and the Persian Gulf oil fires, catastrophic as they were, should yield valuable insights into the resilience of such ecosystems.)

Summary and Recommendations

In the summary section, risk assessors include a discussion of study results in relation to project objectives, study limitations, as well as ideas for risk management decisions including no further action, monitoring, remedial alternatives, or habitat enhancement.

In summary, the risk assessment process seeks to answer the following questions:

- Are ecological receptors currently exposed to site contaminants at levels capable of causing harm, or is future exposure likely?
- If adverse ecological effects are observed or predicted, what are the types, extent, and severity of the effects?
- What are the uncertainties associated with the risk characterization?
- What remedial approaches, if any, are indicated?

Points to Consider

1. As with human health, invest the time up front in planning for the ecological assessment—the purpose, the data needed, data quality objectives, and

the sampling program—rather than try to retrofit generic RI/FS data later. Discuss and obtain agreement with the regulatory agencies and with other data users and stakeholders.

2. Aim for a meaningful and scientifically defensible study (from a risk management point of view) within the time frame and budgetary constraints. Have risk assessments peer reviewed by credible parties.

3. Identify and refine the variables or values that drive the risk, e.g., intake of sediments as a ratio of total food intake by environmental receptors (sediments with high concentrations of metals and pesticides can be a major contributor to total risk estimates). Is there a close correspondence between assessment and measurement endpoints?

4. Identify the most relevant NOAEL or acceptable dose. The values in literature vary by orders of magnitude because of the differences in laboratory vs. field tests, modes of dose administration, assumptions regarding pharmacokinetics, and so on. From the array of values in published literature and databases, select the value closest to the indicator species being studied and the expected exposure scenario for comparison.

5. Consider the costs of overestimating risk (cost of treatment without benefit to society) vs. underestimating risk (potential loss of valuable ecosystem). Are ecological significance, natural fluctuations, and ecosystem resilience adequately considered?

Cases and Examples

1. Chapman et al. (1991) used the Sediment Quality Triad concept to determine if contaminant-induced degradation in marine bottom-dwelling (infaunal benthic) invertebrate communities was occurring in association with an off-shore oil platform. The triad approach used independently derived measures of (a) anthropogenic contamination (bulk sediment chemistry including contaminant concentrations); (b) sediment toxicity (bioassay tests in the laboratory, e.g., LC_{50}); and (c) field measures of benthic community structure (e.g., species richness, evenness, numerical dominance in study area compared with outlying reference areas) at stations radiating outward from the platform. The three measures agreed in showing that stations in the near field, within 25 meters, differed from those beyond. It was shown, however, that high levels of chemical enrichment and associated toxicity did not result in as much degradation in benthic community structure in the near field as might have been expected. The triad allows for graphical representation of large amounts of complex interrelated information to facilitate interpretation, offering a burden-of-evidence approach without a priori assumptions. By their shapes and sizes, the resulting triangles reflect relative differences among sediment chemistry, toxicity, and biotic community structure (the "measurement endpoint").

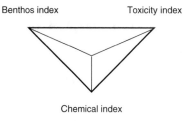

Benthos index   Toxicity index

Chemical index

Sediment Quality Triad

2. Menzie et al. (1992) found that a combination of predictive modeling, laboratory, and field methods was the most effective approach to estimating risks to terrestrial biota at a Superfund site contaminated with pesticides. Predictive methods alone resulted in large uncertainties when extrapolating food chain transfers from the soil to higher trophic levels (birds and mammals). Laboratory and in-field bioassays provided valuable insights on the potential toxicity of soils and the potential for bioaccumulation. Field observations served as an important "reality check" for interpreting the laboratory bioassay results. For example, the soil invertebrate community was found to exhibit vertical and horizontal strata creating exposure regimes quite different from those represented by the laboratory tests. The in-field bioassays with earthworms were especially useful in illustrating subtleties in the spatial distribution of contaminated soils. It was concluded that, if birds and mammals are the ecological receptors of interest, it is much better to examine the animals directly than to rely on modeling to estimate exposures or effects.

3. In an effort to determine which of nearly 500 organic compounds pose the greatest risk to fishery populations in the Great Lakes, Passino and Smith (1987) used a combination of literature review, acute toxicity tests, results of receptor tissue analyses, and information on potential sources. A provisional classification of 19 classes of compounds was established using available information on toxicity, bioaccumulation, occurrence, and source. Following the priorities implied by the provisional rankings, acute toxicity tests were performed with 30 compounds representing the 19 classes. The resulting data, along with information on the chemicals' occurrence in Great Lakes fish and sources, were ranked and weighted for use in calculating revised hazard rankings. The three most hazardous classes, in descending order, were determined to be arene halides (e.g., PCBs, DDT); phthalate esters; and chlorinated camphines (e.g., toxaphene). Toxicity data alone would have produced a different ranking (e.g., phthalate esters would appear much lower in the hierarchy). This study illustrates the value of using multiple sources of information in identifying chemicals of concern.

Habitat Evaluation Procedures (HEP): Overview and Illustration.
This overview, based on the U.S. Fish and Wildlife Service videotape, presents:

(1) objectives and concept of the HEP model; (2) habitat study method; and (3) its uses.

1. *Objectives and Concept.* The HEP effort aims at developing a set of quantitative procedures that can be standardized and applied to a variety of habitats. The concept is simple—a unit of measure based on the value of habitat to fish and wildlife (not the economic value to humans). The habitat unit (HU) is the product of habitat quality and habitat quantity. Habitat quality is expressed in terms of habitat suitability index (HSI), and habitat quantity in terms of acres or hectares.

$$\text{Habitat quality} \times \text{habitat quantity} = \text{habitat unit}$$
$$\text{(HSI)} \qquad\qquad \text{(acres)} \qquad\qquad \text{(HU)}$$

Habitat suitability represents the extent to which the environment satisfied the food, cover, water, and reproductive requirements of the species.

$$\begin{array}{lll} \text{Amounts} & \text{food} & \\ \text{Density} & \text{cover} & \\ \text{Quality} & \rightarrow \quad \text{water} & \rightarrow \quad \text{HSI} \\ \text{Nest sites} & \text{reproduction} & \end{array}$$

HSI ranges from 0 to 1, with 1 representing optimum habitat, defined for each species in terms of density, biomass, and reproductive success. For example, a wetland-upland complex containing dense grass for, say, waterfowl nesting and in-water cover, has a relatively high HSI of 0.6.

$$(0.6 \text{ HSI}) \times (1 \text{ acre}) = 0.6 \text{ HUs}$$

Thus habitat units are equally sensitive to both habitat suitability and area.

2. *Habitat Study.* The study consists of prefield activities, field studies and baseline definition, and future habitat projections.

Prefield activities include:

- Formation of a credible team so that the results will be acceptable to all parties concerned

- Setting study objectives to ensure meaningful results within budget and time frame

- Delineating study boundaries and cover types

- Selecting indicator species based on economic, social, or ecological perspective

- Guilding, i.e., grouping of species with similar habitat requirements; for example, mallard, pintail, and other puddle ducks all need grassy areas near temporary wetlands for nesting and can be represented by any member of the guild.

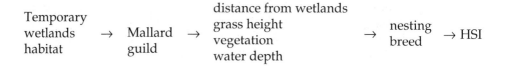

Field activities and baseline studies include:

- Record field data and measure habitat variables (e.g., vegetation density, height)
- Compute HSI values for selected species
- Establish baseline inventory or values

For example, mallard habitat described earlier in a 100-acre area will have 60 habitat units:

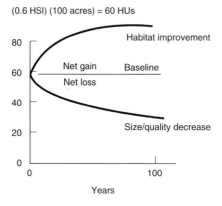

We can project future habitat conditions if changes are expected. For instance, if the 100-acre wetland complex is subjected to drainage and additional cropping, the wetland value for mallard will diminish over time as illustrated above.

3. *Uses of HEP Data.*   We can use the quantitative and qualitative information generated in the habitat study for mitigation to reduce negative impact, for habitat enhancement, and for cost analyses. In this mallard example, it may be possible to recover part of the drained wetlands by simply plugging the drain. The habitat value can be enhanced by planting dense nest cover to improve nest success, and also by fencing the area to control grazing. The HEP studies can similarly be used for different species and for the management of associated aquatic and terrestrial habitats.

Vision for the Next Millennium?

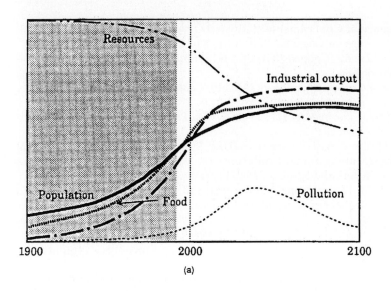

(a)

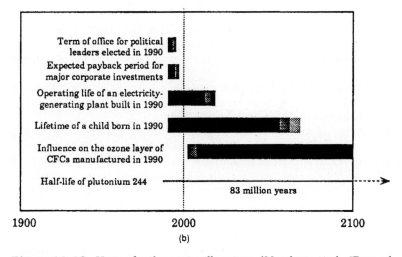

(b)

Figure 11-18. Vision for the next millennium. (*Meadows et al., "Beyond the Limits," 1992; (b) is slightly modified.*)

Globally, we should consider setting aside for posterity ecological treasures not yet overwhelmed by human interference—such as parts of Siberia, Tibet, North America, Australia, rain forests, the oceans, polar regions, and the outer space (the Global Commons).

References and Additional Readings

American Conference of Governmental Industrial Hygienists (ACGIH), 1992–1993. Threshold Limit Values for Chemical Substances and Physical Agents.

American Industrial Health Council (AIHC), 1991. Improving Risk Characterization—Summary of a Workshop.

American Institute of Chemical Engineers (AIChE), Center for Chemical Process Safety (CCPS), New York.

AIChE/CCPS 1992. *Guidelines for Hazard Evaluation Procedures,* 2d ed., with worked examples.

AIChE/CCPS, Health & Safety Executive (UK), European Federation of Chemical Engineering, 1992. International Conference on Hazard Identification and Risk Analysis, Human Factors and Human Reliability in Process Safety (Orlando, Florida).

AIChE/CCPS, 1991. International Conference and Workshop on Modeling and Mitigating the Consequences of Accidental Releases of Hazardous Materials (New Orleans, Louisiana).

AIChE/CCPS, 1989. Guidelines for Chemical Process Quantitative Risk Analysis.

AIChE/CCPS, 1985. Guidelines for Hazard Evaluation Procedures (prepared by Battelle Columbus Division).

Canadian Council of Ministers of the Environment (CCME) National Guidelines for Decommissioning Industrial Sites, 1991.

Casada M., and W. Bridges (JBF Associates), Personal communication on hazard analysis.

Casarett and Doull's *Toxicology, The Basic Science of Poisons,* 4th ed., 1991. Edited by Amdur, Doull, and Klassen. Pergamon Press/McGraw-Hill, New York.

Chapman et al., 1991. "Evaluation of Effects Associated with an Oil Platform, Using the Sediment Quality Triad," *Environmental Toxicology and Chemistry,* vol. 10, pp. 407–424, 1991.

Chechile, R. and S. Carlisle (editors, Tufts University Center for the Study of Decision Making), 1991. Environmental Decision Making—A Multidisciplinary Perspective. Van Nostrand Reinhold, New York.

Chemical Manufacturers Association (CMA), 1989. Evaluating Process Safety in the Chemical Industry: A Manager's Guide to Quantitative Risk Assessment.

Chemical Manufacturers Association Responsible Care: Process Safety Code of Management Practices (1990); Distribution Code of Management Practices (1991).

Chemical Manufacturers Association, 1992. The 1992 CMA Economic Survey: Outlook for 1992 and Beyond.

The Conference Board, 1991. Corporate Stewardship of the Environment, Report 982.

Environmental Protection Agency (EPA/USEPA):

EPA, 1989. Risk Assessment Guidance for Superfund (RAGS), vol. 1, *Human Health Evaluation Manual* (Part A). EPA 540/1-89/002.

EPA, 1991. Risk Assessment Guidance for Superfund: vol. 1, *Human Health Evaluation Manual* (Part B, Development of Risk-Based Preliminary Remediation Goals). EPA 540/R-92/003.

EPA, 1991. Risk Assessment Guidance for Superfund: vol. 1, *Human Health Evaluation Manual* (Part C, Evaluation of Remedial Alternatives). EPA 540/R-92/004.

EPA, 1991. *Human Health Evaluation Manual,* Supplemental Guidance: "Standard Default Exposure Factors." OSWER Directive 9285.6-03.

EPA, 1989. Risk Assessment Guidance for Superfund, vol. 2, *Environmental Evaluation Manual.* EPA 540/1-89/001.

EPA, 1988. *Superfund Exposure assessment Manual.* EPA 540/1-88/001.

EPA, 1988. Guidance for Conducting Remedial Investigations and Feasibility Studies (RI/FS) under CERCLA. EPA 540/G-89/004.

EPA, 1990. *Exposure Factors Handbook.* EPA 600/8-89/043.

EPA, 1986. *Superfund Public Health Evaluation Manual.* EPA 540/1-86/060.

EPA, 1986. Guidelines for Carcinogen Risk Assessment; Guidelines for Mutagenicity Risk Assessment; Guidelines for the Health Risk Assessment of Chemical Mixtures; Guidelines for the Health Assessment of Suspect Developmental Toxicants; Guidelines for Estimating Exposures. *Federal Register,* September 24, 1986.

EPA, 1992. Health Effects Assessment Summary Tables (HEAST) (periodic updates). NTIS PB92-921199.

EPA, 1992. Dermal Exposure Assessment: Principles and Applications. EPA 600/8-91/011B.

EPA, 1992. Guidance for Data Useability in Risk Assessment (Part A). 9285.7-09A.

EPA, 1989. Workshop Report on EPA Guidelines for Carcinogen Risk Assessment. EPA 625/389/015.

EPA, 1992. "Framework for Ecological Risk Assessment," EPA 630/R-92/001.

EPA, 1992. Peer Review Workshop Report on a Framework for Ecological Risk Assessment. EPA 625/3-91/022.

EPA, 1991. Summary Report on Issues in Ecological Risk Assessment. EPA 625/3-91/018.

EPA, 1989. Ecological Assessment of Hazardous Waste Sites: A Field and Laboratory Reference Document. PB89-205967. EPA 600/3-89/013.

EPA, 1991. Eco Update (periodic updates). 9345.0-051.

EPA, 1992. F. Henry Habicht: Guidance on Risk Characterization for Risk Managers and Risk Assessors (February 26, 1992).

EPA, 1992. Larry Reed: "Supplemental Guidance to RAGS: Calculating the Concentration Term" (June 22, 1992).

EPA, 1991. Guidelines for Developmental Toxicity Risk Assessment. *Federal Register,* December 5, 1991.

EPA, 1992. Guidance for Exposure Assessment, Notice. *Federal Register,* May 29, 1992.

EPA, 1992. Personal communication with R. Morgenstern, July 10, 1992.

EPA, 1990. Hazardous Substances in Our Environment, A Citizen's Guide to Understanding Health Risks and Reducing Exposure. EPA 230/09/90/081.

EPA Journal, March/April 1991. Setting Environmental Priorities: The Debate about Risk, vol. 17, no. 2.

EPA, 1987. Unfinished Business: A Comparative Assessment of Environmental Problems, Overview Report. NTIS PB88-127048.

EPA Science Advisory Board, 1990. The Report of the Ecology and Welfare Subcommittee, Relative Risk Reduction Project. Appendix A. EPA SAB-EC-90-021A.

EPA Science Advisory Board, 1990. The Report of the Human Health Subcommittee, Relative Risk Reduction Project. Appendix B. EPA SAB-EC-90-021B.

EPA Science Advisory Board, 1990. The Report of the Strategic Options Subcommittee, Relative Risk Reduction Project. Appendix C. EPA SAB-EC-90-021C.

EPA Region III. Roy Smith. Monte Carlo Risk Assessment: A Regional Science Policy Issue. June 26, 1992.

EPA, 1991. Economic Incentives, Options for Environmental Protection; and EPA 1990. Paying for Progress: Perspectives on Financing Environmental Protection.

EPA and Other Systems, Databases and Models (examples):

EPA IRIS (integrated risk information system).

On-line database containing health risk (slope factors, reference doses) and regulatory information on specific chemicals; available through National Library of Medicine (NLM) MEDLARS Toxnet, and other systems. (Toxnet also provides access to HSDB, RTECS, and TRI databases.)

EPA GEMS/PCGEMS (graphical exposure modeling system)..

Set of models (air, water, soil), programs, and data modules to conduct exposure and risk assessment. Riskpro: commercial version of PCGEMS developed by General Sciences Corp.

EPA UNAMAP Series.

Atmospheric fate models, e.g., BOX, ISCST, ISCLT.

EPA SESOIL (seasonal soil compartment model).

Vadose (unsaturated) zone and groundwater fate model.

CIS (chemical information system).

Toxicology, physical and chemical properties, environmental fate, MSDS, IRIS and other data.

EPA, 1991. NATICH Data Base Report on State, Local, and EPA Air Toxics Activities. EPA 450/3-91/018.

Handbook of Chemical Hazard Analysis Procedures, 1990. Federal Emergency Management Agency (FEMA), U.S. Department of Transportation (DOT) and U.S. Environmental Protection Agency (USEPA).

Harris R. (Environ Corp), and D. Burmaster (Alceon Corp), Restoring Science to Superfund Risk Assessment, 1991.

Harvard School of Public Health, Center for Risk Analysis (J. Graham, director), 1991. OMB vs. the Agencies: The Future of Cancer Risk Assessment.

Hawkins, N., M. Jayjock, and J. Lynch, "A Rationale and Framework for Establishing the Quality of Human Exposure Assessments," *American Industrial Hygiene Association Journal,* vol. 53, January 1992.

Hazardous Materials Control/Superfund '91. Proceedings of the 12th National Conference, Washington, D.C., December 1991.

Health and Welfare Canada, 1989–1990. Canada Health Protection Branch, Health Risk Determination.

James, S., and W. Rish (Woodward-Clyde Consultants), Personal communication on aggregate environmental risk.

Kloman, F., A. Bouska, and W. Gulledge (Tillinghast/Towers Perrin Co.), Personal communication on environmental liability insurance.

Kolluru, R., "Understand the Basics of Risk Assessment," *Chemical Engineering Progress,* March 1991.

Lave, L., and H. Gruenspecht, "Increasing the Efficiency and Effectiveness of Environmental Decisions: Benefit-Cost Analysis and Effluent Fees, A Critical Review," *Journal of Air & Waste Management Association,* May 1991.

Lioy, P., "Assessing Human Exposure to Airborne Pollutants: Advances and Opportunities," *Environmental Science & Technology,* vol. 25, no. 8, August 1991.

Arthur D. Little, Prism Third Quarter 1991, Managing for the Environment.

Marsh and McLennan (M&M, Chicago), 1992. Large Property Damage Losses in the

Hydrocarbon-Chemical Industries, A Thirty Year Review, 14th ed., and related publications.

Meadows et al., *Beyond the Limits*, 1992. Chelsea Green Publishing Co., Post Mills, Vermont.

Menzie et al., 1992. Assessment of Methods for Estimating Ecological Risk in the Terrestrial Component: A Case Study at the Baird & McGuire Superfund Site in Holbrook, Massachusetts, *Environmental Toxicology and Chemistry*, vol. 2, pp. 245–260, 1992.

National Academy of Sciences, National Research Council, 1983. *Risk Assessment in the Federal Government: Managing the Process*, National Academy Press, Washington, D.C.

National Safety Council (Chicago, Illinois): Accident Facts, 1991 edition.

National Wildlife Federation—Corporate Conservation Council, 1990. The Natural Environment: Issues for Management.

Occupational Safety and Health Administration (OSHA) 1989. Air Contaminants—Permissible Exposure Limits.

Occupational Safety and Health Administration 29CFR1910. Hazardous Waste Operations and Emergency Response; Final Rule. *Federal Register*, March 6, 1989.

Occupational Safety and Health Administration. Process Safety Management, OSHA 3132. 1992; and Guidelines for Compliance, OSHA 3133.

Passino, D., and S. Smith, 1987. "Acute Bioassays and Hazard Evaluation of Representative Contaminants Detected in Great Lakes Fish," *Environmental Toxicology and Chemistry*, vol. 6, pp. 901–907, 1987.

Paustenbach, D. (editor), *The Risk Assessment of Environmental and Human Health Hazards: A Textbook of Case Studies*, 1989. Wiley, New York.

Predicting Ecosystem Risk, 1992. Edited by Cairns, Niederlehner and Orvos. Princeton Publishing Co., Princeton, New Jersey.

Project 88—Round II. Incentives for Action: Designing Market-Based Environmental Strategies. A Public Policy Study sponsored by Senators Wirth (Colorado) and Heinz (Pennsylvania). Project Director R. Stavins. Washington, D.C., 1991.

Reilly, W., Aiming Before We Shoot: The Quiet Revolution in Environmental Policy. The National Press Club, Washington, D.C., September 26, 1990.

Risk Analysis: A Guide to Principles and Methods for Analyzing Health and Environmental Risks, 1989. J. Cohrssen and V. Covello, U.S. Council on Environmental Quality, Washington, D.C.

Risk Assessment and Risk Management for the Chemical Process Industry, 1991. Edited by H. Greenburg and J. Cramer, Van Nostrand Reinhold, New York.

Risk Assessment in the Federal Government: Managing the Process, 1983. National Academy of Sciences/National Research Council (NAS/NRC). Washington, D.C.

Ruckelshaus, W., "Risk, Science and Democracy," *Issues in Science and Technology*, Spring 1985.

Salhotra, A., Y. Meeks, R. Thorpe, T. Mckone, and K. Bogen, Application of Monte Carlo Simulation to Estimate Probabilities of Exposure and Human Health Risks. National Research and Development Conference on the Control of Hazardous Materials, Feb. 20–22, 1991, Anaheim, California.

Science, Apr. 17, 1987. vol. 236, pp. 233–364. Several articles on Risk Assessment.

Simons M., R. Hinkle, V. Tomacelli, and W. Heck (Woodward-Clyde Consultants), Personal communication.

Smith, W., Yale University School of Forestry and Environmental Studies, *Air Pollution and Forests: Interaction between Air Contaminants and Forest Ecosystems*, 2d ed., 1990.

Technical Guidance for Hazards Analysis: Emergency Planning for Extremely Hazardous Substances, 1987. USEPA, FEMA, DOT.

Thompson, K., D. Burmaster, and E. Crouch, Monte Carlo Techniques for Quantitative Uncertainty Analysis in Public Health Assessments. *Risk Analysis,* vol. 12, no. 1, 1992.

Travis, C., and C. Doty, Risk Management at Hazardous Waste Sites (1990), Office of Risk Analysis, Oak Ridge National Laboratory, Oak Ridge, Tennessee.

Travis, C., and J. Morris, The Emergence of Ecological Risk Assessment (editorial). *Risk Analysis* (publication of the Society for Risk Analysis), vol. 12, no. 2, 1992.

Uncertainty in Risk Assessment, Risk Management, and Decision Making, 1987. Edited by Covello, Lave, Moghissi, and Uppuluri, Plenum Press, New York.

United Nations Environment Programme (UNEP): APELL (Awareness and Preparedness for Emergencies at Local Level), A Process for Responding to Technological Accidents, 1988. Industry and Environment Program, Paris, France.

U.S. Environmental Protection Agency (USEPA). See EPA.

U.S. Fish and Wildlife Service (personal communication, 1992). Habitat evaluation procedures (HEP), overview with VHS tape.

Wallace, W., and D. Lincoln, How Scientists Make Decisions about Groundwater and Soil Remediation, National Research Council Colloquium, Washington, D.C., 1989.

12

Public Health and Private Initiatives*

Rao V. Kolluru, DrPH
Director, Environmental Health Services,
CH2M Hill†

In this chapter:

- Public Health: Prevention is the Key
- Limiting Exposures: Personal Actions
- Nutrition, Life-style, and Health
- The American Health Care System
- Vision for the Next Millennium

The human health and well-being triad consists of environmental quality, public health, and disease treatment. While the dominant theme of environmental quality is preservation, that of public health is prevention. This chapter complements the previous chapter on Risk Assessment and Management. The focus here is on individual actions that would limit the myriad exposure possibilities indoors and outdoors in concert with the trend toward more active personal involvement in "holistic health." Also discussed are the risk factors, and the means of prevention or control, of major diseases including cardiovascular and cancer diseases, which

*Paul Brandt-Rauf, Sc.D., M.D., Dr.P.H., of Columbia University School of Public Health reviewed this chapter. The author also acknowledges the helpful suggestions of Dr. Michael Utidjian of American Cyanamid Company.

†The chapter was written while the author was at Woodward-Clyde Consultants.

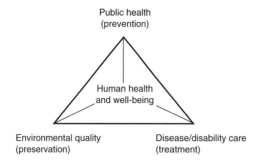

lead to two-thirds of all deaths in the United States. In addition, cases and guidelines are presented for employers to shift emphasis from employee "illness" to "wellness" programs and resource-effective strategies.

Like the weather, people talk about prevention all the time but do little about it. Unlike the weather, much can be done by way of prevention. In this chapter, you will find information on the steps that individuals can take, and employers can promote, to prevent or reduce the risk of disease and to maintain healthy living. The guidelines in this chapter, as well as those presented in other chapters, offer an effective framework for the development and management of corporate environmental, health, and safety (EHS) programs.

Public Health: Prevention Is the Key

In public health there is a hierarchy of preventive measures: primary, secondary, and tertiary. Primary prevention, the most effective strategy, involves the elimination of source or threat of disease before it develops. Secondary prevention is the early detection and treatment to minimize the impact. Tertiary prevention consists of rehabilitation and reduction of residual damage.

A good example of successful primary prevention is the improvement in basic sanitation and hygiene at the turn of the century that, combined with immunizations, virtually eliminated infectious and communicable diseases in the United States and Europe. In the later part of this century, attention shifted to chronic diseases such as heart disease and cancer that became prevalent in industrial societies. (The resurgence of TB, and the AIDS epidemic, as well as the continuing prevalence of sexually transmitted diseases, are grim reminders that there are no grounds for complacency regarding infectious diseases either.)

Examples of secondary and tertiary prevention are screening for breast and cervical cancer for early detection and treatment; and long-term management of chronic diseases such as diabetes, hypertension, and arthritis.

In a broad sense, the "cradle-to-cradle" closed-loop life-cycle concept for products and facilities embodies primary prevention, while the "cradle-to-grave" concept represents secondary prevention. The Superfund and RCRA programs, requiring hundreds of billions of dollars, typify tertiary prevention. A General Accounting Office report on groundwater (GAO, 1992) notes that while EPA's new approach appears to emphasize prevention, it is not accompanied by a meaningful shift in funding priorities. A noteworthy exception is EPA's Wellhead Protection Program; the report estimates that it costs less than 10 million federal dollars to set up such a prevention program, whereas it costs twice that much, $20 million, to clean up groundwater at just one of the over 1200 Superfund NPL sites.

Two of the most important laws in terms of prevention are the Toxic Substances Control Act (TSCA) of 1976 and the Pollution Prevention Act of 1990. TSCA recognized that health and environmental considerations are more easily addressed before rather than after a chemical is produced and introduced into commerce. It requires premanufacture notification (PMN) and significant new use notification. The Pollution Prevention Act represents a dramatic shift of national policy from end-of-pipe control to source reduction that established a hierarchy of prevention or reduction at the source followed by recycling, treatment, and disposal as a last resort.

Why is prevention, especially primary prevention, so critical to us as a nation? The relative value of prevention vs. cure is eloquently expressed by such common folk beliefs as: "An ounce of prevention is worth a pound of cure" and "A stitch in time saves nine." As Professor Bernard Goldstein of UMDNJ–Robert Wood Johnson Medical School stated, "In my view, the most important contribution of EPA has been the prevention of what has not happened at all" (*EPA Journal*, March/April 1991).

Primary ← secondary ← tertiary prevention
_____
← Increasing effectiveness (by an order of magnitude?)

Although difficult to quantify, prevention is particularly effective in situations where, based on our knowledge of cause-effect relationships, we could predict the effects that would occur if actions were not taken to forestall or mitigate such effects. Prevention, encompassing nutritional and lifestyle factors, should be our first line of defense except in emergencies, when drugs and acute treatment, of course, take precedence.

Limiting Exposures: Personal Actions

In daily living, we are all exposed to multitudes of hazardous agents both external (xenobiotics) and internal (endotoxins from natural biological processes). For the sake of discussion, hazard sources are depicted in the following figure by the degree of personal control (Fig. 12-1). The responsibility for limiting these exposures is shared by industry, government agencies, public health professionals, and ultimately the individuals themselves.

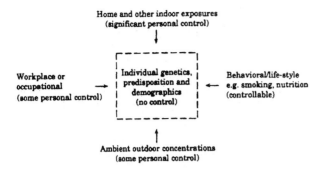

Figure 12-1. Potential exposures and degree of personal control.

The actions suggested in this chapter for preventing or limiting exposures fall into these areas with some overlap:

- Occupational hazards and exposures
- Indoor pollutants and exposures
- Outdoor pollutants and exposures
- Food, nutrition, lifestyle, and health

Occupational Hazards and Exposures

Annual incidence of injury and illness in U.S. manufacturing is about 12 to 13% of full-time employees. The chemical industry which figures prominently in the public view has in fact a lower rate at 6 to 7%, although the data between industries are not exactly comparable because of differences in reporting criteria. An occupational illness is a disease caused by exposure in the work environment. Over 200,000 new cases of occupational illnesses are reported each year; they have been climbing because of both increasing repetitive motion disorders and our growing technical ability to diagnose smaller physiological changes. Lower back injuries and chronic pain complaints constitute the largest source of disability claims. Overall, employers are expected to pay $70 billion in worker's compensation in 1992 for job-related injuries and illnesses. (Worker's compensation is a legal requirement, while health care benefits tend to be an optional program.)

The Occupational Safety and Health Administration (OSHA) was created in 1970 with the primary responsibility to assure safe and healthful working conditions for workers in the workplace. (There have been other major laws and statutes to protect workers such as the Federal Mine Safety and Health Act.) The mandate of the EPA, created the same year as OSHA, has been the protection of the general public outside workplace boundaries, but in recent years this somewhat artificial demarcation has blurred. This is evident from the 1990 Clean Air

Act's Risk Management Plan provisions, including prevention of accidental releases, and OSHA's new rule on process safety management.

In the occupational context, inhalation and skin contact are the predominant routes of exposure while inhalation and ingestion are the dominant routes for the general public. The types of hazards and potential exposures obviously vary with individual occupations (and hobbies), as in the following examples.

Examples of Workplace Hazards

Manufacturing, field work:
  Chemicals and gases (including asphyxiants)
  Dusts and fibers, respirable particulate matter
  Metals, metal dusts, and fumes
  Noise (hearing loss)
  Nonionizing and ionizing radiation
  Heat
  Musculoskeletal problems (e.g., back injuries)
  Repetitive motion trauma/cumulative trauma disorders (CTDs)
  Biological agents

Office:
  Video display terminals (eye strain, musculoskeletal discomfort)
  Repetitive motion trauma, e.g., computer keyboard (tendinitis, carpal tunnel syndrome, CTDs)
  "Sick building syndrome," "tight building syndrome" (see Table 12-1)

Respiratory disorders are among the more common effects of industrial exposures, ranging from temporary discomfort to chronic obstructive pulmonary diseases "COPD" (bronchitis, fibrosis, emphysema) to lung cancer. COPD can result from occupational exposures, ambient air pollutants, or tobacco smoke. Asthma is a well-known immune system response and can be induced or aggravated by allergens such as toluene diisocyanate and platinum salts. Exposure to ozone can increase the sensitivity of asthma patients to subsequent allergen exposure or to inhalation of sulfur dioxide.

Certain occupational groups such as farmers are at increased risk from the sun's uv radiation (because of the amount of time spent outdoors) and exposure to high levels of pesticides. Similarly, health care workers face such hazards as infectious agents (e.g., TB, HIV), cytotoxic agents (e.g., chemotherapeutics, radiation), and toxic gases (e.g., ethylene oxide, anesthetics). Skin disorders, especially contact dermatitis, are also common, accounting for 40 to 50% of all reported cases of occupational disease. Repetitive motion disorders from repeated wrist and hand motions that pinch the median nerve, associated with assembly and similar operations, have emerged as a source of concern in recent years. Nutritional supplements such as vitamin B_6, special exercises, and rest periods have been found to alleviate the symptoms and restore function.

Prevention

Employers have primary responsibility for providing a safe workplace through proper design, engineering controls, administrative practices, and as a last resort, personal protection equipment. Workers can also reduce the risk of exposures through education, training, and personal hygiene (washing hands before eating food and not smoking, for example). Company physicals and screening are helpful, as also is guidance from departments of health of various states and cities. Company physicals can be valuable in affording opportunity for lifestyle counseling. Biological monitoring for specific markers of exposure as part of medical screening and surveillance programs, before clinical manifestation of disease, can also be useful as secondary prevention. Workplace ergonomic programs can prevent or reduce repetitive motion trauma or cumulative trauma disorders.

Illustrative Population Risks in the United States

Hazard	Annual death toll	Degree of uncertainty
Tobacco smoking and chewing	350,000–400,000	Low
Alcohol abuse	150,000	Low
Highway accidents	50,000	Low
Homicides	20,000	Low
Radon	7,000–30,000	Medium
Indoor air toxics	6,000	Medium
Outdoor air toxics	3,000	High
Pesticide residues on foods	3,000	High

SOURCE: Adapted from Harvard School of Public Health, Center for Risk Analysis, Annual Report, 1991.

Estimated Expenditures per Life Year Saved: Selected Programs

	1990 U.S. $
Childhood immunizations	Direct savings
Leaded gasoline phase-out	Direct savings
Safety rules at underground construction sites	52,000
Hemodialysis at a dialysis center	56,000
Coronary artery bypass surgery	68,000
Front seat air bags in new cars	109,000
Dioxin effluent controls at paper mills	5,570,000

SOURCE: Adapted from Harvard School of Public Health, Center for Risk Analysis, Annual Report, 1991.

Indoor Pollutants and Exposures

Most of us spend 75 to 90% of our time indoors, at home or in the workplace. A variety of chemical, biological, and physical hazards may be present indoors in the air, building materials, carpeting and other furnishings, and common household products. Despite some degree of air exchange between indoors and outdoors, indoor levels of some volatile chemicals and other agents are often significantly higher than outdoors, partly a byproduct of the energy saving efforts. Some examples of indoor hazards are:

Chemical	Volatile organic compounds (VOCs), combustion products (CO, NO_x), tobacco smoke, asbestos
Biological	Bacteria, viruses, molds
Physical/radiological	Noise, radon, electromagnetic radiation

A landmark study of indoor exposures, known as the total exposure assessment methodology (TEAM) study, was conducted in the mid-1980s. The purpose of this study was to measure total exposures of populations to selected toxic chemicals (via air, water, and food) and the resulting body burden. Using Tenax personal monitors, the exposures to about 20 prevalent volatile and semivolatile organic compounds of 600 urban residents in New Jersey, North Carolina, North Dakota, and California were measured. Some of the interesting observations and conclusions in this study were:

1. Indoor concentrations (at home and at work) of VOCs, including many common solvents, are almost always higher than outdoor concentrations—mean indoor levels have been found to be 2 to 4 times higher than outdoor levels.

2. Mean indoor personal exposures to the chemicals were almost always higher than outdoor.

3. The elevated indoor concentrations were due to a variety of sources including building materials, consumer products, and personal activities. For example: smoking (benzene, xylenes, ethylbenzene, styrene in breath); passive smoking (same chemicals in indoor air); dry-cleaned clothes (tetrachloroethylene); pumping gas or exposure to auto exhaust gas (benzene in breath); hot water washing and showers (chloroform in air); and use of room fresheners, deodorizers, and mothballs (p-dichlorobenzene in air).

4. The air route provided more than 99% of the exposures for all the chemicals except for trihalomethanes for which drinking water provided nearly all the exposure.

5. In most cases, the above sources far outweighed the impact of major sources (including petrochemical plants) and nonpoint area sources.

In view of these and similar findings from other studies, indoor pollution would seem to be a significant health concern, especially since public perceptions tend to minimize its importance. Table 12-1 summarizes common indoor

Table 12-1. Indoor Pollutants/Hazards and Prevention

Source/hazard	Potential effects/symptoms	Prevention or exposure control
■ Common household chemicals and volatile organic compounds (VOCs), aerosols, e.g., cleansers, disinfectants, air fresheners, paints, solvents, etc., with acetone, toluene, methylene chloride, ammonia, etc.	Eye, nose, and throat irritation Central nervous system depression (narcotic effect) Liver and kidney damage Long-term effects? Propellant/solvent may be inflammable	Follow label directions, use sparingly in ventilated areas; store open containers in detached sheds; substitute less hazardous materials such as water, soap, and borax; replace mothballs and deodorizers containing *p*-dichlorobenzene with baking soda and cedar blocks; substitute aerosol cans with pump dispensers
■ Combustion products Carbon monoxide (CO) Nitrogen oxides (NO_x) Polycyclic aromatic hydrocarbons (PAHs) Stoves, heaters, burners (gas, kerosene, wood, coal) Vehicle exhaust, idling engines	Headache, dizziness, anoxia, angina from high CO levels (odorless) Cough, respiratory discomfort, pulmonary edema from NO_x Cancer risk from some PAHs	Use certified equipment and maintain regularly; install exhaust fans, clean ducts and increase ventilation; don't idle or warm up car in attached garage. Grow pollutant-absorbing house plants, e.g., philodendrons (see also footnote)
■ Ozone (O_3)/smog formed from NO_2 and hydrocarbons (copiers can emit ozone)	Respiratory tract irritation, decreased lung capacity, increased sensitivity to allergens	Don't exercise outdoors when ozone levels are high
■ Tobacco smoke (see also footnote) Active and passive smoking Tobacco chewing Hundreds of constituents including CO, and cancer-causing heavy metals, radionuclides, and polycyclic aromatic hydrocarbons (PAHs)	Lung cancer, oral cancer Pulmonary disorders including bronchitis, asthma; worsening of preexisting conditions; Cardiovascular problems	Avoid smoking, especially indoors; extinguish cigarettes fully; maintain adequate ventilation; do not chew tobacco.
■ Building materials, furniture, and furnishings Asbestos insulation, covering, floor/ceiling tiles, asbestos fibers (not intact asbestos)	If inhaled, restricted pulmonary function, asbestosis, lung cancer, mesothelioma; powerful synergistic effect with smoking'	Don't try to remove friable asbestos; call licensed professional for encapsulation or removal
Formaldehyde gas from particle board, plywood, foam insulation, adhesives, permanent-press furnishings/clothes, and smoke	Eye, nose, and throat irritation, odor, allergy, respiratory cancer	Use materials low in formaldehyde; wash permanent-press clothes before use; maintain adequate air exchange rates

Table 12-1. Indoor Pollutants/Hazards and Prevention (*Continued*)

Source/hazard	Potential effects/symptoms	Prevention or exposure control
Lead in paints, piping, ceramics, and other sources (soil, water, airborne particulates); indoor and outdoor air	Myriad effects including abdominal pain, anemia, reproductive and CNS effects; children at high risk of learning disabilities	Don't attempt to remove lead paint; call licensed contractor; get tap water tested, especially if old home; run tap water 2 or 3 minutes before drinking especially if lead level is higher than 15 μg/L. Minimize use of lead crystal and dinnerware
■ Tap water Chlorination byproducts, e.g., trihalomethanes (THMs) including chloroform and carbon tetrachloride	CNS and liver effects Cancer	Install carbon filters and replace periodically
■ Dry-cleaned clothes Tetrachloroethylene (perchloroethylene)	Eye, nose, and throat irritation; nausea and dizziness; liver damage	Air out dry-cleaned clothes before hanging in closet
■ Skin irritants and allergens/sensitizers Nickel (jewelry), chromates, chlorinated hydrocarbons, isocyanates/urethanes, rubber and leather additives	Skin inflammation (contact dermatitis), hives, acne (contact dermatitis is the most common occupational disease) Respiratory problems, e.g., asthma	Avoid contact with suspected materials; use barrier creams and gloves
■ Pesticides Herbicides, fungicides, insecticides, rodenticides, e.g., organophosphates (malathion, parathion) can be absorbed through the skin	Wide-ranging effects including neurological, respiratory, gastrointestinal, liver, kidney, reproductive; allergy and cancer effects depending on composition, concentration, etc; many accidental or intentional poisonings	Minimize use; follow label directions strictly for use and disposal; buy just the required quantity to minimize storage and disposal. Use biological pesticides if available
■ Radon and its radioactive daughters (see footnote) Earth, rocks, building materials, and other sources—exposure primarily from inhaling airborne particles	Lung diseases such as emphysema, fibrosis, cancer. Smokers are at high risk	According to EPA, if tests show less than 4 picocuries radon per liter of air, no action is necessary; if more than 20 picocuries, consider building foundation vents, sealing floors/joints and other measures to reduce indoor levels
■ Biological agents/microorganisms Bacteria, viruses, fungi/molds, pollen present in air everywhere, e.g., air circulation systems, carpets (dust mites), bathrooms	Respiratory infections Skin diseases Allergies, e.g., asthma Allergic alveolitis ("humidifier fever" attributed to fungi) related to sick building syndrome	Maintain humidity at 40–50%; keep air conditioning system and humidifiers/dehumidifiers and air filters clean

Table 12-1. Indoor Pollutants/Hazards and Prevention (*Continued*)

Source/hazard	Potential effects/symptoms	Prevention or exposure control
■ Outdoor soil contaminants (lead and other metals, pesticides) brought indoors via shoes		Leave shoes out in garage, porch, or in a closet by front door
■ Food-borne diseases Bacteria Viruses Protozoa Fungi	Diarrhea, nausea, abdominal cramps, fever onset in half hour to several days after eating contaminated food	General hygiene such as wash hands before handling foods, store food at proper temperature (cool <40°F or hot >180°F), cook food thoroughly, avoid contact between cooked and raw foods, etc. See Table 12-8
■ Medicines, pesticides, poisons Accidental ingestion	Variety of symptoms including abnormal respiration and behavior	Keep first aid antidote such as ipecac syrup to induce vomiting (usually but not always recommended). Keep original bottles and labels; dispose long time unused per label instructions. Keep poison control center and family physician phone numbers visible and handy
■ Electromagnetic Fields (EMF) Nonionizing radiation Electrical transmission and wiring Electrical appliances, e.g., microwave oven, electric range, fluorescent lamps, television, hair dryer, shaver, electric blanket	Health effects not generally proved; leukemia and reproductive/developmental effects suspected	Field effects proportional to exposure time, declining rapidly with distance; a distance of 1 foot or more from appliance reduces exposure substantially
■ Sun ultraviolet (uv) rays	Skin cancer, cataracts	See Outdoor Exposures in text
■ Fire hazards	Fire, smoke, and heat	Install smoke alarms every level, test and change batteries periodically, keep fire and police phone handy, plan for emergencies
■ Noise (unwanted/undesirable sound) Sound levels >90 dBA; industrial sources, transportation, "music"	Annoyance, physiological changes, loss of hearing	Shut windows to block outside noise, wear ear protectors, limit exposure to short periods

House plants such as philodendrons, palms, corn, and chrysanthemum can help clear the air by absorbing or transforming gaseous pollutants.

Centers for Disease Control (CDC) estimates that 400,000 Americans die from smoking-related diseases, primarily from lung cancer and heart disease. EPA estimates that about 50,000 nonsmokers die from secondhand smoke: 35,000 to 40,000 from heart disease, 3000 to 5000 from cancer, and 5000 to 10,000 from other effects.

Radon is an odorless, invisible radioactive gas present naturally in some rocks and soils. From 200,000 to as many as 8 million houses are estimated to have relatively high radon levels. Radon accounts for about 55% of U.S. population exposure from all sources (360 mrem/year average). EPA estimates that radon exposure causes 7000 to 30,000 deaths each year.

sources and hazards, potential health effects and symptoms, and the actions we can take to prevent or control these exposures.

Outdoor Pollutants and Exposures

The outdoor ambient environment is composed of myriad chemicals, particulates, and radiation, emitted by a variety of sources including industrial facilities, power plants, transportation, waste storage and disposal sites, and natural phenomena. There is sufficient evidence to link chemical air pollutants, as well as natural and biological agents, to such chronic pulmonary diseases as asthma and bronchitis. The lung function suffers when resistance to air flow increases or when a loss of lung surface area reduces the transfer of oxygen to the blood.

The more dramatic and acute effects of air pollution stem from smog and inversion-related episodes. Although smog is a fairly common occurrence even today in some regions, the three classic episodes of air pollution occurred because of inversion caused by meteorologic conditions in which pollutants were trapped at the ground level. These three occurred in Meuse Valley, Belgium, in 1930, where 65 people were reported to have died; Donora, Pennsylvania, in 1948, where 20 people died; and in London, in 1952, where 4000 deaths were attributed to the episode. Most of these deaths were believed to have been caused by preexisting respiratory conditions that were aggravated by the pollution. These episodes undoubtedly spurred much of the subsequent air quality legislation in both the United States and Europe. Although air pollution today is implicated in health and quality of life issues in parts of North America, it tends to be a far more serious public health threat in Eastern Europe and in urban areas in South America and Asia.

Pursuant to the requirements of the Clean Air Act (CAA) Amendments and revisions of 1970 and 1977, the EPA established national ceiling levels for seven ubiquitous pollutants, known as the National Ambient Air Quality Standards (NAAQS). Transportation and power generation directly or indirectly generate the bulk of these pollutants. Two classes of ambient standards were established: primary standards designed to protect public health and secondary standards to protect environment and property, but there was not much difference between these standards (Table 12-2).

The Clean Air Act Amendments of 1990 vastly expanded the scope and coverage of air pollutants and generating sources, including toxic air emissions, acid rain, urban smog, and stratospheric ozone depletion. Title I of this act, "Provisions for Attainment and Maintenance of National Air Ambient Quality Standards," directs EPA to promulgate new or revised national air quality standards. Also of special interest is Title III, which lists 189 hazardous air pollutants (HAPs) to be regulated under the air toxics program. The full implications of these regulations are not yet clear, but a combination of technology-based stan-

Table 12-2. National Ambient Air Quality Standards (NAAQS)

Pollutant	Averaging time	Primary, $\mu g/m^3$	Secondary, $\mu g/m^3$
1. Carbon monoxide	8 hour	10,000	Same
	1 hour	40,000	
2. Sulfur dioxide	Annual	80	None
	24 hour	365	None
	3 hour	1,300	
3. Nitrogen dioxide	Annual	100	Same
4. Ozone	1 hour	235	Same
5. Lead	Quarterly	1.5	Same
6. Particulate matter (PM-10 ≤ 10 μm)	Annual	50	Same
	24 hour	150	

Hydrocarbons standard was revoked in 1983.

dards [e.g., maximum achievable control technology (MACT)] and risk criteria to address residual risk will probably be used in implementing the program.

While the quality of the nation's air is likely to continue to improve, individuals can take steps to reduce their exposure to outdoor air pollutants:

- Pay attention to air quality alerts and warnings—stay indoors with the windows closed during high pollution levels.
- If ozone or smog is a problem in your area, exercise in the early morning or evening.
- On days when pollution levels are high, do not exercise (when exercising an adult inhales 5 to 7 cubic meters of air per hour compared with less than 1 cubic meter while at rest).
- Do not exercise near high-traffic areas (running in urban areas for a half hour is equivalent to inhaling carbon monoxide from a pack of cigarettes).

Hazardous-Waste Sites and Public Health

Perception and Magnitude of Problem

According to public opinion polls, the American public ranks hazardous-waste sites (both active and abandoned) at the top of environmental problems and public health concerns. The wide publicity received by Love Canal (New York), Times Beach (Missouri), Woburn (Massachusetts), and such sites and situations undoubtedly had a strong influence on public perceptions (Fig. 12-2). However, many scientists do not share this view. Despite this divergence, hazardous-waste sites are at the center of intense regulatory effort.

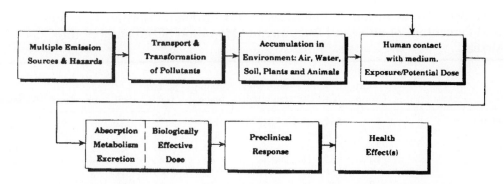

Figure 12-2. Multiple exposures to environmental pollutants and health effects. (*Based in part on Lioy, 1990.*)

Sources of hazardous materials, wastes, and releases are numerous and diverse; an estimated 250 to 300 million tons of hazardous waste are generated each year in the United States (more than 1 ton per capita). Uncontrolled hazardous-waste sites are a legacy of past and present practices. About 1275 hazardous-waste sites have been placed on the Superfund National Priorities List (NPL), and an additional 36,000 sites are in CERCLIS candidate inventory as of March 1992. Overall, there may be as many as a half million sites, including leaking underground storage tanks (LUSTs), mining waste sites, pesticide contaminated sites, underground injection wells, and federal facilities, among others. According to an EPA survey, nearly 4 million people live within 1 mile of a Superfund site. The NPL and other waste sites contain a variety of contaminants ("toxic soup"), but a principal reason for the listing, via the hazard ranking system, is existing or potential impacts on groundwater (Table 12-3). The reason is straightforward and persuasive. Half the U.S. population and 95% of the rural population depend on groundwater as their main source of drinking water. Not so simple is the determination of potential impacts; experience to date indicates that the enormous resources directed at groundwater remediation are grossly out of proportion to the magnitude of risks or expected benefits. However, a National Research Council (NRC) committee makes a counterpoint: "Although current public health burdens from hazardous-waste sites appear to be small, the future risk might be greater insofar as many of the substances involved are highly persistent, and other materials already in the groundwater can migrate into areas where exposure potential is greater." (NRC: Environmental Epidemiology—Public Health and Hazardous Wastes, 1991, p. 20.)

Reported health problems associated with exposure to hazardous-waste site contaminated media include self-reported symptoms, reproductive effects (e.g., fertility, birth defects), congenital cardiac anomalies, neurobehavioral problems, and childhood leukemia. The specific contribution of hazardous-waste sites to these problems is difficult to establish because of many confounding variables such as smoking, alcohol, drugs, diet, occupational exposures, and socioeconomic factors. (Socioeconomic status, including poverty, is generally

Table 12-3. Selected Hazardous Substances at 951 National Priorities List Sites: Number and Percentage of Sites and Documented Migration of Substances into Specific Media

	ATSDR Priority Group	No	%	Sites with migration	Ground-water	Surface water	Soil	Air	Food	Sediment
Metallic elements		564	59	327	234	138	122	37	50	114
Lead	1	404	43	224	159	84	88	28	39	84
Chromium	1	329	35	142	93	55	48	12	15	46
Arsenic	1	262	28	36	92	46	54	16	19	50
Cadmium	1	232	24	112	72	49	45	18	21	44
Mercury	2	129	14	58	29	24	20	6	10	19
Nickel	1	126	13	55	30	24	15	3	8	21
Beryllium	1	21	2	9	2	3	1	0	0	3
Volatile organic compounds (VOCs)		518	54	268	236	88	81	71	31	58
Trichloroethylene	1	402	42	231	204	63	41	44	19	27
Benzene	1	323	34	139	115	41	27	29	9	24
Tetrachloroethylene	1	267	28	125	116	28	22	34	11	17
Toluene	2	256	27	101	78	26	29	26	6	20
Vinyl chloride	1	187	20	87	80	16	14	18	7	9
Methylene chloride	1	183	19	81	61	21	16	17	4	9
Chloroform	1	142	15	74	61	20	8	7	3	9
1,4-Dichlorobenzene	1	31	3	7	6	0	1	1	0	1
Polychlorinated biphenyls (PCBs)	1	162	17	86	43	25	40	11	25	39
Polycyclic aromatic hydro-carbons (PAH)		187	20	75	32	22	31	4	6	38
Benzo(a)pyrene	1	56	6	18	6	6	9	0	2	8
Benzo(a)anthracene	1	32	3	10	3	4	8	0	1	6
Benzo(a)fluoroanthene	1	25	3	10	1	3	5	0	0	4
Chrysene	1	23	2	6	2	1	3	0	1	4
Dibenzo(a,h)anthracene	1	4	<1	1	0	0	1	0	0	0
Phthalates		106	11	35	22	13	17	5	5	16
Bis(2-ethylhexyl)phthalate	1	88	9	35	22	13	16	3	5	16
Pesticides		82	9	25	13	8	17	6	7	12
Dieldrin/aldrin	1	29	3	13	8	2	6	3	2	3
Heptachlor/heptachlor epoxide	1	15	2	4	2	0	1	0	0	1
Dioxins		47	5	21	8	7	16	2	7	11
2,3,7,8-Tetrachloro-dibenzo-*p*-dioxin	1	19	2	15	5	3	8	3	7	10
Other										
Cyanide	1	74	8	23	13	9	7	3	2	8
N-Nitrosodiphenylamine	1	8	1	4	2	1	2	0	1	2

SOURCE: National Research Council: Environmental Epidemiology, 1991. Adapted from ATSDR.

the highest risk factor.) Some estimates of cancer incidence from hazardous-waste site exposure put it on the order of a hundred or so, but there are no reliable data to confirm this estimate.

The Agency for Toxic Substances and Disease Registry (ATSDR, U.S. Public Health Service) was created in 1980 by Superfund legislation. Its mission is to prevent or mitigate adverse human health effects from exposure to hazardous substances in the environment through surveillance, registries, health studies, education, and health advisories. The agency conducts public health assessments for all the Superfund NPL sites; it can also be petitioned to conduct assessments for other sites. The agency uses environmental data (contaminants, toxicity, exposure pathways), health data (communitywide disease compared with state and national rates), and community concerns (quality of life) for the health assessments. EPA and ATSDR have developed a priority list of over 200 hazardous substances found at Superfund sites based on toxicity, frequency of occurrence, and exposure potential. Toxicological profiles have been developed for about half of these and the agency is trying to fill the data gaps in collaboration with the National Institute of Environmental Health Sciences (NIEHS). Basic toxicity data for high-production-volume chemicals are also being developed by Organization for Economic Cooperation and Development (OECD) members under a voluntary program known as Screening Information Data Set or SIDS (see Chap. 11 for more detail). At the Superfund sites, ATSDR issues health advisories such as source removal, access restrictions, resident relocation, and follow-up studies.

Epidemiology

Epidemiology is the study of occurrence of disease, injuries, and other health effects in populations, and the causes and means of prevention. Environmental epidemiology is the study of the effects on human health of biologic, chemical, and physical factors in the external environment.

Epidemiologists conduct two major types of studies to assess the relationship between suspected risk factors and disease: descriptive (e.g., cross-sectional, ecological) and analytical (retrospective, prospective—see Fig. 12-3). Cross-sectional studies provide a snapshot of a given area of both disease and risk factors at one point in time—for example, the National Health Survey that examined the prevalence of heart disease and cholesterol levels, or studies to determine whether there are "pockets" or "clusters" of disease. While easy to conduct, cross-sectional surveys lack the temporal sequence necessary to demonstrate cause-effect relationship. Ecological studies (not to be confused with ecological risk assessment of Chap. 11) generally involve comparisons of disease rates among groups living within specific geographic areas, for example, within a 1-mile radius of a waste site vs. people living farther away. Like cross-sectional studies, ecological studies explore associations and tend to be hypothesis-generating rather than hypothesis-testing in nature.

• Epidemiology: Study of occurrence of disease/injuries in populations, their causes and prevention

• Three basic Study designs: Retrospective, Prospective, Retrospective cohort (historic prospective)

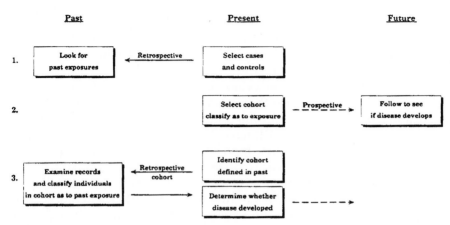

Figure 12-3. Epidemiology study designs.

In retrospective case-control studies, cases with disease are matched against healthy controls drawn from the same population, and past exposures are investigated through records, registries (e.g., cancer, birth defects), questionnaires, and interviews to determine whether past exposures could have resulted in the development of disease. For example, in a case-control study of lung cancer (effect) and smoking (risk factor), cases with lung cancer are compared with controls without lung cancer and their past smoking histories are examined. A measure of relative risk from smoking is provided by the ratio of lung cancer incidence among smokers vs. nonsmokers. Case-control studies need only a few subjects and can be carried out quickly and inexpensively, although past exposures are often difficult to reconstruct, and biased recall and selection of controls pose a problem.

Prospective cohort studies start with a healthy group of exposed and unexposed persons who are tracked into the future for the development of disease, as in the Framingham heart study. (A cohort is a group of people with common experience such as birth year, occupation, or specific exposure to an agent.) Cohort studies can be designed to detect specific outcomes, even with rare exposures, but tend to be costly because of the large number of subjects, long follow-up period, and problems of attrition, and may also be unethical in some situations.

Causation. Several epidemiological studies of hazardous-waste sites (and other risk factors) have been conducted but few, if any, proved conclusive (see, for instance, NRC's Environmental Epidemiology, 1991, and the accompanying box). This is disconcerting, given that epidemiology studies are expensive, cost-

Epidemiological Study of Hazardous-Waste Sites

Environmental epidemiology studies of hazardous-waste sites sometimes succeed in establishing a correlation but seldom a cause-effect relationship. The most common study designs are cross-sectional/ecological and retrospective case-control that usually begin with identification of disease "clusters." An example of the former is a recent study titled "Risk of Congenital Malformations Associated with Proximity to Hazardous Waste Sites" conducted jointly by researchers at Yale University and the Bureau of Environmental and Occupational Epidemiology of New York State Department of Health (Sandra Geschwind et al., *American Journal of Epidemiology*, vol. 135, no. 11, 1992).

An innovative feature of the study is the linking of two large existing databases of NYSDOH, the Congenital Malformation Registry and the Hazardous Waste Site Inspection Program. A total of 9313 newborns with birth defects (cases) and 17,802 healthy controls living in proximity of 590 hazardous-waste sites in New York State were evaluated. The study used an "exposure risk index" incorporating the distance and the hazard ranking score for each site within a 1 mile radius of the birth residence. Birth defects were placed into seven categories using the International Classification of Diseases, ninth revision (ICD-9) and included oral clefts; nervous, integument, musculoskeletal and digestive system defects; chromosomal abnormalities; and syndromes.

Overall, the results indicated a small but statistically significant increase associated with maternal residence proximity to hazardous-waste sites, with an odds ratio of 1:12, i.e., 12% increase, 95% confidence interval (CI 1.06 to 1.18). The results also showed a dose-response relation of malformations associated with waste-site characteristics. The large size of the study population by database linkage increased the statistical power to identify small health effects. Nevertheless, the study shared many of the limitations of cross-sectional studies. Exposure assessment was indirect; no environmental or biological monitoring was conducted to verify exposure. Confounding variables such as smoking, preexisting disease, alcohol, maternal and paternal occupational exposures, and nutritional status were not controlled for. A follow-up study by NYSDOH, with funding from ATSDR, is under way to determine the probability of mothers' exposure through RI/FS pathway data, meteorological conditions, etc. This information could serve to verify the inferences about causality.

ing $1 to $2 million or more. Part of the problem is that they lack the power of statistical significance; by convention, the results should have a likelihood of 5% or less of occurring by chance to be statistically significant. The advent of meta-analyses, a technique that provides a framework for pooling related studies including risk assessments and ATSDR health assessments, may in the future strengthen our ability to draw better inferences about health outcomes. Also, "molecular epidemiology" based on laboratory assays of human tissues and biologic fluids can yield corroborative evidence on exposure—for example, cellular responses or early markers of carcinogen exposure including levels of covalent adducts and micronuclei.

The Need for Action

Available evidence thus suggests that the public health effects from hazardous wastes have been relatively modest to date, but we do not yet have adequate data to conclude that this will remain so (the absence of proof does not necessarily mean the proof of absence). To resolve this predilection and to play it safe, we need to provide insurance for the future and yet not divert resources from proven public health threats. We need to:

- Consider opportunity costs of alternative investments in environment and public health

- Establish a coordinated system of site discovery (and a national inventory of hazardous-waste sites) that integrates public health concerns with the study and remediation aspects

- Develop a surveillance mechanism of sentinel events that provide early warning (including birds or other animals and effects that have a shorter latency than cancers)

- Set up joint task forces of state environmental and health departments, which typically have diverse mandates

- Devise a method to generate and share data in the face of burgeoning toxic tort claims

Ionizing Radiation and Health Effects

Universal Radiation and the Unstable Atom

Radiation, the emission of radiant energy, goes back to the big bang that gave birth to the universe some 20 billion years ago and the earth 4.5 billion years ago. Radioactive materials such as uranium and thorium became part of the earth at its very formation. We are all slightly radioactive since all living tissues contain traces of radioactive substances.

Ionizing radiation is high-frequency, short-wavelength radiation from cosmic rays to ultraviolet rays with sufficient energy to displace electrons from atoms and convert them into ions—charged atoms or molecules (see Fig. 12-4). Nonionizing radiation includes infrared, radio, visible light, and other low frequencies.

One source of radiation is unstable atoms, called radioactive atoms, radionuclides, or radioisotopes. To become more stable, the nuclei eject or emit subatomic particles (alpha and beta) or high-energy photons (gamma rays), in a process called radioactive decay. Unstable atoms of radium and uranium occur naturally, while others are made by human activities as when uranium-235 atoms are split or fissioned in nuclear reactors to release energy.

Different forms of radiation have different energies and penetrating power and hence affect us differently (Fig. 12-5). Alpha particles (helium with two protons and two neutrons) are heavy and energetic but lose energy quickly as they travel and can barely penetrate the outer dead layer of human skin. However, they can be harmful if inhaled or ingested or if they enter the body through open wounds. Beta particles or electrons are fast-moving and may penetrate the outer layers of skin but do less damage than alpha over equal distances. Gamma rays are packets of energy called photons and, traveling at the speed of light, penetrate just about anything short of a slab of lead several inches thick or a few feet of concrete. X-rays are also composed of photons, similar to gamma rays but lower in energy, and originate outside the atomic nucleus. Two measures of radioactivity are Becquerel, corresponding to one disintegration per second, and Curie, corresponding to 3.7×10^{10} disintegrations per second.

Sources of Radiation Exposure, and Health Effects

Natural radiation coming from cosmic rays, naturally occurring radioactive elements, and their decay products (especially radon) represents four-fifths of the exposure of the general population in the United States (Fig. 12-6). Radon-222, an odorless, invisible gas from uranium-238 decay series, accounts for more than half of total radiation and two-thirds of natural radiation. Radon is the second leading cause of lung cancer; EPA estimates that radon causes between 7000 and 30,000 deaths each year. Radon is clearly a significant public health threat that the public is reluctant to concede, but one that can be tackled with relatively modest resources.

A significant part of natural radiation comes from cosmic rays originating deep in interstellar space and some from the sun. People living in high altitudes and airline crews receive relatively high exposures.

Medical applications, including diagnostic and therapeutic x-rays, are the largest source of man-made exposure. Consumer products such as luminous-dial watches and clocks and smoke detectors also contain radioactive materials. Internal dose sources include potassium-40, lead-210, and polonium-210 that enter the body mainly through the food we eat.

Radiation exposure is commonly expressed in rem (roentgen equivalent man) or millirems (mrem). Average exposure in the United States is estimated at 360 mrem per year. There is an interim agreement among international agencies [International Commission on Radiological Protection (ICRIP)] and a number of

EM Phenomena	Examples of Uses	Approximate Frequency Range
Cosmic rays	Physics, astronomy	10^{14} GHz and above
Gamma rays	Cancer therapy	$10^{10} - 10^{13}$ GHz
X-rays	X-ray examination	$10^8 - 10^9$ GHz
Ultraviolet radiation	Sterilization	$10^6 - 10^8$ GHz
Visible light	Human vision	$10^5 - 10^6$ GHz
Infrared radiation	Photography	$10^3 - 10^4$ GHz
Microwave waves	Radar, microwave relays, satellite communication	3–300 GHz
Radio waves	UHF television	470–806 MHz
	VHF television, FM radio	54–216 MHz
	Short-wave radio	3–26 MHz
	AM radio	535–1,605 kHz

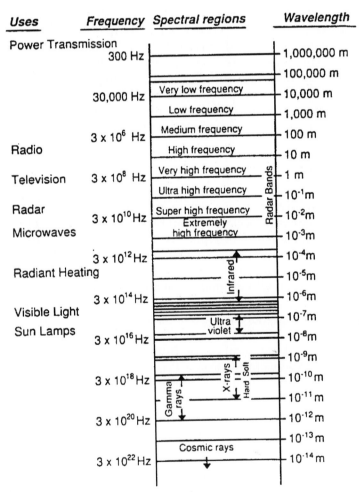

Figure 12-4. Electromagnetic spectrum. (*EPRI.*)

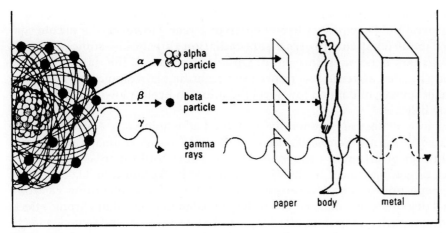

Figure 12-5. Types of radiation and their penetrating power. (*UNEP Radiation, "Doses, Effects, Risks."*)

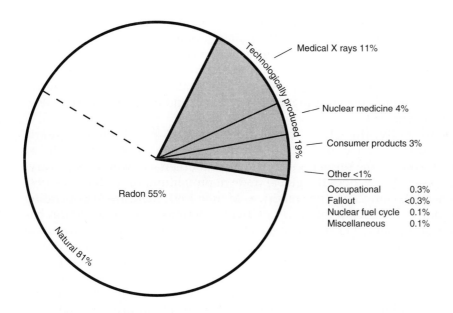

Average individual exposure in the United States 360 mrem/year.

Figure 12-6. Sources of public radiation exposure.

countries that occupational exposures should be limited to 5000 mrem (5 rem) and general public exposure to 500 mrem in a year. However, the debate continues about what constitutes a safe radiation threshold—some scientists believe there is no such threshold. On the other hand, the data published recently by the Lawrence Livermore team regarding Hiroshima and Nagasaki, the main sources of data on low-level radiation, indicate a lower risk than previously believed.

Radiation exposure is generally expressed as whole-body equivalent dose weighted for the differences of different radiations to cause damage and the susceptibilities of different tissues. A dose of 1 rem could increase a person's chance of getting cancer by 0.03% or from 30% background to 30.03%. Large acute exposure to radiation can cause radiation sickness including gastrointestinal disorders, anemia, and electrolyte imbalance; delayed or chronic effects include cataracts, temporary sterility, skin lesions, cancer, and genetic effects. High acute doses can result in death in a few hours or days.

General public exposure to dangerous radiation levels from U.S. nuclear power plants seems unlikely, but significant environmental and public health risks continue from the nuclear weapons facilities such as Savannah River (South Carolina), Rocky Flats (Colorado), and Hanford (Washington). There are also questions and concerns about the building of a repository for high-level waste, and disposal of low-level waste, as well as the decommissioning of old nuclear facilities. (Nuclear power supplied almost 22% of electricity in the United States in 1991. Fossil fuel power generation also poses significant health risks, which point to the need to intensify research and development of renewable energy sources.)

Internationally, the Chernobyl accident in 1986 provided a dramatic reminder that such accidents do not respect national boundaries. The 42 nuclear reactors in the former Soviet Union, and others elsewhere, pose varying degrees of risk, as does the global trade in plutonium. According to a 1991 U.S. General Accounting Office report, as of June 1991, there are 412 operating nuclear power reactors in the world of diverse designs. The United States has the highest number, 111 operating and 8 under construction, followed by France's 55 operating and 7 under construction. The International Atomic Energy Agency, the World Association of Nuclear Operators (established after the Chernobyl accident), and the U.S. Nuclear Regulatory Commission have been involved in efforts to improve international nuclear safety. Moreover, the ironic by-product of the peace process itself presents unprecedented risks involving the destruction of nuclear, chemical, and biological weapons; this will require talent and resources that may well exceed those needed for their creation in the first place.

Sun's Ultraviolet Radiation and Cancer

A second, perhaps more insidious, risk (albeit prized in some circles) is ultraviolet (uv) rays from the sun. Ozone in the upper atmosphere (stratosphere) screens out radiation. As a result of ozone depletion or the "ozone hole," the risks of cancer and cataracts are expected to escalate. Each 1% decrease in ozone layer is believed to result in 3 to 6% increase in skin cancer. Higher exposure to uv radiation can also lower the productivity of sensitive plant species. (Stratospheric ozone that acts as a radiation shield is sometimes referred to as good ozone or "gozone," and the lower atmosphere or troposphere ozone that acts directly as a powerful oxidant and lung irritant is called bad ozone or "bozone.")

In 1991, there were an estimated 600,000 new cases of nonmelanoma skin cancer, and 32,000 cases of the more serious malignant melanoma in the United States. The sun's ultraviolet radiation (in the 280 to 315 nanometer range called uv-B) is thought to damage or mutate gene p53, the same gene damage that is implicated in colon, lung, breast, and other cancers (p53 is one of a class of "guardian genes" that control cell growth). Light-skinned people and children are particularly vulnerable. Here are some protective actions we can take to reduce the risk of cancer and cataracts:

Reducing risk of skin cancer and cataract:

- Avoid excessive exposure to sun, especially in summer between 10 A.M. and 3 P.M.; stay in shade if possible.
- Wear sun screen with a sun protection factor (SPF) of 15 when outdoors.
- Wear hat and long sleeves; cover the body to the extent practical.
- Wear dark eyeglasses specially treated to block uv rays.

Other Public Health Threats

Tobacco Smoking and Chewing

Despite some successes in this arena and the expanding smoke-cessation programs and smoke-free offices, tobacco smoking and chewing remain the number one avoidable public health threat. Smoking has declined among men but has been going up among women and especially teenagers (25 million American women smoke); this portends a more serious problem ahead because of the early start. Smoking has been increasing in much of the rest of the world in men and women as the marketing efforts of tobacco companies have turned to these areas. (Worldwide, more than 3 million die of smoking each year.)

Tobacco smoke contains thousands of hazardous compounds including carbon monoxide, polycyclic aromatic hydrocarbons, heavy metals, radionuclides, etc. Professor Bernard Weinstein of Columbia University Comprehensive Cancer Center calls a pack of cigarettes "Do-It-Yourself Cancer Kit." The multiple and synergistic effects of smoking, both cancer and noncancer, have been well documented. The Centers for Disease Control (CDC) estimates that 400,000 Americans die from smoking-related afflictions each year, primarily from heart disease and lung cancer. The EPA estimates that about 50,000 nonsmokers die from second-hand or passive smoke, 35,000 to 40,000 from heart disease, and the others from cancer and other effects. Passive smoke itself is now considered a carcinogen.

What all this means is that we need to capitalize on the positive momentum and launch a concerted program with the participation of public health professionals, industry, government, educational institutions, the media, and opinion leaders to "catch them young."

Lead

The adverse effects of lead have been known since Roman times. The decline of the Roman empire is sometimes ascribed to the intentional or unintentional contamination of wine by lead or litharge (the acetic acid in sour wine is converted to the sweet-tasting lead acetate). High levels of lead in blood are associated with a variety of ill effects including mental retardation, neurological problems, reproductive effects, hypertension, and brain and kidney damage. Unlike many other metals, there is no known physiological function or safe threshold for lead. Children are particularly vulnerable to lead's toxic effects. Children absorb 40 to 45% of lead from the oral route compared with 5 to 15% by adults; absorption of respirable particles from inhalation is virtually complete.

Lead is distributed throughout the environment in lead-based paint, air, soil and dust, some types of pottery, and food and water. Exposure to lead can thus occur via multiple pathways: air, food, and water and accidental ingestion of peeled paint or soil containing lead. The biggest source of lead in air is vehicle exhaust, although the switch to unleaded gasoline has reduced air concentrations by as much as 90%. Major sources of occupational exposures are battery reclamation, smelting, welding, and lead paint removal. Lead in air is carried by wind and rain and deposited on land and water.

Major sources of lead in drinking water are lead plumbing and solder that connect service lines to the water main. Drinking water accounts for 15 to 20% of total exposure to lead. The EPA drinking water action level at the tap has been reduced to 15 µg lead/liter of water (15 ppb) or 0.015 mg/liter. Steps we can take to reduce exposure to lead in drinking water include: (1) test water from the tap drawn in the morning to determine lead level; (2) let water run from the tap a few minutes before drinking or cooking any time the water was not drawn for several hours; (3) don't cook with hot water from the tap, which dissolves lead more quickly than cold water; (4) drink bottled water; and (5) replace lead plumbing. You may also want to discuss with your pediatrician performing a blood test for lead.

Lead poisoning is one of the most common pediatric health problems, especially among poor children. In 1991, the Centers for Disease Control, citing overwhelming scientific evidence of adverse effects at blood levels as low as 10 µg/dl in children, revised the intervention level downward from 25 to 10 µg/dl.

In the new multitier approach, children with blood lead in the 10 to 14 µg/dl range should receive more frequent screening, and communitywide prevention should be initiated. Children in the 15 to 19 range should receive nutritional and educational intervention. For children with blood lead levels over 45 µg/dl, chelation therapy is suggested; the FDA approved Succimer in 1991 as an oral chelating agent.

In 1992, the Federal Health Care Financing Administration that supervises Medicaid directed the states to screen all children under six for lead poisoning; more than six million children under age six are on Medicaid and half of them may be suffering from some level of lead poisoning. One of the problems in screening is that the old erythrocyte protoporphyrin test is not sensitive or accurate enough for levels below 25 µg/dl and a more sensitive, direct blood lead test is needed. In parallel with this massive screening and treatment effort targeted at high-risk children, we should move forward with primary prevention to eliminate this persistent public health problem (Department of Health and Human Services, "Strategic Plan for the Elimination of Childhood Lead Poisoning," 1991).

Childhood Viral and Bacterial Diseases

Immunizations against such diseases as diphtheria, pertussis, tetanus (DPT), polio, measles, and rubella have made remarkable progress in combating childhood diseases, though it is generally taken for granted. Figure 12-7 shows the different types of diseases and the immunization schedules for primary prevention. Vaccines carry a small risk of undesirable reactions, but the benefits

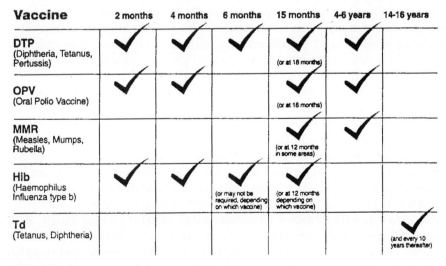

Vaccine	2 months	4 months	6 months	15 months	4-6 years	14-16 years
DTP (Diphtheria, Tetanus, Pertussis)	✓	✓	✓	✓ (or at 18 months)	✓	
OPV (Oral Polio Vaccine)	✓	✓		✓ (or at 18 months)	✓	
MMR (Measles, Mumps, Rubella)				✓ (or at 12 months in some areas)	✓	
Hib (Haemophilus Influenza type b)	✓	✓	✓ (or may not be required, depending on which vaccine)	✓ (or at 12 months depending on which vaccine)		
Td (Tetanus, Diphtheria)						✓ (and every 10 years thereafter)

Figure 12-7. Childhood immunizations. (*Centers for Disease Control.*)

outweigh the risks by far. Following the vaccine product liability crisis of the 1980s, a central fund was created, funded by vaccine sales, to compensate those affected by adverse reactions. Merck and Lederle (division of American Cyanamid) are among the leading suppliers of vaccines, which are an indispensable component of public health.

Nutrition, Lifestyle, and Health

The Dietary Connection

In recent years the growing evidence in support of the role of diet in chronic diseases paralleled public interest in "holistic" health and more active personal involvement. However, the plethora of information and advice that emerged proved confusing and often misleading. To address this issue, and to provide practical guidance to the public, the National Research Council's (NRC) Food and Nutrition Board established a Committee on Diet and Health. (NRC is an arm of the National Academy of Sciences, a nonprofit organization of distinguished scientists and engineers.) The committee conducted a detailed analysis of available scientific data on the role of diet in the etiology and prevention of major chronic diseases, and issued a comprehensive report titled "Diet and Health—Implications for Reducing Chronic Disease Risk" (1989–1990).

Based on a comprehensive review of epidemiological, clinical, and laboratory data, the committee concluded that the evidence for a dietary role is very strong for cardiovascular diseases and highly suggestive for some forms of cancer including colon, prostate, and breast. (For example, the breast cancer rate is relatively low in Japan, where typically 15 to 20% of calories come from dietary fat, but Japanese immigrants to the United States reach the same rate as Americans—one in nine or ten American women develops breast cancer.) Diet and obesity are also found to influence the risk of diabetes mellitus and liver disease. Nutritional factors also play a role in chronic degenerative diseases such as arthritis, and undoubtedly in allergic diseases.

These findings are of immense interest inasmuch as cardiovascular diseases and cancers are the predominant causes of morbidity and mortality in the United States. Of the approximately 2.1 million deaths per year from all causes, cardiovascular diseases (including cerebrovascular incidents such as strokes) account for about 43%, and cancers about 24%, together representing two-thirds of total deaths (Table 12-4). Important to note also is the overlap between the risk factors, e.g., fat intake, obesity, and tobacco smoking. In other words, adoption of better dietary and behavioral patterns can simultaneously reduce the risk of the two leading causes of modern day mortality and morbidity. According to Bruce Ames of the University of California at Berkeley, developer of the Ames Mutagenicity Test, three-fourths of human cancers are preventable through a combination of good dietary and lifestyle practices.

Table 12-4. Causes of Death in the United States, 1990

	Total (thousands)	%	Annual risk (per million)*
All causes	2146	100	8618
■ Cardiovascular diseases (including cerebrovascular)	914	42.6	3671
■ Cancer (malignant neoplasms)	502	23.4	2016
■ Chronic obstructive pulmonary diseases	88	4.1	353
■ Pneumonia	76	3.5	305
■ Diabetes	49	2.3	197
■ Liver diseases	25	1.2	100
■ All other diseases	343	16.0	1374
■ Suicide	31	1.4	124
■ Homicide	25	1.2	100
■ Accidents	93	4.3	373
Motor vehicle	46	2.1	184
Falls	12	0.6	48
Poisons	6	0.3	24
All others	29	1.3	116

SOURCES: National Safety Council, National Center for Health Statistics, U.S. Department of Health and Human Services (provisional data).

*Population in the United States approximately 250 million in 1990. The risk shown is annual risk per million, not individual lifetime risk.

Nutritional Suggestions to Reduce Risk of Chronic Diseases

	Heart disease	Stroke	Cancer	Diabetes	Gastrointestinal diseases*
Reduce fats	x	x	x	x	x
Control total calories	x	x	x	x	x
Increase complex carbohydrates and fiber			x	x	x
Reduce sodium	x	x			
Control alcohol		x	x		x

SOURCE: U.S. Public Health Service.

*Gastrointestinal diseases include gallbladder disease (fat), diverticular disease (fiber), and cirrhosis (alcohol). Although not shown here, smoking is a powerful risk factor for both heart disease and cancer.

The Case for a Step Backward

The body's energy needs depend on many factors including age, gender, and physical activity. Carbohydrates and fats, and to a limited extent protein, provide the energy. Protein and macrominerals are building materials, while vitamins and trace elements catalyze and regulate the numerous biochemical and metabolic processes. The usable energy in food is measured in kilocalories or simply calories. Most adults need 1300 to 1800 calories for basic metabolism such as maintaining body temperature, repairing organs, and maintaining heartbeat and breathing. With age, the basal metabolic rate as well as activity level tends to decline. The caloric requirements for three different groups are shown in the accompanying box.

Energy Requirements

Older adults and sedentary women	1600 calories/day
Teenage girls, active women, sedentary men	2200
Teenage boys and active men	2800

Fats	9 calories/gram
Protein	4 calories/gram
Carbohydrates	4 calories/gram
(Alcohol	7 calories/gram)

On average, American men eat 2360 to 2640 calories a day, and women 1640 to 1800 calories a day. Contrary to popular belief, we are not eating more calories than our forefathers did. In fact we are taking in fewer calories, 10% less on average than in 1970. However, as a nation, we have gained weight and the fat stores have expanded, presumably because of less activity (partly due to the influence of television).

Being overweight is different from being obese. Overweight indicates excess weight for a given height above a standard. Obesity means a high amount of body fat compared with muscle and bone. The distribution of fat may also be important; abdominal fat is believed to pose a higher risk of some cancers than fat deposits elsewhere in the body.

Although we have not increased our total calorie intake, the mix of food sources has shifted. Today, we are consuming some 30% more fat, and more sugars, and less complex carbohydrates than in the early 1900s (see Fig. 12-8). In fact, the NRC and the U.S. Department of Agriculture (USDA) dietary guidelines outlined in the following section appear to have a lot in common with practices at the turn of the century.

Nutritional Guidelines

NRC's nine dietary guidelines, as well as American Heart Association (AHA) and American Cancer Society (ACS) guidelines, are shown in accompanying

Table 12-5. Suggested Weights for Adults, in Pounds

Height	19 to 34 years women–men	35 years and over women–men
5'0"	97–128	108–138
5'1"	101–132	111–143
5'2"	104–137	115–148
5'3"	107–141	119–152
5'4"	111–146	122–157
5'5"	114–150	126–162
5'6"	118–155	130–167
5'7"	121–160	134–172
5'8"	125–164	138–178
5'9"	129–169	142–183
5'10"	132–174	146–188
5'11"	136–179	151–194
6'0"	140–184	155–199
6'1"	144–189	159–205
6'2"	148–195	164–210
6'3"	152–200	168–216
6'4"	156–205	173–222
6'5"	160–211	177–228
6'6"	164–216	182–234

SOURCE: U.S. Department of Health and Human Services and U.S. Department of Agriculture.

Height is without shoes and weight without clothes. The lower weights in the ranges apply to women who tend to have less muscle and bone than men; the higher weights are more applicable to men.

tables and charts for ready reference. The hallmark of good nutrition is still variety, balance, and moderation. The new user-friendly food labels should help consumers plan meals better. The common thread of less fat intake in both AHA and ACS guidelines is obvious. Three major groups of chronic diseases: cardiovascular, cancer, and diabetes, their risk factors, and preventive steps, including diet, are discussed below.

Cardiovascular Diseases

Cardiovascular and cerebrovascular diseases have declined somewhat in recent years but are still the leading cause of death by far in the United States. Several population studies worldwide including the famous Framingham study (Framingham, Massachusetts) amply demonstrated the modern origins and the link between diet and the risk of heart disease.

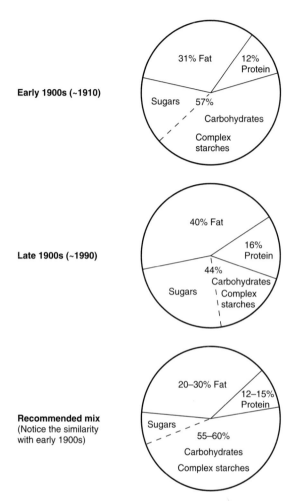

Figure 12-8. Trends in sources of food calories. *Fats:* 20 to 30% (one-third each saturated, monounsaturated, and polyunsaturated fatty acids). *Carbohydrates:* 55 to 60% (mostly complex carbohydrates rather than simple sugars). *Protein:* 10 to 15% (complete protein of plant and animal origin).

Cholesterol as a risk factor has been well publicized, but some confusion still exists about the terminology. Cholesterol, a fat derivative needed by the body, is found only in animal products whereas fats are found in both animal and plant products. About 80% of cholesterol in the human body is actually synthesized by our cells from carbohydrates and is not derived from dietary sources. Cholesterol is transported through the blood by carriers known as low-density lipoproteins (LDL) and high-density lipoproteins (HDL). LDL is the major car-

---

Risk Factors for Heart Disease

Family history (genetic predisposition)

Cholesterol level (>200 mg/dl)

Smoking

Hypertension (blood pressure >140/90 mmHg)

Previous heart attack

Diabetes

Obesity

Male sex (and postmenopausal women with low estrogen levels)

Stress

SOURCE: American Heart Association.

---

rier in blood; some LDL cholesterol is used by the liver (which also makes cholesterol) and some by tissues to form cell membranes, hormones, and other products, but most of it circulates in the bloodstream. Too much LDL cholesterol circulating in the blood, when oxidized, can form plaque and lead to atherosclerosis and clogged arteries—hence its reputation as "bad cholesterol." (Therefore, antioxidants such as vitamins A, beta carotene, C, and E and the mineral selenium can be protective against both vascular disorders and cancers.) HDL tends to carry cholesterol away from arteries to the liver where it is passed from the body and thus is protective against atherosclerosis—hence the "good cholesterol." An HDL level higher than 35 mg/dl and a high HDL/LDL ratio is therefore desirable. Monounsaturated fat (e.g., olive oil) and polyunsaturated fat (e.g., safflower, corn, and fish oils) tend to lower blood cholesterol, whereas saturated fat, usually of animal origin and solid at room temperature (e.g., butter) tends to increase the cholesterol level. In addition to LDL, a high level of triglycerides (most fats exist in this form) may also pose a risk of heart disease.

Blood serum cholesterol, mg/dl	Classification
160–200	Desirable
200–240	Borderline high
>240	High

Optimal cholesterol level (HDL and LDL) is probably in the 160 to 180 mg/dl range; the results of a large Multiple Risk Factor Intervention Trial that came to be known as MR. FIT indicate that lower than 160 mg/dl may increase the risk of some other disorders such as liver disease and hemorrhage. In people with high cholesterol levels, each 1% reduction in cholesterol is expected to lead to a 2% reduction in the risk of heart disease. Although it is generally advisable to limit dietary intake of cholesterol to less than 300 mg a day, there is no direct relationship between dietary intake and blood levels or the incidence of coronary heart disease, since genetics, physical activity, total calorie intake, and other lifestyle factors are also important influences.

Warning signs of heart attack

1. Uncomfortable pressure, fullness, squeezing, or pain in the center of the chest lasting for 2 minutes or more.
2. Pain spreading to the shoulders, neck, jaw, arms, or back.
3. Lightheadedness, fainting, sweating, nausea, and/or shortness of breath.

If you or someone you know shows the symptoms of a heart attack:

1. Call the emergency medical service system. Depending on your community, this could be the fire department or ambulance service.
2. If you can get the victim to the hospital more quickly by driving yourself, do so. If you think you are having a heart attack, don't drive—ask someone to drive you. Go to the nearest medical facility with 24-hour emergency cardiac care.
3. If necessary and if you are properly trained, give CPR (mouth-to-mouth breathing and chest compression) while you are waiting for an emergency vehicle to arrive.

SOURCE: American Heart Association.

National Research Council's Nine Dietary Guidelines

1. Reduce total fat intake to 30% or less of your total calorie consumption. Reduce saturated fatty acid intake to less than 10% of calories. Reduce cholesterol intake to less than 300 milligrams (mg) daily.
2. Eat five or more servings of a combination of vegetables and fruits daily, especially green and yellow vegetables and citrus fruits. Also, increase your intake of starches and other complex carbohydrates by eating six or more daily servings of a combination of breads, cereals, and legumes.
3. Eat a reasonable amount of protein, maintaining your protein consumption at moderate levels.
4. Balance the amount of food you eat with the amount of exercise you get to maintain appropriate body weight.

(Continued)

5. It is not recommended that you drink alcohol. If you do drink alcoholic beverages, limit the amount you drink in a single day to no more than two cans of beer, two small glasses of wine, or two average cocktails. Pregnant women should avoid alcoholic beverages.

6. Limit the amount of salt (sodium chloride) that you eat to 6 grams (slightly more than 1 teaspoon of salt) per day or less. Limit the use of salt in cooking and avoid adding it to food at the table. Salty foods, including highly processed salty foods, salt-preserved foods, and salt-pickled foods, should be eaten sparingly, if at all.

7. Maintain adequate calcium intake.

8. Avoid taking dietary supplements in excess of the U.S. Recommended Daily Allowances (U.S. RDAs) in any one day.

9. Maintain an optimal level of fluoride in your diet and particularly in the diets of your children when their baby and adult teeth are forming.

Ten Ways to a Longer, Healthier Life

1. **Don't smoke.** Avoid the use of tobacco in all forms, including chewing tobacco.

2. **Maintain a desirable body weight.** Be sure your caloric intake is consistent with your energy output. Limit food relatively high in fat, simple sugars, and, of course, calories.

3. **Exercise regularly.** Many forms of exercise—especially walking—are adequate if done vigorously and regularly. All exercise should be preceded by warm-up and followed by cool-down exercises.

4. **Limit your intake of total fats, especially saturated fats.** Approximately 40% of the calories in the typical American diet are derived from fat. The AHF recommends that this be lowered to 25%—or approximately 40 grams of fat per day. Choose foods such as vegetables, fruits, whole grains, fish, poultry, lean meats, and low-fat dairy products. Use a limited amount of fat in food preparation. And avoid packaged goods that have a high fat content.

5. **Maintain your cholesterol level below 200 mg/dl.** Reduce your consumption of high-cholesterol foods, particularly eggs, organ meats such as liver, and whole-milk dairy products. Check labels for contents and, again, avoid the saturated fats found in animal products.

(Continued)

6. **Eat foods high in complex carbohydrates (starch) and fiber.** Select foods that are high in complex carbohydrates such as potatoes, whole-grain pasta, rice, and breads. Increase the fiber in your diet by eating more fruits (apples, citrus fruits, bananas, and berries) and vegetables (with their skin). Include bran, oatmeal, and the whole grains often found in breakfast cereals as well as legumes (beans, peas, and lentils).

7. **Avoid alcohol or drink only in moderation.** To reduce health problems specifically related to the liver, certain types of cancer, high blood pressure, and stroke, avoid or limit your intake of alcoholic beverages (which are high in calories but of no nutritional value) to no more than one or two drinks per day.

8. **Reduce intake of sodium.** Because of the relationship between a high sodium intake and the incidence of high blood pressure and stroke, it is important to maintain your blood pressure at 140/90 or below. Choose foods low in sodium and limit the amount of salt added in food preparation and at the table. Limit smoked foods, cold cuts, and salty snack foods.

9. **Avoid excessive exposure to the sun.** Use a sun screen labeled SPF 15 when outdoors. Wear a hat or other protection. Avoid direct sunlight between the hours of 10 A.M. or 4 P.M. Keep in mind that the best favor you can do for your skin is to avoid the sun as much as possible.

10. **Get adequate rest and be aware of stressful situations.** Everyone needs an adequate amount of sleep to avoid feeling tired and to remain alert and productive. Be prepared to cope with stressful situations. Allow time for relaxation and hobbies to reduce stress.

SOURCE: American Health Foundation (AHF).

Cancer

Cancers are dreaded diseases and the focus of much environmental and work-place legislation. About 1.1 million new cases occur each year in the United States, and more than one-half million deaths (Table 12-6, Fig. 12-9). Worldwide, at least 2 million people die of cancer each year. One in three people in the United States develops some form of cancer; one in four dies from it. Stated another way, the lifetime risk is 1 in 3 (33%) or 1 in 4 (25%). (The regulatory basis generally tends to be one in a million incremental risk, 10^{-6} or 0.000001 vs. 0.25 to 0.33 "background.") Although complex in etiology, the estimated relative importance of major causes or factors is shown in Table 12-7.

The leading cancers in the United States in terms of mortality are lung, breast or prostate, and colorectal, whereas in Africa and Asia stomach, esophageal, cervical, and liver cancers are the dominant types. The leading causes of cancer

Table 12-6. Estimated New Cancer Cases and Deaths
(in Thousands), 1991

	New cases			Deaths		
	Male	Female	Total	Male	Female	Total
Lung	101	60	161	92	51	143
Other respiratory	13	4	17	4	1	5
Total respiratory	114	64	178	96	52	148
Breast	0.9	175	176	0.3	45	45
Colon-rectum	79	79	158	30	31	61
Pancreas	14	14	28	12	13	25
Stomach	15	9	24	8	5	13
Other digestive	17	13	30	15	9	24
Total digestive	125	115	240	65	58	123
Prostate	122	—	122	32	—	32
Uterus	—	46	46	—	10	10
Ovary	—	21	21	—	12	12
Other genital	7	5	12	1		1
Total genital	129	72	201	33	23	56
Bladder, kidney, and other urinary	53	23	76	13	7	20
Leukemia	16	12	28	10	8	18
Other blood and lymph	30	27	57	15	14	29
Oral	21	10	31	5	3	8
Skin* (melanoma)	17	15	32	5	3	8
All other	39	42	81	30	29	59
Total†	545	555	1100	272	242	514

SOURCE: American Cancer Society, Cancer Facts & Figures, 1991.

*Skin new cases are melanoma only; deaths 6500 melanoma and 2000 other skin cancers. Nonmelanoma skin cancer accounts for about 600,000 new cases annually.

†Estimated numbers are rounded.

deaths in American males are lung, prostate, and colorectal; and in females lung, breast, and colorectal.

Prostate cancer, the second most common cancer and cause of death in men, hitherto seems to have suffered from benign neglect. (The prostate is a walnut-sized gland located just below the male urinary bladder.) The risk increases with age; more than 50% of men over age 50 have enlarged prostate, or benign prostatic hyperplasia (BPH), which in itself is not thought to be a risk factor for cancer. The warning signs of prostate cancer are difficult and frequent urination, burning sensation when urinating or ejaculating, and blood or pus in urine. Prevention or early detection includes rectal examination, blood testing for prostate specific antigen (PSA level and rate of increase), or transrectal ultrasound method. Alternatives to BPH surgery are now available, notably Merck's Proscar, approved in 1992 for its treatment. According to some pathologists, virtually all men develop "carcinoma in situ" of the prostate by the age of 70 or 80. However, in the majority of cases, this does not spread or metastasize beyond the gland itself, and the individual dies from other causes. This would mean

Cancer Incidence by Site and Sex*

Male	Female
Prostate 122,000	Breast 175,000
Lung 101,000	Colon & Rectum 78,500
Colon & Rectum 79,000	Lung 60,000
Bladder 37,000	Uterus 46,000
Lymphoma 23,800	Lymphoma 20,800
Oral 20,600	Ovary 20,700
Melanoma of the skin 17,000	Melanoma of the skin 15,000
Kidney 15,800	Pancreas 14,500
Leukemia 15,800	Bladder 13,200
Stomach 14,500	Leukemia 12,200
Pancreas 13,700	Oral 10,200
Larynx 10,000	Kidney 9,500
All sites 545,000	All sites 555,000

Cancer Death by Site and Sex*

Male	Female
Lung 92,000	Lung 51,000
Prostate 32,000	Breast 44,500
Colon & Rectum 30,000	Colon & Rectum 30,500
Pancreas 12,000	Pancreas 13,200
Lymphoma 10,600	Ovary 12,500
Leukemia 9,800	Uterus 10,000
Stomach 8,100	Lymphoma 9,700
Esophagus 7,300	Leukemia 8,300
Bladder 6,400	Liver 5,800
Kidney 6,300	Brain 5,300
Liver 6,300	Stomach 5,300
Brain 6,200	Multiple Myeloma 4,500
All sites 272,000	All sites 242,000

*Excluding nonmelanoma skin cancer and carcinoma in situ.

Figure 12-9. Cancer incidence and deaths by site and sex—1991 estimates.

Table 12-7. Cancer Deaths from Various Factors, Percent of All Cancer Deaths

Factor(s)	Best estimate, %	Range, %
Diet	35	10–70
Tobacco	30	25–40
Alcohol	3	2–4
Food additives*	<1	0.5–2
Reproductive and sexual behavior	7	1–13
Occupation and workplace	4	2–8
Pollution	2	<1–5
Industrial products	<1	<1–2
Medicines and medical procedures	1	0.5–3
Geophysical factors (e.g., sun uv rays)†	3	2–4
Infection	10?	1–?
Unknown	?	?

SOURCE: *FDA Consumer,* June 1990. Original source: Richard Doll and Richard Peto, "The Causes of Cancer: Quantitative Estimates of Avoidable Risks of Cancer in the United States Today," *The Journal of the National Cancer Institute,* June 1981.

*Allowing for a possibly protective effect of antioxidants and other preservatives.

†Exposure to ultraviolet (uv) sunlight is an important factor in causing relatively less dangerous basal cell and squamous cell carcinomas (600,000 new cases each year).

that prostate cancer is of universal incidence and other secondary factors determine whether the individual eventually dies from it—a situation unique in human cancer.

In women, the lung cancer death rate surpassed that of breast cancer in the mid-1980s, as a direct result of increased smoking, with a 20-year time lag common for lung cancer. Several studies are highly suggestive of the relationship between fat intake and colorectal and breast cancers. The connection between smoking and lung cancer has been well established, as also the powerful synergy between smoking and radon and asbestos exposures. (See the accompanying chart on primary and secondary cancer prevention.)

Multistage Carcinogenic Process.   Several synthetic and natural compounds and viruses are capable of inducing cancers in humans. Many, including the polycyclic aromatic hydrocarbon benzo(*a*)pyrene, have to undergo metabolic activation to reactive electrophilic species which can then bind with nucleophilic nucleic acids to form covalent adducts. The converting enzymes, such as Cytochrome P450 or microsomal mono-oxygenase, are normally involved in detoxification and elimination of xenobiotics (hence sometimes referred to as "double-edged sword"). However, human cells are capable of repairing DNA damage unless the defense mechanisms are overwhelmed.

The development of a malignant tumor generally proceeds in three distinct stages: (1) initiation, i.e., DNA binding and gene mutations; (2) promotion, involving cellular membrane damage, epigenetic effects, and development of benign tumors; and (3) progression, i.e., conversion over time to malignant tumor and metastasis. Initiation can occur instantaneously while promotion and progression typically occur over a significant part of a human lifetime. Different agents, mechanisms, and suppressors are involved in the different stages (Weinstein and Groopman, 1991).

Examples of Inhibitors of Carcinogenesis

Vitamin C: Reduces synthesis of carcinogens in body, e.g., nitrosamine formation in stomach

Dietary fiber: Reduces absorption or adsorption of carcinogens

Benzyl isothiocyanate (cruciferous vegetables): Alters metabolism of carcinogens

Selenium, carotene, vitamins C and E: Antioxidants

Flavanoids (fruits and vegetables): Inhibit covalent binding of carcinogens to DNA

Retinoids, B-carotene, α-tocopherol (fruits and vegetables): Inhibit tumor promotion

Organosulfur compounds (garlic, onions), curcumin (turmeric, curry), capsaicin (peppers): Inhibit tumor formation

SOURCE: Adapted from Weinstein and Groopman, 1991.

Trends.   Cancer is undoubtedly a major public health issue, but there is no evidence that we are in the throes of a cancer "epidemic." Lung cancer increased in the last few decades because of smoking, but there has been a marked decrease in stomach and uterine cancer. Breast cancer and colorectal cancer mortality rates remained virtually unchanged. Cancer has become relatively more threatening because of a decline, for example, in cardiovascular diseases and other competing risks, and longer life spans.

In light of this evidence, there seems to be a mismatch between the level of risk posed by certain sources of environmental exposure and the magnitude of resource allocation. The public dread of cancer and the ease of identifying cancer as a clear endpoint could account for the emphasis. Such divergence has been pointed out before by the EPA's Science Advisory Board and others. Some environmentalists think of this as a "diversionary tactic" by industry. Nevertheless, the central tenet of public health policy is the deployment of limited resources where they would best protect or enhance public health, i.e., present the best "leverage." Any deviation from this principle should be articulated and justified and should not happen by default.

Cancer's Warning Signals

Change in bowel or bladder habits

A sore that does not heal

Unusual bleeding or discharge

Thickening or lump in breast or elsewhere

Indigestion or difficulty in swallowing

Obvious change in wart or mole (size, shape, or color)

Nagging cough or hoarseness

Unexplained weight loss

If you have a warning signal, see your doctor.

American Cancer Society Nutritional Guidelines

1. **Avoid obesity**

   Sensible eating habits and regular exercise will help you avoid excess weight gain. Your physician can work with you to determine your best body weight since it depends on your medical condition and body build and an appropriate diet to maintain this weight. If you are 40% overweight, your risk increases for colon, breast, gallbladder, and uterine cancers.

2. **Cut down on total fat intake**

   A diet high in fat may be a factor in the development of certain cancers like breast, colon, and prostate. If you eat less fatty food, you will be able to control your body weight more easily.

3. **Eat more high-fiber foods**

   Regular consumption of cereals, fresh fruits, and vegetables is recommended. Studies suggest that diets high in fiber may help to reduce the risk of colon cancer. And even if not, high-fiber-containing foods are a wholesome substitute for foods high in fat.

4. **Include foods rich in vitamins A and C in your daily diet**

   Choose dark green and deep yellow fresh vegetables and fruits as sources of vitamin A, such as carrots, spinach, sweet potatoes, peaches, apricots; and oranges, grapefruit, strawberries, green and red peppers for vitamin C. These foods may help lower risk for cancers of the larynx, esophagus, and lung.

(Continued)

5. **Include cruciferous vegetables in your diet**

   Certain vegetables in this family—cabbage, broccoli, brussels sprouts, kohlrabi, and cauliflower—may help prevent certain cancers from developing. Research is in progress to determine what in these foods may protect against cancer.

6 **Eat moderately of salt-cured, smoked, and nitrite-cured foods**

   In areas of the world where salt-cured and smoked foods are eaten frequently, there is higher incidence of cancer of the esophagus and stomach. The American food industry has changed to new processes thought to be less hazardous.

7. **Keep alcohol consumption moderate, if you do drink**

   The heavy use of alcohol, especially when accompanied by cigarette smoking or tobacco chewing, increases risk of cancers of the mouth, larynx, throat, and esophagus.

Cancer Prevention	
Avoid those factors that might lead to the development of cancer (primary prevention)	
Smoking	Cigarette smoking is responsible for 85% of lung cancer cases among men and 75% among women—about 83% overall. Smoking accounts for about 30% of all cancer deaths. Those who smoke two or more packs of cigarettes a day have lung cancer mortality rates 15 to 25 times greater than nonsmokers.
Smokeless tobacco	Use of chewing tobacco or snuff increases risk of cancer of the mouth, larynx, throat, and esophagus and is highly habit-forming.
Sunlight	Almost all of the more than 600,000 cases of basal and squamous cell skin cancer diagnosed each year in the United States are considered to be sun-related. Epidemiologic evidence shows that sun exposure is a major factor in the development of melanoma and that the incidence increases for those living near the equator.
Alcohol	Oral cancer and cancers of the larynx, throat, esophagus, and liver occur more frequently among heavy drinkers of alcohol.

Estrogen	Estrogen treatment to control menopausal symptoms increases risk of endometrial cancer. Use of estrogen by menopausal women needs careful discussion by the woman and her physician.
Radiation	Excessive exposure to ionizing radiation can increase cancer risk. Most medical and dental x-rays are adjusted to deliver the lowest dose possible without sacrificing image quality. Excessive radon exposure in homes may increase risk of lung cancer, especially in cigarette smokers. If levels are found to be too high, remedial actions should be taken.
Occupational hazards	Exposure to several different industrial agents (nickel, chromium, asbestos, vinyl chloride, etc.) increases risk of various cancers. Risk from asbestos is greatly increased when combined with cigarette smoking.
Nutrition	Risk for colon, breast, and uterine cancers increases in obese people. High-fat diets may contribute to the development of cancers of the breast, colon, and prostate. High-fiber foods might help reduce risk of colon cancer. A varied diet containing plenty of vegetables and fruits rich in vitamins A and C may reduce risk for a wide range of cancers. Salt-cured, smoked, and nitrite-cured foods have been linked to esophageal and stomach cancer. The heavy use of alcohol, especially when accompanied by cigarette smoking or tobacco chewing, increases risk of cancers of the mouth, larynx, throat, esophagus, and liver.

Actions to diagnose a cancer or precursor as early as possible (secondary prevention/early detection)

Colorectal tests	The American Cancer Society recommends three tests for the early detection of colon and rectal cancer in people without symptoms. A digital rectal examination by a physician during an office visit should be performed every year after the age of 40; the stool blood test is recommended every year after 50; and the proctosigmoidoscopy examination should be carried out every 3 to 5 years, based on the advice of a physician.
Pap test	For cervical cancer, women who are or have been sexually active, or have reached age 18 years, should

(Continued)

have an annual Pap test and pelvic examination. After a woman has had three or more consecutive satisfactory normal annual examinations, the Pap test may be performed less frequently at the discretion of her physician.

Breast cancer detection

The American Cancer Society recommends the monthly practice of breast self-examination (BSE) by women 20 years and older as a routine good health habit. Physical examination of the breast should be done every three years from ages 20 to 40 and then every year. The ACS recommends a mammogram every year for asymptomatic women age 50 and over, and a baseline mammogram between ages 35 and 39. Women 40 to 49 should have a mammogram every one to two years, depending on physical and mammographic findings.

SOURCE: American Cancer Society, Cancer Facts and Figures, 1991.

Diabetes

Diabetes mellitus is a common but somewhat "silent" disorder characterized by abnormal metabolism. About 14 million Americans have some form of diabetes and nearly half of them do not even realize they have it (American Diabetes Association). There are two major types of diabetes; about 1.2 million people, or nearly 10%, have the more serious insulin-dependent type I (also known as juvenile-onset) diabetes that requires daily insulin injections because the insulin-producing pancreatic cells are destroyed, apparently by an autoimmune mechanism triggered by a virus. By far the more common type is the non-insulin-dependent type II diabetes that usually appears in middle or old age. Another kind of diabetes is secondary diabetes caused by damage to the pancreas by certain chemicals, medicines, or diseases of the pancreas or other glands.

In diabetes, insufficient insulin is produced by the pancreas (none or very little in type I), or insulin is not used effectively to convert glucose, a common sugar from food, into energy to fuel the cells. When insulin is insufficient or ineffective, usually as a result of malfunctioning insulin receptor in cells, glucose cannot enter the cells and so accumulates in the bloodstream, resulting in high "sugar" levels. This can, over time, lead to kidney disorders, atherosclerosis, heart attack, stroke, poor circulation, nerve damage, infections, and blindness (retinopathy). Diabetes can increase the risk of heart disease two- to fourfold and is the leading cause of death among diabetics; it is the third major cause of blindness.

Some problems associated with diabetes need immediate attention: hypoglycemia, or low blood sugar, sometimes called insulin reaction or insulin

Looking at the Pieces

The Food Guide Pyramid emphasizes foods from the five food groups shown in the three lower sections of the Pyramid. Each of these food groups provides some, but not all, of the nutrients you need. Foods in one group can't replace those in another. No one food group is more important than another – for good health, you need them all.

USE SPARINGLY

The small tip of the Pyramid shows fats, oils, and sweets. These are foods such as salad dressings and oils, cream, butter, margarine, sugars, soft drinks, candies, and sweet desserts. These foods provide calories and little else nutritionally. Most people should use them sparingly.

2-3 SERVINGS **2-3 SERVINGS**

On this level of the Food Guide Pyramid are two groups of foods that come mostly from animals: milk, yogurt, and cheese; and meat, poultry, fish, dry beans, eggs, and nuts. These foods are important for protein, calcium, iron, and zinc.

3-5 SERVINGS **2-4 SERVINGS**

This level includes foods that come from plants – vegetables and fruits. Most people need to eat more of these foods for the vitamins, minerals, and fiber they supply.

6-11 SERVINGS

At the base of the Food Guide Pyramid are breads, cereals, rice, and pasta — all foods from grains. You need the most servings of these foods each day.

WHAT COUNTS AS A SERVING?

Food Groups

Bread, Cereal, Rice, and Pasta		
1 slice of bread	1 ounce of ready-to-eat cereal	1/2 cup of cooked cereal, rice, or pasta

Vegetable		
1 cup of raw leafy vegetables	1/2 cup of other vegetables, cooked or chopped raw	3/4 cup of vegetable juice

Milk, Yogurt, and Cheese		
1 cup of milk or yogurt	1-1/2 ounces of natural cheese	2 ounces of process cheese

Meat, Poultry, Fish, Dry Beans, Eggs, and Nuts	
2-3 ounces of cooked lean meat, poultry, or fish	1/2 cup of cooked dry beans, 1 egg, or 2 tablespoons of peanut butter count as 1 ounce of lean meat

Figure 12-10. USDA food guide pyramid.

shock caused by too much insulin, too little food, or too much exercise; hyperglycemia, or high blood sugar, occurs with too much food, too little insulin, or during illness or emotional stress; and ketoacidosis, or diabetic coma, that may accompany high blood sugar when the body uses fat instead of glucose, producing high levels of poisonous ketones. (If you are a diabetic, you may want to carry glucose and glucagon in case of a hypoglycemia attack, and wear a "Medic Alert" bracelet.)

Risk Factors for Diabetes

- Family history (especially parents)
- Increasing age
- Obesity (especially abdominal fat)
- Total cholesterol >240 mg/dl, triglycerides >250 mg/dl
- Hypertension

Warning Signs/Symptoms of Diabetes

Insulin dependent (usually occur suddenly)	**Non-insulin-dependent** (usually occur less suddenly)
- Frequent urination	- Any of the insulin-dependent symptoms
- Excessive thirst	- Recurring or hard-to-heal skin, gum, or bladder infections
- Extreme hunger	- Drowsiness
- Dramatic weight loss	- Blurred vision
- Irritability	- Tingling or numbness in hands or feet
- Weakness and fatigue	- Itching
- Nausea and vomiting	

SOURCE: American Diabetes Association.

Prevention and Treatment.   The results of recent studies suggest that type II diabetes can be prevented, managed, or even reversed by early recognition of the risk factors and through a proactive diet and exercise program. This can obviate or reduce the need for insulin injections or oral medications (e.g., sulfonyl ureas, biguanidines) and improve the quality of life. Here are some recommendations:

- Aim for 50% or more of your calories via complex carbohydrates such as whole-grain breads, pasta, rice, and legumes (they break down and are absorbed slowly unlike simple sugars); restrict fat intake to 20% or less; avoid simple sugars; eat regular meals; consider vitamins C and E and minerals chromium and magnesium supplements.

- Exercise regularly, preferably combining different types of exercise such as walking, aerobics, and resistance training; in addition to maintaining cardio-vascular fitness and proper weight, this could increase the number of muscles' insulin receptors and enhance glucose utilization by the cells.

- Maintain weight appropriate to height (Table 12-5).

- Don't smoke; consider joining a support group.

- Maintain blood glucose level in the 70 to 130 mg/dl range by frequent monitoring and a regular regimen. (Try to avoid excessive peaks and valleys and surges of adrenaline and other regulatory hormones by avoiding stress.)

Food-Borne Diseases and Prevention

In the normal scheme of things, four types of microorganisms, bacteria, protozoa, viruses, and fungi, live in and on our bodies in their own niches and are usually harmless and even beneficial. There are two basic varieties: normal resident flora, and transient flora. The normal flora help manufacture nutrients (biotin, pantothenic acid, vitamins B_6 and B_{12}), stimulate the immune system, and stake out a territory that might otherwise be occupied by disease-causing organisms (averting opportunistic infections). The digestive tract especially is full of microbes, which become profuse lower down the tract. The colon harbors some 10 billion bacteria per gram of contents, and the feces is made up of mainly bacteria, about 100 billion per gram, and their by-products.

Biological Agents

Virus. A unit of nucleic acid (RNA or DNA) surrounded by a protein coat. Strictly speaking, not a living organism because it cannot reproduce except through a host's genetic material. It induces the host to replicate more of the virus.

Bacteria. Single cells distinguished by shape (round—cocci, spiral—spirilla, cylindrical—bacilli, curved—vibrios) and whether the cell walls stain purple (Gram-positive) or not (Gram-negative) with the specific Gram stain.

Protozoa. Organisms built of single, complex cells capable of movement.

Fungi and yeasts. A strange breed, unlike animals or plants, built of complex cells but lacking a nervous system or the ability to utilize sunlight. Yeasts are single-celled fungi. (Mushrooms are multicellular macroscopic fungi.)

Food-borne diseases caused by microorganisms are summarized in Table 12-8. The recovery from most of these illnesses is usually quick and complete. An exception is botulism which requires immediate medical attention; botulism is produced by a potent neurotoxin secreted by the bacterium *Clostridium botulinum.* Aflatoxin B1, a food contaminant produced by a fungus mold that infects corn and peanuts, is the most potent carcinogen known. Aflatoxin affects the liver; although rare in the United States, food contaminated with Aflatoxin, probably in combination with Hepatitis B virus infection, is believed to contribute to the high incidence of liver cancer in parts of Africa and Asia.

An old nutritional standby, yogurt, can help with problems stemming from lowered levels of lactobacilli, including yeast infections. Recent studies suggest that consumption of yogurts containing *Lactobacillus acidophilus* cultures helps replace excessive or harmful populations and restore healthy balance.

The ongoing shift from meat to fish consumption is generally a healthy development, but the possibility exists of increased exposure to lipophilic contaminants such as PCBs and pesticides or mercury that tend to bioaccumulate in fish and shellfish. (Biological contamination can of course also pose a risk if food is improperly handled, stored, or cooked.) The risks to recreational and subsistence fishermen can be significant, especially in coastal and inland waters. The FDA is primarily responsible for the safety of food sold across state lines; the states, generally through their departments of health, are responsible for managing risks locally through health advisories and consumption advisories. The health advisories are based on FDA's action levels (e.g., 2 ppm for PCBs) or some type of risk assessment. Consumption advisories and restrictions are based on fish species or location of catch. In addition to being aware of these advisories, the commonsense approach to limiting exposure is to balance the intake of finfish and shellfish and freshwater and saltwater species.

Some foods such as peanuts, eggs, milk, and grains (as well as medicines and insect bites) can cause allergic reactions. A very severe reaction, anaphylactic shock, can occur and may even be life-threatening. To the extent individual allergens can be identified, they should be avoided; epinephrine is helpful for treatment.

Food Additives.   As many as 3000 substances are added intentionally to foods as preservatives, colorants, and taste enhancers. A common preservative in meats is nitrite, which is not a carcinogen by itself but can form nitrosamines that are carcinogenic. Wood smoke also contains nitrosamines. Eating cured and smoked foods increases the risk of stomach cancer.

Two other common preservatives that have been around for some time are BHA (butylated hydroxyanisole) and BHT (butylated hydroxytoluene). There is no convincing evidence that these preservatives or the colorants that are added in small quantities cause cancer or other significant health effects in the vast majority of the population. Sulfites are commonly added to wine, fruit products, and some other foods as a preservative. Some individuals are hypersensitive to sulfites.

Table 12-8. Food-Borne Diseases and Prevention

Disease and organism that causes it	Source of illness	Symptoms
Bacteria:		
Botulism Botulinum toxin (produced by *Clostridium botulinum* bacteria)	Spores of these bacteria are widespread but produce toxin only in an anaerobic (oxygenless) environment of little acidity. Found in a considerable variety of canned foods, such as corn, green beans, soups, beets, asparagus, mushrooms, tuna, and liver pâté. Also, in luncheon meats, ham, sausage, stuffed eggplant, lobster, and smoked and salted fish	Onset: Generally 4–36 hours after eating. Neurotoxic symptoms, including double vision, inability to swallow, speech difficulty, and progressive paralysis of the respiratory system. *Get medical help immediately. Botulism can be fatal*
Campylobacteriosis *Campylobacter jejuni*	Bacteria on poultry and cattle can contaminate meat and milk of these animals. Chief food sources: raw poultry, meat, and unpasteurized milk	Onset: Generally 2–5 days after eating. Diarrhea, abdominal cramping, fever, and sometimes bloody stools. Lasts 7–10 days
Listeriosis *Listeria monocytogenes*	Found in soft cheese, unpasteurized milk, imported seafood products, frozen cooked crabmeat, and cooked shrimp. The *Listeria* bacteria resist heat, salt, nitrite, and acidity better than many other microorganisms. They survive and grow at low temperatures	Onset: From 7–30 days after eating, but most symptoms have been reported 48–72 hours after consumption of contaminated food. Fever, headache, nausea, and vomiting. Primarily affects pregnant women and their fetuses, newborns, the elderly, people with cancer, and those with impaired immune systems. Can cause fetal and infant death
Perfringens food poisoning *Clostridium perfringens*	In most instances, caused by failure to keep food hot. A few organisms are often present after cooking and multiply to toxic levels during cool-down and storage of prepared foods, especially meats. These organisms grow better than other bacteria between 120 and 130°F. So gravies and stuffing must be kept above 140°F.	Onset: Generally 8–12 hours after eating. Abdominal pain and diarrhea, and sometimes nausea and vomiting. Symptoms last a day or less and are usually mild. Can be more serious in older or debilitated people
Salmonellosis *Salmonella* bacteria	Raw meats, poultry, milk and other dairy products, shrimp, frog legs, yeast, coconut, pasta, and chocolate are most frequently involved	Onset: Generally 6–48 hours after eating. Nausea, abdominal cramps, diarrhea, fever, and headache (flulike symptoms). All age groups are susceptible, but symptoms are most severe for elderly, infants, and infirm
Shigellosis (bacillary dysentery) *Shigella* bacteria	Found in milk and dairy products, poultry, and potato salad. Food becomes contaminated when a human carrier does not wash hands and then handles liquid or moist food that is not cooked thoroughly afterward. Organisms multiply in food left at room temperature	Onset: 1–7 days after eating. Abdominal cramps, diarrhea, fever, sometimes vomiting, and blood, pus or mucus in stool

Table 12-8. Food-Borne Diseases and Prevention (*Continued*)

Disease and organism that causes it	Source of illness	Symptoms
Bacteria (*continued*):		
Staphylococcal food poisoning Staphylococcal enterotoxin (produced by *Staphylococcus aureus* bacteria)	Toxin produced when food contaminated with the bacteria is left too long at room temperature. Meats, poultry, egg products, tuna, potato and macaroni salads, and cream-filled pastries are good environments for these bacteria to produce toxin	Onset: Generally 30 minutes–8 hours after eating. Diarrhea, vomiting, nausea, abdominal pain, cramps, and prostration. Lasts 24–48 hours. Rarely fatal
"Septic sore throat" *Streptococcus*	Raw milk or other food contaminated at source	Sore throat, fever
Vibrio infection *Vibrio vulnificus*	The bacteria live in coastal waters and can infect humans either through open wounds or through consumption of contaminated seafood; most numerous in warm weather	Onset: Abrupt. Chills, fever, and/or prostration. At high risk are people with liver conditions, low gastric (stomach) acid, and weakened immune systems
Protozoa: Amebiasis *Entamoeba histolytica*	Exist in the intestinal tract of humans and are expelled in feces. Polluted water and vegetables grown in polluted soil spread the infection	Onset: 3–10 days after exposure. Severe crampy pain, tenderness over the colon or liver, loose morning stools, recurrent diarrhea, loss of weight, fatigue, and sometimes anemia
Giardiasis *Giardia lamblia*	Most frequently associated with consumption of contaminated water. May be transmitted by uncooked foods that become contaminated while growing or after cooking by infected food handlers. Cool, moist conditions favor organism's survival	Onset: 1–3 days. Sudden onset of explosive watery stools, abdominal cramps, anorexia, nausea, and vomiting. Especially infects hikers, children, travelers, and institutionalized patients
Viruses: Hepatitis A virus	Shellfish and mollusks (oysters, clams, mussels, scallops, and cockles) become carriers when their beds are polluted by untreated sewage. Raw shellfish are especially potent carriers, although cooking does not always kill the virus	Onset: Begins with malaise, appetite loss, nausea, vomiting, and fever. After 3–10 days patient develops jaundice with darkened urine. Severe cases can cause liver damage and death

SOURCE: *FDA Consumer*, January–February 1991.

Vitamins and Minerals: Emerging Role

Vitamins and trace minerals are a diverse group of micronutrients that the body needs in small amounts (in microgram or milligram quantities), without which life would be impossible. Vitamins and trace minerals act as catalytic, regulating, and protective agents. Some vitamins are made by the body (vitamin D in skin when exposed to sunlight, K in the intestinal tract by resident bacteria), but most have to be taken in via food and supplements. Vitamin deficiency in the western world is generally rare, although special situations such as dieting, pregnancy, alcoholism, and imbalance in intake rates can lead to deficiencies.

Table 12-9 shows vitamins and minerals considered essential nutrients, recommended daily allowances (RDA) if established, food sources, and health effects. Antioxidant vitamins A, C, and E and the mineral selenium are protective against both cardiovascular diseases and cancers. Vitamins B and C are water-soluble and need to be replenished regularly; vitamins A, D, E and K are fat-soluble and tend to be stored. Water-soluble vitamins are forgiving in terms of safety because excess is excreted; an order of magnitude intake higher than the RDA would not ordinarily be toxic. If you are taking relatively large quantities, it may be better to split into two doses twice a day unless you are taking the controlled-release type. But people should be cautious of fat-soluble vitamin "mega doses" because they accumulate in the body and can be toxic, especially vitamin A, but not water-soluble beta carotene. (The FDA, under the direction of Commissioner David Kessler, is taking a closer look at the "mega-claims" of some vitamin and mineral manufacturers and other proponents, but it would be unfortunate if this resulted in restrictions on micronutrient availability to the general public.) The role of micronutrients has undoubtedly expanded far beyond the traditional disease prevention mode into therapeutic applications together with some tantalizing possibilities—reviving the age-old question: where does a food stop and a drug begin?

The "Health Care System": Disease and Disability Treatment

The expansive policies of the 1960s and the open-ended commitments to health care in the United States led simultaneously to the world's most lucrative industry and an intractable crisis. Between 1970 and 1990, health care expenditures have grown at an annual rate of 11.6%, or almost three percentage points faster than our gross national product (GNP), increasing from 7.3% of GNP in 1970 to 12.3% in 1990 (and to 14% of GNP in 1992). America spends a higher percentage of its GNP, and the expenditures have been growing faster, than any major industrial country. And yet a significant proportion of even the working population does not have health insurance, and the United States ranks near the bottom in many public health measures—below some "third world countries" in infant mortality, for example.

While the dominant theme of environmental quality is preservation, and that of public health prevention, the focus of the American health care system is patient disease treatment. The so-called health care system is not about health or about caring, nor is it really a system. The "system" seeks to "deliver care"— the language is symptomatic of its orientation—like delivering pizza rather than being a partner in the maintenance of people's health and well-being.

Table 12-9. Vitamins and Minerals: Requirements, Functions, and Health Effects

Vitamins and minerals	RDA* and Range		Functions and health effects	Food sources	Possible causes of loss or deficiency†
			Vitamins		
A Retinol (preformed) Fat-soluble	RDA Range	5000 IU 10,000–25,000 IU	Maintains healthy vision, skin, and soft tissue; needed for normal growth and reproduction; prevents night blindness and may retard macular degeneration; antioxidant—protects against cancer of lungs and bladder	Vitamin A: liver, egg yolk, milk, cereals. Carotenoids: body also makes vitamin A from carotenoids in dark green, yellow, and orange vegetables and fruits (e.g., broccoli, carrots, squash)	Diabetes; deficiency of vitamin D and zinc
Beta carotene Provitamin A Water-soluble	Beta carotene Toxic (A) Beta carotene	6 mg >25,000 IU relatively nontoxic			
B₁ Thiamine Water-soluble	RDA Range	1.5 mg 10–50 mg	Helps in nervous system functioning and in obtaining energy from carbohydrates	Meat, eggs, beans, whole grains, and nuts	Some diuretics, pregnancy, niacin deficiency
B₂ Riboflavin Water-soluble	RDA Range	1.7 mg 10–50 mg	Helps gland and digestive system functioning, energy production and metabolism, and other biochemical processes; may reduce risk of esophagus cancer	Milk, whole grains, dark green leafy vegetables, soy foods, brewer's yeast, liver	Antibiotics (deplete gut flora) niacin deficiency
B₃ Niacin Niacinamide Nicotinic acid Water-soluble	RDA Range	20 mg 50–150 mg	Nervous system, heart, liver, sex hormones; aids in energy production and fatty acid synthesis, e.g., cholesterol modulation; prevents pellagra	Grains, meat, poultry, fish, nuts, and beans	Antibiotics (deplete gut flora)
B₆ Pyridoxine Water-soluble	RDA Range Toxic	2.0 mg 10–50 mg >2000 mg	Helps amino acid synthesis and energy production from protein; helps prevent anemia, skin lesions, nerve damage; alleviates carpal tunnel syndrome	Meat, poultry, fish, grains, fruits and vegetables, kidney beans, lentils	Estrogens, oral contraceptives
B₁₂ Cyanocobalamine Water-soluble (but stored in body)	RDA Range	6 µg 20–100 µg	Helps synthesis of DNA and amino acids, and production of energy from fatty acids and carbohydrates; helps prevent pernicious anemia; may protect against heart disease and nerve damage	Meat, milk and milk products, eggs, fish (only foods of animal origin)	B₆, calcium, iron deficiency, laxatives, oral contraceptives. Lack of "intrinsic factor" prevents absorption

482

Vitamin	Measure	Amount	Functions	Food Sources	Depletes/Destroys
Folic acid Folacin B complex Folate Water-soluble	RDA Range Toxic	0.4 mg 0.4–0.8 mg >400 mg	Helps synthesis of genetic material and amino acids; protects against cervical dysplasia, and neural tube birth defects (e.g., anencephaly, spina bifida)	Dark green leafy vegetables (e.g., asparagus, spinach), chick peas, liver	Overeating, oral contraceptives, sulfa drugs, pregnancy
Biotin B complex Water-soluble	RDA Range Toxic	0.3 mg 0.3–0.5 mg >50 mg	Bone marrow, genetic material, glands; aids in energy production and metabolism	Egg yolks, liver, beans, nuts, bananas, legumes	Antibiotics, sulfa drugs
Pantothenic acid B complex Water-soluble	RDA Range Toxic	10 mg 50–200 mg >1000 mg	Adrenal glands, digestion, immunity, nervous system; aids in fatty acid synthesis and energy production and a variety of biochemical processes	Most foods including milk products, eggs, legumes, beans, grains	Alcohol, caffeine
Choline B complex	RDA Range	Not established 100–500 mg	Adrenal and thymus glands, autonomic nervous system, cardiovascular system	Lecithin, eggs, fish, green leafy vegetables, bran, wheat germ, legumes	Alcohol, caffeine, excessive sugar
Inositol B complex Water-soluble	RDA Range	Not established 100–500 mg	Fat and cholesterol metabolism	Citrus fruits, meat, milk, nuts, whole grains, lecithin	Alcohol, caffeine
PABA Para aminobenzoic acid Water-soluble	RDA Range	Not established 10–100 mg	Blood cell formation, intestinal bacterial activity, protein metabolism	Molasses, eggs, milk, bran, whole grains	Alcohol, caffeine, sulfa drugs
C Ascorbic acid Water-soluble	RDA Range Toxic	60 mg 250–3000 mg >5000 mg	Promotes growth of connective tissue (skin, ligaments, bones); prevents scurvy; antioxidant—helps protect against cancer (mouth, esophagus, stomach, cervix) and cataracts; may protect lungs from pollutants and resist viral infections (including common cold); may increase HDL cholesterol in high doses	Citrus fruits, tomatoes, broccoli, green peppers, leafy green vegetables; vitamins destroyed if foods are overcooked	Some drugs, smoking, oral contraceptives, vitamin A deficiency. Foods cooked in high heat, excessive water, and in presence of certain metals, especially copper. Diabetes
Bioflavonoids Vitamin P, citrin Water-soluble	RDA Range	Not established 50–100 mg	Blood vessels, including capillary wall maintenance; augments vitamin C	Same as vitamin C	
D D$_2$ Calciferol (synthetic) D$_3$ Fish liver oils (natural)	RDA Range Toxic	400 IU 400–1000 IU 10,000 IU	Promotes bone growth, and calcium and phosphorus absorption from intestines; prevents rickets and may prevent osteoporosis; augments vitamins A and C	Fish (salmon, tuna), fortified milk, butter, egg yolks, liver; also produced when skin is exposed to sunlight	Laxatives, alcohol

Table 12-9. Vitamins and Minerals: Requirements, Functions, and Health Effects (*Continued*)

Vitamins and minerals	RDA* and Range		Functions and health effects	Food sources	Possible causes of loss or deficiency†
			Vitamins (continued)		
E Tocopherol Fat-soluble	RDA Range Toxic	30 IU 100–800 IU >4000 IU	Antioxidant activity prevents cell damage, lowers risk of cardiovascular disease (hardening of arteries, angina, heart attack, stroke) from LDL cholesterol oxidation, and platelet blood clots; may enhance immune response and reduce cancer risk (breast, stomach, and pancreas); augments vitamins A, B complex, and C	Vegetable oils, peanuts and other nuts, seeds, whole grains, wheat germ, fish liver oils	Environmental pollutants, chlorine, estrogen, laxatives, pregnancy. Diabetes
K Phytonadione Fat-soluble	RDA Suggested	Not established 80 µg	Promotes blood clotting to prevent hemorrhage; may help maintain bone mass by aiding calcium absorption and preventing its loss	Dark green leafy vegetables (turnip, broccoli, lettuce), dairy products, fruits	Aspirin, antibiotics, radiation
			Minerals		
Calcium (Ca) (macromineral)	RDA Range Toxic	1.0 g 1–2 g >12 g	Bones, circulatory and nervous systems; muscle function; most abundant mineral in body, 99% in bones	Dairy products, fish (salmon, sardines), dark green leafy vegetables, e.g., collard, turnip	Inadequate exercise, protein deficiency, excess saturated fats and sugars, some diuretics, phytic acid; vitamin D deficiency
Chloride (Cl) (electrolyte)	RDA	Not established	Component of hydrochloric acid in stomach; helps maintain electrical balance in cells and body fluids	Table salt, milk, eggs, meat	
Chromium (Cr)	RDA Range	Not established 20–200 µg	Glands and circulatory system; works with insulin to metabolize carbohydrates and fats, maintains blood sugar level	Seafood, organ meats, cereals, brewer's yeast, nuts, unrefined cane sugar	
Cobalt (Co)	RDA	Not established	Component of B$_{12}$ (~4%) required for red blood cell production and prevention of pernicious anemia	Naturally present in water, plants, and other foods	Processed and refined carbohydrates, excess iron, insufficient protein

484

Mineral		Amount	Function	Sources	
Copper (Cu)	RDA Range Toxic	2 mg 2–3 mg >100 mg	Required for hemoglobin synthesis and oxidative enzymes for detoxification; helps energy production and iron absorption from digestive tract; forms dark pigment in hair and skin	Nuts, seafood (crabs, oysters), milk, whole grains, legumes	Cadmium, oral contraceptives
Fluoride	RDA Suggested Toxic	Not established <4 mg >4 mg	Strengthens teeth and bones	Natural and fluoridated drinking water, tea	
Iodine (I)	RDA Toxic	0.15 mg >2 mg	Part of thyroid hormones that regulate metabolism; prevents goiter	Iodized table salt, seafood, dairy products	Inland environments deficient in iodine
Iron (Fe)	RDA Toxic	18 mg >100 mg	Component of blood hemoglobin (oxygen carrier in bloodstream); needed to prevent anemia; helps in energy production	Meat, liver, poultry, shellfish, nuts, whole grains, green vegetables	Blood loss (e.g., menstruation), pregnancy, diarrhea, caffeine, copper deficiency, excess intake of other minerals
Magnesium (Mg)	RDA Range Toxic	400 mg 500–1500 mg >6000 mg	Cofactor in many enzymes associated with phosphate; essential for bone formation, neuromuscular activity, and metabolic processes	Grains, nuts (cashews), seafood, poultry, dairy products, green vegetables (chlorophyll)	Alcohol, caffeine, diuretics, oral contraceptives, excessive intake of other minerals
Manganese (Mn)	RDA Range	Not established 3–10 mg	Cofactor in enzymatic reactions, especially phosphorylation, cholesterol and fatty acid synthesis; regulates carbohydrates and other metabolic processes	Cereals, vegetables, fruits, nuts	Excessive intake of refined foods
Molybdenum (MO)	RDA Range	Not established 25–50 µg	Cofactor in enzymatic reactions; aids in energy production	Meat, beans, cereals	
Phosphorus (P) (macromineral)	RDA Range Toxic	1–1.2 g 1–2 g >12 g	Bone and cell formation and repair; energy production and storage; general metabolic processes	Dairy products, fish, poultry, grains, legumes	Aluminum, antacids, excess iron and magnesium
Potassium (K) (electrolyte)	RDA Range	Not established 2–4 g (twice that of sodium)	Transmits nerve signals; maintains fluid balance; important in energy production and muscle contraction (e.g., heartbeat)	Fruits (apricots, bananas, oranges), vegetables, nuts, grains, seeds, milk, fish and shellfish, poultry	Electrolyte loss from diarrhea and strenuous activity and sweating

Table 12-9. Vitamins and Minerals: Requirements, Functions, and Health Effects (*Continued*)

Vitamins and minerals	RDA* and Range		Functions and health effects	Food sources	Possible causes of loss or deficiency
			Minerals (*continued*)		
Selenium (Se)	RDA Range Toxic	Not established 0.1–0.3 mg >1 mg	Part of detoxifying enzyme (glutathione), antioxidant activity protects cell membranes and proteins from oxidant damage; complements vitamin E	Seafood (especially shrimp), meat, milk products, wheat	Some metals and minerals, e.g., arsenic, cadmium, mercury, high fat
Sodium (Na) (electrolyte)	RDA Range Toxic	Not established 1–2 g ~14 g	Cellular fluid balance, cell permeability, nerve signal transmission, muscle contraction and relaxation; augments potassium	Table salt (sodium chloride), seafood, milk products, processed foods with added salt	Most people consume more than necessary amount of salt
Zinc (Zn)	RDA Range Toxic	15 mg 10–25 mg >500 mg	Cofactor in more than 70 enzymes; important for cell reproduction, growth and sexual maturity; carbohydrate and protein metabolism, tissue repair and wound healing	Shellfish (especially oysters), meat, poultry, eggs, dairy products, nuts, whole grain cereal	Alcohol, diuretics, excess manganese and fiber, vitamins A and D, and phosphorus deficiency

SOURCES: Adapted from many sources including National Research Council: Diet and Health, Implications for Reducing Chronic Disease Risk, 1990, and National Academy of Sciences, *Eat for Life*, C. E. Woteki and P. R. Thomas (editors), 1992.

*RDA = recommended daily allowance for adults and children over 4 years (Food and Drug Administration or Department of Agriculture).

†Alcohol, caffeine, tobacco, dieting, inactivity, antibiotics and other drugs, and imbalance in intake can directly or indirectly lead to deficiencies.

Here are some of the system's features and characteristics:

- "Health care" costs totaled $740 billion in 1991 and $830 billion in 1992; health care comprises by far the single largest national outlay (and one that exceeds the gross national product of all but a handful of countries in the world).

- Expenditures as a percentage of GNP amount to 13 to 14% in the United States compared with 6 to 7% in Britain and Japan, and 8% in Canada and Germany. The United States spent about $3000 per capita in 1991, or more than 40% higher than Canada. The United States thus spends a substantially higher proportion than its industrial competitors, possibly diverting resources from investment in research, education, and infrastructure. (U.S. environmental expenditures amounted to about $120 billion in 1991, slightly less than 2% of GNP, within the range of major industrial nations.)

- The system has created national anxiety about health in young and old; 35 to 37 million Americans, most of them working, have no health insurance.

- The system revolves around procedures and payments, instead of patients.

- "Hidden" costs are imposed on employers and employment—average cost per employee in 1991 was $3000 to $3600. Employers are estimated to have paid more than $200 billion for group health insurance in 1991, or about 60% of corporate profits before taxes, and 50% of net earnings on average according to recent surveys.

- What has evolved is a high-tech, fractionated, procedure-oriented medical practice that is exceptionally suited to serve less than 5% of cases and applied liberally to terminal situations. (Some 70% of health care costs are incurred in the last month of life, an appalling indictment of the system.)

- The U.S. health care system ranks with the quarterly bottomline business practices, distorted economic incentives, and the educational system as the factors most responsible for the decline of the American competitive position.

On the positive side:

- High investment in R&D has resulted in a stream of new drugs that are more effective in combating disease and improving the quality of life, as well as substituting for the more costly and risky surgical procedures (on the other hand, the new microsurgical or laparoscopy techniques are also proving to be safer and less traumatic).

- Health care research, and spinoffs into other fields, helped keep America at the forefront, for example, in diagnostics and biotechnology.

- Other countries have drawn upon and benefited from the drugs and techniques developed in the United States.

One segment of the health care sector, the pharmaceutical industry, operates in a competitive environment with sales increasing from about $60 billion in

1991 to $70 billion in 1992 (prescription drugs accounting for about 80%). Pharmaceuticals, prescription and over-the-counter, represent 6 to 10% of health care costs, but despite their modest share, the prices of drugs have come under increasing scrutiny, partly because of high visibility, substantial price differentials in the United States and abroad, and the "unconscionable" prices charged for the AIDS drug AZT and the new bioengineered drugs. The pharmaceutical industry, which invests 10 to 20% of its sales on research and development [five times that of the U.S. industry average; $9.2 billion in 1991 according to the Pharmaceutical Manufacturers Association (PMA)], maintains that the prices are necessary to recoup the high costs of R&D over a limited period of patent protection, to compensate for "dry holes," and to provide incentive for development of new drugs that often save money and improve the quality of life. (Merck, Bristol-Myers Squibb, Pfizer, Roche, and a few others have announced that they would keep the overall price increases of drugs in line with the increase in consumer price index.) The PMA estimates that it takes $231 million and 12 years on average to develop, to gain FDA approval, and to commercialize a new drug. Some critics contend that this is a "bookkeeping trick." One criticism of drug research has been its preoccupation with patentable drugs and profits, ignoring the development of natural, traditional substances with therapeutic properties proved over time though not in a laboratory. Another criticism concerns the amount of spending on drug advertising and marketing relative to research. (Also, many U.S. pharmaceutical companies have a policy not to invest in drugs that do not have a large domestic market, irrespective of worldwide need.) Over the last decade, many leading companies, Merck, Bristol-Myers Squibb, and Johnson & Johnson, among others, have accelerated their research efforts into herbal and other natural ingredients. We may thus be able to look forward to a more "natural balance." In 1992, the National Institutes of Health established an Office for the Study of Unconventional Medical Practices, which should also stimulate interest in alternatives to traditional medicine.

Returning to the runaway costs of the health care modus operandi, how can it be made once again to respond to people's needs? Surprisingly, there is a simple answer: cancel the blank check Congress has created, and set a national budget for health—there is none at present. Here are some thoughts on the subject:

1. Develop a national health care budget, both in dollars and as a percent of GNP.

    Allocate resources by design, not by default. For example, if 8% of GNP is selected as a long-term goal, the present level could be brought in line over a period of 5 to 10 years. Only the budgeted amount would be available for distribution no matter what the reported "costs" are. This will send a clear signal on what the country is willing to pay that would stem the inflationary expectations of the medical establishment and potential entrants. (Governments cannot control the medical costs of an open-ended system except by the direct involvement of the real payer or by allocation. A fixed health care budget could also go a long way toward bridging the national budget deficit.)

2. Earmark a portion of the health care budget, say 20%, for prevention.

This represents the 80–20 urgent vs. important compromise. We do not know exactly how much of the present health care expenditures go into prevention, but probably no more than 3 to 4%. Empirical evidence suggests that prevention is far more resource-effective than treatment—probably by an order of magnitude.

3. Devise a comprehensive, integrated system at the national level.

The system should provide a range of services, encompassing primary care and family services, prevention, acute treatment, and specialists, combining the better features of the American, Canadian, and perhaps Cuban systems. Employers and employees should pay into a fund and have a stake in its performance. Employers, faced with costs spiraling out of their control, might consider transferring retired employee reserves into a national fund that would provide comprehensive care, possibly combining worker's compensation and health care benefits of current employees. (Health care and other obligations to retirees, to be disclosed under the new Financial Accounting Standard 106, can influence corporate credit ratings and interest costs in addition to lower earnings from after-tax charges.) The system administrative costs should be no more than 10 to 15%, which may require the dismantling or restructuring of the archaic and fractionated insurance framework. (There are more than a thousand insurance companies with a thousand different claim forms.)

Buying everyone insurance will not solve the problem—it will only reinforce the open-ended system. Likewise "managed care" will only be a palliative, largely serving to preserve the "privileged franchise" of some groups to impose taxes on present and future generations.

4. Create economic incentives for individual consumers and health care providers pointing in the right direction.

Individual incentives should reward prudent behavior with health care accounts for all Americans, for example. Drawing a parallel from the environmental field, hospitals and other providers should be rewarded for prevention and health care maintenance, similar to the conservation and demand side management (DSM) initiatives of electric utilities.

5. Set up subsystems to address the special needs of the elderly and to serve terminal patients.

Professional judgment, ethical considerations, fixed salaries, and fixed fees should govern these subsystems in order to avoid the excesses of fee-for-service that promote the most expensive treatments in these situations. Quality of life should also be considered in selecting treatments using, for example, a scale such as quality-adjusted life years (QALYs). Health care should be coupled with social support services for the elderly.

6. Establish a health care system focused on people's health—not on disease, insurance, lawyers, technology, politics, or even doctors.

   Technology, lawyers, doctors, and insurance companies have all been blamed in turn for the present state of affairs and high costs, but it is the "system" that needs to be replaced to provide a new public health focus. (Linkages of the components of the system are important but attempts to optimize individual components will seldom result in an optimal system.) Include prevention, nutrition, and wellness training in medical school curriculum, and in grade schools for the general population.

7. Allow medical professionals to practice sound and judicious medicine, and minimize the need for defensive medicine.

   Make rewards and compensation consistent with their contribution to society, but patients should not be viewed as profit centers. "Standard medical practices" do exist as do "standard operating practices" in industries, but the former vary three- or fourfold, notably in diagnostic and surgical procedures (especially in physician-owned facilities).

8. Restructure the malpractice lawsuit framework and the overall tort system.

   Malpractice lawsuits, defensive medicine, and the insurance premiums are estimated to add $40 to $50 billion to the health care costs. This problem should preferably be addressed as part of the overall product liability and the tort system reform.

9. Play a more active role in designing and operating the health care system.

   Employers (private business) pay nearly 30% of the costs of health services and supplies, up from 22% in 1970. In 1990, business health spending amounted to $186 billion, representing 61% of corporate profits before taxes (Health Care Financing Administration). (According to Harold Poling, chairman of Ford Motor Company, Ford spends as much on health care as it does on steel; health care providers comprise Ford's largest supplier.) And yet, employers take a passive role in national health policy, in marked contrast to their active role in the formulation of environmental policies and regulations.

10. Emphasize preventive and wellness services in employee assistance programs (EAP).

    Many leading companies, Johnson & Johnson and Merck, for example, already do. J&J also makes its programs available to other companies. (See Live for Life® case in the following box.) Such employee and family education programs address lifestyle activities, disease and accident prevention, and chronic disease management, as well as becoming informed consumers of medical services.

Live for Life, Johnson & Johnson Wellness Program

The Origins

Corporate health and fitness programs began to appear in the 1970s when scientists, behaviorists, and business leaders concluded that the worksite represents an ideal environment to encourage employees to improve their health and fitness-related practices. In 1979, Johnson & Johnson's research into ways to prevent or forestall avoidable illness resulted in the launch of Live for Life.

A multifaceted work-environment program involving change, risk assessment, and risk reduction, and designed to educate and motivate employees, Live for Life also was designed to provide employees with continuous opportunities to improve their lifestyles. Extensive piloting and testing led to economic and epidemiological studies (published in the *Journal of the American Medical Association* in 1985 and 1986, among others), demonstrating the efficacy and economic return of the Live for Life system.

Interest from other major U.S. corporations and institutions, as well as the successful introduction of Live for Life to virtually all of the 70-plus U.S. units and locations of Johnson & Johnson, led to the creation of Johnson & Johnson Health Management, Inc. (JJHMI) in January 1987. JJHMI's focus is on prevention of disease and injury, an appropriate extension of the corporation's interests in disease detection, treatment, and ongoing health maintenance. As Johnson & Johnson's most focused prevention business, JJHMI works with client companies and institutions to help them improve the health and well-being of their employees through motivation and encouragement of positive and lasting changes in behavior.

What Does the Wellness Program Offer?

Lifestyle activities.   These programs educate and motivate and offer opportunities to participate in various lifestyle improvement areas, including those addressing physical fitness, nutrition, weight reduction, blood pressure control, smoking cessation, stress management, alcohol and drug awareness, or medical self-care.

Screening, monitoring, follow-up.   These involve overall health assessments for individuals, as well as screening for specific conditions, such as high blood pressure, glaucoma, or diabetes.

Safety and accident prevention.   These programs focus on such concerns as defensive driving and seat belt use, home safety and accident prevention, on-the-job safety, first aid, CPR, and choke saving techniques.

(Continued)

Chronic disease management. These programs aid individuals with chronic diseases, such as hypertension, diabetes, and arthritis, in managing their conditions and improving their overall lifestyles.

Employee assistance programs (EAPs). EAPs are offered by employers to help employees manage personal problems that interfere with job performance, such as alcohol and drug abuse and family problems. The programs often include referrals to appropriate professionals outside the company.

Why Another Program?

Employers sponsor health promotion programs to:

- Control costs related to health care
- Improve productivity and morale
- Maintain or improve employee health
- Help in recruitment and retention of employees

Companies first addressed rising health care costs by implementing cost-containment measures—programs for second surgical opinion, higher deductibles, employee copayment. These programs were effective but could be used only *after* an employee became ill. The programs influenced overall costs without affecting the frequency or severity of illness—the underlying cause of increased health care costs. Keeping the employees well was the logical next step for business.

Studies began to pinpoint the costs to business of specific lifestyle risk factors. For example, a Washington Business Group on Health study found that smokers are 50% more likely to be hospitalized and have two times as many on-the-job accidents and 50% greater absenteeism than nonsmokers. On average, smokers at Johnson & Johnson had 45% greater absenteeism and 30% higher major medical expenses than nonsmokers.

Because of the impact of these health risk factors, companies began to realize the business benefits of encouraging employees to make positive changes in their lifestyles.

The Results: Cost Savings

J&J's experience (1991):

	$/employee	Total
Savings from Live for Life (33,000 employees)	$378	$12.5m
Cost of Live for Life program	225	7.4
Net saving (rounded)	$153	$ 5.1m

(J&J's medical insurance in the United States totaled $93 million in 1991.)

Overall program results from studies conducted by J&J:
  Savings per employee (4th year following program implementation)

Inpatient health care costs (4th year)*	$223
Reduced absenteeism (achieved in 3rd year)†	$156
Total savings	$379
Subtract cost of providing health promotion program per employee (1990 dollars)	$225
Net savings per employee	$154

*Live for Life groups experienced lower increases in inpatient hospital costs over a 4-year period compared with control groups. Outpatient costs were not affected by the intervention, however. Live for Life groups experienced additional expense in the first 2 years and cost savings in the final 2 years of the study. During the 4th year, companies with Live for Life saved $223 per employee (1990 dollars).

†Among wage employees, after 1 year of exposure to Live for Life, the control group experienced an increase in absenteeism, while the experimental group showed a decrease. The difference between groups was statistically significant (after adjustment for demographics and baseline differences between experimental and control groups). Differences between groups were not found for salaried employees, however.

SOURCE: Adapted from information provided by Johnson & Johnson.

Vision for the Next Millennium

We return thanks to our mother, the earth, which sustains us…

to the wind, which, moving the air, has banished diseases…

to our grandfather, He-no, that he has protected his grandchildren…

and has given to us his rain…to the sun, that he has looked upon

the earth with a beneficent eye.

IROQUOIS PRAYER OF THANKSGIVING*

References and Additional Readings†

American Cancer Society (Atlanta, Georgia), Cancer Facts and Figures, 1991.

American Diabetes Association (Alexandria, Virginia), What You Need to Know about Diabetes. 12/91 - 200M.

American Health Foundation (New York), various publications.

American Heart Association (Dallas, Texas), various publications on nutrition, diet, smoking, cholesterol, and coronary risk factors.

National Geographic, October 1991.

†See also the References in Chap. 11.

Chemical Manufacturers Association (CMA), Washington, D.C., *U.S. Chemical Industry Statistical Handbook,* 1992.

Electric Power Research Institute (EPRI, Palo Alto, California), Electric and Magnetic Field Fundamentals. EN3012.9.89.

Geschwind, S., J. Stolwijk, M. Bracken, E. Fitzgerald, A. Stark, C. Olsen, and J. Melius, "Risk of Congenital Malformations Associated with Proximity to Hazardous Waste Sites," *Journal of Epidemiology,* vol. 135, no. 11, 1992.

Harvard School of Public Health, Center for Risk Analysis, Annual Report, 1991.

Health Insurance Association of America: Source Book of Health Insurance Data, 1991; and Health Trends Chart Book, 1991.

Institute for Medicine, National Academy of Sciences, 1991. C. Woteki and P. Thomas, editors. Eat for Life: The Food and Nutrition Board's Guide to Reducing Your Risk for Chronic Disease.

Jencks, S., and G. Shieber, "Containing U.S. Health Care Costs: What Bullet to Bite?" *Health Care Financing Review,* 1991, Annual Supplement (Health Care Financing Administration, U.S. Department of Health and Human Services).

Johnson & Johnson Health Management, Inc., information on health programs and services including Live for Life program.

Knapp, R. G., and M. C. Miller, *Clinical Epidemiology and Biostatistics,* Williams & Wilkins, Baltimore, Maryland, 1992.

Kolluru, R., Identifying chemical hazards and controlling health risks: Community and individual initiatives. EPA's First Conference on Public Access to Environmental Information, Washington, D.C., 1989.

Levit, K., and C. Cowan, "Health Care Financing Trends—Business, Households, and Governments: Health Care Costs, 1990," *Health Care Financing Review,* winter 1991 (Health Care Financing Administration, U.S. Department of Health and Human Services).

Mauser & Bahn, *Epidemiology—An Introductory Text,* 1985. Saunders, Philadelphia.

National Research Council (NRC), National Academy of Sciences (NAS) 1989–1990. *Diet and Health: Implications for Reducing Chronic Disease Risk.* National Academy Press, Washington, D.C.

National Research Council, 1990. Valuing Health Risks, Costs, and Benefits for Environmental Decision Making—Report of a Conference. P. Hammond and R. Coppock, editors.

National Research Council, 1991. Frontiers in Assessing Human Exposures to Environmental Toxicants—Report of a Symposium.

National Research Council, National Academy of Sciences, 1991. Environmental Epidemiology: Public Health and Hazardous Wastes.

National Research Council, 1991. Monitoring Human Tissues for Toxic Substances.

National Research Council, 1992. Global Environmental Change: Understanding the Human Dimension.

New York State Department of Health, 1992. Health Advisory—Chemicals in Sportfish and Game, 1992–1993.

Pharmaceutical Manufacturers Association (PMA), Washington, D.C., Modern Medicines: Saving Lives and Money, July 1991; New Drug Approvals in 1991; in development—New Medicines; and other publications. Personal communication.

Physicians Desk Reference (PDR), 1991. Medical Economics Company, Oradell, New Jersey.

Reinert, R., B. Knuth, M. Kamrin, and Q. Stober, "Risk Assessment, Risk Management, and Fish Consumption Advisories in the United States," *Fisheries*, November–December 1991.

Rom, W., *Environmental and Occupational Medicine*. Little, Brown, Boston, 1983.

Sadiku, M., 1989. *Elements of Electromagnetics*. Saunders Publishing/Holt, Rinehart and Winston. Orlando, Florida.

United Nations Environment Programme (UNEP): Radiation—Doses, Effects, Risks (1985). United Nations Publications.

U.S. Department of Agriculture (USDA): USDA's Food Guide Pyramid. *Bulletin* 249, April 1991; and Nutrition and Your Health: Dietary Guidelines for Americans. *Bulletin* 232, November 1990.

U.S. Environmental Protection Agency, 1991. Indoor Air Assessment. EPA600/8-90/044.

U.S. Food and Drug Administration (FDA). *FDA Consumer Magazine*, vol. 26, no. 7, September 1992.

U.S. Food and Drug Administration, "Preventing Food-Borne Illnesses," *FDA Consumer Magazine*, January–February 1991.

U.S. General Accounting Office 1991. Health Care Spending Control—The Experience of France, Germany, and Japan. GAO/HRD-92-9.

U.S. General Accounting Office 1991. Nuclear Power Safety, GAO/NSIAD-92-2B.

Weinstein, B. (Columbia University Comprehensive Cancer Center) and J. Groopman (Johns Hopkins School of Hygiene and Public Health), Environmentally Induced Cancers: Causes, Mechanisms and Prevention, 1991.

Weinstein, B., Symposium on Cell Proliferation, National Institute of Environmental Health Sciences, Research Triangle Park, North Carolina, January 1992.

13

Communicating Risk Information: A Guide to Environmental Communication in Crisis and Noncrisis Situations

Vincent T. Covello, Ph.D.

Division of Environmental Sciences,
School of Public Health
Columbia University

In this chapter:

- Introduction, Definitions
- Science and Perception
- Risk Comparisons
- Conclusions
- Appendix: Principles of Risk Communication in Crisis and Noncrisis Situations

Introduction

Today corporations, government agencies, and other organizations are placing greater emphasis on the need for better environmental communication in crisis and noncrisis situations. Much of the focus is on overcoming problems and difficulties in communicating information about risks of exposures to environmental agents—particularly the risks of exposures to chemicals, heavy metals, and radiation in the air, water, land, and food.

Why so much interest in environmental risk communication? One explanation is the increased number of hazard communication and environmental right-to-know laws relating to exposures to environmental risk agents. Another stems from increased public fear and concern about exposures to environmental risk agents and the corresponding demand for risk information. But a third underlies the first two—the loss of trust in government and industry as trusted and credible sources of information about environmental risks.

Partly in response to this need, researchers have focused their attention on the principles and practice of environmental communication in crisis and noncrisis situations. Environmental communication—commonly known as risk communication—is one of the fastest growing parts of the environmental literature—with hundreds of articles and books published over the last 5 years.

The purpose of this chapter is to review the main findings from this literature. The specific aim is to provide the reader with a general outline of the literature on risk communication and to relate this work to the practical needs of those with risk communication responsibilities. To assist the reader, an appendix is included that lists the main determinants of effective environmental communication in crisis and noncrisis situations.

Definitions

Risk communication can be defined as the exchange of information among interested parties about the nature, magnitude, significance, or control of a risk. Interested parties include government agencies, corporations or industry groups, unions, the media, scientists, professional organizations, special interest groups, communities, and individual citizens.

Information about risks can be communicated through a variety of channels, ranging from media reports and warning labels on products to public meetings or hearings involving representatives from government, industry, the media, and the general public. These communication efforts can be a source of difficulty for both risk communicators and the intended recipients of the information. Industry officials, government officials, and scientists, for example, often express their frustration, arguing that laypeople do not accurately perceive and evaluate risk information. Representatives of citizen groups and individual citizens often express equal amounts of frustration, perceiving risk communicators and risk assessment experts to be uninterested in their concerns and unwilling to take actions to solve seemingly straightforward environmental problems. In this context, the media often serve as transmitters and translators of risk information. But the media have been criticized for exaggerating risks and for emphasizing drama over scientific facts.

Science and Perception

A significant part of the risk communication literature focuses on problems and difficulties in communicating risk information effectively. These problems and difficulties revolve around issues of science and perception and can be organized into four categories: (1) characteristics and limitations of scientific data about risks; (2) characteristics and limitations of government officials, industry officials, and other spokespersons in communicating information about risks; (3) characteristics and limitations of the media in reporting information about risks; and (4) characteristics and limitations of the public in evaluating and interpreting risk information. Each is described below.

1. Characteristics and Limitations of Scientific Data about Risks

One source of difficulty in communicating information about risks is the uncertainty and complexity of data on health, safety, and environmental risks. Risk assessments, despite their strengths, seldom provide exact answers. Owing to limitations in scientific understanding, data, models, and methods, the results of most risk assessments are at best approximations. Moreover, the resources needed to resolve these uncertainties are seldom adequate to the task.

These uncertainties invariably affect communications with the public in the hostile climate that surrounds many environmental issues. For example, uncertainties in environmental risk assessments often lead to radically different estimates of risk. An important factor underlying many debates about risks is the different assessments of risk produced by government agencies, industry, and public interest groups.

Given these uncertainties, a critical need in risk communication is to provide information to the intended audience on the assumptions underlying the calculation of risks. Since many disagreements revolve around these assumptions (e.g., assumptions about doses and exposures), such disclosures could improve public confidence and understanding.

A related flaw is the failure to describe and characterize uncertainties. Risk reports that contain only single risk values or point estimates of risk (e.g., 4000 excess cancers over a lifetime) ignore the true range of risk possibilities. Moreover, they provide an inaccurate picture to the public of the ability of risk assessment to produce precise numbers. A more accurate picture is provided by describing a range of risk estimates based on optimistic or pessimistic (conservative) assumptions.

2. Characteristics and Limitations of Industry Officials, Government Officials, and Other Spokespersons in Communicating Information about Risks

A central question addressed by the literature on risk communication is why some individuals and organizations are trusted as sources of risk information and others are not. This question takes on special importance given that two of the most prominent sources of risk information—industry and government—often lack trust and credibility. In the United States, for example, overall public confidence and trust in government and industry as trusted sources of information has declined precipitously over the past two decades. The majority of people in the United States view industry and government as among the least trusted sources of information about the risks of environmental exposures to chemicals. At the same time, the majority of people view industry and government as among the most knowledgeable sources of information about chemical risks.

Public distrust of government and industry is grounded in several beliefs: that they have been insensitive to public concerns and fears about environmental risks, unwilling to acknowledge problems, unwilling to share information, unwilling to allow meaningful public participation, and negligent in fulfilling their environmental responsibilities. Compounding the problem are beliefs that current environmental laws are too weak, that the environment is worse today than it was 20 years ago, and that government and industry have done a poor job protecting the environment.

Several factors compound these perceptions and problems. First, many officials have engaged in highly visible debates and disagreements about the reliability, validity, and meaning of the results of environmental health risk assessments. In many cases, equally prominent experts have taken diametrically opposed positions on the risks of nuclear power plants, hazardous waste sites, asbestos, electric and magnetic fields, lead, radon, PCBs, arsenic, dioxin, solid waste, and agricultural chemicals such as EDB and ALAR. While such debates may be constructive for the development of scientific knowledge, they often undermine public trust and confidence in industry and government.

Second, resources for risk assessment and management are seldom adequate to meet demands by citizens and public interest groups for definitive findings and rapid action. Explanations by officials that the generation of valid and reliable toxicological or epidemiological data is expensive and time-consuming—or that risk assessment and management activities are constrained by resource, technical, statutory, legal, or other limitations—are seldom perceived to be satisfactory. Individuals facing what they believe is a new and significant risk are especially reluctant to accept such claims.

Third, coordination among responsible authorities is seldom adequate. In many debates about risks, for example, lack of coordination has severely undermined public faith and confidence. Compounding such problems is the lack of consistency in approaches to risk assessment and management by authorities at the local, state, regional, national, and international levels. For example, few requirements exist for regulatory agencies to develop coherent, coordinated, consistent, and interrelated plans, programs, and guidelines for managing risks. As a result, regulatory systems tend to be highly fragmented. This fragmentation often leads to jurisdictional conflicts about which agency and which level of government has the ultimate responsibility for assessing and managing a particular environmental activity or risk. Lack of coordination, different mandates, and confusion about responsibility and authority also lead, in many cases, to the production of multiple and competing estimates of risk. A commonly observed result of such confusion is the erosion of public trust, confidence, and acceptance.

Fourth, many officials in government and industry lack adequate training in community and media relations and in the specific requirements of risk communication. For example, many officials use complex and difficult language and jargon in communicating information about risks and benefits to the media and the public. Technical language or jargon is not only difficult to comprehend but can also create a perception that the official or expert is being unresponsive, dishonest, or evasive.

Finally, many industry and government officials are insensitive to the information needs and concerns of the public. Officials often operate on the assumption that they and their audience share a common framework for evaluating and interpreting risk information. However, this is often not the case. One of the most important findings to emerge from risk perception and communication studies is that people take into consideration a complex array of qualitative and quantitative factors in defining, evaluating, and acting on risk information.

One of the costs of this heritage of mistrust and loss of confidence is the public's reluctance to believe information from government and industry about the risks of exposure to chemicals, heavy metals, and radiation in the workplace and environment.

Programs and plans for overcoming distrust of government and industry require improvements in three areas: in risk assessment, in risk management, and in risk communication. Focusing only on risk communication, better risk communication requires improvements in the credibility of individual spokespeople, in the credibility of organizations with risk assessment and management responsibilities, and enhanced third party support, defined as better collaboration with trust institutions and individuals.

Improving the credibility of individual spokespeople means that those in government and industry who interact with the public on risk issues must develop better communication skills—both verbal and nonverbal. Skill development, in turn, is based on three principles: that perceptions are realities, that the goal of risk communication is to establish trust and credibility when trust and credibility are low, and that effective risk communication is indeed a skill (Box 13-1).

For some audiences, such as the media, spokespersons must develop highly refined skills. But more polished communication skills alone will not solve the problem. Bettering the credibility of spokespeople also calls for improvements in actions by their institutions. People judge others more on their actions than

---

**Box 13-1.   Key Formulas Underlying Effective
Risk Communication**

- $P = R$

  [Perceptions (P) equal realities (R): what is perceived as real will be real in its consequences.]

- $G = T + C$

  [The primary goal (G) of risk communication is to establish high levels of trust (T) and credibility (C); the secondary goal is to convey facts and figures.]

- $C = S$

  [Effective risk communication (C) is a complex skill (S): as with any complex skill, it requires significant amounts of knowledge, training, and practice.]

---

on their words; when their actions fail, they distrust their words. Because spokespeople speak for their institutions, their credibility depends on and will be enhanced only by improvements in the actions of the institutions they represent. Finally, gaining better credibility for spokespeople involves thinking broadly about risk communication and attending to the importance of developing ongoing partnerships with employees and the public. Environmental risk problems are generally long-term, complex problems that require active listening and two-way communication.

Improved credibility for organizations involves making improvements in both environmental performance and outreach efforts, based on a credo of ethical and responsible care. It also involves respect for the differing values and world views that employees and the public use when they evaluate risk information. Their evaluations are often broader than those of experts, and take into account a wide array of considerations, including information about fairness, benefits, control, voluntariness, alternatives, catastrophic potential, familiarity, process, and trust in institutions.

Enhanced third party support includes improvements in coordination and collaboration with organizations and individuals that are perceived by the public to be credible. Surveys indicate that organizations and individuals perceived to be relatively high to medium in credibility on environmental risk issues include physicians and other health professionals, university professors, professional organizations, the media, nonmanagement employees, nonprofit voluntary health organizations, environmental groups, and local citizens who are respected, neutral, and informed on environmental issues (Box 13-2). Better coordination and collaboration with such groups can, in turn, result in alliances, joint communications, and support. It is also important to understand why these professionals and organizations are perceived as credible. Research indicates, for example, that physicians and university professors are credible for two main reasons. First, they are perceived as being motivated by higher goals:

Box 13-2. Indicators of Trust and Credibility

- Perceived caring and empathy

  Perceived sincerity, ability to listen, ability to see issues from the perspective of the other

- Perceived competence and expertise

  Perceived intelligence, training, authoritativeness, experience, educational level, and professional attainment, knowledge, command of information

- Perceived openness and honesty

  Perceived truthfulness, candidness, justness, objectivity, sincerity, disinterestedness

- Perceived dedication and commitment

  Perceived altruism, diligence, self-identification, involvement, hard work

---

physicians are perceived to be dedicated to healing and professors are perceived to be dedicated to truth and knowledge. Second, both groups are perceived to be financially independent of the organizations that hire them as consultants, and thus are not beholden to others for their views. Interestingly, neither physicians nor professors lose significant amounts of credibility with the general public when they do paid work for government or industry.

A common thread in all three strategies is the need to be proactive in establishing high levels of trust and credibility. When trust and credibility are missing or weak, the primary goal of risk communication is to build them up. Only when trust and credibility have been established can other goals, such as education and the sharing of information, follow.

Surveys, case studies, and experimental research all indicate that trust and credibility cannot be built quickly. Instead, they are the result of ongoing partnerships, actions, performance, and skill in communications. Research also indicates that four specific factors influence perceptions of trust and credibility: perceived caring and empathy, perceived competence and expertise, perceived honesty and openness, and perceived dedication and commitment (Box 13-3).

These four factors form the criteria that citizens use to evaluate the credibility of an organization or individual. Risk communication is effective to the degree to which all actions and communications—verbal and nonverbal—convey caring and empathy, competence and expertise, honesty and openness, and dedication and commitment.

Of the four factors, caring and empathy appear to be the most important. In most situations, trust and credibility are determined largely by whether the communicator is perceived as caring and empathetic. For example, does the audience perceive the communicator to be a good listener? Does the audience perceive the communicator to be concerned first and foremost about their con-

---

Box 13-3.   Trust and Credibility of Sources of Environmental Information Based on 1991 Sample Survey of the U.S. Population

Top third

- Physicians and other health or safety professionals
- Professors (especially senior professors from respected local universities)
- Local citizens who are perceived to be neutral, respected, and well informed about the issue
- Nonprofit voluntary health organizations
- Nonmanagement employees

Middle third

- Media
- Environmental groups

Bottom third

- Industry officials
- Federal government officials
- Environmental consultants from for-profit firms

Changes from previous years

Environmental groups—10 to 15% loss of credibility

Media—5 to 10% gain in credibility

Government and industry—10% loss in credibility

---

cerns, be they health, safety, environmental, economic, aesthetic, fairness, or process concerns? Often, people make their initial judgments about caring and empathy within a relatively short period of time, often within the first 30 seconds. Once made, such judgments are extremely resistant to change.

Perceptions of trust and credibility also derive from perceptions of competence and expertise, honesty and openness, and dedication and commitment. Perceptions of competence and expertise are influenced largely by an organization's environmental record and by the spokesperson's merit factors, such as education, track record, experience, knowledge, presentation skills, and professional recognition.

Perceptions of honesty and openness derive largely from actions, words, and nonverbal cues that convey truthfulness and candidness. In oral communica-

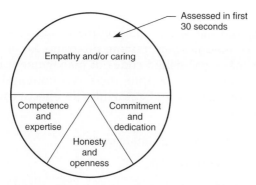

Figure 13-1. Trust and credibility chart. Trust and credibility are difficult to achieve; if lost, they are even more difficult to regain.

tions, nonverbal cues to honesty and openness, such as poor eye contact and physical barriers between the speaker and the audience, play a particularly important role.

Perceptions of dedication and commitment are influenced largely by perceptions of hard work and diligence in the pursuit of health, safety, and environmental goals. An audience will gauge a speaker's hard work and diligence by a number of verbal and nonverbal cues: Is the speaker willing to be available to the community after hours? Does the speaker come to public meetings early and stay late? Is the speaker willing to give a home phone number? Failure to communicate messages of dedication can diminish a speaker's credibility by as much as one-fifth.

Male and female differences on these dimensions of credibility are often pronounced. Women, for example, often receive relatively low initial ratings on competence and expertise. But because women in general receive substantially higher initial ratings than men on the other trust and credibility factors, a woman who is perceived as competent and expert outranks most men in credibility. Further, because men generally are not perceived to be honest, caring, and dedicated to public health and welfare, the rare man who does rank high on all four trust and credibility factors outranks even the most competent woman in credibility.

At the institutional level, prospects for establishing high levels of public trust are modest at best—at least in the short run. They do, however, appear to be better locally than nationally or globally. For example, much of the thrust of the chemical industry's worldwide Responsible Care initiative is to develop, at the local level, an environmental track record of dealing openly, fairly, safely, and responsibly with their employees and neighboring communities.

Government agencies have also initiated programs aimed at increasing public trust. These include enhanced community relations and risk communication programs and extensive field testing of risk communication materials.

Furthermore, several federal and state agencies, including the Environmental Protection Agency (EPA) and the Minnesota Pollution Control Agency, have launched ambitious risk communication training programs for all employees. Finally, several agencies have published codes of management practice for effective risk communication. For example, the Environmental Protection Agency published a set of seven rules and guidelines for effective risk communication in 1988. The rules are:

- Accept and involve the public as a legitimate partner
- Plan carefully and evaluate performance
- Listen to your audience
- Be honest, frank, and open
- Coordinate and collaborate with other credible sources
- Meet the needs of the media
- Speak clearly and with compassion

In introducing the rules, the EPA noted that the goal of risk communication is not to defuse public concern or avoid action but rather to produce an informed public that is involved, interested, reasonable, thoughtful, solution-oriented, and collaborative.

3. Characteristics and Limitations of the Media in Reporting Information About Risks

The mass media play a critical role in transmitting risk information. Given this importance, researchers have focused their attention on the role of the mass media and on characteristics and limitations of the media that contribute to problems in risk communication.

One of the major conclusions to emerge from risk communication research is that the media are biased toward stories that contain drama, conflict, expert disagreements, and uncertainties. The media are especially biased toward stories that contain dramatic or sensational material, such as a minor or major accident at a chemical manufacturing facility or a nuclear power plant. Much less attention is given to daily occurrences that kill or injure far more people each year but take only one life at a time. In reporting about risks, journalists often focus on the same concerns as the public, e.g., potentially catastrophic effects, lack of familiarity and understanding, involuntariness, scientific uncertainty, risks to future generations, unclear benefits, inequitable distribution of risks and benefits, and potentially irreversible effects.

Media coverage of risks is frequently deficient in that many stories contain oversimplifications, distortions, and inaccuracies in reporting risk information.

Media coverage is also deficient not only in what is contained in the story but in what is left out. For example, analyses of media reports on cancer risks show that these reports are often deficient in providing few statistics on general cancer rates for purposes of comparison; providing little information on common forms of cancer; not addressing known sources of public ignorance about cancer; and providing little information about detection, treatments, and other protective measures.

Many of these problems stem from characteristics of the media and the constraints under which reporters work. First, most reporters work under extremely tight deadlines that limit the amount of time for research and for the pursuit of valid and reliable information. Second, with few exceptions, reporters do not have adequate time or space to deal with the complexities and uncertainties surrounding many risk issues. Third, journalists achieve objectivity in a story by balancing opposing views. Truth in journalism is different from truth in science. In journalism, there are only different or conflicting views and claims, to be covered as fairly as possible. Fourth, journalists are source-dependent. Under the pressure of deadlines and other constraints, reporters tend to rely heavily on sources that are easily accessible and willing to speak out. Sources that are difficult to contact, hard to draw out, or reluctant to provide interesting and nonqualified statements are often left out. Finally, few reporters have the scientific background or expertise needed to evaluate the complex scientific data and disagreements that surround many debates about risks. Given these limitations, effectiveness in communicating with the media about risks depends in part on understanding the constraints and needs of the media and adapting one's behavior and information to meet these needs.

4. Characteristics and Limitations of the Public in Evaluating and Interpreting Risk Information

Risk communication research on public attitudes and beliefs parallels in many ways the more general communication research. However, the risk communication literature has several distinctive elements not generally found in the general communication literature. For example, much risk communication research focuses on characteristics and limitations of the public in evaluating and interpreting risk information. These include inaccurate perceptions of levels of risk, lack of interest in risk problems and technical complexities, overconfidence in one's ability to avoid harm, strong beliefs and opinions that are resistant to change, exaggerated expectations about the effectiveness of regulatory actions, desires and demands for scientific certainty, reluctance to make tradeoffs among different types of risks or among risks, costs, and benefits, and difficulties in understanding probabilistic information related to unfamiliar activities or technologies.

An important implication of this literature for risk communication is the distinction between perceptions of risk and judgments of risk acceptability. Even though the level of risk is related to risk acceptability, it is not a perfect correlation. Two factors affect the way people assess risk and evaluate acceptability; these factors modify the correlation.

First, the level of risk is only one among several variables that determines acceptability (Box 13-4). Among the other variables that matter to people in evaluating and interpreting risk information are fairness, benefits, alternatives, control, and voluntariness. In general, a fairly distributed risk is more acceptable than an unfairly distributed one. A risk entailing significant benefits to the parties at risk is more acceptable than a risk with no such benefits. A risk for which there are no alternatives is more acceptable than a risk that could be eliminated by using an alternative technology. A risk that the parties at risk have some control over is more acceptable than a risk that is beyond their control. A risk that the parties at risk assess and decide to accept is more acceptable than a risk that is imposed on them. These statements are true in exactly the same sense in which it is true that a small risk is more acceptable than a large risk. Risk is multidimensional; size is only one of the relevant dimensions.

If one grants the validity of these points, a whole range of risk-management approaches becomes possible. Because factors such as fairness, familiarity, and voluntariness are as relevant as size in judging the acceptability of a risk, efforts to make a risk fairer, more familiar, and more voluntary are as appropriate as efforts to make the risk smaller. Similarly, because control is important in determining the acceptability of a risk, efforts to share power, such as establishing and assisting community advisory committees or supporting third party research, audits, inspections, and monitoring, can be effective in making a risk more acceptable.

Second, deciding what level of risk ought to be acceptable is not a technical question but a value question. People vary in how they assess risk acceptability. They weigh the various factors according to their own values, sense of risk, and stake in the outcome. Because acceptability is a matter of values and opinions, and because values and opinions differ, debates about risk are often debates about values, accountability, and control.

Risk Comparisons

A significant part of the risk communication literature deals with risk comparisons. Interest in risk comparisons derives in part from the perceived difficulties in communicating complex, quantitative risk information to laypersons and the need to put risk information in perspective. Several authors have argued that risk comparisons provide this perspective.

In a typical risk comparison, the risk in question is compared with the risks of other substances or activities. Because comparisons are perceived to be more intuitively meaningful than absolute probabilities, it is widely believed that

Box 13-4.   **Factors Important in Risk Perception and Evaluation**

Factor	Conditions associated with increased public concern	Conditions associated with decreased public concern
■ Catastrophic potential	Fatalities and injuries grouped in time and space	Fatalities and injuries scattered and random
■ Familiarity	Unfamiliar	Familiar
■ Understanding	Mechanisms or process not understood	Mechanisms or process understood
■ Uncertainty	Risks scientifically unknown or uncertain	Risks known to science
■ Controllability (personal)	Uncontrollable	Controllable
■ Voluntariness of exposure	Involuntary	Voluntary
■ Effects on children	Children specifically at risk	Children not specifically at risk
■ Effects manifestation	Delayed effects	Immediate effects
■ Effects on future generations	Risk to future generations	No risk to future generations
■ Victim identity	Identifiable victims	Statistical victims
■ Dread	Effects dreaded	Effects not dreaded
■ Trust in institutions	Lack of trust in responsible institutions	Trust in responsible institutions
■ Media attention	Much media attention	Little media attention
■ Accident history	Major and sometimes minor accidents	No major or minor accidents
■ Equity	Inequitable distribution of risks and benefits	Equitable distribution of risks and benefits
■ Benefits	Unclear benefits	Clear benefits
■ Reversibility	Effects irreversible	Effects reversible
■ Personal stake	Individual personally at risk	Individual not personally at risk
■ Origin	Caused by human actions or failures	Caused by acts of nature or God

they can be used effectively for communicating risk information. A basic assumption of the approach is that risk comparisons provide a conceptual yardstick for measuring the relative size of a risk, especially when the risk is new and unfamiliar.

Risk comparisons have several strengths that address important facets of this problem. They present issues in a mode that appears compatible with intuitive, natural thought processes, such as the use of analogies to improve understanding; they avoid the difficult and controversial task of converting diverse risks into a common unit, such as dollars per life lost or per day of pain and suffering; and they avoid direct numerical reference to small probabilities, which can be difficult to comprehend and evaluate in the abstract.

Many risk comparisons are advanced not only for gaining perspective and understanding but also for setting priorities and determining which risks are acceptable. More specifically, risk comparisons have been advocated as a means for determining which risks to ignore, which risks to be concerned about, and how much risk reduction to seek. A common argument in many risk comparisons, for example, is that risks that are small or comparable to already accepted risks should themselves be accepted. Such claims cannot, however, be defended. Although risk comparisons can provide insight and perspective, they provide only a small part of the information needed for setting priorities or for determining which risks are acceptable.

For example, it is often tempting for industry or government officials to use the following argument when they meet with community groups or members of the public to discuss risks.

> The risk of *a* (emissions from the plant) is lower than the risk of *b* (driving to the meeting or smoking during breaks). Since you (the audience) find *b* acceptable, you are obliged to find *a* acceptable.

This argument has a basic flaw in logic; its use can severely damage trust and credibility. Some listeners will analyze the argument this way:

> I do not have to accept the (small) added risk of living near a chemical plant just because I accept the (perhaps larger, but voluntary and personally beneficial) risk of sunbathing, bicycling, smoking or driving my car. In deciding about the acceptability of risks, I consider many factors, only one of them being the size of the risk—and I prefer to do my own evaluation. Your job is not to tell me about what I should accept but to tell me about the size of the risk and what you are doing about it.

Judgments of acceptability are related not only to annual mortality rates—the focus of most risk comparisons—but also to the broad and diverse set of factors that influence public perceptions of risk and acceptability (Box 13-4). These factors explain, in part, public concerns about the risks of environmental exposures to toxic chemicals. Because of the importance of these factors, comparisons showing that the risks associated with environmental exposures to chemicals are lower than the risks of other activities or technologies may have no effect whatsoever on public perceptions and attitudes. For example, comparing the risk of living near a chemical manufacturing plant with the risk of driving X number of hours, eating X tablespoons of peanut butter, smoking X number of cigarettes a day, or sunbathing X number of hours may provide a perspective but may also be highly inappropriate. Since such risks differ on a variety of qualitative dimensions—e.g., perceived benefits, extent of personal control, voluntariness, catastrophic potential, familiarity, fairness, origin, and scientific uncertainty—it is likely that people will perceive the comparison as irrelevant or meaningless.

The fundamental argument against such comparisons is that it is seldom relevant or appropriate to compare risks with different qualities for risk acceptability purposes, even if the comparison is technically accurate. Several reasons underlie this argument. First, as noted above, there are important psychological and social differences among risks with different qualities. Risks that are involuntary and result from lifestyle choices, for example, are more likely to be accepted than risks that are perceived to be involuntary and imposed.

Second, people recognize that risks are cumulative and that each additional risk adds to their overall risk burden. The fact that a person is exposed to risks resulting from voluntary lifestyle choices does not lessen the impact of risks that are perceived to be involuntary and imposed.

Third, people perceive many types of risk in an absolute sense. An involuntary exposure that increases the risk of cancer or birth defects is perceived as a physical and moral insult regardless of whether the increase is small or whether the increase is smaller than risks from other exposures.

Finally, judgments about the acceptability of a risk can seldom be separated from judgments about the risk decision process. Public responses to risk are shaped both by the characteristics of the risky activity and by the perceived adequacy of the decision-making process. Risk comparisons play only a limited role in such determinations.

These results suggest that risk comparisons, if provided, should have the following characteristics: (1) risks that are compared should be as similar as possible; (2) data sources on risk levels should be credible and identified; (3) limitations of the comparison should be described; (4) all comparisons should have only one purpose—perspective; and (5) all comparisons should be pilot tested with a surrogate for the intended audience.

Conclusions

Given the passage of increasing numbers of right-to-know laws, and given increasing demands by the public for risk information, risk communication will be the focus of increasing attention in years to come. Industry and government officials will continually be asked to provide information about health, safety, and environmental risks to interested and affected individuals and communities. How they answer this challenge will have a profound effect on public perceptions of the risks of modern technology.

The findings reported in this chapter represent only a sampling of results from the emerging area of risk communication research. They suggest, on the one hand, that effective risk communication is a complex art and skill that requires substantial knowledge, training, and practice. They also suggest that there are no easy prescriptions for effective risk communication; that there are limits on what can be accomplished through risk communication alone—no matter how skilled, committed, and sincere an organization or person is. Finally, they suggest that trust and credibility are *the* key factors in successful risk communication.

References

Cohrssen, J., and V. Covello (1989), *Risk Analysis.* Washington, D.C.: White House Council on Environmental Quality.

Conservation Foundation (1985), *Risk Assessment and Risk Control.* Washington, D.C.: Conservation Foundation.

Covello, V. T. (1983), "The Perception of Technological Risks: A Literature Review," *Technological Forecasting and Social Change,* vol. 23, pp. 285–297.

Covello, V. T. (1988), "Informing the Public about Health and Environmental Risks: Problems and Opportunities for Effective Risk Communication," in N. Lind (ed.), *Risk Communication: A Symposium,* Waterloo: University of Waterloo.

Covello, V. T. (1989), "Issues and Problems in Using Risk Comparisons for Communicating Right-to-Know Information on Chemical Risks," *Environmental Science and Technology,* vol. 23, no. 12, pp. 1444–1449.

Covello, V. T. (1991), "Risk Comparisons and Risk Communication," in R. Kasperson, and P. J. Stallen, eds., *Communicating Risks to the Public.* Boston: Kluwer Academic Publishers.

Covello, V. T. (1992), "Risk Communication, Trust, and Credibility," *Health and Environmental Digest,* April 1992, vol. 6, no. 1.

Covello, V. T., and F. Allen (1988), *Seven Cardinal Rules of Risk Communication,* Washington, D.C.: U.S. Environmental Protection Agency, Office of Policy Analysis.

Covello, V. T., D. von Winterfeldt, and P. Slovic (1987), "Communicating Risk Information to the Public," in J. C. Davies, V. Covello, and F. Allen, eds., *Risk Communication.* Washington, D.C.: The Conservation Foundation.

Covello, V. T., P. Sandman, and P. Slovic (1988), *Risk Communication, Risk Statistics, and Risk Comparisons.* Washington, D.C.: Chemical Manufacturers Association.

Covello, V. T., D. McCallum, and M. Pavlova, eds. (1989), *Effective Risk Communication: The Role and Responsibility of Governmental and Non-Governmental Organizations.* New York: Plenum Press.

Covello, V. T., E. Donovan, and J. Slavick (1991), *Community Outreach,* Washington, D.C.: Chemical Manufacturers Association.

Covello, V. T., and M. Merkhofer (1992, in press), *Risk Assessment Methods.* New York: Plenum Press.

Davies, J. C., V. T. Covello, and F. W. Allen, eds. (1987), *Risk Communication.* Washington, D.C.: The Conservation Foundation.

Fischhoff, B. (1985), "Managing Risk Perception," *Issues in Science and Technology,* vol. 2, pp. 83–96.

Fischhoff, B., S. Lichtenstein, P. Slovic, S. L. Derby, and R. L. Keeney (1981), *Acceptable Risk*. Cambridge University Press: New York.

Fischhoff, B. (1987), "Treating the Public with Risk Communications: A Public Health Perceptive," *Science, Technology, and Human Values* 12 (vols. 3 and 4), pp. 13–19.

Hadden, S. (1989), *Citizen Right to Know: Communication and Public Policy*, Boulder: Westview.

Hance, B., C. Chess, and P. Sandman (1987), Improving Dialogue with Communities: A Risk Communication Manual for Government. Trenton, New Jersey, Office of Science and Research, New Jersey Department of Environmental Protection, December 1987.

Johnson, B., and V. Covello, eds. (1987), *The Social and Cultural Construction of Risk: Essays on Risk Selection and Perception*. Boston: Reidel.

Kasperson, R. (1986), "Six Propositions on Public Participation and Their Relevance to Risk Communication," *Risk Analysis*, 1986, vol. 6, pp. 275–282.

Kasperson, R., and J. Kasperson (1983), "Determining the Acceptability of Risk: Ethical and Policy Issues," in J. Rogers and D. Bates (eds.), *Risk: A Symposium*, Ottawa: The Royal Society of Canada, 1983.

Kasperson, R., and P. J. Stallen, eds. (1991), *Communicating Risks to the Public*. Boston: Kluwer Academic Publishers.

Klaidman, S. (1985), "Health Risk Reporting," Washington, D.C.: Institute for Health Policy Analysis, Georgetown University.

Krimsky, S., and A. Plough (1988), *Environmental Hazards: Communicating Risks as a Social Process*. Dover, Massachusetts: Auburn House.

Lowrance, W. W. (1976), *Of Acceptable Risk: Science and the Determination of Safety*. Los Altos, California: Kaufman, 1976.

National Research Council (1983), *Risk Assessment in the Federal Government: Managing the Process*, Washington, D.C.: National Academy Press.

National Research Council (1989), *Improving Risk Communication*, Washington, D.C.: National Academy Press.

Nelkin, D. (1989), "Communicating Technological Risk: The Social Construction of Risk Perception," *American Review of Public Health*, vol. 10, pp. 95–113.

Press, F. (1987), "Science and Risk Communication," pp. 11–17 in J. C. Davies, V. T. Covello, and F. W. Allen (eds.). *Risk Communication*. Washington, D.C.: The Conservation Foundation.

Ruckelshaus, W. D. (1987), "Communicating about Risk," pp. 3–9 in J. C. Davies, V. T. Covello, and F. W. Allen (eds.). *Risk Communication*. Washington, D.C.: The Conservation Foundation.

Sandman, P. M. (1986), *Explaining Environmental Risk*. Washington, D.C.: U.S. Environmental Protection Agency, Office of Toxic Substances.

Sandman, P., D. Sachsman, M. Greenberg, and M. Gotchfeld (1987), *Environmental Risk and the Press*, New Brunswick: Transaction Books.

Slovic, P. (1987), "Perception of Risk," *Science*, vol. 236, pp. 280–285.

Slovic, P., and B. Fischhoff (1982), "How Safe Is Safe Enough? Determinants of Perceived and Acceptable Risk." In L. Gould and C. Walker (eds.), *Too Hot to Handle*, New Haven: Yale University Press, 1982.

Slovic, P., N. Krauss, and V. Covello (1990), "What Should We Know about Making Risk Comparisons," *Risk Analysis*, vol. 10, pp. 389–392.

Thomas, L. M. (1987), "Why We Must Talk about Risk," pp. 19–25 in J. C. Davies, V. T. Covello, and F. W. Allen (eds.). *Risk Communication*. Washington, D.C.: The Conservation Foundation.

Wilson, R. (1979), "Analyzing the Daily Risks of Life." *Technology Review,* vol. 81, pp. 40–46.

Wilson, R. (1984), "Commentary: Risks and Their Acceptability." *Science, Technology and Human Values,* vol. 9, no. 2, spring, pp. 11–22.

Wilson, R., and E. Crouch (1987), "Risk Assessment and Comparisons: An Introduction." *Science,* vol. 236 (April 17, 1987), pp. 267–270.

Appendix
Principles of Effective Risk Communication in Crisis and Noncrisis Situations

This appendix describes strategies and tools for effective environmental communications in crisis and noncrisis situations. The focus is on verbal communications. However, most strategies and tools work equally well for written communications.

Much of the material in the appendix deals with establishing trust and credibility. This is because you cannot communicate effectively without trust and credi-bility.

When trust and credibility are low, the primary goal of communication is to build trust and credibility. The secondary goal is to inform and educate.

Trust and credibility cannot be built quickly. Instead, it is the result of actions, performance, and an ongoing effort to communicate skillfully, openly, and honestly with those who are affected by your operations.

Developing the Message: Do's and Don'ts

Jargon

- Don't use technical terms and acronyms that might be confusing to your audience.
- Do define all technical terms and acronyms; use language that can be understood by a 12- to 14-year-old or that is at least four levels below the average educational grade level of your audience.

Organizational Identity

- Don't take on the corporate identity; never use the name of the organization as a noun or subject of a sentence.
- Do use personal pronouns as much as possible; use the name of the organization only as the subject of a prepositional phrase (in, of, at, for, etc.).

Attacks

- Don't attack the credibility of your critics or opponents if your audience perceives you to have lower credibility.
- Do attack the issue but ignore the person or organization making the attack; quote or enlist the help of someone with equal or higher credibility to criticize your opponents.

Humor

- Don't use humor or sarcasm in discussing health, safety, or environmental issues.
- Do use humor, as appropriate, if directed at yourself.

Risk-Benefit Comparisons

- Don't discuss the benefits of the facility or the product at the same time that you are discussing potential risks, losses, or risk reduction efforts.
- Do discuss risks and benefits in separate communications.

Risk-Cost Relationships

- Don't discuss the costs of risk reduction at the same time that you are discussing risk levels and/or your risk reduction efforts.
- Do discuss risks and costs in separate communications.

Risk Comparisons

- Don't use comparisons of unrelated risks to argue for the acceptability of a risk.
- Do use risk comparisons to help put risks in perspective, but first test their effectiveness with a naive audience.

Benefits

- Don't include information about the benefits of the product or the activity in communications about the risks of the product or activity.

- Do stress and publicize the benefits of the product or the activity in separate communications.

Negative Allegations

- Don't repeat negative allegations.
- Do refute the allegation without repeating it.

Negative Words or Phrases

- Don't use negative or loaded words or phrases: in psychological weight, negatives are equal to five positives and are more likely to be remembered.
- Do use statements, words, and phrases that are positive or neutral; use negative statements only when you want them to be remembered.

Promises

- Don't make promises or commitments without strict deadlines.
- Do what you promise.

Speculation

- Don't speculate about worst cases.
- Do provide positive information on solutions, for example, what is being done to prevent accidents or harm.

Money

- Don't make reference to the amount of money spent on health, safety, and the environment programs.
- Do make reference to the importance you attach to health, safety, and environmental issues, and stress your commitment (e.g., in time and effort) to addressing these issues.

Numbers

- Don't mention or repeat large numbers about negative effects.
- Do stress performance, trend lines, achievements.

Technical Details and Debates

- Don't provide too much technical detail or allow yourself to get drawn into protracted technical debates with critics.

- Do address the facts of the situation but focus your remarks on factors that enhance credibility (e.g., caring, empathy, competence, honesty, openness, dedication).

Guarantees

- Don't state that there are no health, safety, or environmental guarantees.
- Do emphasis achievements to date and the ongoing efforts to minimize risks.

Zero Risk

- Don't state that zero risk is an impossible goal.
- Do emphasize the value of zero risk as a goal.

Comparisons with Others

- Don't compare your organization with other organizations or evaluate their performance.
- Do talk about what you are doing.

Blame

- Don't shift blame or responsibility.
- Do take responsibility for your share of, or contribution to, the problem.

Length of Answers

- Don't give long answers to questions.
- Do attempt to limit your answers to two minutes or less.

Length of Presentations

- Don't give long presentations.
- Do attempt to limit your presentations to 15 minutes or less.

Reliance on Words

- Don't rely entirely on words to carry your risk messages.
- Do use visuals and graphics as much as possible to emphasize key points.

Temper

- Don't allow yourself to get angry or lose your temper.

- Do remain calm and use the question or allegation as a springboard for saying something positive.

Clarity

- Don't assume that you have been understood.
- Do ask whether you have made yourself clear.

Abstractions

- Don't talk only in abstractions.
- Do use examples and analogies to establish a common understanding.

Stories and Facts

- Don't test the patience of your audience with dry facts.
- Do embed your facts in interesting, personal stories.

Nonverbal Messages

- Don't communicate nonverbal messages (e.g., through body language or the setup of a meeting room) that are inconsistent with what you are saying.
- Do be sensitive to the nonverbal messages you are communicating.

Listening

- Don't tell people what they ought to know.
- Do listen closely to what people are saying and the questions they are asking.

Off the Record

- Don't assume that you are not being observed or that you can go off the record.
- Do assume that everything you say or do is part of the public record.

Testing

- Don't present risk messages that haven't been tested with an audience.
- Do practice what you plan to say out loud and test it with an untutored audience.

Absolutes

- Don't state absolutes.
- Do indicate uncertainty.

Quantitative Health Risk Numbers

- Don't expect lay audiences to understand quantitative health risk numbers (e.g., the risk of cancer is only one in a million).

- Do emphasize uncertainties in risk assessment and stress the fact that the true risk ranges between zero and the worst case estimate based on pessimistic assumptions.

Personal Questions

- Don't try to avoid answering personal questions (e.g., would you drink the water?)

- Do indicate your position on the risk in question (including additional personal information as appropriate); if your personal position is not consistent with your organization's position, do not speak on behalf of the organization.

Skills

- Don't expect untrained, unskilled persons to communicate effectively about risk issues.

- Do promote the notion that effective risk communication is a skill that requires training and practice.

Establishing Trust and Credibility

Four factors influence perceptions of trust and credibility:

- Empathy and caring
- Competence and expertise
- Honesty and openness
- Dedication and commitment

The credibility of your communications (print, verbal, electronic) is evaluated against these factors. Message effectiveness is enhanced to the degree to which you communicate messages—verbal and nonverbal—that convey empathy and caring, competence and expertise, honesty and openness, and dedication and commitment.

1. *Empathy and caring.* Over half of your credibility is determined by whether your audience perceives you as empathetic and caring (for example, by whether you are perceived as a good listener or as someone who cares about and shares the concerns of your audience). In most communications, your audience will decide if you are empathetic and caring within the first 30 seconds. Once this judgment is made, it is almost impossible to change.

2. *Competence and expertise.* Approximately 15 to 20 percent of your credibility comes from whether you are perceived as competent and expert on the issue at hand. Perceptions of competence and expertise are influenced by merit factors such as track record, experience, knowledge, education, awards, and performance. Most people assume that industry officials are managerially and technically competent.

3. *Honesty and openness.* Another 15 to 20 percent of credibility comes from whether your audience perceives you to be honest and open. As much as 75 percent of perceptions of honesty and openness come from nonverbal communications. Positive content can be canceled out by negative nonverbal cues such as crossed arms, poor eye contact, or physical barriers between you and your audience (e.g., desks, tables, podiums). Positive content can be enhanced by nonverbal cues such as strong eye contact and outdoor settings.

4. *Dedication and commitment.* The final 15 to 20 percent of credibility comes from whether your audience perceives you to be dedicated and committed to addressing and solving the health, safety, or environmental problem at hand. Perceptions of dedication and commitment are, in turn, influenced by several factors, including whether you are perceived to be hardworking (for example, willing to work overtime or go beyond the call of duty) and diligent in your pursuit of health, safety, or environmental goals.

Answering Difficult Questions

Credibility is enhanced by your ability to answer difficult health, safety, and environmental questions. Difficult questions are best answered using the following five-part structure.

- *Empathy.* In answering difficult questions, you must first show empathy with the person asking the question (examples: "I share your concern about…"; "I agree that…is important"; "If I were in your shoes and reading the same things you've been reading, I would be asking the same questions."). The statement of empathy should be a minimum of 25 percent the length of your answer. This helps to reduce anger or animosity and sets the stage for receiving factual information.

- *Conclusion.* The conclusion is given as the first part of the answer. It contains the key message, the theme that you most want the person asking the question to remember. It should be direct, positive, memorable, concise (less than 10 to 12 seconds in length), and solution-oriented.

- *Supporting facts.* The conclusion is followed by supporting information, usually two or three facts or reasons.

- *Repeated conclusion.* The initial conclusion is repeated using virtually the same words. This drives home the key message so that there is no possible misunderstanding.

■ *Future action.* The last part of the response should describe future actions or ways to obtain additional information. For example, you can emphasize your openness and accessibility by providing your work and home telephone numbers (your home number might be a special dedicated line). Or you can emphasize, with concrete examples, your commitment to safety, prevention, and continuous improvement. By committing yourself to future action, you end the response in a positive manner. Research suggests that about 20 percent of the effectiveness of a response is determined by the "future action" element.

Sample Statements that Express Concern and/or Empathy

"That's a very important question."

"The issue you raised is at the top of my priority list."

"My first priority is…"

"I, too, am concerned about…"

"I think you have a right to be concerned about…"

"I have asked myself that same question…"

"I share your concern about…"

"Looking at this issue from your point of view, I can see why you are concerned about…"

"If I had read and heard the same things you have been reading and hearing, I would ask the same question [have the same concerns] about…"

"As a resident [member of this community; neighbor; parent], I am also concerned about…"

"In listening to you, I can sense your frustration [anger; deep feelings; concerns) about…"

Five Most Frequent Interview Failures

Credibility can be enhanced or lost through interviews. The five most frequent interview failures are:

1. *Failure to take charge.* You must take control of the interview; it must be clear that you are the leader. Your role is not just to answer questions but to communicate effectively one or more key messages.

2. *Failure to anticipate questions.* You should prepare a list of probable questions prior to the interview and practice giving short, concise, well-structured answers.

3. *Failure to develop key messages.* Use the interview as an opportunity to communicate key messages to your audience. Have one to three key messages prepared and ready to use.

4. *Failure to stick to the facts.* Do not speculate or answer hypothetical questions. Avoid "what if" questions by confining your answers to what is known.

5. *Failure to keep calm.* Do not allow the interviewer to upset you. Be courteous but firm. Demonstrate your willingness to cooperate.

Addressing Public Concerns

Credibility is enhanced to the degree to which you correctly identify, anticipate, and empathize with your audiences' concerns. Concerns may be raised in these categories:

- Health concerns
- Safety concerns
- Environmental concerns
- Economic concerns
- Aesthetic concerns (e.g., visual impact, noise, odors)
- Fairness and equity concerns (What benefits does the community receive? Are the risks fairly distributed?)
- Trust and credibility concerns
- Process concerns (Who makes decisions? How do we get more information?)
- Legal concerns

Responses that address each of these concerns should be prepared in advance and tested.

Environmental Vulnerability Analysis

Several factors make you more vulnerable to criticism or attacks by public interest and environmental activists. Knowledge of these factors can help you plan your communications program more effectively.

1. Physical cues to ongoing pollution (e.g., odors, visible air plumes, discolored or foul-tasting water)

2. Reports of mysterious or unusual health or environmental problems by employees, neighbors, reporters, or other external sources of information

3. Large volumes of air or water emissions

4. Large volumes of hazardous waste

5. Poor facility housekeeping

6. Proximity to facilities with health, safety, or environmental problems

7. Presence of dreaded toxic substances (e.g., dioxins, PCBs)

8. Proximity to communities with high levels of education

9. Proximity to large residential communities

10. Proximity to important scenic or cultural sites

11. Presence of organized environmental groups

12. Presence of skilled and/or credible environmental spokespeople

13. Failure to develop an effective community outreach program and "good neighbor" image

A yes answer to all or most of the items is a strong indicator of high vulnerability. Immediate attention may be needed.

Building and Cultivating Allies

Goals

- Coordinate activities and form alliances with other credible sources.
- Issue joint communications with other credible sources.
- Solicit supporting quotable statements from other credible sources.

Targets

- Physicians and other health professionals (on health issues)
- Professors, especially senior faculty members and department chairs (on all issues)
- Local citizens that are respected, neutral, and informed (e.g., clergy, school administrators)
- Public interest groups
- Civic organizations (e.g., League of Women Voters)
- Local experts and professionals
- The media
- Employees and retirees

Key Point.   Build and cultivate alliances with those who have high credibility.

Working Effectively with the News Media

The media play a major role in transmitting and translating risk information. The more effective you are with the media, the more effective will be your communication program.

- Anticipate questions and prepare answers.
- Be helpful.
- Strive to make complicated material as clear as possible.
- Provide leads on additional sources of information.
- Provide written and graphic materials that can be taken away.
- Provide clear analogies and comparisons for difficult concepts.
- Provide background materials on your activities and organization.
- Volunteer to get additional information for the reporter.
- Prepare two or three key messages.
- Prepare several quotable, short (10 to 12 words or less) statements [sound bites] that summarize and state your key messages.
- Identify what you consider to be the most important elements in the story.
- Keep your answers short and concise (maximum: 90 seconds).
- Take charge; answer the reporter's questions but always return to your two or three key positive messages.
- Don't bring up issues or subjects that you don't want to see in a story.
- Keep calm.
- Avoid jargon; define terms in the language of a 10- to 12-year-old.
- Be readily accessible; meet deadlines.
- Do not speak for other organizations; speak only for the organization you represent.
- Always tell the truth; never lie or give misleading or inaccurate information.
- If you can't give information, say why; don't evade the question or say "No comment."
- Stick to the facts; don't speculate or answer "What if" questions.
- Be prepared to answer "personalized" questions.
- Avoid sarcasm.
- Assume that you are always "on the record."
- Provide information promptly—even if it is bad.

- Correct any mistakes.
- Compliment reporters who do a good job.
- Call the reporter to correct inaccuracies.
- Don't hesitate to say "I don't know, but I'll find out the answer and get back to you by…[date, time]." Follow up.
- Develop a reputation as a good source.
- Be proactive.
- Get to know and develop in advance a relationship with reporters, editors, and news directors; don't have your first contact during a crisis or emergency.

Developing Effective Sound Bites

Sound bites are important to the media. They also help any audience remember your key messages. Sound bites should:

- Summarize your conclusion.
- Address the principal underlying concern of the audience, questioner, or listener.
- Be short and concise—10 to 12 words at most.
- Be positive—that is, they should contain no negative words or words with negative connotations.
- Be set apart from the rest of the information presented by a noticeable change in hand gestures or by a change in voice tone, intensity, volume, or pace.
- Be memorable.

Nonverbal Communications

As much as 50 to 75% of message content comes from nonverbal communications. When trust is low, effective nonverbal communication is critical to success. Moreover, when trust is low, nonverbal communications are frequently noticed more often and given a negative interpretation.

Poor Eye Contact.   Messages: dishonest, closed, unconcerned, nervous.

Excellent Eye Contact.   Messages: honest, open, competent, sincere, dedicated, confident, knowledgeable, interested.

Sitting Back in Chair.   Messages: uninterested, unenthusiastic, unconcerned, uncooperative.

Sitting Forward in Chair.   Messages: interested, enthusiastic, concerned, cooperative.

Arms Crossed on Chest.   Messages: uninterested, unconcerned; defiant, not listening, arrogant, impatient, defensive, stubborn.

Infrequent Hand Gestures and Body Movements.   Messages: dishonest, deceitful, nervous, lack of self-confidence.

Rocking Movements.   Messages: nervous, lack of self-confidence.

Frequent Hand-to-Face Contact.   Messages: dishonest, deceitful, nervous.

Hidden Hands.   Messages: deceptive, guilty, insincere.

Open Hands.   Messages: open, sincere.

Buttoned Coat.   Messages: closed, unfriendly, disagreeable.

Unbuttoned Coat.   Messages: open, friendly, agreeable.

Coat On.   Messages: closed, unfriendly, disagreeable, uncooperative.

Coat Removed.   Messages: open, friendly, agreeable, cooperative.

Speaking from Behind Barriers.   Messages: dishonest, deceitful, formality, unconcerned, uninterested, superior.

Speaking Outdoors.   Messages: dedicated, hardworking, involved, concerned.

Speaking from an Elevated Position.   Messages: superiority, dominance, judgmental.

Steepling, Joined Fingertips.   Messages: self-confidence, self-assurance, self-importance, superiority.

Touching and/or Rubbing Nose.   Messages: doubt, disagreement, nervous, deceitful.

Touching and/or Rubbing Eyes.   Messages: doubt, disagreement, nervous, deceitful.

Hands on Hips.   Messages: dedication, self-confidence, cooperative, arrogant.

Pencil Chewing and Hand Pinching.   Messages: lack of self-confidence, doubt.

Jingling Money in Pockets.   Messages: nervous, lack of self-confidence, lack of self-control, deceitful.

Drumming on Table, Tapping with Feet.   Messages: nervous, hostile, impatient, anxiety, boredom.

Head in Hand.   Messages: boredom.

Hand to Chest.   Messages: openness, honesty, dedication, sincerity.

Clenched Hands.   Messages: anger, hostility, determination, uncooperative.

Locked Ankles.   Messages: apprehensive, deceitful, nervous.

Crossed Legs.   Messages: defensive, closed.

Palm to Back of Neck.   Messages: frustration, anger, irritation, hostility.

Straight Posture.   Messages: self-confidence, self-control, assertive, determination.

Slumping Posture.   Messages: nervous, poor self-control.

Glasses on.   Messages: competent, hiding something, deceitful.

Glasses off.   Messages: caring, concerned, confident.

Frequent Blinking.   Messages: nervous, deceitful, inattentive.

Infrequent Blinking.   Messages: self-confidence, honest, listening.

Lowering Voice.   Messages: self-assurance, honesty, caring.

Raising Voice.   Messages: nervous, deceitful.

Shrugging Shoulders.   Messages: unconcerned, indifferent.

Tight-Lipped.   Messages: nervous, deceitful, angry, hostile.

Licking Lips.   Messages: nervous, deceitful.

Indoors, Behind a Desk: Messages: Bureaucratic, uncaring, removed, uninvolved.

Outdoors with Sleeves Rolled Up: Messages: Hardworking, involved, caring, concerned.

Public Meeting/Presentation Guidelines

Note: These guidelines apply primarily to low-trust, low-credibility situations.

- Keep your audience as small as possible (50 people or less; ideally, 20 people or less).
  Comment: Eye contact is critical to perceptions of honesty; eye contact is difficult to accomplish in rooms that hold over 50 people.

- Anticipate questions and concerns; prepare, practice, and test responses.
  Comment: When information gathering is done well, over 90 percent of the questions people ask can be predicted in advance.

- Have a neutral training or experienced moderator.
  Comment: It is difficult to both communicate effectively and control a concerned, unruly, or hostile audience or individual.

- Arrive early at the meeting and leave late.
  Comment: People will notice and appreciate the caring gesture of arriving early and leaving late.

- Agree on ground rules.
  Comment: It is easier to enforce rules of order that are agreed to in advance.

- State how long your presentation will last.
  Comment: People are likely to be more patient if they know how long you will speak.

- Keep your formal presentations short (15 minutes maximum).
  Comment: Attention and retention fall off rapidly after 12 to 15 minutes.

- Have an agenda.
  Comment: People are likely to be more patient if they know how the meeting will be organized.

- Check room setup and logistics (chair and table placement, audiovisual equipment, lighting, heating and air-conditioning).
  Comment: Attention to detail pays off; arrive early so that adjustments can be made.

- Avoid speaking from behind physical barriers such as podiums and tables.
  Comment: Physical barriers can communicate strong nonverbal messages, including dishonesty and lack of openness.

- Allow only one person to speak and be visible at one time; seat all other presenters in the front row.
  Comment: A lineup of speakers can communicate strong nonverbal messages, including the message that it's "my team versus your team."

- Speak from the corner of the room with a flip chart or overhead in the center of the room.
  Comment: Standing in the center of the room makes you a target and identifies you with the problem ("kill the messenger").

- Avoid using slides; use overheads.
  Comment: People will not be able to see your eyes if you dim the lights. Eye contact is critical to establishing trust and credibility.

- Use visuals liberally throughout your presentation.
  Comment: Visuals (graphs, photographs, etc.) increase attention and retention by as much as 50 percent).

- Begin your presentation with strong statement of shared concern, caring, and empathy.
  Comment: Perceptions of trust and credibility are strongly influenced by perceptions of shared concern, caring, and empathy.

- Present only three key points.
  Comment: People have difficulty remembering more than three key messages.

- Write your three key points on a flip chart or overhead.
  Comment: Attention and retention can be improved by keeping the flip chart or overhead containing your three key points visible throughout the presentation.

- State each key message in less than 45 characters.
  Comment: Short messages have greater impact and are more easily remembered.

- Provide a visual for each key message.
  Comment: Visuals (graphs, photographs, etc.) increase attention and retention by as much as 50 percent).

- Go through each key point in turn; provide at least two facts for each key point.
  Comment: At least two credible facts are needed to support messages from low-credibility sources.

- Tell personal stories and anecdotes that illustrate key messages.
  Comment: Personal stories and anecdotes paint word pictures for the listener and aid memory.

- Repeat your three key points at least twice during the presentation.
  Comment: Messages that are repeated are more easily remembered.

- Stay calm.
  Comment: Loss of temper communicates lack of discipline and managerial incompetence.

- Express shared concern, caring, and empathy in response to all questions during the question and answer period.
  Comment: Perceptions of trust and credibility are strongly influenced by perceptions of shared concern, caring, and empathy.

- Be sensitive to all nonverbal communications.
  Comment: As much as 50 to 75% of the information people receive comes from nonverbal communication.

- Keep your answers during the questions and answers to no more than 90 seconds in length.
  Comment: Information attention and retention decreases rapidly after 90 seconds.

- Use at least 30 seconds to answer questions during the questions and answers.
  Comment: Treat all questions as an opportunity to provide your audience with positive information, including details.

- Have all questions handled by a single presenter who acts as the hub of the wheel and who directs questions (if needed) to other presenters and/or experts.
  Comment: Control is maximized by having only one person handle and direct questions as needed.

- Conclude your presentation with information about future actions that will result in continuous progress and improvement: be specific and make a personal commitment.
  Comment: People want to know that the future will be better than the present.

- Conclude your presentation with information about how to obtain more information: be specific and make a personal commitment.
  Comment: People have different information needs and appreciate being given the opportunity to find out more.

Getting Out Ahead

Listed below are questions about chemical risks that are frequently asked by the public and the press. Communication effectiveness can be improved by anticipating which questions might be asked and preparing (and testing) well-structured answers in advance.

Environmental Issues

- Where do all these emissions end up? Where does all the hazardous waste go? Into air, land, water?

- What type of ongoing fence-line monitoring operations do you have in place, and what are you doing to improve your detection program?

- What is the effect of introducing all these man-made chemicals into the environment?
- How will I be notified in a chemical emergency?

Business Issues

- How much would it cost to reduce emissions of chemical X to zero at the plant? Why don't you spend the money to do this?
- How much money does your company make each year from the sale of the chemical(s) being emitted? From the sale of end products which result?
- Can't you substitute some of the hazardous chemicals you use or make with others that are not hazardous?
- Why don't you move your plant to a safer location, some place away from population centers?

Legal/Statutory Issues

- Why didn't your company and others publicize emissions data before the law made you do it?
- How many times in the past year has your plant exceeded your permit limits on chemical X?
- How many times in the past year has your plant been fined for permit violations? How much were the fines?
- Why are you just now telling us the truth about your operations; why did it take you so long?

Health and Safety Issues

- What's the cancer incidence rate among employees at your plant? What's the most common form of cancer found among chemical plant workers?
- If your chemicals are so safe, why do most of your employees and their families live so far away from the plant?
- What have you done to ensure that your plant doesn't create a major tragedy by releasing deadly chemicals that will spill and injure hundreds or thousands of people in the neighborhood? And don't tell me the chances of this happening are low. Tell me what you've done to guarantee it doesn't happen.
- What are the "safe" levels of this chemical?
- How do you know it is safe?
- How do you know what the level is?

- You guess! What are you doing to get a more accurate answer?
- The levels represent average expectations! How do we know that your equipment is typical of the average or is maintained to meet that average? Is there a testing program to ensure this? If so, what are the details of the program—test method, frequency, who performs test?
- Suppose you have an accidental release, does your average go up? If not, why not?
- What are you doing to stop the leaking?
- When can we expect you to stop it?
- What long-term health effects can be expected from low-level exposure to chemicals coming from your plant?
- What is the combined effect of low-level exposure to a multitude of chemicals?
- Why is the quantity of emissions from a chemical plant and/or a combination of plants so high?
- What is the health impact of your chemical plant emissions combined with all the emissions from the other chemical plants?
- What is the no-risk or safe level for long-term exposure?
- What is the effect of exposure on children?
- Will my ability to have children be affected by your chemical emissions?
- Do your products and emissions cause cancer?

Public Policy Issues

- Why should the public allow you to continue to operate in view of the health and environmental hazards you create?
- Why can't you run your business so that it's not a threat to society?
- Why shouldn't the government tax your hazardous emissions by the ton to give your plant some incentive to clean up your act?
- Can't you deodorize the chemicals you spew into the sky so at least they wouldn't stink?
- Why does a chemical plant have the right to expose me to chemicals against my will?

Additional Questions

1. Is anyone in the community at risk?
2. How much of the chemical could have been breathed or ingested by an individual?

3. Are the concentrations safe?

4. What is chemical risk?

5. What is chemical toxicity?

6. What is "exposure"?

7. What were the quantities emitted per day?

8. Were releases continuous, intermittent, or planned?

9. What is the danger of chemicals detected at low concentrations?

10. What is the source of that information?

11. What else is the chemical combined with or in the presence of?

12. How often, when, and how are the releases occurring?

13. At what height are emissions released?

14. At what temperature?

15. Where on the property?

16. What is the predominant daily wind direction? Are releases restricted during certain wind or weather conditions?

17. What are the potential exposure routes (e.g., drinking water, air, or surface water) for the community? Are the air and water safe?

18. How do the chemical risks compare with other risks in the community?

19. What are the symptoms of adverse chemical exposure?

20. Are people who work outdoors at greater risk?

21. Is it risky to sleep in rooms with open windows?

22. Is eating fish from or swimming in local streams risky?

23. Are older people, pregnant women, and children at greater risk than others?

24. Are chemical risks affected by diet, smoking, and other personal choices?

25. Are government standards the best guide to determine "safety" or "purity" of drinking water or contaminant levels?

26. Are "toxic" and "hazardous" the same thing (in regulatory language)?

27. What are "extremely hazardous substances"?

28. Why can't these emissions be stopped entirely?

29. What will the government do about this?

30. Why didn't you tell me this before?

More Questions

- What are the environmental and health effects of the chemicals released? [Reporters should question here whether the effects are chronic or acute.]

- What effects has the particular chemical been tested for, and what effects have not been tested?

- What is the basis of the emissions estimate? Actual measurements provide the most accurate information: when and for what chemicals were they done?

- Has the industry measured or merely estimated human exposure to the chemicals? Do the estimates represent a release over a year, on a daily basis, or in one accident?

- Are air or water monitors (if any) located downwind or downstream of the disposal locations? How far are they from the point of release? How often do the monitors collect samples?

- What concentrations of the chemical have been detected? Is the chemical harmful in that volume? Some substances disperse or degrade; others do not; is their total discharge volume harmful?

- Has the facility provided a quantitative assessment of cancer risks and then compared those figures with the risk associated with natural events or everyday activities?

- Is the reported risk for the most exposed person or a person with average exposure?

- Do the total releases reported include "accidental" spills? If so, what percentage of the total do they represent?

- Has the facility reported its accidental releases to the National Response Center and the Local Emergency Planning Committee (LEPC)?

- Do the major sources of the toxic releases within the facility have pollution controls? Are any additional control measures available? If so, why haven't they been installed?

- Are there less toxic substitutes which could be used?

- Has the company reduced or increased releases from last year? Has it even analyzed what can be done to reduce releases?

- Are there federal, state, or local standards regarding releases of these chemicals?

- Are older people, pregnant women, and children at greater risk than others?

- Are chemical risks affected by diet, smoking, and other personal choices?

- Are government standards the best guide to determine "safety" or "purity" of drinking water or contaminant levels?

- Are "toxic" and "hazardous" the same thing (in regulatory language)?

- What are "extremely hazardous substances"?

- Why can't these emissions be stopped entirely?

- What will the government do about this? [A good additional question here: What is the local emergency planning committee doing with the information it has? How is the LEPC using that information?]
- Why didn't you tell me this before?
- Is the information being reported going to be perennially out of date because it applies to the previous calendar year and not to what is going on today? Are emissions in many cases lower today than they were a year ago?
- Are the numbers merely estimates, based on industries' "assumptions" about their emissions? Is it correct that the numbers do not represent "actual emissions"?

Planning Communications

The step-by-step approach outlined below lays out a process for planning an effective communication program. The steps in the approach constitute a circular process, in which the last step feeds back to the first in a continuous process of planning and improvement.

Step 1: Defining Goals and Objectives

The first step in planning a communications program is to define your goals and objectives.

Key questions to ask yourself at this stage in the process include:

- What are the goals and objectives of the communications program?
- What measurable objectives can be established to define success?
- How can progress be measured?

Step 2: Identifying and Prioritizing Potential Audiences

Identifying and prioritizing potential audiences for your communications program—who you want to reach and influence with your messages—will help you develop relevant messages and materials and identify the channels most likely to reach them.

Key questions to ask yourself at this stage in the process include:

- Who is the target audience?
- What is known about them?

Step 3: Gathering Audience Information

The more you understand about potential audiences the better you can target messages.

Key questions to ask yourself at this stage in the process include:

- What new kinds of information are needed before planning the communications program?

- What budget and time frame do we have for gathering information about the audiences?

Step 4: Selecting Channels: Techniques for Community Outreach

The decisions you make in steps 1 to 3 will guide you in selecting appropriate communication channels and producing effective communication materials.

Key questions to ask yourself at this stage in the process include:

- Are there any existing materials which could be adapted for my communications program?

- Which channels are most appropriate for reaching the target audience? (e.g., mass media, face to face).

- What formats will best suit the channels and the messages? (e.g., pamphlets, videotapes, slide shows, school curricula).

Step 5: Developing Message, Testing, and Delivery

In steps 1 to 4 most program planning is completed; this planning provides the basis for developing messages and other communication materials.

Key questions to ask yourself at this stage in the process include:

- What are the different ways that the message can be presented?

- How does the target audience react to the message concept(s)?

- Does the audience:
  - Understand the message?
  - Recall it?
  - Accept its importance?
  - Agree with the value of the proposed solution or future action?
  - How does the audience respond to the message format?

- Based on responses from the target audience, do changes need to be made in the message or its format?

- How could the message be promoted, the materials distributed, and progress tracked?

Step 6: Broadening Your Base in the Community

In this step, the fully developed program is introduced to the target audience. Key questions to ask yourself at this stage in the process include:

- Is the message making it through the intended channels of communication?
- Is the target audience paying attention, and reacting?
- Do any existing channels need to be replaced, or new channels added?
- Which aspects of the program are having the strongest effect?
- Do changes need to be made to improve program effect?

Step 7: Establishing Dialogue with the Community

This step is where a communications program truly becomes a two-way exchange of information.
Key questions to ask yourself at this stage in the process include:

- How can we institutionalize our communication/community outreach efforts?
- What resources will be needed to establish a continuing dialogue with the community?
- What are the benefits for us and the community in establishing a continuing dialogue on salient issues?
- What is our long-range facility siting communications strategy?

Step 8: Assessing Effectiveness

The specific communications program that you develop should be evaluated by analyzing the results of goal and objective measurements planned in step 1.
Key questions to ask yourself at this stage in the process include:

- Were program objectives met?
- Were the changes which took place the result of the communications program, other factors, or a combination of both?
- How well was each stage of program planning, implementation, and assessment handled?

- Are there program changes or improvements that should be made to increase the likelihood of success or to address changes in the audience or in the nature of the issue?
- Are there lessons learned that could help make future programs more successful?
- Are there lessons learned that should be shared with others in the industry?
- Are there successes by others that we can learn from?

PART 6
Life Cycle Analysis and Environmental Marketing

14

Life Cycle Analysis and Resource Management*

Carl L. Henn, CPL, CFP
Society of Logistics Engineers

James A. Fava, Ph.D.
Roy F. Weston Inc.

In this chapter:

- Life Cycle Analysis in Perspective
- Life Cycle Assessment and Product Stewardship
- Life Cycle Cost and Economic Analysis
- Systems Analysis and Life Cycle Thinking
- Cases and Methodologies

---

*"We don't inherit the earth from our ancestors—
we borrow it from our children."* (AN INDIAN PROVERB)

Life cycle analysis means different things to different people because of its different origins to serve dissimilar purposes, its inherent complexity, and daunting difficulties in its practical application. Worldwide interest in life cycle

*Hans Ebenfelt, chairman, board of directors, Systecom A.B. Sweden, reviewed and contributed to this chapter.

541

thinking and its significance to public policy and private enterprise has nevertheless increased rapidly in recent years in concert with more proactive environmental management. The driving force has been the growing global concern over the increasing consumption of finite material resources and degradation of the earth's life support systems.

The life cycle approach has had two principal and separate development paths, each serving entirely different purposes. Each began in the 1960s, and only recently have there been efforts to bring them together into a more complete systems analysis and decision-making framework. One approach has been product life cycle assessment, a material and energy mass balance methodology designed to reduce environmental releases and waste. The other has been life cycle cost analysis designed to compare bids on large government contracts and subcontracts, especially for military weapons systems.

We describe both the physical and economic approaches and show how these might be integrated into a systems analysis and life cycle management system incorporating environmental impact, economic factors, and product effectiveness.

This chapter presents considerable background material to indicate why current efforts to develop improved methods of analysis and decision making to account for environmental impacts are so important to government, industry, and society.

A basic framework for life cycle thought and action appears to be emerging. "Cradle-to-cradle" life cycle thinking for improved resource management, product design, systems analysis, strategic planning, environmental stewardship, and sustainable development is summarized. The chapter concludes with additional examples of progress in the form of minicases and applied methodologies.

Life Cycle Analysis in Perspective

Life cycle analysis—or assessment, in the context of this chapter—is an evolving management approach for reducing the impact of a product, package, or activity upon human health and the environment. It examines each stage of the life span of manufactured items from extraction of raw materials through production or construction, distribution, use, support, and disposal or recycling.

The term "life cycle" is described and applied in different ways in different industries for different purposes with mixed results and widely varying degrees of enthusiasm. Its relative "newness" and uneven results are inherent in its current state of development and application.

Life cycle analysis, however defined, is a classic example of the great difficulties in applying the emerging sciences of complexity to the real world of industrial management. The sciences of complexity, a group of related disciplines often referred to as system sciences, are an outgrowth of work conducted during and following World War II. During this period breakthroughs occurred in general systems theory, operations research, cybernetics, computer science and information theory, cognitive science and the design, engineering, and management of large, complex technological systems.

These disciplines have been enriched by new discoveries in biology, economics, mathematics, human behavior, and medicine. They have also been influenced by rapid developments in fields of growing importance like artificial intelligence, expert systems, biotechnology, ecology, and decision theory.

Life cycle analysis is only one manifestation of a great transformation currently under way from what might be called Hydrocarbon Man (macho, fossil fuel dependency, and petrochemical proliferation) living in the mechanistic Machine Age, toward Ecological Human Beings moving into the emerging Age of Integrated Systems.

The core concept represented in Fig. 14-1 is the shift already under way from an unsustainable way of thinking and acting to one of sustainability. The challenge we face is how to provide a civilized existence for large numbers of people for an indefinitely long period of time. It does not mean the abandonment of the positive aspects of many of the desirable attributes of the Machine Age. It means a change in emphasis from many undesirable aspects of traditional industrial development to those that will enhance the long-term viability of life on earth.

Biogeophysiological Systems

Our first example is an analogy which suggests that systems thinking conforms more to the nature of life on earth than does mechanistic logic. We begin by comparing the biophysiological system of the human body with the life support system of the earth's ecology. Figure 14-2 shows how three paragraphs from an essay on diabetes can be readily applied to ecological issues with the substitution of a few words.

One of the supreme ironies of civilized life, however, is that although knowledge of how to prevent most diseases already exists, it is not generally heeded even in the most developed countries, despite widespread public information and education. What we know about the health effects of addictive behavior, unhealthy diets, and self-abusive lifestyles tells us that behavioral science and decision theory are crucial to solving problems involving human nature and the quality of life. This is true whether it be human health or ecological health, both of which are inextricably linked. Prevention or cure results not only from scientific knowledge and skills but also from attitudinal consensus building and value judgments on the part of everyone engaged in addressing these problems.

Ill health, it seems, is mostly what keeps doctors in business. But doctors are sworn to "do no harm" in their practice of medicine. Is exploiting natural

Hydrocarbon Man in the Machine Age	Ecological Human Beings in the Age of Integrated Systems
Relative Emphasis ⟶	
Male dominance	Female ascendancy
Specialization	Multidisciplinary holism
Mechanics	Organics
Quantity	Quality
Analysis of parts (reductionism)	Synthesis (symbiosis, synergism)
Form (What is it?)	Function (What does it do and why?)
Linear	Nonlinear, cycles
Measurable internal costs	Total life cycle costs (internal and external)
Authoritarian hierarchies	Interactive networks
Individualism	Communitarianism
Wasteful affluence	Economic sufficiency
Abundance forever	Carrying capacity concerns
Pricing based on internal costs	Full-cost pricing
Shareholder accounting	Stakeholder accounting
Closed systems	Open systems
Materialistic self-interest	Enlightened self-interest
Exploitation	Conservation
Individual rights	Individual and collective responsibilities
Confrontation	Cooperation
Exclusion	Inclusion
Cure	Prevention
Short-term	Longer-term
Rising material expectations	Recognized physical limits
Independence	Interdependence
Collective military security	Collective economic security
Physical growth	Sustainable development
Gross national product	Gross national well-being
Survival of the fittest competition	Competitor alliances for mutual survival
Volume of production output	Quality of input, throughput, and output

Figure 14-1. Hydrocarbon man to ecological human beings.

resources and contaminating our own life support systems necessary to keep industry in business? Or by harmonizing industrial practices with ecological principles, can we achieve sustainable production and consumption, protect the public health, and preserve our natural environment? We believe we can. We believe management science, such as life cycle analysis and clean industrial technologies, will enable us one day to "do no harm" to life on earth.

Mayo Clinic Quotation from Essay on Diabetes	Adaptation of the Mayo Clinic Quotation to Sustainable Development
Today's progress focuses on practical ways you can manage diabetes with medication, exercise, and nutrition. Research efforts include organ transplantation and new technologies to make life easier.	Today's progress focuses on practical ways you can manage environmental damage with pollution prevention, waste reduction, and life cycle analysis. Research efforts include material substitution and new technologies to make life healthier and safer.
Diabetes affects each person differently, but the more you understand your condition, the better your chance of controlling it	Pollution affects each company differently, but the more you understand your condition, the better your chance of controlling or preventing it.
Self-care, education and a partnership with a caring team of professionals are the foundation for living successfully with diabetes.	Responsible care, education, and a partnership with an "eco-efficient" team of professionals are the foundation for living sustainably with industrial technology.
SOURCE: Medical Essay, Supplement to *Mayo Clinic Health Letter*, June 1992.	SOURCE: "Declaration" by the Business Council for Sustainable Development, Stephan Schmidheiny, *Changing Course*, MIT Press, 1992.

Figure 14-2. An analogy of human health to planetary health.

There are sufficient similar characteristics between ecosystems and techno-systems to persuade a growing number of scientists and engineers worldwide that appropriate industrial ecology can coexist compatibly with the natural ecology. Many of these similarities are illustrated in Fig. 14-3, together with important, but not decisive, differences. Human ingenuity is certainly equal to this challenge of industrial redevelopment and can learn a great deal from and about ecological systems in the process. In the long run, there simply is no other choice.

Life Cycle Analysis Is Systems Analysis

Our second example of the practicality of the systems sciences is not an analogy but is related to the projection of past experience. Since life cycle analysis is actually a form of systems analysis, it is instructive to compare the circumstances in which systems analysis came into its own with the circumstances of today.

The enormity and complexity of the Allied mobilization of resources to fight and win World War II was unprecedented in human history. New weapons and equipment, like radar, were developed and placed into wartime operations without any actual combat experience as a guide. Through sheer necessity, tac-

Similarities

Many interactive and integrated variables
Operating components (processors) and subsystems
Structural (nonliving, nonmoving) components
Flow pathways of energy, materials, and information
Complex functional interrelationships
Positive and negative feedback loops, action and reaction
Resource storage capacity
Outside sources of energy
Large-scale waste and dissipation of energy
Diversity through product or species mix
Purposeful action to achieve desired results
Frequent adherence to Pareto's law, i.e., 80/20 rule
Specialist and generalist behavior
Disruption or destruction of system functions by extremes in use or abuse
Ability to optimize resource and energy use through "cost-benefit" trade-offs

Differences

	Natural Ecosystem	*Technological System*
Type of system	Open	Open and closed
Bioregeneration	Yes	No
Energy use	Diffuse	Concentrated
Solar powered	Directly	Indirectly
Energy conversion capacity	Vast	Small to large
Maintenance	Self-maintaining	Needs outside support
Waste recycling	Advanced	Embryonic
Adaptation to intrusive change	Slow, vulnerable, but resilient	Can be fast or nonexistent
Externalities	Few	Many
Entropy	Natural rate	Accelerated rate

Figure 14-3. Features of Ecological Systems and Technological Systems.

tical planning in particular came to rely on techniques such as operations research, theory of games, and linear programming to most effectively deploy air and naval forces. In addition, the magnitude of the combined national resources required to produce and manage the highly technical weaponry and field support of operating forces gave rise to new logistics analysis and management science techniques.

After the war, the economic consequences and high stakes of Cold War defense policies in a new nuclear confrontation became potentially more deadly and far-reaching than ever. Weapons of mass destruction never widely used before, the huge costs of modern national security, and the inherent risks and uncertainty in the resulting complexities of defense planning created a pressing need for better methods of analysis and decision making.

In the early 1960s Defense Secretary McNamara responded to this need with the Planning, Programming, Budgeting System (PPBS) developed by the Rand Corporation. PPBS was based on the art and science of systems analysis. Systems analysis subsequently proved to be a superior method of identifying and evaluating alternative solutions to enormously complex problems. This approach, introduced in the Department of Defense, subsequently was adopted in many areas of government and industry worldwide. Sometimes misrepresented, other times abused, and often misunderstood, systems analysis proved to be a significantly improved tool of policy planning in national security affairs. A "time-phased resource impact" to formulate budgetary requirements and life cycle cost analyses were important elements of PPBS.

This background is instructive because the world is today facing another challenge of great complexity, uncertainty, high cost, and risk. The momentum of destruction and degradation of the earth's life support systems created by the impact of population growth, pollution, and poverty has become a matter of grave concern the world over. Substantial intellectual, moral, and technological resources are required for humankind to change its traditional way of managing the critical relationship between the world economy and the earth's ecology. We believe this includes application of proven and emerging tools, techniques, and methods of problem solving such as systems analysis and life cycle thinking.

Cradle-to-Cradle Management and Strategic Planning

We believe that the ultimate industrial potential of life cycle thinking, in addition to its value in government procurement and regulatory activity, is in its use for the formulation of industrial strategy. Strategic planning in private enterprise will require the systematic integration of life cycle engineering and toxicology with life cycle economics and product performance to satisfy customer needs and achieve long-term company goals. Environmental considerations greatly complicate this process.

The Business Council for Sustainable Development, created to provide industry input to the 1992 Earth Summit in Rio de Janeiro, concluded that a major change required in the management of business involves expansion of the practice of environmental management "from pollution control to an integrated concept for the total life cycle of the product."

This chapter demonstrates how an integrated life cycle approach can contribute to industrial strategic planning and sustainable development. The critical roles of design and quality assurance are also covered to complete the life cycle story.

A primer for the "life cycle story" is presented in Boxes 14-1 and 14-2, which define the life cycle terminology used in this chapter in order to help tighten

---

Box 14-1.   Cradle-to-Grave or Cradle-to-Cradle?

The term "cradle-to-grave" has typically been used to describe a product's "life cycle" from the initial acquisition of raw materials through the stages of production, distribution, use, and phase-out or disposal. In fact, cradle-to-grave is not a *cycle,* in the sense of a circle or loop. It is a life *span.* Cradle-to-grave correctly conveys a sequence of events from beginning to end. These events are the typical stages in a manufactured product's normal lifetime.

With the increasing emphasis on product reuse and recycling, however, use of life *cycle* terminology has become more appropriate than that of life spans. The goal of industrial ecology is to move beyond waste management to minimization of environmental releases and waste and more recycling and reuse, viz., life *beyond* the grave.

"Cradle-to-cradle," therefore, more accurately describes the rebirth, or reincarnation, of the resources being used for a subsequent product's life-time. The cradle-to-cradle process is what environmentally conscious people are talking about and shooting for. It is a natural result of life cycle thinking.

Even the cradle-to-cradle term is not a precise portrayal. What life cycle thinkers really mean to achieve is not only life after death or *instead* of death but also life *before* the cradle. This is the product research and design state that is so critical to the way a product performs and how it affects the environment after it is born and throughout its lifetime. Projected life cycle costing takes place in the design stage.

Cradle-to-cradle should be understood to include the programming of a product's genes on the front end (design) as well as closing the loop on the back end (reuse or recycling). This is not to say that every product or package need be redesigned or recycled but only that a proactive cradle-to-cradle approach can help managers and engineers decide what's best to do.

---

some loose connections between words and actions that have been prevalent in the development of this field.

The important work being performed in life cycle assessment (LCA), described later, does not include market and technological research, design, and development as a stage in the product life span. This physical input-output methodology would have no reason to include design because there are few, if any, chemical or energy inputs or outputs during this initial stage. As a result, a new environmental activity has emerged in many companies, called Design for Environment (DFE), that seeks to fill this void. We consider this design function to be one of the most important developments in enhancing the prospects for life cycle analysis to contribute to pollution prevention and waste reduction. LCA provides for a systematic way of thinking, collecting, and analyzing data to support DFE initiatives.

Box 14-2. All about Life Cycles

Three levels of life cycle activity are discussed here.

The *first level* is conceptual. It is a *way of thinking*. It looks at trees and perceives photosynthesis, transpiration, soil conservation, carbon cycles, food webs, and habitat, not only trunks, branches, leaves, timber, fruit, and seeds. It is an *integrated systems* concept in both space and time. It is also referred to in this chapter as the life cycle "approach." The life cycle approach is *holistic* and *long-term*. It has little directly to do with altruism, the beauty of nature, reverence for life, or other cultural or spiritual values. Life cycle thinking does have a great deal to do with enlightened self-interest,* adaptability, sustainability, survival, ethics, and all the earth and life sciences.

The *second level* is managerial. A life cycle thinking approach to industrial management introduces environmental considerations into all the functions for which business managers are responsible: strategic planning, product and process design, engineering, production, operations, logistics, marketing, finance and accounting, public relations, human resources, and business law, and the like. It recognizes the moral responsibilities and accountability of an enterprise to all its stakeholders (1) to reconcile and protect their health, safety, and other affected interests and (2) to assure productive and efficient management, stewardship, and conservation of energy and the earth's human and material resources. Life cycle management, both public and private, takes an interdisciplinary integrated systems approach to decision making. It looks at all the long-term costs, risks, and benefits of feasible alternatives in planning for the future survival and success of the enterprise in performing its mission.

The *third level* is one of specialized tools, techniques, skills, and methodologies. Various terms are used for life cycle work of this kind, each of which has a meaning and application of its own.

Life cycle analysis is the term most frequently encountered because it has the broadest meaning. It includes any analysis of activities involving product, package, or process life cycles. The analysis can be chemical, toxicological, economic, legal, medical, etc. It is also used in the architectural design and operation of buildings and other structures, however, these specific applications are not within the scope of this chapter.

Life cycle systems analysis is the integration of all the information required to make a decision, policy, plan, or regulation regarding the life cycles of products, packages, systems, or industrial processes. It is a decision support process for planning (life cycle planning), management (life cycle management), industrial design (life cycle engineering, life cycle costing, life cycle

*Term first used to the best of our knowledge by Roy F. Weston.

(Continued)

design for selected attributes), and environmental and health protection (life cycle assessment). Life cycle systems analysis is described in more detail later.

Life cycle assessment (LCA) is the term used by the Society of Environmental Toxicology and Chemistry (SETAC) to describe a three-part methodology being developed for industrial products and processes by a project team of various experts from industry, government, and academia for physical protection of human health, ecological health, and resource consumption.

The life cycle thinking, management, and analysis which comprise the subject matter of this chapter are quite independent from, and very different from, other kinds of "cycle" terminology often used in a business context. For example, the life cycle thinking discussed here has no relation to the traditional economic business cycle. Nor should it be confused with the stages in the market life cycle of a product, viz., introduction, growth, peaking, decline, and phase-out in terms of sales volume.

Design for Environment

The front-end functions of determination of requirements (customer needs), research, design, development, testing, and preproduction evaluation have always been critical to the life cycle performance and costs of military hardware and nondefense capital goods. Product or system design is the result of input from teams of engineers, with their own requirements and criteria for the product attribute(s) for which they are responsible. This is often part of a process called concurrent engineering.

Concurrent engineering is the process of trying to perform all the front-end trade-off design, systems, and product engineering work in parallel as early as possible. The alternative of performing these tasks in some prescribed sequence may require costly changes in the original design at a later time, sometimes even after production has begun.

The efficient translation of customer requirements and design trade-offs to product and process specifications is a vital step in the cradle stage of the life cycle. One of the techniques used by the Japanese to perform this function is called Quality Function Deployment (QFD). QFD provides a framework for assessing competing product attributes and translating them into quantitative engineering terms. It is a proactive or preventive approach to quality assurance and customer satisfaction that can save time and money. The total cost of design errors and other up-front mistakes in the United States is estimated to be sometimes as high as 30% of production costs. It is probably less than 5% in Japan.

Design for specific product attributes is symbolized as DFX, where X can stand for reliability, manufacturability, transportability, supportability, cost, etc. X can also stand for environment (DFE). Until recently, DFE consisted of the test and evaluation of the ability of a product or system to operate properly under harsh environmental conditions. Now DFE is generally associated with the effect of a product on the environment throughout its life cycle rather than vice versa. DFE can mean design for durability, disposability, disassembly, recycling, reuse, or other attributes. French and German auto makers are designing cars for ease of assembly and disassembly with parts and subassemblies coded for materials content in order to facilitate recycling.

The important point to be made here is that designing products and processes for environmental improvement is not a search for a specified set of standard attributes. It is, rather, a systems analysis and decision-making process whose goals depend upon the type of products and processes as well as the specific environmental concerns to be addressed at each stage in the life cycle. Capital goods, consumer goods, commodity-type products, and buildings have very different life cycles, very different materials, very different environmental impacts, very different economics, and consequently very different design solutions. Figure 14-4 shows how product differences can affect the approach and outcome of life cycle analysis and the contribution that can be made by product design or redesign.

Features	Consumable products and packages	Durable goods and large capital projects
Level of technology	Soft or low	Hard and high
Producer size	All sizes	Mostly large
Generation of postconsumer solid waste	Large volumes, widely dispersed	Lesser volumes, fewer sites
Generation of hazardous & solid waste	Widespread	More concentrated
Releases to air and water	Mostly in manufacturing	Throughout life cycle
Recycling and reuse potential:		
Products	Moderate	High
Packages	High	High, when applicable
Life cycle duration	Short	Long
Purchase price of item	Low	High
Cost of ownership	Small and brief	Large and extended
After-sale operation	Little or none	Extensive
After-sale service and support	Little or none	Extensive
Life cycle inventory assessment	Limited or full-scale	Selectively full scale
Full life cycle management	In some cases	In most cases

Figure 14-4. Product differentiation in life cycle analysis.

Front-end environmental impact analysis can pay big dividends in many cases through redesign efforts, but a cost-risk-benefit analysis of most proposed design changes at each stage in the life cycle, and in total, is also essential to a sound environmental strategy. Figure 14-5 is a summation of the multiplicity of impacts on almost every type of business activity by "green product design." Optimizing the many life cycle impacts of products, packages, and processes on producers, consumers, and the environment is a multiattribute challenge to designers that can well enlarge their professional role and responsibilities in the future.

Business Strategy from Cradle to Cradle

Environmental impact is only one factor in strategy development. It is one that has played a minor role in most companies in the past and will play a major role in almost all companies in the future. Strategic environmental initiatives will therefore be required, just as strategic initiatives in the management of total quality, information systems, human resources, international marketing, customer service, and public relations have grown in importance in recent years.

Experience of many environmentally conscious companies thus far has shown that cost-effective pollution prevention and waste reduction has resulted in substantial cost savings and increased profits. We believe the development of clean technology and conservation of resources is the next giant step forward in the industrial revolution. Clean technology is economically more efficient, less hazardous to the public health and safety, and less harmful to the natural environment.

Dutch and Swedish case studies included in the last section of this chapter focus on environmental issues and their physical and economic dimensions throughout the life cycle. These and other methodologies and systems analysis techniques can be adapted to different product lines and processes, but they are mostly suitable for large industrial enterprises, government procurement offices, or government regulatory agencies. Box 14-3 summarizes the evolution to date of life cycle systems analysis for procurement, market, or policy planning. Each of these stages is discussed in more detail later.

Figure 14-6 is a simple Dutch rating system which subjectively scores environmental issues for each stage in the life cycle of a product on a scale of 1 to 5. This Milion-matrix method is used to redesign consumer products by the DUIJF consulting firm in Vught, Holland. It is especially useful for small firms.

Figure 14-7 is our schematic of how life cycle assessment (LCA) and life cycle management can contribute to the development of industrial strategy of larger enterprises. LCA is well along in its development as an environmental input into a life cycle systems analysis that also consists of economic and technical product performance considerations. Physical environmental impacts must be related to full costs and benefits which in turn must be considered in the many

Key development teams	Opportunity	Feasibility	Design	Preproduction	Production	Sales & distribution	Education & regulation	Promotion
Research & development	Identify alternative products and/or applications	Assess existing and alternative products' environmental impact (LCA)	Design for: Least impact Long life Secondary use Recycling Maintenance and repair Disposability	Weigh animal testing vs. alternative testing	Develop packaging recycling infrastructures	Develop product recycling infrastructures	Establish stakeholder alliances and third party endorsement	Certify green products and processes
Manufacturing and technology	Identify alternative materials, energy sources, processing methods	Assess extraction, transporting, processing, and waste disposal environmental impact	Design for pollution prevention and zero waste	Comply with federal and state regulations and local environmental ordinances	Practice quality environmental management	Green audit packing materials, transport vehicles, storage facilities, etc.	Establish stakeholder alliances and third party endorsement	Transfer green technology
Finance and economics	Compare the cost of managing for conformance vs. managing for assurance	Project the cost of impact on: Human and environmental health Liability Resource supply	Institute sustainable development planning	Investigate energy savings and resource conservation incentives	Consider product development partnerships and joint business ventures	Lobby for free market environmentalism	Establish stakeholder alliances and third party endorsement	Budget for environmental education, purchase incentives and stakeholder alliance programs
Marketing	Conduct consumer and customer environmental marketing research	Conduct product purchase, usage, and performance research	Satisfy consumers' and customers' basic needs such as value, price, and performance	Engage support of green suppliers, ecopreneurs, and environmentalists	Be attentive to community relations and community right-to-know	Support trade with environmental education and community outreach programs	Promote consumer environmental education and empowerment	Comply with state green labeling regulations and FTC guidelines

SOURCE: Coddington Environmental Marketing, Inc., New York.

Figure 14-5. Green Product Development: Designing for the Environment.

Box 14-3. Selected Organizations: Life Cycle Systems Analysis

Organizations	Terminology	Description	Not Included in Current Focus
Franklin Associates, et al.	Resource and Environmental Profile Analysis (REPA)	Energy and materials mass balance inventory at each physical stage in product life span	1. Risk assessment 2. Environmental impact 3. Costs
Society of Logistics Engineers (SOLE), et al.	Life Cycle Costing (LCC)	Cost of ownership over entire product life span	1. Measurement of internal compliance, control, and waste management costs 2. External environmental impact
Society of Environmental Toxicology and Chemistry (SETAC), et al.	Product Life Cycle Assessment (LCA)	Assessment of inventory, impact, and improvement at each physical stage in product life span	1. Research, design, and development 2. Costs
ICF, ASTM, EPA	Pollution Prevention, Benefits Analysis, and Total Cost Assessment	Full cost and financial protocol analysis of economic feasibility and benefits of proposed pollution-prevention projects and life span cost estimates, including contingent liabilities	Energy and material input, output, and mass balance analysis
Association of the Dutch Chemical Industry (VNCI)	Integrated Substance Chain Management	Life cycle, full-cost systems analysis and decision-making process to reduce the environmental impact of a substance	Focus is on major factors
Decision Focus/PRECOR Electric Power Research Institute (EPRI)	Beyond Waste Minimization	Full-cost life cycle analysis for procurement of hazardous chemicals by electric utilities, and for optimizing interrelated decisions	Focus is chiefly on procurement decisions and internal cost accounting
Federation of Swedish Industries, et al.	Environmental Priority Strategies in Product Design (EPS System)	Integrated system of LCA, life cycle cost-benefit analysis, and life cycle technical assessment	Focus is on scoring system

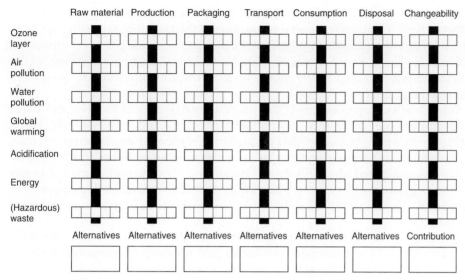

Figure 14-6. Milion-matrix life cycle assessment. (*DUIJF Consultancy, Vught, The Netherlands, 1992.*)

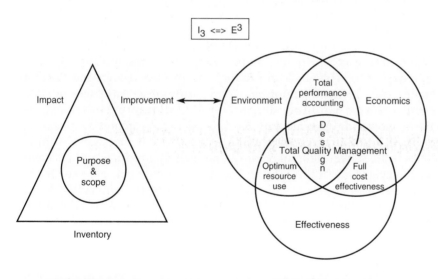

Figure 14-7. The integrated systems of sustainable industrial strategy. (*Copyright August 20, 1992, James A. Fava & Carl L. Henn.*)

trade-off decisions affecting product or system performance, i.e., full cost-effectiveness. Total performance accounting is the tracking, reporting, and full disclosure of the company's performance and accountability for all of its stakeholders. It should be emphasized that this includes future generations, a consideration not included today in any form of traditional economic thought or management theory.

Total Quality Management (TQM) constitutes an umbrella for all of the assurance sciences, i.e., reliability, maintainability, safety, data integrity, etc. It is a customer-inspired, customer-driven, customer-validated engineering, production, and logistic support system from before the cradle to beyond the grave. TQM was conceived, developed, and taught long before environmental issues achieved prominence, yet the philosophy of its most famous proponent, Dr. Edward W. Deming, embodies the very essence of effective environmental management.

Life cycle systems analysis, supported by industry analysis and competitor evaluation, enables a company to devise and implement competitive strategies built on unique strengths in product differentiation, market segmentation, cost leadership, etc., that are responsive to environmentally aware stakeholder concerns.

The management functions and technical disciplines that must be integrated to make life cycle work effective are fairly well identified at this time. The task ahead is to strengthen this integration process so that the three E circles in Fig. 14-7 will indeed overlap more and more as time goes on.

Life cycle thinking is a principal agent of change in the multidisciplinary teamwork required to achieve clean product and process design and development. Quality Management cannot be "Total" without it. Advances in stakeholder performance accounting depend on it. Optimum resource use and sustainable economic development are far less likely to be achieved unless cradle-to-cradle resource strategies are employed. Life cycle management in the final analysis is the stewardship of *resources*, not merely products and packages, A resource life cycle way of thinking and acting is an indispensable key for the use of managers and engineers in their passage into the emerging Age of Integrated Systems. (Professor Ralph Estes, American University, contributed to important parts of this section.)

Life Cycle Assessment and Product Stewardship

Environmental professionals, policy makers, and the general public are intensely interested in having a means to look, holistically, at the environmental consequences associated with the "life cycle" of a process, product, or package. One procedure being developed to accomplish this is termed life cycle assessment (LCA). Life cycle assessments have been used in one form or another

Title	Host	Location	Date
Policy Issues	World Wildlife Fund	Washington, D.C., U.S.A.	May 1990
LCA Workshop	SETAC	Vermont, U.S.A.	August 1990
Practical Aspects	Procter & Gamble	Leuven, Belgium	September 1990
LCA Workshop	SETAC - Europe	Leiden, Netherlands	December 1990
Impact Workshop	SETAC/SETAC-Europe	Sandestin, Florida, U.S.A.	February 1992
LCA Forum	SETAC	Washington, D.C., U.S.A.	March 1992
LCA Symposium	SETAC - Europe	Potsdam, Germany	June 1992
Data Quality	SETAC/SETAC-Europe	Wintergreen, Virginia, U.S.A.	October 1992
Code of Practice	SETAC/SETAC-Europe	Sesimbra, Portugal	March 1993

Figure 14-8. Major forums on LCA.

over the past 25 years or so in Europe, the United States, and a few other countries by industry, government agencies, and other organizations. Interest in this environmental analysis tool has grown substantially in recent years.

This section presents a short history of the development and application of LCA in North America and Europe, originating with efforts in the early 1970s. Recent LCA forums are shown in Fig. 14-8. In addition, a summary of research activities by various industrial and government sectors in North America and Europe is presented. We conclude with an analysis and recommendations as to some specific steps that should be taken in order to enhance the potential application of life cycle as a tool to assist managers and engineers in improving the environmental quality of products, packaging, processes, and activities.

Evolution of Life Cycle Assessments

The history of life cycle assessment can be divided into two periods. The first is the early Development Period from the 1960s to the late 1980s. The second, the Awakening Period, started in 1990 and is continuing today.

Early assessment studies calculated energy requirements associated with various production systems or evaluated chemical inputs and outputs involved with different products, packages, or processes. Since the 1960s, and throughout the energy crises in the 1970s, a number of energy studies have been performed to estimate cost and environmental factors associated with alternative energy sources.

During the 1980s, with the formation of the "green" parties in Europe and with growing concern about solid-waste disposal, there was a renewed interest in life cycle assessment. The solid waste and landfill issues in particular were problems that municipalities and state and national governments increasingly had to face. The emphasis on recyclable materials, recycled products, and the infrastructure associated with recycling also put pressure on organizations to look at potential emissions as well as energy and materials consumption during the entire life cycle of a product. As a result, in the mid- to late 1980s there was increased activity associated with LCA. In many cases the new studies were used to compare products in terms of the energy and materials used and waste and emissions released during each stage of a product's lifetime.

Four primary practitioners during the Development Period concurrently developed analytical tools and life cycle methodologies in the early 1970s: Ian Boustead of the Open University, United Kingdom; Robert Hunt then with Midwest Research Institute and now with Franklin Associates in the United States; the EMPA Program in Switzerland; and Gustav Sundstrom from Sweden.

Since the Awakening Period started in 1990, there has been an increasing number of workshops, studies, and evaluations of methodologies and applications of life cycle work. One of the key drivers of this recent emphasis is recognition of the potential value of life cycle assessment in addressing environmental issues proactively to *prevent* pollution instead of having to control it or clean it up.

A further motivating factor has been the controversies in recent years over marketing claims and product labels citing "scientific studies" like life cycle assessment to promote sales of products allegedly designed to be "environmentally friendly." Even third party endorsements from new organizations like Green Seal and Green Cross (now called Scientific Certification Systems) in the United States and environmental seal organizations in Canada, Europe, and Japan have not escaped criticism of their methods of certification or approval.

Several organizations, industry associations, and private companies have used LCA work to justify claims that appear to be misleading or contradictory. This has led the U.S. Environmental Protection Agency (EPA), the U.S. Federal Trade Commission (FTC), the European Economic Commission (EEC), the International Standards Organization (ISO), several U.S. state governments, the Society of Environmental Toxicology and Chemistry (SETAC), and others to press for acceptable methodologies, available for peer review, upon which process improvements and product advertising claims can reliably be based in order to merit public confidence.

LCA Workshops

This section summarizes the topics covered in several early LCA workshops and identifies key issues and recommendations that address major concerns about applications of LCA.

World Wildlife Fund Policy Forum.   In May 1990, the Conservation Foundation, the EPA, and World Wildlife Fund held a joint workshop on the public policy issues of product life assessments. The objectives of the workshop were to (1) improve the understanding of the potential contributions and limitations of life cycle assessment, (2) identify areas of greatest uncertainty and potential conflict, and (3) contribute to other efforts that are needed to work through various policy and technical issues. The forum was attended by panelists from the United States, Canada, and the Netherlands.

Four major issues were identified during this policy forum:

1. *Nature and scope of LCA.*   It was recognized that there may not be a single methodology but rather multiple approaches to life cycle assessment. In addition, panelists had different views on whether or not risk assessment should be included in the scope of life cycle analysis and, if so, to what degree.

2. *Appropriate use of information.*   Life cycle assessments were perceived as perhaps most useful for specific product comparisons rather than determinations on generic materials. Also, studies were deemed useful for identifying levels of emissions where obvious changes could yield the greatest environmental improvement.

3. *Analytical methods and data.*   Panelists differed concerning the desirability or feasibility of explicitly weighting pollutant loadings to reflect their different environmental impacts. The need for developing common data sources and methodologies for widespread use was discussed. There also was keen interest in developing streamlined product life cycle assessments to meet the demand for timely information. Concerns were expressed over data quality and availability, as well as the high costs of full-blown assessments.

4. *Communicating results of LCA.*   The panelists felt that presenting information to the public that is both understandable and accurate could involve difficult trade-offs. At the same time, it was recognized that LCA work could be of value to a company for internal purposes only and did not need to be communicated to the public in ads or on product labels.

SETAC Technical Framework for Life Cycle Assessment.   In response to the potential application of life cycle assessment as well as some of the concerns about methodology, SETAC sponsored a workshop in August 1990, in Vermont. Its purpose was to develop a consensus on the state of the practice and the research needs for conducting life cycle assessments (SETAC, 1991). The workshop objectives were to clarify definitions and terms associated with LCA; to provide a forum for information exchange between researchers from government, industry, academia, and public interest groups; and to agree on a technical framework of key life cycle assessment components. The workshop participants represented government agencies, universities, public interest groups, industry, consultants, and contract research laboratories in Europe and North America. Japanese observers also attended.

A technical framework for life cycle assessment was developed at this workshop. Life cycle assessment was defined as a technique used to evaluate the environmental burden associated with a product, package, process, or activity during each stage of its lifetime. The analysis begins by identifying and quantifying energy and material usage and environmental releases. These data are used to assess the impact of energy and material usage and releases on the environment and to systematically evaluate and implement opportunities to achieve environmental improvement. LCA includes the entire life cycle from extraction and processing raw materials through manufacturing, transportation, distribution, use/reuse, maintenance, recycling, and final disposition.

A complete life cycle assessment consists of three separate but interrelated components, specifically inventory, impact analysis, and improvement analysis (Box 14-4).

Life Cycle Inventory

The foundation for a product LCA is the inventory component, where energy, raw materials, and environmental releases are measured. Each stage receives inputs of materials and energy and produces outputs of materials, energy, and wastes that are released into the environment. This relationship between the

---

Box 14-4.   Three Components of a Product Life Cycle Analysis

- **Life cycle inventory.** A data-based process of quantifying energy and raw material requirements, air emissions, waterborne effluents, solid waste, and other environmental releases incurred throughout the life cycle of a product, process, or activity.

- **Life cycle impact analysis.** A technical, quantitative and/or qualitative process to characterize and assess the effects of the environmental loadings identified in the inventory component. The assessment should address both ecological and human health considerations, as well as other effects such as habitat modification and noise pollution.

- **Life cycle improvement analysis.** A systematic evaluation of the needs and opportunities to reduce the environmental burden associated with energy and raw materials use and waste emissions throughout the whole life cycle of a product process or activity. This analysis may include both quantitative and qualitative measures of improvements, such as changes in product design, raw materials use, industrial processing, consumer use, and waste management.

SOURCE: SETAC, 1991.

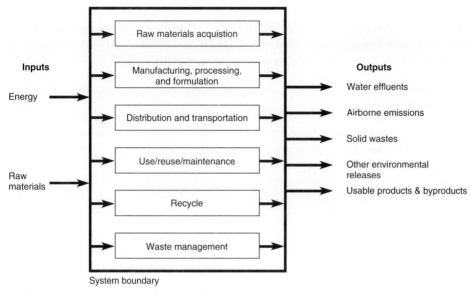

Figure 14-9. Life cycle inventory. (*SETAC, 1991.*)

inputs and outputs and the six stages of a life cycle inventory is shown in Fig. 14-9 and described below.

1. *Raw materials acquisition.*   The boundary for the raw material stage of the inventory begins with all the activities needed for the acquisition of raw materials and energy and ends at the first manufacturing or processing stage that refines the raw material.

2. *Manufacturing, processing, and formulation.*   The processing step of the inventory component analyzes the conversion of feedstocks or raw materials to final products.

3. *Distribution and transportation.*   Transportation is the movement of materials or energy between operations at different locations and can occur at any stage in the life cycle. Distribution is the transfer of the manufactured product from its final manufacturer to its end user. A common attribute of both distribution and transportation is that, although they involve a change in the location or physical configuration of a product, they do not involve a transformation of materials.

4. *Use, reuse, and maintenance.*   The boundary for this stage of the life cycle inventory begins after the distribution of products or materials and ends at the point at which those products or materials are discarded and enter a waste management system.

5. *Recycle.*   The recycling stage encompasses all activities necessary to take material out of the waste management system and deliver it back to the manufacturing/processing stage.

6. *Waste management.* Waste streams are generated at each phase of the life cycle. Waste is any material released to any environmental medium—air, water, or land. Waste management systems include any mechanisms for treating or handling waste prior to its release to the environment.

In summary, the SETAC workshop concluded that the purposes of life cycle inventories were to:

1. Establish a comprehensive baseline of information on a system's overall resource requirements, energy consumption, and emission loadings for further analysis. Resources needed to construct facilities and production equipment, and personal requirements of plant personnel are generally excluded because they are considered insignificant or irrelevant in the lifetime of a particular single product.

2. Identify points within the life cycle as a whole or within a given process, where the greatest reduction in resource requirements and emissions might be achieved at the time of the study.

3. Compare the system inputs and outputs associated with alternative products, processes, or activities on a snapshot basis.

4. Help guide the development of new products, processes, or activities toward a net reduction of resource requirements and emissions.

Considerable research was identified at this workshop to develop the impact and improvement analysis components of LCA. In addition to the six stages illustrated that are common to the life cycle of all products there is an additional life cycle stage of product design and development. Such front-end work can make a substantial contribution to product stewardship and pollution prevention throughout the subsequent stages of a product's life.

Life Cycle Analysis for Packaging

A second workshop, hosted by Procter and Gamble, was held in Leuven, Belgium, in September 1990. Participants were from Belgium, Denmark, Spain, United Kingdom, Switzerland, France, Germany, Austria, the United States, and Sweden. The objective of the workshop was to identify areas of agreement and disagreement among LCA schools of thought in order to create a forum for future discussion and development.

Four major aspects of LCA were discussed during the Leuven workshop:

1. *Applications and limitations.* Participants felt there was a need to ensure the descriptive value of LCA data, i.e., that they must be aggregated correctly and be reproducible and standardized. There was a general feeling that life cycle assessment is not a risk assessment since they are actually different methodologies.

2. *Methodology.*   The workshop addressed issues of functional units, allocation of chemicals and energy among coproducts, and how allocations should be handled in recycling. Other considerations, such as the relationship of inputs and outputs of secondary and primary systems, were also discussed.

3. *Database requirements.*   The workshop participants felt strongly that it was important to develop a systematic approach to gathering data and establishing standardized databases.

4. *Future developments.*   Participants agreed on the need for a greater degree of standardization, recognized authority, and peer review among the practitioners of LCA. The workshop concluded that a specialized organization should be established to provide leadership in the development of LCA research and development, as part of SETAC, the United Nations, or some other institution.

SETAC-Europe LCA Workshop.   A successful workshop was held in December 1991 sponsored by SETAC-Europe in Leiden, Netherlands. This workshop was attended by over 60 individuals from Europe and North America to evaluate the practice of life cycle assessment. Four major topic areas were discussed in considerable depth: inventory issues, classification issues, environmental impact, and databases.

1. *Inventory issues*   Functional product unit and representative processes, system boundaries, product tree definitions, allocation of impacts

2. *Classification issues*   Local vs. superlocal, global environmental problems, potential effects vs. actual effects, identification of headings for classification, organizational aspects of classification

3. *Environmental impact*   Comparative and absolute judgments, methods of evaluation, scoring, perspective

4. *Databases*   Software applications, management of databases, format, data scoring, terminology, implications of different applications, possibilities and limitations of LCA

Impact Assessment Workshop.   A workshop sponsored by SETAC and SETAC-Europe was held in Sandestin, Florida, in February 1992, attended by approximately 50 experts in life cycle assessment and environmental impact analysis. Participants represented state and federal agencies, industries, universities, public interest groups, and research laboratories in the United States, Canada, United Kingdom, Belgium, Denmark, France, Germany, and the Netherlands.

The workshop objectives were to define impact assessment in the context of life cycle assessment, discuss how impact assessment can be applied to LCA, and identify research needs to improve the impact assessment component of LCA.

During the proceedings, workshop participants agreed that a goal definition and scoping steps should be added to the technical framework. These steps define the problem, set the scope of the study to be conducted, select time and spacial boundaries, define boundary conditions and assumptions, and define what is included and excluded in the study. Also, because of the potential complexity of impact analysis, additional scoping activities can occur at various stages throughout a life cycle study.

Participants also defined three major impact categories: human health, ecological health, and resource depletion. Occupational health considerations were included within the human health category. In addition, the group thought social welfare aspects associated with the three primary categories should also be considered.

Current LCA Activities.   In response to the series of workshops, and because SETAC is an international professional society located in North America and Europe as well as in Asia, SETAC formed LCA Advisory Groups in North America and Europe. The mission of the groups is to advance the science, practice, and application of LCA to reduce the environmental burden and resource consumption associated with industrial activities. The group is comprised of representatives from environmental organizations, government, academic community, and industry and it has membership from individuals from North America and Europe. Participants collectively develop plans and interact on a regular basis to seek consensus development of the methodology. To achieve this mission this body will:

- Serve as a focal point to provide a broad-based forum for identification, resolution, and communications of issues regarding LCA
- Facilitate coordination and provide guidance for the development and implementations of LCA

A synopsis of representative LCA activities in North America and Europe is presented in Box 14-5. These activities illustrate accelerated efforts by several organizations and countries to evaluate the application and usefulness of this important management technique. The creation of the new ISO Technical Committee on Environmental Management established a subcommittee on life-cycle analysis under which LCA standards will be developed.

Product Stewardship

Dow Chemical was one of the first to use the term "Product Stewardship" in the early 1970s to convey its commitment to responsible care for products both during manufacturing and in their use by customers. Similar programs have been developed under different names such as Product Responsibility, Product Integrity, or Environmental Quality.

The Chemical Manufacturers Association (CMA) has been promoting a Responsible Care program. One of its management codes of conduct in this program deals with Product Stewardship, which identifies practices to be per-

Box 14-5. Selected LCA Activities in North America and Europe

North America

- U.S. EPA Project Research Program
  - Inventory Guidelines
  - Inventory Case Studies
  - Product/Process Design Manual
  - Impact Analysis Document
- Company-specific studies for strategic planning, design, and improvement
- Trade association–sponsored studies
- Educational forums
  - SETAC conferences—including open forums and training programs
  - Technical conferences
- Networking
  - Department of Defense
  - Professional societies (e.g., SETAC and SOLE)
- ANSI, CSA (through ISO)
- Eco-labeling programs (e.g., environmental choice)
- Environment Canada (e.g., packaging study)

Europe

- European Community
  - Eco-labeling regulations
  - Packaging and packaging waste directive
- Standardization
  - European Standardization Committee CEN:TC 261 Packaging
  - ISO-Strategic Advisory Group on Environment
  - International Association of Packaging Research Institutes (IAPRI)
- Companies are using (partial) LCAs in:
  - Product design
  - Product improvement
  - Product claims
- Conferences
  - CESIO: London
  - SETAC-Europe: Potsdam
  - UNEP

SOURCE: Modified from ISO/SAGE LCA Sub-groups Recommendations to SAGE, October 15, 1992.

formed by a company to develop and implement proactive programs of environmental care.

Regulatory agencies are now looking to on-line changes and modifications to further reduce emissions. Innovations in source reduction and pollution prevention will be the primary focus over the next decade and beyond. There have also been calls for better management of our natural resources to ensure their sustainable use. On balance, the new emphasis will be on increased efficiency through improved resource utilization and reduction of emissions during all stages of a product's life cycle. As a result, companies and organizations have expanded their efforts to better understand and to develop policies and practices to manage the environmental burden and resources used during a product's lifetime. This activity is being referred to by some as Product Stewardship.

What Should Companies Do?

Traditionally, control of environmental pollution has been accomplished on a media-by-media or facility-by-facility basis. One of the weaknesses of this approach is that the relationships among media releases and/or facilities are unclear. Also, not all the environmental releases along the entire life cycle of the products are addressed.

An alternative approach is to identify the environmental releases and resources used by products and/or by product lines. The releases to the environment from the manufacture, use, and disposition of that particular product can then be understood. A manufacturing facility usually manufactures more than one product. The absolute and relative amount of releases to the water, air, and land can be determined for each product or product line at that facility. Collecting environmental release data on a product basis provides a better way of understanding an organization's specific environmental impact. More informed decisions can then be made about that product relative to its contribution to overall releases at a facility.

Let's look at a scenario where a company manufactures three products at its manufacturing facility. The facility releases 10 tons per year of Chemical A according to the SARA Title III TRI Report. Given the increased emphasis on pollution prevention as part of the TRI Form R Reports, the question may be asked: "what product processes contribute to the release of the 10 tons per year of Chemical A?" An inventory analysis of the environmental releases on a product by product basis at the facility reveals that processes and activities associated with Product 1 contributed 8 tons per year, Product 2 contributes 2 tons per year, and Product 3 contributes nothing to the release of Chemical A. Product 1 is an old product that has been losing market share and the product manager had requested a multi-million-dollar investment to improve the product's performance and reestablish market share. However, senior management realizes that this is a high-risk course.

In this simple example, the decision is made to phase out the manufacture and distribution of Product 1. Thus, as a result of understanding the environmental releases associated with each product within a facility, the organization is able to reduce the releases of Chemical A by 80% and at the same time eliminate a potentially risky investment.

This example illustrates alternative ways of collecting and analyzing environmental data to improve the environmental quality of an operation. Based on a product-by-product characterization, several possible decisions could result: (1) A product does not contribute to the environmental releases and should be continued at this time (other things being equal); (2) a product contributes to the release, and research funds can be committed to identify specific actions to reduce the environmental releases; (3) a product contributes significantly to the environmental releases, and technology does not exist to reduce emissions or modify processes. Thus substitution or deletion of the product should be seriously considered.

If a company's accounting system lumps all costs from diverse activities into one category, it has difficulty understanding and managing costs associated with individual products. As companies have begun to better understand their operations and identify the specific sources of operating costs, further cost breakdowns allow management to optimize resources to achieve desired profitability. Similarly, as companies develop additional policies and practices to achieve better environmental performance, improved cost accounting of environmental releases will allow management of long-term environmental liabilities on a product-by-product basis.

Obviously one of the first questions is how and where does one start. Clearly there is no single answer. The approach will depend on the company, its strategies, product lines, and environmental, health, safety, and resource commitment. The following is a systematic approach to product stewardship strategy.

Phase 1.   Overall approach to product stewardship:

Step 1. Establish steering committee with representation from all divisions and relevant functions

Step 2. Conduct initial assessment of existing program

- Review existing practice to ensure compliance with EPA (TSCA, FIFRA, etc), FDA, OSHA, and other regulatory requirements
- Identify environmental, health, safety, and resource issues (real and perceived) relevant to a company's products, packaging, and processes
- Review existing product development process with full life cycle considerations

Step 3. Establish corporate vision and policies

- Improve environmental quality of products, packaging, and processes
- Use resources sustainably
- Eliminate or reduce wastes

- Establish uniform standards worldwide
- Improve continuously
- Ensure products' performance specifications are maintained

Step 4. Implement Policy

- Incorporate measurable actions into business units' and individuals' performance objectives
- Institutionalize life cycle concepts into product, packaging, and process design, development, use, and disposition
- Incorporate environmental policy and practices into existing Total Quality Management program
- Apply life cycle costing practices
- Develop prioritization and screening strategies for products
- Apply training and education programs for company, suppliers, and customers
- Review, audit, and reevaluate implementation process
- Communicate programs and successes

Phase 2.   Implementation and audit plans to ensure compliance with existing environmental, health, and safety requirements:

- Plan to optimize the data and information gathering and regulatory interface component to minimize product licensing time
- Develop data and information management systems
- Prepare regulatory and environmental assessment documents
- Conduct required laboratory and field environmental fate and effects testing

Product Stewardship and LCA

The practice of product life cycle assessment up to now has focused on the inventory component. Two areas to enhance the practice and application of product life cycle assessment are:

1. Establish approaches to bridge the gap between the inventory and assessment components
2. Identify and/or develop accepted approaches to conduct the impact and improvement analyses components

While this research is ongoing, product LCAs can serve a critical role in providing a quantitative catalog of the inputs (energy and raw materials) and outputs for products. Application of life cycle inventories can provide a company with information to help direct its efforts toward areas where immediate reductions in environmental releases can be made. This will help guide the development and evaluation of existing and new products.

Two examples illustrate how companies can utilize the application of product life cycle assessments today to make decisions concerning environmental and resource issues associated with their products or packaging to gain competitive advantage. Procter & Gamble has developed a corporate policy on environmental quality which includes a statement that Procter & Gamble "will develop and use state-of-the-art science and product life cycle assessment, from raw materials through disposal, to assess environmental quality." For example, Procter & Gamble used life cycle assessment conducted on various packaging options for liquid fabric conditioner product to compare the relative resource requirements and environmental releases. Packaging options which offer source reduction opportunities were identified as providing the most efficient use of raw materials and maximum reduction in environmental releases. (See Fig. 14-10.)

The second example is a commitment by Scott Paper Company to apply the concept of product life cycle assessment to their business operations. Scott has developed a strategy to address resource and environmental issues throughout the entire life cycle of their products.

Life Cycle Cost and Economic Analysis

As useful as product life cycle assessment (LCA) has already proved to be in reducing environmental releases, the economic ramifications should be clearly identified. Economic impact and environmental impact are inseparable in the formulation of industrial strategy. In spite of uncertainties and nonquantifiable value judgments, some measure of short- and long-term costs and benefits eventually has to be included to complete a policy analysis. Monetary units of measure are the common denominators typically used by almost every socio-economic system in the world today.

Ironically, the life cycle *assessment* process that has been evolving over the past two decades has no cost methodology, and the life cycle *costing* techniques developed during the same period contain little, if any, environmental impact analysis. True, these analytical tools were designed for quite different purposes, but neither one can provide complete answers without the other.

These life cycle techniques need to be married. However, the attempt at any such merger immediately confronts a significant dilemma: Our present system of economic measurement and decision making doesn't know how to keep meaningful score. If or when it does know how, it doesn't choose to do so. The system simply doesn't count all the costs or assign accountability for all those costs it can count.

New ideas, rules, and frameworks are needed. Life cycle thinking is more than an application of chemical and physical knowledge and conventional financial projections over an extended period of time, i.e., from "cradle to grave." Like sound systems analysis, life cycle analysis must integrate the quantifiable and nonquantifiable costs, risks, and benefits that influence a decision and its most probable outcomes, including so-called negative externalities. This includes public costs as well as private. It includes costs to society, costs to the

LCA Application to Packaging—An Illustration

One of the most important uses of LCAs is to provide companies with a method to ensure that new product formulations or packaging options do indeed result in meaningful environmental improvements. In the following simplified example, an LCA was conducted on various packaging strategies for a liquid fabric conditioner product. Only four of the many options studied are shown here. (For a uniform comparison, the data are based on 1000 liters of single-strength product.)

The table indicates percent decreases for each energy and emission category as compared to a nonrecycled, 64-oz. bottle made of virgin, high-density polyethylene (HDPE).

	Percent decrease in energy usage			Percent decrease in emissions		
	Process	Transport	Feedstock	Solid	Waterborne	Airborne
Strategies for packaging improvement:						
1. Incorporate 25% recycled HDPE into the virgin HDPE bottle	3	0	9	9	(+4)	4
2. Assume 25% consumer recycling of the virgin HDPE bottle	3	2	11	11	(+4)	5
3. Market a concentrated (3X) product in smaller, virgin HDPE bottles	55	53	56	55	54	55
4. Market concentrated (3X) product in virgin paper carton to refill HDPE bottle	53	58	94	91	40	62

These results indicate that the source reductions made possible by product concentration offered greater reductions in life cycle energy requirements and emissions than either incorporation of 25% recycled HDPE or a 25% recycling rate. Product concentration plus the reuse of existing containers offered additional benefits.

Relative to the nonrecycled virgin bottles, each of the four packaging options studied had reduced energy requirements and solid waste emissions. It is important to note that the emissions associated with each packaging option differ in composition and thus require a more detailed examination for meaningful interpretation. This study illustrates the merits of LCA in: (1) providing a baseline as a reference for improvement; (2) guiding product and package development efforts; and (3) lending better understanding of the unique environmental attributes of different packaging strategies.

SOURCE: Data compiled by Franklin Associates, Ltd., and provided courtesy of the Procter & Gamble Company.

Figure 14-10. Evaluating product packaging through LCA.

stakeholders of any economic enterprise, including future generations, as well as costs to the life support systems of our planet. It should also include all the direct and indirect costs of regulation, which can be significant, especially for small firms.

This section explains what life cycle costing is, how and why it got started, its present limitations, and where it must go from here. Illustrations of its uses are provided. Discussions of economic analysis are limited to commonsense microeconomics for use by business managers and engineers. Macroeconomics, national income accounting, and mathematically sophisticated economic analysis are not required for purposes of this discussion.

Origins and Scope of Life Cycle Costing

As mentioned earlier, the initial major impetus for life cycle costing came from the U.S. Department of Defense in the 1960s. The U.S. Navy was a leader in its development. Budgetary processes and the procurement of complex and costly weapons systems required comprehensive analysis and multiyear planning to cope with what had become a massive management challenge. The normal past practice of purchasing military equipment from the lowest bidder no longer made sense, if it ever did, if the lowest-priced hardware was among the most expensive to operate and maintain over its useful lifetime. This "cost of ownership" concept assumed greater importance as the postacquisition costs of facilities, training, operation, maintenance, equipment modification, supply, personnel, and technical service support over many years of use escalated relative to the initial purchase price.

An important early document on life cycle costing was prepared by the Logistics Management Institute, Washington, D.C., in 1965 for the Assistant Secretary of Defense (Installations and Logistics) entitled "Life Cycle Costing in Equipment Procurement." The concept was officially incorporated in Department of Defense policy in 1971 in DOD Directive 5000.1 "Acquisition of Major Defense Systems." During the 1970s life cycle costing was adopted by several state governments, first by Florida in 1974. The U.S. Department of Health, Education and Welfare issued its policy on "life cycle budgeting and costing as an aid in decision making" in 1975. The National Energy Conservation Policy Act, passed in 1978 largely in reaction to the first Arab oil embargo, requires every new federal building to be life cycle cost-effective.

Several factors contributed to relatively sharp increases in ownership costs during the 1970s and 1980s:

- Price and wage inflation over multiyear periods
- A large jump in the cost of energy
- Increasing technological complexity of weapons systems and requirements for their field support

- Slow productivity growth in service sectors
- Greater demands for operational readiness and equipment reliability on a global scale
- Growing problems in the cost of handling and disposal of hazardous wastes and radioactive materials

As a result of these trends, life cycle costing in the military services, in other branches of government, and in industry worldwide has become useful in several areas of planning and procurement:

- Strategic planning
- Evaluating competing programs and projects
- Program and project budgeting
- Awarding contracts among competing bidders
- Selection of logistics support concepts
- Deciding when and how to replace aging equipment, and alternative residual uses of equipment replaced

The basic purposes of life cycle costing are not likely to change a great deal. Methods of computation certainly will. A flurry of federal, state, and local environmental laws and regulations of increasing severity over the past decade have already caused pollution cleanup and control costs to soar. The 1984 amendments to the Resource Conservation and Recovery Act (RCRA), the 1987 amendments to the Clean Water Act, the 1990 amendments to the Clean Air Act, and other second or third generation legislation (1) impose costly requirements upon U.S. manufacturers and many others for waste management and pollution control, as well as (2) create incentives for investment in new equipment, processes, and materials to prevent pollution and minimize waste.

These costs are not trivial. Hundreds of billions of dollars a year in expenses and investments are being incurred worldwide. The costs are reported regularly by the media. The estimated or actual benefits are often not measured and are rarely reported. The reasons are self-evident. Costs are easy to measure. They are real. They hurt. They hurt now. And we know who they hurt. Benefits are difficult to measure. They are controversial. And they help diverse groups in different ways, mostly in the distant future.

Critical cost-benefit-risk analysis issues are involved in the economics of the regulation of health and safety for employees and the public. Should "worst case" standards or "most probable" risks to human health and life be applied in government regulations? What are the direct and indirect regulatory cost savings for each additional projected victim of more lenient standards? The aggregate sums of money involved in such crucial trade-offs are huge. These are not easy questions, especially since the methodology for establishing such standards is still a matter of controversy among toxicologists, epidemiologists, and other experts in the field.

These issues are mentioned here to illustrate that life cycle costing will more and more be wrestling with such difficult questions as the fields of environmental economics, accounting, and law evolve. The element of uncertainty involved in such cost estimates will diminish as a result of gains in scientific knowledge, intelligent regulation and taxation, and case-by-case decisions by our courts of law. Environmental case law not only involves damage to human health but also includes issues of public and private property rights and damages to natural resources. It may some day even include questions of liability for adverse effects on the climate and future generations that may not yet be covered by legislation but require the establishment of contingent liability reserves on the balance sheets of potentially vulnerable companies.

Figure 14-11 portrays the visibility of life cycle costs both from a buyer's standpoint at the time of purchase (far right panels) and from the producer's standpoint at the time of the decision to go into production. Production in this depiction includes research, development, design, testing and acquisition of equipment, raw materials, and working capital. Visibility in this case carries with it the connotation of accuracy. The further into the life span of the product or system the less accurate cost estimates are likely to be.

Visibility also, however, connotes identification of costs and the ability to measure them. Many of the producer's costs of waste management, or mismanagement as the case may be, are buried in indirect overhead accounts. Often, they are not activity-based or product-based. Thus part of the hazardous waste

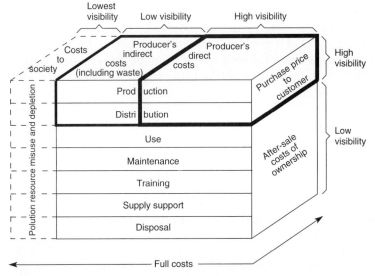

Figure 14-11. Total life cycle cost visibility for durable goods.

costs of an activity or product can be allocated to another product that has no involvement with hazardous materials. In addition, the lowest-visibility costs, i.e., those to society, are downstream costs that are most difficult to measure, become part of some community's general waste management problem, and are not identified on the producer's, consumer's, or anyone else's statement of profit and loss.

It should be noted that Figure 14-11 applies essentially to durable goods with long life spans requiring after-sales service and support. Life cycle *costing* is a concept that has limited application to consumable or semidurable goods because the cost of ownership for these goods consists almost entirely of the purchase price. Life cycle *assessment*, on the other hand, has an important application to consumables because it deals with outputs in the production process that were not being measured heretofore, and with waste management, recycling, and disposal of very large quantities of products and packages.

The schematic in Fig. 14-11 may be misleading in one respect. The "Lowest-Visibility Costs to Society" (externalities) are depicted as essentially constant for each stage of the life cycle (1) relative to other stages and (2) relative to higher-visibility (internally recorded) costs in each stage. This obviously would be quite rare. Environmental impacts vary substantially during each step in a product's life cycle in character, intensity, and cost. Moreover, the cost of ownership to the buyer of a short-lived hazardous consumer item might be negligible but the disposal costs to society relatively high. The ratio of low-visibility externalities to higher-visibility internal costs for each stage of a product's life cycle could have important analytical potential.

Boxes 14-6 and 14-7 illustrate problems associated with full life cycle cost analysis. Minicase examples of the cost of ownership concept in practice are included in the last section of this chapter.

Figure 14-12 represents life cycle industrial economics from a different perspective. It displays the physical ingredients of input and output during the lifetime of manufactured products and identifies the principal players involved in the process. Its purpose is to illustrate how the factors of production and distribution combine to provide goods and services to consumers as well as producing residuals (waste products) in a way that is significant to life cycle economic analysis. This industrial process is basically the same for both capitalist private ownership systems and socialist public ownership systems. This physical process does not concern itself with the sources of investment capital, the measurement and distribution of "profits," or how management of the process is organized, all of which constitute critical differences in the two systems. The physical, functional, and residual processes, however, are similar because they are based on the same hydrocarbon and petrochemical industrial technologies.

Here are some points to consider:

1. *Changes in resource mix.*   Unless present trends are drastically altered, the relative abundance of land, cheap energy, and many raw materials available to smaller populations of the past will be in greater demand and shorter supply for

Box 14-6. Road Salt Economics

It has long been known that road salt causes problems to roads, to automobiles, and to vegetation along roads where salt is used. Road salt has increased the rusting of steel supports and eats away the highways themselves. It hurts trees and vegetation along the roadside and pollutes ground and surface water. The benefits of road salt are obvious in that it reduces the risks of driving under icy road conditions.

A ton of road salt costs approximately $40. This same ton of salt has also been estimated to cause more than $1400 in damage. The added cost of road salt can be broken down as follows:

- Highway corrosion—$650 per ton

- Vehicle corrosion—$525 per ton

- Utilities corrosion—$150 per ton

- Water supply contamination—$100 per ton

Thus a more complete cost associated with use of road salt is estimated to be $1465 ($1425 + $40) per ton.

Environmental impacts also associated with the application of road salt include salt (NaCl) accumulated in soil, foliage dehydration damage, groundwater contamination due to mobile NaCl ions, and heart disease caused by sodium electrolyte. It is difficult to estimate the cost associated with these environmental impacts. If these costs were added, the total cost associated with road salt would be considerably greater than $1465 per ton.

A logical question arises: "Is there a substitute for road salt that performs the same function equally as well but also reduces the impacts on the infrastructure and to the environment?"

In the late 1980s, the Chevron Corporation developed a substitute for road salt. The alternative was calcium magnesium acetate (CMA). It is a white, granular chemical similar in appearance to the vermiculite sold in garden supply stores. Based upon studies completed to date, there does not appear to be any potential for groundwater problems or water damage to flora or fauna. CMA biodegrades in soil, has poor motility in soil, and therefore is unlikely to reach groundwater. It has no effects on Daphnia, an aquatic invertebrate used to measure effects of chemicals on aquatic life.

Further, CMA is about a third as corrosive as road salt. In a dip test performed by the federal government, road salt has a corrosion rate in mils per year of 13.5 compared with 4.8 for CMA. Tap water has a corrosion rate of 3.4 mils per year. However, CMA costs approximately $650 per ton, or more than 15 times the cost of road salt. Consequently, state highway purchasing agents are unlikely to purchase CMA, despite its advantages. While efforts

(Continued)

are under way to reduce the manufacturing costs of CMA, there still exists a problem of how society decides whether to purchase road salt at $40 per ton with long-term damage to roads, cars, and the environment, or to purchase CMA at $650 per ton with a total net savings over an extended period of time.

Clearly, individuals who have responsibility for ensuring that roads are free of ice have primary concern with the best cost-effective product. Their concern would not be for long-term repair and maintenance of the roads and bridges. In that case the traditional road salt is the logical choice.

If the individual responsible for ensuring that roads are free from ice is also responsible for the repair and maintenance of the roads, an alternative choice might be made if a system existed to account for total costs. Today such accounting systems seldom exist. Most decisions are unfortunately based on short-term results which can frequently be harmful in the long run.

SOURCE: Michael B. Lafferty, *Columbus Dispatch*, 1991.

---

the support of much larger human populations in the future. Slow growth in job creation and continued worker and capital migration will put downward pressure on wages, consumer purchasing power, and the per capita rate of increase in resource use. Less hazardous materials will be substituted for harmful ones. Recycling will increase. This changing mix in human and material resource demand and supply will require more sophisticated techniques in life cycle costing, especially for products or systems with long life spans.

2. *Changes in residuals management.*   Source reduction, reuse, and recycling of waste products are on the rise. As waste management costs spiral upward, incentives are created to reduce them. In some cases, waste products from some plants are being used as raw materials for others. In Europe, legislation is emerging to require manufacturers to retrieve their packaging materials and products for remanufacture, recycling, or disposal. The French government's system of "valorization" gives a positive economic value to wastes.

3. *Changes in system cost accounting.*   The creative processes and services employed to produce marketable products add value to those resources that have been rearranged into a new and more useful form. More value can be added if there is less waste of energy and materials, and greater labor productivity. Pollution prevention can achieve greater life cycle improvements in the *net* added value of the entire system.

4. *Changes in business relationships.*   As products and packages move through each stage in their life cycles in a private enterprise system, ownership or custody of these resources can change hands many times. Each exchange is a legal transaction carrying with it rights, responsibilities, and warranties, expressed or implied, of the contractual parties, according to prevailing commercial law. Each owner or custodian has legal responsibilities for the safe use of resources,

---

Box 14-7. Poor Life Cycle Planning Can Be Costly

In June 1992, the Yankee Atomic Electric Company announced that the estimated cost of dismantling its Massachusetts' Yankee Rowe nuclear plant would be $247 million. A previous estimate of dismantling costs in 1989 was $117 million in 1992 dollars. The company has set aside $72 million in a reserve for decommissioning as required by the Nuclear Regulatory Commission. The plant was completed in 1960 at a cost of $39 million.

In August 1992, Portland General Electric announced plans to shut down its Trojan nuclear plant in 1996 when it will have operated only 16 years of its originally planned 40-year lifetime. It has a reserve of $25 million against an estimated decommissioning cost of $200 million to nearly $500 million. Two days after this announcement Portland General Electric stated it would be investing in windmills.

Assuming operating lifetimes of 30 years each, the Worldwatch Institute has estimated that about 60 U.S. nuclear power plants will be candidates for decommissioning by the year 2010. Estimates of dismantling costs now range between $100 million and $2 billion or more per plant. It is uncertain how many, if any, of the 110 reactors now in operation in the United States will continue to operate for their design lifetimes of 40 years.

Disposal costs of this magnitude this soon were never envisioned. If they were, they were never disclosed. Had they been disclosed and included in the calculation of the costs of electricity generated, the early enthusiasm for nuclear power would undoubtedly have been considerably tempered.

Estimates for dismantling the Yankee Rowe plant do not include the full costs of burial of spent fuel rods and other nuclear waste. Concerns here, of course, are not only financial. The U.S. Department of Energy has asked a panel of experts to design a system to warn future civilizations against digging into nuclear waste burial sites which will pose a threat to human health for 300 generations.

SOURCES: *Wall Street Journal,* June 2, 1992; *The New York Times,* August 16, 1992, "Nuclear Power Plants Take Early Retirement" by Mathew L. Wald; *The Futurist,* September–October 1992, "The 10,000-Year Warning" by Gary Kliewer.

---

including labor, land, air, and water, while under his or her care, whether for only a few hours or for a century or longer.

As knowledge about the life cycle environmental impact of products, industrial processes, and packages has grown, environmental laws and regulations have exploded worldwide. This has put pressure, especially upon those furthest along the life cycle chain, to revise their purchasing requirements to reduce their liability for potential environmental damage.

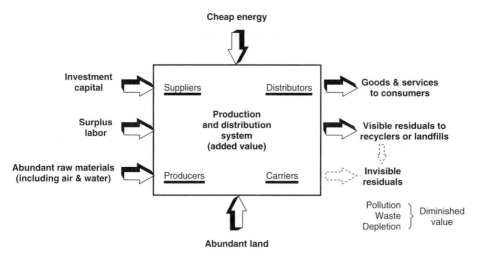

Figure 14-12. Peacetime industrial economy of Hydrocarbon Man.

Life cycle management therefore carries with it inherent legal and social responsibilities, as well as technical and economic requirements, for resource stewardship not only during the ownership or custody of required resources but also, in some measure, during other life cycle stages both upstream and downstream. The legal, societal, financial, and business implications of these evolving boundaries and relationships are tremendous. All the stakeholders have suddenly become virtual partners.

Two Phases of Future Life Cycle Economics

In the life cycle assessment approach we are dealing with the physical balance of chemical and energy input and output. The input is completely under the control of the producer. The output, however, is partly out of control (environmental releases) and potentially harmful. The costs of these releases to health, property, and natural ecology are a negative value of a production and distribution system. These external costs are borne by society. This lack of control on the output side of the chemical mass balance produces an economic disequilibrium which we believe can be reflected in two phases.

Phase I. All internal and appropriate external environmental costs to society should be included in product prices. These would include costs of cleanup, compliance, control, treatment, insurance, fees, penalties, fines, taxes, reserves for contingent liabilities, etc. During this first phase, these added costs would either be passed on to customers in the form of higher prices, or producer profits would decline. Buyers and sellers of products would pay in full, rather than shifting some of their costs to the general public. The cost of polluting products would go up and demand for them would go down.

In the case of products with multiple uses, any particular type of usage that is harmful must be the responsibility of that user since other users who do no harm cannot be expected to pay a price for the product that includes damages inflicted by others. In this phase, regulators and auditors would have to ensure that environmentally irresponsible firms, i.e., those in noncompliance who could underprice those in compliance, were not able to profit by their harmful practices.

Phase II. Competition will steadily put pressure on producers to reduce added costs by making investments in pollution-prevention and waste-reduction measures that will (1) provide a *cleaner* industrial technology, (2) reduce and avoid certain costs in order to produce a *more efficient* industrial technology, and (3) create substantial *new business* opportunities beyond those new goods and services required in Phase I.

Phases I and II can occur in parallel as well as in sequence. Both phases are under way in industry today.

In respect to the full-cost visibility cube in Fig. 14-11, Phase I would ideally render the entire cube fully visible. Phase II would reduce the size of the cube. In this way, producers would be accountable for the *net* added value of their production and distribution systems throughout a product's life cycle. All costs and benefits would be accounted for and controlled on behalf of all stakeholders in a more socially responsive and economically responsible manner. We may never reach this goal in practice, but we can make progress by better understanding the dynamics of the cube and by steadily incorporating more of the "invisible costs" into our economic models and decision making—a matter of simple economic justice.

To more fully appreciate how life cycle costs are presently calculated, the subject of accounting methodologies is presented in the last section of this chapter. Examples of how life cycle costing has been *applied* to environmental questions, however, are considered even more important to an understanding of the range of its uses for different purposes, the direction that life cycle costing is taking, and how it can best be integrated with the product life cycle assessment approach.

Life Cycle Cost Applications

Much life cycle work done by corporations is for proprietary purposes and is not available for public analysis. But the few available cases, mostly developed under contract to government agencies, provide a reasonable picture of the general state of the art of life cycle cost analysis.

Tellus Institute Packaging Study

This recent study (published May 1992), (1) is the only effort in the United States of which we are aware that begins to relate physical life cycle assessment methodology to cost information, and (2) discloses its methodology and the strengths and weaknesses of the findings. The study was prepared for the Council of State Governments (CSG), the U.S. Environmental Protection Agency (EPA), and the New Jersey Department of Environmental Protection and Energy (DEPE).

Packaging materials account for about 30% by weight and 50% by volume of the solid-waste stream in the United States. The useful lifetime of most packages is very short. They are used for containment and protection of contents, as well as for marketing purposes and convenience.

The Tellus researchers and analysts adopted the following approach:

1. *A comprehensive comparison.* Rather than study packages per se, a comparative analysis was made of all major packaging materials: aluminum, glass, steel, five types of paper, and six types of plastic.

2. *Reliance on public information.* It was believed that public data, despite serious limitations in quality and timeliness, was preferable to selective proprietary data that could not be verified or reproduced by independent third parties. However, the data may or may not be representative, given the changes in production processes that have occurred in the interim.

3. *Use of inventory assessment.* The life cycle assessment begins with an "inventory" of energy and raw material inputs and environmental releases associated with each stage in the life cycle of the manufacture, use, and disposal of products, packages, and activities. These inputs and outputs are expressed in units of weight and are not evaluated in terms of relative risks or hazards to human health or the natural environment.

4. *Evaluation of environmental impact.* In the absence of established methodology regarding impact analysis, Tellus employed techniques widely used and debated in energy regulation. Many pollutants were directly assigned cost values equal to the applicable cost of currently required control measures. This method assumes that the societal cost of a pollutant must be at least as great as the costs "society" is willing to pay to control it. This may or may not be true.

This method could not be used for all pollutants. Many toxic and carcinogenic substances were ranked in accordance with their hazards to human health. These hazards were then compared with the health effects of lead and the cost of its removal through air-pollution controls. This assumes, rightly or wrongly, that "society" should be willing to pay twice as much per pound to reduce emissions of a substance twice as dangerous as lead, used as a reference.

5. *Marginal instead of average impacts.* The goal of the study was to identify the change in societal costs resulting from an incremental change in the use of a

given amount of a particular packaging material. Since most policy changes will result in a marginal change in the quantity of one or more packaging materials, the significant impacts of this particular study are the marginal impacts of quantity changes.

The authors of the Tellus report candidly acknowledge certain omissions and weaknesses in their analysis, such as omission of refillable bottles and the life cycle stages of package forming, filling, and transportation, insufficient data on industrial solid waste and recycled plastics production, and some emissions data that are several years old. They further openly discuss the experimental, controversial nature of some of their methods and underlying assumptions. They observe that "We are well aware that we are offering the first word, not the last, on these critical topics," and that some of their efforts at evaluation at least produce a more reasonable basis for measuring economic impact than zero valuation of environmental effects.

The Tellus analysis found, among other things, that both conventional economic costs of disposal and the imputed environmental impact costs of production far exceed the imputed environmental impact costs of disposal. These latter impact costs, however, could actually differ substantially depending on the design, age, condition, and control of landfills or incinerators. These considerations, as well as land use, aesthetics, odor, and other impacts, were not included in the study. Nonetheless, the estimated environmental impact costs of package waste disposal in modern disposal facilities, using the Tellus methodology, are generally only a tiny fraction of the total life cycle impact costs.

The Tellus Study raise analytical issues not covered in the Executive Summary of the report, i.e., the degree of accuracy required or achieved based on the given assumptions, and the sensitivity of the findings to changes in the assumptions. It may be that a range of estimated impact costs for each material rather than single point values could provide a better sense of the degree of uncertainty involved in the findings. On the other hand, it may be that some impact differences are so substantial that a very simple life cycle inventory is all that is required for major improvements at this time. It is ironic that as differences narrow and impact costs are reduced, more sophisticated and costly studies will be required to achieve smaller improvements, and the costs of achieving those improvements might even exceed the uncertain potential benefits.

The purpose of the Tellus Packaging Study was to aid governments in determining regulatory policy. The findings, of course, are of great interest to producers, especially of consumer products and packaging materials. The focus of the study was on marginal costs of environmental impacts of emissions during the principal stages of the material life cycle. It was not the type of full-cost life cycle analysis that might be used for a purchasing or a capital investment decision. For an example of a purchasing decision (solvents used in the electric utility industry) see the case below prepared for the Electric Power Research Institute (EPRI).

An illustration of a capital investment case study appears in another report of the Tellus Institute prepared for the EPA as part of its review of the effect of capital budget accounting on pollution-prevention projects.

Capital Budgeting for Pollution Prevention

In the 1970s it was already apparent to some government regulators and many large industrial firms that measures designed merely to clean up polluted land and water, and to control the levels of harmful releases, constituted a commitment to huge costs of operation. Companies such as 3M, Dow Chemical, Polaroid, and Merck, among others, were already embarking on programs to eliminate pollution in the late 1970s through product and package redesign, materials substitution, and process changes. These early initiatives in pollution prevention typically resulted in waste reduction, energy conservation, and other cost savings that improved the profitability or competitiveness of the companies that undertook them.

Events in the 1980s added additional inducements to industrial pollution-prevention efforts. The "strict, joint and several" liability of Superfund (1980) placed even small contributors to large waste sites at the risk of remediation costs in the millions of dollars. The Community-Right-to-Know provisions of Superfund reauthorization (1986) placed site-specific emissions of toxic chemicals under public scrutiny and added to public pressure for more federal, state, and local regulation. These and other events provided greater incentives for companies to invest in pollution-prevention projects that would benefit their own financial performance in the long run, reduce potential liabilities, and help the environment.

As the more obvious and beneficial steps were taken initially by companies over the first few years, the question slowly emerged as to why more companies and more projects weren't proceeding to invest in capital equipment that promised such favorable results. Organizational and attitudinal barriers have played a role, but economics and capital budget accounting have probably been at least as critical a deterrent as any other reason.

If a project is financed by external borrowing, for example, the cost and availability of capital is a factor. Also, potential lenders may balk at projects that are perceived as too risky, regardless of the projected rates of return. More important to the purposes of this chapter, however, are the internal economic and accounting barriers. These are manifested in thresholds of acceptable profitability, i.e., "hurdle rates" of return that a project must jump over to gain approval. These capital budgeting processes, which calculate costs and benefits over multiyear periods, if not life cycles, are regarded as barriers in many cases of proposed environmental projects because they do not take all the costs and benefits into account.

Recognizing this dilemma, the U.S. EPA requested Tellus Institute to undertake a cooperative project on capital budgeting for environmental projects. The results were published in an EPA document of May 1992 entitled *Total Cost Assessment: Accelerating Industrial Pollution Prevention through Innovative Project Financial Analysis.* Case studies were selected from the pulp and paper industry.

The Total Cost Assessment (TCA) approach used in the Tellus-EPA study consists of four elements:

1. *Expanded cost inventories.* TCA considers a broader range of costs, including probabilistic costs and savings, than are normally included in conventional cost analysis. See Box 14-8.

2. *Expanded time horizon.* TCA uses a time horizon of at least 5 years because many costs and savings from pollution-prevention projects take a long time to materialize.

3. *Long-term financial indicators.* Three standard project financial tools are acceptable for analyzing environmental proposals. These are Net Present Value (NPV), Internal Rate of Return (IRR), and Profitability Index (PI). These techniques identify all positive and negative cash flows over the life of the project, discounting future inflows and outflows at the project's selected cost of capital. For the IRR, the NPV is set at zero and the discount rate is calculated; for the NPV, the discount rate is known and the NPV is calculated. NPV is the preferred approach when comparing projects because under certain conditions the IRR and PI methods fail to identify the most favorable project. It should be noted that the discount rate used is extremely important in environmental projects because projects whose net positive cash flows are further in the future will be substantially lowered by high discount rates, making such investments much less attractive.

4. *Appropriate cost allocation.* Waste management and disposal costs and regulatory compliance costs are often placed in overhead accounts rather than allocated to the particular products and processes responsible for their creation. Such costs need to be assigned to products and their manufacturing activities according to the way in which the type and quantity of waste is generated or controlled. This is necessary to identify and measure the costs and benefits of any actions taken to reduce waste and prevent pollution.

Several TCA methods have been developed to analyze pollution-prevention projects. These methods have been available for several years but have not yet achieved widespread acceptance in industry, despite their ability to compare capital investment options more effectively than conventional accounting procedures.

The Tellus-EPA study applied a TCA approach to two paper mill capital expenditure projects. In both cases the TCA approach was compared with the standard methods the two companies used to evaluate projects.

As might be expected, the TCA approach included costs of waste management, utilities, compliance, and future liability that were not usually considered by the companies in their financial evaluations of capital projects. The results of these comparisons are indicated in Tables 14-1 and 14-2. Clearly, the outcome for environmental projects is more favorable when the heretofore hidden costs of not making the investment are accounted for. The differences in these numbers are not trivial. They are the difference between "go" and "no go." Why, then, has there been a reluctance on the part of most companies to adopt a TCA approach? What are the barriers to more rapid change in the way industry evaluates capital investment projects?

The EPA-Tellus study provides some plausible reasons for this lack of progress.

1. *Need for institutional change.*   Institutional change is perhaps the biggest hurdle of all. Established institutions, with internal cultures and ways of doing business that have made them successful, require enormous threats (e.g., laws with heavy sanctions) or substantial incentives (e.g., quick gains in profitability) to cause them to change the ways they conduct their affairs. Incentives to change—negative or positive—have to be more than reasonable. They must be powerful. They need to overcome the inertia and complacency that tend to develop in every institution.

2. *Excessive complexity.*   Complexity of new methods is a familiar barrier. It is a characteristic of most new technical systems. The TCA approach clearly complicates an already complex process. It introduces factors difficult if not impossible to quantify scientifically, as well as the uncertainties of future economic, regulatory, and legal developments. With the aid of computer technology, decision science, and adequate training, the TCA approach can certainly be mastered and is well justified for large projects. What is needed most for more

Table 14-1. Conventional Capital Project Analysis vs. Total Cost Assessment (Paper Mill Applications)

	Project 1: White water and fiber reuse		Project 2: Conversion to metal-free coating	
	Conventional	TCA	Conventional	TCA
Total capital costs	$1,743,820	$1,743,820	$623,809	$653,809
Annual savings (before interest and taxes)	116,245	658,415	118,112	216,874
Net present value (NPV):				
Years 1 through 10	(702,855)	1,242,536	(98,829)	232,817
Years 1 through 15	(587,346)	1,808,384	13,932	428,040
Internal rate of return (IRR), %:				
Years 1 through 10	0	36	12	24
Years 1 through 15	6	36	16	27
Simple payback, years	11.4	2.0	5.3	3.0

SOURCE: EPA Publication *Total Cost Assessment: Accelerating Industrial Pollution Prevention through Innovative Project Financial Analysis*, May 1992.

Table 14-2. Cost Summary Comparison for Project 2

	Conventional analysis	Total cost assessment	Difference over 15 years	
			Dollars	%
Capital costs	$623,809	$653,809	($30,000)	(4.8)
Net operating savings (costs) before interest and taxes:				
Raw material	18,112	(27,488)	(45,600)	(251.8)
Waste management	121,500	243,871	122,371	100.7
Utilities	(5,000)	(87,029)	(82,029)	(1640.6)
Labor	(8,000)	(8,000)	0	0
Other	(3,500)	84,520	88,020	2514.9
Regulatory compliance	(5,000)	11,000	16,000	320.0
Total	$118,112	$216,874	$98,762	83.6
Intangible benefits not included:				
Liability advance	0	$35,000	$35,000	
Market gain (net profit income)	0	Substantial		

SOURCE: EPA.

Notes on Intangible Benefits: A savings of $35,000 in future liability avoidance is small in this case because it assumes the firm will continue to incinerate its waste, and liability exposure will not occur until year 13. Incineration is presumed to act as a powerful liability safety net for several reasons, an important one of which is that failure of an incinerator facility will leave the facility owner, not the waste generator, liable for personal and property damages.

A significant increase in sales is possible in the European market when lead is removed from the paper coatings.

widespread adoption of TCA is a simplified version for small companies and small projects.

3. *Insatiable data demands.* There is little question of the need for useful data in life cycle assessment, traditional life cycle costing, and systems analysis work as well. Data are costly and time-consuming to collect. However, data are the basic raw materials of the information and communications revolution which is making the Age of Integrated Systems possible. Data feed the software and services that enhance the value added to manufactured products. Data improve the ability to make timely, informed management decisions. Good data are needed to exercise effective financial control and determine how much insurance to carry. Knowledge workers starve without good data. Productivity and competitiveness thrive on it. The power and value of timely and accurate information can far exceed its cost. It can mean the difference between profit and loss, between winning and losing in court, between "go" and "no go." What is needed is a buildup of more cooperative, nonprofit, easily accessible databases and expert systems that can serve as public information utilities. Also needed, of course, is the knowledge of data management economics and decision-making risk assessment to avoid costly information overkill in the search for ever greater certainty. Surely this challenge is not beyond the ability of decision theory and information science and technology to solve, for both small and large users of proprietary systems.

4. *Regulatory impediments.*   Disincentives to adoption of TCA are created by two types of legislation. The end-of-the-pipe regulatory approach, which focuses separately on the control of releases into the air, land, or water, encourages capital investment in the least-cost equipment to comply with these individual requirements. No comprehensive financial analysis is needed to comply with this type of regulation. The states of New York, Oregon, Minnesota, and especially New Jersey have taken steps to encourage a more comprehensive approach to environmental protection.

SEC regulations create an impediment of a different kind. Annual SEC Form 10K filing requirements include disclosure of many actual or potential costs with material effects on a company's performance. Compliance with environmental regulations, and potential losses and environmental liabilities are specifically mentioned. This raises practical issues for TCA in conjunction with public reporting and the disclosure to auditors of uncertain potential liabilities that are used in TCA calculations. It is contended by some legal experts that a company runs the risk of exposing itself to new liability simply by acknowledging and disclosing as yet unknown and contingent environmental liabilities of uncertain dimensions. It is argued further that such action is in potential conflict with its fiduciary responsibilities to its shareholders. This unresolved dilemma is not a positive influence on the ready adoption of TCA methods.

The EPA-Tellus study concludes with observations about TCA that have application to industry in general.

- Application of TCA to capital budgeting is an organizational as well as an analytical challenge.

- No single TCA method is appropriate to all firms.

- Government incentives and disincentives can play an important role in the adoption of TCA.

- Pollution-prevention projects will not always be chosen as the best company strategy as a result of TCA.

- As pollution-prevention projects steadily shed their image as consistent financial losers through use of TCA, its acceptance for cost reduction, cost avoidance, and market expansion goals will channel more investments into capital projects for prevention rather than solely for compliance.

Future Prospects of Life Cycle Costing

Professional participants on the train of environmental awareness appear to be seated as follows:

- Earth, life, and medical scientists are in the locomotive getting jostled by a growing mob of perceptive lawyers.

- Engineers and consultants are seated throughout the train.
- Most economists are in the caboose.
- Most accountants are not on board.

We believe that the term "life cycle costing" is too limited for general application in the emerging Age of Integrated Systems. It is still meaningful only in its original context of estimating total costs of ownership when procuring or investing in capital goods or facilities. Most accountants are still using conventional life cycle costs for purposes of comparing bids and planning budgets.

Even in this special-purpose context, life cycle costing in practice has acquired some critics. We have witnessed inconsistent, noncomparable, "creative" accounting systems and alleged huge discrepancies between original estimates and actual costs incurred. In point of fact, on large government programs actual vs. estimated life cycle costs are rarely, if ever, booked. Disposal and phase-out costs have most often been waived and only now are being addressed in life cycle costing in the U.S. government. Furthermore, costs cannot be considered in isolation. They must be related to product performance and quality. Performance and quality, in turn, are related to environmental impact.

Life cycle costing is an inadequate term even if it were to include environmental costs. As we have seen, more than cost estimating is involved in environmental accounting. It is not only a question of pricing the list of chemical and energy inputs and outputs at each stage in a product's or system's life cycle. Cost avoidance, cost savings, cost accounting, and cost effectiveness play their traditional roles, but so do other measures. Managers must consider economic valuations of nonmarket assets, the economics of risk assessment, discount rates, the monetization of long-term legal liabilities, and the valuation of societal and natural resources, with imputed costs of their degradation and depletion. In these evaluations, values are often more important than costs and outcomes more important than incomes. (See Box 14-8 for more on the subject of accounting.)

Even the term "full life cycle cost" implies that only costs are incurred in protecting public health and the natural environment. "Full life cycle cost-benefit analysis" or "full life cycle cost-effectiveness" would be more accurate descriptions of what life cycle systems analysis, life cycle economics, and life cycle management are about.

In the valuation of environmental impacts there are several competing concepts or methodologies. However, the true test is not found in economic theory or cost accounting principles but in what will stand up in court. The legislation and organizational behavior that will stand up in court in turn will help determine what societal costs (externalities) will eventually become internalized in the prices of goods and services.

It is naive to believe that internalization of environmental societal costs relieves "society" of the burden of payment for clean air and water. Cleanup, control, and certain pollution-prevention costs, penalties, and taxes will be

Box 14-8.   Accounting for Environmental Costs

Two types of environmental accounting are performed by industrial firms in the United States and in many other countries. One system is the physical accounting of chemical releases and waste management. This type of record keeping is mostly in response to environmental regulations, in particular the Toxic Release Inventory (TRI) reported under Right-to-Know legislation in the United States. These data are usually measured in tons against some standard, permit, or company goal.

The other accounting system is the one that counts everything in dollars. Cost accounting is used for internal control. Financial accounting is a management planning and control system, with a primary purpose to inform lenders, investors, regulators, and the public about the financial health of the company.

Life cycle costing is a combination of cost and financial accounting and is performed as often by cost engineers as by cost and financial accountants. Life cycle cost estimates are important in procurement and capital budgeting projects and are increasingly capable of being improved from an environmental standpoint by data from the chemical accounting system.

When environmental costs and savings in waste management, pollution prevention, regulatory compliance, and future liabilities are included in a project analysis, many questions arise that pose difficulties for traditional accounting methods. Such questions as what costs we are dealing with, their magnitude, their probability of occurrence, their time of occurrence, etc., all expand the area of uncertainty and further complicate decision making.

Principal sources of uncertainty are (1) the complexity of assessing risks associated with exposure to different levels and types of hazardous substances during each stage in a product's life cycle, and (2) increasing numbers of complicated, environmental and product liability regulations and court decisions continually affecting costs of control, penalties, fines, and liabilities.

Some regulations require activities that are relatively easy to account for, such as monitoring, training, and manifesting shipments of waste. Others create contingent costs which *may* be incurred *if* certain events occur, such as leaks, spills, and infractions of all kinds. These outcomes are uncertain and depend on many circumstances over which a company has different degrees of control. Such unknowns, as we have seen, are not uncommon in conducting a systems analysis but are a considerable challenge to traditional budgeting and accounting functions. This is why, of course, accountants have typically not been very much involved in life cycle analysis, and precisely why they should be.

The difficulties involved in costing environmental damage do not justify ignoring them, i.e., assigning them a cost of zero. We know there are damages and we know they are at times substantial.

Certain types of uncertainty can be evaluated with the help of legal experience. Economic damages associated with wrongful death and personal injury cases have long been determined in courts of law. Case law and legal handbooks provide guidance for estimating future earnings, life expectancy, work life and probability of employment, nonmarket economic losses, and others. Attorneys are familiar with a wide variety of situations and with key rulings rendered by the courts, as well as the potential impact that changes in key factors can have on an evaluation (sensitivity analysis).

Attempts to reform product liability laws and practices are also instructive. The long battle between consumer groups and trial lawyers vs. manufacturers and insurance companies has produced mountains of studies and data on this subject. As always, much of the information is either flawed or subject to interpretation, and important data required are often nonexistent. It is a mixed bag, therefore, as to when the experience of extensive adversarial proceedings and jury trials reduce or increase the levels of uncertainty in determining the potential costs and risks of product liability.

Potentially useful valuation experience is being gained under the Natural Resource Damage Assessment (NRDA) provision, adopted as an Optional Rule in 1986 under the Comprehensive Environmental Response Compensation and Liability Act (CERCLA). This regulatory procedure can be used (1) to determine the nature and extent of injury to natural resources, including fish and wildlife, caused by a release of hazardous substances or a discharge of oil covered by CERCLA or the Clean Water Act; and (2) to assess compensatory damages for which the responsible party (or parties) is liable.

The procedures to be followed in NRDA cases are prescribed in detail. They require scientific assessments of the degree of injury—past, present, and future—and determination of the dollar value of injuries and costs of restoration by economists and lawyers specializing in natural resource cases. In 1989, the courts upheld this process in rulings on 13 issues from suits challenging these regulations.

The number of NRDA cases is growing, but their value as precedents is limited because individual determinations are based on a unique set of facts and circumstances occurring at specific sites with their own ecological characteristics. However, economic valuation techniques may emerge from litigation of such cases during the years ahead that could prove useful in life cycle economic analysis and financial planning.

For purposes of external financial reporting, contingent costs are a familiar occurrence. Accounting regulations (FAS No. 5, 1975) require reporting of contingencies in the balance sheet or income statement when a firm expects a probable impairment of assets or an operating loss. Until recently, application of this rule has been limited to large probable losses associated with a singular event. Court rulings lately have increasingly required companies to report recurring or longer-term environmental damages not associated with a singular unusual event.

(Continued)

Securities and Exchange Commission (SEC) rules require disclosure of all factors that are "material" to a firm's capital expenditures, earnings, and competitive position. Expenditures on environmental controls, past, present, and future, are included. Any actual or expected governmental proceeding that may affect the financial condition of a company is also included. These accounting and disclosure requirements involve substantial discretion and risk in estimating contingency costs.

If such costs are omitted in analyzing internal capital expenditure projects, investment dollars could be allocated to projects that are vulnerable to continued liability from environmental damage. A habit or policy of such omissions risks a pattern of unanticipated losses to the company. The potential capacity of a pollution-prevention investment to eliminate future liability at its source—its fundamental purpose—can be sacrificed on the altar of accounting convenience and convention.

Accountants are not the people who are required to assess risks. They are part of the team that classifies costs into past, present, future, and contingent dollars. The probabilities, margins of error, and size of future expenditures have to be presented to management for the determination of what options will be selected. Different managers with different risk profiles, or the same managers in different situations, will react differently to the same information.

Customary cost analysis practices also have tended to favor end-of-the-pipe control technologies over pollution-prevention investments. This is because the latter often require more complex changes in production systems which yield benefits in many indirect ways over longer periods of time, including contingency cost savings that are difficult to measure.

Pollution prevention can also create advantages to companies by enhancing their corporate or product images. These are just as real as cost-reduction advantages but again involve benefits that are longer-term and often difficult to measure. Consumers are increasingly sensitive to environmental issues. Capital investment projects that result in "greener" products or packages can help increase sales. Improvements in market performance, however, may never be realized if project financial criteria do not reflect all the costs, liabilities, risks, and benefits that an effective life cycle systems analysis of a large capital investment proposal requires.

A comprehensive report on the issues involved in environmental accounting has been published in the United Kingdom by the Chartered Association of Certified Accountants entitled *The Greening of Accountancy* (1990). This publication is an insightful account of the changes in accounting that appear to be called for by environmental systems thinking and life cycle management. By rethinking the industrial scorekeeping system the profession of finance and accounting can achieve fuller and fairer disclosure and accountability. Total performance accounting can benefit all stakeholders and enhance the long term prospects for both private enterprise and the environment.

passed on to consumers in higher prices of goods and services to the extent that the market will bear them. Lower doctor bills for respiratory diseases may translate into higher costs for cleaner fuel, but not necessarily in equal offsetting amounts.

Calculations to quantify these trade-offs will always be grist for economic argumentation. Less arguable is that companies will voluntarily internalize societal costs only to the extent that it is in their enlightened self-interest to do so. It is obviously in their interests to obey the law and pay their taxes. Beyond that, it is also in their long-term interests to avoid costs, minimize liabilities, satisfy their customers, reduce waste, conserve energy, increase sales, improve their image, carry adequate insurance, and become more competitive.

Life cycle management systems have an important part to play in the evolution of science and technology. It is an exciting challenge for managers and engineers. Success requires important changes in how we think, how we behave, and how we keep score in business and government. This means more accountants will have to get on the train and more economists will have to get better seats. (John R. Barfield, Boeing Defense and Space Group, and Nga T. Anamosa, General Dynamics Electronics Division, reviewed and contributed to this Section.)

Systems Analysis and Life Cycle Thinking

As we have seen, life cycle work is not business as usual. It involves much more than adding items to a management or engineering check-off list, or another column to an accounting or corporate planning spread sheet. A life cycle approach to management and engineering eventually requires considerable rethinking on the part of everyone, including top management. In some companies, dealing constructively with environmental issues with life cycle analysis has had a substantial impact on the corporate culture.

Why is this so? Establishment of goals, management of change, assessment of risk, allocation of resources, resolution of conflict—these are what business and financial management have always been about. Evaluation of the "environment" in which business must operate—social, economic, political, and competitive—is a normal part of market research and strategic planning. Why is the ecological factor any different from all the other changes that business must regularly cope with year after year?

In one sense, it is not. If today's business managers and senior engineers had received an adequate education in earth and life sciences and environmental issues, as young people are beginning to receive today, the surprise factor regarding environmental problems in the business community would be much less. Until the 1970s and 1980s, the combined environmental impact of population growth, use of fossil fuels, petrochemical technology, and Western World consumerism had long been underestimated, or not considered at all, by all but a few "extremists." Today a growing number of the world's largest corporations and respectable top executives regard the management of environmental factors as crucial to the long-term survival of their firms.

So much progress and so many advances in human health and welfare are attributable to science, industrial technology, and market-based economics that it is still difficult for a great many of us to accept evidence of serious trouble as more than an unpleasant annoyance. These "headaches" are often regarded as a small price to pay for the great social and economic benefits bestowed upon us by modern economic growth and development. To discover that the fruits of our labor are not all digestible is upsetting to our traditional ways of thinking and acting.

It is not the purpose of this chapter to make a case one way or the other regarding the ultimate gravity of the adverse health effects and other environmental damage being inflicted by human activities upon the planet. It isn't necessary to do so. The case for life cycle analysis often has merit even when environmental factors are minor. The case grows stronger as our knowledge regarding environmental issues increases and as the level of concern of more and more people everywhere becomes greater. Many companies find a life cycle approach to their resource management and product planning is good business practice purely on the merits of the process.

Our examination of life cycle assessment and life cycle economics leads inexorably to the integrating art and science of systems analysis. Systems analysis is a problem-solving discipline particularly useful for policy planning in government and large industrial enterprises. We focus here on those aspects of life cycle thinking that are most significant in systems analysis when ecological considerations are the greatest.

Proposition 1:   Life cycle work involves all corporate stakeholders and all business functions. Comprehensive life cycle analysis involves the efficiency with which all required resources are used to produce and consume processed goods and services. Therefore, all business management functions are affected, some more or less than others, depending on the kinds of goods and services involved and the stage of the life cycle being addressed. See Fig. 14-13.

Life cycle analysis should therefore not be considered a specialized function. Rather it is a technique, tool, methodology, or way of thinking about the fundamental purpose of an industrial or commercial enterprise. The enduring mission of business has to be the most efficient use of natural, human, and financial resources to produce goods and services needed to sustain and improve the quality of human life on earth. *Not just today or tomorrow, but indefinitely into the future.*

Industrial leaders have only recently begun to address this expanded mission. The typical concept in the capitalist West is that the number one goal of any enterprise is to maximize profits, i.e., provide the best possible financial return to the business owners. To be sure, the majority of business managers acknowledge certain obligations to other constituencies who have a stake in the com-

	Production				Consumption		
Resources (input)	Research, design, and development	Acquisition of raw materials	Production	Distribution	Operation (use)	Support (maintenance and repair)	Recycling, reuse, and disposal

Materials
Renewable
Nonrenewable

Energy
Thermodynamic laws

Labor
Energy
Skills
Manual
Mental

Land

Capital
Private savings
Public expenditures
Cash
Credit

Information

Time

Output (Goods and Services)

Durable goods
Producer hardware and equipment
Consumer durables

Nondurable goods
Products (supplies)
Food (products and packages)

Facilities (buildings, bridges, highways, etc.)

Services (labor, knowledge)

Residuals
By-products
Waste
Liquids
Solids
Gas
Heat (energy)

Figure 14-13. Life cycle systems analysis.

pany, i.e., employees, customers, suppliers, retirees, and the community in which the company's facilities are located. But, in the final analysis, the interests of these stakeholders are almost always subordinated to those of the stockholders as a matter of normal management practice in a capitalistic system.

Environmental factors, among others, have influenced business leaders and socioeconomic thinkers in recent years to think harder about the price of industrial progress. There is a growing realization that our capitalistic economic system, as successful as it has been in many ways, can and must fulfill a more socially responsive and more economically responsible role of resource stewardship and stakeholder equity in the future. We believe that a framework of life cycle thinking can contribute to this goal.

Life cycle management is similar, in its pervasive application, to business ethics and behavioral science. To be operationally effective, knowledge of the latter disciplines and their application cannot be concentrated in the Human Resources Department. They must be practiced throughout the organization. So, too, with life cycle work. Life cycle thinking is enriched, moreover, by the degree to which its practitioners are environmentally literate. We believe environmental literacy will rapidly become as important a professional qualification for managers and engineers in large organizations of the future as computer literacy and information technology are for managers and engineers today.

Proposition 2:   Decision support is the paramount purpose of life cycle systems analysis. Decision support can take many forms, depending on the nature of the problem and the culture of the organization. The level of effort can vary widely. For example:

1. A formal, comprehensive, and data-intensive study by an interdisciplinary team of experts, involving major new products, new processes, large real estate transactions, or construction projects

2. A front-end analysis to identify major issues for further study if appropriate

3. An education and training program in the essentials of life cycle thinking to help managers and engineers incorporate this approach into their normal planning and decision-making activities

4. A combination or modified versions of the above

The value of an environmentally oriented life cycle approach to decision making is that it can expand the boundaries of one's thought processes in space and time. It promotes relationship thinking and can help efforts to make the industrial technosphere more compatible with the natural biosphere. Furthermore, as the costs of cleanup, compliance, and potential liabilities have escalated, new decision tools are needed because environmentally desirable projects often have long-term benefits that are difficult to measure and cannot compete in a short-term, profit-oriented business setting. As the Tellus Institute study on Total

Cost Allocation demonstrates, capital projects that could potentially produce substantial savings through pollution prevention or waste reduction may not be approved using traditional investment criteria.

Life cycle systems analysis can be of great assistance to business managers and engineers in making the important, complex, value-laden decisions often required of them. Boxes 14-9 and 14-10 identify many of the features of a comprehensive study of this kind. Although this full process is obviously not for everybody, it contains a menu of considerations for selective application to a variety of situations, large and small.

The most critical part of this analytical approach in terms of successful outcome is the front-end formulation of the problem. It is more important to choose the right objective(s) and ask the right questions than it is to select the best alternative solution to a poorly structured problem.

Posing the right problem is usually not a job for an expert. Experts can solve problems in their own fields better and faster than others but tend to formulate problems to fit the methods they know for solving them. The risk of defining the wrong problem can be reduced by having goal setting performed by generalists or by a group of experts with a variety of skills and perspectives.

Three aspects of complex decisions are uncertainty, interactive connections, and top management support of change.

Uncertainty.   Formulation and resolution of complex problems contain many areas of uncertainty. This is especially true when there are only small differences in quantitative factors and the focus must be directed to qualitative issues and toward both known unknowns and unknown unknowns. These heighten the uncertainty and controversy involved in many environmental issues. Global warming is a good example.

In the 1960s, someone in the Systems Analysis Office in the Office of the Secretary of Defense came up with this motto: "It is better to be roughly right than exactly wrong." In other words, partial answers to good questions are better than complete answers to poor questions, especially if there are ways to protect yourself against adverse consequences of calculated risks.

Decisions under conditions of uncertainty are made by business managers every day. For example, how much insurance to carry to protect individuals and companies from unpredictable losses resulting from known hazards. This "precautionary principle" of protection is a routine practice in business and personal affairs in the industrialized world. It is a way of being compensated for the cost of being wrong or unlucky.

This same principle was agreed to at the World Industry Conference on Environmental Management in 1984 and subsequently strengthened in 1990 at a meeting of the UN Economic Commission for Europe: "In order to achieve sustainable development, policies must be based on the precautionary principle. Environmental measures must anticipate, prevent and attack the causes of environment degradation. Where there are threats of serious or irreversible

Box 14-9. Life Cycle Systems Analysis

Phase I   Organize a multidisciplinary team of experts with different skills and perspectives

For example, manufacturing, planning, systems engineering, design, marketing, accounting, MIS, etc.

Phase II   Evaluate and clearly state problem(s), objective(s), scope.
Distinguish between site-specific and systemic problems.
State assumptions

What's my role: producer, consumer, regulator?
What's my product: consumer nondurables, technical equipment, buildings, etc.?
The question here is not so much which car I should buy, for example, but should I buy a car at all?

Phase III   Establish appropriate time horizons.
Evaluate how time affects key aspects of the problem and the analysis itself

Is the life cycle of material $\times$ 1 year or 5? What does it depend on?
At what stages of elapsed time in the life cycle are emissions expected to be the greatest? Are emissions large for a short period or small for a long period, or both? Or neither?
When will required information be available relative to the need for an answer?

Phase IV   Identify and define alternatives, their feasibility, constraints, risks, and degree of uncertainty

For example, if we discontinue, modify, or continue to market Product A, how will our customers and competitors react? What will the environmental costs and benefits be?

Phase V   Select the most feasible alternatives for detailed evaluation

Promising alternatives with a high degree of uncertainty should be further evaluated to reduce uncertainty and avoid excluding a feasible option for the wrong reasons

Phase VI   State quality and relative importance of information required. Specify missing data and nonquantitative factors. Evaluate cost, benefit, and time needed to obtain missing data. Consider supporting studies to provide additional facts which may uncover additional alternatives. Search for equivalencies of noncomparable data

The environmental cost envelope with environmental accounting extends beyond the dimensions of the operating envelope and conventional accounting. For example, deicing roads with salt spreaders causes costly damage to cars, soil, etc., that is not normally included in the cost of salt or the cost of spreading.
The relative value and comparability of cost estimates are more important than absolute values.
Wherever possible, use frequency distributions in lieu of averages and distinguish money costs from economic costs.
Can expert opinion substitute for some data?

(Continued)

Box 14-9. Life Cycle Systems Analysis

Phase VII — Compare the most feasible alternatives: Relative life cycle costs and benefits, life cycle cost-effectiveness and sensitivity analyses for each objective, alternative, and major assumption. Restate assumptions, uncertainties, risks, interfaces, interactions, boundaries, trade-offs, and value judgments. Systems integration analysis may be required. The ability to reverse a decision without severe consequences is always important

Use of models, simulations, scenarios, and games. Recycle tentative conclusion in an iterative feedback and learning process. Use of different models for different questions. Certain insensitive variables can be eliminated because they are irrelevant, trivial, or nearly identical in their effects. Examine cost behavior as a result of changes in a system; e.g., costs may be insensitive or correlate well within certain operating parameters and become erratic beyond those parameters.

Cost-effectiveness question: Which car to buy? For a specified performance what is the minimum cost *or* for a specified cost what is the maximum performance? Trade-off question: Buy a car or a sailboat? Noncomparable. Not necessarily either/or. Could be a mix.

---

damage, lack of full scientific certainty should not be used as a reason for postponing measures to prevent environmental degradation."

In April 1992, the International Joint Commission, a government body with responsibility for the environmental quality of the Great Lakes, officially recommended, among other things, that steps be taken to protect against toxics as soon as the "weight of the evidence" indicates the need for such action rather than waiting for scientific certainty to be established. Businesspeople are often quite adept at profiting fron new opportunities created by situations of risk and uncertainty. For example, there are actions that can be taken to reduce heat-trapping greenhouse gases that make sense quite apart from whatever global warming threat they may or may not pose. These are sometimes called "no regrets policies" because they are not investments that may some day prove to have been unnecessary.

Interactive Connections. A second point about life cycle decision making that should be emphasized is the growing realization, from both a scientific and empirical viewpoint, that "everything is connected." Engineers have long understood the importance of interconnections, subsystem interfaces, and systems integration analysis. Yet problems persist. A recent survey of electrical problems in automobiles by Volkswagen revealed that 60% of all failures were due to faulty connections, four times greater than the next most frequent cause. Litigation proceedings often disclose that design, engineering, or production

Box 14-10. Cost-Benefit Notes

1.   The rationale for monetary valuation of nonmarket assets, such as clean air, clean water, or an undamaged atmosphere, is the search for economic efficiency. Not valuing these and other such natural assets classifies them, in effect, as "free goods." Free goods tend to be overused, disregarded, or abused as having no value. Valuation is an effort to correct the economic distortions created by valuing nonmarket assets at zero.

2.   Values are regarded by economists as instrumental; i.e., they are created by wants or preferences of people *for things.* Traditionally, this has meant "value in use" in contrast to "value in exchange." However, "nonuse valuation" has recently gained substantial advocacy, as have "intrinsic values" *in things* that have long been regarded by ecologists as inconsistent with the instrumental values of people; e.g., the value of land used for development is incompatible with use (or "nonuse") of the land as wilderness.

3.   Gains in value are termed benefits. Losses in value are termed costs. The basic cost-benefit decision rule is that a project or policy is acceptable in terms of economic efficiency if the total benefits over time are greater than the total costs (economic resources and environmental impacts) over the same time period, provided the time horizon is long enough to capture all the costs and benefits (life cycle or beyond).

4.   The element of uncertainty over time has created the argument for a new value concept, viz., option value. This value is a kind of insurance premium paid to retain an option of future use of an environmental asset. An environmental cost-benefit model could include not only nonuse option values but also expected use values, environmental impact costs, etc., to weigh the economic merits of a project.

5.   Several methodologies have been developed for establishing monetary measures of environmental costs and benefits in the absence of markets. (*a*) Finding surrogate markets through an inferred preference approach, using hedonic price or travel cost methodologies. (*b*) Creating imaginary markets through preferences expressed in questionnaires. (*c*) Pollution dosage and physical response linked to damage assessment in monetary terms. (*d*) Other polling methods.

6.   Cost-benefit analysis (CBA), also now referred to in Europe as benefit and damage estimation (BDE), involves many methodologies to aid systems analysts and decision makers. For additional information see Benefits Estimates and Environmental Decision-Making, Organization for Economic Cooperation and Development (OECD), 1992.

faults in the interfaces between subsystems are the cause of many aeronautical accidents.

There are several reasons for this that are pertinent to life cycle work.

1. *Inherent interactive complexity.*   Complex interrelationships between and among all the parts of a subsystem not only affect its internal performance but also can directly or indirectly affect the performance of the total system. This is true of all complex systems: mechanical, electronic, biological, chemical, economic, financial, and information systems of all kinds. A drop in the value of the yen in Tokyo can hurt auto stocks in New York and interest rates in London on Monday and have no effect if it happens again on Wednesday under different conditions. So too with ecological systems such as rain forests, the oceans, the biosphere, and the earth's climate. The way systems are tied together can produce multiple and unexpected interactions as a result of an unlikely combination of improbable individual failures, especially under conditions of unusual stress. An unforeseen combination of failures is more probable when interactions are "tightly coupled," i.e., they happen so quickly they can't be turned off or reversed. Conditions of unusual stress can occur when many seemingly unimportant changes over time eventually build to a point where one small intervention can produce a disastrous result, e.g., the moving pebble that starts an avalanche.

2. *Idealistic goal setting.*   Difficulties can arise when well-intentioned goals are established that are too complicated or unrealistic. Well-defined goals themselves may be dissimilar or conflicting. They may set technical or operating requirements that cannot be met without accepting questionable costs and risks associated with unjustifiable complexity. This happens sometimes when we learn that what we want to do can actually be done. So we rise to the challenge. In overly complex designs created to meet highly demanding operating requirements or to accommodate use of hazardous materials, however, problems are more likely to occur. Too many variables may be impractical to fully analyze. Hidden interactive paths have been even known to circumvent safety standards.

3. *Suboptimization trade-offs.*   It is only natural for designers and engineers to want to "brighten the corner" where they are. Their normal goal is to maximize or optimize the performance and reliability of the systems they are individually responsible for. However, suboptimization of these subsystems is often necessary to achieve optimization of the complete system. It is the job of the top designers and chief engineers to assure that this is achieved at the optimum life cycle cost and lowest acceptable risk to the operation of the entire system.

For example, a military supply system designed to support combat forces at a level of 100% operational availability is a luxury because it encourages supply officers to have more than enough of every spare part on hand at all times. Their professional performance ratings and promotions would depend on it. Obviously, the real world of budgetary limitations is different. Trade-offs are required between operations, maintenance and reliability requirements, acceptable stock-out rates for individual parts, inventory levels, safety stocks, reorder points, and transportation lead times—all to suboptimize parts of the system in order to optimize the entire system at a given level of budgetary funding.

This is called integrated logistic support or integrated supply chain management. It integrates all elements of the supply support pipeline. It also integrates support and operational effectiveness over the lifetime of the system. And it must integrate personnel incentive systems and performance evaluations with achievable support criteria and operating goals. How people perform and are motivated, trained, and rewarded are integral parts of any organizational system.

4. *The "life" in life cycle analysis.*   It becomes quickly evident in dealing with environmental issues that coping with Human Nature presents more of a challenge than coping with Mother Nature. Designers, engineers, managers, producers, distributors, and consumers, all the stakeholders, each with their many hopes and fears, are all connected. Their producer and consumer roles in life and their collective impacts on the earth's life support systems give the "life" in life cycle analysis a human behavior dimension.

One of the most vexing of interactions that managers and engineers must contend with is human communications. Engineers in different disciplines often can't even read each other's drawings. This helps to explain why interfaces between subsystems tend to be vulnerable to potential failure. No effort should be spared to assure the integrity of human communications in the interrelated processes of systems analysis, design, and production.

Top Management Support of Change.   Another important aspect of life cycle decision making is the role and attitude of top management in support of ground-breaking work and confidence in the potential results.

Recent survey results from 26 leading U.S. manufacturers of consumer products indicate that a common obstacle to life cycle analysis cited by 14 corporations not active in this work is the "lack of support from senior management." The survey also indicated that the less active companies tend to think about a life cycle approach in terms of risk, potential liability, and regulatory compliance while the companies more active in life cycle work think in terms of market opportunities and innovation.

Top managers who have a defensive mind-set about environmental issues are not likely to see the potential of life cycle analysis or any other technique for converting environmental issues into business opportunities. Environmental protection is often seen by these managers as only an added cost of doing business that reduces profitability and competitiveness. In cases of cleanup and control this is often true. On the other hand, managers who regard outlays for pollution prevention and waste reduction as long-term investments in a cleaner and more sustainable future are more likely to reduce costs and increase efficiency and be the more probable winners in the competitive arena of the twenty-first century.

Proposition 3:   Time is a critical factor. Time is an underestimated and inadequately understood factor of great importance in the analysis and management of environmental issues. Why should the importance of time be any different for environmental issues than for most other management issues?

We believe this is so because the initial time horizons of most business management decisions are normally shorter than the life cycle (i.e., life span) of their products. This occurs even though the impact of those decisions on public health, on the natural environment, and on the lives of future generations can extend chronologically far beyond any single stage in the life cycle and in most cases far beyond the life cycle itself. Future generations are seldom identified in textbooks and business administration courses as stakeholders in a corporate enterprise. This despite the fact that some pollution generated in the production and consumption of manufactured goods, depletion of nonrenewable resources, and lasting damage done in the use, misuse, and abuse of material resources will inevitably affect many people's lives far into the future.

Business managers in the United States have been frequently criticized for their short-term orientation. Even the strongest among them can't seem to withstand the enormous pressures exerted by our capitalist scorekeeping system for short-term performance, even though most of them probably would wish it were otherwise. Full-cost life cycle systems analysis can show us how to keep score and think about consequences in a way that should greatly encourage longer-term thinking. It can provide enhanced credibility to the use of longer time horizons in strategic planning and resource management to help achieve sustained profitability and sustainable development. (See Fig. 14.14 for more on time horizons.)

Managers appreciate the value of time utility. Time is a resource that can work for them or against them. Most of us are less sensitive, however, to the critical relationship between (1) changes and (2) the elapsed time for changes to take place. Study of these relationships is called rate analysis. Rate analysis has grown in importance with environmental concerns because it is a key factor in the performance of ecological systems.

In the evolution, adaptation, accommodation, and survival of different species, many natural changes occur in flora and fauna. Although various changes take place at different rates, the normal rates of change are usually slow. Ecological balances are maintained. Intrusion into these processes, impacting the normal rates of change and their relationships, can be disruptive and destabilizing. Discontinuities and disequilibria occur which interfere with normal system functions. If no corrective feedback mechanisms or effective adaptations restore system balance, partial or complete physical disintegration of the system can result.

Analysis of any system that includes economic and environmental factors must take into account the impact of alternative actions and their relative costs and benefits in both physical and economic terms. Costs and benefits form a dynamic relationship that can vary significantly over time. Costs are often

	Longer-term	Shorter-term
A. Type of decision		
Operating. How to best produce, operate, and support existing assets	X	Source of feedback to planning, development, and investment decisions
Launching. Choice of which product, process, or activity under development to place in production	Return on investment decisions important here	X
Development. Choice of which products, processes, or activities to develop for future operations	Strategic planning for competitive position in future markets	X
B. Factors in analysis		
Range of alternatives	Many	Few
Uncertainty	Great	Less
Risk	Large	Smaller
Information	Poor	Better
Cost emphasis	Comparative	Absolute
Emphasis in estimates	Sensitivity	Accuracy
Estimates	Generalized	Cost engineered
Environment	Prevention	Cleanup and control
Change	More	Less
Life cycle work	Increasing	Limited

Figure 14-14. Effect of time horizon on systems analysis.

incurred at a faster rate than benefits for a short time and later at a much slower rate for a long time. The cost of cleaning up contaminated land sites or initial costs of controlling air or water pollution are examples.

It is vital to appreciate rate analysis of the behavior of both the internal and external costs and benefits of alternative solutions during and even beyond the life cycle of the subject under examination and the system boundaries.

We are consuming many resources and destroying species at an unprecedented rate. If we—managers, engineers, and others—wait too long to change course with life cycle thinking, no global system or braking power now known can prevent an ultimate collision with reality at some time in the foreseeable future.

Proposition 4:   Risk assessment is a major component of life cycle management and systems analysis. Risk assessment deals with the problem of uncertainty. It is therefore inherent in almost all decision making and policy formulation. It becomes even more complex and critical for government regulation, business management, and systems engineering when environmental issues are introduced into the planning process.

How clean is clean? How safe is safe enough? Not even scientific experts and professional consultants can agree on these questions, to say nothing of differences among and between government bureaucrats, politicians, and business interests. The public markedly differs from the experts on risk/benefit trade-offs involving health and safety, especially for threats of low probability but catastrophic consequences.

Nuclear power and associated life cycle mortality risks provide a good example. Fuel cycle deaths in the United States from the mining, production, transport, and use of coal, including pollution, is estimated to be about 10,000 persons a year. Almost no deaths and relatively little pollution are attributable to the construction and operation of nuclear power plants. Yet almost half of the public doesn't want nuclear power.

The fear of the consequences of a nuclear accident, and the recollection of Chernobyl as a case in point, undoubtedly influence the opinion of most persons on this question. The problem of radioactive waste disposal is another negative influence. Although the chance of a Three Mile Island incident, in which there were no known deaths, is calculated by experts to be about 1 in every 300 years, such an accident is obviously possible. People don't want to have to worry about it. Moreover, experts often disagree on the probable causes and remedies in their assessments. In short, experts can be and often are wrong. Fears, even if seemingly irrational, are often justified.

The subjects of risk assessment and risk management are covered extensively in Chap. 11. The challenge of measuring complex physical environmental impacts as part of the life cycle assessment process is described earlier in this chapter.

It is probably safe to say that if all these nonquantifiable, unknown and/or external factors had been considered in a life cycle systems analysis of nuclear power plant construction in the 1950s, fewer nuclear power plants would have been built. There are several reasons for this which are instructive when reflecting on life cycle management principles and practices.

1. *Future costs are normally underestimated.*   Life cycle costs of large complex facilities and highly technical systems are inherently difficult to forecast. In addition, there are almost always powerful incentives to keep estimates low to gain approval of projects, especially for comparison of such proposals with competing alternatives.

2. *Full phase-out costs are often minimized.*   Hazardous materials storage, disposal, and facility dismantling costs to be incurred at the tail end of the life cycle are invariably underestimated. These events are usually so many years in the future that they are sometimes not seriously considered at all. See Box 14-4. This has been routinely the case in the acquisition of defense hardware, hazardous materials, and military facilities.

3. *Many external costs have no identity or visibility.*   External costs associated with contamination of people and property for which the producer, owner, or operator have no accountability or knowledge are not included in conventional accounting and forecasting systems. Such costs are ipso facto omitted from most life cycle planning decisions.

4. *New highly complex projects require intensive risk analysis.*   Extremely complex, advanced technological ventures are subject to unknown internal and external dangers due to their inherent complexity and their lack of operating experience.

5. *Potential accident or pollution victims are stakeholders.*   Designers of systems that have identifiable, predictable victims, established accident rates, or known pollution impacts, such as aircraft, chemical processes, and munitions, are most likely to consider externalities in their work. Those involved in projects where potential victims are anonymous and uncertain and accidents or pollution dangers are judged highly improbable or relatively harmless are less likely to do so.

A systems analysis of a high-risk project that considers all the life cycle costs and benefits can pose several options for regulators or project managers.* For example:

1. Prohibitions and bans, voluntary or involuntary

2. Restrictions in specifications or operations

3. Toleration and risk reduction

In cases 2 or 3, the success of decisions to proceed hinge mainly on one critical function: design. It is here where the internal and external trade-offs are made. It is here where reliability, quality, and sensitivity analyses have their final impact. It is here that customer needs are incorporated and product or system cost-effectiveness is determined, hopefully using internal and external life cycle costs. It is here that legal liabilities and moral responsibilities are born.

System, product, or package designers must consider not only technology but the roles, rights, responsibilities, and interests of all stakeholders, including those in future generations. The industrial design function is the life cycle crucible of all the physical and life sciences, industrial arts, and business economics that go into the production, use, and disposition of processed goods and services. It is indeed where pollution prevention, waste reduction, and the protection of human health and of the earth's life support systems begin.

---

*For an excellent description of a systems approach that incorporates new demands on design imposed by environmental requirements, see the EPA *Life Cycle Design Guidance Manual,* Office of Research and Development, EPA/600/R-92/226, January 1993.

Cases and Methodologies

Case I

Consumer Education and Life Cycle Assessment in Retailing

Life cycle analysis can be applied by distributors of merchandise as well as by manufacturers. Retail chains, for example, can use their purchasing power to influence the type of products and packages they will carry on their shelves. Equally important, they can help educate consumers about the relative environmental merits of what they decide to buy.

Migros, the largest food store and housewares chain in Switzerland, is recognized internationally for its success in fulfilling this role. Migros has had a tradition of socially responsible management, steady growth, and impressive profitability since its founding in 1925. In 1992, the company marketed 30,000 different products. It has exercised a leadership role in Switzerland, working closely with the Swiss government, to promote the sale of products and packages according to their environmental attributes.

The Migros story illustrates several notable points about the use of life cycle analysis. First, it demonstrates how progressive and responsible management in retailing can take the lead in environmental protection for the benefit of its own operating results as well as for the environment. The Home Depot chain in the United States with its tie-in with the Green Cross certification of products based on life cycle analysis is another example. Wal-Mart and Dayton Hudson are two other successful retail chains in the United States who have demanded more environmentally sound products and packages for their customers.

Second, the Migros life cycle system was developed in close cooperation with the Swiss Federal Office of Environment, Forests and Landscape (FOEFL). This cooperative effort has produced one set of commonly accepted data for the waste output from many packaging materials during each stage of their life cycles from raw material extraction to final disposal. It has also resulted in a standard government-approved methodology used by Migros and other Swiss firms in the application of life cycle analysis. Migros shares its computational and graphics computer software with other retailers at cost.

Most of the effort to date by Migros has been on packaging improvement. Only recently has attention been directed by the Swiss government to life cycle analysis for products themselves. Products generally require more specialized analysis. Initial exploration has been conducted on some products marketed by Migros using different system and subsystem boundaries, including those related to employees and transport.

The Migros program was initiated in 1985 with a computer-based environmental information system to report on the results of environmental decisions and help track progress of management actions. This subsequently led to the development of computer graphics which can compare the energy used, the pollution created, and solid waste generated by different packaging materials during all stages of their cradle-to-grave life cycles. The physical amount of waste produced is measured in terms of the weight of each chemical released into the air, water, and land.

The need for a method to compare the impact of the various pollutants on the environment on an equivalent basis led to further development of the current Migros program, called Oekobase 2. This method basically consists of a formula to produce "Ecofactors" for each chemical released by each packaging material at each stage in its life cycle. Ecofactors are then converted to "Ecopoints" for aggregation and comparability. For example:

$$EF = \frac{1}{F_k} \times \frac{F}{F_k} \times C$$

where EF equals the ecofactor for a chemical, F_k represents the government allowance in tons of the chemical which may be released per year based on toxicity and related considerations, F equals the actual number of tons of the chemical released per year in Switzerland, and C is a conversion constant. Also,

$$EP = \frac{EF}{gr} \times Gr$$

where EP equals the number of ecopoints for the chemical, EF is the computed ecofactor for that chemical, gr equals 1 gram, and Gr is the total grams of the chemical released over the life cycle of the material being studied. The higher the number of ecopoints the greater the environmental impact. A high EP is therefore considered a negative rating.

Ecofactors for energy use are calculated by comparing actual energy inputs with energy used in an assigned base year. The theory here is that any increase in energy use is a negative component that will increase the number of ecopoints computed as part of the life cycle analysis.

One dramatic application of this methodology is shown in Fig. 14-15, which is an Oekobase 2 graphic display comparing the number of ecopoints of alternative packaging materials. The polyethylene is in the form of a soft pouch to contain pasteurized liquid milk. The pouch was selected for sale at Migros food markets on the basis of its relatively low number of ecopoints.

This example is also remarkable for its ready consumer acceptance. Despite a radical departure from the more convenient method of delivering fresh milk in bottles or cartons, about half the milk sold was purchased by Swiss consumers in soft plastic pouches within a few months after first being

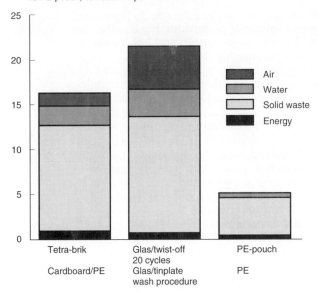

Tetra-brik vs glasbottle multiple use/twist-off
vs PE-pouch, calculations per 1 liter of milk

Legend:
- Air
- Water
- Solid waste
- Energy

Figure 14-15. Ecobalance for milk packaging. [*Database: FOEFL (Swiss Federal Office of Environment, Forests and Landscape), Environmental Series No. 132, Bern, 1991. Included: packaging material production. Not included: transformation (printing, lamination), distribution.*]

introduced. Soft pouches have been used by Procter & Gamble for packaging concentrated fabric conditioners, such as Downy in North America and Lenor in Europe.

The success of milk pouches is a tribute to the effective marketing of an "environmentally friendly" package to a steadily increasing number of environmentally educated and concerned consumers. In this case a substantial saving in material and ease of recycling is readily apparent. Also, the retail price per liter in pouches is the same or slightly less than in other containers.

There are at least two other known cases of marketing liquid milk in plastic pouches. One is the Mini-Sip Pouch, made by DuPont's Canadian unit. The small pillow-shaped pouch is held in the hand and pierced with a sharp straw. The company states this container requires less material to produce and less space to ship and store, and creates 70% less trash by volume than paperboard boxes. About one million U.S. students in a dozen states drink their milk at school in Mini-Sips, DuPont says. Also, thin plastic pouches for milk have been used in Israel for many years, presumably because trees and paper products there are at a premium.

The life cycle system used by Migros does not itself incorporate any considerations of cost. Product managers obtain cost data separately from the results of life cycle analysis for their decision making. Generally, fewer ecopoints mean lower costs as long as substantial savings in materials are being made. However, as pollution approaches zero, investment in new equipment or substitute materials can rise significantly, although these capital outlays may lead to further savings in the long run. In the case of plastic pouches for milk, the cost of material is considerably less than for alternative packages. However, logistics costs to ship and handle plastic pouches are higher. Profit margins are roughly the same.

An important problem still to be resolved by Migros is how to factor all the variable aspects of recycling of materials into their life cycle methodology, especially in the calculation of ecopoints. Nonetheless, the use of life cycle analysis has already proved to be an effective management tool in the improvement of package design to reduce environmental impacts in the manufacture and distribution of many consumer products. This has been accomplished without the use of ecolabeling or "green seals" in a country where change in buying habits does not come easily. Twenty years ago Migros introduced a detergent free of phosphates but nobody bought it. Fifteen years ago the company tried to sell unleaded gas without success, despite obvious environmental benefits in both cases. Today, these and a rapidly increasing number of other environmentally improved products and packages are being sold through the Migros distribution network.

The lesson here is that public education and greater awareness of the growing threats of environmental degradation are as important as analytical tools in environmental progress. The alternative is more comprehensive and burdensome government regulation. The Migros case demonstrates how a pioneering retail company can work constructively with government agencies to promote environmentally responsible action by suppliers and a growing acceptance by consumers, while achieving business goals of the corporation.

References

Interview with Peter Bär, Migros Project Director, Zurich, Switzerland, July 1, 1992.

Schmidheiny, S., *Changing Course*, MIT Press, Cambridge, Massachusetts, 1992.

The Wall Street Journal, December 27, 1991.

Information also was furnished by Asher Derman, Associate Professor, Kean College of New Jersey.

Case II A

The Cost of Ownership, A Unique Service for a Familiar Product

Since 1987, an entrepreneurial company named IntelliChoice Inc., of San Jose, California, has been publishing information on the costs of buying and owning a new car. The company's "Complete Car Cost Guide" provides a wealth of carefully researched and clearly presented data to help car buyers in the United States make a more fully informed economic comparison among over 500 U.S. and other makes and models of passenger vehicles.

Each car's average purchase price is factored into the estimated average costs of depreciation based on average resale value at the end of 5 years. This amortized purchase price is then added to financing, insurance, state fees, fuel costs, maintenance, and repairs over a 5-year period. The resulting data and calculated ratings tell the buyer whether any particular car is a good value compared with other vehicles in its class. Data are updated daily for use in special reports.

The question arises as to how reliable or useful such variable information about such a complex decision can be. Actual purchase decisions by individual buyers in many geographic areas are based on location-specific factors and different vehicle operations, not on national averages. IntelliChoice factors in this complexity. Included in the "Complete Car Cost Guide" are:

1. Car features and options
2. Extensive guidance on purchasing a new car, including many noncost factors such as safety, style, engine power, and feel
3. Clearly stated assumptions and sources on which published costs are based, and definitions of terms and symbols
4. Tables of data to adjust published average costs, as appropriate, to the buyer's location and expected operation of the car
5. General explanation of how certain costs behave beyond a 5-year ownership period

Furthermore, the effort made by the company to apply data to comparable products makes credible the primary goal of the service, i.e., comparisons of *relative* product value at the time of purchase. The precision of total ownership cost projections over a 5-year period is less important since cars will be subject to roughly the same margin of forecasting error.

From the viewpoint of the relative environmental impact of various vehicles, two important factors are included in these ownership costs: (1) the federal "gas guzzler" purchase tax and (2) the fuel cost as a function of energy efficiency, i.e., gallons of fuel consumed per mile driven. However, the IntelliChoice guide is not intended to be a full life cycle analysis of environmental impact.

A full-cost environmental impact study would necessarily include ultimate disposal, ease and extent of materials recycling, motor oil and battery disposal, the societal costs of air pollution, and highway and other subsidies. The major environmental concern obviously is the worldwide use of nonrenewable fossil fuels in enormous volumes, retailing in the United States and many other countries far below their true, full long-term cost in terms of human health and damage to property and the natural environment. A World Resources Institute study concluded that the true cost of gasoline in the United States should be several dollars a gallon to pay for all the hidden costs and benefits of private auto use. Additional taxes on gasoline would curb usage, but such proposals have been very unpopular with the driving public in the United States and consistently resisted by their elected representatives in government.

Significant progress primarily must await the development and use of cleaner-burning hydrocarbon fuels, alternative energy sources, and other measures of pollution prevention and waste reduction in the manufacture, use, and disposal of cars and fuels by auto makers and oil companies.

Major efforts are under way in the United States, Europe, and Japan to develop alternative fuels, improve efficiencies, and reduce emissions. On June 8, 1992, Chrysler, Ford, and General Motors announced the formation of a new consortium to develop technologies for reducing vehicle emissions to meet new federal and state clean air requirements. This is the eighth consortium the big three auto makers have formed. Others include the Vehicle Recycling Partnership, Advanced Battery Research Consortium, Auto/Oil Air Quality Improvement Program, and Environmental Science Research. Life cycle analysis is an integral part of many of these projects.

Chrysler Corporation, for example, is relatively advanced in life cycle management techniques, partly in response to the Clean Air Act and other regulatory requirements. However, Chrysler has elected to emphasize pollution prevention, waste minimization, and other "beyond compliance" measures. Solutions like these are mostly "behind-the-pipe" in lieu of "end-of-the-pipe" controls that are always vulnerable to changes in regulatory requirements. Environmental factors have been folded into many decision-making processes throughout the company, particularly in design, purchasing, production, and painting of vehicles, and waste management.

References

"The Complete Car Cost Guide," 1992, IntelliChoice, Inc., San Jose, California.

Business and the Environment, June 1992.

The Going Rate: What It Really Costs to Drive, June 1992, The World Resources Institute, Washington, D.C.

Presentation by R. J. Kainz and W. C. Moeser, Chrysler Corporation, to the SETAC 13th Annual Meeting, Cincinnati, Ohio, November 11, 1992.

Case II B

The Cost of Ownership, Performance Evaluation of Suppliers

Texas Instruments has developed a unique "cost of ownership" technique for use by its procurement personnel to measure the performance of its suppliers. It is not a life cycle cost analysis as typically used to evaluate bids; rather, it is a method to rate suppliers in terms of a product's (1) price, (2) delivery service, and (3) quality, i.e., meeting specifications required to assure acceptable performance during the product's design lifetime.

Supplier "performance multipliers" are determined for the delivery and quality of selected items and applied to the product price to obtain the "cost of ownership." For example, if an item is purchased for $8, delivered on time, and has zero defects, its cost of ownership is $8. If, however, it is delivered X days late, the *delivery performance multiplier* could be 1.2 instead of the rating of 1.0 awarded for on-time delivery. If the lot acceptance rate, or the rejected parts per million, is less than perfect, the *quality performance multiplier* would be more than 1.0 also, for example, 1.4.

In this case, the "cost" of ownership would be computed as $13.44 instead of $8 ($8 × 1.2 × 1.4). This is, of course, a figurative value in a scoring system, not an actual accounting cost.

In addition to the metrics established separately for delivery and quality, a weighting process also is used to convey the relative importance of on-time delivery and product quality for each rated product. A routine, low-value item, for example, would be assigned a much lower weighting for quality (and therefore a higher weighting for delivery) than a repair part that is critical to the reliability or safety of a piece of equipment where quality would be given a greater weight.

The cost of ownership formula, therefore, is as follows:

$$Price \times Weighted\ delivery\ multiplier \times Weighted\ quality\ multiplier = cost\ of\ ownership$$

Suppliers understand how their products are being rated and have confidence that the rating system is applied consistently to all competitors.

This technique can be applied to as few or as many products as desired. This determination will depend on the availability of the required data and the information system in place for implementing the process.

The significance of this technique to life cycle analysis is its potential for incorporating measures of environmental performance into the formula. For example, an "environmental performance multiplier" could be incorporated into the rating system for types of products where environmental considerations are important and life cycle assessments or other evaluations can be made.

Reference

Presentation by Henry Weissenborn, Texas Instruments, on October 14, 1992, to the Council of Logistics Management, San Antonio, Texas, entitled "Take the EDI Express Train from Requisitioner to Strategic Supplier."

Case II C

The Cost of Ownership, Semiconductor Process Equipment Life Cycle

D. L. Dance

R. W. Burghard

R. J. Markle

SEMATECH, Austin, Texas

Trends in the semiconductor industry show that increasing die sizes, more complex circuits, and smaller device geometries are resulting in increasing wafer cost. A simple economic model has been developed which shows how processing equipment life cycle costs affect finished wafer costs. This model is described in more detail elsewhere.[1] Lifetime cost of ownership per good wafer is highly sensitive to production throughput rates, overall tool reliability, throughput yield, and defect-limited yield. It is relatively insensitive to initial equipment purchase price.

Cost of scrap is a significant part of semiconductor equipment cost of ownership. Scrap losses due to contamination result in lost equipment productivity, and increasing wafer cost. Contamination also requires equipment monitoring and maintenance, which reduces equipment productivity. The measurements required to monitor contamination are costly, requiring the nonproductive use of test wafers and equipment time. Methods of fighting contamination in semiconductor equipment such as filtration and purification also increase equipment cost. Particulate contamination losses, equipment monitoring and maintenance requirements, and equipment and waste-disposal costs are included in the cost of ownership model.

The basic cost of ownership algorithm is described by the following equation:

$$C_W = \frac{C_F + C_V}{TPT \times Y_{TPT} \times U} + C_Y$$

where C_W = cost per wafer
C_F = fixed cost
C_V = variable cost
C_Y = cost due to yield loss
TPT = throughput rate
Y_{TPT} = mechanical throughput yield
U = utilization

Fixed costs include costs such as equipment purchase, installation, and facilities support costs which are normally amortized over the life of the equipment. Contamination-reducing modifications to process equipment including electropolished tubing and ultraclean valves impact the fixed costs of equipment. Variable costs such as material, labor, repair, waste disposal, utility, and overhead expenses are the costs incurred during equipment operation. Contamination-related variable costs include replaceable filters, scheduled equipment cleaning and maintenance, and particle monitoring wafers. Throughput is based on the time to meet a common process requirement such as depositing or etching a nominal film thickness. The maximum throughput rate will be reduced by contamination-related particle monitoring and particle-related rework requirements. Mechanical throughput yield is the operational yield of the tool. This factor is unlikely to be influenced by contamination, but loss of a wafer due to in situ breakage may have a significant effect on other contamination-related factors. Utilization is the ratio of actual production time compared with total available time. Scheduled equipment cleaning and maintenance activities due to contamination will reduce actual production time. Yield loss cost is a measure of the value of wafers lost through operational breakage and defect-limited yield using the following formula:

$$C_Y = (W_{YTPT} \times V_p) + (W_{YD} \times V_f)$$

where C_Y = cost due to yield loss

$\quad W_{YTPT}$ = number of wafers lost owing to the mechanical throughput

$\quad W_{YD}$ = number of wafers lost owing to defects

$\quad V_p$ = value of wafers at process step

$\quad V_f$ = value of wafers at wafer test

The cost of ownership model can estimate how the increased costs due to contamination affect the cost per good wafer shipped over the life of the process tool. These costs include increased fixed costs for preventing contamination, variable costs to address contamination in the tool, and throughput losses due to cleaning, maintenance, and monitoring. The costs of ownership model also considers the cost of scrap, which is a significant part of equipment cost of ownership.[2]

References

1. Carnes, R., and Su, M., "Long Term Cost of Ownership: Beyond Purchase Price," *1991 IEEE/SEMI International Semiconductor Manufacturing Science Symposium*, pp. 39–43.

2. Dance, D. L., Burghard, R. W., and Markle, R. J., "Reducing Process Equipment Cost of Ownership through in Situ Contamination Prevention and Reduction," *Microcontamination*, May 1992, pp. 21–23, 64.

Case III

Electric Utility Chemical Procurement*

Considering full life cycle costs has the potential to help utilities and other firms significantly reduce the overall costs of their operations. The approach can help decision makers minimize the environmental, economic, and legal risks associated with their organizations' selection and use of chemicals and materials. Going a step further, considering the environmental externalities associated with chemicals or materials as a component of the life cycle costs has the potential to reduce the total social cost of their use.

What Are the Decisions?

- Decisions about the acquisition, use, and disposal of chemicals and other materials
- Decisions about products, processes, components, and activities in which chemicals are used

---

*This example of life cycle costing is extracted from a paper "Beyond Waste Minimization: A Life-Cycle Approach to Managing Chemicals and Materials" prepared by David Cohan and Kenneth R. Wapman of Decision Focus Inc., W. Corey Trench, PRECOR Corp., and Mary McLearn, Electric Power Research Institute.

In order to achieve the goal of making better decisions, we need to understand not only the elements of life cycle costs but also the ways in which the decisions influence the costs. Our overall goal is *to optimize the combined results of acquisition, use, and disposal decisions.* Thus a key challenge is to decompose the problem enough to make it feasible to estimate life cycle costs, while appropriately addressing the interrelated nature of the decisions.

To organize our thinking about the range of decisions that may influence life cycle costs, it is helpful to outline a hierarchy of choices as illustrated by the example in Table 14-3, indicating the choice of solvents used in cleaning processes. For this example, three levels of decisions make sense: the choice of chemical or material to use in a given process, the choice of process or product, and the higher-level choice that defines what kinds of products or processes are needed.

Examples of each type of cost element that may be incurred are shown in Table 14-4. Some of these cost elements are currently measured or tracked, while others are not. Others are measured but are typically not considered when decisions are made that will ultimately influence the cost outcomes. These include, for example, many of the indirect costs. Still others, particularly the uncertain and externality costs, are rarely addressed in typical day-to-day decisions regarding the acquisition, use, and disposal of chemicals and materials.

Taking a life cycle cost approach does *not* mean that all these cost elements must be addressed in every decision. Rather the approach requires that the choice of which costs to consider (and which to ignore) be addressed explicitly and that the selection of cost elements be treated *consistently* across interrelated decisions in an organization. Furthermore, the process may not be strictly sequential. With the growth of recycling and reuse, there may be several stages of use, collection or treatment, and reuse, prior to the ultimate disposal of any residuals. Thus the choice of cost elements to address will be determined by practical as well as normative considerations.

Example: Choosing Solvents.   In this example we illustrate the use of life cycle costing techniques to compare two solvents. This illustrative example, although motivated by real considerations and realistic information, is not intended to describe any actual decision at any specific firm.

Consider an electric utility currently using approximately 2000 gallons per year of 1,1,1-trichloroethane (TCA) for a variety of cleaning tasks, including

Table 14-3. Decisions at Several Levels Have Impacts on Life Cycle Costs

Level of choice	Example: solvents
1. Choice of the chemical or material to use in a particular process or product	Use tricholoroethane (TCA) or a citrus-based solvent in a cleaning process?
2. Choice of which process or product to use	Use solvent cleaning or a water-based parts washer?
3. Choice of how to provide the ultimate service or functionality	Use cleaning process or switch to an approach that does not need cleaning?

Table 14-4. A Wide Range of Cost Elements Can Be Addressed Using a Life Cycle Cost Approach

Costs	Acquisition	Use	Disposal and postdisposal
Direct	Purchase cost Taxes Shipping	Labor Equipment Maintenance	Transport and/or storage Recycling, treatment, disposal costs
Indirect	Training Handling and storage Records keeping	Delivery to job site Training Industrial hygiene Regulatory compliance	Training Records keeping EH&S

Uncertain	Cost of spills and acci-
	  dents while handling or
	  in storage
	Legal liabilities
		Costs of spills, leaks while
		  in use
		Equipment failure
		Compliance with new
		  regulations
		Occupational liabilities
			Costs of accidents or spills
			Compliance with new regula-
			  tions
			Legal liabilities
			Post-disposal liabilities

External	Emissions or accidental
	  releases while in storage
		Emissions or accidental
		  releases while in use
			Environmental releases during
			  treatment or after disposal

parts degreasing, in cable splicing operations, and in cleaning up spills on shop floors at a hazardous waste storage facility. Because of concerns about potential health risks and the increasing cost of disposing of spent TCA and TCA-contaminated rags and gloves, the firm began looking for solvents to replace TCA in many applications. Over a period of 3 months, several facilities evaluated the performances of a variety of potential substitute solvents. These evaluations identified one citrus-based solvent as an acceptable substitute for TCA in many applications. Now the utility must decide whether to change to the citrus-based solvent or to continue to use TCA.

In the past, many materials and chemicals, including solvents, were selected primarily on the basis of product efficacy and purchase cost. Little attention was paid to differences in disposal and other costs—primarily because they were thought to be small. Recently, however, the utility has become more aware of the interrelationships among product acquisition, use, and disposal costs. The comparison of these solvents will include all costs incurred from acquisition of the solvents through use, treatment, and disposal. In addition, any legal costs or potential liabilities associated with each solvent will be considered.

The cost elements considered in this example are: acquisition costs including the cost of solvent, any additional transportation or delivery costs, and the costs associated with managing the solvent while it is in inventory. Use costs include the costs of labor incurred to clean equipment, parts, and spills, as well as the costs of any equipment required to complete the cleaning tasks. Use costs also include the costs of managing the solvent after it leaves the storeroom and costs associated with providing product use, health, safety, and emergency training to workers. For this example, the basis for comparing TCA and the citrus-based solvent is the amount of cleaning required during a year. Currently, 37 drums of 55 gallons each are purchased annually for applications in which the citrus-based solvent could be substituted. The shop supervisors estimate that about 1500 labor hours are presently consumed in using TCA to clean parts and equipment.

Treatment and disposal costs include all costs of storing wastes prior to treatment and disposal, and the costs of treating and disposing of these wastes. In this example, wastes include any spent solvent that did not evaporate, and solvent-contaminated rags and gloves. This category also includes any costs incurred to characterize the wastes prior to disposal, and the costs associated with the ultimate treatment and disposal of the wastes. Additional costs may be incurred after the wastes have been disposed of by the utility. Although these postdisposal costs are much less certain than the other costs, in both magnitude and timing, they may vary significantly for these solvents. Postdisposal costs include potential costs incurred to remediate a site where wastes were disposed of, costs of resolving lawsuits related to use or disposal practices, and any public relations costs.

After contacting several suppliers of industrial chemicals, the utility determined that TCA costs about $8 per gallon and the citrus-based substitute costs about $13 per gallon, including all transportation and delivery charges. Currently, about 80 person-hours each year are consumed by instructors and workers reviewing techniques for the proper use of TCA, and for instruction relating to safety and emergency practices applicable to TCA. The health and safety department estimates that much less training would be required to address these issues for a citrus-based solvent, perhaps only 20 person-hours per year. Although the citrus-based solvent is an acceptable substitute for TCA in many applications, obtaining an equivalently clean product typically requires more solvent and more labor. The staff that evaluated the citrus-based solvent estimated that they required 10% more solvent and took 10% longer to complete the cleaning than would have been required if TCA had been used.

Because TCA is a listed hazardous waste, manifesting requirements and general record keeping are greater than would be expected for a citrus-based solvent. Purchasing estimates that the amount of time devoted to managing the solvents would decrease from about 20 hours per year to about 10 hours per year. Currently, purchasing and management allocate about 10 hours per year for the administrative tasks associated with acquiring and storing TCA. Stores staff estimates that they spend an additional 5 hours per year managing TCA, and about 5 hours per year are allocated for managing the spent TCA while it is stored and prepared for disposal. If a citrus-based solvent were used, management would require a total of about 5 hours to manage its acquisition, use, and disposal.

The costs associated with transporting and disposing of spent TCA and TCA-contaminated materials vary considerably, from about $300 per drum to as much as $800 per drum. Typically, this utility pays about $450 per drum to dispose of these wastes. In contrast, because spent citrus-based solvent would not be a listed hazardous waste and because it would not be likely to become characteristically hazardous from the applications in which it would be substituted, it could be disposed of as a nonhazardous waste. Currently, the utility spends about $150 per drum to dispose of similar wastes. However, if the citrus-based solvent must be disposed of as a hazardous

Table 14-5. Estimated Values of Cost Elements

Cost category and component	1,1,1-Trichloroethane (TCA)	Citrus-based solvent
Acquisition costs:		
Administrative costs	10 labor hours/year	1 labor hour/year
Raw material cost, delivered	$8/gallon	$13/gallon
Use costs:		
Worker training costs	80 hours/year	20 hours/year
Product efficacy	2035 gallons/year	2240 gallons/year
	1500 labor hours/year	1650 labor hours/year
Administrative costs	5 labor hours/year	3 labor hours/year
Treatment and disposal costs:		
Administrative costs	5 labor hours/year	1 labor hour/year
Disposal costs	$450/drum	$150/drum

waste, the cost could be as much as $800 per drum. Table 14-5 summarizes the cost information developed for this example.

As shown in Fig. 14-16, based on materials costs alone, TCA is considerably less costly than the citrus-based alternative. However, when full life cycle costs are considered, the total cost associated with providing 1 year of cleaning services is almost identical. The reduced training and disposal costs for the citrus-based solvent balance its greater material cost and slightly lower efficacy.

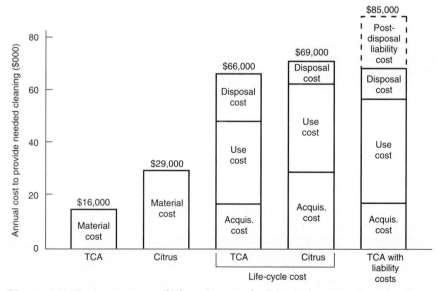

Figure 14-16. Comparison of life cycle costs for TCA and a citrus-based solvent.

Given that the life cycle costs are similar, which solvent is the best choice? Numerous uncertainties are associated with the use of TCA, and with the ensuing costs. For example, the purchase price of TCA is more likely to rise, as could its disposal cost. Owing to its hazardous characteristics, significant potential liabilities may be associated with using and disposing of TCA. Suppose, for example, that the expected value of such (uncertain) liabilities is about $500 per drum of TCA wastes (or, equivalently, that the cost of liability insurance is $500 per drum). The life cycle cost would then increase by about $19,000 to a total of $85,000—well in excess of the cost for the citrus-based solvent.

At this point, the choice seems clear—the known costs for the two options are very close, while TCA has potentially large uncertain costs. However, the ultimate efficacy of the citrus-based solvent is also uncertain. Although estimated to need about 10% more labor and materials to provide equivalent cleaning performance, some evaluators thought that up to 50% more could be required. If so, the life cycle cost would increase to about $91,000 per year, swinging the balance in favor of TCA.

At this point, the utility decided to perform a series of controlled tests for each key cleaning application. These tests confirmed that the citrus-based solvent typically required 5 to 15% more labor and material than did TCA, and never more than a 20% increase. Based on these tests, and a careful review of the potential liabilities, a decision was made to switch to the citrus-based solvent.

This example demonstrates a completely different application and methodology of life cycle costing from the Tellus Packaging Study. It seeks to include consideration of product life cycle costs, potential liability costs, and insurance premiums likely to be incurred directly by the firm as judged by management and the legal staff from a procurement policy point of view. It does not attempt to perform a scientific risk assessment or place an economic value on external environmental impacts per se.

This example does, however, emphasize the interdependent nature and iterative process of multiattribute decision making involved in life cycle analysis. It discusses the goal of system optimization and necessary trade-offs between life cycle costs and product performance. Costs do not stand alone. The ultimate decision is one of life cycle cost-effectiveness, using full costs of environmental impact and referenced criteria for product quality and operating performance, i.e., how well the least-cost option gets the job done or, alternatively, how much it costs to do the job as effectively as we might wish.

Case IV

Integrated Substance Chain Management

The Association of the Dutch Chemical Industry (VNCI) published a study in December 1991 conducted by McKinsey & Company, with others, to examine how to bring the use of chlorine "under full control" to minimize environmental impact. Three pilot products were selected in which chlorine compounds are used as a refrigerant, as a solvent, and in glazing applications. A life cycle methodology was developed to identify and deal with "leakages" into the environment and to examine product substitutes and recycling alternatives. The term "integrated substance chain management" was adopted for this methodology as it is frequently used in similar studies regarding sustainable development conducted pursuant to the Dutch government's National Environment Policy Plan.

This approach consists of three phases:

Phase 1. The initial phase starts with a recycling loop diagram that measures substance volume flows and identifies major environmental issues that could occur now or in the future during the product's total life cycle. Top-down estimates are tested by interviewing key experts, concentrating on those issues where the degree of uncertainty is greatest. In cases where uncertainty cannot be resolved the issue is carried forward to the next step. Sensitivity analysis during subsequent steps will indicate if additional data collection is required to reduce the level of uncertainty.

Options involving material substitution, product redesign, source reduction, process changes, waste management, and recycling are then generated by technical, scientific, and management experts. The most promising of these options are selected, according to a predetermined evaluation process, for further detailed analysis. See Fig. 14-17 for an example of the selection process.

Phase 2.   in the second phase, the most promising options are prioritized on a cost-benefit map consisting of an environmental profile on the horizontal axis and a net economic impact on the vertical axis. Options positioned in the upper right quadrant are clear candidates for early action. Options in the two left-hand quadrants are usually discarded. Options plotted in the lower right quadrant require the most attention of decision makers because of the difficult trade-offs that usually must be made in these cases.

The environmental profile is essentially a physical input-output-impact life cycle assessment. The economic impact is the net short-term and long-term effect of annual changes in direct and indirect operating and capital costs, marketing revenues, and intangible costs throughout the life cycle. External costs to society were not included in this study, but the methodology provides for their inclusion if desired. For best results, the economic impact is a measure of cost-effectiveness which takes into account product performance as well as costs.

The positioning of options, as indicated in Fig. 14-18, is based on facts supplemented by collective informed judgments, including the subjective weighting of facts such as the relative importance of different kinds of environmental damage. An option position may go through several iterations before it is finalized. Key techniques used in this process are cost curves, knowledge enhancement based on reliable information, sensitivity analysis, and application of the 80/20 rule (20% of what elements account for 80% of the total?).

Phase 3. The final phase in the chain management methodology is the development of action plans, including time tables, resources, and responsibilities for implementing the highest-priority options.

The integrated substance chain management approach is a strategic planning technique. It is a comprehensive method of dealing with

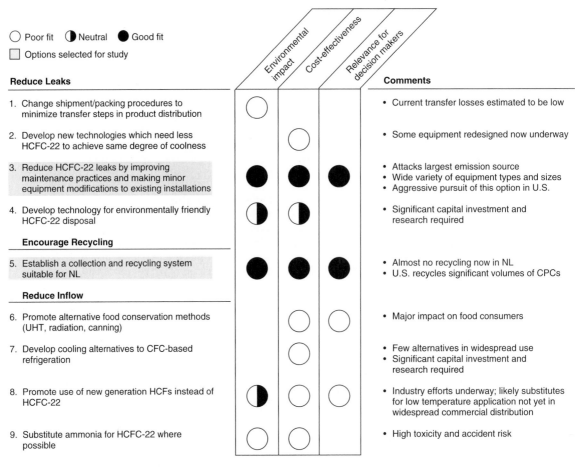

Figure 14-17. Selection of options: HCFC-22-Refrigeration. (*"Integrated Substance Chain Management,"* *Association of the Dutch Chemical Industry, December 1991.*)

fundamental business issues of product development, manufacturing, marketing, use, and recycling or disposal. Product performance, customer requirements, economic results, and the effects on human health and the environment are all systematically considered.

Case V

Environmental Priority Strategies (EPS) in Product Design

In June 1992 the Federation of Swedish Industries published Appendix I to a paper on "International Experiences of Environmentally-Sound Product

Example

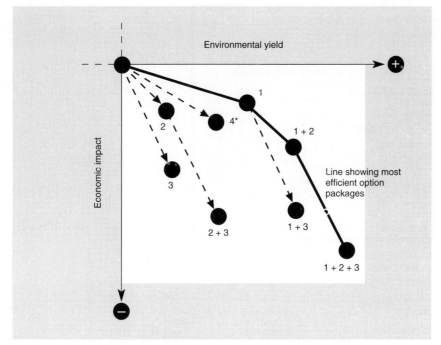

Figure 14-18. Prioritizing options. *Assumption:* Option 4 excludes Options 1, 2, 3, and vice versa. (*"Integrated Substance Chain Management," Association of the Dutch Chemical Industry, December 1991.*)

Development." The appendix is entitled "Background Information on Life-Cycle Assessment (LCA) as a Tool for Eco-design of Products." It provides an approach that emphasizes the shift from pollution control by external regulation to control by internal objectives that are "ecologically motivated, technically feasible and economically reasonable."

The Swedish study recommends procedures that include many of the factors discussed throughout this chapter, i.e., problem identification by a team of experts, potential remedial measures, cost-benefit analysis, evaluation of alternatives, setting of priorities—with life cycle assessment as an essential component of the process. It reviews several European methodologies of life cycle assessment, as well as the SETAC framework, some of which include evaluation of the workplace environment as well as the impact of pollutants on the external environment.

The Swedish paper provides a detailed review of the basic LCA methodology including many of the past and current shortcomings of various approaches. It cites the Swiss "eco-factors" explained in the Migros case in this chapter and the "environmental theme" method, which is used by the Dutch to develop the environmental profile in their option maps for integrated substance chain management, as examples of improved tools for classification and evaluation of LCA results.

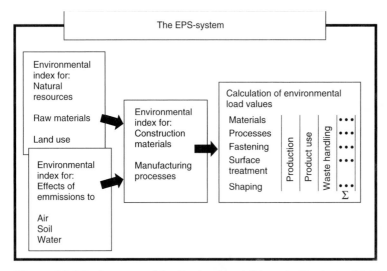

Figure 14-19. Overview of the Environmental Priority Strategies (EPS) system in product design. (*Federation of Swedish Industries; Swedish Environmental Research Institute; Volvo Car Company, 1990.*)

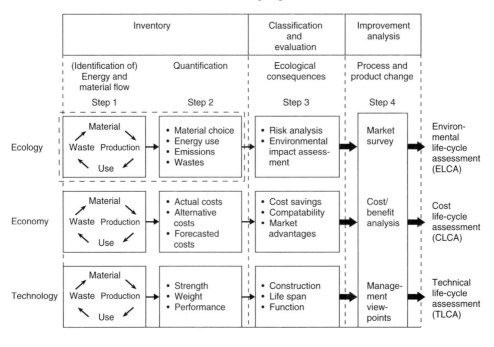

Figure 14-20. A suggested structure of life cycle assessments. (*"Environmental Priority Strategies in Product Design," Federation of Swedish Industries; Swedish Environmental Research Institute, Volvo Car Company, 1990.*)

The Swedish EPS method is an ecological scoring system of assessing environmental impacts on technical, ecological, and socioeconomic systems. EPS calculates an environmental LCA-type inventory "load profile" index for a product to assist in environmental impact assessment.

The goal of the EPS system is to make environmental impacts "visible" through a so-called transparent eco-calculation procedure. The components of the system are illustrated in Fig. 14-19. Energy use is not identified in the exhibit but is included. Environmental load values are expressed as "Environmental Load Units" (ELU) and integrated by combining the indices calculated for the different components of the system.

The indices for substance effects are made up of ecological scores to rate five types of effects on human health and the natural environment during each stage in the life cycle, e.g., intensity, frequency, durability, extent of damage, etc. The higher the score, the more dangerous the product. Sensitivity analysis is used to clarify the influence of uncertainty in the data and to determine what can be deemphasized without disturbing the conclusions.

The system has been incorporated into a simple personal computer (PC) application using standard presentation forms such as histograms, pie charts, and statistical analyses.

The EPS results provide the ecological inputs into an overall structure of life cycle systems analysis which includes economic and technological considerations as illustrated in Fig. 14-20. The economic factors in this structure include four types of valuations:

1. Environmental damage and health costs

2. Costs of site remediation

3. Capital investment and operating costs necessary to maintain ecological quality

4. The economic value of ecological assets

The study concludes by summarizing the advantages of product life information derived from a comprehensive life cycle systems analysis in the listing shown in Fig. 14-21. Product design and strategic planning are included as two advantages among the 11 listed for manufacturers.

Case VI

A. Life Cycle Cost Methodologies

Life cycle costing consists of two basic tasks: (1) methods of estimating costs, a profession of its own, and (2) methods of constructing mathematical models, an important function in systems analysis technology.

A life cycle cost analyst requires skills and knowledge not only in finance, accounting, logistics, statistics, quality control, and cost estimating but also in various engineering disciplines such as reliability, maintainability, and manufacturing. He or she clearly must work closely with specialists in many different engineering fields, and increasingly these days with chemists, toxicologists, and environmental engineers and managers.

Manufacturers could use information from product life assessments in their overall product design and manufacture to:

- compare generic materials
- evaluate resource effects associated with particular products including new products
- compare functionally equivalent products
- compare different options within a particular process with the objective of minimizing environmental impacts
- identify processes, ingredients, and systems that are major contributors to environmental impacts
- supply information for product and procurement audits
- provide guidance in long-term strategic planning concerning trends in product design and materials
- help train product designers in the use of environmentally preferred product materials
- evaluate claims made by other manufacturers
- enhance market competitiveness
- provide information to consumers about the resource characteristics of their products or materials

Public decision makers could use information from product life assessments to:

- supply information needed for legislative or regulatory policy that restricts use of product materials (e.g., bans, taxes, etc.)
- supply information needed to set standards governing product advertising (e.g., defining recycled content, etc.)
- gather environmental information
- identify gaps in knowledge and research priorities
- help evaluate and differentiate among products for labeling programs
- provide information to the public about the resource characteristics of products or materials
- help develop long-term policy regarding overall material use, resource conservation, and reduction of environmental impacts and risks posed by materials and processes throughout the product life cycle
- evaluate claims by manufacturers
- evaluate resource effects associated with source reduction and alternative waste management techniques

Figure 14-21. Potential uses of product life information. (*After World Wildlife Fund and the Conservation Foundation, 1990.*)

Life cycle cost estimates increasingly have played an important role in source selection, particularly for military projects, and in such cases are an integral part of the material acquisition process. The planning for proposals and contracts must include an appropriate organization to manage life cycle cost requirements, specifications, data, customer coordination, proposal preparation, risks, procurement strategy, and contract goals.

An effective life cycle cost program should include the following features:

1. Coordination of life cycle cost and design work.

2. Compatibility of reliability, maintainability, and system safety programs with life cycle cost requirements.

3. Performance of trade-off studies.

4. Identification and management review of principal cost drivers with recommendations for reducing such costs.

5. Communication to all participating parties of their cost goals.

6. Quality of cost estimating database.

7. Soundness of cost estimating methods, including inflation and discount rate factors.

8. Independent validation of principal cost estimates and construction of cost models.

9. Defining of cost priority relative to product delivery schedule, performance, and other requirements by the managements of all contracting parties.

10. Incorporation of life cycle costing requirements into design subcontracts and subcontractors' cost performance reviews.

Methods of estimating costs include not only conventional accounting methods of costing for budgetary purposes but also learning curve costs, internal and external failure costs, quality control costs, environmental costs, prevention costs, warranty costs, etc.

There are several methods for estimating costs and constructing cost models. These include bottom-up estimates, top-down estimates, expert system methods, analogy methods, and algorithmic models. The type of method and model most often depends on the system or type of product involved, so that, in addition to some general-purpose models, there are literally scores of specialized cost models in use for specific purposes. Different cost models are even used for different stages in the life cycle.

The IBIS Associates, Inc. Technical Cost Modeling Approach.

IBIS Associates, Inc., a Wellesley, Massachusetts, management consulting firm, has developed a life cycle cost approach as part of some work it has performed for the U.S. Department of Interior, Bureau of Mines. This work focused on the life cycle costs of a number of consumable and durable goods, including garbage bags, food and beverage containers, plastic drums, and pipes and pipe fittings. The life cycle was defined to be the following:

- Manufacturing

- Transportation

- Storage

- Installation

- Maintenance

- Disposal (including recycling)

For the consumable goods, installation and maintenance were assumed to be zero. In all of the cases, manufacturing costs dominated the other life cycle costs, primarily because the operation costs were low or nonexistent. More recently, IBIS applied life cycle costing to the automobile industry. This work has culminated with a study, Body-in-White Material Systems: A Lifecycle Cost Comparison, completed in 1992 by Jeff Dieffenbach of IBIS Associates. The conclusion of this study is presented to illustrate an application of this methodology.

The methodology for assessing life cycle cost by IBIS Associates is straightforward. The first step is to identify the various life cycle stages. The second is to develop costs for each of these stages. Life cycle stages are represented by the following:

- Raw material extraction and conversion
- Manufacturing
  - Fabrication
  - Assembly and finishing
- Operation
  - Installation
  - Resource consumption
  - Maintenance
  - Repair
- Post-use
  - Disposal
  - Recycling and reuse

In addition, many of these life cycle stages are likely to include transportation and storage. It is important to note that products may not necessarily go through each of the second-level stages (for instance, installation, repair, or recycling). To assess life cycle cost, it is necessary to model each of the relevant stages.

The IBIS LCA methodology treats the four first-level life cycle stages differently. *Raw material extraction and conversion* is represented by the price of the raw material (e.g., sheet metal, plastic resin, etc.). These prices are inputs to *manufacturing*. Manufacturing costs are simulated using Technical Cost Modeling, which is discussed in a bit more detail below. *Operation* costs are dependent on the specific nature of the product and its use. These costs can be estimated directly from factors that include the following: labor rates; installation, maintenance, and repair times; material, fuel and energy prices; and so on. In a manner similar to manufacturing costs, *postuse* costs can be simulated using a model of the process. This "process" might include collection, separation, and purification (in the instance of recycling), and landfilling.

Technical Cost Modeling.   Technical cost models are computer spreadsheets developed and applied for the simulation of manufacturing costs. The foundation of the cost model is a set of algorithms that relate process parameters and cost to a set of user inputs, thereby generating a manufacturing cost breakdown as follows:

- Variable-cost elements
  - Material cost
  - Labor cost
  - Utility cost
- Fixed-cost elements
  - Equipment cost
  - Tooling cost
  - Building cost
  - Maintenance cost
  - Overhead labor cost
  - Cost of capital

Material cost is a function of the amount and price of material in the product, the number of rejected parts, any material scrap generated, and any credits for salvageable material scrap that cannot be fed directly back into the process. Labor cost is a function of the number of laborers, their wages, the production rate, and any process inefficiency. Utility costs include energy, water, and any other process materials such as catalysts or cleaning chemicals that do not end up in the final product.

Equipment, tooling, and building costs include both the total investment as well as the allocation of that investment on a per piece basis. Equipment and building investments are allocated based on the percentage of each that is used for the manufacture of a product, relative to other products that also consume those investments. Tooling investment is allocated based on the total production volume over the life of the product.

Maintenance cost is calculated as a function of the total allocated investment. Overhead labor cost is a semifixed cost that is a function of both direct labor cost and the allocation of investment. The cost of capital is the interest paid on the capital investment.

In a Technical Cost Model, cost is assigned to each *unit operation* in a process flow diagram. Each unit operation represents one or several pieces of equipment that operate at a common production rate. Each operation, or station, can then be characterized by this production rate as well as the number of laborers, equipment and tooling investment, power consumption, and floor space requirement. Collectively, these are called *process parameters*. In addition, each station consumes product and process materials in the form of good parts, rejected parts, and material scrap.

Technical Cost Modeling is implemented on a computer spreadsheet such as Lotus 1-2-3 or Microsoft Excel. The power and flexibility of using a computer spreadsheet facilitates rapid data storage, data manipulation, incorporation of expert review, and output recalculation. A critical component of cost modeling is verification. Any thorough exercise in cost simulation involves a review of results with industry experts. Through this validation process, it is possible to iteratively improve the simulation accuracy.

Technical Cost Model Construction.   Technical Cost Model spreadsheets are composed of two major sections: Inputs and Outputs. The Inputs, entered directly by the user, include the following.

- Product Specifications
  - Material and geometry (mass and dimensions)
- Process Related Factors
  - Downtime, yield, etc.
- Exogenous Cost Factors
  - Wage, salary, investment life, price of electricity, etc.

The model Outputs include Intermediate Calculations and Cost Summaries that correspond to the unit operations of the process. A set of algorithms generate the Outputs based on the user Inputs. The algorithms used by a model can be either *descriptive* or *predictive.*

Descriptive algorithms require the user to directly input process parameters as follows:

- Cycle time or production rate
- Number of laborers
- Equipment and tooling investment
- Floor space
- Power consumption

Once these parameters are established, it is a trivial exercise to allocate cost based on assumptions for product weight, material price, labor wage, and so on. The drawback to a descriptive model, while straightforward in operation, is that the user is required to change parameters each time a new product is costed. An alternative is predictive modeling.

In predictive modeling, the process parameters are calculated as a function of the Product Specifications, which include material type, weight, length, width, thickness, surface area, and so on. The functionality is developed through the reduction of data collected from industry.

Two types of data collection are required for the modeling of a process. The first is from equipment suppliers, the second from manufacturers. From equipment suppliers, data are collected on number of laborers, equipment cost, floor space requirement, and power consumption for each machine size. For each of a range of products, data are collected from manufacturers on the part material and geometry, cycle time or production rate, equipment size, and tool cost.

It is then possible to reduce these data to a set of algorithms:

$$\text{Cycle time} = f(\text{material, geometry})$$

$$\text{Equipment size} = f(\text{geometry})$$

$$\text{Number of laborers} = f(\text{equipment size})$$

$$\text{Equipment investment} = f(\text{equipment size})$$

$$\text{Tooling investment} = f(\text{material, geometry})$$

$$\text{Floor space} = f(\text{equipment size})$$

$$\text{Power consumption} = f(\text{equipment size})$$

Operating and investment costs can be calculated based on these equations and the input assumptions and specifications. Piece cost is then the sum of material cost, operating cost, and investment cost.

$$\text{Piece cost} = f(\text{material, geometry})$$

The result of developing a predictive model is that the user must specify only the material and geometry of the product to simulate its manufacturing cost.

The above methodology was used in a study of alternative materials to be considered for use in the structure and alternative panels of a midsize four-door sedan. In the automobile industry, structure and panels together are often referred to as the "body in white." Table 14-6 shows the summary results of this study.

For the time being, material and process selection decisions are likely to be made on the basis of manufacturing cost. Based on the preceding analysis, the aluminum spaceframe competes favorably with the conventional steel unibody, especially at lower production volumes. This conclusion is based on the critically important assumption that the aluminum spaceframe is technically feasible. While this remains to be seen, there is certainly a compelling incentive to examine it carefully.

From a life cycle cost perspective, the aluminum spaceframe is favored more heavily. At issue then is the value of "life cycle cost" as a motivation for decision making. It is unclear that the manufacturer can realize anything more than intangible benefits to adopting a high manufacturing cost, low life cycle cost design. As markets are driven to lower life cycle cost options, however, there will be a strong impetus.

More directly, there is value in the life cycle perspective for a number of reasons. For instance, the fuel-saving (and therefore emission-reducing) potential of plastics significantly outweighs their landfill penalty. From the point of view of government regulation, it may therefore be desirable to

Table 14-6. Life Cycle Cost Comparison: Automotive Body-in-White

	Steel unibody	Aluminum unibody	Aluminum spaceframe	Composite monocoque
Manufacturing:				
Direct cost	$1336	$1973	$1108	$1798
Indirect cost (value)	($0)	($158)	($153)	($84)
Operation:				
Fuel cost	$956	$563	$572	$748
Repair cost	$277	$277	$277	$277
Postuse:				
Disposal cost (value)	($26)	($187)	($170)	$20
Total life cycle cost	$2543	$2468	$1633	$2759

Annual production volume: 200,000 vehicles per year.
Length of production run: 4 years.

ensure that the landfilling of plastics does not become prohibited. As fuel prices rise for whatever reason, the argument in favor of weight savings becomes stronger still. Eventually, this will translate into demand for more fuel-efficient vehicles. Of course, fuel efficiency can be affected by factors other than weight.

The life cycle cost approach is adopted because it lends insight into the making of decisions. The user of a life cycle study can choose to select or ignore components of life cycle cost, but they are all present. As long as the minimization of cost is considered a desirable end, life cycle cost analysis will be required as an effective means.

Case VI

B. Total Cost Allocation Methodologies for Pollution-Prevention Investments

Several approaches have been developed to take into account environmental factors in the analysis of pollution-prevention investments. None has achieved widespread acceptance in the business community, despite their availability for at least 4 years. This attests to a number of barriers to corporate acceptance, ranging from excessive complexity, intensive data demands, and regulatory impediments, to management inertia. Nonetheless they serve as valuable illustrations of progress to date and as points of reference for formulating additional methods for use in the industrial community.

Three of the more prominent methodologies are outlined below as described in the Environmental Protection Agency (EPA) publication *Total Cost Assessment: Accelerating Industrial Pollution Prevention through Innovative Project Financial Analysis* (May 1992).

The General Electric (GE) Method

Prepared for:	General Electric, Corporate Environmental Programs Richard W. MacLean, Manager
Prepared by:	General Electric and ICF Incorporated
Publication date:	1987
Contents:	Workbook, Worksheets and Financial Calculation Software developed with Lotus 1-2-3, version 2.01.

Description. The GE workbook and software are tools for identifying and ranking waste minimization investment options. The user quantifies direct costs (out-of-pocket cash costs routinely associated with waste management and disposal) and future liability costs (including potential environmental liabilities for remedial action costs, and related costs for personal injury and property damage) of a current waste management practice vs. one or several alternative waste minimization options. To evaluate the profitability of waste minimization investments the user follows three steps outlined in Fig. 14-22.

The workbook employs a system of waste-flow diagrams and detailed checklists to help the user identify (step 1) and estimate the direct capital and

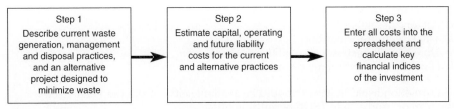

Figure 14-22. Schematic of General Electric methodology.

operating costs (step 2) associated with generation and on- and off-site management of waste streams targeted for reduction. A procedure is presented for estimating the magnitude and timing of future liability costs associated with current and alternative waste management practices (also in step 2). These estimates are based on the type and location of treatment, storage, and disposal facilities (TSDF) utilized, and the quantity and nature of the waste generated. The user first develops a score for the TSDF based on the technology it employs and the location of the facility (i.e., surrounding population density, proximity to water supply, etc.). This score is then used to adjust—up or down—a per-ton cost estimate for corrective actions and claims developed for a base-case, generic hazardous waste landfill. Included in this estimate are the costs of surface sealing, fluid removal and treatment, personal injury, real property claims, economic losses, and natural resource damage claims.

The GE workbook provides step-by-step instructions for entering both direct and future liability cost data and relevant financial parameters into the financial software package or paper worksheets provided in the workbook (step 3). The software calculates streams of after-tax incremental cash flow of the investment, the net present value (NPV) for the current and alternative practice, and the following financial indicators: (1) a break-even point, (2) return on investment (ROI), and (3) discounted cash flow rate of return. The workbook offers recommendations for using the financial indices to identify and rank waste minimization projects.

Data Requirements.   To quantify direct costs of the waste minimization investment, the user needs the following cost data:

1. Estimated capital cost of the waste minimization alternative(s)

2. Operating costs for current waste generation, management, and disposal activities that will be affected by the waste minimization project, including labor, input chemicals, and energy

3. Estimated operating costs for the waste generation, management, and disposal activities under the alternative practice(s)

To estimate future liability costs and the expected year in which a claim may occur, the user must have the following:

1. Information on treatment, storage, and disposal facilities (TSDF)
    a Type of TSDF
    b Population density in surrounding communities

    c Proximity to water supply
    d History of leaks
2. Waste stream information:
    a Quantity of waste sent to TSDF
    b Hazardous constituents of the waste

The information listed in item 1 should be available either from the TSDF used by the firm or from a state TSDF permitting office.

For the financial analysis of the waste minimization investment(s), the user must decide on an inflation rate, discount rate, investment tax credit rate (if applicable), federal tax rate, and depreciation schedule appropriate to the company. This information is generally available from the company accountant, financial officer, or comptroller.

Assessment.   According to GE, approximately 170 industries, consulting firms, government agencies, educational institutions, and other organizations have obtained the workbook and software. Of the 170 approximately 130 are manufacturing industries. No systematic follow-up of these purchasers has been conducted.

Within General Electric the model has not been used exactly as conceived but has been applied to support budgetary analysis of waste management and, more recently, as a communication tool to move management in the direction of waste minimization practices.

The GE system is flexible in that it can serve two principal categories of users. First, a user who is beginning to develop a strategy for waste minimization and is seeking guidance on relevant activities and costs for a TCA would benefit from working through the entire system as summarized in steps 1 to 3 above. By developing the schematic diagrams and utilizing the checklists provided in the workbook, the user is guided in the identification of relevant waste streams and management activities that should be considered in the cost analysis.

Second, users familiar with the full range of activities and costs that should be considered in a TCA may skip steps 1 and 2 and proceed directly to the financial analysis procedure (step 3). In this way, they can expedite the analysis of a specific project by taking only the time necessary to enter the relevant cost items in the worksheets, and examine the financial indices.

The GE financial software is programmed in Lotus, a software package familiar to many people, including small business managers. The system is simple in its design and is user-friendly in its application.

If a user does not wish to include future liability costs for reasons cited earlier, the software can be used to analyze direct costs only. The future liability calculation procedure in the GE workbook can serve as a useful qualitative procedure for assessing, without costing, future liability. It takes the user through a number of additive steps designed to evaluate various key considerations in analyzing this cost component. The process could help the firm qualitatively analyze the risk of a current practice and the effect of a waste minimization alternative.

Because the focus of the workbook is on waste minimization for the purpose of reducing disposal costs and long-term liability, the GE method does not encourage a more comprehensive pollution-prevention approach involving materials substitution and process change. Nor does the workbook provide guidance for the estimation of indirect and less tangible costs and benefits. However, a user can include these items in the evaluation performed with the GE financial analysis software.

Pollution-Prevention Benefits Manual* (EPA Method)

Prepared for: Office of Solid Waste/Office of Policy, Planning and Evaluation, U.S. Environmental Protection Agency

Prepared by: ICF Incorporated

Printing date: October 1990

Contents: Manual and Worksheets

Description. The EPA manual is designed to assist in the cost comparison of one or more pollution-prevention (PP) alternatives to a current industrial practice. The method sets up a hierarchy of costs as follows:

Tier 0—Usual Costs, e.g., equipment, labor, and materials

Tier 1—Hidden Costs, e.g., compliance and permits

Tier 2—Liability Costs, e.g., penalties, fines, and future liabilities

Tier 3—Less Tangible Costs, e.g., consumer responses and employee relations

The hierarchy progresses from the most conventional and certain costs in Tier 0 to the most difficult to estimate and least certain costs in Tier 3. At each tier, the user first analyzes all costs associated with the current and alternative PP project, and then calculates key financial indicators of the economic viability of the PP project. Figure 14-23 illustrates the sequential nature of the method. Financial calculations for each tier are added a tier at a time, until the result concludes that the PP alternative meets the investment criteria (i.e., hurdle rate) of the firm, or all tiers (0 through 3) have been completed. For example, if the results of the Tier 0 financial calculation indicate that the alternative strategy meets the firm's investment criteria, the user may choose not to continue to include Tier 1 to 3 costs. If, however, the result falls short of the investment criteria, then the user may proceed to calculate and add the Tier 1 results to the Tier 0 results, and so on. Even if the Tier 0 or 1 calculation meets the criteria of the firm, a user may want to proceed to estimate Tier 2 and 3 costs to fully analyze the financial implications of the alternative practice.

The manual provides a Regulatory Status Questionnaire, a summary of relevant regulatory programs and cost equations to assist the user in estimating Tier 1 regulatory costs for several compliance activities, including labeling, notification, record keeping, and monitoring. The manual contains numerous cost equations for the estimation of the potential future liability

*The manual has not been officially published; however, copies can be obtained by contacting the EPA, Office of Pollution Prevention, Washington, D.C. 20460.

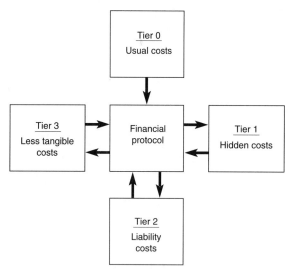

Figure 14-23. Schematic of EPA cost hierarchy methodology.

costs such as groundwater removal and treatment, surface sealing, personal injury, and natural resource damage. In addition, the manual provides guidance for calculating three financial indicators: annualized savings, internal rate of return, and net present value. The manual does not come with software; however, it does contain worksheets that aid in organizing and presenting results from the cost calculations.

Data Requirements.   The following is a summary of the data requirements for each tier included in the manual. While this list is exhaustive, one should keep in mind that (1) not all tiers are necessary to analyze all projects, and (2) not all costs within each tier need to be quantified if data are not available.

Tier 0: Usual Costs

- Depreciable Capital Costs
    - Equipment
    - Materials
    - Utility connections
    - Site preparation
    - Installation
    - Engineering and procurement
- Expenses
    - Start-up costs
    - Permitting costs
    - Salvage value

- Training costs
- Initial chemicals
- Working capital
- Disposal costs
- Raw material costs
- Utilities costs
- Catalysts and chemicals
- Operating and materials (O&M) labor costs
- Operating and materials supplies costs
- Insurance costs
- Operating Revenues
  - From sale of primary products
  - From sale of marketable by-products

Tier 1: Hidden Costs

- Facility's regulatory status under RCRA, CERCLA, SARA Title III, Clean Air Act, OSHA, and relevant state regulatory programs
- Technology-forcing regulatory requirements and the costs associated with them
- Cost components for regulatory activities such as loaded wage rates, frequency of activity, and time required to complete activity, for the following regulatory activities:
  - Notification
  - Reporting
  - Monitoring and testing
  - Record keeping
  - Planning, studies, modeling
  - Training
  - Inspections
  - Manifesting
  - Labeling
  - Preparedness and protective equipment (maintenance)
  - Closure and postclosure assurance
  - Medical surveillance
  - Insurance and special taxes

Tier 2: Liability Costs.   The manual provides cost equations to assist in the calculation of the following future liability costs:

- Soil and waste removal and treatment
- Groundwater removal and treatment
- Surface sealing

- Personal injury
- Economic loss
- Real property damage
- Natural resource damage

Each equation consists of several variables, for which the manual provides suggested values. To illustrate, the equation for real property damage stemming from a hazardous material storage tank or disposal facility is

$$\text{Cost} = a \times b \times c \text{ (in thousands of dollars)}$$

where a = property devaluation factor, 0.15 to 0.30
  b = land value ($000/acre)
  c = area of the off-site plume
  $= [0.33 D^2 + (D \times W) - 0.5 W^2]/4047$

where D = distance to nearest drinking water well (meters), 150 to 3200 m
  W = width of groundwater plume at facility boundary (meters)
Storage tanks: W = 3 to 100 meters
Disposal facilities: W = 500 to 700 meters

A similar equation and set of suggested variable values is provided to predict the expected year in which liabilities may be incurred. While the manual provides a range of suggested values, the user must either choose from the range or use values based on actual information about a facility, the hydrogeologic characteristics of the facility site, distance to nearest drinking water well, and so forth. Since more than one company may be liable for a particular claim, users must estimate their company's share of the potential liability costs.

Tier 3: Less Tangible Costs. The user supplies relevant information to estimate less tangible benefits of pollution prevention resulting from enhanced consumer acceptance, employee and union relations, and corporate image. The manual recommends using the judgment of the analyst and provides some guidance on how to identify and estimate these benefits.

Assessment.   Approximately 600 manuals have been distributed, but no systematic follow-up has been conducted to evaluate the user experience. ICF has also distributed the manual, primarily to consulting firms.

The EPA manual incorporates a wide array of costs—usual, hidden regulatory, liability, and less tangible—which both prompts the user to consider a full range of costs and encourages quantitative analysis. The multitiered structure of this system facilitates step-by-step analysis that starts with the most certain and defensible usual costs and, only if necessary, ends with the less certain, more subtle costs. Therefore, if the investment can be justified on the basis of usual costs, the user does not have to estimate the latter that may generate skepticism within management.

The method provides equations and default values for a number of key costs, which are generally difficult for users to estimate or calculate in the absence of such guidance. Specifically, assistance is provided for the calculation of compliance costs, liabilities resulting from penalties and fines, and liabilities associated with remediation, injury, and property damage. In addition, the method provides useful summaries of relevant federal acts and regulations that assist the user in determining compliance requirements and costs.

The EPA system has no software. Given that some of the equations for calculating costs and financial indices involve long algorithms, a user may have difficulty utilizing these equations without aid from accompanying software. In addition, in the absence of software, users may have difficulty performing screening or scenario analyses to evaluate a number of different alternatives or to experiment with variations on certain alternatives.

PRECOSIS

Prepared for:	U.S. Environmental Protection Agency, Center for Environmental Research Information, Cincinnati, Ohio
Prepared by:	George Beetle, George Beetle Company
Publication date:	1989
Contents:	Manual and Software

PRECOSIS was designed to support the financial analysis of waste reduction projects.* The software is a menu-driven program consisting of 10 data input tables and two output reports containing financial calculations. The programs can be used on any IBM-compatible microcomputer having 512 kilobytes or more of base memory.

Cost data are grouped into three categories:

- Resource effects—costs of labor, material, and facilities
- Revenue or value effects—changes in output quantity and quality, and secondary products and services
- Waste management effects—includes storage, handling, disposal, compliance, insurance, and litigation

The financial assessment of alternative waste reduction strategies is conducted in four steps, as illustrated in Fig. 14-24. First, data describing the baseline (or current) process are entered (step 1). The user enters cost data for labor, materials, facilities, and waste management in unit cost format (e.g., cost per ton of a feedstock material or cost per gallon for waste disposal) and then specifies the number of units needed for the current process (e.g., pounds of feedstock used per year or number of gallons of waste disposed per year). Revenue data are handled in a similar fashion. Using these costs and several financial parameters entered by the user, the system calculates the total cost of the current system.

---

*This system can also be used to evaluate other types of pollution-prevention projects.

Figure 14-24. Schematic of PRECOSIS methodology.

To calculate costs associated with the alternative process, the user must enter an expected increase or decrease (called "effects") in the number of units of resources used, waste generated, and product produced as a result of the process change (step 2). For example, if 500 units of waste are generated by the current system, and 50 units by the alternative system, then the expected decrease in the units of waste is 450.

The software calculates net present value, payback years, internal return on investment, and numerous other financial indicators to evaluate the profitability of the alternative process (step 3). The user can repeat steps 2 and 3 to compare financial differences among alternative waste minimization strategies (step 4). Up to five alternatives can be compared.

Data Requirements. A PRECOSIS user is asked for the following information:

Labor resources:

- Average hourly labor rates
  - Associated fringe benefits by labor class
  - Number of units of each class of labor for the current and alternative processes

Materials:

- Physical units of measurement
- Typical rates of use for the current process and expected change in use for the alternative strategy
- Average delivered costs of materials

Facilities:

- Equipment and building sizes or capacities, average service life, typical salvage value
- Typical rates of use for the current process and expected change in use for the alternative strategy

Revenues:

- Current production rates for primary and secondary products and expected changes in production rates for the alternative strategy

- Current revenue rates for products and expected changes for the alternative strategy

Waste management:

- Waste stream volumes and expected changes for the alternative strategy
- Waste management costs, including waste monitoring and reporting, and expected changes for the alternative strategy
- Insurance for workers and third parties and expected changes for the alternative strategy

Assessment.   Approximately 1000 copies of an older version of the software (uncompiled and more difficult to use than the current version) were distributed at EPA Waste Minimization workshops in 1989. Since May 1990 approximately 100 licenses for the updated version have been sold. No systematic follow-up research has been conducted with firms that received the software at the workshop or those that recently purchased the updated version.

PRECOSIS facilitates analysis of both (1) the economic feasibility of waste minimization projects and (2) the financial differences among waste minimization alternatives. The method is designed to allow side-by-side analysis of the incremental cost effects of up to five alternative projects.

The unit cost method simplifies the estimation of incremental cost effects based on units of raw material and energy used, and quantity of waste generated. It also is well suited to cost sensitivity analysis. For example, once users have entered in sufficient data concerning the current practice, they can easily evaluate the financial effect of reducing an additional unit of waste or raw material, or calculate the effect of changes in waste disposal costs, insurance costs, or the price paid for recovered metals. However, a possible drawback of this sophisticated modeling approach is that PRECOSIS may appear too dissimilar as compared to conventional project financial analyses to which businesses are accustomed. The system may be better suited to financial scenario analysis of waste minimization options, particularly for larger firms with extensive resources committed to evaluating waste minimization opportunities.

The PRECOSIS user likely will need a significant amount of time to learn the method and to understand the way it is structured. This may be a stumbling block for potential users, particularly those with little or no computer experience. Most of the calculations are not explained in the User's Manual nor would the typical user be able to examine formulas in the software. Companies may not be willing to base important investment decisions on the output of a complex model that is not verifiable at this stage.

Bibliography

Allenby, B. R., "Design for the Environment: A Tool Whose Time Has Come," *SSA Journal*, September 1991.

Arthur D. Little, Inc., Consultants, *Seizing Strategic Environmental Advantage, A Life Cycle Approach*, Cambridge, Massachusetts, 1991.

Association of the Dutch Chemical Industry, *Integrated Substance Chain Management*, December 1991.

Blanchard, B. S., and W. J. Fabrycky, *Systems Engineering and Analysis*, Prentice-Hall, Englewood Cliffs, New Jersey, 1990.

Blanchard, B. S., and J. W. Meredith, "Concurrent Engineering, Total Quality Management in Design," Society of Logistics Engineers *Logistics Spectrum*, Winter 1990.

Brimson, J. A., *Activity Accounting*, Wiley, New York, 1991.

Cairncross, F., *Costing the Earth*, Harvard Business School Press, 1992.

Clapham, W. B., Jr., *Natural Ecosystems*, Macmillan, New York, 1973.

Cohan, D., W. C. Trench, and M. McLearn, *Beyond Waste Minimization, A Life Cycle Cost Approach to Managing Chemicals and Materials*, Electric Power Research Institute, 1992.

Dhillon, B. S., *Life Cycle Costing, Techniques, Models and Applications*, University of Ottawa, Gordon and Breach Science Publishers, New York, 1989. (Includes an appendix with a bibliography on life cycle costing and related areas of 65 pages with over 1000 references).

Dollimore, L. S., "A Disciplined Approach to Product Risk Reduction," *Integrated Environmental Management*, Blackwell Scientific Publications, 1992.

Fabrycky, W. J., and B. S. Blanchard, *Life Cycle Cost and Economic Analysis*, Prentice-Hall, Englewood Cliffs, New Jersey, 1991.

Fava, J. A., F. Consoli, and R. A. Denison, Analysis of Product Life Cycle Assessment Applications, SETAC-Europe Workshop on Life Cycle Assessment, Leiden, Netherlands, December 1991.

Fava, J. A., "Product Life Cycle Assessment: Improving Environmental Quality," *Integrated Environmental Management*, Issue 3, Blackwell Scientific Publications, October 1991.

Fava, J. A., "Product Stewardship: A Proactive Approach to Improve Environmental Quality," 1992, Weston Way.

Federation of Swedish Industries, *International Experiences of Environmentally Sound Product Development*, S. Ryding, Appendix I, June 1992.

Fisher, A. C., *Resource and Environmental Economics*, University of California, Berkeley, Cambridge University Press, 1990.

Glantschnig, W. J., "Design for the Environment (DFE): A Systematic Approach to Green Design in a Concurrent Engineering Environment," AT&T Bell Laboratories, Princeton, New Jersey, 1992.

Gray, R. H., *The Greening of Accountancy: The Profession after Pearce*, Certified Accountants Publications, Ltd., London, 1990.

Hauser, J. R., and D. Clausing, "The House of Quality," *Harvard Business Review*, May–June 1988.

Hirschhorn, J. S., and K. U. Oldenburg, *Prosperity without Pollution*, Van Nostrand Reinhold, Princeton, New Jersey, 1991.

Holmes, H., "The Green Police," *Garbage*, September–October 1991.

Kneese, A. V., and B. T. Bower, *Environmental Quality and Residuals Management*, Resources for the Future, Inc., Washington, D.C., 1979.

"Life Cycle Analysis for Packaging Environmental Assessment," Proceedings of the Specialized Workshop, Leuven, Belgium, September 1990. Organized by IMSA and IPRE 1990.

Mackenzie, D., *Design for the Environment*, Rizzoli, New York, 1991.

Odum, E. P., *Ecology and Our Endangered Life Support Systems*, University of Georgia, Sinauer Associates, Inc., 1989.

Odum, H. T., *Environment, Power and Society*, Wiley, New York, 1991.

Office of Technology Assessment, U.S. Congress, *Green Products by Design, Choices for a Cleaner Environment*, September 1992.

Organization for Economic Cooperation and Development (OECD), *Benefits Estimates and Environmental Decision-Making*, 1992.

Perrow, C., *Normal Accidents, Living with High Risk Technologies*, Basic Books, New York, 1984.

Pirocanac, D., "Editor's Notes, Parlez Vous Valorization," *Pollution Engineering*, February 1, 1992.

Pittinger, C., "Global Product Stewardship through Solid Waste Reductions in Consumer Product Packaging," *Changing Course*, Business Council for Sustainable Development, MIT Press, 1992.

Quade, E. S., and W. I. Boucher, *Systems Analysis and Policy Planning, Applications in Defense*, Rand Corporation, American Elsevier Publishing Co., New York, 1970, 3d printing.

Reagan, D., Woodward Clyde Consultants, September 1992 seminar presentation, "Technical Overview of Natural Resource Damage Assessment," Iselin, New Jersey.

Rifkin, J., *Entropy into the Greenhouse World*, rev. ed., Bantam Books, New York, 1989.

Schmidheiny, S., *Changing Course, A Global Business Perspective on Development and the Environment*, Business Council for Sustainable Development, MIT Press, 1992.

Silverstein, M., *The Environmental Factor*, Longman Financial Services Publishing, 1990.

Snow, B. A., *Education in the Systems Sciences*, 1st ed., The Elmwood Institute, Berkeley, California, Winter 1990.

Society of Environmental Toxicology and Chemistry (SETAC), *A Technical Framework for Life-Cycle Assessment*, J. A. Fava, R. Denison, B. Jones, M. A. Curran, B. Vigon, S. Selke, and J. Barnum, Eds. Published by SETAC and SETAC Foundation for Environmental Education, Inc., 1991.

Society of Environmental Toxicology and Chemistry (SETAC), *A Conceptual Framework for Impact Analysis*, J. A. Fava, F. Consoli, R. Denison, K. Dickson, T. Mohin, and B. Vignon, Eds. Published by SETAC Foundation for Environmentla Education, Inc., 1993.

Sullivan, M. S., *Environmental Life Cycle Frameworks: Industry Management of Product Innovation and Environmental Impact*, MIT Master of Science Thesis, May 1992.

Tellus Institute, *CSG/Tellus Packaging Study*, May 1992.

U.S. Environmental Protection Agency (EPA), *Reducing Risks: Setting Priorities and Strategies for Environmental Protection*, 1990.

U.S. EPA *Pollution Prevention Benefits Manual*, October 1989.

U.S. EPA *Total Cost Assessment: Accelerating Industrial Pollution Prevention through Innovative Project Financial Analysis*, May 1992.

U.S. EPA *Life Cycle Design Guidance Manual—Environmental Requirements and the Product System*. EPA 600/R-92/226., January 1993.

World Wildlife Fund and The Conservation Foundation 1990. *Policy Issues on Life Cycle Analysis*, May 1990, Workshop Report.

15

Environmental Marketing*

Carl Frankel, J.D., and Walter Coddington

In this chapter:

- Environmental (ECO) Marketing Overview
- Rationale for Environmental Marketing
- The Business Environment for Environmental Marketing
- Consumer-Product Environmental Marketing Strategies
- Business-to-Business Environmental Marketing Strategies
- Into the Next Millennium

In this chapter, we make the case that it is enlightened and forward-thinking to give the environment a prominent place in your marketing planning. This holds true whether you are marketing to consumer or to commercial and institutional markets. Both markets are receptive to environmental appeals, although their dynamics vis-à-vis environmental issues differ somewhat.

Environmental marketing is not without risks. Ill-conceived programs can backfire. It is critically important for corporate environmental marketing strategies to be planned carefully and knowledgeably. In this chapter, we review the current climate for environmental marketing and provide a set of recommended principles to help marketers make sound environmental marketing decisions.

---

*This chapter was reviewed by Trevor Russel of the Business Council for Sustainable Development.

Environmental (ECO) Marketing Overview

In recent years, the attitudes of both industry and consumers toward the environment have changed appreciably. Businesses are folding a heightened sense of environmental responsibility into their policies and practices, while consumers' green concerns are increasingly being reflected in both their purchase and postpurchase behavior.

These changes are not occurring in a vacuum. The new patterns of conduct reflect an evolution in our society's definition of "environmental responsibility." There is a widespread and growing perception that humans have wrought extensive damage on the planet, that it is our duty to undo that damage in order to secure the welfare of the planet for future generations, and that this can be achieved only through fundamental changes at both the personal and corporate levels. This awareness is causing more and more businesses to adopt the principles of "sustainable development" as a means of safeguarding our environmental future.

We are in an extended period of transition from a relatively low to a relatively high level of environmental awareness. But getting from here to there has not been easy. The road has produced its share of bumps.

In this uncertain, transitional climate, it is important for corporate marketing managers to keep the long term squarely in mind. Ideally, they will position their short-term thinking as a subset of a more expansive awareness, one that looks to a time when the environment has become a substantially higher business priority. *The time has come for corporate marketers to position themselves on the other side of the millennium and to consciously develop strategies that will encourage the emergence of a society that gives greater consideration to environmental issues than is currently the case.*

One foot in the present, one foot in the future: this is difficult but necessary positioning. Difficult because it is never easy to be pragmatic and visionary at the same time. Necessary because the well-being of the planet requires us, both as individual citizens and as businesspeople, to give greater consideration to the environmental impact of our behavior. And necessary, as well, as a matter of long-term business positioning.

Such an approach does more than benefit the environment. As detailed in this chapter, it can also produce palpable business benefits in the form of both short-term payoffs and advantageous long-term market positioning.

Environmental Marketing Defined

1. Environmental marketing consists of the set of core principles and practices that enables companies to put consumers' and others' concerns about the environment to their financial advantage, in an ethically appropriate manner.

2. "Environmental marketing" also defines a changed attitude about, and new context for, making marketing decisions—one in which the environment is a pervasive consideration.

A Set of Principles and Practices

Traditionally, marketers have depended largely on market research, quality and financial controls, trade relations, and promotion to sell their products. Today, a new factor has entered the picture—the environment. Shareholders, consumer activists, environmental groups, regulators, and even retailers are collectively demanding that businesses consider the environmental impact of everything they do.

This puts businesses under tremendous pressure, but it creates substantial opportunities, too. This is why, as per the first part of our definition: "Environmental marketing consists of the set of practices that enables companies to put consumers' and others' concerns about the environment to their financial advantage, in an ethically appropriate context."

The limiting clause ("in an ethically appropriate context...") is important. Environmental marketing is *not* about exploiting people's environmental concerns. Correctly implemented, environmental marketing calls for a company to make a *genuine* commitment to benefiting the environment, one that in turn can be transformed into financial benefit for the company.

It is also important to note our preference for the term "environmental marketing" over "green marketing." Over time, the latter term has become associated with dubious marketing practices. "Green marketing" has come to describe practices that are inappropriate at best and illegal at worst, and it is not our subject here. Indeed, in a public-policy context, "environmental marketing" provides substantial social benefits. To the extent that it encourages companies to compete on the basis of the environmental merits of their processes and products, it decreases the extent to which consumerism damages the environment.

A Change in Attitude

But environmental marketing is about more than a new set of marketing practices. It is also about a change in attitude. The environmentally oriented marketer factors the environment into virtually all business decisions. No matter what the specific subject is—product and packaging design and development, labeling and advertising, or promotional strategies—the environmental marketer takes the environment into account. Thus the second part of our definition: "Environmental marketing" also defines a changed attitude about and new context for making marketing decisions—one in which the environment is a major, indeed ubiquitous, consideration.

Environmentally oriented marketers inevitably spend a substantial amount of time working to increase environmentally responsible behavior within their own organizations. A company should not represent itself as being more environmentally responsible than it is, since it is the environmental marketer's job to help ensure that a company's deeds match its words.

Will environmental marketers always succeed in their efforts to bring senior management around to their point of view? No. Some companies will be receptive to the idea of giving the environment a more prominent place in their strategic thinking, and others will be resistant. Whatever the specific circumstances, it remains the environmental marketer's job to lobby for environmentally enlightened behavior within his or her corporation.

Why Engage in Environmental Marketing?

There are three basic reasons for adopting an environmental marketing strategy.

Competitive Positioning

More and more companies are engaging in environmental marketing, on either an ad hoc or a comprehensive basis. As this becomes standard industry practice, companies which do not engage in environmental marketing will be forced to play a game of catch-up which, by virtue of its timing alone, will invite a perception of shallowness.

Benefiting the Bottom Line

Environmental marketing can produce quantifiable, short-term benefits to the bottom line. Some examples:

- Procter & Gamble's Downy Refill fabric softener went national in fall 1990 after reaching 20% of brand sales in test markets. It currently accounts for 40% of all Downy sales.

- When Procter & Gamble eliminated the outer cartons from its Sure and Secret deodorants, production costs were reduced by 20%, while sales reportedly climbed by 4%.

- In the two years since Church & Dwight Co., Inc., manufacturers of Arm & Hammer baking soda products, launched its environmental marketing program, sales of its baking soda products, which had been flat for many years, grew by several times the rate of population growth. At the same time, the company's laundry detergent solidified its position as the number three selling brand in the United States.

The commercial and institutional side has also produced its share of success stories:

- E.I. DuPont is marketing its internal environmental training program to similarly situated companies.

- Bio T Foam, a nontoxic, noncorrosive degreaser and cleaner designed specifically for the industrial marketing by Colorado-based BioChem Systems, has met with a favorable reception.

- Sunshine Makers (Huntington Harbor, California), makers of Simple Green, a general-purpose cleaning product, reports that its two-and-a-half-year old industrial, institutional, and health care division is the company's fastest-growing unit.

- Ashdun Industries (Englewood Cliffs, New Jersey), makers of a range of green cleaning and paper products, reports that it is receiving "constant calls from the industrial/institutional sector."

Securing the Future

Is "the environment" simply one among many issues, one of many contexts (economic, political, etc.) which it is mankind's unique good fortune to be able to view, as it were, from the outside? Or is "the environment" the overarching context within which all other contexts (including the species *Homo sapiens*) reside? Is the environment *a* context, or is it *the* context?

We believe that the environment is *the* context, that the term describes the biosystem within which we all reside. That is obviously the case if we think about the question in purely physical terms. Yet because we have the unique capability to conceptualize "the environment"—to capture it within our minds—a tendency persists to redefine it as a category of mind, to assume somehow that it is smaller than we are, that we exist beyond and outside it. This is a minor logical lapse, but one with enormous consequences.

If it is indeed the case that we are "inside" the environment, then we harm ourselves whenever we do it harm. This is true whether the "we" refers to us as individuals or in our corporate incarnations. From this perspective, working proactively to benefit the environment is an exercise in enlightened self-interest.

Why Environmental Marketing?

1. Competitive positioning
2. Benefiting the bottom line
3. Securing the future

The Business Environment for Environmental Marketing

The Consumer Market

Green consumerism hit U.S. shores like a tidal wave during the period surrounding Earth Day 1990. Surveys at the time showed very high levels of consumer concern about the environment, as well as a strong stated willingness to translate that concern into buying behavior, up to and including paying significant premiums for "green" products. But then the recession arrived, consumers got tighter with their wallets, and the media rushed in to declare green consumerism dead, or at least moribund.

They were wrong. It is true that consumers' expressed levels of concern exceed their actual buying behavior by a significant margin. It is also the case that consumers are often dubious about green product claims and as a rule unwilling to pay price premiums. These facts notwithstanding, it remains the case that environmentally driven buying behavior is extensive—and growing steadily.

The Roper/S.C. Johnson Surveys.   In 1990, the consumer goods company S.C. Johnson & Son (Racine, Wisconsin) sponsored a study of green consumers by The Roper Organization (New York) which has since come to be viewed as the definitive study on the subject.

The 1990 Roper/Johnson study identified five categories of green (and not-so-green) consumer: (1) True-Blue Greens, (2) Greenback Greens, (3) Sprouts, (4) Grousers, and (5) Basic Browns.

The first two of these segments are clearly green. True-Blue Greens, according to Roper/Johnson, are "true environmental activists and leaders. Their behavior is consistent with strong personal concerns about the environment, and they are convinced that individual actions can make a difference." Greenback Greens "express their commitment to the environment by a willingness to pay significantly higher prices for green products."

Sprouts are a swing group. They "show middling levels of concern about environmental problems, but their involvement in certain kinds of 'environmentally responsible' activities can be rather high."

Two segments are clearly not green. Grousers "are relatively uninvolved in pro-environmental activities, and they justify their indifference by citing factors beyond their control." Basic Browns are "the least environmentally active group of people on virtually all counts. . . . Unlike the Grousers, they do not feel the need to rationalize their lack of effort."

A 1992 update of the landmark Roper/Johnson study has established the increasing strength of green consumerism in the United States.

True-Blue Greens.   Membership in this greenest of categories almost doubled, from 11 to 20%. Writes Roper/Johnson, "Participation in a variety of pro-environmental activities has risen sharply over the past two years, which signals that American society is, indeed, 'greening.'"

Greenback Greens.   This segment shrank sharply, from 11 to 5% of the population. Roper/Johnson's explanation: "The U.S. recession."

Sprouts.   Sprouts climbed from 26 to 31% of the population. Notes Roper/Johnson, "Since the Sprouts are generally the people who move into the 'green' groups as their environmental behavior 'matures,' it appears that . . . the

U.S. (is) poised for further growth in the number of True-Blue Greens, in particular, in the future."

Grousers. The percentage of Grousers in the United States dropped dramatically, from 24 to 9%. Writes Roper/Johnson, "Some Americans are accepting a greater degree of individual responsibility for helping improve the environment; these people have tended to move into the Sprouts group. But on the other hand, a considerable number of Americans have—in the face of the recession—tended to think first of pocketbook issues and, as a result, have felt less of a need to rationalize their lack of environmental involvement. These people have shifted into the Basic Brown group."

Basic Browns. The number of Basic Browns rose sharply, from 28 to 35%. Once again, the culprit, according to Roper/Johnson, was the recession, which has "forced many Americans—especially those with lower incomes—to concentrate more on 'bread-and-butter' issues."

Overall, the percentage of truly green consumers, i.e., the True-Blue Greens and Greenback Greens, climbed from 22 to 25% of the population from 1990 to 1992, with a much higher proportion (80%, compared with the 50% 1990 figure) belonging to the more deeply committed True-Blue Greens. The percentage of "truly browns," i.e., Grousers and Basic Browns, dropped from 52% of the population to 44%, while the Sprouts, the swing group in the middle, climbed from 26 to 31% of the population.

The Roper/Johnson study found that U.S. adults are also exhibiting higher levels of environmental consciousness in their actual behavior.

Figure 15-1 summarizes these findings.

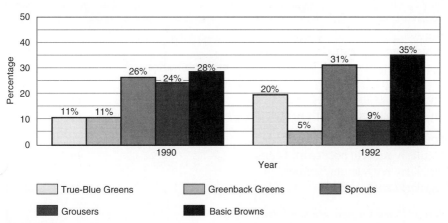

Figure 15-1. Green (and not-so-green) consumers, 1990–1992. (*Roper Organization/S.C. Johnson.*)

In-Store Behavior.   The 1992 Roper/Johnson survey found that green in-store buying behavior is rising steadily. The following types of environmentally conscious behavior rose (the percentages refer to people who "regularly" engage in the activity):

■ *Buy products in refillable packaging*—14% in 1990, 18% in 1992

■ *Buy products made from or packaged in recycled materials*—14% in 1990, 19% in 1992

■ *Avoid buying products in aerosol containers*—23% in 1990, 28% in 1992

■ *Use biodegradable low-phosphate detergents*—24% in 1990, 29% in 1992

An exception to this trend: the percentage of consumers who regularly "avoid buying products from companies which you don't feel are environmentally responsible," which dropped from 16% in 1990 to 12% in 1992.

Post-Purchase Behavior.   Consumers' recycling behavior is rising much more sharply than their in-store behavior, as evidenced by the following findings:

■ Those who "regularly" recycle bottles and cans climbed from 46 to 58%

■ The percentage who "regularly" recycle newspapers rose from 26 to 43%

■ The percentage who "regularly" sort trash increased from 24 to 35%

Figure 15-2 presents the Roper/Johnson data on consumers' purchase and postpurchase behavior.

Q: Which of the following do you do on a regular basis?		
Activity	1990	1992
In-Store:		
Avoid buying products in aerosols, %	23	28
Avoid companies with bad environmental reputations, %	16	12
Buy biodegradable, low-phosphate detergents, %	24	29
Buy products in refillable packages, %	14	18
Buy products made with recycled materials and packaging, %	14	19
Postpurchase:		
Regularly recycle bottles and cans, %	46	58
Regularly recycle newspaper, %	26	43
Regularly sort trash, %	24	35
(*Source: Roper Organization/S.C. Johnson.*)		

Figure 15-2. Consumer Environmental Behavior, 1990 and 1992.

The overall finding of the 1992 Roper/Johnson study: green consumerism is well established and growing slowly but steadily.

Demographics. The Roper/Johnson and other surveys have produced several additional findings about green consumer demographics:

- *Gender.* Women tend to be greener than men.
- *Location.* Green consumerism tends to be highest on the east and west coasts, and lowest in the south.
- *Age.* Children are the greenest group of all. After that, the 36 to 45 cohort tends generally to be the most environmentally conscious, although there are sharp variations from activity to activity—for some activities, younger cohorts are greener, while for others it is the older cohorts who are the most green.
- *Education and income levels.* Levels of green consumerism increase in direct proportion to educational and income levels. The more affluent and better-educated people are, the likelier they are to be green.

Green New Product Activity. The rise in green consumerism has been matched by an increase in the percentage of new products making environmental claims. Although the data showed a slight decline in the first half of 1992, Fig. 15-3 shows how, on balance, green claims have become a familiar component of new product introductions.

The "Four E's." Just how important a role does the environment play in consumers' buy decisions? Bryan Thomlison, director of public affairs for Church

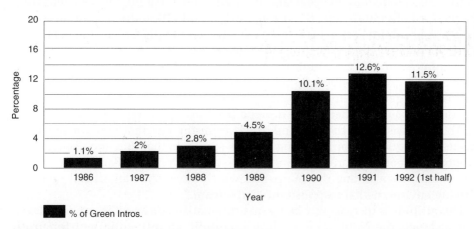

% of Green Intros.

Figure 15-3. Green new product introductions as percent of new product introductions, 1986–1992. (*Marketing Intelligence Service.*)

& Dwight, discusses this issue in terms of "the four 'E's"—efficacy, economy, ease of use, and the environment.

In the furor that surrounded Earth Day 1990, many marketers and market analysts leaped to the conclusion that the environment would be right up there as a buying consideration alongside the "big three" of efficacy, economy, and ease of use. Not so, as it turned out. The environment has settled in at the top of the second tier. It is an important consideration but not yet on a par with price, performance, and convenience (as the "big three" are often known).

Green products which are priced at a premium over nongreen products will generally not do well in the mass marketplace, certainly not until the recession ends and quite possibly beyond. Still, the environment *is* an important buying consideration. We live in an age of parity consumer products. The "big three" being equal, consumers often turn to the second tier to make their purchase decision. *The environment has become the tiebreaker in an age of parity products.*

Commercial and Institutional Markets

Facing short-term lukewarm consumer demand for green products, more and more suppliers are turning their attention to the commercial and institutional side. In large measure, this is an indirect effect of consumers' environmental concerns. One obvious way for companies to respond to the public's demand that they be more environmentally responsible is by using clean processes and green products.

The following are among the many reasons for the commercial market's attractiveness:

1. *Robust demand.* On the whole, demand is strong on the commercial and institutional side. This is true for the two types of green commercial products: (1) products with uniquely commercial and industrial applicability such as Petrofree, a biodegradable vegetable oil–derived drilling fluid for oil wells from Baroid Drilling Fluids, Inc. (Houston, Texas); and (2) products with more universal applicability, such as the abovementioned Simple Green, a general-purpose cleaning product from Sunshine Makers.

Regulatory pressure accounts for much but not all of this demand. Many companies favor green products for reasons that go beyond compliance. Sometimes this reflects genuine environmental commitment, and sometimes the public relations advantages that can be derived from using green products.

Another reason for the demand arises from the fact that many major businesses are requesting or requiring of their suppliers that they too use environmentally responsible products and processes. McDonald's, BankAmerica, and S.C. Johnson are among the companies which have made an official policy of driving environmental responsibility "upstream."

This attitude is increasingly being institutionalized on an intercorporate level. For instance, the National Recycling Coalition, an influential not-for-profit group whose mission is to support the development of a recycling infrastructure, is sponsoring a national Buy Recycling campaign which is built around a Business Advisory Council (BAC) consisting of some 30 major corporations. A key mission of BAC members: lobbying their suppliers to buy recycled.

2. *Price competitiveness.* Another advantage for green products in the commercial and institutional sector is that they tend to be more price competitive with nongreen products than on the consumer side. The reason: the added costs to industry of disposing of cleaning materials containing corrosive, often toxic chemicals.

There is one important caveat to our overall sense of strong demand. Green products *must* be priced competitively with nongreen alternatives—if not on an ounce-for-ounce basis, then on a net cost basis. This is why savings such as those flowing from reduced disposal costs can have such a major influence on the buy decision. Generally, purchasing agents and others in the commercial and institutional sector are more receptive to this sort of "big picture" thinking than consumers, whose thinking tends to be more "micro"—"pennies in, pennies out."

Overseas, there appears to be less resistance to price premiums than in the United States. Natural Chemistry, Inc. (New Canaan, Connecticut), a supplier of green cleaning products, reports that its products, which carry a premium relative to bulk nongreen industrial cleaning products, have done better in Europe and Asia than in the United States.

Interestingly, Natural Chemistry has also made some sales in Russia, a country not usually associated with environmental responsibility. The reason: the so-called Leapfrog Principle. Sometimes, faster progress can be made when there is not a highly developed infrastructure in place that needs to be uprooted (or transcended).

3. *Size of the universe.* The market for commercial and institutional products is enormous: business-to-business transactions account for about 45% of the goods and services sold in the United States.

4. *A streamlined sales process.* Selling to businesses is much more straightforward than selling to consumers. No balky retailers, no expensive advertising.

In addition, marketers get more return for their efforts on the commercial and institutional side. In the words of one marketer, "One positive buy decision, and you've got an entire institution covered."

5. *An optimal educational milieu.* To sell green products to consumers, ongoing education is a must. People need to be brought up to speed about environmental issues, even as they are being asked to buy the product in question. This is not easily achieved in an environment where consumers tend to be distrustful of every corporate pronouncement (studies typically show that only 10 to 15% of consumers find corporate communications on touchy issues such as the environment to be extremely credible), and where the usual mechanisms for communicating information (e.g., advertisements, labels) do not lend themselves to the task of laying out inherently complex environmental information.

These problems do not obtain on the industrial side. Assuming the price is right, many purchasing agents are favorably disposed toward green products, if only because directives have come down from on high to buy green. For much the same reason, i.e., because it is part of their job description, purchasing agents are often relatively well informed about environmental issues. And if they require educating, optimal mechanisms—extended person-to-person discussions, written documentation to which they are prepared to devote real time and attention—are available, as is not the case in consumer channels.

6. *A psychologically straightforward buy decision.*   The industrial-side purchase decision tends to be more cut-and-dried than with consumers. For professional purchasing agents, the buy decision boils down quickly to the essentials—price, performance, and ease of use.

It is not only consumer-products companies which are addressing the commercial green-products market. Industrial-products specialists such as the abovementioned Baroid Drilling Fluids and BioChem Systems are also pursuing commercial green-product opportunities.

Environmental (ECO-) Labeling and Certification

Environmental Labeling Regulation

The rush of environmental energy which accompanied Earth Day 1990 presented marketers with what seemed to be an extraordinary marketing opportunity. By simply touting the environmental performance of a product, increased sales seemed to be virtually guaranteed.

Although most marketers behaved conscientiously, enough questionable environmental claims were made to attract the attention of regulators. An early leader in the attempt to control environmental claims was a Task Force of State Attorneys General headed by Hubert H. Humphrey III, the attorney general of Minnesota (and son of the late senator and vice-president). This group brought legal actions against companies for making false and deceptive environmental claims, and it also produced two reports (*Green Report I* and *Green Report II*) which lay out guidelines for environmental marketing.

The Task Force of State Attorneys General was not alone in attempting to control environmental claims. As of this writing, four states—California, Indiana, New York, and Rhode Island—have comprehensive environmental labeling laws in effect, and a host of other states have statutes and/or regulations in the works.

The fact that regulatory requirements differ from state to state created concern among national marketers about the possible "Balkanization" of the environmental marketing arena. They lobbied the Federal Trade Commission (FTC) for a set of national guidelines, and in the summer of 1992 the FTC responded with a set of recommendations which were widely hailed as fair-minded and reasonable. The Comparison of Environmental Labeling Guides and Regulations chart (pp. 656–659) compares FTC guides to existing regulations and other voluntary guidelines.

After the initial burst of activity (and prior to the issuance of the FTC guides), marketers backed away from environmental claims, often without abandoning them entirely. The standard environmental statement on 2-liter soda bottles at this time was "Please recycle." This formulation was not subject to regulatory scrutiny because it made no claim about the recyclability of the soda bottles. At the same time, however, it cleverly invited the reader to assume that the company in question cared about the nation's solid waste crisis. During this period, of such bobs-and-weaves were environmental claims strategies made.

The issuance of FTC guides is widely expected to bring renewed vigor into the environmental marketing arena. The environmental labeling landscape will probably remain somewhat "Balkanized." However, this is unlikely to deter companies from making environmental claims.

Product Certification

In the United States, environmental labeling claims have been met with suspicion from the public and regulators alike. That is why product certification programs exist—to allow credible third-party organizations to pass judgment on the environmental performance of products and packages rather than leave the assertions to the product manufacturers themselves, who have their own vested interests.

Third-party product certification programs are well advanced in other countries. Germany's Blue Angel program has certified over 3000 products in some 60 product categories. Canada has issued its EcoLogo license to 120 companies offering some 700 products in 34 product categories. Japan, if anything, has done too much too soon in this area: so many certifications have been issued that the legitimacy of the entire program has been thrown into doubt.

The European Community (EC) is also a strong supporter of third-party certification. Although its program is less advanced than the ones in many of its member countries, it is proceeding aggressively with its own plans for an environmental seal.

U.S. consumers strongly support the idea of a product certification authority. In typical surveys, over 80% of consumers indicate that a product certification program would affect their buy decisions.

Despite these strong levels of consumer interest, the United States is lagging behind other countries in the development and deployment of a product certification system. The main reason: the failure of the federal government to put its weight behind the concept. Strapped for funds and lacking formal authorization from either the White House or Congress, the EPA has supported projects to further the state of the art of scientific life cycle analysis (LCA) but has been otherwise inactive in eco-labeling.

It has been left to two competing California-based private organizations, Green Seal and Scientific Certification Systems (SCS, formerly known as Green Cross), to try to bootstrap a product certification system into existence in the United States.

Comparison of Environmental Labeling Guides and Regulations

Law and guidelines	Degradable, biodegradable, photodegradable	Compostable	Recyclable
California	Proven capability to decompose within one year in most common environment where disposed	Not addressed	An article can be conveniently recycled in every county in California with a population over 300,000
Canada	Claims of degradability should not be used for packaging materials. Where appropriate, claims of degradability may be made for products disposed of through the sewage system. In exceptional circumstances, a claim of degradability may be considered for solid products not normally destined to be landfilled. All degradability claims should be appropriately qualified	Not addressed	Claims of recyclability should not be made simply because the material is technically recyclable. Where a reasonable number of recycling facilities exist, "recyclable where facilities exist" is appropriate
Federal Trade Commission	Claim must accurately reflect product or package's ability to decompose into elements found in nature after customary disposal. Examples: A "degradable" claim for a trash bag which is customarily disposed of in a landfill is deceptive, while a qualified claim of "photodegradable—will break into small pieces if left uncovered in sunlight" is not deceptive if substantiated by scientific evidence	An unqualified claim may be deceptive: (1) if municipal composting facilities are not available to a substantial majority of consumers or communities where the package is sold; (2) if the claim misleads consumers about the environmental benefit provided when the product is disposed of in a landfill; or (3) if consumers misunderstand the claim to mean that the package can be safely composted in their home compost pile or device, when it cannot	Claims of recyclability should be qualified to the extent necessary to avoid deception about the limited availability of recycling programs and collection sites. Recyclability claims should clearly state which components of the product or package are recyclable. Example: if recycling programs are available to a significant percentage of consumers or to a significant percentage of the population, but not to a substantial majority of consumers, the claim should be qualified to indicate the limited availability of programs, for example, by stating, "Check to see if recycling facilities exist in your area." In similar circumstances, the statement "Recyclable where facilities exist" *would* be deceptive. Where only a few communities have recycling facilities, language such as "Recyclable in the few communities with facilities…" would *not* be deceptive.

Recycled content	Source reduction	Refillable, reusable	Ozone safe, ozone friendly	Comments
An article's contents contain at least 10%, by weight, postconsumer material	Not addressed	Not addressed	Any chemical or material released into the environment as a result of use or production will not migrate to the stratosphere and cause unnatural and accelerated deterioration of ozone	Currently under attack by various industry associations as violating both commercial and noncommercial free speech
Recycled-content claims should state the specific minimum percentage of recycled content. Both pre- and postconsumer secondary materials qualify as "recycled."	Not addressed	Not addressed	Vague statements such as "ozone friendly" are meaningless statements that imply environmental benefit. Extreme care should be used to make generalized statements like these explicit by providing specific product or packaging characteristics that explain the claimed benefit	Unlike FTC guides, permit "recyclable where facilities exist." Currently under review. New recommendations expected around year-end 1992
May be used for both pre- and postconsumer materials, so long as it would otherwise have entered the solid waste stream. Distinction may (but must not) be made between pre- and postconsumer materials. Example: A package with 20% recycled content by weight that is labeled "20% recycled paper" is *not* deceptive.	Source reduction claims should be qualified to the extent necessary to avoid consumer deception about the amount of the source reduction and about the basis for any comparison asserted.	An unqualified refillable claim should not be asserted unless a system is provided for: (1) the collection and return of the package or refill; or (2) the later refill of the package by consumers with product subsequently sold in another package. A package should not be marketed with an unqualified refillable claim, if it is up to the consumer to find new ways to refill the package	A claim, whether explicit or by inference, that a product does not harm the ozone layer is deceptive if the product contains an ozone-depleting substance. Example: A product labeled "ozone friendly" is deceptive if the product contains any ozone-depleting substance. Example: An unqualified claim that a product "contains no CFCs" is deceptive if the product contains any other ozone-depleting ingredients	The "recyclability" guidelines are somewhat less stringent than the guides in *Green Report II*. The "recycled-content" guides are substantially more generous than those in *Green Report II*. The "ozone safe/ozone friendly" guides do not address the fact that "ozone" has two referents: (1) stratospheric ozone (which the guides do address) and (2) lower-level ozone, i.e., smog (which the guides do *not* address). Under the FTC guides, an "ozone-friendly" claim would appear to be permissible if the product or package contains no stratospheric ozone-producing substances but does produce smog

Comparison of Environmental Labeling Guides and Regulations

Law and guidelines	Degradable, biodegradable, photodegradable	Compostable	Recyclable
Green Report II	Products currently disposed of primarily in landfills should not be promoted as "degradable," biodegradable," or "photodegradable." However, it may be appropriate to make "biodegradability" claims when a product is disposed of in a waste management facility designed to take advantage of biodegradability (such as a municipal solid waste composting facility) *and* the product will safely break down in that environment	Unqualified compostability claims should not be made unless a significant amount of the product is currently being composted everywhere the product is sold. In all other cases, compostability should be accompanied by a clear disclosure about the limited availability of this option. Without further clarification, "compostable where facilities exist" would not be acceptable for a product with limited composting locations	Unqualified recyclability claims should not be made for products sold nationally unless a significant amount of the product is being recycled everywhere the product is sold. Where a product is sold in many areas of the country, a qualified recyclability claim can be made. If consumers have little or no opportunity to recycle a product, recyclability claims should not be made
Indiana	Proven capability to decompose in less than one year in most common environment where disposed	Material will decompose into soil-like material in less than one year under controlled biological circumstances	Can be redeemed or returned at an identifiable recycling location for the purpose of returning the material to the economic mainstream
New York	Not addressed	Not addressed	(1) Access to community recyclable recovery programs available to no less than 75% of population; or (2) a statewide recycling rate of 50% has been achieved; or (3) a manufacturer, distributor, or retailer achieves a statewide recycling rate of 50%, or (4) within specific municipalities where ongoing source separation and recycling provides the opportunity of recycling
Rhode Island	Not addressed	Not addressed	(1) Must be a recyclable material as defined by Rhode Island laws; or (2) must have demonstrated the ability to achieve a minimum 50% recycling rate; or (3) must be entitled to wear the recycling emblem in at least five of the states of the Northeast Recycling Council representing at least 75% of the population of the region, even if the material is not otherwise recyclable in Rhode Island

Recycled content	Source reduction	Refillable, reusable	Ozone safe, ozone friendly	Comments
Recommends that only postconsumer material be referred to as "recycled," and that some other term be used to describe preconsumer secondary material	Source reduction claims should be specific, and where possible include percentages. Comparisons should be clear and complete	Not addressed	In promoting the removal of a single harmful ingredient or a few harmful ingredients from a product or package, care should be taken to avoid the impression that the product is good for the environment in all respects. Example: When the phrase "Contains no CFCs" misleads consumers into believing that the product is "safe for the ozone"	*Green Report II* bars recyclability claims where consumers have little or no opportunity to recycle. The FTC guides permit a heavily qualified recyclability claim in that situation. And whereas *Green Report II* requires advertisers to differentiate between pre- and postconsumer secondary material, the FTC guides make that distinction optional
Contains at least 10% by weight of postconsumer or postmanufacture material	Not addressed	Not addressed	A chemical or material released as a result of the use or production of the package will not migrate to the stratosphere and cause unnatural or accelerated deterioration of ozone	Extremely industry-friendly. Only one site anywhere required for "recyclable." Only 10% recycled content (pre- or postconsumer) required for "recycled-content"
Minimum percentages of pre- and postconsumer material by weight required for different product and packaging types. Example: Paper towels must have 80% secondary material, 40% postconsumer. Example: Plastic packaging must have 30% secondary material, 15% postconsumer.	Not addressed Not addressed	Original product or package can be returned for refilling or reuse a minimum of five times	Not addressed	Legislation governing other environmental labeling terms was introduced this year but not enacted
Percentage by weight of pre- and postconsumer material must be stated		Used or refilled a minimum of five times for its original purpose in a program established by the manufacturer, distributor, or retailer	Not addressed	Does not set minimum standards for recycled content. Instead, requires specific pre- and postconsumer levels to be stated.

SOURCE: *Green MarketAlert* (Bethlehem, Connecticut).

Green Seal and Scientific Certification Systems have similar objectives, but they have taken different approaches reflective of their sharply contrasting organizational identities. Green Seal was launched by Denis Hayes, an ex-lawyer with impeccable activist credentials who is widely viewed as one of the founding fathers of Earth Day.

The roots of SCS are more scientific than activist. Its president, Stanley Rhodes, is a toxicologist by training.

In its public utterances, SCS has tended to stress its scientific expertise, regularly implying that it takes a squadron of Ph.D.'s to deliver the sort of know-how that can make product certification a success. Green Seal has tended to be more market- and consumer-oriented, speaking in less technical language and directing its public comments more to questions of marketplace impact than to issues of technical feasibility.

The competition between the two organizations is reminiscent of the famous race between the tortoise and the hare. Surprisingly, given its heavy emphasis on technical know-how, it is SCS which has played the role of the hare. The organization has moved forward aggressively and erratically. It began by certifying specific aspects of a product's environmental performance—for instance, the recycled content of a package. More extensive "life cycle analyses," it claimed, were not technically feasible. In 1991, however, the organization did an abrupt about-face and came out for life cycle analysis, arguing that breakthroughs by the British specialist Ian Boustead had caused them to change their tune.

Green Seal, meanwhile, has played the tortoise to SCS' hare. The organization has proceeded slowly and steadily toward its goal, enduring substantial criticism along the way for moving too slowly. But by early 1992, proposed certification criteria had begun to flow from Green Seal, with re-refined motor oil, water-efficient fixtures, and toilet and facial tissue among the organization's early proposed standards. In early 1993, Green Seal issued its first seals.

Green Seal's approach to product certification is patterned after Canada's Environmental Choice program. Its so-called environmental impact evaluations do not make any claims to comprehensiveness, as SCS's model for life cycle assessment does. Only selected aspects of a product's life cycle performance (e.g., manufacturing, recycled content, toxic contaminants) are scrutinized by Green Seal. Whereas SCS proposes to examine every letter of the environmental "alphabet," Green Seal is limiting itself to evaluations of specific "letters."

Unlike Green Seal, SCS offers manufacturers a menu of options. In addition to opting for a full-scale LCA, companies can have specific aspects (e.g., recycled content) of the product and packaging combination certified. Or they can opt for a middle ground in which one or more areas of "environmental burden" are measured.

Many smaller manufacturers view third-party product certification more favorably. For them, product certification is a way to create a more level playing field. By and large, the major U.S. consumer goods companies have not been favorably disposed to product certification. For them, third-party certification represents an unwelcome and unnecessary intrusion into a laissez-faire market environment. They are leery about supporting the creation of any independent authority that could take decision-making authority away from them—and when they are being asked to have confidence in organizations as small and as untested as SCS and Green Seal, that makes them all the more resistant.

It will not be easy for SCS and Green Seal to establish product certification in the United States. These two organizations have taken on a task which by all rights belongs to the federal government. Still, there are pluses. For one thing, SCS's and Green Seal's efforts are not occurring in a vacuum. Internationally, the momentum for product certification is very strong, and the United States may not be able to withstand this momentum.

In addition, although many manufacturers resist third-party product certification, consumers support the idea. It is one of capitalism's most fundamental tenets that the company which listens to its customers gains a competitive edge. If one or more consumer goods companies harkens to this fact in the context of product certification, the door to product certification in the United States could open.

And indeed, this may already be happening. Glidden Paint Company, Occidental Chemical Corp., and Stone Container are among the major companies which have received SCS certification, and General Electric is among the companies which have applied for the Green Seal.

Meanwhile, product certification is proving to have another valuable function. Many companies are turning to SCS, Green Seal, and other organizations to audit the environmental performance of their products—not in order to affix a third-party seal to their product labels but in order to better understand how to improve the environmental performance of their products and packages.

Third-party certification is useful both in front of and behind the "corporate curtain." Many companies which are reluctant to use third-party certification as a core marketing strategy are finding it useful to apply the same information "behind the curtain."

Figure 15-4, from *Green Products by Design: Choices for a Cleaner Environment* (Office of Technology Assessment, 1992), displays selected eco-labels from around the world. Eco-labels, such as the government-sponsored ones from various countries shown, help consumers find environmentally preferred products.

The Consumer Goods Product and Supplier Structures

Over time, a clear dichotomy has emerged in the green products marketplace between "deep-green" products and small suppliers on the one hand, and "greened-up" products and major consumer goods companies on the other.

"Deep-green" products build their identity around their claimed environmental assets. These products typically have brand names like *Earth Wise* or *For the Planet*, they are built from the ground up to perform superbly from an environmental perspective, and they are offered by small suppliers.

"Greened-up" products are environmentally improved versions of established brand names. Their environmental appeal is generally secondary, and

Canada (Environmental Choice)   Nordic Countries (White Swan)

West Germany (Blue Angel)   Japan (EcoMark)

United States (Scientific
Certification Systems)*   United States (Green Seal)

Figure 15-4. Eco-labels around the world. (*"Green Products by Design," Office of Technology Assessment, 1992.*)

they are usually offered by major consumer goods companies. Procter & Gamble's Downy Refill is the prototypic example of a greened-up product success story: as noted above, it now accounts for over 40% of all Downy sales.

For a host of reasons (including retailer hesitancy, mixed consumer response, and shallow marketing pockets), "deep-green" products have not succeeded in establishing themselves on supermarket shelves. They are at risk of being relegated to an alternative channel consisting of health and natural product stores, an emerging category known as "earth stores," and other specialty distribution outlets. (However, inroads into mainstream channels *are* occurring. For instance, Earth Rite, a deep-green line of household cleaning products from Benckiser Consumer Products, is available at Wal-Mart's.)

"Greened-up" products, meanwhile, are well established on supermarket shelves. Indeed, they are doing better than many consumers realize, because in what has been a cautious marketing climate, environmental improvements have often gone unmentioned on product labeling.

The major consumer goods companies are controlling the rate of change in the green products marketplace. The changes they implement tend to be incremental, as distinguished from the quantum advances which many small suppliers would prefer.

What is required to shift the green products movement into overdrive is a commitment by a major consumer goods company to a "deep-green" product line. To date, most of the majors have steered away from this option, fearing "cannibalization" of other product lines. But if one or more of these companies decides that it is in their interest to offer deep-green products, the result would probably be a dramatic improvement in the market's receptivity to that product category.

The federal government is encouraging the "greening" of products in a number of ways. Table 15-1 shows a sampling of current projects.

Consumer Product Environmental Marketing Strategies

We now turn to recommended strategies for environmental marketing. There are eight "core principles" for marketing to consumers, and another four for commercial and institutional markets, which we discuss in the following section.

Recommendation 1: Make Sure That Your Program Is Backed by a Genuine Corporate Commitment

Environmental marketing programs that are not backed up by a serious, top-level corporate commitment to the environment should not exist. It is ethically inappropriate to engage in deceptive advertising—and to create an image of

Table 15-1. Federally Funded Programs Related to Green Design

Agency/office	Program/activity	Comments
Department of Energy:		
Office of Industrial Technologies	Industrial Waste Reduction Program	This research and development program aims to identify priority industrial waste streams, assess opportunities for addressing these waste streams through redesigning products and production processes, and technology transfer from national laboratories.
Environmental Protection Agency:		
Office of Research and Development	Environmental Research Guide	Contracted to the American Institute of Architects, this project will provide information to architects on the life-cycle environmental impacts of construction materials.
	Dynamic Case Studies on Environmentally Advanced Product Design	Contracted to the Resource Policy Institute in Los Angeles and the Product Life Institute in Geneva, this project will explore case studies involving green product design.
	Life Cycle Assessment Methodology	Contracted to Battelle, this project will develop standard methodologies for conducting product life-cycle assessments.
	Clean Products Case Studies	Contracted to INFORM, Inc., this project will provide case studies of green design, especially the reduced use of toxic substances in products.
	Safe Substitutes	Contracted to the University of Tennessee, this project will identify priority toxic chemicals and evaluate possible substitutes.
	Life Cycle Design Guidance Manual: Environmental Requirements and the Product System	Contracted to the University of Michigan, this manual will explore how designers can incorporate life-cycle information into their designs.
	National Pollution Prevention Center	Located at the University of Michigan, this center is developing waste prevention information modules for industrial and engineering design courses.
	American Institute for Pollution Prevention	In association with the University of Cincinnati, the institute serves as a liaison to a broad cross-section of industry, with projects involving four aspects of waste prevention; education, economics, implementation, and technology.
Office of Pollution Prevention and Toxics	Design for the Environment	Proposed program to gather, coordinate, and disseminate information on green design.
National Science Foundation:	Engineering Design Research Center	Located at Carnegie Mellon University, the center is organizing a program to explore methods for green design.

SOURCE: Office of Technology Assessment.

environmental commitment when that is in fact not the case is deception, pure and simple.

This is not to suggest that a corporation's track record must be blameless. No company's environmental track record is perfect. What *is* required, however, is genuine commitment at the highest corporate levels.

Insincere environmental marketing programs are also doomed to backfire. At one time it may have been possible to put one over on the public, but no longer. Consumers are on the lookout for deception, and they have an army of journalists and environmental advocacy groups to help them find it.

Recommendation 2: Sell Soft, Not Hard

Much of the public views our environmental crisis as having in large measure been created by selfish, "me-first" thinking on the part of corporations. Consumer-product marketers must take care to ensure that their environmental programs are not couched in terms that feed into this assumption. "Aren't-I-great" horn-tooting carries the same "All-that-matters-is-me" stamp which many consumers view as having contributed so heavily to our environmental predicament in the first place. The company that touts its own superiority is unwittingly feeding into consumers' worst assumptions about our corporate culture.

The best approaches to environmental marketing are indirect and "softer." This in turn boils down to two basic principles:

1. Focus not on "Who Am I?" but on "What Have I Done?" Leap-frog over *image* and discuss *actions*.

2. Discuss not "What Have *I* Done?" but "What Are *We* Doing?" With "me-first" thinking viewed so skeptically by consumers, it makes excellent sense to couch strategies in terms of "us-together"—so long, of course, as it is genuinely collaborative. Whenever possible, environmental marketing language should deemphasize the egocentric and focus on the collective nature of an enterprise.

Here are two real-life examples of "Selling Soft, Not Hard":

- First Brands, makers of Glad brand garbage bags, sponsors annual Glad Bag-a-Thons which bring citizens together to clean up parks and other scenic areas, using (of course) Glad garbage bags.

- In what evolved into a model of environmental labeling, Lever Brothers has used labeling that reads as follows: "PLEASE HELP! We are now using technology that can include recycled plastic in our bottles at levels between 25% and 35%. But to do so consistently, we need more recycled plastic. So please encourage recycling in your community. For more information, call 1-800-544-2002." The Lever Brothers language stands as a model of how to combine the principles of (1) "action, not image," and (2) an emphasis on collective activity.

Recommendation 3: Be Utterly and Indisputably Nondeceptive

In a time when survey after survey shows that consumers deeply distrust corporate communications, it is imperative for environmental communications to be completely above reproach. This requires marketers and public relations executives to do more than simply tell the truth. They must also not play "public-relations-as-usual" with the facts.

Whether a company is environmentally "responsible" or "irresponsible" is usually a matter of opinion, i.e., it tends to be in the eye of the beholder. This is because most corporations have a mixed track record—some positive instances of proactive environmental behavior and other less laudable examples. Old-style "public-relations-as-usual" accentuates the positive while explaining away the negative or sweeping it completely under the rug.

The problem with this approach tends not to be that it violates any laws (it usually doesn't) but that it twists complex truths into simple and favorable ones. Such a strategy is not (to return to the language of our injunction) "indisputably nondeceptive"—and so it should be avoided.

We recommend a more balanced public rendering of the facts. If Company X has some negatives in its history but is making a genuine effort to improve its performance environmentally, the best strategy is simply to say as much.

Recommendation 4: Emphasize Consumer Education

In the introduction to this chapter, we noted the need to approach environmental marketing with "one foot in the present and one foot on the other side of the millennium." The strategy dictated by the view from the other side of the millennium involves *consumer education,* for not until consumers' "depth-of-mind" commitment to the environment has strengthened will environmental consumerism become an embedded aspect of mass behavior.

Consumer education is good for business as well as the environment. It allows corporations to get their name out in front of consumers in a way that bespeaks good corporate citizenship, not blatant self-promotion; i.e., it provides an excellent example of how to "sell soft, not hard."

There are four basic approaches to consumer education:

1. *Sponsoring Environmental Exhibitions. Example:* In 1992, Church & Dwight sponsored an environmental exhibition at the United Nations in New York City immediately prior to the well-publicized United Nations Conference on the Environment and Development (UNCED) in Rio de Janeiro, Brazil.

It is often advisable to develop environmental exhibitions, and other forms of consumer education, in conjunction with environmental groups, which add legitimacy and expertise to the endeavor.

2. *Sponsoring and Developing Environmental Curricula.* This is an increasingly

popular strategy. Children have extremely high levels of environmental interest and sensitivity, and most programs are directed at the K-12 level. Two major retailers, Wal-Mart and Target Stores, have successfully helped launch variations on this theme in the form of national environmental clubs for kids.

In addition, more and more companies are working with business schools, often by providing them with case studies of environmental programs and policies. Corporations which have sponsored or developed environmental curricula for children in recent years include McDonald's, Browning-Ferris, and Procter & Gamble. Dow Chemical went even further: it sponsored a road show called *Recycle This!*—a staged presentation on recycling.

3. *Product-Related Initiatives.* This category ranges from simple labeling messages (e.g., "Please recycle") to single-company in-store displays—Church & Dwight's "Enviro-Centers" carried information about environmentally sensitive cleaning products, including, in Canada, non–Church & Dwight offerings such as lemon juice and vinegar—to complex multiparty promotional campaigns.

In the latter case, the importance of *reach* should not be overlooked. The more people who can be reached with a consumer education program, the better.

4. *Print and Electronic Information.* Another option is simply to deliver environmental information, either as "edu-tisements" (i.e., paid-for advertisements containing general information) or as public service announcements (PSAs).

Recommendation 5: To the Extent Possible, Target Niches

As we have seen, green consumerism is spreading. But although the percentage of dedicated green consumers is rising steadily, an environmentally oriented appeal is currently unlikely to induce a high percentage of middle-of-the-road consumers to try an unknown green product. At this stage of market development, carefully targeted environmental marketing campaigns that single out subgroups of consumers who have particularly high levels of environmental concern are most effective.

An example of such a strategy comes from EarthCare, Inc., a small, North-Carolina–based manufacturer of "eco-apparel." The company initially tried distributing its ValleyCare line of "environmentally friendly" socks in department stores, but demand was not strong enough to keep the products in that channel. The company then shifted its sights to sporting goods and outdoor and earth stores, which attract disproportionately high percentages of environmentally conscious consumers. The result: sharply improved performance for the ValleyCare line.

Down the road, as consumer sensitivity to environmental issues reaches a new level of awareness, broadbrush environmental marketing strategies will become more effective. In the meantime, the more an environmental marketing campaign can be "narrow-casted," the better.

Recommendation 6: Provide Extensive Retailer Support and Education

One of the core principles to have emerged from the early days of environmental marketing is that green products perform in direct proportion to the support they receive from retailers. If retailers understand, believe in, and actively market green products, those products will do well. If retailers ignore them, consumers will ignore them, too.

For this reason, manufacturers and suppliers should devote considerable energy to *retailer* education. Such a campaign should have at least two elements:

- *Pricing.* Many retailers believe that deep-green products must be priced at a premium. This is incorrect: they should be priced at parity. Retailers must be educated about the need for parity pricing.

- *Promotional support.* Retailers must receive substantial promotional support. As we have said, if a green product line is offered without significant retailer support, it will probably not do well. But if that same product is supported by an energetic, visible promotional and educational campaign, the odds for success are excellent. Suppliers must provide retailers with those materials.

Recommendation 7: Work with a Broad Range of Partners

By working with complementary allies, a range of objectives can be achieved which cannot be attained by a company working on its own.

- *Extension of reach.* Strategic alliances expand the reach of product marketers. The most direct way to achieve this is by partnering with the media, but alliances with other corporate partners can achieve the same effect. Let's say a food company partners with an automobile company. That gives the food company access to everyone who comes into the auto manufacturer's dealerships, and vice versa.

- *Access to expertise.* Strategic alliances often provide access to expertise that wouldn't be available in-house.

- *Access to intelligence.* Strategic alliances offer marketers a way to keep their antennae out about relevant developments in the environmental marketing and related arenas.

- *Entree.* Sometimes, strategic partners are also prospective customers. Whether it's the government, another corporation, or even an environmental group, establishing a relationship of trust can pave the way for future sales.

- *Influence.* It is a fact of life that you're likely to be treated better when you're inside the door than when you're outside it. Ask any corporation which has made a donation to an environmental group, and they'll object that heavens no, they haven't done it to influence the environmental group's policy! Still, there's a saying: "Stay close to your detractors." Strategic alliances allow businesses to do just that.

Appropriate candidates for environmental strategic alliances include (1) environmental groups, (2) government agencies, (3) retailers, (4) media, (5) trade associations, and (6) academic institutions.

Recommendation 8: Market to the Environment's Symbolic Meanings

The environment is a psychically charged symbol as well as a source of real-world concern. It is critically important for marketers to factor this often under-appreciated fact into their planning.

The San Francisco–based marketing consultancy American LIVES has elaborated on this hypothesis intriguingly. The company has identified three dominant world views in the United States (there are also a number of ethnic subgroups).

The Heartland Subculture. This group's primary loyalty is to traditionalism in American life. It is a world view nostalgic for the way people lived and believed around the turn of the century. For this group, the environment is a symbol of how the modern world has degraded what they love. They take the human-centered view that the environment warrants protection because it has *use value*—for hunting, boating, and so on.

The Winner Subculture. This group has adopted the dominant views of modern business America. Its most important value is "making it in life." This is typically associated with having a high income and net worth. Winners tend to see the environment in terms of its impact on their financial well-being.

The Person-Centered Green Subculture. This group represents the emerging postindustrial faction of American culture. Its members are well educated and heavily professional. They represent the *culturally* rather than the *technologically* creative part of the population. Cultural changes and reframings of social perception frequently start with them—including environmentalism.

Person-Centered Greens take a more metaphysical approach to the environment than Heartlands or Winners. The environment is not viewed simply as something we'd better take care not to "use up" but as something which should be treated preciously because of its own intrinsic value.

For environmental messages to really hit home with these subcultures, it's not enough simply to talk about the environment. It's also necessary to plug into the specific connotations that each of these groups poses on their idea of the environment. The environment *as symbol* is as important as the environment as fact.

The Eight Recommended Consumer Environmental Marketing Strategies

1. Make sure that your program is backed by a genuine corporate commitment.

2. Sell soft, not hard.

3. Be utterly and indisputably nondeceptive.

4. Emphasize consumer education.

5. To the extent possible, target niches.

6. Provide extensive retailer support and education.

7. Work with a broad range of partners.

8. Market to the environment's symbolic meanings.

Business-to-Business Environmental Marketing Strategies

Recommendation 1: Prioritize Your Targets Carefully

While burgeoning environmental regulation has substantially increased demand for products which enable companies and institutions to "green up" their operations, it is not the case that opportunities in the commercial green-products market are purely regulation-driven. Some companies simply want to do the right thing environmentally. While regulation is a major driver of commercial demand for green products, it is important to identify and pursue opportunities that are not purely regulation-driven.

It is also important to keep in mind that while the overall level of environmental commitment on the part of corporations is rising, it varies sharply from industry to industry and from company to company. Specific needs vary from industry to industry, too. For instance, consumer packaged goods manufacturers have a particularly strong need for recycled materials for their packaging, while the automobile, refrigeration, and computer industries need alternatives to CFCs and other ozone-depleting chemicals.

These particulars notwithstanding, the number of commercial and institutional targets for green products is, for all intents and purposes, limitless. How does one best prioritize among these myriad opportunities? There are two basic keys.

1. By the Level of "Green-ness." Perhaps it goes without saying that companies and industries with established reputations for environmental sensitivity are the ones to target first. However, this is often easier said than done. Some companies are very quiet about their environmental activities; other companies get a lot of positive play for their environmental commitment but don't back it up with their purchasing power. No service currently tracks (much less rates) U.S. companies' environmental performance on anything approaching a comprehensive basis. However, independent resources such as the New York–based Council on Economic Priorities' Shopping for a Better World and the Washington, D.C.–based Investor Responsibility Research Center's Environmental Information Service are useful places to begin.

2. By Public Relations Incentive.   There's a flip side to the truism that it's easiest to sell green products to the companies that are the most green. The use of green products can produce positive public relations play—and often, the companies which most badly need favorable environmental publicity are the ones with the most problematic reputations.

Baroid Drilling Fluids (Houston, Texas) is hoping to capitalize on the public relations benefits offered by its Petrofree environmentally sensitive drilling fluid. Oil companies are under fire from the public, and eager to highlight their environmental commitment.

Green products can also produce public relations benefits for companies that aren't under the gun environmentally. For example, food service companies reap positive publicity from using napkins made from recycled paper.

Even companies that aren't avowedly green can be steered in that direction. One way to do this is by presenting management with evidence (letters, memos, environmental policies, etc.) establishing that more and more companies are favoring suppliers who are themselves green or whose products or processes can help them "green up" their own operations. In such presentations, the focus should be on the fact that a proactive environmental policy is good for business. Benefits to the environment should be positioned as ancillary.

Recommendation 2: Target the Corporate Environmental Conscience

Once your target companies have been identified, the next step is to figure out which individuals inside the company to target with your sales pitch. It's important to keep corporate purchasing agents in the loop, but these individuals are rarely the heart and soul of the corporate environmental conscience. Ideally, the company's environmental leaders (who can often be found on the corporate environmental committee) will be brought into the sales process. But this must be done delicately, so as not to step on the toes of the purchasing agents.

There is no simple algorithm for ensuring that all the needed people are kept in the sales loop on just the right upbeat note. Orchestrating an optimal purchase environment inside a prospect corporation is a subtle business, but well worth the trouble.

Recommendation 3: Price at Parity

Green products *must* be priced competitively with nongreen alternatives—if not on an ounce-for-ounce basis, then on a net cost basis. This is more easily done in commercial than in consumer channels because, as noted above, businesses have to take into account such factors as the costs of disposing materials cleaned with corrosive, often toxic chemicals. But the basic truth still holds that both businesses and consumers are extremely price-sensitive when it comes to green products.

Recommendation 4: Know Your Issues

As we have stressed in this chapter, environmental issues are very complex, and there is a great deal of ignorance about them. In the business-to-business context, it is important for sales representatives to be fully informed about the full array of environmental issues associated with their target companies, with their own company, and with the green products they are selling. The sales process is an information-dissemination process, and better-informed sales representatives outperform those who aren't so well prepared.

Making sure that your sales force is fully informed about all relevant environmental issues requires determination and commitment. A focused, coordinated training program is required. Nor can this be a one-time program. To ensure that your company's representatives are up to date on all the key issues, there must be regular training programs.

In the business-to-business environment, as in consumer channels, education is key. Prospects must be educated—and so must one's own colleagues.

The Four Recommended Business-to-Business Environmental Marketing Strategies

1. Prioritize your targets carefully.
2. Target the corporate environmental conscience.
3. Price at parity.
4. Know your issues.

Into the Next Millennium

Let us now cross the great divide of the year 2000 and paint a portrait of the likely state of green consumerism in the early years of the next century.

Point 1. Environmental consciousness has continued to increase among consumers: the Roper/Johnson Survey for the year 2002, now in its seventh iteration, has identified 33% of the public as True-Blue Greens and another 12% as Greenback Greens, bringing to 45% the percentage of U.S. adults who qualify as truly "green."

Point 2.   "Deep-green" products have made it out of the alternative channels and onto supermarket shelves. The majority of products remain either "brown" or "greened-up," but at least one "deep-green" product is available in virtually every product category—and not just on the east and west coasts, where the levels of green consumerism continue to be highest, but in supermarkets throughout the country.

Point 3.   Product certification programs have much more name recognition than they do today, and they have been shown to aid sales. They are a common but not a universal consumer-product marketing strategy.

Point 4.   Businesses have continued to climb the curve of environmental responsibility. Most significant is their increasing sensitivity to the concept of sustainable development, which has resulted in (1) the more efficient use of environmental "inputs"; (2) greater control of environmental "outputs;" and, at a more philosophical level, (3) an increased appreciation of the merits of cooperation vs. competition. Another consequence: increased demand for green products.

In summary, we envision a business environment in which the growing pains of environmental marketing have largely been worked through and in which businesses are taking their environmental obligations more seriously than ever. In the post-2000 era, principles of interdependence and cooperation will be that much more embedded in the superstructure of corporate values.

Leading Principles

What principles of environmental marketing will dominate the postmillennium era? We anticipate five characteristics in particular:

Environment as a High Priority.   With the current uncertainties regarding what differentiates reprehensible "green marketing" from appropriate "environmental marketing" long since resolved, the environment will be firmly established as a core marketing strategy. Discussions of environmental attributes on products' packaging will be standard operating procedure. The emphasis will be on the specifics of performance—whether of a product or a company—rather than on the generalities of abstract commitment.

Emphasis on Participatory Activities and Relationship Building.   Both at the macro level, with examples such as Japan's hugely successful Ministry of Trade and Industry, and at the more micro level, i.e., at the level of specific strategic alliances, we are currently witnessing a growing appreciation of the benefits of cooperation. An awareness is entering into business's collective consciousness that, all else being equal, it is better to work with than against.

This awareness will be that much more firmly established in the post-2000 time frame, and it will be reflected in corporate environmental marketing strategies by heightened emphasis on participatory activities. On the business-to-business side, there will be more and more strategic alliances. As for the business-consumer connection, here too we expect to see more shared projects, in large measure because it is through shared activities that trust is created—and as we have seen, businesses have a heavy burden of distrust to overcome.

A corollary of this emphasis on participatory activities will be a heightened emphasis on *relationship building*. This, too, is already a coming theme. Here, the guiding philosophy is that companies should position themselves not as "selling to" but as "working with" one's customer base. Instead of a series of static, independent sales "hits," the supplier-customer relationship is an ongoing, dynamic, interactive process, with the parties participating in this process in a spirit of cooperation for their mutual benefit. In the post-2000 time frame, the fundamentally holistic nature of the supplier-customer relationship will be that much more firmly established.

And what better theme to rally around, or to work together on, than the environment? For it is the environment—more specifically, the model of the ecosystem—that has exemplified many of the holistic principles which businesses are now beginning to incorporate into their policies and practices. The inescapable conceptual link between the environment and the holistically oriented emphases on shared activities and relationship building makes it logical to expect the environment to play a central role in the cooperation and partnership marketing strategies of many organizations.

Open Doors, Lowered Walls.   As businesses increasingly come to recognize the extent to which they are interdependent, greater openness will become the norm for corporate communications. Corporations will display a greater willingness to expose hitherto private information to public scrutiny.

In addition to core-level changes in business values, this change will also trace back to the firm hand of government regulation: the SARA Title III Community Right-to-Know laws in particular have forced companies to go public with their environmental releases to air, water, and land.

This attitude will help narrow the credibility gap that currently separates U.S. corporations from consumers—and this, in turn, will make U.S. consumers that much more receptive to environmental marketing strategies.

An Increased Appreciation of "Semiotics."   Most corporate environmental marketing programs focus on the environment as an "external" entity—an appropriate focus, to be sure, but not the only one. In the post-2000 time frame, marketers will increasingly recognize the potency of the environment as an internal *symbol.* Not only will the "semiotics" of the environment be more frequently targeted, but it will increasingly take into account the unique emotions which specific consumer segments overlay on the environment.

Consumer Education—Still a Priority. But with all these changes, one feature will remain the same. Consumer education will continue to be a high priority. We are more in the dark about the environment than we care to admit. We will know more in the post-2000 era, but not so much more that the need for education will have been put behind us. As we move up the environmental learning curve, more light will be shed, but new pockets of darkness will also be uncovered. The need for education is ongoing.

Case Study: Church & Dwight Co., Inc.

Church & Dwight, the $500 million manufacturer of Arm & Hammer baking soda products, operates a comprehensive environmental marketing program whose benefits, in the opinion of Church & Dwight management, have far exceeded the program's relatively modest costs. The program is built on principles which in many ways mirror those espoused in this chapter: (1) a commitment to continuously improving its environmental performance; (2) an emphasis on consumer education; and (3) a preference for strategic alliances, often with multiple partners.

Commitment to Continuous Improvement

Through the vehicle of total quality environmental management (TQEM), Church & Dwight has made a commitment to continuously improving its environmental performance.

Emphasis on Consumer Education

Church & Dwight's primary emphasis has been on consumer education. Among the company's educational activities:

- Funding the national rollout of a volunteer-staffed education effort by the environmental group Clean Water Action to assist consumers in identifying shopping choices that will have a positive impact on the environment.
- Installing "Enviro-Centers" in thousands of supermarkets in the United States. These displays presented Arm & Hammer products, a brochure, *Be an Environmentally Alert Consumer* published by the Environmental Protection Agency, and other literature explaining how consumers could use these basic products. In Canada, they also showed other natural ingredients for household cleaning, such as lemon juice, cornstarch, and vinegar.
- Distributing an "Environmental Use Wheel" which identifies 37 household chores that can be performed with Arm & Hammer products.

A Preference for Strategic Alliances

This policy has led to the creation of several ingenious environmental marketing campaigns, an example of which follows.

UN Environmental Exhibit. Church & Dwight was the main sponsor of a high-visibility multimedia environmental education exhibit which involved numerous partners from both the public and the private sectors. The exhibit was displayed in the lobby of the United Nations in New York City immediately prior to the UN Conference on the Environment and Development (UNCED) in Rio de Janeiro in 1992.

For maximum cost-effective market reach, Church & Dwight recruited as cosponsors a leading retailer and a major publisher. Both organizations offered extensive reach which would not otherwise have been available.

A number of significant public-sector organizations were also involved in the project, including the U.S. Environmental Protection Agency, the U.S. Department of State, and other major national and international organizations including UNEP and UNESCO.

An unexpected, but by no means trivial, benefit of the promotion was that it attracted the attention of the U.S. Department of Defense, which is a significant potential user of Church & Dwight's commercial products. The exhibit thus served as a calling card for the company—in effect, as a letter of introduction.

In Summary

The American public is growing increasingly sensitive to environmental issues, and this is being reflected in their attitudes and buying behavior. Corporations, too, are becoming more and more "green." Slowly but surely, a fundamental change is taking place in how people view their relationship with and responsibilities toward the environment. Because of this enduring transformation, environmental marketing should be a core marketing strategy for the 1990s and beyond.

Four words summarize our recommended approach to consumer-oriented environmental marketing: (1) integrity, (2) information, (3) collaboration, and (4) sensitivity.

1. *Integrity.* Consumers assume the worst of corporate environmental communications. To counterbalance this bias (as well as for straightforward ethical reasons), environmental marketing communications must do more than merely not be deceptive. They must also take pains not to invite a perception of deceptiveness. When it comes to environmental marketing, the most rigorous set of standards imaginable applies.

2. *Information.* Consumers badly need to be educated about environmental issues, and environmental marketing can and should perform this function. In addition to its public policy benefits, consumer education programs allow cor-

porations to put themselves in the favorable position of "working with" rather than "selling to."

3. *Collaboration.* In environmental marketing, partnerships are as a rule advisable. By working with environmental groups, corporations can increase their credibility and expand their expertise. By partnering with media companies, they can extend their reach. By joining forces with consumers, they can create the impression that they are working toward a common goal, rather than exploiting.

4. *Sensitivity.* The environment is not only a physical reality in the external world. It is also a symbol, one that means different things to different people. The most effective environmental marketing strategies will be sensitive to this fact and address the issues which arise out of the environment's symbolic content as well as those which are a function of its physical existence.

As with consumer marketing, education is paramount in business-to-business environmental marketing. Keys to effectively marketing green commercial products include (1) carefully and effectively prioritizing prospects, (2) marketing on a value-oriented basis, i.e., pricing at parity (simply being "green" is not enough), and (3) bringing the "corporate conscience" into the sales loop.

Bibliography

Blueprint for Green Marketing, by Carl Frankel. American Demographics, April 1992.

Environmental Marketing, by Walter Coddington, McGraw-Hill.

Green MarketAlert—A monthly newsletter tracking the marketing implications and business impacts of green consumerism. Published by The Bridge Group, Bethlehem, Connecticut.

Green Products by Design—Choices for a Cleaner Environment, U.S. Congress, Office of Technology Assessment, October 1992.

Guides for the Use of Environmental Marketing Claims, Federal Trade Commission, July 1992.

Hartman Environmental Research & Strategies—A business study containing data about green consumerism, corporate environmentalism, and recommended marketing and communications strategies. Published by The Hartman Group, Newport Beach, California.

PART 7

Environmental Business

16

Environmental Business: Markets and Prospects*

Rao V. Kolluru, DrPH
CH2M Hill

Michael E. Silverstein
Environmental Economics

In this chapter:

- Overview
- Market Segments and Growth Prospects
- Financial Performance
- Key Factors for Success/Environmental Management Consulting
- International Perspectives and Export Opportunities

Overview

"Environmental business" is involved with the protection and preservation of the environment—the air, the water, the land, the energy, the biota—the fundamental resources that sustain human life and economic activity. Paraphrasing a DuPont commercial, one might ask: What in the world isn't environmental?

*Grant Ferrier, publisher of *Environmental Business Journal,* reviewed and contributed to this chapter.

The U.S. environmental industry consists of some 35,000 diverse companies employing about a million people, or 1% of the work force. It is a high-profile industry that presents the opportunity to "do well by doing good." In 1991, revenues of U.S. environmental product and service companies totaled about $120 billion, or 2% of the gross national product, in line with major industrial nations. The global "market," including the United States, is almost $300 billion (Table 16-1).

Driven by the environmental movement, public health concerns, regulatory forces, and liability issues (not to mention the numerous consultants and lawyers), the U.S. environmental industry has been growing at 10 to 20% per year over the last two decades, and in the late 1980s was a Wall Street favorite. The 1990–91 recession, however, proved that even the environmental business is not recession-proof. In addition, the business is showing some signs of maturity and leveling; longer-term, the overall growth rate is projected at a respectable 6 to 10% rather than the phenomenal 10 to 20% of recent years. Some of this change is a matter of definition of what constitutes environmental business but, more remarkably, it will be thanks to the shift from a "linear economy" (mining to manufacture, use to waste) to a "circular economy" that emphasizes reuse and sustainable development. The major portion of environmental expenditures today go toward rectifying results of past practices. We anticipate three related developments: (1) a progressive net decline in the inventory of sites and sources to be remediated or cleaned up; (2) increasing adoption of risk-based criteria in addition to technology that result in more cost-effective courses of action; and (3) the shift of emphasis from controls to prevention and from operating expenses to capital investments that yield financial benefits and competitive advantages in a sustainable economy.

This chapter and the next will provide some insights into the nature of, and prospects for, the environmental industry—the suppliers of products and services to the regulated community. Environmental expenditures of companies as a percent of revenues range from less than 1% for consumer goods, 1 to 2% for

Table 16-1. Global Environmental Market Estimates, Billion Dollars

	1991	1996	Annual growth, %
United States	120	170	7–8
Canada	10	17	11
Mexico	2	4	14
Latin America	6	10	12
Western Europe	82	130	9
Eastern Europe (Russia)	14	27	14
Japan	21	31	8
Australia and New Zealand	3	5	9
Southeast Asia	6	11	14
Rest of the world	16	25	9
Total (rounded)	280	430	9

Primary Source: Environmental Business International

oil and chemicals, to 6% or more for utilities—with an overall industry average of slightly less than 2%. Critical factors for survival and success in the increasingly competitive arena are also identified.

Students and others may find these chapters helpful in planning their careers as well. Among the myriad professionals involved in the environmental industry are chemical, civil, and environmental engineers, biologists, chemists, geologists, hydrogeologists, ecologists, meteorologists, modelers, toxicologists, industrial hygienists, health physicists, epidemiologists and other public health professionals, lawyers, economists, computer systems analysts, urban planners, sociologists, and marketers, with traditional sanitary engineers being in the distinct minority.

The evolution of "environmentalism" in selected countries and the international opportunities presented by recent developments are also discussed here. (See Part 8 for more detailed discussion of international issues.)

Market Segments and Growth Prospects

Transformation of Environmental Business

Definitions of what constitutes the environmental business vary, as also the estimates of market size and growth prospects (Figs. 16-1 and 16-2). The reasons for these differences are manifold:

- Numerous firms in a variety of fields serve this market: pollution-control equipment manufacturers, solid-waste and hazardous-waste management

Figure 16-1. U.S. environmental market pyramid.

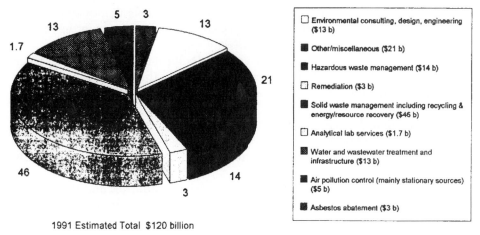

1991 Estimated Total $120 billion

Figure 16-2. U.S. environmental expenditures by segment.

firms, water-treatment companies, chemical producers, consulting and engineering firms, construction contractors, analytical laboratories, recyclers and resource recovery firms, to name a few. There is no specific standard industrial classification (SIC) code to delineate environmental industry products.

- Many environmental firms are privately held (e.g., CH2M Hill, Woodward-Clyde) and offer limited marketing and financial data. In the case of large publicly held companies, a relatively small portion of the total revenues are derived from the environmental field, typically without a clear breakdown of the environmental share.

- Some market estimates include in-house expenditures by regulated companies for environmental compliance and related matters (amounting to about $50 billion), and there is a possibility of some double counting. Yet other estimates include government agency expenditures for administration and enforcement ($10 to $15 billion). Some of the higher estimates include "generic" construction carried out by other than "environmental" firms. Some estimates are in constant dollars whereas others are in current year dollars. Differences also exist in how exports and imports are accounted for.

- Perhaps the most formidable difficulty in defining environmental business is presented by the dramatic shift that is occurring in U.S. industry: from environmental operating expenses to capital outlays, and from predominantly pollution-control compliance costs to investments that yield future revenues and competitive advantages (stimulated by the cradle-to-cradle thinking that is beginning to appear in some circles).

Despite the differences in business definitions and the difficulties in estimating the markets and outlook, the studies we have seen from EPA, consultants, and international organizations point to a U.S. market of about $120 billion in

1991 (Table 16-2). All the estimates and growth projections shown in this chapter are in current year dollars unless noted otherwise.

The Superfund Program

The law that drastically changed and expanded the scope of the environmental business was established by the Comprehensive Environmental Response, Compensation, and Liability Act (CERCLA) of 1980, amended by the Superfund Amendments and Reauthorization Act (SARA) of 1986. (Because of the high proportion of "transaction costs" typical of the program, CERCLA came to be known as the "Comprehensive Employment Rejuvenation for Consultants and Lawyers Act.") The Superfund program was created to clean up "orphaned" and uncontrolled hazardous-waste sites. (The RCRA programs, on the other hand, generally apply to ongoing and operating facilities.)

Sites discovered through citizen reports, federal and state inspections, etc., are investigated by the EPA and ranked by a hazard ranking system based on contamination or migration potential of hazardous substances in groundwater, surface water, soil, and air; explosion or fire hazard; and possibilities for direct human contact at the site. The "worst" sites above the cutoff score (28.5 on a scale of 0 to 100) are included in the National Priorities List (NPL). All sites considered for a Superfund cleanup are included in CERCLIS (Comprehensive Environmental Response, Compensation, and Liability Information System). As of March 1992, the NPL had 1275 sites including federal facilities, and CERCLIS 35,984 sites. The Oil and Hazardous Materials National Contingency Plan (NCP) provides the framework for implementing the Superfund program. One of the key provisions is to compel potentially responsible parties (PRPs) or responsible parties (RPs) to pay for cleanup through joint and several responsibility for contributing to the problem.

Superfund consists of two subprograms: the Removal Program responds quickly to emergencies such as spills and where hazardous materials may have been released or threatened to be released; the Remedial Program is dedicated to long-term cleanup actions. The different stages in a remedial program and the distribution of NPL sites are shown in the table. The remediation market for Superfund and other sites is discussed later.

Stage	Number of sites	Percent
Removals only	17	1.3
Remedial investigations and feasibility studies (RI/FS)	438	35
Records of decision (ROD)	93	7
Remedial designs (RD)	204	16
Remedial actions (RA)	357	28
Construction completed	80	6
Awaiting action	86	7
Total NPL sites	1275	100

SOURCE: EPA, 1992. Superfund Progress—Aficionado's Version: Progress as of March 31, 1992.

Business Segments

The U.S. environmental industry is highly fractionated and has been operating somewhat laissez-faire with thousands of individual consultants, environmental firms, and engineering and construction firms ranging in revenues from thousands of dollars to billions of dollars. The majority of the leading environmental consulting, engineering, and design firms shown in the following tables had their origins actually in other than the "environmental field" but have gravitated toward the business as a natural extension of their expertise and interests.

For the purposes of discussion, the environmental industry can be divided into nine segments, although the definitions are somewhat arbitrary and considerable overlap exists among the different segments. These business segments and their growth prospects are outlined in Table 16-2.

Environmental Consulting, Engineering, and Design

The environmental consulting firms provide front-end services such as assessing the problems, identifying alternative approaches, and designing the preferred alternative for implementation. Typical of these services are CERCLA/Superfund remedial investigation/feasibility studies (RI/FS) and RCRA corrective actions including facility investigation/corrective measures studies (RFI/CMS). The consulting services have been the fastest-growing business segment with annual growth of 20 to 30% that reached an estimated $13 billion market by 1991. Industrial clients account for about 60% of revenues, federal one-third, and municipal and state the balance. Hazardous waste, water, and air have been the main focus of these consulting services.

Table 16-2. U.S. Environmental Expenses and Revenues by Segment, 1991–2001 Estimates, Billion Dollars

Business segment	1991	1996	2001	Annual growth, %
Environmental consulting, design, engineering	13	25	50	10–20
Hazardous-waste management	14	16	18	2–3
Remediation	3	7	20	20–30
Solid-waste management including recycling and energy/resource recovery	46	63	80	5–7
Water and wastewater treatment and infrastructure	13	16	20	3–5
Air-pollution control (mainly stationary sources)	5	10	30	15–30
Asbestos abatement	3	3.5	4	2–3
Analytical lab services	1.7	2.3	3	5–6
Other/miscellaneous	21	27	35	5–6
Total (rounded)	120	170	260	7–10

Adapted from *Environmental Business Journal*, April 1992; A. Farkas and J. Berkowitz of Farkas Berkowitz & Co.; Miller & Associates: Environmental Markets 1992–1995; EPA, 1990. Environmental Investments: The Cost of a Clean Environment.

In the 1990s, the consulting practice is still projected to grow at a strong 10 to 20% annual rate to $25 billion by the late 1990s. The higher end of the range is related to the remediation market. At least half the revenues will be derived from hazardous waste, followed by the rejuvenated air and water quality markets. The share of the federal sector (DOE, DOD) will expand further but is expected to put downward pressure on prices and profit margins. The consulting practice is people-intensive and will remain highly competitive with low capital requirements and few barriers to entry. See Table 16-3 for a list of firms in this field.

Hazardous-Waste Management

This sector consists of off-site facilities to treat, recover, or dispose of hazardous waste, and on-site management of ongoing waste streams. At $14 billion in annual revenues, it is second only to solid waste in market size; chemical waste makes up the largest volume with nuclear and medical waste, accounting for at least $1 billion each. Over the next 10 years, this segment is projected to grow at a modest 2 to 4% because of anticipated decline in hazardous-waste generation as a result of accelerated waste-minimization efforts, spiraling costs of disposal (from $200 or so per ton for secure landfill to $2000 per ton for some incineration processes), surplus capacity, and liability concerns (future Superfunds!).

The leading participants in this segment include:

- Chemical Waste Management—largest and most diversified (Unit of Waste Management, the "mutual fund" of environmental industry)

- Laidlaw Environmental Services—transportation, headquartered in Canada

- Rollins, ENSCO, Ross, Westinghouse—incineration

- DuPont—largest aqueous waste treatment

- Safety-Kleen—solvent and oil recovery, small quantity generators

- USPCI—Union Pacific subsidiary

- Horsehead Resource Development—zinc recovery from electric arc furnace dust

- AETC—research laboratory and small generator waste

- Other firms: metal extraction, polymer and chemical recycling, cement kiln, and other disposal methods

Remediation

Remediation is the actual cleanup phase and includes emergency response actions, e.g., spill cleanup; short-term measures called "interim remedial measures" (IRMs) involving, for example, removal or containment of leaking

Table 16-3. Gross Revenues from Environmental Projects, FY 1991

Leading Environmental Consulting, Engineering, and Design Firms

1. CH2M Hill Cos. Ltd. (Denver, Colorado)	$485 million
2. International Technology Corp. (Torrance, California)	368
3. Metcalf & Eddy Cos. Inc. (Wakefield, Massachusetts)	331
4. Roy F. Weston, Inc. (West Chester, Pennsylvania)	315
5. Camp Dresser & McKee Inc. (Cambridge, Massachusetts)	268
6. Dames & Moore (Los Angeles, California)	245
7. ENSR/American NuKem Corp. (Mahwah, New Jersey)	240
8. The ERM Group (Exton, Pennsylvania)	220
9. J.M. Montgomery Consulting Engineers Inc. (Pasadena, California)	180
SAIC (McLean, Virginia)	180
Ebasco Services, Inc. (New York, New York)	180
10. Black & Veatch (Kansas City, Missouri)	166
11. Radian Corp. (Austin, Texas)	160
12. Groundwater Technology Inc. (Norwood, Massachusetts)	159
13. Engineering-Science Inc. (Pasadena, California)	137
14. Woodward-Clyde Consultants Group Inc. (Denver, Colorado)	131
15. Geraghty & Miller Inc. (Plainview, New York)	127
16. Environmental Science & Engineering Inc. (Peoria, Illinois)	121
17. Malcolm Pirnie Inc. (White Plains, New York)	112
18. Halliburton NUS Environmental Corp. (Gaithersburg, Maryland)	110
19. Law Cos. Group Inc. (Atlanta, Georgia)	108
20. SEC-Donahue Inc. (Greenville, South Carolina)	101
21. Ecology and Environment Inc. (Lancaster, New York)	100
22. Brown & Caldwell Consultants (Pleasant Hill, California)	94
23. McLaren/Hart Environmental Engineering (New York, New York)	86
24. EMCON Associates (San Jose, California)	80
25. Harding Associates Inc. (Novato, California)	77
26. BCM Engineers Inc. (Plymouth Meeting, Pennsylvania)	76
27. URS Consultants Inc. (Paramus, New Jersey)	74
28. Ogden Environmental and Energy Services Co. (Fairfax, Virginia)	70
29. ABB Environmental Services, Inc. (Portland, Maine)	70
30. Golder Associates Corp. (Atlanta, Georgia)	67

Leading Environmental Construction Firms

1. Bechtel Group Inc. (San Francisco, California)	$956 million
2. Fluor Daniel Inc. (Irvine, California)	650
3. The M. W. Kellogg Co. (Houston, Texas)	400
4. Foster Wheeler Corp. and subsidiaries (Clinton, New Jersey)	350
5. United Engineers & Constructors Intl. Inc. (Philadelphia, Pennsylvania)	340
6. Parsons Environmental Services Inc. (Pasadena, California)	322
7. Morrison Knudsen Corp. (Boise, Idaho)	298
8. Jacobs Engineering Group Inc. (Pasadena, California)	259
9. ICF Kaiser Engineers Inc. & affiliates (Oakland, California)	241
10. Stone & Webster Engineering Corp. (Boston, Massachusetts)	227

SOURCE: *Environmental Business Journal,* April 1992. The revenue estimates are approximate and have been compiled from information provided by the companies, industry analysts, and published sources.

drums, fire or explosion sources, and other imminent hazards; and long-term "permanent" solutions (e.g., incineration) that follow the study and design phases.

Principal areas of remedial focus are Superfund and RCRA sites, Department of Energy (DOE) and Department of Defense (DOD) facilities, and the various state-designated sites (Table 16-4). The typical cost range for Superfund-type projects is $20 to $40 million, but by far the majority of remedial projects [e.g., leaking underground storage tanks (LUSTs)] cost less than $5 million.

Given all the publicity about Superfund, RCRA, and other remedial programs, and the high level of public concern about both abandoned and operating hazardous-waste sites, the $3 to 6 billion spent in 1991 seems almost anticlimactic. Unfortunately, in the United States, 80 to 85% of of the money goes into "transaction costs" of the study and argument phase with only 15 to 20% left for actual remediation, in contrast to Canada and Europe, where industry-government cooperation and quick decisions channel 80 to 85% of the funds into remedial actions. The high front-end costs in the United States are a reflection of at least three factors: (1) there has been a heavy emphasis on prolonged study phase in regulatory enforcement; (2) remedial actions cost seven to eight times more than front-end studies, hence organizations are inclined to defer such outlays; and (3) a great deal of uncertainty pervades remedial projects because of a lack of expe-

Table 16-4. Remediation Market Potential, Billion Dollars

	Approx number of sites/units	Market estimates, billions		Long-term cumulative potential ~ 30 years
		1991	1996	
■ Superfund		$1.3	$2.5	>$200 billion
NPL	1,275			
CERCLIS	36,000			
■ RCRA			Included in industrial and other categories	20–60
Sites	2,400			
SWMUs	50,000			
■ Department of Energy (DOE)	67	0.8	2.1	200–400
■ Department of Defense (DOD)	7,200	0.6	1.2	>50–100
■ State programs	22,000	0.8	1.2	40–80
■ USTs, total	~ 500,000 (a fraction to be remediated)	1.0	2.0	20–30
■ Industrial/private		1.5	2.0	?
Total		6	11	$1000 billion ?

Remediation expenditures in 1991 were estimated at $3 to $6 billion. The projected market of $11 billion in 1996 shown here is at the higher end of some estimates, while the $7 billion shown in Table 16-2 is at the lower end of the range.

rience with such projects, which consequently leads to overengineering. In the 12 years of Superfund existence and expenditure of billions of dollars, cleanups have been completed at 80 NPL sites and 40 sites have been deleted. (However, this understates the degree of reduction in public safety and health risks through interim actions and RI/FS or cleanups in progress at most other sites as discussed earlier.)

Examples of major remediation firms are:

Engineering/construction firms: Bechtel, Ebasco, Fluor, Foster-Wheeler, ICF, Jacobs, Parsons, Stone & Webster

Consulting/engineering firms: CH2M Hill, Dames & Moore, Halliburton/Brown & Root Environmental, International Technology, Morrison-Knudson, Roy F. Weston

Chemical company units: AWD Technologies (Dow subsidiary, external focus), DuPont Environmental Remediation Services ("DERS," internal focus)

Defense contractors: Lockheed, TRW, Westinghouse

Other more specialized firms: Canonie, Groundwater Technology, Handex (predominantly USTs), OHM, Riedel, Sevenson

The engineering/construction firms enjoy many advantages in competing for remedial projects: experience in bidding and carrying out large-scale "turnkey" and other construction projects; own labor force to draw from; financial strength to post performance bonds; and substantial liability coverage. Many large consulting firms such as Camp Dresser & McKee (CDM), ERM, and Woodward-Clyde have also been positioning themselves to integrate "downstream" into remedial design and implementation phases and in recent years have strengthened their construction management capabilities. Initially, many consulting/engineering companies are likely to rely on outside subcontractors for actual construction activities.

We foresee an acceleration in remedial activities, expanding from $3 to 6 billion to a $20 billion market in the next 10 years. There are at least three reasons for this optimism: the EPA, responding to criticism about the slow pace of progress, has set specific targets for the remedial action phase; there has been a growing awareness among potentially responsible parties that delaying projects could only mean higher costs in the future and negative publicity; and cleanups facilitate property sale or other asset restructuring. DOE and DOD cleanups will also expand remedial dollar volume. For fiscal 1992–93, DOD received supplemental funds of $448 million for environmental restoration and $432 million for compliance programs.

Solid Waste Management Including Recycling and Energy/Resource Recovery

About 160 million tons of municipal solid waste are produced each year in the United States, 40% by households and the other 60% by commercial and industrial establishments. Solid waste management is the largest and most mature environmental industry segment. It is comprised of the following four operations:

Collection, transportation, and landfill operation	$30 billion
Waste-to-energy operations	2
Recycling (postconsumer)	2
Industrial resource recovery	12
	46

There were about 6000 landfills operating in 1992; half of them may close because of increasing competition and because of RCRA Subtitle D regulation (to be effective October 1993) that mandates stringent design and operating standards. Thousands of local and regional firms participate in this market segment. Waste Management and Browning Ferris Industries (BFI) are the market leaders.

Energy recovery typically means burning solid waste to generate electricity. There are 137 waste-to-energy plants in operation and 11 more under construction. Wheelabrator and Ogden each has about a 20% share, American Ref-Fuel, Westinghouse, ABB, and Foster Wheeler together share 25% (J. Berkowitz).

Postconsumer recycling is the recovery and reuse of salable materials. The recycling market continues to be afflicted by wide price fluctuations. Despite considerable public enthusiasm and cooperation in segregating materials at the source, recycling has not spawned many financially viable ventures within the confines of the present pricing structure. A major exception is aluminum cans. IMCO, Envirosure, and Allwaste are three examples of successful recycling companies. Plastics recycling is gaining momentum, although it has not yet achieved consistent financial viability. One impediment is that the different kinds of plastics cannot usually be mixed. Polyethylene terephthalate (PET) and high-density polyethylene (HDPE) are among the more widely recycled bottles. Biodegradable polymers have also emerged, notably Warner-Lambert's Novon specialty polymers from starch, a renewable resource.

The bulk of industrial resource recovery is in reclamation of spent industrial materials such as scrap steel and aluminum. Advanced resource recovery is a more technology-intensive process that goes beyond simple energy recovery or recycling, but it also suffers from wide price fluctuations for recovered materials. Some examples of resource recovery are Horsehead's recovery of zinc from furnace dust; Regenex's conversion of spent antifreeze and other chemicals into ethylene glycol; and Molten Metal Technology's catalytic extraction of metals from a variety of waste streams.

Overall, with a projected market of $80 billion in 2001, solid waste management will continue to be the largest segment, much of the growth deriving from energy and resource recovery operations.

Water and Wastewater Treatment

The $13 billion market estimate for 1991 shown in Table 16-2 includes industrial and utility capital expenditures of $5 billion; industrial wastewater treatment and maintenance of $5 billion; and the balance municipal sewage treatment. This does not include municipal and private water utilities capital and maintenance expenditures, which probably amount to an additional $20 billion.

It is difficult to draw a line between industrial wastewater and hazardous waste inasmuch as 90% or more of the 250 to 300 billion tons of hazardous waste generated annually is in aqueous form. The key difference is that most industrial wastewater is treated on location and, if the effluent goes to a public treatment works or is discharged under the Clean Water Act's National Pollutant Discharge Elimination System (NPDES) permit, would not be subject to RCRA.

The participants in this market provide equipment, chemicals, and other supplies, and consulting, engineering, and construction services. Among the major participants are:

- CH2M Hill
- CDM
- DuPont
- Foster Wheeler Enviresponse
- Groundwater Technology
- Malcolm Pirnie
- Metcalf & Eddy

The overall market is projected to grow at an average 3 to 5% through the end of the decade. An emerging technological opportunity is natural treatment of wastewater from landfills and hazardous-waste sites using existing or man-made wetlands.

Air-Pollution Control

The 1990 Clean Air Act (CAA) Amendments represent the most comprehensive and far-reaching environmental legislation in recent history. Incorporating market-based incentives, in addition to command-and-control provisions, the act will have an unprecedented impact on industrial and nonindustrial activities, and of course on the environment. In contrast to dialogue under the previous laws that focused mostly on health benefits and costs of compliance, there have been elaborate discussions and studies of the economic benefits of the CAA (see, for instance, EPA's Business Opportunities of the Clean Air Act).

The air-pollution control industry market consists of capital and operating expenditures for:

- Stationary sources (e.g., power plants, manufacturing)
- Mobile sources (transportation)
- Clean alternative fuels and additives [e.g., methanol, methyl tertiary butyl ether (MTBE)]

Total air-pollution control market including construction is about $20 billion. Our estimate of a $5 billion market in 1991 (Table 16-2) is primarily air-pollution control equipment and related speciality services for stationary sources. Mobile sources (catalytic converters) account for an additional $8 billion in annual revenues. Tables 16-5A and 16-5B present a more detailed breakdown by title and industry segment. Note that these projections are year-to-year and cumulative increases (not totals) and are in constant 1990 dollars.

Although some air segments will take time to materialize and expand, air quality (both outdoor and indoor) is undoubtedly a high-growth business over the next two decades. Our projection of a $30 billion market in 2001 may actually understate the market because it does not, for the most part, include mobile sources and investments in alternative fuels and additives such as "gasohol" and MTBE spurred by Title II of the Clean Air Act.

Table 16-5A. Estimates of Increased Revenues from the 1990 Clean Air Act, Billions of 1990 Dollars

	Average annual revenue increase 1992–1995	Average annual revenue increase 1996–2000	Cumulative revenue increase 1992–2000	Equipment and maintenance	Clean fuels	Design and engineering	Instrumentation and monitoring
				Major industry segments benefiting			
Title I (nonattainment)	0.8–1.0	1.0–1.4	8–11	XX	—	X	X
Title II (mobile sources)	1.0–1.5	1.1–1.4	9–13	X	XX	X	X
Title III (air toxics)	1.1–1.4	2.7–3.5	18–23	XX	—	X	X
Title IV (acid rain)	0.8–1.6	2.0–3.0	13–21	XX	XX	X	X
Title VI (stratospheric ozone)	0.3	0.1	2	XX	—	X	X
Total	4.1–5.8	6.6–9.2	50–70				

XX = primary beneficiary; X = significant beneficiary.

Table 16-5B. Air-Pollution Control Industry Growth Potential, Billions of 1990 Dollars

	Current annual revenues	Average annual revenue increase 1992–1995	Average annual revenue increase 1996–2000
Air-pollution control equipment:			
Stationary source	2.0–5.4	2.3–3.4	4.2–5.8
Mobile source	8.3	0.5–0.6	0.6–0.7
	10.3–13.7	2.8–4.0	4.8–6.5
Cleaner-burning and alternative fuels	Not included		
Natural gas		—	0.1
Low-sulfur coal		0.3–0.4	1.2–1.8
Reformulated and oxygenated gasoline		0.3–0.4	0.3–0.4
		0.6–0.8	1.7–2.3
Engineering, design, and construction	Not included	0.4–0.7	0.1–0.2
Instrumentation and emissions monitoring	Not included	0.2–0.4	0.1–0.2
Total (rounded)		4.1–5.8	6.6–9.2

SOURCE: EPA, 1992. Business Opportunities of the New Clean Air Act.

Clean Air Act Amendments and Business Opportunity Overview

Title and provisions	Supplier industries and business opportunities
Title I (Nonattainment): Ozone (1993–2010) CO (1995 and 2000) PM-10 (1995 and 2002)	**Industries:** Air-pollution equipment suppliers, A&E companies, instrument manufacturing, construction companies, oil companies, producers of oxygenated fuel additives, and service stations **Opportunities:** Manufacture, design, development, and construction of technological controls and/or process modifications; production and supply of clean and oxygenated fuels
Title II (Mobile Sources): Reformulated gasoline (beg. in 1995) Oxygenated fuels (beg. November 1992) Fleet program (1998–2001) California pilot program (model years 1996–1999) Tier I tailpipe std. (1994–1998)	**Industries:** Oil companies, producers of oxygenated fuel additives, refineries, chemical manufacturers, A&E companies, and automobile parts suppliers **Opportunities:** Development, production, and supply of reformulated gasoline and oxygenated fuels, and design and production of clean and alternative fueled vehicles, and parts suppliers for motor vehicle emission-control devices
Title III (Air Toxics): Major sources (1992–2000) Area sources (1999) Accidental releases (1993)	**Industries:** Air-pollution control equipment manufacturers, stack testing companies, environmental service firms, and instrumentation manufacturers **Opportunities:** Manufacture, production, design, and construction of air-pollution control equipment and process modifications, and development of accidental release plans
Title IV (Acid Rain): SO_2 provisions (1995 and 2000) NO_x provisions (1995 and 2000) Emissions monitoring (1995 and 2000)	**Industries:** Air-pollution equipment suppliers, A&E companies, and producers and shippers of low-sulfur coal, natural gas, and lime/limestone **Opportunities:** Supply, manufacture, design, and construction of SO_2 and NO_x control equipment and CEMs; and the supply and transport of low-sulfur coal, natural gas, and lime/limestone
Title VI (Stratospheric Ozone): CFC production phase-outs (2000–2015) Recycling and disposal (1992 and 2004) Mobile air conditioners (1991)	**Industries:** Chemical manufacturers, A&E companies, air-pollution control equipment manufacturers, and the environmental service industry **Opportunities:** CFC substitute development and production, manufacture, design, and construction of CFC recovery and recycling equipment including leak-detection equipment, and development and production of non-CFC-containing product substitutes

SOURCE: EPA, 1991. Business Opportunities of the New Clean Air Act.

Leading suppliers of air-pollution control equipment for utilities and manu-facturing industries in descending order of market share are:

- Flakt [Asea Brown Boveri (ABB), Swiss-Swedish firm]
- Air & Water Technologies (Research-Cottrell)
- Wheelabrator
- Joy Technologies
- Environmental Elements

Examples of major consulting and engineering service firms in air quality are:

- ABB
- Air & Water Technologies
- ENSR
- Entropy
- Radian
- TRC

Asbestos Abatement

The asbestos abatement industry experienced a setback in volume and a drastic change in expectations during 1990–92. The market is projected to remain rela-tively flat at $3 to $4 billion over the next several years.

Estimates vary widely, but probably 300,000 to 400,000 commercial and pub-lic buildings contain friable asbestos that poses health risks and are candidates for abatement. (Intact asbestos that is not friable or likely to be airborne is not considered to be hazardous.) A factor that may favor asbestos abatement is an accounting guideline that allows capitalization of asbestos treatment costs, instead of expensing typical of most environmental cleanups.

Recent publications from researchers at Yale University and other institutions suggest that the health risks posed by asbestos do not warrant projected costs of $100 to $150 billion for abatement. EPA policy and scientific opinion seem to be moving toward in-place containment of asbestos coupled with monitoring as an alternative to removal and its associated hazards.

Analytical Laboratory Services

This segment consists of testing laboratories that analyze environmental media samples, e.g., air, soil, water, sediments, and biota samples for pollutants and con-taminants. Sampling is carried out for monitoring purposes, as well as for remedi-ation to determine contaminant levels before, during, and after remedial action.

The environmental analytical services market, estimated at $1.7 billion in 1991, is projected to grow at 5 to 7% over the next decade. This industry plays a far more critical role than the relatively small dollar volume would indicate. The ability to routinely analyze parts per billion or even trillion levels (analogous to detecting one second in 32,000 years—the so-called vanishing zero of analytical chemistry) has led to increasingly stringent environmental regulations.

EPA and state certified laboratories enjoy a competitive advantage. Among the major testing laboratories are:

- CompuChem Laboratories
- Data Chem
- EMS Laboratories
- ENSECO
- Hazleton Environmental Services
- IT Analytical Services
- NET (National Environmental Testing)
- Pace Laboratories
- Savannah Laboratories
- Thermo Analytical

Miscellaneous

This is a catchall that encompasses some major and several minor items: pollution prevention and waste minimization ($6 billion); waste-management supplies and equipment such as protective clothing and storage units ($5 billion); indoor air quality ($5 billion); noise control ($1 billion); radon abatement ($0.2 billion); and others (Miller & Associates, "Environmental Markets 1992–1995"). A rapidly advancing business that is approaching $1 billion sales is environmental information systems and software.

Financial Performance of Environmental Companies

Until about 1989, the chief characteristic of environmental industry was its phenomenal growth. Annual revenues of the entire industry grew more than 20% in the late 1980s and individual companies often doubled in size year after year. The measures of success were frequently just growth rate and the ability to keep up with all the projects.

Operating an environmental business was essentially a technical enterprise with little need for any business management. Marketing was virtually unnecessary as there was a seemingly endless flow of projects and orders for equipment and competition was scarce. Financial planning was underemphasized as strong growth provided strong cash flow. Strategic planning was something the environmental company executive, typically a scientist or engineer, had hardly ever heard of.

In 1989, the growth rate was down to 15%. In 1990, it fell to 10% and by the end of 1991, revenue growth in the environmental industry dropped to just 2%. Companies accustomed to strong growth were unprepared for the shock and many suffered accordingly. The following table contrasts typical pretax operating margins between the late 1980s and 1991.

Business segment	1986–1989 margin, %	1991 margin, %
Solid-waste management	20	17
Hazardous-waste management	20	15
Remediation	10	8
Water and wastewater infrastructure	14	13
Engineering and consulting	8	6
Asbestos abatement	7	7
Equipment	9	9

The recession was a major culprit in the decline of growth and margins for environmental companies but was by no means solely to blame. The domestic market for environmental services has to some extent matured recently and is showing signs of industry adolescence. The industrial community, which provides about 70% of environmental industry revenues (the remainder is from the public sector), has also made some strides in internalizing their own environmental problems and preempting some environmental expenditures by creating solutions more effectively internally and investing in pollution prevention.

The recession also played a major role in the rollercoaster ride of environmental stocks over the past few years. Once perceived as recessionproof, environmental stocks were a favored investment vehicle until mid-1990, when all markets took a plunge. After bouncing back in 1991, however, it became apparent that environmental companies were not immune to the effects of the recession—in fact the contrary was true. The majority of environmental expenditures were proven to be discretionary as cash-strapped companies and governments postponed their projects. The result was a string of poor quarterly results for environmental companies and subsequent drops in share prices.

Figure 16-3 compares the EBJ Index with the Standard and Poors 500 and the NASDAQ OTC Composite from a common reference in the middle of 1988. The EBJ Index is an index of 257 publicly traded environmental firms in North America tracked monthly by *Environmental Business Journal*. After remaining bunched for a year, the three began to divide but basically tracked each other for the next 2 years up to the middle of 1991. The S&P 500 is shown leading (the Dow Jones Industrials exhibit a curve very similar to that of the S&P), followed by the EBJ Index and then the NASDAQ at roughly 10% increments behind. The EBJ briefly popped its head above the S&P in mid-1990 but soon fell back in line.

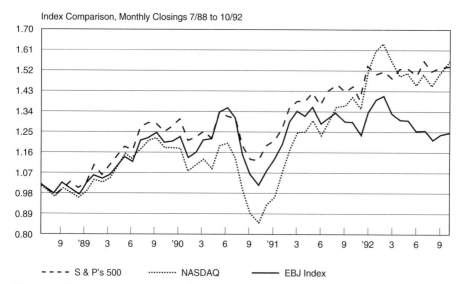

Index Comparison, Monthly Closings 7/88 to 10/92

- - - - S & P's 500   ·········· NASDAQ   —— EBJ Index

Figure 16-3. EBJ Environmental Stock Index vs. S&P 500 and NASDAQ.

The beginning of the end for the EBJ Index was the middle of 1991, when the then-undervalued NASDAQ took off but didn't take its environmental companies with it (the EBJ Index is 63% NASDAQ issues). From mid-1991 until February 1992, the EBJ stayed with the S&P (presumably both were equally victimized by the recession), but then began a precipitous 6-month drop seeing the EBJ fall from 10 to 30% behind the S&P.

In the first phase, the NASDAQ started its run as investors turned to smaller companies because most larger issues had been picked over, and the recession was seen to have a greater impact on big firms. Institutional investors and mutual fund buyers soon followed, sustaining the NASDAQ run into 1992.

In the second phase, the EBJ was impacted by the discovery of accounting irregularities at one firm which had a drag-down effect on others. But that's not the whole story. The persistent recession led to disappointing quarters for environmental service companies, which were further exacerbated by the federal government's efforts to place the economy above the environment. This was symbolized most dramatically by Vice President Quayle's Competitiveness Council and the moratorium on new regulations.

The uncertain legislative and regulatory atmosphere led to further "discretionism" of environmental projects as the Bush administration continued to send the indirect message that environmental compliance may not have to be taken seriously, in spite of the efforts of the EPA.

Presumably, the Clinton administration will reverse the latter, but the enduring economic situation plays a more vital role in driving revenues—and sustaining investor interest—in the environmental industry. If the new administration can combine economic turnaround with environmental reform, a sustained rally for environmental stocks becomes a distinct possibility. The burden does not lie solely with the Clinton administration though. To turn a possibility into a likelihood will take a turnaround in quarterly results—something that can only be accomplished with sound financial management.

The challenge for environmental companies in the 1990s has clearly emerged as a challenge of business management. Whereas most companies grew up practicing only project management, to survive they will need to excel at business management (G. Ferrier).

Key Factors for Success/Environmental Management Consulting

Key factors for success in the environmental market are outlined in the accompanying boxes and in the next chapter. Many of the factors are the same as in other businesses: effective transformation from scientist, founder/entrepreneur to professional management; balancing cash flow requirements (which are inevitably underestimated in a fast-growth mode); strategic planning based on competitive dynamics; fast-response capability to capitalize on short-term opportunities; selective diversification vis-à-vis niche strategies; and leveraging of resources through strategic alliances with key players.

A distinguishing characteristic of the environmental business is that it is primarily regulation-driven, with liability concerns and commercial forces also playing a significant role. Market entry timing is critical and should be in tandem with regulatory enforcement deadlines. Not least is the tyranny of linear thinking and complacency engendered by the phenomenal growth of the last two decades when many sins of commission and omission were forgiven.

The shifting emphasis toward remediation will confer a distinct advantage on contractors that can bid on and manage large-scale construction projects with the ability to post performance bonds; this will accelerate the trend toward "one-stop shops." A 1992 survey of waste generators by the BTI Consulting Group of Boston indicated a reduction in the number of primary environmental service firms from 9 in 1990 to 3 in 1995. The same survey pointed out 22% of environmental services are purchased by corporate headquarters and 78% by plant locations; and that 60% of the waste generators select environmental firms from an approved list. Further, the number of national contracts has been going up, typically incorporating discounts on published fee schedules.

Successful environmental firms also define their business carefully to match their resources with target markets. For example, oil and chemical companies place a high value on consulting services, while utilities are sensitive to the disposal methods and costs of generated waste.

Credibility and good working relationship with governmental agencies and Army Corps of Engineers also represent major assets in the environmental arena. DOE and DOD alone make up a quarter of the remediation market. The ability to serve the federal government market, as well as private industry, without apparent conflict of interest also provides earnings stability from funding fluctuations and business cycles, as does geographic and service diversification.

In order to position themselves to obtain large projects and serve the Fortune 500 and other large clients, many national environmental firms have adopted matrix style practices (e.g., CDM, Geraghty & Miller, Woodward-Clyde). The purpose is to integrate diverse disciplines, deploy professionals across the country as needed, and present a united front, rather than each branch office competing as an independent minicompany. Matrix management is of course not new; in the 1970s and 1980s, a number of multinationals tried the matrix system, linking products, functions, and geographic regions. Some have given it up because of the tendency toward massive bureaucracy with excessive demands on front-line management's time. But there have also been success stories.

Corporate culture is undoubtedly a critical factor in the success of matrix management. CH2M Hill, the largest employee-owned environmental firm, is a case in point. Unlike firms that have one or two large headquarters and regional offices and several satellite offices (such as Black & Veatch) CH2M has a network of more or less medium-sized offices. These offices do not function as "true" profit centers, thus encouraging broader perspective and "corporate team players" rather than "profit center players" (G. Beronja, G. Gunn of CH2M). Although the matrix style seems slow and cumbersome at times, the firm has been able to rapidly mobilize and deploy various disciplines to compete anywhere in the United States and abroad. This same philosophy of shared responsibility enhances professional utilization rates and avoids layoffs by allowing distribution of workloads. In a survey of environmental careers and employer preferences, CH2M has been ranked number one on the preferred list, followed by CDM and Bechtel (*ENR*, September 9, 1991). According to Ralph Peterson, CH2M President, "We have a good nurturing environment—the firm will be resilient because of our basic values" (*ENR* Survey).

An organizational structure that is quite different, but also with a record of business success, is the ERM Group. The various ERM offices operate somewhat independently, almost like franchises—a reminder, once again, that there is no single or simple organizational formula that will ensure universal success.

Environmental Strategic Management Consulting

Environmental management consulting goes beyond compliance to address such pivotal issues as liability management, asset deployment, and strategic business advantage in the overall context of sustainable development. Key aspects of strategic thinking applicable to both industry and consulting firms are identified in the box "Overall Business Strategy." A strategic plan is of course about what and where we want to be and how to get there. A popular misconception is that strategic planning is all about the future. Rather, it is about thinking, actions, and investments *now* to influence the future. Important milestones should be identified in the strategic plan, and it must reflect the lead times.

Overall Business Strategy: Shift of Focus/Expanded Scope

From ⟶	⟶ Toward
■ Narrow client focus	→ Industry, society
■ Single medium/discipline	→ Multimedia/interdisciplinary
■ Single site	→ Worldwide locations, aggregate risk, cross-boundary, global environment
■ Purely technical approach	→ Financial, including market incentives
■ "Cradle-to-grave" thinking	→ "Cradle-to-cradle" or "closed loop" life cycle sustainability
■ Problem-solving, compliance, costs	→ Opportunity seeking, prevention, income, competitive advantage
■ Project management	→ Business management
■ Product stewardship	→ Resource/environmental stewardship
■ Competition, confrontation	→ Collaboration, alliances
■ Efficiency	→ Effectiveness

Traditional environmental service firms view management consulting as a natural extension of their expertise and an opportunity to add value to their services and move into the "boardroom." On the other hand, traditional management consulting firms (e.g., Arthur D. Little, Booz-Allen, McKinsey), accounting/financial firms (e.g., Andersen Consulting, Deloitte and Touche, Price Waterhouse), and law firms (e.g., Sidley & Austin) view the area as their natural turf. A. D. Little, which combines technical and management consulting strengths, has been the leading force in the field; about 20% of its approximately $400 million annual revenues are derived from environmental consulting (*Environmental Business Journal*, December 1992). SRI International is also uniquely positioned to consult in this field. ERM, CH2M Hill, Weston, Law, and Dames & Moore are among the environmental firms that have been involved in management consulting to varying degrees.

The strategic consulting approach combines technical and financial data (from audits, etc.) with database management and decision analysis techniques. The common denominators tend to be risks and dollars that enable ranking and prioritization (including thresholds) to provide a framework for liability management, investments, and resource allocation. Management consultants and financial firms have the advantage of established contacts at the boardroom level, while environmental firms are experienced in developing the basic technical and cost inputs, and decision analysis firms (such as Decision Focus, Strategic Decisions Group, and Applied Decision Analysis) have the capacity to provide a framework for decision making. (See box "The Terrain of Strategic Environmental Management.") Here is a situation that should clearly benefit from alliances and synergy among these types of firms.

The following principles and practices and codes of conduct from international organizations and industry associations can offer guidance for environmental stewardship programs. (See also Appendix C):

- International Chamber of Commerce (ICC): Business Charter for Sustainable Development—Principles for Environmental Management
- Global Environmental Management Initiative (GEMI): based on ICC's principles
- Chemical Manufacturers Association (CMA): Responsible Care
- American Petroleum Institute (API): Strategies for Today's Environmental Partnership (STEP)
- United Nations (UN): Agenda 21
- International Standards Organization (ISO): 9000 series for quality management and quality assurance

In summary, environmental industry is entering a new growth phase with some discontinuities and multiple competitors. Environmental firms that offer strategic management and macro-corporate approaches as "seamless" organizations and demonstrate staying power on a global scale will be tomorrow's leaders.

The Terrain of Strategic Environmental Management

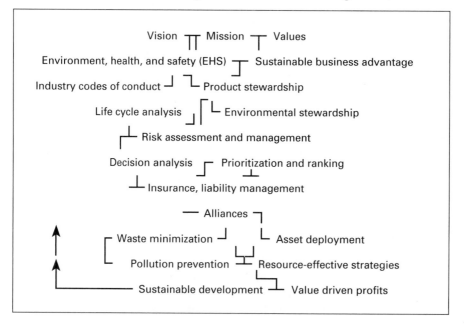

Key Factors for Business Success

- Company culture and vision consistent with client and target markets (e.g., TQEM)

- Existing base of satisfied clients, ongoing relationships, and a high percent of repeat business with national contracts ("base load"); a more complete range of services to select clients (as contrasted with the same service to a wide range of customers)

- Integrated, multimedia cross-boundary environmental consulting and engineering services coupled with remediation/construction capability; local, regional, and international presence (with effective matrix management)

- Track record of delivering quality product on time and on budget (still a necessary though not sufficient condition for success); fast response capabilities; ongoing cross-media/cross-discipline marketing programs

- Ability to translate technical performance and environmental risk into financial and strategic implications, and consult at the "boardroom" level (shift from project management to business management)

- Liability insurance coverage to meet the requirements of large corporate clients

- Positive cash flows and sound balance sheet to seize unexpected opportunities and finance long-term growth

- Entry into a new segment just in time to assure front-end access (not too early or too late); effective leveraging of firm's "unique" strengths

- Ability to recruit, retain, and nurture key professionals

- Credibility and working relationship with federal and state regulatory agencies (especially for DOD and DOE projects)

- Strategic alliances and collaboration with clients, law firms, industry and professional bodies, "competitors," and other major players both in the United States and abroad (benchmarking, partnering, teaming)

- Global thinking—that encompasses markets as well as sources of technologies and qualified professionals (international business not treated as a mere appendage of U.S. market)

Table 16-6 lists leading engineering and design firms.

Table 16-6. Leading Engineering and Design Firms (with Annual Billings More than $50 Million)

Rank Firm	Type of firm	Percent of billings*									
		Gen. building	Industrial and petroleum	Mfg.	Water supply	Sewer and waste	Transportation	Hazardous waste	Power	Other	Foreign billings
Billings totaled $500 million or more											
1. Bechtel Group Inc., San Francisco, California	EC	4	46	1	2	0	9	13	25	0	✓
2. Fluor Daniel Inc., Irvine, California	EC	9	47	20	0	0	3	5	17	0	✓
3. Brown & Root Inc., Houston, Texas	EC	2	81	0	6	1	2	0	2	6	✓
4. Parsons/Main, Pasadena, California	EC	4	61	0	0	2	10	13	5	5	✓
5. Stone & Webster Engineering Corp., Boston, Massachusetts	EC	0	22	4	3	2	8	11	51	0	✓
6. United Engineers & Constructors Intl. Inc., Philadelphia, Pennsylvania	EC	8	47	5	0	0	1	9	30	0	✓
7. John Brown E & C, Houston, Texas	EC	0	100	0	0	0	0	0	0	0	✓
8. ABB Lummus Crest Inc., Bloomfield, New Jersey	EC	0	90	0	0	0	0	5	5	0	✓
9. Services Inc., New York, New York	EC	0	0	0	0	0	0	27	73	0	✓
10. CRSS Inc., Houston, Texas	EC	38	33	10	0	1	8	0	11	0	✓
Billings totaled $499.99 million to $200 million											
11. Foster Wheeler Corp., Clinton, New Jersey	EC	1	79	0	0	1	0	18	1	0	✓
12. Jacobs Engineering Group Inc., Pasadena, California	EC	2	62	13	0	0	0	23	0	0	✓
13. Hill Cos. Ltd., Denver, Colorado	E	0	0	5	9	32	11	34	1	0	✓
14. Black & Veatch, Kansas City, Missouri	EC	1	11	6	15	14	1	9	39	6	✓
15. International Technology Corp., Torrance, California	EC	0	0	0	0	0	0	100	0	0	✓
16. Dames & Moore, Los Angeles, California	E	5	21	12	5	5	8	39	6	0	✓
17. Law Cos. Group Inc./ Sir Alexander Gibb, Atlanta, Georgia	E	21	7	7	5	4	15	32	5	4	✓
18. Parsons Brinckerhoff Inc., New York, New York	EA	15	3	0	1	1	76	1	4	0	✓

#	Company											
19.	Sverdrup Corp., Maryland Heights, Missouri	EAC	8	44	24	2	2	19	1	0	0	√
20.	The Badger Co. Inc., Cambridge, Massachusetts	EC	0	90	0	0	5	0	5	0	0	√
21.	Roy F. Weston Inc., West Chester, Pennsylvania	EC	0	0	0	6	20	0	72	2	0	√
22.	Burns and Roe Enterprises Inc., Oradell, New Jersey	EC	21	12	0	0	0	5	18	44	0	√
23.	ICF Kaiser Engineers, Oakland, California	EC	1	17	3	0	0	22	48	9	0	√
24.	Rust International Corp., Birmingham, Alabama	EC	0	64	15	0	0	0	1	20	0	—
25.	Camp Dresser & McKee Inc., Cambridge, Massachusetts	E	0	0	0	23	39	0	38	0	0	√
26.	NuKem Corp., Mahwah, New Jersey	E	0	0	0	0	0	0	100	0	0	√
27.	Metcalf & Eddy Cos. Inc., Branchburg, New Jersey	EA	0	1	0	9	44	2	42	0	3	√
28.	Woodward-Clyde Group Inc., Denver, Colorado	E	16	18	5	8	10	3	37	4	0	√
29.	Halliburton NUS Environmental Corp., Gaithersburg, Maryland	EA	5	9	0	5	0	0	41	41	0	√
30.	The Austin Co., Cleveland, Ohio	EC	24	14	38	0	0	6	0	0	18	√
31.	PRC Environmental Management, Inc., Chicago, Illinois	E	3	2	26	0	3	4	37	10	16	√
32.	Sargent & Lundy, Chicago Illinois	EA	0	0	0	0	0	0	0	100	0	√
33.	Louis Berger International, Inc., East Orange, New Jersey	EA	2	0	1	7	13	76	2	0	0	√
34.	Daniel, Mann, Johnson & Mendenhall, Los Angeles, California	AE	20	3	6	8	7	40	3	3	11	√
35.	The M.W. Kellogg Co., Houston, Texas	EC	0	87	8	0	0	0	0	0	5	√
	Billings totaled $199.99 million to $100 million											
36.	Howard Needles Tammen & Bergendorf, Kansas City, Missouri	EAP	21	0	0	3	5	71	0	0	0	—
37.	Gilbert/Commonwealth Inc., Reading, Pennsylvania	EA	1	0	6	0	0	0	0	93	0	√
38.	Morrison Knudsen Corp., Boise, Idaho	EC	0	2	24	5	0	22	20	8	19	√
39.	ERM Group, Exton, Pennsylvania	E	0	0	0	1	8	0	91	0	0	√
40.	Professional Service Industries, Inc., Lombard, Illinois	E	35	7	20	2	3	4	20	4	5	—

Table 16-6. Leading Engineering and Design Firms (with Annual Billings More than $50 Million) (*Continued*)

Rank Firm	Type of firm	Gen. building	Industrial and petroleum	Mfg.	Water supply	Sewer and waste	Transportation	Hazardous waste	Power	Other	Foreign billings
41. Groundwater Technology Inc., Norwood, Massachusetts	E	0	0	0	0	0	0	100	0	0	✓
42. Huntingdon Engineering/Environmental, Middleport, New York	E	10	10	15	5	5	5	39	10	0	✓
43. James M. Montgomery Consulting Engineers, Inc., Pasadena, California	E	0	0	0	28	36	0	31	0	2	✓
44. HDR Inc., Omaha, Nebraska	AE	29	0	0	12	19	25	1	3	11	✓
45. Lockwood Greene Engineers, Inc., Spartanburg, South Carolina	EA	3	22	65	1	1	2	3	1	2	✓
46. Day & Zimmerman Inc., Philadelphia, Pennsylvania	EC	1	71	22	0	0	4	0	2	0	✓
47. BE&K Inc., Birmingham, Alabama	EC	10	77	0	0	0	0	2	10	0	✓
48. Michael Baker Corp., Corapolis, Pennsylvania	EA	9	13	1	10	1	40	20	2	5	✓
49. Engineering-Science Inc., Pasadena, California	E	0	0	0	5	19	0	54	0	22	✓
50. Belcan Engineering Group Inc., Cincinnati, Ohio	EA	0	45	55	0	0	0	0	0	0	—
51. CDE Engineering Group, Houston, Texas	EA	1	74	8	0	3	0	2	0	11	✓
52. Hellmuth, Obata & Kassabaum Inc., St. Louis, Missouri	AEP	100	0	0	0	0	0	0	0	0	✓
53. Geraghty & Miller Inc., Plainview, New York	E	0	0	0	10	0	0	90	0	0	—
54. ABB Impell Corp., San Ramon, California	E	0	0	0	0	0	0	0	100	0	✓
55. Environmental Science & Engineering Inc., Peoria, Illinois	E	3	12	3	7	10	4	60	1	0	✓
56. Greiner Engineering Inc., Irving, Texas	EAP	17	0	0	2	2	63	0	0	13	✓
57. Parsons De Leuw Inc., Washington, D.C.	E	0	0	0	0	0	100	0	0	0	✓
58. Golder Associates Corp., Atlanta, Georgia	E	9	2	2	9	2	10	55	4	8	✓

Percent of billings

#	Firm											
59.	Hill International Inc., Willingboro, New Jersey	EA	5	0	0	0	12	22	14	47	0	✓
60.	Holmes & Narver Inc., Orange, California	EA	47	10	0	3	0	15	1	25	0	✓
61.	URS Consultants Inc., Paramus, New Jersey	EA	20	3	2	3	15	26	30	0	2	✓
62.	Malcolm Pirnie Inc., White Plains, New York	E	0	0	0	20	40	0	35	0	5	✓
63.	Ogden Environmental & Energy Services, Fairfax, Virginia	E	3	16	8	5	9	5	43	7	4	✓
64.	Harza Engineering Co., Chicago, Illinois	E	4	1	1	13	4	3	7	61	5	✓
65.	High-Point Group Services, Alexandria, Virginia	E	17	3	0	4	3	64	2	6	0	✓
66.	SEC Donohue Inc., Sheboygan, Wisconsin	EA	3	6	0	5	13	11	47	1	15	✓
67.	Frederic R. Harris Inc., New York, New York	E	1	11	2	2	0	68	3	2	11	✓
68.	Harding Associates, Novato, California	E	2	4	2	3	12	5	65	2	5	—

Billings totaled $99.99 million to $50 million

#	Firm											
69.	Ecology and Environment Inc., Lancaster, New York	E	2	4	0	0	2	0	92	0	0	✓
70.	Burns & McDonnell Engineers Architects-Consultants, Kansas City, Missouri	EA	2	12	4	10	6	25	15	28	0	✓
71.	ATEC Associates Inc., Indianapolis, Indiana	E	12	7	5	1	3	2	70	0	0	—
72.	A. Epstein and Sons International Inc., Chicago, Illinois	AE	45	30	10	0	0	10	0	0	5	✓
73.	S&B Engineers & Constructors Ltd., Houston, Texas	E	0	93	10	0	0	5	2	0	0	—
74.	Skidmore, Owings & Merrill, Chicago, Illinois	AE	100	0	0	0	0	0	0	0	0	✓
75.	Brown and Caldwell Consultants, Walnut Creek, California	E	0	0	0	10	47	0	42	2	0	✓
76.	Post, Buckley, Schuh & Jernigan Inc., Miami, Florida	EP	0	0	0	0	20	60	0	0	10	✓
77.	BCM Engineers Inc., Plymouth Meeting, Pennsylvania	E	1	2	2	10	35	1	51	0	0	✓

Table 16-6. Leading Engineering and Design Firms (with Annual Billings More than $50 Million) (Continued)

Rank Firm	Type of firm	Gen. building	Industrial and petroleum	Mfg.	Water supply	Sewer and waste	Transportation	Hazardous waste	Power	Other	Foreign billings
78. General Physics Corp., Columbia, Maryland	E	0	15	0	5	5	0	15	45	15	—
79. McDermott International Inc., New Orleans, Louisiana	EC	0	100	0	0	0	0	0	0	0	√
80. Ford, Bacon & Davis Cos. Inc., Salt Lake City, Utah	EA	1	59	0	0	0	5	29	0	4	√
81. The Ellerbe Becket Co., Minneapolis, Minnesota	AE	100	0	0	0	0	0	0	0	0	√
82. Dewberry & Davis, Fairfax, Virginia	AEP	20	0	5	8	11	41	3	0	12	√
83. EMCON, San Mateo, California	E	0	0	0	0	0	0	0	0	100	√
84. Barnard and Burk Group Inc., Baton Rouge, Louisiana	EC	0	90	0	0	0	0	0	0	10	—
85. Gensler and Associates/Architects, San Francisco, California	A	56	0	0	0	0	5	0	0	39	√
86. Leo A. Daly, Omaha, Nebraska	AE	60	0	3	5	4	25	2	2	0	√
87. Gannett Fleming, Harrisburg, Pennsylvania	EA	7	5	2	19	25	29	4	2	7	√
88. ABB Environmental Services Inc., Portland, Maine	E	0	0	0	0	0	0	100	0	0	√
89. STV Group, Pottstown, Pennsylvania	EA	24	5	3	0	2	61	5	0	0	√
90. Simons-Eastern Consultants Inc., Greenville, South Carolina	E	0	80	20	0	0	0	0	0	0	√
91. Lester B. Knight & Associates Inc., Chicago, Illinois	AE	9	39	36	0	0	10	0	0	7	√
92. AGRA Engineering Group Inc., Anaheim, California	EA	9	11	1	2	5	10	17	44	0	√
93. Summit Environmental Group Inc., Canton, Ohio	E	6	10	14	4	12	9	38	7	0	—
94. Midwest Technical Inc., Kingsport, Tennessee	EA	1	73	12	0	10	0	2	1	1	—
95. O'Brien & Gere Engineers Inc., Syracuse, New York	E	0	8	7	11	11	3	52	0	9	—
96. The Earth Technology Corp., Long Beach, California	E	0	0	0	1	0	4	53	0	42	√

Percent of billings*

No.	Firm	Type	Water supply	Power	Manufacturing	Building	Transportation	Sewage	Hazardous waste	Petroleum	Industrial process	
97.	Boyle Engineering Corp., Newport Beach, California	EA	15	0	0	44	18	17	0	1	4	✓
98.	RTKL Associates Inc., Baltimore, Maryland	AE	100	0	0	0	0	0	0	0	0	✓
99.	Ammann & Whitney, New York, New York	E	17	0	3	2	2	62	0	2	12	✓
100.	McLaren/Hart Environmental Engrg. Corp., Lester, Pennsylvania	E	0	0	0	0	30	0	70	0	0	—
101.	Greenhorne & O'Mara Inc., Greenbelt, Maryland	EAP	37	0	0	7	16	21	2	1	16	✓
102.	EA Engineering, Science, and Technology, Hunt Valley, Maryland	E	0	0	0	0	1	0	6	3	90	—
103.	HKS Inc., Dallas, Texas	AE	100	0	0	0	0	0	0	0	0	✓
104.	The Kleinfelder Group Inc., Walnut Creek, California	E	0	0	2	5	0	5	40	0	50	—
105.	Tetra Tech Inc., Pasadena, California	AE	5	2	2	1	2	3	82	0	4	—
106.	Heery International Inc., Atlanta, Georgia	AE	97	0	3	0	1	0	0	0	0	✓
107.	Chester Environmental Group, Inc., Pittsburgh, Pennsylvania	E	0	0	0	19	34	0	40	0	7	✓
108.	TAMS Consultants Inc., New York, New York	EA	5	0	0	5	5	66	9	2	8	✓
109.	Wilbur Smith Associates Inc., Columbia, South Carolina	EAP	8	0	0	4	4	80	0	0	5	✓
110.	NBBJ, Seattle, Washington	A	100	0	0	0	0	0	0	0	0	—
111.	Perini Corp., Framingham, Massachusetts	E	8	24	0	0	0	5	8	30	25	✓
112.	The Smith Group, Detroit, Michigan	AEP	85	0	11	0	0	0	0	0	4	✓

SOURCE: *ENR Engineering News-Record.* April 6, 1992.
*Percents may not equal 100% due to rounding.

Key to type of firm: A = architect; E = engineer; P = planner; EC = engineer-contractor; AE = architect-engineer; EA = engineer-architect; G = soils or geotechnical engineer. Other combinations possible. Firms classified themselves.

Key to construction categories: Water supply = dams, reservoirs, transmission lines, distribution mains, irrigation canals, tunnels, treatment plants, pumping stations and desalination plants; Power = thermal and hydroelectric power plants, waste-to-energy plants, transmission lines, substations, cogeneration; Manufacturing = all manufacturing production facilities such as auto assembly plants, electronic assembly, textile, etc.; Building = commercial buildings, offices, stores, shopping centers, educational facilities, government service buildings, hospitals, medical facilities, hotels, residential apartments, housing, other nonresidential buildings; Sewage = sanitary and storm sewers, treatment plants, pumping plants, incinerators; Transportation = airports, bridges, highways, roads, canals and locks, river channelization, dredging, marine and port facilities, piers, railroads, subways, tunnels; Hazardous waste = solid, liquid, chemical, toxic wastes and nuclear wastes; Industrial process = pulp and paper, steel, nonferrous metal refineries, other process plants; Petroleum = refineries, petrochemical, offshore facilities, pipeline, etc.

International Perspectives and Export Opportunities*

Environmental problems are very far from being just an American concern. Serious contamination of air, water, and soil resources is today an endemic reality around the world. While these problems are in evidence everywhere, the manner in which different countries address them varies widely. This is because human institutions—whether they be religious, political, or economic—are products of the histories and the cultural matrices of individual societies. The speed and manner in which a nation's economy responds to new environmental imperatives is therefore largely the product of a nation's own internal dynamics rather than the global initiatives.

Most chapters of this book deal with how this phenomenon is being played out in the United States. About how a combination of market forces, regulations, and changed consumer behavior are gradually transforming a pollution-based American economy into one that is environmentally sensitized. It is also important, however, that American business leaders consider the way in which this phenomenon is playing out in other countries. The international aspects of such transformations, after all, are more than an interesting intellectual exercise. Successes and failures of the greening process in places like Japan, Western Europe, and the old Soviet Union provide important insights and lessons for U.S. government and business planners.

More specifically, they have a very practical, near-term implication for U.S. enterprises. They suggest promising marketing opportunities for U.S. sellers of environmental services and pollution-control equipment; they explain why certain foreign purveyors of these same "green goods" are now penetrating our own domestic waste-handling markets; and they hint at ways in which U.S. government policymakers might work more closely with the American business community to bring about ends which serve to both protect our indigenous environment and promote sustainable economic growth free of down-the-road remediation surprises.

Japan

Japan's move toward a more efficient, hence less polluting economy in recent decades is very strongly grounded in its peculiar history and geography. David Halberstam, in his book *The Next Century*, notes: "There was nothing very ideological about Japanese capitalism....Everything was based on the best use of the nation's limited resources. Like the citizens of most nations, the Japanese might be prisoners of their own myths, but were never prisoners of ideology."

Lack of natural resources always created a predisposition toward less wasteful economic behavior when it came to materials like metals and rubber which

*Part of this section, written by Michael Silverstein, first appeared in the December 1992 issue of *IN BUSINESS* magazine.

were easily recycled. But it did not keep Japanese industry after World War II from being not parsimonious enough when it came to materials that were very cheap in the world market—like petroleum. This changed suddenly after the Arab Oil Embargo of 1973. Japan was hurt more than any other industrialized country by this embargo and subsequent surges in oil prices. The resulting economic fallout led to a rethinking of Japan's overall industrial policies.

What emerged from this rethinking was a concerted effort to make Japan's industry more efficient in its use of *all* materials. The Japanese economy strengthened in consequence as it became better able to sell goods around the world more cheaply than competitors by virtue of using energy and raw materials better. Indeed, depending on whose estimates one chooses to believe, the Japanese now get between two and three times GNP per unit of energy consumed as does the United States.

In the late 1980s and the early part of this decade, Japan's government-industry combine began targeting environmental cleanup and its associated technologies as critical economic growth areas of the future. The country's economy began to reconfigure itself accordingly. Huge contracts for pollution-control equipment and environmental services started to gravitate to the subsidiaries of Japanese firms like Fuji Electric.

Since the late 1980s, Japan's foreign aid programs likewise began to emphasize "environmental" lending. Along with helping boost the country's image in international circles, such an approach is also comparable to the military aid programs so popular with U.S. companies and our government during the Cold War era. U.S. Cold War military lending not only worked to keep countries out of the Soviet sphere of influence; they ultimately generated billions of dollars in new business for American design, engineering, and construction firms. This same result seems a likely beneficial consequence of Japanese green lending for that country's own infrastructure industries.

The Japanese road toward a new environmental economics has thus been very different from that of the United States. It never featured ideological conflicts involving pro- and antibusiness sentiments, or quality-of-life and moralistic predilections. One could even say that it was an environmental economics brought about without environmentalists, a far less potent force in that island nation than in the United States.

Germany

During this century, Germany has been singularly susceptible to the laws of "karma." These laws were clearly operative when it came to that country's evolution toward a new environmental economics. Like every major industrial nation, Germany's first reaction to newly perceived dangers involving toxic wastes was to ship these wastes outside one's own borders. The Italians and French favored sending such material to old colonies in Africa. The Japanese exported much of it to their own old colonies in Asia. The United States tended to export waste materials south of the border.

West Germany, in the 30-year period between 1960 and 1990, made the horrendous miscalculation of using Communist East Germany as its toxic dump of choice. This worked like a charm economically until the Berlin Wall came down and East and West Germany were reunited in 1990. Thereafter, in the best Herman Hesse what goes-around, comes-around tradition, a west-dominated united Germany had to pay the toxic decontamination costs of its newly reintegrated eastern half. Much of present-day Germany's slowing economic growth, its political turmoil, and its radical environmentalism is the direct result of an earlier mistaken belief that environmental problems could be "exported."

Another significant aspect of German environmentalism was its pronounced leftist bent. The "Greens" of West Germany, far more than organized environmentalism in the United States, emerged originally as a kind of last gasp effort by German Socialists to tap into a "pop issue" at the same time populist sentiment in Europe generally was becoming most definitely non-Socialist. Today, there is a more mainstream branch as well as a still highly ideological branch of the Green movement in a united Germany. But unlike the case with Japan, "going green" throughout Germany and much of both east and west Europe generally is still a complex mixture of restructuring along more efficient lines (a purely economic greening for purely economic benefits), and a class and nationalist kulturkampf— between going or not going green for purely political reasons.

Great Britain

Great Britain was the first nation to launch the industrial revolution in the early nineteenth century, and hence the first to fully experience the pollution-related inconveniences and outright horrors that come in its wake. One might suppose this would have inclined its leaders to be especially sensitive to pervasive pollution damages in the late twentieth century, and their economic consequences. But that has not, in fact, proved to be the case.

During the 1980s, while West Germany was passing strong environmental protection measures, a very conservative government in Britain was ignoring such measures in favor of "quick-fix" economic growth. In consequence, Britain was at the receiving end of many kinds of Continental wastes. Its coal industry, though far less politically powerful than in years past, was still sufficiently strong to keep the country from shifting to other less polluting fuels as quickly as some of its European competitors. And an enormous number of sites in the British Isles are today environmentally contaminated in ways that could materially affect the future book value of thousands of British enterprises.

The Old Soviet Union

The failure of the Soviet Union to meet the challenges of a new environmental economics was directly linked to the twin bêtes noires of that nation—a fatal addiction to bureaucratic inertia, and a fascination with economic gigantism.

The years of Brezhnev rule in the Soviet Union, 1964–1982, correspond almost perfectly to the emergence of other parts of the world of growing awareness about how economic activity affects ecosystems, and an appreciation that environmentally sound behavior can be compatible with growth. But neither point of view got a hearing within top councils of the Soviet Union.

This was because environmentalism here was politically associated with the "nationalities question," the attempt of various republics to achieve greater independence within the union. Environmentalism was therefore viewed as a kind of political heresy bordering on treason. The idea that the entire economic system had to be overhauled in ways that would make it more efficient and less polluting met a similar fate. To achieve this end would have required upsetting the communist managerial class and causing temporary unemployment among the working proletariat. This, too, was political heresy bordering on treason.

Even a series of colossal environmental economic disasters like the Chernobyl tragedy could not shake the system into needed change during the 1980s. Marx's disdain for nature as an impediment to historical "progress" and Lenin's fetish for huge and inefficient centralized projects retained their sway. Though the country's mainstream was moving toward a new environmental economic order, its leadership stuck with tried-and-true bureaucratic ways of doing things.

The Soviet model thus ended up a perfect case study in how *not* to mix environmentalism and economics. Russia and other nations of the old Soviet Union emerged in the 1990s as economic and ecological basket cases—and a medical basket case as well. In some especially polluted regions here, children get pneumonia 10 times more frequently than elsewhere, bronchial ailments are five times above the norm, and great numbers are born with deformities resulting from toxemic pregnancies.

The above view of comparative environmental economics consists, of course, of only a few very modest sketches. The various national responses of the above countries (and former countries) to environmental challenges that first began to seriously affect their economic systems in the late 1960s and early 1970s each deserves its own book—and perhaps even series of books. Still, even these sketches suggest some positive and negative things American business and government leaders can learn from the environmental economic experiences of Japan, Germany, Great Britain, and the old Soviet Union:

- Japan has an appalling record of exporting its more toxic manufacturing and deforestation practices to the countries of Southeast Asia, a bias toward gigantic "earth-saving" projects that are positively Leninesque in scope and concept, a growing dependence on plutonium-fueled power plants, and an indigenous "environmentalism" much less geared to protecting nature than to protecting humans from ills associated with toxic discharges.

    None of these approaches is particularly desirable in this country. The chief environmental lesson Americans have to learn from the Japanese is to dispense with ideology when it comes to appreciating how the environment affects the economy, and vice versa. A related lesson is that government, business, and the environmental communities *can* work together in regulatory and other spheres to bring about mutually desirable environmental ends.

- The chief lesson from the Germans is that waste problems cannot be exported, and that when a nation tries to do so, they eventually come back to haunt in very unpleasant ways.

- There are innumerable negative environmental economic lessons to be learned from the old Soviet Union. But perhaps the most poignant one involves "sustainability."

    Sustainability is often presented as a futuristic concept—something that might become a problem if a nation continues to pursue certain presently necessary though unfortunate courses of action. To such a notion, one need only point to the old lands of the Soviet Union. There, the future is today, for those who ignore the dictates of a new environmental economics.

Export Opportunities

Along with viewing the greening of the world economy from the perspective of how different nations are responding to new environmental imperatives, one can also view it from a "green trade among nations" perspective. Gauging the potential for U.S. "environmental exports" in this context, however, is a very difficult proposition. Part of the problem is that we encounter two very distinct sets of numbers in such an exercise. One set includes the amount of money *needed* to clean up the world's dangerously polluted ecosystems. The other consists of the amount of money actually *available* to do the cleaning.

A dramatic example of this economic dichotomy can be seen in Eastern Europe. Environmental conditions in this part of the world are appalling. Air pollution is now cited as the cause of death for one in 17 Hungarians. The Polish government estimates 70% of that country's drinking water is unsafe for human consumption, and about one-quarter of its farmland is too contaminated to raise edible crops. Similar conditions prevail in parts of Czechoslovakia, Rumania, and the Soviet Union.

The same conditions which have undermined east European ecosystems, however, have also undermined the local economies' abilities to correct the problems. An official of the World Resources Institute neatly summed up the economic-ecological conundrum in this region by saying: "How does a country rebuild a shattered economy when it can't breathe its air, till its soil or drink its water?" A report from the Worldwatch Institute reached the corollary conclusion that the "weak economies (of eastern Europe) still preclude major investment in pollution control."

What has come in lieu of real environmental investment in this part of the world is often a sort of Potemkin environmental economic activity. Scores of joint ventures to purchase cleanup equipment or technology are formed—on paper—then simply vanish. A host of problems related to doing business here, ranging from confusing laws on liabilities to currency control to an ingrained suspicion of the profit motive generally, work against boosting real environmental economic activity in the region. Thus, while the theoretical market for environmental goods and services in eastern Europe is vast, actual environmental exports to the region remain quite modest. To date, only a few American environmental consulting firms have derived substantial profits in this part of the world.

The other major difficulty one encounters when trying to put a price tag on present and potential future green exports is defining what, in fact, is an environmental product or service. As whole sectors of the U.S. economy have been environmentally restructured in recent years to accommodate increasingly stringent domestic regulations and enforcement, whole categories of products and services produced by affected industries have become environmentally sensitized.

Chemical makers provide a perfect illustration of how a key U.S. industry has been obliged to change the nature of its product lines in significant ways because of new environmental developments. These same chemical makers are also this country's second largest exporters, trailing only aircraft manufacturers. Are many U.S.-made chemical products, now frequently marketed as being less destructive to ecosystems, "environmental exports"? One could argue that they are—though these exports are never counted as such in official statistics.

An even more striking example of precise definition can be seen in the recently completed cleanup of Kuwaiti oil fields in the wake of war in the Persian Gulf. Should U.S. oil services firms taking part in this sort of cleanup be counted as exporters of "environmental goods and services"? Again, probably not, though given the extraordinary damage to local ecosystems American firms are working to check, the case for doing so seems compelling.

As the above suggests, the extent to which environmental exports *do* contribute or *might* contribute to this country's international trade picture is both easily exaggerated by the size of needed cleanup services in the world generally, and easily underestimated by using traditional methods of defining what is or is not an environmental export. Thus, while knowing we excel in this field and appreciating its vast dimensions conceptually, we are still forced to fall back on generally fuzzy statistics, on the announced long-term government spending plans which may or may not come to fruition, and even on anecdotal evidence when it comes to computing the present and future scope of U.S. green exports. In Eastern Europe, as in the rest of the world outside North America, the immediate emphasis is likely to be on clean water and air, rather than the high-tech and enormously costly reclamation of hazardous-waste sites.

One recent source of data which suggests (if not totally defines) growing spending for pollution control around the world is the OECD's February 1991 study, The Environment Industry: Trends and Issues. It looks at 22 countries in regions around the world (including the U.S. market) and comes up with the following estimates, which are at the lower end of other estimates we have seen.

Pollution-control market	Billions $US		Annual growth, %
	1990	2000	
Water and effluent treatment	60	83	4.0
Waste management	40	63	6.4
Air quality control	30	42	4.4
Environmental services	48	80	7.4
Other pollution-control categories	22	32	5.1

Another, more inclusive, set of estimates of the size of the international pollution-control market, and the export potential for U.S. companies in this international marketplace, was generated by the International Trade Administration of the U.S. Department of Commerce. This preliminary draft report estimated a total 1990 dollar value of this world market (including the United States) of $228 to $370 billion, the world market excluding the United States of $139 to $248 billion, total world exports in this market of $30 to $50 billion, and the U.S. share of these exports in 1990 of $3 to $6 billion.

While the estimates of U.S. prospects for pollution-control exports (even using the traditional, limited definition of "pollution control" goods and services) are significant as a hint of possibilities in this field, it is well worth noting that such projections are subject to dramatic changes—almost always on the upside. As pointed out earlier, for example, the destruction of Kuwaiti oil fields will mean hundreds of millions of dollars in U.S. pollution-control exports to that nation in coming years.

In 1991, Taiwan announced a $300 billion infrastructure upgrade program of which more than $20 billion is to be used for cleaning up its very polluted environment, which should boost opportunities for U.S. exporters. Early in 1991, a trade mission from mainland China purchased considerably more than $50 million in U.S.-made pollution-control equipment in a single buying swing as part of an attempt to improve relations with this country.

Other possible (if not likely) new or much expanded foreign markets for more U.S. pollution-control products and services include badly polluted Iran, should our relations with that country improve; badly polluted India, as that country turns more toward the United States and away from Russia as a source of imports; and Mexico, whose pollution problems, especially along its U.S. border, are now attracting widespread criticism. On the other side of the ledger, should the economy of Russia continue to deteriorate and its trade credits with this country evaporate, its ability to buy U.S. pollution-control technology could diminish as well.

Who Are the U.S. Exporters?

A less statistical, but perhaps equally instructive way to look at how U.S. pollution control and other green exports are currently expanding is to look at how a few individual U.S. companies are benefiting from this export boom.

The growing international operations of environmental services giants like Waste Management, Inc., and Browning-Ferris Industries are well known. But less well-publicized expanded foreign activities by companies like International Technology Corporation and Safety-Kleen are also adding to the credit side of this country's environmental export ledger. The former opened a wholly owned subsidiary in the United Kingdom in 1989, after entering a joint venture with an Italian environmental engineering firm a year earlier. The latter, in recent years, has expanded its solvent recycling operations in Western Europe considerably.

Calgon Carbon, which produces activated carbons used in more than 700 air- and water-cleaning applications, has been expanding its export markets for several years. In 1989, while the company's overall sales were up 12.1%, its sales in Japan were up 53%, and its Canadian sales were up 47%. Company officials predict even stronger demand in Pacific Rim countries during the 1990s.

Isco, Inc., the world's largest producer of wastewater samplers, currently controls about 60% of the world market in this product. Nalco Chemical Company, which calls itself "the world's largest producer of specialty chemicals for water and waste treatment pollution control," increased its exports to Europe to $257 million in 1990, up from $214 million in 1989; and to Latin America $64 million compared to $57 million in 1989.

Export increases like these among U.S. green product and service sellers are becoming commonplace. Already in the 1980s, this fact was reflected in performances like those chalked up by the Plymouth Products division of the Ametek Corporation, which in 1989 won the President's "E" Award for Export Excellence. Plymouth manufactures undersink water filters. Between 1985 and 1988, its export of these filters jumped more than 110%, 70% in 1988 alone.

It is also worth remembering that just as the United States has always exported raw materials from its mines and forests, it is today a major exporter of raw green goods. The most important of these is used paper and cardboard, which is shipped to places like Taiwan, where it is turned into building materials. Recycled waste paper is now the biggest single export by weight from the Port of New York and several other large U.S. ports.

In a pollution control and environmental services marketplace which is becoming increasingly internationalized, it is not at all surprising that just as we are gaining footholds abroad, foreign companies are moving to get a piece of our own huge domestic markets. Toronto-based Laidlaw is one of the largest trash handlers in the United States today, while British-based Atwood plc. controls another substantial part of the U.S. waste market.

As is true with many other industry sectors, foreign corporations are buying large blocks of American waste company stocks, and occasionally buying U.S. companies outright. During 1990, for example, a German holding company, NuKem G.m.b.H, bought up ENSR. Another German entity, Berzelius Unweit-Service AG, bought a large block of Horsehead Resource Company. A French firm, Compagnie Generale des Eaux, bought a large block of Air & Water Technologies stock in 1990 as well.

There is little danger at present that America's lead in the pollution-control market will be sold off to foreign owners the way technology leads in a number of other spheres have been sold off over the years. But clearly, whether through outright acquisition, stock ownership, or development of their own capabilities, non-U.S. corporations are certainly intent on keeping the world environmental market highly competitive.

References

Berkowitz, J. (Farkas Berkowitz & Co.), Outlook for the Industry. *The Environmental Forum*, January/February 1992.

Beronja, G., R. Card, G. Gunn, T. Haislip, M. Mathamel, J. Rogers, and S. Guttenplan (CH2M Hill). Personal communication.

Environmental Business International (San Diego, California). March 1992.

Environmental Business Journal (San Diego, California). April 1992.

Environmental Markets 1992–1995. Richard K. Miller & Associates, Norcross, Georgia.

ENR/Engineering News-Record April 6, 1992. ENR Special Report—The Top 500 Design Firms.

EPA, 1990. Environmental Investments: The Cost of a Clean Environment. Report of the EPA Administrator to U.S. Congress.

EPA Office of Air and Radiation 1992. Business Opportunities of the New Clean Air Act: The Impact of the CAAA of 1990 on the Air Pollution Control Industry. Prepared by ICF Resources Inc. and Smith Barney, Harris Upham and Co.

EPA, 1992. Superfund Progress—Aficionado's Version. Progress as of March 31, 1992.

Farkas, A. (Farkas Berkowitz & Co.), State-of-the-Industry Report '92. Environmental Business '92 Conference, Boston. March 1992.

Ferrier, G. Personal communication.

FitzGerald, C., "More Measurement Tools: GEMI's Environmental Self-Assessment Program." *Total Quality Environmental Management*. Winter 1992/93.

Gorman, G., and V. Bolano (Woodward-Clyde International). Personal communication.

Kidder, Peabody & Co. Environmental/Waste Services Conference, New York, April 1992. Financial and investment summaries by Marc Sulam, Richard Sweetnam, and Andrew Barish.

OECD Environmental Data Compendium 1991. Organisation for Economic Co-operation and Development.

OECD 1991. Environmental Management in Developing Countries. Edited by D. Erocol.

Predpall, D. (Woodward-Clyde). Personal communication.

Silverstein, M. (editor), The Environmental Industry Yearbook and Investment Guide. (New edition published annually by Environmental Economics.)

Silverstein, M., *Environmental Economic Revolution*, St. Martin's Press, New York, 1993.

Whalley, *The Greening of World Trade Issues*. University of Michigan Press, 1992.

17

Environmental Business Strategies*

Vincent A. Rocco, P.E.
Chairman and Chief Executive Officer,
TRC Companies, Inc.

In this chapter:

- Introduction and Scope
- The Environmental Practice, Historical Perspective, Future Challenge
- Business Strength Indicators, Vitality Versus Growth for Growth's Sake
- Strategic Planning for Action and Results
- Lessons Learned During Periods of Adversity
- Effective Marketing and Sales Strategies
- Achieving Real Growth Through Mergers and Acquisitions

Introduction

In the 30-year history of the environmental services business in this country, management decisions which did not factor the full-cost side of the equation into operating plans have been the most prevalent cause of earnings disappointments and business failures. The relative ease of entry into burgeoning new environmental markets coupled with fast revenue growth rates and low

*This chapter was reviewed by Alan L. Farkas of Farkas Berkowitz & Company.

cost of capital have masked the relative immaturity of this industry. More significantly, these factors have obscured the need for attention to sound business policies, plans, and implementation strategies.

This presentation attempts to encapsulate key practices, experience, and lessons learned by several successful companies in the environmental consulting, engineering, and remediation business. These lessons, although instructive in showing the priorities and objectives of well-performing businesses through the 1970s and 1980s, may well become important survival tactics for both technology startups and industry stalwarts during the 1990s and beyond. A profitable, well-managed business is potentially the best differentiator which participants in the environmental services industry can possess in order to enter new markets, capture market share, raise needed capital in a timely manner, undertake strategic initiatives, take advantage of important targets of opportunity, and grow both in the United States and throughout the world in the years to come.

This text cannot be exhaustive on the subject. However, it provides both the outline and the template of business philosophies and practices which have been shown to work in all stages of growth of environmental services businesses. If understood and implemented within the context and environment of the reader's respective business unit or company, these insights may become the foundation of a more sound business practice. This is our objective.

Rather than rely on company-specific case studies to demonstrate salient points, we have freely drawn from personal discussions with the management of several representative environmental services companies—both private and publicly owned. Of special note, the following companies have been instrumental in providing the basis for these general insights:

ABB Environmental Services, Inc.	Tetra Tech
Wheelabrator Technologies, SEC—Donahue	Enseco
Dames & Moore	Bechtel Environmental
EMCON	Fluor Corporation
IT Corporation	Farkas Berkowitz & Company
Roy F. Weston, Inc.	Price Waterhouse
Radian Corporation	Kidder Peabody
EA Engineering, Inc.	Alex. Brown & Sons, Inc.
Air & Water Technologies, Inc.	First Analysis Corporation

Scope

As outlined in the previous chapter, environmental services businesses include a broad range of consulting, engineering, testing, analytical laboratory, emergency response, and remediation services companies. These firms range in size from the individual practitioner to the full-service company with annual sales in the hundreds of millions of dollars—both private and publicly owned.

Additionally, numerous staff organizations and operating divisions of utility, manufacturing, minerals, chemical, pharmaceutical, communications, energy, transportation, and high-technology companies fall into this grouping. These "internal" organizations often offer environmental services both within their parent companies and to third-party buyers.

As a group, environmental services businesses have several characteristics which often differentiate them from environmental product businesses and waste handling, recycling, treatment, and disposal businesses. Typically the former are "people-intensive" businesses which provide specialized services on a transactional or project basis, primarily generating revenue by the selling of their staff's time. Their services are tailored to the specific needs of each client transaction, e.g., are "customized" to some degree, making selling expensive and simple differentiation among competitors difficult.

As an industry, environmental services businesses are very fragmented as to depth of staff, diversity of services, geographic penetration, and client markets. This is primarily because no participants to date have grown to become "market share players." This industry is still relatively young and immature compared with its counterparts in the accounting, legal, investment banking, and advertising professions. Despite their relative reliance on technology, hardware, and remediation equipment, environmental services companies are not "asset-based"—they are not production facilities or factories supported by strong financial backing and large order backlog.

It is generally agreed that at times whole sectors of the environmental services industry have not operated as businesses, but as opportunistic enterprises which exist and survive only because of a burgeoning regulatory-driven demand for the specialized tasks they perform. The historic volatility of the industry, in part, reflects this opinion.

Today, managers of environmental services companies are challenged with one of the most difficult assignments in their career: to build and run a profitable business amid political, economic, and regulatory uncertainty. The scope of this chapter is not to provide the reader a fundamental treatise on the management of service businesses. Instead, it provides a detailed insight as to the previously unpublished vision, strategies, plans, and programs of successful environmental services companies. It focuses on the priorities and tactics used to direct and control the growth of traditionally undercapitalized, people-intensive companies. These materials are predominantly "experience-based," drawing from the actions of seasoned managers which have resulted in demonstrated business successes.

In preparing this guide to effective business policies and practices, we have attempted to describe the historical development of the environmental services industry sector with a candid perspective on the successes and failures and the lessons learned. Indicators of business strength are defined in the context of operating businesses. The pivotal elements of successful business planning are coupled with an appreciation of the management controls required to ensure satisfactory achievement of objectives. Emphasis is placed on development of performance-based operational and strategic plans, marketing and sales strategies which clearly differentiate your company from the competition, and command and control systems for the manager of the 1990s. The careful process of completing successful strategic acquisitions is explored with emphasis on procedure and valuation. Management techniques are discussed which focus on performance measures, communication, and total quality management in the market-driven environment of the environmental services industry of the next decade and beyond.

The Environmental Practice—Historical Perspective—Future Challenge

The management of environmental consulting, engineering, and remediation businesses has historically been fraught with uncertainty. Traditionally, these have always been regulatory driven businesses which, despite the apparent "greening" of the United States and other major industrial nations of the world, remain subject to the stiff winds of change.

From a historical perspective, one can characterize the 1980s as a decade of uncontrolled growth for the industry. But it was growth based upon perceived opportunities which were not realized. Certain market sectors such as real estate development, contaminated site remediation, asbestos abatement, underground storage tank removal, emergency response and spill cleanup, and supporting analytical laboratory services emerged and grew explosively in the wake of the original federal Superfund and RCRA legislation. A vast, newly regulated community of chemical-intensive industries, property owners, and lending institutions was added to traditional buyers such as the U.S. Environmental Protection Agency, states, and local governments. Additionally, the U.S. Department of Energy and Department of Defense were targeted as having tremendous fiscal liability for decades of past waste-mismanagement practices.

An industry of environmental service providers emerged to meet the challenge. In the resource vacuum created by the new legislation, thousands of start-up specialty companies joined the ranks of both established players, predominantly government contractors and infrastructure engineering companies, and well-capitalized industrial corporations attempting to diversify into these new, dream markets. Annual revenue growth rates often exceeded 50 to 100%—fueling voracious recruiting and capital consumption appetites throughout the environmental services industry.

Consequently, the eighties was the "decade of the IPO" (initial public offering) for these "emerging growth companies" with over 100 small to midsized companies ($30 to $250 million in annual sales) raising over $10 billion in public markets. For those companies too small or too early in their technology development stage to raise funds in public markets, venture capital and private debt and equity sources added well over another $2 billion. By the latter half of the eighties, resultant market valuations of many publicly traded environmental services companies exceeded three times their annual revenues and stock prices often soared to more than 25 to 30 times annual after-tax earnings!

To complement these major capital injections, local banks lent heavily at premium rates and onerous covenants to finance private companies who needed growth and working capital as well as desired ownership liquidity through debt-funded employee stock ownership plans (ESOPs)—often without adequate appreciation for longer-term risks and business uncertainties naively assumed by their borrowers during these heady times.

Owners, lenders, and investors alike generally viewed these times as neverending. Even undercapitalized companies could survive on internal funding, e.g., positive cash flow. The great myth of the decade was that environmental companies were "recession-proof" or recession-resistant at the least.

By the end of the decade the tide began to turn. First, it became quite evident that federal, state, and local enforcement policy drives the environmental industry, not regulations alone. Many market sectors declined drastically or became anemic owing to lack of enforcement pressure or protracted delays in regulatory definition, especially with respect to SARA and RCRA—the two principal market drivers for contamination and hazardous-waste management related services.

The national recession which debilitated many industrial client buyers soon affected government markets as well. The administration and legislators challenged regulators to ease up on enforcing debilitating reforms which could cost precious jobs and undercut the country's ability to compete in international markets against foreign competitors with less costly environmental protection ethics in making products and operating plants. Regulatory uncertainty suppressed buyers' interest in spending.

Machinations in the investment community triggered by a complex combination of disappointing earnings announcements and questionable accounting practices in formerly leading companies in the environmental industry significantly reduced investor interest in this sector. Market valuations declined to levels often significantly below annual gross sales. The formerly free-flowing source of public capital became highly restricted. Likewise, banks and traditional lenders, burned by the Savings and Loan scandal and the rapid demise of the real estate development industry, effectively turned their backs on low-asset-based businesses, especially environmental services companies.

By the turn of the decade, most sectors of the environmental services industry faced shrinking markets. Commoditization became evident both in the decline of prices for services and resulting lower profitability of traditional service providers and in the increased number of bidders for any new project opportunity of significant dollar value. Likewise, while the dollar value of major markets shrank, increased competition and the client's growing penchant to pay less by buying locally had effectively caused the geographic range or area of influence of most small to midsized providers of environmental services to also shrink—in southern California and New Jersey, for example, such firms could not compete profitably beyond 50 to 75 miles from their offices.

In the face of this dramatic redefinition of the entire business environment, management of many environmental services companies have found themselves unprepared to grow or even survive. During good times they built significant fixed-cost infrastructures in their companies, overstaffed with expensive professionals, often incurring high salary and benefit costs in order to compete for top talent, expanded into too many disparate businesses, opened too many regional offices, and most importantly, incurred too much debt—oftentimes in anticipation of new markets. For the more conservative companies who waited for the right time to raise capital, today they face a limited audience of interested investors.

Pivotal to the strategies of the successful environmental services companies of the nineties is the realization that markets for services, buying trends, and sources of capital are changing. Management's planning, operating, and business development policies and implementation programs—its basic way of doing business—must change as well.

The good news is, however, that with change comes opportunity. Thankfully, the rejuvenation and maturation of environmental markets now tempered by regulatory uncertainty, recessionary influences, global environmentalism, and limited capital will take time. Adequate time is needed by the environmental services industry to position itself for future growth and continued profitability. This "window of opportunity" may extend through the turn of the century.

A balanced mix—services, cost control, and balance sheet integrity—are integral to running a successful environmental services business in the 1990s. The text to follow describes tactics and strategies used by successful environmental service companies, which possess these valued characteristics, to differentiate themselves from competitors for business, resources, and capital in the changing markets of the next decade and beyond.

Business Strength Indicators—Vitality Versus Growth for Growth's Sake

One principal lesson learned in the past decade is that growth for growth's sake provides little foundation for the competitive marketplace of the 1990s and beyond. Many fast-growth companies without good business strategies for managing growth now face the realities of excess—excess cost and excess debt. In this framework, even providers of value-added services in good markets rapidly become underperformers in the eyes of their owners, investors, bankers, clients, and employees. Going forward, business vitality must be translated into several important and fundamental strength indicators. These business strength indicators are as follows:

1. Strong balance sheet
2. Ample cash balances

3. Positive cash flows

4. Attention to costs

5. Well-defined, yet opportunistic business strategies

6. Market-driven business development programs

7. Balanced mix of services

These indicators have been derived from the commentary of numerous investment analysts, lending institutions, insurers, legal advisers, and company managements. This is a diverse audience, with differing priorities and depth of understanding of environmental services businesses. However, when taken together, their insight must be regarded as valuable, because, in their respective positions, they are closest to the pulse of the environmental industry. A brief discussion on each of these business strength indicators is provided below.

Strong Balance Sheet

As a group, the environmental services industry, primarily comprised of people-intensive consulting, engineering, and remediation companies, is not asset-based. As a result, financial vitality is primarily measured in their degree of debt-free capitalization. For midsized companies in this sector ($50 to $200 million in annual sales), an optimum ratio of debt to capital should not exceed 50%. Even during periods of lower interest rates, experience has shown that service companies typically pay one to two points above the prime lending rate to banks. For these businesses, excessive debt service often becomes a fixed cost, consuming needed working capital which could be utilized more effectively in growing the company. Additionally, annual commitment fees and compensating cash balances tie up needed working capital. During periods of weak or negative cash flow, over-leveraged firms may find that they have insufficient cash to cover debt service and consequently must borrow more—a dangerous situation.

Another indicator of note is the amount of receivables, both billed and unbilled, carried on the balance sheet. Typically, environmental services companies accrue revenues and bill costs and fees on an as-realized basis. Acceptable days receivables should be no greater than 100 days, including unbilled. Obviously, excessive receivables imply that management may not be sufficiently diligent in collection, clients may be dissatisfied with the quality of services, or more troubling, certain receivables may be uncollectible because of the poor financial condition of the client. In any event, receivables management is an important and highly visible indicator of the state of operating and financial controls of a company.

As companies become more sophisticated in management of their assets, other balance sheet items also gain in importance. Reserves for legal actions, bad debts, project cost overruns, uncollectible receivables, etc., are routinely reevaluated and adjusted as needed—often quarterly. Also, at least annually during year-end audit, inventories and work-in-progress are reviewed to ensure that revenues, earnings, and the overall financial condition of the company are correctly stated. Investors and lenders are keenly aware that poorly managed assets consume cash and indicate waste.

Ample Cash Balances

A strong balance sheet should include ample cash balances. This generally translates into sufficient cash in reserve to fund annual growth in working capital, buy needed capital equipment, make strategic investments in technology, markets, and people, provide sufficient cash alone or in combination with equity for strategic acquisitions, and for emergencies.

The definition of the term "ample" varies with the size and growth stage of the individual company. For larger, well-capitalized firms, ready cash may represent as much as 20 to 30% of their net asset value. For smaller, early-growth-stage companies which tend to be net consumers of cash, cash balances must be rejuvenated through periodic capital injection from investors or venture capitalists.

The bottom line is that ample cash on the balance sheet implies resilience, staying power, and the ability to take advantage of strategic, often unplanned business opportunities.

Positive Cash Flows

Services businesses generally live or die based upon cash flow. Positive cash flow is not always achievable during early growth stages of a company when R&D, recruitment, regional expansion, or capital equipment needs and timing exceed cash generated from operations. However, cash-consuming service businesses must either generate increased profits to reverse this trend or maintain a steady stream of investment capital—an unrealistic alternative for smaller companies.

For sophisticated companies in the environmental industry, management of cash flows shares equal priority with achievement of revenue growth and profitability objectives. For positive cash flows to be a meaningful, manageable, and achievable objective of a firm's annual business plan, a cash flow model should be developed as an integral part of the plan. Key cash management practices include pricing strategy, taking into account planned price increases, review of project costing procedures and inclusion of contingencies to avoid cost overruns, contract terms and conditions which address prompt payment, including incentives for early payment as well as penalties for late payment of invoices, formal change order authorizations and "field" change order forms for use by field teams to avoid incurring unauthorized, thereby uncollectible costs, routine project technical, quality, and cost reviews, use of internal contracts staff as well as professional "dunning" services to collect delinquent accounts, etc. Further, all capital improvement, R&D, business expansion, and acquisition programs should be evaluated as to their individual and combined demands for cash. The time factor of cash inputs and outflow is also carefully factored into the equation.

Management has the virtual mandate to generate cash from operations, invest in resources and ventures that offer satisfactory cash on cash returns (in addition to traditional return on investment criteria), and cultivate and maintain private or public financing sources to raise capital at attractive rates well in advance of need.

In a competitive environment, *cash is king!*

Attention to Costs

Whether running a privately owned firm or a public corporation, management must learn to treat corporate assets like their very own. Lack of attention to cost detail has been shown to be one of the greatest weaknesses of the management of environmental services companies of the eighties. There have simply been too many negative surprises! Repeatedly, publicly traded companies have failed to forecast operating costs adequately. Routinely, both the direct, out-of-pocket and indirect costs attributed to new developmental programs, regional expansions, and acquisitions have been underestimated. The key element missing has been the appreciation of the "timing of cost"—the haunting reality that new ventures generally don't turn profits immediately, acquisitions more often than not are dilutive to earnings and most "megaprojects," though potentially very profitable as bid, are often fraught with costly delays.

For smaller firms, lack of size or critical mass often severely limits the opportunity for cost savings. Every dollar spent incrementally has more adverse impact on the financial flexibility of the smaller company.

In most environmental services businesses, the single greatest cost of doing business is the direct and indirect cost of labor. Accurate labor utilization forecasting is the primary challenge to cost control. Second, the appropriate pricing of a firm's labor mix is pivotal. Often, fast-growth companies acquire staff well in advance of supporting contract backlog. This results in unplanned overhead cost. Moreover, the mix of staff may be either too senior to too junior to justify billing fully loaded fees for the work to be performed. This can result in principals working at drastically discounted rates or in work, improperly performed by junior staff, having to be redone at the company's expense. The results are almost always less than planned operating profits or, worse, contract overruns and operating losses.

The message is that, for people-intensive service businesses, time sold alone is generally an insufficient indicator of performance. Effective billing rate and billing multiple must also be factored into the equation in order to properly address revenues vs. costs. Likewise, project staff planning and tracking are pivotal.

Environmental services businesses are generally not technology-driven but are heavy users of expensive technological tools, such as computers and software, CAD systems, analytical testing instrumentation, and field measurement equipment. Progressive companies are now recovering the cost of such investments through rental rates and user fees built into the pricing of their contracts. Maintenance, repair, and refurbishment costs are also considered as a normal client cost. With modern telephone systems, copying machines, and local area network computer systems, companies are making progress in cost recovery and cost containment in these areas as well.

Fundamentally, cost control must be "proactive." Cost projection must be an integral element of short- and long-term business planning. Accounting systems now provide total cost tracking and reporting of fixed and variable costs and cost obligations almost as rapidly as for direct labor. With these tools, management has little excuse to be caught by surprise.

Well-Defined, Yet Opportunistic Business Strategies

The experience of the past 30 years has shown that, early in their development, the most successful companies have defined a clear set of business strategies and have stuck to them, despite changes in the economy and regulatory enforcement. Typically, these strategies embody four principal and often misunderstood objectives for the company:

1. Develop a balanced mix of services
2. Capture a specific market sector and client base
3. Grow profitably and predictably
4. Take advantage of meaningful targets of opportunity

It is beyond the scope of this text to describe the strategic plans of successful companies in detail; however, the common thread in all successful strategic planning appears to be the adherence to a consistent set of long-term goals and objectives which are routinely tested against reality. Strategic planning and the implementation of successful short-term business strategies, embodied in annual business plans, are fundamentally a well-defined and routinely exercised "process." This process includes continuous market assessment, careful appraisal of client needs and the resources needed to serve those needs profitably, corporate structural planning through all stages of a company's growth, simple, routine communication of goals and objectives to all staff, and a timely, unbiased self-appraisal system.

The successful company also exhibits one universal characteristic which allows strategic plans to become more than "shelf documents." This characteristic is a corporate culture which seeks out, rationalizes, and assimilates creative change. It is the unique blend of dogged consistency with respect to long-term goals and objectives and dynamic flexibility in the face of change that appears to create the formula for success in emerging growth companies.

For the 1990s and beyond, the strategic plans of successful environmental services companies will address these topics: horizontal integration, vertical integration, market share, nationalization and internationalization, building financial leverage, and building capital base.

Market-Driven Business Development Programs

The most successful business development strategies will be based on differentiation, e.g., differentiating the firm's image, services, quality, price, and people from that of the competition. Business development programs should be built upon a system of long-term strategies and opportunistic tactics to win new clients and, as importantly, build relationships with existing clients in the face of aggressive competition, evolving technology, changing laws and regulations, and the inevitable cyclical economy.

Let us first characterize the evolution of environmental services markets over the past 20 years. A graphic history of annual average company revenue growth rates depicting the complex market phenomena affecting this industry is shown in Fig. 17-1. New regulation and increased enforcement drive these markets. Some clients, often incredulous about the significance of the enforcement threat and the potential for adverse public pressure, are caught unprepared. Proactive members of the regulated community seek the help of attorneys and specialized consultants early to "buy them time." Others simply wait until a noncompliance order, bad press, or a lawsuit gets their attention.

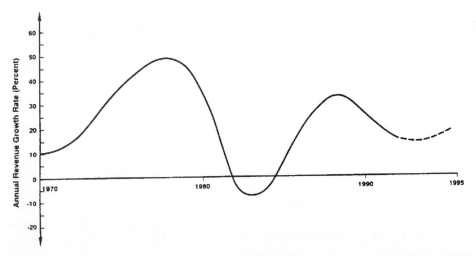

Figure 17-1. Average company annual growth—environmental services industry. (*TRC Companies, Inc.*)

Typically, in the "aftershock" of a new body of environmental regulations, major new service markets are created rapidly because both government regulators and the regulated community need help in planning for and implementing the new requirements. Demand exceeds supply fundamentally because of timing. Initially, direct competition is limited, and pricing is based upon what the market will bear. In this environment, business development often means simply being visible, having key technical skills, if not experience, and answering the telephone. From the resulting milieu of new environmental laws and regulations of the 1970s, well over 5000 new and "retrofitted" environmental services firms evolved.

The regulatory deemphasis of the Reagan administration exacerbated by the recession of the early 1980s brought about the first real "future shock" to the environmental services industry, causing many firms to go out of business or to readapt to the harsher times through downsizing and refocusing. The lessons learned were that environmental markets were not annuities and were very volatile both nationally and locally. Survival for many firms was based upon the retention of existing, quality clients. New client projects were limited and rapidly became targets for numerous competitors. Typically, 10 to 20 "qualified" firms would compete, primarily on price, for each new contract of size that came along.

By the mid-1980s the market for environmental services began to revitalize. SARA and RCRA were well-funded federal environmental programs with substantial monetary and criminal penalties for noncompliance. State and local laws and regulations were promulgated focusing on property transfers, USTs, asbestos, and hazardous air pollutants both in the workplace and in the community. Public awareness and litigiousness became formidable. In addition to thousands of large and small generators and polluters, DOD, DOE, and even local municipalities came under close regulatory scrutiny, both for past improprieties and for continuing operations. These were the stimuli for the rebirth of the pollution-control industry.

In November 1990, the long-awaited Clean Air Act Amendments were passed by Congress. For the first time in the 30-year history of U.S. environmental legislation, Congress passed "regulatory legislation," a technically complex, technology-forcing law which put the burden of compliance clearly on the polluter. Its teeth include stiff monetary penalties and criminal sanctions on management. Its watchdogs become the surrounding communities and employees as well as federal, state, and local regulators. As a very "regulation-like" law, its timetable and effectiveness are somewhat insulated from the politics and policies of the administrative branch of government, and it affords little opportunity for regulatory relief in poor economic times. On the bright side, the Clean Air Act provides market incentives and economically attractive control alternatives for early reductions and conservative control strategies. In its new, rejuvenated form, this legislation could become a model for the reauthorization of other long-standing legislation affecting all pollution media, such as SARA, RCRA, and OSHA.

In the 1990s both in the United States and abroad, the catchword for many environmental initiatives will be "pollution prevention"—that unique combination of product reformulation, waste minimization, resource recovery, and end-of-pipe control technology which ultimately leads to zero pollution discharge. For the U.S. economy, this type of regulatory priority can effectively force changes in how products are made, stored, marketed, transported, consumed, and disposed of. In order to survive, grow, and compete effectively in world markets, U.S. industry must seek economically viable solutions to meet these demands.

Insistence on new technology alone, or simply shutting down facilities in noncompliance, cannot hope to satisfy the balance needed to encourage industrial growth and create jobs while reducing pollution-control costs. Environmental services firms with the formula for solving this problem appear to have the basic tools for differentiating themselves from the competition in the environmental markets of the future.

The effective packaging, communication, and delivery of these "value-added" services become the fundamental elements of the successful marketing and sales program. First, it is important to differentiate between "marketing" and "selling." Marketing is the process of rationalizing the market, gaining visibility among clients as a leading provider of needed products or services, and conditioning the buyer for the sale. Selling is "getting the order," once and then again and again, hopefully with little or no competition after the first assignment.

Effectively, the selling "process" never ends and results in the first transaction's becoming a lasting relationship. Creating a solid "repeat business" base should be a primary objective of the business development process.

In the 1990s investment in and implementation of broad-based business development programs will prove to be pivotal to the environmental services firm's ability to grow profitably. Technical staff typically hate to sell or often fail to listen to a client's statement of real need. Business development must therefore involve a blend of dedicated marketing, sales, and public relations professionals, senior principals, and program managers as well as trained, motivated staff.

Marketing and sales programs should focus on both "boardroom"-level and facility-level penetration. A client's outside legal counsel, accounting firm, lenders, and investment bankers should also be targeted. Public image as well as community involvement are important ingredients and go well beyond presentation of technical papers, leadership in professional societies, and attendance at conferences, symposia, and trade shows.

Market-driven business development programs will become as much of the fiber of the environmental services business in the years to come as the services themselves. They will drive the strategic planning of the firm, test the quality of the services of the firm, focus the attention on where real profits can be made as well as where hidden operating losses are incurred, and equip the well-managed firm with a guidance system to maneuver in a dynamic marketplace.

Balanced Mix of Services

A balanced mix of services is that which a firm can deliver profitably over a sufficient life cycle to justify the investment of time, capital, and human resources to develop each of the services. A service mix is dynamic and changes with time—some service lines reaching maturity ahead of others, some becoming commodities, some evolving through the developmental stage.

Successful companies realize this phenomenon occurs and deal with it head on. By anticipating regulatory or technological changes, they invest early in building or buying capability to support the markets created by these changes. Likewise, they are aggressive in exiting unprofitable or commodity markets by discontinuing certain service lines. Others prefer to be "second first" through strategic mergers, acquisitions, or joint business ventures once the market becomes better defined. Still others maintain a fixed set of traditional business lines and prefer to team with market leaders to get a "piece of the fresh pie." Ultimately, the objective of all types of players is to secure an increasing market share at the national, regional, or local levels depending on their size, capitalization, and appetite.

Buyer preference is a key signal for a firm's management on how to fashion its optimum mix of services. In the seventies, clients emphasized highly specialized firms to help them rationalize their way through the proliferating menu of single-media laws and regulations that had just been promulgated. Environmental impact statements, paper studies, permit applications, field experiments, and massive monitoring programs were the norm during this period. Design and construction of remedial solutions were minimal.

With the passage of SARA, RCRA, and the Clean Air Act Amendments of 1990, a strong multimedia component was required of the environmental services industry. Diversity, size, and depth of staff became an important differentiator among leaders in the industry. Engineers and scientists joined economists, toxicologists, and social scientists in addressing and solving "real world" environmental problems. Studies gave way to plans, designs, construction budgets, and timetables. The product of an assignment was a pollution-control facility or a remediated site. In this environment the "full-service company" was born, offering a broad mix of skills to a wide range of clientele.

As the eighties drew to a close and environmental budgets declined in the recession, many firms redirected themselves to niche markets with longer-term potential. In doing so, they have fashioned their mix of services to offer extensive, "fully integrated" capability, with critical mass and experience directed toward targeted markets such as solid waste, air pollution control, RCRA, hazardous-material management, site remediation, OSHA compliance, testing and laboratory service, etc. This, in part, is in response to the growing demand from U.S. industry to "outsource" specialty services such as environmental to independent contractors rather than employ expensive full-time staff.

Buyers for these services are typically found at the plant or facility level. Projects are smaller and serial in nature, reflecting industry's hesitancy or inability to fix everything at once. Often the buyer's priorities are directed to those issues of greatest regulatory pressure, e.g., immediate financial liability.

Experience and reputation for quality work in servicing one or more specific sectors of industry have become the most valuable credentials both full-service and specialty firms can possess. Going forward, the environmental services industry will become less segmented. Firms or groups of collaborating firms will specialize not only by discipline but also by client industry, offering "full-service solutions" that fix an environmental problem while keeping the client's plant running. "Bundling" of services will also become more common as client's environmental budgets increase and the demand for a broad range of pollution-prevention services increases.

The emerging environmental laws and regulations are placing primary emphasis on "in-plant" solutions. Environmental services firms must recognize that *their real value is in saving clients money and in keeping their plants operating.* This requires a different mind-set than that to address abandoned-waste-site problems. In the future, the environmental services company must have professionals that know firsthand how a plant works and makes profit for its owners. Their recommendations must be cost-effective and work the first time. Additionally, for major sectors of industry both in the United States and abroad, environmental services companies may offer full-time, on-site operating staff to support their clients. This "captive" staff, in effect, becomes the on-site marketing and sales for the other services of the firm.

All these trends will affect the nature and scope of a firm's mix of services. The combinations and permutations may be limitless; however, the result must be the same: *to provide value-added services profitably.*

Strategic Planning for Action and Results

Management's vision, quality, and experience, combined in correct proportions, can produce extraordinary achievements, even in times of adversity. The optimal balance of strategic planning; high-quality, value-added service to clients; and the important assets of both "critical mass" and a strong balance sheet are the keys to success in the nineties. The greatest challenge for management of environmental service companies is to know where they are going, to know their markets, and to be well prepared for the vast changes that are currently taking place in the pollution-control industry.

Effective Business Strategy—A Study in Simplicity

To be effective in the face of the vagaries of this country's fragmented environmental markets, business strategies must be kept simple. Emphasis should be placed on the *unique technical strengths of the firm,* e.g., geotechnical services, air-pollution-control engineering, or remediation. Business development programs should build on long-term client relationships. Good, loyal clients are a firm's best salespeople. Firms should offer integrated services, targeted to key client sector buying trends—following regulatory market drivers and avoiding commodity services. By maintaining a stable base of high-quality contract backlog and emphasizing cost containment at all levels of the company, many firms, using this simple strategy, have stabilized their business even during periods when local or regional markets are adversely impacted by severe economic downturn.

As the company grows, continuing use of this strategy should result in adequate market penetration, regional diversification, and balance between private sector and government contract backlog. The goal is continued visibility and earnings power to grow profitably as the economy improves.

The Total Quality Process

Planning has evolved from a "sometime thing" to an activity that directly affects a company's prospects both in the short term and for the long haul. A key element of planning should be directed to the achievement of "total quality" through an established quality process within the company. Quality, like market share, is a dynamic characteristic; "it waits for no one."

The quality process should encompass the principal ingredients as outlined in the major examination categories of the prestigious Baldridge Award. These include the following:

Leadership and Empowerment.   Top management involvement in creating and building quality begins with the *humility* to accept honest appraisals from employees, clients, and suppliers about *what is wrong—as well as what is right—*with the organization. Management should draw information from multiple sources to create a vision for their company—vision, like corporate goals and objectives, cannot be created in a vacuum. But vision is the first step. Leadership should be demonstrated through *actions, words, time, and dollars* to communicate the vision in such a way that employees are empowered to act.

Empowerment is currently a hot topic. Yet, as often happens with hot topics, the essential meaning gets lost as many scramble to use it. Empowerment in the environmental services industry, in fact, is often so misinterpreted that the real payoffs—shared vision, commitment, efficiency, responsiveness, and the ability to create inspired results—are missed. Too often the term "empowerment" is used to describe something organizations bestow on employees. People talk about "empowering others." When defined this way, empowerment means the same thing as delegation, motivation, participation, teamwork, etc. In reality, these can create opportunity for empowerment, but they are not empowerment. They do not empower. Empowerment is the ability to create what matters most to the members of an organization, independent of the circumstances. It is an orientation to one's profession and life that first happens within each member of an organization as individuals, not the system. More than a set of skills, empowerment is an ethic or philosophy that enables people to claim responsibility for the success of the organization; each participates *proactively* to make change processes, such as strategic quality plans, achieve their intended results.

True empowerment is, in effect, the leadership strategy that directly seeks out and draws upon the values and emotional resources of people and the organization. Traditional management education focuses on problem solving as a central strategy for moving an organization forward—the implied notion being that by eliminating the bad we will end up with the good. It simply doesn't work that way. Empowerment employs a fundamentally different strategy that builds on a shared vision embraced by all members of an organization and equates success with realization of that shared vision. The basis for empowerment is the implementation of a well-defined, clearly communicated strategy for everyone's success which should be management's highest priority.

Information Analysis.   Total quality management is best characterized as the proactive culture in a company that moves from defect detection to defect prevention. Companies must develop a system which generates adequate data, information, and analysis to support a responsive, prevention-based approach to quality. The elements of the system are collection, validation, analysis, dissemination, and monitoring.

Strategic Quality Planning.   To achieve and sustain quality leadership as an important differentiator with respect to competition, management should consider the implementation of a "process approach" to quality improvement. This process approach integrates quality criteria into business planning and utilizes companywide internal, competitive, functional, and generic *benchmarks* to evaluate success.

Human Resource Utilization.   Employee commitment is essential to the success of a total quality program. Successful companies demonstrate the priority of a "people first" philosophy through an emphasis on employee training, continuous open communication, and employee recognition for a job well done. "Making money with people, not out of them" seems to be the philosophy that works best in the environmental services business.

Quality Results.   Defect prevention and continuous quality improvement are built on a foundation of consistently executed quality operations. Every activity of the company should be brought into the program. Top-down commitment, clear lines of authority and accountability at all levels of management, and timely team recognition and corrective action are essential. Routine peer reviews, technical recertification, and performance checks on all staff, serious quality reviews of all projects as part of monthly management reviews, and certification of vendors and subcontractors are typical tools used in a state-of-the-art quality improvement program.

The road to total quality does not end. In dynamic markets, people-intensive companies need interim measures to support continuous improvement and to establish quality milestones and standards. Results could include, for example, better timed market introduction of new services that win clients' acceptance, an appreciable drop in project cost overruns, a significant reduction in unbilled time, and an improved annual repeat business rate with existing clients.

Client Satisfaction.   Receiving timely payment on invoices is far from an indication of client satisfaction. Listening and responding to clients, setting and improving service standards, and gauging client satisfaction are of paramount importance to the success of the total quality process. For the fully integrated or "full-service" environmental services company, the goal is to provide a *total solution* to a client's specialized need. For smaller, more specialized companies, the goal, too, should be to solve the client's problem on time and on budget.

As companies reach beyond mature markets in the hope of pinpointing opportunities for growth in emerging or future markets, they should establish quality standards early. The key to success for early market entrants is understanding what a specific marketplace wants and designing it right the first time.

The quality process requires senior management to become an integral and highly visible part of the "client satisfaction team," the central focal point for collection and analysis of client feedback, channeling results to all key decision makers.

Lessons Learned During Periods of Adversity

Lessons from times of disappointing growth have been discussed earlier. Management techniques for mastering periods of economic adversity are most frequently *learned on the job,* not from textbooks. However, for the environmental services industry, several basic lessons gleaned from the experience of many managers can be very valuable. Listed succinctly, they are as follows:

- *Your people are your most important and valuable resource and asset.* Invest in them, promote their personal and professional development, empower them to be all they can be.

- *Sell what the client needs most,* especially in difficult economic times.

- *Build on long-term client relationships*—satisfied clients are your best salespeople.

- *Build a solid balance sheet*—minimizing reliance on debt.

- Develop internally or package through acquisition or joint venture a *bundle of services* which both differentiate the company from its competition and build market leverage to win new business, maintain profitability, and enter new markets.

- *Emphasize cost control and efficient deployment of corporate resources* at all levels of the company—plan for and reward results through a clear, well-defined Management by Objectives (MBO) program.

- Provide real *employee ownership* of the business and incentivization through an aggressive, performance-driven stock option program, phantom stock program, or ESOP.

- Encourage all employees to *participate in community activities* both to broaden them personally and to "give back" some of the wisdom, work, and wealth needed to help others.

The operating philosophies of "well-seasoned" companies in the industry exhibit certain important "tactics" which evidence that they are aggressive, yet cautious, in running their businesses in adverse times. These tactics, if successful, soon become part of the "culture" of a service organization.

Service businesses in an adverse economy require a "command and control" business planning and performance monitoring system. Management *annually* should prepare a three-year strategic business plan in addition to the annual operating plan. *Monthly* each division of the company should forecast new orders, revenues, and profitability *for the next three months.* This *rolling forecast system* keeps all managers' "eyes on the ball"—to identify problems, maximize profitability, pursue important targets of opportunity, and most importantly, take needed corrective actions in the shortest possible time with the highest level of information for correct decision making.

Selling, general and administration expenses (SG&A) should be controlled tightly, with divisional or subsidiary managers held accountable for their own marketing, sales, contracts, accounting, and human resource functions at levels which optimize subsidiary performance despite recessionary pressures. SG&A functions should be routinely funded or "sold" between subsidiaries to reduce redundancy and total corporate operating cost.

Selling is everyone's job—this is a foundation of corporate culture at market-driven companies—a well-defined responsibility of everyone from the CEO to the receptionist. Such companies sell through a combination of principals and staff but ensure through a corporatewide, new business "lead tracking system" that all key staff possess up-to-date information on every client contact *made daily.* This encourages cross-selling among subsidiaries and divisions and ensures that the company's best professionals are utilized in selling into new situations.

The result is that the cost of selling can be dramatically reduced even in recessionary times. Using this type of program, leads, new orders, and firm contract backlog can be brought to record highs and maintained.

Many publicly owned companies award stock options to their staff. As participants in an "equity building" program of this type, employees see their individual performance and, more importantly, their company performance as the key ingredient to growing their personal estates. This program, beyond salary and other typical benefits, is a key differentiator in motivating staff and in attracting and keeping key staff. Stock options granted annually should vest over a period of three to five years—thereby encouraging longer-term performance standards at all levels of the company and reducing the potential for a competitor "pirating" key employees who are motivated to build a vested interest in the company.

Communication of good news as well as bad should be fast and clear. Weekly companywide, financial performance should be reported on Monday for the previous week. Quarterly unaudited financial reports to management and employees should be routinely issued within two to three weeks after the end of a quarter. The basic lesson is to "keep the staff's and management's eyes on the ball at all times."

Effective Marketing and Sales Strategies of Environmental Services

Favorable developments are emerging in certain U.S. and foreign markets that could offer a potentially significant and extended growth cycle during this decade for the environmental services industry. Following difficulties in the late 1980s and early 1990s, many environmental services firms have reorganized and restructured and are now becoming more productive, better capitalized, and more diversified. Looking ahead, the convergence of political, social, and economic circumstances and events should set the stage for a broad array of environmental consulting, engineering, and remediation firms in the 1990s. Material opportunities are becoming available, slowly at first, but eventually at a more rapid pace, in the hydrocarbon, chemical, federal government, power generation, infrastructure, and international markets, principally Latin America and the Pacific Rim.

Gains in these areas should more than compensate for likely continued sluggishness in the U.S. commercial and industrial construction markets. Environmental services firms should see this activity first and more rapidly with investigative, testing, permitting, and smaller-scale pollution-control projects ($5 to $15 million) getting funding priority, as well as the much-touted DOD and DOE facility remediation and restoration programs.

Government studies project that annual spending in the United States for pollution abatement and control will increase by more than 75% in constant 1990 dollars by the end of the decade. A graphic history and projection of annualized spending by media is shown in Fig. 17-2. Considerable capital is expected to be invested in existing facilities to comply with recent and anticipated environmental requirements, especially those for which capacity expansions are planned. In addition to DOD and DOE restoration and closure assignments, the U.S. Department of Transportation (DOT) Intermodal Surface

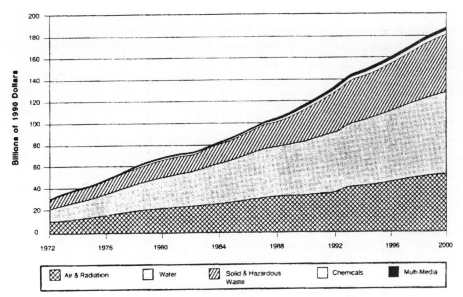

Figure 17-2. Annualized costs for pollution abatement and control by medium. *Note:* Costs for pesticides and toxic substances are included under chemical and multimedia categories. (*EPA, 1990; EPA economic analyses and unpublished data.*)

Transportation Efficiency Act (ISTEA) offers a significant increase in the level of federal funding for transportation projects and their related environmental issues compared to the prior program. Priorities for long-term DOD spending are shown in Fig. 17-3.

Widespread and diverse opportunities are developing for environmental services firms in Latin America and the Pacific Rim, where environmental priorities are rapidly gaining stature and funding. Mexico should attract substantial industrial investment by those seeking access to U.S. markets with the passage of the North American Free Trade Agreement (NAFTA). Environmental compliance costs of such development are expected to be substantial.

In this framework, the adequacy and sophistication of a firm's marketing and sales strategy will be tested to the fullest. For national full-service firms with a foundation of solid industrial experience and an adequate multiple office network and delivery system, *national accounts contracts* with major industry will form the "base load" of high-quality repeat business. Additionally, for experienced specialty firms "sole source" opportunities will drive their business during the early stages of new technology-forcing regulation. For smaller, less differentiated firms, early developing markets will be fragmented and highly competitive.

Players in these emerging markets should recognize that buyers will emphasize several factors in making their buying decisions. These factors become the primary points of "differentiation" which must be emphasized in the successful marketing and sales program:

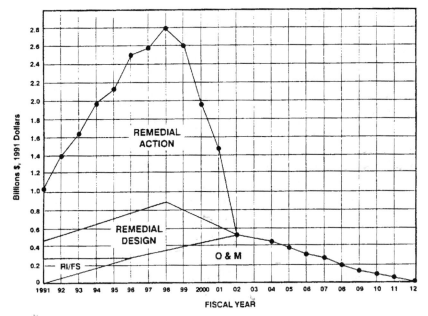

Figure 17-3. DOD Installation Restoration Program (IRP) rate of expenditure, all components. (*TRC Environmental Corporation.*)

- Prior experience with a high repeat business ratio in targeted client sectors
- Depth of staff with strong geographic presence
- Full range of services
- Credibility with local and regional regulators
- Financial staying power and insurability

Firms with these credentials, marketed well, will have a distinct competitive advantage. Maintaining "visibility" in the marketplace is key to exploiting this competitive advantage. This requires emphasis on total quality and staff credentials; fostering a "technical brotherhood" with the client through technical and trade organizations, regional and local business associations and social events; continual outreach through direct contact both on and off the project; technical papers and presentations; and directed promotional programs.

Marketing and sales strategy should strive to build relationships based on proving unique, value-added services that focus on the client's priorities. Services offered should be packaged to provide leverage, both for additional work within the client's organization and, through referral, for work for other clients.

Marketing and sales in the nineties will be expensive—both in time as well as in dollar outlay. Wise use of key staff and bottom line dollars will require careful planning, orchestration, and attention to "getting that order."

Achieving Real Growth Through Mergers and Acquisitions

The rationalization of the markets of the nineties clearly indicates that many private and public firms in the environmental services business may not be adequately equipped to compete effectively. Market pressures will demand adequate size, diversification, capitalization, and staying power. "Market share will wait for no one." This will force "consolidation" throughout the industry, hopefully achieved through well-orchestrated strategic mergers and acquisitions.

The experience in mergers and acquisitions in the environmental services sector is limited, and history has shown that many such transactions have resulted in frustration and disappointment for both parties—the sum of the parts becoming *less* than the whole.

There are several fundamental elements of the merger and acquisition process which, if understood, can better prepare both the buyer and seller for a successful transaction and a productive, enduring relationship. First, it is important to understand what motivates both the buyer and seller. For buyers, the search for merger or acquisition partners is typically driven by the desire to

- Become a "one-stop shop," i.e., fully integrated or full service
- Gain resources, primarily skilled, experienced staff, e.g., "critical mass"
- Enhance profitability, growth, and market share
- Build an asset base and earnings stream to justify raising capital in public markets

  Motivation for sellers is often:

- The need for capital
- Ownership transition
- To compete better
- In trouble

Characteristics of a Successful Transaction

The formula for success in a merger or acquisition is not solely based on agreement on a satisfactory purchase price and acceptable terms of a purchase and sale agreement. It is built on the realization of several pre- and posttransaction characteristics common to both organizations. Some of these can be qualified as follows:

- Both firms should possess a common business philosophy, especially with respect to clients, staff, and quality of service.

- Business plans and sales programs should be integrated as soon as possible. "Earn-outs" tend to force isolation and separation during the critical early stages of a partnership.

- Reporting channels, accountabilities, responsibilities, and authority should be *defined up front.*

- Participants should each possess effective, real-time tracking and control systems.

- Management teams should be *good communicators.*

- A system of cross-company selling should be established up front.

- Both partners should have a *common set of coupled incentives* for key staff to encourage all parties' active participation in achieving common success. The combination should result in *improved earnings* and a solid capital base for the combined company. Earnings "accretion" is essential. Capital markets have become intolerant of transactions which dilute the acquiror's earnings and consume valuable resources. Acquisitions for the purpose of turning around poorly performing companies typically don't work! The acquiror is far better off to pay more for a well-performing company than to take the chance on a "fire sale."

Patience and persistence are essential to the success of any merger or acquisition. The realistic objective of both parties should be to make 2 + 2 = 4 first; the "synergy factor" will take effect in time.

Evaluation of potential partners is the responsibility of *both* the seller and the buyer. A well-orchestrated due diligence period should allow sufficient time for both parties to examine and understand the mutual operational and cultural "fit." In this broader context, due diligence is more than a financial or business liabilities audit. For companies who have not had prior close business relationships, this really is the "mating period."

Preparing for the Transaction

Probably the most frustrating aspect of the acquisition process is to learn, after significant time and effort, that the seller *cannot make the decision* to proceed at any reasonable price, e.g., it is not a "willing seller." Either the seller's valuation expectations are grossly inflated or, in many cases, the seller is not ready to sell at all but is simply getting an "appraisal" of its value and plans to "shop itself around awhile."

This phenomenon should cause potential acquirors to reevaluate their acquisition tactics and ascertain *up front* that the expectations of both parties are compatible. If so, the acquiror should require exclusivity or a "lockout agreement" for a period of 90 to 120 days after a letter of intent is signed to conduct adequate due diligence, settle on price, and establish clear terms and conditions of the sale without having the deal "shopped."

Experience has shown that this process is much more efficient between two publicly owned entities or where the business to be acquired is a division of a larger public company. The reality is that the merger and acquisition process is a "courtship." *The buyer, in effect, becomes the seller*—attempting to convince the potential partner that there is both up front compatibility and great long-term potential if the deal is consummated.

Likewise, the willing seller must also work to bring the transaction to a successful closure. Well before the first potential acquiror knocks on the door, sellers should get their "house in order." Audited financial statements should be prepared for current and at least 2 prior years. A schedule of contract backlog by the client should be prepared and spread by quarter over the length of the contracts. An accurate inventory of capital assets should be prepared. A schedule of receivables, both billed and unbilled, should be prepared along with a candid assessment of their collectibility. Legal liabilities, contract overruns, and environmental problems should be documented. And finally, a 3-year projection of operating revenues, costs and expenses, capital requirements, and profitability should be prepared.

Also, it is important to note that many smaller, privately held companies are Subchapter S corporations, whereas most acquirors are Subchapter C corporations. The differences in accounting treatment require that the seller's financial statements be reconstructed into a format comparable to that of a Subchapter C corporation. In preparing for negotiations to sell their company, owners of a Subchapter S corporation should have their historical financial statements prepared in this alternative manner and should also present pro forma business plans and earnings projections in this format. This will prevent unnecessary confusion and delays in translation during the due diligence and negotiation process. These documents, prepared and presented in a careful and professional manner, greatly add to the efficiency of the process and can support higher valuations.

Valuation Methodology

Valuations today are higher than they have been in recent years. Owner expectations have been significantly influenced by the market valuations of comparable publicly owned companies. Acquirors, on the other hand, have developed valuation formulas which employ a number of differing valuation techniques typically based upon a multiple of pretax earnings or of net annual revenues. Most astute buyers are not prepared to pay public company price-earnings (P/E) multiples for private companies, no matter how profitable they are.

Reliance on public market criteria, however, can still be a very credible means of valuing privately held companies. Financial characteristics of publicly traded companies in comparable businesses can be readily obtained through analyst's reports, industry surveys, company financial statements, newspapers, and the trade press. Key elements for comparison are book value, market capitalization as a percentage of net revenues, and of course, P/E ratio.

One simple approach is based on the use of a weighted formula for valuation of smaller private companies *with consistent historical earnings.* It uses the *average* value of the above elements for comparable publicly traded companies as independent variables.

A = average comparable public companies' price to earnings ratio × private company's earnings for current fiscal year or most recent prior fiscal year

B = average public companies' market capitalization as a percent of annual net revenues × private company's annual net revenues for the same period

C = private company's book value

The valuation formula for this example is as follows:

Private company valuation = (0.5) A + (0.25) B + (0.25) C

Adjustment of variables and weights is judgmental based on consistency of earnings, historical trends, or if the acquired company is undergoing a turnaround. Obviously, for acquirors faced with the prospect of buying future projected earnings, this approach offers little comfort.

Last, it is important to recognize that for publicly owned companies, acquisitions *should add to earnings on an incremental basis.* One of the most effective ways to assure earnings "accretion" is for the buyer to use publicly traded stock to acquire the company, thereby effecting a "pooling" transaction. While the IRS's rules on pooling of interest transactions are complex, it is instructional to recognize that, if a merger or acquisition can be successfully accomplished through pooling, the surviving company can avoid amortizing goodwill, which positively impacts earnings. Typically, by using stock, a public company can pay more for an acquisition than by using valuable cash.

Also, the seller can realize significant advantage in a pooling. A pooling transaction provides stock to the seller *tax-free,* whereas cash would generally be fully taxed on the date of closure. Only on the sale of the stock would the seller be subject to taxation—a timing issue which could give the seller ample time for tax planning. Sellers who accept stock in such a transaction are generally afforded "shelf offering" rights or "piggyback" rights on future public offerings of the acquiring company.

For both parties, a pooling transaction may be a real "win-win" situation; however, both parties would be well advised to seek expert legal, tax, and investment banking assistance before pursuing this approach.

In Conclusion

Experience over the past 30 years demonstrates that environmental services companies must adapt to changing times and develop sound business practices. In the future, capital may be difficult to obtain and markets may remain fragmented and elusive for some time to come. Leading companies in the industry, those with size, diversity, and capital to grow, must think and act like publicly traded companies more than ever before. Accountability for success and failure will be measured more closely and reaction time for decision making will be greatly diminished.

Both the owner and the professional manager must learn and master the skills of strategic management. But as companies grow and merge in this new age, the value of success will be far greater, along with the rewards.

PART 8

Global Perspectives and International Opportunities

18

Environmental Management of Multinational and Transnational Corporations: Policies, Practices, and Recommendations*

Michael W. Hansen

Harris R. Gleckman, Ph.D.
*United Nations Transnational
Corporations and Management Division*

In this chapter:

- The Greening of Corporate Management
- The Benchmark Survey on Corporate Environmental Management
- Recommendations for Responsible Corporate Environmental Management
- United Nations' Role in the Future

---

*Jeffrey Himmelberger, Ph.D., of Clark University reviewed and contributed to this chapter.

The "Greening" of Corporate Management

The question is no longer whether business must change to meet the challenges of the global environment, or even when. The question of the 1990s is how.
      James Gustave Spoeth, President, World Resources Institute

A profound transformation has occurred in corporate management of environmental and occupational matters during the last decade. Increasingly senior corporate managers are directing their attention toward environment, health, and safety (EH&S) issues. A 1991 study by McKinsey & Company reported that 92% of the 400 firms surveyed agreed that "the environmental challenge is one of the central issues of the 21st century."[1] Also, at the 1990 World Economic Forum, 650 industry and governmental leaders ranked the environment as the number one challenge facing business.[2] Many corporations invest substantial resources in developing new and innovative ways of managing their environmental assets and impacts,[3] and overall, companies spent an average 1.1 to 2% of total sales on environmental expenditures and often over 25% of their net income after taxes.

Consequently the international environmental industry has grown at an impressive pace in recent years and is becoming a major, if not *the* major, business opportunity of the future. The industry is valued at almost $300 billion annually with a potential to double by the end of the century. The bulk of this industry is involved in producing and selling pollution-control equipment. But also long-time consulting firms such as Arthur D. Little, Mott MacDonald, and McKinsey are expanding their activities in this field playing key roles in developing new green concepts and in applying them to daily corporate routines.

As more and more corporations engage in environmental management activities, industrial associations such as the International Chamber of Commerce (ICC), the Chemical Manufacturers Association (CMA), and the Japanese industry association, Keidanren, are turning their attention to coordinating and enhancing corporate environmental management. They are producing corporate charters and guidelines on environmental issues which are being adopted by more and more firms.[4] Moreover, business organizations devoted solely to environmental management are being set up, among them the Business Council for Sustainable Development (BCSD) and the Global Environmental Management Initiative (GEMI).

This phenomenon of corporate environmental activism has been called "corporate responsiveness," "responsible care," "corporate self-regulation," "good corporate citizenship," "product stewardship," "proactive management," or "corporate voluntarism." This chapter evaluates the state of corporate environmental management and gives some suggestions on how it can be further improved.

Corporate environmental management has a profound significance for the United Nations discussions on sustainable development. The concept of sustainable development has challenged humankind to stake out new patterns of development based on growth which does not steadily deplete natural resource stocks and the biosphere. For developing countries and economies-in-transition to develop in a sustainable manner, they will need clean technology and managerial experience developed in the industrialized North over two decades of intense environmental regulation. Business in general, and transnational corporations (TNCs) in particular, can work as major vehicles in this transfer of know-how.

The central role that transnational corporations might play is underlined by the fact that TNCs invest more than $225 billion each year outside their home country and that 95% of these investments come from industrialized countries.[5] Moreover, 90% of all technology and product patents worldwide, many of them related to pollution control and resource conservation, are held by TNCs. Consequently, major efforts to attract TNC investments are undertaken by developing countries and economies-in-transition. But often these countries lack the infrastructure, regulatory apparatus, or bargaining power to deal effectively with potential adverse environmental impacts of TNC investments. A Gallup poll conducted in the summer of 1992 found that 35% of the world's population agreed that multinational corporations were "a great deal" responsible for the environmental degradation in developing countries. Whether or not this public perception is accurate, it tends to be reinforced by highly visible examples in developing countries such as the incident at Union Carbide's Bhopal plant in India, unsustainable logging practices by Japanese corporations in Southeast Asia, or the dumping of hazardous waste by European companies in West Africa.

Given this background, it was not surprising that corporate management issues came to play a central and often controversial role at the international conference on sustainable development, the United Nations Conference on the Environment and Development (UNCED) held in Rio in the summer of 1992. Business issues were discussed intensely throughout the preparatory meetings for the conference, and representatives of the business community such as ICC and BCSD participated actively in the discussions, promoting corporate self-regulation as an alternative or supplement to international regulation. Eventually, the conference agreed on a chapter on Business and Industry as part of the Conference's main document, the 800-page Agenda for the 21st Century ("Agenda 21"). The chapter on Business and Industry has two sections, one that deals with "Cleaner Production" and the other that deals with "Responsible Entrepreneurship." Briefly, the chapter calls for corporations to establish worldwide corporate policies on sustainable development (chap. 30.22), report annually on their environmental records (chap. 30.10), promote awareness among employees (chap. 30.14), foster openness and dialogue with employees and the public (chap. 30.26), facilitate the transfer of clean technology to developing countries (chap. 30.22), and in general, ensure ethical and responsible management of products and processes (chap. 30.26). Additional recommendations for business and industry are found scattered throughout the 800 pages of "Agenda 21."[6]

The Benchmark Survey on Corporate Environmental Management

United Nations Transnational Corporations and Management Division (TCMD) [previously, United Nations Centre on Transnational Corporations (UNCTC)] participated actively in the discussions of business issues leading up to UNCED. It was soon realized that although business self-regulation was widely seen as an essential element in sustainable development, in fact very little was known of this phenomenon, apart from anecdotal evidence. Therefore, UNCTC/TCMD conducted a major survey: the Benchmark Survey on Corporate Environmental Management. In addition to providing knowledge of the current state of corporate environmental management, the survey gathered examples of state-of-the-art corporate environmental practices.

This section presents an extract of the final report on the Benchmark Survey,[7] which will be followed by a set of detailed and action-oriented recommendations for transnational corporations in sustainable development. The chapter ends by describing the United Nations' future role in the implementation of UNCED's sustainable development objectives for business.

Survey Design

The data collection for the Benchmark Survey took place in 1990 and 1991. A lengthy questionnaire of more than 200 questions was sent to 800 transnational corporations with sales exceeding $1 billion; 169 transnational corporations responded by filling out the questionnaire and submitting attachments such as corporate policies and annual reports. The sample was divided into three equally large regions/countries: the United States, Japan, and Europe[8]; into four sectors, agricultural products (food processing industry, forestry, and pharmaceutical, 24% of the firms), extractive processing (chemical and oil corporations, 31%), finished products (manufacturing and durables, 36%), and the service sector (9%); and finally into three sales groups, the bottom third ($1 to $2.3 billion), the middle third ($2.3 to $4.9 billion), and the top third group ($4.9 to $50 billion) in terms of annual sales.

The following excerpts from the report on the Benchmark Survey focus on four themes: (1) corporate policy statements and corporate policies; (2) the relationship between corporate environmental management and regulations/international guidelines; (3) the level of international integration of environmental management; and (4) different management communication and control systems. For each theme, the relevant Agenda 21 paragraphs are quoted.

Corporate Policy Statements and Policies/Programs

Policy Statements.   A generalized policy statement on the environment is an important indicator of a corporation's environmental commitment. It sends a message from top management to the employees and the public that the corporation is committed to environmental protection, and it outlines subsequent environmental activities of the corporation.[9] The survey found that 43% of all respondents have a published international policy statement. As seen in Fig. 18-1, 70% of the U.S. respondents have a formal published international policy statement,[10] but only 18% of the Japanese and 41% of the European respondents have such statements. Large TNCs are almost twice as likely to have a policy statement as small TNCs (58 vs. 30%). The extractive sector has such statements more often (60%).

Agenda 21

Recognize environmental management as among the highest corporate priorities and as a key determinant to sustainable development. (30.3)

Ensure responsible and ethical management of processes from the point of view of health, safety and environmental aspects. (30.26)

Looking at the content of the policy statements submitted by the responding TNCs, it was found that the level of detail varied. The decentralized companies, and/or the companies which operate in more than one industrial sector, produce very general, all-encompassing statements such as "will operate in an environmentally friendly manner" or "will pursue best environmental practice" and specify that it is the responsibility of individual subsidiaries to formulate their own policies and programs appropriate to their specific operations and activities. More centralized companies, or those operating in single sectors, tend to produce more detailed statements specifying what is to be achieved, by whom, and when. Those who produce brief policy statements expand them by providing guidelines on how the policy would be implemented. In general, the statements cover the following issues: a definition of environmental protection (preventive, integrative, international validity); research and development; aspects of process and product safety; health protection; production technology; environmental protection technology; control and environmental information

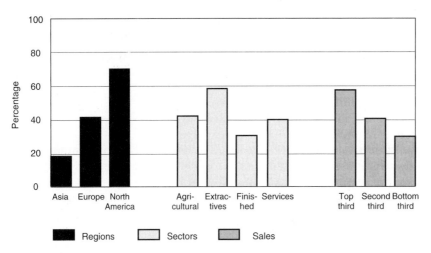

Figure 18-1. Proportion of companies having a formal published international environmental policy statement. (*TCMD/DESD Benchmark Survey, 1990/91.*)

instruments; responsibility of employees; environmental management practices; environmental protection measures; emergency plans; information to the public; and relations with customers.

Amoco Corporation Corporate Policy

To conduct activities in a manner consistent with appropriate safety, health, and environmental considerations; To manufacture and market products and furnish user information on them in a manner consistent with appropriate safety, health, and environmental considerations; To establish and maintain corporate controls, including periodic reviews; To assure that the Company's policy is being properly implemented and maintained; To work with all levels of government in the furtherance and development of appropriate public policies supportive of environmental quality, product safety, and occupational health and safety; To comply with applicable environmental quality, occupational health and safety, and product safety laws and regulation; To build and operate facilities in a manner to protect the health and safety of employees and of individuals in the surrounding communities; To safeguard employees' health through appropriate medical programs.

Policies and Programs.   Environmental policies are internal codes of conduct setting targets and standards for environmental protection in the corporation. Programs are more specific operational guidelines on how the corporation can implement the objectives expressed in corporate policies. Without corporatewide policies, EH&S issues do not gain the benefits of shared knowledge and expertise, and the control with affiliates will tend to be ad hoc and piecemeal.

The Benchmark Survey questionnaire provided a list of 23 specific policies that go beyond national requirements which transnational corporations may have applied throughout the corporation. These are policies on issues such as air, water, and soil pollution, worker health and safety, waste disposal, and sustainable development. Figure 18-2 shows a breakdown of the percentage of firms that have one or more such policies. Generally, the respondents seemed to make an extended use of corporate policies: 75% have policies in place; one-fifth reported having over 15 such policies; and the average respondent has 5.2 companywide policies.

There are significant variations among the corporations. It was found that European corporations, corporations that process agricultural raw materials, and smaller corporations are least likely to have in place any of the 23 specific companywide policies listed in the questionnaire, whereas U.S. and Japanese corporations, corporations in the extractive and finished products sector, and corporations with high sales are most inclined to have such policies.[11]

Table 18-1 has grouped corporate policies and programs into five main categories and shown the percentage of respondents having such policies and programs. It was found that energy-related activities play a central role on the corporate agenda. Clearly, the repeated energy crises of the seventies and early eighties have made corporations highly aware of the importance of stable energy supplies and of the savings to be obtained from energy-conserving activities.

Health- and safety-related policies and programs are more widely adopted than those pertaining to the environment in general. The reason for this finding could be that worker health and safety has a longer regulatory history, and poli-

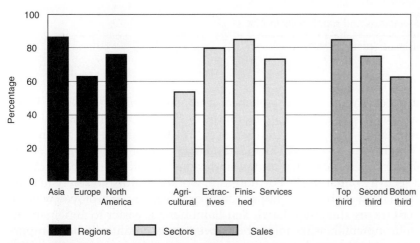

Figure 18-2. Proportion of companies having companywide policies going beyond national regulation. (*TCMD/DESD Benchmark Survey, 1990/91.*)

Table 18-1. Corporate Policy Priorities: Corporate Activities on EH&S and Sustainable Development

Higher-priority areas	Percentage of respondents
Energy-related activities:	
R&D for energy efficient production	70.7
Policies for securing energy supplies	67.7
Policies for conserving nonrenewable resources	54.4
Energy conservation	54.0
Health and safety activities:	
Worker health and safety	67.5
Safety audits	64.7
Accident prevention	60.3
Emergency preparedness	58.0
Hazard assessment procedures	56.9
Traditional environment activities:	
Water quality and pollution	48.1
Air quality and pollution	47.2
Noise pollution	41.1
Soil quality and pollution	31.2
Waste disposal related activities:	
Recycling	84.5
Waste-handling procedures	56.3
Waste disposal	51.6
Waste-reduction technologies	48.7

Lower-priority areas	Percentage of respondents
Predominantly sustainable development activities:	
Greenhouse gas generation reduction	30.1
Renewable energy sources	22.0
Protection of endangered species	15.8
Protection of biodiversity	10.1
Policies for protection of wetlands and rain forests in LDCs	9.2

SOURCE: TCMD/DESD Benchmark Survey, 1990/91.

cies to that effect may be more established in transnational corporations. Bjorn Stigson, head of AB Flakt and a member of the Business Council for Sustainable Development, notes this historical difference: "We treat nature like we treated workers a hundred years ago. We included then no cost for the health and social security of workers in our calculations, and today we include no cost for the health and security of nature."[12] Furthermore, worker health and safety may be perceived to have a more direct impact on operations since employee welfare and productivity are directly related, and liabilities are easier to anticipate. In contrast, environmental issues might be viewed as externalities whose importance declines with distance beyond the factory gate. Firms in the top third sales group are considerably more likely to undertake programs in accident prevention and health and safety than the bottom third group (60 to 80 vs. 35 to 55%). Large corporations have more extensive operations, face greater legal consequences, and possess the needed managerial and financial resources to undertake such programs.

Unilever's Mandatory Health and Safety Policies

Unilever Plc. has mandatory policies, which are implemented worldwide, for product safety and for health and safety at work. Implementation of these policies is a major responsibility of the chairman of each of its operating companies throughout the world and is facilitated by a series of Unilever guidelines and technical policies, including guidelines for environmental protection.

Looking at typical environmental issues such as air, water, or waste, Table 18-1 indicates that waste issues are of particular concern to the responding companies. Soaring expenses for cleanup and waste treatment are likely explanations for this finding.[13] Fewer companies have activities related to air, water, soil, and noise pollution. Interestingly, Japanese corporations are significantly more inclined to have policies on air, water, and noise than European and U.S. corporations. Close to 70% of Japanese respondents have policies on these issues, but only 40 to 50% of U.S. corporations and 20 to 30% of European corporations have them, depending on the activity in question. This difference probably reflects the high salience of those issues in densely populated Japan. In the case of soil contamination, however, North American–based firms tend to have more polices than Japanese and European–based firms, a finding that could be related to the strict U.S. Superfund legislation.

Some activities mentioned in the questionnaire, such as protection of the rain forest and specific less-developed-country (LDC) programs or policies for the reduction of greenhouse-gas emissions, are predominantly related to the international sustainable development discussion. As Table 18-1 indicates, few respondents are engaged in such activities. Nevertheless, one-third of the respondents have policies on greenhouse-gas reduction, a finding probably related to the mandatory phasing out of CFCs as stipulated in the Montreal Protocol.

Environmental Regulations and International Guidelines

Business prefers self-regulation, and much of the management literature treats corporate environmental management as the result of executive decisions alone. Similarly, individual business and industrial associations seem to claim that business to a large extent regulates itself. They support their claim by exhibiting impressive corporate environmental practices.[14] Whatever merits those accounts might have, they tend to disregard that corporate management does not take place in a vacuum but is strongly influenced by regulatory frameworks, international guidelines, and public pressure.

Regulatory Frameworks.   In recent years, the body of regulations for corporations to observe has exploded. For example, the EC Commission has issued more than 300 environmental laws, and in addition European corporations have to comply with national legislation. In the United States, the operations of IBM's Mannassas plant, for example, are covered by some 15,000 pages of state and federal environmental regulation.

Agenda 21

Governments should "establish effective combinations of economic, regulatory and voluntary (self-regulatory) approaches." (8.32)

"Voluntary private initiatives should (also) be encouraged." (30.8)

The survey findings repeatedly showed a close relationship between national regulation and corporate EH&S practices. Respondents were asked which of the following factors had prompted change in companywide environmental policies and programs: consumer protests, negative media publicity, potential legal costs, home country environmental regulation, host country environmental regulations, accidents at their firm, and accidents at other firms. The results are summarized in Fig. 18-3. Sixty-two percent of the respondents said that the development of EH&S laws and regulations in the home country motivated changes in environmental policies and programs. This finding is consistent with the results of a survey conducted among 98 U.S. corporations by Tufts University. This survey identified government laws and regulations as the most influential factor in the development of corporate environmental policies.[15]

The importance of national regulations in influencing corporate environmental management is further supported by the Benchmark Survey's finding of differences between the EH&S practices depending on the location of corporate headquarters. As seen in Fig. 18-2, U.S. and Japanese corporations are significantly more inclined to have environmental policies and programs than their European counterparts.[16] Also, the content of corporate management varies among these three regions in that TNCs in different regions seem to concentrate on different EH&S aspects.

Overall, more than 20% of the respondents stated that environment-related legal actions involving the company influenced change in environmental programs and policies. One-third of the U.S. corporations cited legal action as influ-

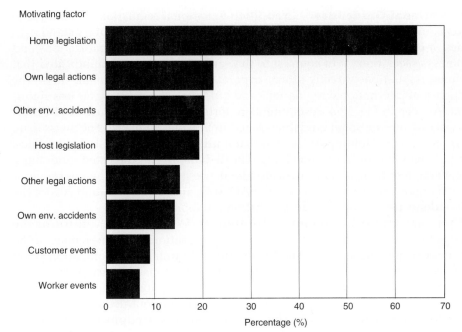

Figure 18-3. Factors influencing change in companywide environmental policies and programs. (*TCMD/DESD Benchmark Survey, 1990/91.*)

ential, but only 18% of the Japanese and 10% of the European corporations. The litigious nature of the North American business environment may be responsible for this sensitivity to legal actions. A survey conducted by Booz-Allen & Hamilton in 1991 among 220 U.S. business executives confirmed that environmental policy in U.S. corporations in most cases was driven by threat, that is, fear of lawsuits and criminal prosecution, rather than opportunity.[17]

In Europe, accidents and malfunctions with ensuing environmental damage are the second most frequently cited reason for change in EH&S management. Major accidents, such as Bhopal, Seveso, and Basel, appear to have influenced the EH&S policies of many companies in this region. For example, a Swiss chemical company, Sandoz, attributes the change of its entire corporate policy to the 1986 accident at its Basel plant. However, smaller-scale incidents at particular TNC subsidiaries, such as leaking storage tanks, also seem to have played an important role in the establishment of EH&S policies in several corporations.

In general, the respondents reported a relatively minor role for consumer- and worker-related events in determining environmental policy. However, a Belgian firm that requested anonymity reported that staff had instigated change by objecting to asbestos materials in the workplace, and Degussa Ag. cited Greenpeace campaigns against the use of CFCs as decisive in shaping its environmental policy.

International Guidelines.   In addition to national regulations, corporations are encouraged to observe and adopt a growing number of voluntary standards, codes of conduct, or guidelines developed by international organizations and business associations.[18] In contrast to the earlier analysis, which indicated that national regulations directly affect corporate environmental management, the influence of international regulations and guidelines seems to be far less significant. As seen in Fig. 18-4, respondents reported only marginal use of 11 different existing international guidelines listed in the questionnaire. The Swiss firm, Alusuisse-Lonza Holding AG, stated that it utilizes nine of the cited guidelines, but less than half of the respondents reported any use of the listed guidelines. In general, less than 10% of the respondents use guidelines set by intergovernmental organizations, such as UNEP, FAO, ILO, and OECD. Around 20% of the respondents use sectorial trade association guidelines.

There are important regional differences: While almost a third of the European and U.S. firms use sectorial trade-association guidelines, none of the Japanese corporations does. The International Standards Organization (ISO) technical environmental guidelines and CMA's Responsible Care program are quite predictably adhered to mainly by European and North American firms, 30 and 39% respectively. Only very few Japanese corporations use any of the mentioned guidelines. However, the questionnaire's predominant focus on

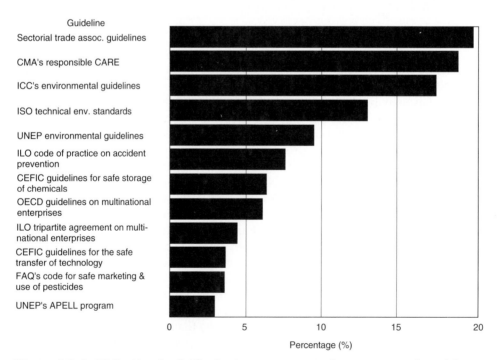

Figure 18-4. Utilization level of voluntary international environmental guidelines. (*TCMD/DESD Benchmark Survey, 1990/91.*)

European and U.S. guidelines may not have done Japanese corporations full justice in this regard. A recent survey among 500 Japanese corporations found that the Keidanren Environmental Charter is being utilized by 70% of the Japanese corporations.[19]

Agenda 21

Business and industry should increase self-regulation, guided by appropriate codes, charters and initiatives integrated into all elements of business planning and decisionmaking. (30.26)

Adopt and report on the implementation of codes of conduct promoting best environmental practice. (30.10)

Asked what role the United Nations should play in the future in regard to international regulation of business and industry, 62% of the respondents want the UN to reduce differences in environmental rules and regulations, and more than half prefers initiatives which would facilitate the development of international policy guidelines. Similarly, the Tufts University study found that 76% of 98 U.S. respondents predicted that the international harmonization of EH&S regulation would lead to improved corporate environmental practices.[20] Clearly, the corporate community wants international coordination of EH&S regulations in order to keep a level playing field. Even if this strong preference for internationally harmonized standards contradicts the present underutilization of such standards, it is a positive signal from a United Nations perspective that corporations, *in principle,* support EH&S boundaries to the international marketplace.

International Integration of Corporate Environmental Management

In recent years, the management literature has discussed a trend toward globalization of corporate management in general, and environmental management in particular.[21] It is claimed that increasingly companies set worldwide standards geared to the toughest laws and conduct assessments to minimize liability and to avoid operating with too many environmental standards. The concept of global environmental management appears to have much in common with the concept of sustainable development. The more TNCs investing in developing countries could apply technologies and practices which are functionally equivalent to their home countries, the less significant the effects of weak environmental regulations and enforcement systems in developing countries would be. Given this background, it is not surprising that UNCED recommended worldwide integration of corporate policies on sustainable development.

Agenda 21

Be encouraged to establish worldwide corporate policies on sustainable development. (30.22)

Introduce policies and commitments to adopt equivalent or not less stringent standards of operation as in the country of origin. (19.52 and 20.30)

Report annually on routine emissions of toxic chemicals to the environment even in the absence of host country requirements. (19.50)

One way of examining the level of worldwide integration achieved by corporations involves analysis of the content of corporate policy statements for explicit international references. Among the 43% of the respondents that reported having a published policy statement, explicit international references were found in only a handful of those statements (see box). This finding is consistent with the Tufts University study of 98 U.S. corporations. Here it was found that less than 20% of the respondents have an explicit statement "to meet or exceed U.S. laws overseas when foreign law is less stringent."[22]

Policy Statements with an Explicit International Aspect

White Consolidated Industries, Inc., makes a statement to "establish and maintain programs to assure that environmental laws and regulations applicable to its products and operations are known and obeyed; *adopt its own standards where laws or regulation may not be adequately protective, and adopt, where necessary, its own standards where laws do not exist*." The policy of a major U.S. based corporation that requested anonymity is in a similar way to "conduct all operations, including the sale and distribution of products and services, in compliance with all applicable environmental laws, regulations and standards." This company goes further when it states "adopt appropriate standards to protect people and the environment *where laws or regulations do not exist or may be inadequate*."

The Swedish automobile manufacturer Volvo has made the following six-point pledge in its environmental policy: (1) Develop products which will meet highest efficiency requirements; (2) opt for manufacturing processes that have least impact on the environment; (3) participate and conduct research and development in the environment field; (4) select consistent raw materials and components; (5) apply a total view regarding impact of products on the environment; (6) *strive to attain a uniform, worldwide environmental standard for processes and products.*

The respondents were asked whether they have formal arrangements between headquarters and overseas affiliates and subsidiaries for coordinating EH&S efforts. Less than half of the firms have such arrangements with their fully controlled affiliates. Even fewer firms (15%) have such arrangements with partially controlled joint-venture affiliates (see Fig. 18-5). Whereas 57% of the U.S. corporations have formal arrangements for allocation of responsibilities on environmental management between corporate headquarters and controlled foreign affiliates, only 32% of the Japanese respondents have such programs. Also, U.S. companies are significantly more likely to have arrangements with noncontrolled affiliates (19% compared with 8% in Japan). This finding is consistent with other findings of the survey, suggesting that U.S. companies are relatively more sensitive and/or aware of the international aspects of their activities than corporations from other regions. For example, U.S. respondents are more inclined to have international policy statements, and more inclined to cite changes in legislation in a host country as the thing prompting overall companywide environmental policies and programs (18 U.S. companies quoted changes in host country legislation as influential, but only 5 Japanese and 9 European companies). Two-thirds of the companies having EH&S arrangements with noncontrolled affiliates are in the extractive based sector. This finding is probably related to the lengthy experiences which many chemical corporations have had with EH&S management in general, and accidents among affiliates and subsidiaries in particular. Given this history, most prefer to control the environmental aspects of the foreign ventures.

Considering that 75% of the respondents have companywide environmental policies and programs of some sort in place, the relatively weak formalization of relations to foreign subsidiaries is striking. But the finding is consistent with the absence of a specific international dimension in all but a few of the policy

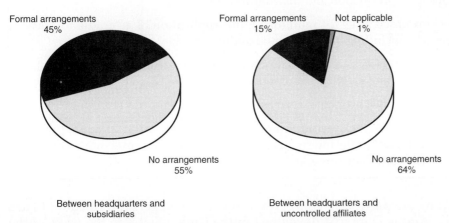

Figure 18-5. Management of subsidiaries. (*TCMD/DESD Benchmark Survey, 1990/91.*)

statements. Three interpretations are possible: (1) companies do not consider control over environmental management in affiliates to be a major issue; (2) companies consider it a major issue, but have been slow to develop formal policies for overseas operations and subsidiaries; and (3) companies consider it a major issue, but choose to address such challenges on an ad hoc, case-by-case basis, rather than through a top-down corporate policy approach.

Management Communications and Control Systems

The focus now shifts from the written policies, regulations, and guidelines that guide corporate environmental management to specific management communications and control activities. This section examines the way corporations control EH&S management on operational levels, and how they communicate environmental issues internally as well as externally.

EH&S Data-Collecting Activities.   The collection of environmental data and the dissemination of this information throughout the corporation is an important first step in improving the firm's impact upon the environment. Information gathering systems, such as EH&S audits or environmental accounting, are important vehicles by which executives become aware of the firm's processes and liabilities and ensure that corporate policies and principles are observed at operational levels.

Agenda 21

Establish environmental management systems, including environmental auditing of production and distribution sites. (20.13)

Develop procedures for monitoring the application of a "cradle to grave" approach, including environmental audits. (20.19)

Conduct environmental audits of existing industries to improve in-plant regimes for the management of hazardous wastes. (20.31)

Give high priority to the hazard assessment of chemicals. (19.15)

Work towards the development and implementation of concepts and methodologies for the internalization of environmental costs into accounting and pricing mechanisms. (30.9)

Audits are particularly important to keep managers informed on EH&S issues. Audits were first developed in the United States in the wake of the Superfund legislation, as a way of identifying liabilities and checking that the corporation complies with regulation. Today many industries see this proce-

Table 18-2. Environmental Data Collection

Higher-priority programs and procedures	Percentage of respondents
Standardized companywide safety audit procedures	64.7
International safety and environmental audits	64.7
Standardized environmental audit procedures	57.8
Standardized hazard assessment procedures	56.9
Monitoring hazardous waste disposal procedures in LDCs	47.8
Environmental bulletin for company managers	44.4

Lower-priority programs and procedures	Percentage of respondents
Standardized pollution monitoring techniques	39.9
Companywide environmental impact assessment	37.2
Standardized environmental impact assessment procedures	39.6
Separate annual environmental statement for the corporate board	37.8
Monitor stacks for air emission components in LDCs	36.6
International environmental accounting	29.7
Survey on biological species on undeveloped lands in LDCs	8.7

SOURCE: TCMD/DESD Benchmark Survey, 1990/91.

dure as absolutely essential, especially before new acquisitions. Remarkably, almost two-thirds of the firms surveyed have enacted standardized procedures and programs for EH&S audits (see Table 18-2).

In addition to auditing, Table 18-2 lists several other EH&S data-collecting procedures such as assessments, monitoring, and accounting. Where hazards are involved, it seems that most respondents have procedures in place. Fifty-seven percent have procedures for hazard assessment. Thirty percent of the respondents reported that they conduct environmental accounting, a notable improvement from a study conducted by UNCTC/TCMD only two years before. Here it was found that less than 10% had established environmental accounting procedures.[23] Other data-collecting procedures, such as environmental impact assessments or surveys in developing countries, are less frequently utilized by the corporations.

There are slight variations between American and Japanese firms. Japanese corporations are more involved with safety audits (82 vs. 69%), whereas U.S. corporations emphasize environment audits (75 vs. 62%). Both U.S. and Japanese corporations are considerably more inclined to utilize environmental data-collection procedures than are European corporations. For example, only 31% of European corporations had environmental audits, and 42% had safety audits.

Looking at sectorial variations, it was found that the extractive sector (oil and chemical TNCs) is approximately 10 to 15% more inclined to utilize EH&S data-collecting procedures than the average corporation.[24] This finding probably reflects the high environmental liabilities which characterize this sector. Interestingly, the service sector is as likely to have audit procedures as any other sector; in fact, 77% of the service companies have safety audit procedures, but only 65% of all respondents. This response suggests a strong corporate desire to keep track of environmental issues, even though the adverse environmental impacts of corporations in this sector presumably are limited.

Innovative Data-Collection Systems in Europe

Five corporations—three Swiss (Ciba-Geigy, Schindler Holding, Sandoz) and one each from Germany (a computer company) and Belgium (Polarcup International)—use risk analysis and environmental auditing in an attempt to filter out at the earliest possible stage future environmental risks resulting from corporate activities. Ciba-Geigy has introduced a "Central Environmental Protection Data Collection" and introduced the environmental audit in 1981. Also a special Energy Commission to set objectives for energy conservation and to propagate information on successful energy saving activities was introduced in 1981.

While there are significant regional and sectorial differences, the central factor in explaining the scope and content of EH&S data-collecting procedures is the corporate size. Those in the top third sales group are generally twice as likely to have such data-collecting procedures in place as is the bottom third group. It is probable that larger corporations require formal procedures effectively to manage environmental performance, whereas smaller corporations can rely on more informal ways of collecting environmental data.

EH&S data-collecting procedures are used less extensively in the context of developing countries. Between 20 and 30% of the respondents repeatedly reported that data are insufficient at headquarters when asked specific questions of their developing countries' activities. Consistent with survey findings on parent-affiliate relations, this finding indicates that information flows between plants in developing countries and corporate headquarters are weak. This observation supports McKinsey & Co.'s study finding that most CEOs outside developing countries are not certain whether the level of knowledge in their industry is adequate to deal with the relevant developing countries' environmental issues effectively.[25]

Ciba-Geigy Acquisitions

Ciba-Geigy has developed a checklist for cases of acquisition, including consideration of the following points:

- Disused landfills
- Groundwater surveys
- Hazardous materials

- Resource research
- Scenario analysis
- Location survey
- Emissions, outflows
- Solvents
- Waste
- Energy
- Storage

Public Relations Activities. Most company publications collected through the Benchmark Survey stress the importance of being good corporate citizens and neighbors, and of supporting various public charities and undertakings. Although public outlook has a long history in corporations, the strong emphasis on the public relations aspects of EH&S issues is a noteworthy trend. Several factors might have made corporations address these aspects. More and more consumers have become environmentally conscious and consider not only the price and quality of the product but also the way in which the product has been produced.[26] Also, the NIMBY factor ("Not in my back yard") makes it increasingly important for corporations to have good community relations in siting situations. Finally, good relations with regulators and environmental groups can help offset adverse consequences of regulations. Thus it seems that corporations stress public relations because public goodwill is a solid business asset.

Agenda 21

Report annually on their environmental record as well as on their use of energy and natural resources. (30.10)

Share their environmental management experiences with local authorities, national governments and international organizations. (30.22)

Table 18-3 lists 15 public relations activities grouped as higher- and lower-priority activities. Between 40 and 50% of the respondents publish reports and brochures on their environmental performance. Nearly two-thirds of the firms publish material safety data sheets (MSDS) for their products, which help users of products and company employees to understand the risks involved. Half the firms engage in product and safety information labeling. The relatively high utilization of these measures reflects recent mandatory requirements such as Right-to-Know legislation, which are becoming common in many countries. Despite the pressure from environmental groups for corporate use of "green"

Table 18-3. Public Relations Activities

Higher-priority activities	Percentage of respondents
Contents of material safety data sheets	63.7
Contents of product labels and safety instructions	52.3
Community participation in emergency planning	51.4
Voluntary financing of environmental organizations	51.0
Annual meeting between headquarters and local environmental officials	50.3
Separate environmental report and environmental section in annual report	47.2
Contributions to local environmental and nature societies	46.1
Formal published international policy and programs	43.1
Toxic education programs for work force or the surrounding communities in developing countries	40.5

Lower-priority activities	Percentage of respondents
Special public briefing or brochure on environmental performance	38.5
Disclosure of product-risk information	32.7
Disclosure of process-risk information	28.5
Public access to environmental R&D results	27.2
Public access to corporate lands for nature walks	25.2
Green labeling	12.3

SOURCE: TCMD/DESD Benchmark Survey, 1990/91.

labeling, it is much less widespread (12%) than legislation-induced labeling practices. Similarly, a recent study of U.S. TNCs by Deloitte & Touche reported only a 20% usage rate for "green" labeling.[27]

Both in the questionnaires and in the information submitted as attachments to the questionnaires, the corporations proved rather reticent in their information policy regarding environmental risks resulting from their products and processes. Only about 30% of the respondents have companywide policies and programs for the disclosure of product and process risks. The general impression of an unwillingness to disclose information on environmental risks has been supported in a recent survey conducted by "The Company Reporting" in Europe. The survey found that only 11% of the corporations disclosed concrete information such as environmental policies or achievements. An additional 12% disclosed information so general as to be virtually meaningless.[28]

Public relations awareness and activities are highest among corporations which have experienced environmental disasters, and more generally, among chemical corporations which apparently have engaged in a collective learning and improvement process in the wake of Bhopal. Thus more than half the corporations in the extractives sector, which consists of oil and chemical industries, disclose product and process risk. Several corporations in this sector also publish information on previous environmental incidents or problems of product and process risk not yet resolved by the corporation. For example, Sandoz International Ltd. has published a special bulletin on the 1986 incident in its Basel plant.

Ciba-Geigy Communications Policy

Ciba-Geigy Ltd. emphasizes the following principles as applicable throughout the corporation:

- Competence
- Openness
- Internal communication
- International communication
- Crisis communication

Looking at community-related activities such as community participation in emergency planning or financing of environmental groups, corporations seem to be quite aware of the importance of good community relations for the operation of the corporation. As shown in Table 18-3, more than half of the corporations responded that headquarters meet annually with local environmental officials and that communities participate in the corporations' emergency planning. More than half the corporations contribute financially to environmental organizations, although seldom is it specified what kind of environmental organizations. A few corporations expressed a very clear community orientation in their policy statements. For example, Borden's "Social Responsibility" subsection of its annual report begins, "Borden, Inc. strives to be a responsible citizen, contributing to the well-being of society in general and to the benefit of the communities in which our people work and live." The subsection then continues to describe Borden's community responsibilities under four headings: (1) Equal Employment Opportunity; (2) Minority Purchasing; (3) Charitable Contributions; and (4) Environmental Protection.

Specific examples of community-related activities identified in the attachments to the questionnaire include maintaining sanctuaries, sponsoring science and environmental fairs, sponsoring ecological campaigns, underwriting environmentally oriented educational programs, and supporting nongovernmental organizations in developing countries.

In general, North American TNCs have more of the procedures and practices for public relations displayed in Table 18-3 than their Japanese and European counterparts. This is again consistent with the tendency of U.S. corporations to have published EH&S policy statements. Furthermore, U.S. companies are almost twice as likely to formally report and inform on environmental performance as Japanese corporations (60 to 70% in the United States vs. 30 to 40% in Japan), with European corporations falling in between. U.S. TNCs are also leading in terms of disclosure procedures and relations with communities. For example, almost half the U.S. corporations disclose product risk, which is twice the percentage of European and Japanese corporations. There are notable exceptions to this trend. Japanese corporations are somewhat more likely to have green labeling programs. And European corporations are more likely than U.S. TNCs to arrange annual meetings with local environmental officials (57 vs. 44% in the United States). The latter difference probably reflects the relatively more *corporatistic* regulatory approach found in many European countries.[29]

Labor Relations Activities.   Historically workers health and safety regulation preceded environmental regulation. Therefore, it is not surprising to find that the respondents reported a high involvement of workers in EH&S activities. Labor communications and training is crucial for effective EH&S management in that it alerts employees to management expectations and gives them the necessary technical skills and procedures to achieve those expectations.

Agenda 21

Industry and business associations should cooperate with workers and trade unions to continuously improve the knowledge and skills for implementing sustainable development operations. (30.13)

Integrate cleaner production principles and case studies into training programmes and organize environmental training programs for the private sector and other groups in developing countries. (20.18)

Survey questions in the area of worker-related issues are listed in Table 18-4. More than 60% of the respondents have worker-related activities, such as training programs and workers participation in developing EH&S procedures. Moreover, more than 80% of the respondents indicated that EH&S responsibilities are a part of the job description, and nearly 70% have environmental performance as part of employees performance record. However, to motivate the staff effectively EH&S objectives may need to be integrated into compensation systems so that EH&S criteria, alongside cost, quality, and profit, influence salaries and promotions. Here, around half the corporations reported that they have incentive schemes to induce staff to contribute to the company's environmental objectives. This result is much higher than previous industry estimates of only 10%.[30] The effectiveness of incentive schemes is stressed by Kodak, which reduced environmental accidents 47% when management compensation became tied to chemical spills.

Despite the importance that corporations seem to devote to labor aspects of EH&S management, only 16 corporations reported worker-related events as influential in formulating their companywide EH&S policies (see Fig. 18-3). Interestingly, one of the companies that responded that worker-related events are influential—a French oil corporation—reported that it views environmental training of its 50,000 employees and their attentiveness in the workplace as its biggest environmental problem.

Table 18-4. Labor Relations Activities

Higher-priority activities	Percentage of respondents
Environmental protection or health and safety responsibilities a part of an employee's job description	82.3
Educating staff on the environmental impact of the firm's operations	68.6
Environmental performance and safety records part of staff's performance evaluations	68.6
Workers' participation in setting EH&S standards	67.8
Worker health and safety as a companywide policy	67.5
Standardized companywide worker safety training programs	67.3
Standardized contents of material and safety data sheets	63.7
Standardized management safety training programs	58.2
Incentive schemes at the plant level to induce staff to contribute to the company's environmental objectives	47.4
Lower-priority activities	**Percentage of respondents**
Adoption of ILO's code of practice on accident prevention	7.5
Adoption of ILO tripartite agreement on multinational enterprises	4.5

SOURCE: TCMD/DESD Benchmark Survey, 1990/91.

Looking at regional variations, the general trend is that Japanese corporations have more EH&S-related activities for workers. For example, nine out of ten Japanese TNCs have worker safety training programs. Moreover, Japanese corporations are considerably more inclined to integrate environmental concerns in personnel policies than their European and U.S. counterparts. Interestingly, though, European firms, which in most other EH&S activities rank third behind the United States and Japan, in the case of labor aspects of EH&S management follow Japanese corporations closely, with U.S. corporations trailing behind. In the case of involving workers in setting EH&S standards, European firms are leading, a fact that probably reflects the relatively high level of unionization in Europe and the historically high degree of institutionalization of labor relations in most European countries.

Ciba-Geigy Involving Employees

In the suggestion scheme an "eco-factor" was introduced for calculating the premium paid for suggestions which improved the environmental performance. The zero error program which allows employees to report environmental problems without proposing a solution was introduced in 1973. "Oekogenda," an environmental management by objectives scheme was introduced in 1990, the "be smart" program for propagating environmental success stories in 1989.

Summary of Survey Findings

The general impression from the analysis of the Benchmark Survey data is that transnational corporations are responding to public and governmental pressures for improved corporate environmental performance. Probably, some changes are largely superficial, initiated only for public relations purposes. But there are indications that in many corporations some level of environmental and especially health and safety considerations are being genuinely incorporated within corporate identities and that the linkages between EH&S and business objectives are beginning to be recognized. Overall, the survey suggests that most corporations are engaged in a kind of environmental management in which short-term costs and liabilities are sought, anticipated, and prevented through environmental management procedures. Thus activities such as audits, safety procedures, waste and recycling policies, and energy-saving programs are well established among the responding corporations. Apparently, 3M's slogan, "Pollution Prevention Pays," is subscribed to by the majority of the respondents. However, more diffuse pollutions, such as air, noise, land, or water pollution, are less frequently addressed than issues that affect health and safety and/or involve immediate savings. Perhaps pollution prevention in those areas pays less.

3M's 3Ps

3M's "pollution prevention pays" (3P) dates back to 1975, and since then more than 3000 projects to prevent pollution at the source have been undertaken. 3M estimates that it has saved $537 million as a result of 3P.

Significant variations were found in the sample: The high environmental liabilities characteristic of the extractive sector are perhaps responsible for its tendency to be considerably more engaged in environmental management than other sectors. Also, corporate size is an important factor in determining the scope and content of environmental programs. Large TNCs usually have more EH&S policies, programs, and procedures. The explanation probably is that "economies of scale" will encourage larger corporations to establish environmental policies. Finally, significant regional variations in the sample were observed. In general, U.S. and Japanese corporations are more inclined to have environmental management activities than European corporations. While the tough enforcement and litigation system in the United States explains much of this finding, the high degree of Japanese engagement is somewhat more surprising, particularly because Japanese management practices traditionally have been described as relatively conservative compared with U.S. practices.

Some corporations still haven't established the most basic procedures for managing their environmental impacts. One-quarter of the respondents have no environmental policies and programs, and often the respondents reported that they don't have information about their EH&S activities or impacts. International guidelines are rarely observed, even though most corporations found international harmonization of environmental standards important. Moreover, relatively inexpensive means of confidence building, such as disclosure of hazards and risks, are utilized by less than one-third of the respondents. Finally, particular sustainable development activities have hardly been undertaken by the responding corporations. In relation to developing countries, only a handful of corporations have specific procedures in place in cases where governmental regulations are absent or weak, and regarding activities related to the global commons such as oceans, the rain forest, or biodiversity only a small minority have policies and activities. The latter finding suggests that the corporate community has just started considering its role in sustainable development, if at all, and that a huge gap between the international community's expectations, as expressed in Agenda 21, and the actual state of corporate environmental management exists in this regard.

The following section presents United Nations suggestions on how transnational corporations can improve their EH&S and sustainable development activities and what international organizations and governments can do to encourage this process.

Recommendations for Responsible Corporate Environmental Management

... I am more convinced than ever before that sustainable development offers the right vision. And a positive approach in converting vision into action is the best alternative. Change will happen, it is inevitable. Two options face us. We can resist change as long as possible, and then suffer the inevitable consequences, or we can accept change as a challenge and be among the leaders in shaping change. It is probably better business to do the latter and it is definitely more fun.
                                                                    Stephan Schmidheiny

There is every reason to believe that the importance of business, and in particular transnational corporations, will increase in the coming years. Transnational corporations' investments, technology, and managerial know-how will grow in importance as the international economy globalizes, as planned economies transform into market economies, and as the developing world becomes more integrated into the international economy. As more nations pursue growth and development objectives through market reform and liberalization of the Foreign Direct Investment (FDI) regimes, transnational corporations will increasingly become engines of capital formation, human resources development, technology transfer, and the exchange of goods and services.

From an environmental perspective, an increasingly global economy—with transnational corporations playing a pivotal role—has both positive and negative implications. The internationalization of economic activity can entail a thrust toward harmonization of national environmental standards and practices and thus strengthening international environmental cooperation; the opening of developing countries to foreign direct investments might lead to the transfer of environmentally sound technology and managerial skills; and the liberalization of trade might give more developing countries access to developed countries' markets. In short, a global economy, with transnational corporations playing a central role, might help break the poverty circle and improve the environment worldwide.

However, a development strategy resting on transnational corporations and trade and investment liberalization might also jeopardize environmental objectives. For example, there is a possibility that countries will use low environmental standards as a way of competing for capital from transnational corporations. Hitherto, there is only scant evidence of this "pollution haven" thesis. But it is likely that growing pollution-abatement costs in the industrialized countries might encourage some corporations to relocate to developing countries.[31] Similarly, such a development strategy might increasingly conflict with national and regional environment and consumer protection policies. Unilateral protection measures could well be perceived as nontariff trade barriers by trade partners, and thus lead to retaliatory action and trade wars. Recent environment-related disputes in the GATT and at the EC Court, as well as the debate over the North American Free Trade Agreement (NAFTA), clearly validate this fear.[32]

In order to prevent adverse environmental consequences of increased trade and FDI, and to utilize the large positive potential of transnational corporations in sustainable development, concerted action from business, governments, and international organizations is absolutely crucial. We suggest that this concerted action should rest on four basic principles: (1) Corporations should manage their environmental assets and liabilities in a globally responsible manner, (2) Governments and international organizations should encourage corporate responsiveness and innovativeness in the area of EH&S protection, (3) Governments and international organizations should set international minimum standards in certain key areas, where human health and safety or intrinsic environmental values are at stake, and (4) International organizations should facilitate the harmonization and adaptation of environmental standards and regulations.

Based on these principles, UNCTC/TCMD developed a set of recommendations for the Preparatory Committee for UNCED on the tasks and responsibilities of transnational corporations, governments, and international organizations.[33] These recommendations were distributed to governments, industry, nongovernmental organizations, and academia and used in the negotiation process. They are the synthesis of a wide range of existing intergovernmental resolutions, conventions and declarations, corporate policy statements, and trade association guidelines, as well as the results of the analysis based on the material collected in connection with the Benchmark Survey, and guidance from expert advisers in business, academia, governments, and nongovernmental organizations. A summary version of the recommendations is presented in the following section.[34]

The Recommendations

UNCTC/TCMD's recommendations are grouped under five key program areas: (A) global corporate environmental management; (B) risk and hazard minimization; (C) environmentally sounder consumption patterns; (D) full-cost environmental accounting; and (E) environmental conventions, standards, and guidelines. The program areas originate from themes identified by the Commission on Transnational Corporations as integral components of sustainable development.[35] For each program area a short introduction is made and the overall objectives of the program area are stated. Then follow detailed and action-oriented recommendations required to meet the overall objectives. As sustainable development management involves responsibilities for business as well as governments and international organizations, the text provides details on steps by which corporations, *in cooperation with governments and international organizations,* can make a significant contribution to sustainable development for each of the five program areas.

A. Global Corporate Environmental Management. Managerial leadership in the adoption of consistently high environmental policies is the key to promoting a global standard of corporate responsibility, even ahead of changes in national and international law. Managerial policies can encourage a corporate culture based upon sustainable development values. In order to institutionalize the corporatewide environment and development policies, however, supportive corporate programs and organizational structures are needed. Corporate efforts to integrate environment, health, and safety goals into performance appraisals, organizational structure, and education and training are the key to linking sustainable development with daily decision making. The overall objectives for corporate environmental policies are:

a. Development of globally applicable corporate policies for the shift toward sustainable development.

b. Establishment or strengthening of global corporate environmental management systems and organizational structures in order to supervise and monitor the adjustment to a sustainable managed corporation.

c. Integration of corporate environmental concerns into the sustainable development needs of host countries.

d. Implementation of the corporate programs and practices required to support environmental and developmental goals in all operations throughout the world.

The managerial tasks for corporations to meet those objectives are to:

a. Recognize sustainable development as among the highest of corporate priorities; develop formal corporatewide policy statement regarding the firm's commitment to sustainable development; establish specific operational policies (e.g., on water, air, and soil protection) and sector-specific policies (i.e., on agriculture, mining, textiles, and electronic production).

b. Adopt a "cradle-to-grave" product life cycle management strategy for overseeing the integration of environmental criteria into the firm's complete range of products, processes, and services.

c. Examine the impact of the firm's activities on the global commons and on the environment and development of host countries.

d. Identify the programs required to support the firm's environment and development policy statement for all operations throughout the world and initiate these programs.

The managerial tasks for governments and international organizations are to:

a. Make sustainable development objectives and aims as clear, stable, and understandable to corporations as possible; adopt sustainable development criteria and guidelines in government regulatory requirements and incentive programs; devise regulatory and/or incentive frameworks in order to encourage a "cradle-to-grave" product life cycle approach.

b. Implement programs for gathering information on corporate operational policies, programs, and technologies conducive to sustainable development; establish an international database and information exchange network as a means of providing corporations and governments with information regarding successful corporate policies, programs, and technologies.

c. Establish an internationally recognized award for the leading sustainable managed corporations.

The data and information tasks for corporations are to:

a. Disseminate the general environmental policy statement and corporatewide operational policies in appropriate languages to all home country plants and affiliates and to joint venture partnerships in host countries and disseminate these policies and statements to licensees, customers, suppliers, and subcontractors.

b. Prepare and perform, on a regular basis, environmental audits covering all home and host country operations; measure the performance of affiliates against both international and internal corporate standards.

Tasks in the area of international and regional cooperation and coordination are to:

a. Develop and implement a formal liaison program between transnational corporate affiliates and host governments for mutual consultation and advice on sustainable development issues; create an international advisory body composed of experts from all concerned parties in order to help promote international policies for the health and safety of workers and for the protection and preservation of the environment.

b. Establish information exchange networks among national, regional, and international research and development institutions; create programs on sustainable development management in academic institutions.

c. Implement cooperative programs for the transfer of environmentally sounder technology between transnational corporations and host country firms and local governments.

The financial and cost evaluation tasks for corporations are to:

a. Establish corporate policies which encourage voluntary contributions in support of nongovernmental organizations undertaking sustainable development projects, particularly in host developing countries.

b. Give preference to corporate investment in funds and investments which are compatible with sustainable growth; establish sustainability factors as a key criterion in determining lending policies for potential investment candidates.

c. Forego activities with firms and other entities which do not meet acceptable local, national, and international environmental, health, and safety standards.

The scientific and technological tasks for corporations are to:

a. Update, every five years, corporatewide policies, programs, and practices in the light of the most recent technological developments and scientific understandings.

b. Conduct sustainable development impact assessments for all prospective investments, divestment, and large management contracts; conduct a periodic assessment of the corporation's impact upon the local economic and social conditions in the host country, in particular in a host developing country.

c. Encourage research and development units to conduct environmental impact assessment studies for new technologies, products, and services both prior to and during the development phase.

The human resource development tasks for corporations are to:

a. Integrate environmental and developmental goals into all corporate incentive and compensation programs.

b. Structure lines of responsibility so as to reflect the critical role of environment and development in managerial decision making; designate, within one year, an executive at headquarters and a senior official at the affiliate level responsible for environmental matters; designate a specific officer or committee at the board of directors level responsible for environmental matters; report to the officer or committee on the progress made by the firm in the implementation of the goals of the United Nations Conference on Environment and Development.

c. Educate senior management throughout the world about corporate sustainable development culture, goals, and policies.

d. Sponsor training programs for host country managers and employees on environmental protection, resource management, and sustainable development; create scholarships for host country employees at technical, trade union, engineering, and management schools in order to build their environmental capabilities.

The capacity-building tasks for corporations are to:

a. Evaluate, within one year, the capacity of affiliates, subcontractors, and suppliers to manage their assigned tasks safely; include in all affiliate, subcontractor, and supplier contracts instructions detailing environmental responsibilities.

b. Engage affiliates in decision making in order to enable them to contribute to the economic and environmental development of the countries in which they operate.

The capacity-building tasks for governments and international organizations are to:

a. Provide technical assistance to host governments on sustainable corporate management techniques, fully utilizing local technical knowledge and experience.

b. Assist small and medium-sized enterprises in developing countries in the education and training of management and employees in sustainable development issues.

c. Identify, within one year, critical issues regarding the local economic and social conditions that need to be considered by an environmental and development impact assessment and devise solutions involving those critical issues.

B. Risk and Hazard Minimization.   Promoting risk minimization in all corporate functions is a requisite for furthering environmental protection and ensuring employee health and safety. In most industrialized countries, enterprises must provide notification of risk in connection with the construction and operation of facilities, toxic chemicals, spills, accidents, and worker fatalities and injuries. Developing countries, however, often lack stringent environmental and worker health and safety regulations. When regulations exist, implementation and enforcement may be ineffective owing to a lack of resources, training, equipment, and staff. Because transnational corporations are familiar with best-practice technologies and comply with regulatory requirements in their home countries, they can make a significant positive contribution to worker health and safety, environmental protection, and resource conservation on a worldwide basis. This contribution is especially valuable in countries where the regulatory regime is below the minimum acceptable standards. The following objectives to minimize risk and hazards should be aimed at:

a. Conduct of environmental practices on a consistently high basis in all operations throughout the world.

b. Reduction of emissions and waste at the source through input and process change, rather than reliance on end-of-pipe treatment.

c. Phasing out or minimization of the use and export of highly hazardous processes, products, and services throughout the enterprise's operations.

The managerial tasks for corporations are to:

a. Assess, on a periodic basis, the environmental and health consequences of corporate operations and make every reasonable effort to restore the environment when it is harmed by the firm's activities. Plan for catastrophic events and outline responses.

b. Adopt the precautionary principle by taking action favoring the protection of the environment in situations where scientific uncertainty cannot be eliminated.

c. Assist workers and union representatives in the identification of potential occupational and environmental hazards and avoid taking discriminatory action against those who report conditions that may create a danger to the environment or pose health and safety hazards.

The managerial tasks for governments and international organizations are to:

a. Establish and maintain a regulatory structure with adequate enforcement capabilities for worker health and safety, pollution prevention and natural resource conservation; ensure that at least one governmental agency is specifically responsible for the protection of the environment and worker safety training; ensure that this agency has adequate resources to perform its functions.

b. Establish and enforce national multimedia (e.g., air, land, and water) environmental standards, zoning ordinances, and permit systems.

The data and information tasks for corporations are to:

a. Maintain up-to-date environmental, health, and safety information for all products and processes used throughout the world and distribute the firm's environmental safety manuals to all employees in all working languages.

b. Follow consistently high practices with regard to product warning labels for transport and storage and instructions for safe use and disposal; survey national disclosure requirements in all operations and ensure compliance.

c. Monitor effluent and emission discharges at all operations throughout the world; publish aggregate data for major pollutants.

d. Establish effective information exchange links between controlled affiliates and local businesses regarding newly discovered environmental hazards and resource conservation methods; make available to affiliates, within an appropriate time frame, environmentally sounder technologies and related discoveries from their introduction elsewhere within the enterprise and, within the same time period, provide information regarding these technologies and discoveries to licensees and joint venture partnerships.

e. Introduce into technology sales and management contracts provisions on accident avoidance and safety standards.

The data and information tasks for governments and international organizations are to:

a. Strengthen national capacities to monitor industrial emissions and discharges; authorize professional bodies to assist in monitoring environmental compliance.

b. Develop safety information networks for consumers, workers, and communities; survey international safety disclosure practices and those of other countries and incorporate them into national legislation.

c. Publicize priority lists of high-hazard chemicals, processes, and services; provide clearinghouse functions for new national regulations governing hazardous and toxic products, processes, and services.

Tasks in the area of international and regional cooperation and coordination are to:

a. Assist in the development of regional and international emergency preparedness and contingency plans to reduce the frequency and impact of large-scale environmental accidents; develop common emergency planning standards and requirements; establish regional centers to support businesses and communities in the preparation of contingency plans for high-risk and high-hazard plants.

b. Establish appropriate consultative mechanisms for the periodic assessment of international environmental standards and regulations in order to keep abreast of advances in scientific and technical knowledge.

c. Provide technical assistance to host country governments on risk assessment, monitoring techniques, hazard analysis, and related specialized skills.

The financial and cost-evaluation tasks for corporations are to:

a. Announce clear financial commitments and achievable target dates for expanded research and development efforts in order to raise the corporation's inventory of nature-sparing and nature-enhancing technologies.

b. Identify existing facilities that are economically and/or environmentally unsound to operate due to resource and energy inefficiencies or the level of hazardous waste generated, and prepare an accelerated schedule to replace or retrofit them to environmentally sounder facilities.

The financial and cost-evaluation tasks for governments and international organizations are to:

a. Provide economic incentives to investors using environmentally sounder technological processes and products while discouraging those who do not support public research and development facilities specifically for the development of environmentally sounder technology.

b. Provide financial resources through multilateral development banks and agencies in order to facilitate the transfer of environmentally sounder technology on concessional terms.

The scientific and technological tasks for corporations are to:

a. Apply risk assessment and hazard analysis techniques to the firm's full range of products, processes, and services; utilize the most recent available scientific knowledge in the design of new products, processes, and services in order to prevent serious or irreversible environmental degradation.

b. Develop materials and energy recovery technologies and practices in order to minimize waste discharges, as well as new techniques and technologies for the repair of environmental damage.

c. Ensure that processes exist to either recycle or safely discard the firm's high-risk and high-volume products.

The scientific and technological tasks for governments and international organizations are to:

a. Assist in the development of risk assessment methodologies, and provide technical assistance and training in their use.

b. Develop uniform classification systems for health, safety, and ecological data, and provide international access thereto.

c. Ensure that the regulations and infrastructure needed to support efficiency in recycling and the use of material and energy, as well as the efficient use of environmentally sounder technologies, are in place.

The capacity-building tasks for corporations are to:

a. Provide all affiliates with adequate knowledge, skills, and equipment in order to minimize the risk of accidents and damage to health and the environment; provide standardized staff training at all local plant sites; at least every three years, audit operations in order to determine if knowledge, skills, and equipment are maintained at a consistently high level.

b. Provide technological know-how to local governments and businesses in order to enhance their ability to adopt environmentally sounder technologies.

c. Utilize fully local technical knowledge and solutions when they are environmentally and/or economically superior.

C. Environmentally Sounder Consumption Patterns. The rapid consumption of natural resources beyond nature's ability to replenish and regenerate them diminishes the quality of life throughout the world. A large volume of these resources are used unwisely. Product information regarding environmentally sounder alternatives can help to transform world consumption patterns. In the industrialized countries, eco-labeling and environmental green seals are two of the newer tools to assist consumers in making environmentally sound choices. In developing countries and countries in transition, consumers should be able to choose products that do not place an unfair burden on their natural resource base. Corporate product development and marketing practices should incorporate these new directions. The following objectives will require the coordinated efforts of corporations, governments, and international organizations:

a. Informing workers, distributors, retailers, consumers, and communities of the actual and possible environmental effects of the firm's products and of the steps that they can take to mitigate any adverse effects.

b. Development and redesign of products and services for the shift toward a sustainable lifestyle.

The managerial tasks for corporations are to:

a. Promote product durability and longevity through companywide quality control programs; emphasize the value-added aspects of products and services over the increased consumption of disposable and/or readily obsolescent products.

b. Alter the firm's product mix in order to support the transition to sustainable lifestyle arrangements in developed countries; avoid introducing, through advertising or other means, unsustainable consumption patterns, particularly in newly developing markets.

c. Establish, when appropriate, a marketing commitment to distribute environmentally sounder products and services in all regions.

The data and information tasks for corporations are to:

a. Ensure effective access to, and dissemination of, key environmental documentation throughout the enterprise as soon as the information becomes available.

b. Disseminate relevant environmental, toxicological, epidemiological, and social data developed from impact assessments.

c. Develop marketing strategies emphasizing the environmental aspects of the firm's products, processes, and services, while maintaining accurate information on any related risks.

The data and information tasks for governments and international organizations are to:

a. Develop common information disclosure standards so that users can receive a comparative assessment of a given product's energy and material efficiency and waste-generation potentials.

b. Provide technical assistance to governments and nongovernmental organizations for the evaluation of safety data submitted for public decision making.

c. Enact and enable standard community right-to-know and right-to-act legislation in order to increase access to environmental information.

d. Harmonize eco-labeling standards and terms.

Tasks in the area of international and regional cooperation and coordination are to:

a. Initiate and maintain liaison among all concerned parties on product safety issues.

b. Establish national and regional cooperative mechanisms for the enhancement of product monitoring, assessment, and hazard forecasting capacities.

The financial and cost-evaluation tasks for governments and international organizations are to:

a. Establish public purchasing requirements that support the growth of environmentally sounder products, processes, and services.

b. Retain the patent rights for environmentally sounder technologies resulting from nationally funded research and development.

c. Develop additional mechanisms (e.g., tariffs, taxes, and purchase requirements) to facilitate the transfer of environmentally sounder technologies.

The scientific and technological tasks for corporations are to:

a. Design new products and services which are safe, energy-efficient, conserve resources, and have extended durability and minimal environmental impact; undertake a survey to identify the aspects of existing products and services for which environmental improvement is necessary.

b. Adapt products and services manufactured or distributed in host countries so as to reflect development needs, geographical conditions, and environmental circumstances; progressively remove from the market products that cannot be used safely.

The human resource development tasks for corporations are to:

a. Provide sufficient data to local communities on risks and safety procedures and related environmental data so that they can make informed decisions.

b. Implement joint research and development programs with local enterprises for new products and services compatible with sustainable development, including those associated with local geographical and socioeconomic conditions (e.g., dry-land farming and small-scale producers).

D. Full-Cost Environmental Accounting.   The failure to account for the depletion and degradation of natural resources distorts product costs and prices and leads to unsustainable production and consumption patterns. Current accounting practices report only market transactions and do not record the full cost of natural resource use. No direct costs are assigned to the consumers of common goods such as air and water. Environmental accounting studies indicate that few corporations have adopted environmental accounting procedures. Internalizing all long-term environmental costs in the accounting and reporting process is a vital operational requirement for sustainable development. Achieving this goal requires the development of new accounting rules and financial statements. There is a need for new valuation methods for quantifying the unrecorded costs of nonsustainable development.

Governments can take supportive steps to ensure that market price signals will reflect full environmental costs. They can adopt the "polluter pays" principle which requires the polluter to internalize the costs of pollution prevention; adopt other economic incentives, such as tradable permits, user fees, and deposit refund systems; and remove price distortions in existing governmental programs that cause natural resources to be underpriced. The following objectives will require the coordinated efforts of corporations, governments, and international organizations:

a. Inclusion of environmental considerations in corporate accounting and reporting in order to relate an enterprise's environmental activities to its financial position and performance.

b. Incorporation of full environmental costs into the production of goods and services in order to send the right price signals to producers and consumers.

c. Development of accounting and reporting methods in order to encompass sustainable development considerations in the calculation of financial results.

The managerial tasks for corporations are to:

a. Provide relevant environmental information in their financial statements to shareholders, creditors, employees, governmental authorities, consumers, and the public; separate environmental expenditure from other expenditures; measure and separate environmental liabilities arising from compliance with environmental regulations from other liabilities; develop a program of environmental auditing.

b. Ensure that compensation is provided to those directly and adversely affected by the environmental harm caused by the enterprise.

c. Redefine asset and liability boundaries in order to include public goods, such as air and water quality and biodiversity, in a manner consistent with sustainable development.

d. Develop and use prototype accounts that measure resource use and link resource use to financial statements through appropriate valuation methods.

e. Utilize the results of sustainable development accounting in order to improve sustainable development management.

The managerial tasks for governments and international organizations are to:

a. Remove price distortions arising from governmental programs affecting land, water, energy, and other natural resources.

b. Review existing accounting and reporting regulations and develop new ones which require more transparent reporting.

c. Develop methods and rules for accounting for sustainable development, including the "polluter pays" principle.

The data and information tasks for governments, international organizations, and corporations are to:

a. Develop a national natural resource inventory based on corporate use of renewable and nonrenewable resources.

b. Prepare, every five years, sustainable development reports at the corporate level, using new prototype accounts and statements showing income on a sustainable basis and include in those reports environmental and development items covering the corporation's impact in developing countries, as well as a statement by the board of directors on the status of the corporation's transition to a sustainable managed corporation.

Tasks in the area of international and regional cooperation and coordination are to:

a. Review investment and trade policies in order to remove distortions in pricing and the barriers that often encourage excessive use and dependence on imports and exports of natural resources.

b. Harmonize accounting rules for financial statements which incorporate environmental considerations.

c. Develop common accounting rules for sustainable development.

The capacity-building tasks for governments and international organizations are to:

a. Support practical research for the development of new prototype statements and methods for valuing all environmental resources.

b. Encourage the retraining of auditors in environmental accounting and reporting so that they can verify that the financial statements give a true and fair view of the enterprise's activities and reflect the full environmental costs of production.

E. Environmental Conventions, Standards, and Guidelines. To support corporate efforts in global environmental management, clear environmental conventions, standards, and guidelines are required. Although an increasing number of international environmental policy declarations, resolutions, guidelines, codes of conduct, and conventions have emerged, national regulations are the dominant influence on corporate environmental policy. As a result of the uneven development of environmental law, the coordination of international, regional, and national policies and instruments is urgently required. Corporations are also able to play an integral role in shaping the future direction of sustainable development through the implementation of industry-agreed environmental standards and guidelines. Corporate self-regulating leadership builds an atmosphere of trust among all concerned parties. Self-regulation in conjunction with supportive governmental efforts is fundamental to building, between business and government, a substantive partnership aimed at sustainable development. The following objectives will require the coordinated efforts of corporations, governments, and international organizations:

a. Compliance with and further development of international and regional environmental guidelines and instruments.

b. Compliance with and further development of national environmental law.

c. Compliance with and further development of industry trade association standards and guidelines.

The managerial tasks for corporations are to:

a. Apply the highest practicable principles and standards for environmental protection equivalently throughout the firm's global operations; survey corporate practices in order to ensure that the highest practicable standards are used consistently in all operations throughout the world.

b. Conform to the provisions of international and regional environmental standards, guidelines, and conventions to the extent that they are applicable to corporate activities, even though not mandatory under national law.

c. Observe all national and local laws and regulations for environmental protection, subject to the overriding responsibility to conform with regional and international standards.

d. Adopt and implement policies and programs in accordance with the highest practicable industry-agreed guidelines.

The managerial tasks for governments and international organizations are to:

a. Develop incentives which encourage corporations to adopt sustainable development policies and programs.

b. Enforce environmental laws and regulations, regardless of forms of ownership.

c. Improve worldwide regulatory consistency through the incorporation of internationally agreed principles and standards in national legislation within five years of their international approval if not explicitly stated in the agreement.

d. Address in future environmental instruments the rights and responsibilities of transnational corporations.

The data and information tasks for governments and international organizations are to:

a. Ensure that transnational corporations have the texts of all appropriate international and regional conventions and guidelines, and national regulations and guidelines.

b. Establish or strengthen a regulatory environment supportive of sustainable development.

c. Assist in the dissemination of information on industry-agreed guidelines and standards, especially to small and medium-sized enterprises.

The financial and cost-evaluation tasks for governments and international organizations are to:

a. Develop and offer incentives for the development and implementation of corporate standards that exceed national and/or internationally agreed standards, laws, and regulations.

b. Encourage and offer incentives for research and development technology that contribute to sustainable development and economic progress.

The scientific and technological tasks for corporations are to:

a. Encourage, every five years, international industry groups to reexamine and update industry guidelines in order to incorporate the most recent scientific understandings and technical developments.

b. Develop standards for accountability on compliance with such updated guidelines.

The scientific and technological tasks for governments and international organizations are to:

a. Survey, within one year, standards established by governments, in order to benefit from a comparative evaluation and, within five years, incorporate the best standards determined by that evaluation in national legislation and regulations.

b. Provide adequate means to ensure protection of the property rights of corporations that transfer environmentally sounder technology.

c. Assist, at the request of host governments, in the development and implementation of environmental standards and guidelines.

d. Establish an independent international monitoring body to monitor the progress made in the development of environmental standards, including industry guidelines.

e. Survey, every five years, industry and corporate guidelines in order to include new and appropriate industry standards, including those related to technological advances, in governmental rules and policies.

The capacity-building task for governments and international organizations is to provide assistance in strengthening the capacity of developing countries to include sustainable considerations in negotiations with foreign investors and technology suppliers.

United Nations Role in the Future

The Benchmark Survey on corporate environmental management revealed that several transnational corporations have already taken steps to establish EH&S policies and programs and are engaged in a broad array of EH&S-related management activities. Furthermore, some corporations have developed highly innovative ways to manage environmental assets and liabilities. This is promising for the prospects of EH&S protection in the future.

However, the potential of corporations to contribute to sustainable development is far from realized. There is still a large gap between the expectations of the UNCED conference, expressed in Agenda 21, and the reality of corporate environmental management. The Benchmark Survey showed that many crucial areas of EH&S management remain unaddressed by corporations, and that international environmental management and sustainable development management is still in its infancy.

UNCTC/TCMD's recommendations were one of many proposals to fill the gap between expectations of the international community and the actual state of corporate environmental management that surfaced throughout the UNCED process.

How does the international community move ahead from here and implement the ideas and visions that were developed during the UNCED process? For its part, the United Nations is presently restructuring in order to give sustainable development a more prominent position in its work. A high-level "Commission on Sustainable Development" is being established, and the scope and nature of this commission's work are being discussed among the relevant UN agencies as well as among governments. One of the factors that will be given special consideration in a more sustainable development-oriented United Nations is the involvement of nongovernmental groups, such as business and industry, in the decision making on, and the implementation of, Agenda 21. It is anticipated that business and industry will respond as energetically to this invitation to dialogue as they did when the United Nations called for the Rio Conference.

Agenda 21 says that business should:

Develop, in cooperation with Governments and sectoral trade associations, guidelines and/or codes of conduct leading to cleaner production. (20.13)

Be full participants in the implementation and evaluation of activities related to Agenda 21. (30.1)

TCMD will continue and strengthen its work on encouraging environmental excellence among transnational corporations and on challenging the corporate community to match or exceed the practices of environmentally leading corporations. Efforts to develop and harmonize international environmental guidelines pertaining to transnational corporations will also be continued. A special effort will be made to clarify the concept of sustainable development in relation to business.[36] In doing this, TCMD will cooperate closely with the business community, convinced that the ingenuity and innovative drive of business is probably one of the best means to meet the joint environmental and developmental challenges of the twenty-first century.

Bibliography

Booz-Allen & Hamilton. *Corporate Environmental Management: An Executive Survey.* 1991.

Bradshaw, Thorton, and D. Vogel, ed. *Corporations and Their Critics: Issues and Answers to the Problems of Corporate Social Responsibility.* New York, McGraw-Hill, 1981.

Brown, Himmelberger, and White. "Development—Environment Interactions in the Export of Hazardous Technologies: A Comparative Study of Three Multinational Affiliates in Developing Countries." In *Technological Forecasting and Social Change* (forthcoming).

Cahan and Smith. The greening of corporate America. *Business Week,* April 23, 1990.

Cairncross, Franches. *Costing the Earth: The Challenge for Governments. The Opportunities for Business.* Boston: Harvard Business School Press, 1992.

Chemical Manufacturers Association. *An Industry Survey of Chemical Company Activists to Reduce Unreasonable Risk.* Washington, D.C.: CMA, February 1983.

Cleaning Up, A Survey of Industry and the Environment. *The Economist,* September 8, 1990.

Deloitte & Touche. *The Environmental Transformation of US Industry: A Survey of US Industrial Corporations' Environmental Strategies, Management Policies and Perceptions.* Stanford: Stanford University Graduate School of Business Public Management Program, 1990.

Peter Dicken. *Global Shift: The Internationalization of Economic Activity.* New York: Guilford Press, 1992.

Dillon and Fisher. *Environmental Management in Corporations: Methods and Motivations.* Massachusetts: The Center for Environmental Management, 1992.

Flaherty, M., and A. Rappaport. *Multinational Corporations and the Environment: A Survey of Global Practices.* Massachusetts: The Center for Environmental Management, 1991.

Gladwin, Tom. *Building the Sustainable Corporation: Creating Environmental Sustainability and Corporate Advantage,* National Wildlife Federation, 1992.

Keidanren. *Towards Preservation of the Global Environment. Results of a Follow Up Survey on the Subject of the Keidanren Global Environmental Charter.* Tokyo: Keidanren, 1992.

Arthur D. Little. *Environmental Health and Safety Policies: Current Practices and Future Trends.* Cambridge, Massachusetts: Arthur D. Little, 1988.

Lund, Leonard. *Corporate Organization for Environmental Policy Making.* New York: The Conference Board, 1974.

Lundqvist, Lennart. *The Hare and the Tortoise: Clean Air Policies in the United States and Sweden.* Ann Arbor: University of Michigan Press, 1980.

McKinsey & Company. *The Corporate Response to the Environmental Challenge.* Amsterdam: McKinsey & Company, 1991.

National Wildlife Foundation. *Building the Sustainable Corporation: Creating environmental sustainability and corporate advantage.* Paper based on "Synergi 92" conference held in California in January 1992.

Pearson, Charles S. *Down to Business: Multinational Corporations, the Environment and Development.* Washington, D.C.: World Resources Institute, 1985.

Sarokin, D. *Toxic Releases from Multinational Corporations: Does the Public Have a Right to Know.* Washington: Friends of the Earth, 1992.

Schmidheiny, Stephan. *Changing Course: A Global Business Perspective on Development and the Environment.* Geneva: Business Council of Sustainable Development, 1992.

Smart, Bruce. *Beyond Compliance: A New Industry View of the Environment.* Washington: World Resources Institute, 1992.

United Nations Centre on Transnational Corporations. *Environmental Aspects of the Activities of Transnational Corporations: A Survey.* New York: United Nations, 1985.

United Nations Centre on Transnational Corporations. *Preliminary results of the Benchmark Survey, report I-IV.* New York: United Nations, 1991.

United Nations Centre on Transnational Corporations. *Transnational Corporations and Sustainable Development: Recommendations of the Executive Director.* (E/C.10/1992/2). New York: United Nations, 1992.

United Nations Conference on Environment and Development. *Agenda for the 21st Century.* A/CONF.151/26 (Vol I-III). New York: United Nations, 1992.

Vogel, David. *National Styles of Regulation: Environmental Policy in Great Britain and the United States.* London: Cornell University Press, 1986.

Willums and Goluke: *From Ideas to Action, Business and Sustainable Development.* Oslo: Gyldendal, 1992.

World Commission on Environment and Development. *Our Common Future.* New York: Oxford University Press, 1987.

References

1. See McKinsey & Company, 1991, p. 4.

2. See Cahan and Smith, 1991.

3. In recent years numerous compilations of examples of innovate corporate EH&S practices have been established. Some of the most interesting recent titles are Willums and Goluke (ICC). *From ideas to action, Business and sustainable development.* (Oslo: Gyldendal, 1992); Smart, Bruce. *Beyond Compliance, A new industry view of the environment.* (World Resources Institute, 1992); Schmidheiny, Stephan (BCSD): *Changing Course: A global business perspective on development and the environment.* (Massachusetts: MIT Press, 1992). Good background articles are Cleaning Up, A survey of industry and the environment. *The Economist, September 8, 1990*; Cahan and Smith. The greening of corporate America. *Business Week, April 23, 1990.*

4. Some of the most interesting industrial guidelines are Keidanren's Global Environmental Charter (4000 Japanese corporations subscribe to this guideline); The German Environmental Management Association's Code of Practices (320 corporate sponsors); ICC's Business Charter for Sustainable Development (more than 1000 corporate subscribers), and the Chemical Manufacturers Association's (CMA) Responsible Care Program (191 U.S. subscribers).

5. Transnational Corporations and Management Division. *World Investment Report: Transnational Corporations as Engines of Growth.* (New York: United Nations, 1992, p. 1.)

6. United Nations Conference on Environment and Development. *Agenda for the 21st Century.* New York: United Nations, 1992.

7. Transnational Corporations and Management Division. *Environmental Management in Transnational Corporations: The Report on the Benchmark Corporate Environmental Survey.* (New York: United Nations, forthcoming.)

8. It should be noted that the U.S. region includes eight Canadian enterprises; that the European region includes two Australian and one New Zealand corporation; and that the Japanese region includes one Indian corporation.

9. For a more detailed discussion of corporate policies, see Arthur D. Little, 1988.

10. This number is fairly high considering that a 1974 study among 516 U.S. corporations conducted by the Conference Board found a formal environmental statement in 40% of the corporations. (Lund, 1974.)

11. A study conducted by Tufts University found that 95% of the responding U.S. corporations had a written EH&S policy in place. (Flaherty and Rappaport, 1991.) The difference between the finding of the Benchmark Survey and this survey can be explained with differences in questions; for example, does the Benchmark Survey ask for *companywide* policies *beyond national requirements?*

12. *The Economist,* September 8, 1990.

13. For example, landfill costs for hazardous waste went from $80 a ton in the early eighties to around $255 a ton by the end, with the main increase being in treatment rather than dumping. According to OECD figures, the price of landfills for asbestos in Europe grew tenfold during the eighties. *The Economist,* September 8, 1990.

14. See, for example, Willums and Goluke (ICC), 1992, or Schmidheiny (BCSD), 1992.

15. Flaherty and Rappaport, 1991.

16. This strong relationship between the home country of the corporation and its environmental practices is sustained even when taking into account that the European respondents typically were somewhat smaller than the Japanese and U.S. respondents. Transnational Corporations and Management Division. *The Benchmark Survey: Transnational Corporations in Sustainable Development.* (New York: United Nations, forthcoming.)

17. Booz-Allen & Hamilton, 1991.

18. Some of the more prominent guidelines are

    - Conseil Europeen des Federations de l'Industrie Chimique (CEFIC). *A guide to safe warehousing for the European Chemical Industry,* Bruxelles, 1987.

    - Conseil Europeen des Federations de l'Industrie Chimique (CEFIC). *Principles and guidelines for the safe transfer of technology.* Bruxelles, 1987.

    - Coalition for Environmentally Responsible Economics (CERES). *The Valdez Principles.* Boston, 1989.

    - Chemical Manufacturers Association (CMA). *Responsible Care.* 1989.

    - Food and Agriculture Organization (FAO). *International Code of Conduct on the Distribution and Use of Pesticides.* Rome, 1986.

- International Chamber of Commerce (ICC): *Business Charter for Sustainable Development,* Paris, 1991.

- International Chamber of Commerce (ICC). *Final Declaration of the Second World Industry Conference on Environmental Management.* Rotterdam, 1991.

- International Labor Organization (ILO). *Tripartite Declaration of Principles concerning Multinational Enterprises and Social Policy.* Geneva, 1977.

- Keidanren: *Global Environmental Charter.* April 1991.

- Organization for Economic Cooperation and Development (OECD). *Guidelines for Multinational Enterprises.* Paris, 1976–1985.

- United Nations Centre on Transnational Corporations (UNCTC). *Criteria for Sustainable Development Management.* New York, 1991.

- United Nations Centre on Transnational Corporations (UNCTC). *Transnational Corporations in Sustainable Development: Recommendations of the Executive Director.* EC/10/1992/2. New York, 1991.

- United Nations Environmental Program (UNEP). *APELL Programme.* Paris, 1988.

19. Keidanren, 1992.

20. See Flaherty and Rappaport, 1991, p. 12. This finding is also supported by McKinsey's Survey, where one of the main conclusions was that whatever happens, policymakers and fellow industrialists should keep the environmental playing field level. (McKinsey, 1991, p. 13.)

21. See, for example, Peter Dicken. *Global Shift: The internationalization of economic activity.* (New York: Guilford Press, 1992) or Reis and Betton. The Environment and Its Effect on Today's Management. *International Management,* February 1992, or Environmental Concerns Gaining Importance in Industry Operations. *Oil and Gas Journal,* July 6, 1992, or Choucri, Nazli. The Global Multinational. *Technology Review,* April 1991 or Prahalad, C.K., and Yves Doz. *The Multinational Mission: Balancing Local Demands and Global Vision.* (New York: The Free Press, 1987) or Brown, Himmelberger, and White. "Development—Environment Interactions in the Export of Hazardous Technologies: A Comparative Study of Three Multinational Affiliates in Developing Countries." In *Technological Forecasting and Social Change.* (Forthcoming) or Castleman, Barry. "Workplace Health in Developing Countries." In Charles Pearson, ed. *Multinational Corporations, Environment, and the Third World: Business Matters.* (Durham: Duke University, 1987) or ESCAP/UNCTC Joint Unit on Transnational Corporations. *Environmental Aspects of Transnational Corporation Activities in Pollution-Intensive Industries in Selected Asian and Pacific Developing Countries.* (Bangkok: ESCAP/UNCTC Publication Series B, No. 15, 1990.)

22. M. Flaherty and A. Rappaport, 1991.

23. In response to a request by the Intergovernmental Working Group of Experts on International Standards of Accounting and Reporting (ISAR), UNCTC undertook two environmental accounting surveys in 1989 and 1990. The surveys' results suggested that "the accounting for environmental expenses was feasible." The study

also noted that: (*a*) despite the heightened awareness, the consideration of environmental issues in annual reports was not widespread; and (*b*) the absence of accounting standards allowed enterprises wide discretion in what they reported and led to a lack of consistency even within the same corporation. *UN. Doc. No. E/C.10/AC.3/1991/5 and E/C.10/AC.3/1990/5.* (New York: United Nations, 1990.)

24. A 1982 survey conducted by the U.S. Chemical Manufacturers Association found that 93% of the responding companies conducted environmental audits. (Chemical Manufacturers Association, 1983.)

25. McKinsey, 1991, p. 14.

26. For example, a recent public opinion poll found that over three-fourths of U.S. consumers said that they are concerned about the environmental impact of the products they purchase, and that they are influenced by the environmental image of the producer; 68% responded that they will pay 5 to 10% more for environmentally acceptable products. (Michael Peters Group, 1990.)

27. Deloitte & Touche, 1991.

28. *Financial Times,* September 16, 1992.

29. "Corporatism" is a term often used in political science literature to describe political systems where the major organized interests such as business and labor are directly incorporated in policymaking and policy implementation. This decision-making style is, according to this literature, common in several European countries, in particular the Scandinavian countries and Germany. In contrast, interest groups in the United States are often described as "pressure groups" far less integrated in political decision making and policy implementation. Good accounts for differences in decision-making and policy implementation styles in European and U.S. environmental politics can be found in Lundqvist, 1982, and Vogel, 1986.

30. Pilko & Associates estimate cited in Cahan and Smith, 1990.

31. TCMD's 1992 World Investment Report concluded that evidence of industrial relocation does exist in certain selected industries, for example, asbestos, heavy metals and leather tanning, but the balance of the research suggests that environmental cost differences have not been a major determinant of foreign direct investment (FDI) and that major shifts have not occurred because of differences in national standards. But there is no doubt that the possibility of industrial flight grows as pollution abatement costs increase and as other elements in TNC investment considerations, such as infrastructure, investment climate, and education, become more favorable to TNCs in many developing countries. [Transnational Corporations and Management Division. *World Investment Report: Transnational Corporations as Engines of Growth* (New York: United Nations, 1992).]

32. For example, the dispute at the EC Court between the Danish government and the EC Commission over the Danish return bottle legislation, the dispute at GATT between Mexico and the United States over a U.S. ban on Mexican tuna product, or the dispute between the EC and the United States over an EC ban on U.S. hormone meat.

33. The Economic and Social Council adopted resolution 1991/55 of 26/July/1991, in which it requested the Executive Director of the United Nations Center on Transnational Corporations, after consultations with international business organi-

zations and other relevant bodies, to prepare action-oriented and practicable recommendations on cooperation for protection and enhancement of the environment in all countries. Subsequently, the Preparatory Committee of the United Nations Conference on Environment and Development requested the full integration of development considerations and needs and realities, in particular of the developing countries, in all Agenda 21 program documents.

34. The original document, Transnational Corporations in Sustainable Development: Recommendations of the Executive Director (EC/10/1992/2) contains, in addition to what is printed in this essay, an introduction, an executive summary, and more than one hundred references to existing guidelines and corporate practices.

35. United Nations Centre on Transnational Corporations. *Transnational Corporations and Issues Relating to the Environment*. (E/C.10/1991/3. New York: United Nations, 1991.)

36. In surveying the sustainable development literature, Tom Gladwin wrote that "the concept of sustainable development is still quite embryonic, generally being discussed and written about in broad conceptual, rather abstract, macrolevel and fuzzy ways." (National Wildlife Federation, 1992, p. 94.)

19

Trade and the Environment: Challenges and Opportunities*

Matthew B. Arnold

Frederick J. Long

In this chapter:

- The Trade and Environment Debate
- Trends in Trade and Environment
- Disputes Between Trade and Environmental Communities
- Progress Toward Solutions
- Outlook and Implications for Corporations
- Appendix: The Danish Bottles Case; German Packaging Legislation

---

*Matthew Arnold is President and Frederick Long is Executive Director of the Management Institute for Environment and Business, an independent, nonprofit organization based in Washington, D.C. The authors give special thanks to Chris Cummings, research assistant, for his contributions to this chapter. Comments on earlier versions of this chapter were provided by Daniel Esty of the U.S. Environmental Protection Agency, Stewart Hudson of the National Wildlife Federation, and Robert Housman of the Center for International Environmental Law. The authors alone are responsible for any factual errors or opinions contained here.

Emerging conflicts between free trade and environmental protection are gaining the attention of policymakers, environmental groups, labor unions, corporations, and other key stakeholders. A 25-year global proliferation of national laws and international environmental agreements, many of which restrict trade and protect domestic markets, has gained the attention of free trade proponents. Conversely, the virtual absence of environmental considerations in trade negotiations, standards setting, and dispute resolution has aroused the ire of environmentalists. Many environmental leaders believe that wide disparities in the stringency of national environmental regulations, when combined with free trade agreements, create "pollution havens" for multinational corporations and thus provide the basis for environmental degradation.

Recent events help define the landscape of trade and environment issues: the Tuna/Dolphin Dispute brought before a GATT panel, an international agreement to reduce use of chlorofluorocarbons, stringent domestic bottling laws in Denmark, and recent negotiations in the European Community and in North America over new free trade agreements. A number of international bodies such as the United Nations, GATT, and the OECD are forming panels to grapple with these challenges. This dizzying pace of change is not likely to slow in the near future. Substantial efforts will be required if trade and environment agendas are ever to be effectively integrated.

This chapter outlines the most important trade and environment issues and establishes their relevance for corporate managers. The second section highlights how changes in trade agreements and increased concern for the environment have heightened our awareness of trade and environment interactions. The third and fourth sections show the various ways in which trade and environmental agreements come into conflict, and how these conflicts might be resolved. Ultimately, we suggest the possible benefits that corporations may derive from proactive engagement in trade and environment debates, and present case studies that enable the reader to work through emerging environmental regulation, its impacts on trade, and its enormous importance for business.

The Trade and Environment Debate

Environment and economy disputes have never been more prevalent than in the past few years. In America's Pacific Northwest, the battle continues over the Endangered Species Act's protection of the spotted owl and the impact this protection will have on jobs in the logging industry. The Brazilian Amazon is the focus of heated domestic and international debate over policies that encourage development of species-rich rain forest areas which leads to deforestation. The UN Conference on Environment and Development (UNCED), known as the "Earth Summit," held in Rio de Janeiro in June 1992 revealed vast differences between countries on virtually every issue up for discussion, including most prominently biodiversity and global warming. These disputes do occur within and among industrialized nations but are particularly pronounced along the North-South axis.

Trade and environment disputes are an important component of these environment and economy disputes. They arise when free trade is perceived to do harm to the environment, or when efforts to protect the environment, whether through international agreements or stringent domestic regulations, impede free flows of trade in goods and services.

The disputes that occur directly between trade and environment advocates are exacerbated by fundamental concerns for protecting sovereign decision making. National priorities have stymied trade advocates in recent efforts to update free trade agreements, and the world system is being undercut by an emerging set of regional trade agreements. Among environmentalists, there is dissension about environmental protection priorities, and how much can be accomplished through collaboration with the business community.

At the center of these disputes is an unmistakable fact: many environmental threats are cross-border in nature. Pollution does not recognize national sovereignty. Hence the only way to solve many environmental problems is through international cooperation. But this cooperation is often hard to achieve, as there are great benefits to "free riders" and limited global policing capacity to keep nations in line with their agreements.

Although international environmental negotiations do not intrinsically need to affect trade flows, there are several reasons why trade measures are perhaps the most effective enforcement tools currently available to negotiators. First, countries differ in the degrees to which they contribute to environmental problems. Regarding global warming, for instance, the countries which have emitted the most CO_2 in the last 50 years are not the same as those which plan to emit the most CO_2 in the next 50 years. Bearing little responsibility for the current state of the problem, countries that are likely to pollute in the future ask, "Why should we forgo the economic benefit of cheap and dirty fuel which is central to our economic development?" This conflict has plagued virtually every major environmental negotiation. The potential threat of trade restrictions gets the immediate attention of those nations which feel no responsibility for a particular problem, and is very effective at bringing negotiators to the table.

The second reason that trade measures are effective is enforcement. In most cases, it pays to be a free rider, to continue a polluting activity while others shoulder the burden of solving the problem. Moreover, effective monitoring of compliance is expensive and cumbersome. Trade measures are an effective means of inducing free riders to participate in problem solving, and they are easy to monitor because of their high transparency.

The interaction of trade and the environment is the subject of research and political initiatives by several United Nations (UN) agencies, the Organization for Economic Cooperation and Development (OECD), the General Agreement on Tariffs and Trade (GATT), and dozens of national governments (see Fig. 19-1). Recently, the Earth Summit, as well as some highly visible disputes, have vaulted the issue into the public domain. Despite these efforts, the ultimate resolution of trade and environment conflicts will require extensive efforts. The radically different cultures and institutional objectives of the two communities, the lack of empirical knowledge about trade and environment interrelation-

General Agreement on Tariffs and Trade (GATT)
  Uruguay Round negotiations
  Working Group on Environmental Measures and International Trade
  Working Group on the Export of Domestically Prohibited Goods and Other Hazardous
  Substances
  GATT Secretariat
Organization for Economic Co-operation and Development (OECD)
  Joint sessions of Trade and Environment Committee
  Joint work by Trade and Environment Directorates
United Nations (UN)
  United Nations Environment Program (UNEP)
  United Nations Development Program (UNDP)
  United Nations Industrial Development Organization (UNIDO)
  United Nations Conference on Trade and Development (UNCTAD)
  United Nations Conference on Environment and Development (UNCED)
U.S. Trade Representatives (USTR)
  Leads interagency task force on trade/environment
  Represents United States at GATT
  Cochairs (with EPA) U.S. delegation to trade/environment discussions at OECD
  Leads negotiations on North American Free Trade Agreement (NAFTA)
Environmental Protection Agency (EPA)
  Participates in interagency trade/environment task force
  Cochairs (with USTR) U.S. delegation to trade/environment discussions at OECD
  Coordinated with Mexico on U.S.–Mexico border environmental matters
  Participates in NAFTA working groups
  Receives recommendations from the Trade and Environment Committee of the National
  Advisory Council for Environmental Policy and Technology
State Department
  Leads U.S. delegation at most international environmental negotiations
  Participates in interagency trade/environment task force
Commerce Department
  Participates in interagency trade/environment task force
  Has administrative units with specialized responsibility, including:
    International Trade Administration
    National Oceanic and Atmospheric Administration (NOAA)
Other departments and agencies with specific missions as relevant:
  Agriculture Department
  Treasury Department
  Justice Department
  Labor Department
  Interior Department
  Energy Department
  Food and Drug Administration
  U.S. International Trade Administration
  Specialized export promotion and foreign assistance agencies:
    U.S. Agency for International Development (USAID)
    Export-Import Bank of the United States
    Overseas Private Investment Corp. (OPIC)
    U.S. Trade and Development Program (US TDP)

Figure 19-1. Organizations and key U.S. federal agencies concerned with trade, development, and environmental matters. [*Source: U.S. Congress, Office of Technology Assessment (OTA). Trade and Environment: Conflicts and Opportunities. ITA-BP-ITE-94 (Washington, D.C.: Government Printing Office, May 1992).*]

ships, and the diffusion of authority among a variety of governments and agencies all make trade and environment uncomfortable, if inevitable, bedfellows.

If these two communities are to get along, experts suggest that each party's objectives should become integral to both. In this sense, movement toward integration parallels the course of a larger international movement toward sustainable development. Advocates of sustainable development argue that economic development and environmental protection are inextricably linked and mutually reinforcing. Economic growth must be undertaken in a way that does not irreversibly damage the earth's pool of natural capital and that protects the right of future generations to enjoy at least the environmental quality that current generations enjoy.

The potential impact of this debate on international business is monumental. The strength, reach, and scope of international environmental agreements, which reached new proportions with the Montreal Protocol, will probably expand if new treaties are signed for issues such as global warming, biodiversity, and sustainable development. Binding international environmental agreements will fuel the expansion of domestic regulatory programs for many years, and continue to encroach upon international trade in goods and services.

The preponderance of domestic environmental regulations will also likely expand on a worldwide basis, presenting daunting compliance challenges for companies and potentially dampening free trade. When nations develop their own approaches to environmental regulations, they usually end up with rules that have different levels of stringency and different application methodologies (e.g., performance vs. technology standards). Product and process standards, procedures and permitting systems, and monitoring and reporting requirements in many instances serve as nontariff barriers to trade. On the other hand, when countries harmonize the stringency and application methodologies of environmental standards, companies can easily transfer compliance systems from one country to another.

Apart from the possible protectionist impact of domestic environmental regulations, stringent regulations are often evaluated in terms of the costs they place on business. Most major regulatory programs in the United States measure the amount of pollution they will keep out of the environment against the cost of equipment and operations required to achieve lower pollution levels. This cost-benefit analysis of regulation fails to consider the potentially powerful boost to competitiveness that results when regulations force companies to focus on the environmental impact of operations. A reexamination of the production process, the elimination of waste, changes in management systems to react more quickly to regulatory changes, and the potential to commercialize products and services developed in response to compliance requirements are all opportunities that can be motivated by stringent regulation. Michael Porter in particular has posited that stringent regulatory requirements may actually improve the competitive position of an industry.[1]

---

[1]M. E. Porter, "America's Green Strategy," *Scientific American,* April 1991, p. 168.

Trends in Trade and Environment

Trends in International Trade

In the trade community, it is an axiom that growth in trade is critical to global economic development and human well-being. Hence increases in trade should make most countries better off. However, the breakdowns of aggregate figures show the potentially insidious effects of trade. Certain countries are benefiting considerably more than others from global free trade. Dissatisfaction with inequitable distribution of welfare from the global free trade system is driving countries to arrange agreements that maximize benefits to a smaller number of participants, at the possible expense of trading partners outside the agreement. Regional trade agreements and bilateral negotiations are becoming more prevalent in almost every region of the world: the European Community (EC), Association of South East Asian Nations (ASEAN), the North American Free Trade Agreement (NAFTA), and U.S.–Japan bilateral agreements are examples. It is unclear whether this trend will damage the global free trade system.

Free trade is conceptually identical to a free market in a closed economy and brings all the same benefits. Countries specialize in production of goods and services in which they have a comparative advantage. The result is that the global costs of production are as low as possible. Consumers reap the benefit when they receive unfettered access to goods that have been produced at the lowest possible cost.

Since the early 1970s, world trade has more than quadrupled, growing from about $800 billion per year in 1974 to nearly $3.5 trillion per year in 1990. Figure 19-2 shows growth between 1985 and 1991.

Growth in international trade has been facilitated by the General Agreement on Tariffs and Trade (GATT), which was established in 1947 to ensure a predictable international trading environment while at the same time fostering greater economic efficiency and growth through trade liberalization. Membership in the agreement has grown significantly and now encompasses over 100 countries. GATT is structured as a flexible document, and it is modified through a periodic negotiation process.

Currently GATT is undergoing its eighth restructuring, and according to *The Economist*, the potential stakes are high.

> The gains within reach are not a theoretical fantasy; they are a matter of cold, hard cash. In sum, the flawed package that the Uruguay Round is poised to deliver would immediately raise global income, according to one careful (and conservative) study, by $120 billion a year—roughly 1/2% of today's gross world product.[2]

Box 19-1 describes key issues in the most recent GATT negotiation process. Negotiations in the Uruguay Round have been highly contentious, especially

---

[2]*The Economist,* June 27, 1992, p. 13.

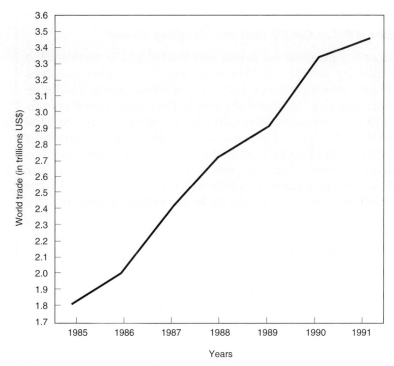

Figure 19-2. Growth in world trade 1985–1991. [*International Monetary Fund (IMF), "Direction of Trade Statistics Yearbook, 1992" (Washington, D.C., IMF, 1992).*]

regarding the level of subsidies that European countries are providing to their agricultural industries. Environmental issues have not been an explicit component of this round of GATT negotiations.

As trade has grown, industrialized nations have gained an increasing share of total trade, at the expense of developing nations. Figures 19-3 and 19-4 indicate the declining share of developing country trade over time. A prominent exception to this is the Asian countries, which have gained an increasing share of world trade in the past decade. In the remainder of the developing world, many countries have either negative or small positive trade balances, allowing them little room for productive investment after payment of interest on foreign debt.[3] For many of these countries, the international trade system serves more to constrain than to liberate; hence their commitment to the system is understandably low.

---

[3]The 10 largest debtor countries in the developing world owe approximately $637 billion. While most would say that the international debt crisis has subsided, foreign interest payments still represent a substantial portion of scheduled payments. See World Bank, *World Development Report 1992: Development and the Environment*. (Oxford: Oxford University Press, May 1992) available from World Bank Publications.

Box 19-1.   GATT and the Uruguay Round

In 1947, the General Agreement on Tariffs and Trade (GATT) established a framework of rules for international trade for over 100 member countries that collectively account for the vast majority of the world's trade. The impetus for GATT was largely a calculated reaction to the problems and failures of the post–World War I world economy, in which trading nations retreated from the international stage and erected tariff walls to protect domestic goods and industries. GATT seeks to promote a liberal trade environment by minimizing nontariff barriers, including environmental regulations, that can severely curtail the free passage of goods. In pursuit of this goal, GATT has been tremendously successful, as world trade has expanded greatly since World War II.

GATT is comprised of a number of core components that have been responsible for trade expansion:

- *Most-Favored Nation (MFN) Treatment (Article I).* Goods imported from or exported to one member country must be treated no differently than like goods imported from or exported to another member country (known as "consistency with like products"). In effect, MFN ensures that a given member country must bestow equivalent trade status upon all member countries.

- *National Treatment (Article III).* Upon importation from another member country, foreign goods must be treated no differently than similar domestic goods. This means trade agencies cannot create taxes or enact stringent regulations solely on imported goods as a protectionist measure. Furthermore, domestically imposed controls cannot be imposed beyond a country's borders (known as "extraterritoriality").

- *Restrictions, Bans, and Quotas (Article XI).* Bans, import quotas, or any other form of quantitative restrictions are prohibited under GATT. Combined, Articles I, III, and XI prohibit the explicit discrimination against foreign goods.

- *General Exceptions (Article XX).* The general exceptions measures permit member countries to enact measures that would otherwise violate GATT, so long as they do not unjustifiably discriminate. Although the article does not specifically mention the environment, the environment has been construed to be included through measures (b), "necessary to protect human, animal or plant life," and (g), "relating to the conservation of exhaustible natural resources if such measures are made effective in conjunction with restrictions on domestic production or consumption."

While these articles have been central to GATT's mission of enabling free trade, there are a number of industries and trade areas that still need clarification and substantial modification.

The latest round of negotiations for changes to GATT, the Uruguay Round, has important implications for the continued success of liberalized trade and for environmental protection and sustainable development. The main goals of this negotiating round are:

- Reduce tariffs overall by one-third

- Reduce and eliminate nontariff measures, including environmental requirements

- Liberalize trade in natural resource–based products

- Reduce and in some cases eliminate agricultural subsidies

- Cut tariff and nontariff barriers on tropical products

- Engineer an agreement on the trade and protection of intellectual property, which could radically alter the future of technology transfer to developing nations

- Harmonize environment and health standards

- Classify subsidies and countervailing measures

While laissez-faire proponents and free traders want to provide an environment in which liberal trade will thrive and realize the estimated $120 billion that is at stake, environmental advocates are concerned that the Uruguay Round's vision of free trade will sacrifice natural resource protection, stimulate resource depletion, and dismantle the ideals of sustainable development. Although most areas are in accord, disagreements between the EC and United States over agricultural subsidies have stalled the negotiations. With the outcome of the rounds uncertain, the extent to which these objectives are reached and implemented remains to be seen.

Sources: C. Arden-Clarke, "The General Agreement on Tariffs and Trade, Environmental Protection, and Sustainable Development," Geneva: World Wildlife Fund (WWF) International, November 1991; R. Housman and D. Zaelke, "Trade, Environment, and Sustainable Development: A Primer," *Hastings International and Comparative Law Review,* vol. 15, no. 4, summer 1992.

While GATT has been faltering in this latest round of negotiations, regional trading blocks have become more active and powerful. The EC, ASEAN, and NAFTA are examples of the trend toward formation of regional trading blocks. These blocks appear to be developing for a number of reasons which are based ultimately on economics and efficiency:

- Blocks can be organized among groups of countries with similar economic, political, environmental, social, and therefore, trade objectives.

- Blocks may deal with individual countries' trade objectives more effectively and efficiently than a broad international regime.

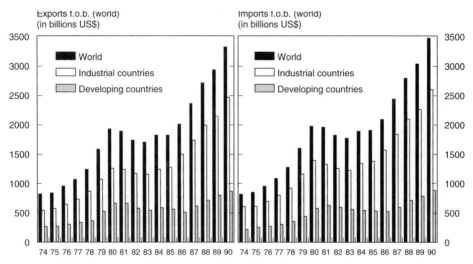

Figure 19-3. Exports and imports, 1974–1990. [*International Monetary Fund (IMF)*, *"International Financial Statistics Yearbook, 1991"* (Washington, D.C., IMF, 1991).]

- Trade issues can be more effectively blended with other economic, political, and social cooperation programs.

- The smaller number of participants makes agreements easier to achieve, and smaller countries can play a more significant role than in larger international arenas.

- Dismantling protective tariff and nontariff barriers can be more readily accomplished with a small number of countries and can be phased in with less short-term economic displacement.

Trends in the Environment Arena

Emission of CFCs and certain other halogenated chemicals has created a large and growing hole in a part of the atmosphere which protects life from harmful solar rays. Burning of forests, combustion of fossil fuels, and emission of other substances may be warming the earth's atmosphere to temperatures that cause massive societal disruptions. The earth's oceans are filling up with debris, both toxic and nontoxic, that may permanently alter certain marine ecosystems. Outer space is a junkyard. Sulfur dioxide emissions in the United States and the United Kingdom are causing acid rain to fall on Canada and Sweden. When one European nation sullies the Rhine or the Danube, others share the cost. Nations that cannot afford to do otherwise are collecting huge payments in exchange for receipt of toxic waste which they are ill-equipped to process.

If the political interdependence of the seventies gave way to the realism of nation-states in the eighties, ecological interdependence may characterize the

Percent of World Export, 1985

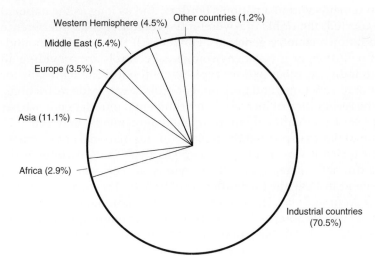

Percent of World Export, 1991

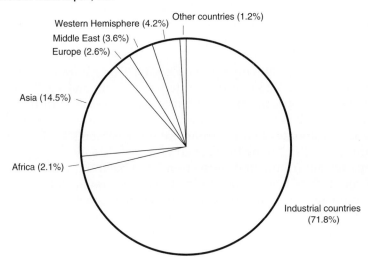

Figure 19-4. Trends in world trade, 1985–1991. [*International Monetary Fund (IMF), "Direction of Trade Statistics Yearbook, 1992" (Washington, D.C., IMF, 1992).*]

post–Cold War nineties. Earth has indeed become a small world in the post-industrial age. Transboundary pollution and serious damage to common resources are causing nations to rethink industrial practices, forge environmental treaties, and make unprecedented changes in free trade systems in order to protect the environment. However, nations possess widely varied natural resource endowments, population densities, national incomes, and socioeconomic priorities, and therefore have different abilities to tolerate pollution. As long as pollution remains within a nation's borders, and as long as the national product is not exported, the rights of sovereignty prohibit outside interference in how much pollution a country generates. However, if there are transboundary spillovers of pollution, or if weak environmental controls are providing an export subsidy to industry, other nations typically will intervene with calls for negotiation, economic sanctions, and unilateral or multilateral trade restrictions.

One result of the recognition of increased environmental interdependence has been a growing list of international environmental agreements. Between 1972 and 1991, the United States expanded the number of international environmental agreements in which it was involved from 50 to 168.[4] The growth over the past 20 years is a dramatic increase over the previous 40 years since the signing of the first agreement in 1933, the *Convention Relative to the Preservation of Fauna and Flora in Their Natural State*. The expansion of international commitments illustrates the increasingly international nature of most environmental problems: pollution in the seas, depletion of fish and whale stocks in common waters, loss of biodiversity, regional and global climate change, and cross-border water pollution.

In the same 20-year period that the United States increased its international treaty obligations on the environment, domestic regulation in the United States and other industrialized nations ballooned. U.S. expenditures on the environment rose from $26 billion to $108 billion in constant dollars.[5] That represents an increase in share of GNP from 0.9 to 2.2%.[6] Comparable increases have occurred in Europe. In 1985, Germany spent 1.5% of GDP on environmental protection vs. 1.1% in France, 1.25% in the United Kingdom, and 1.67% in the United States.[7] These investments are expected to increase at least through the end of the century, which is the longest horizon over which there are projections. The U.S. EPA estimates that environmental investments in the United States will approach 3% of GNP by the year 2000.

As these steps for environmental protection have been implemented, the environmental community has become divided over environmental protection priorities. Environmentalists range from extremists who promote confrontation with industry and government in order to prevent all pollution and environmental degradation, to pragmatists who promote cooperation with companies and policymakers in order to find efficient ways of achieving realistic environ-

---

[4]U.S. Congress, General Accounting Office (GAO), *International Environment: International Agreements Are Not Well Monitored*, GAO RCED-92-43 (Washington, D.C.: Government Printing Office, January 1992).

[5]The most accurate measure of regulation is the cost of compliance, since the actual number of laws do not indicate their significance.

[6]Office of Policy, Planning and Evaluation (OPPE), U.S. Environmental Protection Agency, *Environmental Investments: The Cost of a Clean Environment*, EPA-230-12-90-084 (Washington, D.C.: USEPA, December 1990) p. 2-2.

[7]OPPE, U.S. EPA, op. cit., p. 4–7.

mental protection goals. Extremists are willing to change fundamental aspects of modern society to achieve their objectives and do not recognize the validity of compromise. Pragmatists believe that an industrialized society inevitably generates pollution and degrades the environment; their goal is to minimize these effects. Underlying these disagreements are differences in philosophy that link to religion, the hierarchy of species, and the human condition.

Disputes between Trade and Environmental Communities

Basis for Emerging Conflict

Before presenting several concrete examples of trade and environment conflicts, it may be useful to summarize several viewpoints on the relationship between trade and environmental protection. Not all individuals and organizations fit perfectly into a single category, but the descriptions do outline a spectrum of thinking on trade and the environment.

- *Trade champions: Environmental protection should not interfere with international trade.* Lawrence Summers, chief economist at the World Bank in Washington, D.C., has argued that free trade and resulting economic growth should not be hampered by environmental restrictions. Prohibiting developing countries from using their natural resources freely amounts to protectionism, as it reduces countries' abilities to efficiently allocate their pool of resources in the pursuit of improved living standards.[8] Moreover, in instances where it is generally accepted that environmental standards should exist, standards should be "harmonized" at the international level in order to minimize trade distortions.

- *Environment through trade champions: Unrestricted trade provides the economic base to encourage more vigorous public demand for environmental protection.* In an academic paper presented at a conference on the potential environmental impacts of NAFTA, Gene Grossman and Alan Krueger of Princeton University argue that there is a positive correlation between per capita income and environmental protection.[9] The authors plotted income levels vs. concentrations of a number of pollutants for a number of countries. They

---

[8]In an internal memorandum dated December 1991, Summers argued that allowing movement of toxic waste from developed to developing countries would be efficient from an economic perspective (although he made no argument about the effects of trade on the level of pollution). The memo sparked debate among the international trade and environmental communities. See the February 1992 editions of *The Economist* for a fairly complete account of the debate that ensued.

[9]Gene M. Grossman and Alan B. Krueger, "Environmental Impacts of a North American Free Trade Agreement," paper presented at a conference on U.S.–Mexico Free Trade Agreement, sponsored by the Mexican Secretaria de Comercio y Fomento Industrial, October 8, 1991.

found that pollution levels are greatest when per capita income is approximately $5000. Above and below that level, per capita pollution declines. They suggest that as a country industrializes, pollution increases to a point when the populace has enough wealth to demand higher environmental protection. Although this argument seems valid for the pollutants the authors analyzed—sulfur dioxide and urban particulates—the same trend does not apply to other pollutants. For instance, carbon dioxide emissions increase with GNP per capita beyond the $5000 threshold. (See Box 19-2.)

Other "trade through environment champions" suggest that protected economies are actually worse off environmentally than those open to trade. One reason is that closed economies do not adopt new, often cleaner technology as readily as open economies. In a study of the wood pulp industry, less-distorted economies adopted clean technology more quickly, and reduced their pollution output accordingly.[10]

- *Environment champions: Liberalization of trade directly undermines the pursuit of environmental protection, as free trade often directly results in environmental degradation.* The global environment is critically threatened. In order to assure earth's sustainability, countries must have the freedom to establish stringent domestic regulations, and international environmental agreements must supersede trade agreements when the two conflict. Senior officials of the Sierra Club argue that restrictions on trade are critical to international environmental agreements in order to encourage widespread participation and ensure that parties enforce their provisions.[11] Herman Daly and John Cobb, known for their work in natural resource and environmental economics, argue that rigorous pursuit of free trade tends to weaken community and national standards, including those relating to environmental protection.[12] As stated by another author:

> While the development of international consensus around environmental standards may be a desirable objective, there are several reasons to suspect that the agenda of "free trade" is to lower environmental standards, while removing standard-setting processes to institutions that are less accountable to the community and more amenable to corporate influence and control.[13]

---

[10]D. Wheeler and P. Martin, "Prices, Policies, and the International Diffusion of Clean Technology: The Case of Wood Pulp Production," paper presented at the Symposium on International Trade and the Environment sponsored by the World Bank, November 1991. Several other papers presented at the symposium supported the view that economic growth and free trade have a positive effect on the environment. See also Charles Pearson, "Environmental Control Costs and Border Adjustments," *National Tax Journal*, vol. 28, no. 4, December 1974.

[11]Minutes of the GATT Working Group, Trade and Environment Committee of the National Advisory Council on Environmental Policy and Technology (NACEPT) of the U.S. Environmental Protection Agency, December 4, 1991.

[12]Herman Daly and John Cobb, *For the Common Good* (Boston: Beacon Press, 1989).

[13]Steven Shrybman, "International Trade and the Environment," *Alternatives*, vol. 17, no. 2, 1990.

Box 19-2.   Wealth and the Demand for Environmental Protection

The debate over the relationship between income and environmental quality has recently become more intense and, accordingly, was a central issue at the recent Earth Summit. Two recent studies—one from Princeton Professors Grossman and Krueger, the other from the World Bank—indicate that the effects of income growth on industrial pollution levels is mixed: For certain industrial pollutants, concentrations level off and decrease with income growth; for others, concentrations rise with income growth.

Using trend data on concentrations of two pollutants—sulfur dioxide and suspended particulates—they found that once per capita GDP reaches approximately $5000, concentrations of these pollutants peak. As income continues to rise, concentrations decline significantly. The authors posit that wealth enables people to expand their appetites beyond basic survival to include sanitation and environmental protection. Grossman and Krueger's findings are illustrated in the following graph, which charts sulfur dioxide vs. GDP per capita.

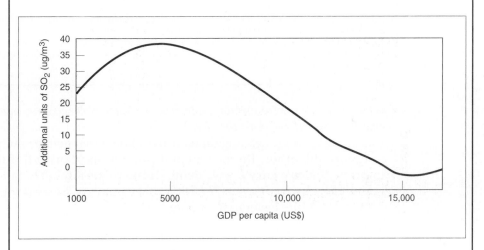

Although Grossman and Krueger's findings have given many free trade advocates the leverage they need to discourage inclusion of environmental protection clauses in trade agreements, World Bank analysts have not found these results to be readily generalizable. Their findings support Grossman and Krueger's conclusions regarding the above air-pollution constituents, yet assessments of other pollutants and media support the opposite conclusion—that there is a positive relationship between pollution and income levels. For example, both per capita generation of municipal wastes and carbon

(Continued)

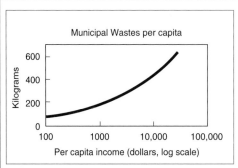

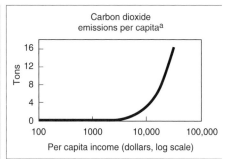

Note: Estimates are based on cross-country regression analysis of data from the 1980s.
[a] Emissions are from fossil fuels.

dioxide emissions rise steadily with income. The above graphs from the World Bank's *World Development Report 1992* document these findings.

Without greater certainty of the links between environmental protection and income, the lessons and implications for the international trade and environment forum are mixed and the debate continues.

Sources: G. M. Grossman and A. B. Krueger, "Environmental Impacts of a North American Free Trade Agreement," presented at a conference on U.S.–Mexico Free Trade Agreement, sponsored by the Mexican Secretaria de Comercio y Fomento Industrial, October 8, 1991; World Bank, World Development Report 1992: Development and the Environment. Oxford: Oxford University Press, May 1992.

- *Integrationists: Environmental protection and trade both serve the cause of sustainable development and must therefore be integrated and given equal emphasis in international agreements.* Leading thinkers have noted that neither camp can afford to ignore the other. Environmental protection plans fail if they do not improve the citizenry's well-being; trade plans similarly fail when they ignore the adverse impacts on the global commons. Stewart Hudson of the National Wildlife Federation has argued:

> To be sure, conflicts between some of the core values of liberalized trade and environmental protection do exist. Nevertheless, an awareness of the mutual benefits of an approach to trade and environmental concerns, based on sustainable development, can help overcome anxiety that this new type of thinking seems to have generated in both the trade and environmental communities.[14]

Officials of the Natural Resources Defense Council, in discussing the North American Free Trade Agreement (NAFTA), have argued for "joining the pursuit of economic prosperity and equity with natural resource protection, cul-

[14]Stewart Hudson, "Trade, Environment, and the Pursuit of Sustainable Development," unpublished paper of the National Wildlife Federation, Washington, D.C., p. 8.

tural diversity and a high quality of environment for current and future generations."[15] The U.S. EPA has taken an approach that appears comparable with those of the integrationists.

Free Traders' Objections

The following sections illustrate a number of the complex problems presented by international trade agreements, international environmental agreements, and domestic environmental regulations that do not account for the concerns of the other communities. The first three sections describe the objections that the trade community typically makes over the infringement by environmental regulations on free trade. It should be pointed out that the historic impact of environmental regulation on trade appears to be quite small. In an excellent review of the competitiveness considerations of U.S. environmental regulation, the Office of Technology Assessment concludes that there may be significant trade impacts within certain industries but that the overall economic impact is not significant.[16] However, the increasing quantity and scope of international environmental agreements and the massive potential impact of a global warming treaty may accelerate the deleterious effect of environmental controls on free trade.

International Environmental Agreements That Impede Free Trade

International environmental agreements which restrict free trade to enforce their provisions have thrust the emerging trade and environment conflict into full public view. Of the 170 or so agreements to which the United States is a party, roughly 20 accords specifically use trade measures as a means of achieving the desired environmental outcome (see Box 19-3). One example is the Convention on International Trade in Endangered Species of Wildlife and Fauna (CITES), created in 1973 to control or eliminate trade in flora and fauna which are now or may become threatened with extinction. Currently, there are 104 signatories to the agreement.

Prior to the formation of CITES, the United States and other countries had unilaterally enacted legislation prohibiting the importation of species they considered endangered. However, by forming a broader agreement, signatories sought to influence practices beyond their borders and further reduce illegal trading. Still, the joint embargo has not worked on every occasion. A prime example is Japan's refusal to end or limit the importation of ivory. The size of the Japanese ivory market provided stimulus to the ivory industry, and contributed to the continued killing of elephant populations across Africa.

[15]Natural Resources Defense Council, et al., "Environmental Safeguards for the North American Free Trade Agreement," (New York: NRDC, June 1992), p. ii.

[16]U.S. Congress, Office of Technology Assessment (OTA), *Trade and Environment: Conflicts and Opportunities,* ITA-BP-ITE-94 (Washington, D.C.: Government Printing Office, May 1992).

Box 19-3.   International Environmental Agreements Utilizing Trade Measures[1]

- Convention Relative to the Preservation of Fauna and Flora in Their Natural State, 1933

- Convention on Nature Protection and Wildlife Preservation in the Western Hemisphere, 1940

- International Convention for the Protection of Birds, 1950

- International Plant Protection Agreement, 1951

- Plant Protection Agreement for the South East Asia and Pacific Region, 1956

- Convention on Conservation of North Pacific Fur Seals, 1957

- Agreement Concerning the Cooperation in the Quarantine of Plants and Their Protection against Pests and Diseases, 1959

- Phyto-sanitary Convention for Africa, 1967

- African Convention on the Conservation of Nature and Natural Resources, 1968

- European Convention for the Protection of Animals during International Transport, 1968

- Benelux Convention on the Hunting and Protection of Birds, 1970

- Convention on International Trade in Endangered Species of Wild Fauna and Flora, 1973

- Agreement on the Conservation of Polar Bears, 1973

- Convention for the Conservation and Management of the Vicuna, 1980

- ASEAN Agreement on the Conservation of Nature and Natural Resources, 1985

- Montreal Protocol on Substances That Deplete the Ozone Layer, 1987

- Basel Convention on the Control of Transboundary Movements of Hazardous Wastes and Their Disposal, 1989

Source: GATT, *International Trade 90–91*, vol. 1, Geneva, GATT, 1992.

[1]The above dates denote the years during which the agreements were signed. These agreements may or may not be in effect at the current time for two reasons: first, signatories must ratify each agreement on the national level and second, many agreements have specific clauses that call for a particular number of parties or certain percentage of countries to participate before they take effect.

In spite of certain failures, CITES experts believe that trade measures are an effective and essential vehicle for wildlife preservation in this instance. Most of the species protected by CITES are found in developing countries and are sold to buyers based in developed countries. The total trade in wildlife (endangered or not) was $5 billion in 1990. Approximately 40% of endangered species are threatened as a result of hunting for trade.[17] Hence trade restrictions can potentially reduce a substantial amount of species loss. The major criticism of CITES is that it prohibits countries from commercially harvesting valuable species and using the profits to protect remaining populations. It contravenes GATT in the use of a ban on trade, although it probably will never be challenged in GATT because of its nearly universal support.

The Basel Convention on the Control of the Transboundary Movements of Hazardous Wastes and Their Disposal also uses trade measures to implement its goals. Initiated in 1989 by 105 countries and the United Nations Environment Program (UNEP), its aim is to limit and more effectively monitor international trade in toxic wastes. The convention requires a potential exporter of hazardous waste to gain the official permission of the importing country and of all countries through which the waste will be transshipped. The intent of these notifications is to ensure that the recipient country understands the risks of the particular wastes in question and has a proper system for treatment and disposal.

A series of politically sensitive transactions and attempted transactions between generators of waste in industrialized countries and recipients in the developing world prompted action on the issue. For instance, three Italian companies offered the government of Guinea Bissau the equivalent of their gross national product in exchange for receipt of several years' volume of waste. The odyssey of the *Khian Sea*, a ship containing incinerator ash from Philadelphia which tried to unload its cargo in numerous ports all over the world, made headlines for several years. The 3000-ton load was finally dumped on a Haitian beach in 1988, where it reportedly still remains.[18] There are numerous other examples of hazardous waste finding its way to places that do not have the technical capability to provide for its safe handling, including Eastern Europe, Africa, and Papua New Guinea.[19] Perhaps the most hysteria-inducing event of this kind was the disappearance of 41 drums of dioxin from a warehouse in Italy after an industrial explosion. The drums were ultimately discovered in an abandoned slaughterhouse in France.[20]

---

[17]Organization of Economic Co-operation and Development (OECD), *The State of the Environment 1992* (Paris: OECD Publications, 1992), p. 277.

[18]See Jane Ives, *The Export of Hazard: Transnational Corporations and Environmental Control Issues* (Boston: Chapman and Hall, 1985). See also Ron Chepesiuk, "From Ash to Cash: the International Trade in Toxic Waste," *E Magazine*, July 1991.

[19]Ives, op. cit.

[20]D. Dickson, "The Embarrassing Odyssey of Seveso's Dioxin," *Science*, June 24, 1983.

The Montreal Protocol on Substances That Deplete the Ozone Layer is one of the most recent and far-reaching examples of an agreement that uses trade measures to enforce its provisions. Designed to reduce the use of chlorofluorocarbons (CFCs) which deplete the stratospheric ozone layer, the Montreal Protocol was initially drafted in 1987 and now has over 80 signatories. Member countries created a timetable for the reduction and ultimate elimination of CFCs from products and production processes. The timetable calls for parties to ban trade in CFCs, CFC technology, products containing CFCs, and ultimately, products that are produced using CFCs.

The initial phase of the protocol restricts trade in CFCs and products that contain them: air conditioning, refrigeration equipment, aerosols, etc. The agreement has created problems because many parties to the agreement trade these products with countries that are not signatories to the protocol. The protocol effectively makes these countries signatories against their will. Of even greater concern to the trade community is the anticipated final phase of the protocol. Starting in 1995, production processes as well as products may become subject to the protocol's restrictions. GATT's rules prohibit trade restrictions based on production methodologies, as this is seen as an infringement on national sovereignty.

If all countries were parties to the agreement, they would effectively exchange national sovereignty (in this case, allowing an international agreement to limit domestic production practices) for the expected environmental benefits. However, since India, Korea, and other developing country exporters have not signed the protocol, their inability to buy and sell products containing CFCs or produced with CFCs is an unacceptable infringement on their right to seek economic development through trade. Certain aspects of the Montreal Protocol may be challenged in the GATT arena by countries such as Korea.

In the recent debates among trade and environmental specialists, the Montreal Protocol has emerged as a "flash point" that has heightened policymakers' interest in possible economic and environmental trade-offs.[21] By making developing countries a party to an agreement they had not signed, the protocol touched a nerve among economists who feel that free trade is the foundation of the international economic system. It further substantiated the view held by many developing countries that the international economic system is skewed against them, as they are not given the opportunity to exploit their natural resources as they see fit. In reviewing environmental agreements like the Montreal Protocol, there are obvious reasons why some of them use trade measures to achieve their goals:

- The environmental problem that the agreement attempts to remedy is a specific result of trade (i.e., CITES and international trade in endangered species).

---

[21]For a complete account of the debate, see Richard Benedick, *Ozone Diplomacy: New Directions in Safeguarding the Planet* (Cambridge: Harvard University Press, 1991).

- International trade is well established and has measurement systems already in place; environmental agreements can use trade to effectively monitor their goals.

- Use of trade measures has the effect of converting nonsignatories into parties to the agreement by limiting their trade with signatory parties. This eliminates free rider problems that have plagued international environmental agreements in the past.

However, resolution of trade and environment disputes requires treaty negotiators to ask:

- Whether the benefits of these agreements exceed trade losses.

- Whether the agreement could achieve its objective without the use of trade measures.

- Whether the use of trade measures is having a positive environmental outcome at all.

One often cited example of how an environmental agreement would disproportionately harm trade involves possible bans on international trade in timber products. It is possible that a ban on trade of tropical timber would actually increase deforestation by eliminating the local value of trees, which increases the relative value of converting the forest to agriculture. In fact, deforestation for agricultural conversion is vastly greater than for export, so a ban on timber export may not only be counterproductive but may not even be focused on the right problem.[22]

Domestic Environmental Laws That Impede Free Trade

Environmental regulation can impact a country's trade and competitiveness in two distinct ways, depending upon whether the standards regulate the production process or the product itself (see Box 19-4). When a country establishes environmental standards for products sold on its markets that exceed the standards of other countries, there may be a reduction in imports of those products. Since domestic industry is usually better able to respond to regulation—because of a more sophisticated understanding of the regulatory process and a greater fixed investment over which to amortize compliance costs—stringent product regulations tend to protect domestic industry. There are numerous examples of

---

[22]General Agreement on Tariffs and Trade (GATT), *International Trade 90–91: Volume I* (Geneva, Switzerland: GATT Secretariat, 1992). See also C. Pearson and R. Repetto, "Reconciling Trade and Environment: The Next Steps," unpublished paper prepared for the GATT Working Group of National Advisory Council on Environmental Policy and Technology (NACEPT) of the U.S. Environmental Protection Agency, December 1991.

this, two of which—the Danish Bottles Legislation and *Verpackungsverordnung*, the German Packaging Law—are detailed as case studies in the Appendix to this chapter.

The Danish Bottles Legislation, enacted in 1981, requires that all beer and soft drink producers selling products in Denmark utilize specific bottle sizes, provide recycling collection facilities, and guarantee reuse of collected bottles. The regulation appears to close the Danish beer and soft drink markets to foreign producers. A single producer, United Breweries, holds 70% of the beer market; the foreign share of the beer market averaged less than 1% during the period covered by the legislation; and a strike at United Breweries in 1985 led to a temporary moratorium on the legislation, inducing imports to jump to more than 3% of the market. On the other hand, the legislation was clearly effective at attaining bottle reuse. Despite complaints about its negative trade impacts, the European Commission was unable to dismantle the legislation in a suit presented before the European Court of Justice.

In spite of this and other examples, it is important to note that domestic producers do not always benefit from stringent product regulation. Japanese automobile manufacturers were quicker than Americans to respond to the U.S. Clean Air Amendments of 1970, which stipulated 90% reductions in hydrocarbon and carbon monoxide emissions from mobile sources. U.S. manufacturers went to court, arguing that such reductions were impossible, while the Japanese improved existing technology to comply with the standards. The Japanese industry's competitive response helped them gain share against the three major American producers throughout the seventies and eighties.

Process regulations impact trade and competitiveness by changing relative production costs of producers in different countries. Stringent process standards enacted in the United States over the last 20 years have required the investment of billions of dollars of environmental controls that are not required in many other countries. The impact on competitiveness of these expenditures is the subject of heated debate and is discussed later.

When examining domestic environmental laws, trade and environment analysts seek answers to the questions below to determine whether or not the environmental benefit justifies the potential impact on trade (the term "proportionality" is used to describe relative trade and environment impacts).

- Does the law protect domestic industry from imports?

- Was it developed based on sound scientific and analytical findings?

- Are the environmental benefits quantifiable with financial or public health measures? How do the results compare with the losses in welfare from reduced trade?

- Does the more stringent regulation provide a basis or standard for harmonization, such that, when other countries' environmental laws become more stringent, they could adopt the same standard and thereby eliminate the disadvantage to foreign producers?

Box 19-4.   Process vs. Product Standards

Environmental protection measures can be simply and fairly built into product standards, such as the U.S. requirement for catalytic converters in automobiles, the prohibition of ozone-depleting aerosols, the removal of lead from gasoline, or restrictions on lobster size. Although the conditions of production are not the same in all countries, product standards are easily applied to all sellers in a market, regardless of the location of production. For instance, the United States currently bans the import of lobsters under a certain size; it reasons that size is correlated to sexual maturity. Harvesting sexually immature lobsters will ultimately destroy lobster populations. However, the Canadians have disputed the ban on the grounds that, owing to the colder waters in Canada, lobsters do not grow very large and achieve sexual maturity at a smaller size than U.S. lobsters. In spite of this biologically compelling argument, a GATT dispute resolution panel upheld the U.S. law because it treats both national and foreign products in the same manner. The consistency and clarity of product standards make them the least discriminatory type of environmental protection and result in their fairly universal acceptance in the trade community.

Neutralizing the differences in process standards presents a more difficult problem, since it is difficult to monitor and measure different production standards in every exporting country. If accurate identification of cost differentials were possible, protection could entail an environmental duty or pollution tax on imports to make up the difference in production costs attributable to environmental controls. Theoretically, exporters could be offered a border payment equivalent to the differential in environmental control costs. In the United States, protection from imports subsidized by lax environmental controls is the goal of the International Pollution Deterrence Act, a Senate bill introduced in 1991 which would apply a countervailing duty on products from countries with weaker standards than those in the United States as a means of internalizing environmental control costs.

A more controversial method of neutralizing different process standards does not rely on countervailing duties but requires foreign-produced goods to be produced in the same manner as domestic goods. For instance, the U.S. Marine Mammal Protection Act (MMPA) seeks to limit the incidental killing of dolphin during tuna fishing operations. The act requires that in order to export tuna to the United States, foreign fleets' dolphin kills must not exceed those of U.S. fleets by 1.25 times. The MMPA and any other national law which stipulates production methodologies outside a country's borders, known in the trade community as "extraterritoriality," are considered to be hostile toward free trade, as they open the door for nations to unilaterally impose domestic standards internationally. As a consequence, they are expressly forbidden in recent GATT panel rulings (see Box 19-5).

Source: S. Hudson, "Trade, Environment and the Pursuit of Sustainable Development," presented at the World Bank Symposium on International Trade and the Environment, Washington, D.C., November 1991.

A critical aspect of any review of domestic environmental laws is who should be responsible for undertaking the review.

Trade Limits to Protect Clean Industry.   Companies that make significant expenditures to clean up their manufacturing process or to produce cleaner products potentially place themselves at a cost disadvantage to competitors that remain dirty. When such expenditures are required by law, assuming effective enforcement, there is a "level playing field" for domestic producers. However, domestic industry is potentially at a disadvantage to producers from countries with weaker environmental regulation. Those companies receive an implicit subsidy in the form of lower environmental control costs. Hence producers from the cleanest country are potentially at the greatest disadvantage.[23] For example, U.S. investment in pollution-abatement equipment as a percentage of total investment in the oil refining industry is nearly four times that in Europe and Japan. See Fig. 19-5 for more information on pollution abatement.

One could therefore develop a compelling rationale for trade protection for a clean country's industries. Many companies in heavily regulated industries, in rare alignment with some environmentalists, argue that they should be afforded protection from dirty imports. Labor is also concerned with the job loss and exportation of jobs they believe will result from differentials in environmental expenditures. The protection could take the form of tariffs, which neutralize the benefits that may accrue to a company from a "dirty" country, quotas, or even complete bans. However, in some cases unabashedly protectionist sentiment has been cloaked in greenery. Here is where the tension lies with free traders: When is environmental protection merely a smokescreen for protectionism?

Sector	Europe	Japan	United States
Food, beverages, tobacco	2.9	—	2.7
Textiles	1.5	5.7	1.6
Pulp and paper	5.3	6.2	4.5
Chemicals	7.0	4.4	7.9
Oil refining	4.3	4.6	16.5
Nonmetallics	4.8	—	3.6
Iron and steel	8.0	4.0	7.1
Machinery	1.9	1.0	0.7

Figure 19-5. Pollution abatement as share of total investment. [*Source: Organization for Economic Co-operation and Development, "The OECD Environment Industry: Situation, Prospects, Government Policies," (Paris, OECD, 1992).*]

---

[23]This argument ignores the potential for increased efficiency, pollution prevention, innovation, and market leadership that may accompany environmental investments. This hypothesis is discussed later under Implications for Corporations.

Environmentalists' Objections

Threats to Domestic Environmental Priority Setting.   While environmentalists are concerned about countries that choose to set standards at levels that are below internationally accepted standards, they also want to ensure that nations (and the state and local governments within these nations) have the ability to select environmental protection standards that exceed these internationally accepted standards.[24] This discussion raises many of the same questions as the Danish Bottles Legislation and *Verpackungsverordnung:* Should a country that has environmental protection goals in mind be allowed to restrict trade in the pursuit of these ends? If so, how can authorities determine when such restrictions are merely unjustifiable protectionism?

The Tuna/Dolphin Dispute provides a challenging case for discussion of this issue (see Box 19-5). Most environmentalists were outraged by the Tuna/Dolphin ruling, as they perceive the outcome as restricting the sovereign right of the United States to establish environmental standards for its own marketplace. Similarly, the ability of individual states to establish regulations that exceed federal standards, while complicating things for businesses that operate in multiple states, is a right that many environmentalists, as well as state governments, consider important.

The environmental policies of the 50 United States represent the most comprehensive array of harmonized standards in the world. The federal government sets minimum standards, which the states have the option of making more, but not less, stringent. A state can gain delegation of a regulatory program by drafting its own rules that meet or exceed federal objectives.

California and the Los Angeles Basin provide a good example. While the federal Clean Air Act Amendments of 1990 established new, more stringent standards for motor vehicle emissions, California produced its own regulatory program on air emissions that will require a percentage of car sales in 1998 to be zero-emission vehicles (likely to be electric vehicles). Since Los Angeles has air quality problems that exceed federally mandated minimum standards by $2\frac{1}{2}$ times, the local agency governing air quality has established rules that dramatically limit the use of volatile organic compounds (VOCs), a primary constituent of urban smog.

In cases where severe environmental conditions or the public demand environmental protection, the environmental community strongly believes that both federal and state governments have the right to act in order to provide for environmental protection. The secondary effects on trade, in such instances, are irrelevant.

Pollution Subsidies.   The flip side of protectionist domestic environmental laws are two forms of pollution subsidies: environmental dumping and pollu-

---

[24]One of the obvious problems of this discussion is the fact that there are not yet any "internationally accepted" environmental standards, whether they be floors or ceilings.

Box 19-5.   The GATT Tuna/Dolphin Dispute

The conflict. The Tuna/Dolphin debate began decades ago with the inception of the U.S. Marine Mammal Protection Act (MMPA) of 1972, which sought to control the incidental killing of marine mammals, particularly dolphin, in commercial fishing operations. Yellowfin tuna, the world's prime commercial tuna, tend to swim beneath pods of dolphin. Using large purse-seine and drift nets to encircle dolphin, fishermen typically trap dolphin as well as the desired catch. Incidental killing of dolphin was common to both the domestic and foreign commercial fishing industry, but the practices were increasingly called into question in the late 1980s. Heightened media coverage of dolphin slaughters elicited strong reactions from the public.

The MMPA banned the selling of tuna in the United States if the number of incidental killing of dolphin exceeded specified limits. Domestically, MMPA called for "the limiting of incidental taking of marine mammals by U.S. commercial fishermen pursuant to a valid permit issued by the National Marine Fisheries Service."[1] Internationally, similar provisions applied. Any country exporting tuna to the United States (both original and intermediary sources) had to ensure that incidental killing levels had not been surpassed.

In 1991, the Earth Island Institute, a nonprofit environmental group, sued Robert Mosbacher, the U.S. Secretary of Commerce, for not enforcing the provisions of MMPA. The institute argued that Mexico was not meeting its obligations under MMPA and called for an embargo on Mexican tuna and tuna products to enter into effect until Mexico could demonstrate that it was meeting MMPA's prescribed requirements. In January 1991 a District Court Judge ruled in favor of Earth Island, and the embargo was scheduled to enter into effect in August of that year. Mexico complained to GATT, arguing that such action violated GATT principles. A three-member GATT panel was convened to hear the case. Thus the debate had begun. Could domestic environmental policies shape international trade policy? Did the United States have the authority to impose extraterritorial measures to control practices beyond its borders? Or was MMPA merely a method to protect domestic industry? Any judgment would have to address these issues.

The arguments. Mexico and a host of other nations, including Venezuela, Vanuatu, Costa Rica, France, Italy, Japan, and Panama, argued that MMPA was illegal under the GATT for a host of reasons:

- It unjustly discriminated against foreign tuna, violating most favored nation principles contained in GATT article I.

- The standard did not apply to the product, tuna, but rather dolphin and hence represented a ban against foreign tuna, violating national treatment principles contained in articles III and XI.

- The ban was not allowable under the general exceptions, article XX.

Mexico further argued that the United States had made no attempt to protect marine mammals internationally, and therefore should seek to establish international agreements and accords to accomplish this object, rather than employ unilateral trade restricting measures.

Conversely, the United States cited the general exceptions provision as justification for MMPA. Sections (b), species preservation measures, and (g), exhaustible natural resource conservation measures, clearly applied to this dispute, and hence the United States had the right to impose process standards in order to ensure the safety of marine mammals.

The ruling. The panel agreed with much of Mexico's argument and struck down the District Court ruling. The panel concluded that MMPA restrictions violated article III and article XI and that the provisions fell outside the scope of article XX, because they were both extraterritorial and not "necessary" within its meaning.

The aftermath. The ruling sent a strong message out into the international trade and environment arenas. First, article III applied only to the treatment of the products, not to "production regulations of the exporting and importing countries." Countries, the panel stated, cannot use domestic environmental regulations as justification for trade restrictions on the production methods of other countries. If such practices were allowed, "each contracting party could (then) unilaterally determine the life or health protection policies (or conservation policies) from which other contracting parties could not deviate without jeopardizing their rights under the General agreement."[2] Hence, the prohibition of production process standards was reaffirmed.

Second, judging the legitimacy of environmental and conservation policies, the panel argued, is beyond its scope; its mandate is merely to judge whether policies violate GATT. As a result, GATT panels are unlikely to invoke the general exceptions provisions on environmental grounds. The panel argued that if environmental measures are to be used in formulating trade policy, then revisions to the GATT text must be arbitrated and accepted by GATT parties. Until then international environmental problems would have to be decided outside the trade policy arena.

Despite the ruling by the panel, the first round of the tuna/dolphin dispute is far from over. The United States has not accepted the panel's interpretation, and the tuna embargo still remains in effect. Moreover, the Earth Island Institute has recently launched a new case which has not yet come before U.S. courts or GATT authorities.

Source: R. Housman and D. Zaelke, "The Collision of the Environment and Trade: The GATT Tuna/Dolphin Decision," *Environmental Law Reporter*, vol. XXII, no. 4, April 1992.

[1]R. Housman and D. Zaelke, "The Collision of the Environment and Trade: The GATT Tuna/Dolphin Decision," *Environmental Law Reporter*, vol. XXII, no. 4, April 1992.

[2]OTA, op. cit., p. 49.

tion havens. Environmental dumping occurs when a nation's exports do not reflect the full environmental costs of production, use, and disposal of products. These nations provide implicit subsidies which could give domestically produced goods a cost advantage in export markets, compared with products from nations with more stringent environmental laws. For instance, requirements to cleanse smokestack emissions of sulfur dioxide represent an internalization of the environmental costs of producing electric power. Nations without such controls will have dirtier air but cheaper power. That trade-off is a national choice until one of two things happens: the sulfur emissions migrate to a neighboring country, causing negative transboundary effects, or attempts are made to export electric power to a nation with more stringent sulfur emission requirements.

Both the migration and electric power export cases result in conflict. In the first case, the nation producing excessive sulfur dioxide will get into trouble with the neighboring governments and the international environmental community. In the second case, the exporting nation will be attacked by the electric power industry of the importing nation.

The pollution haven problem arises from the fact that most developing countries have lower environmental standards than industrialized countries and enforce them with considerably less vigor. The environment ministry is usually underfunded and understaffed, which in many cases reflects low prioritization of environmental protection.[25] A potentially insidious result of pollution havens is the movement of industrialized country multinational companies to these countries, in order to operate with far fewer environmental controls than is required in their home country. Most environmentalists have alleged that multinationals choose locations in underregulated countries as a means of avoiding environmental expenditures. However, older empirical studies suggest that plant siting for most industries is not driven primarily by environmental concerns.[26] Rather, investment decisions are driven by the availability and cost of labor, proximity to major markets, political stability, and other nonenvironmental factors.

Recent sector studies of the U.S.–Mexican border reveal that Mexico's lax standards are a significant consideration within certain industries. For instance, 80% of U.S.-owned wood furniture manufacturers located near the border cited lax air emission standards as a major factor in their plant siting decision.[27] The fact that many of these pollution havens are under pressure to ratchet up their environmental regulations suggests that the benefits of such facility sitings might be temporary.

---

[25]For many countries, the low priority on environmental protection has been influenced by the burden of debt repayment. With the waning of the debt crisis, there are signs—particularly from the June 1992 UN Conference on Environment and Development—that environmental protection will receive higher priority in the future.

[26]Jeffrey H. Leonard, *Pollution and the Struggle for the World Product* (Cambridge: Cambridge Press, 1988).

[27]OTA, op. cit.

The previously mentioned study by Grossman and Krueger suggests a different result from multinationals' movement to a pollution haven.[28] If in fact the pollution haven's citizens become wealthier as a result of the additional foreign investment and job creation, the political momentum generated by environmental welfare preferences may accelerate regulatory development and environmental cleanup (see Box 19-2, Wealth and Demands).

The export of hazardous waste to developing countries serves as a prime example of the potential for wealth generation in this manner. Free traders would argue that developing countries understand the risks associated with accepting these wastes, and choose to do so to receive capital that they can productively use to advance economic development. Environmentalists argue that developing nations rarely understand the health and ecosystem impacts of this waste; since they are technologically unable to manage the waste properly, the likelihood of damage to the global commons increases dramatically. Furthermore, the international transport of hazardous materials is risky, as was demonstrated by the *Exxon Valdez* crisis of 1989.

Disputes Revisited

There appear to be a significant number of instances in which environmental agreements have clearly, whether deliberately or not, contradicted the spirit of current trade agreements. Bans, quotas, and the application of extraterritoriality, as in the Montreal Protocol case, are considered by free traders to be particularly egregious violations of GATT.

On the other hand, it appears that international environment agreements that restrict trade in a manner that is consistent with current GATT provisions are gaining grudging acceptance. Stringent product regulations that are consistently applied, such as the Danish Bottles Legislation, appear to be winning out over the trade community's objections.

However, there appears to be growing dissatisfaction with the current system. The GATT Tuna/Dolphin Dispute is an example of a complex problem in which both sides seem to have legitimate claims. If the boundaries of acceptable trade and environment overlaps are not well defined and the current system for managing these disputes is not sufficient, who should take responsibility for developing a better system?

Progress toward Solutions

Reconciliation of trade and environment conflicts will emerge from mutual understanding of the concepts, institutions, and attitudes of two very distinct cultures. Trade experts will learn the thought process, philosophy, and objectives of environmental institutions. Over time, trade agreements and institu-

---

[28]Grossman and Krueger, op. cit.

tions will reflect environmental priorities, without compromising legitimate free trade. Conversely, environmental standards and international agreements will not abuse trade measures and will utilize them with a fuller understanding of the total economic impact than has been the norm in the past.

As the free world's regulator of liberalized trade, GATT will exert more influence on the resolution of trade and environment tensions than any other single body. It may be that the most strident free-traders have met their match. The one institution that has been most uncompromising in its commitment to free trade is receiving intense political pressure to accommodate legitimate competing interests. Of course, in the mind of a trade proponent, "legitimate" competing interests are nonexistent. There have been numerous environmental disputes heard by GATT panels in recent years, which have been very conservative in allowing exceptions to free trade principles.[29] Regional trade settlements have been more accommodating to environmental interests, notably the EC and the U.S.–Canada Free Trade Agreement.

Largely because of political pressure from certain members, GATT has activated a Working Group on Environmental Measures and International Trade that is exploring how to reconcile trade and environment conflicts. The environmental community is carefully monitoring the activities of this group to ensure that environmental concerns get fair coverage in the group's work. While the environment did not emerge as a focal issue in the Uruguay Round, trade and environment will likely become central to the next round of GATT negotiations.

A particularly consternating factor to the environmental community in dealing with the trade community, in GATT as well as in other trade forums, is the lack of transparency or openness in deliberations. In the United States, the Environmental Protection Agency has fought hard to win a seat at some bargaining tables but has been largely unsuccessful in getting an equal voice in negotiations. In the EC, the environment directorate has been repeatedly neutralized by the trade directorate. The private environmental community has been even more frustrated, as they have been largely excluded from a process in which they are normally fully involved.

Many environmental proponents argue that GATT should be reformed in some way to provide guidance on environmental matters. For instance, some argue that Article XX, the general exceptions provision, should be amended to overtly refer to the environment. Alternatively, the strict prohibition on the use of process standards to restrict trade could be relaxed, with very specific guidance that would not set a broad precedent for other areas. The procedural requirements for amending the GATT, however, are very complicated and require ratification by either two-thirds or unanimous vote by the members, depending upon the issue.[30] Hence, many would-be reformers are looking elsewhere for relief.

---

[29]For a full discussion of GATT environmental dispute panels, see Appendix A in OTA, op. cit.

[30]J. Jackson, *Restructuring the GATT System* (New York: Council on Foreign Relations Press, January 1990).

The OECD began meeting on trade and environment issues in 1991, in order to develop a set of guiding principles for its members in developing trade and environment policies. It was the OECD that first enunciated the Polluter Pays Principle in 1972, which makes the commonsense argument that those who conduct a polluting activity should bear the cleanup costs. The OECD is perceived to be an effective forum for industrialized nations to air views and build consensus on contentious issues prior to introduction in broader UN or GATT forums. For instance, an OECD working group originally structured the Basel Convention, which was subsequently adopted by the UN Environment Programme with only limited modifications. Its focus on industrialized countries may also be its limitation, since developing countries have no opportunity to participate. Based upon discussions that occurred at the Earth Summit, the United Nations is establishing a Commission on Sustainable Development that may play a role in trade and environment matters. The North American Commission on the Environment is another participant in discussions relating to North American trade and environment issues.

While certain academics argue that regional free trade agreements may not ultimately be good for global free trade,[31] they could provide a unique opportunity to resolve potential trade and environment conflicts before they occur. The reduced number of players makes negotiations less complex, while the geographic proximity makes arrival at compromise essential. Both NAFTA and the EC have been attempting to bring domestic environmental standards into convergence, or to develop a time frame under which convergence will occur, as a part of their free trade negotiation processes.

NAFTA provides an interesting case study of the challenges presented by vastly different environmental standards among trading partners (see Box 19-6 for details). Negotiators from the United States, Canada, and Mexico announced in August 1992 that they had achieved an agreement that includes specific minimums for environmental protection, allowability of domestic regulations that exceed these minimums, scientific bases for establishing regulations, and mechanisms for quickly resolving disputes. At this announcement, U.S. EPA Administrator William Reilly claimed:

> NAFTA is the most environmentally sensitive trade agreement ever negotiated anywhere, and it will be seen as a model for other countries. Rejecting NAFTA on environmental grounds would be the environmental mistake of the decade.[32]

Some leading environmental groups dispute Reilly's claim, arguing that too much is left to the good intentions of the Mexican government.

---

[31]See J. Bhagwati, "Regionalism and Multilateralism: An Overview," Columbia University Discussion Paper no. 603. Bhagwati argues that, while regional agreements may provide short-term benefits to the countries involved, they may divert more efficient trading to trading among block members and ultimately complicate the establishment of a single global system.

[32]*Washington Post*, August 13, 1992, p. A12.

Box 19-6. NAFTA

The recent announcement of the North American Free Trade Agreement (NAFTA) marks the establishment of the world's largest regional trade bloc.[1] NAFTA represents over $6.5 trillion in gross domestic product (GDP), $243 billion in intrabloc trade, $760 billion in extrabloc trade, and over 360 million consumers. Although NAFTA clearly represents a boon for free trade and the economies of NAFTA countries, the implications for environmental protection, as well as U.S. employment, are not so readily apparent. The fundamental questions focus on the relationship between trade and the environment. Will natural resource and environmental protection be sacrificed in the name of free trade, or will free trade drive economic performance and lead to enhanced environmental protection and ultimately greater environmental quality? We again refer to the schools of thought described earlier.

Trade champions. NAFTA's promised trade benefits are immense, and many industrialists feel that the agreement is critical to the improvement of American industrial competitiveness. In the words of Carla A. Hills, the U.S. Trade Representative, "Mexico is our fastest growing export opportunity...and this agreement not only locks in the economic reforms and export opportunities that we have secured to date, but builds upon them and creates a real job machine at our back door."[2] The Trade Representative's office is satisfied to let NAFTA's promised economic benefits speak for themselves despite objections from the environmental community.

Environment through trade champions. NAFTA could provide Mexico with both the revenue and inclination to sponsor enhanced environmental protection and enforcement of current environmental standards. Although the Bush Administration has stated that foreign products will have to meet all U.S. product standards based on "sound science," raising Mexico's environmental standards has not been a central part of the negotiating agenda. The administration's position was summarized recently by an EPA official: "The fundamental premise of the NAFTA is: the economic prosperity Mexico should experience under a free trade agreement will enable Mexico to strengthen its existing environmental programs to achieve the rising levels of environmental quality it needs."[3] The Natural Resources Defense Council (NRDC), a New York–based nonprofit institution, summarized the administration's position as "trade equals prosperity equals enhanced environmental protections equals further prosperity equals environmental quality."[4]

Environment champions. Few environmental organizations are readily convinced of the "environment through trade" paradigm. By contrast, groups like the Sierra Club and Public Citizen argue that agreements like NAFTA that promote industrial growth are a major contributor to environmental degradation. They cite the Maquiladora program on the U.S.–Mexico border area as their primary example. Maquiladora industries—assembly plants owned by U.S. companies that are located just over the U.S. border in

Mexico—have devastated the region. Soil contamination from improper hazardous waste disposal practices, and wastewater contamination due to the absence of wastewater treatment plants required under U.S. law, have led to significantly increased rates of birth defects and hepatitis, far beyond the Love Canal tragedy of the early 1980s. The National Toxics Campaign, an Arizona–based nonprofit organization, estimates that over 100 million tons of hazardous waste are housed in plants in the Maquiladora area, posing a severe environmental and human health threat. Despite the recent creation of integrated environmental plans for remediation of the area, the establishment of environmental laws in Mexico and pledges from Mexican President de Gortari that Mexico will not become a "pollution haven," environmental advocates would have preferred to formally codify environmental standards, provisions, and considerations in the text of the accord.

Integrationists. Trade expansion and environmental protection are both valuable and essential contributors to sustainable development. Integrationists seek to evaluate NAFTA based on its ability to support these dual goals. Integrationists, such as the National Wildlife Federation (NWF) and NRDC, argue that while trade must generate revenues to support remediation of past environmental problems and the creation and implementation of new environmental programs, trade must be checked by environmental considerations in order to ensure that environmental degradation does not occur again. However, integrationists disagree over how much weight trade and environmental considerations should be given in environmental programs and agreements. At this point, integrationists appear to disagree over NAFTA's success at balancing trade and environment objectives.

Sources: NRDC et al., Draft Review of U.S.–Mexico Environmental Issues, Washington, D.C., December 1991; U.S. Congress, Congressional Research Service, North American Free Trade Agreement, CRS-IB90140, Library of Congress, Washington, D.C., September 1991; Walter Russell Meade, "Bushism, Found," *Harper's Magazine*, September 1992.

[1]Although NAFTA has been signed by the United States, Canada, and Mexico, it still requires formal ratification by each government before entering into effect.

[2]*Washington Post*, August 13, 1992.

[3]Natural Resources Defense Council (NRDC), et al., "Environmental Safeguards for the North American Free Trade Agreement," New York: NRDC, June 1992.

[4]NRDC, op. cit.

Beyond the discussion of the appropriate forum for resolving grade and environment disputes, we must also ask what rules or models we should follow in attempting to resolve disputes. Harmonization has become a central point of discussion in many trade and environment debates. Genuine harmonization involves not only convergence among countries on the stringency of regulations but also convergence on the structure and enforcement mechanisms for these regulations.

For instance, many U.S. regulations stipulate both acceptable emissions levels and the appropriate technologies for achieving emission reductions, so-called best available technology standards. In order for Mexico to harmonize its regulations with those of the United States, it would have to adopt similar emissions levels and the associated technology standards. While harmonization would be difficult to achieve and may not ultimately be a panacea, it does appear to be the most interesting solution to the impact of environmental restrictions on trade.

Environmentalists' views of harmonization are directly related to their perceptions of the direction in which standards would be harmonized. If harmonization is driven by the lowest common denominator, the effect may be a net reduction in environmental protection at the national level. For instance, U.S. manufacturers may argue that Mexican imports receive a cost advantage from less stringent regulation, and hence U.S. regulators should reduce the stringency of regulation to level the playing field. Alternatively, convergence may go upward, as many believe will be the case with European packaging laws. In this example, both trade effects and environmental effects of the regulation would be positive. The best-case scenario for both communities is characterized by clarity, consistency, and stringency.

The discussion of harmonization brings us back to the aforementioned disparity in the distribution of benefits from trade. Countries have different resource endowments, pollution absorption capacities, and social objectives. Hence absolute consistency in standards may not achieve the optimal outcome for all participants. The successful outcome will be a balance "between the advantages of harmonization—minimizing opportunities for covert protection, and the trade promoting features of internationally uniform standards—with the disadvantages of harmonization—overriding legitimate differences among countries in environmental and economic circumstances, and social preferences, and a standard that is both too high and too low."[33]

Even if conceptually valuable, the notion of harmonizing widely differing environmental standards is not credible unless it also includes technical assistance and funding to help weakly regulated countries adopt desirable control technologies. The Montreal Protocol, as revised in 1990, stipulates the establishment of a technology transfer fund administered by the World Bank to assist firms in developing countries to install non-CFC technologies. In addition, the U.S. EPA and over 15 large users of ozone-depleting solvents formed a technology transfer initiative to exchange ozone-friendly technology among themselves and to transfer it to developing countries. The Industry Cooperative on Ozone Layer Protection (ICOLP) has been extremely successful at assisting these firms and countries to eliminate CFC use in advance of Montreal Protocol deadlines. These inducements to poorer countries not only increase the likelihood that an international agreement will benefit from wide participation but increase the net environmental protection efforts of developing country participants.

---

[33]Pearson and Repetto, op. cit.

Outlook and Implications for Corporations

It is difficult to generalize about the perspective of companies on trade and environment conflicts. To some extent, the impact of new environmental regulations on companies depends on their current competitive positions and the extent to which exports comprise total revenues. Companies that are competitive internationally will oppose protectionist legislation in any market, whereas companies that produce primarily in a single market may support legislation that protects them (e.g., United Breweries in Denmark).[34] Based upon the examples included here, corporations can derive several lessons from these trade and environment conflicts:

■ *Greater infringement on trade by environmental agreements is likely, and confusion over how trade and environment can be integrated will continue, at least for a while.* The resolution of conflicts and the development of institutions that support trade and environment integration will likely be a long time in coming. Without the presence of a well-respected international science group, for example, the resolution between free traders and environmentalists on what constitutes sound science is unlikely. Since many environmental leaders view problems such as global warming and deforestation as both urgent and irreversible, they will not hesitate to use trade measures if they are the most effective means of protecting critical natural resources.

■ *Harmonization of environmental regulations, to the extent that it occurs, is likely to converge upward rather than downward.* It is clear that both industrialized and developing country citizens are demanding stronger environmental protection. In Europe, the Danish bottles and German cases indicate that regulations will indeed converge upward. The German law is being used to develop EC-wide packaging regulations currently under development. However, there is no question that harmonization is difficult to accomplish. Individual countries and, in the United States, individual states continue to construct new, more stringent regulations without consultation from regional and global coordinating bodies. Still, the EC and negotiators of NAFTA have been trying to achieve frameworks for harmonization.

■ *Corporations that anticipate stringency in regulations can gain competitive advantage.* Repeatedly changing business systems to comply with new regulations is costly. It may be more efficient to anticipate regulations, participate in the regulatory process, and influence regulatory structures so that they are easily

---

[34]Witness the disputes over the North American Free Trade Agreement (NAFTA). U.S. financial services and electronics companies argued on behalf of the agreement, as it will likely increase their exports. Major unions representing the steel and automobile industries, in an unusual alliance with environmental groups, fought the agreement on the grounds that both environment and U.S. jobs would be negatively impacted.

implemented.[35] The German packaging law is already creating challenges for business. In order to remain competitive, companies must create (or purchase externally) the capability to collect, sort, and reuse packaging waste at lowest possible cost. In the future, they must redesign their products to reduce packaging waste and its associated costs.

Similarly, one result of the Montreal Protocol's restrictions on the use of ozone-depleting substances is the virtual revolution it has created in electronics, aerospace, refrigeration, dry cleaning, and other industries. Corporations in countries that are parties to the agreement have swiftly developed replacements for CFCs and, in many cases, have phased out CFCs on a quicker schedule than the one mandated by the protocol. Several multinational companies such as AT&T and Northern Telecom have participated in a consortium that has shared and transferred CFC replacement technologies to companies based in developing countries.[36] These companies believe that their proactive efforts in developing countries may be providing them with additional credibility that will be valuable in selling their products.

Consistent with these voluntary efforts, recent initiatives in Germany and the United States have created voluntary regulatory programs to provide companies with flexibility in plant and process upgrades.[37] Many environmental improvements are, in turn, having positive effects on product quality. The lesson to industry is clear: read the regulatory landscape, and design processes to the most stringent standards in order to avoid retooling production processes, operations, and corporate behavior as regulations converge upward.

This proactive stance will require an understanding of how policymakers develop product standards in response to pressures for upward harmonization. At present, firms seeking entry to multiple foreign markets face high costs and confusion in dealing with the complex checkerboard of differing national regulatory approaches and standards toward environmental issues. Using the German Packaging Law example again, imagine the difficulties corporations would face if Germany established a new set of bottle sizes and reuse standards that were different from those in Denmark. This situation theoretically could be reversed at the level of the EC, but the costs of tearing down the systems already built in Denmark and Germany would be astronomical. Uniformity in product standards reduces the negative impacts of environmental regulations on corporate activities.

In order to assist policymakers in making informed decisions, corporations should provide credible input on standards that will accomplish environmental

[35]For instance, BMW played a prominent role in developing recycling standards for the German automotive industry. The ultimate legislation matched BMW's existing system and capability.

[36]The Industry Cooperative for Ozone Layer Protection (ICOLP) was established in 1989. It provides an interesting model of how industrialized country corporations can contribute to the accelerated use of "clean technologies" in developing countries.

[37]The U.S. Environmental Protection Agency's "33/50" program and Germany's vehicle recycling initiatives are both good examples of these programs. The former is a program to motivate companies to eliminate large percentages of toxic chemical discharge, the latter to create a countrywide, multi-industry network for car recycling.

goals at least cost to industry. Perhaps the most credible way that corporations can affect the decisions of policymakers on new forms of environmental regulation is to implement progressive environmental programs, which go beyond compliance and could themselves become the basis for future regulations. Leading multinational corporations that operate in developing countries have already begun discussions about harmonizing both their product standards and production process standards on a voluntary basis.[38]

These discussions are part of a larger corporate effort to determine how the concept of sustainable development can apply to the corporation. While corporate social responsibility is clearly one objective, companies see possible cost advantages in standardizing both their products and the way they make them on a global basis. (This may be especially true when they are producing in developing countries for export to industrialized markets.) GATT papers and various works written by Michael Porter of the Harvard Business School propose that companies operating in markets with more stringent environmental regulations may gain competitive advantage as harmonization occurs. GATT argues:

> The evident international diffusion of environment-consciousness suggests a ladder where those who incur the pollution abatement costs now are likely to be followed later by others. In turn, this means that investment expenditures in abating pollution, and technical changes and innovations induced by environmental policies (more stringent than elsewhere at any point of time), will position the leaders to compete more effectively in the future even if they reduce competitiveness now.[39]

The empirical evidence of the relationship between environmental excellence and competitiveness is not yet conclusive. However, it does appear that most industry leaders also have leading programs in corporate environmental stewardship; this is especially true in industries such as chemicals. The rapid pace of change in the trade and environment arena will reward similar leadership from those firms that move beyond current standards, and attempt to establish their programs and processes as the basis for future domestic regulations and international environmental agreements.

Case Study 2 in the Appendix, entitled *Verpackungsverordnung*, illuminates important trade and environment issues facing companies in the decade ahead and indicates the scope and scale of the challenges to the international business community.

---

[38]See International Chamber of Commerce, *Business Charter for Sustainable Development*, Geneva, Switzerland.

[39]See GATT, *International Trade 90–91*, op. cit., p. 31. M. Porter's *Competitive Advantage of Nations* also makes similar arguments. The Management Institute for Environment and Business (MEB), in examining the interplay between "Environmental Regulation and Industrial Competitiveness," found that companies such as BMW, General Motors, the Pacific Gas and Electric Company (PG&E), and the Northrop Corporation are pursuing new market opportunities through promotion of beyond-compliance environmental standards.

Appendix
Case Study 1:
The Danish Bottles Case*—
Commission of the European
Communities v. Kingdom of Denmark

In September 1988 the Court of the European Communities had to decide whether, by declaring that all containers of beer and soft drinks must be returnable, Denmark had failed to fulfill its free trade duties under the Single European Act (SEA), or whether Denmark's decision was justified on the grounds of environmental protection.

The Conflict

It had long been the practice in Denmark to charge a deposit on the sale of beer and soft drink bottles. This stimulated many consumers to return their bottles voluntarily, helping to keep the environment free of discarded bottles. This system worked well when there were a few different bottle types, and when foreign imports were often made under license or at least bottled in Denmark. However, in the mid-1970s, Danish beer manufacturers began to use cans and different shaped bottles. To ensure that the deposit system continued to be effective, legislation was introduced *"limiting or prohibiting the use of certain materials and types of container...or requiring the use of certain materials and types of container"* (Law No 297, 8th June 1978).

In 1981, as part of the Danish legislation on the reutilization of paper and beverage containers, the Danish Government set new orders for containers of beer and soft drinks (Order 397, 2nd July 1981). The Order said that beers and soft drinks could be marketed only in *"returnable containers."* According to the definition given in the Order, this meant that there had to be a system of collection

*Source: John Clark and the Management Institute for Environment and Business (MEB), "The Danish Bottles Case," case study prepared for the Trade and Environment Committee, the National Advisory Council for Environmental Policy and Technology (NACEPT), U.S. Environmental Protection Agency, January 1992.

and refilling under which a large proportion of used containers were subsequently refilled. With existing technology, this effectively banned plastic and metal containers. Also, the Order required formal approval for returned containers by the Danish National Agency for the Protection of the Environment. The Agency could refuse approval if the planned collection system did not ensure that enough containers were reused, or if a container of equal capacity, already approved and suitable for the same use, was available.

The Setting

Danish brewers had initially been against the recycling regulations introduced in the 1970s. However, they were forced to make significant investments in recycling processes and infrastructure. By the mid-1980s, the Danish industry was in a good position to cope with the strict recycling standards imposed by government. These moves were supported by the Danish firm United Breweries, largely thanks to good market positioning:

- Carlsberg and Tuborg, the firm's two main brands, together accounted for 70% of the Danish market.

- United Breweries was also a major players in the Danish soft drinks market.

- The firm held minority share holdings in most of its local competitors in both markets.

- The firm owned the only glass bottling facility in Denmark.

Outside Denmark the regulations were viewed less kindly. Producers of drinks and containers, and European associations representing the retail trade from other EC member states would have been more concerned, but for the small size of the Danish market. However, the metal packaging industry vigorously complained to the European Commission about the Danish regulations. While the Danish market was small, it might set a precedent for larger markets, such as Germany. It argued that the legislation had the effect of preventing imports of foreign beer and soft drinks into Denmark, because of both administrative difficulties and the costs involved for importers in establishing the required collection system.

The Commission supported this claim and objected to the Danish Order. The Order was amended by the Danes in 1984 (Order 95) to allow the use of nonapproved containers (except metal) if volume was less than 300,000 liters per producer per annum, or if the market was being tested, provided that a deposit and return system was established. Despite this amendment, the Commission considered the measures to be equivalent to a quantitative restriction contrary to Article 30 of the EEC Treaty. The Commission tried to persuade the Danish authorities to modify their position. However, negotiations failed and in December 1986 the Commission brought an action against Denmark before the European Court of Justice.

The Arguments

The Commission's main argument was that by effectively creating a quantitative restriction, Denmark was acting contrary to Article 30 of the EEC Treaty. Article 30 says that *"Quantitative restrictions on imports and all measures having equivalent effect shall...be prohibited between Member States."* These measures of equivalent effect include *"all trading rules enacted by Member States, which are capable of hindering, directly or indirectly, actually or potentially, intra-Community trade."* The Commission argued that the Danish measures could only be justified "if any restrictive effects on trade are not disproportionate to the intended objective of protecting the environment," and that it was possible to encourage recycling by less restrictive means.

The Danes' main argument was that the contested legislation was justified by a legitimate concern to protect the environment, by conserving resources and reducing the volume of waste. The Danish legislation had been very effective: 99% of approved bottles were returned and some of them reused up to 30 times. The Danes also argued than even if the rules might have adverse effects on trade, these effects were small given the size of the market. In 1984 only 0.01% of total Danish beer consumption was accounted for by foreign beers. Ultimately, the Danes' case rested on the following statement: *"...it seems the Commission has not followed the increasing ecological awareness which has arisen in recent years throughout Europe and which has led to the giving of priority to the protection of the environment over the free movement of goods, which, whilst remaining a fundamental objective, is no longer seen as an aim which must be achieved at any price."* Prior voluntary return systems did not achieve satisfactory results, and the impact on trade, they continued, was proportional to the environmental gains.

The Decision

The Court disagreed with much of the Commission's opinion when it announced its verdict in September 1988. It argued that Denmark's case provided *"good grounds for finding that protection of the environment constitutes an imperative requirement which may limit the application of"* the free trade rules. The judgment is the first to permit curbs on free trade on environmental grounds and may have far-reaching implications for other areas of environmental policy. Denmark is planning to impose new vehicle emissions limits beyond those of the EC, and Germany has instituted *Verpackungsverordnung*, a stringent packaging law.

Appendix
Case Study 2:
Verpackungsverordnung
(German Packaging Legislation)

For many years, German officials hesitated to take steps to implement regulations that might better ensure the achievement of the desired recycling and reuse levels, largely because they believed that any mandatory legislation might conflict with EC law and GATT non-tariff-barrier provisions. When the European Court affirmed the Danish bottles legislation, Germany saw an opportunity to enact new legislation to reduce Germany's growing solid-waste stream. The result has been one of the most progressive and ambitious environmental legislative efforts yet known.[1]

Germany has been at the forefront in development of stringent domestic regulations. The Bundeministerium für Umwelt, Naturschutz und Reaktorsicherheit (BMU, or German Ministry of the Environment) led a campaign in the late 1970s and 1980s to reduce one-trip drink containers and pave the way for a collection and reuse system. In an effort to accomplish this objective, Klaus Töpfer, the BMU chief, and his colleagues negotiated a series of voluntary deals with the beverage and recycling industries in 1977 to develop a system for reuse and recycling, but the number of one-trip containers sold and subsequently thrown away continued to rise throughout the 1980s. Without the threat of regulation, the campaign failed to sufficiently motivate industry to engage in the program.

The German Solid-Waste Problem

Although Germany creates less garbage per capita than many other industrialized countries, such as the United States and Japan, it remains a major producer

[1]Frances Cairncross, "How Europe's Companies Reposition to Recycle," *Harvard Business Review*, March–April 1992.

of solid waste.[2] Germany produces on the order of 30 million tonnes of garbage each year. Approximately one-third of this waste is created by households, two-thirds by industrial and commercial practices. Packaging waste represents a significant and steadily growing portion of German waste; it accounts for approximately 30% of German household waste by weight and slightly over 50% by volume of garbage per annum.

Although landfilling and incineration have been the disposal methods of choice, concerns over the environmental sustainability of these methods induced Germany to export a great deal of its waste, in the process becoming Europe's leading waste exporter. In 1988, for instance, West Germany exported 2.1 million tons of garbage to East Germany, an avenue now lost through unification. Moreover, the BMU and parliament enacted legislation banning exportation of waste, which sent German officials looking for answers.

Waste-Disposal Methods

Waste management practices are determined by resource endowments, population densities, and political proclivities. Table 19-A1 indicates Japan's waste efficiency, gauged by its high recycle rate, which is determined by the lack of space for disposal. Germany has a resource and population profile closer to Japan than to the United States, and so must increase its recycle rate as political momentum against landfill and incineration builds.

- *Landfill disposal.* A recent BMU regulatory campaign has led to stricter emissions levels of polychlorinated biphenyls (PCBs) and other constituents from landfill operations. The result has been an increase in the classification of formerly ordinary waste as hazardous. Some sources indicate that Germany will

Table 19-A1. Late 1980s Solid-Waste Management Practices, in Percentage

Management method	Germany	Japan	United States
Landfill	55	27	83
Incineration	30	23	6
Recycle and reuse	15	50	11
Total	100	100	100

SOURCE: The Global Tomorrow Coalition, *The Global Ecology Handbook*, edited by W. H. Corson. Boston: Beacon Press, 1990.

[2]OECD, *State of the Environment, 1991* (Paris: OECD, 1991).

Table 19-A2. German Landfill Prices, 1987–1992

Year	Landfill disposal price (per ton, DM)	Comments
1987	20	Classification as ordinary waste
1988	30	
1989	40	Landfill standards tightening
1990	60	
1991	120	Packaging regulation introduced
1992 (est.)	200	

SOURCE: BMW AG, Munich, Germany.

run out of landfill disposal capacity in 5 years. Landfill costs in Western Europe increased tenfold in the 1980s, and more than that in Germany (see Table 19-A2).

- *Incineration.* Although incineration reduces waste volume by approximately 90%, polychlorinated dibenzodioxin (PCDD) and polychlorinated dibenzofuran (PCDF) in air emissions render incineration a less than optimal disposal option, both environmentally and politically. The political sentiment against incineration, which is not restricted to Germany, has driven the costs of siting new incineration facilities beyond economic viability.

- *Recycling.* Despite currently arcane recycling practices, which require sorting of waste by hand and local drop-off points, Germany has achieved some impressive results. According to the Institut für Praxisorientierte Sozialforschung (Institute for Practice Oriented Social Research) greater progress is being made each year on recycling. At present, 50% of glass, 50% of used paper, and 40% of tinplate packaging are being recovered.[3] However, in order to handle a greater proportion of the nation's waste, recycling firms and facilities will need to expand significantly.

The Public Sector Response

Although Töpfer of the BMU believed the best solution to Germany's and the rest of Europe's solid-waste problems would be an EC-wide directive, he was skeptical about the EC's ability to do anything politically unpopular. In the wake of the European Court's decision on the Danish case, the BMU began tackling Germany's problems on its own. In late 1989, Töpfer targeted his first solid-

[3]S. Swiss, "Too High a Price?" *Environmental Risk,* April 1992.

waste constituent: plastic bottles. In conjunction with environment-minded parliamentarians, he engineered legislation requiring a mandatory deposit on all plastic bottles. Reaction to this, and to several other initiatives in the next two years was mixed, drawing complaints from all sides for going too far and for not going far enough. These early efforts laid the groundwork for the May 1991 ratification of *Verpackungsverordnung,* a severe ordinance that represents a radical departure from historical methods of setting recycling and reuse quotas on packaging materials. In essence, *Verpackungsverordnung* gives consumers the right to return all packaging material directly to the point of sale, with deposits possible on some items and the assurance that the returned packaging must be materially recycled unless it is not technically feasible.

The legislation has a two-part strategy for engaging the problem. In the initial phase, industry must develop an infrastructure for retrieval of different packaging constituents. In the secondary phase, the Ministry of the Environment will determine targets for reuse and recycling of these goods. The retrieval requirements ramp up in three distinct phases between December 1991 and April 1993 on packaging constituents. The materials covered and time frame are as follows:

- *Transport packaging.* Manufacturers and distributors were required to accept all transport packaging, such as crates, drums, styrofoam containers, and pallets, as of December 1991.

- *Secondary packaging.* Manufacturers, distributors, and retailers were obliged to accept all secondary packaging, such as cardboard boxes, cartons, boxes, or shrink wrap, which house products as of April 1992. Secondary packaging is defined as packaging used to prevent theft, clarify the product, or advertise or promote the product.

- *Sales packaging.* Manufacturers, distributors, and retailers are required to accept returned sales packaging as of January 1, 1993. This category is formally defined as all types of packaging necessary to contain and transport goods up to the point of sales or consumption. This includes cans, plastic containers, foil wrapping, and styrofoam and cardboard packaging.

Retrieval of packaging waste, however, is clearly not the end goal of the legislation. Once the retrieved packaging reaches the packaging company, it cannot be landfilled or incinerated (even in waste-to-energy incinerators). *Verpackungsverordnung* also specifies the time frames and collection and recycling/reuse levels that industry will have to meet. These dates and percentages are summarized in Table 19-A3.

The law also prescribes recycling quotas for specific materials, presented in Table 19-A4.

Töpfer has indicated that *Verpackungsverordnung*'s ultimate goal is to develop a "closed loop" system for packaging materials. Accordingly, collection and reuse/recycling levels will rise if the program proves successful.

Table 19-A3. BMU Verpackungsverordnung Implementation Strategy

Implementation date	Collection percentage	Recycle and reuse percentage
January 1, 1993	50	30–70*
July 1, 1995	80	80–90*

SOURCE: Letter from U. Denison, Green Dot licensing manager, DSD GmbH to K. Berhardt, U.S. Trade Office, Düsseldorf, Germany.
*Percentage varies by material.

Table 19-A4. Materials Specific Recycling Quotas

Material	Required recycling percentage
Glass, tin, aluminum	90
Plastic	64
Other packaging (i.e., cardboard)	80
Beverage containers	72*

SOURCE: M. Phillips and F. Steinhoff, "Germany: The World Test Market for Plastics Recycling," Decision Resources, Inc., Burlington, Massachusetts.
*Denotes refillable requirement.

Private Sector Response

Industry is in large part left to its own devices to achieve the goals laid out by *Verpackungsverordnung*. From Germany's past experiences, Töpfer well understands that constructive engagement by industry is critical to the program's operation and ultimate success. In order to put the onus for collection on business, the ministry and parliament made the indication that companies, not municipalities, are to be responsible for handling the problem. Legislators used the logic that, since corporate packaging practices were responsible for the problem, corporations should be responsible for rectifying the problem. If corporations were not held accountable, there would be no incentive to change packaging practices. The legislation does give companies the choice of two paths toward fulfilling their obligations:

Option 1: Retail Network Collection

As is stated in the ordinance's text, consumers can return all packaging to the retailer. Upon receipt of the packaging, the retailer would then ship the packaging back through the retail network to the manufacturer and finally the packaging company.

Option 2: Third-Party Collection

Private industry is free to engage third-party operators to fulfill the requirements of the regulations on their behalf. In essence, private industry could develop, finance, and maintain a private system for the collection and processing of all packaging materials in order to avoid returns to the retailer.

In response to the challenge, the Duales System Deutschland (DSD, or Dual System of Germany), a nonprofit corporation established by more than 400 packaging producers, fillers, and retailers (including multinationals), was established in September 1990 to finance and coordinate a countrywide collection system for all packaging materials. DSD's main objective is to separate the country's waste stream into its nonrecyclable and recyclable, or dual, components. The nonrecyclable waste stream will continue to be handled by municipalities, the recyclable stream by DSD. To date, over 16,000 companies, including a growing number of multinationals, have paid to be parties to the network.

DSD's responsibilities are twofold:

- Coordinating and regulating the packaging waste collection and sorting contracts for all households throughout the country
- Administering and financing the system

The basis of the program is the *der grüne Punkt* or *green dot* (the DSD is often referred to as the *green dot system*), displayed prominently on products and packaging, that signifies that companies are participating in the DSD and ensures that the packaging can be recycled (see Fig. 19-A1).

Figure 19-A1. The Green Dot. (*Source: Duales System Deutschland (DSD), GmbH, Bonn, Germany.*)

The *green dot* also indicates that the packaging may not be returned to the retailer. Instead, households and merchants separate the *green dot* items and place them in yellow receptacles curbside. Contracted collectors transport the contents to any of the 200 sites that are currently under construction throughout the country. These sites are responsible for collecting, sorting, and distributing packaging materials to the original companies. Subsequently, individual materials recycling companies and industries, such as the plastics industry, have developed private companies to process postconsumer materials. For instance, plastics producers, processors, and packaging companies recently established the *Verwertungsgesellschaft für gebrauchte Kunststoffverpackungen* (VGK, or Recycling Company for Used Plastics) to process used plastic containers and promote the recycled plastics market.

DSD will finance its operations by charging a fee for use of the *green dot* on all packages; companies will pay between 1 and 20 pfennigs (1 to 13 U.S. cents) an item for the service, depending on the size and weight of the packaging. The success of the program is virtually guaranteed by the fact that retail store parties claim that they will only carry *green dot* products (as part of their campaign to avoid direct returns). Figure 19-A2 shows the flows of rights, services, and materials in the DSD system.

As was to be expected, the setup and operating costs of the program to industry will be extensive. DSD representatives estimated setup costs to be in the neighborhood of DM15 billion (almost $10 billion), operating costs over DM2 billion (over $1 billion) per annum. To date, DSD has spent over DM7 billion to institute the program.

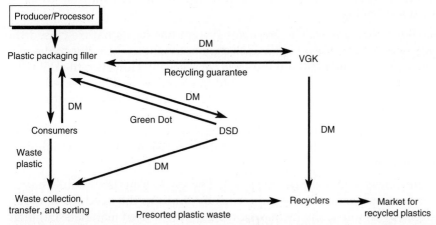

Figure 19-A2. DSD flowchart. (*Source: M. Phillips and P. Steinhoff, "Germany: The World Test Market for Plastics Recycling," Decision Resources, Inc., Burlington, Massachusetts.*)

The DSD Record

Although it is difficult to measure the efficacy of such a program in its early stages, DSD officials are encouraged by the prospects. To date, the transport and secondary packaging operations have been successful, but as the requirements for product packaging come into place, the volume of waste is expected to rise dramatically and operations will expand. DSD currently has pilot programs for total packaging collection running in a number of German cities, and the results have exceeded expectations of DSD officials.

Potential Pitfalls

The response outside of the DSD has been far from encouraging. The EC Commission, the German Trade Ministry, and the BMU have been bombarded by complaints from companies, free trade proponents, and even environmental groups throughout Germany and the Community. A number of issues have been presented:

- *Feasibility.* Although it has been readily demonstrated by local municipalities throughout the world that collection of large amounts of waste is possible, no such demonstration has been made in the recycling or reuse of such a large volume. The plastics industry provides a fine example.[4] Currently, nearly 50,000 tons of plastic are recycled in Germany per annum. However, Germany disposes on the order of 500,000 tons of plastic per annum, over 10 times the current recycled quantity. Simple mathematics indicates that recycling the large volume of currently landfilled plastic waste will require enormous corporate motivation and capital investment. The feasibility of completing an effort of this magnitude within the allotted time frame is highly questionable.

- *Monopoly considerations.* The *green dot* system has by its nature closed the German market to those companies that do not want to subscribe to the new system. Goods retailed without the *green dot* are legal. However, the DSD estimates that 70 to 80% of all products sold in Germany will be covered under its system. Moreover, public statements by retailers, distributors, and importers that are participants in the DSD indicate that they will not accept products, even those with recyclable packaging, without the *green dot.* Hence companies must subscribe to the new system or risk losing access to most of the German market.

- *Economic impacts on materials suppliers.* The packaging laws could have a tremendous impact on some industries by limiting the need for new raw materials. By dramatically increasing the amount of used materials and mandating their use, the ordinance will squeeze many raw materials suppliers.

[4]M. Phillips and F. Steinhoff, "Germany: The World Test Market for Plastics Recycling," Decision Resources, Inc., Burlington, Mass.

For instance, Norway, Europe's leading producer of virgin pulp and paper products, is upset about the potential reduction in demand for its packaging and paper products.

- *Trade barriers and competition.* Although packaging represents only a small fraction of the cost of most products and does not determine the competitive position of firms, the restriction of imports which do not have acceptable packaging presents a significant problem for exporters to Germany and may impede the emergence of a single European market. Many foreign firms complain that the costs of compliance with the legislation are significantly higher than costs to domestic firms. However, it is unclear at this time whether domestic firms will gain any advantage relative to their foreign counterparts.

- *EC implications.* The packaging requirements may be problematic under the provisions of the Single European Act. The issue of extraterritoriality is avoided in this case as the requirement—recyclable packaging—is a physical part of the product; domestic and foreign manufacturers must adhere to the same provisions. However, just as in the Danish bottles case, there may be a question of proportionality: is the *Verpackungsverordnung* program the least restrictive method of achieving the desired environmental outcome? To date, some sixty major international companies have lodged complaints with the European Commission over the new German law through INCPEN (Industry Council for Packaging and the Environment), but the case has not yet come before the court.

- *Environmental benefits.* With the numerous complaints about unnecessary economic and trade impact from the ordinance, it is ironic that even the environmental benefits of the program have come under fire from industry and environmental organizations. Although the DSD is supposed to ensure that all packaging is recyclable and the program is supposed to dramatically reduce the amount of packaging waste in the German waste stream, critics claim that these outcomes are far from obvious or guaranteed, given the numerous problems with the program:

  Qualification requirements. The onus for determining the feasibility of recycling packaging materials is on the packaging company. However, critics question the validity of many of the "recyclable" claims. "It's hair-raising to see some of the packages that have the green dot," according to Jan Bongaerts, head of the Institute for European Environmental Policy in Bonn.[5]

  Environmental impact evaluation. Others complain that the legislation sets forth no criteria for evaluating the environmental impacts of the specific kinds of packaging. Michael Braungert, head of the Hamburg Environmental Institute, states, for instance, that "a paper carton is considered the same packaging as a plastic package with stabilizers."[6] However, the lack of criteria for assessing environmental impacts is a concern.

---

[5]T. Waldrop, "Package Deal," *Tomorrow*, vol. 2, no. 2, 1992.

[6]T. Waldrop, op. cit.

Waste minimization. Although DSD officials argue that the costs per package take the size and weight of package into account, environmental advocates argue that the legislation is more focused on recycling than waste minimization and that market incentives are not strong enough to force companies to minimize packaging and waste.

These potential problems will have to be addressed before the ordinance can gain the full support of environmentalists and foreign companies, both of which are critical to the program's success.

Key Success Factors

The *green dot* program is in its trial stages but will face the ultimate test in 1993 when all packaging waste will have to be collected. While it is not yet far enough along to draw conclusions, a number of success factors will determine the ability of the DSD program to fulfill its stated objectives:

- *Community participation.* Clearly, German citizens will ultimately determine the viability of the program, for they will play the role of supplier. Their willingness to sort recyclable items from nonrecyclable and supply them to DSD contractors is the crucial first stage of the process.

- *Corporate support.* The private sector will bear much of the cost for the implementation and ultimate success of the program. Corporations not only must adhere to recyclable packaging requirements but must ensure that the materials indeed are recycled. For nearly all manufacturers, this will entail making changes in their own activities, helping change the activities of other corporations, and building facilities to meet recycling quotas. The costs to individual firms will be significant. Furthermore, achieving the recycling goals of the ordinance will require substantial cooperation and coordination among firms. Although cooperation is not unprecedented in Germany, it is not a trivial undertaking.

- *Technological innovation.* Some argue that technological advances are necessary to achieve the ambitious goals set forth by the legislation, especially for specific materials such as plastic and cardboard. New processes, products, and technological support will be critical to turning the packaging challenge into a manageable one.

- *Development of waste market.* The public, corporations, and the government will all have to take steps to develop the market for recycled waste and products. As in the United States, the markets for most recycled materials are not strong (e.g., the price for 100 kg of used paper in Germany fell from DM30 to DM1.50 over the course of the last 3 years). Consumer interest in recycled, environmentally friendly goods has grown but remains unstable. For the packaging laws to succeed, increasing and stabilizing the demand for used materials and recycled products is critical.

An Uncertain Future

With the program under way but not yet fully operating, and with many of the recycling quotas yet to be implemented, *Verpackungsverordnung* is still a mystery to the public, government, environmental groups, and the corporate sector:

- *Imports.* Will *Verpackungsverordnung* effect a nontariff barrier for multinationals exporting to Germany?

- *Exports.* Will the laws raise costs to German producers and pose a challenge to their competitiveness on the world market?

- *The European Community.* How will the EC confront tougher national legislation that may pose a threat to the common market in light of the precedent set forth in the Danish bottles case? Will the Community move toward a harmonized packaging ordinance?

- *Corporate behavior.* What strategies will corporations take to confront and adhere to the new legislation? Will they make the substantial investments that are required, cooperate with other firms, develop new processes and technologies, or will they mobilize to strike the new ordinance down? Can they gain business opportunities by developing more effective systems and technologies than their competitors?

- *The solid waste problem.* Will the new ordinance be successful in confronting the solid waste problem? Or is legislation that more directly focuses on minimization necessary in order to ensure the desired environmental benefits?

Bibliography*

Arden-Clarke, C. "The General Agreement on Tariffs and Trade, Environmental Protection, and Sustainable Development." Geneva: World Wildlife Fund (WWF) International, November 1991.

Bhagwati, J. "Regionalism and Multilateralism: An Overview." Columbia University Discussion Paper no. 603. New York: Columbia University Press, 1991.

Center for International Environmental Law (CIEL). "Frictions between International Trade Agreements and Environmental Protections." Unpublished study prepared for the Trade and Environment Committee of the National Advisory Council for Environmental Policy and Technology (NACEPT), U.S. Environmental Protection Agency, January 1992.

Charnovitz, S. "Exploring the Environment Exceptions in GATT Article XX." 25 *Journal of World Trade* 37, October 1991.

Chepesiuk, R. "From Ash to Cash: The International Trade in Toxic Waste." *E Magazine*, July 1991.

Daly, H., and J. Cobb. *For the Common Good.* Boston: Beacon Press, 1989.

Dickson, D. "The Embarrassing Odyssey of Seveso's Dioxin." *Science,* June 24, 1983.

*References for the case studies appear as footnotes in the case studies.

Feketekuzy, G. "U.S. Paper on the Link between Trade and Environment Policy." Unpublished study prepared for the U.S. Environmental Protection Agency's Office of Policy, Planning and Evaluation (OPPE), October 1991.

GATT Press Release. "GATT Rules Are Not an Obstacle to Environmental Protection, but Trade Weapon Could Be Counterproductive." February 1992.

GATT Panel, United States—*Restrictions on Imports of Tuna: Report of the Panel,* 50–51, GATT Doc. DS21/R, September 3, 1991.

General Agreement on Tariffs and Trade (GATT), *International Trade 1990–1991,* vol. 1, Geneva: GATT, 1992.

Grossman, G. M., and Krueger, A. B. "Environmental Impacts of a North American Free Trade Agreement." Paper presented at a conference on U.S.–Mexico Free Trade Agreement, sponsored by the Mexican Secretaria de Comercio y Fomento Industrial, October 8, 1991.

Housman, R., and Zaelke, D. "The Collision of the Environment and Trade: The GATT Tuna/Dolphin Decision." *Environmental Law Reporter,* vol. XXII, no. 4, April 1992.

———. "Trade, Environment, and Sustainable Development: A Primer." *Hastings International and Comparative Law Review,* vol. 15, no. 4, Summer 1992.

Hudson, S. "Trade, Environment and the Pursuit of Sustainable Development." Presented at the World Bank Symposium on International Trade and the Environment, Washington, D.C., November 1991.

Ives, J. *The Export of Hazard: Transnational Corporations and Environmental Control Issues.* Boston: Chapman and Hall, 1985.

Jackson, J. H. "Changing GATT Rules." Unpublished study prepared for the Trade and Environment Committee of the National Advisory Council for Environmental Policy and Technology (NACEPT), U.S. Environmental Protection Agency, November 1991.

———. *Restructuring the GATT System.* New York: Council on Foreign Relations Press, January 1990.

Leonard, J. H. *Pollution and the Struggle for World Product.* New York: Cambridge University Press, 1988.

Management Institute for Environment and Business (MEB). "Montreal Protocol: Science, Trade, and Developing Country Issues." Unpublished study prepared for the Trade and Environment Committee of the National Advisory Council for Environmental Policy and Technology (NACEPT), U.S. Environmental Protection Agency, January 1992.

Management Institute for Environment and Business (MEB) and The London Business School. "The Danish Bottles Case." Unpublished study prepared for the Trade and Environment Committee of the National Advisory Council for Environmental Policy and Technology (NACEPT), U.S. Environmental Protection Agency, January 1992.

National Advisory Council for Environmental Policy and Technology (NACEPT) Trade and Environment Committee. "Committee Briefing Book: An Introduction to the Issues." U.S. Environmental Protection Agency, November 1991.

Natural Resources Defense Council (NRDC), et al. "Environmental Safeguards for the North American Free Trade Agreement." New York: NRDC, June 1992.

Organization for Economic Co-operation and Development (OECD), Environment Committee Secretariat. "Trade and Environment: Major Environmental Issues Note." Paris: OECD, March 1991.

———. "The OECD Environment Industry: Situation, Prospects, Government Policies." Paris: OECD, 1992.

OECD Joint Session of Trade and Environment Experts. "The Applicability of the GATT to Trade and Environment Concerns." Prepared for the "Joint Work Programme on Trade and the Environment," Paris, November 1991.

Pearson, C. "Environmental Control Costs and Border Adjustments." *National Tax Journal*, vol. 28, no. 4, December 1974.

Pearson, C., and Repetto, R. "Reconciling Trade and Environment: The Next Steps." Unpublished study prepared for the Trade and Environment Committee of the National Advisory Council for Environmental Policy and Technology (NACEPT), U.S. Environmental Protection Agency, December 1991.

Porter, M. E., *The Competitive Advantage of Nations*. New York: The Free Press, 1989.

———. "America's Green Strategy." *Scientific American*, April 1991.

Repetto, R. "A Taxonomy Relevant to the Issues." Unpublished note prepared for the Trade and Environment Committee of the National Advisory Council for Environmental Policy and Technology (NACEPT), U.S. Environmental Protection Agency, 1991.

———. "Note on Complementarities between Trade and Environment Policies." Unpublished study prepared for the Trade and Environment Committee of the National Advisory Council for Environmental Policy and Technology (NACEPT), U.S. Environmental Protection Agency, December 1991.

Shrybman, S. "International Trade and the Environment." *Alternatives*, vol. 17, no. 2, 1990.

U.S. Congress, General Accounting Office (GAO). *International Environment: International Agreements Are Not Well Monitored*. GAO RCED-92-43 (Washington, D.C.: Government Printing Office, January 1992).

U.S. Congress, Office of Technology Assessment (OTA). *Trade and Environment: Conflicts and Opportunities*. ITA-BP-ITE-94 (Washington, D.C.: Government Printing Office, May 1992).

Wheeler, D., and Martin, P. "Prices, Policies, and the International Diffusion of Clean Technology: The Case of Wood Pulp Production." Paper presented at the World Bank Symposium on International Trade and the Environment, Washington, D.C., November 1991.

World Bank. *World Development Report 1992: Development and the Environment*. Oxford: Oxford University Press, May 1992.

20

Environmental Strategies for the Developing World

Andrew Steer

Will Wade-Gery
*The World Bank**

In this chapter:

- Environmental Problems/Challenges in Developing Countries
  - Water and Sanitation
  - Air Pollution
  - Land Degradation
- The Strategic Challenge
  - Poverty, Population, and the Environment
  - Strategies for Sustaining Development
- National-Level Environmental Problems: A Three-Part Strategy
  - Building on the Positive Links
  - Breaking the Negative Links
  - Removing Impediments to Action
- Global and Regional Environmental Problems and Strategies
- The Costs of a Sustainable Future
  - Policy Costs
  - Sources of Finance

---

*Andrew Steer is Deputy Director of the World Bank's Environment Department and main author of the *World Development Report 1992*. Will Wade-Gery is a Consultant in the Bank's Environment Department.

Environmental problems in developing countries—including inadequate water and sanitation services, severe air pollution, and land degradation—threaten human health and productivity on a massive scale. Many of these problems are closely related to growing population levels and the high incidence of poverty in developing countries. To achieve sustainable development, a three-part strategy is required.

1. The positive links between economic growth, efficiency, and environmental protection must be fully exploited.
2. Negative links between economic growth and environmental degradation must be broken.
3. Political and institutional obstacles to the adoption of these first two measures must be overcome.

Such a strategy will prove affordable, realistic, and effective. The World Bank is actively involved in assisting borrowing countries with every aspect of this strategy's implementation.

Introduction

Development policies have traditionally been thought to promote growth in human activity, while environmental policies have been seen as restricting it. Released in 1972, the Club of Rome's report on the "predicament of mankind" argued on the basis of the finitude of the earth's physical capacity for deliberately restricting rates of economic growth (Meadows et al., 1972). In recent years, however, the idea of the environment as a constraint to development has given way to an acceptance of the complementarity between development and the environment. As shown by the UNCED process set in motion in Rio in June, 1992, development policymakers increasingly recognize that failing to take the costs of environmental damage into account will prove inefficient and often ineffectual in terms of raising incomes and well-being. Similarly, environmentalists are coming to understand that answers to many problems—especially those that afflict developing country populations—lie in faster, not slower, growth in incomes, along with sound environmental policies.

But if there is now broad agreement at the conceptual level on the need to integrate policies for development and the environment, a large gap between practice and rhetoric remains. Beginning in 1987, the World Bank, an organization which recognizes the alleviation of poverty as its fundamental objective, embarked on a major effort to incorporate environmental concerns into all aspects of its work; previously the bulk of the environmental work undertaken by the Bank (comprising the International Bank for Reconstruction and Development and its affiliated institution, the International Development Association) involved individual projects and sectors, and research or analysis of selected issues. Since 1987, however, a set of principles and policies has evolved to guide the totality of Bank activity. The significant events of 1992—both within the Bank and in the wider international community—can be thought of as marking a transition from a first phase, one of efforts to integrate the goals of environment and development, to a new phase in which particular attention is given to the implementation of integrated policies, so that actions will more consistently correspond to agreed principles.

Agenda 21—UNCED's blueprint for environmental action—gives high priority to the implementation of "win-win" policies that exploit the complementarity between poverty reduction, economic efficiency, and sound environmental management. Additionally, it notes that unregulated economic growth can have profound and sometimes irreversible effects on the environment. These negative impacts need to be addressed by specifically targeted policies, strengthened environmental institutions, and increased allocation of funds for investments in environmental technologies. As emphasized in the *World Development Report 1992* (World Bank, 1992), any strategy that aims at sustainable management of the earth's resources must both build on the positive links between development and the environment and seek to break the negative links between economic growth and environmental degradation. This chapter lays out the outlines of such a strategy and reviews the World Bank's progress in pursuing its implementation.

We begin the chapter with an overview of the specific environmental problems confronting the developing world. At both the national and multilateral level, these problems are sometimes not accorded their rightful place on the environmental agenda, which is instead often focused on international problems of greater concern to developed countries. As a consequence, environmental concerns are sometimes thought—by policymakers and analysts in both the developing and developed worlds—to be a "luxury" only rich countries can afford to address. But once the environmental debate is refocused on the problems that severely affect the welfare of the largest numbers of people, it becomes evident that the imperative of environmental protection is even greater in poor countries than in rich ones.

The next section examines the general relationship between development and the environment. Issues considered include the effects of poverty and population on the environment, and the potential scope for policy to influence the relationship between economic growth and environmental quality. The following section lays out a three-part strategy to achieve sustainable development: first, policies that build on the positive links between development and the environment; second, targeted policies that are designed to correct environmentally damaging forms of behavior; and third, policies that remove obstacles and impediments to sound environmental management. The World Bank's environmental activities, which involve policy dialogue, lending, technical assistance, research, and aid coordination, are examined in the light of this strategy. We also review efforts to address the environmental degradation of the global commons. Such degradation takes a variety of forms: ozone depletion, climate change, biodiversity loss, and the pollution of international waters. Finally, the costs of sound environmental management are estimated, and potential sources of finance are identified and assessed.

Environmental Problems and Challenges in Developing Countries

Environmental degradation has three damaging effects. It harms human health, reduces economic productivity, and leads to a loss of "amenities," a term that describes the many other ways in which people benefit from the existence of an unspoiled environment. Because the interaction of various pollutants with other human and natural factors may be hard to predict, some environmental problems may entail losses in all three areas. The priorities that developing countries set for their own environment will not necessarily be those that dominate the public environmental debate in richer countries. In particular, although some cultures in poor countries may value their natural heritage strongly, most developing countries are understandably likely to give lower priority to forms of amenity damage as long as basic human needs remain unmet. Further, priorities will vary among developing countries. In sub-Saharan Africa, for example, contaminated drinking water and poor sanitation contribute to infectious and parasitic diseases that account for more than 62% of all deaths—twice the level found in Latin America. Such discrepancies notwithstanding, developing countries should give priority to addressing the risks to human health and productivity associated with dirty water, inadequate sanitation, air pollution, and land degradation. All of these cause illness and death on an enormous scale; they are more immediately life-threatening than those environmental problems associated with developed countries, such as carbon dioxide emissions, the depletion of stratospheric ozone, photochemical smogs, acid rain, and hazardous wastes.

Water and Sanitation

Although official data show significant progress in the 1980s, access to uncontaminated water has barely kept pace with population increase; despite a doubling of water supply in rural areas between 1980 and 1990, nearly 1 billion people in the developing world are still without access to clean water. Water quality has continued to deteriorate, with disease-bearing human wastes being the most widespread cause of contamination. More than 1.7 billion people worldwide must contend with inadequate sanitation facilities; and in urban areas the absolute number of people without sanitation has in fact increased during the 1980s by around 70 million. Moreover, even where access to sanitation services has been improved, sewage frequently remains untreated—in Latin America, as little as 2% of sewage receives any treatment.

The use of polluted water for bathing and drinking is one of the principal pathways for infection by diseases that kill millions and sicken more than 1 billion people each year. Unsafe water is a major contributor to the 900 million cases of diarrheal diseases annually, leading to 3 million deaths, most of them children. At any time, 500 million people are suffering from trachoma, 200 million from schistosomiasis or bilharzia, and 900 million from hookworm. Cholera, typhoid, and paratyphoid also continue to stifle human welfare. Many of these conditions have indirect health effects—frequent diarrhea, for instance, can make a child vulnerable to illness and death from other causes. Reducing the health costs of poor water quality often imposes substantial economic costs on individual users. In Jakarta, for instance, households spend more than $50 million each year boiling water—an amount equal to 1% of the city's GDP.

In some locations, these problems are compounded by growing water scarcity, which makes it difficult and expensive to meet increasing demand for drinking water, irrigation, and industrial use. This is a particularly acute problem in arid areas of the Middle East, as well as in places such as northern China, East Java, and parts of India. Groundwater is being depleted, sometimes irreversibly—in Jakarta, over two-thirds of the population relies on groundwater, and the water table has declined dramatically since the 1970s. Excessive groundwater withdrawals also cause salinization (in coastal areas), subsidence, broken sewerage pipes, and flooding. Moreover, existing withdrawals from rivers limit further expansion of irrigation and in-stream uses, such as river transport, sediment flushing, and fish reproduction. Overall, because of their effect on human health and economic growth, deficient water supplies and sanitation pose the most serious environmental problems that face developing countries today. An integrated approach to water management is essential if a crisis is to be avoided in water-short countries over the next decade. The World Bank is now developing explicit procedures for addressing intersectoral water resource issues on a comprehensive basis; a forthcoming Water Resources Management policy paper will examine techniques for protecting and managing water in all its uses, from irrigation to drinking.

Air Pollution

Although consistent monitoring of ambient air pollution is just over a decade old, the evidence clearly indicates that several pollutants—stemming from energy use, vehicular emissions, and industrial production—are frequently over levels considered safe for health. More than 1.2 billion people reside in urban areas in developing countries are exposed to levels of dust and smoke (known collectively as suspended particulate matter, or SPM) that exceed recommended World Health Organization (WHO) standards. Such high SPM levels can cause severe respiratory problems; and poor health and nutrition make developing country populations even more susceptible to the effects of pollution. Rough estimates indicate that if unhealthy levels of SPM were brought down to the annual average level that WHO recommends, between 300,000 and 700,000 premature deaths a year could be averted in developing countries. Moreover, excessive particulate pollution also results in lost productivity: in urban areas with average SPM levels above the WHO guidelines as many as 2.1 working days a year are lost to respiratory illness for every adult in the labor force.

Indoor air pollution from burning wood, charcoal, and dung inside homes—especially in rural Africa and South Asia—seriously endangers the health of 400 to 700 million people, particularly women and children. The pollution levels they are exposed to are often the equivalent of smoking several packs of cigarettes a day, and they contribute to acute respiratory infections that cause an estimated 4 million deaths annually among infants and children. (Biomass burning is also often linked to deforestation, a separate source of environmental degradation.) In addition, high levels of lead, primarily from vehicle emissions, contribute to hypertension and high blood pressure, and hinder neurological development. Estimates for Bangkok suggest that the average child has lost four or more IQ points by the age of seven because of elevated exposure to lead. Finally, more than 1 billion people are exposed to unhealthy levels of sulfur dioxide.

As developing countries grow—which they must if poverty is to be reduced—they will begin to catch up with the levels of energy consumption and industrial production of high-income countries. If current practices and policies continue unchanged, increased energy consumption and industrial production will add enormously to pollution. On current trends, pollution from the fossil fuel generation of electric power will rise tenfold in the next 40 years, from vehicles more than fivefold, and from industrial emissions and wastes also more than fivefold. As the later discussion of national-level environmental problems argues, this challenge can be met; left unaddressed, however, air pollution and its associated costs will rise exponentially.

Land Degradation

As the world's population grows by two-thirds over the next 40 years, demands for food, fuel, and fiber will rise enormously. By 2030 world grain consumption will have increased by about 97%; of this increase, 91% will be in developing countries. Meeting these demands will require more intensive and extensive exploitation of natural resources such as forests and agricultural land. However, both intensification and extensification can cause extensive damage to land resources. Raising yields by increasing the use of chemical inputs, or diverting more water for irrigation purposes can impose severe environmental externalities. Runoff of fertilizer and animal wastes can pollute groundwater and surface water; nutrient depletion and soil erosion may result from mismanaged efforts to raise yields. But agricultural expansion into uncultivated areas, many of which are environmentally fragile, is similarly problematic; already an estimated 60% of the deforestation in developing countries is the result of extensification. Overall, the challenge for the future will be to balance intensive and extensive growth of agriculture so as to avoid the environmental damage and constraints on productivity that each can cause.

Forests.   Nearly 500 million people, most of them poor, live in or near forests, and depend on them for food, fuel, fodder, timber, and income. Over the past decade, developing countries have been converting or degrading their forests, coastal and inland wetlands, and other ecosystems at unprecedented rates. Tropical moist forests, for example, which are the richest ecosystems—in biomass and biodiversity, on land, are being burned and cut at a rate of 17 to 20 million hectares per year, or 1% percent a year—if this continues, these forests will disappear within several generations. Although the international community has focused a great deal of attention on the global environmental ramifications of deforestation, the loss of forests can also pose severe ecological, economic, and social costs at a more local level: soil degradation and watershed destruction; local climate change and disruptions to local hydrological regimes; loss of natural habitat and the valuable biodiversity it protects; and the destruction of the livelihoods and cultural integrity of indigenous forest-dwelling peoples. Sometimes the effects can be dramatic: for instance, in 1991, 5000 villagers were killed by flooding caused in part by deforested hillsides.

Deforestation is caused by farmers, ranchers, logging and mining companies, and fuelwood collectors, each pursuing private interests that are frequently distorted by perverse government policies. Incentives to cut trees are likely to remain strong. The growth of population and income leads to a rising demand for firewood. Falling demand for labor in settled agricultural areas has in some countries prompted numerous migrants to seek new livelihoods and new lands on forest frontiers. These frontiers have become increasingly attractive and accessible in countries such as Brazil, Ecuador, and Indonesia. Often, such settlement has been actively encouraged by governments (with backing from the World Bank and other donors) through cheap credit, land and resettlement grants, provision of infrastructure, and low stumpage fees. The Bank has recently adopted a new series of principles to guide its involvement in the forest sector: among other commitments, the Bank has undertaken not to finance, under any circumstances, commercial logging in primary tropical moist forests.

Soils.   Over 11% of the earth's vegetated surface has undergone moderate or worse soil degradation over the last 40 years. As a result, yields and total harvests of important food crops are declining in a number of areas, particularly in sub-Saharan Africa, even though yields are increasing globally, as well as in developing countries as a whole. Three aspects of soil degradation—desertification, erosion, and salinization and waterlogging—receive the most attention, although desertification does not have as large and pervasive an effect on productivity as the others. (Dramatic images of advancing deserts capture a great deal of media focus; however, satellite imagery of the Sahel shows that during the 1980s vegetation advanced and retreated by up to 200 kilometers between wet and dry years, but did not indicate any underlying desertification trend.)

Soil erosion is often irreversible and it frequently gives rise to serious off-site environmental effects. Even without including such effects, rough estimates suggest that in countries such as Costa Rica, Malawi, Mexico, and Mali, on-farm productivity declines may amount to an annual GDP loss of between 0.5 and 1.5%. The problem is particularly acute in tropical developing countries (especially in their poorer, environmentally fragile areas), where soils, rainfall, and agricultural practices are most conducive to erosion and where rates of soil loss have often been found to exceed the natural rate of soil formation. In addition, salinization now affects nearly one-third of all arable land. Although some of this salinization occurs naturally, about 60 million hectares, or some 24% of all irrigated land, suffer from salinization caused by poor irrigation practices. More than a third of irrigated land in India and a quarter in Pakistan is affected by waterlogging and salinity.

The Strategic Challenge

A failure to address developing countries' environmental problems can directly undercut development in two ways. First, environmental quality—water that is clean and plentiful, air that is healthy—is itself an essential part of the improvement in welfare that development aims to provide. Development will therefore necessarily involve an enhancement of environmental quality: If the benefits from rising incomes are offset by the welfare costs of poor health and other non-pecuniary indicators of "quality of life," then it can make little sense to speak of development in such circumstances. Beyond this inherent connection, however, environmental degradation can undermine productivity and thus retard development. If soils are damaged, aquifers depleted, and ecosystems destroyed, then, regardless of any short-term income benefits that may be achieved, the long-run prospects for development will be undermined. For development to be sustained, environmental quality must be maintained. This will be particularly the case for poorer countries and populations.

Poverty, Population, and the Environment

Because of their poverty, the poor are often forced to live in environmentally fragile areas—on rural land that degrades rapidly, or in crowded squatter settlements—where they are exposed to the greatest environmental health risks. Furthermore, they lack the resources to "buy out of" environmental problems. The recent cholera epidemic in Peru illustrates both these points. Not only were the poorest members of society resident in areas where, because of inadequate sanitation and water services, poor nutrition, and high population density, they were relatively exposed to the disease, but in addition, they were unable to reduce that exposure through simple precautionary measures because of the financial burden involved—the costs of boiling water, for instance, were estimated at 29% of the average poor family's income (a figure which should be considered in conjunction with the fact that more than 60% of the Peruvian population lives at or below subsistence level).

But in the case of many developing country environmental problems, the relationship between development and the environment is a *symbiotic* one. It is not merely that environmental quality and protection are necessary elements of development but that in some cases development is a necessary precondition to effective environmental protection. Inadequate sanitation, shortages of clean water, indoor air pollution from biomass stoves, and many types of land degradation in developing countries *have poverty as their root cause.* Poor land-hungry farmers, for instance, often resort to cultivating environmentally fragile areas: steeply sloped, erosion-prone hillsides; semiarid land where soil degradation is rapid; and tropical forests where crop yields on cleared fields drop after just a few years. Given these fragile and limited resources, poorly defined or nonexistent property rights, limited access to credit and insurance markets, and overwhelming concern with day-to-day survival, such farmers are unable to invest in long-term environmental protection. Rather, they face incentives to maintain or increase short-term benefits at the expense of long-term productivity, particularly during crisis periods. Resources are then "mined" at an unsustainable rate: shortened fallow periods, for instance, may increase agricultural output in the short term but will soon cause soil fertility and yields to decline. Thus underdevelopment causes environmental deterioration which then perpetuates or worsens underdevelopment.

Population.   Population dynamics tend to exacerbate the linkages between underdevelopment and environmental degradation. Poverty generates significant incentives to raise large families and can stimulate migrations to environmentally fragile areas—both outcomes increase pressure on resources and consequently worsen environmental quality, diminish productivity, and reinforce poverty. Environmental degradation can increase the value of children to their parents since they can be put to work gathering firewood, pasturing livestock, or fetching water—all activities which become more time-consuming if tree, range, and drinking water resources are degraded. And rapidly rising population levels increase the demand for goods and services, which, if practices remain unchanged, will necessarily imply worsened environmental damage. Population growth also increases the need for employment and livelihoods; satisfying such a need, particularly in crowded rural areas, will exert additional pressure on natural resources. As Box 20-1 shows, the interactions of the poverty-population-environment nexus are numerous, complex, and mutually reinforcing. Furthermore, they must be considered against a background of persistent poverty and rapidly increasing population levels.

A Worsening Situation?   Over the past 25 years, substantial progress has been made in alleviating poverty. Average consumption per capita in developing countries has increased by 70% in real terms; average life expectancy has

---

Box 20-1. The Africa Nexus Study: Demographic, Environmental, and Economic Interactions

A recently completed World Bank study shows that sub-Saharan Africa's demographic, agricultural, and environmental problems are closely linked (Cleaver and Schreiber, 1991). Key elements of this "nexus" are found in traditional crop production and livestock husbandry methods, traditional land tenure systems and land use practices, traditional responsibilities of women in rural food production and household maintenance, and traditional methods of utilizing dryland and forest resources. These systems and practices have come under increasing strain over the past three decades largely because of rapid population growth and the migration of men from rural to urban areas in search of wage employment.

Traditional land use and forest exploitation practices have become direct causes of environmental degradation and resource depletion. Despite considerable investment in new technologies and agrochemicals, crop yields, especially of food crops, have stagnated or declined in many countries. Slow agricultural growth, which contributes to slow economic growth, has also impeded the ability of these countries to achieve a demographic transition from high to low birthrates. Rapidly expanding rural populations increasingly degrade and mine natural resources in order to ensure their day-to-day survival. Furthermore, continuing rapid population growth ties up scarce resources in order to meet current survival and consumption needs—resources which could otherwise be used to create the base for less resource-intensive, more sustainable development.

The study details numerous other causes of environmental and agricultural deterioration in Africa, including poor rural infrastructure, ineffective agricultural support services, and the inadequacies of education, particularly for women. It lays out a number of policy initiatives and recommends means for their implementation.

---

risen from 51 to 63 years; and primary school enrollment rates have reached 89%. If these gains were evenly spread, much of the world's poverty would be eliminated. Instead, more than one-fifth of humanity still lives in acute poverty. Moreover, during the second half of the 1980s, the incidence of poverty in developing countries actually increased—from slightly more than 1 billion to more than 1.1 billion by 1990. Poverty worsened throughout sub-Saharan Africa, the Middle East and North Africa, and Latin America and the Caribbean; Asian countries were more successful in diminishing its incidence. By 2000, worldwide poverty levels are likely still to exceed 1.1 billion, although the distribution of poverty will change, improving in Asia, stabilizing in Latin America and Eastern Europe, and worsening considerably in sub-Saharan Africa.

Efforts to alleviate poverty and its environmental repercussions will be hampered by projected population increases. Although estimates vary considerably

Billions of people

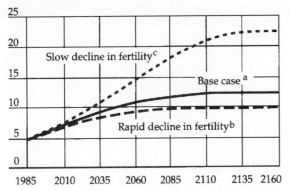

a. Countries with high and nondeclining fertility levels begin the transition toward lower fertility by the year 2005 and undergo a substantial decline - by more than half in many cases - over the next forty years. All countries reach replacement fertility levels by 2060.
b. Countries not yet in transition toward lower fertility begin the transition immediately. For countries already in transition, total fertility declines at twice the rate for the base case.
c. Transition toward lower fertility (triggered when life expectancy reaches 53 years) begins after 2020 in most low-income countries. For countries in transition, declines are half the rate for the base case.
Source: World Bank data.

Figure 20-1. World population projections under different fertility trends, 1985–2160.

(see Fig. 20-1), the World Bank's base case scenario assumes that world population grows from its current level of 5.3 billion to around 9 billion by 2030, stabilizing at around 12.5 billion in the middle of the twenty-second century; 95% of this population growth will be in developing countries. In addition, urban populations are set to expand at a disproportionate rate. In 1990, most people lived in rural areas, but by 2030 urban populations will be twice the size of rural populations. As a group, developing country cities will grow by 160% over the period, exacerbating air and water pollution, increasing energy production and the output of industrial waste, and pushing population densities to unprecedented levels. These environmental problems, known collectively as the "brown agenda," fall particularly heavy on the urban poor, who pay for them in chronic ill health, lower productivity, and reduced income and quality of life.

The 3.7 billion increase in population that will occur over the next 40 years is far greater than in any previous generation and probably much greater than in any subsequent one. The need for increased food production and expanded provision of water and sanitation services is evident, and unprecedented in scale: The potential for environmentally unsustainable agricultural extensification and intensification, large-scale deforestation and destruction of natural habitats, biodiversity loss, extreme water shortages, and incidence of water-related diseases, is similarly unprecedented. At the same time, world consumption of energy and manufactured goods will triple, even under more efficient patterns of use; for developing countries, the increase will be fivefold. These environmental stresses *could* result in tens of millions of premature deaths every year. It is this realization which sometimes generates calls for deliberately limiting rates of economic activity. We believe this conclusion to be mistaken. The key to avoiding environmental collapse is not to produce less but to produce differently.

Strategies for Sustaining Development

All economic activity involves transforming the natural world, but not all economic activity causes excessive environmental degradation. Figure 20-2 shows how rising economic activity can cause certain forms of environmental degradation, but can also, with the right policies and institutions, help address them.[1] Three patterns emerge:

- Some indicators of environmental stress improve as income rises. This is because increasing income provides the resources for public services such as the provision of adequate sanitation and clean water. Rising income can alleviate poverty and thus increase individuals' propensity to invest in environmentally sustainable activities.

- Some environmental problems initially worsen but then improve as incomes rise. Most forms of air and water pollution fit into this category, as do some types of deforestation and encroachment on natural habitats. There is nothing automatic about this improvement; it occurs only when countries deliberately introduce policies to ensure that additional resources are devoted to dealing with environmental problems.

- Other problems continue to worsen with increases in income. The generation of municipal wastes and the emission of carbon and of nitrogen oxides are current examples. In these cases, abatement costs are relatively high, while the costs of environmental damage are often not (yet) perceived to be significant—often because they are borne by someone else. Again the key is policy. In most countries, individuals and firms have little reason to cut back on wastes and emissions until the right incentives—provided by regulations, charges, inducements, or other means—are established.

It is important to realize that the above relationships between income levels and particular environmental problems are not immutable; countries can choose policies that result in much better (or worse) environmental conditions than those in other countries at similar income levels, and technological progress can

---

[1]These points are made in greater detail in *Development and the Environment, World Development Report 1992*, pp. 10–11 and 36–41.

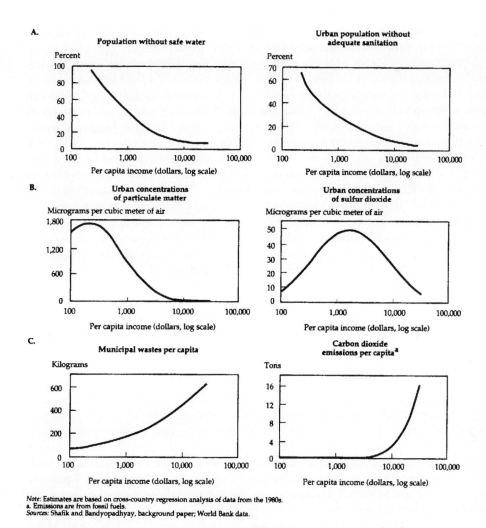

A.

Population without safe water

Percent

100
80
60
40
20
0

100   1,000   10,000   100,000

Per capita income (dollars, log scale)

Urban population without adequate sanitation

Percent

70
60
40
20
0

100   1,000   10,000   100,000

Per capita income (dollars, log scale)

B.

Urban concentrations of particulate matter

Micrograms per cubic meter of air

1,800
1,200
600
0

100   1,000   10,000   100,000

Per capita income (dollars, log scale)

Urban concentrations of sulfur dioxide

Micrograms per cubic meter of air

50
40
30
20
10
0

100   1,000   10,000   100,000

Per capita income (dollars, log scale)

C.

Municipal wastes per capita

Kilograms

600
400
200
0

100   1,000   10,000   100,000

Per capita income (dollars, log scale)

Carbon dioxide emissions per capita[a]

Tons

16
12
8
4
0

100   1,000   10,000   100,000

Per capita income (dollars, log scale)

Note: Estimates are based on cross-country regression analysis of data from the 1980s.
a. Emissions are from fossil fuels.
Sources: Shafik and Bandyopadhyay, background paper; World Bank data.

Figure 20-2. Environmental indicators at different country income levels.

enable countries to develop economically at a lesser environmental cost. The view that greater economic activity inevitably hurts the environment is based on static assumptions about technology, tastes, and environmental investments, and a disregard for the effect that carefully designed and enacted policy can have on all three of these factors. According to this view, as populations and incomes rise, emissions and wastes will ultimately reach levels that exceed the carrying capacity of the planet—with catastrophic consequences. In reality, however, it is not merely the size of the economy that determines environmental quality. Other relevant factors include: the structure of the economy; the efficiency with which inputs are used; the capacity to substitute away from resources that are becoming scarce; and the ability of clean technologies and management practices to reduce environmental damage per unit of input or output.

Significantly, all four of these positive forces—substitution, efficiency gains, innovation, and structural change—can have a powerful effect on the relationship between economic activity and the environment *if the scarcity of natural resources is accurately reflected in decisions about their use.* If resources are correctly valued by those who use them, the prospects are good that the factors above—which tend to limit environmental damage per unit of output—can more than compensate for any negative environmental consequences implied by economic growth. This is not merely a theoretical claim: Empirical data from a cross section of countries, while admittedly not plentiful, support the contention that it is possible to "grow out of" certain environmental problems. For example, Fig. 20-3 shows how, between 1976 and 1985, technological change and environmental awareness demonstrably altered the relationship between income levels and sulfur dioxide, and how, between 1980 and 1985, the relationship between income and urban sanitation levels was similarly changed.

Indeed, incorrect valuation—or more specifically, undervaluation—tends to be associated with the most pressing form of environmental problem—ecosystem deterioration caused by excessive use of renewable resources. Water provides one such example of an undervalued resource, now showing signs of shortage. In Mexico City groundwater is being pumped at rates 40% faster than natural recharge. By the end of the 1990s six East African and all North African countries will have annual renewable water resources below the levels at which societies generally experience water shortage. These situations arise because water's true scarcity value frequently goes unrecognized. In many countries, scarce water is used for low-value agricultural crops, and farmers pay nothing for the water they use. More than half the water supply cannot be accounted for in such cities as Cairo, Jakarta, Lima, Manila, and Mexico City. The contrast with certain nonrenewable resources—like fossil fuels and metals—is clear. Precisely because they are *marketed,* reductions in the stock of these nonrenewables are reflected in rising prices, which in turn induce new discoveries, improvements in efficiency, possibilities for substitution, and technological innovation. Metal price increases during the 1970s, for example, led to the development of fiber optics to replace copper in telecommunications, the recycling of aluminum and other materials, and the production of various synthetic substitutes.

Pointedly, it is the unmarketed side effects associated with the extraction and consumption of metal, mineral, and energy resources that have given rise to environmental problems like local air, river, and groundwater pollution, soil degradation, the destruction of natural habitat, and increased carbon dioxide emissions. These side effects occur because they are external to the existing market framework, and scarcity considerations are therefore not factored into decision making. Similar situations arise with regard to shared resources: users of certain resources, such as the atmosphere or open-access land, do not fully bear the cost of using such resources, which are consequently overused and degraded over time. Wherever environmental problems can be externalized, as

Concentration of sulfur dioxide

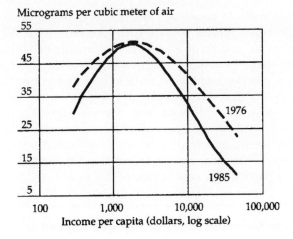

Microgram per cubic meter of air

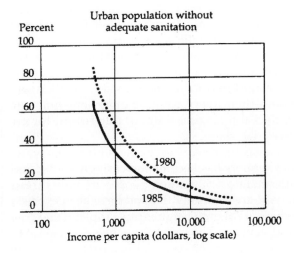

Sources: Shafik and Bandyopadhyay, background paper; World Bank data.

Figure 20-3. Changes in urban sanitation and sulfur dioxide concentrations over time at different country income levels.

with solid wastes and carbon emissions, there are few private incentives to incur the costs of prevention and abatement.

Clearly, then, the policy challenge is to correct for these market imperfections by requiring or inducing actors to take account of scarcity considerations in their behavior. In some cases this will involve extending the reach of market forces—for example, through the elimination of subsidies on the use of scarce resources or the allocation and enforcement of property rights—so that resources are correctly valued. Where market failure cannot be directly overcome, policymakers will have to work to counteract the effects of undervaluation—for example, through restrictions on, or inducements against, environmentally damaging behavior, and through efforts to stimulate behavior that has undervalued environmental benefits. Unfortunately, public policies have often served to exacerbate environmental degradation by distorting the scarcity cost of natural resources. For example, in many developing countries—including Brazil, Ecuador, Cote d'Ivoire, Indonesia, and Nigeria—agricultural incentive policies, timber royalty and concession policies, land tenure, colonization, resettlement, taxation, credit, and trade policies have caused severe deforestation (Sharma and Rowe, 1992). Here market failure is compounded by policy failure (see Box 20-2 for a particularly severe case of this double failing).

Box 20-2.   The Aral Sea: Decision Making without Regard to Scarcity

The Aral Sea is dying. Over the past 30 years, water for irrigation has been abstracted on a massive scale from the Amu Darya and Syr Darya rivers, which feed the sea. Total river runoff into the sea fell from an average 55 cubic meters a year in the 1950s to zero in the early 1980s. Although the irrigation schemes have provided numerous farming jobs throughout the Central Asian republics—Kazakhstan, Kyrghyzstan, Tajikistan, Turkmenistan, and Uzbekistan—their overwhelming environmental cost shows up the deficiencies of decision making without due regard for the value of scarce natural resources like water.

Already the volume of the sea has been reduced by two-thirds; the water in the sea and the surrounding aquifers has become increasingly saline, and the water supplies and health of almost 50 million people are now threatened. As the sea has receded, vast areas of salty flatland have been exposed and salt is being blown from these areas onto neighboring cropland and pastures, causing severe ecological damage. The irrigation schemes themselves have also been mismanaged: overwatering has transformed pastureland into bog; water supplies have become polluted by pesticide and fertilizer residues. Climatic changes in the region have reduced frost-free periods below the minimum necessary to grow cotton, currently the region's main cash crop. If present trends continue unchecked, the sea will eventually shrink to a saline lake one-sixth of its size in 1960.

While it is difficult to find solutions to the prevailing environmental crisis in the Aral Basin, it is not hard to see how such a crisis might have been avoided: incentives to recognize the value of water resources—water charges, for instance—could have allocated water in a sustainable fashion. Ineffective resource valuation contributed substantially to inadequate resource management.

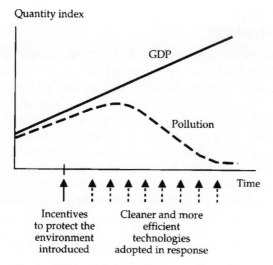

Figure 20-4. Delinking GDP growth and environmental damage.

But if public policy is directed at correcting market failure or countering its effects, it will be possible to "delink" economic growth from environmental damage as environmentally benign practices and technologies are incorporated into the capital stock (see Fig. 20-4). OECD experience since 1970 provides clear evidence of successful "delinking." Access to clean water, adequate sanitation, and municipal waste disposal is now universal. Particulate emissions have fallen by 60% and sulfur dioxides by 38%. Lead emissions declined by 85% in North America and by 50% in most European cities. Although these results involved spending around 0.8 to 1.5% of GDP each year on antipollution policies, OECD countries have seen their economies expand by 80% over the same period. To a large extent, therefore, "delinking" technologies already exist—it is simply a matter of developing countries establishing policy frameworks that can lead to their utilization.

In the next section, the policy outlined above is enlarged into a three-part strategy for development enhancement and environmental protection. Three aspects of this strategy should be stressed from the outset. First, despite the high political and economic cost of different elements of the strategy, its net benefits are substantial, while the net costs of its nonadoption are similarly significant. Second, it is practicable; already, in many countries, some of its elements are being put successfully into practice. Third, if carried through, it is equal to the various environmental challenges laid out above; the threat of catastrophic ecosystem deterioration can be averted.

National-Level Environmental Problems: A Three-Part Strategy

This section discusses the specific policies that will be needed to ensure that decisions—both public and private—better reflect the value of the environment. The purpose of such policies is not, of course, to eliminate all forms of environmental degradation: It is too costly for societies to eliminate air pollution entirely or to preserve all forests intact. Rather, the intention is to balance the costs and benefits of alternative uses for the environment—including conservation—at the margin. Essentially, these policies are of three kinds: first, those that seek to exploit the positive synergies between economic growth, efficiency, and environmental protection; second, targeted policies that seek to break negative links between certain forms of environmental damage and increased economic activity; and third, predominantly institutional policies that aim to eliminate or overcome political and societal obstacles to the successful enactment of the first two policy types.

Building on the Positive Links

There are two main types of policy that are good for both development and the environment (sometimes termed "win-win" policies). The first set yield both increased economic efficiency and reduced environmental damage at no net financial cost to governments, and are illustrated by the horizontally striped area in Fig. 20-5. Key policies of this type include the elimination or reduction of price subsidies, the clarification of property rights, and taxes on urban road

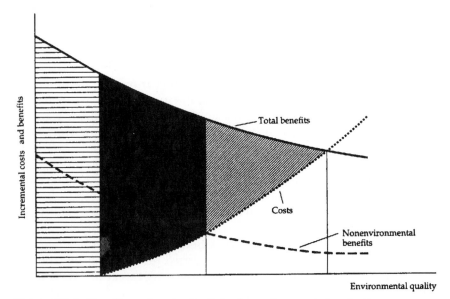

Figure 20-5. Benefits and costs of policies for environmental protection.

congestion. At the macroeconomic level, win-win policies of this type include those directed at promoting more open trade and investment strategies (thus facilitating technology transfer and more efficient allocation of resources) and macroeconomic balance (by developing a longer-term outlook on the part of investors). The second set, illustrated by the black area in Fig. 20-5, also yield economic and environmental benefits but require investment: Examples include improvements in female education, soil conservation, and water supply and sanitation.

Eliminating Subsidies.   Most governments still subsidize the consumption and production of certain natural resources. Energy, water, forests, and pesticides, for example, are often inefficiently used because of misplaced government subsidies, and the result is widespread environmental degradation. If such subsidies are removed, resources will be efficiently allocated and the environment will benefit. Eliminating developing country energy subsidies alone would realize an annual saving of $230 billion—amounting to more than five times total world volume of official development assistance. Estimates for Eastern Europe and the former Soviet Union (which together account for three-quarters of all energy subsidies) suggest that more than half of all energy pollution would be eliminated if energy prices were raised to world levels. In developing countries, electricity prices are, on average, barely more than one-third of supply costs. As a consequence, developing countries use about 20% more electricity than they would if consumers paid the true marginal costs of supply. Further, by undermining the revenue base, low prices reduce the ability of utilities to provide and maintain supplies, and remove their incentive to invest in new, cleaner technologies.

Other distortionary subsidies include logging fees in a sample of five African countries ranging from 1 to 33% of replanting costs; irrigation charges in most Asian countries covering less than 20% of supply costs; and pesticide subsidies in a sample of Latin American, African, and Asian countries ranging between 19 and 83% of costs (see Fig. 20-6 for further details). In Brazil discontinuing the fiscal and credit incentives extended to ranching has saved about $300 million annually while easing pressures for deforestation.

Since distorted incentives are often particularly evident in the behavior of state-owned enterprises, and state-owned enterprises are often concentrated in some of the most polluting sectors of the economy—coal-fired power generation, cement, steel, and mining—there is a strong environmental argument to add to the economic case for exposing such enterprises to competitive forces. Market forces would not only increase prices, but would stimulate necessary improvements in management practices. Some public bodies are simply institutionally unequal to the task of effective pricing policy: many Asian irrigation agencies, for example, currently lack the managerial capacity to develop water pricing policies and collect fees. Furthermore, realistic prices for resources such as irrigation water will tend to reduce excess profits to users and thus reduce the political pressure for public investments that have little economic justification.

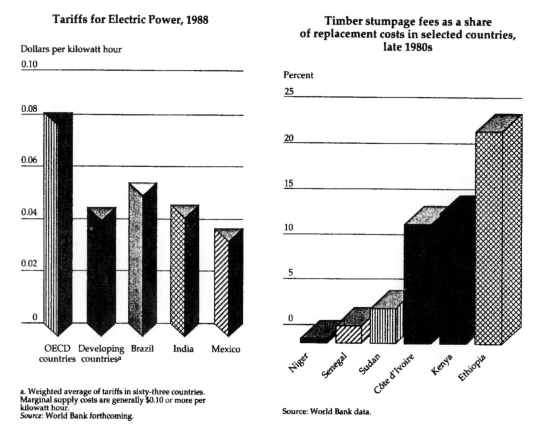

Figure 20-6. Distortionary subsidies whose removal would allow resources to be efficiently allocated and benefit the environment.

In Morocco the financial autonomy of the regional agricultural development office (ORMVAD), achieved through full-cost recovery, was an important reason for the success of the Doukkala irrigation projects. Competitive pressures are also likely to improve accountability, resulting in substantial economic and environmental savings. The current lack of management accountability and transparency that characterize many developing countries' public electric utilities has given rise to massive losses during transmission and distribution: 31% of generation in Bangladesh, 28% in Pakistan, and 22% in Thailand and the Philippines.

The Bank's energy strategy now emphasizes market-based reforms and their capacity to stimulate supply-side efficiency, demand-side conservation, and the modernization of equipment. A recently issued Bank policy paper recommends, among other policies, that the Bank should pursue the commercialization and corporatization of developing country power utilities and in order to encourage private investment in the power sector, should commit some of its own financial resources to underwrite programs that facilitate the involvement of private investors. Several Bank studies indicate that, in combination, pricing and market-oriented institutional reforms could achieve a short-term savings in energy consumed by existing capital stock of around 20 to 25%, without sacrificing the economic benefits of energy use; over the longer term, as investments are made in new capital equipment, larger energy savings are possible, on the order of 30 to 60% over what is possible with current equipment.

IDA credits to Malawi, Burundi, Mauritania, Guinea-Bissau, and Guyana have all been designed to increase efficiency and enhance environmental protection by recovering the costs of electricity production through more realistic pricing policies and improved fee collection. Other Bank projects in a similar vein have supported the use of the private sector for electricity utility management in Cote d'Ivoire and Equatorial Guinea, and for water utility management in Cote d'Ivoire and Guinea-Bissau. In various areas, the Bank has moved to institute improved pricing policies in the water sector: examples include privately metered connections to communal taps and private handpumps, or privatized tubewells. (See Box 20-3.)

Clarification of Property Rights.   Where people have open access to natural resources, such as forests, pastureland, or fishing grounds, they tend to overuse them since no individual user bears the full cost of environmental degradation and there is no mechanism for regulating the use of the resources in question. But, when open access is replaced with some ordered system of use or ownership rights, it is likely that more of the environmental costs of economic activity associated with those resources will become internalized. Individuals will both suffer the consequences of failing to account for environmental factors in their decision making and reap the benefits of successfully investing in environmental protection. The security of their tenure may also make it easier to obtain the credit necessary for such investments. The "tragedy of the commons" is thereby avoided and environmental quality is consequently enhanced.[2]

Thus, for example, the recent assignment of land ownership titles and tenurial rights in Thailand has made it profitable for farmers to invest in soil conservation and land improvement, reducing soil erosion and limiting pressure for agricultural expansion into forested areas. There are numerous other success stories in this regard: providing security of tenure to hill farmers in Kenya has reduced soil erosion; assigning property titles to slum dwellers in Bandung, Indonesia, has tripled household investment in sanitation facilities; clarifying communal land rights in Burkina Faso has sharply improved land management; and allocating transferable rights to fishery resources has checked the tendency to overfish in New Zealand.

It is important to distinguish between open-access regimes and common-property management of natural resources. While the former stimulates excessive

[2]The term is from Hardin, 1968.

Box 20-3.   Willingness to Pay for Water

It is often assumed that eliminating subsidies for resources such as water, in the name of "efficiency," hurts the poor. Such an assumption ignores two key factors: first, the high water prices paid by the poor; and second, the poor's willingness to pay for improved services. Once these factors are noted, it is clear that eliminating subsidies may in fact be of benefit to poor people.

Because the poor often lack piped water facilities, they are obliged to rely on other sources: in rural areas, from sometimes distant rivers; and in urban areas, from vendors. Both sources are costly. For many rural people, obtaining water is time-consuming and heavy work, taking up to 15% of women's time. A review of vending in 16 cities shows that the unit cost of vended water is always much higher than that of water from a piped city supply—from 4 to 100 times higher, with a median of about 12. The situation in Lima is typical; although a poor family uses only one-sixth as much water as a middle-class family, its monthly water bill is three times as large. Subsidized water therefore may not be of financial benefit to the poor.

Second, because poor users are only too aware of the high direct water costs they are currently paying (usually for poor quality services, which have high indirect health and productivity costs), they are willing to pay substantial amounts for easier and improved access. In urban areas, there is substantial evidence that most people, including many of the poor, are willing to pay the full costs of providing on-plot water facilities; in rural areas, recent Bank evidence suggests that people are prepared to pay for yard taps. In both cases, they are prepared to pay substantially more for services that are reliable (see Fig. 20-7a). Willingness to pay can be further increased by making use of innovative financing mechanisms (see Fig. 20-7b). Once users pay for the costs of water services, the increase in revenues obtained from the sale of such services can ensure their maintenance. Contrastingly, with low-quality subsidized water services, revenues are low, and the service further deteriorates.

---

resource use, the latter can result in sound environmental stewardship. In fact, many natural resources—village commons, pastures, water resources, and near-shore fisheries—have been managed by communities, many of them poor, for centuries. Communal management systems have been used for pasture in the Himalayas and the Andes, fisheries in Turkey and the Philippines, irrigation water in southern India, and in many other cases.[3] In all such cases, resource users have developed methods for restricting resource uses by outsiders, allocating use rights among those in the group, and monitoring and enforcing these allocations.

---

[3]Some have argued that even the English medieval commons (which Hardin used to argue his case) was communally managed: access was restricted to certain members of the village, and limits were placed on the number of animals that could be grazed.

Connection rate
(percentage of households)

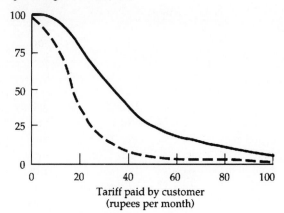

Tariff paid by customer
(rupees per month)

Revenue collected by supplier
(rupees per 100 households per month)

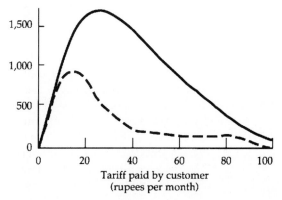

Tariff paid by customer
(rupees per month)

—————— Improved reliability

— — — — Existing reliability

Figure 20-7a. How reliability of supply affects willingness to pay for piped water: Punjab, Pakistan.

Many of these resources are vital to the poorest members of developing countries. Research in seven Indian states has found that common-property resources accounted for between 14 and 23% of poor households' income, and that 84% of poor people's livestock fodder came from grazing on communally held lands; by contrast, wealthy households derived no more than 3% of their income and less than 38% of their animal grazing from common-property lands.

Unfortunately, governments have not always distinguished between communally managed and open-access resources. In the 1950s, Nepal nationalized forests to "protect, manage, and conserve the forest for the benefit of the entire

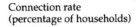

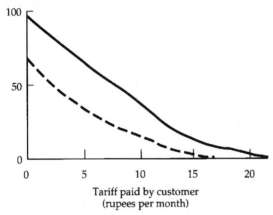

Tariff paid by customer
(rupees per month)

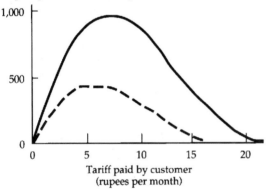

Figure 20-7b. How spreading connection costs over time affects willingness to pay for piped water: Kerala, India.

country." But because the government lacked the resources to regulate use effectively, common property was turned into open-access land in the name of conservation through state control. In the late 1970s, Nepal began to reverse this environmentally destructive policy by returning forests to the control of decentralized administrative units. However, it is not merely the imposition of state ownership that can open access to environmental resources; despite their pervasiveness and effectiveness, common-property regimes are easily eroded since they rely on continuing self-imposed restraints enforced by group members.

These restraints can be eroded by a number of factors including demographic change, technological growth, difficulties in raising capital, and various forms of government interference below the level of outright state control. Thus successful self-management of a fishing village in Sri Lanka was unable to cope with population growth and higher prices, and long-standing cooperative agreements among fishermen in Southern Bahia, Brazil were undermined when nylon nets were introduced under a government program.

The World Bank is actively engaged in efforts to support and enhance communal resource management in the face of such pressures. Governments need to recognize that small organizational units like villages or pastoral associations are better equipped to manage their own resources sustainably than are large institutional authorities. Group action is deeply rooted in many societies—for managing resources, for cooperative marketing and input supply, for running community savings and loan arrangements, and for pooling labor. Successful community management will build on these customary social practices. In the case of Nepalese forestry practice, the Bank has encouraged the devolution of control over particular forest tracts to the villages with which they are closely associated. In the Sahelian region, the Bank has advanced an approach to natural resource management (NRM) that is community-based, participatory, and holistic. Its main instrument is the village land-management plan, which communities design with the help of a multidisciplinary team of technicians. Community "ownership" or acceptance of the plan is crucial, since implementation is the community's responsibility. The plan includes land use rules that govern access to and exploitation of common assets such as rangeland, forests, and water, and it controls specific land improvements on communal as well as individually owned land. The NRM approach has been tested in Burkina Faso, Kenya, Mali, and Senegal (Lusigi and Nekby, 1991).

Of course, misconceived property rights regimes can actually cause environmental degradation: for example, prior to the development of new land zoning laws in Rondônia, forest clearing was one of the criteria for obtaining land title. Moreover, although clear property rights, in inducing private or communal resource users to take into consideration the current and future benefits of their resource use, are likely to effect *on-site* sustainability, they provide no incentive to incorporate external environmental factors. Thus, in certain privately owned forests in the United States, logging may be deemed excessive once biodiversity loss and off-site soil erosion are considered. In such cases additional, specifically targeted environmental controls are often needed.

Investing in Water and Sanitation Services.   Some "win-win" policies, including investments in water and sanitation services, education and family planning programs, and agricultural extension and research, do carry substantial initial financial costs. Overall, however, they yield not only substantial environmental returns but net economic gains also. Aggregate investment in water and sanitation services remained low in the 1980s; public investment accounted for about 0.5% of GDP in developing countries, and investments in sanitation were particularly low. Yet the substantial health and productivity costs of inadequate coverage remain high. The costs of inadequate sanitation investment are especially large, since poor sanitation is a major cause of the degradation of ground and surface water. Economic growth leads to larger discharges of wastewater and solid wastes per capita, and inadequate investments in waste collection and disposal mean that large quantities of water enter both groundwater and surface water. Groundwater contamination is less visible but often more serious because it can take decades for polluted aquifers to cleanse themselves and because large numbers of people drink untreated groundwater.

The economic costs of underinvestment are vividly illustrated by the recent cholera epidemic in Peru. In the epidemic's first 10 weeks, losses in agricultural exports and revenues from tourism were more than three times the amount that the country had invested in sanitation and water supply in the 1980s. One cost-benefit calculation for water facilities in Lima estimates the annual per capita cost borne by households without in-house continuous water connections at $40, and the one-time per capita cost of constructing "easy-access" water facilities and latrines in urban and rural areas at $30.[4]

Between 1966 and 1992, the Bank lent more than $13 billion for water supply and sewerage projects, and in fiscal 1992 lending for water supply and sanitation projects amounted to more than $900 million and funded efforts in 10 countries. Two projects are designed specifically to reduce water pollution by means of improved treatments of wastes: the Ship Waste Disposal Project (assisted by an IDA credit of $15 million and additional GEF financing of $30 million) will assist China to reduce pollution of international waters caused by oily wastes and bilge slops; and Korea's Pusan and Taejon Sewerage Project, assisted by a Bank loan of $40 million, supports the 1990–96 National Wastewater Treatment Plan, which is designed to improve water quality in the country's rivers and coastal waters. Numerous project components address these issues: for example, Tunisia's Municipal Sector Investment Project includes a Bank-financed environmental component of $20.7 million to support a number of ends: improved management of solid and liquid wastes, better sanitation services, and sound disposal of slaughterhouse offal and other food-processing wastes. Improved water resource management is fast becoming one of the key elements of Bank strategy in many regions. In North Africa and the Middle East, for example, the Bank has completed comprehensive country-based water resource assessments in order to review the main aspects of water planning and management, including institutional arrangements, supply and demand management, and investment strategy.

Necessary investment levels may exceed the capacity of the public sector: Several countries—including Argentina, Chile, Cote d'Ivoire, and Guinea—are exploiting the skills of the private sector with great success. One factor such

---

[4]"Easy access" is defined as standpipe facilities less than 1000 meters from each house. The $40 estimate is from UNICEF, 1991. The $30 estimate is from Webb, 1991, and assumes the following per capita values: cost of buying water, $12.50; cost of medication, $6.85; cost of boiling water for drinking, $10; cost of container, $4.00; cost of work days lost, $6.07.

efforts must consider is the public willingness to pay for improved water services—refer back to Box 20-3. Whenever the private benefits of such services are high—as they are for water supply and wastewater collection—then more investment can be financed by charging realistic prices. (Current tariffs in developing countries cover only an average 35% of the costs of supplying water, and services are correspondingly poor.) With other services, such as solid-waste collection and wastewater treatment, the social benefits significantly exceed the benefits to individual users. Then it will rarely be appropriate to charge their full cost, and investments will have to be paid for partly through subsidies. Developing countries need also to concentrate their investment increases in improved *management* of services. Promoting conservation technologies—like wastewater reclamation—and improved demand management may be more worthwhile than investments in new sources of water supply. In sanitation also, investments in innovative sewage *treatment* processes may offer the best returns. Some of these issues are taken up further below.

What might be achieved by increased investment in water and sanitation services? Figure 20-8 shows three possible scenarios. In both graphs, the top curves show that an "unchanged practices" scenario would lead to a rise in the number of people without safe water and adequate sanitation. If the shares of total investment allocated to sanitation (currently 0.6% of gross investment) and to water supply (currently 1.7%) were raised by, say, 50 and 30%, respectively, the numbers unserved might still rise, although not as much (the middle curves in the figure). Far more important (as shown by the bottom curves) is the combination of policy reforms and accelerated investment. By attracting financial, managerial, and skilled labor resources into the sector and by freeing enterprises to invest more and improve maintenance, this new approach, which is already being adopted in some countries, could bring about dramatic increases in access to sanitation and clean water within the next generation.

Accelerating Agricultural Extension and Research. If the doubling in world demand for grain over the next 40 years is to be met in an environmentally sustainable fashion, then investment, particularly in agricultural research, will be required. World grain output will have to grow by 1.6% a year—lower, in fact, than the average 2% a year increase achieved over the last 30 years. The evidence of those same 30 years strongly suggests that the bulk of this increase will have to come from intensification; and experience has also shown that the generation of new knowledge is the most potent and least costly way to improving productivity. If crop yields are to be raised on existing land under cultivation without incurring environmental costs, improved technologies and management practices must be forthcoming. Unfortunately, expenditures on agricultural forestry and forestry research and development are stagnating. In India, for example, expenditure on forestry research amounts to less than 0.01% of the value of forest products consumed each year.

The Bank, however, has long been involved in agricultural research through its support for the Consultative Group on International Agricultural Research,

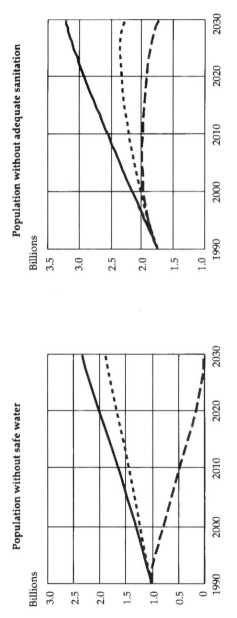

Population without safe water

Population without adequate sanitation

——— "Business as usual" scenario

∙∙∙∙ Scenario with accelerated investment in water supply and sanitation services [a]

– – Scenario with accelerated investment and efficiency reforms [b]

Note: Assumptions are as follows: growth as per Bank base case projections; average per capita income increases by a factor of 3 or more; per capita income elasticity, 0.3; price elasticity, -0.25; initial prices 60 percent of marginal costs, gradually rising to efficiency levels over a twenty-five-year period; initial supply costs 50 percent higher than with good practices (due to managerial inefficiencies), gradually being reduced in step with price efficiency reforms; and marginal costs rising at 3 percent per year.
a. Investment in water supply increases 30 percent, and investment in sanitation services increases 50 percent over the period.
b. To realize this scenario in low-income countries, efficiency reforms - and the resulting increase in investment shares - would need to be greater than average.
Source: World Bank estimates, based on Anderson and Cavendish, background paper.

Figure 20-8. Safe water and adequate sanitation: Three scenarios, 1990–2030.

the Special Program for African Agricultural Research, and the improvement of national agricultural research systems. To date, the agricultural research agenda has tended to focus on integrated land resource management as a subsidiary issue, and the Bank is actively involved in trying to expand and promote research activities relating to environmental aspects of land use, especially soil management and conservation. One research project currently under way examines the experience of a semiarid district in Kenya where, despite a doubling of agricultural productivity per capita and a fivefold increase in population, soil degradation has been significantly reduced over the past two decades. The Bank is exploring the possibility of establishing a research network to examine such issues in collaboration with the International Agricultural Research Centers (IARCs).

Raising productivity in a sustainable manner will require not only research per se but also its active dissemination through education and a strengthening of extension systems. Some environmentally friendly technologies, like integrated pest management, are often information-intensive and, if they are to be effective, require farmers to be well trained. But in many cases, simple, low-cost technologies can dramatically improve yields at no cost to the environment: contour-based cultivation, in particular, can slow water runoff, reduce erosion, and increase the moisture available for crop growth. In India, contour ditches and hedges of vetiver grass have been used to great effect, while in the Sahel, rock bunds have performed a similar role. In dry years, bunded fields in Burkina Faso yield up to 50% more than traditional fields. In itself, of course, the availability of these kinds of technologies will be insufficient to generate the necessary productivity increases. For these practices to be *adopted and invested in*, farmers must face the correct set of incentives: extension, infrastructural, credit, and marketing services may all require improvement. Further, they are only likely to prove effective in conjunction with the allocation or clarification of tenurial rights and the removal of price distortions against farmers.

The Bank is also assisting in the expansion of forestry research and the integration of forestry into the work of the IARCs. Special efforts are being directed toward agroforestry technologies that can help improve soil fertility, conserve soil moisture, and increase crop and livestock yields. The Bank is also committed to financing pilot experimental forest management operations aimed at expanding knowledge regarding sustainable utilization of degraded forest areas. Of course, improved agricultural intensification can also reduce the pressures on forests, especially where research focuses specifically on maintaining productivity on already deforested land. Farm trials conducted in Peru show that for every additional hectare with sustainable and high productivity, an estimated 5 to 10 hectares a year of tropical rain forest could be saved from destruction by shifting cultivators. Similar trial transitions from shifting to continuous cultivation are being promoted in Indonesia and Brazil.

Accelerating Education and Family Planning Programs.   Better education can fulfill a multiplicity of developmental and environmental goals: It enables the adoption of more sustainable practices in agriculture, industry, and household management and helps accelerate a transition from subsistence to intensive agriculture and off-farm employment. Providing increased access to education in Thailand was found to be the single most effective policy for reducing pressure on forests. But education's single most significant impact is demographic: Investments in female education, particularly at the secondary level, have some of the highest returns for development and the environment. Evidence from a cross section of countries shows that where no women are enrolled in secondary education, the average woman has seven children, but where 40% of all women have had a secondary education, the average drops to three children, even after controlling for factors such as income. Investments in schools, teachers, and materials must be accompanied by policies designed to increase enrollment, such as scholarship programs.

Family planning programs have already contributed to reduced population growth and will continue to offer substantial returns in the future. However, despite an increase in the rate of contraceptive use from 40% in 1980 to 49% in 1990, unmet demand for contraceptives remains high, ranging from about 15% of couples in Brazil, Colombia, and Indonesia to more than 35% in Bolivia, Ghana, and Kenya. This demand will have to be met to achieve even the Bank's base case population projections. Moreover, the demand for family planning services must be boosted via improvements in infant and maternal health and in women's status. The provision of family planning services is now regularly augmented by programs to improve maternal and child health care, nutrition interventions, health and education, and income-generating activities to women. The Bank's emphasis on reducing population growth is part of an overall effort to address environmental concerns, attack poverty, and spur economic growth. Lending for population, health, and nutrition activities have grown from $305 million in 1988 to nearly $1 billion today. During fiscal 1991, ten IDA projects with population components were approved, compared to four in fiscal 1990 and one in fiscal 1989. In fiscal 1992, $103 million was lent specifically for population programs, and this sum is expected to increase to about $250 million in fiscal 1993.

Breaking the Negative Links

Unfortunately, positive policies of the kind laid out above are not by themselves likely to achieve sustainable development. Returning to Fig. 20-5, the diagonally striped area represents the set of policies that have a net economic cost, but an overall benefit once environmental factors are correctly taken into account. There are two critical aspects to the selection of such policies. First, valuation must be employed to determine the costs and benefits of different targeted measures and hence the correct priorities for action and the appropriate level of environmental protection. As the figure shows, although it will be possible to enhance environmental quality even beyond this point, it will not be worthwhile—the marginal costs of the necessary policy measures will outweigh their marginal benefit. A second critical aspect is the *design* of such policies: what policy method or approach can target and alter environmentally destructive behavior in the most cost-effective manner possible?

Assessing Priorities and Trade-Offs

To fix the correct priorities for action, policymakers must be able to identify and evaluate the environmental impacts of human behavior. Since the analysis in the 1950s and 1960s of hydroelectric projects in the United States, good progress has been made in incorporating environmental concerns into project analysis. But only a few governments have used such techniques to set environmental priorities and make decisions about trade-offs. Estimating the costs of environmental damage—as well as the costs of preventing such damage—may be technically so complex as to be beyond the institutional capacity of many developing countries. At the same time, it needs to be recognized that whenever policymakers make choices about environmental priorities or standards—even if only by omission—they are implicitly placing values on different environmental costs and benefits. Since imperfect analysis is better than none, decision makers cannot afford to forgo the effective and systematic assessment of policy trade-offs.

Research and investment are urgently required in three areas: gathering basic data on environmental conditions and trends; evaluating the impacts of economic activity on resources and the environment; and identifying alternative means of raising incomes while protecting the environment. At the micro level, this requires effective environmental assessment of development projects and effective use of environmental data; at the macro level, sound environmental management will depend on a comprehensive understanding of the costs and benefits of economywide and sectoral policies. World Bank research is now increasingly aimed at improving environmental information and developing economic techniques for analyzing such information.[5]

Environmental Assessment. Much damage to the biosphere has been caused by an inadequate assessment of potential environmental degradation, an underestimation of the costs of environmental damage, and a consequent failure to consider alternative investments. Environmental assessment (EA) is designed to address these deficiencies; it identifies ways of making development projects more sustainable by preventing, minimizing, mitigating, or compensating for adverse environmental impacts. The World Bank now employs the EA process as a key decision-making tool in the project cycle, and for EA

---

[5]This research agenda is sometimes labeled, somewhat misleadingly, "environmental economics."

purposes all projects are now placed in one of three categories. Category A projects—dams, reservoirs, industrial estates, land clearance, large-scale irrigation, and flood control—have potentially large environmental impacts and require a full environmental assessment. Several category A projects have been modified following EAs: in Ecuador, a channel was rerouted to avoid disruption to a lagoon; a road in Botswana was rerouted to avoid an archeological site; and in Uganda the ability of ranges to support livestock was analyzed before augmenting cattle herds. Projects are assigned to Category B when their impacts are not likely to be as sensitive, numerous, or as diverse as Category A, and therefore undergo less rigorous analysis. No EA is required for Category C projects such as family planning, education, and health and nutrition projects.

The costs of not carrying out adequate environmental assessment are vividly illustrated by a number of ill-conceived and poorly implemented development projects. For example, the Polonoreste rural development and highway projects in Brazil, funded in part with a loan from the World Bank, failed to anticipate the extent to which its infrastructure developments would stimulate in-migration, and consequently large-scale deforestation. Of course, a failure to consider environmental benefits can also result in an inefficient distribution of resources; and conversely, valuing such benefits can improve decision making. A Bank-funded forestry project in northern Nigeria was found to have three times the rate of return once environmental factors, such as reduced soil erosion, were taken into account.

EA, both within the Bank and externally, is a relatively recent innovation: the Bank's first review of its environmental assessment process—which has been in operation for 3 years—stresses the need to strengthen borrowing countries' capacities to conduct effective environmental assessment. Significantly, the review recommends strengthening sectoral and regional EA approaches, since these can help development institutions and borrowers evaluate the state of resource stocks; identify development options with minimal environmentally adverse impacts; and provide a better link between country economic planning and the EA process. Several Bank projects or project components have begun to address these concerns. In Brazil, the Water Sector Modernization Project includes $8 million for institutionalizing environmental assessment of water and sewerage projects and promotes a better balance between investments in water supply and sewerage. Mexico's Irrigation and Drainage Sector Project includes a component to institutionalize environmental assessment as a necessary element in the development of the government's investment program for the irrigation sector. And in Trinidad and Tobago, the Business Expansion and Industrial Restructuring Project is partly designed to strengthen the government's capacity to review environmental impact assessments. Beginning in mid-1992, and under the terms of Bank technical cooperation agreement with the Commonwealth of Independent States, training in environmental impact assessment has been offered to a number of specialists from the former Soviet republics.

Environmental Information Systems.   For environmental assessment and policymaking—at either micro or macro levels—to be effective, adequate environmental data must be available. Unfortunately, such data are often incomplete or site-specific, making it difficult to extrapolate results. And although remote-sensing techniques are improving rapidly, providing scientists with a more complete understanding of environmental deterioration at the regional and global level, it is still hard to obtain a full picture of environmental degradation at local or project levels without carrying out extensive and expensive baseline studies on the ground.

Policymaking in the absence of adequate analysis of costs and benefits can be highly inefficient. Researchers in Bangkok, in examining the health impacts of pollution, found that the greatest threats were generated by particulate matter, lead, and microbiological diseases, while other environmental problems that traditionally receive a great deal of attention—contamination of groundwater and surface water; air pollutants such as nitrogen and sulfur dioxides, and ozone; and hazardous wastes—were much less dangerous. (In fact the gravest threats were found to be at least 100 times more serious than the lowest risks.) With this kind of information, cost-effective pollution-control policies can be developed. Similarly for Mexico City, new data have recently shown that the health costs associated with suspended particulates are potentially as high as $800 million annually—more than eight times greater than those associated with ozone, which was previously assumed to be the most serious air-pollution threat in the metropolitan area. More surprising still, perhaps, the health costs associated with polluted water and inadequate sanitation in Mexico City have been estimated at three times greater (about $3 billion) than the costs associated with all forms of urban air pollution in the same area.

In order to evolve realistic and sustainable management strategies, economists, and planners must have detailed knowledge of a country's natural resource base. Of particular importance in this regard is the collection and processing of information on land use patterns, including soil and hydrological conditions, vegetation cover, climate, and the results of past and present human activities. To this end, the Bank supports the establishment of national environmental information systems (EIS). For example, in 1990 the Bank initiated an EIS program in sub-Saharan Africa. Its goal is to help countries in the region create environmental information systems that are tailored for resource users, planners, and decision makers. The program helps countries identify their needs for environmental information and analyze the technical, institutional, legal, and economic factors that prevent them from meeting those needs. It aids them in finding long-term solutions, partly by learning from existing information systems. Many countries have participated in the program, sharing information among themselves. They include Benin, Botswana, Burkina Faso, Cote d'Ivoire, Ghana, Lesotho, Madagascar, Mali, Senegal, Tanzania, Uganda (see Box 20-4), Zambia, and Zimbabwe.

To respond to emerging environmental policy priorities, the Bank has developed an environmental indicators' database of more than 400 time series, which draws from both in-house and external sources. The database will provide a foundation for combining environmental and economic information in policy development—for example, in the context of national environmental action

---

Box 20-4. Improving Environmental Information in Uganda

In Uganda, the Environmental Information System (EIS) program has acted as a catalyst for improving the quality of environmental data and information. In conjunction with the Environmental Action Plan process, it has reinforced awareness among high-level government staff of the need for better environmental information.

Work at the National Environment Information Center (NEIC), which began operating in September 1990, has focused on identifying the users of environmental information and understanding their priority needs in relation to natural resource management. A long-term environment information strategy and 5-year investment program are being prepared. The demand for environmental information in Uganda was analyzed by means of a questionnaire encompassing five main groups of users at the local, urban, district, national, and project levels. The results have shown that the following types of data are prerequisites for the conservation and rational use of the country's resource base: demographic, agricultural, energy resources, soils, protected areas, intersectoral (e.g., climate change), and biological diversity.

In the long term, the NEIC plans to establish and maintain a reliable and up-to-date database on natural resources and the state of the environment through effective cooperation with ministries and institutions responsible for information, as well as universities, research institutes, NGOs, and the private sector. It intends to serve as the hub for an entire network of environmental databases, thereby ensuring data compatibility and efficient exchange of information, and to carry out data modeling and analysis.

---

plans (EAPs). Other information sources include the Global Environmental Monitoring System (GEMS), managed by UNEP, which monitors air and water quality in 142 countries, and compiles internationally comparable data. Currently, the GEMS is underfunded relative to its potential value in improving decision making. The Bank is engaged in many information-gathering exercises: for example, to generate more comprehensive data on the state of marine biodiversity, the Bank, in collaboration with the World Conservation Union (IUCN), is heading a global effort to map out areas rich in marine life.

To overcome the costs of assembling and analyzing data, countries can use estimates of the impact of pollution on health and productivity calculated in other countries, coupled with similar calculations based on domestic circumstances. Some results can be generalized: Particulate emissions from electricity generation and industrial processes, which are a major cause of disease and cost little to solve (around 1 to 2% of capital costs), should be targeted vigorously; sulfur dioxide emissions, which cost much more to reduce and cause less damage in most places, are a lower priority; and lead emissions from transportation, which have very high health costs, should be reduced quickly in cities with dense vehicular traffic. Generalizations are less straightforward in other areas, but for land resource management, most serious studies suggest that the value to local communities and regions is often surprisingly high and the value of the land for agriculture, particularly over the longer term, is usually lower than anticipated. Careful analysis can help clarify not only how much should be protected, but also who should pay. A study in Cameroon found that protecting the Korup National Park was hard to justify in terms of narrow national interest but easy to justify when worldwide benefits were taken into account.

Recently efforts have been taken to incorporate environmental data into national environmental indicators: GNP statistics or other indicators based on the United Nations System of National Accounts are altered so as to account for natural resource depreciation and other costs associated with environmental degradation. Disaggregated to the sectoral level, indicators of this kind can assist in generating policy priorities, but in aggregate form they are of little practical use; while they may remind policymakers of potential trade-offs between economic growth and environmental quality, they do not provide any indication of whether a country's use of its natural capital is suboptimal, or what actions might be taken to correct any suboptimalities.

Impact of Economywide and Sectoral Policies.   A final form of environmental information assesses the impact of macroeconomic and sectoral policy. This kind of information effectively expands the scope of environmental assessment so that it can benefit policy at the macro level. Liberalized trade policy, for instance, is sometimes thought to give rise to environmentally damaging behavior: recent controversies have concerned the negative effects of the North American Free Trade Agreement on air and water quality in Mexico and the southwestern United States, of liberalized cassava exports to the EC on soil erosion in Thailand, and of exchange rate depreciation on deforestation in Ghana. But in these and other cases, the primary cause of environmental damage is not liberalized trade but a failure of markets and governments to price environmental resources appropriately. Trade restrictions are therefore an unnecessarily blunt and indirect means to environmental protection. Moreover, by promoting competition and specialization and encouraging technological progress, open trade and investment policies can raise productivity and improve efficiency—including the efficient use of environmental resources. The resultant diffusion of environmentally benign technologies and the growth of cleaner industrial structures can in fact *lower* pollution levels. Available evidence indicates that fast-growing economies with liberal trade policies have experienced less pollution-intensive trade growth than closed economies, and that national differences in environmental regulations have not been a major explanatory factor in the changing international patterns of "dirty" industry location.

Another area of focus that is particularly relevant to the World Bank's policy dialogue is the environmental impact of adjustment lending. Bank research to date has utilized a series of country case studies to identify two basic patterns that characterize policy-environment linkages in the context of adjustment-related reforms: the unanticipated production and substitution effects that economic reforms have on resource use, and the poverty and environmental degradation associated with inappropriate policies and programs. Further case studies will focus on adjustment-related economic reform and forestry management in Bolivia, air pollution in Mexico, and wildlife management in Zimbabwe. A next step will be to synthesize the results of these studies and assess the incorporation of environmental components into adjustment operations.

The Bank's public economics research program is also increasingly focused on issues of environmental economics. For example, one project assesses the economic costs of different policy instruments—taxes and regulations—used to address local pollution problems; it develops an analytical framework for evaluating alternative measures and applies it to several cases, including Indonesia, Mexico, and Poland. The Polish case study is an important component of the Bank's continuing assistance in preparing a central and eastern European action program for submission to the Conference of the European Environment Ministers in 1993. The program is designed to identify investment priorities in the region, selected on the basis of health impacts and cost-effectiveness criteria, for addressing local, transboundary, and global environmental problems; and to establish the policy and institutional prerequisites for its successful implementation.

Policy recommendations are also being developed on the basis of two other valuation case studies. In Madagascar, both conventional and innovative economic techniques have been used to evaluate the various impacts of national parks management on the country's tropical forests: damage to forests and watersheds, timber and nontimber benefits, health benefits, impacts on biodiversity, and ecotourism benefits. The other case study considers the incorporation of environmental impacts into energy sector decision making in the context of Sri Lanka's electric power expansion plan. Multiple criteria evaluation techniques were used to supplement conventional cost-benefit analyses of the trade-offs among coal, oil, hydroelectric, and nonconventional energy sources, as well as reduction of system losses, end-use conservation, pricing policy, and demand management. These and other research projects (on such issues as integrated land resource management, and the management of water and marine resources) indicate the potential for environmental valuation. As analytical tools, data, and scientific knowledge improve, decisions about environmental priorities, standards, and policies can become better informed. A number of current and planned Bank-supported projects, among them recent loans to Chile and Mexico, include funding to support economic analysis of major environmental problems and policy issues.

Targeting Policies to Change Behavior

Environmentally destructive forms of behavior can be targeted in one of two ways: first, behavioral changes can be *induced* by market-based *incentives*; second, behavioral changes can be *required* by governmental *regulations*. The former tax or charge polluters according to the damage they do, while the latter—known sometimes as "command and control" policies—rely on quantitative restrictions. In selecting which type of policy to adopt, resource-poor developing countries should be guided principally by the cost of effective implementation. In general, the cost-effective policy mix depends on the characteristics of the environmental problem in question as well as the capabilities of available regulatory institutions. Although historically the regulatory approach has been dominant in most countries, in most circumstances a combination of policies—regulatory and market-based—will be most cost-effective. A recent study of air pollution from transport in Mexico City conducted by the Bank and the Mexican regulatory authorities recommended a mix of policies: mandated emission standards, fuel improvements, and a gasoline tax. The city has already begun to implement some of these policies, including gas retrofits for high-use vehicles; emissions standards and inspection programs for all vehicles; replacement of older taxis by newer catalyst-equipped models; introduction of unleaded gas; and prices for unleaded and leaded gas both increased by about 50%. A similar study is now under way for Bangkok.

In some circumstances regulatory instruments are most appropriate. Where there are a small number of public enterprises and/or noncompetitive private firms, market-based incentives are unlikely to take effect. Moreover, when technologies for controlling pollution or resource use are relatively uniform and can easily be specified and enforced by policymakers, quantitative measures may be cost-effective, as has been shown in the case of the Brazilian industrial town of Cubatao. In Cubatao the main sources of pollution were few and readily identifiable: steel, fertilizer, petrochemical, and cement plants. From a crisis stage in the mid-1980s—involving mass evacuations and hospitalizations—conditions have improved, mostly as a result of an aggressive stance by the local environmental agency, which regularly closes plants down in order to force the installation of abatement technology. The government has also initiated a series of civil action suits seeking restoration of damaged wetlands, waterways, and other natural resources—thus demonstrating that regulations will be enforced against violators. Regulatory approaches will also be appropriate whenever it is imperative that certain thresholds of degradation not be crossed, as with emissions of radioactive and toxic wastes or intrusions on unique habitats. In cases such as these, the need to control levels of environmental damage strictly and reliably outweighs the risk that price-based instruments might not have such high costs.

In many cases, however, and particularly in developing countries with limited administrative capacities, market-based measures may be more appropriate than regulatory instruments. The advantages of market-based measures are several. They are difficult to evade: Resource users essentially face a choice of reduced resource use or higher financial costs. As a result, enforcement costs will tend to be low; if the policy is self-enforcing—like deposit refund schemes—enforcement costs will be practically zero. They are relatively flexible: For example, under a system of nonlinear fees and fines recently introduced in Eastern Europe, the charge is increased—in Poland by ten times—if discharges exceed some specified level. They are doubly efficient since they allow environmental problems to be addressed by those polluters able to do so at least cost, and they encourage polluters to develop innovative and cost-effective pollution abatement technologies. Finally, tax-based incentives generate revenues. Such revenues may themselves contribute to efficiency if they replace revenues generated from more distortionary sources, such as trade tariffs and corporate taxes; they can also be allocated to pollution abatement, thus enhancing environmental quality still further.

To date the most widely used market-based instruments have targeted behavior only indirectly related to environmental damage. These include fuel and vehicle taxes (in most industrial countries), congestion charges (in Singapore), and surcharges on potentially damaging inputs such as pesticides and plastics (Denmark and Sweden). Recently, however, more direct instruments—such as the newly introduced carbon taxes in Europe, deposit-refund schemes for batteries (in several European countries), hazardous waste charges and performance bonds (under consideration in Bangkok), surcharges on stumping fees to pay for replanting (Indonesia), effluent charges (in São Paulo, and in Tianjin and other Chinese cities)—have been growing in importance. Indirect policies are relatively blunt, in that they have few points of administrative application. Taxes on polluting inputs or area-based forestry charges, for example, can be implemented through the existing tax system. More direct policies, such as emission taxes, are administratively more demanding since they target individual polluters or resource users. Given their administrative constraints, developing countries may find blunter policies more attractive.

Several Bank project components seek to expand the use of market-based instruments. A $32.8 million IDA credit for Yemen's Land and Water Conservation Project aims to establish a number of strong fiscal incentives, including not only the elimination of environmentally harmful subsidies but also the imposition of appropriate water charges. The $50 million loan for Mexico's Environmental Project includes financing for further studies to explore the use of market-based instruments in encouraging environmental protection. The Mediterranean Environmental Technical Assistance Program, a joint initiative of the World Bank and the European Investment Bank, contains several such components: in Tunisia, a Pilot Wastewater Reuse program is looking at the feasibility of marketing wastewater, sludge, and compost; and in Cyprus, an Environmental Fiscal Instruments policy study is developing appropriate fiscal mechanisms for implementing sound land-use policies and coastal zone management practices.

Removing Impediments to Action

Although the principles of sound environmental management are relatively straightforward, and a range of effective policies are clearly discernible, a number of obstacles—political, managerial, organizational, institutional, informational—have in too many cases prevented or held back necessary reform. Effective sustainable development strategies must overcome these obstacles.

Policy Coordination.   Given the intersectoral nature of effective environmental management, there is an overwhelming need for developing countries to be able to set priorities and ways of achieving them *in a coordinated fashion*. National environmental action plans (or EAPs) allow developing countries to incorporate all aspects of environmental management. The EAP process starts with a complete review of environmental issues to determine national priorities, which are then addressed through a series of policy actions, investment proposals, and institutional changes, coordinated across all economic and societal sectors. Moreover, an EAP integrates strategies for environmental management with overall national development policy and decision making. Because many forms of environmental degradation are intersectoral, appropriate policy responses will often cut across normal bureaucratic jurisdictions. In São Paulo, Brazil, for instance, the metropolitan area has a planning agency, while the state has agencies with responsibilities for environmental protection, water, and sanitation. A consequence of this divided responsibility is that programs for controlling industrial pollution have not been integrated with investments in wastewater treatment, while sewage treatment plants have been constructed but not the needed interceptor and trunk line sewers. The coordination and integration aspects of action plans are therefore of paramount importance.

The Bank's role in the preparation and implementation of an EAP is primarily to advise and provide technical assistance, at the request of the government in question. The degree of Bank involvement depends on the capacity of the government to design and manage the process; Bank support may be substantial in some countries and minimal in others.[6] As an EAP is developed, the Bank incorporates information from the EAP into its own country assistance strategy and economic and sector work. EAPs also facilitate donor coordination at the country level by specifying environmental priorities, and help mobilize appropriate resources and expertise to tackle identified problems. Overall, they therefore provide an exceptionally powerful means to incorporate environmental concerns into the mainstream of the Bank's work and into the development process within borrowing countries. In Africa in particular, the EAP has become the cornerstone of Bank policy toward the environment and development.

To date, seven EAPs have been completed—Burkina Faso, Ghana, Lesotho, Madagascar, Rwanda, Egypt, and Sri Lanka. Several others—including the Seychelles, Bangladesh, China, Cyprus, and Pakistan—are near completion. In other countries—in China and throughout Eastern Europe—the Bank has prepared—or, in the case of Indonesia, the Philippines, and Thailand, is preparing—comprehensive environmental strategies papers (ESPs) that fulfill a role very like that of EAPs. In China, for instance, the ESP will serve as the basis for the government's expanded environmental work program over the next 3 to 5 years. All told, about 50 other countries are currently preparing EAPs or their

---

[6]A new Operational Directive (OD 4.02: Environmental Action Plans, July 1992) provides guidance to Bank staff for assisting borrowers in preparing such plans.

functional equivalents. Additionally, in a number of cases, Bank staff are actively facilitating and participating in the formulation of strategic *regional* environmental action plans. These include a regional Environmental Action Program for Central and Eastern Europe and an Environmental Program for International Waters (EPIW), which comprises the Danube, Baltic, Black Sea, and Mediterranean Environmental Management Programs. All of these contain extensive institutional components.

Institution Building.   Given their limited administrative resources, developing countries must think carefully about the institutional and organizational components of environmental management: one recent review of 40 years of World Bank experience in the water and sanitation sectors identified institutional failure as the most frequent and persistent cause of poor performance. In many cases there is a great deal of scope for developing countries to improve the capacity of their institutions to assess trade-offs and set priorities, coordinate activities, resolve conflicts, and enforce compliance with the policies that are established. In addition to the obvious needs—improved technical skills, adequate finance, and a clarification of environmental priorities—institutional capacity must be enhanced in two main ways. First, all parties—public and donor agencies—need to be held accountable for the environmental impact of their actions. Making regulatory and monitoring functions independent is one effective means to this end. Second, the EAP process or its equivalent needs to contain an effective institutional component. In some countries—Brazil, China, and Nigeria—a formal high-level agency has proved useful in coordinating policy across diverse sectors.

In conjunction with the EAP process, the Bank supports a growing number of stand-alone environmental and technical assistance projects, which are specifically designed to reform the policy and institutional frameworks for national environmental decision making. Fiscal 1992 saw the approval of 19 projects that were primarily environmental, of which six were primarily concerned with building institutional capacity to formulate and implement environmental strategies and action plans.[7] Typical of these is the Nigeria Environmental Management Project (an IDA credit of $25 million), under which support is provided to the Federal Environmental Protection Agency, the Natural Resources Coordinating Council, the Ecological Fund, federal ministries, and state environmental agencies to plan and implement environmental policy and to monitor and enforce environmental systems. Almost all primarily environmental projects, and many projects with significant environmental components, include some element of institution building or capacity enhancement. It seems likely that in the future, more lending will go to institutional development proj-

[7]Bank-financed projects are deemed "primarily" environmental, or "free-standing," if either the costs of environmental protection measures or the environmental benefits accruing from the project exceed 50% of total project costs or benefits.

ects, and that components to strengthen environmental management units will be increasingly incorporated into other lending operations. During fiscal 1992 in the Latin American region alone, institution-building and -reinforcing projects were under development in Bolivia, China, Colombia, and Ecuador; and proposed future lending for the same purposes includes projects in Nicaragua and Venezuela among others. Some institution-building programs are sector-specific and are directed at more than one borrowing country: Box 20-5 provides a case study of managerial and institutional innovation in an urban context.

Box 20-5.   Innovative Institutional Approaches to Improving Urban Environments

Asian cities have grown rapidly over the past 30 years and their growth continues to accelerate. If current trends continue, 60% of Asia's projected population of 2.9 billion people will live in towns and cities by 2025—a tripling of the number of urban dwellers in 1985. Such rapid urban growth and industrialization have led to pervasive pollution of air, water, and land, undermining the benefits of development and imposing a heavy burden on urban residents, especially the poor.

The Metropolitan Environmental Improvement Program (MEIP), established in 1989 to assist Asian governments' efforts to enhance their environmental management capabilities, is administered by the World Bank, with basic funding for core programs provided by the UNDP. Its first phase concentrates on five cities: Beijing, Bombay, Colombo, Jakarta, and Manila. MEIP holds a unique mandate to combine the planning and monitoring of the more traditional sectoral donor activities in metropolitan areas in, for example, water supply and sanitation, solid-waste management, transport, and industry to achieve an integrated view of the impact of these activities on land, air, and water. To facilitate this, Environmental Management Strategies (EMS) are being prepared in all five cities; most will be completed by early 1993.

Work in each city is guided by a steering committee composed of representatives from central and local government agencies responsible for economic planning, environmental protection, sectoral development, land use, and urban planning, as well as from the private sector and NGOs. Working groups are formed to oversee technical aspects of specific projects. MEIP's practice of working with and bringing together government agencies, NGOs, community groups, and the private sector has earned it widespread support in the participating cities. To strengthen the capabilities of government agencies, MEIP helps bolster their institutional relationships and improve their environmental management capacities. MEIP also assists the five cities in preparing feasibility studies to address high-priority environmental issues, which are then incorporated into Bank projects.

Overcoming Political Pressures.   Stopping environmental damage often involves taking rights away from people who may be politically powerful. Industrialists, farmers, loggers, and fishermen fiercely—and in many cases, successfully—defend their assumed rights to pollute or exploit natural resources. In contrast, the poorer members of society, who tend to have the most to gain from an improved environment, tend to play little part in setting the environmental agenda. At the least, the distributional impacts of environmental degradation (and of efforts to address them) may distort the setting of priorities. For example, wealthy city dwellers, who may be able to protect themselves from unsafe water, may persuade governments to assign higher priority to air pollution, which has impacts that are harder to escape. Yet water investments may have a much larger immediate health benefit.

A number of other political pressures work against sound environmental management. These include the tendency to make policy in response to high-visibility environmental crises. Powerful images of oil spills or leaking toxic wastes can capture the public imagination and consequently play a role in initiating policy change. The danger here is that priorities can be distorted away from environmental issues like poor-quality drinking water which, while less dramatic in terms of imagery, actually puts more lives at risk. A further pressure against sound policy is the self-regulation of what is usually among the most pollution-intensive sectors of the economy—publicly owned enterprises. We have already noted that such enterprises often price environmental resources incorrectly and that a number of countries, some of them in the developing world, have begun to experiment with privatization in an effort to improve accountability and efficiency. Independent regulatory "watchdog" agencies may also have a valuable role to play. The state of the environment in Eastern Europe—where environmental standards are often stricter than in the European Community or the United States—demonstrates the public sector's limited capacity for self-regulation.

To overcome these political impediments to sustainable development, governments should build constituencies for change and thus alter the political economy of environmental degradation. To some extent, the latter is already changing, as evidenced by the growing public support for sound environmental policy. As voters, protestors, consumers, and even, in some cases producers, people in many countries show a similar interest in environmental causes. Worldwide, the move toward more democratic forms of government has coincided with an increase in popular environmental consciousness. But to overcome political impediments more completely, governments will have to take further steps.

Involving Local People.   Good environmental data are of benefit not only to policymakers. Environmentally educated and aware publics are likely to put pressure on governments to implement sound policies, and they are more likely to accept the costs and inconveniences of environmental policies. Results can be dramatic. In Curitiba, Brazil, a well-informed and involved public, together with a committed mayor and municipal government, have given rise to numerous environmental innovations and an improved quality of life in this city of 2 million: public transport is used by most of the population, green spaces have been expanded, recycling is widely practiced, and industrial location and product mix are carefully chosen to minimize pollution. In the slums of Karachi, after months spent trying to have sewerage systems installed by public authorities, community organizers decided to take matters into their own hands and, with a small amount of core external funding, the Orangi Pilot Project (OPP) was started. By eliminating corruption, educating community members, and making use of their labor, the costs of installing in-house latrines and underground sewers were cut drastically to around $50 per household. As the project began to prove its worth, other communities, and eventually other municipalities in Pakistan, began to duplicate its methods; over half a million poor people in Karachi now have sewerage as a direct result of the OPP.

The World Bank recognizes that communities will only support environmental programs that reflect local beliefs, values, and ideology. As a consequence, it tries to promote local participation to the fullest extent possible. The preparation of EAPs, for example, involves a broad process of popular participation, organized through various levels of government, including local authorities, and through civic groups, research and academic institutions, nongovernmental organizations, and other private sector organizations. This kind of participation helps to broaden policymakers' understanding of cross-sectoral issues and to develop a national consensus on the EAP's priorities for action and means of implementation. Extensive local participation in EAP preparation is both time-consuming and expensive; but, unless an action plan is developed in conjunction with those who will have to implement it, it is likely to be regarded as an "external" product and consequently be ignored. Popular participation in policymaking can change the political economy of environmental degradation from the bottom up.

Similarly, the Bank's environmental assessment procedure stipulates that a borrowing country must solicit and take into account the views of affected groups and local nongovernmental organizations (NGOs). Where Bank-supported projects affect indigenous people, efforts are made to ensure their informed participation in the preparation of development plans and in project design, implementation, and evaluation. Many indigenous peoples, such as those in the tropical rain forests of Southeast Asia and the Amazon, have developed a valuable understanding of complex ecosystems. Ignoring local sources of knowledge can prove costly. In Bali, when a large internationally financed agricultural project tried to replace traditional rice varieties with high-input imported varieties, the result was a sudden increase in insect pests, followed by declining crop yields. A subsequent project that built on the long-established Balinese production system has proved much more successful.

Many other Bank-related activities now incorporate local participation. The Metropolitan Environmental Improvements Program, for instance, supports a number of local efforts through NGOs and community groups, including on-site waste collection in Bombay; the Clean Settlements Program in Colombo, which works to help low-income communities manage their own environments; composting and recycling in Jakarta; and pilot programs in Metro Manila to expand public sanitation services and upgrade the Balikatan women's movement resource recovery model. To establish environmental priorities in five different cities, the Bank's Urban Management Program employed locally designed questionnaires to generate information on important indicators such as land use, energy use, transport, wastes, and air, water, and noise pollution. Results were subsequently elaborated during consultations with citizens in each city, culminating in an "environmental town meeting." In each city, the process produced consensus on one or more environmental priorities.

Global and Regional Environmental Problems and Strategies

Thus far the analysis has focused on national-level environmental problems and strategies with a few cross-boundary issues. Although less immediately threatening, global and regional forms of environmental degradation are still of significance for developing countries. Several classes of environmental problems can be classified as global: first, environmental degradation of the "global commons"—ozone depletion, global warming, or the pollution of international waters; and second, degradation of resources that, while they belong to one country, have a value for the international community that is not reflected in the market. The latter category includes tropical rain forests, other special ecological habitats, and individual species, termed collectively "biodiversity." The impact of many of these global environmental problems is uncertain, but potentially severe; and it is therefore a matter of some controversy whether developing countries should include these problems' resolution or alleviation as being among their most urgent priorities. Box 20-6 details the three major global environmental problems threatening developing countries.

In addition to global environmental problems, a number of other forms of environmental degradation take effect at the regional level. Where resources are regionally shared, environmental externalities may spread across borders in the form of water pollution, reduced river flow, or acid rain. Countries therefore become environmentally interdependent. As with global degradation, international cooperation may be required to resolve these issues. However, it is important to realize that despite the need for cooperation, solutions will necessarily have to be enacted at the national level. Country-level policies are not therefore altered by the transboundary nature of an environmental problem. Interdependence does require cooperative approaches—whose generation faces a series of obstacles—but once cooperation has been achieved or agreed upon, policies at the national level should still follow the same basic policy prescriptions outlined above.

Box 20-6. Principal Global Environmental Challenges Facing Developing Countries

While much environmental damage and loss is all too evident today, other sources of potential danger—particularly the three global environmental problems laid out below—may not show their ill effects for some time. Moreover, the potential seriousness of these problems is disputed.

- **Stratospheric ozone depletion.** This is the most immediate global commons problem; scientists continue to record alarmingly high atmospheric levels of ozone-destroying substances—primarily carbon monoxide, which originates from chlorofluorocarbons (CFCs). Ozone in the stratosphere protects life on earth by absorbing much of the ultraviolet radiation that causes skin cancer and cataracts, and may damage the human immune system; uv radiation also reduces the productivity of microscopic marine organisms that are at the base of the ocean's food chain. The effects of increased uv radiation on agriculture and forestry are still only partially understood; some crops have shown a capacity to adapt to increased uv exposure, while the growth and photosynthetic capacity of others have been affected.

- **Global warming.** Increasing emissions of carbon dioxide and other greenhouse gases (GHGs)—including CFCs—reduce the earth's net emission of energy to space and therefore raise average temperatures on earth. The exact size of the greenhouse effect remains unclear, as do the timing of the purported increase, the location of the resultant changes in climate, and the seriousness of its consequences. However, average world temperatures may rise by 1.5 to 4.5°C by the second half of the next century. Potentially significant effects are more likely to result from related changes in soil moisture, storms, and sea level than from temperature as such, and these changes are even harder to predict. Unfortunately, just as it is difficult to rule out costly climatic effects of greenhouse gas accumulations, it is hard to demonstrate compellingly that they are likely to occur.

- **Biodiversity loss.** Not only does biological diversity—a composite of genetic information, species, and ecosystems—provide material wealth—both now and in the future—in the form of food, fiber, medicine, and industrial inputs, it also supports complex ecosystems in ways that are only partially understood. The complex web of interactions that maintains the vitality of ecosystems may unravel if only a small number of key species become extinct. In the 1970s, the Malaysian fruit industry, worth some $100 million annually, came under threat when trees producing a popular local fruit, the durian, began to bear less fruit. Eventually, this was

(Continued)

> linked to a decline in the population of a single bat species, which was responsible for pollinating the durian trees. Subsequent conservation efforts to protect the bats' habitat led to the recovery of the animals and the durian industry. A failure to protect biodiversity—and the current rate of species extinction is unprecedentedly high—therefore risks squandering resources whose value is incompletely understood.

Strategies

Generating International Cooperation.   For two reasons, resolving or alleviating global or regional environmental problems requires effective international cooperation. First, in an international system of sovereign states, no single authority can lay down and enforce appropriate policies. Within individual countries, as we have seen, sound environmental management strategies have recourse to regulatory controls, economic incentives, a common legal framework, and—where necessary—the coercive powers of a governing authority at the national or subnational level. But solutions to international environmental problems must evolve consensually, backed up by persuasion and negotiation. This can be a slow process: the United Nations Convention on the Law of the Sea, for instance, took 10 years to negotiate and, a decade after the end of negotiations, still has not come into force. Second, the scope for unilateral action is limited. No one country acting alone is likely to affect significantly the overall trend of global environmental deterioration. In this sense, the global commons suffers Hardin's "tragedy."

These two factors together create the *demand* for international cooperation to protect the global commons. Unfortunately, they do not guarantee its *supply*, since any given solution is liable to generate unequal distributions of costs and benefits. The costs of international inaction may not be borne, or borne equally, by all countries; the gains from policies may not accrue to those who take the biggest steps. Perhaps as important, the perception of unequal gains and losses can hinder the development of consensus. Some countries may be understandably unwilling to invest in solutions to global environmental problems, given substantial and immediate national-level environmental concerns. The key to supplying international agreement will often be side payments—to secure action, rich countries may sometimes need to pay poor ones. In particular, the issue of how to give weight to the interests of the poor and politically weak lays an especially heavy burden on the world's more powerful countries.

The threat of greenhouse warming illustrates many of these problems. Any form of international cooperation on this issue will have to address the following factors, all of which affect the distributional impact of global warming and possible means of addressing it.

- Climate change, and the rate of climate change, will differ across countries. Even where the pattern of climate change is similar, it may affect countries differently because of differences in ecology, economic activity, or the values placed on environmental resources.

- Countries have emitted, and continue to emit, very different quantities of greenhouse gases. Industrial countries have contributed a disproportionate share of accumulated gases in the atmosphere.

- The costs of preventive measures—such as reducing emissions—will vary across countries. Some estimates suggest that the costs (relative to GDP) of stabilizing emissions at present levels could be almost twice as high as the world average (Manne and Richels, 1992; Whalley and Wigle, 1991). Moreover, the costs of preventive measures may differ relative to the costs of adaptive responses—such as improved coastal defenses—across countries.

These disparities illustrate clearly the difficulties of achieving international consensus on issues relating to the degradation of the global commons. Even if the concept of side payments is accepted, the scope for disagreement is still significant. In the context of global warming, for instance, a payment system might depend on preset targets for emission levels, in turn dependent on a preceding allocation of emission rights. The latter, of course, can have major distributional effects: allocating rights by population would produce very different results to allocating them by income. In the context of biodiversity, external payments to a developing country for improved habitat and species conservation may prove ineffective if that country's overall policy framework conflicts with conservationist ends. But payments conditioned on an overall policy direction may represent to developing countries an excessive sacrifice of autonomy.

Despite these difficulties, steps have been taken by the international community toward multilateral cooperation on the issues of climate change and biodiversity. The Global Environment Facility (GEF), designated as the interim funding mechanism for the Biodiversity and Climate Change Conventions, is designed to allocate funds to developing countries in ways that offset the unequal distribution of costs and benefits resulting from international agreements. As such, the GEF's overarching aim is to finance measures *in the interests of the world at large*; it does not fund activities that address purely national issues, although its actions are intended to harmonize with the developmental and environmental goals of the countries involved.

The Global Environment Facility.   The GEF was established in 1990 as a 3-year pilot program to provide grants for investment projects, technical assistance and—to a lesser extent—research. GEF resources are to be used to explore ways of assisting developing countries to protect the global environment, including the transfer of environmentally benign technologies. The pilot facility assists developing countries in the demonstration of solutions to four main global environmental problems: (1) global warming, particularly the effects on the world's climate of greenhouse gas emissions resulting from the use of fossil fuels and the destruction of carbon-absorbing forests; (2) pollution of international water through, for example, oil spills and the accumulation of wastes in oceans and international river systems; (3) destruction of biological diversity through the degradation of natural habitats and the "mining" of natural resources; and (4) the depletion of the stratospheric ozone layer by emissions of chlorofluorocarbons (CFCs), halons, and other gases. Although projects must fall into one of these four priority areas, not all projects that benefit the global environment automatically qualify for support from the GEF. Projects financed by the facility must also be innovative and demonstrate the effectiveness of a particular technology or approach. Given its pilot nature, other criteria include the contribution a project makes to human development (for instance, through education and training), and the provision for evaluation and dissemination of results.

Responsibility for implementing the GEF is shared between UNDP, the UNEP, and the World Bank. UNDP is responsible for technical assistance, capacity building, and project preparation; UNEP plays a central role in strategic planning and provides environmental advice on specific projects[8]; and the World Bank administers the GEF, acts as the repository for GEF funds, and is responsible for implementing investment projects. In total, the facility has some $1.3 billion to commit over the 3-year pilot phase that began in 1990. By June 1992, 28 countries (11 of them in the developing world) had pledged contributions to the GEF.

As of July 1992, the GEF portfolio consisted of more than 70 projects amounting to $580 million. Six investment projects totaling $80 million have been approved: conserving the environment in Bhutan; preserving biodiversity in Poland; displacing fossil fuels with bagasse for energy production in Mauritius; conserving biodiversity in Mexico; handling and disposing of ships' waste in six Chinese ports, and an afforestation project in Ecuador. The projects in Bhutan and Poland were free-standing, financed entirely by the GEF; the other four were Bank-supported projects in which the GEF funded a component. In attempting to balance the portfolio both thematically and geographically, a determined effort has been made to fill important gaps and utilize experience gained from the pilot phase to maximum effect. As of June 1992, 47% of resources from the core fund had been earmarked for biodiversity, 36% for global warming, and 17% for international waters.

The pilot phase of the GEF comes to an end in late 1993, and efforts are currently under way to restructure the GEF for a longer-term role. Participating countries have agreed on a set of principles to guide the evolution of the GEF, including its availability to serve as the funding mechanism of global environmental conventions; a broadened scope to include land degradation issues, such as desertification and afforestation, as they relate to the four focal areas; universal membership; a decision-making process designed to ensure an equitable

---

[8]UNEP also provides the secretariat for the Scientific and Technical Advisory Panel (STAP), a group of 16 eminent scientists from industrial and developing countries. This independent group has formulated criteria for eligibility and priorities for selection of GEF projects. STAP members also review project proposals and coordinate research and data collection.

representation of the interests of developing and donor countries; and a single funding mechanism to be periodically replenished. This agreement on the restructuring of the GEF was instrumental in forging international consensus on the designation of the GEF as the financial mechanism for the Climate Change and Biodiversity conventions, and for the incremental costs of measures outlined in Agenda 21 for the achievement of global environmental benefits. Several countries have supported a two- to threefold increase in resources for the GEF once the pilot phase ends in 1993.

The Costs of a Sustainable Future

Policy Costs

We have argued that sound environmental strategies have affordable costs, given their economic and environmental benefits, although some may carry a stiff political price. However, as Fig. 20-5 makes clear, despite their evident cost-effectiveness over the long term, many sound strategies have substantial initial investment requirements. Exact costs will depend on standards chosen, the time path for reaching them, and the policy instruments used. Below, we lay out some very approximate estimates for particular environmental problems in developing countries. These figures (1990 prices) should be treated as orders of magnitude only, and they assume that new technologies and management practices are phased in over a generation.

Water and Sanitation.   The scenarios in Fig. 20-8 assumed an investment increase from 0.6 to 0.8% of GDP. If universal provision is to be achieved by 2030, the share might have to be larger in low-income countries, even allowing for the effects of price and institutional reforms.

Electric Power.   Assuming that reasonable efficiency improvements and pricing policies are achieved over the next 25 years, and that the best control technologies in current use are applied to all new investments, then investment levels will have to increase from about $120 billion today to about $200 billion a year by the end of the 1990s for developing country demand to be met. Controlling particulates will raise investment costs by about 0.04% of GDP; where necessary, controls on sulfur dioxide and nitrogen oxides would add another 0.5%.

Vehicle Emissions.   Assuming that cleaner fuels and emission control practices are phased in over 25 years, the costs of moving to a low-pollution strategy (where total emissions are below current levels) would be about 0.2% of GDP by 2000 and about 0.5% by 2010.

Industrial Emissions and Wastes.   If manufacturers' spending on pollution controls—both end-of-pipe and in-plant measures—were to approach 2 to

3% of investment costs, then developing countries could appreciably reduce industrial pollution and avoid the costs of cleanup later. The extra costs would amount to about 0.2 to 0.3% of GDP by the end of the decade.

Agriculture and Forestry.   The costs of preventing soil erosion and degradation are comparatively small, while the costs of rehabilitating degraded areas can be large. Investment of around 0.2 to 0.3% of GDP would probably be sufficient to extend the coverage of improved soil-management practices by up to 100 million hectares. Capital costs will have to be augmented with expenditure on research, extension, training, education, and support for infrastructure and afforestation.

Population and Female Education.   To achieve a rapid decline in fertility rates, family planning expenditures will have to rise to about 0.2% of GDP by 2000. It will also require improved progress on reducing poverty and increasing access to education. Eliminating educational discrimination at the primary and secondary levels would cost about 0.25% of GDP.

Overall, the additional costs of needed investments could amount to around 2 to 3% of GDP by 2000, or about $100 billion in 1990 prices. Relative to the potential for economic growth in developing countries, these sums are modest; they are also much less than the potential savings from efficiency gains that are an integral element of sound environmental strategies. Moreover, much of this expenditure would add to employment and income growth in developing countries.

Sources of Finance

Most of these investments will be paid by private and public enterprises and thus by consumers. This is as it should be—unless environmentally damaging activities become less profitable to producers and less attractive to consumers, it will be hard to effect a convergence of the private and social interests in environmental protection. But additional financing will still be required from private and official sources. Three sources in particular should be stressed. First, environmental investment costs can be met by increased export earnings. A successful conclusion to the current Uruguay GATT round would generate additional annual export earnings in developing countries of $65 billion by the end of the decade. In this context, industrial country growth can also help; a 1 percentage point increase in OECD growth over a 4-year period would generate more than $80 billion in annual foreign exchange earnings by developing countries. Second, since so many environmental investments have profitable rates of return, it is imperative that developing countries obtain access to commercial finance and obtain foreign investment. Over the last 2 years, commercial flows to Chile, Mexico, and Venezuela have been restored, and they should now be extended to a much wider range of countries. Debt relief may be required in some cases. Increased savings rates—especially in the public sector—would help also.

Third, it is essential that additional development assistance be forthcoming to tackle local environmental problems, and that existing aid flows provide support for sound environmental management. The GEF and IDA were both identified at UNCED as suitable vehicles for increased concessional funding at the national and global levels, respectively. Increased funding reinforces the need for improved institutional capacities within developing countries. Innovations such as the EAP process can greatly facilitate the coordination of additional flows by both donors and borrowers. Tables 20-1 and 20-2 indicate the total disbursements of different types of aid by multilateral and regional organizations; precise figures for the environmental components of these totals are not available.

Table 20-1. Net Disbursements of Concessional Flows by Multilateral Organizations, 1980, 1985, and 1990 ($ million)

	Concessional flows		
	1980	1985	1990
Major financial institutions:			
IDA	1543	2599	3,912
IBRD	107	34	
IDB	326	351	155
African Development Fund	96	210	603
Asian Development Fund	149	393	1,101
IFAD	54	270	120‡
Subtotal	2274	3857	5,891
United Nations:			
WFP	539	779	933
UNDP	660	635	1,130
UNHCR	465	418	466
UNWRA	157	187	293
UNICEF	247	279	584
UNTA	35	295	230
UNFPA	150	127	179
Other UN	235	327	683
Subtotal	2487	3047	4,497
Other sources:			
IMF*	1636	−298	321
EEC	1061	1287	2,896
Arab Funds	286	133	156
Other institutions†	46	29	40‡
Subtotal	3029	1151	3,413
Total concessional (rounded)	7790	8174	13,801

SOURCE: OECD, *Development Co-operation, 1991 Report*, December 1991.
*IMF Trust Fund, SAF, and ESAF.
†Caribbean Development Bank and Council of Europe.
‡Estimates.

Table 20-2. Net Disbursements of Nonconcessional Flows by Multilateral Organizations, 1980, 1985, and 1990 ($ million)

	Nonconcessional flows		
	1980	1985	1990
Major financial institution:			
IBRD	3166	5041	5,009
IFC	295	94	1,385
IDB	567	1398	1,060
African Development Bank	97	235	1,001
Asian Development Bank	328	400	1,197
Others	10	306	237
Subtotal	4463	7474	9,889
EEC	257	152	299
Arab Funds	128	286	
Total Nonconcessional	4848	7912	10,188

SOURCE: OECD, *Development Co-operation, 1991 Report,* December 1991.

References

Principal Sources

World Bank. 1992. *World Development Report 1992: Development and the Environment.* New York: Oxford University Press.

World Bank. 1992. *The World Bank and the Environment, Fiscal 1992.* Washington, D.C.

World Development Report Background Papers[9]

Dennis Anderson. 1992. "Economic Growth and the Environment." Policy Research Working Paper 979, World Bank, Washington, D.C.

Dennis Anderson and William Cavendish. 1992. "Efficiency and Substitution in Pollution Abatement: Simulation Studies in Three Sectors." Industry and Energy Department, World Bank, Washington, D.C.

William Ascher. 1992. "Coping with the Disappointing Rates of Return of Development Projects with Environmental Aspects." Policy Research Working Paper 965, World Bank, Washington, D.C.

Edward B. Barbier and Joanne C. Burgess. 1992. "Agricultural Pricing and Environmental Degradation." Policy Research Working Paper 960, World Bank, Washington, D.C.

Robin W. Bates and Edwin A. Moore. 1992. "Commercial Energy Efficiency and the Environment." Policy Research Working Paper 972, World Bank, Washington, D.C.

Wilfred Beckerman. 1992. "Economic Development and the Environment: Conflict or Complementarity?" Policy Research Working Paper 961, World Bank, Washington, D.C.

[9]The following papers are available from the World Development Report Office, room T-7101 (202/473-1393).

Richard E. Bilsborrow. 1992. "Rural Poverty, Migration, and the Environment in Developing Countries: Three Case Studies." Policy Research Working Paper 1017, World Bank, Washington, D.C.

Charles R. Blitzer, R. S. Eckaus, Supriya Lahiri, and Alexander Meeraus. 1992. (a) "Growth and Welfare Losses from Carbon Emission Restrictions: A General Equilibrium Analysis for Egypt." Policy Research Working Paper 963, World Bank, Washington, D.C. (b)"How Restricting Carbon Dioxide and Methane Emissions Would Affect the Indian Economy." Policy Research Working Paper 978, World Bank, Washington, D.C.

Pierre Crosson and Jock Anderson. 1992. "Resources and Global Food Prospects: Supply and Demand for Cereals to 2030." World Bank Technical Paper 184, Washington, D.C.

Shelton H. Davis. 1993. "Indigenous Views of Land and the Environment." Discussion Paper 188, World Bank, Washington, D.C.

Judith M. Dean. 1992. "Trade and the Environment: A Survey of the Literature." Policy Research Working Paper 966, World Bank, Washington, D.C.

David O. Hall. 1992. "Biomass." Policy Research Working Paper 968, World Bank, Washington, D.C.

John B. Homer. 1992. "Natural Gas in Developing Countries: Evaluating the Benefits to the Environment." Discussion Paper 190, World Bank, Washington, D.C.

Ravi Kanbur. 1992. "Heterogeneity, Distribution and Cooperation in Common Property Resource Management." Policy Research Working Paper 844, World Bank, Washington, D.C.

Arik Levinson and Sudhir Shetty. 1992. "Efficient Environment Regulation: Case Studies of Urban Air Pollution." Policy Research Working Paper 942, World Bank, Washington, D.C.

Robert E. B. Lucas, David Wheeler, and Hemamala Hettige. 1992. "Economic Development, Environmental Regulation and the International Migration of Toxic Industrial Pollution: 1960–1988." Forthcoming.

Robert E. B. Lucas, 1992. "Toxic Releases by Manufacturing: World Patterns and Trade Policies." Policy Research Working Paper 964, World Bank, Washington, D.C.

Stephen Mink. 1992. "Poverty, Population and the Environment." Discussion Paper 189, World Bank, Washington, D.C.

Ashoka Mody and Robert Evenson. 1992. "Innovation and Diffusion of Environmentally Responsive Technologies." Forthcoming.

David Pearce. 1992. "Economic Valuation and the Natural World." Policy Research Working Paper 988, World Bank, Washington, D.C.

Nemat Shafik and Sushenjit Bandyopadhyay. 1992. "Economic Growth and Environmental Quality: Time Series and Cross-Country Evidence." Policy Research Working Paper 904, World Bank, Washington, D.C.

Anwar Shah and Bjorn Larsen. 1992. (a) "Carbon Taxes, the Greenhouse Effect, and Developing Countries." Policy Research Working Paper 957, World Bank, Washington, D.C. (b) "World Energy Subsidies and Global Carbon Emissions." Policy Research Working Paper 1002, World Bank, Washington, D.C.

Margaret E. Slade. 1992. (a) "Environmental Costs of Natural Resource Commodities: Magnitude and Incidence." Policy Research Working Paper 991, World Bank, Washington, D.C. (b) "Do Markets Underprice Natural Resource Commodities?" Policy Research Working Paper 962, World Bank, Washington, D.C.

Piratta Sorsa. 1992. "The Environment—A New Challenge to GATT?" Policy Research Working Paper 980, World Bank, Washington, D.C.

Sheila Webb and Associates. 1992. "Waterborne Diseases in Peru." Policy Research Working Paper 959, World Bank, Washington, D.C.

Additional References[10]

Cleaver, Kevin, and Gotz Schreiber. 1991. "The Population, Environment and Agriculture Nexus in Sub-Saharan Africa." Africa Region Technical Paper, World Bank, Washington, D.C.

Eskeland, Gunnar. 1992. "Demand Management in Environmental Protection: Fuel Taxes and Air Pollution in Mexico City." World Bank, Country Economics Department, Washington, D.C.

Garrett Hardin. 1968. "The Tragedy of the Commons," *Science.*

Low, Patrick (ed.). 1992. *International Trade and the Environment.* World Bank Discussion Paper no. 159, Washington, D.C.

Lusigi, Walter J., and Bengt A. Nekby. 1991. "Dryland Management in Sub-Saharan Africa: The Search for Sustainable Development Options." World Bank, Africa Technical Department, Environment Division, Washington, D.C.

Manne, A. S., and R. G. Richels, 1992. "Global CO_2 Emission Reductions—The Impacts of Rising Energy Costs." *Energy Journal,* vol. XII, no. 1.

Martin, Paul, et al. 1992. "The Industrial Pollution Projection System: Concept, Initial Development and Critical Assessment." World Bank, Environment Department, Assessments and Programs Division, Washington, D.C.

Meadows, Donella H., Dennis L. Meadows, Jorgen Randers, and William W. Behrens III. 1972. *The Limits to Growth.* New York: Universe Books.

Rogers, Peter. 1992. "Comprehensive Water Resources Management: A Concept Paper." Policy Research Working Paper 879. World Bank, Water and Sanitation Division, Infrastructure and Urban Development Department, Washington, D.C.

Sharma, Narendra, and Raymond Rowe. 1992. "Managing the World's Forests," *Finance and Development,* June 1992, vol. 29, no. 2, World Bank, Washington, D.C.

UNICEF. 1991. "Plan de Accion Por La Infancia." Programa de Apoyo Sectorial de Agua y Saneamiento.

Whalley, John, and Randall Wigle. 1991. "The International Incidence of Carbon Taxes." In Roger Dornbusch and James M. Poterba, eds. *Global Warming: Economic Policy Responses,* Cambridge, Massachusetts: MIT Press.

World Bank. 1991. *The Forest Sector.* A World Bank Policy Paper. Washington, D.C.

——— 1991. *Environmental Assessment Sourcebook:* World Bank Technical Papers 139, 140, and 154.

——— 1992. "The Bank's Role in the Electric Power Sector: Policies for Effective Institutional, Regulatory, and Financial Reform." Industry and Energy Department, Washington, D.C.

---

[10]For a more complete bibliography, see *The World Bank and the Environment, Fiscal 1992,* pp. 144–152, and *Development and the Environment, World Development Report 1992,* pp. 183–191.

21

Population, Environment, and Health*

Allan Rosenfield, M.D.

Dean, Columbia University School of Public Health

In this chapter:

- Population: definitions and history
- Projected population growth trends
- Impact on development and environment
- Family planning programs
- The prospects

Among the many problems impacting adversely on both the environment and the social and economic development efforts of countries are those resulting from their current high rates of population growth. With an average growth rate of 1.7%, world population is doubling every 38 years. The world currently is adding more than 90 million people every year (approximately the population of Mexico), causing significant stress in many of the world's poorest countries. In addition to socioeconomic and environmental consequences, high fertility also has adverse effects on the health of infants, young children, and women.[1,2]

*Adapted from Reference 1.

Introduction

During the second half of the twentieth century, problems secondary to the high rates of population growth that currently exist in much of the developing world have been recognized as being among the most complex of the challenges facing society. The large increases in the numbers of people during the last 40 or 50 years have resulted in an ever-increasing utilization of both renewable and nonrenewable resources, including food, topsoil, forests, and minerals. In many countries, grazing lands are being overused, fishing areas are being depleted, and forests are being destroyed.

It is possible that the world already is living well beyond its physical means, related in large part both to rapid rates of population growth in most developing countries and to excessively high rates of consumption of natural resources in most developed countries, most conspicuously in the United States.[3] Robert McNamara, the former head of the World Bank, was quoted some years ago as saying that "short of nuclear war itself [population growth] is the gravest issue that the world faces over the decades immediately ahead."[4]

An opposing view—one that suggests that rather than being a problem, population growth is a good thing—has also received much attention in recent years. Advocates of this position argue that younger, growing societies are more likely to be innovative and creative, and that the prospect of constantly expanding markets fuels economic growth. They suggest that people are our most important resources and that technological advances will solve any perceived problems related to current or future rates of population growth.[5]

There is no question that the world rate of population growth and, more specifically, the rates in many developing countries recently are at higher levels than the world has ever seen in the past. Increasingly, governments throughout the developing world have taken the position that these high rates of growth are an impediment to their overall social, health, and economic development efforts, contribute to environmental degradation, and as well have a negative impact on the health of both women and young children.

An extensive literature is available on all facets of this issue. No attempt is made here to resolve the debates nor is there an exhaustive review of the literature; instead current available data are summarized and various important issues related to, and resultant from, population growth are discussed.

Population: Definitions and History

Population Growth.   The rate of population growth (or the rate of natural increase of a population), expressed as a percentage, is calculated by subtracting the death rate from the birthrate (both expressed as rates per 1000) and dividing by 10. However, it is worth noting that a country's growth rate can be more complex than the simple subtraction of death rates from birthrates would indicate. Immigration and emigration also may play an important role in the rate at which a nation's population grows. For example, the rate of natural increase in the United States today is only about 0.7%, but the actual U.S. population is growing at a more rapid rate than this because of both legal and illegal immigration. Unfortunately, because accurate data for illegal immigration simply are not available, we can only guess at the full impact these factors have on an individual country's population growth.

Emigration was an important factor in Europe during the late nineteenth and early twentieth centuries in slowing population growth within these countries as death rates fell. North and South America and Australia, for example, received large numbers of people from Europe during the late nineteenth and early twentieth centuries. For most countries in the developing world today, however, migration is a minor factor in overall growth rates and thus we will look only at rates of natural increase and will not consider local emigration or immigration.

History.   The world's population in A.D. 1 is estimated to have been only about 250 million.[6] Historically, human populations increased in size at a very slow rate. Because of such factors as famine, war, disease, poor sanitation, and poor nutrition, death rates remained at about the same level as birthrates for a very long period of time, thus resulting in very low population growth rates. Throughout most of human history, the annual average rate of growth never reached even 0.1%, as compared with a worldwide rate today of 1.7% and rates in some developing countries of 3% or higher.

It was not until the early nineteenth century that the world's population reached 1 billion people, as death rates in the developed countries of Europe and North America began to fall (Fig. 21-1). This decline in mortality was primarily a result of the many changes brought about by the Industrial Revolution,

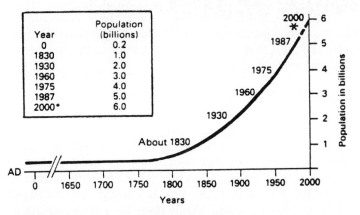

Year	Population (billions)
0	0.2
1830	1.0
1930	2.0
1960	3.0
1975	4.0
1987	5.0
2000*	6.0

Figure 21-1. World population: estimates and projections, years 0–2000. * = projected figures. [*From Rosenfield, A., "Population Growth, Development and Health," in Rosenfield, A., and Fathalla, M. (eds.), "FIGO Manual on Human Reproduction," Park Ridge: Parthenon Press, 1990, p. 26, with permission.*]

including improvements in education, nutrition, and sanitation. Thus population growth rates began to increase and it took only about 100 more years for the world to add a second billion people. As the growth rate continued to accelerate, a third billion was added by 1960, only 30 years later, and an additional billion by 1975. Only 12 years were needed to reach a total of 5 billion in 1987, and it is projected that the 6 billion mark will be reached before the turn of the century. By the year 2000, the world's population will be approximately 6.2 billion, and it will total about 8.5 billion in 2025.[7-9]

Population Growth Rates. While rates of growth in the developed world currently average approximately 0.6%, rates in the developing world, outside of China, average about 2.1%, with several countries having rates of 3% or higher.[10] The resultant world rate of growth is between 1.7 and 1.8%, slightly lower than the peak reached a few years ago of 2%. Both rates are unprecedented in human history and occur at a time when the world has the largest population base ever—over 5 billion persons. Because, as discussed below, these rates of growth lead to a doubling of the population in relatively short periods of time, it is clear that these levels of growth cannot continue indefinitely.

The world is currently adding about 93 million people per year, approximately the size of Mexico, the tenth largest country in the world. To put it more vividly, the world's population in 1993 is increasing by approximately 170 people per minute, or about 250,000 people every day, the equivalent of creating a large new city daily.[10]

Growth rates appear to be relatively low, with an average rate of increase for the world being only 1.7% per year. However, as with banking rate increases, it is easier to understand the implications of these rates by calculating the time it takes a population to double its size at various rates of growth. At a growth rate of 3% per year (a rate that is not uncommon in some parts of the developing world), the size of a population will double in just 23 years. Even at an annual growth rate of 1% per year, the population size doubles in 69 years. Simple mathematical calculations suggest that there clearly is a limit to the number of times a population can continue to double.

The Demographic Transition. The countries of Europe and North America passed through a slow process of death and birthrate declines, called the "demographic transition," that took approximately 150 years (Fig. 21-2).[11] Beginning in the early nineteenth century, death rates began to fall gradually from levels of approximately 30 to 40 per 1000 people to a low of 10 or less per 1000 by the mid-twentieth century. During the same period of time, birthrates also began to decline, from levels close to 40 per 1000 to current levels of 15 per 1000 or less in much of the developed world. While there have been debates as to whether the decline in birthrates in some developed countries preceded or followed the death rate decline, over the course of 150 years both rates have reached their current low levels, without the prolonged period of very high population growth rates currently seen in developing countries.

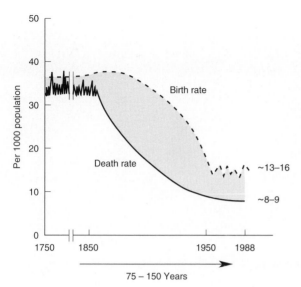

Figure 21-2. Demographic transition in the developed world. [*From Rosenfield, A., "Population Growth, Development and Health," in Rosenfield, A., and Fathalla, M. (eds.), "FIGO Manual on Human Reproduction," Park Ridge: Parthenon Press, 1990, p. 26, with permission.*]

An important characteristic of the demographic transition in western nations was that it occurred at a point in time when the base population was relatively small and land was relatively plentiful. Furthermore, emigration to the sparsely populated Americas helped ease population pressure in many western European nations during periods of increasing rates of population growth. Finally, the demands on natural resources in countries undergoing the transition were much less than today, so that the growth in population could be absorbed somewhat more easily than is the case today in the developing world.

These concurrent declines in birth and death rates in Europe are thought to have stemmed from a variety of factors. Perhaps the most important influence was the Industrial Revolution, which brought improvement in education, income, nutrition, public sanitation, and general standards of living. Interestingly, much of the birthrate decline took place before the advent of modern contraception. Couples wishing to have fewer children practiced a variety of traditional methods, with coitus interruptus probably being the most common. Abortion and, in some cases, infanticide are also thought to have been practiced.[11]

In the developing world, birth and death rates remained quite high until the period following World War II.[12] In the ensuing 25 years, death rates fell quite precipitously, from levels of approximately 40 per 1000 to a low of about 12 per 1000 (Fig. 21-3). While death rates had declined rather slowly in western European nations, death rates in developing nations declined rapidly as a result

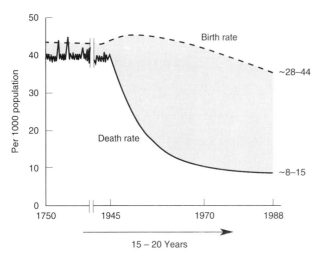

Figure 21-3. Demographic transition in the developing world. [*From Rosenfield, A., "Population Growth, Development and Health," in Rosenfield, A., and Fathalla, M. (eds.), "FIGO Manual on Human Reproduction," Park Ridge: Parthenon Press, 1990, p. 28, with permission.*]

of a variety of factors such as immunization programs (with, for example, the eradication of smallpox), improved sanitation, access to modern drugs (usually, however, through the traditional health system), better nutrition, and various other public health measures. Unfortunately, birthrate declines followed only very slowly and could not match, at least initially, the speed of the decline in mortality. However, changes are beginning to occur more rapidly in many countries as they enter the demographic transition.

Current and Projected Levels of Population Growth

Current Levels of Growth.   As of mid-1992, the world's population was estimated to be 5.5 billion people, three-quarters of the total being located in the developing world, with rates of population growth differing widely around the world.[10] The less developed, nonindustrialized nations are expanding at a much more rapid rate than are the more developed areas. Even within the developing world there are sharp contrasts in rates of population growth, with fertility rates falling rather rapidly in East Asia, somewhat more slowly in Latin America, and most slowly in South Asia (the Indian subcontinent) and sub-Saharan Africa.

Although the world growth rate in mid-1992 was 1.7%, Africa and Latin America grew at rates of 2.9 and 2.0%, respectively, while the European and North American populations increased at rates of only 0.4 and 0.7%, respectively. India's growth rate hovers at about 2.0%. The rate of population growth in China has fallen to 1.5% over the last two decades, a remarkable decline in the world's largest nation. In a few other Asian countries, such as South Korea, Taiwan, and Thailand, growth rates also have declined to relatively low levels (between 1.0 and 1.5%) during the same period of time. With varying degrees of economic development taking place in these countries, a common factor in the declines has been active national family planning program efforts.

Projected Growth. Projections of future population size have been made, based on a variety of demographic and statistical sources.[7-9] Because of uncertainties about birthrates and death rates, however, a range of projections is usually made—low, medium, and high estimates—based on different criteria. Current medium-level projections are that the world's population will reach 6 billion shortly before the year 2000, at which time the more developed nations will have about 1.3 billion inhabitants, while the less developed countries will have a population just under 5 billion.

Asia (which contains both the People's Republic of China and India, the two largest countries in the world) accounts for more than 50% of the world's population, with a total of 3.2 billion people. China's current population of over 1 billion is equal to that of the entire world some 150 years ago. By the year 2000, India will also have more than 1 billion people, and by 2025 it is estimated that both India and China will each have approximately 1.4 to 1.5 billion inhabitants.

Replacement Fertility. At a point known as replacement level, each couple has only two children, on average, thus providing exactly the number of people to replace themselves in the population. Some western industrialized countries have actually reached a point at which couples are having fewer than two children. As a result, in those countries death rates exceed birthrates, and eventually the population size will begin to decline.

Although fertility in developing countries has begun to decline, it is almost impossible for fertility in these nations to fall to replacement level by the year 2000. Even when replacement fertility has been reached, most developing countries will continue to grow for many more years because of the age structure of their populations, in which there are far more young people than old people. Thus the lowest estimate for the world's population total once replacement fertility has been reached is 8.1 billion people, although World Bank and United Nations projections suggest that the world may eventually have between 9.8 and 11.0 billion people, with the highest projection being 15 billion people, three times the current size of the world.[9,13]

Age Structure. Estimating when population stabilization will occur relates to the age structure of a population. In most developing countries, because high fertility is now coupled with rapidly declining mortality, as much as 40 to 50% of the people in these countries are children under the age of 15, compared with

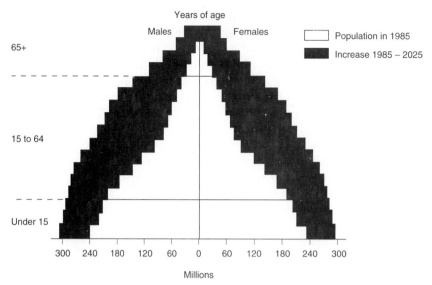

Figure 21-4. Population by age and sex, developing countries. [*From Rosenfield, A., "Population Growth, Development and Health," in Rosenfield, A., and Fathalla, M. (eds.), "FIGO Manual on Human Reproduction," Park Ridge: Parthenon Press, 1990, p. 31, with permission.*]

fewer than 25% in developed countries.[10] The age structure resembles a pyramid, with many more young people than there are older people (Fig. 21-4).

Most developed countries, in contrast, currently have both low fertility and low mortality; because of increases in the life span, there are relatively more older people, and because recent fertility levels are lower than in the past, there are relatively fewer young people. The resulting age structure is almost rectangular in appearance, with roughly equal percentages of people in each of the age cohorts (Fig. 21-5). Thus, while the size of the young adult population (those aged 20 to 39) will increase by only about 17 million in developed countries between now and the end of the century, it will grow by a staggering 600 million in the developing world. The need for jobs in these regions of the world will be expanding at an extraordinary rate during that time. What is perhaps most important to note is that these figures are not projections; rather they are based on numbers of children already born.

Momentum of Population Growth.   The age structure in most developing countries is closely related to the "momentum of population growth," in which there is a significant, continued increase in population even after replacement fertility has been attained. As the population pyramid for a typical developing country demonstrates, with far more young people than older people, the society will continue to produce more births than deaths until the pyramid, after many years, becomes more rectangular in shape, as in the Western world today.

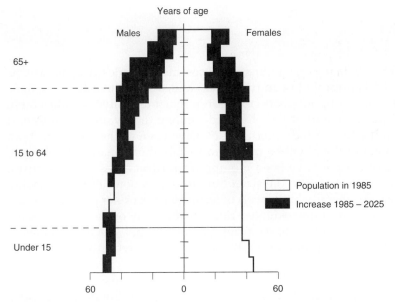

Figure 21-5. Population by age and sex, developed countries. [*From Rosenfield, A., "Population Growth, Development and Health," in Rosenfield, A., and Fathalla, M. (eds.), "FIGO Manual on Human Reproduction," Park Ridge: Parthenon Press, 1990, p. 31, with permission.*]

Even if the world achieved replacement fertility in about the year 2000, the population at that time would be approximately 6.2 billion, but it would not stabilize until a total of about 8.4 billion is reached.[14] If, on the other hand, replacement level is not reached until 2040, the world's population would stand at that time at 12 billion and would continue growing until it reached 15.5 billion. It now appears essentially impossible for the world to reach a level of replacement fertility by the year 2000; there is hope, however, that it will happen before 2040.

For some countries, however, it will take much longer than this average. Bangladesh, India, and Indonesia, for example, will need at least 125 years before the population stops growing. In Nigeria and Egypt, nearly a century will be required.

It is impossible to state categorically the optimal population size for the planet earth. Many believe that we have already passed the point at which people can be sustained with a reasonable standard of living, particularly in the poorer countries. Others argue that with modern technology, many billions more "could be" accommodated reasonably. The reality may lie somewhere between these two extremes, but exponential population growth clearly cannot continue indefinitely. There is a limit to the carrying capacity of the earth, and at some point population growth must return to a level close to zero, as has been the case throughout most of human history.

Impact of Population Growth on Development and the Environment

Urban Growth.   In many developing countries, most people (in some cases as high as 80 to 90%) currently live in rural areas and work primarily as farmers. However, with increasing numbers of children remaining alive, families often have an inadequate amount of land to divide among their various children. If the farms continue to be subdivided as they have been in the recent past, an increasing number of them will be unable to sustain their tenants. As a result, large numbers of people have been moving from rural areas into the cities, thereby adding even further to the size of urban populations already growing steadily because of generally high levels of fertility. Thus urban populations are increasing in size at an unprecedented rate, creating one of the world's most dramatic and difficult shifts, one requiring urgent action.[16] The environmental impact of this burgeoning urban growth is immense, as recently described in United Nations documents.[17,18]

In 1930, only one of the world's ten largest cities (Buenos Aires) was in a developing country. By 1950, three of the ten (Shangai, Buenos Aires, and Calcutta) were in the developing world. By the year 2000, as Fig. 21-6 shows, it is projected that 12 of the 15 largest cities of the world will be located in developing countries. In 1950, the tenth largest city, Calcutta, had 4.4 million people; in 2000, it is projected that the tenth largest city will have 16.3 million people. Most of the cities listed for the year 2000 were relatively small in 1950. Mexico City, for example, had 3 million people in 1950, but it is projected to have close to 30 million in 2000. Similarly, Jakarta had 1.6 million in 1950, but it is projected to have 16.6 million in 2000. In 1950, there was only one developing country which had a city with more than 5 million people, as compared with five such cities in the developed world. By the year 2000, however, it is estimated that

Actual population, 1950		Projected population, 2000	
City	Population (millions)	City	Population (millions)
New York	12.3	Mexico City	31.0
London	10.4	São Paulo	25.8
Rhein-Ruhr	6.9	Tokyo	24.2
Tokyo	6.7	New York	22.8
Shanghai	5.8	Shanghai	22.7
Paris	5.5	Beijing	19.9
Buenos Aires	5.3	Rio de Janeiro	19.0
Chicago	4.9	Bombay	17.1
Moscow	4.8	Calcutta	16.7
Calcutta	4.4	Jakarta	16.6

Adapted from van der Tak J, Haub C, Murphy E: Our population predicament: A new look.

Figure 21-6. The world's 10 largest urban areas—1950 (actual) and 2000 (projected).

while the developed world will have 12 cities with populations in excess of 5 million, the developing world will have over 40 such cities.

Even in the developed world, most nations have not learned to cope with the range of social problems afflicting large cities, despite having relatively affluent societies. Inner-city blight is an increasingly common problem throughout large industrialized countries, perhaps most dramatically seen in the United States. In poorer countries, there is little hope of providing adequate housing, sanitation, clean water, schools, health services, and other social services for the exploding urban populations.

The extraordinary problems resulting from the massive population shifts occurring in many developing countries are already being felt. Large slums have developed in the areas surrounding the central cities, secondary to the large influx of recent migrants from rural communities. The so-called marginal areas surrounding Mexico City provide examples of some of the most devastating poverty and squalor seen anywhere in the world. Even with these conditions, Mexico City's marginal areas continue to grow at a rapid rate, suggesting that despite its problems the city somehow seems more attractive to many people than the difficult life and lack of opportunity in the rural communities from which they emigrate.

Social and Economic Impacts.   With the decline in mortality and the ever-increasing numbers of children born and remaining alive, countries are faced with a number of problems that adversely affect the development process. Both the age structure and the rate of growth have important influences on development. In a very simple sense, 100 persons of working age in a developed country support approximately 32 children under the age of 15; in a developing country, on the other hand, 100 persons of working age may have to support as many as 90 children under the age of 15.

A significant problem in most developing countries is the provision of adequate education for the growing numbers of children. While at least 7 years of education is desirable, or even mandatory in many developing countries, a high percentage of children in fact drop out of school long before finishing an elementary education, often before reaching even the fourth grade. In these countries, considerable financial outlay is necessary to expand the number of school buildings, classrooms, and teachers just to maintain present enrollment percentages. Where there are rapidly increasing numbers of children, the possibility for expanding enrollment to make schooling available for all young people becomes much more difficult.

Impact on the Environment

Increases in the number of people significantly aggravate such problems as the declining amounts of arable land per person and deforestation (secondary to the constant search for firewood and more land for farming), which in turn leads to a loss of topsoil. These processes, together with climatic factors, are leading to an annual worldwide rate of desertification equivalent in land area to the state of Maine.[19] A recent report, entitled "The Environment and Population Growth: Decade for Action," states in its introduction:

> The signs of environmental stress grow as the world's population increases: worn-out farmlands, eroded hillsides, polluted water, parched grasslands, smoke-laden air, depleted ozone and treeless ranges. Each year about 17 million hectares of tropical forest vanish—an area the size of Tunisia or Uruguay. Fish catches are leveling off. Cities clogged with refuse. Water and air, instead of sustaining life, cause disease.

The problem is indeed a serious one. Some have suggested that the current generation is stealing from its own children.[19] We are polluting at an unprecedented rate and utilizing both renewable and nonrenewable resources. Usable agricultural land is being degraded, forests destroyed, biodiversity is being threatened and there is a misuse of fresh water supplies. We need action on a number of fronts, such as resource conservation, new economic approaches, pollution control, and a much broader family planning effort.

A U.S. government report, entitled *Global 2000*, published in 1980 suggested that rapid deterioration would take place in a number of areas of the world in the first half of the twenty-first century.[19] This report was based on the work of researchers from agencies throughout the government whose task was to assemble as much information as possible on a broad range of topics, from which projections were made of the problems that could be expected in the future. For example, the report predicted an Asian food crisis in about 2010, as the amount of land available for expanded agricultural development ran out. It also projected that non-OPEC African countries will suffer massive famine somewhere shortly after the year 2000. Unfortunately, serious famine is already being seen in many areas south of the Saharan desert.

The report also predicted that this food crisis will occur despite the advances in technology that led to the so-called Green Revolution of the late 1960s and early 1970s. The production of higher-yielding rice, wheat, and other grains was indeed a significant technological advance, but such grains require significant input of energy and use of fertilizer. The costs in developing countries even for current levels of use of oil and gas for electricity, heavy industry, automobiles, consumer goods, and a variety of other needs already are significant drains on the budgets of these countries. The energy requirements of the new agricultural technologies are simply beyond the budgetary reach of many countries. Furthermore, because of poorly developed transportation and distribution systems, many rural areas have never received the benefits of those grains and fertilizers that were affordable.

Finally, based on work done for the report by the National Academy of Sciences, it was suggested that a world population of 10 billion people is close to, if not above, the maximum that "an intensively managed world might hope to support with some degree of comfort and individual choice."[19]

An editorial on population growth some years ago in *Lancet* concluded:

> The 26 countries nearing replacement level...all are situated in the more prosperous northern half of the world and correspond roughly to what has been called the rich man's club—that minority of the human race which has access to a disproportionately large share of the resources. The situation for the remaining three quarters of the world's population is very different. The pressure of (population) increase in numbers, mainly confined to the poorer countries of the world, compounds enormously the task they face. Possibly 80 percent of the children in developing countries have some degree of malnutrition. Millions will spend their lives uneducated, unemployed, ill-housed and without access to the most elementary health, welfare, and sanitary services, and unchecked population increases is a major causal factor.[20]

Impact on Health and Mortality

While much of the interest of governments in lowering population growth rates relates to the presumed negative impact of rapidly increasing population size on various aspects of social and economic development and on the environment, decreases in current high birthrates also can have a dramatic public health impact on currently high levels of maternal, infant, and childhood (under age 5) morbidity and mortality.[21] Although mortality rates in the developing world, particularly for infants and young children, have declined in recent decades, they remain significantly higher than those in developed nations. As a result of these high rates, as many as 14 million infants and young children are estimated to die each year from preventable causes.

An important component of the current "child survival" initiatives is to increase the use of family planning for the purpose of birth spacing. The data are clear that spacing of 2 years or less between births significantly increases infant mortality rates as compared with a spacing period of greater than 2 years.[22,23] In addition to the effect of a short spacing interval on the newborn infant, there is also a negative effect on the previously born child. Estimates have been made of the potential reduction in infants' deaths if all children were born after birth intervals of 2 years or longer, with reductions in some countries of 16 to 40%.

Maternal mortality rates in the West are in the range of 7 to 15 deaths per 100,000 live births, while in developing countries the ratio ranges from 100 to over 1000 deaths per 100,000 live births.[24,25] This differential is even greater for maternal mortality than it is for infant mortality rates, and results in approximately 500,000 pregnancy-related deaths each year, a high percentage of which are preventable. Particularly tragic is the fact that, according to World Health Organization estimates, 20 to 40% of these deaths are secondary to complications of an illegal abortion.

At the ratio of 1000 per 100,000, a woman faces a 1% chance of death, and if she has ten pregnancies, her overall risk of death is nearly one in ten, a risk of death that is even higher in high-risk groups. Thus women over the course of their reproductive lifetime face a significant risk of death each time they are pregnant.

Maternal mortality ratios are highest in remote rural areas of sub-Saharan Africa and of South Asia. A woman's risk of a pregnancy-related complication is increased if she already has had four or more children and is either under age 18 or over 35. Among these high-risk women, the practice of contraception to limit childbearing can have a very important positive impact on their health.

Family Planning Programs

The response of most developing countries to both the demographic and health imperatives has been the implementation of national family planning programs. India was the first country to declare a national population policy aimed at reducing population growth rates in the late 1950s. In the 1960s and 1970s many other countries followed suit so that presently almost all of the world's larger developing countries have national population and/or family planning programs aimed at lowering population growth rates and improving the health of women and children.

Successful implementation of these programs has varied. Some countries in Asia, including China, Thailand, South Korea, Taiwan, and Indonesia have been remarkably successful in providing family planning services to increasingly large percentages of reproductive age couples.[26] Starting more recently than these Asian countries, family planning services in a number of Latin American countries have become widely available and used. Less successful have been parts of the Indian subcontinent and most of sub-Saharan Africa.

While some of the most successful programs, in which 60% or more of women aged 15 to 45 are using some method of family planning, occur in countries in which socioeconomic development efforts also have been most successful, there are impressive records of family planning acceptance in poor areas of the world in which development efforts are progressing very slowly. Perhaps the best example is in rural Bangladesh, one of the poorest countries in the world.[27,28] Despite many difficulties in making services available in this extraordinarily poor and crowded country, an effective effort in recent years has resulted in a dramatic rise in contraceptive prevalence levels (to over 30%), well above the expectation of most experts.

Over the last 20 years, there has been an impressive international effort to collect comparative demographic data from most of the developing world.[29,30] These surveys, initially called the World Fertility Survey and more recently the Demographic and Health Surveys, have demonstrated significant interest among both women and men in limiting the size of their families, with very high percentages of those women who already have four or more children already saying that they wish no more. In much of the world, over 50% of women state that they do not wish any additional children. The surveys, however, have demonstrated a much greater desire for family planning than actual use of a family planning method, with as much as 50% of married women of reproductive age in some countries stating that they want no more children but are not using a contraceptive method. A country-by-country assessment demonstrates remarkable expansion of family planning efforts but also shows how much more will be needed in the future if both the expressed wishes of women are to be met and population growth slowed.[26,31]

Over the past 2 decades there has been significant investment in population programs, with a particular emphasis on family planning programs, by the international donor community, including the World Bank, various United Nations agencies, individual developed country governments, and a number of private foundations, predominantly from the United States. In addition, increasing amounts of limited developing country government funds are being invested in these programs. Nonetheless it has been suggested that much more funding is needed over the next decades if the world is to have any hope of meeting the desired needs of developing world couples and of slowing growth rates sufficiently so that the eventual size of the world's population will be 10 billion or less, rather than close to 15 billion.[26,32] While one cannot, with assurance, state the ultimate carrying capacity of the world, the numbers of people currently being projected for the future will place major strains on the planet, with devastating impact on those already living in poverty.

The Prospects

It is certainly clear that much more investment needs to be made in broad development efforts throughout the developing world and equally clear that slowing population growth alone will not result in a solution to the multiple problems faced by the poor countries of the world. Nonetheless, among the multiple problems facing developing countries today, high rates of population growth rank among the most important. And yet only about 1% of all development expenditures currently are devoted to population and family planning program efforts. A significant increase in the allocation of resources in this area still would be only a fraction of overall efforts. But making family planning services universally accessible to all women could increase worldwide prevalence significantly, which is essential if stabilization of population growth is to occur in a reasonable period of time.

Over the past 30 years, total fertility per family has decreased from 6.0 to 3.9 today, a dramatic decline. Despite a truly significant increase in the practice of contraception during this period of time, thanks to increasing numbers of national family planning program efforts, much still remains to be done. International surveys have demonstrated that large numbers of women state that they do not wish any further children or that they wish to space the next birth and are not currently using any modern contraceptive method. Currently, of the 747 million married women of reproductive age in the developing world, 366 million are not using contraception. A sizable percentage of this number do not wish to be pregnant, at least at present. International donors currently contribute about $1 billion to family planning programs; at least a doubling of this amount is thought to be essential to meeting the unmet need for family planning.

If these advances are coupled with other development and environmental efforts, such as decreasing pollution, replanting forests, improving the status of women, expanding educational and job opportunities, and improving health, a stable population would contribute significantly to an improved life for all people.

In addition, there is an urgent need to better link groups concerned about population with those whose main concern is the environment and/or development. There is much overlap of interest and, working together, these groups should accomplish more than either can do alone. Effective linkages should be developed between the donor community, both private and public, leading to a much more coordinated development effort. Funds are needed to encourage research on the linkages between global environmental issues and population, with such research serving to help us all better understand the social and cultural context of the extraordinary challenges and embark on timely action.

References

1. Rosenfield A: "Population growth: Implications and problems." *Infectious Disease Clinics North America*, 1991, 5 (2):277–296.

2. Rosenfield A: "Population growth: Development and Health" in Rosenfield A, Fathalla M: *FIGO Manual in Human Reproduction* 1990. Parthenon Publishing Group, Park Ridge.

3. The Global 2000 Report to the President: Entering the Twenty-first Century, vol. 1, Washington DC, Government Printing Office, 1980.

4. McNamara RS: Address to the Board of Governors, World Bank. Belgrade, Yugoslavia, Washington DC, World Bank, 1979.

5. Simon JL: *The Ultimate Resource*. Princeton, NJ, Princeton University Press, 1981.

6. Berelson B: "World population: Status report, 1974." In *Reports on Population/Family Planning*. New York, Population Council, 1974.

7. United Nations: *UN Demographic Yearbook*, 1988. New York, United Nations, 1990.

8. United Nations Population Division: World Population Prospects as Assessed in 1988. New York, United Nations, 1990.

9. World Bank: *World Development Report*, 1984. New York, Oxford University Press. 1984.

10. United Nations Population Division: "World Population 1992." United Nations, New York.

11. Knodel J, van de Walle E: "Lessons from the past: Policy implications of historical fertility studies." *Popul Dev Rev* 5:217, 1979.

12. Rosenfield A: Population: A global problem. *Curr Probl Obstet Gynecol* V(6):1–39, 1982.

13. Population Crisis Committee: Report on Progress towards Population Stabilization. Washington DC, Population Crisis Committee, 1990.

14. van der Tak J, Haub C, Murphy EG: Our population predicament: A new look. *Popul Bull* 34:3–48, 1979.

15. World Bank: World Development Report, 1979. London, England, Oxford University Press, 1979.

16. United Nations Population Division: The prospects of world urbanization, revised as of 1984, populations studies no. 101. New York, United Nations, 1987.

17. Shaw RP: The impact of population growth on environment: The debate heats up. Environmental Impact Assessment Review (World Bank) 1992, 12:11–36.

18. Cruz MC, Mayer CA, Repetto R, Woodward R: *Population Growth, Poverty and Environmental Stress: Frontier Migration in the Philippines and Costa Rica*, 1992. World Resources Institute, Washington.

19. The Global 2000 Report to the President: Entering the Twenty-first Century, vol. 1. Washington DC, Government Printing Office, 1980.

20. "Zero population growth—for whom [editorial]?" *Lancet* 2:824, 1978.

21. Maine D: *Family Planning: Its Impact on the Health of Women and Children*. New York, Center for Population and Family Health, Columbia University, 1981.

22. Maine D, McNamara R: *Birth Spacing and Child Survival*. New York, Columbia University, 1985.

23. Pebley AR, Millman S: Birthspacing and child survival. *Int Fam Plann Perspect* 12(3):69, 1986.

24. Rosenfield A: Maternal mortality in developing countries. *JAMA* 262:376, 1989.

25. Rosenfield A, Maine D: Maternal mortality—A neglected tragedy. *Lancet* 2:83, 1985.

26. Potts M, Rosenfield A: The fifth freedom, revisited. *Lancet* 1990, in press.

27. Menken J, Phillips J: Population change in a rural area of Bangladesh. *Ann Am Acad Polit Sci* 510:87, 1990.

28. Phillips J, Simmons R, Koenig M, et al: Determinants of reproductive change in a traditional society. *Stud Fam Plann* 19(6):318, 1988.

29. Arnold F, Blanc AF: Fertility Levels and Trends, Demographic and Health Surveys Comparative Studies Series. Columbia, Maryland, Institute for Resource Development, 1990, in press.

30. Cleland J, Hobcraft J, Dinesen B: *Reproductive Change in Developing Countries: Insights from the World Fertility Survey*. London, England, Oxford University Press, 1985.

31. Ross JA, Rich M, Molzan JP, et al: Family Planning and Child Survival: 100 Developing Countries. New York, Center for Population and Family Health, Columbia University, 1988.

32. Population Crisis Committee: Report on Progress toward Population Stabilization. Washington DC, Population Crisis Committee, 1990.

22

Global Environmental Issues and Sustainable Resource Management*

Walter H. Corson, Ph.D.
Global Tomorrow Coalition

In this chapter:

- Global Ecology and Human Impacts on the Environment
- Strategies for Sustainable Development
- Progress Toward Sustainable Management: Case Studies
- Innovative Rural Communication System

You will find in this chapter a summary of the principles of global ecology from a systems perspective; a review of current global trends in population growth, resource use, and environmental quality; evidence that these trends cannot be maintained over the long run; and strategies for moving to a more sustainable path. The chapter summarizes the major environmental issues and presents case studies of how businesses are, and could be, responding to these issues. Also included is a model of an innovative low-cost communication system for resource and program management in developing countries.

---

*Bruce Smart of World Resources Institute reviewed this chapter. Henry Norman of Volunteers in Technical Assistance (VITA) wrote the last section "Innovative Rural Communication System."

Global Ecology and Human Impacts on the Environment

Principles of Ecology

Ecology is the study of relations between organisms—forms of life—and their living and nonliving environment. The key lesson of ecology is that organisms are directly or indirectly dependent on one another and on their nonliving environment. Because living and nonliving parts of the earth are highly interdependent, any change caused by humans in earth systems is likely to result in many effects, often unexpected and unpredictable.

Whereas the biosphere is made up of the living and dead organisms found near the earth's surface on land, in water, and in the atmosphere, the ecosphere consists of organisms and their nonliving environment. (An estimated 10 to 80 million species of animals, plants, and microorganisms inhabit the earth.) Life on earth depends on concentrated high-quality *energy* from the sun that passes through the ecosphere and then radiates back into space as degraded, dilute, low-quality heat. Organisms could not survive without the cycling of *nutrients*—chemical compounds needed to sustain life—that occurs through parts of the ecosphere in *biogeochemical cycles*. The water, carbon, oxygen, nitrogen, phosphorus, and sulfur cycles are the principal ways that nutrients pass through the ecosphere to sustain life. Human activities such as agriculture and the burning of fossil fuels are increasingly altering these cycles.

Ecosystems are communities of organisms interacting with one another and with their local environment; they can be natural (such as a marsh) or manmade (a waste-treatment pond). Natural ecosystems perform many valuable functions for humans—for example, a wetland can convert municipal waste to usable water, and a forest can absorb rainfall and prevent flooding. Major land ecosystems include forests, grasslands, and deserts; major water ecosystems include lakes, rivers, and oceans.

The principal living parts of ecosystems are classified as "producers"—primarily green plants that make nutrients by photosynthesis, "consumers"—animals that feed on living organisms, and "decomposers"—organisms that feed on wastes and the remains of dead plants and break them down into simpler compounds for reuse by green plants.

The flow of nutrients and energy in an ecosystem from producers to consumers to decomposers comprises food chains and food webs (interwoven food chains). Nutrients continually cycle through the living and nonliving parts of ecosystems as part of biogeochemical cycles. In contrast to nutrients, energy moves only one way through food chains. Most of the available energy is lost at each stage or trophic level, because each organism uses much of it in its own life processes, and because when energy is used, it is degraded to lower-quality, less-available forms. On average, only about a tenth of the energy present at each stage in a food chain is available to the next consumer (see Fig. 22-1).

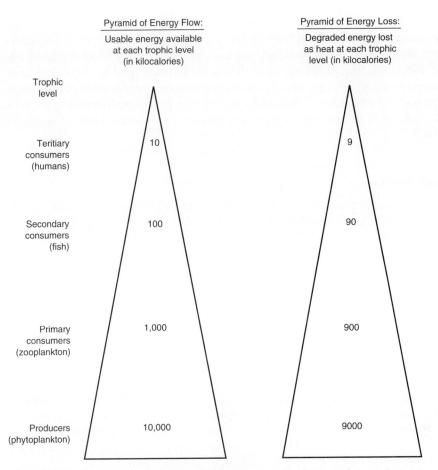

Figure 22-1. Energy pyramids. Generalized pyramids of energy flow and energy loss, showing the decrease in usable high-quality energy available at each succeeding trophic level in a food chain. (*Adapted from G. Tyler Miller, "Living in the Environment: An Introduction to Environmental Science," 6th edition, Belmont, California: Wadsworth, 1990, p. 89.*)

Energy Efficiency

Many devices can produce work by converting energy from one form to another, such as a motor that uses the higher-quality potential energy in a liquid fuel to produce lower-quality mechanical or kinetic energy to propel a vehicle. Such energy conversion devices and processes differ in their energy efficiency, or the percentage of energy input that performs useful work—such as moving a vehicle—relative to the total energy input. Less energy is wasted by making motors, appliances, and other energy-conversion devices as efficient as possible, and by not using higher-quality energy (such as electricity generated with high-temperature steam) to carry out tasks that can be done with lower-quality energy (such as space heating that can be accomplished with low-temperature waste heat). We can also improve the efficiency of energy use by sealing and insulating buildings to slow the loss of low-quality degraded heat to the environment. Because energy use is depleting nonrenewable energy supplies such as oil and natural gas and causing environmental damage, we will soon have to shift to nonpolluting, renewable energy sources such as sunlight and wind.

The Earth's Energy System

Each year the earth receives about 178,000 terawatts (10^{12} watts) of solar radiation from the sun, or about 15,000 times the world's current energy use. Of this amount, 30% is immediately reflected into space, and 50% is absorbed by the earth, changed to heat, and reradiated. The remaining 20% creates the movement of air in the atmosphere, evaporates water, generates climate, causes the circulation of ocean waters, and powers photosynthesis by which plants produce carbohydrates from carbon dioxide and water. Without solar energy, life on earth as we know it could not exist.

Solar energy consists of radiation that forms a continuous electromagnetic spectrum, ranging from long, low-frequency radio waves of low-energy radiation through standard and short-wave radio waves, microwaves, infrared radiation (heat), the visible light spectrum, ultraviolet radiation, x-rays, and finally gamma rays with the highest frequency and energy level. Much of the harmful radiation, such as ultraviolet radiation and x-rays, is filtered out by the atmosphere. The stratospheric ozone layer absorbs most of the ultraviolet radiation, which can harm all forms of life. The small amount of ultraviolet radiation that does penetrate the ozone layer can cause sunburn and skin cancer.

The earth's energy balance is affected by the composition of the atmosphere. Some gases in the atmosphere—including water vapor, carbon dioxide, and methane—absorb more infrared radiation from the earth's surface than other gases. As the amounts of atmospheric carbon dioxide and other heat-trapping "greenhouse" gases increase as a result of human activities, the earth's surface and lower atmosphere become warmer. Any major changes in the earth's atmosphere or surface, or in the abundance and distribution of life on earth, will affect the absorption and reflection of heat and light. Such changes could alter the earth's heat balance and change its temperature and climate.

Atmosphere and Climate

The *atmosphere* surrounding the earth consists mostly of nitrogen (78%), oxygen (21%), argon (0.9%), and carbon dioxide (0.03%). The water vapor content of the atmosphere varies from zero to about 4%; also present are small amounts of other compounds including methane, ozone, hydrogen sulfide, carbon monoxide, oxides of nitrogen and sulfur, and hydrocarbons.

The *climate* of a particular region is determined in part by its latitude (distance north or south from the equator) and its relation to land masses and oceans. Climate is defined by a region's characteristic atmospheric conditions in various seasons, such as temperature, precipitation and moisture, and wind. Characteristic climate types include tropical, subtropical, continental, desert, subarctic, and arctic; within these types, variations in moisture produce subtypes such as moist and dry tropical. The nature and variability of a region's climate strongly influence the kinds of organisms that live there; for example, a moist tropical climate is likely to produce copious vegetation and rich biological diversity.

Over the past several million years, the earth's climate has changed many times. Climate changes range in scope from local to global, and in duration from a few years to a few million years. More than two-thirds of the earth's surface is water, and oceans have a major effect on climate. Short-term oscillations in ocean currents and temperatures have caused regional changes in temperature and precipitation lasting for several years, while longer-term changes in global temperatures lasting hundreds or thousands of years have produced cooling and warming trends accompanied by the advance and retreat of glaciers and polar ice caps. Since about 1750, global temperatures have risen steadily, except for a moderate cooling trend between 1940 and the late 1970s. (The rise over the last 100 years has been about 0.5°C, which may be within the range of natural variation.)

Many factors have been considered as causes of climatic variation in the past, including irregularities in the earth's orbit, changes in the earth's inclination toward the sun, variations in solar radiation, and changes in the composition of the atmosphere. Most climatologists believe that the increase in atmospheric concentrations of heat-trapping "greenhouse" gases that began around 1750 with the increasing use of fossil fuels during the Industrial Revolution will eventually cause a global warming. In addition to carbon dioxide, other major greenhouse gases produced by human activity are methane, ozone, nitrous oxide, and chlorofluorocarbons (Table 22-1).

Table 22-1. Contributions to Global Warming

Activity	Greenhouse gas					Percent warming by activity
	Carbon dioxide	Methane	Ozone	Nitrous oxide	Chloro-fluorocarbons	
Energy use	35	4	6	4	x	49
Deforestation	10	4	x	x	x	14
Agriculture	3	8	x	2	x	13
Industry	2	x	2	x	20	24
Percent warming by gas	50	16	8	6	20	100

SOURCE: World Resources Institute, *World Resources 1990–91* (New York: Oxford University Press, 1990), p. 24.
x = contribution small or not known.

The data show that carbon dioxide and energy use each accounts for about half of global warming. Some scientists maintain that the 0.5°C increase in global temperatures that has occurred since 1890 is evidence that emissions of carbon dioxide and other heat-absorbing gases are already warming the earth through the "greenhouse" effect.

Properties of Systems

In the ecosphere, a variety of different systems can be identified. A system has a number of parts or components that function together and behave as a whole, with identifiable inputs and outputs. Examples of systems include a single organism, a pond, a waste-treatment plant, a nation's economy, the earth's atmosphere, and the ecosphere.

A system may be open in regard to some factor that it exchanges with other systems, or closed in relation to a factor not exchanged with other systems. For example, the earth is an open system with respect to solar energy, which it receives from the sun and radiates back into space; but earth is essentially a closed system with respect to minerals. Systems respond to inputs and produce outputs or responses.

When a system's output also serves as an input that leads to changes in the system, it is called feedback. If the system's response reinforces the output, the feedback is "positive"; if the response is in the opposite direction to the output, the feedback is "negative." Global warming could cause both positive and negative feedback. Rising temperatures could produce thin high clouds that reflect heat back to the earth's surface, tending to warm it—an example of positive feedback. However, higher temperatures could also create thick lower-level clouds that block incoming solar heat, tending to cool the earth's surface—a case of negative feedback. Negative feedback is generally desirable because it stabilizes a system and keeps it in a steady-state condition. Positive feedback, sometimes called a "vicious circle," is destabilizing in this context.

These examples of possible positive and negative feedbacks affecting the atmospheric system illustrate an important aspect of complex systems: Elements of a system are highly interdependent, and it is very difficult, if not impossible, to predict all or even most of the effects of a change in one aspect of the system. Even small changes in one part of a system will often cause secondary and tertiary effects within the system—for example, higher global temperatures would be very likely to change rainfall patterns and crop yields. And changes in one system are likely to affect other related systems—for example, higher temperatures would alter temperature-dependent ecosystems. Computer models of the global climate system indicate that as concentrations of greenhouse gases in the atmosphere increase, rainfall patterns will shift, causing wetter conditions in some areas and drier conditions in others.

In summary, the earth and its ecosystems are extremely complex entities in which even minor change may cause many effects that are extremely difficult to predict. It would be very hard to forecast in any detail how global warming would affect regional rainfall patterns or populations of individual plant and animal species, but it is certain that substantial warming would cause many significant changes.

Exponential Growth of Human Activity

An important example of positive feedback is represented by the exponential growth of some aspect of a system, such as the population of a species or the consumption of a resource. In exponential growth, the increase occurs at a constant rate or percentage of the current amount, such as a 2% annual growth in human population. For growth rates up to about 10%, the doubling time is roughly equal to the number 70 divided by the growth rate in percent. Thus a population that continues to grow at 2% a year will double in 35 years; at 3% annual growth it will double in only 23 years. Currently, the world's human population of 5.5 billion is growing at 1.8% a year; if that rate continued, total population would exceed 10 billion in less than 40 years. Not only the population but also the growth of many aspects of human activity has increased greatly since the Industrial Revolution, and especially since the mid-twentieth century (Table 22-2).

The environmental impact of human activity is largely the product of three quantities: the number of people, the amounts of resources each person uses, and the environmental pollution and degradation caused by that resource use (Ehrlich and Ehrlich, 1990). Estimates of how much these three quantities grew between 1950 and 1990 follow:

Growth factor for world population = 2.1

Growth factor for the number of units of resources used per person (the increase per person calculated as the average growth in the use of wood, water, food, energy, metals, and chemicals) = 5.8 divided by 2.1 = 2.8

Very rough estimate of the growth factor for pollution and other environmental impacts per unit of resource used (based on the average of estimated changes in environmental impacts worldwide resulting from changes in the production and use of wood, water, food, energy, metals, and chemicals) = 1.1

Increase in environmental impact = 2.1 × 2.8 × 1.1 = 6.5

These rough estimates suggest that there could have been a sixfold increase in the overall environmental impact of human activity on the global environment over the 40-year period. The United states, with less than 5% of world population, uses roughly 20% of the earth's resources and accounts for about a quarter of many pollutants.

Earth Cycles and Human Impacts

Since the earth was formed, materials in its crust have been undergoing continuous change, including the creation and breakdown of minerals and rock for-

Table 22-2. Global Growth of Human Activity, 1950–1990

Activity	1950	1990	Growth factor
Human population, billions	2.6	5.3	2.1
Domestic livestock population, billions	2.3	4.1	1.8
Wood production, billion cubic meters	1.5	3.5	2.4
Water consumption, thousand cubic kilometers	1.4	3.8	2.7
Grain production, million tons	631	1780	2.8
Domestic fowl production, billions	3.0	10.9	3.6
Carbon emissions from fossil fuels, billion tons	1.6	5.8	3.6
Meat production, million tons	46	171	3.7
Fish catch, million tons	22	97	4.4
Gross world product, trillion 1987 U.S. dollars	3.8	18.8	4.9
Energy use, billion tons of coal equivalent	2.4	11.9	5.0
Metal consumption, billion tons	0.45	2.55	5.7
Soybean production, million tons	18	104	5.8
Industrial production index, 1963 = 100	45	310	6.9
Registered motor vehicles, millions	67	486	8.8
Fertilizer use, million tons	14	138	9.9
Aluminum production, million tons	1.7	18.1	10.6

SOURCES: Brown, Flavin, and Kane, 1992; Meadows, Meadows, and Randers, 1992; Food and Agriculture Organization; Population Reference Bureau; World Resources Institute; Worldwatch Institute.

mations. These processes are collectively known as earth cycles, and include the tectonic cycle, the rock cycle, the hydrologic or water cycle, and the biogeochemical cycles. The time required for material to move through these cycles varies greatly—from as little as a few hours for the water cycle to less than a year to decades for some of the biogeochemical cycles, up to millions of years for the rock cycle and tens or hundreds of millions of years for the tectonic cycle.

The Biogeochemical Cycles. Elements and chemicals required as nutrients for life on earth are continuously recycled through the ecosphere and changed from one form to another by a combination of biological, geological, and chemical processes. These biogeochemical cycles are driven directly or indirectly by energy from the sun, and include six elements that form the major building blocks of living matter: carbon, hydrogen, oxygen, nitrogen, phosphorus, and sulfur. These elements make up about 95% of the mass of all living matter on earth. Human activity has significantly altered the cycling of these elements, especially the cycling of carbon, nitrogen, and sulfur. Some of the major impacts of human activity on the earth's basic cycles and systems are summarized in Tables 22-3 and 22-4. The data show that energy use, agriculture, and industrial manufacturing all have important impacts on the earth's basic life-support systems and cycles.

Human Impacts and Ecological Thresholds

Human impacts on the land, water, air, forests, and other natural resources and ecosystems that support life on earth are causing changes in the earth's physical condition that are to varying degrees irreversible—that is, causing permanent or long-term loss of resources, or long-term alteration of ecosystems. Among such changes are:

   Destruction of tropical forests and other habitats

   Loss of plant and animal species

   Conversion of fertile land to desert

   Erosion of topsoil

   Depletion and contamination of groundwater

   Depletion of some energy and mineral resources

   Buildup of atmospheric carbon dioxide and other greenhouse gases

   Depletion of the stratospheric ozone layer

In many cases, such changes appear to be pushing resources and systems over thresholds beyond which they cannot absorb such impacts without permanent damage. Some of the major changes are summarized below.

Changes in the Earth's Physical Condition*

Forest Cover.   Nearly half of the world's original expanse of biologically rich tropical forests has been cleared for timber, agriculture, and development. Tropical forests are shrinking by about 17 million hectares (42 million acres) per year, an area the size of Missouri. Some 31 million hectares of temperate-zone forest in industrial countries have been damaged, apparently by air pollution.

Oceans.   Pollution of ocean and coastal waters by oil, industrial and municipal wastes, agricultural runoff, and acid precipitation is harming marine life in many regions. Mangroves, coral reefs, estuaries, and other biologically rich marine ecosystems are being damaged by pollution and coastal development.

*SOURCES: Worldwatch Institute, World Resources Institute, and Global Tomorrow Coalition.

Table 22-3. Summary of Major Human Impacts on Earth Cycles

Human activity	Impacts
Carbon cycle:	
Burning of fossil fuels and biomass, destruction of forests and other vegetation, manufacture of cement, production of food and livestock, release of chlorofluorocarbons	Since 1890, atmospheric CO_2 has risen about 20% and atmospheric CH_4 nearly 80%; increased atmospheric concentrations of heat-trapping carbon compounds may already have begun to raise global temperatures
Oxygen cycle:	
Burning of oxygen-consuming fuels and destruction of oxygen-producing plants	Could significantly reduce oxygen content of the atmosphere over the long term
Increased levels of carbon dioxide in the atmosphere, and nitrates and phosphates in the oceans	Could significantly reduce dissolved oxygen in the oceans and harm marine life
Emissions of chlorine and bromine compounds from industry and biomass burning	Alteration of oxygen-ozone balance and depletion of stratospheric ozone layer
Nitrogen cycle:	
Burning of fuels and industrial processes release 3–5 times as much nitrogen as soil bacteria convert to ammonia	Airborne nitrogen oxides form acids can damage vegetation and aquatic ecosystems
Extraction of nitrogen from the air to make fertilizers, production of food crops and livestock, discharge of municipal sewage	Agriculture depletes soil nitrogen; waterborne nitrates from fertilizers, livestock wastes, and sewage contaminate groundwater and disrupt aquatic ecosystems, causing growth of algae, oxygen depletion, and fish kills
Phosphorus cycle:	
Production of food crops and livestock, and use of phosphates in detergents and other products release 5–8 times the amount of phosphorus released naturally	Agriculture depletes soil phosphorus; waterborne phosphates from fertilizers and detergents disrupt aquatic ecosystems, causing growth of algae, oxygen depletion, and fish kills
Sulfur cycle:	
Burning of fossil fuels to produce electricity, and industrial processes such as oil refining and ore smelters release as much sulfur as amounts released naturally	Airborne sulfur oxides form acids, damage vegetation and aquatic ecosystems, and may alter the earth's heat balance
Biologic cycle:	
Cutting of forests and clearing of land for timber, firewood, agriculture, livestock, and human settlements; degradation of fertile land to less fertile dryland and desert; emission of toxic substances	Degradation and loss of habitats cause extinction of at least 140 plant and animal species a day; removal of vegetation causes loss of fertile soil through water and wind erosion, and releases billions of tons of CO_2 to the atmosphere each year; humans appropriate about 25% of the earth's net primary biological productivity

Table 22-3. Summary of Major Human Impacts on Earth Cycles (*Continued*)

Human activity	Impacts
Hydrologic cycle:	
Clearing of land for timber, firewood, agriculture, and human settlements; overgrazing of land by livestock	Increased surface water runoff reduces water retained by the land for evaporation to the air and for recharge of underground water supplies
Withdrawal of surface and underground water for agriculture, industry, and cities	Depletion of surface and underground water supplies in many areas
Discharge of wastes from agriculture, cities, mining, and other industries	Pollution of surface and underground water supplies in many areas

Table 22-4. Summary of Major Human Impacts on Earth Systems

Human activity	Impacts
Atmospheric system:	
Energy use	Accounts for about 49% of global warming; is a major source of acid precipitation
Deforestation	Accounts for about 14% of global warming; contributes to acid precipitation
Agriculture	Accounts for about 13% of global warming
Industry/mining	Accounts for most of stratospheric ozone depletion and about 25% of global warming; sulfur oxides from ore smelting account for a significant amount of acid precipitation
Energy system:	
Energy use, deforestation, agriculture, and industry	Increase in atmospheric concentrations of heat-trapping gases may already have begun to raise global temperatures
Loss of vegetation through deforestation, desertification, and development	Decrease in solar energy absorbed by vegetation; increase in energy reflected back to the atmosphere

Ocean Fisheries.   Yields from a number of the world's major ocean fisheries have leveled off or are falling, and some have collapsed because of overfishing. Many fish species are declining as overfishing becomes chronic in most of the world's seas.

Species Diversity.   Habitat destruction for agriculture and development, especially in the tropics, is causing the extinction of at least 140 species of plants and animals each day, hundreds of thousands of species will disappear over the next 10 years.

Grasslands.   Millions of acres of the world's grasslands have been over-grazed by livestock; some, especially in Africa and the Middle East, have become desert. Almost two-thirds of U.S. rangeland is in poor to fair condition.

Topsoil.   An estimated 25 billion tons are lost annually from cropland; some 77 billion tons are lost each year from all land areas by water erosion. Since 1945, about 11% of the earth's vegetated soils have been seriously degraded.

Fresh Water.   Underground water tables are falling in parts of Africa, China, India, and North America as demand for water, especially for agriculture, rises above aquifer recharge rates. In the United States, one-fourth of the groundwater withdrawn each year is not replenished.

Groundwater Quality.   In industrial nations, groundwater supplies are threatened by pesticides and nitrates from agriculture, by leaking underground storage tanks for gasoline and other chemicals, and by many thousands of industrial and municipal waste-disposal sites, including thousands of toxic waste dumps. More than 50 pesticides contaminate groundwater in 39 American states.

Wetlands.   Between 25 and 50% of the world's coastal and inland wetlands have been drained, built upon, or seriously polluted.

Lakes.   Thousands of lakes in the industrial north have been acidified by air pollution and acid rain and are now nearly biologically dead; thousands more are dying.

Atmosphere.   Air pollution threatens health in hundreds of cities; emissions of sulfur and nitrogen compounds are altering the earth's basic sulfur and nitrogen cycles.

Climate.   Emissions of carbon dioxide, methane, chlorofluorocarbons, and other heat-absorbing gases are altering the earth's carbon cycle and may be responsible for a rise in global temperatures of about 0.5°C (nearly 1°F) over the last 100 years. Six of the seven warmest years in over a century occurred in the 1980s, and 1990 was the warmest year on record. Mean temperature is projected to rise another 1.5 to 4.5°C between now and 2050 and is expected to disrupt global weather patterns. Rising ocean temperatures are already melting arctic ice packs and harming coral reefs in the tropics.

Sea Level.   Over the last 100 years, warmer temperatures and melting ice have caused sea levels to rise about 0.3 meter in some areas; they are projected to rise between 1.4 and 2.2 meters and threaten many coastal communities by 2100.

Ozone Layer in the Upper Atmosphere.   Emissions of ozone-destroying gases have depleted the earth's protective ozone layer by more than 3% worldwide; depletion has reached 50% during the spring over Antarctica. Each 1% drop increases harmful ultraviolet radiation by 2%, and elevated radiation levels have been detected at several locations in the Southern Hemisphere. This radiation poses a serious threat to life on earth.

Primary Causes of Human Impacts

Changes in the earth's physical condition resulting from human activity can be grouped into four categories of human impact:

1. Loss of habitats and species

2. Degradation of land and soil

3. Depletion of nonrenewable energy, mineral, and water resources

4. Pollution of water and air

Among the primary causes of these human impacts are:

1. Unsustainable population growth

2. Unsustainable agriculture, energy use, and industrial production

3. Poverty and inequalities (that is, unequal access to factors such as food, shelter, land, health care, education, employment, and political power)

"Unsustainable" means that these activities diminish the earth's long-term capacity to support life, or endanger natural ecosystems that support life. There is evidence that unsustainable population growth is the single most important causal factor for all four categories of human impact listed above. Analysis suggests that unsustainable food production may be the next important cause for all impacts, followed by unsustainable energy use, unsustainable industrial production, and poverty and inequalities. Population growth exacerbates the impacts of all the other causal factors. Growth of affluent populations with high levels of consumption is an especially important cause of air and water pollution, and depletion of nonrenewable energy, minerals, and fresh water (Corson, 1990).

Summary*

There is persuasive evidence that human impacts are beginning to alter the energy and atmospheric systems, are affecting the basic biogeochemical cycles, and are causing significant harm to important parts of the hydrologic and biologic cycles. Continued emissions of heat-absorbing and ozone-depleting gases

*Primary sources for the material in this section are Botkin and Keller, 1987; Miller, 1990; and Corson, 1990. Additional sources include Brown and Postel, 1987; Ehrlich and Ehrlich, 1990; Meadows and others, 1992; and Vitousek and others, 1986.

could destabilize the climate system and endanger living organisms. Analysis suggests that unsustainable population growth and food production, along with unsustainable energy use and industrial production, as well as poverty, are all important causes of these impacts.

Strategies for Sustainable Development

The term *sustainable development* covers a variety of strategies for ensuring the future habitability of the earth. It includes the concept of meeting the needs of today's population without compromising the ability of future generations to meet their needs and without endangering the atmosphere, water, soil, and ecosystems that support life on earth. Sustainable development can also mean the management of financial, natural, and human assets to increase long-term wealth and well-being, as well as a way of living on the earth's income instead of depleting its natural capital. (World Commission on Environment and Development, 1987.)

Many ecologists, systems analysts, and others feel that if current trends in population growth, resource use, and environmental degradation continue, they will cause serious and irreversible damage to the earth's critical life-support systems and will undercut prospects for improving human welfare or even maintaining current levels of economic well-being, ultimately threatening the survival of human civilization. For example, the authors of *Beyond the Limits* conclude that unless population growth, resource consumption, and pollution are scaled back, the world's economy will suffer serious consequences within a few decades (Meadows et al., 1992). (See also Ehrlich and Ehrlich, 1990; and Gore, 1992.) On the other hand, many economists and business leaders believe that limiting growth is not the way to overcome poverty or correct environmental problems. Lawrence Summers, chief economist at the World Bank, maintains that continued economic growth is essential for solving environmental problems in developing countries, and the Business Council for Sustainable Development, an international body consisting of 48 corporate heads, believes that economic incentives will work better than curbs on growth to protect the environment (Ember, 1992; Schmidheiny, 1992).

A growing number of analysts are working to bridge the gap between ecological and economic approaches to the problems of resource depletion and environmental degradation. Members of the recently formed International Society for Ecological Economics are developing ways to estimate the monetary value of human and natural resources, and the costs of harm to those resources. By seeking to estimate the "true" or "full" costs of pollution and resource depletion, this approach provides a rationale for passing these costs on to producers and consumers, thus "internalizing externalities" and encouraging more sustainable ways of producing goods and services. (See, for example, Costanza, 1991; Daly, 1991, Daly and Cobb, 1989; Repetto, 1990.)

As the costs of resource degradation become known, societies can create economic and other incentives to lessen the damage to resources and can develop the means to move governments, businesses, and individuals toward sustainable paths of economic and social progress. Business firms, as the world's foremost creators of wealth, technology, and employment, have a unique opportunity and a special responsibility to use their vast human and financial resources to help make the transitions necessary to achieve sustainable development (Schmidheiny, 1992; International Chamber of Commerce, 1989).

Business leaders are coming to recognize the close links between economic growth and environmental quality, and there is growing evidence that innovative business firms can combine growth and environmental protection in ecologically sustainable modes of economic development. Many companies have already demonstrated that environmental protection can be good for business as well as beneficial for society generally. (See, for example, Council on Economic Priorities, 1991; Smart, 1992.)

Needed Transitions to Sustainable Societies

Many studies have considered the kinds of changes necessary to reverse current trends and shift to a course of sustainable economic and social development that would meet present needs without jeopardizing the well-being of future generations. (For example, see Brown and others, 1991; Milbrath, 1989; Schmidheiny, 1992; Speth, 1990; and World Commission on Environment and Development, 1987.) These changes include a wide range of economic, technological, social, political, institutional, and ethical factors and, if made, would represent a major paradigm shift—a change in the dominant beliefs, ideas, and values underlying behavior and public policy.

The current dominant social paradigm is largely based on the assumptions of neoclassical economics: The free market will maximize social welfare, and there are unlimited supplies of natural resources and "sinks" for disposing of the wastes resulting from resource use (Porter and Brown, 1991). Beginning in the 1960s with events such as the publication of Rachel Carson's *Silent Spring* (1962), the dominant paradigm has been questioned as public concern about air and water pollution has grown. During the 1970s and 1980s the assumptions of "frontier economics" were increasingly challenged, and by the late 1980s the concept of sustainable development had emerged as the basis of an alternative paradigm (World Commission on Environment and Development, 1987; Porter and Brown, 1991).

A real transition to sustainable development will involve much more than environmental protection and will require basic changes in economic, social, and political systems. Among the needed changes are a transition to economies that encourage sustainable enterprise and discourage harmful activity, and a shift to efficient, environmentally benign technologies for energy use, transportation, and food production. Population size must become compatible with resource and environmental constraints, and lifestyles should stress quality rather than quantity of consumption.

In addition to these changes, a broad range of shifts in other areas will be needed to move societies to a sustainable path. These include transitions in social organization, governance, information management, education, and ethics and world views. More emphasis will be needed on living in harmony with nature, respecting other forms of life, and protecting natural resources for future generations.

Sustainable Development Accounting

Ecologists, economists, and others are developing a broad range of innovative economic practices to help lessen environmental degradation and make the production of goods and services more sustainable. These include the use of environmental indicators, full-cost accounting, economic incentives, life cycle analysis, environmental auditing, and forums to facilitate progress toward sustainable development.

Natural resources such as forests, soil, fresh water, and wildlife clearly have economic value and are essential for economic development and for human survival. They are economic assets because they can generate future income. Yet under current national income accounting procedures, natural resources are not valued as productive assets and depreciated over time as are assets such as buildings and equipment. National budgets and other annual audits rarely consider the depletion of natural resources. The standard national income accounting system used by all market economies for economic analysis and planning fails to distinguish between the creation of income and the destruction of natural resource assets.

This gross discrepancy between how we measure economic activity and how we appraise the use of natural resources that ultimately sustain the economy often results in a distorted view of economic health and sends misleading signals to policymakers. Ironically, when we destroy forests, deplete the fertility of croplands, and pollute air and water, income as measured by the gross national product shows an increase. The absence of natural resource accounting supports and appears to validate the notion that rapid economic growth can be realized and sustained by exploiting natural resources; the result is deceptive temporary gains in current income at the expense of permanent losses in economic wealth. In short, we fail to view our natural resources and environment as productive capital, even though we use them as such, and we are rapidly consuming our natural resource capital instead of living within the income derived from it. (See Daly and Cobb, 1989; Pearce and Turner, 1990; and Repetto, 1989.)

Sustainable Development Indicators

Social, economic, and natural resource indicators can include both monetary and nonmonetary measures, and generally fall into three types:

1. Monetary measures such as income or revenue from the sale of goods or natural resources, and expenditures for raw materials or pollution control

2. Nonmonetary measures of quantities such as life expectancy, rate of unemployment, and concentration of air pollutants

3. Nonmonetary estimates of variables such as adequacy of transportation services, effectiveness of waste treatment, and frequency of disease caused by air pollution, often ranked on a scale of 1 to 5 or 1 to 10

Some aspects of indicators in 2 and 3 can be monetized, for example, costs attributable to pollution-caused disease, or costs related to time and energy wasted in traffic congestion.

Examples of social and human resource indicators include population size, density, and growth rate; infant mortality; and life expectancy.

Examples of economic indicators include average income per person, rate of unemployment or inflation, energy consumption per unit of economic output, and budgetary surplus or deficit.

Examples of natural resource indicators include air and water quality, area of fertile land or forest cover, number and populations of plant and animal species, and releases of toxic substances.

Internalizing External Costs

Sustainable development accounting (SDA) offers an alternative to standard accounting procedures that measure only the value of goods and services produced and the direct costs of raw materials, labor, and other inputs that are traditionally contained in financial statements and included in statistics such as the gross national product or gross domestic product. To augment these quantities, SDA attempts to account for indirect costs and benefits that affect human welfare and the natural resources on which all human and economic activities ultimately depend. SDA "internalizes" or includes factors such as the cost of harm to people and natural ecosystems caused by air and water pollution, and the value of lost or damaged natural resources such as forests, wetlands, fertile cropland, and groundwater—quantities traditionally ignored or considered as "external" costs and not included in conventional accounting systems.

Economic Incentives

Sustainable development accounting provides a basis for developing a range of positive and negative incentives that can help reduce, prevent, or correct social and environmental damage, and encourage sustainable resource use. Negative incentives include taxes, surcharges, price increases, user fees, deposits, regulations, transferable rights and permits, and fines and other penalties designed to discourage harmful activity and cover the costs resulting from it. Positive incentives include tax credits or reductions, refunds, rebates, subsidies, price reductions, improved technologies, research and development support, and other positive inducements and innovations designed to encourage less harmful or benign activity. By shifting the tax burden from individual and corporate income taxes to activities that degrade natural resources and the environment, productive enterprise can be encouraged and harmful activities discouraged. In summary, by making prices and incentives compatible with long-term sustainability, people and organizations receive meaningful inducements to protect the earth's life-support systems.

Indicators for Business Firms

A variety of indicators can help business firms determine the full economic, social, and environmental costs of their activities and help them develop sustainable policies.

- Financial balance sheet indicators: income and expenditures, profit and loss, assets and liabilities

- Productivity indicators: output per employee, output per production unit

- Contributions to human welfare per unit of output

- Harm to human welfare from goods and services not accounted for by other indicators (for example, harm to human health from unsafe products)

- Record of compliance with health and safety standards for workers and the local public

- Record of compliance with environmental regulations

- Energy and raw material consumption per unit of product

- Air, water, and land pollution per unit of product (for example, emissions of carbon dioxide, sulfur and nitrogen oxides, toxic chemicals, and heavy metals, expressed as pounds of waste per pound of product)

- Depletion and degradation of natural resources per unit of product (for example, fossil fuels, other minerals, topsoil, timber, groundwater, wetlands, and other natural habitats)

Life Cycle Analysis

Life cycle analysis (LCA) is an accounting method that allows comparison of resource requirements and environmental impacts for different product options. (See also Chap. 14.) A complete LCA includes three parts:

- An inventory of resource requirements and environmental emissions at each stage of the product's life cycle, including raw material procurement, manufacturing, distribution, use, disposal, and possible reuse

- Assessment of the environmental impacts of resource use and emissions

■ Assessment of opportunities for improvement in each stage of the life cycle

Life cycle analyses provide a means for resolving the complex environmental issues associated with every product. Procter & Gamble has used LCA widely, for example, to evaluate the relative merits of disposable diapers and cloth diapers, and to compare different packaging options.

Environmental Auditing

The U.S. Environmental Protection Agency has defined environmental auditing as "a systematic, documented, periodic and objective review by regulated entities of facility operations and practices related to meeting environmental requirements." Environmental auditing can include not only efforts to prevent pollution of air, land, and water but also monitoring of health and safety standards for workers and the local public. The auditing helps companies avoid compliance violations, and reveals less expensive ways to comply with environmental regulations. The audits can lead to cost cuts through waste reduction and avoidance of expensive mistakes.

Facilitating Progress toward Sustainability

Many changes will be necessary to move societies toward the sustainable use of global resources. In addition to innovations such as natural resource accounting, new economic incentives, and environmental auditing, many changes must occur in all aspects of societies—from how we produce goods and services to how we view our place in nature and the needs of future generations. The details of needed changes and the strategies for achieving them should be discussed as part of a public dialogue. The dialogue should involve all sectors of society—community groups, labor, business, public and private agencies, the media, and educational, religious, ethnic, and minority organizations. Concepts and ideas related to sustainability must be discussed and debated in order to arrive at a consensus on what actions and policies are necessary.

The Business Role

Business firms should extend their traditional concern with minimizing costs to the social and environmental costs attributable to their products. Companies can begin to keep environmental accounts and include in product prices the costs they incur for pollution control, waste disposal, and resource depletion. Such procedures can help give firms economic incentives to use less energy and other resources per unit of production, and will help ensure that the social and environmental costs of their products are borne by current consumers rather than future generations. The next section contains a number of examples of how companies are working to promote sustainable development.

A Checklist for Companies

To help take advantage of the opportunities in environmental protection, Frances Cairncross, environment editor for *The Economist*, has drawn up this list of suggestions for company management:

- Put the most senior person possible in charge of environmental policy.
- Draft an environmental policy; then make it public.
- Measure the amount of wastes you are creating and what energy you are using.
- Institute a regular environmental audit to check on what is happening.
- Consider ways to reduce the range of materials you use that could do environmental harm.
- Try to make a business opportunity out of disposing of your product when the customer has finished with it.
- Accept that environmental regulations will tend to increase; accept the highest standards before they become compulsory (Cairncross, 1992).

Other important factors for company management to consider include:

- Public commitment to environmental protection by the company's chief executive officer.
- Responsibility for environmental concerns by line managers.
- The need to set quantitative, timed environmental goals and to measure and report progress.
- The need to consider the benefits from cooperation among businesses, environmentalists, and governments (Bruce Smart, personal communication).

Guidelines for Environmental Responsibility

Following the *Exxon Valdez* oil spill in 1989, a coalition of environmental organizations and investment groups formed Project CERES (Coalition for Environmentally Responsible Economies) and developed guidelines for a code of conduct that business firms could follow to show their commitment to environmental responsibility. These guidelines are known as the "Valdez Principles"; they include several important prerequisites for sustainable development, but some of the principles are considered too extreme for most businesses to accept:

1. Protection of the biosphere: Minimize the release of pollutants that may cause environmental damage.

2. Sustainable use of natural resources: Conserve nonrenewable natural resources through efficient use and careful planning.

3. Reduction and disposal of wastes: Minimize the creation of waste, especially hazardous waste, and dispose of such materials in a safe, responsible manner.

4. Wise use of energy: Make every effort to use environmentally safe and sustainable energy sources to meet operating requirements.

5. Risk reduction: Diminish environmental, health, and safety risks to employees and surrounding communities.

6. Marketing of safe products and services: Sell products that minimize environmental impact and that are safe for consumers.

7. Damage compensation: Accept responsibility for any harm the company causes to the environment; conduct bioremediation, and compensate affected parties.

8. Disclosure: Public dissemination of information on incidents relating to operations that harm the environment or pose health or safety hazards.

9. Environmental directors and managers: Appoint at least one board member who is qualified to represent environmental interests.

10. Assessment and annual audit: Produce and publicize each year a self-evaluation of progress toward implementing the principles and meeting all applicable laws and regulations worldwide. Environmental audits will also be produced annually and distributed to the public.

SOURCE: The 1990 CERES Guide to the Valdez Principles, as published in Henderson, 1991.

The Business Charter for Sustainable Development

The International Chamber of Commerce's Business Charter for Sustainable Development, announced in April 1991, encourages companies to improve their environmental performance in accord with 16 principles (International Chamber of Commerce, 1991):

1. Corporate priority: To recognize environmental management as among the highest corporate priorities and as a key determinant to sustainable development; to establish policies, programs, and practices for conducting operations in an environmentally sound manner.

2. Integrated management: To integrate these policies, programs, and practices fully into each business as an essential element of management in all its functions.

(Continued)

3. Process of improvement: To continue to improve corporate policies, programs, and environmental performance, taking into account technical developments, scientific understanding, consumer needs, and community expectations, with legal regulations as a starting point; and to apply the same environmental criteria internationally.

4. Employee education: To educate, train, and motivate employees to conduct their activities in an environmentally responsible manner.

5. Prior assessment: To assess environmental impacts before starting a new activity or project and before decommissioning a facility or leaving a site.

6. Products and services: To develop and provide products or services that have no undue environmental impact and are safe in their intended use, that are efficient in their consumption of energy and natural resources, and that can be recycled, reused, or disposed of safely.

7. Customer advice: To advise, and where relevant, educate customers, distributors, and the public in the safe use, transportation, storage, and disposal of products provided; and to apply similar considerations to the provision of services.

8. Facilities and operations: To develop, design, and operate facilities and conduct activities taking into consideration the efficient use of energy and materials, the sustainable use of renewable resources, the minimization of adverse environmental impact and waste generation, and the safe and responsible disposal of residual wastes.

9. Research: To conduct or support research on the environmental impacts of raw materials, products, processes, emissions, and wastes associated with the enterprise and on the means of minimizing such adverse impacts.

10. Precautionary approach: To modify the manufacture, marketing, or use of products or services or the conduct of activities, consistent with scientific and technical understanding, to prevent serious or irreversible environmental degradation.

11. Contractors and suppliers: To promote the adoption of these principles by contractors acting on behalf of the enterprise, encouraging and, where appropriate, requiring improvements in their practices to make them consistent with those of the enterprise; and to encourage the wider adoption of these principles by suppliers.

12. Emergency preparedness: To develop and maintain, where significant hazards exist, emergency preparedness plans in conjunction with the emergency services, relevant authorities, and the local community, recognizing potential transboundary impacts.

13. Transfer of technology: To contribute to the transfer of environmentally sound technology and management methods throughout the industrial and public sectors.

14. Contributing to the common effort: To contribute to the development of pubic policy and to business, governmental, and intergovernmental programs and educational initiatives that will enhance environmental awareness and protection.

15. Openness to concerns: To foster openness and dialogue with employees and the public, anticipating and responding to their concerns about the potential hazards and impacts of operations, products, wastes, or services, including those of transboundary or global significance.

16. Compliance and reporting: To measure environmental performance; to conduct regular environmental audits and assessments of compliance with company requirements, legal requirements, and these principles; and periodically, to provide appropriate information to the board of directors, shareholders, employees, the authorities, and the public.

By late 1992 these principles had been adopted by some 1000 business firms worldwide (International Chamber of Commerce, personal communication).

Progress toward Sustainable Resource Management: Case Studies

This section summarizes the major global environmental problems and provides brief case studies or illustrations of how innovative business firms are addressing the problems and in the process conserving resources, protecting health and the environment, and often saving money. The issues covered include energy, transportation, climate, air and water pollution, water supply, hazardous and solid waste, mining, agriculture, forestry, and wildlife.

Improving Energy Efficiency

Since World War II, the world's annual energy consumption has increased about fivefold—from 2.4 to nearly 12 billion tons of coal equivalent. Fossil fuel use has grown rapidly, and has enabled many nations to achieve higher living standards. Yet most energy is used inefficiently, and widespread use of coal and oil produces pollution that threatens air quality, human health, vegetation, and climate stability. The burning of fossil fuels releases most of the air pollutants that are damaging forests in Europe and North America, and accounts for roughly half of the greenhouse gas emissions expected to cause global warming.

When consumers purchase fossil fuels or electricity, they pay only a fraction of their total social, economic, and environmental costs. The United States spends more than $400 billion a year in direct energy costs, and one study estimates that the additional indirect costs could be between $100 and $300 billion

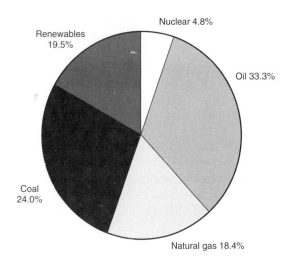

Total: 9300 million tons oil equivalent

Figure 22-2. World energy use, oil equivalent, 1989. (*Christopher Flavin and Nicholas Lennsen, "Beyond the Petroleum Age: Designing a Solar Economy." Worldwatch Paper 100, Washington, D.C.: Worldwatch Institute, December 1990.*)

annually. These costs include military expenditures to protect oil supplies in the Middle East, federal subsidies to energy producers, health care costs and lost employment from pollution-related disease, and environmental degradation (Hubbard, 1991).

Nuclear power accounts for about 5% of global energy production. Worldwide, about 430 nuclear power plants are in operation; the United States has just over a hundred plants in service, supplying 22% of the electric energy. Nuclear power causes much less air pollution than power from fossil fuels, but high costs, accidents, and concern about proliferation of nuclear weapons, radiation risks, safe disposal of nuclear wastes, and decommissioning of closed power plants have caused a number of countries to curtail or forgo nuclear programs.

In view of the wide range of uncertainties, costs, and risks associated with energy obtained from oil, coal, gas, and nuclear materials, it is essential to improve the efficiency of energy use and to develop a variety of renewable, solar-based energy sources as soon as possible. Government and private incentives to conserve energy and use it more efficiently can slow or even reverse growth in energy consumption and can yield important environmental, economic, and social benefits. Such incentives include efficiency standards for vehicles and appliances, and taxes and fees that make the price of energy sources and energy use reflect their true social and environmental costs.

Many methods exist to improve energy efficiency in transportation and industry, and for buildings and appliances. Technologies now commercially available can reduce energy consumption in these sectors from 20 to 60% or more. If the United States were to fully implement existing energy-efficient technologies, it could save one-third to one-half of the more than $400 billion it now spends annually on energy. Energy-efficiency improvements can save up to 85% of the cost of providing new energy supply.

In spite of recent improvements, some industrial nations still use energy inefficiently. For example, compared with West Germany and Japan, the United States uses about twice as much energy to produce a dollar of gross national product. U.S. industry, which accounts for 36% of all U.S. energy consumption, could lower its fuel consumption by 25% or more through improvements in energy efficiency.

Case Studies

In the United States, a number of utilities have developed innovative programs to conserve electricity, including Consolidated Edison, Duke Power, New England Electric, Pacific Gas and Electric, and Southern California Edison. Two of these programs are summarized below, along with a case in which the Swedish government stimulated an efficient appliance design.

New England Electric's Energy Conservation Program.   In the early 1980s, New England Electric (NEE) began to help its commercial customers save energy by investing in more efficient lighting systems, electric motors, and heating and cooling systems. Initially the programs were experimental and inexpensive. However, as the program expanded, costs rose, and since the prevailing regulatory system linked profitability to electricity generation and sales, it created a disincentive to further increasing investment in conservation.

In 1987, by working with the Conservation Law Foundation (CLF) and state regulatory agencies, NEE showed that efforts to reduce energy demand could only continue if the company could profit from its conservation efforts. NEE and CLF developed a plan whereby NEE agreed to increase its investments in energy conservation in return for a share of the generated savings.

In 1990, NEE spent $71 million for energy conservation, saving 194,300 megawatthours of electricity, worth $161 million. Of its net savings of $90 million, NEE retained $8.4 million (9%), and its customers kept the balance. NEE now devotes a larger relative share of its revenues to conservation than any other U.S. utility. The company plans to reduce by 20% its emissions of greenhouse gases by the year 2000 through greater use of natural gas and purchase of electricity generated by hydropower, as well as through energy conservation (Schmidheiny, 1992; Smart, 1992).

Holderbank Cement Company's Energy-Efficient Program.   The Swiss-based Holderbank group of companies produces cement and related products in 24 countries around the world. Electrical and thermal energy costs account for nearly half of total cement production costs. Concern about rising energy costs and environmental impacts led Holderbank to initiate an intensive energy-conservation program in 1990, which set targets for energy use per unit of product and developed a six-stage implementation plan. The plan includes plant surveys, workshops and training sessions, and introduction of energy control devices.

To test the program, Holderbank implemented it at two Mexican pilot plants. Within 5 months the two plants had saved $440,000. The Mexican experience showed that greater employee involvement was needed to identify energy-conservation opportunities. As a result, interdisciplinary energy management teams were created at each plant, with members drawn from all relevant departments and coordinated by an energy manager. Based on initial results, Holderbank believes it can achieve overall energy savings of 3 to 13% with little investment, and 17 to 28% savings with investment of more time and money (Schmidheiny, 1992).

Electrolux's Energy-Efficient Refrigerator.   In 1989, the Swedish National Board for Industrial and Technical Development decided to promote development of more efficient refrigerators by sponsoring a competition. Representatives of major refrigerator purchasers helped set the terms of the competition, which included an energy-consumption limit of 1 kilowatthour per liter (kWh/liter) per year. This compared with an average energy consumption of 1.4 kWh/liter for new units and 2.0 kWh/liter for units already installed. The winner was guaranteed an order of at least 500 units and was offered a reward of $80 per unit if electrical consumption did not exceed 0.9 kWh/liter.

Five companies, two of which were Swedish, entered the competition. In December 1990, the Swedish-based Electrolux Company was announced as the winner; the firm had developed a model that uses only 0.79 kWh/liter a year. Although this unit costs 10 to 20% more than a standard Electrolux model, the cost will be recovered in about 4 years due to lower energy consumption. The competition helped change the attitude and plans of a major company. For the company, consumers, and society, the main benefit of the competition is the creation of a market for energy-efficient appliances. The case study shows that environmentally beneficial product improvements can be accelerated by innovative government action to stimulate the market (Schmidheiny, 1992).

Promoting Renewable Energy

The sun's energy makes possible a number of promising renewable energy technologies, including solar thermal, solar photovoltaic, wind, ocean thermal, small-scale hydropower, biomass, and hydrogen produced from renewable energy. Geothermal energy is another renewable source that draws on the earth's interior heat. Some of these sources are now nearly competitive in cost with fossil-fuel energy. Renewable technologies could be competitive in meeting 80% of U.S. energy needs within 20 years if given adequate support through economic incentives and funding of applied research, development, and demonstration projects.

Renewable energy sources can offer a number of advantages over nonrenewable fossil fuels, including lessened dependence on petroleum imports, lower vulnerability to supply interruptions, reduced air pollution and carbon dioxide emissions, greater diversity of supply sources, and suitability for small-scale energy systems. Taken together, renewable energy sources offer great potential for eventually replacing energy from fossil fuels and nuclear power. Hydropower now produces more than a fifth of the world's electricity, and in a few areas such as California, solar thermal and wind energy already generate significant amounts of electricity. Norway, Brazil, and the Philippines obtain at least half of their energy from renewable sources.

Case Studies

In the United States, both private companies and public utilities are carrying out innovative programs to develop renewable energy sources. Several of these programs have demonstrated that some solar and wind energy technologies are close to being cost-competitive with conventional energy sources, especially if the full costs are taken into account.

Luz International's Solar Electric Generating Systems.   Using parabolic trough collectors, Luz International's solar generating plants in southern California produce nearly 275 megawatts of electricity, about a quarter of that produced by a large conventional power plant. Luz generates about 90% of the world's solar electricity. When completed, the program will produce almost 680 megawatts, enough electricity to serve the residential needs of nearly a million people. Except for relatively low emissions from the natural gas backup system, the process releases no air pollutants. The company's innovations in design and manufacturing have lowered the cost of solar thermal power by more than two-thirds to between 7 and 8 cents per kilowatthour. This cost is about one-third of competing solar technologies, and nearly competitive with many conventional fossil-fuel power plants (Renew America, 1990: Luz International, 1990).

U.S. Windpower's Altamont Electric Generating Project.   U.S. Windpower is the world's leading manufacturer of wind turbines and the largest supplier of wind-generated electricity. Their Altamont-Solano project includes more than 3000 turbines located in the Altamont Pass and Montezuma Hills of California. In 1989, the project produced 600 million kilowatts, enough electricity to power 100,000 homes. Windpower is a promising energy source for the North Central and Northwest United States, and is already supplying significant amounts of energy in northern Europe and elsewhere (Renew America, 1990).

Pacific Gas and Electric's Green Resource Plan.   Pacific Gas and Electric (PG&E) is combining energy-efficiency improvements and development of renewable energy sources to meet its customers' growing energy needs. PG&E already obtains nearly half of its energy from renewable technologies, including hydropower, geothermal wind, biomass, and solar power. PG&E's Resource Plan includes development of new energy supply resources to support long-term needs. Between now and the year 2000, new supplies will come from renewable and high-efficiency energy technologies, including hydropower, wind power, and efficient gas turbines. Beyond the year 2000, PG&E plans to emphasize technologies such as wind, solar thermal, advanced gas turbines, fuel cells, and energy storage systems (Renew America, 1992).

Improving Transportation Efficiency

Worldwide, transportation accounts for about 20% of energy use, and in industrial nations, transportation's share is more than 30%. The current global fleet of some 600 million motor vehicles consumes half the world's oil; the number of vehicles could double by the year 2030. In the United States, over 190 million motor vehicles travel more than 2 trillion miles each year, an average of 12,000 miles per person, almost double the rate in most industrial countries. Motor vehicles account for nearly two-thirds of U.S. petroleum use and about 60% of urban air pollution. While the fuel efficiency of U.S. automobiles rose from 13 miles per gallon (mpg) in 1973 to 27 mpg in the late 1980s, it is still below the 30 to 33 mpg level achieved in other industrial nations. And prototype vehicles exist that can achieve 60 to 100 mpg without sacrificing passenger space or safety.

Among the fuel-related social costs of motor vehicle use are air pollution, which is a significant health threat in some urban areas; dependence on oil imports, an important security problem; and emissions of gases that contribute to global warming and depletion of the ozone layer. Other social costs include traffic congestion in urban areas, traffic accidents, highway noise, and loss of productive land. A recent study estimates that the full costs of driving motor vehicles in the United States may involve as much as $300 billion annually in indirect expenses not paid by the drivers. These include costs for road building and maintenance; highway patrols and traffic management; harm from air pollution; and time, fuel, and other losses resulting from traffic congestion (MacKenzie and others, 1992).

Employers contribute to traffic congestion by not charging for parking and not encouraging ride sharing and use of public transportation. About 86% of the U.S. work force commutes to work by car, and over 90% of all commuters pay no parking fee at work.

While there is no single answer to transportation problems, there are several priorities. One is to adopt an integrated, systems approach to regional and local transit needs, including better land-use planning to minimize commuting distances. Another priority is to provide alternatives to motor vehicles such as bicycles, heavy and light rail systems, and electric-powered personal rapid transit systems. For motor vehicles, promising energy options include using alternative energy sources to reduce pollution, such as natural gas, methanol, electricity, and hydrogen; and doubling or tripling fuel efficiency through the use of fuel cell–powered electric vehicles. Additional measures include encouraging van pooling and carpooling, eliminating parking subsidies, levying taxes on commuting to recover the full costs of vehicle use, and facilitating telecommuting through technologies such as telephones, facsimile machines, and computer modems that allow employees to work at home.

Case Studies

Portland Regional Transportation Plan.   Local, regional, and state governments in the Portland, Oregon, area have designed a system to control urban and regional growth and protect the environment and quality of life. The program provides close coordination between land use and transportation planning, and includes development of a light rail system and a transit mall (Renew America, 1992).

AT&T—State of Arizona Telecommuting Pilot Program.   In response to growing air pollution in the Phoenix metropolitan area, AT&T and the state of Arizona have developed a public-private partnership for a pilot telecommuting program in Phoenix to reduce employee travel. AT&T and the Arizona Energy Office identified and trained employees with job responsibilities compatible with telecommuting. Participants work from home one day a week, reducing their commuting mileage by 20%. During the first 6 months of the program, 134 telecommuters achieved these benefits: 97,078 fewer miles driven to and from work, prevention of about 1.9 tons of vehicle-related air pollutants, savings of about $10,400 in travel expenses, and avoidance of 3705 hours of stressful driving time.

The telecommuting program has improved employee productivity and morale, and reduced stress and turnover. AT&T and the state of Arizona have distributed more than 500 information packets describing the program, and many U.S. and foreign companies have shown interest in starting similar programs (Renew America, 1992).

RoadRailer's Rail Truck Technology.   RoadRailer has developed a unique detachable "rail truck" vehicle design that allows cargo to be moved by both rail and highway without repackaging. The technology reduces fuel consumption by 25 to 50% while saving time and money. Originally developed through a

New York State Energy Research and Development Authority program, the rail truck replaces the conventional rail flatcar with a trailer unit, saving 13 tons of weight.

By 1990, some 1000 rail truck units were operating in 10 U.S. states. The RoadRailer design reduces diesel fuel requirements and also cuts energy and operating costs by eliminating the need for large gantry cranes and the complex loading and unloading required for flatcars. The rail truck costs only $17,000 compared with the $25,500 price of a rail-compatible trailer (Renew America, 1990).

Slowing Climate Change

Carbon dioxide and certain other trace gases in the atmosphere—including chlorofluorocarbons (CFCs), methane, ozone, and nitrous oxide—act somewhat like glass in a greenhouse, transmitting solar radiation but retaining some of the heat from earth that would otherwise radiate back into space. Fossil-fuel use and loss of vegetation are increasing the amount of carbon dioxide in the atmosphere. The concentration has risen from its preindustrial level of about 280 parts per million (ppm) to more than 350 ppm today. About four-fifths of the increase now comes from the burning of fossil fuels; the rest is released when forests are cut and other vegetation is destroyed. This increase in carbon dioxide, along with growing concentrations of other heat-absorbing gases—especially CFCs and methane—may be increasing the "greenhouse effect" and raising global temperatures, which have risen 0.5°C since 1890. Seven of the eight warmest years on record occurred between 1980 and 1990.

Many scientists agree that the increasing concentrations of greenhouse gases will warm the earth on average about 1.3°C by the year 2020, and about 3°C by 2070. A 3° rise would make the earth warmer than it has been during the last 2 million years and would occur so rapidly that many plant and animal species would be unable to survive.

Energy use accounts for about 50% of greenhouse gas emissions, CFCs and other industrial effluents contribute roughly 25%, and deforestation and agriculture each account for between 10 and 15%. The United States is the largest single contributor to global warming, emitting about 1 billion metric tons of carbon dioxide equivalents each year.

The impact of global warming on rainfall patterns and crop harvests could be especially disruptive. While some northern countries could benefit, crop yields in the U.S. Midwest could drop by a third, and areas that are already arid, such as eastern Brazil, much of Africa, and parts of Asia, will probably become drier.

There are many ways to reduce emissions of greenhouse gases and curb global warming. Measures to improve energy efficiency include mandated standards for motor vehicles, appliances, and buildings; and taxes on polluting energy sources. Increased use of solar energy would lower carbon dioxide emissions, as would curbing deforestation and increasing reforestation. Less use of energy- and chemical-dependent agricultural practices would lower greenhouse gas emissions from petroleum consumption and chemical fertilizers. Consuming less meat and more grains would save energy, water, and fertilizers, thus reducing greenhouse gas emissions. And a phaseout of CFCs would eliminate a major greenhouse gas. At the June 1992 United Nations Conference on Environment and Development (the "Earth Summit") in Brazil, over 150 countries signed the Climate Convention, which calls for nations to limit their emissions of carbon dioxide and other greenhouse gases, with the goal of returning to 1990 emissions levels by the year 2000.

Case Study

Most programs to improve energy efficiency and to replace fossil fuels with solar-based energy sources contribute to reducing greenhouse gas emissions and stabilizing the climate. Programs to plant trees and other vegetation, which use carbon dioxide also help to prevent global warming.

AES Corporation's Carbon Offset Programs.   Because of concern that its fossil-fueled power facilities were contributing to global warming, the Virginia-based AES Corporation has worked with World Resources Institute on a way to offset its carbon emissions and avoid any net impact on the global carbon dioxide balance. AES's program seeks to balance carbon released from its new power plants by increasing the amount of carbon stored in trees and plants. Because carbon dioxide emissions circulate throughout the atmosphere, AES can locate a carbon offset project anywhere in the world.

AES's Thames power plant in Connecticut is expected to release about 16 million tons of carbon over its 40-year life. To offset these emissions, AES has provided $2 million to support the Guatemalan Agroforestry Project, created to regain lost vegetation and control soil erosion through reforestation and soil conservation. The project is designed to generate enough biomass to absorb 18 million tons of carbon over the same 40-year period (Smart, 1992).

Protecting the Ozone Layer

Chlorofluorocarbons (CFCs) and other airborne pollutants are depleting the earth's stratospheric ozone layer, and ozone is the only atmospheric gas that effectively blocks the damaging ultraviolet rays of the sun. In some regions ozone depletion has significantly increased the amount of harmful ultraviolet radiation that reaches the earth's surface. CFCs are stable at ground level, but when they are exposed to ultraviolet rays in the stratosphere, they break down and release chlorine. Each chlorine molecule can destroy some 100,000 ozone molecules. CFCs are used as refrigerants, solvents, aerosol propellants, and blowing agents in foam production.

Between 1979 and 1990, average ozone levels worldwide declined by 3.5%. During the spring, ozone levels over Antarctica have dropped as much as 50%. Each 1% drop in stratospheric ozone increases ultraviolet radiation by 2%, may raise the rate of skin cancer by 5 to 7%, and could double deaths from skin cancer in the United States above the current toll of some 8000 a year.

Industrial nations have already made significant progress in reducing CFC emissions. As a result of the 1987 Montreal Protocol and subsequent international initiatives, some 93 countries have agreed to stop CFC production by the year 2000.

Case Studies

Many business firms are working to phase out CFCs and other ozone-depleting substances, including companies such as AT&T, Dow Chemical, Du Pont, Electrolux, IBM, Northern Telecom, Xerox, and Zytec. IBM has pledged a worldwide CFC phaseout in electronics production by 1993. Northern Telecom helped found the Industry Cooperative for Ozone Layer Protection, a Washington, D.C.–based association of 17 multinational corporations augmented by governments and industry associations from Japan, Mexico, the former Soviet Union, Sweden, and the United States (Smart, 1992). Many electronics companies are beginning to use water-based solutions in place of CFCs to clean printed circuit boards.

Du Pont's Program to Recycle and Phase Out CFCs.   Du Pont helped develop CFCs in the 1930s, and historically was the world's largest CFC manufacturer. In 1988 when a scientific consensus emerged that CFCs were depleting the ozone layer, Du Pont decided to phase out the chemicals. In 1990 the company announced a pioneering program to recycle CFCs. Du Pont now buys back used Freon and other CFCs from hundreds of thousands of customers who use the chemicals in refrigerators and air conditioners. The company provides CFC containers and pays for the freight. Du Pont's goal is to end CFC production by the year 2000 at the latest, and replace the chemicals with safe alternatives. The company says that its CFC production is 45% below the allowable limit set by the 1987 Montreal Protocol. Du Pont's decision to phase out CFCs stimulated the company to find substitutes and provided an opportunity for it to become the leader in developing alternative chemicals (Council on Economic Priorities, 1991; Smart, 1992).

AT&T's Program to Eliminate CFC Use.   In 1988, AT&T joined a group of companies working to develop substitutes for chlorofluorocarbons that it uses as a solvent to clean electronic equipment. AT&T had previously purchased up to one-third of all CFCs used in the United States, about half of which were released into the environment. AT&T formed a partnership with another company to develop an alternative to CFC use, and in 1989 announced the availability of a fluxing process that eliminates the need to use CFC-113 to make electronic parts. In 1989, AT&T also announced it would eliminate all CFC use by 1994. By the end of 1990, the company had cut its CFC emissions by 50% and had saved more than $4 million during the year in avoided CFC purchases (AT&T, 1991).

Controlling Hazardous Substances

Hazardous substances—including toxic waste, industrial chemicals, pesticides, and nuclear waste—enter the workplace, the marketplace, and the environment. Through pollution of air, soil, and water supplies, hazardous substances pose both short- and long-term threats to human health and natural resources. Exposure to toxic substances can occur at worksites such as farms and industrial plants, and in homes from residues on food and contaminated drinking water.

The bulk of hazardous and toxic wastes is generated by process industries; the largest sources are chemical production and mineral and metal processing. In industrialized countries, the chemical and petrochemical industries produce nearly 70% of hazardous wastes. Between 1950 and the late 1980s, output of synthetic organic compounds increased more than ninefold in the United States and more than twentyfold worldwide.

The Organization for Economic Cooperation and Development (OECD) estimates that the world generates about 340 million metric tons of hazardous waste each year. The United States produces about 250 to 300 million metric tons annually, more than a ton for each citizen. Louisiana generates over 3 tons per person each year, and West Virginia, Tennessee, and Texas each produce more than 2 tons per person. About two-thirds of U.S. hazardous waste is disposed of on land, 22% is discharged into waterways, and only about 11% is recycled or treated to detoxify it before discharge. Other countries treat a larger part of their hazardous waste; for example, West Germany detoxifies about 35% of its waste and incinerates 15%.

For Western industrial nations, the cost of hazardous waste disposal averages around $50 to $100 or more per ton. For certain wastes, such as those containing PCBs (polychlorinated biphenyls), disposal costs can be as high as $4500 per ton. In the United States, more than 10,000 hazardous waste disposal sites may need to be cleaned up; the task could take as long as 100 years and cost hundreds of billions of dollars.

Hazardous substances can cause a wide range of harmful effects on human health and the environment. Protracted exposure to some organic compounds has been linked to a variety of health problems, including birth defects; gastrointestinal, neurological, and liver damage; cancer; and death. Heavy metals such as lead, cadmium, and mercury can cause brain, liver, and kidney damage. Exposure to radioactive materials can cause various forms of cancer. Hazardous substances can also accumulate and cause long-term or permanent damage to streams, rivers, lakes, wetlands, coastal estuaries, forests, and other ecosystems.

Because of the increased expense and regulation associated with hazardous waste in Western nations, some industries are exporting toxic materials. Much of this waste goes to areas less capable of handling it properly than the industry's home country. In a recent 2-year period, about 3 million tons of hazardous waste were shipped from the United States and western Europe to countries in Africa and eastern Europe. In recognition of growing concern over illegal traffic in toxic waste, 50 countries adopted the Basel Convention in 1989. The treaty restricts international traffic in hazardous materials—especially their export from rich to poor states.

In addition to waste treatment, several methods are being developed to slow the proliferation of hazardous substances. These include reduction and recycling of toxic waste production in industry, the use of integrated pest management in agriculture to lessen dependence on pesticides, and methods to improve the storage of nuclear wastes and limit their future production. The best way to avoid the hazards of toxic waste is not to produce the waste in the first place. Source reduction that prevents waste generation is far less expensive than traditional waste-management strategies. In the United States, emissions of toxic chemicals declined from 7.0 billion pounds in 1987 to 4.8 billion pounds in 1990.

Case Studies

A growing number of chemical companies are saving money, preventing pollution more effectively, and even increasing productivity by eliminating waste emissions at the source rather than managing them after they are produced (Dorfman, 1992). Successful waste-reduction programs have been implemented by companies such as Allied-Signal, Aristech Chemical, AT&T, Chevron, Dow Chemical, Du Pont, Exxon, Johnson Wax, Merck, 3M, Monsanto, Unocal, and Xerox.

3M's Pollution Prevention Pays (3P) Program.   In 1975, the Minnesota-based 3M company made pollution prevention an integral and permanent part of its operations. The 3P program views all forms of pollution—air, water, and land—as a wasteful, inefficient use of resources. The program's guiding principles are listed in order of priority:

- Prevent pollution at the source.
- Recover and recycle manufacturing by-products and other assets for internal use or external sale.
- Treat wastes that cannot be prevented or recycled, using control equipment and other methods to reduce toxicity and volume.
- Dispose of treatment residue through appropriate methods.

Since 1975, more than 3000 3P projects have been implemented, preventing the release of over 575,000 tons of pollutants and saving 3M more than $530 million. (See Chap. 6.)

Dow Chemical's Waste Reduction Always Pays (WRAP) Program. As part of its WRAP program, in 1986, the Michigan-based Dow Chemical Company adopted the standard waste-management hierarchy of waste reduction as top priority, followed by recycling and reuse of waste by-products, waste treatment, and landfill storage. As a result of the WRAP program, less than 1% of Dow's hazardous waste now goes to landfills. All Dow plants are required to maintain an inventory of process emissions to the air, land, and water, which is used to evaluate each operation using an index of pounds of waste per pound of product. The WRAP program relies on a combination of management commitment and employee initiative. Employees propose waste-reduction projects that may involve equipment alterations or changes in maintenance, operation, or administration. Payoffs may include higher yields, recovery of materials previously lost, savings in disposal costs, and reduced emissions. Since 1985, Dow has lowered its air emissions by at least half.

At one Dow facility, a project team found ways to recover and reuse much of a reactant used to produce agricultural products, thus cutting its consumption by 80%. The change eliminated 2.5 million pounds of waste a year, and saved Dow $8 million annually through lower costs for labor, raw materials, and pollution control. At another Dow plant, a waste-reduction team modified a resin process to allow recovery of methanol that had previously been treated as waste. The changes saved 660,000 pounds of methanol a year, which when combined with avoided waste-treatment costs, resulted in total annual savings of about $90,000. Dow Chemical's experience suggests that successful waste-reduction programs depend on employee creativity and enthusiasm, and that waste reduction should be seen as an opportunity rather than a burden (Schmidheiny, 1992).

Du Pont's Waste-Minimization Program. Du Pont, the largest U.S. chemical company, has set a number of waste-reduction goals to be met by the year 2000 or earlier. These include:

- Reduce hazardous waste by 35% compared to 1990 levels.

- Reduce toxic air emissions by 60% compared to 1987 levels (by 1993).

- Reduce carcinogenic air emissions by 90% compared to 1987 levels.

- Eliminate, or render nonhazardous, all toxic discharges to the ground or surface waters.

At its Beaumont, Texas, plant, Du Pont makes acrylonitrile, a material used to produce plastics. Each year this process produced more than 110 million pounds of ammonium sulfate waste. By modifying the process, the company was able to reduce waste generation substantially and save almost $1 million a year through decreased raw material use and lower hazardous-waste disposal costs.

One Du Pont plant that manufactures fluorelastomers recently projected the need for an incinerator to reduce about 200,000 pounds of air emissions a year, at a purchase cost of $2 million and with yearly operating costs of $1 million. By making engineering changes that cost only $3000, Du Pont was able to cut air emissions by 50% and save $400,000 in annual costs. Another series of engineering changes that cost $250,000 will lower emissions by another 30%. By spending just over $250,000, the company will reduce emissions by 80%, save $400,000 a year, and avoid a $2 million investment and $1 million in annual operating costs (Smart, 1992).

Unocal's Program to Reduce Urban Air Pollutants.   As a way to decrease hazardous air pollutants from motor vehicles in the Los Angeles area, Unocal developed its novel South Coast Recycled Auto Program (SCRAP). Motor vehicles emit about 60% of ozone-forming emissions (including hydrocarbons and nitrogen oxides), and older, pre-1971 vehicles account for only 3% of miles driven but about 24% of these emissions. In 1990, Unocal announced a demonstration program to eliminate several thousand of these older vehicles through a voluntary plan. Unocal offered to pay $700 for each car, and then send it to a scrap yard to be crushed and recycled.

By allocating $5 million to purchase and scrap 7000 pre-1971 vehicles, Unocal estimated it would prevent the release of about 6 million pounds of air pollutants. Other groups contributed enough funds to the project to pay for scrapping another 1400 vehicles and avoid additional pollution (Smart, 1992).

Managing Solid Waste

Solid waste disposal is a gigantic global issue, especially in industrial countries. Wastes are generated at every stage in our use of materials, from their extraction and processing to their abandonment as used items. In 1990, the 24 industrial nations that comprise the Organization for Economic Cooperation and Development (OECD) handled an estimated 9 billion metric tons of waste materials of all kinds. This included nearly 1.5 billion tons of industrial wastes (of which about 340 million tons were classified as hazardous) and about 420 million tons of municipal wastes. The remaining 7 billion tons of material included wastes from energy production, agriculture, mining, demolition of structures, dredging, and sewage facilities (OECD, 1991).

The United States produces 160 to 180 million tons of municipal solid waste each year, most of which is dumped in landfills. In 1978, there were about 20,000 landfills, but now less than 6000 remain unfilled and open. Between now and 1994, some 2000 landfills will be filled and closed, and few new sites are available. The situation is already critical in many urban areas, and the Environmental Protection Agency (EPA) estimates that the volume of U.S. municipal solid waste will increase 20% by the year 2000. Landfill costs are climbing rapidly, reflecting the growing expense of creating and maintaining landfills.

Solid waste disposal is causing serious pollution problems in the United States and other industrial countries. Waste disposal in landfills can cause contamination of groundwater and surface waters when rainfall leaches hazardous substances from materials in the waste. And as organic waste decays, methane can accumulate and create the potential for explosions. If waste is improperly incinerated, effluent gases can contain dioxins and other hazardous air pollutants. The ash from incineration can also be hazardous unless stored in secure landfills.

One preferred waste-management hierarchy includes, in descending order of preference: waste reduction, recycling, incineration, and landfilling. Source reduction and recycling are the favored options for reducing the amount and toxicity of waste that must be incinerated or placed in landfills. A substantial amount of solid waste can be recovered and recycled or reused as secondary resources—materials that can replace primary (virgin) resources, which would otherwise have to be extracted from the earth or obtained from forests or other sources, at greater cost.

In many countries, important opportunities for waste reduction and for recycling and recovery of valuable materials are being missed. In the United States, nearly 80% of municipal solid waste is dumped in landfills, and only about 13% is recycled, though this represents an increase from less than 7% in the 1960s. A number of industrial nations have effective programs to recycle components of municipal waste and minimize the waste that goes to landfills. Utilizing consumer sorting, western Europe recovers some 30% of its waste, and estimates for Japan range between 26 and 39%. The former West Germany reuses or incinerates about 45% of its solid waste, while Japan recycles or burns more than 70%.

Waste recycling saves energy and materials and reduces air and water pollution, water use, and mining wastes. When paper is recycled, savings on energy, pollution, and water use range from 23 to 74%; savings from steel recycling range from 40 to 85%; and when aluminum is recycled, energy use and pollution are cut by at least 90%.

In the United States, state and local initiatives play a central role in improving solid-waste management. A number of states are implementing mandatory recycling legislation covering glass, aluminum, plastic, and paper. Local communities use a variety of means to cut waste generation and increase recycling; these include developing markets for recycled materials, designing systems for collecting and sorting materials, encouraging composting for yard and food wastes, and levying taxes or surcharges on products, packaging, and disposal methods that contribute heavily to the waste stream. Success in reducing the volume of waste will require major changes by manufacturers and consumers, combined with concerted efforts at all levels of government.

Case Studies

Many companies have programs to reduce the volume of solid waste resulting from the production and use of their products. Among them are Amoco, AT&T, Du Pont, General Mills, IBM, S.C. Johnson Wax, Kellogg, McDonald's, Procter & Gamble, Rubbermaid, and Volkswagen.

S.C. Johnson's Environmentally Responsible Packaging Program.   By 1990, S.C. Johnson Wax, a Wisconsin-based manufacturer of household cleaning products, had commercialized reduced-waste packaging of its consumer products. These innovations include their "enviro-box," with 92% less packaging material; more recyclable material in packaging for floor care products; a 90% reduction of packaging for the laundry product, Shout; and fully recyclable packaging for carpet cleaning materials and other products. In 1992, Johnson announced a series of goals that includes a 50% reduction in the total volume of packaging material to be achieved by the year 2000 (Schmidheiny, 1992).

Procter & Gamble's Use of Life Cycle Analysis to Reduce Solid Waste. Procter & Gamble is a major producer of household and personal care products. P&G has applied life cycle analysis to a number of products, including diapers, packaging for detergent and personal care products, and surfactants used in detergents and other cleaning products. In a study of seven different packaging options for a fabric conditioner, P&G concluded that the use of soft pouches or paper cartons in place of plastic bottles can reduce packaging waste by up to 95% (Schmidheiny, 1992).

Volkswagen's Program to Build Recyclable Cars.   Spurred by rapidly diminishing landfill capacity, German car manufacturers are now redesigning their products with more emphasis on ease of disassembly and reuse of materials. Some manufacturers are seeking to make their products nearly 100% recyclable. At Volkswagen, 62% of the total production material goes into the product and 32% is recycled; only 6% is now considered waste. Nearly all of VW's plastic waste is recycled; the different plastic polymers are separated and remolded for reuse.

Since early 1990, VW has operated a pilot car recycling plant; by the end of 1991, over 2000 cars had been processed. As each car is dismantled, the various materials are separated. Oils and other liquids are drained off. Batteries are removed and acid, plastics, and metals are recovered. Plastic parts are separated and sent to suppliers. Valuable precious metals are taken out of catalytic converters. After the glass and rubber have been collected, the remaining steel is shredded for reuse. VW is using its experience in this pilot plant to design a future car recycling system (Schmidheiny, 1992).

Other Business Recycling Initiatives.   Rubbermaid, Amoco, and McDonald's are collaborating to recycle polystyrene plastic materials. An Amoco-owned plant in Brooklyn, New York, converts used McDonald's food trays into flakes that Rubbermaid uses in some products. McDonald's also uses recycled paper for some of its packaging.

Many companies are using recycled or recyclable packaging material. Kellogg has used recycled paperboard packaging for its cereals since 1906, and General Mills reports that 98% of its packaging is made of either recycled paper or recyclable plastic (Council on Economic Priorities, 1991).

Mining Minerals Sustainably

Minerals are a foundation of modern industrial society and are essential raw materials for economic growth and progress. Minerals are indispensable for providing food, water, and energy and for meeting other basic human needs.

Industry depends heavily on some 80 minerals. A number of these, including aluminum and iron, are relatively abundant and widely distributed, although bauxite (aluminum ore) deposits are located mainly in the tropics and subtropics. The United States is highly dependent on imports of strategic minerals such as manganese and platinum, and is particularly vulnerable to supply interruptions.

In agriculture, minerals containing phosphorus, potassium, and nitrogen are used throughout the world to increase crop yields and maintain soil fertility. Many countries depend on imports of mineral fertilizers, including phosphates, potash, nitrates, and ammonium compounds, to sustain the productivity of croplands.

In the past two generations, the world has consumed more minerals than were used in all of previous human history. Between 1950 and 1987, while world population doubled, production of the three most used metals increased far more; copper nearly threefold, steel almost fourfold; and aluminum more than ninefold.

Land must be disturbed to extract minerals from the earth, and provisions for land reclamation must be part of plans for mining operations. When minerals are processed and refined, complex and expensive technologies are often required to minimize water and air pollution and damage to ecosystems.

Recycling of materials from both manufacturing and consumer waste can conserve minerals and reduce environmental damage. Metal recycling can save money, create jobs, conserve energy and water, and reduce air and water pollution and other environmental impacts. For example, when aluminum is recycled instead of produced from virgin ore, energy use and air and water pollution are all cut by 90% or more.

Case Study

ALCOA's Sustainable Bauxite Mining in Australia. In ecologically sensitive western Australia, mineral extraction requires protection of water supplies, forests, and other natural resources. ALCOA, a U.S.–based aluminum producer, has used a comprehensive approach to mining bauxite ore that includes all stages of the operation—planning, mineral extraction, and site rehabilitation. Before mining is begun, drainage characteristics and existing water quality are assessed, and plant and animal surveys provide a basis for postmining rehabilitation design. Each year about 450 hectares (1125 acres) are mined to an average depth of about 4 meters, and then restored and replanted.

ALCOA's experience suggests that environmental disruption from mining operations can be limited if initial environmental research findings are used to plan the mineral extraction and subsequent site rehabilitation, and if management demonstrates proper commitment to ecological restoration and provides appropriate training, resources, and motivation to its employees (Schmidheiny, 1992).

Protecting Water Supplies

Unlike fossil fuels, fresh water is a renewable resource. If water is efficiently used and carefully protected, the hydrologic cycle can provide enough fresh water to meet current global needs for the foreseeable future. However, many human activities have high water use rates, and population growth and rising requirements for energy and food are placing growing demands on both the quantity and the quality of fresh water supplies. Total water use more than tripled between 1950 and 1990, and is now estimated at more than 3500 cubic kilometers per year. Pollution of surface and underground water supplies is a growing problem in many areas. Inefficient use, inadequate conservation, pollution, drought, and rapid local increases in water demand are creating shortages of clean water in a number of countries.

Increasing use of water for agriculture, industry, and municipalities, and environmental degradation all contribute to fresh water shortages. About 2 billion people live in regions with chronic water shortages. Most of Africa, much of the Middle East and South Asia, parts of Central America, and the western United States are already short of water. Groundwater supplies are rapidly declining in parts of China, India, the United States, and many other countries. In many regions, future water shortages are likely to limit growth in agriculture and industry, and could jeopardize health and economic development.

Irrigation for agriculture accounts for about 73% of the world's water use; 21% goes to industry and the other 6% to domestic use. In the United States, agriculture accounts for over 80% of total water use; much of this water goes to produce fodder for livestock. Most cropland irrigation is highly inefficient, since a large part of the water is not absorbed by crops and is lost by evaporation or seepage into the ground. Worldwide, irrigation systems, on average, are only about 37% efficient.

In developed nations, surface and underground water supplies are being polluted by industrial, mining, and municipal wastes, and by surface runoff from urban and agricultural areas. Most industrial processes produce potential water pollutants; these processes include the production of petroleum, petrochemicals, and other commercial chemicals; pesticides; fertilizers; steel and other metals; and paper products. In the United States, damage from water pollution is estimated at $20 billion annually.

In North America and Europe, many lakes have become eutrophic—overburdened with nitrates and phosphates from fertilizers, animal wastes, and municipal sewage. Excessive nitrate concentrations in water supplies, especially when combined with pesticide residues, can cause a variety of serious health problems. In the United States, some 15 million people drink from potentially unsafe water supplies.

To ensure adequate water supplies, major priorities include proper protection and management of watershed areas; creation of incentives for water conservation and recycling, such as water prices that reflect the real costs of supply; and reduction of subsidies for water used to irrigate crops, especially fodder for livestock. To ensure acceptable water quality, high priority should go to reducing the generation of solid, liquid, and airborne wastes by industry, agriculture, and municipalities. Wastes that cannot be eliminated must be adequately contained and treated.

Wastewater reuse and recycling in industry can help curb growth in water demand. In the United States, where water use declined 11% between 1980 and 1985, industrial waste reduction is saving water and reducing pollution. In Israel, farmers already reuse a third of urban wastewater to irrigate crops, and plans call for recycling four-fifths of it by the year 2000. Between 1965 and 1974, Japan raised the proportion of recycled water use in industry from a third to two-thirds.

Case Studies

HENKEL's Substitutes for Phosphates in Detergents.   HENKEL is a German-based company that makes consumer products and specialty chemicals. Its detergents and household cleaners account for nearly a third of its total annual sales of about $8 billion. In 1973, after investing nearly $80 million in research and development over a decade, HENKEL began consumer testing of its phosphate substitute, Sasil. By 1982, tests had shown that Sasil was both environmentally safe and effective as a cleaning agent. Sales of HENKEL's phosphate-free detergent increased steadily, and the old phosphate product was phased out in 1989. In Germany, the amount of phosphates in laundry detergents dropped from 275,000 tons in 1978 to zero by 1991. Nonphosphate powder detergents now have a 100% market share in several European countries and Japan (Schmidheiny, 1992).

Ocean Arks International's Solar Aquatic Wastewater Purification Process.   Located in Falmouth, Massachusetts, Ocean Arks has developed a series of new technologies to protect surface water and groundwater. These methods purify liquid wastes, including sewage and discharges from food processing operations, without using the hazardous chemicals required in conventional waste-treatment systems. The procedure relies on solar-powered greenhouses stocked with a variety of plants and aquatic organisms, and utilizes processes found in complex natural ecosystems to neutralize toxic substances and kill harmful bacteria. The treatment system is both economical and effective compared with conventional methods (Meadows, 1988; Renew America, 1990).

Practicing Sustainable Agriculture

Between 1950 and 1984, world grain production rose more rapidly than population, increasing 2.6-fold and boosting output per person by 40%. This remarkable growth resulted from a variety of factors, including expansion of grain acreage; increased use of irrigation, agricultural chemicals, and high-yield crop varieties; and improved management techniques.

Between 1984 and 1990, however, world grain output per person declined by 4%. The scarcity of fresh water and other factors are beginning to limit crop production in many regions, and the backlog of unused agricultural technology is diminishing.

In addition to 5.5 billion people, the earth's farms and rangelands must now provide food for more than 4 billion livestock, including nearly 1.3 billion cattle, and for about 11 billion chickens and other domestic fowl. *The world's cattle now consume food equivalent to the caloric needs of nearly 9 billion people.*

Unsustainable production of crops and livestock is an important cause of land and soil degradation, loss of wildlife and habitats, and both depletion and pollution of surface and underground water supplies. Unsustainable agricultural practices are seriously degrading and eroding croplands in most of the world's important agricultural regions, and erosion of fertile topsoil is increasing as more marginal land is farmed.

Growing use of agricultural chemicals—fertilizers and pesticides—is polluting water supplies and affecting people and wildlife in many countries. Between 1950 and 1990, global use of chemical fertilizers increased 11.6-fold, and pesticide use grew more than 30-fold. Nitrates from chemical fertilizers have polluted many wells, lakes, and rivers in the United States and Europe. Pesticides are becoming less effective as more species develop immunity to them. In the 1940s, only a few insects were known to be resistant to pesticides; now there are more than 450 resistant species. In addition, a number of weed species have become resistant to herbicides.

Farmers in a number of countries are beginning to use low-input, regenerative agricultural methods that reduce expensive and environmentally harmful material inputs of pesticides and inorganic fertilizers and that increase the use of organic fertilizers, biological pest controls, integrated pest management, and other ecologically sound crop management techniques. In most cases, such methods result in a net economic gain for the farmer, compared with more costly high-input methods, and in greater long-term productivity of the land.

Case Study

Low-Input Sustainable Agriculture (LISA) in the United States.   The U.S. Department of Agriculture's LISA program is designed to help U.S. farmers substitute improved management, scientific information, and on-farm resources for some of the purchased agricultural chemicals that they rely on. The program stems from public concern about groundwater contamination and health risks associated with the use of pesticides and nitrate fertilizers, from farmers' concerns with the growing costs of high-input agriculture, and from their desire to increase net returns while reducing risks and making food production and environmental goals more compatible.

Results of the program have been encouraging. For example, during the 1987 drought, studies in North Carolina showed that experimental corn plots grown using conventional methods averaged a net loss of $422 per hectare, compared with a net loss of only $235 per hectare for plots using low-input agriculture. In 1986, soybeans grown using conventional techniques yielded a net profit of $64 per hectare, compared with a profit of $116 per hectare under low-input management. In a South Dakota study during the 1988 drought, a conventional farming system with chemical inputs incurred a net loss of $25,000, while a comparable low-input system earned about $5000—a difference between the two systems of $30,000. Not all of the low-input methods being tested are effective or profitable, but in general the outlook is positive in terms of long-term productivity and sustainability (Madden and O'Connell, 1989).

Conserving Forests

Since the beginning of agriculture some 10,000 years ago, nearly 35% of the earth's original forest cover has been converted to cropland, pasture, human settlements, and other uses. In recent decades, forest and woodland cover in the tropics has declined rapidly, while temperate forest area has shown a slow net increase due to the expansion of tree plantations.

One of the earth's most important coniferous forests, stretching from northern California to Alaska, is rapidly disappearing. About 60% of the Canadian part of this ancient forest has been felled, and 90% of the U.S. portion has been cut. While tropical forests support a greater variety of wildlife species, this ancient coniferous forest contains on average more than twice as much wood as a tropical forest, and includes the largest and most of the oldest trees on earth.

Tropical moist forests, or rain forests, cover only 7% of the earth's land surface, yet they contain more than half of all plant and animal species. These forests are our richest source of raw materials for agriculture and medicines, and yield many products of industrial and commercial value. In addition to timber, tropical forests provide nuts and fruits, edible oils, steroids, rubber, resins, waxes, gums, tannins, latexes, and lubricants. Tropical forests also perform many essential functions. They moderate air temperature, absorb carbon dioxide, generate oxygen, recycle nutrients, absorb rainfall and release moisture to the atmosphere, regulate water flow, and control soil erosion.

Tropical forests are rapidly being cleared for farming, timber, cattle ranching, and large-scale development projects. Government policies that encourage forest exploitation, especially excessive logging and clearing for farms and ranches, are a major cause of tropical forest destruction. Each year, 16 to 20 million hectares of tropical forest are lost, an area roughly the size of Missouri.

Deforestation rates increased rapidly during the 1980s in many tropical countries. Many other countries have already lost large areas of their tropical forests. Latin America has lost nearly 40%, while the loss for Asia is more than 40%, and for Africa over 50%. In Central America, more than 60% of the original forest cover is gone, with two-thirds of the loss occurring since 1950.

Deforestation is frequently related to poverty and debt. Poor, landless farmers often cut forests because they have no alternatives. Developing countries encourage forest clearing to provide land for cattle production and plantation crops that they can export for revenue to help manage heavy foreign debts.

Forest destruction is causing the loss of many valuable forest products and could alter regional and even global climate. Tropical deforestation accounts for a significant part of global greenhouse gas emissions and is a leading cause of the decline and extinction of plant and animal species. Loss of tropical forests already affects hundreds of millions of people through increased flooding, soil erosion and silting of waterways, drought, shortages of fuelwood and timber, displacement of societies, and destruction of cultures.

Deforestation can be slowed by establishing forest reserves, improving management of exploited forests for sustainable use, preventing unsustainable development projects, increasing reforestation, and reducing pressures for forest clearing through land reform, improved agriculture, and population planning. Studies in Brazil and Peru demonstrate that net revenues from long-term harvesting of nontimber forest products are two to three times greater than revenues from commercial logging or clearing the forest for cattle ranching. In Central America, the potential value of medicinal plants harvested from tropical forests greatly exceeds revenues from clearing the land for other agricultural uses.

Case Studies

Mitsubishi's Initiatives to Support Reforestation.

Japan is the world's largest importer of tropical timber, and 92% of its imports come from Malaysia. The Mitsubishi Corporation is a major Japanese trading company with logging operations in Malaysia. Although Mitsubishi is not a major timber importer, it was apparently chosen for criticism by environmentalists of its role in deforestation because of its high name recognition.

In response to the criticism, Mitsubishi created a 10-person environmental affairs department to supervise environmental audits within the corporation and to support research beneficial to the environment. The department concluded that there was inadequate knowledge about how to regenerate tropical forests, and that conventional reforestation programs had both economic and ecological faults. To improve knowledge about reforestation, the company created a 50-hectare experimental rain forest ecosystem in Malaysia by planting tree species native to the region. Planting began in March 1991, and the company has organized three tropical forest seminars involving academic, government, and business participants to exchange information about the project (Schmidheiny, 1992).

Aracruz Celulose's Sustainable Forestry Program. Most of Brazil's southeastern coastal forests have been cut, and land degradation and unemployment in the region are widespread. Aracruz Celulose, one of Brazil's leading companies, specializes in producing pulp for paper manufacture. The company has combined government financial support with entrepreneurship in a reforestation project using fast-growing eucalyptus trees.

Aracruz's project covers 203,000 hectares and includes a modern pulp mill, a port for shipping the product, and extensive infrastructure for the local community. The company is conserving 27% of the region that is still covered with original forest, and it is planting 1.5 million native trees, including 60,000 fruit trees to increase the bird population. Each year Aracruz distributes millions of free eucalyptus trees to local farmers for planting; later harvesting helps reduce local pressures to cut the native forest for lumber or charcoal (Schmidheiny, 1992).

Smith & Hawken's Promotion of Sustainable Forestry Products. Smith & Hawken is a California-based company specializing in garden equipment and outdoor furniture. The furniture formerly included teak from Southeast Asian countries known to be experiencing rapid deforestation. In 1988, customers became concerned about the origins of its teak furniture, and asked for assurance that the company was not contributing to deforestation. In response, Smith & Hawken sought a way to guarantee that its teak suppliers were practicing sustainable forestry. The company could not verify that teak supplied from Thailand and Burma was produced by sustainable practices, so it switched to suppliers in Java, Indonesia, where teak plantations were first established in the 1870s.

Smith & Hawken worked with the Rainforest Alliance to create an independent program for certifying sustainably harvested tropical wood products. To be certified, a supplier must minimize environmental impacts, provide social benefits to local communities, and follow a long-term management plan. Through its efforts, Smith & Hawken has helped change the rules of the U.S. furniture business and has induced other companies to examine their sources of supply (Schmidheiny, 1992).

Weyerhaeuser's Forestry Management Program. In 1966, Weyerhaeuser Company began an intensive, high-yield forest management strategy designed to:

- Dramatically increase per-acre productivity of usable wood fiber.
- Provide an attractive investment opportunity.
- Help meet increasing demand for forest products.
- Relieve pressures on public lands that were increasingly being managed to emphasize nontimber resources values.

Weyerhaeuser now finds that timber on its most productive land grows twice as fast as in unmanaged forests. Weyerhaeuser nurseries grow 300 million seedlings a year; one-third go to company forests and the rest are sold to other landowners. On each acre harvested, the company plants 300 to 600 new trees. Weyerhaeuser believes that through intensive management of its forest lands, it can reduce the need to harvest timber from less productive public land and from virgin forests (Smart, 1992).

Protecting Wildlife and Biological Diversity

Preserving the earth's diversity of plant and animal species is a critical issue. The genetic variety contained in wild species can relieve human suffering and improve the quality of life, yet the activities of human populations are rapidly destroying natural habitats. As habitats are lost, biodiversity is irreversibly diminished through extinction of wild species. Critical habitats with rich biodiversity include tropical forests, wetlands, and coastal aquatic environments such as mangroves and coral reefs. Farming, timber and energy production, industry, and human settlements all contribute to habitat loss.

Over the last several thousand years, about 30% of the earth's forests and woodlands have been cleared. Half of the world's species-rich wetlands have been drained or degraded, and biologically diverse ocean coral reefs are being destroyed throughout the tropics. Future climate changes from projected global warming could disrupt plant and animal communities worldwide.

Current estimates of the number of plants, animals, and other organisms on earth range from 10 to 80 million or more; species that have evolved over millions of years are disappearing at rates of at least 140 species a day, or 50,000 per year. If current rates of habitat destruction continue, a quarter of all known species could be gone within 50 years.

Wild plants and animals produce foods, medicines, and essential raw materials and are important for future improvement of crops and livestock and for development of new medicines and industrial products. Plants and animals also provide valuable services such as pest control and flood control, maintenance of soil productivity, and the natural recycling of waste.

Worldwide sales of medicines derived from wild plants total about $40 billion a year. Some 1400 tropical forest plants and 500 marine organisms contain potential anticancer agents. Agriculture is highly dependent on genetic resources. Three crop species—wheat, rice, and maize—provide half the world's food supply. These and other crops are vulnerable to pests and disease, and the only effective way to counter these threats is to interbreed crops with pest- and disease-resistant varieties, including wild ones. Wild plant species provide industry with raw materials for a wide variety of products, including wood, rubber, oils, and gums. Much less than 1% of the world's botanical species has been analyzed for potential uses in medicine, agriculture, and industry.

A number of initiatives are helping to protect wildlife and biologically rich habitats. These include laws and treaties, creation of parks and reserves, "debt-for-nature" exchanges that provide economic incentives for conservation, and policies by development banks designed to protect biodiversity. Many species and ecosystems have been saved from extinction by concerted human efforts. The bison, sea otter, American alligator, peregrine falcon, whooping crane, and brown pelican were all on the way to extinction and are now recovering, with human assistance.

Case Studies

Du Pont's Wildlife Enhancement Program.   Du Pont has made promoting wildlife around its facilities an important environmental commitment. Through its collaboration with the United States–based Wildlife Habitat Enhancement Council (WHEC), Du Pont works to protect wildlife on more than 66,000 hectares at 140 corporate locations in the United States.

In 1989, Du Pont announced it would build a major facility at Asturias, Spain, and engaged WHEC to help design the project. The Asturias facility is located on 320 hectares of land and will include a number of units to produce fibers and related products. The areas around these units—about half the total area—are dedicated to wildlife. Working with local university faculty and conservationists, Du Pont and WHEC are developing a plan to protect wildlife, improve water management, and preserve local culture. The plan includes provisions to end clear-cutting of trees, conduct an inventory of plant and animal species, and develop a wetland zone for migratory waterfowl. The facility will use state-of-the-art pollution-control technology to prevent groundwater pollution; it will serve as a demonstration project for other companies in Europe (Schmidheiny, 1992).

Southern California Edison's Endangered Species Alert Program.   As part of Edison's commitment to help reverse the loss of plant and animal species in California, the company developed a program to help protect endangered species and their habitats. Edison produced a detailed field manual that helps its employees anticipate possible threats to species before they develop. The manual provides information about both federal and California Endangered Species Acts.

Other Edison wildlife programs help protect birds of prey. To prevent large birds from being electrocuted by touching two power lines at once, Edison has installed elevated perches on its power poles well above the power lines. The company also tries to avoid locating power lines and structures in areas with high bird concentrations.

Monsanto.   Many other companies have implemented wildlife protection programs. For example, in Tennessee the Monsanto Company has drained and decontaminated a series of chemical waste ponds at a closed manufacturing facility, restored over 5000 acres of woodland, and is planting several million cypress trees to attract wildlife (Renew America, 1992).

Summary

Business and industry have critical responsibilities and roles to play in preserving the global environment and moving toward a sustainable future. The case studies in this chapter provide evidence that many business firms are adopting bold policies and practices to protect natural resources and environmental quality, and are often saving money in the process. The extensive financial, technological, and organizational resources available to business can become powerful forces for promoting sustainable development.

Innovative Rural Communication System: Getting Information to Those Who Need It

Henry Norman, President

Volunteers in Technical Assistance (VITA)

"Knowledge is power!" That ancient wisdom is getting a new twist these days from a dedicated group of scientists, engineers, and technicians who believe information is the key to sustainable economic development.

For the 5000 men and women of VITA—Volunteers in Technical Assistance—finding solutions to problems like food production, water supply, and soil erosion is only part of the answer. Often the big question is how to get this information out to those who need it in a form they can use.

This is where VITA has been able to make a contribution. VITA staff and volunteers design simple, inexpensive applications of sophisticated technologies and train people to use technology to solve problems. In its 33-year history, VITA has helped design technologies as disparate as fuel-efficient wood-burning cookstoves and low-cost satellite communications systems. The aim is to provide Third World clients with the information they need to make intelligent choices among the various technologies available.

The sought-after technologies range from food production, storage, and processing to renewable energy to housing and sanitation. Also in demand is information on subjects like enterprise development, credit programs, and marketing programs.

To aid in the delivery of such information, VITA has developed a low-cost communications system, VITACOMM. This makes use of low-earth-orbiting satellites, a system known as VITASAT, a digital radio system called VITAPAC, and VITANET, a message delivery system that makes use of existing telephone networks (Fig. 22-3).

A Disaster Information Center operated as part of VITANET provides voluntary organizations and government agencies with up-to-the-minute information on natural disasters as well as listing of companies and individuals offering assistance.

Rural decision makers are the real environmental and economic managers in the developing world. Thus addressing their needs for hands-on technical and economic information should meet one of the most pressing requirements of development.

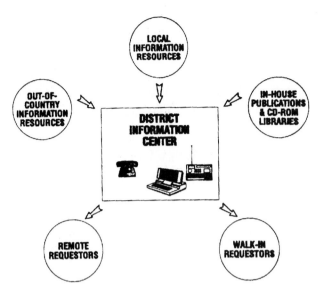

Figure 22-3. Innovative rural communication system.

Local decision makers—whether farmers, entrepreneurs, village leaders, or elders—must identify and balance economic opportunities and social pressures on limited natural resources. If resources are to be managed sustainably, decisions must be made by rural institutions and constituencies. If these local leaders are to make sound choices, they must have access to information that is appropriate to their needs and in a form that is digestible. Where this is the case, rural communities have shown they can develop their own wise resource management policies and their own sound economic, public health, and educational solutions.

Although some of the systems mentioned above might strike the reader as rather "high tech," the hardware and software for the different technologies have been carefully integrated for ease of use and durability and to provide for smooth interconnection between the different communication systems.

Rural Information Hubs

VITA is now working to develop a system of self-sustaining district communications centers that would provide principally rural areas of developing countries with access to information now usually available only in urban areas. As envisaged, and the concept is still being refined, the district communications centers represent the convergence of all of VITA's activities in the developing world.

Equipped with inexpensive computer and communication technologies, and simple technical manuals and maps, the district centers would help meet the information needs of rural communities in agriculture, education, business, environment, health, and other disciplines. The centers would help pay their own way by charging customers for electronic message and inquiry or transfer services to distant information sources, markets, and suppliers. With the help of such message services, agriculturalists and entrepreneurs could keep track of distant commodity prices and potential buyers for the goods they produce. They also could discover the best buys on needed goods and equipment. Or they could use the message system to find the best way to get their goods to market.

Electronic Message Centers

For both space-borne and terrestrial network capabilities, the primary communication technologies to be relied on are the computer, the printer, editing software, and the packet radio. The message services would rely heavily on VITAPAC, a relatively inexpensive digital packet radio system which allows computers to talk to each other by radio. Each station in a VITAPAC network consists of a computer or terminal, a two-way radio, a modem-like device called a terminal node controller (TNC), a printer, and an antenna.

Messages entered into the computer or terminal are sent to the TNC, which breaks them down into small pieces or packets for transmission. The receiving station's TNC decodes the messages and sends them on to the computer or terminal for viewing and printing. Packet radio systems can be especially helpful in areas presently without telephones services or with telephone services that cannot carry the digital signals now used for a variety of electronic information transfers.

With a packet radio system protected from signal interference, rural areas could have access to banking and credit services approaching those now usually available only in urban areas. District centers, of course, could be "hubs" with "spokes" to local banks to create a national banking system.

With packet radio, a district center could also become an important source of information for the national government. With proper training, the equipment could be operated by indigenous district information center personnel—making it an added source of local employment and income.

Regional Resource Centers

The district centers would also serve as libraries and storage points for all kinds of information on available technologies. For example, the centers would be stocked with VITA's popular "Understanding Technology" series of technical manuals. The 74 titles currently available in this series range from "Understanding Agroforestry Techniques" to "Understanding Water Wells" and cover such topics as solar energy, evaporative cooling, integrated pest management, wind energy, and vegetable drying. These and other manuals available from VITA have been specially edited to reflect local social and cultural realities.

The manuals and visual information provided must be geared to local problems and conditions. District center managers would have access to large-scale maps detailing a district's resource potential and the risks involved for a variety of human activities. There would also be information on local ecological conditions such as soil suitability for particular crops, susceptibility to erosion, or the presence of disease vectors or pests. With such information at their fingertips, district center personnel would be in a position to offer timely advice on proposed ventures or problems that arise.

At present, map resources are limited in many developing countries, especially those in Africa. However, with the help of experts, soil and geologic data could be derived from archived Landsat imagery. Climate data could also be compiled with the help of automated sensing devices and sent by packet radio to meteorologic centers. State-of-the-art techniques for analyzing such information could be used to produce maps showing conditions in the district. They could be also used to tailor technical manuals to local conditions.

Fortunately, with the end of the Cold War, mapping resources once tightly controlled because of security considerations have "gone public." For example, Russian Soyuz satellite imagery with resolutions all the way down to 2 meters, along with the tools for analyzing it, are now available from a private company in Moscow.

With the guidance of district center managers, clients could find useful information for remedying many of the problems that plague them. Farmers could select seed based on monitored soil fertility and could experiment with other methods for raising crop yields. In this way, the center would strengthen the capacities of rural constituents to discover and develop locally appropriate solutions to their development problems.

Information Unlimited

The possibilities opened by the district center approach are boundless. Once the centers have electronic communication capability, technical queries could, when needed, be directed to expert groups in other countries. A question about a VITA technical manual, for example, might be passed on to the volunteer who wrote the manual. The facilities would make possible a continuing dialogue among field sites and laboratories, health practitioners and disease control experts and teachers, students, and other knowledge sources.

Some Advantages of District Centers

- **For farmers.**   Data on local ecological conditions, e.g., soil suitability, susceptibility to erosion, disease vectors, pests. Up-to-date market and supplies information. Access to banking, credit facilities.
- **For merchants, businesspeople.**   Message services to distant markets, suppliers. Banking, credit services. Information on new products, technologies.
- **For environmentalists, health workers.**   Easy access through VITA-COMM, VITAPAC to out-of-country experts on virtually any topic. Access also to information stored in worldwide databanks on environmental, health problems.

Incorporated in the information center concept is the hope and expectation that the functions of each center will be shaped and molded by the community it serves. As preferences for types of information or services are identified, information center managers will have to respond to the interests in their "info-marketplace" if they are to succeed financially and in other ways. As local information needs are defined, centers may decide to "upgrade" from basic information roles to new services such as offering classes for high-demand technical subjects or creating mobile outreach programs.

District information centers might also be used to meet various specific needs—for example, to help set up enterprises for transportation of produce and supplies, to help with census enumeration and family planning, or to assist in property records management for local governments. With additional information management technologies, the potential of each center could be increased significantly. A CD-Rom Disk drive and associated educational materials would greatly broaden educational opportunities for both children and adults.

Shared use of global positioning technology would allow district centers to carry out inexpensive but precise field research for laboratories investigating disease vectors or to study the potential for new crops. Data obtained in this way could also be used to survey for engineering firms planning new roads or sewer lines.

Creating wealth—that is, using technology to add value to products—has been an essential element in the philosophy of VITA since its founding in 1959. Protection of the environment through sustainable development is another key element of that philosophy.

Getting Started

Setting up district information centers will require careful planning. Developing nations are littered with technologies and projects that failed largely because project need assessments had low priorities in the planning process. Too often, perception of development needs represents the thinking of project planners, directors, and some direct beneficiaries but not rural constituents themselves.

One of the first decisions, of course, involves selection of the site. Ideally, the choice would be made on the basis of need. Where is the need for such services greatest and where could one expect the greatest impact for the money invested? Among factors to be considered are the current state of standard communication services and the potential for improvement, the level of educational or training facilities, and the possibilities for creating a self-sufficient marketing area.

On the technical side, one of the first steps in establishing district information centers is to create a district-level resource inventory index. These data, supplemented by maps showing both resource potential and risks, would permit technical assistance tailored to local realities—i.e., soil condition, climate, terrain, cultural factors, available technology, etc. Next is the task of installing computer and communications gear and training local personnel to use them. VITA is now working on a package of recommended equipment.

How to Get Started

Establishing a district information center involves, first of all, drawing up a business plan. In the short term, external support in the form of international funding may be required, but if the project is to survive over the long term, consideration must be given from the start to achieving self-sufficiency.

The critical component is demand—whether there is sufficient demand for the services and whether the services can be provided at rates the "customers" can pay. Determining effective demand may require meeting with potential requesters. In this, sample surveys may be a useful tool for gauging the breadth of the "market shed" and determining whether it could become self-supporting.

Financial support is likely to be available from international agencies only to the extent they are convinced their planned projects in a given country can be undertaken more efficiently with the help of district information centers. Once they are convinced of this, international lenders, hopefully, will encourage government recipients of aid to contract with the district centers for their services.

One major consideration in establishment of a district information center is the political climate in the host country. What sort of agricultural, economic, education, health, and human service policies are in effect? How amenable are government officials likely to be to changes in the way things are done? What other political or ethnic issues are there that could hamper operations?

Funding can also be a major problem. Despite the growing attention now focused on the need to promote sustainable development, money for such efforts remains hard to come by. Nevertheless, there is also cause for hope. For one thing, there is increasing recognition in the multinational banking community that information is infrastructure every bit as much as roads and rail lines are infrastructure. Hopefully, this new awareness will translate into loans needed for improvements in information infrastructure.

There is yet another major problem: Communication ministries in some developing countries look upon packet radio systems as a potential competitor in providing telephone service. VITA's response to such fears is to point out that its packet radio services are not intended as substitute for government phone service but as a means of extending and enhancing that service. Where the packet radio system is integrated with government telephone lines, the profitability of the government service might increase as new service areas and new customers are added.

The Philippines Example

All the technologies needed for setting up district information centers are now readily available. Indeed, many of the technologies are already in use for various applications.

Apart from the financial backing that must be found, what is needed now is sufficient push to get things rolling. This can only come from understanding how important information and communication are to achieving sustainable economic development. In this, we can take heart from an experience in the Philippines that shows not only the need for such services but how they could become self-sustaining.

The Philippines story began with a visit to VITA headquarters outside Washington, D.C., by a Filipino group. Impressed with the information it found, the group returned to Manila with copies of everything VITA produced and opened an office and reading room stocked with this information. For a fee, users could make copies of material of particular interest to them. Now, in response to popular demand, for-fee courses are being offered at the Manila center on some of the topics covered.

The Philippines example, along with similar experiences in other countries served by VITA, is further proof not only that is there a demand for such services but that people in developing countries are willing to pay for these services. What better yardstick is there for assessing the importance of information in economic development strategy!

Bibliography

American Telephone and Telegraph. (1991). "AT&T Environment and Safety Report on Activities, 1990." New York.

Botkin, D. B., and E. A. Keller. (1987). "Environmental Studies: Earth as a Living Planet." Merrill, Columbus, Ohio.

Brown, L. R., and others. (1992). "State of the World, 1992." W. W. Norton, New York.

Brown, L. R., C. Flavin, and H. Kane. (1992). "Vital Signs 1992: The Trends That Are Shaping Our Future." W. W. Norton, New York.

Brown, L. R., C. Flavin, and S. Postel. (1991). "Saving the Planet: How to Shape an Environmentally Sustainable Global Economy." W. W. Norton, New York.

Brown, L. R., and S. Postel. (1987). Thresholds of change. In "State of the World 1987" (L. R. Brown and others). W. W. Norton, New York.

Cairncross, F. (1992). "Costing the Earth: The Challenge for Governments, The Opportunities for Business." Harvard Business School Press, Cambridge, Massachusetts.

Carson, R. (1962). "Silent Spring." Houghton Mifflin, Boston.

Commoner, B. (1990). "Making Peace with the Planet." Random House, New York.

Corson, W. H., ed. (1990). "The Global Ecology Handbook." Beacon Press, Boston.

Corson, W. H. (1992). "Priorities for Sustainable Societies." Global Tomorrow Coalition, Washington, D.C.

Costanza, R., ed. (1991). "Ecological Economics: The Science and Management of Sustainability." Columbia University Press, New York.

Council on Economic Priorities. (1991). "The Better World Investment Guide." Prentice-Hall Press, New York.

Daly, H. E. (1991). "Steady-State Economics." 2d Edition. Island Press, Washington, D.C.

Daly, H. E., and J. B. Cobb, Jr. (1989). "For the Common Good: Redirecting the Economy Toward Community, the Environment, and a Sustainable Future." Beacon Press, Boston.

Dorfman, M. H., and others. (1992). "Environmental Dividends: Cutting More Chemical Wastes." INFORM, New York.

Ehrlich, P. R., and A. H. Ehrlich. (1990). "The Population Explosion." Simon and Schuster, New York.

Ember, L. R. (1992). Limits to growth of resource use, population, pollution urged again. *Chemical & Engineering News*, April 27.

Gore, A., Jr. (1992). "Earth in the Balance: Ecology and the Human Spirit." Houghton Mifflin, Boston.

Henderson, H. (1991). "Paradigms in Progress: Life Beyond Economics." Knowledge Systems, Indianapolis, Indiana.

Hubbard, H. W. (1991). The real cost of energy. *Scientific American*, April.

International Chamber of Commerce. (1989). ICC: The business approach to sustainable development. *Development*, Journal of the Society for International Development 2(3), 37–39.

International Chamber of Commerce. (1991). "The Business Charter for Sustainable Development." Paris, France.

Luz International, Ltd. (1990). "The Luz Record." Los Angeles.

MacKenzie, J. J., R. C. Dower, and D. D. Chen. (1992). "The Going Rate: What It Really Costs to Drive." World Resources Institute, Washington, D.C.

Madden, J. P., and P. F. O'Connell. (1989). "Early Results of the LISA Program." U.S. Department of Agriculture, Washington, D.C.

Meadows, D. H. (1988). The new alchemist. *Harrowsmith*, November–December.

Meadows, D. H., D. L. Meadows, and J. Randers. (1992). "Beyond the Limits: Confronting Global Collapse, Envisioning a Sustainable Future." Chelsea Green, Post Mills, Vermont.

Milbrath, L. W. (1989). "Envisioning a Sustainable Society: Learning Our Way Out." State University of New York Press, Albany.

Miller, G. T. (1990). "Living in the Environment: An Introduction to Environmental Science." 6th Edition. Wadsworth, Belmont, California.

Pearce, D. W., and R. K. Turner. (1990). "Economics of Natural Resources and the Environment." The Johns Hopkins Press, Baltimore, Maryland.

Porter, G., and J. W. Brown. (1991). "Global Environment Politics." Westview Press, Boulder, Colorado.

Renew America. (1992). "Environmental Success Index." Washington, D.C.

Renew America. (1990). "Searching for Success." Washington, D.C.

Repetto, R. (1990). "Promoting Environmentally Sound Economic Progress: What the North Can Do." World Resources Institute, Washington, D.C.

Repetto, R., and others. (1992). "The Kindest Cut: Paying for Tax Reductions with Pollution Charges." World Resources Institute, Washington, D.C.

Repetto, R., and others. (1989). "Wasting Assets: Natural Resources in the National Income Accounts." World Resources Institute, Washington, D.C.

Schmidheiny, S. (1992). "Changing Course: A Global Business Perspective on Development and the Environment." The MIT Press, Cambridge, Massachusetts.

Smart, B., ed. (1992). "Beyond Compliance: A New Industry View of the Environment." World Resources Institute, Washington, D.C.

Speth, J. G. (1990). Six steps toward environmental security. *Christian Science Monitor*, January 22.

Vitousek, P. M., P. R. Ehrlich, A. H. Ehrlich, and P. Matson. (1986). Human appropriation of the products of photosynthesis. *Bioscience* 36(6), 368–373.

World Commission on Environment and Development. (1987). "Our Common Future." Oxford University Press, New York.

Appendix A
Selected Environmental and Health Organizations, Professional and Industry Associations, and Government Agencies

Agency for Toxic Substances and Disease Registry (ATSDR)
Centers for Disease Control (CDC)
(U.S. Public Health Service, Department of Health and Human Services)
1600 Clifton Road, NE
Atlanta, GA 30333
Phone (404) 639-0700
William L. Roper, MD, MPH,
  Administrator
Barry L. Johnson, PhD,
  Asst. Administrator

Air & Waste Management Association
Three Gateway Center, Four West
P.O. Box 2861
Pittsburgh, PA 15230
Phone (412) 232-3444
Fax (412) 232-3450
Martin E. Rivers, Exec. V.P.

American Association of Engineering Societies (AAES)
1111 19th Street, NW
Washington, DC 20036
Phone (202)296-2237
Fax (202) 296-1151
Ernest L. Daman, President
Mitchell H. Bradley, Executive Director

American Cancer Society
1599 Clifton Road, NE
Atlanta, GA 30329
Phone (404) 320-3333/(800) 227-2345
William M. Tipping, Exec. V.P.

American Chemical Society (ACS)
1155 16th Street, NW
Washington, DC 20036
Phone (202) 872-4600
Joseph A. Dixon, Chairman of the Board
Paul G. Gassman, President

American Conference of Governmental Industrial Hygienists (ACGIH)
6500 Glenway Avenue
Cincinnati, OH 45211
Phone (513) 661-7881

American Forest and Paper Association
1250 Connecticut Avenue, NW
Washington, DC 20036
Phone (202) 463-2700

American Heart Association
7272 Greenville Avenue
Dallas, TX 75231
Phone (800) 242-8721

American Industrial Health Council (AIHC)
1330 Connecticut Avenue, NW
Washington, DC 20036
Phone (202) 659-0060
Fax (202) 659-1699
Ronald A. Lang, President

American Industrial Hygiene Association (AIHA)
2700 Prosperity Avenue
Fairfax, VA 22031
Phone (703) 849-8888
Fax (703) 207-3561
Henry J. Muranko, CIH. President

American Institute of Chemical Engineers (AIChE)
345 East 47th Street
New York, NY 10017
Phone (212) 705-7338
Fax (212) 752-3297
Richard E. Emmert, PhD Exec. Dir.

American Lung Association
American Thoracic Society
1740 Broadway
New York, NY 10019
Phone (212) 315-8700
Lee B. Reichman, M.D., President
John R. Garrison, Mng. Dir.

American Management Association (AMA)
135 West 50th Street
New York, NY 10020
Phone (212) 586-8100
David Fagiano, President

American Petroleum Institute (API)
1220 L Street, NW
Washington, DC 20005
Phone (202) 682-8000
Fax (202) 682-8232
Charles J. DiBona, President

American Public Health Association (APHA)
1015 Fifteenth Street, NW
Washington, DC 20005
Phone (202) 789-5600
Wm H. McBeath, M.D., Exec. Dir.

Business Council for Sustainable Development
World Trade Center Building
Route de Aeroport 10
CH-1215 Geneva 15, Switzerland
Phone 011/4122/788-3202
Stephan Schmidheiny, Chairman

Center for Science in the Public Interest
1501 16th Street, NW
Washington, DC 20036
Phone (202) 332-9110
Michael F. Jacobson, Exec. Dir.

Chemical Industry Institute of Toxicology (CIIT)
6 Davis Drive, P.O. Box 12137
Research Triangle Park, NC 27709
Phone (919) 541-2070
Fax (919) 541-9015
Roger O. McClellan, DVM, President

Chemical Manufacturers Assoc. (CMA)
2501 M Street, NW
Washington, DC 20037
Phone (202) 887-1100
Robert A. Roland, President

Columbia University School of Public Health
Division of Environmental Sciences &
Occupational Medicine
60 Haven Avenue, B-1
New York, NY 10032
Phone (212) 305-3464
Fax (212) 305-4012
Vincent T. Covello, PhD
Director, Center for Risk Communication

The Conference Board
845 Third Avenue
New York, NY 10022
Phone (212) 759-0900
Fax (212) 980-7014
Preston Townley, President and CEO

The Conservation Foundation
1250 24th Street, NW
Washington, DC 20037
Phone (202) 293-4800
Russell E. Train, Chairman

Council on Economic Priorities Inc.
30 Irving Place
New York, NY 10003
Phone (212) 420-1133/(800) 822-6435
Fax (212) 420-0988
Alice Tepper Marlin, President

Council on Environmental Quality
(CEQ)
President's Commission on Environmental
Quality (PCEQ)
722 Jackson Place, NW
Washington, DC 20503
Phone (202) 395-5750
Fax (202) 395-3745
Michael R. Deland, Chairman

Ecological Society of America
Center for Environmental Studies
Arizona State University
Tempe, AZ 85287
Phone (602) 965-3000/8087
Duncan T. Patten, PhD,
Business Mgr.

Environment Canada
10 Wellington Street
Hull, Quebec K1A0H3
Canada
Phone (819) 997-2800

Environmental Defense Fund (EDF)
257 Park Avenue South
New York, NY 10010
Phone (212) 505-2100
Frederic D. Krupp, Executive Director

Environmental Protection Agency
(EPA/USEPA)
401 M Street, SW
Washington, DC 20460
Phone (202) 260-2090
William K. Reilly, Former Administrator
Carol M. Browner, Administrator

Federal Emergency Management Agency
(FEMA)
500 C Street, SW
Washington, DC 20472
Phone (202) 646-2500

Food and Drug Administration (FDA)
Dept. of Health and Human Services
5600 Fishers Lane
Rockville, MD 20857
Phone (301) 443-1544
David A. Kessler, M.D., Commissioner
200 C Street, SW
Washington, DC 20204

4-H Program
Extension Service
U.S. Department of Agriculture
Washington, DC 20250
Phone (202) 447-5853
Leah Hooper, Deputy Administrator

Friends of the Earth, Environmental Policy
Institute, The Oceanic Society
Executive Offices, 218 D Street, SE
Washington, DC 20003
Phone (202) 544-2600
Jane Perkins, President

Global Environmental Management
Initiative (GEMI)
2000 L Street, NW
Washington, DC 20036
Phone (202) 296-7449
Fax (202) 296-7442
George D. Carpenter, Chairman
Susan F. Vogt, Executive Director

Greenpeace U.S.A.
1436 U Street, NW
Washington, DC 20009
Phone (202) 462-1177
Peter Bahouth, Exec. Dir.

Harvard School of Public Health
677 Huntington Avenue
Boston, MA 02115
Phone (617) 432-4343
Fax (617) 432-2494
John D. Graham, PhD
Director, Center for Risk Analysis

Hazardous Substance Management Research Center (HSMRC)
Center for Haz. & Toxic Substance Mgt.
NJ Institute of Technology (NJIT)
Newark, NJ 07102
Phone (201) 596-3006/3233
Richard S. Magee, ScD, Exec. Dir.

Health and Welfare Canada
Tunnui's Pasture
Ottawa, Ontario K1A0K9
Canada
Phone (613) 957-2991

INFORM
381 Park Avenue South
New York, NY 10016
Phone (212) 689-4040
Joanna D. Underwood, President

International Chamber of Commerce (Paris)
38 Cours Albert 1er
75008 Paris, France
Phone (33) (1) 4953-2828
Fax (33) (1) 4225-8663
American affiliate:
U.S. Council for International Business
1212 Avenue of the Americas
New York, NY 10036
Phone (212) 354-4480
Fax (212) 575-0327
Allen F. Jacobson, Chairman
Abraham Katz, President

Investor Responsibility Research Center
1755 Massachusetts Avenue, NW
Washington, DC 20036
Phone (202) 234-7500
Frank Minard, Chairman of the Board
Margaret Carroll, Executive Director

Management Institute for Environment and Business (MEB)
1220 Sixteenth Street, NW
Washington, DC 20036
Phone (202) 833-6556
Fax (202) 833-6228
Matthew B. Arnold, President

National Academy of Sciences (NAS)
National Research Council (NRC)
2101 Constitution Avenue, NW
Washington, DC 20418
Phone (202) 334-2000
Bruce M. Alberts, PhD, President

National Association of Environmental Professionals (NAEP)
5165 McArthur Blvd., NW
Washington, DC 20016
Phone (202) 966-1500
Susan Eisenberg, Executive Director

National Association of Manufacturers (NAM)
1331 Pennsylvania Ave., NW
Washington, DC 20004
Phone (202) 637-3000
Dexter F. Baker, Chairman
Jerry J. Jasinowski, President

National Audubon Society
950 Third Avenue
New York, NY 10022
Phone (212) 832-3200
Peter A. Berle, President

National Fire Protection Association (NFPA)
1 Battery March Park
Quincy, MA 02269
Phone (800) 344-3555

National Ground Water Association
(formerly **National Water Well Association**)
Association of Ground Water Scientists and Engineers
6375 Riverside Drive
Dublin, OH 43017
Phone (614) 761-1711
Fax (614) 761-3446
David Schmitt, Executive Director

National Institute for Occupational Safety and Health (NIOSH)
4676 Columbia Parkway
Cincinnati, OH 45226
Phone (800) 356-4674
J. Donald Millar, M.D., Director and Asst.
 Surgeon General
Administrative Offices:
NIOSH/Centers for Disease Control (CDC)
1600 Clifton Road, NE
Altanta, GA 30333
Phone (404) 639-3311

National Institute of Environmental Health Sciences (NIEHS)
National Toxicology Program (NTP)
111 T.W. Alexander Drive
P.O. Box 12233
Research Triangle Park, NC 27709
Phone (919) 541-3454
Kenneth Olden, PhD, Director

National Institutes of Health (NIH)
Department of Health and Human
 Services
9000 Rockville Pike
Bethesda, MD 20892
Phone (301) 496-4000/2433
Bernadine Healy, M.D., Director

National Library of Medicine
8600 Rockville Pike
Bethesda, MD 20894
Phone (301) 496-1131

National Oceanic and Atmospheric Administration (NOAA)
U.S. Department of Commerce
14th St. and Constitution Ave., NW
Washington, DC 20230
Phone (202) 482-2985

National Safety Council
444 North Michigan Avenue
Chicago, Illinois 60611
Phone (800) 621-7619

National Science Foundation
1800 G Street, NW
Washington, DC 20550
Phone (202) 357-5000
Frederick Bernthal, Acting Director

National Technical Information Service (NTIS)
U.S. Department of Commerce
5285 Port Royal Road
Springfield, VA 22161
Phone (703) 487-4650
Fax (703) 321-8547

National Wildlife Federation
Corporate Conservation Council
1400 Sixteenth Street, NW
Washington, DC 20036-2266
Phone (202) 797-6800
Jay D. Hair, President

Natural Resources Defense Council
40 West Twentieth Street
New York, NY 10011
Phone (212) 727-2700
John Adams, Executive Director

The Nature Conservancy
1815 North Lynn Street
Arlington, VA 22209
Phone (703) 841-5300
John C. Sawhill, President

Oak Ridge National Laboratory
P.O. Box 2008
Oak Ridge, TN 37831
Phone (615) 576-2107
Fax (615) 574-9887
Curtis C. Travis, PhD
Director, Center for Risk Management

Occupational Safety and Health Administration (OSHA)
(U.S. Department of Labor)
200 Constitution Avenue, NW
Washington, DC 20210
Phone (202) 219-8576
David C. Ziegler, Dir. Admin. Programs

Office of Environmental Policy
Old Executive Office Building
17 Street and Pennsylvania Avenue, NW
Washington, DC 20501
Phone (202) 456-6224
Fax (202) 456-2710
Kathleen McGinty, JD, Director

Office of Technology Assessment (OTA)
U.S. Congress
600 Pennsylvania Ave., SE
Washington, DC 20510
Phone (202) 224-3695
Roger C. Herdman, M.D., Director

**Pharmaceutical Manufacturers Association
  (PMA)**
1100 Fifteenth Street, NW
Washington, DC 20005
Phone (202) 835-3400
Gerald J. Mossinghoff, President

Resources for the Future
1616 P Street, NW
Washington, DC 20036
Phone (202) 328-5000
Robert W. Fri, President
Paul R. Portney, Vice President

Sierra Club
730 Polk Street
San Francisco, California 94109
Phone (415) 776-2211
Michael L. Fischer, Exec. Dir.

**Smithsonian Environmental
  Research Center**
P.O. Box 28
Edgewater, MD 21037
Phone (301) 261-4190
David L. Correll, Director

Society for Risk Analysis (SRA)
8000 Westpark Drive
McLean, VA 22102
Phone (703) 790-1745
Fax (703) 790-9063
Richard J. Burk, Exec. Sec.

**Society of Environmental Toxicology and
  Chemistry (SETAC)**
1010 North Twelfth Ave.
Pensacola, FL 32501
Phone (904) 469-1500
Fax (904) 469-9778
Rodney Parrish, Executive Director

Society of the Plastics Industry (SPI)
1275 K Street, NW
Washington, DC 20005
Phone (202) 371-5200
Fax (202) 371-1022
Larry L. Thomas, President

Society of Toxicology
1101 Fourteenth Street, NW
Washington, DC 20005
Phone (202) 371-1393

**Synthetic Organic Chemical Manufacturers
  Association Inc. (SOCMA)**
1330 Connecticut Avenue, NW
Washington, DC 20036
Phone (202) 659-0060
Fax (202) 659-1699
Ronald A. Lang, President

**United Nations Environment Programme
  (UNEP)**
Headquarters and Regional Office
P.O. Box 30552
Nairobi, Kenya
Phone 2542230800
Mostafa K. Tolba, Exec. Dir.

UNEP New York Liaison Office
Room DC2-0816
New York, NY 10017
Phone (212) 963-8138
Noel J. Brown, PhD, Special Representative

U.S. Bureau of Mines
Division of Mineral Commodities
Washington, DC 20241
Phone (202) 501-9649

U.S. Chamber of Commerce
1615 H Street, NW
Washington, DC 20062
Phone (202) 659-6000

U.S. Department of Agriculture (USDA)
14th Street and Independence Ave., SW
Washington, DC 20250
Phone (202) 447-2791

U.S. Department of Commerce
14th Street and Constitution Ave., NW
Washington, DC 20230
Phone (202) 377-2000

U.S. Department of Energy (DOE)
1000 Independence Ave., SW
Washington, DC 20585
Phone (202) 586-5000

U.S. Department of Transportation (DOT)
400 Seventh Street, SW
Washington, DC 20590
Phone (202) 426-4000

U.S. Environmental Protection Agency (EPA/USEPA)
401 M Street, SW
Washington, DC 20460
Phone (202) 260-2090
William K. Reilly, Former Administrator
Carol M. Browner, Administrator

U.S. Fish and Wildlife Service
U.S. Department of the Interior
1849 C Street, NW
Washington, DC 20240
Phone (202) 208-5634
John F. Turner, Director

U.S. Public Interest Research Group
215 Pennsylvania Avenue, SE
Washington, DC 20003
Phone (202) 546-9707
Gene Karpinski, Exec. Dir.

Volunteers in Technical Assistance (VITA) and **World Environment Center (WEC)**
1600 Wilson Blvd.
Arlington, VA 22209
Phone (703) 276-1800
Fax (703) 243-1865
Henry R. Norman, JD, President (VITA)

Water Environment Federation (formerly **Water Pollution Control Federation**)
601 Wythe Street
Alexandria, VA 22314
Phone (703) 684-2400
Fax (703) 684-2492

The Wilderness Society
900 Seventeenth Street, NW
Washington, DC 20006-2596
Phone (202) 833-2300
George T. Frampton, Jr., President

World Bank—Environmental Department
1818 H Street, NW
Washington, DC 20433
Phone (202) 473-3202
Fax (202) 477-0565
Mohammed El-Ashry, PhD, Director

World Engineering Partnership for Sustainable Development (WEPSD); Global Environment & Technology Foundation (GETF)
7010 Little River Turnpike
Annandale, VA 22003
Phone (703) 750-6401
Fax (703) 750-6506
William J. Carroll, Chairman (WEPSD)
William L. Robertson, President (GETF)

World Environment Center (WEC)
419 Park Avenue South
New York, NY 10016
Phone (212) 683-4700
Fax (212) 683-5053
Antony G. Marcil, President

World Federation of Engineering Organizations (WFEO)
201 Amersham Road
High Wycombe, Bucks HP135AJ England
300 North Lake Avenue
Pasadena, CA 91101
Phone (818) 568-6669
Fax (818) 568-6619
William (Bud) Carroll, President

World Health Organization (WHO)
Avenue Appia CH-1211
Geneva 27, Switzerland
Phone 4122/791-2111
Hiroshi Nakajima, General Director

WHO Office at UN
2 UN Plaza, DC2-0970
New York, NY 10017
Phone (212) 963-6001

World Resources Institute (WRI)
1709 New York Avenue, NW
Washington, DC 20006
Phone (202) 638-6300
Fax (202) 638-0036
Jonathan Lash, JD, President

World Wildlife Fund
1250 Twenty-fourth Street, NW
Washington, DC 20037
Phone (202) 293-4800
Kathryn S. Fuller, President

Worldwatch Institute
1776 Massachusetts Avenue, NW
Washington, DC 20036
Phone (202) 452-1999
Lester R. Brown, President

Zero Population Growth
1400 Sixteenth Street, NW
Washington, DC 20036
Phone (202) 332-2200
Susan Weber, Exec. Dir.

Appendix B
Acronyms and Glossary

ACGIH	American Conference of Governmental Industrial Hygienists
ACS	American Chemical Society (or American Cancer Society)
AIChE	American Institute of Chemical Engineers
AIHA	American Industrial Hygiene Association
AIHC	American Industrial Health Council
AIME	American Institute of Mining, Metallurgical, and Petroleum Engineers
ALARA	As Low As Reasonably Achievable
AMA	American Management Association (or American Medical Association)
ANSI	American National Standards Institute
AOC	Area of Concern
APELL	Awareness and Preparedness for Emergencies at Local Level (UN)
APHA	American Public Health Association
API	American Petroleum Institute
AQUIRE	Aquatic Toxicity Information Retrieval database
ARARs	Applicable or Relevant and Appropriate Requirements
ARCS	Alternative Remedial Contracting Strategies
ASCE	American Society of Civil Engineers
ASEAN	Association of Southeast Asian Nations
ASME	American Society of Mechanical Engineers
ASTM	American Society for Testing and Materials
ATSDR	Agency for Toxic Substances and Disease Registry (CDC)
AWMA	Air & Waste Management Association
AWQC	Ambient Water Quality Criteria
BACT	Best Available Control Technology
BADT	Best Available Demonstrated Technology
BAF, BCF	Bioaccumulation Factor, Bioconcentration Factor
BANANA	"Build Absolutely Nothing Anywhere Near Anyone" (syndrome)
BAT	Best Available Treatment/Technology

BCSD	Business Council for Sustainable Development
BLEVE	Boiling Liquid Expanding Vapor Explosion
BPT	Best Practicable (Control) Technology
BRA	Baseline Risk Assessment
BTAG	Biological/Ecological Technical Assistance Group (EPA)
CAA	Clean Air Act
CAAA	Clean Air Act Amendments
CAD/CAM	Computer Assisted Design/Computer Assisted Manufacturing
CAER	Community Awareness and Emergency Response (CMA)
CAMEO	Computer-Aided Management of Emergency Operations
CAMU	Corrective Action Management Unit
CAS(RN)	Chemical Abstract Service (Registry Number)
CDC	Centers for Disease Control (HHS)
CDI	Chronic Daily Intake
CEO, COO	Chief Executive Officer, Chief Operating Officer
CEQ	Council on Environmental Quality
CERCLA	Comprehensive Environmental Response, Compensation, and Liability Act of 1980
CERCLIS	Comprehensive Environmental Response, Compensation, and Liability Information System
CFCs	Chlorofluorocarbons
CFR	Code of Federal Regulations
CHEMTREC	Chemical Transportation Emergency Center
CIIT	Chemical Industry Institute of Toxicology
CITES	Convention on International Trade in Endangered Species of Wildlife and Fauna
CLP	Contract Laboratory Program
CMA	Chemical Manufacturers Association
CMS/CMI	Corrective Measures Study/Corrective Measures Implementation (RCRA)
COCs	Chemicals (or Contaminants) of Concern (Indicator Chemicals)
COD	Chemical Oxygen Demand
COPD	Chronic Obstructive Pulmonary Diseases
CPR	Cardiopulmonary Resuscitation
CPSC	Consumer Product Safety Commission
CTC	Cradle-to-Cradle (concept)
CTDs	Cumulative Trauma Disorders
CWA	Clean Water Act (FWPCA)
DCF	Discounted Cash Flow

DNA	Deoxyribonucleic acid
DOD	U.S. Department of Defense
DOE	U.S. Department of Energy
DOT	U.S. Department of Transportation
DPT	Diphtheria, Pertussis, Tetanus (immunization)
EA	Environmental Assessment
EC	European Community (Common Market)
EDF	Environmental Defense Fund
EHS	Extremely Hazardous Substance
EHS/EH&S	Environmental, Health and Safety (policies, plans, programs)
EIA	Environmental Impact Assessment
ELCA	Environmental Life-Cycle Assessment
EMF	Electromagnetic Fields
EPA	U.S. Environmental Protection Agency
EPCRA	Emergency Planning and Community Right to Know Act (SARA Title III)
EPRI	Electric Power Research Institute
ERA	Ecological Risk Assessment
ERPG	Emergency Response Planning Guideline (AIHA)
F&EI	Fire and Explosion Index (Dow)
FASB	Financial Accounting Standards Board
FDA	U.S. Food and Drug Administration
FEMA	Federal Emergency Management Agency
FIFRA	Federal Insecticide, Fungicide, and Rodenticide Act
FMEA	Failure Mode and Effects Analysis
FOIA	Freedom of Information Act
FONSI	Finding of No Significant Impact (NEPA)
FR	Federal Register
FS	Feasibility Study
FTA/ETA	Fault Tree Analysis/Event Tree Analysis
FTC	Federal Trade Commission
FWPCA	Federal Water Pollution Control Act (Clean Water Act)
GAAP	Generally Accepted Accounting Principles
GAO	General Accounting Office
GATT	General Agreement on Tariffs and Trade
GEMI	Global Environmental Management Initiative
GEMS	Global Environmental Monitoring System (UNEP)
GIS	Geographic Information System

GMPs	Good Manufacturing Practices
GNP, GDP	Gross National Product, Gross Domestic Product
HASP	Health and Safety Plan
HAZOP	Hazard and Operability Study
HEAST	Health Effects Assessment Summary Tables (EPA)
HEP	Hazard Evaluation Procedure (or Habitat Evaluation Procedure)
HHS	Department of Health and Human Services (formerly HEW)
HI	Hazard Index
HIAA	Health Insurance Association of America
HMCRI	Hazardous Materials Control Resources Institute
HQ	Hazard Quotient (or Headquarters)
HRA	Human Reliability Analysis
HRS	Hazard Ranking System
HSDB	Hazardous Substance Database
HSWA	Hazardous and Solid Waste Amendments
HVAC	Heating, Ventilation, and Air Conditioning (System)
IARC	International Agency for Research on Cancer
ICC	International Chamber of Commerce
ICRP	International Commission on Radiological Protection
IDLH	Immediately Dangerous to Life or Health
IEEE	Institute of Electrical and Electronics Engineers
ILSI	International Life Sciences Institute/Risk Science Institute
IPCS	International Program on Chemical Safety (United Nations)
IPM	Integrated Pest Management
IRIS	Integrated Risk Information System (EPA)
IRMs	Interim Remedial Measures
ISCLT	Industrial Source Complex Long Term Model
ISCST	Industrial Source Complex Short Term Model
ISO	International Standards Organization (Geneva, Switzerland)
ITP	Industrial Toxics Reduction Project
LCA	Life Cycle Analysis/Assessment
LC50/LD50	Median Lethal Concentration/Lethal Dose
LDCs	Less Developed Countries
LDL, HDL	Low Density Lipoproteins, High Density Lipoproteins (cholesterol)
LDRs	Land Disposal Restrictions
LEL	Lower Explosive Limit
LEPC	Local Emergency Planning Committee
LLW	Low Level (radioactive) Waste

LOAEL	Lowest Observed Adverse Effect Level
LUSTs	Leaking Underground Storage Tanks (current usage omits the "L")
MACT	Maximum Achievable Control Technology
MCL	Maximum Contaminant Level
MCLG	Maximum Contaminant Level Goal
MEI	Maximum Exposed Individual
MOA/MOU	Memorandum of Agreement/Memorandum of Understanding
MSDS	Material Safety Data Sheet
MSHA	Mine Safety and Health Administration
MTBE	Methyl Tertiary Butyl Ether
MTD	Maximum Tolerated Dose
NAAQS	National Ambient Air Quality Standards (CAA)
NAFTA	North American Free Trade Agreement
NAM	National Association of Manufacturers
NAS	National Academy of Sciences
NATICH	National Air Toxics Information Clearinghouse
NCP	National Contingency Plan (National Oil and Hazardous Substances Pollution Contingency Plan)
NEPA	National Environmental Policy Act
NGOs	Nongovernmental Organizations
NESHAPs	National Emissions Standards for Hazardous Air Pollutants (CAA)
NFPA	National Fire Protection Association
NHANES	National Health and Nutrition Examination Study
NIEHS	National Institute of Environmental Health Sciences
NIH	National Institutes of Health
NIMBY	"Not in My Backyard" (syndrome)
NIOSH	National Institute for Occupational Safety and Health (CDC)
NLM	National Library of Medicine
NOAA	National Oceanic and Atmospheric Administration (Commerce Department)
NOAEL	No Observed Adverse Effect Level
NPDES	National Pollutant Discharge Elimination System (CWA)
NPL	National Priority List (CERCLA)
NRC	National Research Council or Nuclear Regulatory Commission
NRDA	Natural Resource Damage Assessment
NRDC	Natural Resources Defense Council
NSF	National Science Foundation
NTIS	National Technical Information Service

NTP	National Toxicology Program (NIEHS)
OECD	Organization for Economic Cooperation and Development
OMB	Office of Management and Budget
OSHA	Occupational Safety and Health Administration/Act
OSWER	Office of Solid Waste and Emergency Response (EPA)
OTA	Office of Technology Assessment (US Congress)
PAHs	Polycyclic (or Polynuclear) Aromatic Hydrocarbons
PB-PK	Physiologically Based Pharmacokinetics
PCBs	Polychlorinated Biphenyls
PCEQ	President's Council on Environmental Quality
pCi/l	picocuries per liter
PDF	Probability Density/Distribution Function
PEL	Permissible Exposure Limit (OSHA)
PHA	Preliminary Hazard Analysis
PHS	U.S. Public Health Service
PM10	Particulate Matter, nominally 10 microns or less
PMA	Pharmaceutical Manufacturers Association
POTW	Publicly Owned Treatment Works
ppb	Parts per Billion (micrograms per kilogram)
ppm	Parts per Million (milligrams per kilogram)
PRGs	Preliminary Remediation Goals
PRP	Potentially Responsible Party (CERCLA)
PSM	Process Safety Management (OSHA)
QA/QC	Quality Assurance/Quality Control
QAPP	Quality Assurance Program (or Project) Plan
RA	Risk Analysis/Assessment
RACT	Reasonably Available Control Technology
RAD	Radiation Absorbed Dose (unit of measurement of radiation absorbed by humans)
RAGS	Risk Assessment Guidance for Superfund (EPA)
RCRA	Resource Conservation and Recovery Act
RD, RA	Remedial Design, Remedial Action
R&D	Research and Development
RDA	Recommended Daily Allowance
rDNA	Recombinant DNA
REL	Recommended Exposure Limit (NIOSH)
REM	Roentgen Equivalent Man
RFA/RFI	RCRA Facility Assessment/RCRA Facility Investigation
RfC	Reference Concentration

RfD	Reference Dose (virtually safe dose)
RI/FS	Remedial Investigation/Feasibility Study
Risk	A measure of probability and magnitude of adverse consequences
RME	Reasonable Maximum Exposure
RMPP	Risk Management and Prevention Program (California)
RNA	Ribonucleic Acid
ROD	Record of Decision (CERCLA)
RPM	Remedial Project Manager (CERCLA)
RTECS	Registry of Toxic Effects of Chemical Substances
SAB	Science Advisory Board
SARA	Superfund Amendments and Reauthorization Act of 1986
SARs	Structure-Activity Relationships
SBA	Small Business Administration
SDWA	Safe Drinking Water Act
SEC	Securities and Exchange Commission
SERC	State Emergency Response Commission
SETAC	Society of Environmental Toxicology and Chemistry
SF	Slope Factors for Carcinogens
SHI	Substance Hazard Index
SIDS	Screening Information Data Set (OECD Chemical Testing)
SIP	State Implementation Plan (CAA)
SITE	Superfund Innovative Technology Evaluation
SOCMA	Synthetic Organic Chemical Manufacturers Association
SOPs	Standard Operating Procedures
SPCC	Spill Prevention, Containment, and Countermeasure (CWA)
SPDES	State Pollutant Discharge Elimination System
SPI	Society of the Plastics Industry
SPM	Suspended Particulate Matter
SRA	Society of Risk Analysis
STAR	Stability Wind Rose
STEL	Short-Term Exposure Limit
Superfund	The fund and program operated under CERCLA and SARA
SWMU	Solid Waste Management Unit
TBC	To Be Considered
TCDD	Tetrachlorodibenzo-p-dioxin
TCLP	Toxicity Characteristic Leachate Procedure
TLV	Threshold Limit Value (ACGIH)
TNC	Transnational Corporation

TPQ	Threshold Planning Quantity
TQEM	Total Quality Environmental Management
TQM	Total Quality Management
TRI	Toxic Release Inventory
TRV	Toxicity Reference Value
TSCA	Toxic Substances Control Act
TSDF	Treatment, Storage, and Disposal Facilities
TSP	Total Suspended Particulates
UCL	Upper Confidence Limit
UF/MF	Uncertainty Factor/Modifying Factor
UL	Underwriters' Laboratories
UN	United Nations
UNAMAP	Users' Network for Applied Modeling of Air Pollution
UNCED	United Nations Conference on Environment and Development (also known as "Earth Summit" held in Brazil, 1992)
UNEP	United Nations Environment Programme
U.S./USA	United States of America
USDA	United States Department of Agriculture
USEPA	United States Environmental Protection Agency
USGS	United States Geological Survey
USTs	Underground Storage Tanks
UV	Ultraviolet rays/radiation
VITA	Volunteers in Technical Assistance
VOCs	Volatile Organic Compounds
WFEO	World Federation of Engineering Organizations
WHO	World Health Organization (UN)

Appendix C
Environmental Guiding Principles and Codes of Conduct

Industry association	Title of principal charter/code of conduct	Guidelines and other complementary documents
	1. Cross-Sector Industry Associations	
International		
Business Council on Sustainable Development (BCSD)	Declaration of the Business Council on Sustainable Development (1992)	Changing Course: A Global Business Perspective on Development and Business
International Chamber of Commerce (ICC)	The Business Charter for Sustainable Development (1990)	Environmental Guidelines for World Industry (includes supplementary guidelines on wastes) (1990) ICC Guide to Effective Environmental Auditing (1991) ICC Code on Environmental Advertising (1991) Position papers on "Environmental labelling systems" (1990) and "Environmental Advertising" (1992) Business Briefs: Economics and the environment; Toxic chemicals; Hazardous wastes; Energy and protection of the atmosphere; Biodiversity conservation; Forests: Technology cooperation; Education for sustainable development From Ideas to Action—Business and Sustainable Development
Business and Industry Advisory Committee to the OECD (BIAC)	Statement on the Environment (1990)	Guides for manufacturers and traders exporting chemicals (1985)
Belgium		
Fédération des entreprises de Belgique (FEB)	ICC Business Charter for Sustainable Development	Guidelines for an Environmental Policy (1982)

Industry association	Title of principal charter/code of conduct	Guidelines and other complementary documents
	1. Cross-Sector Industry Associations (*Continued*)	
Finland		
Confederation of Finnish Industries (CFI)	Guidelines for Environmental Care and Protection in Finnish Industry (1988)	Handbook on Environmental Protection in Industry (1992)
	ICC Business Charter for Sustainable Development	Handbook of Main Issues of Environmental Protection for SMEs (1992)
		Checklist of Environmental Protection for SMEs (1992)
		Guidelines for Environmental Arguments in Marketing (1990)
Germany		
Bundesverband der Deutschen Industrie e.V. (BDI)		Initiative of German Business for Worldwide Precautionary Action to Protect the Climate (1991)
Japan		
Japan Federation of Economic Organizations (Keidanren)	Keidanren Global Environmental Charter (1991)	Environmental Guidelines for Japanese Enterprises Operating Abroad
Sweden		
Federation of Swedish Industries	Industrial Environmental Policy (1987)	Environmental Management Handbook (1991, '90, '89)
	ICC Business Charter for Sustainable Development	Environmental Auditing Handbook (1990)
United Kingdom		
Confederation of British Industries (CBI)		Guidelines on the Disclosure of Safety, Health and Environmental Information to the Public
		Managing Waste—Guidelines for Business
		Efficient Water Management—Guidelines for Business
		Guidelines on the Responsible Disposal of Wastes (1982)
		Narrowing the Gap: Environmental Auditing Guidelines for Business
		Corporate Environmental Policy Statements
		Towards a Recycling Culture
		Environmental Register—Incorporating managing waste guidelines for business
		The Greenhouse Effect and energy efficiency
		Managing The Greenhouse Effect—A Business Perspective
		Environment Means Business: A CBI action plan for the 1990s
		Several others
USA		
Global Environmental Management Initiative (GEMI)	ICC Business Charter for Sustainable Development	An Environmental Self-Assessment Program (1992)

Industry association	Title of principal charter/code of conduct	Guidelines and other complementary documents
2. Sector-Specific Industry Associations		

2.1 Chemical

International

International Council of Chemical Associations (ICCA)		Environmental Health & Safety Principles

Europe

European Chemical Industry Council (CEFIC)	Responsible Care Program	Guidelines on Improving Energy Efficiency (1992) Guidelines on Transfer of Technology (Safety, Health and Environmental Aspects) (1991) Guidelines on Occupational Health Management (1991) EN29001/ISO9001—Guidelines for Use by the Chemical Industry (1991) Guidelines on Waste Minimization (1990) Checklist for On-Site Emergency Plans (1990) The "CICERO Book of Experience" on Risk Communication (1990) Industrial Waste Management: A CEFIC approach to the issue (1989, 1984) Guidelines for the Communication of Environmental Information to the Public (1989) Recommendations on the Safety Auditing of Road Haulers (1988) Guidelines for the Protection of the Environment (1987) A Guide to Safe Warehousing for the European Chemical Industry (1987) Information on Hazards of Substances at the Individual Workplace (1987)

Australia

Australian Chemical Industry Council (ACIA)	Responsible Care Program 8 Codes of Practices (3 *completed; 5 others planned*)	

Austria

Federation of Austrian Chemical Industry	Responsible Care Program	

Belgium

Belgian Federation of Chemical Industries (FIC/FCN)	Responsible Care Program	5 major guidelines planned: ■ *Guidelines for protection of the environment* ■ *Guidelines for communication to the public* ■ *Safe Distribution guidelines* ■ *Process Safety guidelines*

Brazil

Associacao Brasileira Da Industria Quimica De Productos Derivados (ABIQUM)	Responsible Care Program (*Atuacao Responsavel*)	

Industry association	Title of principal charter/code of conduct	Guidelines and other complementary documents
	2. Sector-Specific Industry Associations (*Continued*)	
Canada Canadian Chemical Producers Association (CCPA)	Responsible Care Program 6 Codes of Practices ■ *Community Awareness and Emergency Response* ■ *Research & Development* ■ *Manufacturing* ■ *Transportation* ■ *Distribution* ■ *Hazardous Waste Management*	
Finland Chemical Industry Federation of Finland	Responsible Care Program (*Vastuu Huomisesta/Ansvar for Morgondagen*) Codes of Management Practice ■ *Process Safety Code* ■ *Waste Management Code* ■ *Distribution Code* ■ *Product Stewardship Code* ■ *Environmental Protection (under preparation)*	Checklists and Guidance Notes
France Union des Industries Chimique (UIC)	Responsible Care Program 4 Codes of practice ■ *Safe employment of contractors* ■ *Handling and transfer of liquid chemicals in bulk* ■ *Safe use of chemicals* ■ *Used packaging*	30 published documents
Germany Verband der Chemischen industrie (VCI)	Responsible Care Program Code of Conduct on Exporting Dangerous Chemicals	Guidance notes and recommendations in: ■ *protection of the environment* ■ *health and safety* ■ *product stewardship* ■ *communication*
Ireland Federation of Irish Chemical Industries (FICI)	Responsible Care Program	
Italy Federchimica	Responsible Care Program	Guides on "Environmental Auditing" and "Emergency Preparedness" being prepared.
Japan Japan Chemical Industry Association (JCIA)	Responsible Care Program	
Mexico Asociation National de la Industria Quimica (ANIQ)	Responsible Care Program (*Responsabilidad Integral*)	

Industry association	Title of principal charter/code of conduct	Guidelines and other complementary documents
	2. Sector-Specific Industry Associations (*Continued*)	
Mexico (*Continued*)	7 codes of practice being developed: ■ *Community protection* ■ *Pollution Prevention* ■ *Safety Process* ■ *Transportation and Distribution* ■ *Employee Health and Safety* ■ *Research and Development* ■ *Product Safety*	
New Zealand New Zealand Chemical Industry Council (NZCIC)	Responsible Care Program Codes of practice ■ *Workplace Injuries—Quarterly Safety Performance Review* ■ *Environmental Performance Indicators*	
The Netherlands Vereniging Van de Nederlandse Chemische Industrie (VNCI)	Responsible Care Program Various codes of practice	CEFIC Guidelines for the Protection of the Environment
Spain Federacion Empresarial de la Industria Quimica Espanola (FEIQUE)	Responsible Care Program (*Compromiso de Progreso*)	
Sweden Association of Swedish Chemical Industries	Responsible Care Program (*Responsibility & Care*) CEFIC Guidelines for the Protection of the Environment	Manuals (in Swedish) ■ *Responsibility and care* ■ *The environment protection law: responsibility, organization, administration* ■ *The environment protection law: information and consultation* ■ *Environmental safety assessment: a model* ■ *The company and the media* ■ *Safety chemicals (under preparation)* ■ *Safe transportation (under preparation)* ■ *Product stewardship (to be planned)*
Switzerland Swiss Society of Chemical Industries (SSCI)	Responsible Care Program	Guide for the reduction of environmental impact of packaging (under preparation)
United Kingdom Chemical Industries Association (CIA)	Responsible Care Program	Responsible Care Reports (May 1992, Issue 1) Responsible Care management systems—guidelines for certification to ISO 9001 health, safety and environmental management systems (and BS 7750 environmental management systems) in the chemical industry (1992)

Industry association	Title of principal charter/code of conduct	Guidelines and other complementary documents
	2. Sector-Specific Industry Associations (*Continued*)	
United Kingdom (Continued)		Responsible Energy—a practical guide to energy efficiency (1992)
		Proceedings of Responsible Care seminars (September 1991, February 1991, June 1990, October 1989)
		Guidance on safety, occupational health and environmental protection auditing (1991)
		Be prepared for an emergency—guidelines on emergency planning (1991)
		Code of conduct to protect against the diversion of chemicals into the illicit production of drugs and chemical weapons (1991)
		Guidance for chief executive officers on Responsible Care (1990)
		Guidance on procedures for organizing and monitoring road transport of dangerous substances in bulk (1990)
		Guidance on transfer connection for the safe handling of anhydrous ammonia in the UK (1990)
		Guidelines for bulk handling of chlorine at customer installations (1983)
		Guidelines for bulk handling of ethylene oxide (1983)
		Guidelines for safe warehousing of substances with hazardous characteristics (1983)
		Safe Exportation of Chemicals: An Industry Approach to the Issue (1988)
		Videos
		Responsible to the Community (1992 training version also available)
		Several other videos
USA Chemical Manufacturers Association (CMA)	Responsible Care Program 6 Codes of Management Practices (CMA) ■ *Community Awareness and Emergency Response* ■ *Distribution* ■ *Process Safety* ■ *Pollution Prevention* ■ *Employee Health and Safety* ■ *Product Stewardship Code*	
2.2 Agrochemical		
International International Fertilizer Industry Association (IFA)	Vancouver Communique (1990) Code of Best Agricultural Practices to Optimize Fertilizer Use (1990)	World Fertilizer Use Manual Booklets and safety recommendations for the storage, handling and use of fertilizers and intermediates
International Group of National Associations of Agrochemical Manufacturers (GIFAP)	FAO International Code of Conduct on the Distribution and Use of Pesticides	A Guide to Implementation for Traders and Formulators

Industry association	Title of principal charter/code of conduct	Guidelines and other complementary documents
	2. Sector-Specific Industry Associations (*Continued*)	

2.2 *Agrochemical (Continued)*

International

Industry association	Title of principal charter/code of conduct	Guidelines and other complementary documents
International Group of National Associations (GIFAP) (*Continued*)		Prior Informed Consent (PIC): A Guide to its Working
		Guidelines for the safe handling of pesticides during their formulation, packing, storage and transport (1982)
		Guidelines for the safe and effective use of pesticides (1983)
		Guidelines for emergency measures in cases of pesticide poisoning (1984)
		Guidelines for quality control of pesticides during formulation and packing (1985)
		Guidelines for the avoidance, limitation, and disposal of pesticide waste on the farm (1987)
		Guidelines for safe warehousing of pesticides (1988)
		Guidance for Field Testing of Genetically Modified Microorganisms and Plants (1991)
		Guidelines for the Safe Transport of Pesticides (1987)
		Guidelines for Personal Protection when Using Pesticides in Hot Climates (1989)
		Guidelines for Writers of Pesticide Labels and Literature (1989)
		Disposal of Unwanted Pesticides Stocks— Guidance on the Selection of Practical Options (1991)
		Safe Use News

Europe

Industry association	Title of principal charter/code of conduct	Guidelines and other complementary documents
European Fertilizer Manufacturers Association	Code of Best Agricultural Practices to Optimize Fertilizer Use (1990)	

Philippines

Industry association	Title of principal charter/code of conduct	Guidelines and other complementary documents
Agricultural Pesticide Institute of the Philippines (APIP)	Code of Ethics (1990)	

2.3 *Mining and metals*

International

Industry association	Title of principal charter/code of conduct	Guidelines and other complementary documents
International Iron and Steel Institute (IISI)	Environmental Principles (1992) (revised Statement on the Environment—1972)	
Lead Development Association		Control of lead at work: guidelines for plumbers and plumbing lecturers (1981)
Lead Industries Association	Product Stewardship Program	

Canada

Industry association	Title of principal charter/code of conduct	Guidelines and other complementary documents
The Mining Association of Canada	Guide for Environmental Practice (1990)	

USA

Industry association	Title of principal charter/code of conduct	Guidelines and other complementary documents
American Iron and Steel Institute (AISI)	Environmental Policy Statement	

Industry association	Title of principal charter/code of conduct	Guidelines and other complementary documents
	2. Sector-Specific Industry Associations (*Continued*)	

2.4 *Petroleum and Energy*

International
International Petroleum Industry Environmental Conservation Association (IPIECA)

Guidelines on Biological Impacts of Oil Pollution
Management of Oil Spill Response: A Petroleum Industry Guide

Europe
CONCAWE

Regulatory guidelines of environmental concern to the oil industry in Western Europe (1976–79)
Guidelines for the determination of atmospheric concentrations of oil mists (1981)
Guidelines for recording industrial hygiene data (1983)

European Committee of Electricity Supply Undertakings	Statement of Environmental Policy and Code of Conduct	
European Petroleum Industry Association (EUROPIA)	Environmental Guidelines	

Canada

Canadian Petroleum Association (CPA)	Environmental code of practice (1989)	Environmental operating guidelines for the Alberta petroleum industry (1988)
Petroleum Association for Conservation of the Environment (PACE)	Mission statement (1992)	Guidelines for updating the petroleum industry inventory of equipment, materials, and contractors for oil spill control, using the national emergency equipment locator system (1977) Guidelines for handling gasoline spills on land and water surface (1976) Guidelines for the continuing operation of local oil spill co-operatives (1977) Bulk plant guidelines for oil spill prevention and control (1980) Underground tank operations: review of state of the art and guidelines (?)

United Kingdom

The Institute of Petroleum	Mission Statement (1992)	Code of practice for the use of oil slick dispersants (1979)

USA

American Petroleum Institute (API)	Strategies for Today's Environmental Partnership (STEP) Program	Environmental Mission and Guiding Environmental Principles (1990) Management Practices, Self-Assessment Process and Resource Materials (RP 9000) (1992)

2.5 *Leather*

International

International Council of Tanners	Statement of the International Leather Industry Principles for Improved Environmental, Health and Safety Performance (Draft 1990)	

Industry association	Title of principal charter/code of conduct	Guidelines and other complementary documents
2. Sector-Specific Industry Associations (*Continued*)		

2.6 *Pulp and paper*

Japan
Japan Federation for Paper Industries — — Guidelines to reduce PCDD/PCDF discharge in pulp mill effluent (1990)

USA
American Paper Institute — — Environmental Guiding Principles

2.7 *Tourism*

International
World Travel and Tourism Council (WTTC) — — Environmental Guidelines

Alliance Internationale de Tourisme (AIT)/ Federation Internationale de l'Automobile (FLA) — Charter of Ethics for Tourism and the Environment (1992)

Canada
Pacific Asia Travel Association (PATA) — Code for Environmentally Responsible Tourism

Tourism Industry Association of Canada — Code of Ethics for the Industry / Code of Ethics for Tourists — Guidelines for the Tourism Industry Association / Guidelines for Accommodation / Guidelines for Foodservice / Guidelines for Tour Operators / Guidelines for Ministries of Tourism

United Kingdom
The Prince of Wales Business Leaders Forum — Charter for Environmental Action in the International Hotel and Catering Industry (1992)

| 3. Professional Associations | | |

International
World Federation of Engineering Organizations (WFEO) — Code of Environmental Ethics for Engineers (1985)

International Federation of Consulting Engineers (FIDIC) — Environmental Policy for FIDIC Members

World Enginering Partnership for Sustainable Development (WEPSD) — Vision, Mission, Goals statement (1993)

PRIMARY SOURCE: United Nations Environment Programme (UNEP).

Index